THE
unofficial **GUIDE**®
TO Walt Disney
World®

2013

Also available from John Wiley & Sons, Inc., and John Wiley & Sons Ltd:

Beyond Disney: The Unofficial Guide to Universal Orlando, SeaWorld, and the Best of Central Florida

Mini-Mickey: The Pocket-Sized Unofficial Guide to Walt Disney World

The Unofficial Guide Color Companion to Walt Disney World

The Unofficial Guide to Britain's Best Days Out: Theme Parks and Attractions

The Unofficial Guide to Cruises

The Unofficial Guide to Disneyland

The Unofficial Guide to Disneyland Paris

The Unofficial Guide to Dubai

The Unofficial Guide to Las Vegas

The Unofficial Guide to Walt Disney World with Kids

The Unofficial Guide to Washington, D.C.

THE *unofficial* GUIDE®

TO Walt Disney World®

2013

BOB SEHLINGER *and* LEN TESTA

(Walt Disney World® is officially known as Walt Disney World® Resort.)

Please note that prices fluctuate in the course of time and that travel information changes under the impact of many factors that influence the travel industry. We therefore suggest that you write or call ahead for confirmation when making your travel plans. Every effort has been made to ensure the accuracy of information throughout this book, and the contents of this publication are believed to be correct at the time of printing. Nevertheless, the publishers cannot accept responsibility for errors or omissions, for changes in details given in this guide, or for the consequences of any reliance on the information provided by the same. Assessments of attractions and so forth are based upon the authors' own experiences; therefore, descriptions given in this guide necessarily contain an element of subjective opinion, which may not reflect the publisher's opinion or dictate a reader's own experience on another occasion. Readers are invited to write the publisher with ideas, comments, and suggestions for future editions.

Published by:
John Wiley & Sons, Inc.
111 River St.
Hoboken, NJ 07030-5774

Produced by Menasha Ridge Press

Cover design by Paul Dinovo

Interior design by Vertigo Design

For information on our other products and services or to obtain technical support, please contact our Customer Care Department from within the United States at 800-762-2974, from outside the United States at 317-572-3993, or by fax at 317-572-4002.

John Wiley & Sons, Inc., also publishes its books in a variety of electronic formats. Some content that appears in print may not be available in electronic formats.

ISBN 978-1-118-27756-0

Manufactured in the United States of America

5 4 3 2 1

CONTENTS

LIST *of* MAPS *and* DIAGRAMS

INTRODUCTION

WHY "UNOFFICIAL"?

DECLARATION OF INDEPENDENCE

THE AUTHORS AND RESEARCHERS of this guide specifically and categorically declare that they are and always have been totally independent of the Walt Disney Company, Inc.; of Disneyland, Inc.; of Walt Disney World, Inc.; and of any and all other members of the Disney corporate family not listed.

The material in this guide originated with the authors and researchers and has not been reviewed, edited, or approved by the Walt Disney Company, Inc.; Disneyland, Inc.; or Walt Disney World, Inc.

This guidebook represents the first comprehensive *critical* appraisal of Walt Disney World. Its purpose is to provide the reader with the information necessary to tour Walt Disney World with the greatest efficiency and economy and with the least hassle.

In this guide, we represent and serve you. If a restaurant serves bad food, or a gift item is overpriced, or a ride isn't worth the wait, we say so, and in the process we hope to make your visit more fun and rewarding.

DANCE TO THE MUSIC

A DANCE HAS A BEGINNING and an end. But when you're dancing, you're not concerned about getting to the end or where on the dance floor you might wind up. In other words, you're totally in the moment. That's the way you should be on your Walt Disney World vacation.

You may feel a bit of pressure concerning your vacation. Vacations, after all, are very special events—and expensive ones to boot. So you work hard to make your vacation the best that it can be. Planning and organizing are essential to a successful Walt Disney World vacation, but if they become your focus, you won't be able to hear the music and enjoy the dance.

So think of us as your dancing coaches. We'll teach you the steps to the dance in advance so that when you're on vacation and the music plays, you'll dance with effortless grace and ease.

THE IMPORTANCE OF BEING GOOFY

EGBERT HOOFNAGEL, who coordinates the calendar for all Walt Disney World parks and venues, sits puzzling over an event to be held at the ESPN Wide World of Sports Complex. . . .

"MacDermott, can you come here for a minute?"

"Aye, boss?"

"There's a, ahem, 'ferret-legging' contest scheduled next month at the Wide World of Sports. Is this something that involves the Disney characters?"

MacDermott looks surprised. "Nae, sir, it doesn't. But as far as characters go, it will draw some of the strangest you'll ever see."

"So what *is* ferret-legging?" Hoofnagel inquires, more confused than ever.

"It's sort of a test of endurance where you stuff a live ferret down your trousers. The ferrets are quite, um, *lively* when they get in there. Whoever can suffer the beast the longest is the winner."

"Good grief! Have you ever tried ferret-legging?"

"Nae, sir, ferret-legging is for girlie-men in England and Wales. In Scotland we use the noble wolverine. Tuck it right up under our kilts, we do."

Hoofnagel's eyebrows take the elevator to the top floor and stick there, afraid to descend. "Well, do you have anything on under there— like, you know, *underpants*?" he stammers.

"You'll hafta ask the wolverine. That's a Scottish national secret."

"This doesn't sound very Disney-like," Hoofnagel says. "Do you think it's appropriate for the Wide World of Sports?"

After mulling it over a bit, MacDermott responds, "Well, it depends, but my honest opinion is that Americans are too soft for this sport. Then there are those great, baggy britches yer lads wear. The seat of the pants hangs down around the knees, it does. A proper ferret could get lost in there for a fortnight."

Hoofnagel demurs. "Americans can't stand to watch a sport where they don't win. I think we should cancel."

"Either that or start small for the Yanks, maybe mouse-legging. Works well with our corporate symbol, it does. We could call it 'Mickey's in Yer Knickies.' "

"That's *appalling*! I'd be fired on the spot!"

"How about 'Parrots in Yer Pants'? 'Weasels in Yer Y-Fronts'?"

Enter Vilmos Paprikash, a recent immigrant who's heard the whole conversation while changing the air-conditioner filter. "In East Vovodyodo, ve put chicken in pants and keep her there until she lay egg. You could try, perhaps?"

Hoofnagel groans. "You're both giving me a migraine. I *won't* sign off on anything that involves putting live animals in your clothing!"

"Easily solve!" Paprikash announces cheerily. "Ve have other game vhere you run 1-mile race vith dead sturgeon strapped to calf. That vould be perfect, yes?"

"NOOOOOOOOOOOOO!!!"

And so it goes. . . .

What really makes writing about Walt Disney World fun is that the Disney people take everything so seriously. Day to day, they debate momentous decisions with far-ranging consequences: Will Pluto look silly in a silver cape? Have we gone too far with the Little Mermaid's cleavage? With the nation's drug problem a constant concern, should we have a dwarf named Dopey?

Unofficially, we think having a sense of humor is important. This guidebook has one, and it's probably necessary that you do, too—not to use this book, but to have the most fun possible at Walt Disney World. Think of the *Unofficial Guide* as a private trainer to help get your sense of humor in shape. It will help you understand the importance of being Goofy.

HONEY, I BLEW UP THE BOOK!

THE FIRST EDITION OF *The Unofficial Guide to Walt Disney World* was fewer than 200 pages, a mere shadow of its current size. Since that edition, Disney World has grown tremendously. The *Unofficial Guide* has grown to match this expansion. (Truth be told, Bob has put on a little weight himself. Len's rate of metabolism, on the other hand, is so high that his body is incapable of producing fat.)

A mom from Streator, Illinois, was amazed by the size of the *Unofficial Guide,* writing not unsympathetically:

> It had been 10 years since we have been to WDW, and I was shocked by how the size of your book grew. After going, I'm surprised that it's so small.

We have no idea where it will all end. In 30 years we may be selling an alphabetized, 26-volume edition, handsomely packaged in an imitation-oak bookcase. In the meantime, we offer a qualified apology for the bulk of this edition. We know it may be too heavy to carry comfortably without the assistance of a handcart or Sherpa, but we defend the inclusion of all the information presented. Not every diner uses ketchup, A.1. sauce, or Tabasco, but it's nice to have all three on the table.

Concerning *Unofficial Guide* content, a mom from Vallejo, California, requests that we include a map of the Orlando airport. Other reader ideas for new content included these suggestions:

- *I think your guide should have a list of attractions that provide (1) seats, (2) air-conditioning, and (3) at least 15 minutes off your feet.*

- *I feel your* Unofficial Guide *should include a claustrophobia rating for each attraction.*

- *I wish you'd discuss restrooms more in the next edition. I found myself constantly searching for one.*

- *We think you need a rating system regarding water [i.e., how wet you can expect to get on specific attractions]. EW = Extreme Water; SW = Some Water; M = Mist.*

- *A touring plan for wimpy teens would be helpful.*

- *I'd like to see a more adult version of the one-day touring plan for the Magic Kingdom—one that doesn't include Fantasyland, the Country Bears, or Tom Sawyer Island. Title this plan "I hate those damn bears!"*

These comments are representative in that many of you would like more detailed coverage of one thing or another. Believe me, we've debated adding an airport map, as well as hundreds of other things, but haven't done so. Why? Because we don't have an infinite number of pages with which to work, and we felt other information was more important. You'd be amazed by the wealth of worthwhile material that doesn't make the cut. What if we put it all in? Well, the book would look more at home in your hayloft than on your bookshelf.

YOUR *UNOFFICIAL* WALT DISNEY WORLD TOOLBOX

YOU NEED DIFFERENT TOOLS to work on your car than you do to fix a leaky faucet or trim your azaleas. It's much the same with a Walt Disney World vacation. If we think of information as tools, a couple with two toddlers in diapers will need different tools than a party of seniors going to the Epcot International Flower & Garden Festival. Likewise, adults touring without children, families with kids of varying ages, and honeymooners all require their own special tools.

To meet the varying needs of our readers, we've created the very comprehensive guide before you. We call *The Unofficial Guide to Walt Disney World,* at about 850 pages, the "Big Book." It contains the detailed information that anyone traveling to Walt Disney World needs to have a super vacation. It's our cornerstone.

But as thorough as we try to make the main guide, there still isn't sufficient space for all the tips and resources that may be useful to certain readers. Therefore, we've developed four additional guides, each designed to work in conjunction with the Big Book and provide information tailored to specific visitors. Although some advice from the Big Book, such as arriving early at the theme parks, is echoed in these guides, most of the information is unique. You might think of the Big Book as a vacuum cleaner and the other guides as specialized attachments that certain users might need for a particular job (back to tools, you see).

Here's what's in the toolbox:

The Unofficial Guide Color Companion to Walt Disney World, by Bob Sehlinger and Len Testa, is a visual feast that proves a picture is worth a thousand words. In the Big Book, for instance, you can learn about the best guest rooms to request at the Wilderness Lodge, but in the *Color Companion* you can *see* the rooms, along with the pool and the magnificent lobby. For the first time, full-color photos illustrate how long the lines get at different times of day, how wet riders get on Splash Mountain, and how the parks are decked out for various holidays. The *Color Companion* will whet your appetite for Disney fun, picture all the attractions, serve as a keepsake, and, as always, help make your vacation more enjoyable. Most of all, the *Color Companion* is for fun. For the first time, we're able to use photography to express our zany *Unofficial* sense of humor. Think of it as Monty Python meets Walt Disney in Technicolor.

The Unofficial Guide to Walt Disney World with Kids, by Bob Sehlinger and Liliane J. Opsomer with Len Testa, presents detailed planning and touring tips for a family vacation, along with more than 20 family touring plans that are exclusive to this book.

Mini-Mickey: The Pocket-Sized Unofficial Guide to Walt Disney World, by Bob Sehlinger, Len Testa, and Ritchey Halphen, is a portable CliffsNotes-style version of *The Unofficial Guide to Walt Disney World.* It distills information from the Big Book to help short-stay or last-minute visitors decide quickly how to plan their limited hours at Disney World.

Beyond Disney: The Unofficial Guide to Universal, SeaWorld, and the Best of Central Florida, by Bob Sehlinger and Robert N. Jenkins, is a guide to non-Disney theme parks, attractions, restaurants, outdoor recreation, and nightlife in Orlando and Central Florida.

THE DEATH OF SPONTANEITY

ONE OF OUR ALL-TIME FAVORITE LETTERS came from a man in Chapel Hill, North Carolina:

> *Your book reads like the operations plan for an amphibious landing: Go here, do this, proceed to Step 15. You must think that everyone is a hyperactive, type-A theme park commando. What happened to the satisfaction of self-discovery or the joy of spontaneity? Next you'll be telling us when to empty our bladders.*

As it happens, *Unofficial Guide* researchers are a pretty existential crew. We're big on self-discovery, if the activity is walking in the woods or watching birds. Some of us are able to improvise jazz, and others can whip up a mean pot of chili without a recipe. When it comes to Disney World, however, we all agree that you need either a good plan or a frontal lobotomy. The operational definition of self-discovery and spontaneity at Walt Disney World is the "pleasure" of heat prostration and the "joy" of standing in line.

Let's face it: Walt Disney World is not a very existential place. In many ways it's the quintessential system, the ultimate in mass-produced entertainment, the most planned and programmed environment anywhere.

We aren't saying that you can't have a great time at Walt Disney World. What we *are* saying is that you need a plan. You don't have to be compulsive or inflexible; just think about what you want to do before you go. Don't delude yourself by rationalizing that the information in this guide is only for the pathological and the superorganized. Ask not for whom the tome tells, Bubba—it tells for thee.

DON'T LET THE TAIL WAG THE DOG

SOME FOLKS BECOME SO INVESTED in their plan that it becomes the centerpiece of the vacation. A Columbia, Missouri, mom, obviously intent on making every second count, offers time-saving advice that makes *Unofficial* strategies look flat-out amateurish:

> *Getting to the park when it opens is the key to beating the lines. To make that happen: (1) Pack breakfast on the go—you can eat your Pop-Tarts once you're on the shuttle bus, then drink your juice while you wait in line for Dumbo. (2) Send the fastest runner in your party to jump on the bus or boat; the driver will wait if he sees you coming and one of your kids is already hanging on. (3) Showering wastes precious park and rest time; the pool will do. (4) Braid your daughter's hair. Seriously. My 8-year-old never had to brush her hair in the*

morning (worst case: do her hair on the shuttle bus—don't waste time in your room). (5) Ball caps for boys also avoid hair brushing and help with the sun.

It's hard to imagine keeping up with this woman, but she apparently derived great satisfaction from creating and executing her plan. For most, however, the stress and doggedness of this approach would push them over the edge. Remember the basics: Know thyself, nothing to excess, and concentrate on having fun.

CORRECTIONS, UPDATES, AND BREAKING NEWS

CORRECTIONS AND UPDATES can be found online at the *Unofficial Guide* website, **touringplans.com.** Also available on the site are the WDW Crowd Calendar; more than 140 touring plans; our mobile app, Lines; trip-planning and -organizing tools; a Ticket Calculator; research reports; and breaking Walt Disney World news.

WE'VE GOT ATTITUDE

SOME READERS DISAGREE about our attitude toward Disney. A woman from Golden, Colorado, lambastes us:

I read your book cover to cover and felt you were way too hard on

Disney. It's disappointing when you're all enthused about going to Walt Disney World to be slammed with all these criticisms.

A reader from Little Rock, Arkansas, takes us to task for the opposite prejudice:

Your book was quite complimentary of Disney, perhaps too complimentary. Maybe the free trips you travel writers get at Disney World are chipping away at your objectivity.

And from a Williamsport, Pennsylvania, mother of three:

Reading your book irritated me before we went to Disney World because of all the warnings and cautions. I guess I'm used to having guidebooks pump me up about where I'm going. But once I arrived, I found I was fully prepared and we had a great time. In retrospect, I have to admit you were right on the money. What I regarded as you being negative was just a good dose of reality.

unofficial **TIP**
Check out experienced Disney World visitors' opinions of the parks in this book, and apply them to your own travel circumstances.

Finally, a reader from Phoenixville, Pennsylvania, prefers no opinions at all, writing:

While each person has the right to his or her own opinion, I didn't purchase the book for an opinion.

For the record, we've always paid our own way at Walt Disney World: hotels, admissions, meals, the works. We don't dislike Disney, and we don't have an ax to grind. We're positive by nature and much prefer to praise than to criticize. Personally, we have enjoyed the Disney parks immensely over the years, both experiencing them and writing about them. Disney, however, as with all corporations (and all people), is better at some things than others. Because our readers shell out big bucks to go to Walt Disney World, we believe they have the right to know in advance what's good and what's not. For those who think we're overly positive, please understand that the *Unofficial Guide* is a guidebook, not an exposé. Our aim is for you to enjoy your visit. To that end, we report fairly and objectively. When readers disagree with our opinions, we, in the interest of fairness, publish their viewpoints alongside ours. To the best of our knowledge, the *Unofficial Guides* are the only travel guides in print that do this.

THE SUM OF ALL FEARS

EVERY WRITER WHO EXPRESSES an opinion is accustomed to readers who strongly agree or disagree: It comes with the territory. Extremely troubling, however, is the possibility that our efforts to be objective have frightened some readers away from Walt Disney World or made others apprehensive.

A mom from Avon, Ohio, was just such a person, writing:

After reading parts of the Unofficial Guide, *I seriously reconsidered going to WDW at all. We've been to other theme parks before, and I felt that WDW required too much planning. It actually stressed me out to read your guide (at first), because it seemed that WDW had too many pitfalls—too many things to plan for that could go wrong, too many horrible outcomes (like waiting for hours in scorching heat with kids), etc. My friend convinced me it wouldn't be that bad, however, so I kept on with planning the trip.*

We certainly understand the reader's feelings, but the key point was that, though apprehensive, she stayed the course. Here's what she said after returning home:

Let me tell you, your guide and touring plans were dead-on accurate! We didn't wait more than 10 or 15 minutes for almost every attraction in two days!

For the record, if you enjoy theme parks, Disney World is as good as it gets, absolute nirvana. If you arrive without knowing a thing about the place and make every possible mistake, chances are about 90% that you'll have a wonderful vacation anyway. In the end, guidebooks don't make or break great destinations. Rather, they're simply tools to help you enhance your experience and get the most for your money.

As wonderful as Walt Disney World is, however, it's a complex destination. Even so, it isn't nearly as challenging or difficult as, say, New York, San Francisco, or Paris. And, happily, there are numerous ways to save money, minimize hassle, and make the most of your time. That's what this guide is about: giving you a heads-up regarding potential problems and opportunities. Unfortunately, some *Unofficial Guide* readers add up the warnings and critical advice and conclude that Walt Disney World is too intimidating, too expensive, or too much work. They lose track of the wonder of Disney World and focus instead on what might go wrong.

Our philosophy is that knowledge is power (and time and money, too). You're free to follow our advice or not at your discretion. But you can't exercise that discretion if we fail to present the issues.

With or without a guidebook, you'll have a great time at Walt Disney World. If you let us, we'll help you smooth the potential bumps. We're certain we can help you turn a great vacation into an absolutely superb one. Either way, once there, you'll get the feel of the place and quickly reach a comfort level that will allay your apprehensions and allow you to have a wonderful experience.

TOO MANY COOKS IN THE KITCHEN?

WE RECEIVED THIS QUERY from a Manchester, Vermont, reader and feel it deserves a serious response:

> *I read a review on the Internet criticizing the* Unofficial Guide *because it was "written by a team of researchers." The reviewer doesn't say why he thinks the team approach is inferior, but the inference is along the lines of "too many cooks spoil the soup." Why do you use this approach?*

There are several reasons. Foremost is that the team approach enables us to undertake much more sophisticated and extensive research. Collecting waiting-time data for our touring plan software (see page 68), for example, requires that more than a dozen researchers visit the Disney parks for several days at eight or more different times of year.

unofficial **TIP**
Researching and writing this book as a team results in a more objective guidebook for you.

Another project, monitoring the Disney transportation system, requires riding and timing every bus, boat, and monorail route, a task that takes four researchers almost a week to complete. In covering lodging, the *Unofficial Guide* reviews, rates, and ranks about 250 Disney World–area hotels, more than four times as many as other guidebooks. On any research trip, we have one or two teams of hotel inspectors checking hotels all day long.

No other guides do this, nor can they, because the scope of the research and processing of data require time, experience, and resources beyond the capabilities of a single author or even several coauthors. An entire organization collects and compiles the information for the *Unofficial Guide*, an organization guided by individuals with extensive training and experience in research design, as well as data collection and analysis. Known and respected in both the travel industry and academe, *Unofficial Guide* research has been recognized by *USA Today,* the BBC, *The New York Times,* the *Dallas Morning News,* the Travel Channel, and CNN, as well as by numerous academic journals.

Not all *Unofficial Guide* research relates to the parks and resorts. We also conduct extensive research on you, the reader. From the concept up, you see, *Unofficial Guides* are different from other guidebooks. Other guides are researched and developed by individual authors or coauthors, usually travel writers. Thus, everything is filtered through the lens of those authors' tastes, preferences, and opinions. Publishers of these guides hope the information the author presents is compatible with the needs of the reader, but if it is, the compatibility is largely accidental. In *Unofficial Guides,* by contrast, it's your tastes, preferences, and opinions that dictate the content of the guides. In other words, we start with the needs of our readers, identified through exhaustive research, and build a book that meets those needs.

Another reason for using a team approach is to minimize author bias. As discussed earlier, a single author incorporates his or her own tastes and opinions in his work. Our researchers, by contrast, include individuals ranging in age from 12 to 70 and sometimes, for special assignments, children as young as 8. Thus the opinions and advice in the *Unofficial Guide* are informed by the perspectives of a diverse group of researchers—a process that, we believe, achieves the highest level of objectivity.

Finally, understand that no individual author can possibly be qualified to write about every topic in the vast range of important subjects that make up a good guide to Walt Disney World. Thus, our chapter on Walt Disney World with Kids (Part Six) was developed in consultation with three nationally respected child psychologists and an advisory group of parents. Similarly, we have professional culinary experts dedicated to the task of rating restaurants. Our golf coverage, likewise, is handled by pro-golf writer Larry Olmsted, and our database and touring plan program are developed and managed by programmer and software developer Len Testa. When you cover shopping, you want a local who lives to shop and knows where to find every back-counter deal within 50 miles. Guess what? We've got her! In a nutshell, there are more of us so that we can do more for you. We (Bob and Len) put the fruits of our research into words, but behind us is an organization unequaled in travel publishing.

THE *UNOFFICIAL* TEAM

SO WHO ARE THESE FOLKS? Allow us to introduce them all, except for our dining critic, who shall remain anonymous:

Our website stays running with the talents of Scarlett Litton, who runs the blog and leads our social-media team; statisticians Steve Bloom and Brian McNichols; web developer Brad Huber; Todd Perlmutter, who develops our touring plan software; David Davies, our jack-of-all-trades; and Gerelyn Reaves, who answers e-mail, keeps up with park hours, and generally keeps us running. Henry Work created our Lines app.

Finally, we'd like to thank the following folks for their proofreading and fact-checking assistance: Patricia Arnold, Caroline Baggerly, Brandon Baker, Johnny Bean, Jennifer Bearden, Scott Berry, Shiraz Biggie, Isabelle Boivin, Chris Bowers, Jennifer Bowles, Annette Broskie, Steven Cantafio, Gerald Carpenter, Ann Caugh, Karen Chappell, Scott and JC Chupack, Robyne Clement, Mary Jo Collins, Tanya Conklin, Jennifer B. Davis, Diana Drummond, Ann Dunnington, Annette Forde, Rich Gairing, James Garfield, Ashley Graham, Shane Grizzard, Mary Hagedorn, Jamie Hagel, Marie Hillin, Jacquelyn M. Howard, Lisa Johnson, Kimberly Knight, Susan Kometz, Andrea Kurczewski,

BOB SEHLINGER Author and executive publisher
LEN TESTA Coauthor, **touringplans.com**
software developer, data-collection director
RITCHEY HALPHEN Managing editor
FRED HAZELTON Statistician
SARAH KELLETH **touringplans.com** webmaster,
Lines developer
KRISTEN HELMSTETTER Survey collator

KAREN TURNBOW, PhD
Child psychologist
JIM HILL Disney historian
PAM BRANDON Shopping guru
LARRY OLMSTED Golf expert
TAMI KNIGHT Cartoonist
LAUREL STEWART
Fact-checking supervisor

DATA COLLECTORS
Rob Sutton *Supervisor*
Chantale Brazeau
Kai Brückerhoff
Kenny Cottrell
Guy Garguilo
Shane Grizzard
Scarlett Litton
Lillian Macko
Richard Macko
Kristen Mitchell
Megan Parks
Cliff Myers
Robert Pederson
Jeff "Fred" Reisdorf
Julie Saunders
Darcie Vance
Rich Vosburgh
Kelly Whitman

CONTRIBUTING WRITERS
Rich Bernato
J. L. Knopp
Liliane J. Opsomer
Sue Pisaturo
Laurel Stewart
Darcie Vance
Mary Waring
Deb Wills

HOTEL INSPECTORS
Ritchey Halphen
Kristen Helmstetter
Lillian Macko
Richard Macko
Myra E. Merkle
Darcie Vance

EDITORIAL & PRODUCTION
Annie Long *Typesetter*
Steve Jones, Scott McGrew
Cartographers
Ann Cassar *Indexer*

Proofreaders
Susan Cullen Anderson
Ashley M. Arthur
Emily C. Beaumont
Julie Hall Bosché
Taryn Chase Jackson
Kate McWhorter Johnson
Carolyn Acree Jones
Ashley Leath
Gabriela Oates
L. Amanda Owens
Susan Roberts
Terri Robertson
Vanessa Rusch
Laura Shauger
Andy Sloan
Lady Vowell Smith

John Kutey, Gene Langenberger, Jen Langenberger, Rebeccah Linder-Murray, Amy Morell Lucas, Carol Lyons, Sarah Maisel, Christa Martin, Mary Martin, Tanya Mathis, Shari Matz, Chris G. Maxwell, Patti McCumber, Rebecca Noun McDermott, Graeme "OzGuff" McGufficke, Gretchen McKinley, Robert McKinnon, Heather Melito-Dezan, Richard Mercer, Marvin Miller, Michelle E. Miller, Sara Moore, Sue Motroni, Kim Mullins, Jill Odice, Kimberly Oehrlein, Jason Osinski, Jennifer Paolino, Jeff Pincus, Eric and Tracy Raymond, Jennifer Reall, Dan Record, Ashley A. Reeve, Chris W. Ridgeway, Trina Rowe, Dr. Roger T. Sauer, Saundra Schmidt, Andy Scott, Anna Scott, Joi Scott, Kelly Bryant Seymore, Jol Silversmith, Betsy Silvestri, Teri Sizemore, Glenn Sonoda, Kristen Sprague, Paige Steel, Lauren Stewart, Raymie Summey, Kurt Sutton, Bob Thomas, Erin Vick, Ingrid Vinson, Susan K. Van Vleet, Rich Vosburgh, Kevin Wallace, Tracy Wentz, George Robert White, Katina Williams, and Connie Wolosyk.

THE HOW AND THE WHY OF IT

A DAYTON, OHIO, READER offers the following comment:

> I used several guides preparing for our Disney World trip. One of them dumped on the Unofficial Guide for referring to Dumbo as a "cycle ride." Though my kids are totally infatuated with Dumbo, I found your section about how the various types of rides work to be both interesting and useful. Dumbo's charm and appeal don't change the fact that it's a cycle ride. Get a life!

Most guidebooks do a reasonably good job with what and where. *Unofficial Guides* add the how and why. Describing attractions or hotels or restaurants (the what) at a given destination (the where) is the foundation of other travel guidebooks. We know from our research, however, that our readers like to know how things work. Take hotels, for example. In the *Unofficial Guide,* we not only provide hotel choices (rated and ranked, of course) but also explain the economic and operational logic of the lodging industry (the why) and offer instructions (the how) that enable the reader to take advantage of opportunities for hotel discounts, room upgrades, and the like. In this and all our *Unofficial Guides,* whether we're discussing cruise ships, theme parks, ski resorts, casinos, or golf courses, we reveal the travel industry's inner workings and demonstrate how to use such insight in selecting and purchasing travel and for planning itineraries. For the reader, knowledge is power, which translates into informed decisions and confidence.

THIS IS NOT A NOVEL!

THOUGH THIS GUIDE IS FULL OF CHARACTERS—and was created by a few more—it is at heart a reference work, and many readers do not read it cover-to-cover, as they would a piece of fiction. For some this causes problems—witness this angry reader who identified him/herself as "None of Your Business":

> *This e-mail is in regards to* The Unofficial Guide to Walt Disney World, *which I purchased last year for our trip to Disney World this year. I am very disappointed that the book doesn't mention that an additional fee is required to access the touring plans and crowd-level information on your website. Here is an excerpt from the book:*
>
> **If you decide to splurge and burn a pass on a half-day or less, refer to our** *Unofficial Guide* **Crowd-Level Calendar at touringplans.com.**
>
> *The book refers to this website in other sections as well but does not mention that a fee is involved! I don't mind paying, but I am disgusted that you would not mention it in your book.*
>
> *You are hypocrites, and I will not purchase another* Unofficial Guide. *Shame on me for assuming this information would be free, even though I shelled out $23.99 [Canadian] for the book.*
>
> *Print this in your guide, Len and Bob.*

Don't you hate it when people hide their true feelings just to be polite? In any event, None of Your Business's complaint illustrates how readers use the guide in different ways. Here's our reply to NOYB:

> *Dear None,*
>
> *Thanks for your letter. Here's the thing:*
>
> The Unofficial Guide to Walt Disney World *is used by many readers as a reference work as opposed to a cover-to-cover read. Consequently, a reader might miss something, say, at the beginning of the guide, that provides information necessary for understanding references to the same subject elsewhere. For several editions, we've been explaining in Part One, Gathering Information, specifically what*

readers can access on our website at no cost and what they can access only with a paid subscription.

In the last edition, this information read as follows:

Much of our web content, including our computer-optimized touring plans, the resort photos and video, and the Ticket Calculator, is completely free for anyone to use. Access to part of the site, most notably the Crowd Calendar, additional touring plans, and in-park wait times, requires a small subscription fee (current-book owners get a substantial discount). This nominal charge helps keep us online and costs less than a sandwich at Flame Tree Barbecue in Disney's Animal Kingdom. Plus, **touringplans.com** offers a 45-day money-back guarantee—something we don't think the Flame Tree can match.

In an 850-page book, it's unrealistic for us to think everyone will read every word. On the other hand, when it comes to something that's mentioned a number of times throughout the book, it's totally impractical to explain it again and again each time it's referenced. So we don't blame you for being angry—you probably were using the guide as a reference and just missed the explanation.

All the best,
Bob and Len

To sum up: If you use the guide like an encyclopedia or dictionary —for example, you look something up in one of the indexes, then go to the cited page—you may overlook information presented in previous sections that is vital to understanding the subject. Likewise, if you skip or skim over explanatory material in the introductory chapters, that might lead to a misunderstanding later on.

THE *UNOFFICIAL GUIDE* PUBLISHING YEAR

WE RECEIVE MANY QUERIES asking when the next edition of the *Unofficial Guide* will be available. Usually our new editions are in stores by late August or early September. Thus, the 2014 edition will be on the shelves in August or September 2013.

LETTERS AND COMMENTS FROM READERS

MANY WHO USE *The Unofficial Guide to Walt Disney World* write us to comment or share their own strategies for visiting Disney World. We appreciate all such input, both positive and critical, and encourage our readers to continue writing. Their comments and observations are frequently incorporated into revised editions of the *Unofficial Guide* and have contributed immeasurably to its improvement. If you write us or return our reader-survey form, rest assured that we won't release your name and address to any mailing-list companies, direct-mail advertisers, or other third party. Unless you instruct us otherwise, we'll assume that you don't object to being quoted in the *Unofficial Guide*.

unofficial **TIP**
If you're up for having your comments quoted in the guide, please be sure to tell us your hometown.

Reader Survey and Restaurant Survey

At the back of this guide is a questionnaire you can use to express opinions about your Walt Disney World visit. The questionnaire allows every member of your party, regardless of age, to tell us what he or she thinks. Use the separate restaurant survey to describe your Disney World dining experiences. Clip the questionnaire and restaurant survey and mail them to: Reader Survey, The *Unofficial Guide* Series, P.O. Box 43673, Birmingham, AL 35243. For your convenience, an electronic version of both surveys can be found online at **touringplans.com/walt -disney-world/survey.**

How to Contact the Authors

Bob Sehlinger and Len Testa
The Unofficial Guide to Walt Disney World
P.O. Box 43673
Birmingham, AL 35243
unofficialguides@menasharidge.com

When you write, put your address on both your letter and envelope; the two sometimes get separated. It's also a good idea to include your phone number. If you e-mail us, please tell us where you're from. Remember, as travel writers, we're often out of the office for long periods of time, so forgive us if our response is slow. *Unofficial Guide* e-mail isn't forwarded to us when we're traveling, but we'll respond as soon as possible after we return.

WALT DISNEY WORLD: *An* OVERVIEW

IF YOU'RE CHOOSING A U.S. TOURIST DESTINATION, the question is not whether to visit Walt Disney World, but how to see its best offerings with some economy of time, effort, and finances.

WHAT WALT DISNEY WORLD ENCOMPASSES

WALT DISNEY WORLD COMPRISES 43 square miles, an area twice as large as Manhattan. Situated strategically in this vast expanse are the **Magic Kingdom, Epcot, Disney's Hollywood Studios,** and **Disney's Animal Kingdom** theme parks; 2 swimming theme parks; a sports complex; 5 golf courses; 36 hotels and a campground; more than 100 restaurants; 4 interconnected lakes; a shopping complex; 8 convention venues; a nature preserve; and a transportation system consisting of four-lane highways, elevated monorails, and a network of canals.

Walt Disney World has around 62,000 employees, or "cast members," making it the largest single-site employer in the United States. Keeping the costumes of those cast members clean requires the equivalent of 16,000 loads of laundry a day and the dry cleaning of 30,000 garments daily. (Mickey Mouse alone has 290 different sets of duds, ranging from a scuba wet suit to a tux; Minnie boasts more than 200 outfits.) Each year, Disney restaurants serve 10 million burgers, 6 million hot dogs, 75 million Cokes, 9 million pounds of French fries, and 150 tons of popcorn. In the state of Florida, only Miami and Jacksonville have bus systems larger than Disney World's. The Disney monorail trains have logged mileage equal to more than 30 round-trips to the moon.

DISNEY-SPEAK POCKET TRANSLATOR AND GUIDE TO COMMON ABBREVIATIONS

IT MAY COME AS A SURPRISE to many, but Walt Disney World has its own somewhat peculiar language. See the charts below and on page 17 for some terms and abbreviations you're likely to bump into, both in this guide and in the larger Disney (and Universal) community.

DISNEY-SPEAK	English Definition
ADVENTURE	Ride
ATTRACTION	Ride or theater show
ATTRACTION HOST	Ride operator
AUDIENCE	Crowd
BACKSTAGE	Behind the scenes, out of view of customers
BULL PEN	Queuing area
CAST MEMBER	Employee
CHARACTER	Disney character impersonated by an employee
COSTUME	Work attire or uniform
DARK RIDE	Indoor ride
DAY GUEST	Any customer not staying at a Disney resort
FACE CHARACTER	A character who doesn't wear a head-covering costume (Snow White, Cinderella, Jasmine, and the like)
GENERAL PUBLIC	Same as day guest
GREETER	Employee positioned at an attraction entrance
GUEST	Customer
HIDDEN MICKEYS	Frontal silhouette of Mickey's head worked subtly into the design of buildings, railings, golf greens, attractions, and just about anything else
IN REHEARSAL	Operating, though not officially open
LEAD	Foreman or manager, the person in charge of an attraction
ON STAGE	In full view of customers
PRESHOW	Entertainment at an attraction before the feature presentation
RESORT GUEST	A customer staying at a Disney resort
ROLE	A cast member's job
SECURITY HOST	Security guard
SOFT OPENING	Opening a park or attraction before its stated opening date
TRANSITIONAL EXPERIENCE	An element of the queuing area and/or preshow that provides a storyline or information essential to understanding the attraction

THE MAJOR THEME PARKS

The Magic Kingdom

When people think of Walt Disney World, most think of the Magic Kingdom, opened in 1971. It consists of the adventures, rides, and shows featuring the Disney cartoon characters, and Cinderella Castle. It's only one element of Disney World, but it remains the heart.

The Magic Kingdom is divided into six "lands," with five arranged around a central hub. First you come to **Main Street, U.S.A.,** which

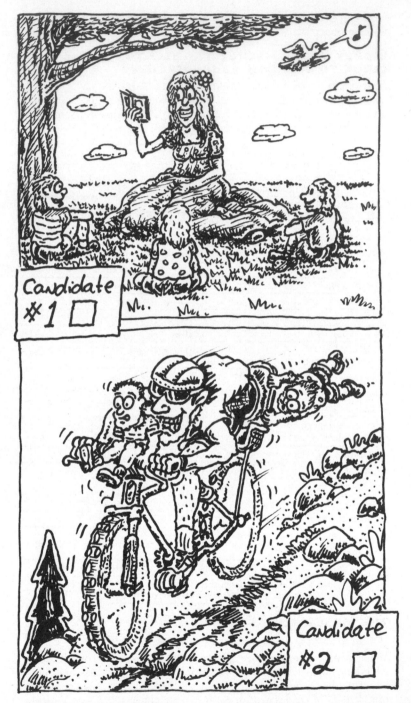

SURVEY: *Which author do you prefer to write your guidebooks?*
(Guess which one you got?)

ABBREVIATION	WHAT IT STANDS FOR
CM	Cast member
CRS	Central Reservations System
DCL	Disney Cruise Line
DDRA	Downtown Disney Resort Area
DDV	Disney Deluxe Villas
DHS	Disney's Hollywood Studios
DTS	Disney Transportation System
DVC	Disney Vacation Club
EMH	Extra Magic Hours
I-DRIVE	International Drive (major Orlando thoroughfare)
IOA	Universal's Islands of Adventure theme park
OTA	Online travel agency
TTC	Ticket and Transportation Center
WDI	Walt Disney Imagineering
WDTC	Walt Disney Travel Company
WDW	Walt Disney World
WWOHP	The Wizarding World of Harry Potter (at IOA)

connects the Magic Kingdom entrance with the hub. Clockwise around the hub are **Adventureland, Frontierland, Liberty Square, Fantasyland,** and **Tomorrowland.** Five hotels (**Bay Lake Tower;** the **Contemporary, Polynesian,** and **Grand Floridian** resorts; and the **Grand Floridian Disney Vacation Club** complex) are connected to the Magic Kingdom by monorail and boat. Two other hotels, **Shades of Green** and **Wilderness Lodge & Villas,** are nearby but aren't served by the monorail.

Epcot

Opened in October 1982, Epcot is twice as big as the Magic Kingdom and comparable in scope. It has two major areas: **Future World** consists of pavilions concerning human creativity and technological advancement; **World Showcase,** arranged around a 40-acre lagoon, presents the architectural, social, and cultural heritages of almost a dozen nations, each country represented by replicas of famous landmarks and settings familiar to world travelers.

The Epcot resort hotels—the **BoardWalk Inn & Villas, Caribbean Beach Resort, Dolphin, Swan,** and **Yacht & Beach Club Resorts and Beach Club Villas**—are within a 5- to 15-minute walk of the International Gateway (back-door) entrance to the theme park. The hotels are also linked to Epcot and Disney's Hollywood Studios by canal. Epcot is connected to the Magic Kingdom and its hotels by monorail.

Disney's Hollywood Studios

Opened in 1989 as Disney-MGM Studios and a little larger than the Magic Kingdom, Disney's Hollywood Studios has two areas. The first is a theme park focused on the past, present, and future of the motion picture and television industries. This section contains movie-theme rides and shows and covers about half of the complex. Park highlights include a re-creation of Hollywood and Sunset boulevards from Hollywood's Golden Age, stunt demonstrations, a children's play area, shows on sound effects, and four high-tech rides.

The second area, a (mostly idle) motion picture and television production facility, encompasses soundstages, a backlot of streets and sets, and support services. Public access is limited to tours that, among others, take visitors behind the scenes for crash courses on Disney animation and moviemaking.

Disney's Hollywood Studios is connected to other Walt Disney World areas by highway and canal but not by monorail. Guests can park in the Studios' pay parking lot or commute by bus. Guests at Epcot resort hotels can reach the Studios by boat or on foot.

Disney's Animal Kingdom

About five times the size of the Magic Kingdom, Disney's Animal Kingdom combines zoological exhibits with rides, shows, and live entertainment. The park is arranged somewhat like the Magic Kingdom, in a hub-and-spoke configuration. A lush tropical rainforest serves as Main Street, funneling visitors to **Discovery Island,** the park's hub. Dominated by the park's central icon, the 14-story-tall, hand-carved **Tree of Life,** Discovery Island offers services, shopping, and dining. From there, guests can access the themed areas: **Africa, Asia, DinoLand U.S.A.,** and **Camp Minnie-Mickey.** Discovery Island, Africa, Camp Minnie-Mickey, and DinoLand U.S.A. opened in 1998, followed by Asia in 1999. Africa, the largest themed area, at 100 acres, features free-roaming herds in a re-creation of the Serengeti Plain. Guests tour in open-air safari vehicles.

Disney's Animal Kingdom has its own parking lot and is connected to other Walt Disney World destinations by the Disney bus system. Although no hotels lie within Animal Kingdom proper, the **All-Star Resorts, Animal Kingdom Lodge & Villas,** and **Coronado Springs Resort** are all nearby.

THE WATER PARKS

DISNEY WORLD HAS TWO MAJOR water parks: **Typhoon Lagoon** and **Blizzard Beach.** Opened in 1989, Typhoon Lagoon is distinguished by a wave pool capable of making 6-foot waves. Blizzard Beach is newer, having opened in 1995, and it features more slides. Both parks are beautifully landscaped, and great attention is paid to atmosphere and aesthetics. Typhoon Lagoon and Blizzard Beach have their own adjacent parking lots and can be reached by Disney bus.

OTHER WALT DISNEY WORLD VENUES

Downtown Disney (Downtown Disney Marketplace and Downtown Disney West Side)

Downtown Disney is a large shopping, dining, and entertainment complex that encompasses **Downtown Disney Marketplace** on the east,

Downtown Disney West Side on the west, and **Pleasure Island** in the middle. Downtown Disney Marketplace contains the world's largest Disney-character-merchandise store, upscale resort-wear and specialty shops, and several restaurants, including the tacky-but-popular **Rainforest Cafe** and its equally tacky cousin, **T-REX**. Downtown Disney West Side, which opened in 1997, combines nightlife, shopping, dining, and entertainment. The **House of Blues** serves Cajun-Creole dishes in its restaurant and electric blues in its music hall. **Bongos Cuban Cafe,** a nightclub and cafe created by Gloria Estefan and her husband, Emilio, offers Cuban rhythms and flavors. **Wolfgang Puck Grand Cafe,** sandwiched among pricey boutiques, is the West Side's prestige eatery. For entertainment, you'll find a 24-screen cinema; a permanent showplace for the extraordinary 70-person cast of **Cirque du Soleil** *La Nouba;* and **DisneyQuest,** an interactive virtual reality and electronic-games venue. Access Downtown Disney via Disney buses from most Disney World locations.

BoardWalk

Near Epcot, the BoardWalk is an idealized replication of an East Coast 1930s waterfront resort. Open all day, the BoardWalk features upscale restaurants, shops and galleries, a brewpub, and an ESPN sports bar. In the evening, a nightclub with dueling pianos and a DJ dance club join the lineup. There's no admission fee for the BoardWalk, but some individual clubs levy cover charges at night. In addition to the public facilities are a 371-room Deluxe hotel and a 532-unit time-share development. The BoardWalk is within walking distance of the Epcot resorts and Epcot's International Gateway. Boat transportation is available to and from Epcot and Disney's Hollywood Studios; buses serve other Disney World locations.

ESPN Wide World of Sports Complex

The 220-acre Wide World of Sports is a state-of-the-art competition and training facility consisting of a 9,500-seat ballpark, two field houses, and venues for baseball, softball, tennis, track and field, beach volleyball, and 27 other sports. The spring-training home of the Atlanta Braves, the complex also hosts a mind-boggling calendar of professional and amateur competitions. Walt Disney World guests are welcome as paying spectators but can't use the facilities unless they're participating in a scheduled competition.

Disney Cruise Line

In 1998, the Walt Disney Company launched (literally) its own cruise line with the 2,400-passenger *Disney Magic.* Its sister ship, the *Disney Wonder,* first sailed in 1999. Cruises depart from Port Canaveral, Florida (about a 90-minute drive from Walt Disney World), on three-, four-, and seven-night itineraries. Caribbean and Bahamian cruises include a day at **Castaway Cay,** Disney's private island. Cruises can be packaged with a stay at Disney World. Although the cruises are family-oriented, extensive children's programs and elaborate child-care facilities allow parents plenty of opportunity for time away from the kids. In 2011 and 2012, respectively, two new ships, the *Disney Dream* and the *Disney Fantasy*, joined the fleet, enabling the Disney Cruise Line to expand sailings to the Caribbean, Alaska, the Mexican Riviera, and the Mediterranean. For more on the Disney Cruise Line, see Part Five.

THE PEOPLE

HOW YOU'RE TREATED BY THE CAST MEMBERS you encounter at Walt Disney World can make or break a vacation. Fortunately, Disney staff often go the extra mile to make your visit special, as the following three readers report. First, from a New York City man:

> I lost my glasses during the trip and had to go 24 hours awaiting a spare pair to be sent by overnight mail. Went to Sunshine Seasons for lunch; found a cast member and explained my situation. Said I couldn't read the menu displays and asked for a printed menu. He said they didn't have those but offered to tell me what was available. I said that would be too much bother; his response: "You're why I'm here." He took me to each of the four stations and described every dish. When I had my order, he took me to the dessert station and told me every option. Then he got my drink for me along with napkins, utensils, and a straw, then escorted me to the cashier.

A family from St. Joseph, Michigan, has this to relate:

> We had a very unexpected and wonderful surprise waiting in our stroller after the Country Bear Jamboree. Out of nearly 30 strollers, ours had been visited by Santa Mickey while we were in the show. We came out to a stroller decorated with silly bands, Christmas ornaments, and a snowman Mickey plush toy. Our 5-year-old son was delighted, not to mention the rest of our party. Just another way that WDW goes one more step to make a magical experience.

Finally, from a suburban Philadelphia family:

> At Expedition Everest, I witnessed expert handling of a group of teenage line-jumpers by Disney staff. Once they reached the loading area, cast members ushered them aside in a very calm and friendly fashion, causing no apparent disruption. I didn't see where they were ushered or what happened next, but I did not see them board the ride. It was as if they were never there.

"No, no . . . really, it's OK. It's just not what I expected."

South Orlando & Walt Disney World Area

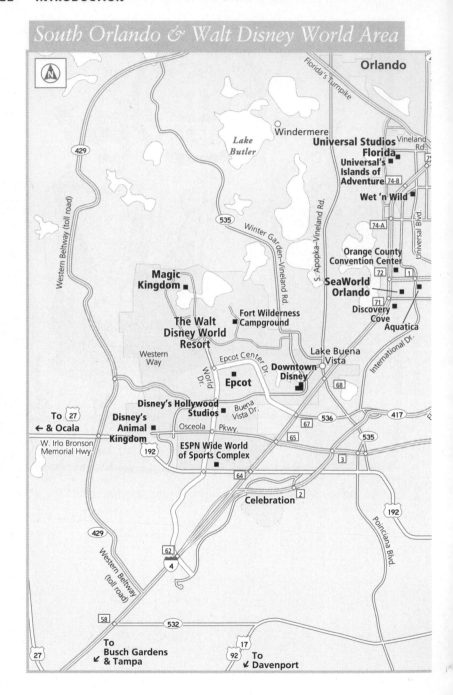

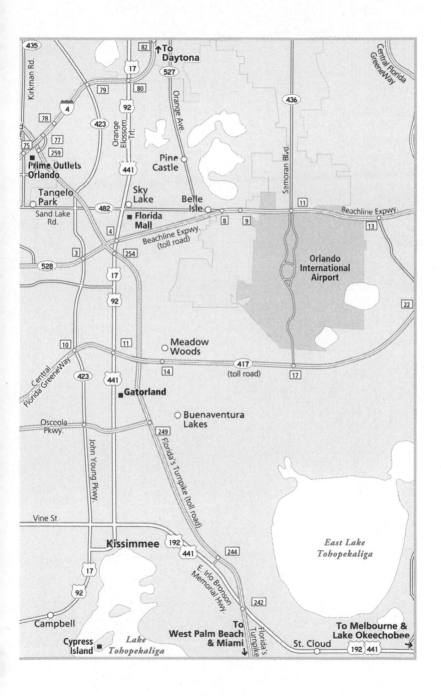

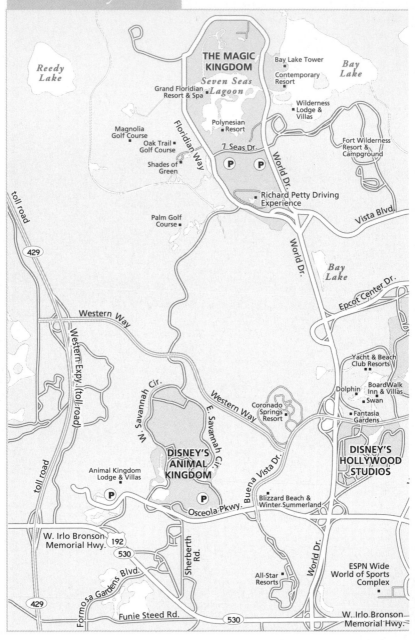

Walt Disney World

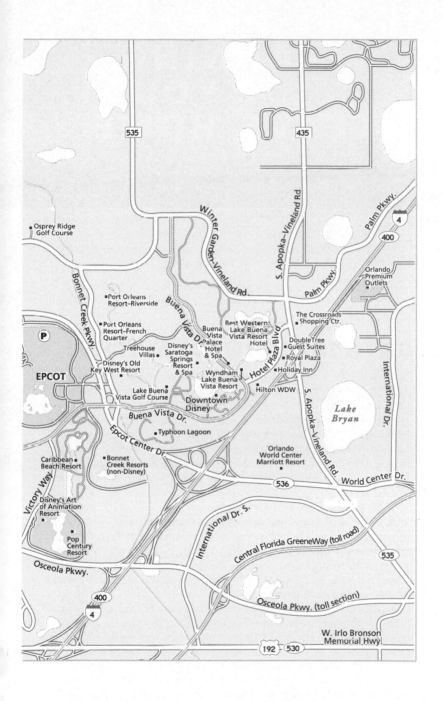

PART ONE

PLANNING *before* YOU LEAVE HOME

Visiting Walt Disney World is a bit like childbirth—you never really believe what people tell you, but once you have been through it yourself, you know exactly what they were saying!

—Hilary Wolfe, a mother and
Unofficial Guide reader from Swansea, Wales

GATHERING INFORMATION

IN ADDITION TO USING THIS GUIDE, we recommend that you visit our website, **touringplans.com,** which offers essential tools for planning your trip and saving you time and money.

One of the most popular parts of touringplans.com is our **Crowd Calendar,** which shows crowd projections for each Disney and Universal theme park for every day of the year. Look up the dates of your visit, and the calendar will not only show the projected wait times for each day but will also indicate for each day which theme park will be the least crowded.

We've launched two new website features since the last edition of this book. First, with our **computer-optimized touring plans,** you choose the attractions you want to experience, including character greetings, parades, fireworks, meals, and midday breaks, and we'll give you a step-by-step itinerary for doing all those things while minimizing your wait in line. It's great for figuring out how much you can realistically see in the amount of time you have available.

A particularly cool feature of the software is that you can use it to update your plans as your needs change. Let's say your touring plan calls for riding The Haunted Mansion next but your family *really* needs an ice-cream break and 30 minutes out of the sun. Get the ice cream and take the break; when you're done, just click the "Optimize" button on your phone, and your plan will be updated with what to do next. Want to add another ride on Space Mountain? Tell the software and click the "Optimize" button, and another updated plan will appear. Nifty, no?

We've also added **complete dining menus** for all of Walt Disney World. We spent more than a month collecting menus from every food cart, stand, kiosk, counter-service restaurant, and sit-down restaurant in Walt Disney World. Then we entered everything—more than 11,000 items—into a giant database and put it online. The whole thing is searchable, too, so you can find every restaurant in Epcot that serves steak (and its prices), or see which snacks at the Main Street Bakery are eligible for the Disney Dining Plan. Updated constantly, these menus represent the most accurate collection of Disney dining information available anywhere.

Both the computer-optimized touring plans and menus are available in **Lines,** our mobile application, which provides continuous real-time updates on wait times at Walt Disney World and Disneyland. Using a combination of our in-park research and updates sent in by readers, Lines shows you the current wait and Fastpass-distribution times at every attraction in every park, as well as our estimated wait times for these attractions for the rest of today and tomorrow. For example, Lines will tell you that the posted wait time for Space Mountain is 60 minutes, and that based on what we know about how Disney manages Space Mountain's queue, the actual time you'll probably wait in line is 48 minutes. Lines is the only Disney app that shows you both posted and actual wait times.

Lines is available free to touringplans.com subscribers for the Apple iPhone and iPad at the iTunes Store (search for "TouringPlans"; requires iOS 3.2 or later) and for Android devices at the Google Play Store (requires Android 2.1 Eclair or later); owners of other phones can use the web-based version at **m.touringplans.com.**

As long as you've got that smartphone handy while visiting the World, we and your fellow *Unofficial Guide* readers would love it if you could report on the wait times you see while you're there. Run Lines, log in to your user account, and click "+Time" in the upper right corner to help everyone out.

Lines has been extremely well received—so well, in fact, that some users can't wean themselves off of it when they return home. A Deerfield, New Hampshire, wife writes:

We absolutely LOVED Lines. We've been home from vacation for several days, and my husband is still checking the wait times and loving the fact that we got out of there before the Thanksgiving rush.

From a Philadelphia reader:

Your app is amazing! I took my iPad with me to the parks, and it was very helpful. Several times the posted wait for the standby line at an attraction was long, but Lines said it wasn't. I took a chance and used the standby line, and you were right—I walked on without any more wait than the Fastpass users.

A Clinton, Massachusetts, mom using Lines discovered an unexpected benefit:

The phone app was also great for occupying my 9-year-old son. He loved checking wait times! At night, back at the hotel, he would ask to borrow my phone so he could see how long people at MK were waiting for Splash Mountain.

A big money-saving feature of the website is our **Disney Ticket Calculator** (see page 50), which tells you the most economical combination of tickets to buy (and where to buy them) to see everything you want in the theme parks and water parks.

Much of our web content, including the computer-optimized touring plans, menus, resort photos and video, Ticket Calculator, and updates and changes to this guide, is completely free. Access to part of the site, most notably the Crowd Calendar, additional touring plans, and in-park wait times, requires a small subscription fee (current-book owners get a substantial discount). This nominal charge helps keep us online and costs less than a sandwich at Flame Tree Barbecue in Disney's Animal Kingdom. Plus, **touringplans.com** offers a 45-day money-back guarantee—something we don't think Flame Tree can match.

Next, we recommend that you obtain the following:

1. **THE WALT DISNEY TRAVEL COMPANY FLORIDA VACATIONS BROCHURE AND DVD** These cover Walt Disney World in its entirety, list rates for all Disney resort hotels and campgrounds, and describe Disney World package vacations. They're available from most travel agents, by calling the Walt Disney Travel Company at ☎ 407-828-8101 or 407-934-7639, or by visiting **disneyworld.com.** Be prepared to hold. When you get a representative, ask for the DVD vacation planner.

2. **THE DISNEY CRUISE LINE BROCHURE AND DVD** This brochure provides details on vacation packages that combine a cruise on the Disney Cruise Line with a stay at Disney World. Disney Cruise Line also offers a free DVD that tells you all you need to know about Disney cruises and then some. To obtain a copy, call ☎ 800-951-3532 or order at **disneycruise.com.**

3. **ORLANDO MAGICARD** If you're considering lodging outside Disney World or if you think you might patronize out-of-the-World attractions and restaurants, obtain an Orlando Magicard, a Vacation Planner, and the Orlando Official Vacation Guide (all free) from the Orlando Official Visitor Center. The Magicard entitles you to discounts for hotels, restaurants, ground transportation, shopping malls, dinner theaters, and non-Disney theme parks and attractions. The Orlando Magicard can be conveniently downloaded for printing at **orlandoinfo.com/magicard.** To order the accommodations guide, call ☎ 800-643-9492. For more information and materials, call ☎ 407-363-5872 weekdays during business hours and 9 a.m.–3 p.m. Eastern time weekends, or go to **visitorlando.com.**

4. ***FLORIDA ROOMSAVER GUIDE*** Another good source of discounts on lodging, restaurants, and attractions statewide is *Florida RoomSaver,* published by Trader Publishing Company. You can sign up at **roomsaver .com** to have a free monthly guide sent to you by e-mail, or you can view the guide online. If you prefer a hard copy over a digital version, you can request one by calling ☎ 800-222-3948 Monday–Friday, 8 a.m.–5 p.m. Eastern time. To order by mail, write to 13709 Progress Blvd., Box 14, Alachua, FL 32615. The guide is free, but you pay $3 for handling ($5 if it's shipped to Canada).

unofficial **TIP**
Request information as far in advance as possible, and allow four weeks for delivery. Follow up if you haven't received your materials within six weeks.

Important Walt Disney World Addresses

COMPLIMENTS, COMPLAINTS, AND SUGGESTIONS Walt Disney World Guest Communications P.O. Box 10040 Lake Buena Vista, FL 32830-0040
CONVENTION AND BANQUET INFORMATION Walt Disney World Resort South P.O. Box 10000 Lake Buena Vista, FL 32830-1000
MERCHANDISE MAIL ORDER (Guest Service Mail Order) P.O. Box 10070 Lake Buena Vista, FL 32830-0070
WALT DISNEY WORLD CENTRAL RESERVATIONS P.O. Box 10100 Lake Buena Vista, FL 32830-0100
WALT DISNEY WORLD EDUCATIONAL PROGRAMS P.O. Box 10000 Lake Buena Vista, FL 32830-1000
WALT DISNEY WORLD INFO / GUEST LETTERS / LETTERS TO MICKEY MOUSE P.O. Box 10040 Lake Buena Vista, FL 32830-0040
WALT DISNEY WORLD TICKET MAIL ORDER P.O. Box 10140 Lake Buena Vista, FL 32830-0140

5. **KISSIMMEE VISITOR'S GUIDE** This full-color guide is one of the most complete resources available and is of particular interest to those who intend to lodge outside of Disney World, featuring ads for hotels, rental houses, time-shares, and condominiums, as well as a directory of attractions, restaurants, special events, and other useful info. For a copy, call the Kissimmee Convention and Visitors Bureau at ☎ 800-327-9159 or 407-944-2400, or view it online at **floridakiss.com.**

6. **GUIDEBOOK FOR GUESTS WITH DISABILITIES** Available at Guest Relations when entering the theme/water parks, at resort front desks, and wheelchair-rental areas (listed in each theme park chapter). More-limited information is available at **disneyworld.disney.go.com/plain-text.**

WALT DISNEY WORLD ON THE WEB

SEARCHING THE INTERNET for Disney information is like navigating an immense maze for a very small piece of cheese: There's a lot of information available, but you may have to wade through list after list until you find the Internet addresses you want and need.

Many individuals maintain elaborate Disney-related sites and chat groups, but the information they provide isn't always accurate.

Recommended Websites

Unofficial Guide coauthor Len Testa has combed the web looking for the best Disney sites. His picks follow.

BEST OFFICIAL THEME PARK SITE The official **Walt Disney World website** (**disneyworld.com** or **disneyworld.disney.go.com**) still has the most information, even if you sometimes have to hunt for it. It remains more useful than the official sites for Universal Studios (**universal orlando.com**) and SeaWorld (**seaworld.com**). All three websites contain

Walt Disney World Phone Numbers

General Information	☎ 407-824-4321 or 407-824-2222
General Information for the Hearing-Impaired (TTY)	☎ 407-827-5141
Accommodations/Reservations	☎ 407-W-DISNEY (934-7639)
All-Star Movies Resort	☎ 407-939-7000
All-Star Music Resort	☎ 407-939-6000
All-Star Sports Resort	☎ 407-939-5000
AMC Downtown Disney 24 Theatres	☎ 888-262-4386
Animal Kingdom Lodge & Villas (*Jambo House & Kidani Village*)	☎ 407-938-3000
Art of Animation Resort	☎ 407-938-7000
Beach Club Resort	☎ 407-934-8000
Blizzard Beach Information	☎ 407-560-3400
BoardWalk Inn	☎ 407-939-5100
Caribbean Beach Resort	☎ 407-934-3400
Celebration Realty Office	☎ 407-361-2555
Centra Care	☎ 407-200-2273
Formosa Gardens	☎ 407-397-7032
Kissimmee	☎ 407-390-1888
Lake Buena Vista	☎ 407-934-2273
Universal–Dr. Phillips	☎ 407-291-9960
Cirque du Soleil	☎ 407-939-7600
Contemporary Resort–Bay Lake Tower	☎ 407-824-1000
Convention Information	☎ 407-828-3200
Coronado Springs Resort	☎ 407-939-1000
Dining Advance Reservations	☎ 407-WDW-DINE (939-3463)
Disabled Guests Special Requests	☎ 407-939-7807
Disney Institute	☎ 407-824-7997 or 321-939-4600
DisneyQuest	☎ 407-828-4600
Disney's Old Key West Resort	☎ 407-827-7700
Disney's Saratoga Springs Resort & Spa, Treehouse Villas	☎ 407-827-1100
Downtown Disney Information	☎ 407-827-2281
ESPN Wide World of Sports Complex	☎ 407-939-GAME (4263)
Fantasia Gardens Miniature Golf	☎ 407-560-4753
Fort Wilderness Resort & Campground	☎ 407-824-2900
Golf Reservations and Information	☎ 407-WDW-GOLF (939-4653)

Grand Floridian Resort & Spa	☎ 407-824-3000
Group Camping	☎ 407-939-7807 (press 4)
Guided-Tour Information	☎ 407-WDW-TOUR (939-8687)
Guided VIP Solo Tours	☎ 407-560-4033
House of Blues Tickets & Information	☎ 407-934-2583
Lost and Found (for articles lost):	
Today at Disney's Animal Kingdom	☎ 407-938-2785
Today at Disney's Hollywood Studios	☎ 407-560-4668
Today at Epcot	☎ 407-560-7500
Today at the Magic Kingdom	☎ 407-824-4521
Today at Universal Orlando (Universal Studios, Islands of Adventure, and CityWalk)	☎ 407-224-4233
Yesterday or before (at all Disney parks)	☎ 407-824-4245
Merchandise Guest Services	☎ 407-363-6200
Ocala/Marion County Chamber of Commerce	☎ 352-629-8051
Outdoor Recreation Reservations & Information	☎ 407-WDW-PLAY (939-7529)
Polynesian Resort	☎ 407-824-2000
Pop Century Resort	☎ 407-938-4000
Port Orleans French Quarter Resort	☎ 407-934-5000
Port Orleans Riverside Resort	☎ 407-934-6000
Resort Dining	☎ 407-WDW-DINE (939-3463)
Security:	
Routine	☎ 407-560-7959
Urgent	☎ 407-560-1990
Shades of Green Resort	☎ 407-824-3400
Telecommunication for the Deaf Reservations	☎ 407-939-7670
Tennis Reservations & Lessons	☎ 407-621-1991
Walt Disney Travel Company	☎ 407-939-6244
Walt Disney World Dolphin	☎ 407-934-4000
Walt Disney World Speedway	☎ 407-939-0130
Walt Disney World Swan	☎ 407-934-3000
Walt Disney World Ticket Inquiries	☎ 407-566-4985
Weather Information	☎ 407-827-4545
Wilderness Lodge & Villas	☎ 407-824-3200
Winter Summerland Miniature Golf	☎ 407-560-3000
Wrecker Service (if closed, call Security, above)	☎ 407-824-0976
Yacht Club Resort	☎ 407-934-7000

information on ticket options, park hours, height requirements for attractions, disabled-guest access, and the like. Disney's site also allows you to make dining reservations online, which is really useful when you don't have enough time to do so by phone. As an added bonus, you can make online reservations starting at 6 a.m. Eastern, an hour before the phone lines open. On the minus side, however, be aware that when making hotel reservations, Disney's website will automatically select the more expensive options, such as a water-view room instead of a standard view or a Park Hopper and Water Park Fun and More admission instead of a base ticket. You have to manually undo each of those options every time you change your search criteria, too. That Disney condones this sneakiness is an embarrassment to its corporate culture.

BEST OFFICIAL MOM'S SITE Who knew? Walt Disney World has a Mom's Panel composed of almost four dozen moms and a few red herrings—er, dads—all chosen from among 10,000-plus applicants. The panelists have a website, **disneyworldmoms.com,** where they offer tips, discuss how to plan a Disney World vacation, and answer questions about how those guys got into the henhouse. The parents are unpaid and are free to speak their minds. One mom actually went from fan to cast member when Disney recruited her to head the panel.

BEST GENERAL UNOFFICIAL WALT DISNEY WORLD WEBSITE Besides touringplans.com, Deb Wills's **allears.net** is the first website we recommend to friends who want to make a trip to Disney World. It contains information on virtually every hotel, restaurant, and activity in the World. Want to know what a room at a Disney resort looks like before you book one? This site has photos—sometimes for each floor of a resort. Updated several times a week, the site includes menus from Disney restaurants, ticketing information, maps, and more.

BEST MONEY-SAVING SITE Mary Waring's **MouseSavers** (**mousesavers.com**) is the kind of site for which the web was invented. It keeps an updated list of discounts and reservation codes for use at Disney resorts. The codes are separated into categories such as "For the general public" and "For residents of certain states." Anyone who calls the Disney Reservation Center at ☎ 407-W-DISNEY (934-7639) can use a current code and get the discounted rate. Savings can be considerable—up to 40% in many cases. Two often-overlooked site features are the discount codes for rental cars and non-Disney hotels in the area.

BEST WALT DISNEY WORLD PREVIEW SITE If you want to see what a particular attraction is like, visit **YouTube** (**youtube.com**). Enter the name of the desired attraction in the search bar at the top of the page, and multiple videos should come up. Videos of indoor ("dark") rides are usually inferior to those of outdoor rides due to poor lighting, but even the videos of indoor rides generally provide a good sense of what the attraction is about.

SOCIAL MEDIA Facebook and **Twitter** are popular places for Disney fans to gather online and share comments, tips, and photos. Following fellow Disneyphiles as they share their in-park experiences can make you feel like you're there, even as you're stuck in a cubicle at work.

BEST INTERNET RADIO STATION MouseWorld Radio (mouseworld radio.com) plays everything from attraction themes and hotel background music to old sound clips from Disney resort TV ads. What makes MouseWorld Radio special is that the tracks match what the Disney parks are playing at the time of day you're listening. So every morning at 8 a.m., you'll hear essentially the same music that's currently playing at the Magic Kingdom before it opens, and every night at 9 p.m. you'll hear *IllumiNations* just as if you were at Epcot.

BEST THEME-PARK-INSIDER SITE If *The E! True Hollywood Story* ever did an episode on theme park development, the result would be something like **jimhillmedia.com.** Well researched and supplied with limitless insider information, Jim Hill's columns guide you through the internal squabbles, shareholder revolts, and outside competition that have made (and that still make) Walt Disney World what it is.

BEST TRIVIA SITES Lou Mongello's excellent *Walt Disney World Trivia Book* has an equally good online companion; check it out on iTunes and at **wdwradio.com.** You'll find message boards, Disney-theme-park news, and more. Lou hosts live chats at his site, usually on Wednesdays. Lou also hosts the very popular *WDW Radio Show* podcast.

Fans of Steve Barrett's *Hidden Mickeys* book now have an online destination where they can keep updated on the latest tri-circle sightings at **hiddenmickeysguide.com.** Steve also writes the *Hassle-Free Walt Disney World Vacation* guidebook, chock-full of touring plans and Disney advice that he's developed for family and friends over the years. Aside from the *Unofficial Guide,* Steve's probably got the most thorough and thoughtful touring advice around.

BEST SITES FOR TRAFFIC, ROADWORK, CONSTRUCTION, AND SAFETY INFORMATION Visit **expresswayauthority.com** for the latest information on roadwork in the Orlando and Orange County areas. The site also contains detailed maps, directions, and toll-rate information for the most popular tourist destinations. Check **flhsmv.gov/fhp/cps** to learn about state child-restraint requirements. Finally, we like **mapquest.com** for driving directions.

> *unofficial* **TIP**
> You can't pick a less crowded time to visit Walt Disney World than the period between Labor Day and October 1.

WHEN *to* GO *to* WALT DISNEY WORLD

Why do they call it tourist season if we can't shoot them?
—Palatka, Florida, outdoorsman

SELECTING THE TIME OF YEAR FOR YOUR VISIT

WALT DISNEY WORLD IS BUSIEST Christmas Day through New Year's Day. Also extremely busy are Thanksgiving weekend, the week of Presidents Day, the first full week of November, spring break for colleges, and late March through the third week of April. On just a single day in these peak times, as many as 92,000 people have toured the Magic

Kingdom! This level of attendance isn't typical—only those who simply cannot go at any other time should tackle the parks at their peak.

The least busy time is from Labor Day in September through the beginning of October. Next slowest are the second full week of November through the weekend preceding Thanksgiving, the week after Thanksgiving until the week before Christmas, January 4 through the first week of February (except the Martin Luther King Jr. holiday weekend and the weekend of the Disney World Marathon), and the last week of April through early June. Late February, March, and early April are dicey. Crowds ebb and flow according to spring-break schedules and the timing of Presidents Day weekend. Though crowds have grown in September and October as a result of promotions aimed at locals and the international market, these months continue to be good for weekday touring at the Magic Kingdom, Disney's Hollywood Studios, and Disney's Animal Kingdom, and for weekend visits to Epcot.

A family who vacationed during the slow period following the Thanksgiving holiday had this to say:

> *My family went down when the Christmas decorations were up, and it was AMAZING! The decorations were incredible and put you in just the right mood for the holidays. It leaves you speechless, especially when you see the castle at the Magic Kingdom lit up at night.*

The Downside of Off-Season Touring

Though we strongly recommend going to Disney World in the fall, winter, or spring, there are a few trade-offs. The parks often open late and close early during the off-season. When they open as late as 9 a.m., everyone arrives at about the same time. A late opening coupled with an early closing drastically reduces touring hours. Even when crowds are small, it's difficult to see big parks such as the Magic Kingdom between 9 a.m. and 7 p.m. Early closing (before 8 p.m.) also usually means no evening parades or fireworks. And because these are slow times, some rides and attractions may be closed. Finally, Central Florida temperatures fluctuate wildly during late fall, winter, and early spring; daytime highs in the 40s and 50s aren't uncommon.

unofficial **TIP**
In our opinion, the risk of encountering colder weather and closed attractions during an off-season visit to Walt Disney World is worth it.

Given the choice, however, smaller crowds, bargain prices, and stress-free touring are worth risking cold weather or closed attractions. Touring in fall and other "off" periods is so much easier that our research team, at the risk of being blasphemous, would advise taking children out of school for a Disney World visit.

Most readers who've tried Disney World at various times agree. A father of two from Reynoldsburg, Ohio, writes:

> *Taking your kids out of school—is it worth it? Yes! It used to be true that missing a week of school would place your child so far behind it could take months for him or her to regain that lost week. Not so today. With advance preparation, this was no problem. With less than an hour of homework after dinner, our kids went back to school with*

assignments completed and no makeup work. But it was all those other hours with no lines and no heat that were the real payoff.

There's another side to this story, and we've received some well-considered letters from parents and teachers who don't think taking kids out of school is such a hot idea. From a father in Fairfax, Virginia:

My wife and I are disappointed that you seem to be encouraging families to take their children out of school to avoid the crowds at WDW during the summer months. My wife is an eighth-grade teacher of chemistry and physics. She has parents pull their children, some honor-roll students, out of school for vacations, only to discover when they return that the students are unable to comprehend the material. Parents' suspicions about the quality of their children's education should be raised when children go to school for 6 hours a day yet supposedly can complete this same instruction with "less than an hour of homework" each night.

unofficial **TIP**
Instead of taking the kids out of school, consider scheduling your Disney World trip immediately following the last week of school in the spring or during the week before school starting in the fall. The crowds will be well below summer peak.

A Martinez, California, teacher offers this compelling analogy:

There are a precious 180 days for us as teachers to instruct our students, and there are 185 days during the year for Disney World. I have seen countless students during my 14 years of teaching struggle to catch up the rest of the year due to a week of vacation during critical instructional periods. The analogy I use with my students' parents is that it's like walking out of a movie after watching the first 5 minutes, then returning for the last 5 minutes and trying to figure out what happened.

But a teacher from Penn Yan, New York, sees things differently:

I've read the comments by teachers saying that they all think it's horrible for a parent to take a child out for a vacation. As a teacher and a parent, I disagree. If a parent takes the time to let us know that a child is going to be out, we help them get ready for upcoming homework the best we can. If the child is a good student, why shouldn't they go have a wonderful experience with their family? I also don't understand when teachers say they can't get something together for the time the student will be out. We all have to plan ahead, and we know what we are teaching days, if not weeks, in advance. Take 20 minutes out of your day and set something up. Learn to be flexible!

BE UNCONVENTIONAL The Orange County Convention Center in Orlando hosts some of the largest conventions and trade shows in the world. Rooms anywhere near Walt Disney World are hard to find when there's a big convention, and as this Toronto, Ontario, reader points out, are also expensive:

If saving money on accommodations is an important part of your trip, be sure to check rates on the Net before you settle on a date. Trade shows at the Orange County Convention Center can host over

Annual Attendance Patterns at the Magic Kingdom

Visitors per day (thousands) **100**

— **80**

Christmas   New Year's

Easter

Thanksgiving   Presidents   Memorial   **60**
Day   Day

Labor   College   —
Day   Spring Break   **40**

20

0

Sept   Oct   Nov   Dec   Jan   Feb   Mar   Apr   May   Jun   Jul   Aug

100,000 attendees, with most of them staying one to a room. This drives rates on even average properties to two or three times normal rates. Since all large conventions are scheduled over one year out, these spikes in room rates should be visible up to 12 months prior.

You can check the convention schedule at the Orlando Orange County Convention Center for the next seven months at **occc.net /global/calendar.**

DON'T FORGET AUGUST Kids go back to school pretty early in Florida (and in a lot of other places, too). This makes mid- to late August a good time to visit Walt Disney World for families who can't vacation during the off-season. A New Jersey mother of two school-age children spells it out:

The end of August is the PERFECT time to go (just watch out for hurricanes, it's the season). There were virtually no wait times, 20 minutes at the most.

A mom from Rapid City, South Dakota, agrees:

School starts very early in Florida, so our mid-August visit was great for crowds, but not for heat.

And from a family from Roxbury, New Jersey:

I recommend the last two weeks of August for anyone traveling there during the summer. We have visited twice during this time of year and have had great success touring the parks.

HIGH-LOW, HIGH-LOW, IT'S OFF TO DISNEY WE GO Though we recommend off-season touring, we realize that it's not possible for many families. We want to make it clear, therefore, that you can have a wonderful experience regardless of when you go. Our advice, irrespective of season, is to arrive early at the parks and avoid the crowds by using one of our touring plans. If attendance is light, kick back and forget the touring plans.

WE'VE GOT WEATHER! Long before Walt Disney World, tourists visited Florida year-round to enjoy the temperate tropical and subtropical climates. The best weather months generally are October, November, March, and April. Fall is usually dry, whereas spring is wetter. December, January, and February vary, with average highs of 72°–73°F intermixed with highs in the 50°–65°F range. May is hot but tolerable. June, July, August, and September are the warmest months. Rain is possible anytime, usually in the form of scattered thunderstorms. An entire day of rain is unusual.

Walt Disney World Climate

	JAN	FEB	MAR	APR	MAY	JUN	JUL	AUG	SEP	OCT	NOV	DEC
AVERAGE DAILY LOW (°F)												
	49°	50°	55°	60°	66°	71°	73°	73°	73°	65°	57°	51°
AVERAGE DAILY HIGH (°F)												
	72°	73°	78°	84°	88°	91°	92°	92°	90°	84°	78°	73°
AVERAGE DAILY TEMPERATURE (°F)												
	61°	62°	67°	72°	77°	81°	82°	82°	82°	75°	68°	62°
AVERAGE DAILY HUMIDITY PERCENTAGES												
	74%	71%	71%	69%	72%	77%	79%	80%	80%	77%	76%	76%
AVERAGE RAINFALL PER MONTH (INCHES)												
	2.1"	0.8"	3.2"	2.2"	3.9"	7.4"	7.8"	6.3"	5.6"	2.8"	1.8"	1.9"
NUMBER OF DAYS OF RAIN PER MONTH												
	6	7	8	6	9	14	17	16	14	9	6	6

CROWD CONDITIONS AND THE BEST AND WORST PARKS TO VISIT FOR EACH DAY OF THE YEAR We receive thousands of e-mails and letters inquiring about crowd conditions on specific dates throughout the year. Readers also want to know which park is best to visit on each day of their stay. To make things easier for you (and us!), we provide at **touringplans.com** a calendar covering the next year (click "Crowd Calendar" on the home page). For each date, we offer a crowd-level index based on a scale of 1–10, with 1 being least crowded and 10 being most crowded. Our calendar takes into account all holidays, special events, and more, as described on the next page. The same calendar lists the best and worst park(s) to visit in terms of crowd conditions on any given day. Collecting data for the Crowd Calendar requires us to have researchers in the parks year-round. Thus, to keep the calendar current on a daily basis, we have to charge a modest subscription fee. The same fee also provides access to additional touring plans and other features. Owners of the current edition of the guide are eligible for a substantial discount on the subscription.

A Bristol, Tennessee, couple had good luck with the calendar:

> *The UG Crowd Calendar is 100% accurate. We love it and will continue to use it every trip. We even tested it in heavy-duty crowds just to see if it worked, and you were dead-on correct!*

But a Braintree, Massachusetts, woman cautions:

It should be emphasized that parks can still feel really crowded on a low-crowd day, especially the Magic Kingdom. But you will notice the difference when you see the wait times for the rides. Anyone expecting to have room to roam freely in certain parts of the Magic Kingdom on a low attendance day will be disappointed. The same is true for Animal Kingdom: We went there on a "low" attendance day in the afternoon, and it was extremely congested and difficult to walk through some areas of the park.

HOW WE DETERMINE CROWD LEVELS AND BEST DAYS A number of factors contribute to the models we use to predict both crowd levels and the best days to visit each theme park.

Data we use to predict crowd levels:

- Historical theme park hours from the same time period in past years
- Disney's special-events calendar (for example, Mickey's Not-So-Scary Halloween Party)
- Legal holidays in the United States
- Public-school schedules (including spring-break schedules for the 50 largest public-school districts east of the Mississippi, plus Massachusetts and Connecticut)
- Weekly historical occupancy rates for Orlando-area hotels
- Central Florida tourism demographics

Historical park hours include the actual operating hours for all of the theme parks over the past five years. Special events include everything from official Walt Disney World–sanctioned events to such independent events as Gay Days. Our hotel data contains weekly occupancy rates for seven different areas within the Orlando market, including the key Disney-area hotels in Lake Buena Vista, in the greater International Drive–Universal Orlando area, in Kissimmee, and along US 192 (Irlo Bronson Memorial Highway). Our Central Florida tourism demographics cover everything from where Orlando visitors come from and how long they stay to how many people make up each party and which theme parks they visit.

Data we use to determine the best days for each park:

- Actual wait-time statistics gathered in the parks
- Our own surveys of Disney guests' touring habits
- Disney's Extra Magic Hours schedule
- Special events calendars
- U.S. legal holidays
- Outside sources (such as the U.S. Department of Transportation and *Consumer Reports*)

SOME EXCEPTIONS You'll occasionally see a particular recommendation in the calendar that contradicts general advice given in this guide. As an example, we've recommended Epcot on the Tuesday before Christmas in the past, even though Tuesday is typically Epcot's morning Extra Magic Hour day. Why? Because Epcot is the best park to be in when crowds are large, as they are around Christmas. The effect of

TOP 10 AMERICAN THEME PARKS

	THEME PARK	2011 ATTENDANCE	CHANGE FROM 2010
1.	Magic Kingdom (WDW)	17.1 million	+1%
2.	Disneyland	16.1 million	+1%
3.	Epcot	10.8 million	–
4.	Disney's Animal Kingdom	9.8 million	+1%
5.	Disney's Hollywood Studios	9.7 million	+1%
6.	Universal's Islands of Adventure	7.7 million	+29%
7.	Disney California Adventure	6.3 million	+1%
8.	Universal Studios Florida	6.0 million	+2%
9.	SeaWorld Orlando	5.2 million	+2%
10.	Universal Studios Hollywood	5.1 million	+2%

Source: *Themed Entertainment Association/AECOM Global Attractions Attendance Report 2012*

additional crowds from Epcot's morning Extra Magic Hours pales in comparison to the effect of holiday crowds in the other parks, especially the Magic Kingdom. In this case, Epcot is not so much a "good" choice as it is the proverbial lesser evil.

Likewise, we'll occasionally recommend the Magic Kingdom on a Thursday or Monday, especially during the slower months, even if there's a special event like Mickey's Not-So-Scary Halloween Party scheduled there. This is because we're trying to recommend each park at least once in any seven-day period so that families taking a week-long vacation can be sure to visit each park on at least one day. When all the other rules used don't fulfill this requirement, we're forced to make another of those lesser-evil recommendations.

EXTRA MAGIC HOURS

EXTRA MAGIC HOURS is a perk for families staying at a Walt Disney World resort, including the Swan, Dolphin, and Shades of Green, and the Hilton in the Downtown Disney resort area. On selected days of the week, Disney resort guests will be able to enter a Disney theme park 1 hour earlier or stay in a selected theme park about 2 hours later than the official park-operating hours. Theme park visitors not staying at a Disney resort may stay in the park for Extra Magic Hour evenings, but cannot experience any rides, attractions, or shows. In other words, they can shop and eat.

unofficial **TIP**
You'll need to have a Park Hopper option on your admission ticket to take advantage of the Extra Magic Hours at more than one theme park on the same day.

Because Extra Magic Hours figure so prominently in our Crowd Calendar calculations, and because Disney is constantly rearranging the Extra Magic Hours schedule for each theme park, we've been forced to withdraw the calendar from the guidebook. Fortunately we can make daily changes to our Crowd Calendar on our website, **touringplans.com,** and thus keep the calendar totally updated for you.

We should also mention that the swimming theme parks, Typhoon Lagoon and Blizzard Beach, also offer Extra Magic Hours.

WHAT'S REQUIRED? A valid admission ticket is required to enter the park, and you must show your Disney Resort ID when entering. For evening Extra Magic Hours, show your Disney Resort ID if you want to experience any of the rides or attractions, or just show up at the park turnstiles at any time after evening Extra Magic Hours begin.

WHEN ARE EXTRA MAGIC HOURS OFFERED? The regular Extra Magic Hours schedule is subject to constant change, especially during holidays and other periods of peak attendance. Gone are the days when you could be certain which park was running Extra Magic Hours.

You can phone Walt Disney World Information at ☎ 407-824-4321 or 407-939-6244 (press 0 for a live representative), check the parks calendar at **disneyworld.com,** or check the Crowd Calendar at **touringplans.com** for the dates of your visit.

We seriously hope that Disney will adopt a permanent schedule, but if it doesn't, use the information available from Walt Disney World Information, the official website, or **touringplans.com** to discover any schedule changes that might affect you. To avoid the most crowded park, simply steer clear of the one(s) offering Extra Magic Hours.

WHAT DO EXTRA MAGIC HOURS MEAN TO YOU? Crowds are likely to be larger when the theme parks host an Extra Magic Hours session. If you're not staying at a Disney resort, the *Unofficial Guide* suggests avoiding the park hosting Extra Magic Hours, if at all possible.

TYPICAL EXTRA MAGIC HOURS SCHEDULE *(frequently varies)*

MORNING

MON	TUES	WED	THUR	FRI	SAT	SUN
Animal Kingdom	Epcot	—	Magic Kingdom	Animal Kingdom	DHS	—

EVENING

MON	TUES	WED	THUR	FRI	SAT	SUN
DHS	—	—	—	Epcot	—	Magic Kingdom

If you're staying at a Disney resort, there are a couple of strategies you can employ to cut down on your wait in lines. One strategy is to avoid the park hosting Extra Magic Hours entirely, if possible.

If you can be at the park when it opens, a second strategy would be to visit the park offering a morning Extra Magic Hours session until lunchtime, then visit another, less-crowded park in the afternoon. This strategy would allow you to take advantage of smaller morning crowds to visit the headliner attractions in one park, then take a slower, more relaxed tour of another park in the afternoon. For example, you might visit the Magic Kingdom Thursday morning, seeing as much of Tomorrowland or Fantasyland as possible during Extra Magic Hours, then visit the rest of the park until lunch. Before the Magic Kingdom crowds peaked in the early afternoon, you'd leave for Epcot and spend the rest of the day there.

Consider two things if choosing between morning or evening Extra Magic Hours sessions: first, whether your family functions better getting up early or staying up late, and second, the time at which the parks close to day guests. If you can handle those early mornings, you'll find shorter lines during morning Extra Magic Hours. Evening Extra Magic Hours are most useful when the crowds are low and the parks close relatively early to the general public, so your family doesn't have to stay up past midnight to take advantage of the perk.

EARLY ENTRY (a.k.a. Morning Extra Magic Hours)

THE EARLY-ENTRY PROGRAM APPLIES to the Magic Kingdom, Epcot, Disney's Animal Kingdom, Disney's Hollywood Studios, and Blizzard Beach and Typhoon Lagoon water parks. Several days of the week, Disney resort guests are invited to enter a designated theme park 1 hour before the general public. During the early-entry hour, guests can enjoy attractions opened early just for them.

How Early Entry Affects Attendance at the Theme Parks

Early entry strongly affects attendance at the theme parks, especially during busier times of year. Vast numbers of Disney resort guests tour whichever park is designated for early entry. If the Magic Kingdom is tapped for early entry on Thursday, for example, it'll be more crowded that day, while Epcot, Disney's Animal Kingdom, and Disney's Hollywood Studios will be less crowded. Epcot, Animal Kingdom, and the Studios will be more crowded when those parks are slated for early entry.

During holiday periods and summer, when Disney hotels are full, early entry makes a tremendous difference in crowds at the designated park. The program funnels so many people into the early-entry park that it fills by about 10 a.m. and is practically gridlocked by noon.

unofficial **TIP**
Whatever edge resort guests gain by taking advantage of early entry is offset by horrendous crowds later in the day. During busier times of year, regardless of your hotel, avoid any park on the day it's scheduled for early entry.

If you elect to use your early-entry privileges, be among the first early entrants. A mother of three from Lee's Summit, Missouri, writes:

> *Our first full day at WDW, we went to the Magic Kingdom on an early-entry day for resort guests. We were there at 7:30 a.m. and were able to walk onto all the rides in Fantasyland with no wait. At 8:45 a.m. we positioned ourselves at the Adventureland rope and ran toward Splash Mountain when the rope dropped. We were able to ride Splash Mountain with no wait and then Big Thunder with about a 15-minute wait. We then went straight to the Jungle Cruise and the wait was already 30 minutes, so we skipped it. The park became incredibly crowded as the day progressed, and we were all exhausted from getting up so early. We left the park around noon. After that day, I resolved to avoid early-entry days and instead be at a non-early-entry park about a half-hour before official opening time.*

This note from a North Bend, Washington, dad emphasizes the importance of arriving at the beginning of the early-entry period.

> *We only used early entry once—to Disney's Hollywood Studios. We*

got there 20 minutes after early entry opened, and the wait for Tower of Terror was 1½ hours long without Fastpass. We skipped it.

A Baltimore mother of a 3-year-old reports:

We chuckled to ourselves on our first day when we watched hordes of people attempt to pack onto an Animal Kingdom shuttle for Extra Magic Hours. We were the only family on the Epcot shuttle that morning and didn't wait for any rides the entire day!

But a Winston-Salem, North Carolina, mom evidently had the worst experience of all:

Disney Hollywood Studios was a MADHOUSE. Do NOT go on Extra Magic Hours days. After spending about 3 hours to ride three rides, I just wanted to trample the people stampeding to the exit.

Early Entry and Park-Hopping

An alternative strategy for Disney resort guests is to take advantage of early entry, but only until the designated park gets crowded. At that time, move to another park. This plan works particularly well at the Magic Kingdom for families with young children who love the attractions in Fantasyland. However, it will take you about an hour to commute to the second park of the day. If, for example, you depart the Magic Kingdom for Disney's Hollywood Studios at 10 a.m., you'll find the Studios pretty crowded when you arrive at about 11 a.m. Keeping these and other considerations in mind, here are some guidelines:

1. Use the early-entry–park-hopping strategy during the less busy times of year when the parks close early. You'll get a jump on the general public and add an hour to what, in the off-season, is an already short touring day.

2. Use the early-entry–park-hopping strategy to complete touring a second park that you've already visited on a previous day, or specifically to see live entertainment in the second park.

Never hop to Disney's Animal Kingdom—it's almost always the first park to close each evening, so arriving later than 2 p.m. for the handful of remaining hours is not generally a good use of time, plus it will be too crowded by the time you arrive.

On any day except the park's Extra Magic Hours days, hopping to Epcot is usually good. Epcot is able to handle large crowds better than any other Disney park, minimizing the effects of a midday arrival. Also, World Showcase has a large selection of interesting dining options, making it a good choice for evening touring.

Don't hop to the park with early entry (Extra Magic Hours). The idea is to avoid crowds, not join them.

Limit your hopping to two parks per day. Hopping to a third park in one day would result in more time spent commuting than saved by avoiding crowds.

A Texas mom who park-hopped during the busy season learned a lesson:

We made the mistake of doing a morning at the Magic Kingdom and an afternoon at the Studios. Worst idea ever. By the time we got to the Studios, all the Fastpasses were gone for Toy Story Mania!, the Tower of Terror, and Rock 'n' Roller Coaster. And all three rides had at least 90-minute waits.

Nighttime Version of Extra Magic Hours

The Evening Extra Magic Hours program lets Disney resort guests enjoy a different theme park on specified nights for about 2 hours after it closes to the general public. Guests pay no additional charge to participate but must show their resort IDs at each ride or attraction they wish to experience. You can also show up at the turnstiles at any point after evening Extra Magic Hours have started. Note that if you've been in another park that day, you'll need the Park Hopper feature on your admission ticket to enter. Evening Extra Magic Hours are offered at the Magic Kingdom, Epcot, and Disney's Hollywood Studios, but not at Disney's Animal Kingdom.

During busier times of year, families seem to take more advantage of evening Extra Magic Hours at the Magic Kingdom and the Studios than at Epcot. Evening Extra Magic Hour crowds can be every bit as large as those throughout the day during busier times of the year, even when the evening EMH session extends into the wee hours of the morning. A mom from Fairhaven, Massachusetts, doesn't mince words:

I say steer clear of a park that is open late. There are only a few attractions open and tons of people trying to get on them.

More attractions operate during the extended evening period than during the early-entry hour in the morning. Certain fast-food and full-service restaurants remain open as well. The program is presumably in response to perks extended to Universal Orlando hotel guests that allow them to go to the front of the line at any Universal attraction. Disney has thus far maintained a level playing field, rejecting programs that extend line-breaking privileges to resort guests.

SUMMER AND HOLIDAYS

A READER FROM COLUMBUS, OHIO, once observed, "The main thing I learned from your book is not to go during the summer or at holiday times. Once you know that, you don't need a guidebook."

While we might argue with the reader's conclusion, we agree that avoiding summer and holidays is a wise strategy. That said, we also understand that many folks have no choice concerning the time of year they visit Disney World. Much of this book, in fact, is dedicated to making sure those readers who visit during busier times enjoy their experience. Sure, off-season touring is preferable, but, armed with knowledge and some strategy, you can have a great time whenever you visit.

To put things in perspective, early summer (up to about June 15) and late summer (after August 15) aren't nearly as crowded as the intervening period. And even midsummer crowds pale in comparison to the hordes during holiday periods. If you visit in midsummer or during a holiday, the first thing you need to know is that the theme parks' guest capacity is not infinite. In fact, once a park reaches capacity, only Disney resort guests arriving via the Disney transportation system are allowed to enter. If you're not a Disney resort guest, you may find yourself in a situation similar to this Boise, Idaho, dad's:

This is the worst of it. The Magic Kingdom and Disney's Hollywood Studios were so full they closed the parks. For three days we could not enter those parks, so we were forced to go to Epcot and use up two days of our four-day pass. We decided to pay for another night at our hotel to see if the crowds would let up, but no luck. All we could do was just drive around Orlando and sightsee.

We hasten to point out that this reader would've had no difficulty gaining admission to the parks of his choice had he committed to being at the turnstiles 35–60 minutes before official opening time.

Packed-Parks Compensation Plan

The thought of teeming throngs jockeying for position in endless lines under the baking Fourth of July sun is enough to wilt the will and ears of the most ardent Mouseketeer. Disney, however, feeling bad about those long lines and challenging touring conditions on packed holidays, compensates patrons with a no-less-than-incredible array of first-rate live entertainment and events.

Shows, parades, concerts, and pageantry continue throughout the day. In the evening, so much is going on that you have to make tough choices. Concerts, parades, light shows, laser shows, fireworks, and dance productions occur almost continually. No question about it: You can go to Walt Disney World on the Fourth of July (or any crowded extended-hours day), never get on a ride, and still have a good time.

Disney provides colorful decorations for most holidays, plus special parades and live entertainment for Christmas, New Year's, Easter, and Fourth of July, among others. Regarding Christmas, we advise visiting in early December when you can enjoy the decorations and festivities without the crowds. If you must tour during the holidays and New Year's, skip the Magic Kingdom; consider visiting Epcot or Disney's Hollywood Studios instead.

If you visit on a nonholiday midsummer day, arrive at the turnstile 30–40 minutes before the stated opening on a non-early-entry day. If you visit during a major holiday period, arrive 1 hour before. Hit your favorite rides early using one of our touring plans, then go back to your hotel for lunch, a swim, and perhaps a nap. If you're interested in the special parades and shows, return to the park in late afternoon or early evening. Assume that unless you use Fastpass, early morning will be the only time you can experience the attractions without long waits. Finally, don't wait until the last minute in the evening to leave the park. The exodus at closing is truly mind-boggling.

Epcot is usually the least crowded park during holidays. Expect the others to be mobbed. To save time in the morning, buy your admission in advance. Also, consider bringing your own stroller or wheelchair instead of renting one of Disney's. If you're touring Epcot or the Magic Kingdom and plan to spend the day, try exiting the park for lunch at a nearby resort hotel. Above all, bring your sense of humor, and pay attention to your group's morale.

THE WALT DISNEY WORLD CALENDAR

JANUARY Usually held the second weekend after New Year's, the **Walt Disney World Marathon** pulls in more runners and their families every year. In 2012, some 24,000 athletes participated in the event—enough people to affect crowd conditions and pedestrian traffic throughout Disney World. In the spirit of participatory journalism, *Unofficial Guide* coauthor and podcaster Len Testa usually runs the marathon, the half-marathon, or both. Check the **wdwtoday.com** podcast archives for all of Disney's running events.

FEBRUARY **Black History Month** is celebrated throughout Walt Disney World with displays, artisans, storytellers, and entertainers. There's no extra charge for the activities, and the celebration's effect on crowd levels is negligible.

Mardi Gras and **Presidents Day** both increase attendance in the first half of the month. At the end of February is the **Princess Half-Marathon** (February 22–24 in 2013), drawing around 15,000 participants. The schedule for the weekend includes a health expo, kid races, and a family 5K in addition to the big race. Like the January races, the Princess increases park attendance and affects vehicular and pedestrian traffic.

MARCH The **Epcot International Flower & Garden Festival** runs annually from mid-March to mid-May or June. Expert horticulturists showcase exotic floral displays and share gardening tips. The 30 million blooms from some 1,200 species will make your eyes pop, and, best of all, the event doesn't seem to affect crowd levels at Epcot.

APRIL Disney doesn't need much to boost attendance, what with **Easter** and some spring-break vacations happening this week (Easter is on March 31 in 2013).

MAY Disney's Hollywood Studios hosts *Star Wars* **Weekends** annually beginning this month, with appearances from that franchise's actors and technicians. These events draw mainly local sci-fi fans, but some come from all over the country. While the impact on regular Disney World crowds is low, you'll find long lines if you want to meet any of the celebrity guests. Also this month: the **Expedition Everest Challenge,** a 5K race at Disney's Animal Kingdom. Impact on crowds is low, but traffic is affected by the runners getting to and from the park.

JUNE Events this month include both *Star Wars* Weekends and **Gay Days.** Since 1991, gay, lesbian, bisexual, and transgendered (GLBT) people from around the world have converged on and around the World in early June for a week of events centered around the theme parks. Today, Gay Days attracts more than 140,000 GLBT visitors and their families and friends. Universal Studios and Wet 'n Wild also participate. For additional information, visit **gaydays.com.**

SEPTEMBER Radio personality Tom Joyner hosts an extremely popular party at Walt Disney World. Usually held during Labor Day weekend, the **Tom Joyner Family Reunion** typically features live musical performances, comedy acts, and family-oriented discussions. For more information, visit **blackamericaweb.com.**

Night of Joy, a Christian-music festival, is staged at the Magic Kingdom this month, usually the second weekend in September. About

16 nationally known acts perform concerts on Friday and Saturday evenings after the park has closed. For information or to purchase tickets, call ☎ 407-W-DISNEY (934-7639) or visit **tinyurl.com/night -of-joy.** (Prices for the 2013 event were unavailable at press time; 2012 tickets ran $50–$60 per night, or around $100 for both nights.)

Those who say Christmas is the most wonderful time of year have never been to the **Epcot International Food & Wine Festival.** Held in the World Showcase from late September through mid-November, the celebration represents 30 nations and includes demonstrations, wine seminars, tastings, and opportunities to see some of the world's top chefs. Although many activities are included in Epcot admission, the best workshops and tastings are by reservation only and cost extra. Call ☎ 407-WDW-DINE well in advance for more information. We think the culinary demonstrations (around $11–$13) and wine-and-beverage seminars ($10–$12) are some of the best values at the festival. Because most of the food kiosks are set up around World Showcase, it can be difficult to walk through the crowds around some of the popular spots. Wait times at Epcot's attractions, however, are affected only slightly.

Held two dozen or so nights each year from mid-September through October 31 (and occasionally into November), **Mickey's Not-So-Scary Halloween Party** runs from 7 p.m. to midnight at the Magic Kingdom. The event includes trick-or-treating in costume, parades, live music, storytelling, and a fireworks show. For reservations and details, call ☎ 407-W-DISNEY. (Prices for the 2013 event were unavailable at press time.)

Finally, Disney's Hollywood Studios hosts the **Twilight Zone Tower of Terror 10-Miler** road race in September. See **rundisney.com** for details.

NOVEMBER Moved from its original early-October date, the **Wine and Dine Half-Marathon** weekend revolves around a 13.1-mile race that ends with a party amid Epcot's International Food & Wine Festival. The number of runners and their "cheer squads"—combined with the guests who descend upon Epcot for the food festival alone—blows up the crowd levels like an agitated pufferfish. Again, vehicular and pedestrian traffic is disturbed by the running courses throughout Disney property.

Christmas and New Year's at the Theme Parks

Don't expect to see all the attractions in a single day of touring at any park. Skip the Magic Kingdom, if possible, if you tour the week between Christmas and New Year's. Epcot, on the other hand, is at its best during the holidays. Touring in the evening will reward you with stunning displays of holiday decorations and slightly smaller crowds than during the day. Disney's Hollywood Studios is also a good choice for evening touring. Crowds will be larger than normal, but the decorations make up for it. One must-see is the **Osborne Family Spectacle of Dancing Lights,** featuring a staggering 5 million Christmas lights.

A Bridgewater, Massachusetts, mom loves Disney World during the holidays but warns that it's not the best time for everyone:

Having just completed our first holiday trip, I would never recommend a Christmas-week vacation for first-time visitors. But for anyone who's visited enough to navigate the parks without a map, the opportunity to experience the beauty and joy of the holiday season outweighs the huge crowds. You must accept that access to rides and shows will be limited and instead concentrate on the unique offerings such as the Osborne lights at the Studios and the parades and fireworks at the Magic Kingdom. Allow yourself time to visit the resorts—the gingerbread house at the Grand Floridian must be seen to be believed. And arrive early: We were in the MK by 7:10 a.m. on New Year's Eve and enjoyed all of the parades, shows, and fireworks, as well as all the major rides (except Splash Mountain— it was too cold).

The Magic Kingdom stages the New Year's Eve fireworks on both December 30 and 31 for those who either wish to see fireworks in multiple parks or who don't wish to be caught in the largest crowds of the year on New Year's Eve.

MICKEY'S VERY MERRY CHRISTMAS PARTY This event is staged 7 p.m.–midnight (after regular hours) on several evenings in November and December. For dates and prices, call ☎ 407-W-DISNEY. (Prices for the 2013 event were unavailable at press time.) Included in the cost is the use of all attractions during party hours, holiday-themed stage shows featuring Disney characters, cookies and hot chocolate, performances of Mickey's Once Upon a Christmastime Parade, carolers, "a magical snowfall on Main Street," white lights on Cinderella Castle, and fireworks.

A reader from Pineville, Louisiana, tried the Very Merry Christmas Party and found the guest list too large for her liking:

Another thing I will not do again is go to the Very Merry Christmas Party. We went in early December to avoid crowds and were taken by surprise to find wall-to-wall people. They offered some great shows, but we could not get to them. The parade at 9 p.m. and the fireworks at 10 p.m., then fighting our way back to the parking lot, was all we could muster.

PART TWO

MAKING *the* MOST *of* YOUR TIME *and* MONEY

ALLOCATING MONEY

Did Walt really intend for it to be so expensive that the average family couldn't afford it?

—*Unofficial Guide* reader from Amarillo, Texas

EVEN IF YOU STOP AT DISNEY WORLD for only an afternoon, be prepared to drop a bundle. In Part Three, we'll show you how to save money on lodging, and in Part Ten, you'll find tips for economizing on meals. This section will give you some sense of what admission costs, as well as which admission options best meet your needs.

DISNEY AND THE ECONOMY

WITH THE U.S. NO LONGER in what economist Paul Krugman calls the "Oh God, we're all gonna die!" phase of the Great Recession, Disney has cut back the size and scope of its discounts to the general public. Its current strategy is to charge more for hotels, food, and tickets, even if that means slightly fewer families decide to visit. In other words, Disney's goal is to increase revenue through price hikes rather than attendance.

Imagine you're running an upscale lemonade stand that caters to families with disposable income. When the recession hit, you discounted your premium lemonade to $1 per glass, the lowest price to ensure you had enough money to pay expenses and keep the stand open. At $1 per glass, you had 100 customers per day, and your gross revenue per day was $100.

Now, with an economic recovery under way but still uneven, you've decided to increase the price of your lemonade to $1.05, figuring that the vast majority of people who want fine lemonade can still afford it. And you're right: 98 people buy your lemonade the next day, and you make $102.90. Your revenue increased by almost 3% even though you lost a couple of customers. Even better, you need fewer lemons because you sold fewer lemonades, so the cost of your raw materials has dropped and your profits have increased.

That strategy is essentially what Disney's doing with its hotels, restaurants, and park admissions. Year-over-year attendance at the theme parks has been more or less flat recently, so Disney has increased revenue by raising costs on the people who can afford to go—that is, Disney would rather charge 5% more to the 98% who can make it to the World. Discounts are still available during slower times such as September, but they're smaller and more narrowly focused to specific dates. And keep in mind that with its Magical Express airport-shuttle service, Disney has created a captive audience for its restaurants. Prices there continue to increase much faster than inflation, because those guests have literally nowhere else to go.

It's a different story for off-site hotels, which lack services like free shuttles and proximity to theme parks. Outside the Disney bubble, you can still find substantial savings at three- and four-star hotels, even during peak season, and restaurant meals up to 40% less expensive than Disney's. It helps considerably if you've got a car, even if you factor in the cost of gas.

WALT DISNEY WORLD ADMISSION OPTIONS

IN AN EFFORT TO ACCOMMODATE various vacation needs, Disney offers a number of different admission options. These range from the humble One-Day Base Ticket, good for a single entry into one Disney theme park, to the top-of-the-line Premium Annual Pass, good for 365 days of admission into every Disney theme or water park, plus DisneyQuest.

The sheer number of ticket options available makes it difficult and, yes, daunting to sort out which option represents the least expensive way to see and do everything you want. An average family staying for a week at an off-World hotel and planning a couple of activities outside the theme parks has about a dozen different ticket options to consider. To complicate matters, comparing options requires detailed knowledge of the myriad perks included with specific admissions. Finding the optimum admission, or combination of admissions, however, could save the average family a nice little bundle. Many families, we suspect, become overwhelmed trying to sort out the different options and simply purchase a more expensive ticket with features they will probably not use. Adding to the frustration, Disney's reservation agents are trained to avoid answering subjective questions about which ticket option is "best."

HELP IS ON THE WAY!

TO SIMPLIFY THINGS, we've tried to define guidelines to help you choose the best ticket options for your vacation. Eight hours into this project, we sounded like a theme park version of Forrest Gump. Remember that scene where Bubba rattles off 7,000 different ways to prepare shrimp? Well, that was kinda like us, babbling about tickets. Even saying some of the ticket names ("Adult Internet-Only Seven-Day Base Ticket with Park Hopper Option") made us sound like our local Starbucks barista, only not as perky.

After a day or so, we realized that coming up with a handful of general guidelines was an impossible task, so we built a tool to figure it

> *unofficial* **TIP**
> Try touringplans.com's **Disney Ticket Calculator** before purchasing your park tickets. It's free and considers almost every ticket combination available.

WDW Theme Park Ticket Options

	1-day	2-day	3-day	4-day	5-day
BASE TICKET AGES 3–9					
	$88.40	$174.66	$240.69	$254.54	$266.25
	–	($87.33/day)	($80.23/day)	($63.63/day)	($53.25/day)
BASE TICKET AGE 10 AND UP					
	$94.79	$187.44	$257.73	$272.64	$285.42
	–	($93.72/day)	($85.91day)	($68.16/day)	($57.08/day)

Base Ticket admits guest to one theme park each day of use.

	1-day	2-day	3-day	4-day	5-day
FOR PARK HOPPER, ADD:					
	$37.28	$60.71	$60.71	$60.71	$60.71
	–	($30.35/day)	($20.24/day)	($15.18/day)	($12.14/day)

Park Hopper option entitles guest to visit more than one theme park on each day of use.

	1-day	2-day	3-day	4-day	5-day
FOR WATER PARK FUN AND MORE, ADD:					
	$60.71	$60.71	$60.71	$60.71	$60.71
	2 visits	2 visits	3 visits	4 visits	5 visits

Water Park Fun and More option entitles guest to a specified number of visits (between 2 and 10) to a choice of entertainment and recreation venues.

	1-day	2-day	3-day	4-day	5-day
FOR PARK HOPPER *PLUS* WATER PARK FUN AND MORE, ADD:					
	$84.14	$84.14	$84.14	$84.14	$84.14
	–	($42.07/day)	($28.05/day)	($21.03/day)	($16.83/day)
FOR NO EXPIRATION, ADD:					
	–	$31.95	$42.60	$90.53	$138.45
	–	($15.98/day)	($14.20/day)	($22.63/day)	($27.69/day)

No Expiration means unused admissions on a ticket have no expiration date.

out. Visit **touringplans.com** and try out the **Disney Ticket Calculator** (choose it from the "Walt Disney World" pull-down menu at the top of the page). It aggregates ticket prices from a number of online ticket vendors, including Disney itself. Just answer a few simple questions relating to the size of your party and the theme parks you intend to visit, and the calculator then identifies your four least expensive ticket options.

The program will also make recommendations for considerations other than price. For example, Annual Passes, although they might cost more, make sense in certain circumstances because Disney often offers substantial resort discounts and other deals to Annual Pass holders. Those resort discounts, especially during off-season times, can more than offset a small incremental charge for the Annual Pass.

MAGIC YOUR WAY

WALT DISNEY WORLD OFFERS AN ARRAY of theme park ticket options, grouped into a program called Magic Your Way. The simplest option, visiting one theme park for one day, is called a **One-Day Base**

(*Note:* All ticket prices include 6.5% sales tax)				
6-day	**7-day**	**8-day**	**9-day**	**10-day**
BASE TICKET AGES 3–9				
$276.90	**$287.55**	**$298.20**	**$308.85**	**$319.50**
($46.15/day)	($41.08/day)	($37.28/day)	($34.32/day)	($31.95/day)
BASE TICKET AGE 10 AND UP				
$296.07	**$306.72**	**$317.37**	**$328.02**	**$338.67**
($49.35/day)	($43.82/day)	($39.67/day)	($36.45/day)	($33.87/day)
Park choices are Magic Kingdom, Epcot, Disney's Hollywood Studios, or Disney's Animal Kingdom.				
$60.71	**$60.71**	**$60.71**	**$60.71**	**$60.71**
($10.12/day)	($8.67/day)	($7.59/day)	($6.75/day)	($6.07day)
Park choices are any combination of Magic Kingdom, Epcot, Disney's Hollywood Studios, or Disney's Animal Kingdom on each day of use.				
$60.71	**$60.71**	**$60.71**	**$60.71**	**$60.71**
6 visits	7 visits	8 visits	9 visits	10 visits
Choices are Disney's Blizzard Beach water park, Disney's Typhoon Lagoon water park, DisneyQuest, Oak Trail Golf Course, or ESPN Wide World of Sports Complex.				
$84.14	**$84.14**	**$84.14**	**$84.14**	**$84.14**
($14.02/day)	($12.02/day)	($10.52/day)	($9.35/day)	($8.41/day)
$175.73	**$202.35**	**$228.98**	**$266.25**	**$292.88**
($29.29/day)	($28.91/day)	($28.62/day)	($29.58/day)	($29.29/day)

Note: Check **touringplans.com** for the latest ticket prices, which are subject to change. All tickets expire 14 days after first use unless No Expiration is purchased.

Ticket. Other features, such as the ability to visit more than one park per day ("park-hopping"), or the inclusion of admission to Disney's minor venues (Typhoon Lagoon, Blizzard Beach, DisneyQuest, and the like), are available as individual add-ons to the Base Ticket.

The more days of admission you purchase, the lower the cost per day. For example, if you buy an adult five-day Base Ticket for $285.42 (taxes included), each day will cost $57.08, compared with $94.79 a day for a one-day pass. Base Tickets can be purchased from 1 up to 10 days and admit you to exactly one theme park per day.

unofficial **TIP**
Unlike Disney's previous multiday tickets, Base Tickets can't be used to visit more than one park per day.

Disney says that Base Tickets expire within 14 days of the first day of use. In practice, they really mean 13 days after the first day of use. If, say, you purchase a four-day Base Ticket on June 1 and use it that day for admission to the Magic Kingdom, you'll be able to visit a single Disney theme park on any of your three remaining days between June 2 and June 15. After that, the ticket expires and any unused days will be lost. Through another add-on, however, you can avoid the 14-day expiration and make your ticket valid forever. More on that later.

BASE-TICKET ADD-ONS

NAVIGATING THE MAGIC YOUR WAY PROGRAM is like ordering dinner in an upscale restaurant where all menu selections are à la carte: many choices, mostly expensive, virtually all of which require some thought.

Three add-on options are offered with the Magic Your Way Base Ticket, each at an additional cost:

PARK HOPPER Adding this feature to your Base Ticket allows you to visit more than one theme park per day. The cost is $37.28 (including tax) on top of the price of a one-day Base Ticket and $60.71 added to the price of multiday Base Tickets—exorbitant for one or two days, but it becomes more affordable the longer your stay. As an add-on to a seven-day Base Ticket, the flat fee would work out to $8.67 per day for park-hopping privileges. If you want to visit the Magic Kingdom in the morning and eat at Epcot in the evening, this is the feature to request.

NO EXPIRATION Adding this option to your ticket means that unused admissions to the major theme parks and the swimming parks, as well as other minor venues, never expire. If you added this option to a 10-day Base Ticket and used only 4 days this year, the remaining 6 days could be used for admission at any date in the future. The No Expiration option ranges from $31.95 with tax for a 2-day ticket to $292.88 for a 10-day Base Ticket. This option is not available on single-day tickets.

WATER PARK FUN AND MORE (WPFAM) This option gives you a single admission to one of Disney's water parks (Blizzard Beach and Typhoon Lagoon), DisneyQuest, Oak Trail Golf Course, or the ESPN Wide World of Sports Complex. The cost is a flat $60.71 (including tax). Except for the single-day WPFAM ticket, which gives you two admissions, the number of admissions equals the number of days on your Base Ticket. If you buy an 8-day Base Ticket, for example, and add the WPFAM option, you get eight WPFAM admissions. What you can't do is, say, buy a 10-day Base Ticket with only three WPFAM admissions or a 3-day Base Ticket with four WPFAM admissions. You can, however, skip WPFAM entirely and buy an individual admission to any of these minor parks. This last option is almost always the best deal if you want to visit only one of the venues above.

In 2012 Disney began offering a **Park Hopper–WPFAM combo** for $84.14 including tax. If you plan to spend a lot of time at the water parks and other WPFAM venues, the combo will save you $37 over buying the two options separately.

The foregoing add-ons are available for purchase in any combination (except for the No Expiration add-on on one-day tickets). If you buy a Base Ticket and then decide later on that you want one or more of the options, you can upgrade the Base Ticket to add the feature(s) you desire.

Annual Passes

An **Annual Pass** provides unlimited use of the major theme parks for one year; a **Premium Annual Pass** also provides unlimited use of the minor parks. Annual Pass holders also get perks, including free parking and seasonal offers such as room-rate discounts at Disney resorts. The Annual Pass is not valid for special events, such as admission to Mickey's Very Merry Christmas Party. Tax included, Annual Passes run $611.31 for both adults and kids age 3 and up. A Premium Annual Pass, at $744.44 for adults and kids age 3 and up, provides unlimited admission to Blizzard Beach, Typhoon Lagoon, DisneyQuest, and Oak Trail Golf Course, in addition to the four major theme parks. In addition to Annual Passes, Florida residents are eligible for discounts on one-day theme park Base Tickets (about 10%) as well as on various add-on options.

Florida Resident Passes

Disney offers several special admission options to Florida residents. The **Florida Resident Annual Pass** ($452.63 for adults and kids age 3 and up) and the **Florida Resident Premium Annual Pass** ($595.34 for adults and kids age 3 and up) both offer unlimited admission and park-hopping priv-

unofficial **TIP**
Magic Your Way offers significant incentives for taking a longer vacation or buying more days of admission.

ileges to the four major theme parks. The Florida Resident Premium Annual Pass also provides unlimited admission to Blizzard Beach, Typhoon Lagoon, DisneyQuest, and Oak Trail Golf Course, in addition to the four major theme parks. AAA offers some nice discounts on these passes. And the **Florida Resident Seasonal Pass** ($318.44 for adults and kids age 3 and up) provides unlimited admission to the four major theme parks except on select blackout dates.

One final note: It doesn't cost as much to renew an Annual Pass as it does to buy it in the first place. When you renew any Annual Pass, you get an 8–9% savings from the cost of the original pass.

A CLOUD IS JUST A CLOUD

THIS SECTION WAS FORMERLY TITLED "Every Cloud Has a Polyester Lining." In it we explained the few ways that Magic Your Way could save you money. Well, forget that—almost all good deals have gone the way of the dinosaur. The only exception is for folks who don't intend to

unofficial **TIP**
In our estimation, considering the time value of money, buying the No Expiration option is pretty much a sucker play.

park-hop and will require four or more days' admission, all to be used during a single vacation. If this describes your situation, you can realize some significant economies of scale. As you can see from our admissions chart, the more days you buy, the more you save: The cost of an adult 10-day Base Ticket ($338.67) is only $81 more than the cost of an adult 3-day Base Ticket ($257.73). If you buy the 10-day ticket, you can whittle your admission cost per day, tax included, down to $33.87 for adults and $31.95 for children. So what's changed for everybody else?

Consider that most guests need only four or five days' admission; the most cost-effective strategy would seem to be to buy a 10-day Base Ticket plus the No Expiration option so you could roll over any unused admission days to a subsequent trip. When Disney first rolled out Magic Your Way, the No Expiration option actually was pretty reasonable.

Well, they couldn't let *that* continue, could they?

If you buy an adult 10-day Base Ticket for $338.67 plus No Expiration for $292.88, you'll pay $631.55 including tax, or $63.15 a day—$5 more a day compared with simply buying a 5-day Base Ticket each time you visit Walt Disney World. While it's true that admission prices might go up before you visit again, in which case No Expiration would be to your benefit, it's equally true that you might misplace the tickets you bought in the previous scenario, or that you might have some better use for the $292.88 you shelled out on top of your ticket purchase.

BIG BROTHER IS WATCHING

ALL MAGIC YOUR WAY TICKETS are personalized, with the ticket holder's name and biometric information stored on the ticket. This doesn't mean, however, that you have to provide a DNA sample when you plunk down your cash. Recording the biometric information requires a quick and painless measurement of one finger from your right hand, taken the first time you use the ticket. It's been used without incident for a number of years on Disney's Annual Pass.

The advantages of the bio scan are not altogether clear, though it's doubtless intended to prevent the original purchaser of the pass from selling unused days to a third party. If you're purchasing admission for your entire family and are worried about the difficulty in keeping everyone's tickets straight, we're told that Disney's computer system will link every family member's data to every ticket, allowing anyone to enter with anyone else's ticket. We've confirmed this by having a platoon of *Unofficial Guide* researchers (including men, women, and children) swap passes with each other; all were admitted.

This new scanning process is so cumbersome that it has taken guests more than 30 minutes to enter some parks during peak periods, and sometimes more than an hour. In response to this, Disney frequently turns off the scanning process entirely (usually at Disney's Animal Kingdom).

HOW TO GET THE MOST FROM MAGIC YOUR WAY

FIRST, HAVE A REALISTIC IDEA of what you want out of your vacation. As with anything, it doesn't make sense to pay for options you won't use. A seven-day theme park ticket with seven WPFAM admissions might seem like a wonderful idea when you're snowbound and planning your trip in February. But actually trying to visit all those parks in a week in July might end up feeling more like Navy SEAL training. If you're going to make only one visit to a water park, DisneyQuest, or ESPN Wide World of Sports, you're almost always better off purchasing that admission separately rather than in the WPFAM option. If you plan to visit two or more WPFAM venues, you're better off buying the add-on.

Next, think carefully about paying for No Expiration. An inside source reports that fewer than 1 in 10 admission tickets with unused days are ever used at a Disney theme park. The rest are misplaced, discarded, or forgotten. Unless you're absolutely certain you'll be returning to the World within the next year or two and have identified a safe place to keep those unused tickets, we don't think the additional cost is worth the risk. (We've lost a few of these passes ourselves.)

GOTCHA!

DISNEY HAS HISTORICALLY INCREASED admission prices about a month after the *Unofficial Guide* goes to press. (For this edition and the previous one, Disney raised its prices while the *Guide* was still in production. Go figure.) Price hikes have generally run about 3–4% a year, but as discussed previously, specific ticket categories are frequently bumped much more. In 2012, the average increase across all admissions was a greedy 14%, and children's prices on Annual Passes were eliminated altogether. In any event, if you're putting a budget together, assume at least a 3% increase—but know that it could be *much* higher.

WHERE TO PURCHASE MAGIC YOUR WAY TICKETS

YOU CAN BUY YOUR ADMISSION PASSES on arrival at Walt Disney World or purchase them in advance. Admission passes are available at Walt Disney World resorts and theme parks. Passes are also available at some non-Disney hotels and shopping centers, as well as through independent ticket brokers. Because Disney admission prices are only marginally discounted in the Walt Disney World–Orlando area, the chief reason for you to purchase from an independent broker is convenience. Offers of free or heavily discounted tickets abound, but they generally require you to attend a time-share sales presentation.

Magic Your Way tickets are available at Disney Stores and at **disney world.com** for the same prices listed in the chart on pages 50 and 51.

If you're trying to keep costs to an absolute minimum, consider using an online ticket wholesaler, such as **Undercover Tourist, Kissimmee Guest Services, Maple Leaf Tickets,** or the **Official Ticket Center,** especially for trips with five or more days in the theme parks. All tickets sold are brand-new, and the savings can range from $2 to more than $41, depending on the ticket and options chosen. We've spoken with representatives from each company, and they're well versed in the pros and cons of the various tickets and options. If the new options don't make sense for your specific vacation plans, the reps will tell you so.

unofficial **TIP**
If you order tickets in advance of your trip, be sure to allow enough time for the tickets to be mailed to your home.

All four companies offer discounts on tickets for almost all Central Florida attractions, including Disney, Universal, SeaWorld, and Cirque du Soleil. Discounts for the major theme parks range from about 6% to 8.5%. Tickets for other attractions are more deeply discounted. **Undercover Tourist** (U.S.: ☎ 800-846-1302; Monday–Friday, 9 a.m.–4 p.m. Eastern time; U.K.: ☎ 0800 081 1702; Monday–Friday, 2 p.m.–9 p.m. Greenwich mean time; worldwide: ☎ +1 386-239-8624; fax +1 386-252-3469; **undercovertourist.com**) offers free delivery and has a sweetheart relationship with **MouseSavers** (**mousesavers.com**). If you subscribe to the MouseSavers e-newsletter, you can access Undercover Tourist through a special "secret" link that provides additional savings on top of the normal discount. **Kissimmee Guest Services** (950 Celebration Blvd., Suite H, Celebration; ☎ 321-939-2057; Monday–Friday, 8 a.m.–8 p.m., Saturday, 8 a.m.–5 p.m., Sunday, 8 a.m.–noon, all Eastern time; U.K.: ☎ 0208 432 4024; **kgs tickets.com**) offers a lowest-price guarantee and $10 delivery to any Orlando-area hotel (orders over $5 only). The **Official Ticket Center** (3148 Vineland Road, Kissimmee; daily, 8 a.m.–8:30 p.m. Eastern time; ☎ 407-396-9029 or 877-406-4836; fax 407-396-9323; **official ticketcenter.com**) offers U.S. Priority Mail shipping for a flat $8 fee or $10 for delivery to Orlando-area hotels; it's of course free if you pick up at their office. **Maple Leaf Tickets** (4647 W. Irlo Bronson Highway [US 192], Kissimmee; daily, 8 a.m.–6 p.m. Eastern time; ☎ 407-396-0300 or 800-841-2837; fax 407-396-4127; **mapleleaftickets.com**) offers the same deal on pickup at their store and for $6.95 delivery to Orlando-area hotels; U.S. Priority Mail service is a flat $6.95 per order.

You can also save money on Disney World tickets just by planning ahead and watching the calendar, as this mom from Broomfield, Colorado, explains:

> *If you're planning a trip in advance, buy your passes before the end of the year. Our travel agent recommended this because Disney usually increases its prices in the new year. So we bought our tickets for June back in December and sure enough, I found the price of a pass had increased $20 per person. That's an $80 savings for our family.*

Finally, if all this is too confusing, our website will help you navigate all of the new options and find the least expensive ticket options for your vacation. Visit **touringplans.com** for more details.

FOR ADDITIONAL INFORMATION ON PASSES

IF YOU HAVE A QUESTION OR CONCERN regarding admissions that can be addressed only through a person-to-person conversation, call **Disney Ticket Inquiries** at ☎ 407-566-4985, or e-mail **ticket.inquiries@disneyworld.com.** If you call, be aware that you may spend a considerable time on hold; if you e-mail, be aware that it can take up to three days to get a response. If you just need routine information, call ☎ 407-824-4321 for recorded info. If the recorded information doesn't answer your question, return to the main menu and press *0* to reach a live Disney representative. Information is also available at **disneyworld.com.**

unofficial **TIP**
What to do with the kid's pass you bought long before your 6-foot-tall teenager hit puberty? Go to Guest Relations and ask to have it changed into a regular-admission pass for the number of days left on the ticket.

WHERE THE REAL DEALS ARE

BOTH GREAT THEME PARKS, **Universal Studios Florida** and **Universal's Islands of Adventure** routinely offer admission discounts and specials. At one time, for example, you could score a free two-day, two-park park-hopping ticket for the kids (ages 3–9) for every adult two-day, two-park ticket you bought online at **universalorlando.com.** For a family of four—say, Mom, Dad, and two kids under age 10—the total cost to visit both Universal parks was $290, including tax. For the same family to spend two days at Disney parks with park-hopping privileges during the same period, it cost a whopping $967, tax included. Even in the absence of any discounts, two days of park-hopping at Universal for our family of four cost $409 less than the same admission at Walt Disney World.

THE BRITISH ARE COMING!

IN THE UNITED KINGDOM, DISNEY offers advance-purchase tickets not available in the United States. The **Five-Day Premium Ticket** costs £231 for adults and £204 for children. It provides unlimited admission as well as park-hopping privileges to the major theme parks, and five admissions to the minor venues. The **Seven-Day Premium Ticket** (£236 for adults and £209 for children) provides the same features except that it includes seven admissions to the minor venues. Both expire 14 days from the date of first use.

Ultimate Tickets are priced at £236 for adults and £209 for kids for 14-day passes, and £274 and £247 for 21-day passes. The Ultimate Tickets provide unlimited admission to both major and minor parks along with park-hopping privileges to the major parks. The 14-day Ultimate Ticket expires 14 days after first use, and the 21-day Ultimate Ticket expires 21 days after first use. For additional information call ☎ 0870-242-4900 U.K. or ☎ 407-566-4985 U.S., or see **disneyworld .co.uk** or the **Disney Information Bulletin Board** at **thedibb.co.uk.**

MORE DISCOUNTS ON ADMISSIONS

Admission Discounts Available to Certain Groups and Individuals

AAA Members can buy passes for a discount of 3–5%.

DISNEY VACATION CLUB Members get a discount on Annual Passes.

DISNEY CORPORATE SPONSORS If you work for a Disney World corporate sponsor, you might be eligible for discounted admissions or preferential treatment at the parks. Ask your employee-benefits office.

MILITARY, DEPARTMENT OF DEFENSE, CIVIL SERVICE Active-duty and retired military, Department of Defense (DOD) civilian employees, some civil-service employees, and dependents of these groups can buy Disney multiday admissions at a 9–10% discount. At most military and DOD installations, the passes are available from the Morale, Welfare, and Recreation office. Civil-service employees should contact their personnel office to see if they're eligible. Military personnel can buy a discounted admission for nonmilitary guests as long as the military member accompanies the nonmilitary member. If a group seeks the discount, at least half must be eligible for the military discount.

Special Passes

Walt Disney World offers a number of special and situational passes that are not known to the general public and are not sold at any Disney World ticket booth. The best information we've found on these passes is available on the Internet at **mousesavers.com.**

HOW MUCH DOES IT COST PER DAY?

A TYPICAL DAY WOULD COST $623.92, excluding lodging and transportation, for a family of four—Mom, Dad, 12-year-old Tim, and

8-year-old Sandy—driving their own car and staying outside the World. They plan to stay a week, so they buy five-day Base Tickets with Park Hopper Option.

HOW MUCH DOES A DAY COST?	
Breakfast for four at Denny's with tax and tip	$29.50
Epcot parking fee (free for pass holders and resort guests)	$14.00
Four day admission on a 5-day Base Ticket with Park Hopper Option	$273.08
Dad: *Adult 5-day with tax is $346.13 divided by five days = $69.23*	
Mom: *Adult 5-day with tax is $346.13 divided by five days = $69.23*	
Tim: *Adult 5-day with tax is $346.13 divided by five days = $69.23*	
Sandy: *Child 5-day with tax is $326.96 divided by five days = $65.39*	
Morning break (soda or coffee)	$13.50
Fast-food lunch (sandwich or burger, fries, soda), no tip	$38.00
Afternoon break (soda and popcorn)	$21.50
Dinner at Italy (no alcoholic beverages) with tax and tip	$195.34
Souvenirs (Mickey T-shirts for Tim and Sandy) with tax*	$39.00
One-day total (without lodging or transportation)	**$623.92**
* *Cheer up—you won't have to buy souvenirs every day.*	

The cost of a Disney vacation almost always increases at a rate higher than either the rate of U.S. inflation (as measured by the Consumer Price Index) or the rate of the average U.S. worker's wages (as measured by the federal Bureau of Labor Statistics). The largest price hikes lately have occurred at Disney's full-service restaurants. Our typical dinner at Epcot's Italy Pavilion—two shared appetizers, median-priced entrees for the adults, a child's dinner, two shared sides, two shared desserts, and four sodas—has increased by 8% in the past year. That's more than three times the rate of inflation (currently around 2.2%) and the average U.S. worker's wages increase (about 1.7%). By way of comparison, the one-day total also increased by about 3.4% since our last edition's update.

A Birmingham, Alabama, mom of two begs to differ with our budget recommendation above for souvenirs:

> *Sorry, but Uncle Bob is totally out of touch when he says "you won't have to buy souvenirs every day." In my experience, you'll head home with several sets of character ears; enough dress-up costumes to outfit the neighborhood; and countless pins, toys, and knickknacks.*

▮▮ ALLOCATING TIME

DURING DISNEY WORLD'S FIRST DECADE, a family with a week's vacation could enjoy the Magic Kingdom and the now-closed River Country and still have several days left for the beach or other area attractions. Since Epcot opened in 1982, however, Disney World has steadily been enlarging to monopolize the family's entire vacation.

Today, with the addition of Blizzard Beach, Typhoon Lagoon, Disney's Hollywood Studios, Disney's Animal Kingdom, and Downtown Disney, you should allocate 6 days for a whirlwind tour (7–10 if you insist on a little relaxation during your vacation). If you don't have that much time, be prepared to make some hard choices.

The theme parks and water parks are huge and require a lot of walking and, sometimes, a lot of waiting in lines. Approach Walt Disney World the same way you would an eight-course Italian dinner: with plenty of time between courses. Don't cram too much into too little time.

WHICH PARK TO SEE FIRST?

THIS QUESTION IS LESS ACADEMIC than it appears, especially if your party includes children or teenagers. Children who see the Magic Kingdom first expect the same type of entertainment at the other parks. At Epcot, they're often disappointed by the educational orientation and serious tone (many adults react the same way). Disney's Hollywood Studios offers some wild action, but the general presentation is educational and more adult. Though most children enjoy zoos, animals can't be programmed to entertain. Thus, children may not find Animal Kingdom as exciting as the Magic Kingdom or DHS.

First-time visitors should see Epcot first; you'll be able to enjoy it without having been preconditioned to think of Disney entertainment as solely fantasy or adventure.

See Disney's Animal Kingdom second. Like Epcot, it's educational, but its live animals provide a change of pace.

Next, see Disney's Hollywood Studios, which helps all ages transition from the educational Epcot and Animal Kingdom to the fanciful Magic Kingdom. Also, because DHS is smaller, you won't walk as much or stay as long.

Save the Magic Kingdom for last.

The foregoing advice notwithstanding, we know that most readers make a beeline for the Magic Kingdom, mostly for the reason that this North Carolina reader asserts:

> Although you recommend sort of a reverse order for park visitation, ending up at the Magic Kingdom last, I disagree. We went to the Magic Kingdom first, which is Disney World for many of us.

OPERATING HOURS

DISNEY RUNS A DOZEN OR MORE SCHEDULES each year. Call ☎ 407-824-4321 for the exact hours before you arrive. Off-season, parks may be open as few as 8 hours (9 a.m.–5 p.m.). At busy times (particularly holidays), they may operate from 8 a.m. until 2 a.m. We maintain easily readable park hours and entertainment and Extra Magic Hour schedules at **touringplans.com** and through our mobile app, **Lines** (**touringplans.com/lines**).

OFFICIAL OPENING VERSUS REAL OPENING

WHEN YOU CALL, you're given "official hours." Sometimes, parks open earlier. If the official hours are 9 a.m.–9 p.m., for example, Main

Street in the Magic Kingdom might open at 8:30 a.m., and the remainder of the park at 9 a.m.

Disney surveys local hotel reservations, estimates how many visitors to expect on a given day, and opens the theme parks early to avoid bottlenecks at parking facilities and ticket windows and to absorb crowds as they arrive.

Rides and attractions shut down at approximately the official closing time. Main Street in the Magic Kingdom remains open 30 minutes to an hour after the rest of the park has closed.

THE VACATION THAT FIGHTS BACK

VISITING DISNEY WORLD REQUIRES levels of industry and stamina more often associated with running marathons. A mother from Middletown, New York, spells it out:

> A vacation at WDW is not a vacation in the usual sense. Rather, it's a vacation that's frankly exhausting, but definitely worth doing. WDW is a magical place, where the visitor feels welcomed from the minute they arrive at their accommodations to the last second before boarding the shuttle bus back to the airport.

A British gentleman, thinking we exaggerated about the walking required, measured his outings using a pedometer. His discovery:

> I decided to wear a pedometer for our recent visit to WDW. Our visits to the theme parks were spread over five days, during which my wife and I (ages 51 and 55) walked a total of 68 miles for an average of 13 miles per day!

The point is, at Walt Disney World less is more. Take the World in small doses, with plenty of swimming, napping, reading, and relaxing in between. If you don't see everything, you can always come back!

Also, you can prepare. An Ohio reader discovered this too late:

> I fly a desk for a living and don't get near enough walking or standing exercise to prepare myself for the rigors of the World. My wife and I have determined that before we go to Disney World again, we will be able to walk at least 5 miles without a rest or feeling any pain the next day. After pounding the pavement for hours on end, we were so exhausted that we had no choice but to spend two of our vacation days just recovering from the previous day's walking.

Hitting the Wall

As you plan your time at Disney World, consider your physical limitations. It's exhausting to rise at dawn and run around a theme park for 8–12 hours day after day. Sooner or later (usually sooner), you hit the wall. Every Disney World vacation itinerary should include days when you don't go to a theme park and days when you sleep in and take the morning off. Plan these to follow unusually long and arduous days, particularly those when you stay in the parks to see the evening parades or fireworks.

A Suwanee, Georgia, reader makes this suggestion:

*The one area that I think you can expand on in your book is pre-
paring people for the overall pace that this type of vacation war-
rants. My initial plan for the family entailed a day at MK, one day
each at Epcot, Animal Kingdom, Disney's Hollywood Studios, Universal Studios, and Islands of Adventure, one down day, and a left-
over day for a second visit to something we hadn't finished. By day
two, I became acutely aware that there was no way we would be able
to keep up that pace.*

A La Grange, Illinois, mom sidestepped our advice to stay rested:

*As I was planning, I was very sure we wouldn't be taking a swim/nap
break in the middle of the day. No way! On the very first day of touring (at the Magic Kingdom), my 7-year-old said (at 9:30 a.m.—after
only 2 hours at the park), "I'm hot—when can we go back to the hotel
and swim?" Needless to say, we took that little break every day.*

THE PRACTICALITY OF RETURNING TO YOUR HOTEL FOR REST

MANY READERS WRITE ABOUT the practicality of departing the
theme park for a nap and swim at the hotel. A dad from Sequim,
Washington, made the following request:

*I would like to see nearness to the parks emphasized in your accom-
modation guide, taking traffic and hotel access into account. We tried
going back to the hotel for midday breaks, but it was too time-consuming. By the time you got to the car, negotiated traffic, rested, and
reversed the process to get back to the park, it took 2–3 hours for a
short rest and was not worth it!*

First, in response to the reader's request, we publish a chart in
Part Three, Accommodations, that provides the commuting times to
each of the Disney theme parks from virtually every hotel within 20
miles of Walt Disney World. But to address the larger issue, we think
the reader was overly anxious about the time away from the parks.
Two to three hours really won't cut it. Had he resigned himself to a
4- to 5-hour break, his family would've stayed rested and relaxed.

Here's the scoop: At Disney's Animal Kingdom, Disney's Hollywood
Studios, and Epcot, you can get to your car in the parking lot in about
15–20 minutes. From the Magic Kingdom, it will take you 30–35 minutes. Obviously, if you're at the farthest point from the park entrance
when you decide to return to the hotel, or you barely miss a parking-
lot tram, it will take longer. But from most places in the parks, the
previous times are correct. Once in your car, you'll be able to commute to most US 192 hotels, all Disney World hotels, all Lake Buena
Vista hotels, and most hotels along the Interstate 4 corridor and south
International Drive ("I-Drive") in 20 minutes or less. It will take about
the same time to reach hotels on I-Drive north of Sand Lake Road and
in the Universal Orlando area.

So, for most people, the one-way commute will average 30 minutes.
But here's what you get for your time: a less-expensive lunch at a restaurant of your choosing; a swim; and a 1½- to 2-hour nap. If you add
up the times, you'll be away from the parks about 4–5 hours, counting

the commute. If you want, eat dinner outside the World before returning. Clearly, this won't work during times of year when the parks close early, but these aren't times when most families go to Disney World. If you visit when the parks close early, you'll see more attractions in less time, owing to reduced attendance, and you'll be able to leave the parks earlier and take your break in the late afternoon or early evening. Not ideal, but neither are the crowds and heat of summer.

A corollary to this discussion is what you do the next day. If you're getting a 3- to 5-hour break each day and not keeping late hours, you'll be fine. If you forgo the break, you'll need to alternate full days with very easy, sleep-late days in order to recharge your batteries. If you do neither, you'll say hello to the wall by your third day.

A Boston mom shares her experience:

> *The tip about taking the break is an absolute must! The days we didn't take the break were a nightmare. Don't make that decision when the kids are doing fine at noon. Think about that tired, cranky, sweaty child in about 3 hours. Then imagine that same child at 5 p.m.!*

ARRIVAL- AND DEPARTURE-DAY BLUES: WHAT TO DO WHEN YOU HAVE ONLY HALF A DAY

unofficial **TIP**
You may want to forgo a half-day at the Disney parks for other area attractions that are smaller and require less visiting time—or to just unpack and gear up for your first full Disney day.

ON ARRIVAL AND DEPARTURE DAYS, you probably will have only part of a day for touring or other recreational pursuits. It's a common problem: You roll into the World about 1 p.m., excited and ready to go—but where?

The first question: Do you feel comfortable using a full day's admission to the parks when you have less than a full day to tour? The incremental cost to add another day of admission is small when you're visiting for three or more days, but significant if you're there for only a long weekend.

Your arrival time and the parks' closing times are also considerations, but so is the touring disadvantage you suffer by not being on hand when a park opens. **Fastpass,** a reservation system for popular attractions (discussed starting on page 80), provides some relief from long afternoon lines, but it isn't available for every attraction, nor is there an unlimited supply of passes.

Opting for a Partial Day at the Theme Parks

If you decide to use one day's admission on a half-day or less, refer to our *Unofficial Guide* Crowd Calendar at **touringplans.com.**

One option, if you can reach the park before 1 p.m. and stay until closing (5–8 p.m., depending on season), is Disney's Animal Kingdom, which requires the least time to tour. Because guests who arrive at opening frequently complete their tour by about 3 p.m., crowds thin in late afternoon. As a bonus, Fastpass is offered for the most popular attractions. If you arrive after 1 p.m., however, the daily allocation of Fastpasses, especially for Kilimanjaro Safaris or Expedition Everest, might be exhausted. And Animal Kingdom closes earlier than the other parks.

Whenever you arrive at a theme park (including Universal parks) after 10 a.m., you should go to higher-capacity attractions where waiting time is relatively brief, even during the most crowded part of the day. In Disney parks, you can also cut your time in line by using Fastpass. Another time-saver at Test Track in Epcot, at Expedition Everest in Disney's Animal Kingdom, and Rock 'n' Roller Coaster in Disney's Hollywood Studios, and at several Universal Studios and Islands of Adventure attractions is the **singles line,** a separate line for individuals who are alone or don't mind riding alone. The objective is to fill odd spaces left by groups that don't quite fill the entire ride vehicle. Because there aren't many singles and most groups are unwilling to split up, singles lines are usually much shorter than regular lines.

Disney parks are better for partial-day touring than Universal parks because Disney parks generally operate more high-capacity attractions than Universal does. We like the Universal parks and admire their cutting-edge technology, but the best way to see them is to be there at opening and follow our touring plans.

Our clip-out Touring Plan Companions (in the back of this book) list attractions in each Disney park that require the least waiting during the most crowded part of the day. Although the queues for these attractions may seem humongous, they move quickly. Also check out parades, stage shows, and other live entertainment. Popular attractions generally stay packed until an hour or so before closing; however, they often require little waiting during evening parades, fireworks, or, in the case of Disney's Hollywood Studios, *Fantasmic!*

Alternatives to the Theme Parks on Arrival Day

Before you head out for fun on arrival day, you must check in, unpack, and buy admissions, and you probably will detour to the grocery or convenience store to buy snacks, drinks, and breakfast food. At all Disney resorts and many non-Disney hotels, you cannot occupy your room until after 3 p.m.; however, many properties will check you in, sell you tickets, and store your luggage before that hour.

The least expensive way to spend your arrival day is to check in, unpack, do your chores, and relax at your hotel swimming pool.

Other daytime options include a trip to a local water park. Because the Disney water parks are so crowded (during summer you need to be on hand for opening, just as you do at the other Disney parks), we recommend **Wet 'n Wild** (**wetnwildorlando.com**) on International Drive, which is generally less crowded than Disney's water parks but more expensive. What's great about Wet 'n Wild is that it stays open late in summer. Any water park that stays open past 5 p.m. is worth a look, because crowds at all parks clear out substantially after 4 p.m. If the park is open late and you get hungry, you'll find ample fast food. No matter which water park you choose, slather on broad-spectrum sunscreen. (For details on water parks, see Part Twenty.)

If you want something drier, we heartily recommend **Gatorland,** a quirky attraction on US 441 near Kissimmee (about 20 minutes from Walt Disney World). Gatorland, a slice of pre-Disney Florida, is exceptionally interesting and well managed. It's perfect for a half-day outing, provided you like alligators, snakes, and lizards. For information, call ☎ 800-393-JAWS or go to **gatorland.com**.

If none of the previous fires your boiler, consider miniature golf (expensive in the World; more reasonable outside it) or **DisneyQuest,** a venue at Downtown Disney West Side featuring interactive games and simulator technology. Alas, like the Disney parks, DisneyQuest is expensive and doesn't handle crowds particularly well. Late mornings and early afternoons are the best times to go.

In the Evening

Dinner provides a great opportunity to plan the next day's activities. If you're hungry for entertainment too, take in a show at or after dinner. If you go the show route, we recommend **Cirque du Soleil** *La Nouba* at Downtown Disney West Side. Cirque is expensive, but we think it's the single best thing in all of Walt Disney World. Disney also offers some dinner shows, of which the *Hoop-Dee-Doo Musical Revue* is our pick of the litter. Both Cirque and *Hoop-Dee-Doo* are extremely popular; make reservations far in advance. A dozen or so non-Disney dinner shows are advertised in visitor magazines.

If you're not up for Cirque or a dinner show, consider **CityWalk,** Universal's nighttime-entertainment complex. Other options include **Jellyrolls,** a dueling-pianos club at the BoardWalk, and **Raglan Road,** an Irish pub with live music and good food at Downtown Disney. All are best appreciated by adults—energetic adults, at that.

Departure Days

Departure days don't seem to cause as much consternation as arrival days. If you want to visit a theme park on your departure day, get up early and be there when it opens. If you have a lot of time, check out and store your luggage with the bell desk or in your car. Or, if you can arrange a late checkout, you might want to return to your hotel for a shower and change of clothes before departing. Some hotels are quite lenient regarding late checkouts; others assess a charge.

THE CARDINAL RULES FOR SUCCESSFUL TOURING

MANY VISITORS DON'T HAVE SIX DAYS to devote to Disney. Some are en route to other destinations or may wish to sample additional Central Florida attractions. For these visitors, efficient touring is a must.

Even the most time-effective touring plan won't allow you to comprehensively cover two or more major theme parks in one day. Plan to allocate an entire day to each park (an exception to this is when the parks close at different times, allowing you to tour one park until closing, then proceed to another).

One-Day Touring

A comprehensive one-day tour of the Magic Kingdom, Epcot, Disney's Animal Kingdom, or Disney's Hollywood Studios is possible but requires knowledge of the park, good planning, good navigation, and plenty of energy and endurance. One-day touring leaves little time for sit-down meals, prolonged browsing in shops, or lengthy breaks. One-day touring can be fun and rewarding, but allocating two days per park, especially for the Magic Kingdom and Epcot, is preferable.

Successfully touring the Magic Kingdom, Epcot, Animal Kingdom, or Disney's Hollywood Studios hinges on three rules:

1. Determine in Advance What You Really Want to See

Which attractions appeal to you most? Which ones would you like to experience if you have time left? What are you willing to forgo?

To help you set your touring priorities, we describe the theme parks and every attraction in detail in this book. In each description, we include the authors' evaluation of the attraction and the opinions of Disney World guests expressed as star ratings. Five stars is the highest rating.

Finally, because attractions range from mid-way-type rides and horse-drawn trolleys to high-tech extravaganzas, we have developed a hierar-chy of categories to pinpoint an attraction's magnitude:

unofficial **TIP**
If your schedule permits only one day of touring, concentrate on one theme park and save the others for another visit.

SUPER-HEADLINERS The best attractions the theme park has to offer. Mind-boggling in size, scope, and imagination. Represent the cutting edge of attraction technology and design.

HEADLINERS Multimillion-dollar, full-scale, themed adventures and theater presentations. Modern in technology and design and employing a full range of special effects.

MAJOR ATTRACTIONS More modestly themed adventures, but ones that incorporate state-of-the-art technologies. Or larger-scale attractions of older design.

MINOR ATTRACTIONS Midway-type rides, small "dark" rides (cars on a track, zigzagging through the dark), small theater presentations, transportation rides, and elaborate walk-through attractions.

DIVERSIONS Exhibits, both passive and interactive. Includes playgrounds, video arcades, and street theater.

Though not every attraction fits neatly into these descriptions, the categories provide a comparison of attraction size and scope. Remember that bigger and more elaborate doesn't always mean better. Peter Pan's Flight, a minor attraction in the Magic Kingdom, continues to be one of the park's most beloved rides. Likewise, for many young children, no attraction, regardless of size, surpasses Dumbo.

2. Arrive Early! Arrive Early! Arrive Early!

This is the single most important key to efficient touring and avoiding long lines. First thing in the morning, there are no lines and fewer people. The same four rides you experience in 1 hour in early morning can take as long as 3 hours after 10:30 a.m. Eat breakfast before you arrive; don't waste prime touring time sitting in a restaurant.

The earlier a park opens, the greater your advantage. This is because most vacationers won't rise early and get to a park before it opens. Fewer people are willing to make an 8 a.m. opening than a 9 a.m. opening. On those rare occasions when a park opens at 10 a.m., almost everyone arrives at the same time, so it's almost impossible to beat the crowd. If you visit during midsummer, arrive at the turnstile

30–40 minutes before opening. During holiday periods, arrive 45–60 minutes early.

Many readers share their experiences about getting to the parks before opening. From a 13-year-old girl from Bloomington, Indiana:

> Please stress this to your readers: If you want to ride anything with a short wait, you have to get up in the morning! If this is a sacrifice you aren't willing to make, reconsider a Disney World vacation. If you take a break at the hot part of the day, you'll be fine.

An Owasso, Oklahoma, reader followed our advice, with great results:

> Every time we got to the park before opening time as suggested by the guide, we were able to do every attraction as many times as we wanted to. It also allowed us to relax when it got hot later in the day.

A Pennsylvania mom of two found that slacking didn't pay:

> This is emphasized in the guide multiple times, but I want to say it again: Be at rope drop. I went during one of the slowest times of the year, and the morning I didn't wake up for rope drop I was able to experience less than half of what I did the other days.

Likewise, from a Tecumseh, Ontario, reader:

> There were a couple of days that we did not want to be tied to a schedule and tried to take it easy a bit, starting out with breakfast at a restaurant. Well, we sure made a mistake on those days! It made us late for park opening and really messed up the whole day.

A Minneapolis mother of three managed a compromise:

> Getting there early meant we could do the popular things without a long wait. That way I got my type-A "get things done" stuff out of the way in the morning and my husband got to indulge his "let's wander without a plan" personality the rest of the day.

Most touring plans are compromised if you're not on hand for park opening, as this dad from Whitehouse, New Jersey, attests:

> We were astonished at the number of people who show up at the parks after 11 a.m. and are surprised to learn how long it takes to do things. We've met people who seem to wake up one morning and decided to go to Disney World without knowing anything about the place. It's as if they were showing up at a church fair.

If getting the kids up earlier than usual makes for rough sailing, don't despair: You'll have a great time no matter when you get to the park. Many families with young children have found that it's better to accept the relative inefficiencies of arriving at the park a bit late than to jar the children out of their routine. In our guide especially for families, *The Unofficial Guide to Walt Disney World with Kids,* we provide a number of special touring plans (including touring plans for sleepyheads) that we don't have room for in this guide.

3. Avoid Bottlenecks

Helping you avoid bottlenecks is what the *Unofficial Guide* is about. This involves being able to predict where, when, and why they occur.

Concentrations of hungry people create bottlenecks at restaurants during lunch and dinner; concentrations of people moving toward the exit near closing time cause gift shops en route to clog; concentrations of visitors at new and popular rides, and at rides slow to load and unload, create logjams and long lines.

Our solution for avoiding bottlenecks is touring plans for the Magic Kingdom, Epcot, Disney's Animal Kingdom, Disney's Hollywood Studios, and the two Disney water parks. We also provide detailed information on rides and performances, enabling you to estimate how long you may have to wait in line and allowing you to compare rides for their crowd capacity.

All touring plans are in the back of this book, following the indexes. Plans for the Magic Kingdom begin on page 818 and for Epcot on page 824. One-day touring plans for Animal Kingdom and Disney's Hollywood Studios follow, on pages 829 and 830, respectively. Next come one-day touring plans for Universal Studios Florida and Universal's Islands of Adventure, on pages 831 and 832, respectively. Finally, touring plans for Blizzard Beach and Typhoon Lagoon water parks are found on pages 833 and 834, respectively.

WHAT'S A QUEUE?

ALTHOUGH IT'S NOT COMMONLY USED in the United States, *queue* (pronounced "cue") is the universal English word for a line, such as one in which you wait to cash a check at the bank or to board a ride at a theme park. Queuing theory, a mathematical area of specialization within the field of operations research, studies and models how lines work. Because the *Unofficial Guide* draws heavily on this discipline, we use some of its terminology. In addition to the noun, the verb *to queue* means to get in line, and a *queuing area* is a waiting area that accommodates a line. When guests decline to join a queue because they perceive the wait to be too long, they're said to *balk*.

OF UTMOST IMPORTANCE: READ THIS!

IN ANALYZING READER SURVEYS, we were astonished by the percentage of readers who *don't* use our touring plans. Scientifically tested and proven, these plans can save you **4 entire hours** or more of waiting in line in a single day—4 fewer hours of standing, 4 hours freed up to do something fun. Our groundbreaking research that created the touring plans has been the subject of front-page articles in the *Dallas Morning News* and *The New York Times* and has been cited in numerous scholarly journals. So why would you *not* use them?

We get a ton of reader mail—98% of it positive—commenting on our touring plans. First, from an Albany, New York, reader:

> I used the One-Day Touring Plan for Adults for the Magic Kingdom, and I was shocked by how well it worked. I even took about a 3-hour break to go to Downtown Disney (via the Contemporary), and I was still able to do everything on the plan. Incredible.

A Danville, Pennsylvania, mom overcame a doubting spouse:

> My husband thought the touring plans were a product of an overly obsessive-compulsive mind. He laughed at me for wanting to use

them, but he finally conceded on Christmas Eve at the Magic King-dom. He wasn't laughing anymore by noon, when we had already ridden all of the rides with really long lines!

On the other hand, a somewhat irritated Washington, West Virginia, wife reports:

I saw several people with the Unofficial Guide *and had to ask if the plans really work. They all said yes. Unfortunately, my husband had his own plans . . . which didn't include following anyone else's.*

An Ohio family felt the wind in their sails:

The whole time we were in the Magic Kingdom, following the tour-ing plan, it seemed that we were traveling in front of a hurricane—we'd wait 10 minutes or so for an attraction (or less—sometimes we just walked right on), but when we got out and started moving on to the next one, we could see the line building for what we just did.

For a Glasgow, Scotland, reader, touring the *Unofficial* way con-tributed to family harmony:

Trying to decide where to go next wasn't something we had to worry about. There was none of that "Whatever you think"/"I don't mind"–type discussion that can haunt even the best of holidays.

For two readers, our touring plans had unexpected benefits. A 30-something mom of two from Oconomowoc, Wisconsin, found that they fanned the flames of *amour:*

My husband was a bit doubtful about using a touring plan, but on our first day at Magic Kingdom, after we'd done all the Fantasyland attrac-tions and ridden Splash Mountain twice before lunch, he looked at me with amazement and said, "I've never been so attracted to you."

Meanwhile, to a young, Gardner, Massachusetts, reader's delight, the plans boosted her popularity:

I went with my school for the Magic Music Days (we performed in the Main Street Electrical Parade and the Candlelight Processional). I've been to Disney before several times, and my parents have always used the Guide. I looked crazy to my friends, with my huge book well worn and marked with Post-its and a stack of clip-out touring plans in my hand. The group who traveled around with me were amazed—as soon as we would leave a ride we had walked on with no wait min-utes before, there'd be a line with a wait of 15–20 minutes! Thank you for helping me impress my friends!

TOURING PLANS: WHAT THEY ARE AND HOW THEY WORK

See More, Do More, Wait Less

From the first edition of the *Unofficial Guide,* minimizing our readers' waits in line has been a top priority. We know from our research and that of others that theme park patrons measure overall satisfaction based on the number of attractions they're able to experience during a visit: the more attractions, the better. Thus, we developed and offered our readers field-tested touring plans that allow them to experience as many attractions as possible with the least amount of waiting in line.

Our touring plans have always been based on theme-park-traffic flow, attraction capacity, the maximum time a guest is willing to wait (called a *balking constraint*), walking distance between attractions, and waiting-time data collected at specific intervals throughout the day and at various times of year. The plans derived from a combinatorial model (for anyone who cares) that married the well-known assignment problem of linear programming with queuing (waiting-line) theory. The model approximated the most time-efficient sequence in which to visit the attractions of a specific park. After we created a preliminary touring plan from the model, we field-tested it in the park, using a test group (who followed our plan) and a control group (who didn't have our plan and who toured according to their own best judgment).

The two groups were compared, and the results were amazing. On days of heavy attendance, the groups touring without our plans spent an average of 4 hours more in line and experienced 37% fewer attractions than did those who did use the plans.

Over the years, this research has been recognized by both the travel industry and academe, having been cited by such diverse sources as *The New York Times, USA Today, Travel Weekly, Bottom Line, Money, Operations Research Forum*, CBS News, Fox News Channel, the BBC, the Travel Channel, and the *Atlanta Journal-Constitution*. The methodology behind our touring plans was also used as a case study in the 2010 book *Numbers Rule Your World*, by Kaiser Fung.

unofficial **TIP**
The facts and figures in our books come from years of data collection and analysis by expert statisticians, programmers, field researchers, and lifelong Disney enthusiasts.

John Henry and the Nail-Driving Machine

As sophisticated as our model may sound, we recognized that it was cumbersome and slow, and that it didn't approximate the "perfect" touring plan as closely as we desired. Moreover, advances in computer technology and science, specifically in the field of genetic algorithms, demonstrated that it wouldn't be long before a model, or program, was created that would leave ours in the dust.

Do you remember the story of John Henry, the fastest nail driver on the railroad? One day a man appeared with a machine he claimed could drive spikes faster than any man. John Henry challenged the machine to a race, which he won, but which killed him in the process. We felt a bit like John Henry. We were still very good at what we did but knew with absolute certainty that sooner or later we'd have to confront the touring plan version of a nail-driving machine.

Our response was to build our own nail-driving machine. We teamed up during the mid-1990s with Len Testa, a scientist and programmer who was working in the field of evolutionary algorithms and who, coincidentally, was a Disney junkie. Marrying our many years of collecting Walt Disney World observations and data to Len's vision and programming expertise, we developed a state-of-the-art program for creating nearly perfect touring plans.

Several university professors, many of them leaders in their fields, have contributed research or ideas to the software program. Findings from early versions of the software have been published in peer-reviewed academic journals. The most recent versions of the program are protected through pending patent applications. Special thanks go to Albert C. Esterline, PhD, and Gerry V. Dozier, PhD, of North Carolina A&T State University. Credit is also due to Nikolaos Sahinidis, PhD, as well as his graduate students at the University of Illinois at Urbana-Champaign, who have contributed a number of exceptionally helpful studies. Chryssi Malandraki, PhD, of United Parcel Service and Robert Dial, PhD, of the Volpe National Transportation System Center have likewise provided assistance and encouragement over the years.

It has been a process of evolution and refinement, but in each year of its development, the new program came closer to beating the results of our long-lived model. In 2002 at field trials during the busy spring-break period, the new program beat the best touring plan generated by the traditional *Unofficial* model by 90 minutes at the Magic Kingdom. This was in addition to the 3 hours saved by the earlier model. Getting there, however, wasn't easy.

The Challenge

One thing that makes creating good touring plans difficult is that there are many different ways to see the same attractions. For example, if we want to visit Space Mountain, Pirates of the Caribbean, and Splash Mountain as soon as the Magic Kingdom opens, there are six ways that we can do so:

1. First ride Space Mountain, then Pirates of the Caribbean, then Splash Mountain.

2. First ride Space Mountain, then Splash Mountain, then Pirates of the Caribbean.

3. First ride Splash Mountain, then Space Mountain, then Pirates of the Caribbean.

4. First ride Splash Mountain, then Pirates of the Caribbean, then Space Mountain.

5. First ride Pirates of the Caribbean, then Splash Mountain, then Space Mountain.

6. First ride Pirates of the Caribbean, then Space Mountain, then Splash Mountain.

Some of these combinations make better touring plans than others. Because the queue for Space Mountain increases rapidly, it's best to ride this particular attraction first thing in the morning. For similar reasons, it would be better to ride Splash Mountain before Pirates. In this example, Touring Plan 2 would probably save us the most time standing in line. Touring Plan 5 would probably result in the most waiting in line.

As we add attractions to our list, the number of possible touring plans grows rapidly. Adding a fourth attraction would result in 24 possible touring plans, since there are four possible variations for each of the 6 plans listed previously. In general, the number of possible touring plans for n attractions is $n \cdot (n-1) \cdot (n-2) \ldots \cdot 1$. (Don't let the mathematical notation throw you. If we plug real numbers in, it's quite simple.) For five attractions, as an example, there are $5 \times 4 \times 3 \times 2 \times 1$ possible touring plans. If you don't have a calculator handy, that adds up to 120 potential plans. For six attractions, there are $6 \times 5 \times 4 \times 3 \times 2 \times 1$, or

720 possible plans. A list of 10 attractions has more than 3 million possible plans. The 21 attractions in the Magic Kingdom One-Day Touring Plan for Adults have a staggering 51,090,942,171,709,440,000 possible touring plans. That's more than 51 billion billion combinations, or roughly six times as many as the estimated number of grains of sand on Earth. Adding in complexities such as Fastpass, parades, meals, and breaks further increases the combinations.

Scientists have been working on similar problems for years. Companies that deliver packages, for example, plan each driver's route to minimize the distance driven, saving time and fuel. In fact, finding ways to visit many places with minimal effort is such a common problem that it has its own nickname: the traveling-salesman problem.

For more than a small number of attractions, the number of possible touring plans is so large it would take a very long time for even a powerful computer to find the single best plan. A number of proposed techniques give very good, but not necessarily exact, solutions to the traveling-salesman problem in a reasonable amount of time.

The *Unofficial Guide* touring plan program contains two algorithms that allow it to quickly analyze tens of millions of possible plans in a very short time. (An algorithm is to a computer what a recipe is to a chef. Just as a chef takes specific steps to make a cake, a computer takes specific steps to process information. Those steps, when grouped, form an algorithm.) The program can analyze Fastpass distribution patterns at all attractions, for example, and suggest the best times and attractions to use Fastpass. The software can also schedule rest breaks throughout the day. If you're going to eat lunch in the park, the software can suggest restaurants near where you'll be at lunchtime that will minimize the time you spend looking for food. Numerous other features are available, many of which we'll discuss in the next section.

The program, however, is only part of what's needed to create a good touring plan. Good data is also important. For more than 14 years, we've been collecting data in the theme parks at every conceivable time of year. With the introduction of our Lines mobile app in 2010, we've been able to collect wait times from every theme park every day of the year—more than 500,000 to date. We supplement this data with additional numbers from researchers in the parks. For example, one test we did involved comparing Disney's posted wait time at Space Mountain with the actual time guests were waiting in line. To do this, we had eight researchers get in line at Space Mountain every 15 minutes, from park opening to park closing, for days on end. Then we compared those actual wait times with Disney's posted wait times and used the results to calibrate our touring plan models.

So how good are the touring plans in the *Unofficial Guide*? Our computer program typically gets within about 2% of the optimal touring plan and finds an optimal plan for most straightforward situations around 70% of the time. To put this in perspective, if the hypothetical "perfect" Adult One-Day Touring Plan took about 10 hours to complete, the *Unofficial* touring plan would take around 10 hours and 12 minutes. Since it would take about 30 years for a really powerful computer to find that "perfect" plan, the extra 12 minutes is a reasonable trade-off.

In the 2003 edition of this guidebook, we noted the possibility of using our touring plan software to see all of the 40-plus attractions in the Magic Kingdom in one day. We dubbed this the Ultimate Magic Kingdom Touring Plan and offered it free to anyone up for the challenge. Several people have completed this plan since that time, and many others have come close. The current record-holders are Jordyn and Kenny White of Gun Barrel City, Texas, who saw 75 attractions in 17 hours and 26 minutes on June 17, 2011. That works out to roughly 1 attraction every 14 minutes. The Whites' record surpassed the effort of Graeme and Megan McGufficke of Asheville, North Carolina, who saw 60 attractions in 13 hours and 39 minutes on June 12, 2010. Drop us a line or visit **touringplans.com/ultimate** if you're up for the challenge. Ultimate Touring Plans are available for the other Disney World theme parks, too. Note that these plans aren't intended for families, first-time visitors, or anyone simply wanting a nice day in the parks. To the contrary, they're like running a marathon.

Make Your Own Touring Plans—Free

If you've never been to Walt Disney World, we suggest using the plans in this book. Besides being the best our program can produce, these plans have been field-tested by tens of thousands of families. They'll ensure that you see the best Disney attractions with as little waiting in line as possible.

If you're a return visitor who knows exactly what you want to see, go to **touringplans.com** to create your own touring plans, free of charge. Tell the software the date, time, and park you've chosen to visit, along with the attractions you want to see. The plan will tell you, for your specific travel date and time, the exact order in which to visit the attractions to minimize your waits in line. Besides attractions, you can schedule meals, breaks, character greetings, and more.

You can follow your touring plans on **Lines.** As you walk around the park, the app can automatically adjust your plan based on what's happening around you. If, say, a ride breaks down or a large tour group suddenly jumps in line at Space Mountain, your touring plan will be adjusted to make your overall wait in line as small as it can be. It's like a GPS for theme parks!

OVERVIEW OF THE TOURING PLANS

OUR TOURING PLANS ARE STEP-BY-STEP guides for seeing as much as possible with a minimum of standing in line. They're designed to help you avoid crowds and bottlenecks on days of moderate-to-heavy attendance. On days when attendance is lighter (see "Selecting the Time of Year for Your Visit," page 33), the plans will save time, but they won't be as critical to successful touring.

What You Can Realistically Expect from the Touring Plans

Though we present one-day touring plans for each theme park, be aware that the Magic Kingdom and Epcot have more attractions than you can reasonably expect to see in one day. Because the two-day plans for the Magic Kingdom and Epcot are the most comprehensive, efficient, and relaxing, we strongly recommend them over the one-day plans. However, if you must cram your visit into a single day, the one-day plans will allow you to see as much as is humanly possible. Although Disney's Hollywood Studios has grown considerably since its 1989 debut, seeing everything in one day is still possible. Likewise, Disney's Animal Kingdom is a one-day outing.

Variables That Affect the Success of the Touring Plans

The plans' success will be affected by how quickly you move from ride to ride; when and how many refreshment and restroom breaks you take; when, where, and how you eat meals; and your ability (or lack thereof) to find your way around. Smaller groups almost always move faster than larger groups, and parties of adults generally cover more ground than families with young children. Switching off (page 334), also known as "The Baby Swap" or child swapping, among other things, inhibits families with little ones from moving expeditiously among attractions. Plus, some folks simply cannot conform to the plans' "early to rise" conditions, as this reader from Cleveland Heights, Ohio, recounts:

> Our touring plans were thrown totally off by one member who could not be on time for opening. Even in October, this made a huge difference in our ability to see attractions without waiting. Zen-like patience and appreciating the moment are useful for group travel with varying ages and traveling styles.

And a family from Centerville, Ohio, says:

> The toughest thing about your touring plans was getting the rest of the family to stay with them, at least to some degree. Getting them to pass by attractions in order to hit something across the park was no easy task (sometimes impossible).

If you have young children in your party, be prepared for character encounters. The appearance of a Disney character usually stops a touring plan in its tracks. While some characters stroll the parks, it's equally common that they assemble in a specific venue where families queue up for photos and autographs. Meeting characters, posing for photos, and collecting autographs can burn hours of touring time. If your kids collect character autographs, you need to anticipate these interruptions and negotiate some understanding with your children about when you'll follow the plan and when you'll collect autographs. Our advice is to go with the flow or set aside a specific morning or afternoon for photos and autographs. Note that queues for autographs, especially in the Magic Kingdom and at Camp Minnie-Mickey in Disney's Animal Kingdom, are sometimes as long as the queues for major attractions. The only time-efficient ways to collect autographs are to use Fastpass where available (such as for Mickey Mouse and the Disney princesses at the Town Square Theater) or to line up at the character-greeting areas first thing in the morning. Early morning is also the best time to experience the popular attractions, so you may have some tough choices to make.

While we realize that following the plans isn't always easy, we nevertheless recommend continuous, expeditious touring until around noon. After noon, breaks and diversions won't affect the plans significantly.

Some variables that can profoundly affect the plans are beyond your control. Chief among these are the manner and timing of bringing a particular ride to capacity. For example, Big Thunder Mountain Railroad, a roller coaster in the Magic Kingdom, has five trains. On a given morning, it may begin operation with two of the five, then add the other three when needed. If the waiting line builds rapidly before operators go to full capacity, you could have a long wait, even in early morning.

Another variable relates to the time you arrive for a theater performance. You'll wait from the time you arrive until the end of the presentation in progress. Thus, if a show is 15 minutes long and you arrive 1 minute after it has begun, your wait will be 14 minutes. Conversely, if you arrive as the show is wrapping up, your wait will be only a minute or two.

Finally, the Disney Dining Plan's required restaurant reservations impose a rigid schedule that can derail a touring plan, as this Wichita, Kansas, mom attests:

The touring plans were impractical if used with the dining plan. The hour-long meals wreaked havoc on the itinerary, and we never seemed to be able to get back on track, even with low crowd levels and rainy afternoons!

Flexibility

The attractions included in the touring plans are the most popular ones as determined by more than 39,000 reader surveys. Even so, your favorite attractions might be different. Fortunately, the touring plans are flexible. One way to customize them is to use our touring plan software at **touringplans.com.** Just choose the attractions you really want to see, and the software will create a plan just for you.

Alternatively, some changes are simple enough to make on your own. If a plan calls for an attraction you don't wish to experience, simply skip it and move on to the next one. You can also substitute similar attractions in the same area of the park. If a plan calls for, say, riding Dumbo and you're not interested but you'd enjoy the Mad Tea Party (which is not on the plan), then go ahead and substitute it for Dumbo. As long as the substitution is a similar attraction—substituting a show for a ride won't work—and is pretty close to the attraction called for in the touring plan, you won't compromise the plan's overall effectiveness.

A family of four from South Slocan, British Columbia, found they could easily tailor the touring plans to meet their needs:

We amended your touring plans by taking out the attractions we didn't want to do and just doing the remainder in order. It worked great, and by arriving before the parks opened, we got to see everything we wanted, with virtually no waits!

As did a Jacksonville, Florida, family:

We used a combination of the Two-Day Touring Plan for Parents with Small Children and the Two-Day Touring Plan for Adults. We were able to get on almost everything with a 10-minute wait or less.

Our longest wait was on our second day for the Jungle Cruise, but the wait was still only 20 minutes.

What to Do if You Lose the Thread

Anything from a blister to a broken attraction can throw off a touring plan. If unforeseen events interrupt a plan:

1. Skip a step on the plan for every 20 minutes' delay. If, for example, you lose your wallet and spend an hour hunting it, skip three steps and pick up from there.

2. Forget the plan and organize the remainder of your day using the Walt Disney World standby wait times listed in our mobile application, **Lines** (**touringplans.com/lines**).

unofficial **TIP**
If you're following a touring plan in **Lines,** our mobile app, just press the "Optimize" button when you're ready to start touring again. The software will figure out the best possible plan for the remainder of your day, regardless of what just happened.

What to Expect When You Arrive at the Parks

Because most touring plans are based on being present when the theme park opens, you need to know about opening procedures. Disney transportation to the parks begins 1½–2 hours before official opening. The parking lots open at around the same time.

Each park has an entrance plaza outside the turnstiles. Usually, you're held there until 30 minutes before the official opening time, when you're admitted. What happens next depends on the season and the day's crowds.

1. **LOW SEASON** At slower times, you'll usually be confined outside the turnstiles or in a small section of the park until the official opening time. At the Magic Kingdom you might be admitted to Main Street, U.S.A.; at Disney's Animal Kingdom, to The Oasis and sometimes to Discovery Island; at Epcot, to the fountain area around Spaceship Earth; and at Disney's Hollywood Studios, to Hollywood Boulevard. Rope barriers supervised by Disney cast members keep you there until the "rope drop," when the barrier is removed and the park and its attractions are opened at the official start time.

2. **HIGH-ATTENDANCE DAYS** When large crowds are expected, you'll usually be admitted through the turnstiles up to 30 minutes before official opening, and the entire park will be operating.

3. **VARIATIONS** Sometimes Disney will run a variation of those two procedures. In this, you'll be permitted through the turnstiles and find that one or several specific attractions are open early. At Epcot, Spaceship Earth and sometimes Test Track or Soarin' will be operating. At Animal Kingdom, you may find Kilimanjaro Safaris and *It's Tough to Be a Bug!* running early. At Disney's Hollywood Studios, look for Tower of Terror, Toy Story Mania!, and/or Rock 'n' Roller Coaster. The Magic Kingdom almost never runs a variation. Instead, you'll usually encounter number 1, or occasionally 2.

For many years at all four parks, Disney cast members would dive for cover when the rope was dropped as hordes of adrenaline-crazed guests stampeded to the parks' most popular attractions. This ritual insanity no longer exists—at least not in the tumultuous versions of years past. Disney has increased the number of cast members supervising the rope drop in order to suppress the melee. In some cases, the rope isn't even "dropped." Instead, it's walked back: Cast members lead you with the rope at a fast walk toward the attraction you're straining to reach, forcing you (and everyone else) to maintain their pace. Not until they near the attraction do cast members step aside. A New Jersey mom described it thus:

> *You're no longer allowed to sprint to these attractions because of people being trampled. Now there's a phalanx of cast members lined up at the rope who instruct you in friendly but no uncertain terms that when the rope drops they will lead you to the rides at a fast walk. However, you're not allowed to pass them. (No one ever said what would happen if you did pass.) To my surprise, every-one followed the rules and we were splish-splashing within 5 min-utes after 9 a.m.*

When Disney walks the rope back, the only way you can gain an advantage is to arrive early enough to be up front near the rope. Be alert, though; cast members sometimes step out of the way after about 50 yards. If this happens, walk quickly but safely for the remaining distance to your destination.

Clip-Out Touring Plans

For your convenience, we've prepared graphical clip-out copies of all touring plans. These pocket versions combine touring plan itineraries with maps and directions. Select the plan appropriate for your party, and get familiar with it. Then clip the pocket version from the back of this guide and carry it with you as a quick reference at the theme park.

Will the Plans Continue to Work Once the Secret Is Out?

Yes! First, all the plans require that a patron be there when a park opens. Many Disney World patrons simply won't get up early while on vaca-tion. Second, less than 1% of any day's attendance has been exposed to the plans—too few to affect results. Last, most groups tailor the plans, skipping rides or shows according to taste.

How Frequently Are the Touring Plans Revised?

Because Disney is always adding new attractions and changing opera-tions, we revise the plans every year, and updates are always available at **touringplans.com.** Most complaints we receive come from readers using out-of-date editions of the *Unofficial Guide.* Even if you're up to date, though, be prepared for surprises. Opening procedures and show-times may change, for example, and you can't predict when an attrac-tion might break down.

Tour Groups from Hell

We've discovered that tour groups of up to 200 people sometimes use our plans. A woman from Memphis, Tennessee, writes:

> *When we arrived at the Land Pavilion at Epcot, a tour guide was holding your book and shouting into a bullhorn, "Step 7—proceed to Journey into Imagination!" With this, about 65 Japanese tourists in red T-shirts ran out the door.*

Unless your party is as large as the Japanese group, this develop-ment shouldn't alarm you. Because tour groups are big, they move slowly and have to stop to collect stragglers. The tour guide also has to accommodate the unpredictability of five dozen or so bladders.

"Bouncing Around"

Many readers object to crisscrossing a theme park as our touring plans sometimes require. A lady from Decatur, Georgia, said she "got dizzy from all the bouncing around." We empathize, but here's the rub, park by park.

In the Magic Kingdom, the most popular attractions are positioned across the park from one another. This is no accident. It's a method of more equally distributing guests throughout the park. If you want to experience the most popular attractions in one day without long waits, you can arrive before the park fills and see those attractions first (requires crisscrossing the park), or you can enjoy the main attractions on one side of the park first, then try the most popular attractions on the other side during the hour or so before closing, when crowds presumably have thinned. Using Fastpass lessens the time you wait in line but tends to increase the bouncing around because you must visit the same attraction twice: once to obtain your Fastpass and again to use it.

> *unofficial* **TIP**
> We've revised the Epcot plans to eliminate most of the "bouncing around" and have added instructions to minimize walking.

The best way to minimize "bouncing around" at the Magic Kingdom is to use the Two-Day Touring Plan (see pages 821 and 822), which spreads the more popular attractions over two mornings and works beautifully even when the park closes at 8 p.m. or earlier.

Disney's Animal Kingdom is arranged in a spoke-and-hub configuration like the Magic Kingdom, simplifying crisscrossing the park. Even so, the only way to catch various shows is to stop what you're doing and troop across the park to the next performance.

Disney's Hollywood Studios is configured in a way that precludes an orderly approach to touring, or to a clockwise or counterclockwise rotation. Orderly touring is further confounded by live entertainment that prompts guests to interrupt their touring to head for whichever theater is about to crank up. At the Studios, therefore, you're stuck with "bouncing around" whether you use our plan or not. In our opinion, when it comes to Disney parks, it's best to have a plan.

Touring Plans and the Obsessive-Compulsive Reader

We suggest sticking to the plans religiously, especially in the mornings, if you're visiting during busy times. The consequence of touring spontaneity in peak season is hours of standing in line. When using the plans, however, relax and always be prepared for surprises and setbacks.

If you find your type-A brain doing cartwheels, reflect on the advice of a woman from Trappe, Pennsylvania:

> *You cannot emphasize enough the dangers of those with compulsive personalities using your touring plans. I had planned for this trip for two years and researched it by use of guidebooks, computer programs, videotapes, and information received from WDW. On night three of our trip, I ended up taking an unscheduled trip to the emergency room. When the doctor asked what seemed to be the problem, I responded, "I don't know, but I can't stop shaking, and I can't stay*

here very long because I have to get up in a couple hours to go to Disney's Hollywood Studios." Diagnosis: an anxiety attack caused by my excessive itinerary.

An Omaha, Nebraska, couple devised their own way to cope:

We created our own 4.25 x 5.5 guidebook for our trip that included a number of pages from the **touringplans.com** *website. This was the first page:*

The Type-A Spouse's Bill of Rights
1. We will not see everything in one vacation, and any attempt to do so may be met with blunt trauma.
2. Len Testa will not be vacationing with us. His plans don't schedule time for benches. Ours may.
3. We may deviate from the touring plans at some point. Really.
4. Even if it isn't on the Disney Dining Plan, a funnel cake or other snack may be purchased without a grouchy face from the nonpurchasing spouse.
5. Sometimes, sitting by the pool may sound more fun than going to a park, show, or other scheduled event. On this vacation, that will be fine.
6. "But I thought we were going to . . ." is a phrase that must be stricken from the discussion of any plans that had not been previously discussed as a couple.
7. Other items may be added as circumstances dictate at the parks.

It was a much happier vacation with these generally understood principles in writing.

Touring Plan Rejection

Some folks don't respond well to the regimentation of a touring plan. If you encounter this problem with someone in your party, roll with the punches as this Maryland couple did:

The rest of the group was not receptive to the use of the touring plans. I think they all thought I was being a little too regimented about planning this vacation. Rather than argue, I left the touring plans behind as we ventured off for the parks. You can guess the outcome. We took our camcorder with us and watched the movies when we returned home. About every 5 minutes or so there's a shot of us all gathered around a park map trying to decide what to do next.

A reader from Royal Oak, Michigan, ran into trouble by not getting her family on board ahead of time:

The one thing I will suggest is if one member of the family is doing most of the research and planning (like I did), that they communicate what the book/touring plans suggest. I failed to do this and it led to some, shall we say, tense moments between my husband and me on our first day. However, once he realized how much time we were saving, he understood why I was so bent on following the plans.

Finally, as a Connecticut woman alleges, the plans are incompatible with some readers' bladders and personalities:

I want to know if next year when you write those "day" schedules you could schedule bathroom breaks in there, too. You expect us to be at a certain ride at a certain time, with no stops in between. What were you thinking when you made these schedules?

Note that our mobile app, **Lines,** can be used to find attractions with low wait times, even if you're not using a structured touring plan.

Touring Plans for Low-Attendance Days

We receive a number of letters each year similar to the following one from Lebanon, New Jersey:

The guide always assumed there would be large crowds. We had no lines. An alternate tour for low-traffic days would be helpful.

If attendance is low, you don't need a touring plan. Just go where your taste and instinct direct, and glory in the hassle-free touring. Having said that, however, there are attractions in each park that bottleneck even if attendance is low. These are Space Mountain, Splash Mountain, Dumbo, The Many Adventures of Winnie the Pooh, Under the Sea: Voyage of the Little Mermaid, Peter Pan's Flight, and the Seven Dwarfs Mine Train in the Magic Kingdom; Test Track, Soarin', and Mission: SPACE at Epcot; Kilimanjaro Safaris and Expedition Everest at Disney's Animal Kingdom; and Rock 'n' Roller Coaster, Star Tours—The Adventures Continue, *The Twilight Zone* Tower of Terror, and *Toy Story* Mania! at Disney's Hollywood Studios. Most of these are Fastpass attractions. Experience them immediately after the parks open, or use Fastpass. Remember that crowd size is relative and that large crowds can gather at certain attractions even during less-busy times. We recommend following a touring plan through the first five or six steps. If you're pretty much walking onto every attraction, feel free to scrap the remainder of the plan.

EXTRA MAGIC HOURS AND THE TOURING PLANS

IF YOU'RE A DISNEY RESORT GUEST and use your morning Extra Magic Hours privileges, complete your early-entry touring before the general public is admitted, then position yourself to follow the touring plan. When the public is admitted, the park will suddenly swarm. A Wilmington, Delaware, mother advises:

The early-entry times went like clockwork. We were finishing up the Great Movie Ride when Disney's Hollywood Studios opened to the public, and we had to wait in line quite a while for Voyage of the Little Mermaid, which sort of screwed up everything thereafter. Early-opening attractions should be finished up well before regular opening time so you can be at the plan's first stop as early as possible.

In the Magic Kingdom, early-entry attractions currently operate in Fantasyland and Tomorrowland. At Epcot, they're in the Future World section. At Disney's Animal Kingdom, they're in DinoLand U.S.A., Asia, Discovery Island, and Africa. At Disney's Hollywood Studios, they're dispersed. Practically speaking, see any attractions on the plan that are open for early entry, crossing them off as you do. If you finish all early-entry attractions and have time left before the general public is admitted, sample early-entry attractions not included in the plan. Stop touring about 10 minutes before the public is admitted, and position yourself for the first attraction on the plan that wasn't open for early entry. During early entry in the Magic Kingdom, for example, you can almost always experience Peter Pan's Flight and It's a Small World in Fantasyland, plus Space Mountain and *Stitch's Great Escape!* in Tomorrowland. As official opening nears, go to the boundary between Fantasyland and Liberty Square and be ready to blitz Splash and Big Thunder mountains according to the touring plan when the rest of the park opens.

Evening Extra Magic Hours, when a designated park remains open for Disney resort guests 2 hours beyond normal closing time, have less effect on the touring plans than early entry in the morning. Parks are almost never scheduled for both early entry and evening Extra Magic Hours on the same day. Thus a park offering evening Extra Magic Hours will enjoy a fairly normal morning and early afternoon. It's not until late afternoon, when park hoppers coming from the other theme parks descend, that the late-closing park will become especially crowded. By that time, you'll be well toward the end of your touring plan.

FASTPASS

THIS RIDE-RESERVATION SYSTEM was designed by Disney to moderate the high wait times at some of its most popular attractions. There's no extra charge to use Fastpass, and you can use it even if you're not staying at a Disney resort. (For details on Disney's future plans for this system, see "Coming Soon: Fastpass Plus," on page 85.)

Here's how it works: Your handout park map and signage at attractions will tell you which attractions are included. Attractions operating Fastpass will have a regular line and a Fastpass line. A sign at the entrance will tell how long the wait is in the regular line. If the wait is acceptable to you, hop in line. If it seems too long, insert your admission pass into a Fastpass machine and receive an appointment time to return and ride later in the day. When you return at the designated time, you enter the Fastpass line and proceed with minimal waiting to the attraction's preshow or boarding area. The system works well and can save a lot of waiting time.

The effort to accommodate Fastpass holders makes anyone in the regular line feel second-class. And a telling indication of their status is that they're called "standby guests." Disney is sending a message here: Fastpass is heaven; anything else is limbo at best and probably purgatory. In any event, you'll think you've been in hell if you're stuck in the regular line during the hot, crowded part of the day.

Fastpass doesn't eliminate the need to arrive early at a theme park. Because each park offers a limited number of Fastpass attractions, you still need an early start if you want to see as much as possible in one day. Plus, there's a limited supply of Fastpasses available for each attraction on any day. If you don't arrive at a given theme park until midafternoon, you might find that no more Fastpasses are available. Fastpass does make it possible to see more with less waiting, and it's a great benefit to those who like to sleep late or who choose an afternoon or evening at the parks on their arrival day. It also allows you to postpone wet rides, such as Kali River Rapids at Disney's Animal Kingdom or Splash Mountain at the Magic Kingdom, until a warmer time of day.

Understanding the Fastpass System

The purpose of Fastpass is to reduce the wait for designated attractions by distributing guests at those attractions throughout the day. This is accomplished by providing an incentive (a shorter wait) for guests willing to postpone experiencing the attraction until later in the day. The system also, in effect, imposes a penalty (standby status) on those who don't use it. However, spreading out guest arrivals sometimes also decreases the wait for standby guests.

When you insert your admission pass into a Fastpass time clock, the machine spits out a slip of paper about two-thirds the size of a credit card—small enough to fit in your wallet but also small enough to lose easily. Printed on it are the attraction's name and a time window during which you can return to ride— for example, 2:15 p.m.–3:15 p.m.

Obtaining a Fastpass

You can ordinarily obtain a Fastpass anytime after a park opens (some attractions are a little tardy getting their Fastpass system up), but the Fastpass return lines don't usually begin operating until 35–90 minutes after opening.

Whenever you obtain a Fastpass, you can be assured of a period of time between when you receive your Fastpass and when you report back. The interval can be as short as 30 minutes or as long as 3–7 hours, depending on park attendance and the attraction's popularity and hourly capacity. Generally, the earlier in the day you obtain a Fastpass, the shorter the interval before your return window. If the park opens at 9 a.m. and you obtain a Fastpass for Splash Mountain at 9:25 a.m., your appointment for returning to ride would be 10–11 a.m. or 10:10–11:10 a.m. The exact time will be determined by how many other guests have obtained Fastpasses before you.

To more effectively distribute guests over the day, Fastpass machines bump the 1-hour return period back a few minutes for a set number of passes issued (usually about 6% of the attraction's hourly capacity). For example, when Splash Mountain opens at 9 a.m., the first 125 people to obtain a Fastpass may get a 9:40–10:40 a.m. return window. The next 125 guests are issued Fastpasses with a 9:45–10:45 a.m. window. And so it goes, with the time window dropping back 5 minutes for every 125 guests. The fewer guests who obtain Fastpasses for an attraction, the shorter the interval between receipt of your pass and the return window. Conversely, the more guests issued Fastpasses, the longer the interval. If an attraction is exceptionally popular and/or its hourly capacity is relatively small, the return window might be pushed back to park closing time. When this happens, the Fastpass machines shut down and a sign is posted indicating that

FASTPASS ATTRACTIONS AT WALT DISNEY WORLD		
MAGIC KINGDOM	• Big Thunder Mountain • Buzz Lightyear's Space Ranger Spin • Dumbo • Jungle Cruise	• Peter Pan's Flight • Seven Dwarfs Mine Train • Space Mountain • Splash Mountain • Winnie the Pooh
EPCOT	• Living with the Land* • Maelstrom • Mission: SPACE	• Soarin' • Test Track
ANIMAL KINGDOM	• DINOSAUR • Expedition Everest	• Kali River Rapids • Kilimanjaro Safaris
DHS	• Rock 'n' Roller Coaster • Star Tours—The Adventures Continue	• Toy Story Mania! • The Twilight Zone Tower of Terror
		Available seasonally

all Fastpasses are gone for the day. It's not unusual, for example, for Soarin' at Epcot to have exhausted its Fastpasses by 1 p.m. or for Toy Story Mania! at the Studios to have distributed all available Fastpasses by 11 a.m.

Rides routinely exhaust their daily Fastpass supply, but shows almost never do. Fastpass machines at theaters try to balance attendance at each show so that the audience for any given performance is divided about evenly between standby and Fastpass guests. Consequently, standby guests for shows aren't discriminated against to the degree experienced by standby guests for rides. In practice, Fastpass *diminishes* the wait for standby guests.

unofficial **TIP**
With few exceptions, the standby line at theater attractions requires less waiting than using Fastpass.

So why not just run around the park first thing in the morning, collecting Fastpasses for every attraction? Because Disney won't let you. To keep guests from abusing the system, Disney requires them to wait a certain amount of time between obtaining passes. That time span varies based on the attraction and time of year, but it's usually either the beginning of your Fastpass return time or 2 hours, whichever comes first. The actual time is usually printed near the bottom of your most recent pass. Also, you don't have to use your most recent Fastpass before getting another—the Fastpass computer monitors only the distribution of passes, ignoring whether or when a pass is used.

Let's say, for example, you get a Fastpass for Toy Story Mania! at 9 a.m. and the return-time window is 10:05–11:05 a.m. You should be able to get another Fastpass for any attraction (including Toy Story Mania!) at 10:05 a.m. Alternatively, if you get a Fastpass for the same attraction at 10 a.m. and the return-time window is 4:05–5:05 p.m., you should be able to get another Fastpass for any attraction (including Toy Story Mania!) around noon.

Returning to Ride

Disney officially enforces the ride return time printed on the Fastpass. If your return time for Space Mountain is between 8:05 a.m. and 9:05 a.m., then Disney expects you to return between those times to ride. *Unofficially,* Disney will usually allow you to show up 5 minutes early or up to 15 minutes late and still use the pass (8 a.m.–9:20 a.m. in our example). If you arrive late to the Fastpass line because of a lengthy meal, ride breakdown, or other unforeseen circumstance, you can explain the issue to the cast member working the line, and he or she will decide whether you can still use your pass.

When the cast member has validated your Fastpass, you'll enter a line marked FASTPASS RETURN that routes you more or less directly to the boarding or preshow area. Each person in your party must have his own Fastpass and be ready to show it at the entrance of the Fastpass return line. Before you enter the boarding area or theater, another cast member will collect your Fastpass.

Cast members are instructed to minimize waits for Fastpass holders. Thus, if the Fastpass return line suddenly becomes inundated (something that occurs by chance), cast members will intervene to shorten the line. As many as 25 Fastpass holders will be admitted for each standby guest until the Fastpass line is reduced to an acceptable length.

WHEN TO USE FASTPASS Except as discussed below, there's no reason to use Fastpass during the first 30–40 minutes a park is open. Lines for most attractions are manageable during this period, and this is the only time of day when Fastpass attractions exclusively serve those in the regular line.

> *unofficial* **TIP**
> Although Fastpass usually eliminates 85% or more of the wait you'd experience in the standby line, you can still expect a short wait—usually less than 15 minutes and frequently less than 10 minutes.

Using Fastpass requires two trips to the same attraction: one to obtain the pass and another to use it. You must invest time to obtain the pass, then interrupt your touring later to backtrack in order to use it. The additional time, effort, and touring modification are justified only if you can save more than 30 minutes.

Eight Fastpass attractions build lines so quickly in the morning that failing to queue up within the first 6 or so minutes of operation will all but guarantee a long wait: Soarin' and Test Track at Epcot; Expedition Everest and Kilimanjaro Safaris at Disney's Animal Kingdom; Space Mountain at the Magic Kingdom; and Rock 'n' Roller Coaster, Toy Story Mania!, and The Twilight Zone Tower of Terror at Disney's Hollywood Studios. With these, you should race directly to the attractions when the park opens or obtain a Fastpass.

Another four Fastpass attractions—Splash Mountain, Winnie the Pooh, Peter Pan's Flight, and the Seven Dwarfs Mine Train in the Magic Kingdom—develop long queues within 30–50 minutes of park opening. If you can make your way to them before the wait becomes intolerable, lucky you. Otherwise, your options are Fastpass or a long time waiting in line.

At a number of Fastpass attractions, the time gap between getting your pass and returning to ride can range from 3–7 hours. If you think you might want to use Fastpass on the following attractions, obtain it before 11 a.m.:

MAGIC KINGDOM	EPCOT	ANIMAL KINGDOM	DHS
Buzz Lightyear's Space Ranger Spin	Mission: SPACE	Expedition Everest	Rock 'n' Roller Coaster
Peter Pan's Flight	Soarin'		Toy Story Mania!
Space Mountain	Test Track		
Splash Mountain			
Winnie the Pooh			

In case you're wondering how Fastpass waits compare with waits in the standby line, here's what we observed at Space Mountain during spring break on a day when the park opened at 9 a.m. From 9 to 10 a.m., both sides of Space Mountain served standby guests (there are two identical roller coasters in the Space Mountain building). At 10 a.m., the entire right side was cleared and became dedicated to Fastpass. At 10:45 a.m., the posted standby wait time was 45 minutes, for Fastpass only 10 minutes. At 1:45 p.m., the posted standby wait time was 1 hour, with 10 minutes for Fastpass. These observations document the benefit of Fastpass and, interestingly, also reveal shorter waits in the regular line than those observed at the same time of day before the advent of Fastpass.

unofficial **TIP**
Regardless of the time of day, if your wait in the regular line at a Fastpass attraction is 25–30 minutes or less, join the regular line.

TRICKS OF THE TRADE It's possible to acquire a second Fastpass before you use the first one (and sooner than 2 hours after getting it). When obtaining Fastpasses, it's quicker and more considerate if one person obtains passes for your entire party. This means entrusting one individual with your valuable park-admission passes and your Fastpasses, so choose wisely.

Obtain Fastpasses for all members of your party, including those who are too short, too young, or simply not interested in riding, as this family of four recommends:

Utilize the Fastpasses of people in your group who don't want to ride. Our 6-year-old didn't want to ride anything rough. All four of us got Fastpasses for each ride. When the 6-year-old didn't want to ride, my husband and I took turns riding with the 12-year-old. It was our version of the Fastpass child swap, and the 12-year-old got double rides.

A reader from Kettle Falls, Washington, shares his technique:

When I went to a park, I headed for my favorite ride and got in the standby line while I sent my companion to get us Fastpasses. So we were able to ride twice with almost no wait.

Our mobile wait-times app, **Lines,** will show you which Fastpass attractions still have passes available and when we estimate they'll run out. See Lines in action before you go at **touringplans.com/lines.**

Fastpass Guidelines

- Don't mess with Fastpass unless it can save you 30 minutes or more.
- If you arrive after a park opens, obtain a Fastpass for your preferred attraction first thing.
- Check the Fastpass return time before obtaining a Fastpass. Make sure you'll be in the park and able to ride during your time window.
- You can obtain a second Fastpass at the time printed at the bottom of your first Fastpass.
- Make sure everyone in your party has his or her own Fastpass.
- Obtain Fastpasses for Peter Pan's Flight, Space Mountain, Splash Mountain, and Winnie the Pooh at the Magic Kingdom; Mission: SPACE, Soarin', and Test Track at Epcot; Expedition Everest at Disney's Animal Kingdom; and Rock 'n' Roller Coaster and Toy Story Mania! at Disney's Hollywood Studios as early in the day as possible.
- Try to obtain Fastpasses for rides not mentioned previously by 1 p.m.
- Don't depend on Fastpasses being available after 2 p.m. during busier times.
- Don't obtain a Fastpass for a theater attraction until you've experienced all the Fastpass rides on your itinerary. (Using Fastpass at theater attractions usually requires more time than using the standby line.)

Coming Soon: Fastpass Plus

At press time, Disney wasn't telling anyone anything specific about how its next-generation ride-reservation system will work. Even the formal name of the system isn't known, but we'll refer to it for now as "Fastpass Plus." Enough bits have leaked, however, for us to form a general sense of its operation.

One major new change is that guests will be able to select their own return-time windows for attractions. For example, the Big Thunder Mountain Railroad Fastpass machine will display a list of 1-hour time windows (1–2 p.m, 2–3 p.m., etc.) for you to choose from. This solves the problem of not being able to use Fastpasses whose return times end up in the middle of meals or naps—an important consideration now that Disney is enforcing return-time windows.

You'll also be able to reserve Fastpasses days or weeks in advance from your computer or smartphone. You'll be able to schedule rides on Pirates of the Caribbean just as you'd schedule dinner at Cinderella's Royal Table.

In addition, Disney should greatly expand the number of Fastpass-enabled attractions from the current set of 28 attractions to more than 70 over the next few years. Popular attractions on the schedule include Dumbo, Pirates of the Caribbean, and Spaceship Earth. We hear some great parade- and fireworks-viewing spots will also be reserved for Fastpass Plus, and some of these spots may be created just for the new system. (One idea we've heard is extending a seating area into World Showcase Lagoon for *IllumiNations*.)

The most important development, however, isn't exactly a welcome one: Fastpass will be tied to how much money you're spending at

Disney. This is sure to outrage many guests, who will no doubt object to paying extra to avoid hours-long waits for attractions on top of premium prices just to get into the parks. But with Disney facing pressure from shareholders to increase its earnings every year, charging for Fastpass was probably inevitable.

So how will Disney make money on Fastpass? By limiting the number of Fastpasses you can get per day, with guests at expensive hotels getting the most. The actual scheme hasn't been determined, but what we hear goes something like this: Day guests (i.e., those not staying at a Disney hotel) will get one Fastpass per day, guests at Value resorts will get two Fastpasses per day, guests at Moderate resorts will get three Fastpasses per day, and guests at Deluxe resorts will get four to six Fastpasses per day.

This is how Disney plans to make money on Fastpass while still claiming it's free for everyone. While technically true, this conveniently overlooks the fact that guests staying at $50-per-night Kissimmee hotels could get Fastpasses for six or more attractions in one day under the old system if they were willing to do the walking. Now the thing that matters most is how much money you've spent.

But spending $500 per night at the Grand Floridian may still not be enough to get you the Fastpasses you want. Like tables at a restaurant, Fastpasses are available only in limited quantities at any hour, for any attraction. Passes for popular attractions running at popular times may be unavailable if you wait too long to reserve them. For example, Fastpasses for the Magic Kingdom fireworks may be popular enough that you'll have to reserve them 180 days in advance—just as you must do to reserve an 8 a.m. spot at Cinderella's Royal Table.

We're also told that the number of Fastpasses you'll be able to reserve will be reduced if you wait too long to book your trip. Make a deposit six months in advance and you'll get the full complement of Fastpasses; wait to book until three weeks before your trip and you may only get half that number. Why? By getting lots of guests to book earlier, Disney has a better idea of how many people will be in the parks on any given day. This allows Disney to fine-tune everything from how many employees it needs to staff rides on those days to how many cupcakes it needs to bake for its restaurants. Eliminating even a couple of percentage points of waste from a budget the size of Disney World's saves millions of dollars annually.

Finally, we hear that Disney will limit how many Fastpasses guests can obtain for headliner attractions in a single park. Disney's rules may allow a guest to obtain Fastpasses on only two of the Magic Kingdom's three "mountains" on any given day, for example, or otherwise restrict which combination of attractions you can reserve.

When will all of this happen? The new Fantasyland attractions already have elements of the new system built in, and we should see an announcement from Disney sometime in late 2012 or early 2013, with an initial set of attractions debuting around then, too. Full rollout may happen in phases spread over one or more years, possibly stretching into 2015.

UNDERSTANDING WALT DISNEY WORLD ATTRACTIONS

DISNEY WORLD'S PRIMARY APPEAL IS IN ITS rides and shows. Understanding how these are engineered to accommodate guests is interesting and invaluable to developing an efficient itinerary.

All attractions, regardless of location, are affected by two elements: capacity and popularity. Capacity is how many guests the attraction can serve at one time. Popularity shows how well visitors like an attraction. Capacity can be adjusted at some attractions. It's possible, for example, to add trams at the Studio Backlot Tour at Disney's Hollywood Studios or put extra boats on the Magic Kingdom's Jungle Cruise. Generally, however, capacity remains relatively fixed.

Designers try to match capacity and popularity as closely as possible. A high-capacity ride that isn't popular is a failure. Lots of money, space, and equipment have been poured into the attraction, yet there are empty seats. Journey into Imagination at Epcot fits this profile.

It's extremely unusual for a new attraction not to measure up, but it's fairly common for an older ride to lose appeal. Some attractions, such as Space Mountain at the Magic Kingdom, have sustained great appeal years beyond their debut, while others declined in popularity after a few years. Most attractions, however, work through the honeymoon, then settle down to handle the level of demand for which they were designed. When this happens, there are enough interested guests during peak hours to fill almost every seat, but not so many that long lines develop.

Sometimes Disney correctly estimates an attraction's popularity but fouls the equation by mixing in a third variable such as location. Spaceship Earth, the ride inside the geosphere at Epcot, is a good example. Placing the ride squarely in the path of every person entering the park assures that

it will be inundated during morning when the park is filling. On the flip side, *The American Adventure,* at the opposite end of Epcot, has huge capacity but plays to a partially filled theater until midafternoon, when guests finally reach that part of the park.

If demand is high and capacity is low, large lines materialize. The Studios' Toy Story Mania! is the only headliner attraction without a minimum height requirement that is open during morning Extra Magic Hours. Thus, it's the only headliner many families can experience, so demand quickly outstrips the ride's capacity. The result of this mismatch is that children and parents often suffer hour-long waits for a 6½-minute ride.

Capacity design is predicated on averages: the average number of people in the park, the normal distribution of traffic to specific areas, and the average number of staff needed to operate the ride. On a holiday weekend, when all the averages are exceeded, all but a few attractions operate at maximum capacity, and even then they're overwhelmed by the huge crowds. On days of low attendance in the fall, capacity is often not even approximated, and guests can ride without having to wait.

Only the Magic Kingdom and Disney's Animal Kingdom offer low-capacity midway rides and spook-house "dark" rides. They range from state-of-the-art to antiquated. This diversity makes efficient touring of the Magic Kingdom much more challenging. If guests don't understand the capacity–popularity relationship and don't plan accordingly, they might spend most of the day in line.

Although Epcot, Animal Kingdom, and Disney's Hollywood Studios have fewer rides and shows than the Magic Kingdom, almost all their attractions are major features on par with the Magic Kingdom's Pirates of the Caribbean and The Haunted Mansion in scope, detail, imagination, and spectacle. All but one or two Epcot, Animal Kingdom, and DHS rides are fast-loading, and most have large capacities. Because Epcot, Animal Kingdom, and DHS attractions are generally well engineered and efficient, lines may appear longer than those in the Magic Kingdom but usually move more quickly. There are no midway rides at Epcot or DHS, and fewer attractions at those parks are intended for children.

unofficial **TIP**
The Magic Kingdom offers the greatest variety in capacity and popularity, with vastly differing rides and shows.

In the Magic Kingdom, crowds are more a function of the popularity and engineering of individual attractions. At Epcot and Animal Kingdom, traffic flow and crowding are more affected by park layout. For touring efficiency, it's important to understand how Magic Kingdom rides and shows operate. At Epcot and Animal Kingdom, this knowledge is less important.

To develop an efficient touring plan, it's necessary to understand how rides and shows are designed and function. We'll examine both.

CUTTING YOUR TIME IN LINE BY UNDERSTANDING THE RIDES

WALT DISNEY WORLD HAS MANY TYPES OF RIDES. Some, such as The Great Movie Ride at Disney's Hollywood Studios, can carry more than 3,000 people an hour. At the other extreme, TriceraTop Spin at Animal Kingdom can handle only around 500 people an hour. Most rides fall somewhere in between. Many factors figure into how long you'll wait to experience a ride: its popularity; how it loads and unloads; how many persons can ride at once; how many units (cars, rockets, boats, flying elephants, and the like) are in service at a time; and how many cast members are available to operate the ride. Let's take the factors one by one.

1. How Popular Is the Ride?

Newer rides such as the Magic Kingdom's Under the Sea: Voyage of the Little Mermaid and Seven Dwarfs Mine Train attract a lot of people, as do such longtime favorites as the same park's Big Thunder Mountain Railroad. If a ride is popular, you need to know how it operates in order to determine the best time to ride. But a ride need not be especially popular to generate long lines; in some cases, such lines are due not to a ride's popularity but to poor traffic engineering. This is the case at the

Mad Tea Party and Prince Charming Regal Carrousel (among others) in Fantasyland. Both rides serve only a small percentage of any day's attendance at the Magic Kingdom, yet because they take so long to load and unload, long lines form regardless.

2. How Does the Ride Load and Unload?

Some rides never stop. They're like conveyor belts that go around and around. These are "continuous loaders." The Magic Kingdom's Haunted Mansion and Epcot's Spaceship Earth are continuous loaders. The number of people that can be moved through in an hour depends on how many cars—"doom buggies" or whatever—are on the conveyor. The Haunted Mansion and Spaceship Earth have lots of cars on the conveyor, and each consequently can move more than 2,000 people an hour.

Other rides are "interval loaders." Cars are unloaded, loaded, and dispatched at set intervals (sometimes controlled manually, sometimes by computer). Space Mountain in Tomorrowland is an interval loader. It has two tracks (the ride has been duplicated in the same facility). Each track can run as many as 14 space capsules, released at 36-, 26-, or 21-second intervals. (The bigger the crowd, the shorter the interval.)

In one kind of interval loader, empty cars, as in Space Mountain's space capsules, return to where they reload. In a second kind, such as Splash Mountain, one group of riders enters the vehicle while the previous group departs. Rides of the latter type are referred to as "in and out" interval loaders. As a boat docks, those who have just completed their ride exit to the left; at almost the same time, those waiting to ride enter the boat from the right. The reloaded boat is released to the dispatch point a few yards down the line, where it's launched according to the interval being used.

Interval loaders of both types can be very efficient people-movers if (1) the dispatch (launch) interval is relatively short and (2) the ride can accommodate many vehicles at one time. Since many boats can float through Pirates of the Caribbean at one time, and since the dispatch interval is short, almost 3,000 people can see this attraction each hour.

The least efficient rides, in terms of traffic engineering, are "cycle rides," also called "stop and go" rides. On cycle rides, those waiting to ride exchange places with those who have just ridden. Unlike in-and-out interval rides, cycle rides shut down during loading and unloading. While one boat is loading and unloading in It's a Small World (an interval loader), many other boats are advancing through the ride. But when Dumbo the Flying Elephant touches down, the whole ride is at a standstill until the next flight launches (ditto Prince Charming Regal Carrousel and the Mad Tea Party).

In cycle rides, the time in motion is "ride time." The time the ride idles while loading and unloading is "load time." Load time plus ride time equals "cycle time," or the time from the start of one run of the ride until the start of the next. The only cycle rides in Disney World are in the Magic Kingdom and Disney's Animal Kingdom.

3. How Many Persons Can Ride at One Time?

This figure expresses "system capacity," or the number of people who can ride at one time. The greater the carrying capacity of a ride (all other things being equal), the more visitors it can accommodate per hour. Some rides can add extra units (cars, boats, and such) as crowds build, to increase capacity; others, such as the Astro Orbiter in Tomorrowland, have a fixed capacity (it's impossible to add more rockets).

4. How Many Units Are in Service at a Given Time?

Unit is our term for the vehicle in which you ride. At the Mad Tea Party the unit is a teacup, at Peter Pan's Flight a pirate ship. On some rides (mostly cycle rides), the number of units operating at one time is fixed. There are always 32 flying elephants at Dumbo and 90 horses on Prince Charming Regal Carrousel. There's no way to increase the capacity of such rides by adding units. On a busy day, the only way to carry more people each hour on a fixed-unit cycle ride is to shorten the loading time or decrease the ride time. The bottom line: On a busy day for a cycle ride, you'll wait longer and possibly be rewarded with a shorter ride. This is why we steer you away from cycle rides unless you're willing to ride them early in the morning or late at night. These are the cycle rides:

THE MAGIC KINGDOM Astro Orbiter, Dumbo the Flying Elephant, Mad Tea Party, The Magic Carpets of Aladdin, Prince Charming Regal Carrousel, The Barnstormer

DISNEY'S ANIMAL KINGDOM TriceraTop Spin

Many other rides throughout Disney World can increase their capacity by adding units as crowds build. For example, if attendance is light, Big Thunder Mountain Railroad in Frontierland can start the day by running only one of its five mine trains from one of two available loading platforms. If lines build, the other platform is opened and more mine trains are placed into operation. At capacity, the five trains can carry about 2,400 persons an hour. Likewise, Star Tours at Disney's Hollywood Studios can increase its capacity by using all its simulators, and the Maelstrom boat ride at Epcot can add more Viking ships. Sometimes a long queue will disappear almost instantly when new units are brought online. When an interval loader places more units into operation, it usually shortens the dispatch intervals, allowing more units to be dispatched more often.

5. How Many Cast Members Are Available to Operate the Ride?

Adding cast members to a ride can allow more units to operate or additional loading or holding areas to open. In the Magic Kingdom, Pirates of the Caribbean and It's a Small World can run two waiting lines and loading zones. The Haunted Mansion has a 1½-minute pre-show staged in a "stretch room." On busy days, a second stretch room can be activated, permitting a more continuous flow of visitors to the actual loading area.

Additional staff makes a world of difference to some cycle rides. Often, the Mad Tea Party has only one attendant. This person alone must clear visitors from the ride just completed, admit and seat visitors for the upcoming ride, check that each teacup is secured, return to the control panel, issue instructions to the riders, and finally activate the ride (whew!). A second attendant divides these responsibilities and cuts loading time by 25–50%.

CUTTING YOUR TIME IN LINE BY UNDERSTANDING THE SHOWS

MANY FEATURED ATTRACTIONS AT DISNEY WORLD are theater presentations. While they aren't as complex as rides, understanding them from a traffic-engineering standpoint may save you touring time.

Most theater attractions operate in three phases:

1. Guests are in the theater viewing the presentation.

2. Guests who have passed through the turnstile wait in a holding area or lobby. They will be admitted to the theater as soon as the show in progress concludes.

Several attractions offer a preshow in their lobby to entertain guests until they're admitted to the main show. Examples include *Enchanted Tiki Room* and *Stitch's Great Escape!* in the Magic Kingdom; *Honey, I Shrunk the Audience/Captain EO* at Epcot; and *Muppet-Vision 3-D* at Disney's Hollywood Studios.

3. A line waits outside. Guests in line enter the lobby when there's room, and will ultimately move into the theater.

Theater capacity, the presentation's popularity, and park attendance determine how long lines will be at a theater attraction. Except for holidays and other days of heavy attendance, and excluding one particularly popular show (see below), the longest wait for a show usually doesn't exceed the length of one performance. As almost all theater attractions run continuously, stopping only long enough for the previous audience to leave and the waiting audience to enter, a performance will be in progress when you arrive. *O Canada!* at Epcot's Canada Pavilion lasts 18 minutes; your longest wait under normal circumstances is about 18 minutes if you arrive just after the show has begun.

All theaters (except a few amphitheater productions) are very strict about access. You can't enter during a performance. This means you'll always have at least a short wait. Most theaters hold a lot of people. When a new audience is admitted, any outside line will usually disappear. An exception is *Beauty and the Beast—Live on Stage* at Disney's Hollywood Studios. Because this show is so popular, you may have to wait through more than one show before you're admitted (unless you go early in the morning or after 4:30 p.m.).

A WORD ABOUT DISNEY THRILL RIDES

READERS OF ALL AGES should try to be open-minded about Disney "thrill rides." In comparison with those at other theme parks, the Disney attractions are quite tame, with more emphasis on sights, atmosphere, and special effects than on the motion, speed, or feel of the ride. While we suggest you take Disney's pre-ride warnings seriously, we can tell you that guests of all ages report enjoying rides such as Tower of Terror, Big Thunder Mountain, and Splash Mountain.

A Washington State reader sums up the situation well:

When I thought of Big Thunder Mountain and Space Mountain, what came to mind was gigantic hills, upside-down loops, huge vertical drops, etc. I actually hate roller coasters, especially the unpleasant sensation of a long drop, and I have never taken a ride that loops you upside down.

In fact, the Disney thrill rides are all tame in comparison. There are never any long and steep hills (except Splash Mountain, and it's there for anyone to see, so you have informed consent going on the ride). I was able to build up courage to go on all of them, and the more I rode them, the more I enjoyed them.

Seniors who experience Disney thrills generally enjoy the smoother rides like Splash Mountain, Big Thunder Mountain, and Tower of Terror and tend to dislike more jerky attractions. This letter from a Gig Harbor, Washington, woman is typical:

I am a senior woman of small stature and good health. I am writing my comments on Space Mountain, Splash Mountain, Big Thunder Mountain, and Star Tours. My experience is that all of the rides, with the exception of Star Tours, were wonderful rides. Star Tours is too jerky and fast, the music is too loud, and I found it to be unacceptable.

Notwithstanding this letter, most comments we receive from seniors about Star Tours are positive. The Rock 'n' Roller Coaster and Expedition Everest, however, are a different story. Both are serious coasters that share more in common with Revenge of the Mummy at Universal Studios than they do with Space Mountain or Big Thunder Mountain.

Mission: SPACE, a high-tech simulation ride at Epcot, is a toss-up (pun intended). It absolutely has the potential to make you sick. Disney, however, tinkered with it throughout its first year of operation to minimize the likelihood of motion sickness without compromising the thrill. The ride vehicles are constructed with an easy-clean design that allows cast members to quickly hose down any mess that occurs. But don't worry: Disney is as interested in avoiding this unpleasant exercise as you are in keeping your cookies right where they belong. A no-spin version, launched in 2006, is less likely to launch your lunch.

ATTRACTION-BREAKDOWN RATES

NOTHING CAN PUT A DAMPER on touring more than arriving at an attraction only to find that it has closed temporarily. Modern theme park attractions have complicated engineering with electrical, computer, and mechanical systems designed to shut down when they sense the ride is performing outside its intended parameters.

Some attractions, such as high-speed roller coasters or water-based rides, are more sensitive than others. The chart below shows how often, on average, an attraction experiences at least one temporary shutdown on any given day. Attractions at the top of the list are also more likely to experience several breakdowns in a single day.

ATTRACTION	BREAKDOWN FREQUENCY
SPACE MOUNTAIN*	Every other day
SPLASH MOUNTAIN*	Every other day
PIRATES OF THE CARIBBEAN	3 days per week
TEST TRACK*	3 days per week
BIG THUNDER MOUNTAIN RAILROAD	2 days per week
EXPEDITION EVEREST	2 days per week
ROCK 'N' ROLLER COASTER*	2 days per week
THE HAUNTED MANSION	1 day per week
JUNGLE CRUISE	1 day per week
THE MANY ADVENTURES OF WINNIE THE POOH	1 day per week
TOY STORY MANIA!	1 day per week
TOWER OF TERROR	1 day per week
Indicates that the attraction is likely to break down more than once per day.	

It usually takes Disney about 30 minutes to get an attraction working again. If you arrive at the attraction and discover it isn't open, check with a cast member to make sure the shutdown is temporary,

The Top 16 Central Florida Roller Coasters

COASTER	HOST PARK	CENTRAL FLORIDA RANK	INTER-NATIONAL RANK
MANTA	SeaWorld	1	30
EXPEDITION EVEREST	Animal Kingdom	2	91
CHINESE FIREBALL	Islands of Adventure	3	40
CHEETAH HUNT	Busch Gardens	4	N/A
MONTU	Busch Gardens	5	20
THE INCREDIBLE HULK COASTER	Islands of Adventure	6	43
KUMBA	Busch Gardens	7	34
HUNGARIAN HORNTAIL	Islands of Adventure	8	46
KRAKEN	SeaWorld	9	39
SHEIKRA	Busch Gardens	10	23
HOLLYWOOD RIP RIDE ROCKIT	Universal Studios	11	71
ROCK 'N' ROLLER COASTER	DHS	12	136
GWAZI	Busch Gardens	13	87
REVENGE OF THE MUMMY	Universal Studios	14	73
SPACE MOUNTAIN	Magic Kingdom	15	131
BIG THUNDER MOUNTAIN	Magic Kingdom	16	173

Source: **bestrollercoasterpoll.com**

and skip that step in your plan. If you can stay in the area, you may find that lines will be short when the attraction opens again.

No attractions are immune to temporary shutdowns. Those not on the list tend to break down about once or less per month, on average.

CENTRAL FLORIDA ROLLER COASTERS

IF YOU EVER GO TO A PARTY where guests are discussing Immelmanns, batwings, heartline rolls, dive loops, rollovers, lift hills, and LIM launchers, don't mistake the guests for fighter pilots. Incredibly, you'll be among the intelligentsia of roller-coaster aficionados. This growing population, along with millions of other not-quite-so-fanatical coaster lovers, is united in the belief that roller coasters are—or ought to be—the heart of every theme park.

Though Disney pioneered the concept of super-coasters with the **Matterhorn Bobsleds** at Disneyland in 1959, it took them 16 years to add another roller coaster, **Space Mountain** at Walt Disney World, to their repertoire. In relatively quick succession followed Space Mountain at Disneyland and **Big Thunder Mountain Railroad** at both Disneyland's and Walt Disney World's Magic Kingdoms. Irrespective of the Mountains' popularity, Disney didn't build another coaster in the United States for almost 20 years. In the interim, coasters enjoyed

TYPE	LENGTH (FEET)	HEIGHT (FEET)	INVERSIONS	SPEED (MPH)	RIDE TIME	RIDE FEEL
Steel/inverted	3,359	140	4	56	2:35	Very smooth
Steel/sit-down	4,424	112	0	50	3:45	Very smooth
Steel/inverted	3,200	125	5	60	2:25	Very smooth
Steel/sit-down	4,429	102	1	60	3:30	Smooth
Steel/inverted	3,983	150	7	60	3:00	Smooth
Steel/sit-down	3,700	110	7	67	2:15	Smooth
Steel/sit-down	3,978	143	7	60	2:54	Slightly rough
Steel/inverted	3,200	125	5	55	2:25	Very smooth
Steel/sit-down	4,177	149	7	65	2:02	Smooth
Steel/sit-down	3,188	200	1	70	3:00	Very smooth
Steel/sit-down	3,800	167	2	65	2:30	Rough
Steel/sit-down	3,403	80	3	57	1:22	Very smooth
Wood/sit-down	3,508	91	0	51	2:30	Very rough
Steel/sit-down	2,200	45	0	40	3:00	Very smooth
Steel/sit-down	3,196	90	0	27	2:35	Rough
Steel/sit-down	2,780	45	0	36	3:30	Smooth

a technical revolution that included aircraft carrier–type launching devices and previously unimaginable loops, corkscrews, vertical drops, and train speeds. Through all this, Disney sat on the sidelines. After all, Disney parks didn't offer "rides" but, rather, "adventure experiences" in which the sensation of the ride itself was always secondary to storylines and visuals. But when archrival Universal announced plans for its Islands of Adventure theme park, featuring an entire arsenal of thrill rides, Disney—spurred by competition—went to work.

The upshot was a banner year in 1999 for Central Florida coasters, with **The Incredible Hulk Coaster, Dueling Dragons: Fire** and **Ice** (now **Dragon Challenge: Chinese Fireball** and **Hungarian Horntail**) opening at Universal's Islands of Adventure, the **Rock 'n' Roller Coaster** coming online at the Disney's Hollywood Studios, and **Gwazi,** a wooden coaster, premiering at Busch Gardens Tampa. Close on their heels in early 2000 was **Kraken** at SeaWorld. These six coasters made Space and Big Thunder mountains look like cupcakes and wienie buns. All except Gwazi featured inversions, corkscrews, and rollovers. Best of all for coaster lovers, none of the players were content to rest on their laurels. Universal Studios came back with **Revenge of the Mummy** in 2004, followed by **SheiKra** at Busch Gardens in 2005 and the awe-inspiring **Expedition Everest** at Disney's Animal Kingdom in 2006.

The spring and summer of 2009 witnessed the unveiling of two new coasters: **Manta** at SeaWorld Orlando and **Hollywood Rip Ride Rockit** at Universal Studios. Manta is an inverted flying steel coaster on which riders are suspended under the tracks, prone and facedown, from a carriage shaped like a giant manta ray.

Like Manta, Hollywood Rip Ride Rockit at Universal Studios is a steel coaster, only here you sit as opposed to being suspended. The first hill is a 16-second *vertical* climb, followed by a 65-mph plunge.

Today there are 14 big-time roller coasters in Central Florida, 18 if you want to include the measurably tamer Space Mountain and Big Thunder Mountain rides as well as Flying School and Coastersaurus at Legoland. The Incredible Hulk, Cheetah Hunt, Rock 'n' Roller Coaster, and Revenge of the Mummy feature accelerated launch systems in which the train is hurled as opposed to ratcheted up the first hill; Rock 'n' Roller Coaster and Revenge of the Mummy are indoor coasters augmented by mind-blowing visuals, special effects, and soundtracks. Expedition Everest is the most fully realized attraction of the 14, with a storyline, astounding attention to detail, and a track that plunges in and out of the largest (albeit artificial) mountain in Florida. Expedition Everest shares with Revenge of the Mummy the distinction of constantly surprising you and catching you off-guard. Kraken, Cheetah Hunt, and Expedition Everest are the longest of the lot, their tracks exceeding 4,000 feet long. **Montu** at Busch Gardens, along with Dragon Challenge at Universal, are inverted coasters, meaning that the track is overhead and your feet dangle.

Having ridden all the coasters until we could no longer walk straight, we rank them as follows. (For a glossary of roller-coaster terminology, see **ultimaterollercoaster.com/coasters/glossary**.)

1. MANTA, SEAWORLD There are coasters you barely survive and coasters you savor. Manta is clearly among the latter: a supersmooth experience that leaves you grinning from ear to ear. An inverted flying steel coaster, Manta gently lowers you into a suspended Superman position and you, well, fly. Many coaster fans consider the most memorable moments a sweeping loop in the first half of the ride and near-misses of a pond or rock wall (depending where you're sitting) in the second half. Technically, Manta has it all. After a first drop of 113 feet, it zooms through a pretzel loop, a 360-degree incline roll, and two corkscrews while reaching a height of 140 feet and speeds of 55 mph.

2. EXPEDITION EVEREST, DISNEY'S ANIMAL KINGDOM This coaster offers such a complete package, with something to dazzle each of the senses, that it overcomes its lack of loops and inversions. The segment on Expedition Everest where the train corkscrews downward in the dark may be the most unusual in roller-coaster annals. Though you begin the segment in reverse, you soon succumb to an almost disembodied and dreamlike state of drifting in a void, with an exhilarating sense of speed but with no certain sense of direction. "Are we still going backwards?" my companion screamed, totally lost in the whirl of motion. When you can see, there's plenty to look at. The mountain, with its caverns, cliffs, and crags, is a work of art; then there's that pesky yeti who menaces you throughout the ride. And for those of you who hate rough coasters, Expedition Everest is oh-so-smooth. Die-hard coaster junkies, who are often ill-tempered unless they're upside down and shaken like a ketchup bottle, give short shrift to the great ride Expedition Everest provides.

3. DRAGON CHALLENGE: CHINESE FIREBALL, UNIVERSAL'S ISLANDS OF ADVENTURE Previously called Dueling Dragons, Dragon Challenge was given a new theme and incorporated into The Wizarding World of Harry Potter, which opened at Universal's Islands of Adventure in June 2010. The number-three ranking was disputed within our research group, with several of us placing Montu at Busch Gardens third. Dragon Challenge has two trains, Chinese Fireball and Hungarian Horntail (formerly Fire and Ice), that are launched in short succession, creating a sense of chase between the two. Though both trains have identical lift hills, their respective layouts are different, and Chinese Fireball offers the superior ride. The action is unrelenting yet very smooth, with a 115-foot drop, five inversions, and speeds of 60 mph. Because this is an inverted coaster, your feet dangle throughout.

4. CHEETAH HUNT, BUSCH GARDENS With a 4,429-foot track, Cheetah Hunt is the longest coaster in Florida. A complete experience both tactilely and visually, Cheetah Hunt hurls you through the scenic, wildlife-rich Serengeti Plain section of the park. The ride emulates the hunting style of the cheetah with sudden bursts of speed. This is accomplished with linear-synchronous-motor launches similar to the accelerated launch systems of The Incredible Hulk Coaster at Universal and Rock 'n' Roller Coaster at DHS. With Cheetah Hunt, however, you're launched three times—once at the start of the ride and twice more during the circuit. The layout includes a 130-foot drop into a shallow canyon, overbanked turns, parabolas, and a heartline-roll inversion. The linear out-and-back course allows more opportunity for viewing the animals than would the more common concentric, twisting layouts from which it's almost impossible to take in your surroundings (assuming you have your eyes open).

5. MONTU, BUSCH GARDENS Montu is a little longer than Chinese Fireball and features seven inversions—including loops of 104 and 60 feet and a 0-g roll—on a layout distinguished by its very tight turns. With an initial drop of 128 feet, Montu posts top speeds of 60 mph and pulls 3.8 g's. Also inverted, Montu is intense and exhilarating but less visually interesting than and not as smooth as Chinese Fireball. Like some of our researchers, the coasterfanatics.com and bestrollercoaster poll.com polls rank Montu ahead of the Fireball.

6. THE INCREDIBLE HULK COASTER, UNIVERSAL'S ISLANDS OF ADVENTURE Hulk doesn't have any weak points. A tire-propelled launch system takes you from 0 to 40 mph in 2 seconds up the first hill, hurling you into a twisting dive of 105 feet. From there it's two loops, two flat-spin corkscrews, a cobra roll, and a plunge through a 150-foot-long tunnel to the end. You hit speeds of 67 mph and pull as many as 4 g's. Unequivocally, the Hulk has the best start of any roller coaster in Central Florida. The ride, however, is not quite as smooth as Chinese Fireball's, and it's not inverted like Chinese Fireball and Montu, which is why we've ranked it sixth.

7. KUMBA, BUSCH GARDENS With a track of almost 4,000 feet, seven inversions, a 135-foot first drop, g-forces of 3.8, a top speed of 60 mph, and a very tight layout, Kumba can hold its own with any coaster. Features include a 114-foot-tall vertical loop, two rolls, and interlocking corkscrews, among others. We find Kumba a little rough, but sitting toward the back of the train mitigates the problem somewhat.

8. DRAGON CHALLENGE: HUNGARIAN HORNTAIL, UNIVERSAL'S ISLANDS OF ADVENTURE Hungarian Horntail is Chinese Fireball's slightly less evil twin, with speeds of 55 mph and a first drop of 95 feet, compared with Chinese Fireball's 60 mph and 115 feet. So too Hungarian Horntail's design elements are different, though both coasters hit you with five inversions bundled in a mix of rolls, corkscrews, and a loop. Like Chinese Fireball, Hungarian Horntail is an inverted coaster.

9. KRAKEN, SEAWORLD Based on ancient myth, the Kraken was a ferocious sea monster kept caged by Poseidon, Greek god of the sea. Much of Kraken's track is over water, and the ride takes a number of sweeping dives into subterranean caverns. A very fast coaster, Kraken hits speeds of 65 mph with one drop of 144 feet, and it boasts loops, rolls, and corkscrews for a total of seven inversions. Though not inverted, the cars are open-sided and floorless.

10. HOLLYWOOD RIP RIDE ROCKIT, UNIVERSAL STUDIOS "The Triple R," as some locals call it, opened in August 2009 as Universal's second roller coaster. A steel sit-down coaster, RRR trades full inversions for steep dives and tight corkscrew turns. The ride is a lot more jarring than we expected, with a fair amount of lateral shaking. The gimmick here is that you can select your own music to accompany the ride. Views from the top of the 167-foot lift hill are killer. The Triple R reaches top speeds of 65 mph.

11. SHEIKRA, BUSCH GARDENS While the higher-rated coasters do a lot of things well, SheiKra is pretty much one-dimensional—it drops like a rock straight down (a sheikra is an African hawk known for diving vertically on its prey). That's right: a no-slope, 90-degree free fall. After scaling the 200-foot lift hill, the coaster descends over the lip of the first drop and brakes to a stop. There you're suspended, dangling for a few anxious moments until the train is released. On the way down, you hit speeds of 70 mph—a very high speed for roller coasters—and enjoy the best airtime of any Florida coaster. (Airtime is the sensation of floating when your body is forced up from the seat bottom, creating air between the seat and your body. The phenomenon is most commonly experienced on a drop or while cresting hills.) Following a loop, the drill is repeated on a second, more modest drop. The cars on SheiKra are the widest we've seen, seating eight people across in each of three rows. Accordingly, the track is very wide. This width, among other things, makes for a plodding, uninspiring ride except during the two big drops. More compelling is the view of downtown Tampa from the top of the lift hill.

12. ROCK 'N' ROLLER COASTER, DISNEY'S HOLLYWOOD STUDIOS This wasn't a unanimous ranking either. The Rock 'n' Roller Coaster reaches a height of only 80 feet, lasts only 1 minute and 22 seconds, and incorporates just a couple of design elements, but that 0- to 57-mph launch in 2 seconds is totally sweet. Rock 'n' Roller Coaster is a dark ride (that is, it's indoors) and the story is that you're on your way to an Aerosmith concert in Hollywood in a big stretch limousine. Speakers in each car blast a soundtrack of the group's hits synchronized with the myriad visuals that erupt out of the gloom. The ride is smooth. Not the biggest or baddest coaster in the realm, but like Expedition Everest, it'll put a big grin on your face every time.

13. GWAZI, BUSCH GARDENS As the only traditional wooden coaster of the 16 rides ranked, Gwazi at first looked like a snore: no inversions, corkscrews, loops, barrel rolls, or any of the other stuff that had been rearranging our innards. Wrong! This coaster serves up an unbelievably wild ride that seems literally out of control most of the time. Teeth-rattlingly rough, with much side-to-side lurching, Gwazi reaches a top speed of 51 mph but feels twice that fast. In the best wooden-coaster tradition, riders attempt to hold their arms in the air, but on Gwazi it's impossible. The track is hard to read, and the way the train shifts and banks surprises you constantly. Gwazi's coaster trains were replaced in 2011, making the ride marginally smoother (*marginally* being the operative word). Gwazi is a racing coaster (a dual-track roller coaster whose trains leave the station at the same moment and race each other through the circuit) with two trains, Lion/Yellow and Tiger/Blue. Of the two, Tiger/Blue gives you the biggest bang for your buck.

14. REVENGE OF THE MUMMY, UNIVERSAL STUDIOS If we were ranking attractions as opposed to roller coasters, this one would rank much higher. Revenge of the Mummy is a super-headliner hybrid and, in Disney parlance, a full-blown "adventure experience," of which its coaster dimension is only one aspect. A complete description of the attraction can be found starting on page 663; for the moment, however, we can tell you that Revenge of the Mummy is a dark ride full of tricks and surprises, and in roller-coaster mode only for about a third of the ride. The ride is wild enough, but the visuals and special effects are among the best you'll find.

15. SPACE MOUNTAIN, THE MAGIC KINGDOM When you strip away the theme of this beloved Disney favorite (renovated in 2009), you're left with a souped-up version of the Wild Mouse, a midway staple with sharp turns and small, steep drops that runs with two- or four-passenger cars instead of trains. But when you put a Wild Mouse in the dark—where you can't anticipate the turns and drops—it's like feeding the mouse steroid-laced cheese. With Space Mountain, Disney turned a dinky coaster with no inversions and a top speed of 27 mph into a fairly robust attraction that set the standard for Disney thrill rides until the debut of The Twilight Zone Tower of Terror. Space Mountain may be close to the bottom of our ranking, but in the hearts of many theme park guests, it remains number one.

16. BIG THUNDER MOUNTAIN RAILROAD, THE MAGIC KINGDOM With its runaway-mine-train storyline, Big Thunder is long on great visuals but ranks as a very innocuous roller coaster. Though many riders consider it jerky and rough, it's a Rolls-Royce compared with the likes of Gwazi and Kumba at Busch Gardens. Unlike on Gwazi, it's not only possible but easy to ride with your arms in the air. Though a steel coaster, Big Thunder offers no inversions and a top speed of only 36 mph. Then again, the higher-ranked coasters don't offer falling boulders, flash floods, possums, buzzards, and dinosaur bones.

ACCOMMODATIONS

The BASIC CONSIDERATIONS

LOCATING A SUITABLE HOTEL OR CONDO is critical to planning any Walt Disney World vacation. The basic question is whether to stay inside the World. Luxury lodging can be found both in and out of Disney World. Budget lodging is another story. In the World, hotel-room rates range from about $84 to more than $900 per night during high season. Outside, rooms are as low as $35 a night.

Beyond affordability is convenience. We've lodged both in and out of Disney World, and there's special magic and peace of mind associated with staying inside the World. "I feel more a part of everything and less like a visitor," one guest writes.

There's no real hardship in staying outside Disney World and driving or taking a hotel shuttle to the theme parks. Meals can be less expensive, and rooming outside the World makes you more receptive to other Orlando-area attractions and eating spots. **Universal Studios** and **Universal's Islands of Adventure, Kennedy Space Center Visitor Complex, SeaWorld,** and **Gatorland** are well worth your attention.

Because Walt Disney World is so large, some off-property hotels are closer in time and distance to many of the theme parks than are some Disney resorts. Check our Hotel Information Chart on pages 261–279, which lists commuting times from both Disney and non-Disney hotels. Lodging prices are subject to change, but our researchers lodged in an excellent (though not plush) motel surrounded by beautiful orange groves for half the cost of staying in the least-expensive Disney hotel. Our one-way commute to the Magic Kingdom or Epcot parking lots was 17 minutes.

If you have young children, read Part Six, Walt Disney World with Kids, before choosing lodging. Seniors, couples on a honeymoon or romantic holiday, and disabled guests should read the applicable sections of Part Seven, Special Tips for Special People, before booking.

THE TAX MAN COMETH

SALES AND LODGING TAXES can add a chunk of change to the cost of your hotel room. Cumulative tax in Orange County is 12.5% and in adjacent Osceola County, 13%. Lake Buena Vista, the Universal Studios area, International Drive, and all the Disney resorts except the All-Star Resorts are in Orange County.

ABOUT HOTEL RENOVATIONS

WE INSPECT SEVERAL HUNDRED HOTELS in the Disney World area to compile the *Unofficial Guide*'s list of lodging choices. Each year we call each hotel to verify contact information and inquire about renovations or refurbishments. If a hotel has been renovated or has refurbished its guest rooms, we reinspect it, along with any new hotels, for the next edition of the *Guide*. Hotels reporting no improvements are rechecked every two years. We inspect most Disney-owned hotels every 6–12 months, and not less than once every two years.

unofficial **TIP**
Request a renovated room at your hotel—these can be much nicer than the older rooms.

Many hotels more than five years old, both in and out of the World, refurbish 10–20% of their guest rooms each year. This incremental approach minimizes disruption but makes your room assignment a crapshoot—you might luck into a newly renovated room, or you might be assigned a threadbare one.

Disney resorts won't guarantee specific rooms but will note your request for a recently refurbished room and will try to accommodate you. Non-Disney hotels will often guarantee you an updated room when you book.

unofficial **TIP**
Power shoppers, rejoice: If you're staying on Disney property, you can charge theme park and Downtown Disney purchases to your hotel room.

BENEFITS OF STAYING IN THE WORLD

DISNEY RESORT HOTEL AND CAMPGROUND GUESTS have privileges and amenities unavailable to those staying outside the World. Though some of these perks are advertising gimmicks, others are real and potentially valuable.

Here are the benefits and what they mean:

1. CONVENIENCE If you don't have a car, commuting to the parks is easy via the Disney transportation system. This is especially advantageous if you stay in a hotel connected by monorail or boat service. If you have a car, however, dozens of hotels outside Disney World are within 5–10 minutes of theme-park parking lots.

2. EXTRA MAGIC HOURS AT THE THEME PARKS Disney World lodging guests (excluding guests at the independent hotels of the Downtown Disney Resort Area, except the Hilton) are invited to enter a designated park 1 hour earlier than the general public each day or to enjoy a designated theme park for about 2 hours after it closes to the general public in the evening. Disney guests are also offered specials on admission, including discount tickets to the water parks. These benefits are subject to change without notice.

Early entry can be quite valuable if you know how to use it. It can also land you in gridlock. (See our detailed discussion of early entry, starting on page 41.)

3. BABYSITTING AND CHILD-CARE OPTIONS Disney hotel and campground guests have several options for babysitting, child care, and children's programs. Disney's **Polynesian** and **Grand Floridian** resorts, along with several other Disney hotels, offer "clubs"—themed child-care centers where potty-trained children ages 3–12 can stay while the adults go out.

Though somewhat expensive, the clubs are highly regarded by children and parents. On the negative side, they're open only in the evening, and not all Disney hotels have them. If you're staying at a Disney hotel without a club, you're better off using a private in-room babysitting service (see page 350). In-room babysitting is also available at hotels outside Disney World.

4. DISNEY'S MAGICAL EXPRESS SERVICE If you arrive in Orlando by commercial airliner, Disney will collect your checked baggage and send it by bus directly to your Walt Disney World resort, allowing you to bypass baggage claim. The service is available daily from 5 a.m. to 10 p.m.; there's also a bus waiting to transport you to your hotel, but if you arrive after 10 p.m., you'll have to collect your baggage yourself and take it with you on the bus. This complimentary service still has occasional hiccups, and your bus may stop at other Disney resorts before you're deposited at your hotel, but you can't beat free.

When it's time to go home, you can check your baggage and receive your boarding pass at the front desk of your Disney resort. This service is available to all guests at Disney hotels (excluding the Swan, the Dolphin, Shades of Green, and hotels of the Downtown Disney Resort Area), even those who don't use Magical Express (folks who have rental cars, for example). Resort check-in counters are open from 5 a.m. until 1 p.m., and you must check in no later than 3 hours before your flight (within the U.S. and Puerto Rico only). Participating airlines are **AirTran, Alaska, American, Delta, JetBlue, Southwest, United,** and **US Airways.** All of the preceding airlines have restrictions on the number of bags, checking procedures, and related items; consult your carrier before leaving home for specifics. For an in-depth discussion of Disney's Magical Express, see Part Eight, Arriving.

5. PRIORITY THEME PARK ADMISSIONS On days of unusually heavy attendance, Disney may restrict admission into the theme parks for all customers. When deciding whom to admit into the parks, priority is given to guests staying at Disney resorts. In practice, no guest is turned away until a park's parking lot is full. When this happens, that park will be packed to gridlock. Under such conditions, you'd exhibit the common sense of an amoeba to exercise your priority-admission privilege.

6. CHILDREN SHARING A ROOM WITH THEIR PARENTS There's no extra charge per night for children younger than 18 sharing a room with their parents. Many hotels outside Disney World also offer this.

7. FREE PARKING Disney resort guests with cars pay nothing to park in theme park lots. This saves $14 per day.

8. RECREATIONAL PRIVILEGES Disney guests get preferential treatment for tee times at the golf courses.

STAYING IN OR OUT OF THE WORLD: WEIGHING THE PROS AND CONS

1. COST If cost is a primary consideration, you'll lodge much less expensively outside Disney World. Our ratings of hotel quality, cost, and commuting times to the theme parks encompass hotels both in and out of the World (see "How the Hotels Compare" and the Hotel Information Chart, both later in this chapter).

2. EASE OF ACCESS Even if you stay in Disney World, you're dependent on some mode of transportation. It may be less stressful to use the Disney transportation system, but with the single exception of commuting to the Magic Kingdom, the fastest, most efficient, and most flexible way to get around is usually a car. If you're at Epcot, for example, and want to take the kids back to Disney's Contemporary Resort for a nap, forget the monorail. You'll get back much faster by car.

A reader from Raynham, Massachusetts, who stayed at the Caribbean Beach Resort writes:

> Even though the resort is on the Disney bus line, I recommend renting a car if it fits one's budget. The buses don't go directly to many destinations, and often you have to switch buses. Getting a bus back to the hotel after a hard day can mean a long wait in line.

Readers complain about problems with the Disney transportation system more than almost any other topic. These comments from a Havertown, Pennsylvania, dad are representative:

> WDW bus transportation is quite inefficient. When traveling from the BoardWalk to anywhere else, we had to pick up other passengers at the Swan, Dolphin, and Yacht and Beach Clubs before heading off to the parks. Same story upon return.

Although it's only for the use and benefit of Disney guests, the Disney transportation system is nonetheless public, and users must expect inconveniences: conveyances that arrive and depart on their schedule, not yours; the occasional need to transfer; multiple stops; time lost loading and unloading passengers; and, generally, the challenge of understanding and using a large, complex transportation network.

Relatively few Americans use public transportation frequently, but guests who do—as did this Heswall, England, reader—tend to be more satisfied with Disney's bus system:

> I really feel that you are a bit hard on the Disney transport service. This may be an American thing, but we Brits are more used to buses. We were told buses were running every 20 minutes, but in practice we never waited more than 10.

If you plan to have a car, consider this: Disney World is so large that some destinations within the World can be reached more quickly from off-property hotels than from Disney hotels. For example, guests at lodgings on US 192 (near the so-called Walt Disney World Maingate) are closer to Disney's Hollywood Studios, Animal Kingdom, and Blizzard Beach water park than guests at many hotels inside Disney World.

A Kentucky dad overruled his family about staying at a Disney resort and is glad he did:

> My wife read in another guidebook that it can take 2 hours to commute to the parks if you stay outside Walt Disney World. I guess it could take 2 hours if you stayed in Tampa, but from our hotel on US 192 we could commute to any of the parks except the Magic Kingdom and have at least one ride under our belt in about an hour. (We

found out later that the writer of the other guidebook worked for Disney Magazine.)

For commuting times from specific non-Disney hotels, see our Hotel Information Chart on pages 261–279.

3. YOUNG CHILDREN Although the hassle of commuting to most non-World hotels is only slightly (if at all) greater than that of commuting to Disney hotels, a definite peace of mind results from staying in the World. Regardless of where you stay, make sure you get your young children back to the hotel for a nap each day.

4. SPLITTING UP If you're in a party that will probably split up to tour (as frequently happens in families with teens or children of widely varying ages), staying in the World offers more transportation options and, thus, more independence. Mom and Dad can take the car and return to the hotel for a relaxed dinner and early bedtime while the teens remain in the park for evening parades and fireworks.

5. FEEDING THE ARMY OF THE POTOMAC If you have a large crew that chows down like cattle on a finishing lot, you may do better staying outside the World, where food is far less expensive.

6. VISITING OTHER ORLANDO-AREA ATTRACTIONS If you'll be visiting SeaWorld, Kennedy Space Center Visitor Complex, Universal Orlando, or other area attractions, it may be more convenient to stay outside the World.

The **DISNEY RESORTS**

DISNEY RESORTS 101

BEFORE YOU MAKE ANY DECISIONS, understand these basics regarding Disney resorts.

1. RESORT CLASSIFICATIONS Disney loves to categorize, so it's not surprising that they've developed a hierarchy of resort classifications. **Deluxe resorts** are Disney's top-of-the-line hotels. **Disney Deluxe Villa (DDV) resorts** (also known as **Disney Vacation Club [DVC] resorts**) offer suites, some with full kitchens. These resorts equal or surpass Deluxe resorts in quality; several are attached to Deluxe resorts. (Be aware that all Disney resorts except DDV resorts levy a nightly surcharge for every additional adult in a room beyond the standard two.) **Moderate resorts** are a step down in guest-room quality, amenities, and cost. Anchoring the bottom of the list are **Value resorts,** with the smallest rooms, most limited amenities, and lowest rates of any Disney-owned hotels. Standard rooms at the these resorts are generally the smallest on-property, but two-room "family suites" are available at certain Value resorts. Finally, there's **Fort Wilderness Resort & Campground,** which offers both campsites and fully equipped cabins.

unofficial **TIP**
Understand that Disney Reservation Center and Walt Disney Travel Company representatives don't have detailed personal knowledge of resorts.

2. MAKING RESERVATIONS Whether you book through Disney, a travel agent, online, with a tour operator, or through an organization like AAA, you'll frequently save by booking the room exclusive of any vacation package. This is called a *room-only reservation*. Though later in this chapter we'll scrutinize the advantages and disadvantages of buying a package, we'll tell you now that Disney World packages at list price rarely save you money (though sometimes they're worthwhile for the convenience and peace of mind).

In dealing with Disney for rooms only, call the Disney Reservation Center (DRC) at ☎ 407-W-DISNEY (934-7639). Because of some administrative and operational consolidation, reservationists at the DRC are now trained to sell only Walt Disney Travel Company packages. Even if you insist that you want only a room, they'll try to bundle it with some small extra, like a miniature-golf pass, so that your purchase can be counted as a "basic" package. This seems innocuous enough, and you might even appreciate the mini-golf passes, but classifying your reservation as a package allows Disney to apply numerous restrictions and cancellation policies that you won't be saddled with if you buy a room only. In regard to cancellation policies, however, be aware that there are trade-offs. If you book a package and cancel less than 45 days before arrival, you lose your $200 deposit. If you book only a room and cancel less than a week before arrival, you lose your deposit of one night's room charge, which can easily be more than $200 if you stay at a Deluxe resort or DDV resort. Also, Disney dining plans cannot be booked with a room-only reservation.

When you call, tell the agent what you want in terms of lodging and obtain a room-only rate quote. Then tell the agent what you're looking for in terms of admissions. When you've pinned down your room selection and lodging costs, ask the agent if he or she can offer any packages that beat the à la carte prices. But don't be swayed by little sweeteners included in a package unless they have real value for you. If the first agent you speak to isn't accommodating, hang up and call back. There are a couple hundred agents, some more helpful than others.

When dealing with Disney reservations, a careful shopper from West Lafayette, Indiana, advises both wariness and toughness:

> *Making reservations through* W-DISNEY *is like buying a car: You need to know the sales tricks, have a firm idea of what you want, and be prepared to walk away if you don't get what you want at a price you want to pay.*

If you need specific information, call the resort directly, ask for the front desk, and pose your question before phoning the DRC. If your desired dates aren't available, keep calling back or check online at **disneyworld.com.** Something might open up.

3. A MOST CONFUSING VIEW Rates at Disney hotels vary from season to season (see the next section) and from room to room according to view. Further, each Disney resort has its own seasonal calendar. Seasons such as "Regular," "Value," "Peak," and "Holiday" vary depending on the resort instead of that tired old January–December calendar that the rest of us use. But confusing as Disney seasons are, they're logic personified

unofficial **TIP**
Avoid calling the DRC between 11 a.m. and 3 p.m.—this is its busiest time of day.

compared to the panoply of guest-room views the resorts offer. Depending on the resort, you can choose standard views, water views, pool views, lagoon views, garden views, or savanna views, among others. "Standard view," the most ambiguous category, crops up at about three-fourths of Disney resorts. It's usually interpreted as a view that doesn't fit any other view classification the hotel offers. At Animal Kingdom Lodge, for example, you have savanna views, pool views, and standard views. Savanna views overlook the replicated African savanna, pool views overlook the swimming pool, and standard views offer stunning vistas of other stuff . . . whatever that might be.

With a standard view, however, you can at least pinpoint what you *won't* be seeing. Every resort defines water views differently. According to a manager at the Grand Floridian Resort & Spa, for example, a water view is a direct, unobstructed frontal view of Seven Seas Lagoon. Views of swimming pools or sideways views of the lagoon don't count. If the Grand Floridian sells you a water-view room, by George, you're gonna see some water. Scoring a room with a view of the Magic Kingdom is a different matter, as a mom from Pontefract, England, attests:

unofficial **TIP**
If you book a king room at a Moderate resort, you can request a water-view room at no extra charge (this isn't guaranteed, though).

> We stayed at the Grand Floridian, which was lovely. However, I paid extra for a Magic Kingdom view. I was soooo disappointed when all I could see from the balcony was Space Mountain (unless I hung out so far I risked falling over). I was so looking forward to sitting on the balcony with a glass of wine and watching the fireworks. I know that next time I will have to ask for a view of Cinderella Castle, not just a Magic Kingdom view.

Zip over to the Yacht Club Resort, another Deluxe property, and the definition of "water view" is completely different. Like the Grand Floridian, the Yacht Club is on a lake, but booking a water-view room doesn't guarantee you'll see the lake. At the Yacht Club, anything wet counts, whether it's in front of you or so far to the side you have to crane your neck. If somehow you can glimpse the lake, a creek, or a swimming pool, you have a water view.

Our favorite water views are at the Contemporary Resort's Garden Building, which extends toward Bay Lake to the east of the giant A-frame. Rooms in this three-story structure afford some of the best lake vistas in Walt Disney World. Many rooms are so near the water, in fact, you could spit a prune pit into the lake from your window. And their category? Garden views.

unofficial **TIP**
Disney will guarantee connecting rooms if your party includes more children than adults.

We could go on and on, but pinning Disney down on precisely what will be outside your window is the point. In our discussion of individual resorts later in this chapter, we'll tell you which rooms have the good views.

4. HOW TO GET THE ROOM YOU WANT Disney will not guarantee a specific room when you book but will post your request on your reservation record. Our experience indicates that making a request by room number confuses the Disney reservationists; as a result, they're unsure where to place you if the room you've asked for is unavailable. To increase your odds of getting the room you want, tell the reservationist exactly what characteristics and amenities you desire—for example: "I'd like a room with a balcony on the second or third floor of the Contemporary Resort's Garden Building with an unobstructed view of the lake." (It's unnecessary to ask for a nonsmoking room at a Disney resort, as all rooms were designated smoke-free in 2007.)

Be direct and politely assertive when speaking to the Disney agent. Port Orleans Resort, for example, offers either standard or water view rooms . . . but "water view" could mean a view of the river or a swimming pool. If you want to overlook the river, say so; likewise, if you want a pool view, speak up. Similarly, state clearly such preferences as a particular floor, a corner room, a room near restaurants, a room away from elevators and ice machines, or a room with a certain type of balcony. If you have a laundry list of preferences, type it in order of importance, and e-mail, fax, or mail it to the DRC. Include your contact information and reservation confirmation number.

unofficial **TIP**
Three to four days before you arrive, call the resort front desk. Call late in the evening when they're not so busy, and reconfirm the requests that by now should be appearing in their computers.

It will be someone from the resort who actually assigns your room. Call back in a few days to make sure your preferences were posted to your record.

We'll provide info needed for each resort to frame your requests, including a resort layout map and our recommendations for specific rooms or buildings. We'll use a dash (–) to indicate a range of rooms. Thus, "Rooms 2230–2260" refers to the 31 rooms within that range. Sometimes we'll specify even- or odd-numbered rooms within a range, for example, "odd-numbered rooms 631–639." In this case we're referring to Rooms 631, 633, 635, 637, and 639, eliminating intervening even-numbered rooms.

HOW TO GET DISCOUNTS ON LODGING

THERE ARE SO MANY GUEST ROOMS in and around Disney World that competition is brisk, and everyone, including Disney, wheels and deals to fill them. Disney, however, has its own atypical way of managing its room inventory. To uphold the brand integrity of its hotels, Disney prefers to use inducements rather than discounts per se. For example Disney might offer a fifth night free with four nights booked at the standard rate, or include free dining if you reserve a certain number of nights. Consequently, many of the strategies for obtaining discounted rates in most cities and destinations don't work well for Disney hotels. We'll explore these strategies in-depth when we discuss booking non-Disney hotels near Walt Disney World; for the moment, though, here are some tips for getting price breaks at Disney properties:

1. SEASONAL SAVINGS Save from $15 to $50 per night or more on a Disney hotel room by visiting during the slower times of year. However, Disney uses so many adjectives ("Regular," "Holiday," "Peak," "Value," and the like) to describe its seasonal calendar that it's hard to keep up. Plus, the dates for each "season" vary among resorts. If you're set on staying at a Disney resort, order a copy of the Walt Disney Travel Company Florida Vacations video/DVD brochure.

Disney seasonal dates aren't sequential like spring, summer, fall, and winter. That would be way too simple. For any specific resort, there are often two or more seasonal changes in a month. To add to this complexity, Disney also varies the price of its hotel rooms with the day of the week, charging more for the same room on Friday and Saturday nights. The increased rates typically apply only during busier times of the year, such as holidays, and range from $10 to $20 or more per room per night.

2. ASK ABOUT SPECIALS When you talk to Disney reservationists, ask specifically about specials. For example, "What special deals or discounts are available at Disney hotels during the time of our visit?" Being specific and assertive paid off for a Warren Township, New Jersey, dad:

> Your tip on asking Disney employees about discounts was invaluable. They will not volunteer this information, but by asking we saved almost $500 on our hotel room using a AAA discount.

Another New Jersey reader takes a high-calorie approach:

> My husband and I begin planning each WDW vacation the same way: Call the famous 407-W-DISNEY number and speak to someone with a ridiculous name (this time it was Flower and Buffy). I present my vacation plan to the operator, which consists of my specific date, WDW resort, and ticket choice. She quotes me a price; I thank her for her help and hang up. I call again and present my exact same plan to a new operator, who quotes me a totally different price! I repeat the phone process again and obtain another price for the same plan. After three years, my husband and I feel like we're playing "Spin the Wheel to Get a Price for the WDW Vacation." Now, instead of getting disgusted, we make it a night of calling with coffee and dessert.

A family from West Springfield, Massachusetts, discovered that if you keep on shopping even after you've booked, your efforts can really pay off:

> I booked our trip online with Disney using a special-offer discount we had received in the mail. Two months before our trip, and after I had already paid in full, Disney ran a special that was actually better than the one I had booked. I gave them a call, and they politely, quickly, and efficiently credited me with the difference.

3. "TRADE-UP" OR "UPSELL" RATES If you request a room at a Disney Value resort and none is available, you may be offered a discounted room in the next category up (Moderate resorts, in this example). Similarly, if you ask for a room in a Moderate resort and none is available, Disney will usually offer a deal for Disney Deluxe Villa rooms or a Deluxe resort. You can angle for a trade-up rate by asking for a resort category that's more likely to be sold out.

4. KNOW THE SECRET CODE The folks at **MouseSavers** (**mousesavers .com**) maintain an updated list of discounts and reservation codes for

Disney resorts. The codes are separated into categories such as "for anyone," "for residents of certain states," and "for Annual Pass holders." For example, the site once listed code CVZ, published in an ad in some Spanish-language newspapers and magazines, offering a rate of $65 per night for Disney's All-Star Resorts from April 22 to August 8. Anyone calling the Disney Reservation Center at ☎ 407-W-DISNEY can use a current code and get the discounted rate.

Be aware that Disney targets people with PIN codes in e-mails and direct mailings. PIN-code discounts are offered to specific individuals and are correlated with a given person's name and address. When you try to make a reservation using the PIN, Disney will verify that the street or e-mail address to which the code was sent is yours.

MouseSavers has a great historical list of when discounts were released and what they encompassed at **mousesavers.com/historical wdwdiscounts.html.** You can also sign up for the MouseSavers news-letter, with discount announcements, Disney news, and exclusive offers not available to the general public.

To get your name in the Disney system, call the Disney Reservation Center at ☎ 407-W-DISNEY and request that written info or the free trip-planning DVD be sent to you. If you've been to Walt Disney World before, your name and address will of course already be on record, but you won't be as likely to receive a PIN-code offer as you would by calling and requesting to be sent

unofficial **TIP**
To enhance your chances of receiving a PIN-code offer, you need to get your name and street or e-mail address into the Disney system.

information. On the web, go to **disneyworld.com** and sign up (via the trip-planning DVD) to automatically be sent offers and news at your e-mail address. You might also consider getting a **Disney Rewards Visa Card,** which entitles you to around two days' advance notice when a discount is released (visit **disney.go.com/visa** for details).

Our blog, **blog.touringplans.com,** often provides advance notice on discount details and their dates of availability. Two other sites, **allears .net** and **wdwinfo.com,** also have discount codes.

5. INTERNET SELLERS Online travel sellers **Expedia (expedia.com), Travelocity (travelocity.com),** and **One Travel (onetravel.com)** sell Disney hotels, but usually at a price approximating the going rate obtainable from the Walt Disney Travel Company or Walt Disney World Central Reservations. Most breaks are in the 7–25% range, but they can go as deep as 40%. Disney also places its hotel rooms on **Priceline (priceline .com).** While still abstaining from the "Name Your Own Price" aspect of the site, Disney's hotel rooms are now in Priceline's inventory and available through its conventional booking engine at a discounted rate.

6. WALT DISNEY WORLD WEBSITE Particularly in the postrecession economy, Disney has become more aggressive about offering deals when it sees lower-than-usual future demand. Go to **disneyworld.com** and look for "Special Offers" or "Save 25% on Stays" on the home page. In the same place, also look for seasonal discounts, usually listed as "Summertime Savings" or "Fall Savings" or something similar. You can also go to "Tickets and Packages" at the top right of the home page, where you'll find a link to Special Offers. You must click on the particular special to get the discounts: If you fill out the information on

"Price Your Dream Vacation," you'll be charged the full rack rate. Reservations booked online are subject to a $200 penalty if canceled less than 45 days before arrival. Before booking rooms on Disney's or any website, click on "Terms and Conditions" and read the fine print.

7. RENTING DISNEY VACATION CLUB POINTS The Disney Vacation Club (DVC) is Disney's time-share-condominium program. DVC resorts (a.k.a. Disney Deluxe Villa resorts) at Walt Disney World are **Bay Lake Tower** at the Contemporary Resort, **Disney's Old Key West Resort, Disney's Saratoga Springs Resort & Spa, Treehouse Villas at Saratoga Springs,** the **Beach Club Villas,** the **Villas at Wilderness Lodge, Animal Kingdom Villas,** and the **BoardWalk Villas.** Each resort offers studios and one- and two-bedroom villas (some resorts also offer three-bedroom villas). All accommodations are roomy and luxurious. The studios are equipped with kitchenettes, wet bars, and fridges; the villas come with full kitchens. Most accommodations have patios or balconies.

DVC members receive a number of "points" annually that they use to pay for their Disney accommodations. Sometimes members elect to "rent" (sell) their points instead of using them in a given year. Though Disney is not involved in the transaction, it allows DVC members to make these points available to the general public. The going rental rate is usually in the range of $12–$13 per point. A studio for a week at the BoardWalk Villas would run you $3,150 with tax for regular season if you booked through the Disney Reservation Center. The same studio costs the DVC member 83 points for a week (106 during peak season). If you rented his points at $13 per point, the BoardWalk Villas Studio would cost you $1,468 with tax—almost $1,700 less.

You have two options when renting points: locate and deal directly with the selling DVC member, or go through a company that specializes in DVC points rental.

The popular Disney-discussion site **Disboards** (**disboards.com**) has a specific forum for matching DVC sellers and renters. When you deal directly with the selling DVC member, you pay him or her directly, such as by certified check (few members accept credit cards). The DVC member makes a reservation in your name and pays Disney the requisite number of points. Arrangements vary, and some trust is required from both parties. Usually your reservation is documented by a confirmation sent from Disney to the owner and then passed along to you. Though the deal you cut is strictly up to you and the owner, you should always insist on receiving the aforementioned confirmation before making more than a one-night deposit.

Finding a seller yourself can sometimes yield good deals, but takes time and effort with no guarantees you'll find a match. For a fixed rate of around $13 per point, the folks at **dvcrequest.com** will act on your behalf as a points broker, matching your request for a specific resort and dates to their available supply. They'll also take requests months in advance and notify you as soon as something becomes available—a big benefit to those who can't surf the web every day. Plus they accept major credit cards.

We suggest using the discussion boards if you're going during the off-season, you could stay at any of several resorts, and you've got the time and skills to invest in finding a seller at a low rate. If you're trying to book a particular resort, especially during a busy time of year, there's something to be said for the low-hassle approach of a points broker.

8. TRAVEL AGENTS are active players and particularly good sources of information on limited-time programs and discounts. We believe a good travel agent is the best friend a traveler can have. And though we at the *Unofficial Guide* know a thing or two about the travel industry, we always give our agent a chance to beat any deal we find. If she can't beat it, we let her book it anyway if it's commissionable. We nurture a relationship that gives her plenty of incentive to roll up her sleeves and work on our behalf.

As you might expect, there are travel agents and agencies that specialize, sometimes exclusively, in selling Walt Disney World. These agents have spent an incredible amount of time at the resort, and they have also completed extensive Disney-education programs. They're usually the most Disney-knowledgeable agents in the travel industry. Most of these specialists and their agencies display the "Earmarked" logo stating that they're Authorized Disney Vacation Planners.

These Disney specialists are so good we use them ourselves. The needs of our research team are many, and our schedules are complicated. When we work with an Authorized Disney Vacation Planner, we know we're dealing with someone who knows Disney inside and out, including where to find the deals and how to use all tricks of the trade that keep our research budget under control. Simply stated, they save us time and money, sometimes lots of both.

Each year we ask our readers to rate the travel agent who helped plan their Disney trip. The best of the best include **Sue Pisaturo** of **Small World Vacations,** whom we've used many times and who contributes to this guide (**sue@wdwvacations.com**); **Lori Bandera,** who's been at the top of this list twice (**banderawdwtravel@aol.com**); **Coleen Bolton** (**coleenbolton@earthlink.net**); **Deb Chambers** (**deb@themagic forless.com**); **Michelle Cunningham** (**mcmick3@gmail.com**); **Leslie Henson** (**lesliehhenson@gmail.com**); and **Karen Nunn** (**karen.nunn@ gmail.com**).

Our reader-survey results indicate that for Walt Disney World, you'll be much more satisfied using a travel agent who specializes in Disney and much more likely to recommend those agents to a friend. While the agents above are the ones most consistently recommended in our surveys, you'll find good Disney specialists throughout the country if you prefer to work with someone close to home.

9. ORGANIZATIONS AND AUTO CLUBS Disney has developed time-limited programs with some auto clubs and organizations. AAA, for example, can often offer discounts on hotels and packages comparable to those Disney offers its Annual Pass holders. Such deals come and go, but the market suggests there will be more. If you're a member of AARP, AAA, or any travel or auto club, ask whether the group has a program before shopping elsewhere.

10. ROOM UPGRADES Sometimes a room upgrade is as good as a discount. If you're visiting Disney World during a slower time, book the least expensive room your discounts will allow. Checking in, ask very politely about being upgraded to a "water view" or "pool view" room.

A fair percentage of the time, you'll get one at no additional charge. Understand, however, that a room upgrade should be considered a favor. Hotels are under no obligation to upgrade you, so if your request is not met, accept the decision graciously. Also, note that suites (such as the Art of Animation Suites) are exempt from discount offers.

11. MILITARY DISCOUNTS The **Shades of Green Armed Forces Recreation Center,** near the Grand Floridian Resort & Spa, offers luxury accommodations at rates based on a service member's rank, as well as attraction tickets to the theme parks. For rates and other information, call ☎ 888-593-2242 or see **shadesofgreen.org.**

12. YEAR-ROUND DISCOUNTS AT THE SWAN AND DOLPHIN RESORTS Government workers, teachers, nurses, military, and AAA and Entertainment Coupon Book members can save on their rooms at the Dolphin or the Swan resort (when space is available, of course). Call ☎ 800-227-1500.

CHOOSING A WALT DISNEY WORLD HOTEL

IF YOU WANT TO STAY IN THE WORLD but don't know which hotel to choose, consider these factors:

1. COST Consider your budget. Hotel rooms start at about $84 a night at the **All-Star** and **Pop Century** resorts during Value Season and top out near $900 at the **Grand Floridian Resort & Spa** during Holiday Season. Suites, of course, are more expensive than standard rooms.

Animal Kingdom Villas, Bay Lake Tower, Beach Club Villas, BoardWalk Villas, Disney's Old Key West Resort, Disney's Saratoga Springs Resort & Spa, and **Wilderness Lodge Villas** offer condo-type accommodations with one-, two-, and (at Saratoga Springs, BoardWalk Villas, Disney's Old Key West, Animal Kingdom Villas, and Bay Lake Tower) three-bedroom units with kitchens, living rooms, DVD players, and washers and dryers. Prices range from $300 per night for a studio suite at Animal Kingdom Villas to more than $2,600 per night for a three-bedroom villa at BoardWalk Villas. Fully equipped cabins at **Fort Wilderness Resort & Campground** cost $285–$455 per night. A few suites without kitchens are available at the more expensive Disney resorts.

For any extra adults in a room (more than two), the nightly surcharge for each extra adult is $26.63 per night with tax at all resorts but DDV resorts, which levy no surcharge.

Before you choose a resort based on price alone, consider this: Our reader surveys indicate you'll be more satisfied with your hotel choice if it's slightly more expensive than the hotels you typically stay at.

Our Disney survey asks readers to name the kinds of hotels they generally choose when on vacation somewhere other than Disney. We list the top hotel chains in every category, from budget choices such as Days Inn and Super 8 through high-end resorts including Four Seasons and Ritz-Carlton, and we provide a space for folks to name other resorts.

Next, we calculate how satisfied our readers are at their Disney hotel based on the kinds of hotels they typically stay at on trips excluding Walt Disney World. For example, if you typically stay at a mid-priced hotel such as Holiday Inn, how satisfied are you likely to be with Disney's moderate resorts? The following chart shows the results.

IF YOU TYPICALLY STAY AT THIS TYPE OF HOTEL . . .	YOU'RE MOST LIKELY TO BE SATISFIED BY THIS TYPE OF DISNEY RESORT
Budget-priced	Moderate (98%)
Midpriced	DDV (96%) or Moderate (93%)
Upscale	Deluxe (97%)
Luxury	Deluxe (98%)
Vacation home/condo	Moderate (98%) or DDV (82%)

In general, readers report that they're most satisfied staying at a hotel one category up from their typical non-Disney choices. The Disney Moderate resorts do particularly well overall. Note that these results explicitly take into account the price differences among the resorts. That is, even after taking into account that moderately priced resorts are more expensive than budget resorts, readers who typically stay at budget resorts are still more satisfied at a Moderate than a Value when at Disney.

We think that measuring satisfaction based on a reader's background is more meaningful than simply reporting the satisfaction of all readers. On the web, you typically don't know the basis by which other people judge hotels. The result is a jumble of ratings that often make little sense in aggregate. At press time, for example, TripAdvisor .com's reader rankings placed Disney's Pop Century—a Value resort— one spot higher than Disney's Contemporary Resort, the Swan, and the Dolphin—all Deluxe resorts. TripAdvisor's users also rated every Value resort as a four-star hotel. While there's certainly nothing wrong with Pop Century, no objective review would place it at the same level as the Contemporary.

Also at Disney World are the seven hotels of the **Downtown Disney Resort Area (DDRA).** Accommodations range from fairly luxurious to motel-like. While the DDRA is technically part of Disney World, staying there is like visiting a colony rather than the motherland. Free parking at theme parks isn't offered—nor is early entry, with one exception, the Hilton—and hotels operate their own buses rather than use Disney transportation. For more information on DDRA properties, see page 196.

WHAT IT COSTS TO STAY IN THE DOWNTOWN DISNEY RESORT AREA	
Best Western Lake Buena Vista Resort Hotel	$104–$250
Buena Vista Palace Hotel & Spa	$179–$1,009
DoubleTree Guest Suites	$82–$505
Hilton in the WDW Resort	$95–$329
Holiday Inn in the WDW Resort	$94–$159
Royal Plaza	$109–$249
Wyndham Lake Buena Vista Resort	$77–$399

2. LOCATION Once you determine your budget, think about what you want to do at Disney World. Will you go to all four theme parks or concentrate on one or two?

COSTS PER NIGHT OF DISNEY RESORT HOTEL ROOMS (rack rate)	
All-Star Resorts	$84–$184
All-Star Music Resort Family Suites	$198–$375
Animal Kingdom Lodge	$265–$635
Animal Kingdom Villas (Jambo House, Kidani Village)	$300–$2,345
Art of Animation Resort	$94–$425
Bay Lake Tower	$415–$2,605
Beach Club Resort	$335–$2,730
Beach Club Villas	$345–$1,265
BoardWalk Inn	$345–$2,905
BoardWalk Villas	$345–$2,345
Caribbean Beach Resort	$159–$314
Contemporary Resort	$315–$3,730
Coronado Springs Resort	$164–$1,330
Disney's Old Key West Resort	$315–$1,795
Disney's Saratoga Springs Resort & Spa	$315–$1,795
Dolphin (Sheraton)	$274–$564
Fort Wilderness Resort & Campground (cabins)	$285–$455
Grand Floridian Resort & Spa	$460–$3,210
Polynesian Resort	$405–$3,140
Pop Century Resort	$89–$194
Port Orleans Resort (French Quarter, Riverside)	$159–$319
Swan (Westin)	$274–$564
Treehouse Villas	$595–$980
Wilderness Lodge	$265–$1,540
Wilderness Lodge Villas	$355–$1,260
Yacht Club Resort	$335–$2,915

If you'll be driving a car, your Disney hotel's location isn't especially important unless you plan to spend most of your time at the Magic Kingdom. (Disney transportation is always more efficient than your car in this case because it bypasses the Transportation and Ticket Center, the World's transportation hub, and deposits you at the theme park entrance.) If you haven't decided whether you want a car for your Disney vacation, see "How to Travel around the World" (page 383).

Most convenient to the Magic Kingdom are the three resorts linked by monorail: the **Grand Floridian, Contemporary–Bay Lake Tower,** and **Polynesian.** Commuting to the Magic Kingdom via monorail is quick and simple, allowing visitors to return to their hotel for a nap, swim, or meal.

Contemporary Resort–Bay Lake Tower, in addition to being on the monorail, is only a 10- to 15-minute walk to the Magic Kingdom. Guests reach Epcot by monorail but must transfer at the Transportation and Ticket Center. Buses connect the resort complex to Disney's Hollywood Studios and Animal Kingdom. No transfer is required, but the bus makes several stops before reaching either destination.

The Polynesian Resort is served by the Magic Kingdom monorail and is an easy walk from the transportation center. At the center, you can catch an express monorail to Epcot. This makes the Polynesian the only Disney resort with direct monorail access to both Epcot and the Magic Kingdom. To minimize your walk to the transportation center, request a room in the Rapa Nui, Tahiti, or Tokelau guest buildings.

Wilderness Lodge & Villas, along with **Fort Wilderness Resort & Campground,** are linked to the Magic Kingdom by boat, and to everywhere else in the World by somewhat convoluted bus service.

Most convenient to Epcot and Disney's Hollywood Studios are the **BoardWalk Inn, BoardWalk Villas, Yacht & Beach Club Resorts, Beach Club Villas,** the **Swan,** and the **Dolphin.** Though all are within easy walking distance of Epcot's International Gateway, boat service is also available. Vessels also connect Epcot hotels to DHS. Epcot hotels are best for guests planning to spend most of their time at Epcot or DHS.

Centrally located are **Caribbean Beach Resort, Pop Century Resort,** and **Art of Animation Resort.** Along Bonnet Creek, **Disney's Old Key West** and **Port Orleans** resorts also offer a central location. Also along Bonnet Creek, pretty much surrounded by Walt Disney World, is a parcel of land that Disney was unable to acquire and that went undeveloped for decades. Now that property is home to three non-Disney hotels: the **Waldorf Astoria Orlando,** the **Hilton Orlando Bonnet Creek,** and the **Wyndham Bonnet Creek Resort.** None of the three is technically in Walt Disney World, but you can access them only via Disney property and roads—a real sore point with Disney. The hotels are as close to the theme parks as Disney's own and offer transportation to the parks and Downtown Disney. Because these are neither Disney hotels nor located on Disney property, we do not cover them in full. We do, however, profile the Waldorf Astoria and the Wyndham Bonnet Creek Resort later in this chapter in "Hotels outside of Walt Disney World."

Though they're not centrally located, the **All-Star, Coronado Springs,** and **Animal Kingdom Lodge & Villas** resorts have very good bus service to all Disney World destinations and are closest to Animal Kingdom. **Wilderness Lodge & Villas** and **Fort Wilderness Resort & Campground** have the most convoluted transportation service.

If you plan to play golf, book **Disney's Old Key West Resort** or **Disney's Saratoga Springs Resort & Spa,** both built around golf courses. The military-only **Shades of Green** resort is adjacent to two courses. Near but not on a golf course are the **Grand Floridian, Polynesian,** and **Port Orleans** resorts. For boating and water sports, try the **Polynesian, Contemporary,** or **Grand Floridian** resorts, **Fort Wilderness Resort & Campground,** or **Wilderness Lodge & Villas.** The lodge and campground are also great for hikers, bikers, and joggers.

unofficial **TIP**
If you plan to use Disney transportation to visit all four major parks and one or both of the water parks, book a centrally located resort that has good transportation connections. The Epcot resorts and the Polynesian, Caribbean Beach, Art of Animation, Pop Century, and Port Orleans resorts fill the bill. Disney's Old Key West Resort is centrally located but offers limited bus service between noon and 6 p.m.

3. ROOM QUALITY Few Disney guests spend much time in their hotel rooms, though these rooms are among the best designed and most well appointed anywhere. Plus, they're meticulously maintained. At the top of the line are the luxurious rooms of the **Contemporary, Grand Floridian,** and **Polynesian** resorts; bringing up the rear are the small rooms of the **All-Star Resorts.** But even these economy rooms are sparkling-clean and quite livable.

The chart opposite shows how Disney hotels (along with the **Swan** and **Dolphin,** which are Westin and Sheraton hotels) stack up for quality.

4. THE SIZE OF YOUR GROUP Larger families and groups may be interested in how many persons a Disney resort room can accommodate, but only Lilliputians would be comfortable in a room filled to capacity. Groups requiring two or more guest rooms should consider condo or villa accommodations in or out of the World. The most cost-efficient Disney lodgings for groups of five or six persons are the cabins at **Fort Wilderness Resort & Campground.** They sleep six adults plus a child or toddler in a crib. If your party includes more than six people, you'll need either two hotel rooms, a suite, or a condo. The Disney room-layout schematics on the following pages show the rooms' relative sizes and configurations, along with the maximum number of persons per room.

5. THEME All Disney hotels are themed. Each is designed to make you feel you're in a special place or period of history.

Some resorts carry off their themes better than others, and some themes are more exciting. **Wilderness Lodge & Villas,** for example, is extraordinary, reminiscent of a grand national-park lodge from the early 20th century. The lobby opens eight stories to a timbered ceiling supported by giant columns of bundled logs. One look eases you into the Northwest-wilderness theme. The lodge is a great choice for couples and seniors and is heaven for children.

Animal Kingdom Lodge & Villas replicates grand safari lodges of Kenya and Tanzania and overlooks its own African game preserve. By far the most exotic Disney resort, it's made to order for couples on romantic getaways and for families with children. The **Polynesian,** likewise dramatic, conveys the feeling of the Pacific Islands. It's great for romantics and families. Many waterfront rooms offer a perfect view of Cinderella Castle and the Magic Kingdom fireworks across Seven Seas Lagoon.

Grandeur, nostalgia, and privilege are central to the **Grand Floridian** and **Yacht & Beach Club Resorts** and the **BoardWalk Inn & Villas.** Although modeled after Eastern-seaboard seaside hotels of different eras, the resorts are similar. **Disney's Saratoga Springs Resort & Spa,** supposedly representative of an upstate New York country retreat, looks like what you'd get if you crossed the Beach Club with the Wilderness Lodge. For all the resorts inspired by northeastern resorts, thematic distinctions are subtle and lost on many guests.

Port Orleans French Quarter Resort lacks the mystery and sultriness of the real New Orleans French Quarter but captures enough of its architectural essence to carry off the theme. **Port Orleans Riverside Resort** likewise succeeds with its plantation and bayou setting. **Disney's Old Key West Resort** gets the architecture right, but cloning Key West

HOTEL	ROOM-QUALITY RATING
1. BAY LAKE TOWER	95
2. CONTEMPORARY RESORT	93
3. GRAND FLORIDIAN RESORT & SPA	93
4. POLYNESIAN RESORT	92
5. ANIMAL KINGDOM VILLAS	91
6. SHADES OF GREEN	91
7. BEACH CLUB RESORT	90
8. BEACH CLUB VILLAS *(studios)*	90
9. BOARDWALK VILLAS *(studios)*	90
10. DISNEY'S SARATOGA SPRINGS RESORT & SPA *(studios)*	90
11. DISNEY'S OLD KEY WEST RESORT *(studios)*	90
12. DOLPHIN	90
13. SWAN	90
14. TREEHOUSE VILLAS *(studios)*	90
15. WILDERNESS LODGE VILLAS *(studios)*	90
16. ANIMAL KINGDOM LODGE	89
17. BOARDWALK INN	89
18. YACHT CLUB RESORT	89
19. FORT WILDERNESS CABINS	86
20. WILDERNESS LODGE	86
21. PORT ORLEANS FRENCH QUARTER	84
22. CORONADO SPRINGS RESORT	83
23. PORT ORLEANS RIVERSIDE	83
24. CARIBBEAN BEACH RESORT	80
25. ART OF ANIMATION RESORT	78
26. ALL-STAR RESORTS	73
27. POP CENTURY RESORT	71
N/A GRAND FLORIDIAN DVC *(too new to rate)*	N/A

on such a large scale totally glosses over Key West's idiosyncratic patchwork personality. The **Caribbean Beach Resort**'s theme is much more effective at night, thanks to creative lighting. By day, it looks like a Miami condo development.

Coronado Springs Resort offers several styles of Mexican and southwestern American architecture. Though the lake setting is lovely and the resort is attractive and inviting, the theme (with the exception of the main swimming area) isn't especially stimulating—more like a Scottsdale, Arizona, country club than a Disney resort.

The **All-Star Resorts** comprise 30 three-story, T-shaped hotels with almost 6,000 guest rooms. There are 15 themed areas: 5 celebrate sports (surfing, basketball, tennis, football, and baseball), 5 recall Hollywood movies, and 5 have musical motifs. The resort's design, with entrances shaped like giant Dalmatians, Coke cups, footballs, and the like, is pretty adolescent, sacrificing grace and beauty for energy and nov-elty. Guest rooms are small, with decor reminiscent of a teenage boy's

HOTEL	THEME
ALL-STAR RESORTS	Sports, music, and movies
ANIMAL KINGDOM LODGE & VILLAS	African game preserve
ART OF ANIMATION RESORT	Disney's animated films
BAY LAKE TOWER	Upscale, ultramodern urban hotel
BEACH CLUB RESORT & VILLAS	New England beach club of the 1870s
BOARDWALK INN	East Coast boardwalk hotel of the early 1900s
BOARDWALK VILLAS	East Coast beach cottage of the early 1900s
CARIBBEAN BEACH RESORT	Caribbean islands
CONTEMPORARY RESORT	Future as perceived by past, present generations
CORONADO SPRINGS RESORT	Northern Mexico and the American Southwest
DISNEY'S OLD KEY WEST RESORT	Key West
DISNEY'S SARATOGA SPRINGS RESORT & SPA	1880s Victorian lake
DOLPHIN	Modern Florida resort
GRAND FLORIDIAN RESORT & SPA	Turn-of-the-20th-century luxury hotel
POLYNESIAN RESORT	Hawaii–South Seas islands
POP CENTURY RESORT	Icons from various decades of the 20th century
PORT ORLEANS FRENCH QUARTER RESORT	Turn-of-the-19th-century New Orleans
PORT ORLEANS RIVERSIDE RESORT	Antebellum Louisiana plantation, bayou-side retreat
SWAN	Modern Florida resort
TREEHOUSE VILLAS	Rustic vacation homes with modern amenities
WILDERNESS LODGE & VILLAS	National-park grand lodge of the early 1900s
YACHT CLUB RESORT	New England seashore hotel of the 1880s

bedroom. Despite the theme, there is no sports, music, or movies at All-Star Resorts. **Pop Century Resort** is pretty much a clone of All-Star Resorts, only this time the giant icons symbolize decades of the 20th century (Big Wheels, 45-rpm records, silhouettes of people doing period dances, and such), and period memorabilia decorate the rooms. Across the lake from Pop Century Resort is the **Art of Animation Resort,** with icons and decor based on four animated features: *Cars, Finding Nemo, The Lion King,* and *The Little Mermaid.*

Pretense aside, the **Contemporary, Swan,** and **Dolphin** are essentially themeless though architecturally interesting. The original Contemporary Resort is a 15-story A-frame building with monorails running through the middle. Views from guest rooms here and in Bay Lake Tower are among the best at Disney World. Swan and Dolphin are massive yet whimsical. Designed by Michael Graves, they're excellent examples of "entertainment architecture." The two resorts' guest rooms, originally avant-garde bordering on garish, have been totally

DISNEY DELUXE RESORTS ROOM DIAGRAMS

Contemporary Resort

Typical room, 394 square feet
*Rooms accommodate 5 guests,
plus 1 child under age 3 in a crib.*

Polynesian Resort

Typical room, 415 square feet
*Rooms accommodate 5 guests,
plus 1 child under age 3 in a crib.*

Grand Floridian Resort & Spa

Typical room, 440 square feet
*Rooms accommodate 5 guests,
plus 1 child under age 3 in a crib.*

BoardWalk Inn

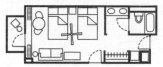

Typical room, 371 square feet
*Rooms accommodate 4 guests,
plus 1 child under age 3 in a crib.*

Beach Club Resort

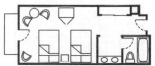

Typical room, 381 square feet
*Rooms accommodate 5 guests,
plus 1 child under age 3 in a crib.*

Yacht Club Resort

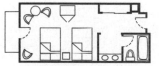

Typical room, 381 square feet
*Rooms accommodate 5 guests,
plus 1 child under age 3 in a crib.*

Wilderness Lodge

Typical room, 344 square feet
*Rooms accommodate 4 guests,
plus 1 child under age 3 in a crib.*

Animal Kingdom Lodge

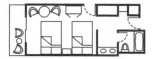

Typical room, 344 square feet
*Rooms accommodate 2–5 guests,
plus 1 child under age 3 in a crib.*

redesigned. Although still visually interesting, they're now more restful and easier on the eye.

6. DINING The best resorts for dining quality and selection are the Epcot resorts: the **Beach Club Villas, BoardWalk Inn & Villas, Dolphin, Swan,** and **Yacht & Beach Club Resorts.** Each has good restaurants and is within easy walking distance of the others and of the 14 restaurants

Continued on page 122

DISNEY DELUXE VILLA RESORTS ROOM DIAGRAMS

Disney's Old Key West Resort

Studio (gray): 376 square feet
One-bedroom: 942 square feet
Two-bedroom: 1,333 square feet
Grand Villa: 2,202 square feet

Animal Kingdom Villas (Jambo House & Kidani Village)

Studio (gray): 316–365 square feet (Jambo House),
366 square feet (Kidani Village)
One-bedroom: 629–710 square feet (Jambo House),
807 square feet (Kidani Village)
Two-bedroom: 945–1,075 square feet (Jambo House),
1,173 square feet (Kidani Village)
Grand Villa: 2,349 square feet (Jambo House),
2,201 square feet (Kidani Village)

Bay Lake Tower

Studio (gray): 339 square feet
One-bedroom: 803 square feet
Two-bedroom: 1,152 square feet
Grand Villa: 2,044 square feet

BoardWalk Villas

Studio (gray): 412 square feet
One-bedroom: 814 square feet
Two-bedroom: 1,236 square feet
Grand Villa: 2,491 square feet

Treehouse Villas at Disney's Saratoga Springs Resort & Spa

Standard Plan
Three-bedroom:
1,074 square feet

DDV guest-occupancy limits: studios, 4 persons; one-bedroom villas, 5 at Old Key West, Animal Kingdom Lodge (Kidani Village and some Jambo House), 4 everywhere else; two-bedroom villas, 9 at Animal Kingdom Lodge (Kidani Village) and Bay Lake Tower, 8 everywhere else; three-bedroom Grand Villas, 9 at Saratoga Springs Treehouse Villas, 12 everywhere else. *Note:* To all these limits you may add 1 child under age 3 in a crib.

DISNEY DELUXE VILLA RESORTS
ROOM DIAGRAMS *(continued)*

Wilderness Lodge Villas

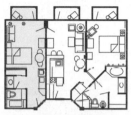

Studio (gray): 356 square feet
One-bedroom: 727 square feet
Two-bedroom: 1,080 square feet

Disney's Saratoga Springs Resort & Spa

Studio (gray): 355 square feet
One-bedroom: 714 square feet
Two-bedroom: 1,075 square feet
Grand Villa: 2,113 square feet

Beach Club Villas

Studio (gray): 356 square feet
One-bedroom: 726 square feet
Two-bedroom: 1,083 square feet

DISNEY MODERATE RESORTS ROOM DIAGRAMS

Coronado Springs Resort

Typical room, 314 square feet
*Rooms accommodate 4 guests,
plus 1 child under age 3 in a crib.*

Port Orleans French Quarter Resort

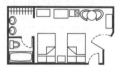

Typical room, 314 square feet
*Rooms accommodate 4 guests,
plus 1 child under age 3 in a crib.*

Caribbean Beach Resort

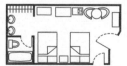

Typical room, 314 square feet
*Rooms accommodate 4 guests,
plus 1 child under age 3 in a crib.*

Port Orleans Resort Riverside

Typical room, 314 square feet
*Rooms accommodate 4 guests,
plus 1 child under age 3 in a crib.
Alligator Bayou has trundle bed for
extra child (54" long) at no extra charge.*

DISNEY VALUE RESORTS ROOM DIAGRAMS

All-Star Resorts Family Suite

Sleeper
TV
Safe
A/C
Safe
TV Desk A/C
Walkway
Queen
Refrig.

Typical suite, 520 square feet
*Suites accommodate 6 guests,
plus 1 child under age 3 in a crib.*

All-Star Resorts

Typical room, 260 square feet
*Rooms accommodate 4 guests,
plus 1 child under age 3 in a crib.*

Pop Century Resort

Typical room, 260 square feet
*Rooms accommodate 4 guests,
plus 1 child under age 3 in a crib.*

Art of Animation Resort,
Finding Nemo Family Suite

Typical room, 565 square feet
*Rooms accommodate 6 guests,
plus 1 child under age 3 in a crib.*

Art of Animation Resort,
Little Mermaid Standard Room

Typical room, 277 square feet
*Rooms accommodate 4 guests,
plus 1 child under age 3 in a crib.*

FORT WILDERNESS RESORT CABIN DIAGRAM

Fort Wilderness Resort & Campground

WH
Bunk beds
Double bed
Murphy bed
Living room & Dining room
Booth bench
Table

Cabins, 504 square feet
*Cabins accommodate 6 guests,
plus 1 child under age 3 in a crib.*

Continued from page 119

in Epcot's World Showcase section. If you stay at an Epcot resort, you have a total of 31 restaurants within a 5- to 12-minute walk.

The only other place in Disney World where restaurants and hotels are similarly concentrated is in the **Downtown Disney Resort Area.** In addition to restaurants in the hotels themselves, the **Hilton, Holiday**

Inn at Walt Disney World, Wyndham Lake Buena Vista Resort, and **Buena Vista Palace Hotel & Spa,** as well as **Disney's Saratoga Springs Resort & Spa,** are within walking distance of restaurants in Downtown Disney.

Guests at the **Contemporary, Polynesian,** and **Grand Floridian** can eat in their hotels, or they can commute to restaurants in the Magic Kingdom (not recommended) or in other monorail-linked hotels. Riding the monorail to another hotel or to the Magic Kingdom takes about 10 minutes each way, plus waiting for the train.

All the other Disney resorts are somewhat isolated. This means you're stuck dining at your hotel unless (1) you have a car or (2) you're content to eat at the theme parks or Downtown Disney.

Here's the deal. Disney transportation works fine for commuting from hotels to theme parks and Downtown Disney, but it's hopeless for getting from one hotel to another. If you're staying at Port Orleans and want to dine at the Swan, forget it. It can take you up to an hour and a half each way by bus. You could take a bus to the Magic Kingdom and catch a train to one of the monorail-served hotels for dinner. That would take "only" 45 minutes each way. When all is said and done, your best strategy for commuting from hotel to hotel by road is to use your car or pony up for a cab.

Of the more-isolated resorts, **Wilderness Lodge & Villas** and **Animal Kingdom Lodge & Villas** serve the best food. **Coronado Springs, Port Orleans, Disney's Old Key West,** and **Caribbean Beach** resorts each have a full-service restaurant, and all but Old Key West have a food court and pizza delivery. None of the isolated resorts, however, offer enough variety for the average person to be happy eating in his/her hotel every day. **Pop Century Resort, Art of Animation Resort,** and the **All-Star Resorts** (Disney's most isolated hotel complex) have nearly 10,500 guest rooms and suites, but no full-service restaurants. There are four food courts, but you have to get to them before 11 p.m. in most cases.

7. AMENITIES AND RECREATION Disney resorts offer a staggering variety of amenities and recreational opportunities (see charts on the following pages). All provide elaborate swimming pools, themed shops, restaurants or food courts, bars or lounges, and access to five Disney golf courses. The more you pay for your lodging, the more amenities and opportunities are at your disposal. **Animal Kingdom Lodge & Villas, BoardWalk Inn, Wilderness Lodge,** and the **Contemporary, Grand Floridian, Polynesian,** and **Yacht & Beach Club** resorts, for example, all offer concierge floors.

For swimming and sunning, the **Contemporary–Bay Lake Tower, Polynesian, Wilderness Lodge & Villas,** and **Grand Floridian** offer both pools and white-sand nonswimming beaches on Bay Lake or Seven Seas Lagoon. **Caribbean Beach Resort,** the **Dolphin,** and the **Yacht & Beach Club** also provide both pools and nonswimming beaches. Though lacking a lakefront beach, **Disney's Saratoga Springs Resort & Spa, Animal Kingdom Lodge & Villas, Port Orleans** and **Coronado Springs** resorts, and **BoardWalk Inn & Villas** have exceptionally creative pools. See the bottom chart on page 126 for our rankings of the swimming facilities at each Disney resort.

Bay Lake and Seven Seas Lagoon are the best venues for boating. Resorts fronting these lakes are **Contemporary–Bay Lake Tower,** the **Polynesian, Wilderness Lodge & Villas,** the **Grand Floridian,** and **Fort Wilderness Resort & Campground.** Though on smaller bodies of water, **BoardWalk Inn & Villas, Caribbean Beach, Coronado Springs,** the **Dolphin, Old Key West, Port Orleans, Saratoga Springs,** and the **Yacht & Beach Club** also rent watercraft.

Most convenient for golf are **Shades of Green, Saratoga Springs, Old Key West, Contemporary–Bay Lake Tower,** the **Polynesian,** the **Grand Floridian,** and **Port Orleans.** Tennis is available at the resorts indicated with bullets (•) in the chart on the facing page. Disney resorts with fitness and weight-training facilities are rated and ranked in the top chart on page 126 (resorts not listed don't have such facilities).

Disney Resort Amenities

RESORT	SUITES	CONCIERGE FLOOR	NUMBER OF ROOMS	ROOM SERVICE (FULL)	BROAD- BAND INTERNET	FREE IN-ROOM WI-FI	FRIDGE/ MINI- FRIDGE
ALL-STAR RESORTS	•	—	5,406	—	—	•	•
ANIMAL KINGDOM LODGE	•	•	972	•	—	•	•
ANIMAL KINGDOM VILLAS	•	•	458	•	—	•	•
ART OF ANIMATION RESORT	•	—	1,984	—	—	•	•
BAY LAKE TOWER	•	—	295	•	—	•	•
BEACH CLUB VILLAS	•	—	282	•	—	•	•
BOARDWALK INN	•	•	371	•	—	•	•
BOARDWALK VILLAS	•	—	532	•	—	•	•
CARIBBEAN BEACH RESORT	—	—	2,112	—	—	•	•
CONTEMPORARY RESORT	•	—	655	•	—	•	•
CORONADO SPRINGS RESORT	•	•	1,915	•	—	•	•
DISNEY'S OLD KEY WEST RESORT	•	—	761	—	—	•	•
DISNEY'S SARATOGA SPRINGS RESORT & SPA	•	—	1,260	—	—	•	•
DOLPHIN	•	—	1,509	•	—	•	•
FORT WILDERNESS CABINS	—	—	409	—	•	•	•
GRAND FLORIDIAN RESORT & SPA	•	•	867	•	—	•	•
POLYNESIAN RESORT	•	•	847	•	—	•	•
POP CENTURY RESORT	—	—	2,880	—	—	•	•
PORT ORLEANS RESORT	—	—	3,056	—	—	•	•
SHADES OF GREEN	•	—	586	•	—	•	•
SWAN	•	—	758	•	—	•	•
TREEHOUSE VILLAS	•	—	60	—	—	•	•
WILDERNESS LODGE & VILLAS	•	—	863	•	—	•	•
YACHT & BEACH CLUB RESORTS	•	•	1,197	•	—	•	•

Disney Resort Recreation

	FITNESS CENTER	WATER SPORTS	MARINA	BEACH	TENNIS	BIKING
ALL-STAR RESORTS	—	—	—	—	—	—
ANIMAL KINGDOM LODGE & VILLAS	•	—	—	—	•*	—
ART OF ANIMATION RESORT	—	—	—	—	—	—
BAY LAKE TOWER	•	•	•	•	–	–
BEACH CLUB VILLAS	•	•	•	•	•	—
BOARDWALK INN	•	•	•	—	•	•
BOARDWALK VILLAS	•	•	•	—	•	•
CARIBBEAN BEACH RESORT	—	•	•	•	—	•
CONTEMPORARY RESORT	•	•	•	•	—	—
CORONADO SPRINGS RESORT	•	•	•	•	•	•
DISNEY'S OLD KEY WEST RESORT	•	•	•	—	•	•
DISNEY'S SARATOGA SPRINGS RESORT & SPA, TREEHOUSE VILLAS	•	—	—	—	•	•
DOLPHIN	•	•	•	•	•	—
FORT WILDERNESS RESORT	—	•	•	•	•	•
GRAND FLORIDIAN RESORT & SPA	•	•	•	•	•	—
POLYNESIAN RESORT	—	•	•	•	—	•
POP CENTURY RESORT	—	—	—	—	—	—
PORT ORLEANS RESORT	—	•	•	•	—	•
SHADES OF GREEN	•	—	—	—	•	•
SWAN	•	—	—	•	•	—
WILDERNESS LODGE & VILLAS	•	•	•	•	—	•
YACHT & BEACH CLUB RESORTS	•	•	•	•	•	—

Kidani Village only

While there are many places to bike or jog at Disney World (including golf-cart paths), the best biking and jogging are at **Fort Wilderness Resort & Campground** and the adjacent **Wilderness Lodge & Villas. Caribbean Beach Resort** offers a lovely hiking, biking, and jogging trail around the lake. Also good for biking and jogging is the area along Bonnet Creek extending through Port Orleans and Old Key West toward Downtown Disney. Epcot resorts offer a lakefront promenade and bike path, as well as a roadside walkway suitable for jogging.

On-site child-care programs are offered at **Animal Kingdom Lodge & Villas, BoardWalk Inn & Villas,** the **Dolphin, Grand Floridian Resort & Spa,** the **Hilton in the Walt Disney World Resort,** the **Polynesian,** the **Swan, Wilderness Lodge & Villas,** and the **Yacht & Beach Club Resorts.** All other resorts offer in-room babysitting (see page 350 for details).

Disney offers free public Wi-Fi at all resorts as well as at the water parks, the ESPN Wide World of Sports Complex, and several other public areas on-property. Wi-Fi is not provided in the theme parks. The free Wi-Fi is convenient if you want a quick peek at an e-mail or glance

HOTEL	FITNESS-CENTER RATING
1. DISNEY'S SARATOGA SPRINGS RESORT & SPA, TREEHOUSE VILLAS	☆★★★★
2. GRAND FLORIDIAN RESORT & SPA	★★★★½
3. ANIMAL KINGDOM LODGE & VILLAS	★★★★
4. BOARDWALK INN & VILLAS	★★★★
5. YACHT & BEACH CLUB RESORTS (shared facility)	★★★★
6. CONTEMPORARY RESORT–BAY LAKE TOWER (shared facility)	★★★½
7. CORONADO SPRINGS RESORT	★★★½
8. WILDERNESS LODGE & VILLAS	★★★½
9. DOLPHIN	★★★
10. SHADES OF GREEN	★★★
11. SWAN	★★★
12. DISNEY'S OLD KEY WEST RESORT	★½

HOTEL	POOL RATING
1. YACHT & BEACH CLUB RESORTS & BEACH CLUB VILLAS (shared complex)	★★★★★
2. ANIMAL KINGDOM VILLAS (Kidani Village)	★★★★½
3. PORT ORLEANS RESORT	★★★★½
4. DISNEY'S SARATOGA SPRINGS RESORT & SPA, TREEHOUSE VILLAS	★★★★½
5. WILDERNESS LODGE & VILLAS	★★★★½
6. ANIMAL KINGDOM LODGE & VILLAS (Jambo House)	★★★★
7. BAY LAKE TOWER	★★★★
8. CORONADO SPRINGS RESORT	★★★★
9. DOLPHIN	★★★★
10. POLYNESIAN RESORT	★★★★
11. SWAN	★★★★
12. BOARDWALK INN & VILLAS	★★★½
13. CONTEMPORARY RESORT	★★★½
14. GRAND FLORIDIAN RESORT & SPA	★★★½
15. ALL-STAR RESORTS	★★★
16. ART OF ANIMATION RESORT	★★★
17. CARIBBEAN BEACH RESORT	★★★
18. DISNEY'S OLD KEY WEST RESORT	★★★
19. FORT WILDERNESS RESORT & CAMPGROUND	★★★
20. POP CENTURY RESORT	★★★
21. SHADES OF GREEN	★★★

at tomorrow's weather, but in our experience it's too slow and unreliable if you have to do serious work. On a recent stay at Port Orleans Riverside, for example, it was virtually impossible to get even a single web page to load at 7:30 a.m., but afternoon downloads at the Yacht Club reached speeds comparable to those of basic broadband. With the introduction of Wi-Fi, Disney is slowly removing wired high-speed Internet access from its hotel rooms.

8. NIGHTLIFE The boardwalk at **BoardWalk Inn & Villas** has an upscale dance club (albeit one that has never lived up to its potential), a club with dueling pianos and sing-alongs, a brewpub, and a sports bar. BoardWalk clubs are within easy walking distance of all Epcot resorts. Most non-Disney hotels in the **Downtown Disney Resort Area,** as well as **Disney's Saratoga Springs Resort & Spa,** are within walking distance of Downtown Disney nightspots. Nightlife at other Disney resorts is limited to lounges that stay open late.

> *unofficial* **TIP**
> The best lounges are **Narcoossee's** at the Grand Floridian, **Kimonos** at the Swan, and the **California Grill Lounge** at the Contemporary. Honorable mention goes to the **Territory Lounge** at Wilderness Lodge, where you can sometimes order from the menu of the adjacent Artist Point restaurant.

At the Contemporary Resort's **California Grill Lounge,** you can relax over dinner and watch the fireworks at the nearby Magic Kingdom.

All the Goodies without the Big Bucks

A Roanoke, Virginia, couple share how they enjoyed Disney's luxury resorts on the cheap:

> *One thing I think you should emphasize in your guide is how lovely it is to enjoy the Deluxe resorts without having to pay to stay there. We had a rental car, so it was easy for us to drive to Animal Kingdom Lodge, the Grand Floridian, and Wilderness Lodge for dinner. We allowed enough time before our reservation to explore the resort, have a drink in the bar, and then be shown to our table. We felt very thrifty enjoying these expensive resorts so much and then going back to our moderately priced resort just to sleep.*

RESEARCHING WALT DISNEY WORLD HOTELS

THE *UNOFFICIAL GUIDE* HOTEL TEAM inspects hundreds of hotel rooms each year throughout North America and stays abreast of current trends and issues in the lodging industry. One such issue is the list of frequent complaints hotel guests make regarding their rooms. Over the past few years, the most common complaints include excessive noise, uncomfortable beds, poor lighting, outdated furnishings, high phone charges, and substandard towels. Because these complaints are ongoing concerns, the hotel team undertook a complete reevaluation of every Walt Disney World resort (including the **Swan** and **Dolphin**) in each of these areas.

In the Lab with Dr. Fluffy

Our tests included everything from the quality of the bed linens to the age of the mattresses to the fluffiness (loft) of the pillows. While evaluation criteria for linens and mattresses are fairly well known, we couldn't find any standard test to measure pillow fluffiness. A search of *Consumer Reports'* website failed to find anything, and fear of another restraining order kept us from making all the phone calls to the magazine that we wanted. So we had to invent our own.

The method we came up with is based on measuring how far a half-filled gallon jug of water sank into the middle of a pillow. (Two quarts of water weigh between one-third and one-half as much as a typical human head, according to most estimates. Also, a gallon jug is easy to find, and no one thinks twice if you bring one into a hotel lobby. Not so with a replica of a human head—trust us.)

Key to this experiment was determining the proper range of support a good pillow should provide. A test bottle that sank too deep into a pillow would indicate not enough support; on the other hand, a bottle that sank very little might indicate an experience akin to sleeping on a brick. We therefore evaluated a wide range of pillows before the test to establish the proper range of support.

The best pillows are found at the non-Disney-owned **Swan** and **Dolphin** resorts. It's probably no coincidence that these are the only hotels using pillows made with goose feathers and down; all of the Disney-owned resorts use either polyester fill or foam. Other good pillows were found at Disney's **Wilderness Lodge** and **Wilderness Lodge Villas.** The pillows at the **Grand Floridian, Port Orleans French Quarter and Riverside,** and **Fort Wilderness Cabins** did poorly in our tests.

Mattresses at all the Walt Disney World resorts come from brand-name manufacturers such as Sealy and Simmons. Value resorts typically have either two full-size mattresses or one king; Moderate and Deluxe resorts have two queen beds (each about 20% larger than a full) or one king. One notable exception is the Swan, which uses the aptly named Heavenly Bed mattresses. Throughout the resorts, almost all the mattresses we inspected were less than 2 years old, and about half were less than a year old. The oldest mattress we found on Disney property—in service for 8 years—was at Disney's **Fort Wilderness Cabins.** (Outside Disney, we've seen 17-year-old mattresses still in use.)

Disney's Value and Moderate resorts use the same brand of 180-thread-count sheets for their bed linens. Disney's Deluxe and DDV resorts (except the **Contemporary**) and the independent **Swan** and **Dolphin** resorts all use 250-thread-count sheets.

Pipe Down Out There

Noisy rooms rank near the top of hotel guests' complaints every year. A well-designed room blocks both the noise coming from an adjacent room's television and from the swimming pool across the resort. Based on our initial tests of both interior and exterior soundproofing, and for the reasons outlined on page 130, we believe that a room's exterior door is the critical component in keeping sound out.

Our test equipment consisted of a digital sound meter, a portable CD player, and a copy of The Who's greatest hits. We first calibrated the volume of the CD player until Roger Daltrey's ear-piercing wail in "Baba O'Riley" reached 70 decibels on the sound meter. Next, we took the CD player outside the room and placed the meter on top of the pillow of the bed closest to the exterior door. We replayed "Baba

Disney Hotels: Complaints and Comparisons

	SOUND	LIGHTING	PILLOWS	OVERALL
ALL-STAR MOVIES	D	D	B	C–
ALL-STAR MUSIC	A	D	C	C+
ALL-STAR SPORTS	A	D	B	B
ANIMAL KINGDOM LODGE & VILLAS (Jambo House)	F	A	B	C+
ANIMAL KINGDOM VILLAS (Kidani Village)	C	C	B	C
ART OF ANIMATION RESORT *(too new to rate)*				
BAY LAKE TOWER	A	C	B	B+
BEACH CLUB RESORT & VILLAS	B	D	B	C+
BOARDWALK INN	B	F	B	C
BOARDWALK VILLAS	B	D	B	C+
CARIBBEAN BEACH RESORT	B	C	B	B
CONTEMPORARY RESORT	D	A	A	B+
CORONADO SPRINGS RESORT (studios)	B	B	B	B+
DISNEY'S OLD KEY WEST RESORT	A	D	C	C+
DISNEY'S SARATOGA SPRINGS RESORT & SPA	B	C	C	C+
DOLPHIN	A	D	A	B+
FORT WILDERNESS RESORT (cabins)	C	D	D	D
GRAND FLORIDIAN DVC *(too new to rate)*				
GRAND FLORIDIAN RESORT & SPA	F	A	D	C–
POLYNESIAN RESORT	F	A	B	C+
POP CENTURY RESORT	B	F	B	C
PORT ORLEANS FRENCH QUARTER	B	C	D	C
PORT ORLEANS RIVERSIDE	A	C	D	C+
SWAN	A	F	A	B
TREEHOUSE VILLAS AT DISNEY'S SARATOGA SPRINGS RESORT & SPA	A	B	B	B+
YACHT CLUB RESORT	B	F	B	C
WILDERNESS LODGE	D	A	A	B+
WILDERNESS LODGE VILLAS	F	A	A	B

O'Riley" and recorded the decibel reading on the sound meter. For good measure, we also recorded the sound level in the room with and without the AC running, and around the resort in general.

Surprisingly, six of the seven worst results came from Disney Deluxe resorts, with **Animal Kingdom Lodge (Jambo House)**, the **Grand Floridian**, the **Polynesian**, and **Wilderness Lodge Villas** making up the bottom four. Eight hotels earned top marks: **All-Star Music**,

All-Star Sports, Bay Lake Tower, the **Dolphin, Disney's Old Key West Resort, Port Orleans Riverside Resort,** the **Swan,** and **Treehouse Villas.** In addition to the Deluxe resorts mentioned previously, the **Contemporary** and **Wilderness Lodge** were near the bottom of the list, along with the Value **All-Star Movies** resort.

Illustration: Chris Eliopoulos

Overall, Value and Moderate resorts did much better than Deluxe resorts when it came to blocking out exterior noise, with Disney's All-Star Music and All-Star Sports, both Value resorts, being the overall winners (the Art of Animation Resort was not yet open). That certainly runs counter to what consumers would expect, so we set about trying to find an explanation. Like any good detective, we looked for an economic motive first.

The explanation turns out to be fairly simple, and it does come down to money—Disney's money. At Disney's Value and Moderate resorts (and, notably, Disney Vacation Club resorts), each room's exterior door opens onto the great outdoors, just as the average home's exterior door opens to the outside world. These exterior doors must have extensive weather stripping to keep out wind and rain. Also, exterior-facing walls tend to be thicker and better insulated than interior walls, as these measures reduce Disney's costs to heat and cool the rooms. Such walls also work really well at blocking noise.

QUIETEST ROOMS IN WALT DISNEY WORLD
ALL-STAR MUSIC Buildings 5 and 6, rooms facing west; Building 4, rooms facing northwest
ALL-STAR SPORTS Building 3, rooms facing west; Building 2, rooms facing north
BAY LAKE TOWER Any room is good here—rooms are the quietest in WDW
BEACH CLUB Easternmost buildings, rooms facing east
BEACH CLUB VILLAS Southernmost wings, rooms facing north-northwest
BOARDWALK INN All rooms facing courtyard, just east of main lobby
CARIBBEAN BEACH Trinidad South, Buildings 35 and 38, rooms facing lake; Barbados, Buildings 11 and 12, facing south
PORT ORLEANS RIVERSIDE Alligator Bayou, Buildings 26 and 28, rooms facing east; Acadian House, north wings, rooms facing west
PORT ORLEANS FRENCH QUARTER Building 1, rooms facing water; Building 7, north wing, rooms facing water; Building 6, north wing, rooms facing water
TREEHOUSE VILLAS Any room is good here
WILDERNESS LODGE Northernmost wing, rooms facing northwest (woods)
WILDERNESS LODGE VILLAS Southernmost building, water-view rooms facing east

In contrast, Deluxe rooms typically have doors that open onto an interior hallway that Disney is already paying to heat and cool. Thus, there's little economic incentive for Disney to put the same materials into the outward-facing doors and walls of some Deluxe resorts, since the temperature range outside the room is relatively constant and there's no need to keep rain or wind out. (In fact, many Deluxe resorts have a small gap of ¼–¾ inch at the bottom of their doors to aid in getting fresh air *into* the rooms.) Unfortunately, this permits more sound to enter. Finally, the interior hallways themselves can function as giant echo chambers, allowing sounds to bounce off the walls back and forth, up and down the hallway. Not so at the other resorts, where many sounds bounce off an exterior wall and out into space.

Room soundproofing, however, is only half of the story. The other half, as any good real estate agent knows, is location; despite the resort's relatively good performance, a pool-view room at All-Star Sports is likely to pick up a lot more noise than an upper-floor corner room at the Grand Floridian, because the former faces a heavily used public space. So our next task was to determine the amount of external noise affecting every single room at the Walt Disney World Resort.

We assigned *Unofficial Guide* researcher Rich Vosburgh to the task. Using a combination of resort maps, aerial photography, and a whole lot of old-fashioned legwork, Rich created an External Noise Potential metric for each hotel room on Disney property, taking into account factors including the floor level, pedestrian traffic, proximity to public spaces, and number of nearby hotel rooms. Finally, the research team revisited every building in every resort to verify our rankings. For the most part, we were spot on. But there were a couple of surprises that we're sure we would've overlooked had we not reviewed every single room. For example, the southwest-facing rooms in Buildings 7 and 8 of Disney's **All-Star Music** resort are situated well away from most public spaces in the resort and overlook the extreme end of a parking lot. There's not a lot of pedestrian traffic around, and the rooms themselves tested well for soundproofing—hey, these should be some quiet rooms, right? Well, when we visited the resort, we discovered that this particular section of parking lot, because it was away from most guest rooms, is where Disney decides to warm up its diesel buses in the morning before servicing the three All-Star Resorts. At 6 a.m., the area around these buildings sounded like Daytona International Speedway on race day.

Our research indicates that quiet rooms can be found in almost any resort. For readers who put peace and quiet at the top of their list, we've listed the 10 quietest spots among all WDW resorts in the chart on the facing page.

Let There Be Light

As with noise, poor lighting generally ranks near the top of hotel guests' complaints. Of particular concern is the lighting in the bathroom and grooming area, the head of the bed (for reading), and the desk or table area (for working). In fact, lighting here is so important that professional associations publish standards listing the minimum amount of lighting needed for each area. Our evaluations incorporate the standards and recommendations of the Illuminating Engineering Society of North America (IESNA), a leading institution for lighting research, technology, and its applications.

Our test equipment was an industrial-grade digital light meter, able to detect a wide range of light levels. In addition to testing the lighting at the grooming, desk, and bed areas, we also tested the bath/shower area, the armchair or sitting area (if the room had one), and the overall light level in the room. The results were weighted to emphasize the quality of light in the grooming, desk, and bed areas.

The rooms with the best lighting were found at **Animal Kingdom Lodge & Villas (Jambo House),** the **Contemporary,** the **Grand Floridian,** the **Polynesian,** and **Wilderness Lodge & Villas,** all Deluxe resorts. **Coronado Springs** was the highest-scoring Moderate resort. No Value resort posted acceptable scores in lighting.

Rooms at the Polynesian exceeded the IESNA's minimum recommendations in every area, and the Contemporary's new rooms exceeded the recommendations in all except the armchair reading area. Disney seems to be giving special attention to room lighting when doing its resort rehabs, and it's paying off.

Outside the Contemporary and Polynesian, the **Caribbean Beach** and **Grand Floridian** scored high with their grooming-and-bath-area lighting, while the **Wilderness Lodge Villas** and **Coronado Springs** had the best lighting in the desk/work area, with Coronado Springs using a specially designed ceiling lamp to ensure bright work surfaces; and **Wilderness Lodge** and **Port Orleans Riverside** had the best bed lighting. The worst scores were recorded at the **BoardWalk Inn,** the **Swan, Pop Century Resort,** and the **Yacht Club Resort.** How bad is the lighting? Rooms this dim are fertile ground for Barry White music as you put the moves on your sweetie.

Check-in and Checkout

Up to 10 days before you arrive, you can log on to **mydisneyreservation .com** to complete the check-in process, make room requests, and note events such as birthdays and anniversaries you're celebrating during your trip. Provide a credit card number and your arrival and departure times, and Disney will send you an e-mail confirmation that your check-in is complete. When you arrive at your resort, you'll bypass the regular check-in desk and head for another desk reserved for those who've already done so online.

If you're unable to check in online before your trip, then check-in processing is another area of guest service where you'd expect the more highfalutin resorts to shine, but our research shows that the Value resorts are by far the most efficient. The best of the best is the **Pop Century Resort,** where it's rare to wait in line for more than a couple of minutes. The Pop Century has the largest registration desk as well as the most agents manning it. What's more, a front-desk supervisor paces the registration lobby, directing guests and ensuring minimum waits. Even when a Magical Express bus deposits 45 people at one time, they're quickly processed. Almost as good is check-in efficiency at the Value **All-Star Resorts.**

Deluxe resorts have smaller front desks and fewer agents, but then guests generally arrive in smaller numbers than at the Value and Moderate resorts. A line of four or five waiting guests is not unusual, but the wait is usually less than 15 minutes. The arrival of a busload of guests can overwhelm the front desk of Deluxe resorts, but this is the exception rather than the rule. The least efficient of the Deluxe resorts' front desks is that of the **Polynesian Resort.**

By far the longest registration lines occur at the Moderate resorts, with the **Caribbean Beach Resort** being the worst of the worst.

If your room is unavailable when you arrive, Disney will either give you a phone number to call to check on the room or will offer to call or send a text message to your cell phone when it's ready.

A Cleveland mom shares her family's strategy for being content until their room is ready:

> My husband and I can't believe how people complain about the downtime people have while waiting for their room to be ready. We pack our bathing suits, cover-ups, and sunscreen in our carry-ons. We arrive, check in, and leave our cell number for a text when the room is ready and head to the pool. By the time our room is ready, we're rarin' to go!

Checking out is a snap at all Disney resorts. Your bill will be prepared and affixed to your doorknob or slipped under your door the night before you leave. If everything is in order, you have only to pack up and depart. If there's a problem with your bill, however, you'll have to resolve it at the front desk, where the previous order of most efficient to least efficient is a good gauge of the probable hassle you're in for.

UNOFFICIAL GUIDE READERS SPEAK OUT

MANY READERS SHARE with us their experiences and criticisms regarding Disney hotels through our survey questionnaire (in the back of this book and online at **touringplans.com/walt-disney-world/survey**). Some copy us on letters of complaint sent to Disney. If you've written or copied us about a bad experience, you might be surprised that we haven't quoted your letter. Any business can have a bad day, even a Disney hotel, and a single incident might not be indicative of the hotel's general level of quality and service. In our experience, if a problem is endemic the same complaint will usually surface in a number of letters. But even with our voluminous reader mail, your comments often paint a mixed picture. For instance, for every letter we get that's critical of Disney's Grand Floridian Resort & Spa, it's not unusual for us to receive another letter telling us it's the best place the reader ever stayed.

We tend to hear more often from readers when things go badly than when things go well. Whether your experience was positive or negative, we encourage you to share it with us. The more comments we receive, the more accurate and complete a picture we can provide.

READERS' 2012 DISNEY RESORT REPORT CARD

EACH YEAR, SEVERAL THOUSAND READERS send in their responses to the survey at the end of this guide. Found on pages 134–137, the Reader Report Card documents their opinions of the Disney resorts as well as the Swan, the Dolphin, and Shades of Green. **Room quality** reflects readers' satisfaction with their rooms, while **Check-in efficiency** rates the speed and ease of check-in. **Quietness of room** measures how well, in the guests' perception, their rooms are insulated from external noise. **Shuttle service** rates Disney bus, boat, and/or monorail service to and from the hotels. **Pool** reflects reader satisfaction with the resorts' swimming pools. **Staff** measures the friendliness

WOULD YOU RECOMMEND THIS HOTEL TO A FRIEND?

RESORT NAME	definitely recommend
Wilderness Lodge	89%
Port Orleans French Qtr.	87%
Animal Kingdom Lodge	86%
Contemporary Resort	86%
Yacht Club Resort	82%
BoardWalk Villas	80%
Wilderness Lodge Villas	79%
Animal Kingdom Villas	78%
Shades of Green	78%
Beach Club Resort	76%
Pop Century Resort	76%
Saratoga Springs Resort	76%
Polynesian Resort	75%
BoardWalk Inn	73%
Caribbean Beach Resort	70%
All-Star Music	69%
Dolphin	68%
Port Orleans Riverside	68%
Grand Floridian Resort	67%
Old Key West Resort	66%
All-Star Movies	65%
Bay Lake Tower	65%
Coronado Springs Resort	56%
All-Star Sports	50%
Saratoga Springs–Treehouse Villas	50%
Fort Wilderness Cabins	47%
Swan	33%
Grand Floridian DVC	–
Art of Animation	–
Average for WDW hotels	76%
Average for off-site hotels	57%

WOULD YOU STAY AT THIS HOTEL AGAIN?

RESORT NAME	would stay again
Bay Lake Tower	100%
Beach Club Resort	100%
BoardWalk Inn	100%
Saratoga Springs–Treehouse Villas	100%
Swan	100%
Wilderness Lodge	100%
Yacht Club Resort	100%
Port Orleans French Qtr.	98%
All-Star Music	97%
Contemporary Resort	97%
Coronado Springs Resort	97%
BoardWalk Villas	96%
Polynesian Resort	95%
Animal Kingdom Lodge	94%
Animal Kingdom Villas	94%
Dolphin	94%
Grand Floridian Resort	92%
Pop Century Resort	91%
Saratoga Springs Resort	90%
Caribbean Beach Resort	89%
Old Key West Resort	86%
Wilderness Lodge Villas	85%
Port Orleans Riverside	83%
Fort Wilderness Cabins	82%
All-Star Movies	80%
All-Star Sports	80%
Shades of Green	78%
Grand Floridian DVC	–
Art of Animation	–
Average for WDW hotels	90%
Average for off-site hotels	86%

Readers' Disney Resort Report Card

	HOTEL
	ALL-STAR MOVIES
	ALL-STAR MUSIC
	ALL-STAR SPORTS
	ANIMAL KINGDOM LODGE–JAMBO HOUSE
	ANIMAL KINGDOM LODGE–KIDANI VILLAGE
	ART OF ANIMATION RESORT
	BAY LAKE TOWER
	BEACH CLUB RESORT
	BEACH CLUB VILLAS

and helpfulness of the resort's employees, and **Food court** rates resorts' counter-service-dining facilities and food value.

Readers ranked Disney resorts about the same in this year's survey and the previous year's, giving the majority of Disney properties an overall B rating. Bus transportation and dining options are the areas where Disney scores lowest; check-in efficiency and hotel staff are Disney's strongest suits. While reader satisfaction with Disney hotels last year was essentially the same as with off-site hotels, this year's results show readers slightly more satisfied with Disney resorts than the average off-site property. (Interestingly, off-site properties tend to score lowest on bus transportation and dining, too.)

Putting It All Together:
Reader Picks for Best and Worst Resorts

Among Deluxe resorts, **Wilderness Lodge** and **Animal Kingdom Lodge** did better than average in all three surveys. The **Yacht Club Resort** also did well this year, which is interesting because it had placed near the bottom of the surveys for the past three years. Having stayed at the Yacht Club recently, we haven't been able to pinpoint exactly what's changed, but we do note that the resort gets high marks for check-in efficiency and staff friendliness. The **BoardWalk Villas** did well among DDV/DVC resorts.

Port Orleans French Quarter is the highest-ranking Moderate hotel. We suspect it rates highly with guests because it's smaller than all other Disney Moderate resorts and is well themed. Among Value resorts, **Pop Century** tops the list. We suspect, however, that the new rooms at the **Art of Animation Resort** will put it high up on next year's list.

As in years past, readers tended to be tougher than the *Unofficial Guide* hotel inspectors when it came to ratings. (For example, we really like the Polynesian Resort.) But remember that readers are rating one guest room during a specific visit, while our inspectors provide a comparative rating of more than 250 Disney and non-Disney hotels in and around Walt Disney World. For our ratings, see "How the Hotels Compare," on pages 254–260.

ROOM QUALITY	CHECK-IN EFFICIENCY	QUIETNESS OF ROOM	SHUTTLE SERVICE	POOL	STAFF	FOOD COURT	OVERALL RATING
B–	B	B–	B	B	C	C	B–
B–	A	C	B–	B	B	C–	B–
C	A	C	B	C	A	C	B
B+	A	A	C	B	A	C	B
A	B+	B–	C	B	B+	D	B
–	–	–	–	–	–	–	–
B	B–	A	B	B	B	C	B
B	B	B	B	A	B	D	B
A	A	B	C+	A–	A	D	B

Readers' Disney Resort Report Card *(continued)*

HOTEL
BOARDWALK INN
BOARDWALK VILLAS
CARIBBEAN BEACH RESORT
CONTEMPORARY RESORT
CORONADO SPRINGS RESORT
DOLPHIN
FORT WILDERNESS
GRAND FLORIDIAN DVC
GRAND FLORIDIAN RESORT & SPA
OLD KEY WEST RESORT
POLYNESIAN RESORT
POP CENTURY RESORT
PORT ORLEANS FRENCH QUARTER
PORT ORLEANS RIVERSIDE
SARATOGA SPRINGS RESORT & SPA
SARATOGA SPRINGS–TREEHOUSE VILLAS
SHADES OF GREEN
SWAN
WILDERNESS LODGE
WILDERNESS LODGE VILLAS
YACHT CLUB RESORT
AVERAGE FOR DISNEY HOTELS
AVERAGE FOR OFF-SITE HOTELS

WALT DISNEY WORLD HOTEL PROFILES

FOR THOSE OF YOU WHO'VE PLOWED through the foregoing and remain undecided, here are our profiles of each Disney resort. For photos, video, and up-to-date information on the Walt Disney World resorts, check out our website, **touringplans.com**.

THE MAGIC KINGDOM RESORTS

Grand Floridian Resort & Spa

Walt Disney World's flagship hotel is inspired by Florida's grand Victorian seaside resorts from the turn of the last century. A complex of four- and five-story white frame buildings, the Grand Floridian integrates verandas,

ROOM QUALITY	CHECK-IN EFFICIENCY	QUIETNESS OF ROOM	SHUTTLE SERVICE	POOL	STAFF	FOOD COURT	OVERALL RATING
A	A	A	B	C	A	D	B
A	A	B	C+	A–	A	D	B
B	B+	B+	B	B	B	C	B
B	A	B	C+	B	A–	D	B
B	B	B	B	R	B	D	B
A–	B	A	C	B	C+	D	B–
B	B	A	C+	B	B	F	C
–	–	–	–	–	–	–	–
B	A	C	B	A–	A	D	B
B	B	B	B	C+	C	D	B
B	B	B	B	B	B	C	B
C	B	C	B	B	B	C	B
B	A	B	B	B	A–	D+	B
B	B	B	B	B	B	C	B–
B	A–	B+	C	B	A	C–	B
A	A	A	D–	N/A	A–	N/A	B
B	B	B+	F	D	B–	D+	C
B	C	B	C	C	D	D	C
B	A	B	B	B	B+	C	B
A–	B–	A	B+	B	B+	B	B
B+	A	C	B	B+	A	D	B
B	B	B	B	B	B	C–	B
B	C+	C+	F	B	C	D	C

intricate latticework, dormers, and turrets beneath a red shingle roof to capture the most memorable elements of 19th-century ocean-resort architecture. A five-story domed lobby encircled by enameled balustrades and overhung by crystal chandeliers establishes the resort's understated opulence. Covering 40 acres along the Seven Seas Lagoon, the Grand Floridian offers lovely pools, white-sand beaches, and a multifaceted marina.

The 867 guest rooms, with wood trim and soft goods (curtains, linens, towels, and the like) in beachy tones, are luxurious yet warm and inviting rather than stuffy or overly feminine. Armoires, marble-topped sinks, and ceiling fans amplify the Victorian theme. Large by any standard, the typical room is 440 square feet (dormer rooms are smaller) and furnished with two queen beds, a daybed, a reading chair, and a table with two side chairs. Many rooms have a balcony.

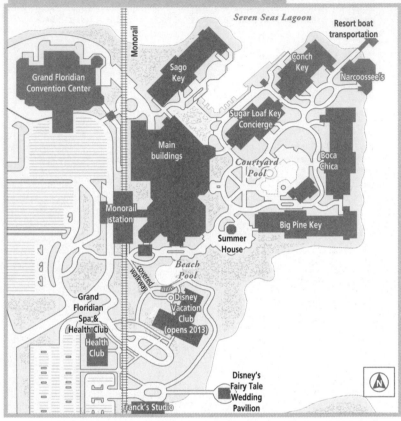

Grand Floridian Resort & Spa

With a high ratio of staff to guests, service is outstanding. The resort has several full-service restaurants, and others are a short monorail ride away. The hotel is connected directly to the Magic Kingdom by monorail and to other Disney World destinations by bus. Walking time to the monorail and bus-loading areas from the most remote guest rooms is about 7–10 minutes.

The Grand Floridian is scheduled to open a DVC wing sometime in early 2013. This new T-shaped building, between the existing main building and the Polynesian Resort along the shore of Seven Seas Lagoon, should comprise around 147 villas in studio, one-, two-, and three-bedroom configurations. A separate parking lot will go up next to the building (partially overlooking the lagoon), and a quarter-acre kids' pool will be added adjacent to the existing main pool. The DVC building will probably have no separate restaurants or dining—just as with Bay Lake Tower, you'll have to head to the mother resort to get your grub.

Most reader comments concerning the Grand Floridian are positive. First, from a Durham, North Carolina, mother of two preschoolers:

Grand Floridian Resort & Spa	
STRENGTHS	**WEAKNESSES**
On Magic Kingdom monorail	Imposing, rather formal public areas
Ferry service to Magic Kingdom	Overly large physical layout
Excellent guest rooms	Children don't get theme
Children's programs, character meals	Only one on-site restaurant suitable for younger children
Excellent children's pool	Distant guest self-parking
Beach	
Diverse recreational options	
Good restaurant selection via monorail	
On-site child care	

The Grand Floridian pool with the waterslide was a big hit with our kids. They also loved taking the boat across the lagoon to return from the Magic Kingdom. The resort's location and transportation services were unbeatable.

A Lexington, Kentucky, mom makes the case for kids at the Grand Floridian:

I wouldn't rule out the Grand Floridian by assuming kids won't get the theme. My 5-year-old daughter was mesmerized when we pulled up to its entrance and saw its grandeur—her mouth fell open and she exclaimed, "Oooh, fancy, Mommy, just like where a real princess lives!" As a matter of fact, she believes that Cinderella herself sleeps at the Grand Floridian when she isn't at the castle.

GOOD (AND NOT-SO-GOOD) ROOMS AT THE GRAND FLORIDIAN The resort is spread over a peninsula jutting into Seven Seas Lagoon. In addition to the main building, there are five dispersed, rectangular buildings also hosting guests. Most rooms have a balcony, and most balconies are enclosed by a rail that affords good visibility. Rooms just beneath the roof in each building (dormer rooms) have smaller, inset, solidly enclosed balconies that limit visibility when you're seated. Most dormer rooms, however, have vaulted ceilings and a coziness that compensates for the less-desirable balconies.

If you want to be near the bus and monorail stations, most of the restaurants, and shopping, ask for a room in the main building (all concierge rooms). The best rooms are 4322–4329 and 4422–4429, which have full balconies and overlook the lagoon in the direction of the beach and the Polynesian Resort. Other excellent main-building rooms are 4401–4409, with full balconies overlooking the marina and an unobstructed view of Cinderella Castle across the lagoon.

Of the five lodges, three (Conch Key, Boca Chica, and Big Pine Key) have one long side facing the lagoon and the other facing inner courtyards and swimming pools. At Conch Key, full-balcony rooms 7228–7231, 7328–7331, and 7425–7431 offer vistas across the lagoon to the Magic Kingdom and castle. Less-expensive rooms in the same building that offer good views are 7211, 7311, and 7411;

7413, 7415, 7417, 7419, and 7421; 7212, 7312, and 7412; and 7414. (Grand Floridian room numbers are coded. Take Room 7213: 7 is the building number, 2 is the floor, and 13 is the room number.) In Boca Chica and Big Pine Key, ask for a lagoon-view room on the first, second, or third floor. Many garden-view rooms in Big Pine Key, and a few in Boca Chica, have views obstructed by a poolside building. These are the worst views from any Grand Floridian room.

The two remaining buildings, Sugar Loaf Key (concierge only) and Sago Key, face each other across the marina. The opposite side of Sugar Loaf Key faces a courtyard, while the other side of Sago Key faces a finger of the lagoon and a forested area. All these views are pleasant but not in the same league as those from the rooms listed previously. Exceptions are end rooms in Sago Key (Rooms 5139, 5144, 5145, 5242–5245, 5342–5345) that have a view of the lagoon and Cinderella Castle.

Polynesian Resort

South Pacific tropics are re-created at this Deluxe resort. The Polynesian consists of 11 two- and three-story Hawaiian "longhouses" situated around the four-story Great Ceremonial House. Buildings at the Polynesian feature wood tones, with exposed-beam roofs and tribal-inspired geometric inlays in the cornices. The Great Ceremonial House contains restaurants, shops, and a rainforest atrium lobby with a rocky waterfall and more than 70 species of tropical plants. Spread across 39 acres along Seven Seas Lagoon, the resort has three white-sand beaches, some with volleyball courts. Its pool complex likewise captures the South Pacific theme. The Polynesian has no on-site fitness center, but its guests are welcome at the Grand Floridian's facility a short quarter-mile walk or 2-minute monorail ride away. Landscaping is superb, with periodic refurbishment, so garden-view rooms are generally superior to garden- or standard-view rooms at other resorts.

Polynesian Resort	
STRENGTHS	**WEAKNESSES**
Relaxed and casual ambience	Overly large and confusing layout
Ferry service to Magic Kingdom	Walkways exposed to rain
Romantic atmosphere	Noise from nearby motor speedway and ferry
Exotic theme that children love	Front-desk inefficiency
On Magic Kingdom monorail	
Epcot monorail within walking distance	
Transportation and Ticket Center adjoins resort	
Redecorated rooms, among the nicest at WDW	
Child care, children's programs, and character meals	
Beach and marina	
Excellent swimming complex	
Recreational options	

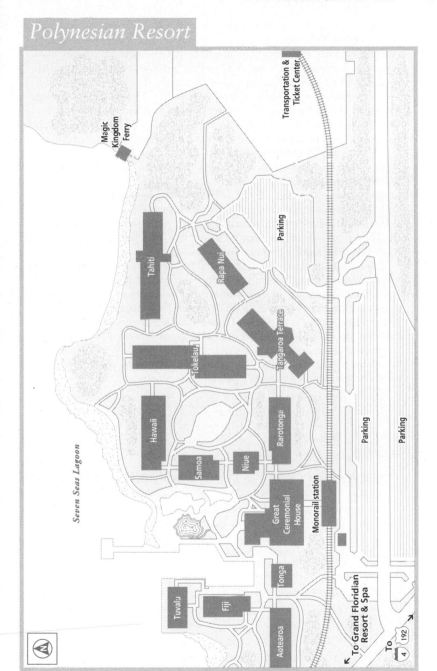

Polynesian Resort

Although the Polynesian is one of Disney's oldest resorts, periodic refurbishments keep it well maintained. A two-year rehab completed in 2007 brought new carpet, paint, and soft goods to all rooms. That refurbishment also included high-speed Internet access (additional fee), flat-panel televisions, and built-in closets. Each dresser includes two horizontal shelves above and below the TV for extra storage capacity—a big improvement in both form and function over previous designs. Similarly, the closets are spacious, light, and eminently functional. A nice touch on most of the new furniture and woodwork is the addition of textured surfaces (some of them carved). Lighting throughout the rooms, including the desk/work areas and beds, is among the best on Disney property.

Bathrooms are well designed, albeit somewhat small. Shelves above and below sinks allow plenty of storage. Outward-curving shower rods were installed during refurbishment, adding substantial elbow room to the shower without increasing its size. New light fixtures in the bathrooms have brought a tremendous improvement in usability.

Easily accessible by monorail are full-service restaurants at the Grand Floridian and Contemporary resorts, as well as restaurants in the Magic Kingdom. The Polynesian has a monorail station on-site and is within easy walking distance of the Transportation and Ticket Center. Bus service is available to other Disney destinations. Walking time to the bus- and monorail-loading areas from the most remote rooms is 8–11 minutes.

Some readers wouldn't stay anywhere else, as a family from Summerville, South Carolina, attests:

> *Polynesian was WONDERFUL. We were in the Tahiti building and could walk to the Transportation and Ticket Center to get on the buses to Disney's Hollywood Studios and Animal Kingdom without getting on the monorail. From now on, we will ONLY stay at the Polynesian. Well worth the extra $.*

A family of four from Portsmouth, New Hampshire, writes:

> *Loved the Polynesian. Room was clean, and "mousekeeping" was always done before noon. The pool was fun, and having the monorail in the hotel made getting to the Magic Kingdom and Epcot very easy. The bus service to the other parks did seem rather slow, though—we waited 20–25 minutes for buses on at least three occasions.*

A Holliston, Massachusetts, reader advises:

> *For people who stay at the Polynesian: Take your shower in the evening or at night. Early-morning showers were cold, and the water never fully warmed up. Also, the heated pool doesn't feel heated on cool days.*

A Maryland family of four found the guest-room soundproofing somewhat lacking:

> *Connecting rooms at the Polynesian were noisy. We took towels from the pool and stuffed them under the door to deaden the noise coming from the other room.*

GOOD (AND NOT-SO-GOOD) ROOMS AT THE POLYNESIAN RESORT The Polynesian's 11 guest-room buildings, called *longhouses,* are spread over a long strip of land bordered by the monorail on one side and Seven Seas Lagoon on the other. All the buildings, except for the more recently added Tahiti, Rapa Nui, and Tokelau, were part of the original hotel, which opened with the Magic Kingdom in 1971. All buildings feature first-floor patios and third-floor balconies. The older buildings, comprising more than half the resort's rooms, have fake balconies on their second floors. (The newer buildings offer full balconies on both the second and third floors, and patios on the first.) A small number of patios in the first-floor rooms have views blocked by mature vegetation, but these patios provide more room than do the balconies on the third floor. If view is important and you're staying in one of the eight older longhouses, ask for a third-floor room.

Within the Great Ceremonial House are most restaurants and shops, as well as the resort lobby, guest services, and bus and monorail stations. Longhouses most convenient to the Great Ceremonial House (Fiji, Tonga suites, Rarotonga, Niue, and Samoa) offer views of the swimming complex, a small marina, or inner gardens. There are no lagoon views except for oblique views from the upper floors of Fiji and Samoa, Aotearoa, and Tokelau, and a tunnel view from Tonga (suites only). Samoa, however, by virtue of its proximity to the main swimming complex, is a good choice for families who plan to spend time at the pool. If your children are under age 8, request a first-floor room on the Nanea Volcano Pool side of Samoa.

You can specifically request a lagoon- or Magic Kingdom–view room at the Polynesian, if you're willing to pay extra. The best of these rooms are on the second and third floors in Tahiti, the third floor in Tuvalu, and, if you're staying in a concierge room, the first and third floors in Hawaii.

One family's experience in a concierge room proved advantageous:

> *The view was spectacular. Every night the Electrical Water Pageant was pulled across the lake right in front of our room. My kids loved it. Then, after the parade, we had a perfect view of the fireworks over Cinderella Castle.*

There are some quirks in the way Disney categorizes room views at the Polynesian, though, and it's possible to get a view of the castle and fireworks while staying in a garden-view room. Second- and third-floor rooms in Tokelau (Rooms 2901–2913, 2939–2948, 3901–3913, and 3939–3948) offer you the best shot at sideways views of the castle and fireworks, although readers say some taller palm trees may block even these upper rooms. First-floor rooms (1901–1913 and 1939–1948) may also have landscaping blocking some of the Magic Kingdom views, but the patio provides more room to move to find a better spot, too.

In addition to second-floor rooms in the older buildings (the buildings with fake balconies), also avoid the monorail-side rooms in Rarotonga and the parking-lot side of Rapa Nui. Garden-view rooms in Aotearoa are especially nice, but the monorail, though quiet, runs within spitting distance.

If you plan to spend a lot of time at Epcot, Tahiti and Rapa Nui are within easy walking distance of the Transportation and Ticket Center (TTC) and the Epcot monorail. Even if you're going to the Magic Kingdom, it's a shorter walk from Tahiti and Rapa Nui to the TTC and Magic Kingdom monorail than to the monorail station at the Great Ceremonial House. Tuvalu, Fiji, and Aotearoa are the most distant accommodations from the Polynesian's bus stop. For large strollers or wheelchair access, take the ferry to the Magic Kingdom.

Wilderness Lodge & Villas

STRENGTHS	WEAKNESSES
Magnificently rendered theme	No character meals
The favorite resort of children	Must take boat or bus to get to off-site dining options
Romantic setting, architecture	
Good on-site dining	
Great views from guest rooms	
Extensive recreational options	
Elaborate swimming complex	
Health and fitness center	
On-site child care	

This Deluxe resort is inspired by national-park lodges of the early 20th century. The Wilderness Lodge & Villas ranks with Animal Kingdom Lodge as one of the most impressively themed and meticulously detailed Disney resorts. Situated on the shore of Bay Lake, the lodge consists of an eight-story central building augmented by two seven-story guest wings and a wing of studio and one- and two-bedroom condominiums. The hotel features exposed timber columns, log cabin–style facades, and dormer windows. The grounds are landscaped with evergreen pines and pampas grass. The lobby boasts an 82-foot-tall stone fireplace and two 55-foot Pacific Northwest totem poles. Timber pillars, giant tepee chandeliers, and stone-, wood-, and marble-inlaid floors accentuate the lobby's rustic luxury. Although the resort isn't on vast acreage, it does have a beach and a delightful pool modeled on a mountain stream.

The lodge's 727 rooms have darkly stained Mission-style furniture accented by earth tones in the soft goods. The Native American–patterned bedspreads, rough-hewn armoires, and faux-calfskin fixtures create a sort of log-cabin coziness. Typical rooms have two queen-size beds, and some have one queen bed and bunk beds. All rooms have a table and chairs and a vanity outside the bathroom. Most rooms have balconies. Guest rooms were refurbished in 2006 with new wall coverings, carpeting, and fixtures.

Part of the DVC time-share program, the 136 adjoining Wilderness Lodge Villas are studio and one- and two-bedroom units in a freestanding building to the right of the lodge. Studios offer kitchenettes; one- and two-bedroom villas come with full kitchens. The lodge's rustic

Wilderness Lodge & Villas

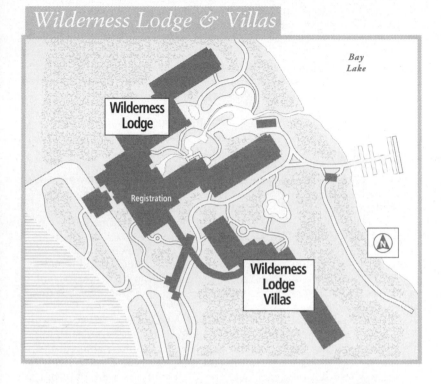

decor extends to the villas, which can be booked by non-DVC members as space allows. The villas share restaurants, pools, and other amenities with Wilderness Lodge.

Service at Wilderness Lodge & Villas is excellent. There are two full-service restaurants, with several more a boat ride away. The resort is connected to the Magic Kingdom by boat and to other Disney parks by bus. Boat service may be suspended during thunderstorms, so if it's raining or looks like it's about to, Disney will provide buses. Walking time to bus- and boat-loading areas from the most remote rooms is about 5–8 minutes.

A Westminster, Maryland, family is high on the Wilderness Lodge:

> The Wilderness Lodge is one of the best resorts we have stayed at EVER. The hotel is gorgeous, and the theming is beautiful and realistic without being overdone.

Two adult couples from Fort Smith, Arkansas, think the Wilderness Lodge is great, with one reservation (pardon the pun):

> The ambience of the lodge makes up for a lot of the transportation problems, but there has been a real downturn in my opinion in the efficacy of the bus transportation.

GOOD (AND NOT-SO-GOOD) ROOMS AT WILDERNESS LODGE & VILLAS The lodge is shaped like a very blocky V. The main entrance and lobby are at the closed end of the V. Next are middle wings that connect the lobby to the parallel end sections, which extend to the open part of the V. The V's open end flanks pools and gardens and overlooks Bay Lake directly or obliquely. Avoid rooms on the fourth, fifth, and sixth floors numbered 70–99; these overlook the main lobby and pick up every whoop, holler, and shout from the boisterous Whispering Canyon Cafe downstairs. The noise makes it difficult to get to sleep before Whispering Canyon closes, usually at 10 p.m.

The better rooms are on floors 4, 5, and 6, toward the V's open end. On the very end of the V, rooms 4000–4003, 4166–4169, 5000–5003, 5166–5169, 6000–6003, and 6166–6169 offer a direct frontal view of the lake. Toward the end of the V on the parallel wings, but facing inward, odd-numbered rooms 4005–4023, 4147–4165, 5005–5023, 5147–5165, 6005–6023, and 6147–6165 face the courtyard, but with excellent oblique lake views. Even-numbered rooms 5004–5030 and 6004–6030 front a woodland northwest of the lodge, and beyond the woodland, the Magic Kingdom. Odd-numbered rooms 5035–5041, 5123–5129, 6035–6041, and 6123–6129, on the lake end of the parallel middle wings, offer a direct but distant view of the lake, with pools and gardens in the foreground. Rooms looking southeast face the Wilderness Lodge Villas, a garden area, and woods. The map suggests that these rooms offer a lake view, but the trees block the line of sight.

Only a handful of rooms at the lodge overlook parking lots, service areas, and such. The rooms listed above afford the most desirable views, but if you can't score one of them, you're pretty much assured of a woodland view or a room fronting the faux rocks and creek in the V's inner courtyard. Concierge rooms on the seventh floor aren't recommended. Only those facing the Magic Kingdom have nice views, and even those have a service area in the foreground. Almost all rooms at the lodge have balconies.

Except for a few rooms overlooking the pool, rooms at Wilderness Villas offer woodland views. The best are odd-numbered rooms 2531–2563 and 3531–3563, which open to the northeast, or lakeside, of the resort (though you can't see the lake). Rooms on the opposite side of the same wing offer similar views, but with some roads and parking lots visible, and with traffic noise.

Contemporary Resort and Bay Lake Tower

This Deluxe resort on Bay Lake is the least themed of the Disney-owned properties. The 655-room Contemporary is unique in that its A-frame design permits the Magic Kingdom monorail to pass through the structure's cavernous atrium. The only real source of color in the atrium is a 90-foot mosaic depicting Native American children and nature. The off-white central tower is augmented by a three-story Garden Building fronting Bay Lake to the south and by Bay Lake Tower, a 295-room, 15-story Disney Deluxe Villa development, to the north.

Standard rooms in the A-frame afford fantastic views of Bay Lake or the Magic Kingdom, and all have balconies. At 394 square feet each, they're only slightly smaller than equivalent rooms at the Grand Floridian.

The Contemporary's rooms are quite stunning and, in our opinion, the nicest of any Disney resort. Perhaps for the first time since the early

Contemporary Resort & Bay Lake Tower

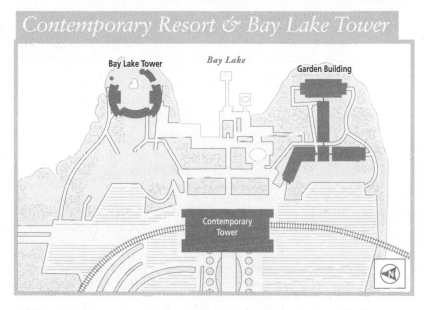

1970s, the room decor lives up to the resort's name. Amenities include wall-mounted flat-screen plasma TVs, built-in closets, new soft goods, and high-speed Internet (Wi-Fi is free; wired access, while it's still available, costs extra). Wood accents, in a warm red tone, are a welcome relief from the beige that dominated so many hotel palettes over the past decade. Orange and yellow accent pieces add just the right splash of color. The flat-screen TV is surrounded by a modern interpretation of the traditional family hearth: Two expansive curved shelves (perfect for storing small items) serve as the hearth's mantel, while a colorful

Contemporary Resort and Bay Lake Tower	
STRENGTHS	**WEAKNESSES**
On Magic Kingdom monorail	Sterility of theme and decor in public areas
10-minute walk to Magic Kingdom	
Interesting A-frame architecture	
Nicest guest rooms at WDW	
Great views of the Magic Kingdom or Bay Lake	
Character meals	
Excellent children's pool	
Marina	
Recreational options, including super games arcade	
Restaurant selection via monorail	
On-site child care	

tiled display underneath simulates the fireplace. Functional, attractive, and clever, it's the furniture equivalent of George Clooney.

A lot of thought went into the bathroom design, too. You enter the bath through a sliding pocket door instead of a traditional hinged model. The pocket door provides plenty of room and makes it easy to move around inside. (It's such a great idea, Len has adopted it in his own home.) The curved shower-curtain rod (also found in the Polynesian's renovated bathrooms) is inspired. Combined with the pocket door, the curtain rod makes the bathroom feel much bigger than it is. Another thoughtful touch: A small motion sensor detects when you're up and moving at night, and turns on a dimmed bathroom light to help you find your way.

Bathroom sinks have an avant-garde flat-bottom design. If you can name a single Belgian architect or you own shoes made in Scandinavia, you'll probably love them; other folks think they look like lab equipment. When brushing your teeth, spit directly over the drain; otherwise, the toothpaste glob doesn't move. One minor gripe: You have to scoot around one of the sinks to get in the shower. (We're sure George Clooney has his quirks, too.)

The work area is vastly improved, with ample surface space provided by an L-shaped, glass-topped desk; it looks high-tech, but rounded corners perfectly soften the piece. Lighting is superb, with top scores in the bathroom grooming, reading, and work areas. Small, stylish overhead lights are more than ample for reading in bed, assuming you're not exhausted.

The Contemporary's beds are topped with 250-thread-count sheets. Down-filled pillows replace Disney's ubiquitous polyester-filled. Sadly, the air-conditioning system was not included in the upgrade, and it's a little noisier than most. If you like to sleep with a bit of white noise in the background, however, you'll be in heaven.

Dining options abound. On the first floor is The Wave . . . of American Flavors, a 220-seat "health-conscious 21st-century" restaurant. What does "health-conscious" mean in Disney-speak? You can still get bacon for breakfast, but the coffee it comes with is certified organic and bird-friendly. The Contempo Cafe, a counter-service restaurant on the fourth floor's Grand Canyon Concourse, serves upscale sandwiches, salads, and flatbread pizzas throughout the day. Chef Mickey's, also on the fourth floor, hosts a popular character buffet at breakfast and dinner. On the 15th floor, the award-winning California Grill serves contemporary American cuisine.

The pool has slides, and the resort has around a half-dozen shops. The Contemporary is within easy walking distance of the Magic Kingdom; monorail transportation is available to both the Magic Kingdom and Epcot. Other destinations can be accessed by bus or boat. Walking time to transportation loading areas from the most remote rooms is 6–9 minutes.

While we think the Contemporary is fabulous, an Eden, New York, couple could've used a little more peace and quiet in their newly renovated room:

We thought the Internet-connected PC was a great feature and used it quite a bit at first, until at 6:13 a.m. the first morning the computer

*turned itself on with a great bit of noise and fanfare alerting us that
we had messages, which were basically ads for various Disney events
and resort features. We turned it off only to have it wake back up
with more messages 10 minutes later. I finally unplugged it from the
wall. (Ugh!) The worst part of the Contemporary, though, was the
blaring M-I-C-K-E-Y from Chef Mickey's just below our room—the
noise started promptly at 8 a.m. and repeated every 30 minutes.*

**GOOD (AND NOT-SO-GOOD) ROOMS AT THE CONTEMPORARY
RESORT** There are two guest-room buildings at the Contemporary: the
A-frame tower and the Garden Building. Rooms in the A-frame overlook
either Bay Lake and the marina and swimming complex on one side, or
the parking lot with Seven Seas Lagoon and the Magic Kingdom in the
background on the other. Except for most second- and third-floor rooms
in the Garden Wing, each guest room has a balcony with two chairs and
a table. If you stay on the Magic Kingdom side of the A-frame, ask for a
room on the ninth floor or higher. The parking lot and connecting roads
are less distracting there. On the Bay Lake side, the view is fine from all
floors, though higher floors are preferable.

In the Garden Building, all ground-floor rooms have patios. Only
end rooms on the second and third floors facing Bay Lake have full
balconies; all other rooms have balconies only a foot deep. The
Garden Building is a fair walk from the restaurants, shops, front
desk, guest services, and monorail station in the A-frame. This isolation, however, is a plus when it comes to the scenery and tranquility
offered by some guest rooms.

There's a lot of boat traffic in the lake and canal alongside the
Garden Building. Nearest the lake and quietest are Rooms 6116–
6123, 6216–6223, and 6316–6323. At the water's edge but noisier are
Rooms 6107–6115, 6207–6215, and 6307–6315. Flanking the canal
connecting Bay Lake and Seven Seas Lagoon are Rooms 5128–5143,
5228–5251, and 5328–5351. All these have nice canal and lake views,
but they're subjected to a lot of noise from passing watercraft.

The Garden Building also has rooms facing the marina, pool, and
playground; these work well for families with young children. The
view isn't comparable to views from the rooms previously listed, but
ground-floor rooms 5110–5125 provide easy access to the pool.

In addition to offering some of the most scenic and tranquil guest
rooms in Disney World, the Garden Building likewise contains some
of the most undesirable ones. Avoid rooms ending with numbers 52
through 70—almost all of these look directly onto a parking lot.

BAY LAKE TOWER Opened in 2009, Bay Lake Tower is a 15-story,
295-unit DDV resort featuring studios and one-, two-, and three-bedroom villas, as well as two-story, three-bedroom Grand Villas with
spectacular views of Bay Lake and the Magic Kingdom. Laid out in a
semicircle, Bay Lake Tower is connected to the Contemporary Resort
by an elevated, covered walkway and shares the Contemporary's
monorail service.

Rooms at Bay Lake Tower are well appointed, with flat-panel TVs,
DVD players, mini-fridges, microwaves, and coffeemakers. Brightly
colored accessories and paintings complement a neutral gray color

scheme. Wood tables and granite countertops add a natural touch to the surroundings. Each room features a private balcony or patio. The rooms we've stayed in tested as the quietest on Disney property, and average for lighting and bedding.

Studios sleep up to four people and include one queen-size bed and one double sleeper sofa. The part of the studio with the bed, sofa, and television measures about 170 square feet and feels small with just two people; four would be an adventure. The studio's layout also puts the bathroom sink and vanity in the same small area as the kitchen, but on opposite walls. Negative reactions from guests prompted change. Disney plans upcoming refurbishments to move one of the sinks into the bathroom and add a full-length mirror to the kitchenette.

One-bedroom villas sleep five and provide a formal kitchen, a second bathroom, and a living room in addition to the studio bedroom. The living room's chair and sofa fold out to provide beds for three more people.

Two-bedroom villas sleep nine and include all of the kitchen amenities found in a one-bedroom, plus an extra bathroom. One of the baths is attached to a second bedroom with two queen beds or a queen bed plus a sleeper-sized sofa. As with the one-bedrooms, a sofa bed and sleeper chair in the living room provide extra places to snooze, though they're best suited to small children. Bathrooms in the two-bedroom villas are laid out a bit better than those in the one-bedrooms, with more room to move about. One odd feature in these (also found at other DVC resorts) is a folding door separating the tub from the master bedroom. Nevertheless, we think the two-bedroom villas are the best of Bay Lake Tower's standard offerings.

The two-story Grand Villas sleep 12 and include four bathrooms, the same master-bedroom layout, and two bedrooms with two queen beds apiece. An upstairs seating area overlooking the main floor provides a sleeper sofa and chair. These rooms have two-story windows that offer unparalleled views of either Bay Lake or the Magic Kingdom—with unparalleled prices to match.

Unofficial Guide reader opinions of Bay Lake Tower have been mostly positive. A Minnesota family of four loved it:

> *We had a studio with a Magic Kingdom view. The balcony was a private oasis where my husband and I would relax and watch the fireworks together after the kids were asleep. On our second night he looked at me and said, "We're always going to stay here."*

But an Atlanta dad is lukewarm:

> *I'm not sure I can recommend Bay Lake Tower to non–Disney Vacation Club members. The lack of a lobby and other amenities was a drag. Also, we had a studio (regular view) and it was very small. For the money, the Polynesian is far better.*

Bay Lake Tower has a pool and pool bar for its own private use. Plans are also in place to add a jogging path as well as a fire pit specifically for Bay Lake Tower guests; however, dining, transportation, and other recreational activities are shared with the Contemporary Resort.

Shades of Green

STRENGTHS	WEAKNESSES
Large guest rooms	No interesting theme
Informality	Limited on-site dining
Quiet setting	Limited bus service
Views of golf course from guest rooms	
Convenient self-parking	
Swimming complex, fitness center	
Video arcade	
Game room with pool tables	
Ice-cream shop	

This Deluxe resort is owned and operated by the U.S. Armed Forces and is open to U.S. military personnel (including members of the National Guard and reserves, retired military, and employees of the U.S. Public Health Service and the Department of Defense) and their families, foreign military personnel attached to U.S. units, and some civilian contractors. Shades of Green consists of one three-story building nestled among three golf courses, which are open to all Disney guests.

At 455 square feet each, the 586 guest rooms at Shades of Green are larger than those at the Grand Floridian. Decor is pleasant though thoroughly unremarkable—pretty much the same as at any midpriced hotel. Most rooms have two queen-size beds, a daybed, and a table and four chairs, as well as a television in an armoire. All rooms have a patio or balcony.

A Minot AFB, North Dakota, father of three thinks Shades of Green is the way to go (mostly):

> As an active-duty military member, I can tell you there's no better deal on a WDW vacation than at Shades of Green. A couple of drawbacks, though, were the midlevel quality of the food at the Italian restaurant and the lack of a place to get a drink. Our first visit to this hotel was in 1996 just after it opened; if you haven't been since it was overhauled—wow. You're in for a treat.

A reader from Austin, Texas, raises the issue of hidden costs:

> Although Shades of Green is a good deal, there are several hidden costs associated with staying there. While guests at other Disney resorts park free, self-parking at SOG costs $5 a day, which is in addition to the $14-a-day parking fee at the Disney parks. Plus, the daily cost of in-room Internet or Wi-Fi is $6.95 or $8.95, depending on the service you choose.

Finally, a mom from Winchester, Virginia, weighs in:

> Shades of Green has an AAFES [Army & Air Force Exchange Service] on-site. In addition to carrying everything one might find in a hotel gift/sundries shop, this small store carries Disney merchandise. It's also a Class Six [a military version of a package store]. We were

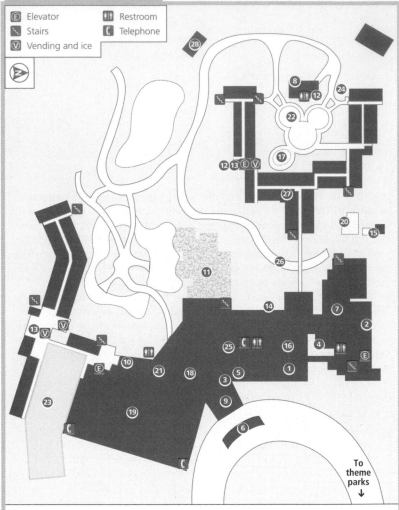

Shades of Green

Key:
- E Elevator
- ↕ Stairs
- V Vending and ice
- ⊮ Restroom
- ☏ Telephone

1. AAFES Shopette
2. America Ice Cream Shoppe
3. ATM
4. Attraction Ticket Sales
5. Bell stand & front desk
6. Bus stop
7. East Meets West
8. Evergreens Sports Bar & Grille
9. Express Café
10. Fitness Center
11. The Garden Gallery Restaurant
12. Game rooms
13. Guest laundry
14. Guest Services
15. Hot tub & Magnolia Pool Grille
16. Java Café
17. Kiddie Pool
18. Lobby
19. Magnolia Ballroom
20. Magnolia Pool Area
21. Mangino's Bistro
22. Mill Pond Pool Area
23. Parking garage
24. Playground
25. Registration
26. Remember the Fun Walkway
27. Sales & Marketing
28. Tennis courts

To theme parks ↓

*able to purchase everything we needed there and never had to leave
WDW in search of a grocery store. Plus there's no tax on purchases.
A huge time- and hassle-saver!*

Even though the resort isn't operated by Disney, service is comparable to that at Disney Deluxe properties. Transportation to all theme
parks is by bus, with a transfer required to almost all destinations.
Walking time to the bus-loading area from the most remote rooms is
about 5 minutes. The resort is immensely popular; make reservations
seven months in advance.

You don't have to worry much about bad rooms at Shades of
Green. Except for a small percentage that overlook the entrance road
and parking lot, most offer views of the golf courses that surround the
hotel, or the swimming area. When you book your reservation, make
your preference known. Shades of Green has its own website, **shades
ofgreen.org.**

THE EPCOT RESORTS

THE EPCOT RESORTS ARE ARRAYED around Crescent Lake
between Epcot and Disney's Hollywood Studios (but closer to Epcot).
Both theme parks are accessible by boat and on foot. No Epcot resort
offers transportation to Epcot's main entrance. As a Greenville, South
Carolina, mom reports, this can be a problem:

> *The only transportation to Epcot is by boat or foot. There's no bus
> available to take you to the front gates. We had to walk through the
> International Gateway and all the way to the front of Epcot to ride
> Future World attractions. And if we finished Epcot at the end of the
> day near the front entrance, the only way back home was a long hike
> through Future World and the International Gateway.*

A reader from Emporia, Kansas, didn't let the transportation problem get her down:

> *We had no transportation to the front gate of Epcot for arrival before
> opening. So we decided to do the early entry at Magic Kingdom
> (7 a.m.), take in one popular attraction, and then catch the monorail
> to Epcot. Worked like a charm. We were at Epcot by 8:20 a.m.*

Yacht & Beach Club Resorts and Beach Club Villas

These adjoining five-story Deluxe resorts are similarly themed. Both
have clapboard facades with whitewashed-wood trim. The Yacht Club
is painted a subdued gray, while the Beach Club is painted a brighter
blue. The Yacht Club has a nautical theme with model ships and antique
navigational instruments in public areas. The Beach Club is embellished
with beach scenes in foam green and white. Both resorts have themed
lobbies, with a giant globe in the Yacht Club's and sea-horse fixtures in
the Beach Club's. The resorts face 25-acre Crescent Lake and share an
elaborate swimming complex.

There are 621 guest rooms at the Yacht Club, 576 guest rooms at
the Beach Club, and 282 studio and one- and two-bedroom villas at
the Beach Club Villas, part of the DVC time-share program. Most of
the hotel rooms are 381 square feet and have two queen-size beds,

Yacht & Beach Club Resorts & Beach Club Villas

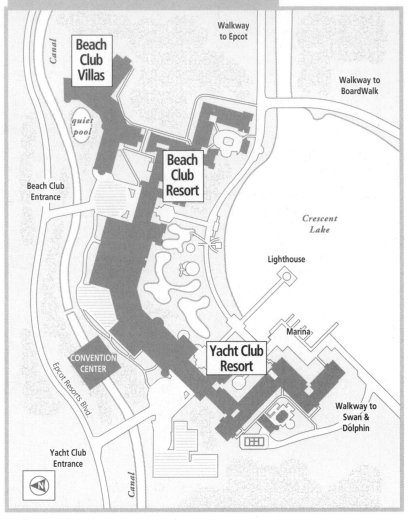

a daybed, and a desk and a chair. Like the Grand Floridian's, rooms have a lot of drawer space. Yacht Club rooms are decorated in blue and white; Beach Club offers soft green and blue tones. Some rooms have balconies.

The Beach Club Villas evoke seaside Victorian cottages. Studio accommodations offer kitchenettes; one- and two-bedroom villas have full kitchens. Subject to availability, villas are open to the public as well as to DVC (time-share) members. The villas share restaurants, pools, and other amenities with the Yacht & Beach Club Resorts. A small business center serves guests' work needs for both the Yacht and Beach Clubs and Beach Club Villas.

Yacht & Beach Club Resorts and Beach Club Villas	
STRENGTHS	**WEAKNESSES**
Nautical/New England theme	No transportation to Epcot main entrance except by taxi
Attractive guest rooms	No convenient counter-service food
Good on-site dining	Poor room-to-hall soundproofing
Kids' programs, character meals	
Excellent selection of nearby off-site dining	
Boat service to Disney's Hollywood Studios and Epcot	
10-minute walk to rear entrance of Epcot	
10-minute walk to BoardWalk	
15-minute walk to Disney's Hollywood Studios	
Best resort swimming complex at WDW	
Health and fitness center	
Convenient self-parking	
View from waterside guest rooms	
On-site child care	

As Disney Deluxe resorts, the Yacht Club and Beach Club provide excellent service. They offer nine restaurants and lounges and are within walking distance of Epcot and the BoardWalk. Transportation to other destinations is by bus or boat. Walking time to the transportation loading areas from the most remote rooms is 7 minutes.

Although the Yacht & Beach Club Resorts are arrayed along Crescent Lake opposite the BoardWalk, a relatively small percentage of guest rooms actually overlook the lake. Many additional rooms have an oblique view of the lake but face a courtyard or garden. To complicate matters, the resorts don't differentiate between a room with a lake view and one overlooking a swimming pool, pond, or canal. All are considered water views. We receive letters each year from readers complaining that their "water view" was a distant, sidelong peek at a swimming pool.

The Beach Club consists of a long main building with several wings protruding toward Crescent Lake. Looking at the resort from Crescent Lake, the Beach Club adjoins the Yacht Club on the left and spreads toward Epcot on the right. The main building and the various wings range from three to five stories. Most rooms have balconies or, on the ground floor, patios. Balconies are either big enough for a couple of chairs, or about 6 inches deep (stand at the rail or sit in a chair inside the room). Top-floor rooms often have enclosed balconies inset into the roof. Unless you're standing, visibility is somewhat limited from these dormer balconies.

We receive a lot of mail about the Yacht & Beach Club Resorts, most of it positive. First, these remarks from a Wayland, Massachusetts, mother of two:

This was the first time we stayed at the Beach Club, and for us the amazing pool complex was worth the extra money. Several nights we climbed up to the top of the waterslide as the sun was setting, and it was an incredible sight—truly a memorable experience!

This mom from Brownsville, Texas, however, has some issues with the Beach Club:

The room doors at the Beach Club don't fit very snugly, so any noise from the hall was practically broadcast into our room. The room was close to the elevators, so it sounded like everyone in the hotel was stampeding past our door in the morning. I like the Beach Club very much, but if we go back I'll ask for a more remote room way at the end of the hall.

From a Norman, Oklahoma, mom who visited during the summer:

Beach Club was great, but swimming facilities close at 8 p.m., leaving nothing to do in the evening if you choose not to tour a park at night. For $400+ a day, you'd think the swimming pool would be open at least until sunset!

GOOD (AND NOT-SO-GOOD) ROOMS AT THE BEACH CLUB RESORT The Beach Club's better views are from rooms with full balconies, and from those that overlook the lake. Other good rooms include those facing woods, with Epcot in the background. The latter are the resort's quietest, most peaceful rooms, in terms of both noise and scenery. They're also nearest to Epcot's International Gateway entrance if you're walking, but farthest from the resort's main pool area, lobby, and restaurants. Of the remaining rooms, most face courtyards, with some of these providing oblique views of the lake, and others overlooking parking lots and the resort's front entrance.

Here are our recommendations for good Beach Club rooms. All room numbers are four digits, with the first digit specifying the floor and the remaining three digits the room number.

Water-view rooms with full balconies facing the lake Odd-numbered rooms 2641–2647, 3501–3511, 3683–3691, 3725–3795, 5607–5623, 5683–5691, and 5725–5795. (The Beach Club will charge you for a water-view room if there's so much as a birdbath in sight. If you're going to pay the price, get a real water view.)

Standard-view rooms with full balconies facing the woods and Epcot Even-numbered rooms 3512–3536 and 4578–4598.

GOOD (AND NOT-SO-GOOD) ROOMS AT THE YACHT CLUB RESORT When you look at the Yacht Club from Crescent Lake, the resort is connected to the Beach Club on the right and angles toward the Dolphin hotel on the left. All Yacht Club rooms offer full balconies or, on the ground floor, patios. Rooms with the best views are as follows (the higher the last three digits in the room number, the closer to lobby, main pool area, and restaurants):

Fifth-floor rooms with full balconies directly facing the lake, with the BoardWalk Inn in the background Rooms 5161, 5163, 5207, and 5241.

Fifth-floor rooms directly facing Epcot Rooms 5171–5185.

Some other rooms face the BoardWalk or Epcot across Crescent Lake, but they're inferior to the rooms just listed.

Avoid standard-view rooms at either resort except for Rooms 3512–3536 and 4578–4598 at the Beach Club; these overlook a dense pine thicket. In addition to offering a nice vista for a standard-view rate, these are the closest rooms to Epcot available at any resort on Crescent Lake.

BEACH CLUB VILLAS This Disney Deluxe Villa property is supposedly inspired by the grand Atlantic seaside homes of the early 20th century. We'll bet the villas don't resemble any seaside home you ever saw. Thematically, there's little to differentiate the Beach Club Villas from the Yacht & Beach Club Resorts, or from the parts of the BoardWalk Inn & Villas that don't front the BoardWalk.

Configured roughly in the shape of a fat Y or slingshot, the Beach Club Villas are away from the lake adjoining the front of the Beach Club Resort. Arrayed in connected four- and five-story taffy-blue sections topped with cupolas, the villas are festooned with white woodwork and slat-railed balconies. The effect is clean, breezy, and evocative, though we're not certain of what. Accommodations include studios, with a kitchenette, one queen bed, and a sofa sleeper; and one- and two-bedroom villas with full kitchens. The rooms are a bit small but attractively furnished in pastels with New England–style summer-home furniture. Patterned carpets and seashore-themed art complete the package.

We don't like the Beach Club Villas as well as the Wilderness Lodge Villas (more visually interesting) or the villas of Disney's Old Key West Resort (roomier, more luxurious, more private). The Beach Club Villas have their own modest pool but otherwise share the restaurants, facilities, and transportation options of the adjoining Yacht & Beach Club Resorts. The villas' strengths and weaknesses include all of those listed for the Yacht & Beach Club Resorts. Additional strengths include laundry and kitchen facilities in the one- and two-bedroom units, and self-parking directly adjacent to the building. The villas' one additional weakness is that they offer no lake view.

GOOD (AND NOT-SO-GOOD) ROOMS AT THE BEACH CLUB VILLAS Though the studios and villas are attractive and livable, the location of the Beach Club Villas, between parking lots, roads, and canals, leaves much to be desired. Rooms facing the pool offer a limited view of a small canal but are subject to traffic noise. Ditto the rooms on the northeast side, but they don't face the pool. Only southeast-facing rooms provide both a scenic landscape (woods) and relative relief from traffic noise. The nearby road is only two-lane, and traffic noise probably won't bother you if you're indoors with the balcony door closed, but for the bucks you shell out to stay at the villas, you can find nicer, quieter accommodations elsewhere on Disney property. If you elect to stay at the Beach Club Villas, go for odd-numbered rooms 229–251, 329–351, 429–451, and 529–551.

BoardWalk Inn & Villas

On Crescent Lake across from the Yacht & Beach Club Resorts, the BoardWalk Inn is another of the Walt Disney World Deluxe resorts. The

BoardWalk Inn & Villas

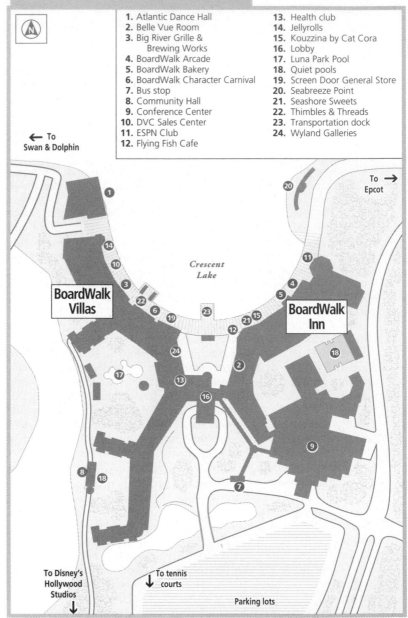

1. Atlantic Dance Hall
2. Belle Vue Room
3. Big River Grille & Brewing Works
4. BoardWalk Arcade
5. BoardWalk Bakery
6. BoardWalk Character Carnival
7. Bus stop
8. Community Hall
9. Conference Center
10. DVC Sales Center
11. ESPN Club
12. Flying Fish Cafe
13. Health club
14. Jellyrolls
15. Kouzzina by Cat Cora
16. Lobby
17. Luna Park Pool
18. Quiet pools
19. Screen Door General Store
20. Seabreeze Point
21. Seashore Sweets
22. Thimbles & Threads
23. Transportation dock
24. Wyland Galleries

← To Swan & Dolphin

To → Epcot

Crescent Lake

BoardWalk Villas

BoardWalk Inn

To Disney's Hollywood Studios ↓

To tennis courts ↓

Parking lots

complex is a detailed replica of an early-20th-century Atlantic coast boardwalk. Facades of hotels, diners, and shops create an inviting and exciting waterfront skyline. In reality, the BoardWalk Inn & Villas are a single integrated structure behind the facades. Restaurants and shops

STRENGTHS	WEAKNESSES
Lively seaside and amusement-pier theme	No restaurants within easy walking distance suitable for children
Newly refurbished guest rooms	No restaurants in hotel
10-minute walk to Epcot rear entrance	Limited children's activities and no character meals
15-minute walk to Disney's Hollywood Studios	No transportation to Epcot main entrance
Boat service to Disney's Hollywood Studios and Epcot	Distant guest self-parking
Well-themed swimming complex	Boardwalk-view rooms noisy
3-minute walk to BoardWalk midway and nightlife	
Good selection of off-site dining within walking distance	
Health and fitness center	
Good views from waterside guest rooms	
On-site child care	

occupy the boardwalk level, while accommodations rise up to six stories above. Painted bright red and yellow along with weathered pastel greens and blues, the BoardWalk resorts are the only Disney hotels that use neon signage as architectural detail. The complex shares a pool having an old-fashioned amusement-park theme (there are also two quiet pools).

The BoardWalk Inn's 371 Deluxe rooms measure 371 square feet each. Most contain two queen-size beds with hardwood headboards, an upholstered sleeper sofa, a cherry desk and chair, an iPod-capable alarm clock, and ceiling fans. Decor includes yellow-and-white-striped wallpaper and striped green curtains. Closet space exceeds that in other Disney Deluxe rooms. Most rooms have balconies.

The 532 BoardWalk Villas are decorated in warmer tones and primary colors, with bright tiles in the kitchens and bathrooms. Villas range from 412 to 2,491 square feet (studio through three-bedroom), and sleep 4–12 people. Many villas have full kitchens, laundry rooms, and whirlpool tubs. The villas tend to be more expensive than similar accommodations at other Disney resorts—you pay for the address.

The inn and villas are well staffed and offer excellent service. They're also home to some of Disney World's finest restaurants and shops. The complex is within walking distance of Epcot and is connected to other destinations by bus and boat. Walking time to transportation loading areas from the most remote rooms is 5–6 minutes.

Reader comments about the BoardWalk Inn & Villas include the following. From an Iowa City, Iowa, family:

We were surprised that so relatively few rooms at the BoardWalk Inn have interesting views. We were in a group staying there before a Disney cruise, and the one couple who actually had a view of the boardwalk said it was noisy.

A number of readers have complained about the bus service at the BoardWalk Inn. This comment is typical:

Regarding the BoardWalk, the transportation by bus (Animal King-
dom and Magic Kingdom) was the worst. We waited at least 40 min-
utes every time and almost missed a dinner reservation (for which we
left 1½ hours early). I also didn't like having multiple stops.

**GOOD (AND NOT-SO-GOOD) ROOMS AT THE BOARDWALK INN &
VILLAS** The complex comprises several wings that radiate from the
lobby complex, roughly in the shape of a giant *H*. Crescent Lake and
the Promenade (pedestrian boardwalk) are to the north, the entrance is
to the south, and the canal that runs to Disney's Hollywood Studios is
to the west. At the BoardWalk, the "water" part of "water view" can
mean Crescent Lake, the canal, or a small pool. There are two concierge
floors for those wanting extra service.

Most rooms at the inn and villas have a balcony or patio, though
balconies on the standard upper-floor rooms alternate between large
and medium. The BoardWalk Inn & Villas each share about half the
frontage on the Promenade, which overlooks Crescent Lake. The
Promenade's clubs, stores, and attractions are spread about equally
between the two sections, leading to similar levels of noise and com-
motion. However, the inn side is closer to Epcot and the nearby access
road; this provides better views of Epcot fireworks and easier access
to that park, but it also means more road noise.

Otherwise, the inn is actually less noisy than the more expensive villas; there's one tranquil, enclosed courtyard, and another half-enclosed
area with a quiet pool (where BoardWalk's Garden Suites are). There
are many rooms to avoid at the inn, starting with rooms overlooking
access roads and parking lots, and rooms looking down on the unat-
tractive roof of the adjacent conference center. And although the aforementioned quiet rooms face courtyards, the views are pretty ho-hum.
When you get right down to it, the only rooms with decent views are
those fronting the Promenade and lake, specifically odd-numbered
rooms 3213–3255 and 4213–4255. We're told by Disney insiders that
most of these rooms are reserved more than 10 months in advance, so
snagging one requires advance planning and a lot of luck. As for the
others, you're more likely to get a better view at the far less expensive
Port Orleans, Caribbean Beach, or Coronado Springs resorts.

The villas are somewhat better. Most overlook a canal to the west
with the Swan resort and its access road and parking lots on the far
side. Worse are the rooms that front BoardWalk's entrance and car
lots. As at the inn, the villas offer only a handful of rooms with good
views. Odd-numbered rooms 3001–3033, 4001–4033, and 5001–
5033 afford dynamic views of the Promenade and Crescent Lake,
with Epcot in the background. They're a little noisy if you open your
balcony door but otherwise offer a glimpse of one of Disney World's
more happening places. Unless you bag one of these rooms, however,
you'll spend a bundle for a very average (or worse) view.

Promenade-facing villa rooms have noise issues identical to their
inn counterparts. The midsection of the canal-facing villas look out
on Luna Park Pool, a carnival-themed family-pool complex that gets
extremely noisy during the day. Some of the quieter villas are away
from the Promenade with views of the canal and a partially enclosed
quiet pool. Noise is practically nonexistent; the only downside is

that the rooms are relatively distant from the Promenade and Epcot. Rooms on the opposite side of this wing are almost as quiet, but they face BoardWalk's parking lot and thus are less desirable.

The Swan and Dolphin

STRENGTHS	WEAKNESSES
Exotic architecture	Confusing layout
Extremely nice guest rooms	No transportation to Epcot main entrance
Good on-site and nearby dining	Self parking distant, requires daily fee
Health and fitness center	Resorts don't qualify for Disney's Magical Express service
Excellent beach, swimming complex	
Best WDW resort for business travelers	
Business center	
On-site child care	
Children's programs, character meals	
Varied recreational offerings	
View from guest rooms	
10-minute walk to BoardWalk nightlife	
Boat service to Disney's Hollywood Studios and Epcot	
Participates in Extra Magic Hours program	

Although these resorts are inside the World and Disney handles their reservations, they're owned by Sheraton (Dolphin) and Westin (Swan) and can be booked directly through their parent companies, too. The resorts face each other on either side of an inlet of Crescent Lake. The Dolphin is a 27-story triangular turquoise building. On its roof are two 56-foot-tall fish balanced with their tails in the air. The Swan has a 12-story main building flanked by two seven-story towers. Two 47-foot-tall swans adorn its roof, paralleling their marine counterparts across the way. Both the Swan and the Dolphin have been described as bizarre and stylistically disjointed. At the very least, they're eclectic in their theming. Disney says you'll step into a "fantasy world." We think the experience is more akin to Art Deco gone haywire. The giant swans look swanlike, but the Dolphin's fish are more like catfish from outer space. The atmosphere at these properties could be described as adventurous or confusing, depending on how much you value the work of a good interior decorator.

The Dolphin's restyled lobby is the more ornate, featuring a rotunda with spokelike corridors branching off to shops, restaurants, and other public areas. At the other end of the spectrum, the Swan's lobby is so small that it seems an afterthought. Both resorts feature art of wildly different styles and eras (from Matisse to Roy Lichtenstein). The Dolphin's Grotto Pool is shaped like a seashell and has a waterfall, while the Swan's pool is a conventional rectangle.

The Dolphin's rooms underwent a complete redesign several years back; soft goods and televisions were updated in 2010. Where garish

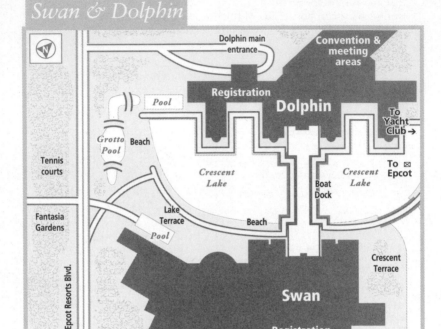

Swan & Dolphin

decor had characterized (some say branded) the hotel's rooms for years, the current design incorporates light-colored woods, floral earth-tone carpeting, and pastel-blue draperies. The plush Heavenly Beds are buttressed by oversize wood headboards adorned with abstract murals. A sleek, contemporary dresser-desk combo and a reading chair complete the furnishings. Some rooms have balconies.

The Swan's guest rooms feature restful earth-tone pastels and handsome Scandinavian-modern blond bedsteads and dressers. Westin's Heavenly Beds make for ultracomfy sleeping. The rooms have great light for reading, in or out of bed. A huge, round mirror framed in blond wood hangs above the dresser. The bath, though small for a Disney World hotel, is elegantly appointed.

Because the Swan and the Dolphin aren't run by Disney, service is less sugarcoated than at other Disney resorts. They'll also nickel-and-dime you to death. For example, both tack on a $14 per day "resort fee" and another $10 per day for self-parking. Even more shocking is the price the Dolphin's gift shop charges for sundries: We paid almost $10 for a single pint of Ben & Jerry's ice cream—roughly $3 more than Disney charges in its gift shops (and twice as much as Publix). Whatever rate you're quoted at the Swan and the Dolphin, temper your expectations by adding another $30 per day in miscellaneous costs.

The two hotels collectively house more than a dozen restaurants and lounges and are within easy walking distance of Epcot and the BoardWalk. They're also connected to other destinations by bus and boat. Walking time from the most remote rooms to the transportation loading areas is 7–9 minutes.

Reader comments about the Swan and Dolphin touch on the same several themes. The following remarks from an El Paso, Texas, reader are representative:

> *Since I was able to score a really great deal through MouseSavers, we gave the Swan a try. The swimming-pool setup was super, and our room was beautiful and had a great view looking toward Epcot. Taking the two hotels together, the restaurant selection was the best I've seen in or out of the World. On the downside, both hotels are really spread out, and it was quite a hike from self-parking to the entrance of the Swan.*

A couple from Nashua, New Hampshire, also tout the Swan and Dolphin:

> *We stayed at the Dolphin and found that neither the Disney nor the Swan and Dolphin websites, nor anything else, depict how great the pool complex is. Not only are there multiple pools, a sandy beach, swan boats, whirlpools, a waterfall, a waterslide, and maybe the best poolside bar in all of Disney World, there's also a wonderfully green, restful grotto-in-tropical-forest theme.*

GOOD (AND NOT-SO-GOOD) ROOMS AT THE SWAN AND THE DOLPHIN
These sprawling hotels are configured very differently, and their irregular shapes mean it's easier to discuss groups of rooms in relation to exterior landmarks and compass directions rather than by room numbers. When speaking with a Disney reservationist, use our tips to ask for a particular view or area.

THE SWAN East-facing rooms offer prime views, particularly in the upper half of the seven-story wing above the Il Mulino New York Trattoria. From this vantage point, guests overlook a canal and the BoardWalk, with Epcot in the distance. *IllumiNations* fireworks enliven the view nightly. Balcony rooms are available on floors 5, 6, and 7. However, rooms in the wing nearest the hotel's main section have the southern portion of their view obscured by the building's easternmost portion, which juts east beyond the seven-story wing. There are some east-facing rooms on that portion of the main section, sans balconies. Lofty palm trees obscure the view from east-facing rooms below the fourth floor. The best rooms with an Epcot view are 626 and 726.

North-facing rooms afford views of the Dolphin and (generally) of the courtyard. Exceptions are the north-facing rooms on the easternmost portion of the main section, which look across Crescent Terrace to the BoardWalk. These afford angled views of Epcot and are buffered by palms on the lowest three floors. The few north-facing rooms at the end of the Swan's two eight-story wings directly overlook Crescent Lake. However, the bulk of north-facing rooms are in the main section and overlook the courtyard, with greenery, fountains, and an indoor cafe in its center. Courtyard-facing rooms are subject to noise from below, though never much.

Above the eighth floor, north-facing rooms in the main section overlook roofs of the shorter wings. In these rooms, height enhances the vista from your window, but only near the center of the hotel is the view not seriously marred by rooftops below.

North-facing main-section rooms have a more direct view of the Dolphin across the lake than the courtyard-facing rooms in either eight-story wing. However, most wing rooms can view the lake at an angle. Those on the northern edge of the western wing also view the BoardWalk at an angle.

Most courtyard-facing rooms have balconies; 224 rooms are so equipped, and these balconies offer panoramic 180-degree views. Of course, from most rooms at the Swan, part of any 180-degree view will include another section of the hotel.

The Swan's worst views are from west-facing rooms above the fourth floor, which overlook the unsightly roof of the hotel's western wing. The northernmost rooms in the wing directly above Kimonos restaurant are an exception to this, as their balconies overlook the pool and the beach on Crescent Lake's western shore. Rooms 680–691 offer nice pool views.

Above the Swan's main entrance, south-facing rooms overlook the parking lot, with forest and Disney's Hollywood Studios in the distance. However, the canal is also visible to the east. These rooms lack balconies.

THE DOLPHIN Consisting of a central A-frame with large wings jutting off each side and four smaller arms extending from the rear of the building, the Dolphin is attached to a large conference center, which means that the majority of guests are ostensibly there on business. The same amenities found at Disney Deluxe resorts are found at the Dolphin. All parks are accessible from a shuttle stop or a boat dock between the Dolphin and the Swan.

If you want a room with easy access to shopping, dining, and transport to and from the parks, almost any Dolphin room will do. The shuttle (outside the main entrance) and the boat dock are equidistant from the main front and rear exits. Restaurants and shopping are primarily on the first and third floors. If you also want a view of something other than parking-lot asphalt, your choices narrow considerably. Rooms in the Dolphin with pleasant views are in the four arms on the rear of the building. Rooms on all the arms sport balconies from the first through fourth floors, then offer balconies or windows alternately on floors five through nine.

One of the Dolphin's best views overlooks the Grotto Pool on the far west side of the building. An artificial beach with a small waterfall is visible from rooms at the very end of the large west wing. None of these rooms has a balcony, but that might be a blessing, since the pool comes with canned tiki music and a bar. A better bet would be to ask for a room on the far west side of the first rear arm. These outer rooms have balconies and are more removed from the pool. Rooms on the inner, west part of that arm overlook a bladderwort-encrusted reflecting pool; these aren't recommended. Nor are the facing rooms on the next arm.

Between the second and third arms looms the monstrous Dolphin fountain, and the better choices here are on the top two floors. Here, from arm two you can see the BoardWalk (including any nighttime fireworks), and from arm three you can see the Grotto Pool. Otherwise, you may find you have a view of massive green-concrete fish scales. The noise from the water is loud, and the fountain gushes continuously. Depending upon your temperament, you will find this either soothing or maddening.

Arms three and four are situated around a reflecting pool. A concern for rooms in this area is that the ferry toots its horn every time it approaches and departs the dock. Its path runs right by these rooms, and the horn blows just as it passes. The first time that happens, it's quaint. By the 117th, your hair will be coming out in clumps.

The Crescent Lake side of arm four, and the small jut of the large Dolphin wing perpendicular to it, offer arguably the best views. You have an unobstructed view of the lake and Epcot fireworks, a fine BoardWalk view for people-watching, and, from higher floors, a view of the beach at Beach Club. There's ferry noise, but these rooms still have the most going for them. The best of the best in this arm are Rooms 8015, 7015, 5015, 4015, and 3015. Balcony rooms at the Dolphin generally run $30 a day more than rooms without balconies.

Caribbean Beach Resort

STRENGTHS	WEAKNESSES
Attractive Caribbean theme	Large, confusing layout
Children's play areas	Long lines to check in
Convenient self-parking	Lackluster on-site dining
Walking, jogging, biking	No easily accessible off-site dining
Lakefront setting	No character meals
	Extreme distance of many guest rooms from dining and services
	Occasionally poor bus service

The Caribbean Beach Resort occupies 200 acres surrounding a 45-acre lake called Barefoot Bay. This midpriced resort, modeled after resorts in the Caribbean, consists of the registration area ("Custom House") and six two-story "villages" named after Caribbean islands. Each village has its own pool, laundry room, and beach. The Caribbean motif is maintained with blue metal roofs, widow's walks, and wooden railed porches. The atmosphere is cheerful, with buildings painted blue, lime green, and sherbet orange. In addition to the six village pools, the resort's main swimming pool is themed as an old Spanish fort, complete with slides and water cannons.

Most of the 2,112 guest rooms are 314 square feet and contain two double beds and a table and two chairs. Some are decorated with bright tropical colors, while others are decorated with neutral beach tones. All are outfitted with the same light-oak furniture. Rooms don't have balconies, but the access passageways are external and have railings. Many of the rooms have been refurbished and rethemed to

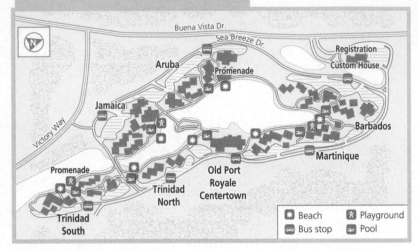

include characters from Disney/Pixar's *Finding Nemo*. In addition, rooms in Trinidad South have recently been rethemed to a *Pirates of the Caribbean* motif. These rooms cost about $30 more than comparable ones elsewhere in the resort.

One of the most centrally located resorts, the Caribbean Beach offers transportation to all Disney World destinations by bus. Though it has one full-service restaurant and a food court, food service is woefully inadequate for a resort of this size. Walking time to the transportation loading area from the most remote rooms is 7–9 minutes, so guests should seriously consider having a car.

Despite these limitations, many readers love the Caribbean Beach. An Edgewater, Colorado, couple comes to its defense:

> *Caribbean Beach was great. The hotel was full, but we saw very few people. It's laid out so that you have some privacy, even though there was a bit of walking. However, the food court didn't prepare food on-site—it was always served at the same temperature and degree of staleness.*

A Philadelphia dad with two tots in tow also had a mostly positive review:

> *The Caribbean Beach Resort was beautiful. Our island (Barbados) was very quiet and relaxing on the courtyard/garden side, but the walk to the bus stop with a child was a bit of a haul. The bus service was also slower than in my past experiences.*

A family of four from Gretna, Louisiana, found everything a bit spread out:

> *Too far around resort for convenience. To main desk to solve key problems—45-minute round-trip by shuttle. To food court—40 minutes, plus 3-minute walk in rain to and from bus stop.*

From a Ridgeway, Virginia, mother of one:

The Caribbean Beach Resort was great—especially the housekeeping staff, who creatively rearranged my daughter's toys every day. Made coming back to the room much more fun. My only complaint with CBR was the inefficiency of checkout—although express checkout was available, someone had to be present to have luggage moved from the room to the main house for transport via Magical Express. We had scheduled a late-afternoon flight on our last day so we could all spend one last morning in the park—I missed most of it because I had to go and sit with the luggage. I was not happy AT ALL.

A mom from Fenton, Michigan, found bus service lacking:

We loved the Caribbean Beach Resort for the most part, but we recommend renting a car and/or paying for a preferred room location— especially if you're going in the hotter months or are impatient. The buses just take way too long with all the stops, and we thought it was a long hike to the food court and pools in the heat.

GOOD (AND NOT-SO-GOOD) ROOMS AT THE CARIBBEAN BEACH RESORT The resort's grounds are quite pleasant. Landscaping—lots of ferns and palm trees—is verdant, especially in the courtyards. The six "islands," or groups of buildings clustered around Barefoot Bay, are identical. The two-story motel-style structures are arranged in various ways to face courtyards, pools, the bay, and so forth. The setup is similar to Disney's Coronado Springs Resort in nearly every way but theme.

In general, corner rooms at Caribbean Beach Resort are preferable since they have more windows. Standard-view rooms face either the parking lots or courtyards, and the usual broad interpretation of water views is in play here. Beyond that, your main choices will revolve around your preference for proximity to (or distance from) the Custom House, pools, parking lots, or beaches on Barefoot Bay. Each island has direct access to at least one beach, playground, bus stop, and parking lot.

The island of Barbados is nearest the Custom House, but its central location guarantees that it also experiences the most foot traffic and road noise. It also shares its only beach and playground with Martinique, which probably is the best area for families. (Martinique has access to two beaches, is adjacent to the main pool and playground at Old Port Royale Centertown, and yet is removed enough from the Custom House to offer a little serenity for parents.) The islands of Aruba and Jamaica are similar in character to Martinique, but each has only one beach, and guests must cross a footbridge to reach Old Port Royale center. Trinidad North comprises three buildings, and its thin layout means that noise penetrates its courtyard from surrounding roads and from rambunctious kids at Old Port Royale next door. The quietest island is Trinidad South, which is most remote from resort facilities. It has its own playground and beach, and the beach has a bonus—the view across Barefoot Bay is of wild, undeveloped Florida forest, a rarity on Disney property.

After you've sorted out your convenience and location priorities, think about the view. Avoid the standard-view rooms; all look onto a parking lot, road, or tiny garden. Water views at the Caribbean overlook swimming pools or Barefoot Bay. Pool views are less than enchanting, and there's lots of noise and activity around the pools. Bay views are the pick of the litter at the Caribbean. Such rooms in Barbados, Martinique, Trinidad North, and Trinidad South catch the afternoon sun. Bay-view rooms in Aruba and Jamaica catch the morning sun. Because we like the sun at our back in the evening, we always go for Rooms 4245–4252 in Jamaica or Rooms 5253–5264 and 5541–5548 in Aruba. If you don't mind the sun in your eyes during cocktail time, Rooms 2245–2256 and 2413–2416 in Martinique, 1246–1248 in Barbados, and all lake-facing second-story rooms in Buildings 35, 38, and 39 in Trinidad South are good bets. We're not crazy about any room in Trinidad North. Be aware that the aging air-conditioning units for individual buildings are pretty loud. One room with an especially nice bay view (2525 in Martinique) is nonetheless not recommended because of its proximity to a clunky air-conditioner.

THE BONNET CREEK RESORTS

(Note: *There are three non-Disney hotels along Bonnet Creek on private property adjacent to Walt Disney World. These are covered later in this chapter in "Hotels outside Walt Disney World."*)

Disney's Saratoga Springs Resort & Spa, Treehouse Villas

STRENGTHS	WEAKNESSES
Extremely nice studio rooms and villas	Traffic congestion at resort's southeast exit
Lushly landscaped setting	Small living areas in villas
Best fitness center at WDW	Distance of some accommodations from dining and services
Convenient self-parking	Limited dining options
Close to Downtown Disney	No character meals
Best spa at Walt Disney World	Limited dining options
Golf on-property	No character meals
Hiking, jogging, water recreation	Limited dining options
Excellent themed swimming complex	No character meals
	Theme and atmosphere not kid-friendly
	Spotty bus service

This Disney Deluxe Villa resort features a theme wordily described by Disney as recalling an "1880s, Victorian, upstate New York lakeside retreat" amid "pastoral landscapes, formal gardens, bubbling springs, and natural surroundings." Saratoga Springs comprises 1,260 studio and one-, two-, and three-bedroom villas across the lake from Downtown Disney. Housed in 12 buildings, most accommodations are of recent vintage, while the fitness center, check-in building, and spa are retooled vestiges of the erstwhile Disney Institute. An adjacent 60-unit DDV complex, Treehouse Villas at Disney's Saratoga Springs Resort & Spa, opened in 2009.

The fitness center is by far the best at Walt Disney World. Surrounded on three sides by golf courses, Saratoga Springs is the only Disney-owned resort that affords direct access to the links (the military-only Shades of Green also provides golf on-property).

The main pool is the resort's focal point. Called High Rock Spring, it tumbles over boulders into a clear, free-form heated pool. A waterslide winds among the rocks, two whirlpool spas, and an interactive wet-play area for children. Two quiet pools serve villas far from the main pool. One of these underwent a major expansion in 2011, tripling its size and adding a 140-foot waterslide, children's play area, and quick-service-dining location. Other recreational features include tennis courts, playgrounds, and paths for jogging, walking, and biking. Disney buses provide transportation to the theme parks. Downtown Disney is accessible by boat or by foot from some accommodations.

Furnishings and soft goods in the villas and studios are less whimsical and a little more upscale and masculine than in other Disney resorts. Chairs, sofas, and tables are quite substantial, perhaps a little too large for the rooms they inhabit. The overall effect, however, is sophisticated and restful. A Gulf Shores, Alabama, family, however, takes a slight exception to the restful part:

> *Saratoga Springs Resort was beautiful, comfortable, and exactly what we needed for our family of five. It was VERY quiet . . . except for the toilets. When you flushed, it sounded like the space shuttle launching.*

A couple from Peru, Indiana, takes a more critical tack:

> *Saratoga Springs is our least favorite resort. We didn't enjoy the theming, and unless you have a car, getting around by the bus system is a real hassle. The food court is very small for the size of the resort, and the food is expensive for what you get. Also, the checkout process was very slow, and our room seemed smaller than comparable rooms at BoardWalk Villas and Old Key West.*

A Cartersville, Georgia, reader echoes the previous complaint about bus service:

> *No matter what time we attempted to leave a park for Saratoga Springs, there were no buses. Forty-five minutes was the norm. We loved Saratoga Springs, but why pay the premium when we ended up driving or taking cabs so as not to waste 2–3 hours per day?*

But a visitor from Whitney, England, says bus service is improving:

> *I think the bus service at Saratoga Springs has an undeserved negative reputation. There has been a dramatic improvement. During our most recent visit (we stayed on-site for 25 nights), our bus wait was less than 10 minutes on all occasions apart from two.*

GOOD (AND NOT-SO-GOOD) ROOMS AT DISNEY'S SARATOGA SPRINGS RESORT & SPA This resort's sprawling size puts some of its best rooms very far away from the main lobby, restaurants, and shops. If you don't

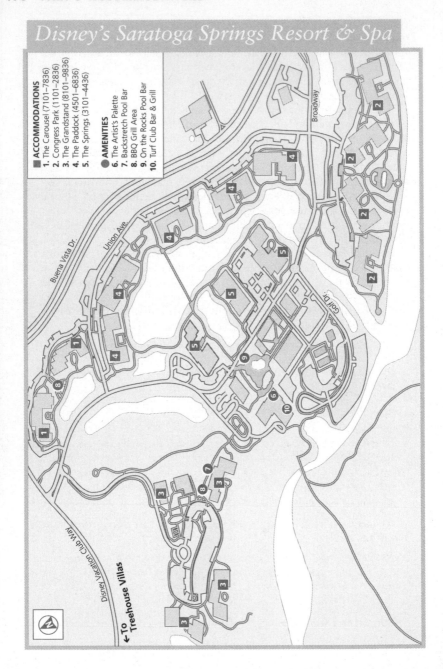

Disney's Saratoga Springs Resort & Spa

ACCOMMODATIONS
1. The Carousel (7101–7836)
2. Congress Park (1101–2836)
3. The Grandstand (8101–9836)
4. The Paddock (4501–6836)
5. The Springs (3101–4436)

AMENITIES
6. The Artist's Palette
7. Backstretch Pool Bar
8. BBQ Grill Area
9. On the Rocks Pool Bar
10. Turf Club Bar & Grill

have a car, the best rooms are those in The Springs, numbered 3101–3436 and 3501–3836. Ask for a room toward the northeast side of these buildings (away from the lobby), as the southwest rooms border a well-traveled road. Avoid Rooms 4101–4436 in Building 14; a pedestrian walkway

Treehouse Villas at Disney's Saratoga Springs Resort & Spa

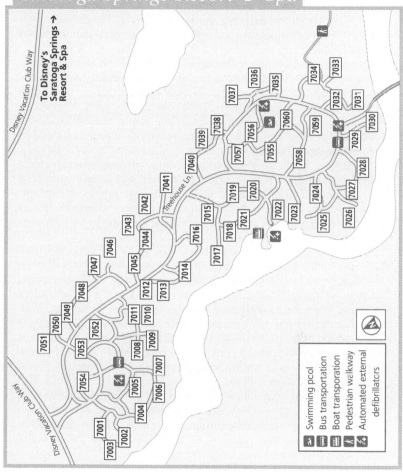

runs behind the patios of this building and gets a lot of use early in the morning from guests headed to breakfast.

If you've got a car or you don't mind a couple of extra furlongs' walk to the lobby, Rooms 1101–1436 and 2501–2836 in Congress Park offer quietness, a view of Downtown Disney, and a relatively short walk to the bus stop. Also good are Rooms 4501–4826, 6101–6436, and 6501–6836 in The Paddock. Avoid rooms on the northeast side of the 5101–5435 building of The Paddock, as well as the northwest side of the 5501–5836 building; these border a swimming pool and bus stop.

In addition to being quiet, Rooms 1101–1436 of Congress Park and Rooms 6101–6436 and 6501–6836 of The Paddock afford the closest walks to Downtown Disney shops, restaurants, and entertainment.

TREEHOUSE VILLAS AT DISNEY'S SARATOGA SPRINGS RESORT & SPA Opened in 2009, this complex of 60 three-bedroom villas lies between Disney's Old Key West Resort and the Grandstand section of Saratoga Springs proper, with a separate entrance off Disney Vacation Club Way. The treehouses are bordered by Lake Buena Vista Golf Course to the northeast and a waterway to the southwest that feeds into Village Lake.

True to their name, the villas stand on stilts 10 feet off the ground (ramps provide wheelchair access) and are surrounded by a densely wooded landscape. Each villa is an eight-sided structure with three bedrooms and two full bathrooms in about 1,074 square feet—about the same size as two-bedroom villas at the Wilderness Lodge, Beach Club, and Saratoga Springs but smaller than those at Animal Kingdom, BoardWalk, and Old Key West.

Each villa holds nine people, one more than comparably sized rooms at the other DDV resorts. The master and second bedrooms have queen beds, and the third bedroom has bunk beds. A sofa bed and sleeper chair in the living room round out the mattress lineup. As with other sleeper sofas and chairs, we think these are more appropriate for kids than adults.

Because of their size, the treehouses cost about the same as a two-bedroom villa elsewhere at Saratoga Springs. When we stayed here, however, we didn't notice the missing space because the layout of the kitchen, dining areas, and living areas was so open. Thus, the extra bedroom might be a good value. Beware the master bathroom, however: The shower and tub are side-by-side in an enclosed glass wall. If you're tilting down in the shower to shave your legs or grab a bottle of shampoo, you could whack your head on the side of the tub if you're not careful. Not good for housekeeping to find you passed out and prunelike on the shower floor.

The interior of each villa is decorated with natural materials, such as stone floors in the kitchen, granite countertops, and stained wood furniture. End tables, picture frames, and bunk beds are made from rustic logs. Bathrooms, outfitted in modern tile, have showers and tubs plus a decent amount of counter space.

Because of its location, Treehouse Villas has few amenities of its own: Each villa has a large wooden deck with charcoal grill, and all villas share a small central pool with spa. A walking path connects the complex to the main Saratoga Springs grounds, and Treehouse Villas guests can use all of the facilities at Saratoga Springs. Two dedicated bus stops serve the villas.

A family from Columbus, New Jersey, thinks a stay at the Treehouse Villas is money well spent:

> *I give them five stars for value. We were trying to be economical, as there were nine people in our party and it saved us approximately $700–$1,000 per night. Our villa had three rooms and a pull-out couch that comfortably housed our group. It had a great eat-in kitchen as well, which further helped us save money on breakfast. All that said, it was not easy traveling to the theme parks—it took approximately 45 minutes to an hour.*

Treehouses 7024–7034 and 7058–7060 are closest to one of the villas' two dedicated bus stops and the walkway to Saratoga Springs; 7026–7033 also have water views. Treehouses 7001–7011 and 7052–7054 are closest to the other bus stop. Finally, Treehouses 7035–7037, 7055, 7056, and 7060 surround the pool.

Disney's Old Key West Resort

STRENGTHS	WEAKNESSES
Extremely nice studios and villas	Large, confusing layout
Full kitchens in villas	Substandard bus service
Quiet, lushly landscaped setting	Limited on-site dining
Convenient self-parking	No easily accessible off-site dining
Small, private swimming pools	Extreme distance of many guest rooms from dining and services
Recreation options	No character meals

This was the first DDV property. Although the resort is a time-share property, units not being used by owners are rented on a nightly basis. Disney's Old Key West Resort is a large aggregation of two- to three-story buildings modeled after Caribbean-style residences and guesthouses of the Florida Keys. Set subdivision-style around a golf course and along Bonnet Creek, the buildings are arranged in small, neighborhood-like clusters. They feature pastel facades, white trim, and shuttered windows. The registration area is in Conch Flats Community Hall, along with a full-service restaurant, modest fitness center, marina, and sundries shop. Each cluster of accommodations has a quiet pool; a larger pool is at the community hall. (A new waterslide in the shape of a giant sandcastle has been installed at the main pool.)

This resort offers some of the roomiest accommodations at Walt Disney World. Studios are 376 square feet; one-bedroom villas, 942; and two-bedroom villas, 1,333. Studios contain two queen-size beds, a table and two chairs, and an extra vanity outside the bathroom. One-bedroom villas have a king-size bed in the master bedroom, a queen-size sleeper sofa in the living room, a laundry room, and a full kitchen. Two-bedroom villas feature a king-size bed in the master bedroom, a queen-size sleeper sofa and foldout chair in the living room, and two queen beds in the second bedroom. All villas have enough closet space to contain your entire wardrobe. Studios and villas are tastefully decorated with wicker and upholstered furniture and peach and light-green color schemes. Each villa has a private balcony that opens onto a delightfully landscaped private courtyard.

Transportation to other Disney World destinations is by bus. Walking time to transportation loading areas from the most remote rooms is about 6 minutes.

An Erie, Pennsylvania, reader thinks Old Key West is Walt Disney World's most well-kept secret:

Old Key West has the most spacious rooms and villas and the easiest access to your car (right outside your door!). It's in a great location and built around a gorgeous golf course. There are a number of

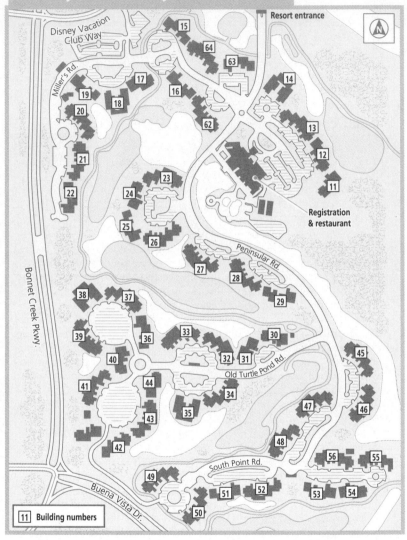

Disney's Old Key West Resort

small, almost private pools, so you don't have to go to the main pool to swim. You don't hear much about Old Key West, but if you go there you won't want to stay anywhere else.

GOOD (AND NOT-SO-GOOD) ROOMS AT DISNEY'S OLD KEY WEST RESORT Old Key West is huge, with 49 three-story villa buildings. Each contains a mix of studio and multiroom villas. Views are nice from almost all villas. To enhance the view, all multiroom villas and some studios have a large balcony furnished with a table and chairs. Though nice vistas are easy to come by, quiet is more elusive. Because the resort is bordered by busy Bonnet Creek Parkway and even busier Buena Vista Drive, the best villas are those as far from the highway noise as possible. For quiet isolation and a lovely river view, ask for Building 46 or 45, in that order. For a lake and golf-course view away from road noise but closest to restaurants, recreation, the marina, the main swimming complex, and shopping, ask for Building 13. Nearby, Buildings 12 and 11 are likewise quiet and convenient but offer primarily golf-course views. Next-best choices are Buildings 32 and 34. Building 32 looks onto a lake with the golf course in the background, while 34 faces the golf course with tennis courts to the left and a lake to the right. None of the buildings recommended is more than a 2- to 5-minute walk to the nearest bus stop or pool. Avoid Buildings 19–22, 38 and 39, 41 and 42, and 49–51.

Ground-floor villas make lugging in suitcases and groceries less taxing. Though the top floor requires a three-story climb, views from on high are superior. The top floor also ensures that you'll have no noisy neighbors clomping above you.

Port Orleans Resort

STRENGTHS	WEAKNESSES
Creative swimming areas	Large, confusing layout
Nice guest rooms, especially in French Quarter	Extreme distance of many guest rooms from dining and services
Beautiful landscaping and grounds	Insufficient on-site dining
Pleasant setting along Bonnet Creek	No easily accessible off-site dining
Food courts	No character meals
Convenient self-parking	Congested bus-loading areas
Children's play areas	Erratic bus service
Varied recreational offerings	
Boat service to Downtown Disney	

A Moderate resort, Port Orleans is divided into two sections. The smaller, southern part is called the French Quarter; the larger section is labeled Riverside.

PORT ORLEANS FRENCH QUARTER RESORT The 1,008-room French Quarter section is a sanitized Disney version of New Orleans's Vieux Carré. Consisting of seven three-story guest-room buildings next to the Sassagoula River, the resort suggests what New Orleans would look like if its buildings were painted every year and garbage collectors never went on strike. There are prim pink-and-blue guest buildings with wrought-iron filigree, shuttered windows, and old-fashioned iron lampposts. In keeping with the Crescent City theme, the French Quarter is landscaped with magnolia trees and overgrown vines. The centrally located Mint contains the registration area and food court and is a reproduction of a turn-of-the-19th-century building where Mississippi Delta farmers sold their harvests. The registration desk features a vibrant Mardi Gras mural and old-fashioned bank-teller windows. The section's

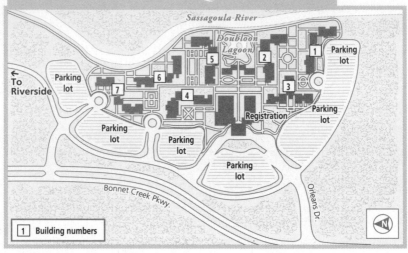

Port Orleans French Quarter Resort

"Doubloon Lagoon" surrounds a colorful fiberglass creation depicting Neptune riding a sea serpent.

French Quarter rooms measure 314 square feet. Most contain two queen beds, a table and two chairs, a dresser-credenza, and a vanity outside the bathroom. We think French Quarter has the most attractive and tasteful rooms of any of the Disney Moderate resorts. With their cherry headboards, Mardi Gras–pastel bedspreads, cherry-wood credenzas with oak inlays, and dark-blue floral carpet, the rooms rival those of several Deluxe resorts. No rooms have balconies, but ornamental iron-railed accessways on each floor provide a good (though less private) substitute.

There's a food court but no full-service restaurant. The closest full-service eatery is in the adjacent Riverside section of the resort, about a 15-plus-minute walk. The commute to restaurants in other hotels may be 40–60 minutes each way. The Disney bus system links the French Quarter to all Disney World destinations. Walking time to bus-loading areas from the most remote French Quarter rooms is 7–10 minutes.

Most readers really like Port Orleans French Quarter. This comment from a Wynnewood, Pennsylvania, father of two is typical:

I highly recommend Port Orleans French Quarter. We stayed at All-Star Movies on our last trip and didn't think it made sense to stay anywhere else. Well, we were wrong. The price difference wasn't that big, and what we got for the difference was well worth it: uncrowded pool, bellhop service, front-door greeters with great tips for touring, and a bigger, more comfortable room. Totally worth the extra money.

A Milford, Connecticut, mom had transportation problems:

We had a wonderful time at Disney, but I do wish Port Orleans French Quarter and Riverside didn't share a bus route. After the

Port Orleans Riverside Resort

French Quarter bus stop, there are four stops at Riverside. You always got a seat, but sometimes it took upwards of an hour to get to the parks after waiting for the bus, then stopping at all four Riverside depots.

One Philadelphia Gen Xer wasn't exactly flush with joy about his Port Orleans stay:

The in-room toilets seem to be powered by jet thrusters. We were woken up far too many times in the night when someone in a neighboring room would flush.

An unidentified e-mailer backs him up:

The reader comment about the toilets is 100% correct. They're air-pressure-forced rather than water-flow-and-gravity-operated. It's similar to what happens when you flush a toilet on an airplane, only MUCH louder. Every morning I was woken up at 7:30 a.m. with an hour's worth of whooooshing. If I stay there again, I'll invest in a portable sound machine to try to mask the noise.

GOOD (AND NOT-SO-GOOD) ROOMS AT PORT ORLEANS FRENCH QUARTER RESORT Seven guest-room buildings flank the pool and Guest Relations building and bus stop. The best views are from rooms directly facing the river and natural pine forest on the opposite bank. Wings of Buildings 1, 2, 5, 6, and 7 flank the river and provide the best river views in either the French Quarter or Riverside sections of Port Orleans. River-view rooms in Buildings 1, 6, and 7 are a long walk from French Quarter public facilities, but they're the most tranquil. Families with children should request river-view rooms in Buildings 2 and 5, nearest the swimming complex. Make sure the reservationist understands that you're requesting a room with a river view, not just a water view. All river-view rooms are also water-view rooms, but not vice versa.

Following are the best river-view rooms in each building:

Building 1	Rooms 1127–1132, 1227–1232, 1327–1332
Building 2	Rooms 2127–2132, 2227–2232, 2327–2332
Building 5	Rooms 5117–5122, 5217–5222, 5317–5322
Building 6	Rooms 6123–6126, 6223–6226, 6323–6326, 6133–6140, 6233–6240, 6333–6340, 6141–6148, 6241–6248, 6341–6348
Building 7	Rooms 7141–7148, 7241–7248, 7341–7348

Standard-view rooms look onto a courtyard or a parking lot. There are no private balconies, but you can bring a lawn chair and sit on the exterior accessway. You'll have to make way for fellow guests coming and going to their rooms, but most of the time you'll be undisturbed.

PORT ORLEANS RIVERSIDE RESORT Riverside draws on the lifestyle and architecture of Mississippi River communities in antebellum Louisiana. Spread along the Sassagoula River, which encircles "Ol' Man Island" (the section's main swimming area), Riverside is subdivided into two more themed areas: the "mansion" area, which features plantation-style architecture, and the "bayou" area, with tin-roofed rustic (imitation) wooden buildings. Mansions are three stories tall, while bayou guesthouses are a story shorter. The river-life theme is augmented by groves of azalea and juniper. Riverside's food court houses a working cotton press powered by a 32-foot waterwheel.

Each of Riverside's 2,048 rooms is 314 square feet. Most provide one king or two queen beds, a table and two chairs, and two pedestal sinks outside the bathroom. Rooms in the Alligator Bayou section of Riverside feature brass bathroom fixtures, hickory-branch bedposts, trundle beds, and quilted bedspreads. Rooms in the plantation-themed Magnolia Bend section of Riverside are more conventional, with light-yellow walls, dark wood furnishings, and teal carpets with dark-blue floral patterns. All rooms feature two queen beds or one king bed.

Two Riverside buildings contain exclusively Disney character–themed rooms—512 in all—similar in concept to the *Pirates of the Caribbean* and *Finding Nemo* ones at Caribbean Beach. Riverside's rooms are themed to *Aladdin, Beauty and the Beast,* and *The Princess and the Frog.* Features include new bedspreads, artwork, and fixtures carrying the theme of each movie.

Many readers have written asking us to emphasize that, aside from the differences in guest rooms described previously, all the rooms are more or less the same regardless of the facade of your building. In other words, if your building looks like a mansion, that doesn't mean your guest room will look like it belongs in one.

Riverside has one full-service restaurant and a food court. The restaurant is a 15-minute walk from many of the guest buildings. The Disney bus system links the resort to all Disney World destinations. The commute to restaurants in other hotels may be 40–60 minutes each way. Walking time from the most remote rooms to the transportation loading areas is 10 minutes.

A multigenerational family from Little Rock, Arkansas, shares the following:

We loved Port Orleans. The cast members were very friendly and helpful. The grounds were absolutely beautiful. The rooms were also very quiet. The only downside was the shuttle service: It was standing-room-only much of the time, and this was the off-season—we wonder how bad it would be in July! However, we liked the resort so much, we can't wait to stay there again.

A family of adults from Boston agrees about the scenery:

Riverside was very nice. You downplayed how beautiful the grounds and wildlife are.

But a New York City reader doesn't think the atmosphere lives up to its promise:

Although the Riverside section is modeled after mansions of the Old South, this will have no bearing on one's stay. The outside decor of each building is simply a "shell"—there's little or no decor inside your guest room that corresponds to the theme.

Finally, a Lexington, Kentucky, mom touts Riverside's counter-service food:

Hands-down, the counter service at Riverside was the most convenient, efficient, and spacious of any we have experienced at Disney. Their create-your-own/made-to-order pasta bar was one of the most enjoyable meals we experienced—and we had counter service at the Grand Floridian, the Polynesian, and the Contemporary, plus we ate at Cinderella's Royal Table, Chef Mickey's, The Crystal Palace, the Biergarten, and Akershus.

GOOD (AND NOT-SO-GOOD) ROOMS AT PORT ORLEANS RIVERSIDE RESORT Riverside is so large that we use bicycles whenever we work there. All told, there are 20 guest-room buildings (not counting flanking wings on two buildings). Divided into two sections, Alligator Bayou and Magnolia Bend, the resort is arrayed around two pine groves and a watercourse that Disney calls the Sassagoula River. Magnolia Bend consists of four three-story, grand plantation–style complexes named Acadian House, Magnolia Terrace, Oak Manor, and Parterre Place. Though Magnolia Bend is on the river, only about 15% of the guest rooms have an unobstructed view of the water. The vast majority of rooms overlook a courtyard or parking lot. Trees and other vegetation block the view of many rooms actually facing the river. The best views in Magnolia Bend are from the third-floor river side of Acadian House (Building 80), which overlooks the river and Ol' Man Island.

To the south are Magnolia Terrace (Building 85) and Oak Manor (Building 90), each in an *H* shape. In them, only second- and third-floor rooms on the very top of the *H* (facing the river) have an unobstructed water view. Ask for Rooms 9416, 9417, 9039, 9042, and 9239–9242. Both H-shaped buildings, however, are nearer the front desk, restaurant, lounge, and shopping complex than is Acadian House. Continuing south, Parterre Place (Building 95) has a number of rooms overlooking the river, but they also overlook the parking lot on the far shore. In general, with the few exceptions described above, if you really want a nice river view, opt for Port Orleans French Quarter downriver.

Alligator Bayou, the other part of Port Orleans Riverside, forms an arch around the resort's northern half. Sixteen smaller, two-story guest-room buildings, set among pine groves and abundant gardens, offer a cozy, tranquil alternative to the more-imposing structures of the Magnolia Bend section of Riverside and Port Orleans French Quarter. If you want a river view, ask for a second-story water-view room in Building 27 or 38. Building 14 also offers some river-view rooms and is convenient to shops, the front desk, and the restaurant, but it's in a noisy, high-traffic area. A good compromise building for families is Building 18. It's insulated from traffic and noise by landscaping, yet is next to a satellite swimming pool and within an easy walk of the Guest Relations building.

Disney's Port Orleans Riverside map shows two lakes north of the river bend, suggesting additional water views in Alligator Bayou. But these are dried-up lakes now forested with pine. This area, however, is richly landscaped to complement the "pine islands," and though out of sight of water, it offers the most peaceful and serene accommodations in the Port Orleans resort. In this area, we recommend Buildings 26, 25, and 39, in that order. Note that these buildings are somewhat distant from the resort's central facilities, and there's no adjacent parking. In Alligator Bayou, avoid Buildings 15, 16, 17, and 24, all of which are subject to traffic noise from nearby Bonnet Creek Parkway.

Remember: All Port Orleans guest buildings have exterior corridors. When you look out your window, a safety rail will be in the foreground, and other guests will periodically walk past.

THE ANIMAL KINGDOM RESORTS

Animal Kingdom Lodge & Villas

STRENGTHS	WEAKNESSES
Exotic theme	Remote location
Uniquely appointed guest rooms	Spotty bus service
Most rooms have private balconies	
Views of savanna and animals from guest rooms	
Themed swimming area	
Excellent on-site dining, including a buffet	
On-site nature programs and storytelling	
Health and fitness center	
Child-care center on-site	
Proximity to non-Disney restaurants on US 192	

Animal Kingdom Lodge & Villas

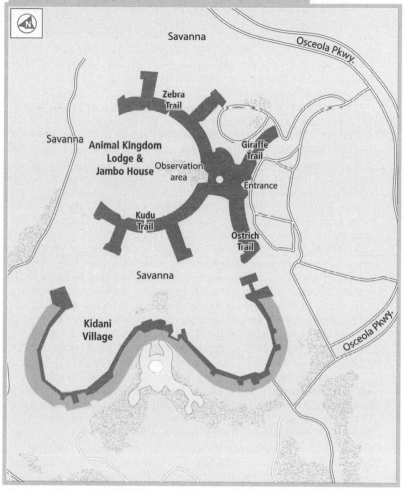

In the far southwest corner of the World and adjacent to Animal Kingdom theme park, Animal Kingdom Lodge opened in 2001. Designed by Peter Dominick of Wilderness Lodge fame, Animal Kingdom Lodge fuses African tribal architecture with the exotic, rugged style of grand East African national-park lodges. Five-story, thatched-roof guest-room wings fan out from a vast central rotunda housing the lobby and featuring a huge mud fireplace. Public areas and about half of the rooms offer panoramic views of a private 43-acre wildlife preserve, punctuated with streams and elevated *kopje* (rock outcroppings) and populated with some 200 free-roaming animals and 130 birds. Most of the 972 guest rooms measure 344 square feet and boast hand-carved furnishings and richly colored soft goods. Almost all have full balconies.

In 2007, in the first of two phases, Disney converted 134 rooms of the original hotel into DDV accommodations. Disney opened part of the second phase, called Kidani Village, in the spring of 2009, and the remaining portion in late 2009. To avoid the confusion of having to differentiate two separate DDV buildings with "Animal Kingdom Villas" in their names, Disney has christened the units in the original hotel—as well as the building itself—as Jambo House. Thus, if you're staying in a DDV unit at Animal Kingdom Lodge you're at Jambo House, and if you're staying in the new building you're at Kidani Village. The entire complex, classified by Disney as a Deluxe resort, is called Animal Kingdom Lodge & Villas.

Jambo House offers fine dining in a casual setting at Jiko—The Cooking Place. Twin wood-burning ovens are the focal point of the restaurant, which serves meals inspired by the myriad cuisines of Africa. Boma—Flavors of Africa, the family restaurant, serves a buffet with food prepared in an exhibition kitchen featuring a wood-burning grill and rotisserie. Tables are under thatched roofs. The Mara, a quick-service restaurant with extended hours, and Victoria Falls, a delightful mezzanine lounge overlooking Boma—Flavors of Africa, round out the hotel's food-and-beverage service. Other amenities include an elaborate swimming area and a village marketplace. Children ages 6–14 can explore African culture through games and crafts. Cost is $70 per child; reservations must be made using a credit card.

Consisting of a separate freestanding building shaped like a backwards 3, Kidani Village comprises 324 units, a dedicated savanna, a new pool, and Sanaa, a sit-down restaurant combining Indian and African cuisines. Other features include a fitness center, an arcade, a gift shop, and tennis, shuffleboard, and basketball courts. Kidani Village is connected to the original hotel by a half-mile walking trail; DDV guests at either resort can use the facilities at both buildings.

Both Jambo House and Kidani Village have studios and one-, two-, and three-bedroom villas. Most rooms at Kidani Village are larger, however, and the difference is anywhere from 50 square feet for a studio to more than 200 square feet for a two-bedroom unit. (The three-bedroom Grand Villas at Jambo House, 148 square feet larger than those in Kidani Village, are the exception.) Because of the difference in area, one-bedroom units in Kidani Village can accommodate up to five people and two-bedroom units can hold up to nine via a sleeper chair in the living room. At Jambo House, one-bedroom "value" rooms sleep four, while standard, savanna, and Club Level rooms sleep five.

Having stayed at Kidani Village shortly after its opening, we think it's a quiet, relaxed resort. The lobby and rooms have a smaller, more personal feel than Jambo House's. The building exterior isn't anything special—essentially a set of green rectangles with oversize African-themed decorations attached. Kidani's distance from Jambo House makes it feel even more remote than the latter. The bus stops are a fair distance from the main building, too, and it's easy to head in the wrong direction when you're coming back from the parks at night.

Animal Kingdom Lodge & Villas is connected to the rest of Disney World by bus, but because of the resort's remote location, you should seriously consider having a car if you stay there.

A family of four from Lincoln, England, gives Animal Kingdom Lodge a mixed, though mostly positive, review:

We had a fab holiday, but we wouldn't recommend people paying the extra money to have a savanna room. The animals are scarce, and you don't really spend much time in your room. The pool and the kids' club were fantastic and the hotel stunning. The food court was fine, although we wished they'd change the menu, as after two weeks you're fed up of the same choices.

A Portage, Indiana, family begs to differ with us:

We disagree with your assessment that the Giraffe Trail is the least desirable wing of Animal Kingdom Lodge. We stayed in a pool view room and loved it. The view was beautiful, even without the animals (which you can view elsewhere). The proximity to the pool, lobby, and restaurants was great, and a bonus was the direct exits from the hallway to the outside, which were very close to where Disney transportation picks up. And we saved about $500 over what we would've spent on a savanna view.

GOOD (AND NOT-SO-GOOD) ROOMS AT ANIMAL KINGDOM LODGE & VILLAS A glance at the resort map tells you where the best rooms and villas are. Kudu Trail and Zebra Trail, two wings branching from the rear of Jambo House, form a semicircle around the central wildlife savanna. Along each wing are seven five-story buildings, with accommodations on floors 2–5. Five buildings on each wing form the semicircle, while the remaining two buildings jut away from the center. The best rooms—on floors 3 and 4, facing into the circle—are high enough to survey the entire savanna yet low enough to let you appreciate the ground-level detail of this amazing wildlife exhibit; plus, these rooms offer the easiest access to the lobby and restaurants. Second-floor rooms really can't take in the panorama, and fifth-floor rooms are a little too high for intimate views of the animals. Most of the fourth-floor rooms in Jambo House are reserved for concierge guests, and the fifth and sixth floors house the DDV units.

Most rooms in the outward-jutting buildings, as well as rooms facing away from the interior, also survey a savanna, but one not as compelling as that of the inner circle. On the Zebra Trail, the first two buildings plus the first jutting building provide savanna views on one side and look onto the swimming complex on the other.

Less attractive still are two smaller wings, Ostrich Trail and Giraffe Trail, branching from either side of the lodge near the main entrance. Some rooms in Ostrich Trail, on the left, overlook a small savanna. Rooms on the opposite side of the same buildings overlook the front entrance. Least desirable is Giraffe Trail, extending from the right side of the lobby. Rooms in this wing overlook either the pool (water view) or the resort entrance (standard view).

The best views in Kidani Village are the north-facing rooms near the bottom and middle of the backwards 3. Try rooms numbered 7X38–7X44, 7X46–7X52, 7X04–7X11, 7X68–7X7, and 7X60–7X67 (X = numbers 0–9). These overlook the savanna next to the lodge's Kudu Trail rooms and beyond into undeveloped woods. West- and south-facing rooms in the bottom half of the Kidani building overlook the parking lot, while west-facing rooms in the top half have either pool or savanna views.

Coronado Springs Resort

STRENGTHS	WEAKNESSES
Nice guest rooms	Insufficient on-site dining
Good view from waterside guest rooms	Extreme distance of many guest rooms from dining and services
Food court	No character meals
Themed swimming area with waterslides	
Fitness center	
Business center	
Convenient self-parking	

Coronado Springs Resort, near Animal Kingdom, is Disney's only mid-priced convention property. Inspired by northern Mexico and the American Southwest, the resort is divided into three separately themed areas. The two- and three-story Ranchos call to mind southwestern cattle ranches, while the two-story Cabanas are modeled after Mexican beach resorts. The multistoried Casitas embody elements of Spanish architecture found in Mexico's great cities. The lobby, part of the Casitas, features a mosaic ceiling and tiled floor. The vast resort surrounds a 22-acre lake, and there are three small pools as well as one large swimming complex. The main pool features a reproduction of a Mayan steppe pyramid with a waterfall cascading down its side.

Most of the resort's 1,915 guest rooms measure 314 square feet and contain two queen beds, a table and chairs, and a vanity outside the bathroom. Rooms are decorated with sunset colors and feature hand-painted Mexican wall hangings. All have coffeemakers. No room has its own balcony.

Perhaps because Coronado Springs is geared to conventions, getting work done here is easier than at any other Disney Moderate resort. A specially designed light fixture above the desk holds a halogen bulb and provides excellent illumination of the work area. Wi-Fi is available throughout the resort, and the business-center staff is friendly and knowledgeable.

Coronado Springs offers one full-service restaurant as well as Disney World's most interesting food court. Unfortunately, there's not nearly enough food service for a resort this large and remote. If you book Coronado Springs, we suggest you have a car to expand your dining options. The resort is connected to other Disney destinations by bus only. Walking time from the most remote rooms to the bus stop is 8–10 minutes.

Disney has converted Cabana 9B to Club Level rooms, with access to a private lounge for serving breakfast and snacks throughout the day. These rooms cost around $100–$130 more than standard rooms, per night, depending on the season.

Reader opinions concerning Coronado Springs are split. A family from Cumming, Georgia, was disappointed:

The convention center really interferes with a family vacation—everyone we met there was working and wanted to talk about work while we were trying to get away from work!

Coronado Springs Resort

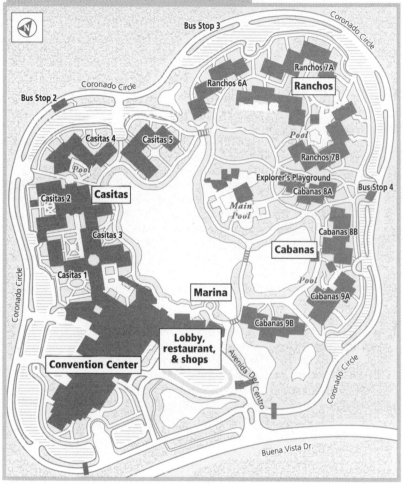

A Portsmouth, England, mother had a very different experience:

The rooms were spotless and very spacious. The concierge team and staff were amazingly helpful. Although there were many conferences at the time we stayed there, it never interfered with our stay or enjoyment of the resort.

A St. Catharines, Ontario, mom says, "Enough walking already!"

This resort was far too big. It was a 10-minute walk to get to the main pool and a 10-minute walk in a different direction to get to the food court.

A family from Indianapolis had no complaints about the swimming pools:

The pool at Coronado Springs was excellent—the kids loved the slide! Also utilized smaller pool close to our room—was good for kids to relax before bedtime.

Finally, from a Canvey Island, England, reader:

We stayed at the Coronado Springs Resort and were very satisfied overall. The Pepper Market food court was overly complicated (stamping tickets to pay at the end, multiple tickets per party), but the quality was good. The Maya Grill was a disappointment, overpriced for the quality of the food. The walk around the lake on a nice day is a delight.

As a convention hotel, Coronado Springs is peculiar. Unlike most convention hotels, where everything is centrally located with guest rooms in close proximity, rooms at this resort are spread around a huge lake. If you're assigned a room on the opposite side of the lake from the meeting area (and restaurants!), plan on an 11- to 15-minute hike every time you leave your room. If your organization books Coronado Springs for a meeting, consider having your meals catered. The hotel's restaurants simply don't have the capacity during a large convention to accommodate the breakfast rush or to serve a quick lunch between sessions.

GOOD (AND NOT-SO-GOOD) ROOMS AT CORONADO SPRINGS RESORT
Coronado Springs encircles a large artificial lake called Lago Dorado. In addition to the main building (El Centro), which contains shopping venues, restaurants, and a conference center, there are three communities of accommodations, each different in appearance and layout. Moving clockwise around the lake, the Casitas are near the lobby, restaurants, shops, and convention center. Standard-view rooms face parking lots or a courtyard. Water-view rooms cover pools, lake, birdbaths, and so on. For a good view of Lago Dorado, try to book one of these rooms:

3220–3287 (except 3224, 3230, 3260, 3261, 3265–3267, and 3274)

3320–3387 (except 3324, 3330, 3360, 3361, 3365–3367, and 3374)

3420–3487 (except 3424, 3430, 3460, 3461, 3465–346/, and 3474)

4230–4266

5200–5213, 5223–5263 (except 5250)

5300–5313, 5323–5363 (except 5350)

5400–5413, 5423–5463 (except 5450)

Next in our rotation are the Ranchos, set back from the lake. The desert theme translates to plenty of cactus and gravel, not much water or shade, and almost no good views. Though near the main swimming facility, Ranchos are a hike from everything else. The following rooms afford the best views:

6103, 6203, 6303, 6225, 6226, 6325, 6326, 6245, 6246 (water views);

6600–6604, 6610 (water views); 6750–6760 (woods views)

Next are the Cabanas, which offer some very nice lake views. Cabana 9B is our favorite, near restaurants and the convention center, and only a moderate walk to the main pool. Rooms with the best views are 9500–9507, 9600–9611, and 9650–9657, with lake views, and 4640–4647 and 9640–9647, with a view of a small lagoon. Rooms that overlook the lake are subject to some generally tolerable traffic noise.

Other lake-view rooms we recommend include:

8120, 8121, 8124–8126, 8128–8131, and 8140–8147

8500–8511, 8550–8553, 8571, and 8573

8600–8611, 8650–8653, 8671, and 8673

9108–9110, 9150–9153, 9170–9173, 9203–9210, 9250–9253, and 9270–9273

As at Port Orleans and the Caribbean Beach Resort, external railed walkways to guest rooms double as balconies. Because there's not a lot of traffic along them, you can pull a chair from your room onto the walkway and enjoy the view. We always bring lawn chairs expressly for "balcony" use when we stay at Coronado Springs.

All-Star Sports, All-Star Music, and All-Star Movies Resorts

STRENGTHS	WEAKNESSES
Kid-friendly theme	Remote location
Low (for Disney) rates	Small guest rooms (except family suites)
Large swimming pools	No full-service dining
Food courts	Large, confusing layout
Convenient self-parking	Congested bus-loading areas
	No character meals
	Limited recreation options

Disney's version of a budget resort features three distinct themes executed in the same hyperbolic style. Spread over a vast expanse, the resorts comprise 30 three-story motel-style guest-room buildings. Although the three resorts are neighbors, each has its own lobby, food court, and registration area. The All-Star Sports Resort features huge sports icons: bright football helmets, tennis rackets, and baseball bats— all taller than the buildings they adorn. Similarly, the All-Star Music Resort features 40-foot guitars, maracas, and saxophones, while the All-Star Movies Resort showcases giant popcorn boxes and icons from Disney films. Lobbies of all are loud (in both decibels and brightness) and cartoonish, with checkerboard walls and photographs of famous athletes, musicians, or film stars. There's even a photo of Mickey Mouse with Alice Cooper. Each resort has two main pools; Music's are shaped like musical instruments (the Piano Pool and the guitar-shaped Calypso Pool), and one of Movies' is star-shaped. All six pools feature plastic replicas of Disney characters, some shooting water pistols.

At 260 square feet, guest rooms at the All-Star Resorts are very small. They're so small that a family of four attempting to stay in one room might redefine *family values* by week's end. Each room has two double beds or one king bed, a separate vanity area, and a table and chairs. Most bedspreads feature athletes, movie stars, or musicians; most light fixtures are star-shaped. No rooms have balconies.

All-Star Resorts

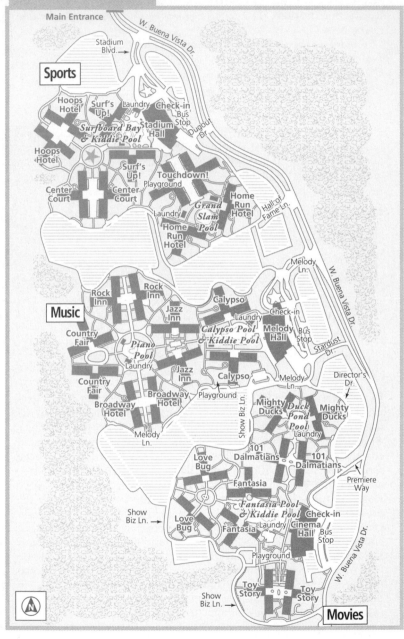

Main Entrance

W. Buena Vista Dr.

Stadium Blvd. →

Sports

Hoops Hotel
Surf's Up!
Laundry
Check-in
Bus Stop
Dugout Dr.

Surfboard Bay & Kiddie Pool
Stadium Hall

Hoops Hotel

Surf's Up!
Touchdown!
Playground
Center Court
Center Court

Grand Slam Pool
Home Run Hotel
Hall of Fame Ln.

Laundry
Home Run Hotel

Melody Ln.

W. Buena Vista Dr.

Rock Inn
Rock Inn
Jazz Inn
Calypso

Music

Calypso Pool & Kiddie Pool
Laundry
Check-in
Melody Hall
Bus Stop

Country Fair
Piano Pool
Stardust Dr.

Laundry
Jazz Inn
Calypso

Country Fair

Broadway Hotel
Playground
Melody Ln.
Director's Dr.

Broadway Hotel
Melody Ln.

Mighty Ducks
Duck Pond Pool
Mighty Ducks

Show Biz Ln.
Laundry

Premiere Way

Love Bug
101 Dalmatians
101 Dalmatians

Fantasia

Fantasia Pool & Kiddie Pool
Check-in

Show Biz Ln. →
Love Bug
Fantasia
Laundry
Cinema Hall
Bus Stop

Playground

W. Buena Vista Dr.

Toy Story
Toy Story

Show Biz Ln. →

Movies

If you're planning to save for a Disney vacation, you may want to save enough for a bigger room at another resort if space is an important consideration. Also, the All-Stars are the noisiest Disney resorts, though guest rooms are well soundproofed and quiet.

Due to the low staff-to-guest ratio, service is not the greatest. Also, there are no full-service restaurants, and the bus ride from the remote All-Stars to a sit-down restaurant at another resort is about 45 minutes one-way (there is, however, a McDonald's about a quarter-mile away). Bus service to the theme and water parks is pretty efficient. Walking time to the bus stop from the most remote guest rooms is about 8 minutes.

> *unofficial* **TIP**
> If you're going to stay at an All-Star Resort, stay at Sports. The sole reason is that the shuttle buses pick up at the All-Stars in this order: Sports, Music, Movies. That little difference can mean a lot when you're traveling with kids or with a group.

Occasionally, all three All-Star Resorts will share a bus going to the same park. When this happens, All-Star Sports guests are usually picked up first on the Disney bus route. It's possible for Sports passengers to completely fill the first bus dispatched, resulting in longer waits at the other All-Star Resorts. Each All-Star generally has its own separate bus for the return trip.

We receive a lot of letters commenting on the All-Star Resorts. From a family group of 13 from East Greenbush, New York:

> *The All-Star Resorts are perfectly family-oriented. Some nice touches that were not mentioned in your guide—a small amphitheater set up in the lobby to occupy the kids while you check in, and soft sidewalk material surrounding the kiddie pool, which is only about 10 inches deep. And the playground has two separate jungle gyms—one for older kids and one for younger kids.*

A Canadian family had this experience:

> *The guide didn't prepare us for the large groups of students who take over the resorts. They're very noisy and very pushy when it comes to getting on buses. Our scariest experience was when we tried getting on a bus and got mobbed by about 100 students.*

From a Massachusetts family of four:

> *I would never recommend the All-Star for a family. It was like dormitory living. Our room was about 1 mile from the bus stop, and the room was tiny—you needed to step into the bathroom, shut the door, then step around the toilet that blocked half the tub.*

But a Baltimore family had a very positive experience:

> *We were pleasantly surprised by All-Star Movies. Yes, the rooms are small, but the overall magic there is amazing. The lobby played Disney movies, which is perfect if you get up early and the buses aren't running yet. There are great photo ops everywhere (Donald and Daisy were awesome). Customer service was impeccable.*

Finally, a dad from Rogers, Arkansas, had this to say:

> *Make sure that people understand how inconvenient the shuttle service becomes when you have to share one bus for all three All-Star*

Resorts. This one issue ruined what was an otherwise very pleasant experience. For this reason alone, I will never stay at the All-Star Resorts again.

ALL-STAR FAMILY SUITES To the rejoicing of parents everywhere, Disney opened 192 family suites at its All-Star Music Resort. In the Jazz and Calypso buildings, these suites measure roughly 520 square feet, slightly larger than the cabins at Fort Wilderness. Each suite, formed from the combination of two formerly separate rooms, includes a kitchenette with mini-refrigerator, microwave, and coffeemaker. Sleeping accommodations include a queen bed in the bedroom, plus a pullout sleeper sofa and two chairs that convert to beds in the family room. We're not sure we'd let adult friends (ones we want to keep, anyway) on the sofa bed or those chair beds, but they're probably fine for children. A hefty door separates the two rooms.

The suites also feature flat-screen televisions in each room, plus two bathrooms—one more than the Fort Wilderness cabins. The suites cost anywhere from 25% to 40% less than the cabins, but they don't have the kitchen space or appliances to prepare anything more than rudimentary meals. If you're trying to save money by eating in your room, the cabins are your best bet. If you just want a little extra space and somewhere to nuke your Pop-Tarts in the morning, go with the All-Star suites.

Reader comments concerning the family suites have been generally positive, though measured. First, from a North Carolina family of five:

The family suites at All-Star Music were great! It was so nice to have a place to unwind without the kids at night, along with two bathrooms and extra space for breakfast/snack/drinks in the kitchen area. My only issue was that we weren't comfortable leaving the kids on the foldouts because they're right next to the front door, plus my husband and I didn't want to be confined to the bedroom from the time we put the kids to bed, so we slept on a foldout. The first night was hell, but the second night we took the mattresses off the pullout chair and ottoman and put them on top of the mattress on the couch—MUCH better!

A North Adams, Massachusetts, dad is more enthusiastic:

We opted for the All-Star Music Family Suite this trip and were really pleased. The biggest advantage was the two full bathrooms. We were thinking about going to the Fort Wilderness Resort and renting a cabin (for the full kitchen and homey atmosphere), but between having a meal plan and then realizing that there would be two bathrooms in the Family Suite, we decided on that. It was about $300 less expensive than Fort Wilderness as well.

From a Skokie, Illinois, family of five:

We found the All-Star Music Family Suite to be very roomy for the six of us. Our teenagers and preteen were quite comfortable on the pullout sofa, chair, and ottoman. Having the two bathrooms was a must, and the kitchen area was great; lots of shelf space for the food we had delivered from GardenGrocer (they're excellent, by the way) [see page 409]. Our only complaint about the resort is that from 7:30 a.m. until midnight there's always music playing—it can get annoying to always have that beat going in the background. The rooms are soundproofed but not enough; had to use earplugs.

GOOD (AND NOT-SO-GOOD) ROOMS AT THE ALL-STAR RESORTS
Though the layouts of All-Star Resorts' Movies, Music, and Sports sections are different, the buildings are identical three-story, three-winged structures. The T-shaped buildings are further grouped into pairs, generally facing each other, and share a common subtheme. For example, there's a *Toy Story* pair in the Movies section. In addition to being named by theme, such as *Fantasia,* buildings are numbered 1–10 in each section. Rooms are accessed via a motel-style outdoor walkway, but each building has an elevator.

Parking is plentiful, all of it in sprawling lots buffering the three sections. A room near a parking lot means easier loading and unloading but also unsightly views of the lot during your stay. The resort offers a luggage service, but it often takes up to an hour for your bags to arrive.

The sure way to avoid a parking-lot vista is to request a room facing a courtyard or pool. The trade-off is noise. The sound of cars starting in the parking lot is no match for shrieking children or hooting teenagers in the pool. But don't count on a good view of the pool, even if your room faces it directly. The buildings' themed facade decorations are placed on their widest face—the top of the *T*—which is also the side facing the pool or courtyard. In some cases, as with the surfboards in the Sports section, these significantly obstruct the view from nearby rooms. Floodlights are trained on these facades and if you step out of your room at night to view the action below, looking down may result in temporary blindness.

The sort of traveler you are should dictate the room you request at All-Star Resorts. If you choose the resort because you'd rather spend time and money at the parks, opt to be near the bus stop, your link to the rest of the World. Note that buses leave from the central public buildings of each section, which are near the larger, noisier pools. If you're planning to return to your room for an afternoon nap, request a room farther from the pools. Also consider an upper-story room to minimize foot traffic past your door. On the other hand, if you choose All-Star for its kid-friendly aspects, consider roosting near the action. A bottom-floor room provides easy pool access, and a room looking out on a courtyard or pool allows you to keep an eye on children playing outside.

For travelers without young children (infants excluded), the best bets for privacy and quiet are buildings that overlook the forest behind the resort, Buildings 2–4 in All-Star Sports and 4–7 in All-Star Music. Interior-facing rooms in these buildings (and their partners) also fill the bill, since they overlook courtyards farthest from the large pools. The courtyards vary with theme but are generally only mildly amusing.

If you're traveling with children, opt for a section and building with a theme that appeals to your kids. Often, that will be a film— movies are the lifeblood of the Disney empire—but it might be a sport. If you're staying in Home Run Hotel, don't forget the ball and gloves to maximize the experience (just keep games of catch away from the pool). Older elementary- and middle-school children probably will want to spend hotel time in or near the bigger pools or arcades in nearby halls. Periodically, cadres of teenagers—too cool for their younger siblings—effectively commandeer the smaller secondary pools. Playgrounds are tucked behind Building 9 in All-Star Music and behind Building 6 in All-Star Sports. Rooms facing these are ideal for families with children too young or timid for the often-chaotic larger pools. In All-Star Movies, the playground is nearer to the food court than to any rooms.

The following tip from a former All-Star Resorts cast member from Fayetteville, Georgia, illustrates just how big these resorts are:

> *Please tell your readers that rooms at the far end of the Mighty Ducks building of All-Star Movies are closer to the All-Star Music food court, pool, and buses than to All-Star Movies' own facilities. Follow the walkway from the Ducks building north to All-Star Music's Melody Hall.*

Pop Century Resort

STRENGTHS	WEAKNESSES
Kid-friendly theme	Small guest rooms
Low (for Disney) rates	No full-service dining
Large swimming pools	Large, confusing layout
Food court	No character meals
Convenient self-parking	Limited recreation options
Fast check-in	

On Victory Way near the ESPN Wide World of Sports Complex is Disney's Pop Century Resort. Originally designed to be completed in phases, the first section opened in 2004. The long-planned second phase of Pop Century was canceled in favor of a new Value resort, Art of Animation (see profile on page 195).

Pop Century is an economy resort; rooms run $82–$174 per night. In terms of layout, architecture, and facilities, Pop Century is almost a clone of the All-Star Resorts (that is, four-story, motel-style buildings built around a central pool, food court, and registration area). Decorative touches make the difference. Where the All-Star Resorts display larger-than-life icons from sports, music, and movies, Pop Century draws its icons from decades of the 20th century. Look for such oddities as building-sized Big Wheels, hula hoops, and the like, punctuated by silhouettes of people dancing the decade's fad dance.

The public areas at Pop Century are marginally more sophisticated than the ones at the All-Star Resorts, with 20th-century period furniture and decor rolled up in a saccharine, those-were-the-days theme. A food court, a bar, a playground, pools, and so on emulate the All-Star Resorts model in size and location. A Pop Century departure from the All-Star precedent has merchandise retailers thrown in with the

Pop Century Resort & Art of Animation Resort

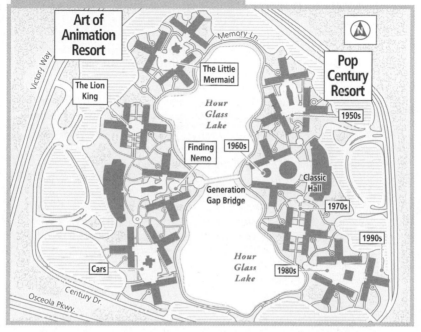

fast-food concessions in a combination dining-and-shopping area. This apparently is what happens when a giant corporation tries to combine selling pizza with hawking Goofy hats. (You just know the word *synergy* was used like cheap cologne in those design meetings.) As at the All-Star Resorts, there's no full-service restaurant. The resort is connected to the rest of Walt Disney World by bus, but because of the limited dining options, we recommend having a car.

Guest rooms at Pop Century are small at 260 square feet. The decor is upbeat, with print bedspreads and wall art depicting pop memorabilia from decades past. Light-finish wood-inlaid furniture and dark, patterned carpet provide an upscale touch, but these are not rooms you'd want to spend a lot of time in. Bathrooms are tiny and counter space a scarce commodity. Worst of all, we've received many complaints from readers that the soundproofing between rooms is inadequate. A lake separating Pop Century from the Art of Animation Resort offers water views not available at the All-Star Resorts.

A reader from Dublin, Georgia, thinks we're underrating the Pop Century Resort:

> I can't believe you don't like Pop Century. (1) It's far superior to the All-Stars but the same price. (2) There's a lake at a Value resort and a view of fireworks. (3) The courtyards have Twister games, neat pools, and a Goofy "surprise fountain" for little children. (4) The memorabilia is interesting to us over 18 years old. (5) I love the gift shop,

food court, and bar combo. The shrimp lo mein is the best bargain and among the best food anywhere. (6) There are frozen Cokes in the refillable-mug section. (7) Bus transportation is better than anywhere else, including Grand Floridian! (8)You can rent surrey bikes. (9) The rooms have real soap instead of the All-Stars' yucky, globby stuff. (10) The layout is more convenient to the food court. (11) I never hear construction noise, and the noise from neighbors is not worse than anywhere else. (12) Where else do the cast members do the shag to oldies?

Don't know what it is about Pop Century fans, but they seem to have a propensity for making lists—take this Waukee, Iowa, family:

We loved Pop Century Resort; it was perfect for our family: (1) It was cheap enough that we had plenty of money left over for other fun things at Disney. (2) The shrimp lo mein was one of the most awesome fast-food items we've had at Disney. (3) Although the rooms are a little small and the lighting isn't the best, the resort is affordable enough that without tax two rooms at the Pop Century are in the same price range as one room at other resorts. (4) It's not far from any park at Disney, nor from Downtown Disney. (5) The combo food court–shopping area really works: My grandparents can eat breakfast in the food court while my brother, sister, parents, and I shop. (6) Food is actually pretty affordable for Disney. (7) Great pools that are not too far from our rooms. (8) You can request a room on the first floor, near the parking lot. They were really accommodating when we explained that I had to have a rather heavy oxygen tank brought to our room, so it would be easier on us to stay on the first floor. (9) Check-in takes probably the least amount of time that I have ever seen at a Disney resort.

But a Springfield, Illinois, father of three gives Pop Century a mixed review:

We wanted something different from All-Star Movies (two stays in the previous three years), so we gave Pop Century a shot. Believe the noise complaints—they're true. It's like the walls were made of papier-mâché, and we were staying in a block of rooms reserved for some sort of hillbilly family reunion. Although the bus service was great and the pool (and splash pools) were nice for a Value resort, we'll be back at All-Star Movies the next time around.

From a Kentucky family of four:

The Pop Century food court seemed to run out of ice early in the evening, and they'd shut down drink dispensers early. There were still lots of people up late coming back from the parks, and it created huge bottlenecks for drinks.

And, finally, a reader named Melanie (who didn't mention where she was from) had the following experience:

We decided to stay at the Pop Century. I called them directly to ask a few questions so I would be prepared when I called Disney reservations. I told the person who answered that I had heard the hotel was noisy. She said, "The hotel is not noisy, just the kids who stay here." HA!

GOOD (AND NOT-SO-GOOD) ROOMS AT POP CENTURY RESORT Guest rooms don't have private patios or balconies. If you bring a lawn chair, however, you can sit on the railed walkway that serves as the guest-room access corridor on each floor. The best rooms for both view and convenience are the lake-view rooms in Buildings 4 and 5, representing the 1960s. These rooms are subject to noise from neighboring Victory Way and Osceola Parkway; through the end of 2012, they're also subject to construction noise from work on the new Art of Animation Resort across the lake. A safer short-term bet, though with a less compelling view, would be east-facing rooms in the same building, that is, rooms facing the registration and food-court building. Next-best choices would be the east-facing rooms of Building 3 in the 1950s, and of Building 6 in the 1970s. Avoid south-facing rooms in 1980s Building 7 and 1990s Building 8. Both are echo chambers for noise from nearby Osceola Parkway. Finally, so-called "preferred" rooms at Pop Century, which are closer to the main pool and lobby, cost about $15–$20 more than others. They're definitely closer, but they probably save only 5–10 minutes of walking per day and probably subject you to more noise from guests walking past your room. We don't think these rooms are worth the extra cost.

Disney's Art of Animation Resort

Opened in May 2012, Disney's Art of Animation is a Value resort across Hour Glass Lake from Pop Century. It was originally designed to be part of Pop Century and represent the years 1900–1949, but recessions and an abundance of hotel capacity prevented Disney from ever completing construction. When the time came for a new Value resort, Disney switched the theme to its animated movies, which still fit in well with the pop-culture motif across the lake.

Like Pop Century, Art of Animation consists of four-story buildings and exterior-facing rooms, a series of themed swimming pools, and a food court. However, most of Animation's accommodations are suites similar to those at Disney's All-Star Resorts. All told, there are 864 standard rooms and 1,120 suites. Some of the buildings feature interior hallways to the guest rooms instead of the exterior walkways found at Disney's other Value resorts. Free public Wi-Fi is available.

Art of Animation's suites are around 565 square feet, the result of combining two value rooms into one suite. Each suite has a master bedroom, a living room, two full bathrooms, and a kitchenette with mini-fridge, microwave, and coffeemaker. Sleeping accommodations include a queen bed in the bedroom, a sleeper sofa, and a living-room table that converts into a full-size bed. The bedroom and living room have flat-screen TVs.

Slightly larger than rooms at other Value resorts, standard rooms are 277 square feet and include one king or two double beds, a flat-screen TV, a mini-fridge, and a table and chairs.

The resort's theme incorporates characters from four Disney films: *Cars, Finding Nemo, The Lion King,* and *The Little Mermaid.* All but the *Mermaid*-themed rooms are suites. As at Pop Century, large, colorful icons are placed in the middle of each group of buildings; here, though, they represent the films' characters rather than pop-culture touchstones. An interesting departure from the other Value resorts is the outside paint schemes: Rather than using pastels, Disney has decorated the exteriors with giant murals stretching the length of each structure. The *Cars* buildings, for example, each display a four-story panoramic vista of the American desert, with the movie's character icons in the middle, while the *Lion King* buildings capture a single verdant jungle scene. It's a great idea.

Three of the four sets of themed buildings have pools; the *Lion King* complex has a playground instead. Like the other Value resorts, Art of Animation has a central building—here called Animation Hall—for check-in and bus transportation; it also holds the resort's food court, Landscape of Flavors; a gift shop; and a video-game arcade.

Speaking of check-in, the wall behind the front desk is a dazzling rainbow of colors from floor to ceiling. In sharp contrast to the faded paints and photos at, say, the All-Stars, Art of Animation's backlight displays and wall art are bright and vibrant and should stand up well to Florida's weather.

INDEPENDENT HOTELS OF THE DOWNTOWN DISNEY RESORT AREA

THE SEVEN HOTELS OF THE DOWNTOWN DISNEY RESORT AREA (DDRA) were created in the days when Disney had far fewer of its own resorts. The hotels—the **Best Western Lake Buena Vista Resort Hotel,** the **Buena Vista Palace Hotel & Spa, DoubleTree Guest Suites,** the **Hilton in the Walt Disney World Resort,** the **Holiday Inn in the Walt Disney World Resort, Royal Plaza,** and **Wyndham Lake Buena Vista Resort**—are chain-style hotels with minimal or nonexistent theming, though the Buena Vista Palace, especially, is pretty upscale. All were hit hard by the recession, and several of the larger properties shifted their focus to convention and business travelers.

AMENITIES AT DOWNTOWN DISNEY RESORT AREA HOTELS					
HOTEL	CHILDREN'S PROGRAMS	DINING	KID-FRIENDLY	POOL(S)	RECREATION
Best Western LBV Resort	None	★★½	★★★	★★½	★★
Buena Vista Palace	★★★★	★★★★	★★★½	★★★½	★★★★
DoubleTree Guest Suites	None	★★	★★★	★★½	★★½
Hilton WDW Resort	None	★★½	★★½	★★★	★★½
Holiday Inn WDW Resort	None	★★	★★	★★★	★★
Royal Plaza	★★½	★★	★★½	★★½	★★★
Wyndham LBV Resort	★★½	★★½	★★★	★★★	★★★

The main advantage to staying in the DDRA is being in Disney World and proximal to Downtown Disney. Guests at the Hilton, Wyndham Lake Buena Vista Resort, Buena Vista Palace, and Holiday Inn are an easy 5- to 15-minute walk from the Marketplace on the east side of Downtown Disney. Guests at the Royal Plaza, Best Western Lake Buena Vista, and DoubleTree Guest Suites are about

10 minutes farther by foot. Disney transportation can be accessed at Downtown Disney, though the Disney buses take a notoriously long time to leave due to the number of stops throughout the shopping and entertainment complex. Although all DDRA hotels offer shuttle buses to the theme parks, the service is provided by private contractors and is somewhat inferior to Disney transportation in frequency of service, number of buses, and hours of operation. Get firm details in advance about shuttle service from any DDRA hotel you're considering. All these hotels are easily accessible by car and are only marginally farther from the Disney parks than several of the Disney resorts (and DDRA hotels are quite close to Typhoon Lagoon water park).

All DDRA hotels try to appeal to families, even the business and meeting hotels. Some have pool complexes that rival those at any Disney resort, whereas others offer a food court or all-suite rooms. A few sponsor Disney-character meals and organized children's activities; all have counters for buying Disney tickets, and most have Disney gift shops.

A Difficult Value Proposition

To update this section, we stayed at every DDRA hotel in 2011 and 2012. With the exception of the Buena Vista Palace, the Hilton, and perhaps the Holiday Inn, we find it difficult to recommend any of these hotels. The rooms at many, such as the Wyndham and Best Western, are in need of refurbishment. Further, for much of the year there's little price difference between these rooms and those at Disney's Value resorts, especially when Disney offers discounts.

Speaking of prices, all of the DDRA resorts tack on daily charges for self-parking or Internet access, or a cockamamy "resort fee." These fees add $7–$28 per night to your stay, plus tax.

ADDITIONAL FEES AT THE DDRA RESORTS				
HOTEL	SELF-PARKING	RESORT FEE	INTERNET	TOTAL PER DAY
BEST WESTERN LBV RESORT	Free	$7	Free	$7
BUENA VISTA PALACE	Free	$17	$10	$27
DOUBLETREE GUEST SUITES	$10	None	$10	$20
HILTON WDW RESORT	$12	None	$10	$22
HOLIDAY INN WDW RESORT	$10	None	Free	$10
ROYAL PLAZA	$10	$8	$10	$28
WYNDHAM LBV RESORT	$12	$16	N/A	$28

Heaven knows we think Disney's Deluxe resorts are overpriced, but it's hard to see how any of the DDRA properties can compete with the value proposition of Disney's inexpensive hotels, which offer free airport transportation, better bus service, free parking, and extra time at the theme parks. We suspect that most readers who choose the DDRA resorts do so either because they've earned enough "rewards points" at the chain to qualify for a free stay or the Disney resorts are sold out. We'd be hard-pressed to think of another reason to stay at these hotels, especially if we had a car.

Descriptions of each DDRA resort follow. Also take a peek at the combined website for the DDRA hotels at **downtowndisneyhotels .com**. Finally, check the comparative chart on page 196.

Best Western Lake Buena Vista Resort Hotel ★★★

2000 Hotel Plaza Blvd.
☎ 407-828-2424 or
800-348-3765
lakebuenavista
  resorthotel.com

THE 18-STORY, 325-ROOM Best Western Lake Buena Vista has relatively few of the extras common to most other DDRA properties. The rooms are starting to become dated, and we think they're in need of refurbishment. Parking is a hike from many rooms, and to get to them you pass through hallways and areas that could use a good scrubbing with hot water and soap. The most surprising thing was the attitude of general indifference from several of the staff when we needed help checking in.

A breakfast buffet and dinner service of American fare are available in the Trader's Island Grill, while the Parakeet Café offers sandwiches and snacks. The poolside Flamingo Cove Lounge provides its own menu of pub standards as well as alcoholic refreshment. The pool is small though pleasantly landscaped, and there's a kiddie pool as well. Other amenities include a fitness room and game room. Although there are no organized children's programs, the resort can arrange child care.

Buena Vista Palace Hotel & Spa ★★★½

1900 E. Buena Vista Dr.
Lake Buena Vista
☎ 407-827-2727 or
866-397-6516
buenavistapalace.com

IN THE DOWNTOWN DISNEY RESORT AREA, the Buena Vista Palace is upscale and convenient. Surrounded by an artificial lake and plenty of palms, the spacious pool area contains three heated pools, the largest of which is partially covered (nice for when you need a little shade); a whirlpool and sauna; a basketball court; and a sand volleyball court. Plus, a pool concierge will fetch your favorite magazine or fruity drink. On Sunday, the Watercress Café hosts a character brunch ($22 for adults and $10 for children). The 897 guest rooms are posh and spacious; each comes with desk, coffeemaker, hair dryer, satellite TV with pay-per-view movies, iron and board, and mini-fridge. There are also 117 suites. In-room babysitting is available through All About Kids (see page 351). One lighted tennis court, a European-style spa offering 60 services, a fitness center, an arcade, a playground, and a beauty salon round out amenities. Two restaurants and a mini-market are on-site. And if you aren't wiped out after time in the parks, consider dropping by the Lobby Lounge or the full-menu sports bar for a nightcap. *Note:* All these amenities and services come at a price—a $17-per-night resort fee will be added to your bill.

DoubleTree Guest Suites ★★★½

2305 Hotel Plaza Blvd.
☎ 407-934-1000
doubletreeguestsuites.com

THIS GIANT WHITE BUNKER of a hotel is the only all-suite establishment on Disney World property. What DoubleTree Guest Suites lacks in atmosphere and creative attributes, it makes up for in convenience and comfort. Within walking distance of Downtown Disney, the 229 suites are spacious for a family, although the decor is startling, with no apparent theme. No rooms have balconies, though ground floors offer patios.

Amenities include a safe, hair dryer, refrigerator, microwave, coffeepot, fold-out bed, and two TVs (bedroom and living room).

Children will enjoy the kids' check-in desk, the complimentary chocolate-chip cookie, and the small playground. The heated pool, children's pool, and whirlpool spa are moderate in size; a minus is that traffic noise from Interstate 4 can faintly be heard from the pool deck. The tiny fitness center (more like a fitness closet), pool table, four tennis courts, and outdoor bar are adjacent to the pool. High-speed Internet and a business center in the lobby (includes fax, printer, two computers, and copier) are convenient for those on working holidays. The Market (open 7 a.m.–midnight) offers groceries, drinks, ice cream, and sundaes for those late-night munchies; the EverGreen Cafe serves breakfast, lunch, and dinner. Babysitting service is available.

Hilton in the Walt Disney World Resort ★★★★

THE HILTON IS THE ONLY DDRA HOTEL offering Disney's Extra Magic Hours program to its guests. Although the rooms are becoming dated, they're comfortable and nicer than most others in the DDRA.

1751 Hotel Plaza Blvd.
☎ 407-827-4000
hilton-wdwv.com

On-site dining includes Covington Mill Restaurant, offering American sandwiches and pasta; Andiamo, an Italian bistro; and Benihana, a Japanese steakhouse and sushi bar (the last two are reviewed in Part Ten, Dining in and around Walt Disney World). Covington Mill hosts a Disney-character breakfast on Sundays. The two pools are matched with a children's "spray pool" and a 24-hour fitness center. An exercise room and a game room are available, as is a 24-hour market. Babysitting is available, but there are no organized children's programs.

A Denver family of five found the Hilton's shuttle service lacking:

> Transportation from the Hilton, provided by a company called Mears, was unreliable. They did a better job of getting guests back to the hotel from the park than getting them to the park from the hotel. Shuttles from the hotel were randomly timed and went repeatedly to the same parks—skipping others and leaving guests to wait for up to an hour.

Holiday Inn in the Walt Disney World Resort ★★★½

CLOSED DUE TO HURRICANE DAMAGE in 2004, the Holiday Inn finally reopened in February 2010 after a $35 million renovation. The layout remains the same, with tower rooms grouped around an atrium and wing rooms overlooking the pool. The feel of

1805 Hotel Plaza Blvd.
☎ 407-828-8888
or 888-465-4329
hiorlando.com

the hotel is modern and contemporary yet relaxed and comfortable. Downtown Disney is just a short walk away.

The totally upgraded rooms feature pillow-top beds with triple sheeting and firm or soft pillows. Each room has a 32-inch flat-screen HDTV and free high-speed Internet. The bathrooms are clean and well designed—the nicest in any DDRA resort. Amenities include granite countertops and showerheads with a choice of comfort sprays.

The Palm Breezes Restaurant and Bar serves breakfast, lunch, and dinner at reasonable prices. A breakfast buffet is available, as well as à la carte items. The Grab n Go Outlet in the lobby offers quick snacks and sandwiches. Other amenities include a large and well-kept zero-entry pool, along with a Jacuzzi in the pool area. A separate entrance brings you into the convention center, ballroom, and meeting room areas, with a business center nearby.

Royal Plaza ★★★½ (tower rooms); ★★★ (garden rooms)

1905 Hotel Plaza Blvd.
☎ 407-828-2828 or
800-248-7890
royalplaza.com

WE LIKE THE ROYAL PLAZA quite a bit, but it has to be one of the most star-crossed hotels we've ever seen. One owner had to sell the place as part of a divorce settlement in the late 1990s. Then it remained closed for years after it was damaged by two different hurricanes in 2004. Later it was foreclosed upon. The new owners, B Hotels and Resorts, announced a complete overhaul in mid-2012, to be completed in late 2013. The hotel will remain open during the renovation, which promises to give the property a decidedly upscale yet family-friendly feel.

As for the current decor, it's stylish, with muted blues prevailing in standard rooms and vibrant yellows, rich reds, and warm wood tones dominating in tower rooms. Bathroom space in the standard rooms is on the small side, while tower rooms have more than enough elbow room. Each room has a small sitting area, a desk, and high-speed Internet. Soft goods, including towels, curtains, and pillow-top mattresses, are upgrades from previous versions.

The Giraffe Café serves American breakfast, lunch, and dinner; the attached Giraffe Lounge is the main hotel bar, though Sips is open seasonally poolside. The pool itself is comfortable and pleasant, though not flashy or particularly kid-oriented. Four lighted tennis courts and an exercise room are available.

On the first and second floors of the garden wing, ask for Rooms X49–X64. Tower rooms X02–X07, X14, X16, and X17 are also good. The other rooms on the first two levels are subject to more foot traffic, noise from public spaces, and guests entering and leaving the main building. While they'll have less traffic, tower rooms not listed previously can pick up noise from the elevators and ice machines on each floor. Discounts are often available at **mousesavers.com.**

Wyndham Lake Buena Vista Resort ★★★½

1850 Hotel Plaza Blvd.
☎ 407-828-4444
or 800-624-4109
wyndhamlakebuena
vista.com

ACROSS FROM DOWNTOWN DISNEY, the Wyndham Lake Buena Vista was formerly known as Regal Sun Resort. The lobby is bright and airy and check-in service friendly. Rooms are larger than most and have in-room refrigerators. Pool-facing rooms in the hotel's wings have exterior hallways that overlook the pool and center courtyard; these hallways can be noisy during summer months. Elevators are available, but they're unusually slow—it's probably faster to walk to the second and third floors, assuming you're up for the exercise. Disney-character breakfasts take place on Tuesdays, Thursdays, and Saturdays at LakeView Restaurant.

CAMPING AT WALT DISNEY WORLD

FORT WILDERNESS RESORT & CAMPGROUND is a spacious area for tent and RV camping. Fully equipped, air-conditioned prefabricated log cabins are also available for rent.

STRENGTHS	WEAKNESSES
Informality	Isolated location
Children's play areas	Complicated bus service
Best recreational options at WDW	Confusing campground layout
Special day and evening programs	Lack of privacy
Campsite amenities	Very limited on-site dining options
Shower and toilet facilities	Limited automobile traffic
Hoop-Dee-Doo Musical Revue show	Crowding at beaches and pools
Convenient self-parking	Small baths in cabins
Off-site dining via boat at Magic Kingdom	Extreme distance to store and restaurant facilities from many campsites

Tent/Pop-Up campsites provide water, electricity, and cable TV and run from $46 to $93 depending on season. **Full Hook-Up** campsites have all of the previous amenities, accommodate large RVs, and run from $61 to $108 per night. **Preferred Hook-Up** campsites for tents and RVs add sewer connections and run from $66 to $115 per night. **Premium** campsites add an extra-large concrete parking pad and run from $76 to $125 a night.

All sites are level and provide picnic tables, waste containers, grills, and high-speed Internet (additional fee). Fires are prohibited except in the grills. Pets are permitted in some Premium and Preferred loops.

Campsites are arranged on loops accessible from one of three main roads. There are 28 loops, with Loops 100–2000 for tent and RV campers, and Loops 2100–2800 offering cabins at $275–$450 per night. RV sites are roomy by eastern-U.S. standards, with the Premium and Full Hook-Up campsites able to accommodate RVs more than 45 feet long, but tent campers will probably feel a bit cramped. (Note that tent stakes cannot be put into the concrete at the Premium sites.) On any given day, 90% or more of campers are RV-ers.

Fort Wilderness Resort & Campground arguably offers the most recreational facilities and activities of any Disney resort. Among them are two video arcades; nightly campfire programs; Disney movies; a dinner theater; two swimming pools; a beach; walking paths; bike, boat, canoe, golf-cart, and water-ski rentals; a petting zoo; horseback riding; hayrides; fishing; and tennis, basketball, and volleyball courts. There are two convenience stores, a restaurant, and a tavern. Comfort stations with toilets, showers, pay phones, ice machine, and laundry facilities are within walking distance of all campsites.

Access to the Magic Kingdom is by boat from Fort Wilderness Landing and to Epcot by bus, with a transfer at the Transportation and Ticket Center (TTC) to the Epcot monorail. Boat service may be suspended during thunderstorms, so if it's raining or looks like it's about to, Disney will provide buses. An alternate route to the Magic

Fort Wilderness Resort & Campground

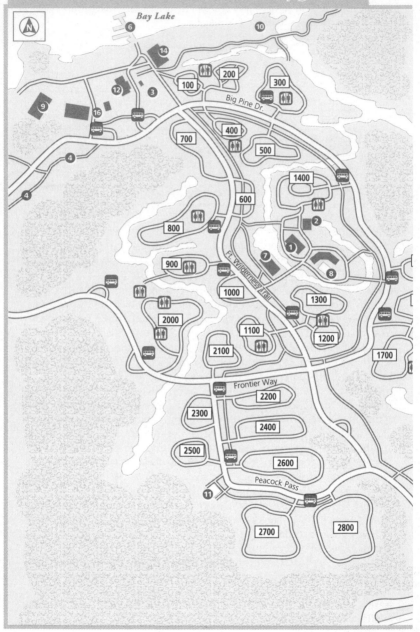

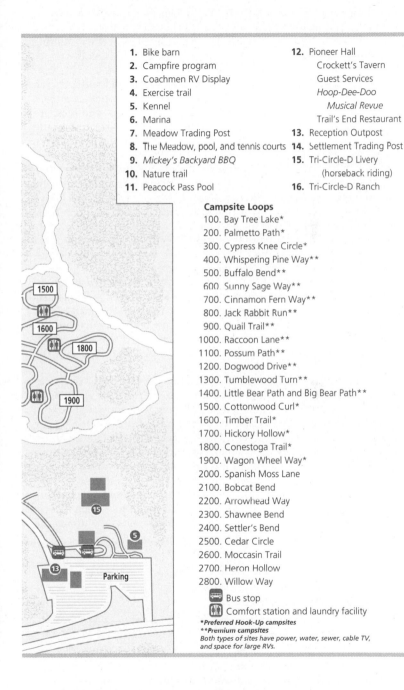

1. Bike barn
2. Campfire program
3. Coachmen RV Display
4. Exercise trail
5. Kennel
6. Marina
7. Meadow Trading Post
8. The Meadow, pool, and tennis courts
9. *Mickey's Backyard BBQ*
10. Nature trail
11. Peacock Pass Pool

12. Pioneer Hall
    Crockett's Tavern
    Guest Services
    Hoop-Dee-Doo
      Musical Revue
    Trail's End Restaurant
13. Reception Outpost
14. Settlement Trading Post
15. Tri-Circle-D Livery
      (horseback riding)
16. Tri-Circle-D Ranch

Campsite Loops
100. Bay Tree Lake*
200. Palmetto Path*
300. Cypress Knee Circle*
400. Whispering Pine Way**
500. Buffalo Bend**
600. Sunny Sage Way**
700. Cinnamon Fern Way**
800. Jack Rabbit Run**
900. Quail Trail**
1000. Raccoon Lane**
1100. Possum Path**
1200. Dogwood Drive**
1300. Tumblewood Turn**
1400. Little Bear Path and Big Bear Path**
1500. Cottonwood Curl*
1600. Timber Trail*
1700. Hickory Hollow*
1800. Conestoga Trail*
1900. Wagon Wheel Way*
2000. Spanish Moss Lane
2100. Bobcat Bend
2200. Arrowhead Way
2300. Shawnee Bend
2400. Settler's Bend
2500. Cedar Circle
2600. Moccasin Trail
2700. Heron Hollow
2800. Willow Way

Bus stop
Comfort station and laundry facility
Preferred Hook-Up campsites
Premium campsites
Both types of sites have power, water, sewer, cable TV,
and space for large RVs.

Kingdom is by internal bus to the TTC, then by monorail or ferry to the park. Transportation to all other Disney destinations is by bus. Motor traffic within the campground is permitted only when entering or exiting. Get around within the campground by bus, golf cart, or bike, the latter two available for rent.

For tent and RV campers, there's a fairly stark trade-off between sites convenient to pools, restaurant, trading posts, and other amenities, and those that are most scenic, shady, and quiet. RV-ers who prefer to be near guest services, the marina, the beach, and the restaurant and tavern should go for Loops 100, 200, 700, and 400 (in that order). Loops near the campground's secondary facility area with pool, trading post, bike and golf-cart rentals, and campfire program are 1400, 1300, 600, 1000, and 1500, in order of preference. If you're looking for a tranquil, scenic setting among mature trees, we recommend Loops 1800, 1900, 1700, and 1600, in that order, and the backside sites on the 700 loop. The best loop of all, and the only one to offer both a lovely setting and proximity to key amenities, is Loop 300. The best loops for tents and pop-up campers are 1500 and 2000, with 1500 being nearest a pool, a convenience store, and the campfire program.

With the exception of Loops 1800 and 1900, avoid sites within 40 yards of the loop entrance. These sites are almost always flanked by one of the main traffic arteries within Fort Wilderness. Further, sites on the outside of the loop are almost always preferable to those in the center of the loop. RV-ers should be forewarned that all sites are back-ins and that although most sites will accommodate large rigs, the loop access roads are pretty tight and narrow.

Rental cabins offer a double bed and two bunk beds in the only bedroom, augmented by a Murphy bed (pulls down from the wall) in the living room. There's one rather small bathroom with shower and tub.

The prefab log cabins (classified as Moderate resorts in the Disney hierarchy) are warm and homey, but the stem-to-stern interior wood paneling and smallish windows make for pretty dark accommodations at night. Neither the lighting fixtures provided nor the wattage of their bulbs are up to the job of lighting the cabins once the sun goes down.

All cabins offer air-conditioning, color televisions with DVD players and/or VCRs, fully equipped kitchens, and dining tables. Housekeeping is provided daily. Most readers are crazy about the cabins. Some representative comments follow.

A Wappingers Falls, New York, family writes:

We stayed at Fort Wilderness in a cabin because

- *We wanted a separate bedroom area.*
- *We wanted a kitchen.*
- *Our kids are very lively and the cabins were apart from each other so we wouldn't disturb other guests.*
- *We thought the kids might meet other children to play with.*

The cabins worked out just right for us. Although the kids didn't meet any other children to play with, they had a ball chasing the little lizards and frogs, kicking around pinecones, sitting on the deck to eat ice pops, and sleeping in bunk beds. We went to the campfire twice (we brought our own marshmallows and sticks).

From a Downers Grove, Illinois, family of five:

While we all enjoyed the cabins and resort, we spent a LOT of time waiting for buses and ferries, more than we remember waiting a few years ago. They've recently made some changes to the bus routes, and while we liked having a stop at the Meadow area, there was always a long wait for a purple bus to take us back to the cabin when returning from the parks (from both depots). They need a separate bus route just for the cabins.

A Rochester, New York, dad agrees:

If you're staying at Fort Wilderness Cabins, we would highly recommend getting a golf cart. There's a lot going on at the campground itself, and the bus system can be cumbersome. Also, our 3-year-old wasn't always up for the walk—just getting from our cabin to the main loop was a lot for her.

This Mechanicsville, Virginia, mom concurs on the golf cart:

Loved the cabins at Fort Wilderness. The location was perfect with the boat transportation to the Magic Kingdom. A golf cart is a must, though it drives the daily cost to stay at the cabins up into the Deluxe price range.

A mother of two from Albuquerque, New Mexico, offers this:

We stayed in a cabin and liked having all the space and the full kitchen. I was very disappointed in the pools, however. I had expected a Disney resort pool, and instead there were only two relatively small concrete holes in the ground. The pool nearest our cabin (still a quarter-mile away!) never even had a lifeguard. I had hoped to be able to send the kids to swim when we needed some time to ourselves, but with the distance and lack of lifeguards, there was no way to do that.

Though the cabins are especially popular, RV and tent campers love Fort Wilderness, too. First from a Marietta, Georgia, multi-generational family:

I do wish you'd stress more the advantages of Fort Wilderness. With sites for any size/type of camper/tent, it's FAR more affordable than any hotel inside the park. Additionally, you could theoretically (although not likely) prepare all of your own meals. We usually had breakfast, packed snacks, and returned for lunch and dinner every day. We were able to decrease our food budget and devote it to a character lunch and tea at the Grand Floridian.

A mother of two from Mechanicsville, Virginia, puts Fort Wilderness on a pedestal as well:

The most important thing—the family time. This is the only resort where you're encouraged to go outside and play! Your kids are not stuck in a hotel room, at the pool, or at an arcade. You can bike, swim, visit two arcades, hike the nature trail, ride a horse, rent a boat, play volleyball, go to the beach, attend a free character sing-along and marshmallow roast followed by a classic Disney movie that many younger families never knew existed (we were introduced to Snowball Express and Robin Hood), enjoy multiple playgrounds, play tennis, rent a golf cart, walk around at night to see the festively decorated campsites (many Disney-themed), take a romantic carriage ride, take your first pony ride, find the armadillo that lives next to the bathrooms in the 1300 loop, and see a wild turkey. Don't forget the fishing or the great view of the fireworks from the beach or the up-close water light parade.

With all of this stuff, much of it free or very affordable, who needs the parks? We visited last June and never set foot in a park.

Bus service at Fort Wilderness leaves a lot to be desired, so much in fact that we wouldn't stay there unless we had our own car. To go anywhere you first have to catch an internal bus that makes many, many stops. If your destination is outside Fort Wilderness, you then have to transfer to a second bus. To complicate things, buses serving destinations outside the campground depart from two locations, the Reception Outpost and Pioneer Hall. This means that you have to keep track of which destinations each transfer center serves.

Finally, if you rent a cabin or camp in a tent or RV, particularly in fall or spring, keep abreast of local weather conditions. This is not the place to be in a tornado.

A number of independent campgrounds are within 30 miles of Walt Disney World. Here are the closest:

Kissimmee-Orlando KOA ☎ 407-396-2400; **kissorlandokoa.com.**
96 licensed sites; about 6 miles to Walt Disney World US 192 (Maingate) entrance

Sherwood Forest RV Resort ☎ 800-548-9981; **rvonthego.com.**
531 licensed sites; about 4 miles to Walt Disney World US 192 (Maingate) entrance

Tropical Palms Resort ☎ 407-396-4595; **tropicalpalmsrv.com.**
365 licensed sites; about 2.5 miles to Walt Disney World US 192 (Maingate) entrance

HOW *to* EVALUATE *a* WALT DISNEY WORLD TRAVEL PACKAGE

HUNDREDS OF WALT DISNEY WORLD PACKAGE VACATIONS are offered each year. Some are created by the Walt Disney Travel Company, others by airlines, independent travel agents, and wholesalers. Almost all include lodging at or near Disney World plus theme park admissions. Packages offered by airlines include air transportation.

Prices vary seasonally; mid-March through Easter, summer, and holiday periods are the most expensive. Off-season, forget packages: There are plenty of empty rooms, and you can negotiate great discounts, especially at non-Disney properties. Similarly, airfares and rental cars are cheaper off-peak.

Almost all package ads are headlined "5 Days at Walt Disney World from $645" (or such). The key word is *from:* The rock-bottom price includes the least desirable hotels; if you want better or more-convenient digs, you'll pay more—often much more.

Packages offer a wide selection of hotels. Some, like the Disney resorts, are very dependable. Others run the gamut of quality.

Checking two or three independent sources is best. Also, before you book, ask how old the hotel is and when the guest rooms were last refurbished. Locate the hotel on a map to verify its proximity to Disney World. If you won't have a car, make sure that the hotel has an adequate shuttle service.

Packages with non-Disney lodging are much less expensive. But guests at Disney-owned properties get Extra Magic Hours privileges, free parking, and access to the Disney transportation system. These privileges (except Extra Magic Hours for Hilton guests) don't apply to guests at the Downtown Disney Resort Area hotels (Best Western Lake Buena Vista Resort Hotel, Buena Vista Palace Hotel & Spa, DoubleTree Guest Suites, Hilton in the Walt Disney World Resort, Holiday Inn in the Walt Disney World Resort, Royal Plaza, and Wyndham Lake Buena Vista Resort).

Packages should be a win–win proposition for both buyer and seller. The buyer makes only one phone call and deals with one sales-person to set up the whole vacation (transportation, rental car, admissions, lodging, meals, and even golf and tennis). The seller, likewise, deals with the buyer only once. Some packagers also buy airfares in bulk on contract, not unlike a broker playing the com-modities market. By buying a large number of airfares in advance, the packager saves significantly over posted fares. The practice is also applied to hotel rooms. Because selling packages is efficient and the packager often can buy package components in bulk at discount, the seller's savings in operating expenses are sometimes passed on to the buyer, making the package not only convenient but also an exceptional value.

In practice, however, the seller may realize all the economies and pass on no savings. Packages sometimes are loaded with extras that cost the packager almost nothing but run the package's price sky-high. Savings passed on to customers are still somewhere in Fantasyland.

Choose a package that includes features you're sure to use. You'll pay for all of them whether you use them or not. If price is more important than convenience, call around to see what the package would cost if you booked its components on your own. If the package price is less than the à la carte cost, the package is a good deal. If costs are about equal, the package probably is worth it for the convenience. Much of the time, however, you'll find you save significant-ly by buying the components individually.

unofficial **TIP**
If you consider a non-Disney hotel, check its quality as reported in independent travel references such as the *Unofficial Guides,* AAA directories, *Forbes* guides, or *Frommer's* guides.

CUT TO THE CHASE

WHEN YOU PHONE THE DISNEY reserva-tions number (☎ 407-W-DISNEY), you'll be subjected to about 5–10 minutes of recorded questions (many just fish-ing for nonrelevant personal information). If you actually want to make a reservation, slog on through. (When the question "Have you called us before?" pops up, answer "yes" unless you want to be corralled into an additional survey for "first-timers.") If you just want to ask a question or speak to a live person, touch 0 to bypass all the recorded stuff.

WALT DISNEY TRAVEL COMPANY MAGIC YOUR WAY PACKAGES

DISNEY'S MAGIC YOUR WAY travel-package program mirrors the admission-ticket program of the same name. Here's how it works: You begin with a base package room and tickets. Tickets can be customized to match the number of days you intend to tour the theme parks, and range in length from 1 to 10 days. As with theme park admissions, the package program offers strong financial incentives to book a longer stay. "The longer you play, the less you pay per day," is the way Disney puts it, borrowing a page from Sam Walton's concept of the universe. A one-day adult Base Ticket (with tax) costs $90.53, whereas if you buy a seven-day ticket, the average cost per day drops to $40.62. You can purchase options to add on to your Base Tickets, such as hopping between theme parks; visiting water parks, DisneyQuest, or ESPN Wide World of Sports; and buying your way out of an expiration date for any unused ticket features.

With Magic Your Way packages, you can avoid paying for features you don't intend to use. You need not purchase a package with theme park tickets for the entire length of your stay. With Magic Your Way you can choose to purchase as many days of admission as you intend to use. On a one-week vacation, for example, you might want to spend only five days in the Disney parks, saving a day each for Universal Studios and SeaWorld. With Magic Your Way you can buy only five days of admission on a seven-day package. Likewise, if you don't normally park-hop, you can now purchase multiday admissions that don't include the park-hopping feature. If you don't use all your admissions, you can opt for the No Expiration add-on, and the unused days will be good forever. Best of all, you can buy the various add-ons at any time during your vacation.

Before we deluge you with a boxcar of options and add-ons, let's define the basic components of Disney's Magic Your Way package:

- One or more nights of accommodations at your choice of any Disney resort. Rates vary with lodging choice: The Grand Floridian is the most expensive, and the All-Star, Pop Century, and Art of Animation resorts are the least expensive.
- Magic Your Way Base Ticket for the number of days you tour the theme parks
- Unlimited use of the Disney transportation system
- Free theme park parking.
- Official Walt Disney Travel Company luggage tag (one per person)

Magic Your Way Dining Plans

Disney offers dining plans to accompany its Magic Your Way ticket system. They're available to all Disney resort guests except those staying at the Swan, the Dolphin, the hotels of the Downtown Disney Resort Area, and Shades of Green, none of which are Disney-owned or -operated. Guests must also purchase a Magic Your Way package from Disney (not through an online reseller), have Annual Passes, or be members of the Disney Vacation Club (DVC) to participate in the plan. Except for DVC members, a three-night minimum stay is typically also required. Overall cost is determined by the number of nights you stay at a Disney resort.

As a family of five from Waldron, Michigan, learned, you must purchase a Disney package vacation to be eligible for a dining plan:

> We read through the Unofficial Guide *and noticed that it said not to book a package during slow season. We were overwhelmed with the decisions that we had to make, so we booked the resort first, then the tickets, and then we wanted the dining plan. Well, they wouldn't add the dining plan on because we had already booked everything.*

MAGIC YOUR WAY PLUS DINING PLAN This plan provides, for each member of your group, for each night of your stay, one counter-service meal, one full-service meal, and one snack at participating Disney dining locations and restaurants, including room service at some Disney resorts (type "Disney Dining Plan Locations 2013" into your favorite Internet search engine to find sites with the entire list). The plan also includes one refillable drink mug per person, per package, but it can be filled only at Disney resort counter-service restaurants. For guests age 10 and up, the price is $56.94 during summer and holidays and $55.59 per night during off-peak times; for guests ages 3–9, the price is $18.16 per night during summer and holidays and $17.16 off-peak, tax included. Children younger than age 3 eat free from an adult's plate.

The counter-service meal includes a main course (sandwich, dinner salad, pizza, or the like), dessert, and nonalcoholic drink, or a complete combo meal (a main course and a side dish—think burger and fries), dessert, and nonalcoholic drink, including tax. The full-service sit-down meals include a main course, dessert, nonalcoholic drink, and tax. If you're dining at a buffet, the full-service meal includes the buffet, a nonalcoholic drink, and tax. The snack includes items normally sold from carts or small stands throughout the parks and resorts: ice cream, popcorn, soft drinks, fruit, chips, apple juice, and the like.

For instance, if you're staying for three nights, each member of your party will be credited with three counter-service meals, three full-service meals, and three snacks. All those meals will be put into an individual "meal account" for each person in your group. Meals in your account can be used on any combination of days, so you're not required to eat every meal every day. Thus, you can skip a full-service meal one day and have two on another day.

Disney's top-of-the-line restaurants (dubbed "Disney Signature" restaurants in the plan), along with Cinderella's Royal Table, all the dinner shows, regular room service, and in-room pizza delivery, count as two full-service meals. If you dine at one of these locations, two full-service meals will be deducted from your account for each person dining.

In addition to the preceding, the dining plan comes with several other important rules:

Disney Lodging for Less

Mary Waring, *Webmaster at* **MouseSavers** (mousesavers.com; *see page 32), knows more about Disney hotel packages than anyone on the planet. Here are her money-saving suggestions.*

BOOK "ROOM-ONLY." It's frequently a better deal to book a room-only reservation instead of buying a vacation package. Disney likes to sell vacation packages because they're easy and profitable. When you buy a package, you're typically paying a premium for convenience. You can often save money by putting together your own package. It's not hard: Just book room-only at a resort and buy passes, meals, and extras separately.

Disney now prices its standard packages at the same rates as if you had purchased individual components separately at full price. However, what Disney doesn't tell you is that components can usually be purchased separately at a discount—and those discounts are not reflected in the brochure prices of Disney's packages. (Sometimes you can get special-offer packages that do include discounts; see below.)

Keep in mind that Disney's packages often include extras you're unlikely to use. Also, packages require a $200 deposit and full payment 45 days in advance; plus, they have stringent change and cancellation policies. Generally, booking room-only requires a deposit of one night's room rate with the remainder due at check-in. Your reservation can be changed or canceled for any reason until five days before check-in.

Whether you decide to book a Disney vacation package or create your own, there are a number of ways to save:

- **USE DISCOUNT CODES TO REDUCE YOUR ROOM-ONLY OR PACKAGE RATE.** Disney uses these codes to push unsold rooms at certain times of year and occasionally offers packages that include resort discounts or value-added features. Check a website like mousesavers.com to learn about codes that may be available for your vacation dates. Some codes are available to anyone, while others are just for Florida residents, Annual Pass holders, and so on.
    Discount codes aren't always available for every hotel or every date, and they typically don't appear until two to six months in

- Everyone staying in the same resort room must participate in the plan.
- Children ages 3–9 must order from the kids' menu, if available. This rule is occasionally not enforced at Disney's counter-service restaurants, enabling older children to order from the regular (adult) menu.
- Alcoholic beverages and some bottled nonalcoholic drinks are not included in the plan.
- A full-service meal can be breakfast, lunch, or dinner. The greatest savings occur when you use your full-service-meal allocations for dinner.

advance. The good news is that you can usually apply a code to an existing room-only reservation. Simply call the Disney Reservation Center at ☎ 407-W-DISNEY (934-7639) (or contact a Disney-savvy travel agent) and ask whether any rooms are available at your preferred hotel for your preferred dates using the code.

- **BE FLEXIBLE.** Buying a room or package with a discount code is a little like shopping for clothes at a discount store: If you wear size XX-small or XXXX-large, or you like green when everyone else is wearing pink, you're a lot more likely to score a bargain. Likewise, resort discounts are available only when Disney has excess rooms. You're more likely to get a discount during less-popular times (such as value season) and at larger or less-popular resorts. Animal Kingdom Lodge and Disney's Old Key West Resort seem to have discounted rooms available more often than the other resorts do.

- **BE PERSISTENT.** This is the most important tip. Disney allots a certain number of rooms to each discount. Once the discounted rooms are gone, you won't get that rate unless someone cancels. Fortunately, people change and cancel reservations all the time. If you can't get your preferred dates or hotel with one discount code, try another one (if available) or keep calling back first thing in the morning to check for cancellations—the system resets overnight, and any reservations with unpaid deposits are automatically released for resale.

- **SPRING FOR "FREE DINING."** One of Disney's biggest package bargains, this promotion has been offered since 2005 during less-busy times of year. When you purchase a full-price room and full-price tickets for each person in the room, you get a Disney Dining Plan for your entire stay. The trick is to choose one of Disney's cheapest rooms and enjoy all that free food: If you choose a Value resort, you get the Quick-Service Dining Plan; if you choose a Moderate resort, you get the standard Disney Dining Plan. You can also book a Value resort and pay the difference to upgrade from Quick-Service to the regular plan. Free Dining is always offered in late August and throughout September (a slow time due to heat, humidity, hurricane season, and kids going back to school); sometimes it's offered at other times during the year.

- The meal plan expires at midnight **on the day you check out** of the Disney resort. **Unused meals are nonrefundable.**
- The dining plan is occasionally unavailable when using certain room-only discounts.

QUICK-SERVICE DINING PLAN This plan includes meals, snacks, and nonalcoholic drinks at most counter-service eateries in Walt Disney World. The cost (including tax) is $37.58 per day for guests age 10 and up, $14.32 per day for kids ages 3–9. The plan includes two counter-service meals and one snack per day, in addition to one refillable drink mug per person, per package (eligible for refills only at counter-service locations in your Disney resort). The economics of the plan are difficult to justify unless you're drinking gallons of soda or coffee to offset Disney's inflated prices.

MAGIC YOUR WAY DELUXE DINING PLAN This plan offers a choice of full- or counter-service meals for three meals a day at any participating restaurant. In addition to the three meals a day, the plan also includes two snacks per day and a refillable drink mug. The Deluxe Plan costs $102.27 for adults and $28.91 for children for each night of your stay during peak season, and $99.97 per adult and $26.84 per child off-peak (prices include tax). Cranking it up another notch, there are even more extravagant dining plans associated with Magic Your Way Premium and Platinum packages, both described a little later.

In addition to food, all the plans include deal sweeteners such as a free round of miniature golf, a certificate for a 5 x 10–inch print from Disney's PhotoPass, a sort of two-for-one certificate for use of Sea Raycers watercraft, a "commemorative" luggage tag, and such.

Disney ceaselessly tinkers with the dining plans' rules, meal definitions, and participating restaurants. For example, it's possible (though not documented) to exchange a sit-down-meal credit for a counter-service meal, although doing this even once can negate any savings you get from using a plan in the first place.

THINGS TO CONSIDER WHEN EVALUATING THE PLUS DINING PLAN The dining plan has been one of the most requested of Disney's package add-ons since its introduction; families report that their favorite aspect is the peace of mind that comes from knowing their meals are paid for ahead of time, rather than having to keep track of a budget while they're in the parks. Families also enjoy the communal aspect of sitting down together for a full meal, without having to worry about who's picking up the food or doing the dishes.

Costwise, however, it's difficult for many families to justify using the plan. If you prefer to always eat at counter-service restaurants, you'll be better off with the Quick-Service plan. You should also avoid the Plus plan if you've got finicky eaters, you're visiting during holidays or summer, or you can't get reservations at your first- or second-choice sit-down restaurants. In addition, if you've got children age 10 and up, be sure that they can eat an adult-sized dinner at a sit-down restaurant every night; if not, you'd probably come out ahead just paying for everyone's meals without the plan.

*un*official **TIP**
The Plus dining plan costs $56.94/day for adults and $18.16/day for kids ages 3–9 (peak season). Combining two of your table-service options, you can eat one meal higher on the hog at Disney's more upscale eateries.

If you opt for the plan, skipping a single full-service meal during a visit of five or fewer days can mean the difference between saving and losing money. In our experience, having a scheduled sit-down meal for every day of a weeklong vacation can be mentally exhausting, especially for kids and teens. One option might be to schedule a meal at a Disney Signature restaurant, which requires two full-service credits, and have no scheduled sit-down meal on another night in the middle of your trip, allowing everyone to decide on the spot if they're up for something formal.

As already noted, many of the most popular restaurants are fully booked as soon as their reservation windows open. If you're still interested in the dining plan, book your restaurants as soon as possible, typically 90–180 days before you visit. Then decide whether the plan makes economic sense. For more on Advance Reservations—the term is Disney-speak (hence the capital letters) and not exactly what it implies—see Part Ten.

If you're making reservations to eat at Disney hotels other than your own, a car allows you to easily access all the participating restaurants. When you use the Disney transportation system, dining at the various resorts can be a logistical nightmare. Those without a car may want to weigh the immediate services of a taxi—typically $10–$12 each way across Disney property, versus a 50- to 75-minute trip on Disney transportation each way.

For an in-depth discussion of the various plans, including number crunching (with algebra, even!), visit **touringplans.com** (click "Dining" on the home page, then "Disney Dining Plan").

Readers who tried the Disney dining plan had varying experiences, but frustration seems to be a common refrain. A St. Louis family of three comments:

> We purchased the dining plan and would never do it again. Far too expensive, far too much food, and then you have to tip on top of the expense. Additionally, table-service meals were hard to use for us, reservations hard to obtain. Much easier to purchase what you want, where and when you want. Food is a "gotcha" at Disney, but the dining plan proved to be a poor choice for us.

A New Hampshire family concurs:

> Dining plans are NOT for us. Keeping track of the meals, figuring out what you can and can't buy, and rushing around on the last day trying to use up what's left is just too stressful. We'd rather just buy what we want, when and where we want it.

A reader from The Woodlands, Texas, laments that the plan has altered the focus of her vacation:

> For me, the Disney Dining Plan has taken a lot of the fun out of going to Disney World. Now, dining for each day must be planned months in advance unless one is to eat just hot dogs, pizza, and other walk-up items. I want to have fun. I don't want to be locked into a tight schedule, always worrying about where we need to be when it's time to eat, and I don't want to eat when I'm not hungry just because I have a reservation somewhere. As heretical as it may sound, I'm actually less inclined to go to WDW now.

A Toronto family says gratuities add up:

> Families should be warned that tips in Disney table-service restaurants can add up quickly in a week. The tip for our party of five at Le Cellier alone was $45.

A father of two from Danbury, Connecticut, however, gives the plan a thumbs-up:

We had the dining plan, so all of our meals were on the property. We were pleasantly surprised at both the service and quality of food. The entertainment during the meals, especially at the 50's Prime Time Cafe and Whispering Canyon, really added to the meals.

And a Belmont, Massachusetts, dad is a fan of the Quick Service Dining Plan:

If you intend to eat Disney food, the counter-service meal plan is a good option. We didn't want the full plan because the restaurants seemed overpriced, and the necessity of reservations months in advance seemed crazy and a bar to flexibility. You get two counter-service meals (entree/combo, dessert, drink) and two snacks (food item or drink) per person per day as part of the plan, and even though kids' meals are cheaper, there's no distinction when you order—kids can order [more-expensive] adult meals.

A mom from Orland Park, Illinois, comments on the difficulty of getting Advance Reservations:

I purchased the dining plan for this trip and must say I will never do it again. It's impossible to get table reservations anywhere good—the restaurants that are available are available for a reason. We found ourselves taking whatever was open and were unhappy with every sit-down meal we had, except for lunch at Liberty Tree Tavern. I don't enjoy planning my day exclusively around eating at a certain restaurant at a certain time, but that is what you must do six months in advance if you want to eat at a good sit-down restaurant in Disney. That is ridiculous.

As this reader from San Jose, California, explains, guests who are not on the dining plan need to know how the plan has affected obtaining Advance Reservations:

The Disney Dining Plan has almost eliminated any chance of spontaneity when visiting any of the sit-down restaurants. When planning 90 days out for the off-season, I was told by the Disney rep to make all my reservations then because the restaurants are booked by people on the dining plan. In fact, I was told that most of the sit-down restaurants don't even take walk-ins anymore. Sure enough, even though I was well over 90 days away from my vacation, a lot of my restaurant choices were unavailable. I had to rearrange my entire schedule to fit the open slots at the restaurants I didn't want to miss.

A family from Wilmington, Massachusetts, shared this:

We found the basic dining plan somewhat limiting, and it provided way too much food. Dessert came with both the counter-service and table-service meals. If you tell the server that you don't want dessert at either of these meals, he or she will try hard to convince you that you are making a life-altering mistake because you aren't getting your money's worth. I understand that the dining plan is a great value for many people, but we aren't a "strap on the feedbag" kind of group.

Pesky Technicalities and Administrative Problems

Readers report experiencing a host of problems with both understanding and using the Disney Dining Plan. A family of four from Mount Pleasant, South Carolina, observes:

> The impact of the Disney Dining Plan was amazing. It created longer lines at the registers because they were programmed to ring up each thing individually, or so it seemed. For instance, for a Mickey Meal, the checkout guy had to push buttons for chicken nuggets, applesauce, milk, and fries—not just one button for the entire meal. It took the guy about 7 minutes to figure it and process us. Meanwhile, people stood there gazing up at the menu trying to figure out how they could fit their meals into their dining plans. It was incredibly frustrating for those of us who paid with cash. One mother did say that with her three boys, she was spending more time in the restaurants eating than on the rides, so hey—maybe it isn't such a bad thing after all!

A woman from Atco, New Jersey, warns:

> The Disney Dining Plan doesn't always work for snacks, even though vendors have signs posted stating they accept the card. We were told many times, "Oh, the machine isn't working today."

Many readers report that Disney cast members are more knowledgeable about the dining plan these days. A Washington, D.C.–area couple writes:

> The kinks are worked out, and everyone at the parks we talked to seemed to get it, but we still spent $40 or more at most sit-down dinners on drinks and tips.

Many families purchase the dining plan without understanding how limited the menu choices are for kids age 9 and under. First from a West Chester, Ohio, mom:

> All three of our girls are under 9 and had to choose "Kid's Picks" wherever offered. We didn't come across anything like burgers, hot dogs, or pizza the whole time we were there. They were so sick of mac-and-cheese and chicken nuggets after day two that going out to eat wasn't that exciting for them. We were given a hard time when we asked about substituting something different, and we were turned down 50% of the time. On our last day, a sympathetic employee told us we could get any counter-service food we wanted and just not tell the cashier that it was for a child (apparently, for counter service, Disney doesn't keep track of who it's for).

A Pittsburgh mother of three recounts a similar experience:

> I have one negative comment about the Disney Dining Plan: There was no variety at all in the children's menus at the table-service and counter-service restaurants. The amount of food they get is also very small—OK for my 4-year-old but not for my 9-year-old, who ended up eating off my plate; otherwise, I would've had to buy something extra to fill him up. Plus, we went to Pizzafari in Animal Kingdom, and there was NO PIZZA on the dining plan's kids' menu.

From a Midwestern reader:

We could almost relate our dining experience to that of a person who receives food stamps—very restricted and always at the mercy of someone else for food selection.

From a Wisconsin father of two:

On the last day of our visit, we were still learning about acceptable substitutions. For example, at breakfast you can have two drinks (coffee and OJ). You can also do this for lunch, but you have to give up your dessert. In the 90-degree heat, I would've gladly given up my fattening dessert to have a bottle of cold water to bring along.

The dining plan left a family of five from Nashville, Tennessee, similarly dazed and confused:

What was annoying was the inconsistency. You can get a 16-ounce chocolate milk on the kids' plan, but only 8 ounces of white milk at many places. At Earl of Sandwich, you can get 16 ounces of either kind. A pint of milk would count as a snack (price $1.52), but they wouldn't count a quart of milk (price $1.79) because it wasn't a single serving. However, in Animal Kingdom, my husband bought a water-bottle holder (price $3.75) and used a snack credit.

Reader Tips for Getting the Most Out of the Plan

A mom from Radford, Virginia, shares the following tip:

Warn people to eat lunch early if they have dinner reservations before 7 p.m. Disney doesn't skimp on food—if you eat a late lunch (where, by the way, they feed you the same ungodly amount of food), you WILL NOT be hungry for dinner.

A mom from Brick Township, New Jersey, found that the dining plan streamlined her touring:

We truly enjoyed our Disney trip, and this time we purchased the Dining Plan. This was great for the kids because we did a character-dining experience every day. This helped us in the parks because we didn't have to wait in line to see the characters. Instead, we got all of our autographs during our meals.

A Saskatoon, Saskatchewan, father of three says you have to watch vendors like a hawk:

We had a problem with a vendor who charged us meal service for each of the ice-cream bars we purchased. This became evident at our final sit-down meal, when we didn't have any meal vouchers left. Check the receipts after every purchase!

Finally, a Brooklyn family of four warns that the plan doesn't always eliminate the need to use cash:

We ate dinner at Jiko—we each ordered a salad and a main course and skipped dessert—and while the food was good, we ended up leaving annoyed by Disney's cheapness. We were on the dining plan and were told that our meals would be two credits each. This translates to *about $80 apiece. Fine. But when the check came, we were not only charged the two credits each, we were charged $12 each for the salads. Plus tips. I asked why we had been charged extra, and I was told that dessert was included in the meal plan but not first courses. It's pretty annoying to pay $80 per person for a one-course dinner and STILL have to put down more cash.*

Magic Your Way Premium Package

With the Magic Your Way Premium Package you get lodging; Magic Your Way Base Tickets; breakfast, lunch, and dinner (including two snacks per day plus gratuities and one refillable resort drink mug per person), character meals, and dinner shows; unlimited golf, tennis, fishing excursions, and water sports; select theme park tours; Cirque du Soleil show tickets; unlimited use of child-care facilities—everything you can think of except for alcoholic beverages. The Premium Package costs $189 for adults and $139 for kids ages 3–9 (tax included) in addition to the cost of the standard Magic Your Way package. *Note:* A minimum three-night stay at Walt Disney World is required in order to book the Premium Package.

> *unofficial* **TIP**
> For all Magic Your Way plans, everyone in the room must be on the same package and ticket options. All tickets must be used within 14 days of first use, unless the No Expiration option is purchased.

Disney, needless to say, has built a nice profit into every component of the Magic Your Way Premium Package. If you don't use all the features and didn't purchase the No Expiration option on your tickets, Disney makes out even better.

PLATINUM PACKAGE The favorite of high rollers who want to prepay for everything they might desire while at Walt Disney World, the Platinum Package gets you lodging; Base Tickets; breakfast, lunch, and dinner in full-service restaurants; unlimited golf, tennis, boating, and recreation; unlimited dinner shows and character breakfasts; primo Cirque du Soleil seats; private in-room child care; unlimited use of child-care facilities; personalized itinerary planning; the Richard Petty Ride-Along Experience; a spa treatment; a fireworks cruise; admission to select tours; reserved seating for *Fantasmic!*; and (here's the kicker) nightly turndown service! Everything you can think of, in other words, except alcoholic beverages. Per diem prices (including tax) for the Platinum Package are $249 for adults and $180 for kids in addition to the cost of a standard Magic Your Way package—but anyone who buys this package doesn't give a Goofy fart what the prices are anyway. As with the Premium Package, a minimum three-night stay is required.

NUMBER CRUNCHING

COMPARING A MAGIC YOUR WAY PACKAGE with purchasing the package components separately is a breeze.

1. Pick a Disney resort and decide how many nights you want to stay.

2. Next, work out a rough plan of what you want to do and see so you can determine the admission passes you'll require.

3. When you're ready, call the Disney Reservation Center (DRC) at ☎ 407-W-DISNEY and price a Magic Your Way package with tax for your selected resort

and dates. The package will include both admissions and lodging. It's also a good idea to get a quote from a Disney-savvy travel agent (see page 111).

4. Now, to calculate the costs of buying your accommodations and admission passes separately, call the DRC a second time. This time, price a room-only rate for the same resort and dates. Be sure to ask about the availability of any special deals. While you're still on the line, obtain the prices, with tax, for the admissions you require. If you're not sure which of the various admission options will best serve you, consult our free Ticket Calculator at **touringplans.com.**

5. Add the room-only rates and the admission prices. Compare this sum to the DRC quote for the Magic Your Way package.

6. Check for deals and discounts for packages, room-only rates, and admission.

When you upgrade to a Magic Your Way Premium Package, you load the plan with so many features that it's extremely difficult to price them individually. For a rough comparison, price the plan of your choice using the previous steps. To complete the picture, work up a dining budget, excluding alcohol. Add your estimated dining costs to the room-only quote and admissions quote, and compare this to the price of the plan.

THROW ME A LINE!

IF YOU BUY A PACKAGE FROM DISNEY, don't expect reservation-ists to offer suggestions or help you sort out your options. Generally, they respond only to your specific questions, ducking queries that require an opinion. A reader from North Riverside, Illinois, complains:

> I have received various pieces of literature from WDW, and it's very confusing to figure out everything. My wife made two telephone calls, and the representatives from WDW were very courteous. However, they only answered the questions posed and were not eager to give advice on what might be most cost-effective. I feel a person could spend 8 hours on the phone with WDW reps and not have any more input than you get from reading the literature.

If you can't get the information you need from Disney, contact a good travel agent. Chances are the agent can help you weigh your options.

PACKAGES FROM A DIFFERENT PERSPECTIVE

WE'VE ALWAYS EVALUATED PACKAGES from a dollars-and-cents point of view, paying scant attention to other considerations such as time, economy, and convenience. A reader from Westchester County, New York, finally got our attention, writing:

> I fully understand your position not to recommend the Premium plans in your guide, because they're expensive. However, when one books six rooms, as I have, with guests ages 4–59, including a wife, grandchildren, children, sons- and daughters-in-law, and a nanny, the thought of trying to find out what way each family segment would like to go and then arranging for it on a daily basis is a scary scenario.

With the Premium Plan, they can go where they want, eat where they want, and Gramps and his roommate don't have the hassle.

A Mobile, Alabama, couple also liked the Premium Plan, although they had some reservations (pardon the pun) about dining:

While we had plenty of time to see and do things, had we been there for a week or less we probably would've been frustrated with how much time it took to eat three table-service meals a day, once you calculate the secondary time expense of traveling to the restaurant (which may or may not be in the park you're in at the moment). There was one time in particular where we finished eating lunch and basically had to go check in for dinner almost immediately!

Purchasing Room-Only Plus Passes versus a Package

Sue Pisaturo of **Small World Vacations** (**smallworldvacations.com**), a travel agency that specializes in Disney, also thinks there's more involved in a package-purchase decision than money.

Should you purchase a Walt Disney World package or buy all the components of the package separately? There's no single answer to this confusing question.

A Walt Disney World package is like a store-bought prepackaged kids' meal, the kind with the little compartments filled with meat, cheese, crackers, drink, and dessert: You just grab the package and go. It's easy, and if it's on sale, why bother doing it yourself? If it's not on sale, it still may be worth the extra money for convenience.

Purchasing the components of your vacation separately is like buying each of the meal's ingredients, cutting them up into neat piles and packaging the lunch yourself. Is it worth the extra time and effort to do it this way? Will you save money if you do it this way?

You have two budgets to balance when you plan your Disney World vacation: time and money. Satisfying both is your ultimate goal. Research and planning are paramount to realizing your Disney vacation dreams. Create your touring plans before making a final decision with regard to the number of days and options on your theme park passes. Create your dining itinerary (along with Advance Reservations, if possible) to determine if Disney's dining plan can save you some money.

HOTELS *outside* WALT DISNEY WORLD

SELECTING AND BOOKING A HOTEL OUTSIDE WALT DISNEY WORLD

LODGING COSTS OUTSIDE DISNEY WORLD vary incredibly. If you shop around, you can find a clean motel with a pool within 5–20 minutes of the World for as low as $40 a night. Because of hot competition, discounts abound, particularly for AAA and AARP members.

Continued on page 224

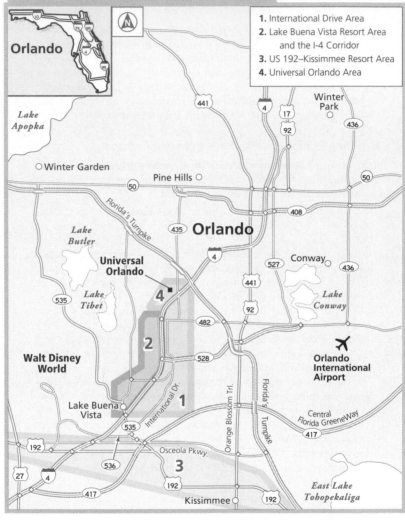

Hotel Concentrations around Walt Disney World

1. International Drive Area
2. Lake Buena Vista Resort Area and the I-4 Corridor
3. US 192–Kissimmee Resort Area
4. Universal Orlando Area

International Drive & Universal Areas

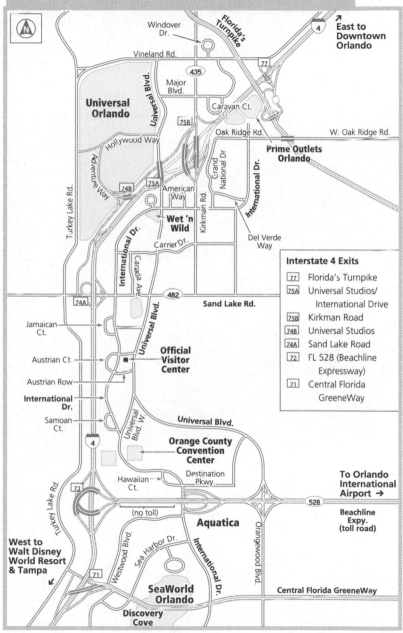

Lake Buena Vista Resort Area & the I-4 Corridor

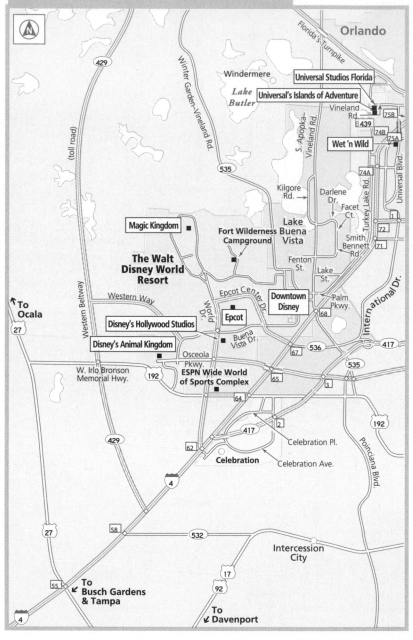

US 192–Kissimmee Resort Area

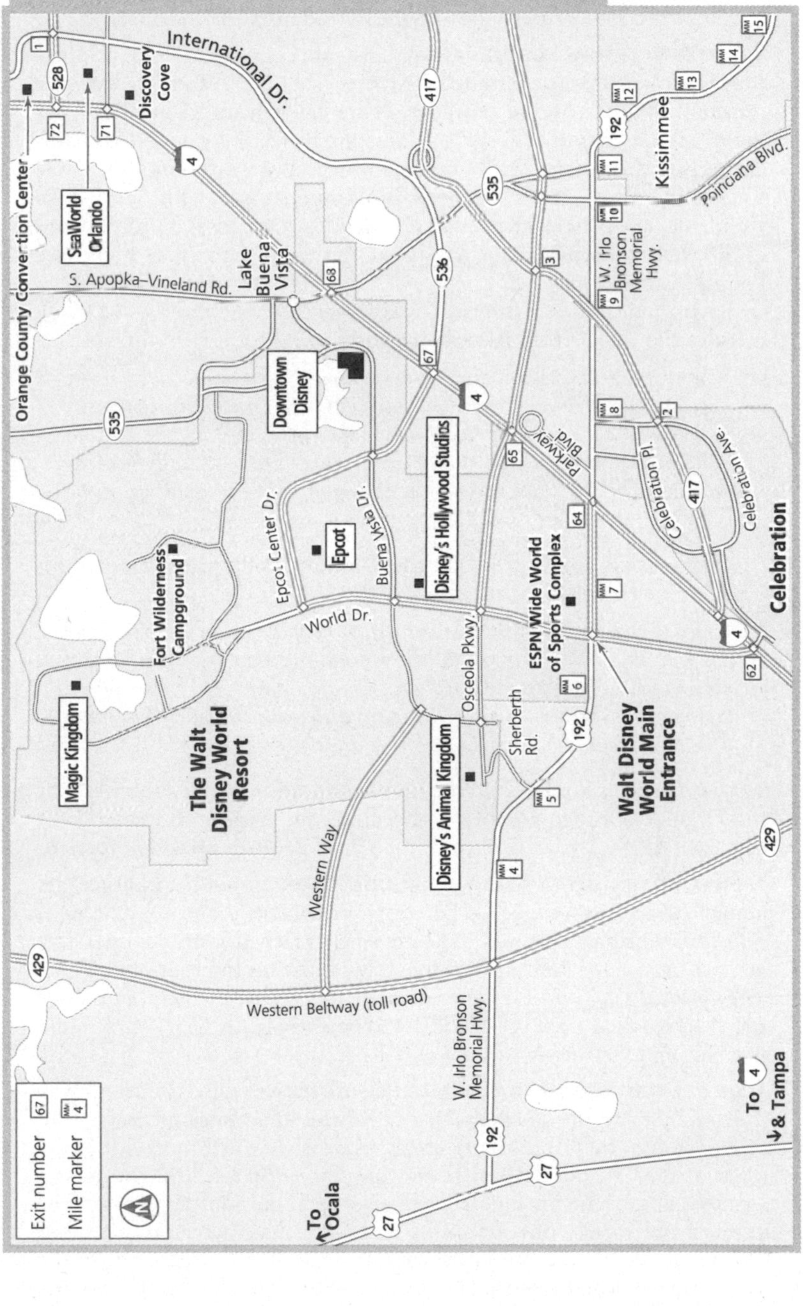

Continued from page 219

There are four primary out-of-the-World areas to consider:

1. INTERNATIONAL DRIVE AREA This area, about 15–25 minutes northeast of the World, parallels I-4 on its eastern side and offers a wide selection of hotels and restaurants. Prices range from $56 to $400 per night. The chief drawbacks of this area are its terribly congested roads, countless traffic signals, and inadequate access to westbound I-4. While International's biggest bottleneck is its intersection with Sand Lake Road, the mile between Kirkman and Sand Lake roads is almost always gridlocked. We provide tips for avoiding this traffic in Part Eight (see "Sneak Routes," page 387).

Regarding traffic on International Drive (known locally as I-Drive), a convention-goer from Islip, New York, weighed in with this:

> *When I visited Disney World with my family last summer, we wasted huge chunks of time in traffic on International Drive. Our hotel was in the section between the big McDonald's [at Sand Lake Road] and Wet 'n Wild [at Universal Boulevard]. There are practically no left-turn lanes in this section, so anyone turning left can hold up traffic for a long time.*

Traffic aside, a man from Ottawa, Ontario, sings the praises of his I-Drive experience:

> *International Drive is the place to stay when going to Disney. Your description of this location failed to point out that there are several discount stores, boutiques, restaurants, mini-putts, and other entertainment facilities, all within walking distance of remarkably inexpensive accommodations and a short drive away from WDW.*

I-Drive hotels are listed in the *Official Vacation Guide,* published by the Orlando–Orange County Convention and Visitors Bureau. For a copy, call ☎ 800-972-3304 or 407-363-5872, or see **orlandoinfo.com.**

2. LAKE BUENA VISTA AND THE I-4 CORRIDOR A number of hotels are along FL 535 and west of I-4 between Disney World and I-4's intersection with Florida's Turnpike. They're easily reached from the interstate and are near many restaurants, including those on International Drive. The *Official Vacation Guide* (see above) lists most of them. For some traffic-avoidance tips, see "The I-4 Blues" (page 371) in Part Eight, Arriving and Getting Around.

3. US 192 (IRLO BRONSON MEMORIAL HIGHWAY) This is the highway to Kissimmee to the south of Disney World. In addition to large, full-service hotels, there are many small, privately owned motels that are often a good value. Several dozen properties on US 192 are nearer Disney parks than are more expensive hotels inside the World. The number and variety of restaurants on US 192 has increased markedly, compensating for the area's primary shortcoming. Locally, US 192 is called Irlo Bronson Memorial Highway. The section to the west of I-4 and the Disney "Maingate" is designated Irlo Bronson Memorial Highway West, while the section from I-4 running southeast toward Kissimmee is Irlo Bronson Memorial Highway East.

A senior citizen from Brookfield, Connecticut, was pleased with lodging in the US 192–Kissimmee area:

> We were amazed to find that from our cheaper and superior accommodations in Kissimmee it took only 5 minutes longer to reach the park turnstiles than it did from the Disney accommodations.

Hotels on US 192 and in Kissimmee are listed in the *Kissimmee Visitor's Guide*. Order a copy by calling ☎ 800-327-9159, or view it online at **floridakiss.com**.

4. UNIVERSAL STUDIOS AREA In the triangular area bordered by I-4 on the southeast, Vineland Road on the north, and Turkey Lake Road on the west are Universal Orlando and the hotels most convenient to it. Running north–south through the middle of the triangle is Kirkman Road, which connects to I-4. On the east side of Kirkman are a number of independent hotels and restaurants. Universal hotels, theme parks, and CityWalk are west of Kirkman. Traffic in this area is not nearly as congested as on nearby International Drive, and there are good interstate connections in both directions.

DRIVING TIME TO THE PARKS FOR VISITORS LODGING OUTSIDE WALT DISNEY WORLD

OUR HOTEL INFORMATION CHART on pages 261–279 shows the commuting time to the Disney theme parks from each hotel listed. Those commuting times represent an average of several test runs. Your actual time may be shorter or longer depending on traffic, road construction (if any), and delays at traffic signals.

The commuting times in our Hotel Information Chart show conclusively that distance from the theme parks is not necessarily the dominant factor in determining commuting times. Among those we list, the hotels on Major Boulevard opposite the Kirkman Road entrance to Universal Orlando, for example, are the most distant (in miles) from the Disney parks. But because they're only one traffic signal from easy access to I-4, commuting time to the parks is significantly less than for many closer hotels.

Note that times in the chart differ from those in the Door-to-Door Commuting Times chart in Part Eight. The door-to-door chart in Part Eight compares using the Disney transportation system and driving your own car *inside* Walt Disney World. These times include actual transportation time plus tram, monorail, or other connections required to get from the parking lots to the entrance turnstiles. The hotel chart's commuting times, by contrast, represent only the driving time to and from the parks, with no consideration for getting to and from the parking lot to the turnstiles.

Add to the commuting times in the Hotel Information Chart a few minutes for paying your parking fee and parking. Once you park at the Transportation and Ticket Center (Magic Kingdom parking lot), it takes 20–30 minutes more to reach the Magic Kingdom via monorail or ferry. To reach Epcot from its parking lot, add 7–10 minutes. At Disney's Hollywood Studios and Animal Kingdom, the lot-to-gate transit is 5–12 minutes. If you haven't purchased your theme park admission in advance, tack on another 10–20 minutes.

GOOD NEIGHBOR HOTELS

SOME HOTELS PAY DISNEY a marketing fee to display a "Good Neighbor" designation. Usually there is a ticket shop in the lobby that sells full-price Disney tickets. Other than that, the designation means nothing for the consumer. It doesn't guarantee quality—some Good Neighbor hotels are very nice, others not so much. Some are close to Walt Disney World, while others are quite far away. Disney requires Good Neighbor hotels to provide free shuttle service to Walt Disney World but prohibits them from offering shuttle service to Universal or SeaWorld.

HOTEL SHOPPING ON THE INTERNET: WELCOME TO THE WILD WEST

UNMATCHED AS AN EFFICIENT and timely distributor of information, the Internet has become the primary resource for travelers seeking to shop for and book their own air travel, hotels, rental cars, entertainment, and travel packages. It's by far the best direct-to-consumer distribution channel in history.

INTERNET ECONOMICS 101 The evolution of selling travel on the web has radically altered the way airlines, hotels, cruise lines, rental-car companies, and the like do business. Before the Internet, these entities depended on travel agents or direct contact with customers by phone. Transaction costs were high because companies were obligated to pay commissions and fund labor-intensive in-house reservations departments. With the advent of the Internet, inexpensive e-commerce transactions became possible: Airlines and rental-car companies began using their own websites to effectively cut travel agents out of the sales process. Hotels also developed websites but continued to depend on wholesalers and travel agents as well.

It didn't take long before independent websites sprang up that sold travel products from a wide assortment of suppliers, often at deep discounts. These sites, called **online travel agencies (OTAs),** include such familiar names as Travelocity, Orbitz, Priceline, Expedia, Hotels .com, and Hotwire. Those mentioned and others like them attract huge numbers of customers shopping for hotels.

OTAs AND THE MERCHANT MODEL In the beginning, hotels paid OTAs about the same commission that they paid travel agents, but then the OTAs began applying the thumbscrews, forcing hotels to make the transition from a simple commission model to what's called a *merchant model.* Under this model, hotels provide an OTA with a deeply discounted room rate that the OTA then marks up and sells. The difference between the marked-up price and the discounted rate paid to the hotel is the OTA's gross profit. If, for example, a hotel makes $120 rooms available to an OTA at a 33% discount, or $80, and the OTA sells the room at $110, the OTA's gross profit is $30 ($110 − $80).

The merchant model, originally devised for wholesalers and tour operators, has been around since long before the Internet. Wholesalers and tour operators, then and now, must commit to a certain volume of business, commit to guaranteed room allotments, pay deposits, and bundle the discounted rates with other travel services so that the actual hotel rate remains hidden within the bundle. This is known as *opaque pricing*. The merchant model costs the hotel two to three times the normal travel-agent commission—considered justifiable because the wholesalers and tour operators also promote the hotel through brochures, websites, trade shows, print ads, and events.

OTAs now demand the equivalent of a wholesale commission or higher but are subject to none of the requirements imposed on wholesalers and tour operators. For instance, they don't have to commit to a specified volume of sales or keep discounted room rates opaque. In return, hotels give up 20–50% of gross profit and are rewarded by having their rock-bottom rates plastered all over the Internet, with corresponding damage to their image and brand. (This last is why it's very rare to see a Disney hotel advertised on an OTA site at a price lower than what you can obtain from Disney itself.)

What's more, doing business with OTAs is very expensive for hotels. A hotel's cost of a multiday booking on its own website is $10–$12, including site hosting and analytics, marketing costs, and management fees. This is 10–20 times cheaper than the cost of the same booking through an OTA. Let's say a hotel sells a $100 room for six nights on its own website. Again, the booking would cost the hotel around $12, or $2 per night. If an OTA books the same room having secured it from the hotel at a 30% discount, the hotel receives $70 per night from the OTA. Thus the hotel's cost for the OTA booking is $30 per night, or $180 for six nights—15 times as costly as selling the room online with no middleman.

In the hotel industry, occupancy rates are important, but simply getting bodies into beds doesn't guarantee a profit. A more critical metric is *revenue per available room* (RevPAR). For a hotel full of guests booked through an OTA, RevPAR will be 20–50% lower than for the same number of guests who booked the hotel directly, either through the hotel's website or by phone.

It's no wonder, then, that hotels and OTAs have a love–hate relationship. Likewise, it's perfectly understandable that hotels want to maximize direct bookings through their own websites and minimize OTA bookings. Problem is, the better-known OTAs draw a lot more web traffic than a given hotel's (or even hotel chain's) website. So the challenge for the hotel becomes how to shift room-shoppers away from the OTAs and channel them to its website. A number of hotel corporations, including Choice, Hilton, Hyatt, InterContinental, Marriott, and Wyndham, have risen to that challenge by forming their own OTA called **Room Key** (**roomkey.com**). The participating chains hope that working together will generate enough visitor traffic to make Room Key competitive with the Expedias and Travelocities of the world.

MORE POWER TO THE SHOPPER Understanding the market dynamics we've described gives you a powerful tool for obtaining the best rates for the hotel of your choice. It's why we tell you to shop the web for the lowest price available and then call your travel agent or the hotel itself to ask if they can beat it. Any savvy reservationist knows that selling you the room directly will both cut the hotel's cost and improve gross margin. If the reservationist can't help you, ask to speak to his or her supervisor. (We've actually had to explain hotel economics to more than a few clueless reservation agents.)

As for travel agents, they have clout based on the volume of business they send to a particular hotel or chain and can usually negotiate a rate even lower than what you've found on the Internet. Even if the agent can't beat the price, he or she can often obtain upgrades, preferred views, free breakfasts, and other deal sweeteners. If you enjoy cybershopping, have at it, but hotel shopping on the Internet isn't as quick or convenient as handing the task to your travel agent. When we bump into a great deal on the web, we call our agent. Often she can beat the deal or improve on it, perhaps with an upgrade. *Reminder:* Except for special arrangements agreed to by you, the fee or commission due to your travel agent will be paid by the hotel.

THE SECRET The key to shopping on the Internet is, well, shopping. When we're really hungry for a deal, there are a number of sites that we always check out (see below):

OUR FAVORITE ONLINE HOTEL RESOURCES
mousesavers.com Best site for hotels in Disney World
dreamsunlimitedtravel.com Excellent for both Disney and non-Disney hotels
2000orlando-florida.com Comprehensive hotel site
valuetrips.com Specializes in budget accommodations
roomsaver.com Provides discount coupons for hotels
floridakiss.com Primarily US 192–Kissimmee area hotels
orlandoinfo.com Good info; not user-friendly for booking
orlandovacation.com Great rates for condos and home rentals

We scour these sites for unusually juicy hotel deals that meet our criteria (location, quality, price, amenities). If we find a hotel that fills the bill, we check it out at other websites and comparative travel search engines such as **Kayak** (**kayak.com**) and **Mobissimo** (**mobissimo.com**) to see who has the best rate. (As an aside, Kayak used to be purely a search engine but now sells travel products, raising the issue of whether products not sold by Kayak are equally likely to come up in a search. Mobissimo, on the other hand, only links potential buyers to provider websites.) Your initial shopping effort should take about 15–20 minutes, faster if you can zero in quickly on a particular hotel.

Next, armed with your insider knowledge of hotel economics, call the hotel or have your travel agent call. Start by asking about specials. If there are none, or if the hotel can't beat the best price you've found on the Internet, share your findings and ask if the hotel can do better. Sometimes you'll be asked for proof of the rate you've discovered online—to be prepared for this, go to the site and enter the dates of your stay, plus the rate you've found to make sure it's available. If it is, print the page with this information and have it handy for your travel agent or for when you call the hotel. (*Note:* Always call the hotel's local number, not its national reservations number.)

INDEPENDENT AND BOUTIQUE HOTEL DEALS While chain hotels worry about sales costs and profit margins, independent and so-called boutique hotels are concerned about discoverability—making themselves known to the traveling public. The market is huge and it's increasingly hard for these hotels to get noticed, especially when they're competing with major chains. Independent and boutique hotels work on the premise that if they can get you through the front door, you'll become a loyal customer. For these hotels, substantially discounting rates is part of their marketing plan to build a client base. Because such hotels get lost on the big OTA sites and on search engines like Kayak and Google, they've jumped on the flash-sale bandwagon. Offering almost irresistible rates on daily-coupon sites like **Groupon** and **LivingSocial,** the independents can get their product in front of thousands of potential guests.

These offers are very generous but also time-limited. If you're in the market, though, you'll be hard-pressed to find better deals. While an OTA such as Expedia generally obtains rooms at a 20–35% discount off the hotel's published rate, flash sites cut deals at an extra-deep discount. This allows their subscribers to bid on or secure coupons for rooms that are often as much as 50% lower than the hotel's standard rate, and that frequently include perks such as meals, free parking, waived resort fees, shopping vouchers, spa services, and entertainment. On Groupon's home page, click "Getaways" or just wait for Getaway coupons by e-mail as part of your free subscription. On LivingSocial you have to specifically subscribe to "Adventures" and "Escapes"; otherwise, you'll receive only non-travel-related offers.

ANOTHER WRINKLE Finally, a quick word about a recent trend: bidding sites. On these sites you enter the type of accommodation you desire and your travel dates, and hotels will bid for your reservation. Some sites require that you already have a confirmed booking from a hotel before you can bid. A variation is that you reserve a room at a particular hotel (including Disney hotels) for a set rate. If the rate drops subsequently, you get money back; if the rate goes up, your original rate is locked in.

Late 2011 and early 2012 saw the launch of TripAdvisor's **Tingo** (**tingo.com**), Silicon Valley–based **Guestmob** (**guestmob.com**), and Montreal-based **BackBid** (**backbid.com**), all claiming to be able to beat rates offered by hotel websites and OTAs.

Simply put, bidding sites work best when hotels are dumping inventory—something that almost never happens with Disney resorts and is rare among the better non-Disney properties. Two-star hotels can always be booked for two-star prices, so nobody bids on hotels with fewer than three stars.

IS IT WORTH IT? You might be asking yourself if it's worth all this effort to save a few bucks. Saving $10 on a room doesn't sound like a big deal, but if you're staying six nights that adds up to $60. Earlier we referred to unusually juicy deals, deep discounts predicated by who-knows-what circumstances that add up to big money. They're available every day, and with a little perseverance you'll find them—not often for Disney hotels, but for hotels that are just as good. Good hunting!

Two Other Discount Sources Worth Mentioning

1. ORLANDO MAGICARD Orlando Magicard is a discount program sponsored by Visit Orlando. Cardholders are eligible for discounts of 12–50% at about 50 hotels. The Magicard is also good for discounts at some area attractions, three dinner theaters, museums, performing-arts venues, restaurants, shops, and more. Valid for up to six persons, the card isn't available for larger groups or conventions.

To obtain a free Magicard and a list of participating hotels and attractions, call ☎ 800-643-9492 or 407-363-5872. On the web, go to **orlandoinfo.com/magicard;** the Magicard and accompanying brochure can be printed from a personal computer. If you miss getting one before you leave home, obtain one at the Convention and Visitors Bureau Information Center at 8723 International Drive. When you call for your Magicard, also request the *Official Vacation Guide.*

2. *FLORIDA ROOMSAVER* GUIDE This book of coupons for discounts at hotels statewide is free in many restaurants and motels on main highways leading to Florida. Because most travelers make reservations before leaving home, picking up the book en route doesn't help much. To view it online or sign up for a free monthly guide sent by e-mail, visit **roomsaver.com.** For a hard copy ($3 for handling, $5 if shipped to Canada), write to 13709 Progress Blvd., Box 14, Alachua, FL 32615, or call ☎ 800-222-3948 Monday–Friday, 8 a.m.–5 p.m. Eastern time.

CONDOMINIUMS AND VACATION HOMES

VACATION HOMES ARE FREESTANDING, while condominiums are essentially one- to three-bedroom accommodations in a larger building housing a number of similar units. Because condos tend to be part of large developments (frequently time-shares), amenities such as swimming pools, playgrounds, game arcades, and fitness centers often rival those found in the best hotels. Generally speaking, condo developments don't have restaurants, lounges, or spas. In a condo, if something goes wrong, there will be someone on hand to fix the problem. Vacation homes rented from a property-management company likewise will have someone to come to the rescue, though responsiveness tends to vary vastly from company to company. If you rent directly from an owner, correcting problems is often more difficult, particularly when the owner doesn't live in the same area as the rental home.

In a vacation home, all the amenities are contained in the home (though in planned developments there may be community amenities available as well). Depending on the specific home, you might find a small swimming pool, hot tub, two-car garage, family room, game room, and even a home theater. Features found in both condos and vacation homes include full kitchens, laundry rooms, TVs, DVD players/VCRs, and frequently stereos. Interestingly, though almost all freestanding vacation homes have private pools, very few have backyards. This means that, except for swimming, the kids are pretty much relegated to playing in the house.

Time-share condos are clones when it comes to furniture and decor, but single-owner condos and vacation homes are furnished and decorated in a style that reflects the taste of the owner. Vacation homes, usually one- to two-story houses in a subdivision, very rarely afford interesting views (though some overlook lakes or natural areas), while condos, especially the high-rise variety, sometimes offer exceptional ones.

The Price Is Nice

The best deals in lodging in the Walt Disney World area are vacation homes and single-owner condos. Prices range from about $65 a night for two-bedroom condos and town homes to $200–$500 a night for three- to seven-bedroom vacation homes. Forgetting about taxes to keep the comparison simple, let's compare renting a vacation home to staying at one of Disney's Value resorts. A family of two parents, two teens, and two grandparents would need three hotel rooms at Disney's Pop Century Resort. At the lowest rate obtainable, that would run you $82 per night, per room, or $246 total. Rooms are 260 square feet each, so you'd have a total of 780 square feet. Each room has a private bath and a television.

Renting at the same time of year from **All Star Vacation Homes** (no relation to Disney's All-Star Resorts), you can stay at a 2,053-square-foot, four-bedroom, three-bath vacation home with a private pool 3 miles from Walt Disney World for $269—not quite as economical as Disney's Value resorts, but plenty of value all the same: With four bedrooms, each of the teens can have his or her own room. Further, for the dates we checked, All Star Vacation Homes was running a special in which they threw in a free rental car with a one-week home rental.

But that's not all—the home comes with the following features and amenities: a big-screen TV with PlayStation, DVD player, and VCR (assorted games and DVDs available for complimentary checkout at the rental office); a CD player; a heatable private pool; five additional TVs (one in each bedroom and one in the family room); a fully equipped kitchen; a two-car garage; a hot tub; a laundry room with full-size washer and dryer; a fully furnished private patio; and a child-safety fence.

The home is in a community with a 24-hour gated entrance. At the community center are a large swimming pool; a whirlpool; tennis, volleyball, and half-court basketball courts; a children's playground; a gym and exercise room; a convenience store; and a 58-seat cinema.

One thing we like about All Star Vacation Homes is that its website (**allstarvacationhomes.com**) offers detailed information, including a dozen or more photos of each specific home. When you book, the home you've been looking at is the actual one you're reserving. (If you want to see how the home previously described is furnished, for instance, go to the home page, scroll down to "Select Code," and choose property code **2-8137 SP-WP** in the pull-down menu. You'll be taken to another page with a description of the home, a slide show, a floor plan, a virtual tour, and more.)

On the other hand, some vacation-home companies, like rental-car agencies, don't assign you a specific home until the day you arrive. These companies provide photos of a "typical home" instead of making information available on each of the individual homes in their inventory. In this case, you have to take the company's word that the typical home pictured is representative and that the home you'll be assigned will be just as nice.

How the Vacation-Home Market Works

In the Orlando–Walt Disney World area, there are more than 25,000 rental homes, including stand-alone homes, single-owner condos (that is, not time-shares), and town homes. The same area has about 114,000 hotel rooms. Almost all the rental homes are occupied by their owners for at least a week or two each year; the rest of the year, the owners make the homes available for rent. Some owners deal directly with renters, while others enlist the assistance of a property-management company.

Incredibly, about 700 property-management companies operate in the Orlando–Walt Disney World market. Most of these are mom-and-pop outfits that manage an inventory of 10 homes or less (probably fewer than 70 companies oversee more than 100 rental homes).

Homeowners pay these companies to maintain and promote their properties and handle all rental transactions. Some homes are made available to wholesalers, vacation packagers, and travel agents in deals negotiated either directly by the owners or by property-management companies on the owners' behalf. A wholesaler or vacation packager will occasionally drop its rates to sell slow-moving inventory, but more commonly the cost to renters is higher than when dealing directly with owners or management companies: Because most wholesalers and packagers sell their inventory through travel agents, both the whole-saler/packager's markup and the travel agent's commission are passed along to the renter. These costs are in addition to the owner's cut and/or the fee for the property manager.

Along similar lines, logic may suggest that the lowest rate of all can be obtained by dealing directly with owners, thus eliminating middlemen. Although this is sometimes true, it's more often the case that property-management companies offer the best rates. With their marketing expertise and larger customer base, these companies can produce a higher occupancy rate than can the owners themselves. What's more, management companies, or at least the larger ones, can achieve economies of scale not available to owners regarding maintenance, cleaning, linens, even acquiring furniture and appliances (if a house is not already furnished). The combination of higher occupancy rates and economies of scale adds up to a win–win situation for owners, management companies, and renters alike.

Location, Location, Location

The best vacation home is one that is within easy commuting distance of the theme parks. If you plan to spend some time at SeaWorld and the Universal parks, you'll want something just to the northeast of Walt Disney World (between the World and Orlando). If you plan to spend most of your time in the World, the best selection of vacation homes is along US 192 to the south of the park.

Walt Disney World is mostly in Orange County but has a small southern tip that dips into Osceola County, which, along with Polk County to the west of the World, is where most vacation homes and single-owner condos and town houses are. Zoning laws in Orange County (which also includes most of Orlando, Universal Studios, SeaWorld, Lake Buena Vista, and the International Drive area) used to prohibit short-term rentals of homes and single-owner condos, but in recent years the county has loosened its zoning restrictions in a few predominantly tourist-oriented areas. So far, practically all of the vacation-rental homes in Orange County are in the **Floridays** and **Vista Cay** developments.

By our reckoning, about half the rental homes in Osceola County and all the rental homes in Polk County are too far away from Walt Disney World for commuting to be practical. That said, an entrance to Walt Disney World off the FL 429 four-lane toll road halves the commute from many of the vacation-home developments arrayed around the intersection of US 192 and US 27. FL 429 runs north–south from I-4 south of Walt Disney World to Florida's Turnpike. You might be able to save a few bucks by staying farther out, but the most desirable homes to be found are in Vista Cay and in developments no more than 4 miles from Disney World's main entrance on US 192 (Irlo Bronson Memorial Highway), in Osceola County.

To get the most from a vacation home, you need to be close enough to commute in 20 minutes or less to your Walt Disney World destination. This will allow for naps, quiet time, swimming, and dollar-saving meals you prepare yourself. Though traffic and road conditions are as important as the distance from a vacation home to your Disney destination, we recommend a home no farther than 5 miles away in areas northeast of Walt Disney World and no farther than 4.5 miles away in areas south of the park. Bear in mind that rental companies calculate distance from the vacation home to the absolute nearest square inch of Disney property, so in most instances you can expect to commute another 3 or more miles within Walt Disney World to reach your ultimate destination.

Shopping for a Vacation Home

The only practical way to shop for a rental home is on the web. This makes it relatively easy to compare different properties and rental companies; on the downside, there are so many owners, rental companies, and individual homes to choose from that you could research yourself into a stupor. There are three main types of websites in the home-rental game: those for property-management companies, which showcase a given company's homes and are set up for direct bookings; individual owner sites; and third-party listings sites, which advertise properties available through different owners and sometimes management companies as well. Sites in the last category will usually refer prospective renters to an owner's or management company's site for reservations.

We've found that most property-management sites are not very well designed and will test your patience to the max. You can practically click yourself into old age trying to see all the homes available or figure out where on earth they are. Nearly all claim to be "just minutes from Disney." (By that reasoning, we should list our homes; they're also just minutes from Disney . . . 570 minutes, to be exact!)

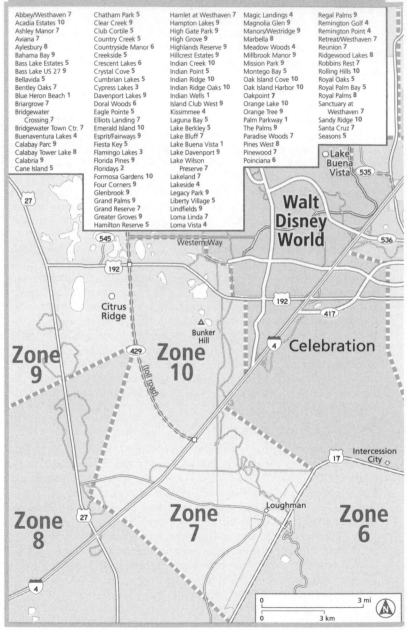

Rental-Home Developments near WDW

Abbey/Westhaven 7
Acadia Estates 10
Ashley Manor 7
Aviana 7
Aylesbury 8
Bahama Bay 9
Bass Lake Estates 5
Bass Lake US 27 9
Bellavida 5
Bentley Oaks 7
Blue Heron Beach 1
Briargrove 7
Bridgewater
 Crossing 7
Bridgewater Town Ctr. 7
Buenaventura Lakes 4
Calabay Parc 9
Calabay Tower Lake 8
Calabria 9
Cane Island 5

Chatham Park 5
Clear Creek 9
Club Cortile 5
Country Creek 5
Countryside Manor 6
Creekside 5
Crescent Lakes 6
Crystal Cove 5
Cumbrian Lakes 5
Cypress Lakes 3
Davenport Lakes 9
Doral Woods 6
Eagle Pointe 5
Elliots Landing 7
Emerald Island 10
Esprit/Fairways 9
Fiesta Key 5
Flamingo Lakes 3
Florida Pines 9
Floridays 2
Formosa Gardens 10
Four Corners 9
Glenbrook 9
Grand Palms 9
Grand Reserve 7
Greater Groves 9
Hamilton Reserve 5

Hamlet at Westhaven 7
Hampton Lakes 9
High Gate Park 9
High Grove 9
Highlands Reserve 9
Hillcrest Estates 9
Indian Creek 10
Indian Point 5
Indian Ridge 10
Indian Ridge Oaks 10
Indian Wells 1
Island Club West 9
Kissimmee 4
Laguna Bay 5
Lake Berkley 5
Lake Bluff 7
Lake Buena Vista 1
Lake Davenport 9
Lake Wilson
 Preserve 7
Lakeland 7
Lakeside 4
Legacy Park 9
Liberty Village 5
Lindfields 9
Loma Linda 7
Loma Vista 4

Magic Landings 4
Magnolia Glen 9
Manors/Westridge 9
Marbella 8
Meadow Woods 4
Millbrook Manor 9
Mission Park 9
Montego Bay 5
Oak Island Cove 10
Oak Island Harbor 10
Oakpoint 7
Orange Lake 10
Orange Tree 9
Palm Parkway 1
The Palms 9
Paradise Woods 7
Pines West 8
Pinewood 7
Poinciana 6

Regal Palms 9
Remington Golf 4
Remington Point 4
Retreat/Westhaven 7
Reunion 7
Ridgewood Lakes 8
Robbins Rest 7
Rolling Hills 10
Royal Oaks 5
Royal Palm Bay 5
Royal Palms 8
Sanctuary at
 Westhaven 7
Sandy Ridge 10
Santa Cruz 7
Seasons 5

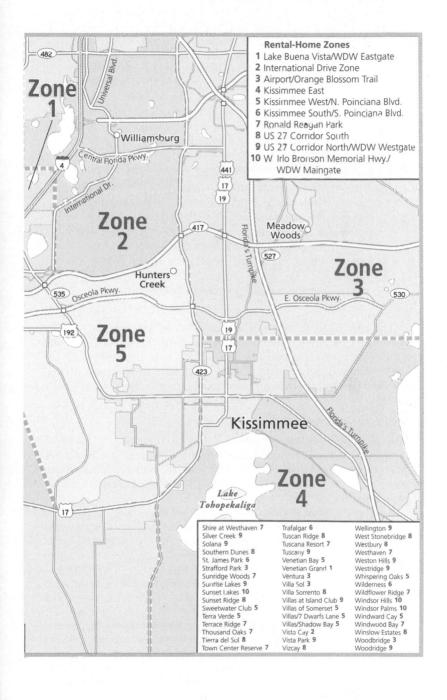

Rental-Home Zones

1 Lake Buena Vista/WDW Eastgate
2 International Drive Zone
3 Airport/Orange Blossom Trail
4 Kissimmee East
5 Kissimmee West/N. Poinciana Blvd.
6 Kissimmee South/S. Poinciana Blvd.
7 Ronald Reagan Park
8 US 27 Corridor South
9 US 27 Corridor North/WDW Westgate
10 W. Irlo Bronson Memorial Hwy./
   WDW Maingate

Shire at Westhaven 7
Silver Creek 9
Solana 9
Southern Dunes 8
St. James Park 6
Strafford Park 3
Sunridge Woods 7
Sunrise Lakes 9
Sunset Lakes 10
Sunset Ridge 8
Sweetwater Club 5
Terra Verde 5
Terrace Ridge 7
Thousand Oaks 7
Tierra del Sol 8
Town Center Reserve 7

Trafalgar 6
Tuscan Ridge 8
Tuscana Resort 7
Tuscany 9
Venetian Bay 5
Venetian Grand 1
Ventura 3
Villa Sol 3
Villa Sorrento 8
Villas at Island Club 9
Villas of Somerset 5
Villas/7 Dwarfs Lane 5
Villas/Shadow Bay 5
Vista Cay 2
Vista Park 9
Vizcay 8

Wellington 9
West Stonebridge 8
Westbury 8
Westhaven 7
Weston Hills 9
Westridge 9
Whispering Oaks 5
Wilderness 6
Wildflower Ridge 7
Windsor Hills 10
Windsor Palms 10
Windward Cay 5
Windwood Bay 7
Winslow Estates 8
Woodbridge 3
Woodridge 9

Many websites list homes according to towns (such as Auburndale, Clermont, Davenport, Haines City, and Winter Garden) or real estate developments (including Eagle Pointe, Formosa Gardens, Indian Ridge, and Windsor Palms) in the general Disney area, none of which you're likely to be familiar with. The information that counts is the distance of a vacation home or condo from Walt Disney World; for that you often must look for something like "4 miles from Disney" embedded in the home's description. If you visit a site that lists homes by towns or real estate developments, begin by looking at our map on the previous pages, which shows where all these places are in relation to Walt Disney World. If the map is unhelpful in determining distance, we suggest that you find another location for your stay.

The best websites provide the following:

- Numerous photos and in-depth descriptions of individual homes to make comparisons quick and easy
- Overview maps or text descriptions that reflect how far specific homes or developments are from Walt Disney World
- The ability to book the specific rental home of your choice on the site
- An easy-to-find phone number for non-Internet bookings and questions

The best sites are also easy to navigate, let you see what you're interested in without your having to log in or divulge any personal information, and list memberships in such organizations as the Better Business Bureau and the Central Florida Vacation Rental Managers Association (visit **cfvrma.com** for the association's code of ethics).

Recommended Websites

After checking out dozens upon dozens of sites, here are the ones we recommend. All of them meet the criteria listed above. If you're stunned that there are so few of them, well, so were we. (For the record, we elected not to list some sites that met our criteria but whose homes are too far away from Walt Disney World.)

All Star Vacation Homes (allstarvacationhomes.com) is easily the best of the management-company sites, with easily accessible photos and plenty of details about featured homes. All the company's rental properties are within either 4 miles of Walt Disney World or 3 miles of Universal Studios.

#1 Dream Homes (floridadreamhomes.com) has a good reputation for customer service and now has photos of and information about the homes in its online inventory.

Orlando's Finest Vacation Homes (orlandosfinest.com) represents both homeowners and property-management companies. Offering a broad inventory, the Orlando's Finest website features photos and information on individual homes. Although the info is not as detailed as that offered by the All Star Vacation Homes site, friendly sales agents can fill in the blanks.

Vacation Rentals by Owner (vrbo.com) is a nationwide vacation-homes listings service that puts prospective renters in direct contact with owners. The site is straightforward and always lists a large number of rental properties in Celebration, Disney's planned community situated about 8–10 minutes from the theme parks. Two similar listings services with good websites are **Vacation Rentals 411 (vacation rentals411.com)** and **Last Minute Villas (lastminutevillas.net)**.

The website for **Visit Orlando (visitorlando.com)** is the place to go if you're interested in renting a condominium at one of the many time-share developments (click on "Places to Stay" at the site's home page). You can call the developments directly, but going through this website allows you to bypass sales departments and escape their high-pressure invitations to sit through sales presentations. The site also lists hotels and vacation homes. For all types of accommodations, you can sort by distance from where you'll spend your touring time. Distance-sorting categories include Walt Disney World, Universal, the Orange County Convention Center, and downtown Orlando, among others. If you select Universal, for example, the list of accommodations will be ordered from the closest to the most distant.

Making Contact

Once you've found a vacation home you like, check around the website for a Frequently Asked Questions (FAQ) page. If there's not a FAQ page, here are some of the things you'll want to check out on the phone with the owner or rental company.

1. How close is the property to Walt Disney World?
2. Is the home or condominium that I see on the Internet the one I'll get?
3. Is the property part of a time-share development?
4. Are there any specials or discounts available?
5. Is everything included in the rental price, or are there additional charges? What about taxes?
6. How old is the home or condo I'm interested in? Has it been refurbished recently?
7. What is the view from the property?
8. Is the property near any noisy roads?
9. What is your smoking policy?
10. Are pets allowed? This consideration is as important to those who want to avoid pets as to those who want to bring them.
11. Is the pool heated?
12. Is there a fenced backyard where children can play?
13. How many people can be seated at the main dining table?
14. Is there a separate dedicated telephone at the property?
15. Is high-speed Internet access available?
16. Are linens and towels provided?
17. How far are the nearest supermarket and drugstore?
18. Are child-care services available?
19. Are there restaurants nearby?

20. Is transportation to the parks provided?

21. Will we need a car?

22. What is required to make a reservation?

23. What is your change/cancellation policy?

24. When is checkout time?

25. What will we be responsible for when we check out?

26. How will we receive our confirmation and arrival instructions?

27. What are your office hours?

28. What are the directions to your office?

29. What if we arrive after your office has closed?

30. Whom do we contact if something breaks or otherwise goes wrong during our stay?

31. How long have you been in business?

32. Are you licensed by the state of Florida?

33. Do you belong to the Better Business Bureau and/or the Central Florida Vacation Rental Managers Association?

We frequently receive letters from readers extolling the virtues of renting a condo or vacation home. This endorsement by a family from Ellington, Connecticut, is typical:

Our choice to stay outside Disney was based on cost and sanity. We've found over the last couple of years that our children can't share the same bed. We have also gotten tired of having to turn off the lights at 8 p.m. and lie quietly in the dark waiting for our children to fall asleep. With this in mind, we needed a condo/suite layout. Anything in Disney offering this option [BoardWalk Villas, Beach Club Villas, Old Key West, and the like] was going to cost $400–$500 a night. This was not built into our Disney budget. We decided on the Sheraton Vistana Resort. We had a two-bedroom villa with full kitchen, living room, three TVs, and washer/dryer. I packed for half the trip and did laundry almost every night. The facilities offered a daily children's program and several pools, kiddie pools, and "playscapes." Located on FL 535, we had a 5- to 10-minute drive to most attractions, including SeaWorld, Disney, and Universal.

A St. Joe, Indiana, family also had a good experience, writing:

We rented a home in Kissimmee this time, and we'll never stay in a hotel at WDW again. It was by far the nicest, most relaxing time we've ever had down there. Our rental home was within 10–15 minutes of all the Disney parks, and 25 minutes from SeaWorld. We had three bedrooms, two baths, and an in-ground pool in a screened enclosure out back. We paid $90 per night for the whole shootin' match. We did spring for the pool heating, $25 per night extra in February. We used AAA Dream Homes Rental Company and they did a great job by us. They provided us with detailed info before we went down so we'd know what we needed to bring.

From a New Jersey family of five:

I cannot stress enough how important it is if you have a large family (more than two kids) to rent a house for your stay! We had visited WDW several times in the past by ourselves when we were newlyweds. Fast-forward to 10 years later, when we took our three kids, ages 6 years, 4 years, and 20 months. We stayed at Windsor Hills Resort, which I booked through **globalresorthomes.com.** *I was able to see all the homes and check availability when I was reserving the house. This development is 1 5 miles from the Disney Maingate. It took us about 10 minutes to drive there in the a.m., and we had no traffic issues at all.*

THE BEST HOTELS FOR FAMILIES OUTSIDE WALT DISNEY WORLD

WHAT MAKES A SUPER FAMILY HOTEL? Roomy accommodations, in-room fridge, great pool, complimentary breakfast, child-care options, and programs for kids are a few of the things the *Unofficial Guide* hotel team researched in selecting the top hotels for families from among hundreds of properties in the Disney World area. Some of our picks are expensive, others are more reasonable, and some are a bargain. Regardless of price, be assured that these hotels understand a family's needs.

Though all of the following hotels offer some type of shuttle to the theme parks, some offer very limited service. Call the hotel before you book and ask what the shuttle schedule will be when you visit. Since families, like individuals, have different wants and needs, we haven't ranked the following properties here; they're listed by zone and alphabetically.

INTERNATIONAL DRIVE & UNIVERSAL AREAS

CoCo Key Hotel and Water Resort–Orlando
★★★★½

Rate per night $83–$268. **Pools** ★★★★. **Fridge in room** Yes. **Shuttle to parks** Yes (Aquatica, SeaWorld, Universal, Wet 'n Wild). **Maximum number of occupants per room** 4. **Special comments** Daily $19 room fee for use of the water park; day guests may use the water park for $22.95/person Monday–Friday ($24.95 on weekends and $17.95 for Florida residents).

THE COCO KEY HOTEL AND WATER RESORT is on International Drive, not far from the Universal Orlando theme parks. It combines a tropical-themed hotel with a canopied water park featuring 3 pools and 14 waterslides, as well as poolside food and arcade entertainment. A full-service restaurant serves breakfast and dinner; a food court offers family favorites such as burgers, chicken fingers, and pizza.

7400 International Dr.
Orlando
☎ 407-351-2626 or
877-875-4681
cocokeyorlando.com

A unique feature of the resort is its cashless payment system, much like that on a cruise ship. At check-in, families receive bar-coded wristbands that allow purchased items to be easily charged to their room.

The unusually spacious guest rooms include 37-inch flat-screen TVs, free Wi-Fi, granite showers and countertops, and plenty of accessible outlets for guests' electronics.

DoubleTree by Hilton Orlando at SeaWorld ★★★★½

Rate per night $107–$599. **Pools** ★★★½. **Fridge in room** Standard in some rooms; available in others for $10/day. **Shuttle to parks** Yes. **Maximum number of occupants per room** 4. **Special comments** Good option if you're visiting SeaWorld or Aquatica. Pets welcome (1 per room, 25-pound limit, $75).

10100 International Dr. Orlando
☎ 407-352-1100 or 800-327-0363
doubletreeorlando idrive.com

FORMERLY THE INTERNATIONAL PLAZA RESORT & SPA, this hotel has undergone a comprehensive $35 million renovation. On 28 lush, tropical acres with a Balinese feel, the DoubleTree is adjacent to SeaWorld and Aquatica water park. All 1,094 rooms and suites—classified as "resort" or "tower"—have been completely refurbished and are equally suitable for business travelers or families. We recommend the tower rooms for good views and the resort rooms for maximum convenience. The Bamboo Grille serves steak and seafood, along with breakfast; you can also get a quick bite at Bangli Lounge, the deli, or the pool bar. Relax and cool off at one of the three pools (there are two more just for kids), or indulge in a special spa treatment. A fitness center, mini-golf course and putting green, children's day camp, and game area afford even more diversions. The resort is about a 15-minute drive to Walt Disney World, a 12-minute drive to Universal, or a short walk to SeaWorld.

Hard Rock Hotel ★★★★½

Rate per night $225–$520. **Pool** ★★★★. **Fridge in room** $15/day. **Shuttle to parks** Yes (Universal, SeaWorld, Discovery Cove, Aquatica, and Wet 'n Wild). **Maximum number of occupants per room** 5 (double-queen) or 3 (king). **Special comments** Microwaves available for $15/day.

5800 Universal Blvd. Orlando
☎ 407-503-2000 or 888-464-3617
hardrockhotel orlando.com

ON UNIVERSAL PROPERTY, the 650-room Hard Rock Hotel is nirvana for kids older than 8, especially those interested in music. Architecture is California Mission–style, and rock memorabilia is displayed throughout. If you plan to spend at least a few days at Universal parks, this is an excellent upscale option. Guests receive theme park privileges such as all-day access to the Universal Express line-breaking program, as well as delivery of packages to their rooms and priority seating at select Universal restaurants. The music-filled pool area has a white-sand beach, a 260-foot waterslide, a 12,000-square-foot pool, an underwater audio system, and an ultrahip pool bar. You'll also find four restaurants and lounges, including the Palm Restaurant, a chic lounge, a fitness center, and a Hard Rock merchandise store. Guest rooms are ultrahip, too, with cutting-edge contemporary decor, CD sound system, TV with pay-per-view movies and video games, coffeemaker, iron and board, minibar, robes, hair dryer, and two phones. A supervised activity center, Camp Lil' Rock, serves kids ages 4–14. Pet-friendly rooms are available.

Holiday Inn Resort Orlando–The Castle   ★★★½

Rate per night $89–$245. **Pool** ★★★. **Fridge in room** Yes ($15/day). **Shuttle to parks** Yes (Universal, SeaWorld, and Wet 'n Wild). **Maximum number of occupants per room** 4. **Special comments** For an additional fee ($13.95 for adults, free for kids), up to 4 people receive a full breakfast. Small pets welcome for an additional $75.

YOU CAN'T MISS THIS ONE; it's the only castle on I-Drive. Inside you'll find royal colors (purple predominates), opulent fixtures, European art, Renaissance music, and a mystic Castle Creature at the door. The 216 guest rooms also receive the royal treatment in decor, though some guests may find

8629 International Dr.
Orlando
☎ 407-345-1511 or
877-317-5753
thecastleorlando.com

them gaudy. All, however, are fairly large and well equipped with TV, minibar (fridge is available at an extra charge), free Wi-Fi, coffeemaker, iron and board, hair dryer, and safe. The Castle Café off the lobby serves full or Continental breakfast. For lunch or dinner, you might walk next door to Vito's Chop House (dinner only) or Café Tu Tu Tango (an *Unofficial* favorite). The heated circular pool is 5 feet deep and features a fountain in the center, a poolside bar, and a whirlpool. There's no separate kiddie pool. Other amenities include fitness center, gift shop, lounge, valet laundry service and facilities, and guest-services desk with park passes for sale and babysitting recommendations. Security feature: Elevators require an electronic key card.

Loews Portofino Bay Hotel   ★★★★½

Rate per night $209–$526. **Pools** ★★★★. **Fridge in room** Minibar; fridge available for $15/day. **Shuttle to parks** Yes (Universal, SeaWorld, Discovery Cove, and Wet 'n Wild). **Maximum number of occupants per room** 4. **Special comments** Character dinner on Friday.

IN UNIVERSAL ORLANDO, the 750-room Portofino Bay Hotel is themed like an Italian Riviera village. Guests receive theme park privileges such as all-day access to the Universal Express line-breaking program, as well as delivery of packages to their rooms and priority seating at select Universal restaurants. The rooms

5601 Universal Blvd.
Orlando
☎ 407-503-1000 or
888-464-3617
tinyurl.com/
  portofinobay

are ultraluxurious, with Italian-style furnishings, opulent bathrooms, and soothing neutral hues. Standard guest-room amenities include minibar, coffeemaker, iron and board, hair dryer, safe, and TV with pay-per-view movies. Microwaves are available ($15 per day). Campo Portofino offers supervised activities (movies, video games, crafts, and such) for children ages 4–14. The cost is $15 per hour plus $15 per meal, per child; hours vary. Trattoria del Porto restaurant offers a character dinner from 6:30 until 9:30 p.m. on Friday, with characters such as Scooby Doo and Woody Woodpecker in attendance. Portofino has four other Italian restaurants (each with a children's menu), an Italian bakery (also serves gelato), and two bars. Three elaborate pools, gardens, jogging trails, pet-friendly rooms, and a spa and fitness center round out major amenities. If you have the bank account to pay for it and plan to spend time at Universal, you can't go wrong here.

Nickelodeon Suites Resort   ★★★½

Rate per night $139–$649. **Pools** ★★★★. **Fridge in room** Yes. **Shuttle to parks** Yes. **Maximum number of occupants per room** 8. **Special comments** Daily character breakfast; resort fee of $25/night.

14500 Continental
   Gateway
Orlando
☎ 407-387-5437 or
877-NICK-111
nickhotel.com

SPONGEBOB SQUAREPANTS, eat your heart out. This resort is as kid-friendly as they come. Decked out in all themes Nickelodeon, the hotel is sure to please any fan of TV shows the likes of *SpongeBob, Dora the Explorer, Avatar: The Last Airbender,* and *iCarly,* to name a few. Nickelodeon characters from the channel's many shows hang out in the resort's lobby and mall area, greeting kids while parents check in. Guests can choose from among 777 suites—one-bedroom Family Suites and two- and three-bedroom KidSuites—executed in a number of different themes—all very brightly and creatively decorated. All suites include kitchenettes or full kitchens; also standard are microwave, fridge, coffeemaker, TV, iron and board, hair dryer, and safe. KidSuites feature a semiprivate kids' bedroom with bunk or twin beds, pull-out sleeper bed, 32-inch TV, CD player, and activity table. The master bedroom offers ample storage space that the kids' bedroom lacks. Additional amenities include a high-tech video arcade, Studio Nick—a game-show studio that hosts several game shows a night for the entertainment of a live studio audience, a buffet (kids age 3 and younger eat free with a paying adult), a food court offering Subway and other choices, the full-service Nicktoons Cafe (offers character breakfasts), a convenience store, a lounge, a gift shop, a fitness center, a washer and dryer in each courtyard, and a guest-activities desk (buy Disney tickets and get recommendations on babysitting). Not to be missed—don't worry, your kids won't let you—are the resort's two pools, Oasis and Lagoon. Oasis features a water park complete with water cannons, rope ladders, geysers, and dump buckets, as well as a hot tub for adults (with a view of the rest of the pool so you can keep an eye on little ones) and a smaller play area for younger kids. Kids will love the huge, zero-entry Lagoon Pool with 400-gallon dump bucket, plus a nearby basketball court and nine-hole mini-golf course. Pool activities for kids are scheduled several times a day, seasonally; some games feature the infamous green slime. Whatever you do, avoid letting your kids catch you saying the phrase "I don't know" while you're here—trust us.

Rosen Shingle Creek   ★★★★

Rate per night $111–$285. **Pools** ★★★★. **Fridge in room** Yes. **Shuttle to parks** Yes (Universal, Wet 'n Wild, Discovery Cove, Aquatica, and SeaWorld only). **Maximum number of occupants per room** 4.

9939 Universal Blvd.
Orlando
☎ 407-996-9939
or 866-996-6338
rosenshinglecreek.com

BEAUTIFUL ROOMS (east-facing ones have great views) and excellent restaurants distinguish this mostly meeting- and convention-oriented resort. The pools are large and lovely and include a lap pool, a family pool, and a kiddie wading pool. There's an 18-hole golf course on-site as well as a superior spa and an adequate fitness center. Child care is provided as well. Though a state-of-the-art video arcade will gobble up your kids' pocket change, the real kicker, especially for the 8-years-and-up crowd, is a natural area encompassing lily ponds, grassy wetlands, Shingle Creek, and an adjacent cypress swamp. Running through the area is a nature trail complete with signs to help you identify wildlife. Great blue herons, wood storks, coots, egrets, mallard ducks, anhingas, and ospreys are common, as are sliders (turtles), chameleons, and skinks (lizards). Oh yeah, there are alligators and snakes, too—real ones, but that's part of the fun. If you stay at Shingle Creek and plan to visit the theme parks, you'll want a car. Shuttle service is limited, departing and picking up at rather inconvenient times and stopping at three other hotels before delivering you to your destination.

LAKE BUENA VISTA & I-4 CORRIDOR

Buena Vista Palace Hotel & Spa ★★★½

Rate per night $121–$449. **Pools** ★★★½. **Fridge in room** Yes. **Shuttle to parks** Yes (Disney only). **Maximum number of occupants per room** 4. **Special comments** Sunday character brunch available.
See full profile on page 198.

Hilton in the Walt Disney World Resort ★★★★

Rate per night $99–$340. **Pools** ★★★½. **Fridge in room** Minibar; mini-fridge available free on request. **Shuttle to parks** Yes (Disney theme and water parks only). **Maximum number of occupants per room** 4. **Special comments** Sunday character breakfast and Disney Extra Magic Hours program.
See full profile on page 199.

Holiday Inn Resort Lake Buena Vista ★★★½

Rate per night $71–$200. **Pool** ★★★. **Fridge in room** Yes. **Shuttle to parks** Yes (Disney only). **Maximum number of occupants per room** 4–6. **Special comments** The first hotel in the world to offer KidSuites; resort fee of $11.95/night entitles guests to numerous perks, including use of fitness center and daily fountain drinks for kids.

THE BIG LURE HERE IS KIDSUITES—405-square-foot rooms, each with a separate children's area. Themes include a tree house, jail, space capsule, and fort, among others. The kids' area sleeps two to four children in one or two sets of bunk beds. The separate adult area has its own TV, safe, hair dryer, and mini-kitchenette with fridge, microwave, sink, and coffeemaker. Standard guest rooms offer these adult amenities. Other kid-friendly amenities include the tiny Castle Movie Theater, which shows movies all day, every day; a playground; an arcade with video games and air hockey, among its many games; and a basketball court. Other amenities include a fitness center for the grown-ups and a large free-form pool complete with kiddie pool and two whirlpools. Applebee's serves breakfast and dinner and offers an à la carte menu for dinner. There's also a minimart. More perks: Kids age 12 and younger eat free from a special menu when dining with one paying adult (maximum four kids

13351 FL 535
Orlando
☎ 407-239-4500 or
866-808-8833
hiresortlbv.com

per adult), and "Dive-Inn" poolside movies are shown on Saturday nights. Finally, pets weighing 30 pounds or less are welcome for an additional $40 nonrefundable fee.

Hyatt Regency Grand Cypress ★★★★½

Rate per night $144–$369. **Pool** ★★★★★. **Fridge in room** Yes, plus minibar. **Shuttle to parks** Yes (Disney, Universal, SeaWorld). **Maximum number of occupants per room** 4. **Special comments** Wow, what a pool!

1 Grand Cypress Blvd.
Orlando
☎ 407-239-1234
grandcypress.hyatt.com

THERE ARE MYRIAD REASONS to stay at this 1,500-acre resort, but the pool ranks as number one. The 800,000-gallon tropical paradise has two 45-foot waterslides, waterfalls, caves and grottoes, and a suspension bridge. The Hyatt also is a golfer's paradise. With 45 holes of Jack Nicklaus–designed championship golf, a 9-hole pitch-and-putt course, and a golf academy, there's something for golfers of all abilities. Other recreational perks include a racquet facility with hard and clay courts, a private lake with beach, a fitness center, and miles of trails for biking, walking, and jogging. (*Note:* A daily $22 resort fee applies.) The 769 standard guest rooms are 360 square feet and have a Florida ambience, with green and reddish hues, touches of rattan, and private balconies. Amenities include minibar, iron and board, safe, hair dryer, ceiling fan, and cable/satellite TV with pay-per-view movies and video games. Suite and villa accommodations offer even more amenities. Camp Hyatt provides supervised programs for kids ages 3–12; in-room babysitting is available. Six restaurants offer dining options. Four lounges provide nighttime entertainment. If outdoor recreation is high on your family's list, Hyatt is an excellent high-end choice.

Marriott Village at Lake Buena Vista ★★★

Rate per night $69–$159. **Pools** ★★★. **Fridge in room** Yes. **Shuttle to parks** Disney only, $7. **Maximum number of occupants per room** 4 (Courtyard and Fairfield) or 5 (SpringHill). **Special comments** Free Continental breakfast at Fairfield and SpringHill.

8623 Vineland Ave.
Orlando
☎ 407-938-9001 or
800-761-7829
marriottvillage.com

THIS GATED HOTEL COMMUNITY INCLUDES a 388-room Fairfield Inn (★★★½), a 400-suite SpringHill Suites (★★★), and a 312-room Courtyard (★★★½). Whatever your budget, you'll find a room here to fit it. If you need a bit more space, book SpringHill Suites; if you're looking for value, try the Fairfield Inn; if you need limited business amenities, reserve at the Courtyard. Amenities at all three properties include fridge, cable TV, iron and board, hair dryer, and microwave. Cribs and roll-away beds are available at no extra charge at all locations. Swimming pools at all three hotels are attractive and medium-sized, featuring children's interactive splash zones and whirlpools; in addition, each property has its own fitness center. The incredibly convenient Village Marketplace food court includes Pizza Hut, Village Grill, Village Coffee House, and a 24-hour convenience store. Bahama Breeze and Golden Corral full-service restaurants are within walking distance. Other services and amenities include a Disney planning station and ticket sales, an arcade, and a Hertz car-rental desk. Shoppers will find the Orlando Premium Outlets adjacent. You'll get plenty of bang for your buck at Marriott Village.

Sheraton Lake Buena Vista Resort ★★★★

Rate per night $90–$351. **Pool** ★★★★. **Fridge in room** Yes. **Shuttle to parks** Yes (Disney only). **Maximum number of occupants per room** 4–6. **Special comments** Dogs 80 pounds and under allowed; $9.95/day resort fee.

FORMERLY THE SHERATON SAFARI HOTEL & SUITES, this resort recently underwent a $25 million renovation. The entire property, including the 400 guest rooms and the 90 family junior suites, has gotten major upgrades that give it a sleek, modern feel. The family junior suites provide bunk beds for children, but gone are the kitchenettes. Amenities in each room include Sheraton Sweet Sleeper beds, free Wi-Fi, 42-inch HDTV, refrigerator, coffeemaker, hair dryer, safe, clock-radio, and iron and board. Microwaves are available at an extra charge. The relaxing pool area now features cabanas with food service (for a fee), and youngsters can enjoy the cascading waterfall and waterslide (sorry, kids—the python is gone). The Top of the Palms Spa offers massages, facials, manicures, and pedicures. Also on-site are two restaurants, a business center, a fitness center, an arcade, and a gift shop.

12205 S. Apopka–Vineland Rd.
Orlando
☎ 407-239-0444 or 800-325-3535
sheratonlakebuena vistaresort.com

Sheraton Vistana Resort Villas ★★★★½

Rate per night $119–$189. **Pools** ★★★½. **Fridge in room** Yes. **Shuttle to parks** Yes (Disney free; other parks for a fee). **Maximum number of occupants per room** 4–8. **Special comments** Though time-shares, the villas are rented nightly as well.

THE SHERATON VISTANA IS DECEPTIVELY LARGE, stretching across both sides of Vistana Centre Drive. Because Sheraton's emphasis is on selling the time-shares, the rental angle is little known. But families should consider it; the Vistana is one of Orlando's best off-Disney properties. If you want a serene retreat from your days in the theme parks, this is an excellent base. The spacious villas come in one-bedroom, two-bedroom, and two-bedroom-with-lock-off models (which can be reconfigured as one studio room and a one-bedroom suite). All are decorated in beachy pastels, but the emphasis is on the profusion of amenities. Each villa has a full kitchen (including fridge/freezer, microwave, oven/range, dishwasher, toaster, and coffeemaker, with an option to prestock with groceries and laundry products), clothes washer and dryer, TVs in the living room and each bedroom (one with DVD player), stereo with CD player in some villas, separate dining area, and private patio or balcony in most. Grounds offer seven swimming pools (three with bars), four playgrounds, two restaurants, game rooms, fitness centers, a mini-golf course, sports equipment rental (including bikes), and courts for basketball, volleyball, tennis, and shuffleboard. A mind-boggling array of activities for kids (and adults) ranges from crafts to games and sports tournaments. Of

8800 Vistana Centre Dr.
Orlando
☎ 407-239-3100 or 866-208-0003
tinyurl.com/vistanaresort

special note: Vistana is highly secure, with locked gates bordering all guest areas, so children can have the run of the place without parents worrying about them wandering off.

Waldorf Astoria Orlando ★★★★½

Rate per night $297–$3,710. **Pool** ★★★★. **Fridge in room** Yes. **Shuttle to parks** Yes (Disney only). **Maximum number of occupants per room** 4, plus child in crib. **Special comments** A good alternative to Disney's Deluxe properties.

14200 Bonnet Creek
   Resort Lane
Orlando
☎ 407-597-5500
waldorfastoria
   orlando.com

OPENED IN 2009, the Waldorf Astoria is between I-4 and Disney's Pop Century Resort, near the Hilton Orlando at the back of the Bonnet Creek Resort property. Getting here requires a GPS or good directions, so be prepared with those before you travel. Once you arrive, however, you'll know the trip was worth it. Beautifully decorated and well manicured, the Waldorf is more elegant than any Disney resort. Service is excellent, and the staff-to-guest ratio is far lower than at Disney properties.

At just under 450 square feet, standard rooms feature either two queen beds or one king. A full-size desk allows you to get work done if it's absolutely necessary, and rooms also have flat-screen televisions, high-speed Internet, and Wi-Fi. The bathrooms are spacious and gorgeous, with cool marble floors, glass-walled showers, separate tubs, and enough counter space for a Broadway makeup artist. This space is so nice, we've debated whether we'd rather stay at Pop Century with three others or sleep in a Waldorf bathroom by ourselves.

Amenities include a fitness center, a spa, a golf course, six restaurants, and two pools (including one zero-entry pool for kids). Poolside cabanas are available for rent. The resort offers shuttle service to the Disney parks about every half-hour, but check with the front desk for the exact schedule when you arrive. Runners will enjoy the relative solitude—it's about a 1-mile round-trip to the nearest busy road, and the route is flat as a pancake.

Wyndham Bonnet Creek Resort ★★★★½

Rate per night $191–$329. **Pool** ★★★★. **Fridge in room** Yes. **Shuttle to parks** Yes (Disney only). **Maximum number of occupants per room** 4–12 depending on room/suite. **Special comments** A non-Disney suite hotel within Walt Disney World.

9560 Via Encinas
Lake Buena Vista
☎ 407-238-3500 or
   888-743-2687
wyndham
   bonnetcreek.com

THIS CONDO HOTEL lies on the south side of Buena Vista Drive, about a quarter-mile east of Disney's Caribbean Beach Resort. The property has an interesting history: When Walt Disney began secretly buying up real estate in the 1960s under the names of numerous front companies, the land on which this resort stands was the last holdout and was never sold to Disney, though the company tried repeatedly to acquire it through the years. (The owners reportedly took issue with the way Disney went about acquiring land and preferred to see the site languish undeveloped.) The 482-acre site was ultimately bought by Marriott, which put up a Fairfield Inn time-share development in 2004. The Wyndham is part of a luxury-hotel complex on the same site that includes a 500-room Waldorf Astoria (see facing page) and a 1,000-room Hilton. The development is surrounded on three sides by Disney property and on one side by I-4.

The Bonnet Creek Resort offers upscale, family-friendly accommodations: one- and two-bedroom condos with fully equipped kitchens, washers and dryers, jetted tubs, and balconies. Activities and amenities on-site include two outdoor swimming pools, a "lazy river" float stream, a children's activities program, a game room, a playground, and miniature golf. Free scheduled transportation serves all the Disney parks. One-bedroom units are equipped with a king bed in the bedroom and a sleeper sofa in the living area; two-bedroom condos have two double beds in the second bedroom, a sleeper sofa in the living area, and an additional bath.

US 192 AREA

Clarion Suites Maingate ★★★½

Rate per night $51–$126. **Pool** ★★★. **Fridge in room** Yes. **Shuttle to parks** Yes (Disney, Universal, and SeaWorld). **Maximum number of occupants per room** 6 for most suites. **Special comments** Free Continental breakfast daily.

THIS PROPERTY HAS 150 SPACIOUS one-room suites, each with double sofa bed, microwave, fridge, coffeemaker, TV, hair dryer, and safe. The suites aren't lavish, but they're clean and contemporary, with muted deep-purple and beige tones. Extra bathroom counter space is especially convenient for larger families. The heated pool is large and has plenty of lounge chairs and moderate landscaping. A kiddie pool, whirlpool, and poolside bar complete the courtyard. Other amenities include an arcade and a gift shop. But Maingate's big plus is its location next door to a shopping center with about everything a family could need. There, you'll find 10 dining options, including Outback Steakhouse, Red Lobster, Subway, T.G.I. Friday's, and Chinese, Italian, and Japanese eateries; a Winn-Dixie Marketplace; a liquor store; a bank; a dry cleaner; and a tourist-information center with park passes for sale, among other services. All this a short walk from your room.

7888 W. Irlo Bronson
    Memorial Hwy.
Kissimmee
☎ 407-390-9888 or
888-390-9888
clarionsuites
    kissimmee.com

Gaylord Palms Hotel and Convention Center
★★★★½

Rate per night $161–$319. **Pool** ★★★★. **Fridge in room** Yes. **Shuttle to parks** Yes (Disney only). **Maximum number of occupants per room** 4. **Special comments** Probably the closest you'll get off-World to Disney-level extravagance. Resort fee of $15/day.

THIS DECIDEDLY UPSCALE RESORT has a colossal convention facility and caters strongly to business clientele, but it's still a nice (if pricey) family resort. Hotel wings are defined by the three themed, glass-roofed atriums they overlook. Key West's design is reminiscent of island life in the Florida Keys; Everglades is an overgrown spectacle of shabby swamp chic, complete with piped-in cricket

6000 W. Osceola Pkwy.
Kissimmee
☎ 407-586-2000
gaylordpalms.com

noise and a robotic alligator; and the immense, central St. Augustine harks back to Spanish Colonial Florida. Lagoons, streams, and waterfalls cut through and connect all three, and walkways and bridges abound. Rooms reflect the colors of their respective areas, though there's no particular connection in decor (St. Augustine atrium-view rooms are the most opulent, but they're not Spanish). A fourth wing, Emerald Bay Tower, overlooks the Emerald Plaza shopping and dining area of the St. Augustine atrium. These rooms are the nicest and the most expensive, and they're mostly used by convention-goers. Though rooms have fridges and alarm clocks with CD players (as well as other perks such as high-speed Internet access), the rooms themselves really work better as retreats for adults than for kids. However, children will enjoy wandering the themed areas, playing in the family pool (with water-squirting octopus). In-room child care is provided by Kid's Nite Out (see page 351).

Orange Lake Resort ★★★★½

Rate per night $67–$270. **Pools** ★★★★. **Fridge in room** Yes. **Shuttle to parks** Yes (fee varies depending on destination). **Maximum number of occupants per room** Varies. **Special comments** This is a time-share property, but if you rent directly through the resort (as opposed to the sales office), you can avoid time-share sales pitches.

8505 W. Irlo Bronson Memorial Hwy. Kissimmee ☎ 407-239-0000 or 800-877-6522 orangelake.com

YOU COULD SPEND YOUR ENTIRE VACATION never leaving this property, about 6–10 minutes from the Disney theme parks. From its 10 pools and two mini–water parks to its golfing opportunities (36 holes of championship greens plus two 9-hole executive courses), Orange Lake offers an extensive menu of amenities and recreational opportunities. If you tire of lazing by the pool, try waterskiing, wakeboarding, tubing, fishing, or other activities on the 80-acre lake. There's also a live alligator show, exercise programs, organized competitive sports and games, arts-and-crafts sessions, and miniature golf. Activities don't end when the sun goes down. Karaoke, live music, a Hawaiian luau, and movies at the resort cinema are some of the evening options.

The 2,412 units are tastefully decorated and comfortably furnished, ranging from suites and studios to three-bedroom villas, all containing fully equipped kitchens. If you'd rather not cook on vacation, try one of the seven restaurants scattered across the resort: two cafes, three grills, one pizzeria, and a fast-food eatery. If you need help with (or a break from) the kids, babysitters are available to come to your villa, accompany your family on excursions, or take your children to attractions for you.

Radisson Resort Orlando-Celebration ★★★★

2900 Parkway Blvd. Kissimmee ☎ 407-396-7000 or 800-634-4774 radissonorlando resort.com

Rate per night $75–$221. **Pool** ★★★★½. **Fridge in room** Yes. **Shuttle to parks** Yes (Disney only). **Maximum number of occupants per room** 5. **Special comments** $12.50/day resort fee; kids age 10 and younger eat free with a paying adult at Mandolin's restaurant.

THE POOL ALONE IS WORTH A STAY HERE, but the Radisson Resort gets high marks in all areas. The free-form pool is huge, with a waterfall and waterslide surrounded by palms and flowering plants, plus a smaller heated pool, two whirlpools, and a kiddie pool. Other outdoor amenities include two lighted tennis courts, sand volleyball, a playground, and jogging areas. Kids can also blow off steam at the arcade, while adults might visit the fitness center. Rooms are elegant, featuring Italian furnishings and marble baths. They're of ample size and include minibar (some rooms), coffeemaker, TV, iron and board, hair dryer, and safe. Dining options include Mandolin's for breakfast (buffet) and dinner, and a 1950s-style diner serving burgers, sandwiches, shakes, and Pizza Hut pizza, among other fare. A sports lounge with a 6 x 11–foot TV offers nighttime entertainment. Guest services can help with tours, park passes, car rental, and babysitting. While there are no children's programs per se, there are plenty of activities such as face painting by a clown, juggling classes, bingo, and arts and crafts at the pool.

HOTELS *and* MOTELS:
Rated and Ranked

IN THIS SECTION, WE COMPARE HOTELS in four main areas outside Walt Disney World (see page 224) with those inside the World.

In addition to Disney properties, we rate hotels in the four lodging areas defined earlier in this chapter. Additional hotels can be found at the intersection of US 27 and I-4, on US 441 (Orange Blossom Trail), and in downtown Orlando. Most of these require more than 30 minutes of commuting to Disney World and thus are not rated. We also haven't rated lodging east of Siesta Lago Drive on US 192.

WHAT'S IN A ROOM?

EXCEPT FOR CLEANLINESS, state of repair, and decor, travelers pay little attention to hotel rooms. There is, of course, a clear standard of quality and luxury that differentiates Motel 6 from Holiday Inn, Holiday Inn from Marriott, and so on. Many guests, however, fail to appreciate that some rooms are better engineered than others. Making the room usable to its occupants is an art that combines both form and function.

Decor and taste are important. No one wants to stay in a room that's dated, garish, or ugly. But beyond decor, how "livable" is the room? In Orlando, for example, we've seen some beautifully appointed rooms that aren't well designed for human habitation. Even more than decor, your room's details and design elements are the things that will make you feel comfortable and at home.

ROOM RATINGS

TO EVALUATE PROPERTIES FOR THEIR QUALITY, tastefulness, state of repair, cleanliness, and size of their standard rooms, we have grouped the hotels and motels into classifications denoted by stars—the overall star rating. Star ratings in this guide apply only to Orlando-area properties and don't necessarily correspond to ratings awarded by *Frommer's*, Mobil, AAA, or other travel critics. Because stars have little relevance when awarded in the absence of recognized standards of comparison, we have tied our ratings to expected levels of quality established by specific American hotel corporations.

Overall star ratings apply only to room quality and describe the property's standard accommodations. For most hotels, a standard accommodation is a room with one king bed or two queen beds. In an all-suite property, the standard accommodation is either a studio or a one-bedroom suite. In addition to standard accommodations, many hotels offer luxury rooms and special suites, which aren't rated in this guide. Star ratings for rooms are assigned without regard to whether a property has restaurant(s), recreational facilities, entertainment, or other extras.

In addition to stars (which delineate broad categories), we use a numerical rating system—the room-quality rating. Our scale is 0–100, with 100 being the best possible rating and zero (0) the worst. Numerical ratings show the difference we perceive between one property and another. For instance, rooms at both the Hawthorn Suites Universal and the Clarion Suites Maingate are rated 3½ stars (★★★½). In the supplemental numerical ratings, the former is an 82 and the latter a 76. This means that within the 3½-star category, Hawthorn Suites has slightly nicer rooms than Clarion Suites.

The location column identifies the area around Walt Disney World where you'll find a particular property. The designation **WDW** means the property is inside Walt Disney World. A **1** means it's on or near International Drive. Properties on or near US 192 (a.k.a. Irlo Bronson Memorial Highway, Vine Street, and Space Coast Parkway) are indicated by a **3,** and those in the vicinity of Universal Orlando as **4.** All others are marked with **2** and for the most part are along FL 535 and the I-4 corridor, though some are in nearby locations that don't meet any other criteria.

LODGING AREAS *(see map on page 220)*	
WDW	Walt Disney World
1	International Drive
2	Lake Buena Vista and I-4 Corridor
3	US 192 (Irlo Bronson Memorial Highway)
4	Universal Orlando Area

Names of properties along US 192 also designate location (for example, Holiday Inn Maingate West). The consensus in Orlando seems to be that the main entrance to Disney World is the broad interstate-type road that runs off US 192. This is called the **Maingate.** Properties along US 192 call themselves Maingate East or West to differentiate their positions along the highway. So, driving southeast from Clermont or Florida's Turnpike, the properties before you reach the Maingate turn-off are called Maingate West, while the properties after you pass the Maingate turnoff are called Maingate East.

Cost estimates are based on the hotel's published rack rates for standard rooms. Each **$** represents $50. Thus a cost symbol of **$$$** means that a room (or suite) at that hotel will be about $150 a night; amounts over $200 are indicated by **$ x 5** and so on.

OVERALL STAR RATINGS		
★★★★★	Superior rooms	Tasteful and luxurious by any standard
★★★★	Extremely nice rooms	What you'd expect at a Hyatt Regency or Marriott
★★★	Nice rooms	Holiday Inn or comparable quality
★★	Adequate rooms	Clean, comfortable, and functional without frills—like a Motel 6
★	Super-budget	These exist but are not included in our coverage

We've focused on room quality and excluded consideration of location, services, recreation, or amenities. In some instances, a one- or two-room suite is available for the same price or less than that of a single standard hotel room.

If you've used an earlier edition of this guide, you'll notice that new properties have been added and many ratings and rankings have changed, some because of room renovation or improved maintenance or housekeeping. Failure to maintain rooms or lax housekeeping can bring down ratings.

Before you shop for a hotel, consider this letter from a man in Hot Springs, Arkansas:

We canceled our room reservations to follow the advice in your book and reserved a hotel highly ranked by the Unofficial Guide. *We wanted inexpensive, but clean and cheerful. We got inexpensive, but also dirty, grim, and depressing. The room spoiled the holiday for me aside from our touring.*

This letter was as unsettling to us as the bad room was to the reader—our integrity as travel journalists is based on the quality of the information we provide. When rechecking the hotel, we found our rating was representative, but the reader had been assigned one of a small number of threadbare rooms scheduled for renovation.

unofficial **TIP**
The key to avoiding disappointment is to snoop in advance. Ask how old the hotel is and when its guest rooms were last renovated.

Be aware that some chains use the same guest-room photo in promotional literature for all their hotels and that the rooms at a specific property may not resemble the photo. When you or your travel agent calls, ask how old the property is and when the guest room you're being assigned was last renovated. If you're assigned a room inferior to expectations, demand to be moved.

Note: The following hotels listed in the 2012 *Unofficial Guide* have declined so precipitously in quality that we have eliminated them from our ratings:

- **Central Motel** 4698 W. Irlo Bronson Memorial Highway, Kissimmee
- **Golden Link Resort Motel** 4914 W. Irlo Bronson Memorial Highway, Kissimmee
- **Key Motel** 4810 W. Irlo Bronson Memorial Highway, Kissimmee

The Top 30 Best Deals

	HOTEL	LOCATION	OVERALL QUALITY	ROOM QUALITY	($ = $50)
1.	MONUMENTAL HOTEL	1	★★★★½	94	$+
2.	RODEWAY INN MAINGATE	3	★★½	59	$−
3.	LIKI TIKI VILLAGE	3	★★★★½	90	$$−
4.	HOLIDAY INN MAIN GATE EAST	3	★★★★½	90	$$−
5.	CHAMPIONS WORLD RESORT	3	★★★	66	$
6.	HOMESUITEHOME EASTGATE	3	★★½	57	$−
7.	RAMADA MAINGATE WEST KISSIMMEE	3	★★★	65	$
8.	BAYMONT INN & SUITES CELEBRATION	3	★★★	72	$
9.	SHADES OF GREEN	WDW	★★★★½	91	$$
10.	CONTINENTAL PLAZA HOTEL KISSIMMEE	3	★★½	60	$−
11.	EXTENDED STAY DELUXE ORLANDO CONVENTION CENTER	1	★★★★	84	$$−
12.	HILTON GRAND VACATIONS CLUB AT SEAWORLD	1	★★★★½	95	$$
13.	EXTENDED STAY DELUXE ORLANDO LAKE BUENA VISTA	2	★★★★	83	$$−
14.	ORLANDO VISTA HOTEL	2	★★★★	83	$$−
15.	RADISSON RESORT ORLANDO-CELEBRATION	3	★★★★	86	$$−
16.	MAINGATE LAKESIDE RESORT	3	★★★	67	$
17.	HILTON GARDEN INN LAKE BUENA VISTA/ORLANDO	2	★★★★	88	$$−
18.	EXTENDED STAY AMERICA UNIVERSAL	4	★★★½	75	$+
19.	DAYS INN ORLANDO/I-DRIVE	1	★★½	61	$−
20.	MYSTIC DUNES RESORT & GOLF CLUB	3	★★★★	87	$$−
21.	FOUR POINTS BY SHERATON ORLANDO STUDIO CITY	1	★★★★½	90	$$
22.	HOLIDAY INN RESORT LAKE BUENA VISTA	2	★★★½	82	$$−
23.	SUPER 8 KISSIMMEE/MAINGATE	3	★★★	70	$
24.	MOTEL 6 ORLANDO–I-DRIVE	1	★★½	61	$−
25.	KNIGHTS INN MAINGATE KISSIMMEE/ORLANDO	3	★★	55	$−
26.	VACATION VILLAGE AT PARKWAY	3	★★★★½	91	$$+
27.	DESTINY PALMS MAINGATE WEST	3	★★½	60	$−
28.	EXTENDED STAY DELUXE ORLANDO UNIVERSAL	4	★★★½	75	$+
29.	ROYAL CELEBRATION INN	3	★★½	60	$−
30.	SERALAGO HOTEL & SUITES MAIN GATE EAST	3	★★★	71	$+

- **Monte Carlo Motel** 4733 W. Irlo Bronson Memorial Highway, Kissimmee
- **Quality Inn & Suites** 2945 Entry Point Blvd., Kissimmee

A WORD ABOUT TOLL-FREE TELEPHONE NUMBERS

AS WE'VE REPEATED SEVERAL TIMES in this chapter, it's essential to communicate with the hotel directly when shopping for deals and stating your room preferences. Most toll-free numbers are routed directly to a hotel chain's central reservations office, and the customer-service agents there typically have little or no knowledge of the individual hotels in the chain or of any specials those hotels may be offering. In our Hotel Information Chart (pages 261–279), therefore, we list the toll-free number only if it connects directly to the hotel in question; otherwise, we provide the hotel's local phone number. We also provide local numbers for the Disney resorts in the Hotel Information Chart and in the Walt Disney World Phone Numbers chart on pages 30 and 31, but note that these hotels must be booked through the Disney Reservation Center (☎ 407-W-DISNEY). After you've reserved your room, however, it's a good idea to call the hotel directly about two weeks before you arrive to make sure the reservation is in order.

THE 30 BEST HOTEL VALUES

IN THE CHART ON THE FACING PAGE, we look at the best combinations of quality and value in a room. Rankings are made without consideration for location or the availability of restaurant(s), recreational facilities, entertainment, and/or amenities.

A reader wrote to complain that he had booked one of our top-ranked rooms in terms of value and had been very disappointed in the room. We noticed that the room the reader occupied had a quality rating of ★★½. Remember that the list of top deals is intended to give you some sense of value received for dollars spent. A ★★½ room at $40 may have the same value as a ★★★★ room at $115, but that doesn't mean the rooms will be of comparable quality. Regardless of whether it's a good deal, a ★★½ room is still a ★★½ room.

For example, the Magic Castle Inn and Suites is a clean, reasonably comfortable motel with an exceptionally friendly staff, within 15 minutes of every Disney theme park. During one Christmas season they had available basic rooms for around $54 per night when every other hotel within 20 miles of Walt Disney World was charging $150. The catch? They're right next door to a place that gives helicopter tours of Orlando . . . all day long. You won't notice a thing if you don't plan on midday breaks, but our midafternoon naps were filled with visions of *M*A*S*H* and *Apocalypse Now*. We'd still stay there again, but our significant others have different opinions.

How the Hotels Compare

HOTEL	LOCATION	OVERALL QUALITY	ROOM QUALITY	COST ($ = $50)
Omni Orlando Resort at ChampionsGate	2	★★★★★	96	$$$$+
Hilton Grand Vacations Club at SeaWorld	1	★★★★½	95	$$
Sheraton Vistana Resort Villas	2	★★★★½	95	$$$–
Rosen Centre Hotel	1	★★★★½	95	$$$$
Disney's Animal Kingdom Villas (*Kidani Village*)	WDW	★★★★½	95	$ x 7
Bay Lake Tower at Contemporary Resort	WDW	★★★★½	95	$ x 10–
Monumental Hotel	1	★★★★½	94	$+
Gaylord Palms Hotel & Convention Center	3	★★★★½	94	$$$$
The Ritz-Carlton Orlando, Grande Lakes	1	★★★★½	94	$ x 7–
Westgate Town Center	2	★★★★½	93	$$+
Renaissance Orlando SeaWorld	1	★★★★½	93	$$$$–
JW Marriott Orlando Grande Lakes	1	★★★★½	93	$ x 5–
Orange Lake Resort	3	★★★★½	93	$ x 5–
Hard Rock Hotel	4	★★★★½	93	$ x 6+
Contemporary Resort	WDW	★★★★½	93	$ x 7
Waldorf Astoria Orlando	2	★★★★½	93	$ x 10–
Grand Floridian Resort & Spa	WDW	★★★★½	93	$ x 11–
DoubleTree by Hilton Orlando at SeaWorld (resort)	1	★★★★½	92	$$$–
DoubleTree by Hilton Orlando at SeaWorld (tower)	1	★★★★½	92	$$$–
Hyatt Regency Grand Cypress	2	★★★★½	92	$$$–
Marriott's Grande Vista	1	★★★★½	92	$$$
Westgate Lakes Resort & Spa	2	★★★★½	92	$$$
Hilton Orlando	1	★★★★½	92	$ x 5–
Marriott's Sabal Palms	2	★★★★½	92	$ x 5–
Villas of Grand Cypress	2	★★★★½	92	$ x 5+
Loews Portofino Bay Hotel	4	★★★★½	92	$ x 9–
Polynesian Resort	WDW	★★★★½	92	$ x 9+
Shades of Green	WDW	★★★★½	91	$$
Vacation Village at Parkway	3	★★★★½	91	$$+
Disney's Animal Kingdom Villas (*Jambo House*)	WDW	★★★★½	91	$ x 7
Holiday Inn Main Gate East	3	★★★★½	90	$$–
Liki Tiki Village	3	★★★★½	90	$$–
Four Points by Sheraton Orlando Studio City	1	★★★★½	90	$$
Westgate Vacation Villas	2	★★★★½	90	$$+

How the Hotels Compare

HOTEL	LOCATION	OVERALL QUALITY	ROOM QUALITY	COST ($ = $50)
CoCo Key Water Resort–Orlando	1	★★★★½	90	$$$–
Marriott's Harbour Lake	2	★★★★½	90	$$$–
Lighthouse Key Resort & Spa	3	★★★★½	90	$$$
Bohemian Celebration Hotel	2	★★★★½	90	$$$$–
Polynesian Isles Resort (*Diamond Resorts*)	3	★★★★½	90	$$$$–
Rosen Plaza Hotel	1	★★★★½	90	$$$$–
Wyndham Bonnet Creek Resort	2	★★★★½	90	$ x 5–
Dolphin	WDW	★★★★½	90	$ x 5+
Swan	WDW	★★★★½	90	$ x 5+
Grand Beach	1	★★★★½	90	$ x 6–
Peabody Orlando	1	★★★★½	90	$ x 6
Disney's Old Key West Resort	WDW	★★★★½	90	$ x 7+
Disney's Saratoga Springs Resort & Spa	WDW	★★★★½	90	$ x 7+
Loews Royal Pacific Resort at Universal Orlando	4	★★★★½	90	$ x 7+
Beach Club Resort	WDW	★★★★½	90	$ x 8
Beach Club Villas	WDW	★★★★½	90	$ x 8+
BoardWalk Villas	WDW	★★★★½	90	$ x 8+
Wilderness Lodge Villas	WDW	★★★★½	90	$ x 8+
Treehouse Villas at Disney's Saratoga Springs Resort & Spa	WDW	★★★★½	90	$ x 15–
Courtyard Orlando Lake Buena Vista at Vista Centre	2	★★★★	89	$$+
DoubleTree Universal	4	★★★★	89	$$+
Hilton Orlando Bonnet Creek	1	★★★★	89	$$$+
Orlando World Center Marriott Resort	2	★★★★	89	$ x 5+
Disney's Animal Kingdom Lodge	WDW	★★★★	89	$ x 7–
Yacht Club Resort	WDW	★★★★	89	$ x 8
BoardWalk Inn	WDW	★★★★	89	$ x 8+
Hilton Garden Inn LBV/Orlando	2	★★★★	88	$$–
Sheraton Lake Buena Vista Resort	2	★★★★	88	$$
Hilton Grand Vacations Club on I-Drive	1	★★★★	88	$$+
Caribe Royale All-Suite Hotel & Convention Center	1	★★★★	88	$$$$–
WorldQuest Orlando Resort	1	★★★★	88	$$$$–
Rosen Shingle Creek	1	★★★★	88	$$$$+
Mystic Dunes Resort & Golf Club	3	★★★★	87	$$–
Hawthorn Suites Lake Buena Vista	2	★★★★	87	$$+
Wyndham Cypress Palms	3	★★★★	87	$$$
The Westin Imagine Orlando	1	★★★★	87	$$$$–

How the Hotels Compare

HOTEL	LOCATION	OVERALL QUALITY	ROOM QUALITY	COST ($ = $50)
Hilton in the Walt Disney World Resort	WDW	★★★★	87	$$$$+
Radisson Resort Orlando-Celebration	3	★★★★	86	$$−
Floridays Resort Orlando	1	★★★★	86	$$$
Marriott Cypress Harbour Villas	1	★★★★	86	$ x 5+
Wilderness Lodge	WDW	★★★★	86	$ x 6+
Fort Wilderness Resort (cabins)	WDW	★★★★	86	$ x 7−
Marriott Imperial Palm Villas	1	★★★★	86	$ x 9−
Barefoot'n Resort	3	★★★★	85	$$
Marriott Residence Inn Orlando SeaWorld/International Center	2	★★★★	85	$$
Caribe Cove Resort Orlando	3	★★★★	85	$$$−
Homewood Suites by Hilton LBV-Orlando	2	★★★★	85	$$$−
Legacy Vacation Club LBV	2	★★★★	85	$$$−
Marriott's Royal Palms	1	★★★★	85	$ x 5−
Extended Stay Deluxe Orlando Convention Center	1	★★★★	84	$$−
Hyatt Place Orlando/Universal	4	★★★★	84	$$
Star Island Resort & Club	3	★★★★	84	$$$+
Port Orleans Resort (French Quarter)	WDW	★★★★	84	$$$$−
Extended Stay Deluxe Orlando LBV	2	★★★★	83	$$−
Orlando Vista Hotel	2	★★★★	83	$$−
Wyndham Orlando Resort	1	★★★★	83	$$
Buena Vista Suites	1	★★★★	83	$$+
Coronado Springs Resort	WDW	★★★★	83	$$$$−
Port Orleans Resort (Riverside)	WDW	★★★★	83	$$$$−
Country Inn & Suites Orlando Maingate at Calypso	3	★★★½	82	$$−
Holiday Inn Resort LBV	2	★★★½	82	$$−
Courtyard Orlando LBV in Marriott Village	2	★★★½	82	$$+
Hawthorn Suites Universal	1	★★★½	82	$$+
Holiday Inn Resort Orlando–The Castle	1	★★★½	82	$$+
Nickelodeon Suites Resort	1	★★★½	82	$$+
Radisson Hotel Orlando LBV	2	★★★½	82	$$+
Parkway International Resort	3	★★★½	82	$$$−
The Point Orlando Resort	1	★★★½	82	$$$+
Westgate Towers	2	★★★½	81	$$
Embassy Suites Orlando–LBV	2	★★★½	81	$$+
Homewood Suites by Hilton I-Drive	1	★★★½	81	$$$

How the Hotels Compare

HOTEL	LOCATION	OVERALL QUALITY	ROOM QUALITY	COST ($ = $50)
Hampton Inn & Suites Orlando–South Lake Buena Vista	3	★★★½	80	$$
Hilton Garden Inn Orlando at SeaWorld	1	★★★½	80	$$
Legacy Vacation Club Orlando	3	★★★½	80	$$
Fairfield Inn & Suites Near Universal Orlando Resort	4	★★★½	80	$$+
Hilton Garden Inn Orlando I-Drive North	1	★★★½	80	$$+
Holiday Inn Express LBV	2	★★★½	80	$$+
Orbit One Vacation Villas	3	★★★½	80	$$+
Residence Inn Orlando Convention Center	1	★★★½	80	$$+
SpringHill Suites Orlando Convention Center	1	★★★½	80	$$+
Buena Vista Palace Hotel & Spa	WDW	★★★½	80	$$$–
Hawthorn Suites Orlando Convention Center	1	★★★½	80	$$$–
Lucaya Village Resort	3	★★★½	80	$$$–
DoubleTree Guest Suites	WDW	★★★½	80	$$$
Embassy Suites Orlando I-Drive/Jamaican Court	1	★★★½	80	$$$+
Caribbean Beach Resort	WDW	★★★½	80	$$$$–
Holiday Inn in the Walt Disney World Resort	WDW	★★★½	79	$$$–
Fairfield Inn & Suites Orlando LBV (rooms)	2	★★★½	78	$$
Art of Animation Resort	WDW	★★★½	78	$$+
Fairfield Inn & Suites Orlando LBV (suites)	2	★★★½	78	$$+
Courtyard Orlando I-Drive	1	★★★½	78	$$$
WorldGate Resort	3	★★★½	77	$$$+
Clarion Suites Maingate	3	★★★½	76	$$–
Palms Hotel & Villas	3	★★★½	76	$$–
Grand Lake Resort	1	★★★½	76	$$
Hampton Inn Orlando/LBV	2	★★★½	76	$$
Royal Plaza (tower)	WDW	★★★½	76	$$+
Extended Stay America Universal	4	★★★½	75	$+
Extended Stay Deluxe Orlando Universal	4	★★★½	75	$+
Best Western Plus Universal Inn	4	★★★½	75	$$–
Fairfield Inn & Suites Orlando LBV in Marriott Village	2	★★★½	75	$$–
Holiday Inn & Suites Orlando Universal	4	★★★½	75	$$
Quality Suites Royale Parc Suites	3	★★★½	75	$$
Wyndham Lake Buena Vista Resort	WDW	★★★½	75	$$

How the Hotels Compare

HOTEL	LOCATION	OVERALL QUALITY	ROOM QUALITY	COST ($ = $50)
Residence Inn Orlando I-Drive	1	★★★½	75	$$+
Residence Inn Orlando LBV	2	★★★½	75	$$+
Rosen Inn at Pointe Orlando	1	★★★½	75	$$+
Staybridge Suites Orlando	1	★★★½	75	$$+
Embassy Suites Orlando I-Drive	1	★★★½	75	$$$−
Galleria Palms Kissimmee Hotel	3	★★★	74	$+
Quality Suites Orlando	2	★★★	74	$+
Best Western LBV Resort Hotel	WDW	★★★	74	$$−
Quality Suites Orlando LBV	2	★★★	74	$$−
Orlando Hotel & Suites	1	★★★	74	$$+
La Quinta Inn Orlando I-Drive	1	★★★	73	$+
All-Star Resorts	WDW	★★★	73	$$+
International Palms Resort & Conference Center	1	★★★	73	$$+
Royal Plaza (garden)	WDW	★★★	73	$$+
Baymont Inn & Suites Celebration	3	★★★	72	$
Extended Stay America Orlando Convention Center	1	★★★	72	$+
Ramada Plaza Resort and Suites Orlando I-Drive	1	★★★	72	$$−
Staybridge Suites Lake Buena Vista	2	★★★	72	$$+
Seralago Hotel & Suites Main Gate East	3	★★★	71	$+
Ramada Gateway Kissimmee (tower)	3	★★★	71	$$−
Pop Century Resort	WDW	★★★	71	$$+
SpringHill Suites Orlando LBV in Marriott Village	2	★★★	71	$$+
Super 8 Kissimmee/Maingate	3	★★★	70	$
Comfort Suites Universal	4	★★★	70	$$−
Hampton Inn I-Drive/Convention Center	1	★★★	70	$$−
Holiday Inn Express West of Theme Park Area	3	★★★	70	$$−
Best Western Orlando Gateway Hotel	1	★★★	70	$$$−
Monumental MovieLand Hotel	1	★★★	68	$+
Westgate Palace	1	★★★	68	$$$$−
Maingate Lakeside Resort	3	★★★	67	$
The Enclave Hotel & Suites	1	★★★	67	$$−
Hampton Inn Universal	4	★★★	67	$$
Champions World Resort	3	★★★	66	$
Comfort Inn Universal Studios Area	1	★★★	66	$
Ramada Convention Center I-Drive	1	★★★	65	$
Ramada Maingate West Kissimmee	3	★★★	65	$

How the Hotels Compare

HOTEL	LOCATION	OVERALL QUALITY	ROOM QUALITY	COST ($ = $50)
Quality Inn International Hotel	1	★★★	65	$$–
Best Western I-Drive	1	★★★	65	$$+
Ramada Gateway Kissimmee (*garden*)	3	★★½	64	$+
Clarion Inn & Suites at I-Drive	1	★★½	64	$$–
Clarion Inn Lake Buena Vista	2	★★½	64	$$–
Hampton Inn South of Universal	1	★★½	64	$$+
Silver Lake Resort	3	★★½	64	$$+
The Floridian Hotel & Suites	1	★★½	63	$
Orlando Metropolitan Express	1	★★½	63	$
La Quinta Inn Orlando–Universal Studios	4	★★½	63	$+
Country Inn & Suites Orlando Universal	1	★★½	63	$$–
Econo Lodge Inn & Suites I-Drive	1	★★½	62	$
Days Inn Orlando/I-Drive	1	★★½	61	$–
Motel 6 Orlando–I-Drive	1	★★½	61	$–
Rodeway Inn Universal Studios Area	1	★★½	61	$+
Celebration Suites	3	★★½	61	$$–
Continental Plaza Hotel Kissimmee	3	★★½	60	$–
Destiny Palms Maingate West	3	★★½	60	$–
Royal Celebration Inn	3	★★½	60	$–
Super 8 Kissimmee	3	★★½	60	$
Clarion Hotel Maingate	3	★★½	60	$+
Comfort Inn I-Drive	1	★★½	60	$+
Days Inn Orlando/Convention Center	1	★★½	60	$+
Days Inn Orlando/Universal Maingate	4	★★½	60	$+
Lexington Suites Orlando	1	★★½	60	$+
Howard Johnson Inn Orlando I-Drive	1	★★½	59	$–
Rodeway Inn Maingate	3	★★½	59	$–
Claremont Hotel Kissimmee	3	★★½	59	$+
Howard Johnson Enchanted Land Hotel	3	★★½	59	$$–
Red Roof Inn Orlando Convention Center	1	★★½	58	$+
Extended Stay Deluxe Pointe Orlando	1	★★½	58	$$–
HomeSuiteHome Eastgate	3	★★½	57	$–
Knights Inn Maingate Kissimmee/ Orlando	3	★★	55	$–
Masters Inn Kissimmee	3	★★	55	$–

How the Hotels Compare

HOTEL	LOCATION	OVERALL QUALITY	ROOM QUALITY	COST ($ = $50)
Quality Inn & Suites Eastgate	3	★★	55	$+
Travelodge Suites East Gate Orange	3	★★	55	$+
Motel 6 Main Gate West	3	★★	52	$−
Rosen Inn	1	★★	51	$+
America's Best Inn Main Gate East	3	★★	50	$−
Magic Castle Inn & Suites	3	★★	50	$−
Howard Johnson Express Inn & Suites	3	★★	50	$
La Quinta Inn Orlando I-Drive North	1	★★	50	$+
HomeSuiteHome Kissimmee Maingate	3	★★	48	$−
Motel 6 Main Gate East	3	★★	47	$−
Orlando Continental Plaza Hotel	1	★★	47	$−
Red Roof Inn Kissimmee	3	★★	47	$$−
Days Inn Clermont Theme Park West	3	★½	41	$+

Hotel Information Chart

All-Star Resorts ★★★
1701–1901 W. Buena Vista Dr.
Lake Buena Vista, FL 32830
☎ 407-934-7639
tinyurl.com/disneyvalueresorts

LOCATION	WDW
ROOM RATING	73
COST ($ = $50)	$$+

commuting times to parks (*in minutes*)
MAGIC KINGDOM	6:15
EPCOT	5:45
ANIMAL KINGDOM	4:15
DHS	5:15

America's Best Inn Main Gate East ★★
5150 W. US 192*
Kissimmee, FL 34746
☎ 407-396-1111
americasbestinnmge.com

LOCATION	3
ROOM RATING	50
COST ($ = $50)	$–

commuting times to parks (*in minutes*)
MAGIC KINGDOM	15:45
EPCOT	15:15
ANIMAL KINGDOM	13:45
DHS	15:00

Art of Animation Resort ★★★½
1850 Animation Way
Lake Buena Vista, FL 32830
☎ 407-938-7000
tinyurl.com/disneyvalueresorts

LOCATION	WDW
ROOM RATING	78
COST ($ = $50)	$$+

commuting times to parks (*in minutes*)
MAGIC KINGDOM	8:30
EPCOT	6:30
ANIMAL KINGDOM	6:15
DHS	5:00

Barefoot'n Resort ★★★★
2750 Florida Plaza Blvd.
Kissimmee, FL 34746
☎ 407-589-2127
barefootn.com

LOCATION	3
ROOM RATING	85
COST ($ = $50)	$$

commuting times to parks (*in minutes*)
MAGIC KINGDOM	16:30
EPCOT	14:00
ANIMAL KINGDOM	14:00
DHS	12:30

Bay Lake Tower at Contemporary Resort ★★★★½
4600 N. World Dr.
Lake Buena Vista, FL 32830
☎ 407-824-1000
tinyurl.com/baylaketower

LOCATION	WDW
ROOM RATING	95
COST ($ = $50)	$$$$$$$$$–

commuting times to parks (*in minutes*)
MAGIC KINGDOM	ON MONORAIL
EPCOT	11:00
ANIMAL KINGDOM	17:15
DHS	14:15

Baymont Inn & Suites Celebration ★★★
7601 Black Lake Rd.
Kissimmee, FL 34747
☎ 407-396-1100
tinyurl.com/baymontcelebration

LOCATION	3
ROOM RATING	72
COST ($ = $50)	$

commuting times to parks (*in minutes*)
MAGIC KINGDOM	8:30
EPCOT	8:15
ANIMAL KINGDOM	5:30
DHS	7:45

Beach Club Resort ★★★★½
1800 Epcot Resorts Blvd.
Lake Buena Vista, FL 32830
☎ 407-934-8000
tinyurl.com/beachclubresort

LOCATION	WDW
ROOM RATING	90
COST ($ = $50)	$$$$$$$

commuting times to parks (*in minutes*)
MAGIC KINGDOM	7:15
EPCOT	5:15
ANIMAL KINGDOM	6:45
DHS	4:00

Beach Club Villas ★★★★½
1900 Epcot Resorts Blvd.
Lake Buena Vista, FL 32830
☎ 407-934-2175
tinyurl.com/beachclubvillas

LOCATION	WDW
ROOM RATING	90
COST ($ = $50)	$$$$$$$$+

commuting times to parks (*in minutes*)
MAGIC KINGDOM	7:15
EPCOT	5:15
ANIMAL KINGDOM	6:45
DHS	4:00

Best Western I-Drive ★★★
8222 Jamaican Ct.
Orlando, FL 32819
☎ 407-345-1172
tinyurl.com/bwidrive

LOCATION	1
ROOM RATING	65
COST ($ = $50)	$$+

commuting times to parks (*in minutes*)
MAGIC KINGDOM	8:30
EPCOT	8:15
ANIMAL KINGDOM	11:15
DHS	10:45

Best Western LBV Resort Hotel ★★★
2000 Hotel Plaza Blvd.
Lake Buena Vista, FL 32830
☎ 407-828-2424
lakebuenavistaresorthotel.com

LOCATION	WDW
ROOM RATING	74
COST ($ = $50)	$$–

commuting times to parks (*in minutes*)
MAGIC KINGDOM	16:00
EPCOT	11:15
ANIMAL KINGDOM	15:15
DHS	13:00

Best Western Orlando Gateway Hotel ★★★
7299 Universal Blvd.
Orlando, FL 32819
☎ 407-351-5009
bworlando.com

LOCATION	1
ROOM RATING	70
COST ($ = $50)	$$$–

commuting times to parks (*in minutes*)
MAGIC KINGDOM	20:30
EPCOT	15:45
ANIMAL KINGDOM	18:45
DHS	18:30

Best Western Plus Universal Inn ★★★½
5618 Vineland Rd.
Orlando, FL 32819
☎ 407-226-9119
tinyurl.com/bwuniversal

LOCATION	4
ROOM RATING	75
COST ($ = $50)	$$–

commuting times to parks (*in minutes*)
MAGIC KINGDOM	17:30
EPCOT	13:00
ANIMAL KINGDOM	16:00
DHS	15:30

* Irlo Bronson Memorial Highway

Hotel Information Chart (continued)

BoardWalk Inn ★★★★
2101 Epcot Resorts Blvd.
Lake Buena Vista, FL 32830
☎ 407-939-5100
tinyurl.com/boardwalkinn

LOCATION	WDW
ROOM RATING	89
COST ($ = $50)	$$$$$$$$+

commuting times to parks (*in minutes*)
MAGIC KINGDOM	7:15
EPCOT	5:30
ANIMAL KINGDOM	7:00
DHS	3:00

BoardWalk Villas ★★★★½
2101 Epcot Resorts Blvd.
Lake Buena Vista, FL 32830
☎ 407-939-5100
tinyurl.com/boardwalkvillas

LOCATION	WDW
ROOM RATING	90
COST ($ = $50)	$$$$$$$$+

commuting times to parks (*in minutes*)
MAGIC KINGDOM	7:15
EPCOT	5:30
ANIMAL KINGDOM	7:00
DHS	3:00

Bohemian Celebration Hotel
★★★★½
700 Bloom St.
Celebration, FL 34747
☎ 407-566-6000
celebrationhotel.com

LOCATION	2
ROOM RATING	90
COST ($ = $50)	$$$$–

commuting times to parks (*in minutes*)
MAGIC KINGDOM	13:30
EPCOT	13:00
ANIMAL KINGDOM	13:00
DHS	12:30

Caribe Cove Resort Orlando
★★★★
9000 Treasure Trove Ln.
Kissimmee, FL 34747
☎ 407-997-4444
caribecove.com

LOCATION	3
ROOM RATING	85
COST ($ = $50)	$$$–

commuting times to parks (*in minutes*)
MAGIC KINGDOM	22:30
EPCOT	22:00
ANIMAL KINGDOM	13:00
DHS	18:00

Caribe Royale All-Suite Hotel & Convention Center
★★★★
8101 World Center Dr.
Orlando, FL 32821
☎ 407-238-8000
cariberesorts.com

LOCATION	1
ROOM RATING	88
COST ($ = $50)	$$$$–

commuting times to parks (*in minutes*)
MAGIC KINGDOM	9:15
EPCOT	4:45
ANIMAL KINGDOM	7:45
DHS	8:15

Celebration Suites ★★½
5820 W. US 192*
Kissimmee, FL 34746
☎ 407-396-7900
suitesatoldtown.com

LOCATION	3
ROOM RATING	61
COST ($ = $50)	$$–

commuting times to parks (*in minutes*)
MAGIC KINGDOM	11:15
EPCOT	11:00
ANIMAL KINGDOM	9:15
DHS	10:30

Clarion Inn & Suites at I-Drive ★★½
9956 Hawaiian Ct.
Orlando, FL 32819
☎ 407-351-5100
tinyurl.com/clarionidrive

LOCATION	1
ROOM RATING	64
COST ($ = $50)	$$–

commuting times to parks (*in minutes*)
MAGIC KINGDOM	19:30
EPCOT	14:15
ANIMAL KINGDOM	17:15
DHS	16:45

Clarion Inn LBV ★★½
8442 Palm Pkwy.
Lake Buena Vista, FL 32836
☎ 407-996-7300
clarionlbv.com

LOCATION	2
ROOM RATING	64
COST ($ = $50)	$$–

commuting times to parks (*in minutes*)
MAGIC KINGDOM	13:15
EPCOT	8:30
ANIMAL KINGDOM	11:30
DHS	11:00

Clarion Suites Maingate
★★★½
7888 W. US 192*
Kissimmee, FL 34747
☎ 407-390-9888
clarionsuiteskissimmee.com

LOCATION	3
ROOM RATING	76
COST ($ = $50)	$$–

commuting times to parks (*in minutes*)
MAGIC KINGDOM	10:00
EPCOT	9:15
ANIMAL KINGDOM	7:00
DHS	9:00

Comfort Suites Universal
★★★
5617 Major Blvd.
Orlando, FL 32819
☎ 407-363-1967
tinyurl.com/csuniversal

LOCATION	4
ROOM RATING	70
COST ($ = $50)	$$–

commuting times to parks (*in minutes*)
MAGIC KINGDOM	17:45
EPCOT	13:15
ANIMAL KINGDOM	16:15
DHS	15:15

Contemporary Resort
★★★★½
4600 N. World Dr.
Lake Buena Vista, FL 32830
☎ 407-934-7639
tinyurl.com/contemporarywdw

LOCATION	WDW
ROOM RATING	93
COST ($ = $50)	$$$$$$$

commuting times to parks (*in minutes*)
MAGIC KINGDOM	ON MONORAIL
EPCOT	11:00
ANIMAL KINGDOM	17:15
DHS	14:15

Continental Plaza Hotel Kissimmee ★★½
7785 W. US 192*
Kissimmee, FL 34747
☎ 407-396-1828
continentalplazahotels.com

LOCATION	3
ROOM RATING	60
COST ($ = $50)	$–

commuting times to parks (*in minutes*)
MAGIC KINGDOM	9:15
EPCOT	8:45
ANIMAL KINGDOM	6:30
DHS	8:30

* Irlo Bronson Memorial Highway

Buena Vista Palace Hotel & Spa ★★★½
1900 Buena Vista Dr.
Lake Buena Vista, FL 32830
☎ 407-827-2727
buenavistapalace.com

LOCATION	WDW
ROOM RATING	80
COST ($ = $50)	$$$–

commuting times to parks (*In minutes*)

MAGIC KINGDOM	16.00
EPCOT	11:15
ANIMAL KINGDOM	15:15
DHS	13:00

Buena Vista Suites ★★★★
8203 World Center Dr.
Orlando, FL 32821
☎ 407-239-8588
bvsuites.com

LOCATION	1
ROOM RATING	83
COST ($ = $50)	$$+

commuting times to parks (*in minutes*)

MAGIC KINGDOM	9:15
EPCOT	4:30
ANIMAL KINGDOM	7:30
DHS	8:15

Caribbean Beach Resort ★★★½
900 Cayman Way
Lake Buena Vista, FL 32830
☎ 407-934-3400
tinyurl.com/caribbeanbeachresort

LOCATION	WDW
ROOM RATING	80
COST ($ = $50)	$$$$–

commuting times to parks (*in minutes*)

MAGIC KINGDOM	8:00
EPCOT	6:00
ANIMAL KINGDOM	7:15
DHS	4:15

Champions World Resort ★★★
8660 W. US 192 *
Kissimmee, FL 34747
☎ 407-396-4500
championsworldresort.com

LOCATION	3
ROOM RATING	66
COST ($ = $50)	$

commuting times to parks (*in minutes*)

MAGIC KINGDOM	13:45
EPCOT	13:45
ANIMAL KINGDOM	10:45
DHS	13:00

Claremont Hotel Kissimmee ★★½
6051 W. US 192 *
Kissimmee, FL 34747
☎ 407-396-1748
claremontkissimmee.com

LOCATION	3
ROOM RATING	59
COST ($ = $50)	$+

commuting times to parks (*in minutes*)

MAGIC KINGDOM	11:15
EPCOT	11:00
ANIMAL KINGDOM	8:15
DHS	10:30

Clarion Hotel Maingate ★★½
7675 W US 192 *
Kissimmee, FL 34747
☎ 407-396-4000
clarionhotelmaingate.com

LOCATION	3
ROOM RATING	60
COST ($ = $50)	$+

commuting times to parks (*in minutes*)

MAGIC KINGDOM	8:30
EPCOT	8:00
ANIMAL KINGDOM	5:30
DHS	7:30

CoCo Key Water Resort–Orlando ★★★★½
7400 International Dr.
Orlando, FL 32819
☎ 407-351-2626
cocokeywaterresort.com

LOCATION	1
ROOM RATING	90
COST ($ = $50)	$$$–

commuting times to parks (*in minutes*)

MAGIC KINGDOM	21:00
EPCOT	16:30
ANIMAL KINGDOM	19:00
DHS	19:30

Comfort Inn I-Drive ★★½
8134 International Dr.
Orlando, FL 32819
☎ 407-313-4000
tinyurl.com/comfortidrive

LOCATION	1
ROOM RATING	60
COST ($ = $50)	$+

commuting times to parks (*in minutes*)

MAGIC KINGDOM	20:00
EPCOT	15:30
ANIMAL KINGDOM	18:30
DHS	18:00

Comfort Inn Universal Studios Area ★★★
6101 Sand Lake Rd.
Orlando, FL 32919
☎ 407-363-7886
tinyurl.com/comfortuniversal

LOCATION	1
ROOM RATING	66
COST ($ = $50)	$

commuting times to parks (*in minutes*)

MAGIC KINGDOM	22:15
EPCOT	17:30
ANIMAL KINGDOM	20:30
DHS	20:00

Coronado Springs Resort ★★★★
1000 W. Buena Vista Dr.
Orlando, FL 32830
☎ 407-939-1000
tinyurl.com/coronadosprings

LOCATION	WDW
ROOM RATING	83
COST ($ = $50)	$$$$–

commuting times to parks (*in minutes*)

MAGIC KINGDOM	5:30
EPCOT	4:00
ANIMAL KINGDOM	4:45
DHS	4:45

Country Inn & Suites Orlando Maingate at Calypso ★★★½
5001 Calypso Cay Way
Kissimmee, FL 34746
☎ 407-997-1400
countryinns.com/orlandofl_maingate

LOCATION	3
ROOM RATING	82
COST ($ = $50)	$$–

commuting times to parks (*in minutes*)

MAGIC KINGDOM	13:30
EPCOT	13:00
ANIMAL KINGDOM	11:30
DHS	12:30

Country Inn & Suites Orlando Universal ★★½
7701 Universal Blvd.
Orlando, FL 32819
☎ 407-313-4200
countryinns.com/orlandofl_universal

LOCATION	1
ROOM RATING	63
COST ($ = $50)	$$–

commuting times to parks (*in minutes*)

MAGIC KINGDOM	21:00
EPCOT	16:15
ANIMAL KINGDOM	19:15
DHS	18:45

Hotel Information Chart (continued)

Courtyard Orlando I-Drive
★★★½
8600 Austrian Ct.
Orlando, FL 32819
☎ 407-351-2244
tinyurl.com/courtyardidrive

LOCATION	1
ROOM RATING	78
COST ($ = $50)	$$$

commuting times to parks (*in minutes*)
MAGIC KINGDOM	21:45
EPCOT	17:00
ANIMAL KINGDOM	20:00
DHS	19:30

Courtyard Orlando LBV at Vista Centre ★★★★
8501 Palm Pkwy.
Lake Buena Vista, FL 32836
☎ 407-239-6900
tinyurl.com/courtyardlbv

LOCATION	2
ROOM RATING	89
COST ($ = $50)	$$+

commuting times to parks (*in minutes*)
MAGIC KINGDOM	13:15
EPCOT	8:30
ANIMAL KINGDOM	11:30
DHS	11:00

Courtyard Orlando LBV in Marriott Village ★★★½
8623 Vineland Ave.
Orlando, FL 32821
☎ 407-938-9001
marriottvillage.com

LOCATION	2
ROOM RATING	82
COST ($ = $50)	$$+

commuting times to parks (*in minutes*)
MAGIC KINGDOM	12:00
EPCOT	7:15
ANIMAL KINGDOM	10:15
DHS	9:45

Days Inn Orlando/ Universal Maingate ★★½
5827 Caravan Ct.
Orlando, FL 32819
☎ 407-351-3800
tinyurl.com/daysinnuniversal

LOCATION	4
ROOM RATING	60
COST ($ = $50)	$+

commuting times to parks (*in minutes*)
MAGIC KINGDOM	18:45
EPCOT	14:00
ANIMAL KINGDOM	17:00
DHS	16:30

Destiny Palms Maingate West
★★½
8536 W. US 192*
Kissimmee, FL 34747
☎ 407-396-1600
destinypalmshotel.com

LOCATION	3
ROOM RATING	60
COST ($ = $50)	$−

commuting times to parks (*in minutes*)
MAGIC KINGDOM	13:45
EPCOT	13:15
ANIMAL KINGDOM	11:00
DHS	13:00

Disney's Animal Kingdom Lodge ★★★★
2901 Osceola Pkwy.
Lake Buena Vista, FL 32830
☎ 407-938-3000
tinyurl.com/aklodge

LOCATION	WDW
ROOM RATING	89
COST ($ = $50)	$$$$$$$−

commuting times to parks (*in minutes*)
MAGIC KINGDOM	8:15
EPCOT	6:15
ANIMAL KINGDOM	2:15
DHS	6:00

Disney's Saratoga Springs Resort & Spa ★★★★½
1960 Broadway
Lake Buena Vista, FL 32830
☎ 407-827-1100
tinyurl.com/saratogawdw

LOCATION	WDW
ROOM RATING	90
COST ($ = $50)	$$$$$$$+

commuting times to parks (*in minutes*)
MAGIC KINGDOM	14:45
EPCOT	8:45
ANIMAL KINGDOM	18:15
DHS	14:30

Dolphin ★★★★½
1500 Epcot Resorts Blvd.
Lake Buena Vista, FL 32830
☎ 407-934-4000
swandolphin.com

LOCATION	WDW
ROOM RATING	90
COST ($ = $50)	$$$$$+

commuting times to parks (*in minutes*)
MAGIC KINGDOM	6:45
EPCOT	5:00
ANIMAL KINGDOM	6:15
DHS	4:00

DoubleTree by Hilton Orlando at SeaWorld (*resort*)
★★★★½
10100 International Dr.
Orlando, FL 32821
☎ 407-352-1100
doubletreeorlandoidrive.com

LOCATION	1
ROOM RATING	92
COST ($ = $50)	$$$−

commuting times to parks (*in minutes*)
MAGIC KINGDOM	17:45
EPCOT	13:00
ANIMAL KINGDOM	16:00
DHS	15:30

Econo Lodge Inn & Suites I-Drive ★★½
8738 International Dr.
Orlando, FL 32819
☎ 407-345-8195

LOCATION	1
ROOM RATING	62
COST ($ = $50)	$

commuting times to parks (*in minutes*)
MAGIC KINGDOM	22:00
EPCOT	17:15
ANIMAL KINGDOM	20:15
DHS	19:45

Embassy Suites Orlando I-Drive ★★★½
8978 International Dr.
Orlando, FL 32819
☎ 407-352-1400
embassysuitesorlando.com

LOCATION	1
ROOM RATING	75
COST ($ = $50)	$$$−

commuting times to parks (*in minutes*)
MAGIC KINGDOM	22:00
EPCOT	17:15
ANIMAL KINGDOM	20:15
DHS	19:45

Embassy Suites Orlando I-Drive/ Jamaican Court ★★★½
8250 Jamaican Ct.
Orlando, FL 32819
☎ 407-345-8250
orlandoembassysuites.com

LOCATION	1
ROOM RATING	80
COST ($ = $50)	$$$+

commuting times to parks (*in minutes*)
MAGIC KINGDOM	20:15
EPCOT	15:30
ANIMAL KINGDOM	18:30
DHS	18:00

* Irlo Bronson Memorial Highway

Days Inn Clermont Theme Park West ★½
9240 W. US 192*
Kissimmee, FL 34711
☎ 863-424-6099
tinyurl.com/daysinnclermont

LOCATION	3
ROOM RATING	41
COST ($ = $50)	$+

commuting times to parks (in minutes)
MAGIC KINGDOM	14:00
EPCOT	13:15
ANIMAL KINGDOM	11:00
DHS	13:00

Days Inn Orlando/ Convention Center ★★½
9990 International Dr.
Orlando, FL 32819
☎ 407-352-8700
daysinnorlandohotel.com

LOCATION	1
ROOM RATING	60
COST ($ = $50)	$+

commuting times to parks (in minutes)
MAGIC KINGDOM	18:45
EPCOT	14:00
ANIMAL KINGDOM	17:00
DHS	16:30

Days Inn Orlando/I-Drive ★★½
5858 International Dr.
Orlando, FL 32819
☎ 407-351-4410
tinyurl.com/daysinnidrive

LOCATION	1
ROOM RATING	61
COST ($ = $50)	$−

commuting times to parks (in minutes)
MAGIC KINGDOM	20:30
EPCOT	16:00
ANIMAL KINGDOM	19:00
DHS	18:30

Disney's Animal Kingdom Villas (Jambo House) ★★★★½
2901 Osceola Pkwy.
Lake Buena Vista, FL 32830
☎ 407-938-3000
tinyurl.com/akjambo

LOCATION	WDW
ROOM RATING	91
COST ($ = $50)	$$$$$$$

commuting times to parks (in minutes)
MAGIC KINGDOM	8:15
EPCOT	6:15
ANIMAL KINGDOM	2:15
DHS	6:00

Disney's Animal Kingdom Villas (Kidani Village) ★★★★½
2901 Osceola Pkwy.
Lake Buena Vista, FL 32830
☎ 407-938-3000
tinyurl.com/akkidani

LOCATION	WDW
ROOM RATING	95
COST ($ = $50)	$$$$$$$

commuting times to parks (in minutes)
MAGIC KINGDOM	8:15
EPCOT	6:15
ANIMAL KINGDOM	2:15
DHS	6:00

Disney's Old Key West Resort ★★★★½
1510 North Cove Rd.
Lake Buena Vista, FL 32830
☎ 407-827-7700
tinyurl.com/oldkeywest

LOCATION	WDW
ROOM RATING	90
COST ($ = $50)	$$$$$$$+

commuting times to parks (in minutes)
MAGIC KINGDOM	10:45
EPCOT	6:00
ANIMAL KINGDOM	14:30
DHS	10:30

DoubleTree by Hilton Orlando at SeaWorld (tower) ★★★★½
10100 International Dr.
Orlando, FL 32821
☎ 407-352-1100
doubletreeorlandoidrive.com

LOCATION	1
ROOM RATING	92
COST ($ = $50)	$$$−

commuting times to parks (in minutes)
MAGIC KINGDOM	17:45
EPCOT	13:00
ANIMAL KINGDOM	16:00
DHS	15:30

DoubleTree Guest Suites ★★★½
2305 Hotel Plaza Blvd.
Lake Buena Vista, FL 32830
☎ 407-934-1000
doubletreeguestsuites.com

LOCATION	WDW
ROOM RATING	80
COST ($ = $50)	$$$

commuting times to parks (in minutes)
MAGIC KINGDOM	13:00
EPCOT	8:30
ANIMAL KINGDOM	12:30
DHS	10:00

DoubleTree Universal ★★★★
5780 Major Blvd.
Orlando, FL 32819
☎ 407-351-1000
doubletreeorlando.com

LOCATION	4
ROOM RATING	89
COST ($ = $50)	$$+

commuting times to parks (in minutes)
MAGIC KINGDOM	19:00
EPCOT	14:15
ANIMAL KINGDOM	17:15
DHS	16:45

Embassy Suites Orlando–LBV ★★★½
8100 Lake Ave.
Orlando, FL 32836
☎ 407-239-1144
embassysuiteslbv.com

LOCATION	2
ROOM RATING	81
COST ($ = $50)	$$+

commuting times to parks (in minutes)
MAGIC KINGDOM	12:45
EPCOT	8:00
ANIMAL KINGDOM	11:00
DHS	10:30

The Enclave Hotel & Suites ★★★
6165 Carrier Dr.
Orlando, FL 32819
☎ 407-351-1155
enclavesuites.com

LOCATION	1
ROOM RATING	67
COST ($ = $50)	$$−

commuting times to parks (in minutes)
MAGIC KINGDOM	20:45
EPCOT	16:15
ANIMAL KINGDOM	19:15
DHS	18:45

Extended Stay America Orlando Convention Center ★★★
6451 Westwood Blvd.
Orlando, FL 32821
☎ 407-352-3454
tinyurl.com/esorlando

LOCATION	1
ROOM RATING	72
COST ($ = $50)	$+

commuting times to parks (in minutes)
MAGIC KINGDOM	17:30
EPCOT	12:45
ANIMAL KINGDOM	15:45
DHS	15:30

Hotel Information Chart (continued)

Extended Stay America Universal ★★★½
5620 Major Blvd.
Orlando, FL 32819
☎ 407-351-1788
tinyurl.com/esuniversal

LOCATION	4
ROOM RATING	75
COST ($ = $50)	$+

commuting times to parks (*in minutes*)
MAGIC KINGDOM	18:00
EPCOT	14:15
ANIMAL KINGDOM	18:00
DHS	16:00

Extended Stay Deluxe Orlando Convention Center ★★★★
6443 Westwood Blvd.
Orlando, FL 32821
☎ 407-351-1982
tinyurl.com/esdorlando

LOCATION	1
ROOM RATING	84
COST ($ = $50)	$$–

commuting times to parks (*in minutes*)
MAGIC KINGDOM	17:30
EPCOT	12:45
ANIMAL KINGDOM	15:45
DHS	15:30

Extended Stay Deluxe Orlando LBV ★★★★
8100 Palm Pkwy.
Orlando 32836
☎ 407-239-4300
tinyurl.com/esdlbv

LOCATION	2
ROOM RATING	83
COST ($ = $50)	$$–

commuting times to parks (*in minutes*)
MAGIC KINGDOM	13:45
EPCOT	9:00
ANIMAL KINGDOM	12:00
DHS	11:30

Fairfield Inn & Suites Orlando LBV (*rooms*) ★★★½
12191 S. Apopka–Vineland Rd.
Lake Buena Vista, FL 32836
☎ 407-239-1115
tinyurl.com/fairfieldlbv

LOCATION	2
ROOM RATING	78
COST ($ = $50)	$$

commuting times to parks (*in minutes*)
MAGIC KINGDOM	14:00
EPCOT	9:15
ANIMAL KINGDOM	12:15
DHS	11:45

Fairfield Inn & Suites Orlando LBV (*suites*) ★★★½
12191 S. Apopka–Vineland Rd.
Lake Buena Vista, FL 32836
☎ 407-239-1115
tinyurl.com/fairfieldlbv

LOCATION	2
ROOM RATING	78
COST ($ = $50)	$$+

commuting times to parks (*in minutes*)
MAGIC KINGDOM	14:00
EPCOT	9:15
ANIMAL KINGDOM	12:15
DHS	11:45

Fairfield Inn & Suites Orlando LBV in Marriott Village ★★★½
8615 Vineland Ave.
Orlando, FL 32821
☎ 407-938-9001
marriottvillage.com

LOCATION	2
ROOM RATING	75
COST ($ = $50)	$$–

commuting times to parks (*in minutes*)
MAGIC KINGDOM	12:00
EPCOT	7:15
ANIMAL KINGDOM	10:15
DHS	9:45

Four Points by Sheraton Orlando Studio City ★★★★½
5905 International Dr.
Orlando, FL 32819
☎ 407-351-2100
fourpointsorlandostudiociy.com

LOCATION	1
ROOM RATING	90
COST ($ = $50)	$$

commuting times to parks (*in minutes*)
MAGIC KINGDOM	20:30
EPCOT	15:45
ANIMAL KINGDOM	18:45
DHS	18:15

Galleria Palms Kissimmee Hotel ★★★
3000 Maingate Ln.
Kissimmee, FL 34747
☎ 407-396-6300
galleriapalmsorlando.com

LOCATION	3
ROOM RATING	74
COST ($ = $50)	$+

commuting times to parks (*in minutes*)
MAGIC KINGDOM	8:15
EPCOT	7:30
ANIMAL KINGDOM	5:15
DHS	7:15

Gaylord Palms Hotel & Convention Center ★★★★½
6000 W. Osceola Pkwy.
Kissimmee, FL 34746
☎ 407-586-0000
gaylordpalms.com

LOCATION	3
ROOM RATING	94
COST ($ = $50)	$$$$

commuting times to parks (*in minutes*)
MAGIC KINGDOM	9:00
EPCOT	8:45
ANIMAL KINGDOM	7:00
DHS	8:15

Hampton Inn & Suites Orlando–South LBV ★★★½
4971 Calypso Cay Way
Kissimmee, FL 34746
☎ 407-452-3126
tinyurl.com/hamptonsouthlbv

LOCATION	3
ROOM RATING	80
COST ($ = $50)	$$

commuting times to parks (*in minutes*)
MAGIC KINGDOM	20:30
EPCOT	15:00
ANIMAL KINGDOM	17:00
DHS	16:00

Hampton Inn I-Drive/Convention Center ★★★
8900 Universal Blvd.
Orlando, FL 32819
☎ 407-354-4447
tinyurl.com/hamptonocc

LOCATION	1
ROOM RATING	70
COST ($ = $50)	$$–

commuting times to parks (*in minutes*)
MAGIC KINGDOM	21:30
EPCOT	17:00
ANIMAL KINGDOM	20:00
DHS	19:30

Hampton Inn Orlando/LBV ★★★½
8150 Palm Pkwy.
Orlando, FL 32836
☎ 407-465-8150
tinyurl.com/hamptonlbv

LOCATION	2
ROOM RATING	76
COST ($ = $50)	$$

commuting times to parks (*in minutes*)
MAGIC KINGDOM	12:45
EPCOT	8:00
ANIMAL KINGDOM	11:00
DHS	10:30

Extended Stay Deluxe Orlando Universal ★★★½
5610 Vineland Rd.
Orlando, FL 32819
☎ 407-370-4428
tinyurl.com/esduniversal

LOCATION	4
ROOM RATING	75
COST ($ = $50)	$+

commuting times to parks (in minutes)
MAGIC KINGDOM	18:00
EPCOT	14:15
ANIMAL KINGDOM	18:00
DHS	16:00

Extended Stay Deluxe Pointe Orlando ★★½
8750 Universal Blvd.
Orlando, FL 32819
☎ 407-903-1500
tinyurl.com/esdpointe

LOCATION	1
ROOM RATING	58
COST ($ = $50)	$$−

commuting times to parks (in minutes)
MAGIC KINGDOM	17:45
EPCOT	13:00
ANIMAL KINGDOM	17:00
DHS	15:30

Fairfield Inn & Suites Near Universal Orlando Resort
★★★½
5614 Vineland Rd.
Orlando, FL 32819
☎ 407-581-5600
tinyurl.com/fairfielduniversal

LOCATION	4
ROOM RATING	80
COST ($ = $50)	$$+

commuting times to parks (in minutes)
MAGIC KINGDOM	17:30
EPCOT	12:45
ANIMAL KINGDOM	15:45
DHS	15:15

Floridays Resort Orlando
★★★★
12562 International Dr.
Orlando, FL 32821
☎ 407-238-7700
floridaysresortorlando.com

LOCATION	1
ROOM RATING	86
COST ($ = $50)	$$$

commuting times to parks (in minutes)
MAGIC KINGDOM	14:30
EPCOT	9:45
ANIMAL KINGDOM	12:45
DHS	12:15

The Floridian Hotel & Suites
★★½
7531 Canada Ave.
Orlando, FL 32819
☎ 407-202-3021
thefloridianhotel.com

LOCATION	1
ROOM RATING	63
COST ($ = $50)	$

commuting times to parks (in minutes)
MAGIC KINGDOM	20:15
EPCOT	15:45
ANIMAL KINGDOM	18:45
DHS	18:15

Fort Wilderness Resort
(cabins) ★★★★
4510 N. Fort Wilderness Trail
Lake Buena Vista, FL 32830
☎ 407-824-2900
tinyurl.com/ftwilderness

LOCATION	WDW
ROOM RATING	86
COST ($ = $50)	$$$$$$$−

commuting times to parks (in minutes)
MAGIC KINGDOM	13:15
EPCOT	8:30
ANIMAL KINGDOM	20:00
DHS	14:00

Grand Beach ★★★★½
8317 Lake Bryan Beach Blvd.
Orlando, FL 32821
☎ 407-238-2500
diamondresorts.com/grand-beach

LOCATION	1
ROOM RATING	90
COST ($ = $50)	$$$$$$−

commuting times to parks (in minutes)
MAGIC KINGDOM	16:00
EPCOT	10:30
ANIMAL KINGDOM	18:00
DHS	13:00

Grand Floridian Resort & Spa ★★★★½
4401 Floridian Way
Lake Buena Vista, FL 32830
☎ 407-824-3000
tinyurl.com/grandflresort

LOCATION	WDW
ROOM RATING	93
COST ($ = $50)	$$$$$$$$$$$−

commuting times to parks (in minutes)
MAGIC KINGDOM	ON MONORAIL
EPCOT	4:45
ANIMAL KINGDOM	11:45
DHS	6:45

Grand Lake Resort ★★★½
7770 W. US 192*
Kissimmee, FL 34747
☎ 407-396-3000
dailymanagementresorts.com

LOCATION	1
ROOM RATING	76
COST ($ = $50)	$$

commuting times to parks (in minutes)
MAGIC KINGDOM	9:15
EPCOT	8:30
ANIMAL KINGDOM	6:15
DHS	8:30

Hampton Inn South of Universal ★★½
7110 S. Kirkman Rd.
Orlando, FL 32819
☎ 407-345-1112
tinyurl.com/hamptonkirkman

LOCATION	1
ROOM RATING	64
COST ($ = $50)	$$+

commuting times to parks (in minutes)
MAGIC KINGDOM	21:15
EPCOT	16:45
ANIMAL KINGDOM	19:45
DHS	19:15

Hampton Inn Universal
★★★
5621 Windhover Dr.
Orlando, FL 32819
☎ 407-351-6716
tinyurl.com/hamptonuniversal

LOCATION	4
ROOM RATING	67
COST ($ = $50)	$$

commuting times to parks (in minutes)
MAGIC KINGDOM	19:00
EPCOT	14:15
ANIMAL KINGDOM	17:15
DHS	16:45

Hard Rock Hotel ★★★★½
5800 Universal Blvd.
Orlando, FL 32819
☎ 407-503-2000
hardrockhotelorlando.com

LOCATION	4
ROOM RATING	93
COST ($ = $50)	$$$$$$+

commuting times to parks (in minutes)
MAGIC KINGDOM	21:45
EPCOT	17:00
ANIMAL KINGDOM	20:00
DHS	19:30

Hotel Information Chart (continued)

Hawthorn Suites LBV
★★★★
8303 Palm Pkwy.
Orlando, FL 32836
☎ 407-597-5000
hawthornlakebuenavista.com

LOCATION	2
ROOM RATING	87
COST ($ = $50)	$$+

commuting times to parks (in minutes)
MAGIC KINGDOM 20:15
EPCOT 15:30
ANIMAL KINGDOM 18:30
DHS 18:00

Hawthorn Suites Orlando Convention Center ★★★½
6435 Westwood Blvd.
Orlando, FL 32821
☎ 407-351-6600
hawthornsuitesorlando.com

LOCATION	1
ROOM RATING	80
COST ($ = $50)	$$$−

commuting times to parks (in minutes)
MAGIC KINGDOM 17:30
EPCOT 12:45
ANIMAL KINGDOM 15:45
DHS 15:30

Hawthorn Suites Universal ★★★½
7601 Canada Ave.
Orlando, FL 32819
☎ 407-581-2151
hawthornsuitesuniversal.com

LOCATION	1
ROOM RATING	82
COST ($ = $50)	$$+

commuting times to parks (in minutes)
MAGIC KINGDOM 20:15
EPCOT 15:45
ANIMAL KINGDOM 18:45
DHS 19:15

Hilton Grand Vacations Club at SeaWorld ★★★★½
6924 Grand Vacations Way
Orlando, FL 32821
☎ 407-239-0100
tinyurl.com/hgvseaworld

LOCATION	1
ROOM RATING	95
COST ($ = $50)	$$

commuting times to parks (in minutes)
MAGIC KINGDOM 17:00
EPCOT 12:30
ANIMAL KINGDOM 16:30
DHS 15:30

Hilton Grand Vacations Club on I-Drive ★★★★
8122 Arrezzo Way
Orlando, FL 32821
☎ 407-465-2600
tinyurl.com/hgvidrive

LOCATION	1
ROOM RATING	88
COST ($ = $50)	$$+

commuting times to parks (in minutes)
MAGIC KINGDOM 16:15
EPCOT 14:00
ANIMAL KINGDOM 17:00
DHS 16:30

Hilton in the Walt Disney World Resort ★★★★
1751 Hotel Plaza Blvd.
Lake Buena Vista, FL 32830
☎ 407-827-4000
hilton-wdwv.com

LOCATION	WDW
ROOM RATING	87
COST ($ = $50)	$$$$+

commuting times to parks (in minutes)
MAGIC KINGDOM 15:15
EPCOT 10:30
ANIMAL KINGDOM 14:30
DHS 12:15

Holiday Inn Express LBV ★★★½
8686 Palm Pkwy.
Orlando, FL 32836
☎ 407-239-8400
tinyurl.com/hiexpresslbv

LOCATION	2
ROOM RATING	80
COST ($ = $50)	$$+

commuting times to parks (in minutes)
MAGIC KINGDOM 14:15
EPCOT 9:45
ANIMAL KINGDOM 12:45
DHS 12:15

Holiday Inn Express West of Theme Park Area ★★★
105 Summer Bay Blvd.
Clermont, FL 34711
☎ 407-239-8315
tinyurl.com/hiexpressclermont

LOCATION	3
ROOM RATING	70
COST ($ = $50)	$$−

commuting times to parks (in minutes)
MAGIC KINGDOM 14:00
EPCOT 9:15
ANIMAL KINGDOM 11:30
DHS 13:15

Holiday Inn in the Walt Disney World Resort ★★★½
1805 Hotel Plaza Blvd.
Lake Buena Vista, FL 32830
☎ 407-828-8888
hiorlando.com

LOCATION	WDW
ROOM RATING	79
COST ($ = $50)	$$$−

commuting times to parks (in minutes)
MAGIC KINGDOM 15:30
EPCOT 10:45
ANIMAL KINGDOM 12:30
DHS 14:45

HomeSuiteHome Eastgate ★★½
5565 W. US 192*
Kissimmee, FL 34746
☎ 407-396-0707
homesuitehome.com

LOCATION	3
ROOM RATING	57
COST ($ = $50)	$−

commuting times to parks (in minutes)
MAGIC KINGDOM 13:30
EPCOT 13:15
ANIMAL KINGDOM 11:30
DHS 12:15

HomeSuiteHome Kissimmee Maingate ★★
7300 W. US 192*
Kissimmee, FL 34747
☎ 407-396-7300
homesuitehome.com

LOCATION	3
ROOM RATING	48
COST ($ = $50)	$−

commuting times to parks (in minutes)
MAGIC KINGDOM 8:15
EPCOT 8:00
ANIMAL KINGDOM 5:00
DHS 7:45

Homewood Suites by Hilton I-Drive ★★★½
8745 International Dr.
Orlando, FL 32819
☎ 407-248-2232
homewoodsuitesorlando.com

LOCATION	1
ROOM RATING	81
COST ($ = $50)	$$$

commuting times to parks (in minutes)
MAGIC KINGDOM 21:45
EPCOT 17:00
ANIMAL KINGDOM 20:00
DHS 19:30

* Irlo Bronson Memorial Highway

Hilton Garden Inn LBV/Orlando ★★★★
11400 Marbella Palm Ct.
Orlando, FL 32836
☎ 407-239-9550
tinyurl.com/hgilakebuenavista

LOCATION	2
ROOM RATING	88
COST ($ = $50)	$$–

commuting times to parks (in minutes)
MAGIC KINGDOM	17:30
EPCOT	12:00
ANIMAL KINGDOM	18:00
DHS	15:00

Hilton Garden Inn Orlando at SeaWorld ★★★½
6850 Westwood Blvd.
Orlando, FL 32821
☎ 407-354-1500
tinyurl.com/hgiseaworld

LOCATION	1
ROOM RATING	80
COST ($ = $50)	$$

commuting times to parks (in minutes)
MAGIC KINGDOM	15:30
EPCOT	11:00
ANIMAL KINGDOM	14:00
DHS	13:30

Hilton Garden Inn Orlando I-Drive North ★★★½
5877 American Way
Orlando, FL 32819
☎ 407-363-9332
hiltongardenorlando.com

LOCATION	1
ROOM RATING	80
COST ($ = $50)	$$+

commuting times to parks (in minutes)
MAGIC KINGDOM	21:15
EPCOT	16:30
ANIMAL KINGDOM	19:30
DHS	19:00

Hilton Orlando ★★★★½
6001 Destination Pkwy.
Orlando, FL 32819
☎ 407-313-4300
thehiltonorlando.com

LOCATION	1
ROOM RATING	92
COST ($ = $50)	$$$$$–

commuting times to parks (in minutes)
MAGIC KINGDOM	19:30
EPCOT	14:30
ANIMAL KINGDOM	20:00
DHS	17:00

Hilton Orlando Bonnet Creek ★★★★
14100 Bonnet Creek Resort Ln.
Orlando, FL 32821
☎ 407-597-3600
hiltonbonnetcreek.com

LOCATION	1
ROOM RATING	89
COST ($ = $50)	$$$+

commuting times to parks (in minutes)
MAGIC KINGDOM	8:00
EPCOT	6:00
ANIMAL KINGDOM	7:15
DHS	4:15

Holiday Inn & Suites Orlando Universal ★★★½
5905 Kirkman Rd.
Orlando, FL 32819
☎ 407-351-3333
hiuniversal.com

LOCATION	4
ROOM RATING	75
COST ($ = $50)	$$

commuting times to parks (in minutes)
MAGIC KINGDOM	19:00
EPCOT	14:15
ANIMAL KINGDOM	17:15
DHS	16:45

Holiday Inn Main Gate East ★★★★½
5711 W. US 192*
Kissimmee, FL 34746
☎ 407-396-4222
holidayinnmge.com

LOCATION	3
ROOM RATING	90
COST ($ = $50)	$$–

commuting times to parks (in minutes)
MAGIC KINGDOM	12:15
EPCOT	12:00
ANIMAL KINGDOM	10:15
DHS	11:30

Holiday Inn Resort LBV ★★★½
13351 FL 535
Orlando, FL 32821
☎ 407-239-4500
hiresortlbv.com

LOCATION	2
ROOM RATING	82
COST ($ = $50)	$$–

commuting times to parks (in minutes)
MAGIC KINGDOM	10:45
EPCOT	6:00
ANIMAL KINGDOM	9:00
DHS	8:30

Holiday Inn Resort Orlando–The Castle ★★★½
8629 International Dr.
Orlando, FL 32819
☎ 407-345-1511
thecastleorlando.com

LOCATION	1
ROOM RATING	82
COST ($ = $50)	$$+

commuting times to parks (in minutes)
MAGIC KINGDOM	22:30
EPCOT	17:45
ANIMAL KINGDOM	20:45
DHS	20:15

Homewood Suites by Hilton LBV-Orlando ★★★★
11428 Marbella Palm Ct.
Orlando, FL 32836
☎ 407-239-4540
tinyurl.com/homewoodsuiteslbv

LOCATION	2
ROOM RATING	85
COST ($ = $50)	$$$–

commuting times to parks (in minutes)
MAGIC KINGDOM	17:30
EPCOT	12:00
ANIMAL KINGDOM	18:00
DHS	15:00

Howard Johnson Enchanted Land Hotel ★★½
4985 W. US 192*
Kissimmee, FL 34746
☎ 407-396-4343
howard-johnson-enchanted.h-rez.com

LOCATION	3
ROOM RATING	59
COST ($ = $50)	$$–

commuting times to parks (in minutes)
MAGIC KINGDOM	16:15
EPCOT	16:00
ANIMAL KINGDOM	15:45
DHS	14:15

Howard Johnson Express Inn & Suites ★★
4836 W. US 192*
Kissimmee, FL 34746
☎ 407-396-4762
tinyurl.com/hojolakefrontpark

LOCATION	3
ROOM RATING	50
COST ($ = $50)	$

commuting times to parks (in minutes)
MAGIC KINGDOM	16:30
EPCOT	16:15
ANIMAL KINGDOM	14:30
DHS	15:45

Hotel Information Chart (continued)

Howard Johnson Inn Orlando I-Drive ★★½
6603 International Dr.
Orlando, FL 32819
☎ 407-351-2900
tinyurl.com/hojoidrive

LOCATION	1
ROOM RATING	59
COST ($ = $50)	$–

commuting times to parks (*in minutes*)
MAGIC KINGDOM	21:00
EPCOT	16:30
ANIMAL KINGDOM	19:30
DHS	19:00

Hyatt Place Orlando/ Universal ★★★★
5895 Caravan Ct.
Orlando, FL 32819
☎ 407-351-0627
orlandouniversal.place.hyatt.com

LOCATION	4
ROOM RATING	84
COST ($ = $50)	$$

commuting times to parks (*in minutes*)
MAGIC KINGDOM	19:00
EPCOT	14:15
ANIMAL KINGDOM	17:45
DHS	16:45

Hyatt Regency Grand Cypress ★★★★½
1 Grand Cypress Blvd.
Orlando, FL 32836
☎ 407-239-1234
grandcypress.hyatt.com

LOCATION	2
ROOM RATING	92
COST ($ = $50)	$$$–

commuting times to parks (*in minutes*)
MAGIC KINGDOM	13:30
EPCOT	8:45
ANIMAL KINGDOM	11:45
DHS	11:15

La Quinta Inn Orlando I-Drive ★★★
8300 Jamaican Ct.
Orlando, FL 32819
☎ 407-351-1660
tinyurl.com/lqidrive

LOCATION	1
ROOM RATING	73
COST ($ = $50)	$+

commuting times to parks (*in minutes*)
MAGIC KINGDOM	21:45
EPCOT	17:15
ANIMAL KINGDOM	20:15
DHS	19:45

La Quinta Inn Orlando I-Drive North ★★
5825 International Dr.
Orlando, FL 32819
☎ 407-313-4100
tinyurl.com/lqidrivenorth

LOCATION	1
ROOM RATING	50
COST ($ = $50)	$+

commuting times to parks (*in minutes*)
MAGIC KINGDOM	20:30
EPCOT	16:00
ANIMAL KINGDOM	19:00
DHS	18:30

La Quinta Inn Orlando– Universal Studios ★★½
5621 Major Blvd.
Orlando, FL 32819
☎ 407-313-3100
tinyurl.com/lquniversal

LOCATION	4
ROOM RATING	63
COST ($ = $50)	$+

commuting times to parks (*in minutes*)
MAGIC KINGDOM	18:00
EPCOT	13:15
ANIMAL KINGDOM	16:15
DHS	16:00

Lighthouse Key Resort & Spa ★★★★½
8545 W. US 192*
Kissimmee, FL 34747
☎ 321-329-7000
lighthousekeycondos.com

LOCATION	3
ROOM RATING	90
COST ($ = $50)	$$$

commuting times to parks (*in minutes*)
MAGIC KINGDOM	20:00
EPCOT	21:00
ANIMAL KINGDOM	14:00
DHS	17:00

Liki Tiki Village ★★★★½
17777 Bali Blvd.
Winter Garden, FL 34787
☎ 407-856-7190
likitiki.com

LOCATION	3
ROOM RATING	90
COST ($ = $50)	$$–

commuting times to parks (*in minutes*)
MAGIC KINGDOM	9:00
EPCOT	8:45
ANIMAL KINGDOM	5:15
DHS	8:15

Loews Portofino Bay Hotel ★★★★½
5601 Universal Blvd.
Orlando, FL 32819
☎ 407-503-1000
tinyurl.com/portofinobay

LOCATION	4
ROOM RATING	92
COST ($ = $50)	$$$$$$$$$–

commuting times to parks (*in minutes*)
MAGIC KINGDOM	21:45
EPCOT	17:15
ANIMAL KINGDOM	20:15
DHS	19:45

Maingate Lakeside Resort ★★★
7769 W. US 192*
Kissimmee, FL 34747
☎ 407-396-2222
maingatelakesideresort.com

LOCATION	3
ROOM RATING	67
COST ($ = $50)	$

commuting times to parks (*in minutes*)
MAGIC KINGDOM	9:15
EPCOT	8:30
ANIMAL KINGDOM	6:30
DHS	8:30

Marriott Cypress Harbour Villas ★★★★
11251 Harbour Villa Rd.
Orlando, FL 32821
☎ 407-238-1300
tinyurl.com/cypressharbourvillas

LOCATION	1
ROOM RATING	86
COST ($ = $50)	$$$$$+

commuting times to parks (*in minutes*)
MAGIC KINGDOM	17:45
EPCOT	13:15
ANIMAL KINGDOM	17:45
DHS	16:15

Marriott Imperial Palm Villas ★★★★
8404 Vacation Way
Orlando, FL 32821
☎ 407-238-6200
tinyurl.com/imperialpalmvillas

LOCATION	1
ROOM RATING	86
COST ($ = $50)	$$$$$$$$$–

commuting times to parks (*in minutes*)
MAGIC KINGDOM	9:45
EPCOT	5:00
ANIMAL KINGDOM	8:00
DHS	7:30

* Irlo Bronson Memorial Highway

International Palms Resort & Conference Center ★★★
6515 International Dr.
Orlando, FL 32819
☎ 407-351-3500
internationalpalms.com

LOCATION	1
ROOM RATING	73
COST ($ = $50)	$$+

commuting times to parks (*in minutes*)
MAGIC KINGDOM	21:15
EPCOT	16:45
ANIMAL KINGDOM	19:45
DHS	19:15

JW Marriott Orlando Grande Lakes ★★★★½
4040 Central Florida Pkwy.
Orlando, FL 32837
☎ 407-206-2300
jw-marriott.grandelakes.com

LOCATION	1
ROOM RATING	93
COST ($ = $50)	$$$$$–

commuting times to parks (*in minutes*)
MAGIC KINGDOM	23:00
EPCOT	18:15
ANIMAL KINGDOM	21:30
DHS	20:45

Knights Inn Maingate Kissimmee/Orlando ★★
7475 W. US 192 *
Kissimmee, FL 34746
☎ 407-396-4200
tinyurl.com/knightsinnmgk

LOCATION	3
ROOM RATING	55
COST ($ = $50)	$

commuting times to parks (*in minutes*)
MAGIC KINGDOM	8:15
EPCOT	7:45
ANIMAL KINGDOM	5:45
DHS	7:30

Legacy Vacation Club LBV ★★★★
8451 Palm Pkwy
Lake Buena Vista, FL 32836
☎ 407-238-1700
legacyvacationresorts.com

LOCATION	2
ROOM RATING	85
COST ($ = $50)	$$$–

commuting times to parks (*in minutes*)
MAGIC KINGDOM	13:15
EPCOT	8:30
ANIMAL KINGDOM	11:30
DHS	11:00

Legacy Vacation Club Orlando ★★★½
2800 N. Poinciana Blvd.
Kissimmee, FL 34746
☎ 407-997-1900
legacyvacationresorts.com

LOCATION	3
ROOM RATING	80
COST ($ = $50)	$$

commuting times to parks (*in minutes*)
MAGIC KINGDOM	16:30
EPCOT	16:15
ANIMAL KINGDOM	14:30
DHS	15:30

Lexington Suites Orlando ★★½
7400 Canada Ave.
Orlando, FL 32819
☎ 407-363-0332
lexingtonhotelorlando.com

LOCATION	1
ROOM RATING	60
COST ($ = $50)	$+

commuting times to parks (*in minutes*)
MAGIC KINGDOM	20:30
EPCOT	15:45
ANIMAL KINGDOM	18:45
DHS	18:15

Loews Royal Pacific Resort at Universal Orlando ★★★★½
6300 Hollywood Way
Orlando, FL 32819
☎ 407-503-3000
tinyurl.com/royalpacific

LOCATION	4
ROOM RATING	90
COST ($ = $50)	$$$$$$$+

commuting times to parks (*in minutes*)
MAGIC KINGDOM	20:00
EPCOT	15:15
ANIMAL KINGDOM	18:15
DHS	17:45

Lucaya Village Resort ★★★½
2941 Lucayan Harbour Cir.
Kissimmee, FL 34746
☎ 407-397-0700
lucayavillageresort.com

LOCATION	3
ROOM RATING	80
COST ($ = $50)	$$$–

commuting times to parks (*in minutes*)
MAGIC KINGDOM	18:30
EPCOT	14:00
ANIMAL KINGDOM	15:00
DHS	14:00

Magic Castle Inn & Suites ★★
5055 W. US 192 *
Kissimmee, FL 34746
☎ 407-396-2212
themagiccastleinn.com

LOCATION	3
ROOM RATING	50
COST ($ = $50)	$–

commuting times to parks (*in minutes*)
MAGIC KINGDOM	14:15
EPCOT	13:45
ANIMAL KINGDOM	12:15
DHS	13:30

Marriott Residence Inn Orlando SeaWorld/ International Center ★★★★
11000 Westwood Blvd.
Orlando, FL 32821
☎ 407-313-3600
tinyurl.com/residenceinnseaworld

LOCATION	2
ROOM RATING	85
COST ($ = $50)	$$

commuting times to parks (*in minutes*)
MAGIC KINGDOM	15:45
EPCOT	11:15
ANIMAL KINGDOM	14:15
DHS	13:45

Marriott's Grande Vista ★★★★½
5925 Avenida Vista
Orlando, FL 32821
☎ 407-238-7676
tinyurl.com/marriottsgrandevista

LOCATION	1
ROOM RATING	92
COST ($ = $50)	$$$

commuting times to parks (*in minutes*)
MAGIC KINGDOM	15:00
EPCOT	12:45
ANIMAL KINGDOM	15:45
DHS	15:15

Marriott's Harbour Lake ★★★★½
7102 Grand Horizons Blvd.
Orlando, FL 32821
☎ 407-465-6100
tinyurl.com/harbourlake

LOCATION	2
ROOM RATING	90
COST ($ = $50)	$$$–

commuting times to parks (*in minutes*)
MAGIC KINGDOM	18:00
EPCOT	13:30
ANIMAL KINGDOM	18:00
DHS	16:30

Hotel Information Chart (continued)

Marriott's Royal Palms
★★★★
8404 Vacation Way
Orlando, FL 32821
☎ 407-238-6200
tinyurl.com/marriottsroyalpalms

LOCATION	1
ROOM RATING	85
COST ($ = $50)	$$$$$–

commuting times to parks (*in minutes*)
MAGIC KINGDOM	9:45
EPCOT	5:00
ANIMAL KINGDOM	8:00
DHS	7:30

Marriott's Sabal Palms
★★★★½
8805 World Center Dr.
Orlando, FL 32821
☎ 407-238-6200
tinyurl.com/marriottssabalpalms

LOCATION	2
ROOM RATING	92
COST ($ = $50)	$$$$$–

commuting times to parks (*in minutes*)
MAGIC KINGDOM	14:00
EPCOT	9:00
ANIMAL KINGDOM	16:00
DHS	11:00

Masters Inn Kissimmee ★★
5367 W. US 192*
Kissimmee, FL 34746
☎ **407-396-4020**

LOCATION	3
ROOM RATING	55
COST ($ = $50)	$–

commuting times to parks (*in minutes*)
MAGIC KINGDOM	13:45
EPCOT	13:30
ANIMAL KINGDOM	11:45
DHS	13:00

Motel 6 Main Gate West ★★
7455 W. US 192*
Kissimmee, FL 34747
☎ 407-396-6422
tinyurl.com/motel6mgw

LOCATION	3
ROOM RATING	52
COST ($ = $50)	$–

commuting times to parks (*in minutes*)
MAGIC KINGDOM	7:15
EPCOT	6:45
ANIMAL KINGDOM	4:45
DHS	6:30

Motel 6 Orlando–I-Drive
★★½
5909 American Way
Orlando, FL 32819
☎ 407-351-6500
tinyurl.com/motel6idrive

LOCATION	1
ROOM RATING	61
COST ($ = $50)	$–

commuting times to parks (*in minutes*)
MAGIC KINGDOM	20:15
EPCOT	16:00
ANIMAL KINGDOM	19:00
DHS	18:30

Mystic Dunes Resort & Golf Club ★★★★
7600 Mystic Dunes Ln.
Kissimmee, FL 34747
☎ 407-396-1311
mystic-dunes-resort.com

LOCATION	3
ROOM RATING	87
COST ($ = $50)	$$–

commuting times to parks (*in minutes*)
MAGIC KINGDOM	10:45
EPCOT	10:30
ANIMAL KINGDOM	7:45
DHS	10:00

Orbit One Vacation Villas
★★★½
2950 Entry Point Blvd.
Kissimmee, FL 34741
☎ 407-396-1000
tinyurl.com/orbitonevillas

LOCATION	3
ROOM RATING	80
COST ($ = $50)	$$+

commuting times to parks (*in minutes*)
MAGIC KINGDOM	14:30
EPCOT	14:30
ANIMAL KINGDOM	7:00
DHS	10:00

Orlando Continental Plaza Hotel ★★
6825 Visitors Cir.
Orlando, 32819
☎ 407-352-8211
orlandocontinental
plazahotel.com

LOCATION	1
ROOM RATING	47
COST ($ = $50)	$–

commuting times to parks (*in minutes*)
MAGIC KINGDOM	20:30
EPCOT	15:45
ANIMAL KINGDOM	18:45
DHS	18:30

Orlando Hotel & Suites
★★★
8214 Universal Blvd.
Orlando, FL 32819
☎ 407-581-9001
orlandohotelandsuites.com

LOCATION	1
ROOM RATING	74
COST ($ = $50)	$$+

commuting times to parks (*in minutes*)
MAGIC KINGDOM	23:00
EPCOT	18:15
ANIMAL KINGDOM	21:15
DHS	20:45

Palms Hotel & Villas ★★★½
3100 Parkway Blvd.
Kissimmee, FL 34747
☎ 407-396-2229
thepalmshotelandvillas.com

LOCATION	3
ROOM RATING	76
COST ($ = $50)	$$–

commuting times to parks (*in minutes*)
MAGIC KINGDOM	8:30
EPCOT	8:15
ANIMAL KINGDOM	6:30
DHS	7:45

Parkway International Resort ★★★½
6200 Safari Trail
Kissimmee, FL 34746
☎ 407-396-6600
parkwayresort.com

LOCATION	3
ROOM RATING	82
COST ($ = $50)	$$$–

commuting times to parks (*in minutes*)
MAGIC KINGDOM	8:30
EPCOT	8:15
ANIMAL KINGDOM	6:15
DHS	7:45

Peabody Orlando ★★★★½
9801 International Dr.
Orlando, FL 32819
☎ 407-352-4000
peabodyorlando.com

LOCATION	1
ROOM RATING	90
COST ($ = $50)	$$$$$$

commuting times to parks (*in minutes*)
MAGIC KINGDOM	19:30
EPCOT	15:15
ANIMAL KINGDOM	18:15
DHS	17:45

* Irlo Bronson Memorial Highway

Monumental Hotel
★★★★½
12120 International Dr.
Orlando, FL 32821
☎ 407-239-1222
monumentalhotelorlandofl.com

LOCATION	1
ROOM RATING	94
COST ($ = $50)	$+

commuting times to parks (*in minutes*)
MAGIC KINGDOM	14:45
EPCOT	10:00
ANIMAL KINGDOM	13:00
DHS	12:30

Monumental MovieLand Hotel ★★★
6233 International Dr.
Orlando, FL 32819
☎ 407-351-3900
monumentalmovielandhotel.com

LOCATION	1
ROOM RATING	68
COST ($ = $50)	$+

commuting times to parks (*In minutes*)
MAGIC KINGDOM	20:30
EPCOT	15:45
ANIMAL KINGDOM	18:45
DHS	18:15

Motel 6 Main Gate East ★★
5731 W. US 192*
Kissimmee, FL 34746
☎ 407-396-6333
tinyurl.com/motel6mge

LOCATION	3
ROOM RATING	47
COST ($ = $50)	$−

commuting times to parks (*in minutes*)
MAGIC KINGDOM	12:30
EPCOT	12:00
ANIMAL KINGDOM	10:30
DHS	11:45

Nickelodeon Suites Resort
★★★½
14500 Continental Gateway
Orlando, FL 32821
☎ 407-387-5437
nickhotel.com

LOCATION	1
ROOM RATING	82
COST ($ = $50)	$$+

commuting times to parks (*in minutes*)
MAGIC KINGDOM	9:45
EPCOT	5:00
ANIMAL KINGDOM	8:00
DHS	7:30

Omni Orlando Resort at ChampionsGate ★★★★★
1500 Masters Blvd.
ChampionsGate, FL 33896
☎ 407-390-6664
omnihotels.com

LOCATION	2
ROOM RATING	96
COST ($ = $50)	$$$$+

commuting times to parks (*in minutes*)
MAGIC KINGDOM	15:30
EPCOT	15:00
ANIMAL KINGDOM	15:00
DHS	14:30

Orange Lake Resort
★★★★½
8505 W. US 192*
Kissimmee, FL 34747
☎ 407-239-0000
orangelake.com

LOCATION	3
ROOM RATING	93
COST ($ = $50)	$$$$$

commuting times to parks (*in minutes*)
MAGIC KINGDOM	8:45
EPCOT	8:30
ANIMAL KINGDOM	5:30
DHS	8:00

Orlando Metropolitan Express ★★½
6323 International Dr.
Orlando, FL 32819
☎ 407-351-4430
orlandometropolitanexpress.com

LOCATION	1
ROOM RATING	63
COST ($ = $50)	$

commuting times to parks (*in minutes*)
MAGIC KINGDOM	20:45
EPCOT	16:00
ANIMAL KINGDOM	19:00
DHS	18:30

Orlando Vista Hotel ★★★★
12490 S. Apopka–Vineland Rd.
Orlando, FL 32836
☎ 407-239-4646
orlandovistahotel.com

LOCATION	2
ROOM RATING	83
COST ($ = $50)	$$−

commuting times to parks (*in minutes*)
MAGIC KINGDOM	13:00
EPCOT	8:30
ANIMAL KINGDOM	11:30
DHS	11:00

Orlando World Center Marriott Resort ★★★★
8701 World Center Dr.
Orlando, FL 32821
☎ 407-239-4200
marriottworldcenter.com

LOCATION	2
ROOM RATING	89
COST ($ = $50)	$$$$$+

commuting times to parks (*in minutes*)
MAGIC KINGDOM	9:45
EPCOT	5:00
ANIMAL KINGDOM	8:00
DHS	7:30

The Point Orlando Resort
★★★½
7389 Universal Blvd.
Orlando, FL 32819
☎ 407-956-2000
thepointorlando.com

LOCATION	1
ROOM RATING	82
COST ($ = $50)	$$$+

commuting times to parks (*in minutes*)
MAGIC KINGDOM	22:00
EPCOT	17:00
ANIMAL KINGDOM	22:30
DHS	19:30

Polynesian Isles Resort (Diamond Resorts)
★★★★½
3045 Polynesian Isles Blvd.
Kissimmee, FL 34746
☎ 407-396-1622
polynesianisle.com

LOCATION	3
ROOM RATING	90
COST ($ = $50)	$$$$−

commuting times to parks (*in minutes*)
MAGIC KINGDOM	14:30
EPCOT	14:15
ANIMAL KINGDOM	12:30
DHS	14:00

Polynesian Resort ★★★★½
1600 Seven Seas Dr.
Lake Buena Vista, FL 32830
☎ 407-824-2000
tinyurl.com/polynesianresort

LOCATION	WDW
ROOM RATING	92
COST ($ = $50)	$$$$$$$$$+

commuting times to parks (*in minutes*)
MAGIC KINGDOM	12:00
EPCOT	8:00
ANIMAL KINGDOM	16:15
DHS	12:30

Hotel Information Chart (continued)

Pop Century Resort ★★★
1050 Century Dr.
Lake Buena Vista, FL 32830
☎ 407-938-4000
tinyurl.com/disneyvalueresorts

LOCATION	WDW
ROOM RATING	71
COST ($ = $50)	$$+

commuting times to parks (*in minutes*)

MAGIC KINGDOM	8:30
EPCOT	6:30
ANIMAL KINGDOM	6:15
DHS	5:00

Port Orleans Resort (French Quarter) ★★★★
2201 Orleans Dr.
Lake Buena Vista, FL 32830
☎ 407-934-5000
tinyurl.com/portorleansfq

LOCATION	WDW
ROOM RATING	84
COST ($ = $50)	$$$$–

commuting times to parks (*in minutes*)

MAGIC KINGDOM	12:00
EPCOT	8:00
ANIMAL KINGDOM	16:15
DHS	12:30

Port Orleans Resort (Riverside) ★★★★
1251 Riverside Dr.
Lake Buena Vista, FL 32830
☎ 407-934-6000
tinyurl.com/portorleansriverside

LOCATION	WDW
ROOM RATING	83
COST ($ = $50)	$$$$–

commuting times to parks (*in minutes*)

MAGIC KINGDOM	12:00
EPCOT	8:00
ANIMAL KINGDOM	16:15
DHS	12:30

Quality Suites Orlando LBV ★★★
8200 Palm Pkwy.
Orlando, FL 32836
☎ 407-465-8200
qualitysuiteslbv.com

LOCATION	2
ROOM RATING	74
COST ($ = $50)	$$–

commuting times to parks (*in minutes*)

MAGIC KINGDOM	13:45
EPCOT	9:15
ANIMAL KINGDOM	12:15
DHS	11:45

Quality Suites Royale Parc Suites ★★★½
5876 W. US 192 *
Kissimmee, FL 34746
☎ 407-396-8040
royaleparcsuitesorlando.com

LOCATION	3
ROOM RATING	75
COST ($ = $50)	$$

commuting times to parks (*in minutes*)

MAGIC KINGDOM	11:15
EPCOT	11:00
ANIMAL KINGDOM	9:15
DHS	10:30

Radisson Hotel Orlando LBV ★★★½
12799 Apopka–Vineland Rd.
Orlando, FL 32836
☎ 407-597-3400
tinyurl.com/radissonlbv

LOCATION	2
ROOM RATING	82
COST ($ = $50)	$$+

commuting times to parks (*in minutes*)

MAGIC KINGDOM	13:45
EPCOT	9:00
ANIMAL KINGDOM	12:00
DHS	11:30

Ramada Gateway Kissimmee (tower) ★★★
7470 W. US 192 *
Kissimmee, FL 34747
☎ 407-396-4400
tinyurl.com/ramadakiss

LOCATION	3
ROOM RATING	71
COST ($ = $50)	$$–

commuting times to parks (*in minutes*)

MAGIC KINGDOM	8:15
EPCOT	8:00
ANIMAL KINGDOM	6:00
DHS	7:45

Ramada Maingate West Kissimmee ★★★
7491 W. US 192 *
Kissimmee, FL 34747
☎ 407-396-6000
tinyurl.com/ramadamgw

LOCATION	3
ROOM RATING	65
COST ($ = $50)	$

commuting times to parks (*in minutes*)

MAGIC KINGDOM	8:15
EPCOT	7:30
ANIMAL KINGDOM	5:00
DHS	7:15

Ramada Plaza Resort and Suites Orlando I-Drive ★★★
6500 International Dr.
Orlando, FL 32819
☎ 407-345-5340
tinyurl.com/ramadaplazaidrive

LOCATION	1
ROOM RATING	72
COST ($ = $50)	$$–

commuting times to parks (*in minutes*)

MAGIC KINGDOM	21:30
EPCOT	16:45
ANIMAL KINGDOM	19:45
DHS	19:15

Residence Inn Orlando Convention Center ★★★½
8800 Universal Blvd.
Orlando, FL 32819
☎ 407-226-0288
tinyurl.com/resinnconventioncenter

LOCATION	1
ROOM RATING	80
COST ($ = $50)	$$+

commuting times to parks (*in minutes*)

MAGIC KINGDOM	22:00
EPCOT	17:30
ANIMAL KINGDOM	20:30
DHS	20:00

Residence Inn Orlando I-Drive ★★★½
7975 Canada Ave.
Orlando, FL 32819
☎ 407-345-0117
tinyurl.com/residenceinnidrive

LOCATION	1
ROOM RATING	75
COST ($ = $50)	$$+

commuting times to parks (*in minutes*)

MAGIC KINGDOM	20:00
EPCOT	15:15
ANIMAL KINGDOM	18:15
DHS	17:45

Residence Inn Orlando LBV ★★★½
11450 Marbella Palm Ct.
Orlando, FL 32836
☎ 407-465-0075
tinyurl.com/residenceinnlbv

LOCATION	2
ROOM RATING	75
COST ($ = $50)	$$+

commuting times to parks (*in minutes*)

MAGIC KINGDOM	15:40
EPCOT	11:00
ANIMAL KINGDOM	14:00
DHS	13:30

*Irlo Bronson Memorial Highway

Quality Inn & Suites Eastgate ★★
4960 W. US 192[*]
Kissimmee, FL 34746
☎ 407-396-1376
tinyurl.com/qieastgate

LOCATION	3
ROOM RATING	55
COST ($ = $50)	$1

commuting times to parks (*in minutes*)

MAGIC KINGDOM	15:45
EPCOT	15:30
ANIMAL KINGDOM	13:45
DHS	14:45

Quality Inn International Hotel ★★★
7600 International Dr.
Orlando, FL 32819
☎ 407-996-1600
orlandoqualityinn.com

LOCATION	1
ROOM RATING	65
COST ($ = $50)	$$−

commuting times to parks (*In minutes*)

MAGIC KINGDOM	19:45
EPCOT	15:00
ANIMAL KINGDOM	18:00
DHS	17:30

Quality Suites Orlando ★★★
9350 Turkey Lake Rd.
Orlando, FL 32819
☎ 407-351-5050
qualitysuites-lbv.com

LOCATION	2
ROOM RATING	74
COST ($ = $50)	$+

commuting times to parks (*in minutes*)

MAGIC KINGDOM	20:45
EPCOT	16:00
ANIMAL KINGDOM	19:00
DHS	18:30

Radisson Resort Orlando-Celebration ★★★★
2900 Parkway Blvd.
Kissimmee, FL 34747
☎ 407-396-7000
tinyurl.com/radissonoc

LOCATION	3
ROOM RATING	86
COST ($ = $50)	$$−

commuting times to parks (*in minutes*)

MAGIC KINGDOM	8:30
EPCOT	8:00
ANIMAL KINGDOM	6:30
DHS	7:45

Ramada Convention Center I-Drive ★★★
8342 Jamaican Ct.
Orlando, FL 32819
☎ 407-363-1944
tinyurl.com/ramadaidrive

LOCATION	1
ROOM RATING	65
COST ($ = $50)	$

commuting times to parks (*in minutes*)

MAGIC KINGDOM	20:15
EPCOT	15:30
ANIMAL KINGDOM	18:30
DHS	18:00

Ramada Gateway Kissimmee (garden) ★★½
7470 W. US 192[*]
Kissimmee, FL 34747
☎ 407-396-4400
tinyurl.com/ramadakiss

LOCATION	3
ROOM RATING	64
COST ($ = $50)	$+

commuting times to parks (*in minutes*)

MAGIC KINGDOM	8:15
EPCOT	8:00
ANIMAL KINGDOM	6:00
DHS	7:45

Red Roof Inn Kissimmee ★★
4970 Kyng's Heath Rd.
Kissimmee, FL 34746
☎ 407-396-0065
tinyurl.com/redroofocc

LOCATION	3
ROOM RATING	47
COST ($ = $50)	$$−

commuting times to parks (*in minutes*)

MAGIC KINGDOM	16:45
EPCOT	16:15
ANIMAL KINGDOM	14:45
DHS	16:00

Red Roof Inn Orlando Convention Center ★★½
9922 Hawaiian Ct.
Orlando, FL 32819
☎ 407-352-1507
tinyurl.com/redroofkiss

LOCATION	1
ROOM RATING	58
COST ($ = $50)	$+

commuting times to parks (*in minutes*)

MAGIC KINGDOM	19:00
EPCOT	14:15
ANIMAL KINGDOM	17:15
DHS	16:45

Renaissance Orlando SeaWorld ★★★★½
6677 Sea Harbor Dr.
Orlando, FL 32821
☎ 407-351-5555
tinyurl.com/renorlandoseaworld

LOCATION	1
ROOM RATING	93
COST ($ = $50)	$$$$−

commuting times to parks (*in minutes*)

MAGIC KINGDOM	16:45
EPCOT	12:15
ANIMAL KINGDOM	15:15
DHS	14:45

The Ritz-Carlton Orlando, Grande Lakes ★★★★½
4012 Central Florida Pkwy.
Orlando, FL 32837
☎ 407-206-2400
grandelakes.com

LOCATION	1
ROOM RATING	94
COST ($ = $50)	$$$$$$$−

commuting times to parks (*in minutes*)

MAGIC KINGDOM	23:00
EPCOT	18:15
ANIMAL KINGDOM	21:30
DHS	20:45

Rodeway Inn Maingate ★★½
5995 W. US 192[*]
Kissimmee, FL 34747
☎ 407-396-4300
tinyurl.com/rodewaymaingate

LOCATION	3
ROOM RATING	59
COST ($ = $50)	$−

commuting times to parks (*in minutes*)

MAGIC KINGDOM	11:15
EPCOT	11:00
ANIMAL KINGDOM	9:15
DHS	10:30

Rodeway Inn Universal Studios Area ★★½
7050 S. Kirkman Rd.
Orlando, FL 32819
☎ 407-351-2000
tinyurl.com/rodewayuniversal

LOCATION	1
ROOM RATING	61
COST ($ = $50)	$+

commuting times to parks (*in minutes*)

MAGIC KINGDOM	22:00
EPCOT	16:30
ANIMAL KINGDOM	19:30
DHS	19:00

Hotel Information Chart (continued)

Rosen Centre Hotel ★★★★½
9840 International Dr.
Orlando, FL 32819
☎ 407-996-9840
rosencentre.com

LOCATION	1
ROOM RATING	95
COST ($ = $50)	$$$$

commuting times to parks (*in minutes*)
MAGIC KINGDOM	19:45
EPCOT	15:15
ANIMAL KINGDOM	18:15
DHS	17:45

Rosen Inn ★★
6327 International Dr.
Orlando, FL 32819
☎ 407-996-4444
rosenhotels.com

LOCATION	1
ROOM RATING	51
COST ($ = $50)	$+

commuting times to parks (*in minutes*)
MAGIC KINGDOM	21:00
EPCOT	16:15
ANIMAL KINGDOM	19:15
DHS	18:45

Rosen Inn at Pointe Orlando ★★★½
9000 International Dr.
Orlando, FL 32819
☎ 407-996-8585
rosenhotels.com

LOCATION	1
ROOM RATING	75
COST ($ = $50)	$$+

commuting times to parks (*in minutes*)
MAGIC KINGDOM	22:15
EPCOT	17:30
ANIMAL KINGDOM	20:30
DHS	20:00

Royal Plaza (garden) ★★★
1905 Hotel Plaza Blvd.
Lake Buena Vista, FL 32830
☎ 407-828-2828
royalplaza.com

LOCATION	WDW
ROOM RATING	73
COST ($ = $50)	$$+

commuting times to parks (*in minutes*)
MAGIC KINGDOM	15:45
EPCOT	11:00
ANIMAL KINGDOM	15:00
DHS	12:45

Royal Plaza (tower) ★★★½
1905 Hotel Plaza Blvd.
Lake Buena Vista, FL 32830
☎ 407-828-2828
royalplaza.com

LOCATION	WDW
ROOM RATING	76
COST ($ = $50)	$$+

commuting times to parks (*in minutes*)
MAGIC KINGDOM	15:45
EPCOT	11:00
ANIMAL KINGDOM	15:00
DHS	12:45

Seralago Hotel & Suites Main Gate East ★★★
5678 W. US 192 *
Kissimmee, FL 34746
☎ 407-396-4488
seralagohotel.com

LOCATION	3
ROOM RATING	71
COST ($ = $50)	$+

commuting times to parks (*in minutes*)
MAGIC KINGDOM	12:15
EPCOT	12:00
ANIMAL KINGDOM	10:15
DHS	11:30

Silver Lake Resort ★★½
7751 Black Lake Rd.
Kissimmee, FL 34747
☎ 407-397-2828
silverlakeresort.com

LOCATION	3
ROOM RATING	64
COST ($ = $50)	$$+

commuting times to parks (*in minutes*)
MAGIC KINGDOM	8:15
EPCOT	8:00
ANIMAL KINGDOM	4:30
DHS	7:30

SpringHill Suites Orlando Convention Center ★★★½
8840 Universal Blvd.
Orlando, FL 32819
☎ 407-345-9073
tinyurl.com/shsconventioncenter

LOCATION	1
ROOM RATING	80
COST ($ = $50)	$$+

commuting times to parks (*in minutes*)
MAGIC KINGDOM	22:30
EPCOT	17:50
ANIMAL KINGDOM	20:45
DHS	20:20

SpringHill Suites Orlando LBV in Marriott Village ★★★
8601 Vineland Ave.
Orlando, FL 32821
☎ 407-938-9001
marriottvillage.com

LOCATION	2
ROOM RATING	71
COST ($ = $50)	$$+

commuting times to parks (*In minutes*)
MAGIC KINGDOM	12:00
EPCOT	7:15
ANIMAL KINGDOM	10:15
DHS	9:45

Super 8 Kissimmee ★★½
1815 W. Vine St.
Kissimmee, FL 34741
☎ 407-396-8883
tinyurl.com/super8kiss

LOCATION	3
ROOM RATING	60
COST ($ = $50)	$

commuting times to parks (*in minutes*)
MAGIC KINGDOM	11:45
EPCOT	11:15
ANIMAL KINGDOM	11:00
DHS	9:45

Super 8 Kissimmee/ Maingate ★★★
5875 W. US 192 *
Kissimmee, FL 34746
☎ 407-396-8883
tinyurl.com/super8maingate

LOCATION	3
ROOM RATING	70
COST ($ = $50)	$

commuting times to parks (*in minutes*)
MAGIC KINGDOM	8:30
EPCOT	8:00
ANIMAL KINGDOM	7:45
DHS	5:45

Swan ★★★★½
1200 Epcot Resorts Blvd.
Lake Buena Vista, FL 32830
☎ 407-934-3000
swandolphin.com

LOCATION	WDW
ROOM RATING	90
COST ($ = $50)	$$$$$+

commuting times to parks (*in minutes*)
MAGIC KINGDOM	6:30
EPCOT	4:45
ANIMAL KINGDOM	6:15
DHS	4:00

* Irlo Bronson Memorial Highway

Rosen Plaza Hotel ★★★★½
9700 International Dr.
Orlando, FL 32819
☎ 407-996-9700
rosenplaza.com

LOCATION	1
ROOM RATING	90
COST ($ = $50)	$$$$–

commuting times to parks (*in minutes*)
MAGIC KINGDOM	20:45
EPCOT	16:15
ANIMAL KINGDOM	19:15
DHS	18:45

Rosen Shingle Creek ★★★★
9939 Universal Blvd.
Orlando, FL 32819
☎ 407-996-9939
rosenshinglecreek.com

LOCATION	1
ROOM RATING	88
COST ($ = $50)	$$$$+

commuting times to parks (*in minutes*)
MAGIC KINGDOM	21:00
EPCOT	16:15
ANIMAL KINGDOM	19.30
DHS	18:45

Royal Celebration Inn ★★½
4944 W. US 192*
Kissimmee, FL 34746
☎ 407-396-4455
royalcelebrationorlando.com

LOCATION	3
ROOM RATING	60
COST ($ = $50)	$–

commuting times to parks (*in minutes*)
MAGIC KINGDOM	15:45
EPCOT	15:30
ANIMAL KINGDOM	13:45
DHS	15:00

Shades of Green ★★★★½
1950 W. Magnolia Palm Dr.
Lake Buena Vista, FL 32830
☎ 407-824-3400
shadesofgreen.org

LOCATION	WDW
ROOM RATING	91
COST ($ = $50)	$$

commuting times to parks (*in minutes*)
MAGIC KINGDOM	3:30
EPCOT	4:45
ANIMAL KINGDOM	9:30
DHS	6:15

Sheraton LBV Resort ★★★★
12205 S. Apopka–Vineland Rd.
Orlando, FL 32836
☎ 407 239-0444
**sheratonlakebuenavista
resort.com**

LOCATION	2
ROOM RATING	88
COST ($ = $50)	$$

commuting times to parks (*in minutes*)
MAGIC KINGDOM	13:45
EPCOT	9:00
ANIMAL KINGDOM	12:00
DHS	11:30

Sheraton Vistana Resort Villas ★★★★½
8800 Vistana Centre Dr.
Orlando, FL 32821
☎ 407-239-3100
tinyurl.com/vistanavillas

LOCATION	2
ROOM RATING	95
COST ($ = $50)	$$$–

commuting times to parks (*in minutes*)
MAGIC KINGDOM	11:15
EPCOT	6:30
ANIMAL KINGDOM	9:30
DHS	9:00

Star Island Resort & Club ★★★★
5000 Avenue of the Stars
Kissimmee, FL 34746
☎ 407-997-8000
star-island.com

LOCATION	3
ROOM RATING	84
COST ($ = $50)	$$$+

commuting times to parks (*in minutes*)
MAGIC KINGDOM	15:45
EPCOT	15:15
ANIMAL KINGDOM	14:15
DHS	13:30

Staybridge Suites LBV ★★★
8751 Suiteside Dr.
Orlando, FL 32836
☎ 407-238-0777
tinyurl.com/staybridgelbv

LOCATION	2
ROOM RATING	72
COST ($ = $50)	$$+

commuting times to parks (*in minutes*)
MAGIC KINGDOM	14:15
EPCOT	9:30
ANIMAL KINGDOM	12:30
DHS	12:00

Staybridge Suites Orlando ★★★½
8480 International Dr.
Orlando, FL 32819
☎ 407-352-2400
tinyurl.com/staybridgeidrive

LOCATION	1
ROOM RATING	75
COST ($ = $50)	$$+

commuting times to parks (*in minutes*)
MAGIC KINGDOM	21:15
EPCOT	16:30
ANIMAL KINGDOM	19:30
DHS	19:00

Travelodge Suites East Gate Orange ★★
5399 W. US 192*
Kissimmee, FL 34746
☎ 407-396-7666
tinyurl.com/travelodgeego

LOCATION	3
ROOM RATING	55
COST ($ = $50)	$+

commuting times to parks (*in minutes*)
MAGIC KINGDOM	13:30
EPCOT	13:15
ANIMAL KINGDOM	11:45
DHS	12:45

Treehouse Villas at Disney's Saratoga Springs Resort & Spa ★★★★½
1960 Broadway
Lake Buena Vista, FL 32830
☎ 407-827-1100
tinyurl.com/saratogawdw

LOCATION	WDW
ROOM RATING	90
COST ($ = $50)	$$$$$$$$$$$$$$$–

commuting times to parks (*in minutes*)
MAGIC KINGDOM	12:45
EPCOT	7.15
ANIMAL KINGDOM	16:45
DHS	12:30

Vacation Village at Parkway ★★★★½
2949 Arabian Nights Blvd.
Kissimmee, FL 34747
☎ 407-396-9086
dailymanagementresorts.com

LOCATION	3
ROOM RATING	91
COST ($ = $50)	$$+

commuting times to parks (*in minutes*)
MAGIC KINGDOM	8:30
EPCOT	8:15
ANIMAL KINGDOM	6:45
DHS	7:45

Hotel Information Chart (continued)

Villas of Grand Cypress
★★★★½

1 N. Jacaranda
Orlando, FL 32836
☎ 407-239-4700
grandcypress.com

LOCATION	2
ROOM RATING	92
COST ($ = $50)	$$$$$+

commuting times to parks (*in minutes*)
MAGIC KINGDOM	13:30
EPCOT	12:30
ANIMAL KINGDOM	20:30
DHS	16:30

Waldorf Astoria Orlando
★★★★½

14200 Bonnet Creek Resort Ln.
Lake Buena Vista, FL 32830
☎ 407-597-5500
waldorfastoriaorlando.com

LOCATION	2
ROOM RATING	93
COST ($ = $50)	$$$$$$$$$$–

commuting times to parks (*in minutes*)
MAGIC KINGDOM	8:00
EPCOT	6:00
ANIMAL KINGDOM	7:15
DHS	4:15

Westgate Lakes Resort & Spa
★★★★½

10000 Turkey Lake Rd.
Orlando, FL 32819
☎ 407-345-0000
westgateresorts.com/lakes

LOCATION	2
ROOM RATING	92
COST ($ = $50)	$$$

commuting times to parks (*in minutes*)
MAGIC KINGDOM	17:30
EPCOT	14:30
ANIMAL KINGDOM	19:15
DHS	18:00

Westgate Vacation Villas
★★★★½

4000 Westgate Blvd.
Kissimmee, FL 34747
☎ 407-239-0510
**westgateresorts.com/
vacation-villas**

LOCATION	2
ROOM RATING	90
COST ($ = $50)	$$+

commuting times to parks (*in minutes*)
MAGIC KINGDOM	8:45
EPCOT	8:30
ANIMAL KINGDOM	5:45
DHS	8:00

The Westin Imagine Orlando
★★★★

9501 Universal Blvd.
Orlando, FL 32819
☎ 407-233-2200
westinimagineorlando.com

LOCATION	1
ROOM RATING	87
COST ($ = $50)	$$$$–

commuting times to parks (*in minutes*)
MAGIC KINGDOM	19:45
EPCOT	15:00
ANIMAL KINGDOM	18:15
DHS	17:30

Wilderness Lodge ★★★★
901 Timberline Dr.
Lake Buena Vista, FL 32830
☎ 407-824-3200
tinyurl.com/wildernesslodge

LOCATION	WDW
ROOM RATING	86
COST ($ = $50)	$$$$$$+

commuting times to parks (*in minutes*)
MAGIC KINGDOM	N/A **
EPCOT	10:00
ANIMAL KINGDOM	15:15
DHS	13:30

Wyndham Bonnet Creek Resort ★★★★½
9560 Via Encinas
Lake Buena Vista, FL 32830
☎ 407-238-3500
wyndhambonnetcreek.com

LOCATION	2
ROOM RATING	90
COST ($ = $50)	$$$$$–

commuting times to parks (*in minutes*)
MAGIC KINGDOM	8:00
EPCOT	6:00
ANIMAL KINGDOM	7:15
DHS	4:15

Wyndham Cypress Palms
★★★★

5324 Fairfield Lake Dr.
Kissimmee, FL 34746
☎ 407-397-1600
cypresspalms.com

LOCATION	3
ROOM RATING	87
COST ($ = $50)	$$$

commuting times to parks (*in minutes*)
MAGIC KINGDOM	15:15
EPCOT	15:00
ANIMAL KINGDOM	14:45
DHS	14:45

Wyndham LBV Resort
★★★½

1850 Hotel Plaza Blvd.
Lake Buena Vista, FL 32830
☎ 407-828-4444
wyndhamlakebuenavista.com

LOCATION	WDW
ROOM RATING	75
COST ($ = $50)	$$

commuting times to parks (*in minutes*)
MAGIC KINGDOM	15:15
EPCOT	10:45
ANIMAL KINGDOM	14:45
DHS	12:15

---

* Irlo Bronson Memorial Highway
** Primary transportation to Wilderness Lodge and Wilderness Lodge Villas is by ferry rather than by car.

Westgate Palace ★★★
6145 Carrier Dr.
Orlando, FL 32819
☎ 407-996-6000
westgateresorts.com/palace

LOCATION	1
ROOM RATING	68
COST ($ = $50)	$$$$–

commuting times to parks (*in minutes*)
MAGIC KINGDOM	20:45
EPCOT	16:15
ANIMAL KINGDOM	19:15
DHS	18:45

Westgate Towers ★★★½
7600 West US 192*
Kissimmee, FL 34747
☎ 407-396-2500
westgateresorts.com/towers

LOCATION	2
ROOM RATING	81
COST ($ = $50)	$$

commuting times to parks (*in minutes*)
MAGIC KINGDOM	8:45
EPCOT	8:30
ANIMAL KINGDOM	5:45
DHS	8:00

Westgate Town Center ★★★★½
4000 Westgate Blvd.
Kissimmee, FL 34747
☎ 407-396-2500
westgateresorts.com/town-center

LOCATION	2
ROOM RATING	93
COST ($ = $50)	$$+

commuting times to parks (*in minutes*)
MAGIC KINGDOM	8:45
EPCOT	8:30
ANIMAL KINGDOM	5:45
DHS	8:00

Wilderness Lodge Villas ★★★★½
901 Timberline Dr.
Lake Buena Vista, FL 32830
☎ 407-824-3200
tinyurl.com/wlvillas

LOCATION	WDW
ROOM RATING	90
COST ($ = $50)	$$$$$$$$+

commuting times to parks (*in minutes*)
MAGIC KINGDOM	N/A**
EPCOT	10:00
ANIMAL KINGDOM	15:15
DHS	13:30

WorldGate Resort ★★★½
3011 Maingate Ln.
Kissimmee, FL 34747
☎ 407-396-1400
wgtresort.com

LOCATION	3
ROOM RATING	77
COST ($ = $50)	$$$+

commuting times to parks (*in minutes*)
MAGIC KINGDOM	8:15
EPCOT	7:45
ANIMAL KINGDOM	5:45
DHS	7:45

WorldQuest Orlando Resort ★★★★
8849 Worldquest Blvd.
Orlando, FL 32821
☎ 407-387-3800
worldquestorlando.com

LOCATION	1
ROOM RATING	88
COST ($ = $50)	$$$$–

commuting times to parks (*in minutes*)
MAGIC KINGDOM	16:30
EPCOT	11:00
ANIMAL KINGDOM	17:00
DHS	14:00

Wyndham Orlando Resort ★★★★
8001 International Dr.
Orlando, FL 32819
☎ 407-351-2420
wyndham.com/hotels/MCOWD

LOCATION	1
ROOM RATING	83
COST ($ = $50)	$$

commuting times to parks (*in minutes*)
MAGIC KINGDOM	19:45
EPCOT	15:00
ANIMAL KINGDOM	18:15
DHS	17:30

Yacht Club Resort ★★★★
1700 Epcot Resorts Blvd.
Lake Buena Vista, FL 32830
☎ 407-934-7000
tinyurl.com/yachtclubwdw

LOCATION	WDW
ROOM RATING	89
COST ($ = $50)	$$$$$$$$

commuting times to parks (*in minutes*)
MAGIC KINGDOM	7:15
EPCOT	5:15
ANIMAL KINGDOM	6:45
DHS	4:00

PART FOUR

SERENITY NOW!
A Look at Disney-Area Spas

YOU'VE JUST SUGGESTED another theme park mini-marathon to your spouse, and from her barely audible murmur you realize she's debating which relative should get the kids when she stands trial for murdering you.

We've all been there. Fortunately, Orlando is awash in spas ready to rub, wrap, and restore your loved one to domestic tranquility.

Note that the cost of a basic 1-hour massage is well over $100 before tip at most of these places. Even midpriced hotels seem eager to tack "Resort and Spa" onto their names to get a cut of that action, regardless of whether they actually know how to run either. In an effort to get you the most inner peace for your money, we sent the *Unofficial Guide* research team to evaluate nine Walt Disney World–area spas.

At each resort, our team had a standard massage, a basic facial, and a manicure–pedicure combination. Each service was scheduled during a different week to ensure that one person's bad day didn't mar the whole evaluation. Also, we used the same small group of researchers throughout the tests to ensure the most consistent comparisons of what is admittedly a somewhat subjective experience.

unofficial **TIP**
When you pay, check whether a gratuity has already been added to your bill. Most spas we visited (but not those at Disney resorts) tack on a tip of 18–20%.

We rated each spa on a scale of one star (poor) to five stars (excellent) in three areas. **Customer service** includes our interactions with the spa staff on everything from scheduling appointments to the actual treatments to follow-up questions after the visit. **Facilities** rates the amenities, functionality, and decor of the locker rooms, waiting areas, and equipment used before and after the services. **Amenities** rates secondary spa offerings such as food, pools, fitness centers, and the like. In addition, **sales pressure** (rated from low to high) indicates how hard the spa staff pushes you to buy its products after your treatment. (Underlying our star system is a numerical scale of 0–100, so spas with the same overall star rating may have different numerical ratings.)

For this edition, **The Waldorf Astoria Spa by Guerlain** joins **The Ritz-Carlton Spa, Orlando** at the top of our rankings. These spas compare favorably to high-end spas found anywhere else in the United

States, and we recommend them even though they're about a 20-minute drive from some Disney resorts. The best spa directly on Disney property is **The Spa at Disney's Saratoga Springs Resort**, which earned better marks than Disney's more-well-known **Grand Floridian Spa & Health Club.**

A fabulous money-saving idea is to find out if the spa you're interested in offers a day pass. These inexpensive tickets ($8–$35 among the spas we reviewed) typically allow use of the spa's fitness center, pool, sauna, steam room, and showers for an entire day. Complimentary fresh fruit and tea are usually included. The Spa at Disney's Saratoga Springs Resort offers passes only to Disney resort guests, but the other spas we checked—except the one at Orlando World Center Marriott Resort, which doesn't offer passes at all—will accommodate anyone regardless of whether they're staying at that resort.

ORLANDO SPAS RATED & RANKED	
SPA	**OVERALL RATING**
1. Tie between THE RITZ-CARLTON SPA, ORLANDO and THE WALDORF ASTORIA SPA BY GUERLAIN	★★★★★
3. RELÂCHE SPA AT GAYLORD PALMS	★★★★
4. THE SPA AT DISNEY'S SARATOGA SPRINGS RESORT	★★★★
5. THE SPA AT THE BUENA VISTA PALACE	★★★★
6. MANDARA SPA AT LOEWS PORTOFINO BAY HOTEL	★★★½
7. Tie between GRAND FLORIDIAN SPA & HEALTH CLUB and MANDARA SPA AT THE DOLPHIN	★★★½
9. THE SPA AT ORLANDO WORLD CENTER MARRIOTT RESORT	★★½

SPA PROFILES

Grand Floridian Spa & Health Club ★★★½
(spa closed for renovations until early 2013)

Grand Floridian Resort, 4111 N. Floridian Way, Lake Buena Vista;
☎ 407-824-2332; relaxedyet.com

Customer service ★★★½. **Facilities** ★★½. **Amenities** ★★★. **Sales pressure** Medium. **Price range** $75–$375 spa services; $25–$110 nail services; $35–$70 kids' services (ages 4–12); 10% off for Disney Annual Pass holders, Disney Vacation Club members, and guests with military ID.

COMMENTS Operated by Niki Bryan Spas, the spa at Walt Disney World's flagship resort is in a separate building between the resort and the wedding pavilion, along the walking path to the Polynesian Resort.

The Grand Floridian, Disney's oldest spa, is currently closed for some long-overdue renovations, which we hope will bring its facilities up to the level of luxury found at other high-end spas. Pre-renovation, robes and lockers were self-serve, and the only private place to change was in the bathroom stalls. All but one nail-drying machine was broken during two of our visits several weeks apart, and much of the other equipment seemed to be showing its age. On a positive note, some of the best conversations we had with other guests happened in the Grand Floridian's lounge.

Our researchers had mixed feelings about the Grand Floridian. One thought it felt like a "high school locker room," while another praised the friendly service she received despite arriving for her appointment on the wrong day. We did get some pressure at checkout to buy products used during several of our treatments. Until we find out how the spa's upgrades shake out, we recommend The Spa at Disney's Saratoga Springs Resort instead (see page 284) if you're staying in the World.

Mandara Spa at Loews Portofino Bay Hotel ★★★½

Universal Studios, 5601 Universal Blvd., Orlando; ☎ 407-503-1244; mandaraspa.com

Customer service ★★★★★. **Facilities** ★★★★½. **Amenities** ★★★. **Sales pressure** Medium. **Price range** $50–$650 spa services; $15–$160 hair and nail services; $25–$200 kids' services (ages 13–17); 10–20% discount for Universal Annual Pass holders; 20% service charge.

COMMENTS The Universal Studios Mandara has an edge over its sister spa in Walt Disney World (see next profile). Both locations are well themed with Eastern influences, such as Buddha statues and silk drapes or wall hangings, but the Portofino location has some pluses, such as blankets offered while waiting.

The Portofino Bay Mandara Spa has a soothing, unmistakably Asian theme. Waiting areas are decorated in comfortable earth tones; treatment rooms feature silk-draped ceilings. Changing and bathroom areas are spacious and clean, but they also include less-than-subtle advertisements for products sold on premises.

The emphasis on tranquility extends to the stellar spa services, which included free self-heating oil for our massages. Men and women enjoy separate steam and sauna facilities. The Portofino's sand-bottom pool is conveniently located near the entrance to the spa, as are nail services. The fitness center is on the other side of the glass wall, however, so you may feel a bit like that doggie in the window.

Mandara Spa at the Dolphin ★★★½

Walt Disney World Dolphin, 1500 Epcot Resorts Blvd., Lake Buena Vista; ☎ 407-934-4772; mandaraspa.com

Customer service ★★★★★. **Facilities** ★★★. **Amenities** ★★★. **Sales pressure** High. **Price range** $50–$650 spa services; $15–$160 hair and nail services; $25–$200 kids' services (ages 13–17); Disney Annual Pass holders get 10% off; 20% service charge.

COMMENTS Although the Mandaras at the Dolphin and the Portofino Bay Hotel share an Asian theme, everything is dialed down a notch at the Dolphin spa, starting with the waiting areas, of which there are two: the Meditation room, stocked with teas, water, and fruit; and the Consultation room, which is so close to the treatment rooms that voices occasionally disrupt the clients' treatment experience.

Gone are the comfy sofas and chairs found at the Portofino Bay Mandara Spa: At the Dolphin, it's standing-room-only. And we were surprised that both of this spa's two waiting rooms are unisex, mixing robe-clad men and women.

The treatment rooms, though pleasant, are also not on par with the Portofino Mandara's. Instead of silk-draped ceilings, an Asian-inspired wall hanging decorates one wall. Trappings aside, the Dolphin's spa also lacks a sauna, offering patrons only a coed steam room.

The one important asset that both Mandara Spas have in common is exceptional treatments delivered by skilled staff. The Dolphin's employees seemed to be the most talkative of any we encountered.

Relâche Spa at Gaylord Palms ★★★★

Gaylord Palms Hotel & Convention Center, 6000 W. Osceola Parkway, Kissimmee; ☎ 407-586-4772; gaylordpalms.com/spa

Customer service ★★★★. Facilities ★★★★½. Amenities ★★★★. Sales pressure Low. Price range Price range $70–$390 spa services; $40–$100 nail services; $25–$50 kids' services (ages 4–10); 10% discount for Florida residents Monday–Friday.

COMMENTS *Relâche* means "relax" in French, and the name is no exaggeration. The staff's courtesy and professionalism were apparent from our initial phone call to our reception upon arrival to the technicians and assistants who worked on us. A complete tour of the facilities is given when you arrive, and you're encouraged to show up early to enjoy everything.

After changing into a comfy robe and slippers in a spacious and clean locker room, you're ushered into either the men's or women's waiting room, where lemon water, delicious teas, and fresh and dried fruits and nuts are provided. From there you move into the coed Tea Room, with more refreshments, very comfortable seating, and soft lights and music.

The soft lights and music continue in the immaculate treatment rooms. A facial includes neck, décolleté, hand, and foot massages. Luscious, fruity creams and serums are applied and are available for purchase afterward, but sales pressure is kept low.

Our manicure was just as enjoyable, with the same refreshments available. The nail salon is clean and comfortable. As with our facial, the products used during our treatments were waiting on a tray as we checked out, but there was no sales pressure.

The Ritz-Carlton Spa, Orlando ★★★★★

4012 Central Florida Parkway, Orlando; ☎ 407-393-4200; ritzcarlton.com/en/properties/orlando/spa

Customer service ★★★★★. Facilities ★★★★★. Amenities ★★★★★. Sales pressure Low–medium. Price range $75–$3,000 (!) spa services; $35–$175 nail services; $35–$120 kids'/teens' services; 15% discount for Florida residents Sunday–Friday; 20% service charge.

COMMENTS You'll enter the Ritz asking yourself whether you can afford the spa. You'll leave wondering why you're not staying at the hotel. So good are the services and facilities that you won't even mind the commute from Walt Disney World property.

The spa is housed in a separate three-story building behind the main hotel. Guests are given a full tour when they arrive, showing them where each amenity is. Every level is tastefully and elegantly decorated, including locker rooms, treatment rooms, and waiting rooms. Both unisex and coed waiting areas are available.

Spa-goers also have the use of a separate whirlpool tub, sauna and steam rooms, and an outside lap pool where an attendant supplies complimentary towels, water, and sunscreen. All the equipment we used and observed was in working order during our visits. The only criticism our researchers had during any of our treatments was that the Ritz's atmosphere might seem too formal to some folks. But there's no doubt that it's luxurious and professional.

The Ritz was one of the few spas that offered a variety of massage oils, and the only one that adjusted the massage table's headrest to ensure our comfort. Sales pressure after the treatments was fairly low; no one followed us around as we browsed the spa store.

The Spa at Disney's Saratoga Springs Resort ★★★★

1490-A Disney Vacation Club Way, Lake Buena Vista; ☎ 407-827-4455; relaxedyet.com

Customer service ★★★★. **Facilities** ★★★★. **Amenities** ★★★★. **Sales pressure** Low. **Price range** $75–$490 spa services; $35–$110 nail services; $35–$70 kids' services (ages 4–12); 10% off for Disney Annual Pass holders, Disney Vacation Club members, and guests with military ID.

COMMENTS Also operated by Niki Bryan Spas, the spa at this Disney Deluxe Villa resort outshines the spa at the Grand Floridian. This is likely due to the newness of this location, with Saratoga Springs Resort having opened its first phase in May 2004.

Decorated in soothing shades of green, with a beach-themed waiting room, this multilevel spa is the real thing. Locker rooms, sauna, and fitness center are on the first floor, while the treatment rooms are a private elevator ride away on the second. Overall, the spa is more spacious than the Grand Floridian's, with the exception of similar small treatment rooms. They also have an ultracool machine that extracts all of the water from your bathing suit, if you decide to wear one! Our one complaint: During busier times, attendants don't always provide tours of the facilities, leaving you to navigate the lockers and changing areas on your own.

A wide variety of Niki Bryan Spa products are available for purchase during checkout, yet sales pressure was lower than that at the Grand Floridian.

The Spa at Orlando World Center Marriott Resort ★★½

8701 World Center Drive, Orlando; ☎ 407-238-8705; marriottworldcenter.com/spa

Customer service ★★★★. **Facilities** ★★. **Amenities** ★★★. **Sales pressure** High. **Price range** $100–$450 spa services; $30–$110 nail services.

COMMENTS In a small, separate building at the back of a sprawling hotel complex, The Spa at Orlando World Center Marriott Resort requires a hike from your room, or a really good set of directions if you're coming by car.

The women's locker room has no private changing areas; however, the bathroom stalls are big enough to make do. Spa-goers have the use of steam rooms and fitness facilities. Women should know that once they're in their spa robes, they're directed to a coed quiet room to await treatments. (On our visit, the spa was rife with male bonding.)

A staffer pressured us insistently to buy expensive oils and lotions after our treatments. Worse yet, the nail-drying equipment was either broken or nonexistent when we visited for our manicure: After shelling out $35 (plus tip), we were told to sit in the quiet room and blow on our nails to dry them.

The Spa at the Buena Vista Palace ★★★★

1900 E. Buena Vista Drive, Lake Buena Vista; ☎ 407-827-3200; buenavistapalace.com

Customer service ★★★★★. **Facilities** ★★★½. **Amenities** ★★★★. **Sales pressure** Low. **Price range** $25–$354 spa services; $15–$65 nail services; $15–$60 kids' services (ages 6–11); $100 teen facial (ages 12–17); 15% discount for Florida residents weekdays.

COMMENTS Plush, swallow-you-whole robes are the first of the pleasures awaiting guests at The Spa at the Buena Vista Palace. Locker rooms offer two small, private changing rooms and a posh, nicely lit vanity area. Treatment rooms are small and nondescript, but clean. Separate waiting rooms are provided for men and women. On the downside, the facilities are older and in need of updating. Treatments were top-notch; staff encouraged the use of the sauna, steam room, and other facilities, and took time to explain the benefits of each. All services were performed with care and professionalism.

Water was from a cooler, and no fruit or other snacks were offered during our visits. Sales pressure after our visits was low, with no attempt to sell any of the oils, lotions, robes, or WD-40 (joke!) applied to our bodies. A tip was included in the service, so read the receipt before adding a gratuity. Children's treatments are available, but the money's better spent on you and your sanity.

The Waldorf Astoria Spa by Guerlain ★★★★★

Waldorf Astoria Orlando, 14200 Bonnet Creek Resort Lane, Orlando; ☎ 407-597-5360; waldorfastoriaorlando.com/spaandfitness/spa

Customer service ★★★★★. **Facilities** ★★★½. **Amenities** ★★★★★. **Sales pressure** Low. **Price range** $149–$350 facials; $149–$450 massages; $45–$90 manicure/pedicure; $45–$250 other services; Florida residents receive discounts of up to 25%.

COMMENTS There's no sign on the spa's entrance, but finding it is worth the effort. (Turn left once inside the hotel, walk past the gift store, and you'll see the door.) After a warm welcome from the front desk and a tour of the facilities, you begin by choosing one of three scents for your treatment room and a flavored water for your post-treatment recovery.

The spa has separate men's and women's lounges, decorated in earth tones and each with a Jacuzzi, steam room, and tea lounge with healthy snacks. Treatment rooms are impeccably clean and have a small locker area to store your robe and slippers.

While the prices seem high, many treatments include options that cost extra elsewhere. Our facial, for example, included eyebrow waxing and trimming. Our therapist was attentive without disrupting our rest.

A gratuity is automatically added to all treatments. Spa-facility passes are available for $30 per day. Guerlain products are available for purchase but without heavy sales pressure.

PART FIVE

The DISNEY CRUISE LINE

The MOUSE at SEA

THE WALT DISNEY COMPANY has been in the cruise business with two almost identical ships, the **Disney Magic** and the **Disney Wonder,** since 1998 and 1999, respectively. Two new, larger ships, the **Disney Dream** and **Disney Fantasy,** entered service in 2011 and 2012. Though the foundation of its business is built on Bahamian and Caribbean cruises out of Port Canaveral (about 90 minutes from Walt Disney World) and Miami, the Disney Cruise Line (DCL) also offers Alaskan, Canadian, and European cruises as well as repositioning cruises. All Bahamian cruises originating in Port Canaveral and Miami make at least one port call at Disney's private island, **Castaway Cay.** DCL's Alaskan and European itineraries are as well conceived and interesting as its Bahamian and Caribbean itineraries are unimaginative and prosaic (more about that later).

From the outset, Disney has put together a team of respected cruise-industry veterans, dozens of the world's best-known ship designers, and Disney's own unrivaled creative talent. Together, they've created the Disney ships, recognizing that every detail is critical to the line's success. Their task: to design a product that makes every guest feel that the vacation is intended for him or her.

unofficial **TIP**
All Disney East Coast cruise itineraries can be bundled with a stay at Walt Disney World.

The first surprise is the ships' appearance. They're simultaneously classic and innovative. Exteriors are traditional, reminiscent of great ocean liners of the past, but even in that you'll find a Disney twist or two. Inside, they're up-to-the-minute technologically, and full of novel ideas for dining, entertainment, and cabin design. For Port Canaveral and Miami cruises, Disney's private island, Castaway Cay, was chosen in order to avoid the hassle of tendering. As for dining, each evening you dine in a different restaurant with a different motif, but your waiters and dining companions move with you.

The company targets first-time cruisers, counting on Disney's reputation for quality, service, and entertainment to dispel novices' doubts about cruise vacations. Much time and effort has been spent to ensure

Disney Cruise Line Standard Features

OFFICERS	American and international
STAFF	American and international
DINING	Three themed family restaurants with "rotation" dining; alternative adults-only restaurants; indoor/outdoor cafe for buffet breakfast and lunch, snacks, and buffet dinner for children; pool bar/grill for burgers, pizza, and sandwiches; ice-cream bar
SPECIAL DIETS	On request at the time of booking; health-conscious-cuisine program
ROOM SERVICE	24 hours
DRESS CODE	Casual by day; casual–semiformal in the evenings
CABIN AMENITIES	Direct-dial telephone with voice mail; tub and shower; TV; safe; hair dryer; mini-fridge or cooling box
ELECTRICAL OUTLETS	110 AC
WHEELCHAIR ACCESS	Yes
SMOKING	Only in designated areas
TIPPING	In 2012, DCL began automatically charging tips for servers and cabin stewards to guests' onboard accounts (see **tinyurl.com/dcltipping** for details). If you didn't prepay these gratuities when you booked or made your final payment, you'll receive a letter upon check-in explaining the charges. You may change the amounts or pay in cash by visiting your ship's Guest Services desk. Tips for dining managers and room service are at your discretion. A 15% service charge is added automatically to bar bills.
CREDIT CARDS	All major cards for cruise payment and onboard charges

that the ships appeal to adults—with or without children—as much as to children and families. Adults are catered to in myriad ways and presented with an extensive menu of adult-oriented activities. For example, the ships have adults-only alternative restaurants, swimming pools, and nightclubs; entertainment ranges from family musicals to adults-only variety performances. Meanwhile, almost from sunrise to midnight, children are offered equally varied programs. Because all programs are offered à la carte, families can choose how much time to spend together or pursuing separate interests.

The children's programs are excellent. In fact, they're rated the best in the industry by Bob and cruise-guide author Kay Showker. Thus, it's no surprise that many parents see their kids only at breakfast and dinner. But while adults can easily get a breather from children, it's tougher to escape Disney's syrupy, wholesome, cuter-than-a-billion–Beanie Babies entertainment, which permeates every cruise. In other words, to enjoy a Disney cruise, you'd better love Disney.

To Boldly Go Where Everyone Has Gone Before

To say that Disney's Bahamian and Caribbean ports of call are trite is an understatement. The cruises ply the same waters on pretty much the same itineraries as every other ship. On any given day, you'll see other

2013 DCL Cruise Areas and Ports of Call

ALASKA

- **7-NIGHT ALASKAN CRUISE** Seattle or Vancouver, Tracy Arm, Skagway, Juneau, Ketchikan, Victoria, Seattle or Vancouver

BAHAMAS

- **3-, 4-, AND 5-NIGHT BAHAMIAN CRUISES** Port Canaveral, Nassau, Castaway Cay, Port Canaveral
- **4-NIGHT BAHAMIAN CRUISE** Miami, Key West, Nassau, Castaway Cay, Miami

CARIBBEAN

- **7-NIGHT EASTERN CARIBBEAN CRUISE** Port Canaveral, St. Maarten (or San Juan), St. Thomas, Castaway Cay, Port Canaveral
- **7-NIGHT WESTERN CARIBBEAN CRUISE** Port Canaveral, Grand Cayman, Costa Maya, Cozumel, Castaway Cay, Port Canaveral
- **7-NIGHT WESTERN CARIBBEAN CRUISE** Galveston, Grand Cayman, Costa Maya, Cozumel, Galveston
- **5-NIGHT CARIBBEAN CRUISE** Miami, Cozumel, Castaway Cay, Miami
- **5-NIGHT CARIBBEAN CRUISE** Miami, Grand Cayman, Cozumel, Miami

EUROPE

- **4-NIGHT MEDITERRANEAN CRUISE** Barcelona, Nice (Villefranche), Palma de Mallorca, Barcelona
- **7-NIGHT MEDITERRANEAN CRUISE** Barcelona, Nice (Villefranche), Florence (La Spezia), Rome (Civitavecchia), Naples, Barcelona
- **12-NIGHT MEDITERRANEAN CRUISE WITH GREECE** Barcelona, Nice (Villefranche), Florence (La Spezia), Rome (Civitavecchia), Athens (Piraeus), Ephesus (Kusadasi), Mykonos, Valetta, Barcelona
- **12-NIGHT MEDITERRANEAN CRUISE WITH VENICE** Barcelona, Nice (Villefranche), Florence (La Spezia), Rome (Civitavecchia), Naples, Venice (overnight), Dubrovnik, Valetta, Barcelona

MEXICAN RIVIERA

- **6-NIGHT MEXICAN RIVIERA CRUISE** Los Angeles, Cabo San Lucas, Puerto Vallarta, Los Angeles
- **7-NIGHT MEXICAN RIVIERA CRUISE** Los Angeles, Puerto Vallarta, Mazatlán, Cabo San Lucas, Los Angeles

PACIFIC COAST

- **7-NIGHT PACIFIC COAST CRUISE** Los Angeles, San Francisco, San Diego, Ensenada, Los Angeles

megaliners disgorging thousands of vacationers onto once-sleepy little islands, now reincarnated as giant sprawling malls dedicated entirely to cruise-ship passengers. Incidentally, our perspective here is more green than jaded—the cruise industry has taken a terrible toll on the culture and lifestyle of the Caribbean.

The three- and four-night Bahamian cruises offer an easy introduction to cruising, but the ports of call are lackluster. **Nassau,** aside from some lovely beaches, just isn't very interesting. Adjacent (via a bridge) **Paradise Island** offers a huge, upscale casino, but you probably didn't take a Disney cruise because you were hot to play blackjack. Then, of course, there's the obligatory "native market." The second "port," **Castaway Cay,** is Disney's own private island, where you can sunbathe, swim, and enjoy a barbecue. There are also some well-conceived organized programs for children. While Disney's done a good job with the island, you won't find much to see or explore, though your choices of how to explore (hike, snorkel, kayak, bike) are plentiful. You'll love it if you're a sun worshiper or water puppy; most others get their fill in an hour or two. Clearly, on the three- and four-night itineraries, the ship itself is the main attraction.

On the seven-night Western Caribbean itinerary, **Grand Cayman** is a real snore except for a shore excursion during which you swim and snorkel with stingrays. **Cozumel** is the best port of call on the itinerary, with a world-famous scuba and snorkeling reef, Xelha Mayan ruins, and excursions to more-celebrated Mayan ruins on the mainland. The last port is Castaway Cay.

Of all Cape Canaveral Disney cruises offered, the seven-night Eastern Caribbean itinerary is the pick of the litter. The first port of call is **St. Maarten,** the smallest island in the world ever to have been partitioned between two different nations, shared by the French and the Dutch in a spirit of neighborly goodwill for almost 200 years. **St. Thomas** in the U.S. Virgin Islands is the most beautiful, varied, and interesting port of call in Disney's Caribbean–Bahamian mix, though it lacks the mystique of being in a foreign country. Once again, Castaway Cay completes the itinerary.

THE FUTURE IS NOW

IN 2007, DISNEY CRUISE LINE PLACED ORDERS for two new 4,000-passenger ships with the Meyer Werft shipyard in Papenburg, Germany. Now in service, the vessels more than double the line's passenger capacity. The new ships sport the same black hulls as the older *Disney Wonder*'s and *Disney Magic*'s and, like those two ships, draw their inspiration from the classic transoceanic liners of the 1930s. In addition to carrying more passengers, the new ships are two decks taller than the *Wonder* and *Magic*. Before the liners debuted, our suggested names for them included the *Walter E. Disney* and the *Roy O. Disney;* the *Chip* and the *Dale;* and the *Beavis* and the *Butt-head* (hey, cartoon characters rule when it comes to anything Disney). Ultimately, Disney named them the *Disney Dream,* launched in 2011, and the *Disney Fantasy,* which entered service in March 2012.

The SHIPS

DISNEY MAGIC, DISNEY WONDER, DISNEY FANTASY, AND *DISNEY DREAM* are modern cruise ships with sleek lines, twin smokestacks, and nautical styling that calls to mind classic ocean liners, but with instantly recognizable Disney signatures. The colors—black, white, red, and yellow—and the famous face-and-ears silhouette on the stacks are clearly those of Mickey Mouse. Look closely, and you'll see that *Magic*'s stern ornamentation is a 15-foot Goofy hanging by his overalls.

Interiors combine nautical themes with Art Deco inspiration. Disney images are everywhere, from Mickey's profile in the wrought-iron bal-

ustrades to the bronze statue of Helmsman Mickey at the center of the three-deck Grand Atrium. Disney art is on every wall and in every stairwell and corridor. A grand staircase sweeps from the atrium lobby to shops selling Disney Cruise Line–themed clothing, collectibles, jewelry, sundries, and more. (The shops are always full of eager buyers; some observers speculate that the cruise line will derive as much revenue here as other lines do from their casinos, which Disney ships don't have.)

The ships have two lower decks with cabins, three decks with dining rooms and show rooms, then three upper decks of cabins (five on the Dream and Fantasy). Two sports and sun decks offer separate pools and facilities for families, and for adults without children. Signs point toward lounges and facilities, and all elevators are clearly marked forward, aft, or midships.

Our main complaint concerning the ships' design is that outdoor public areas focus inward toward the pools instead of seaward, as if Disney wants you to forget you're on a cruise liner. On the *Magic* and the *Wonder*, there's no public place where you can curl up in the shade and watch the ocean—at least not without a Plexiglas wall between you and it. On Deck 4 of the *Dream* and the *Fantasy*, however, there's an open promenade, complete with comfy deck chairs, that circles the ship. It's shady and fairly well protected from wind, and it offers the opportunity to sit back and enjoy the sea without looking through Plexiglas barriers.

Speaking of Plexiglas, a predictable but nonetheless irritating design characteristic is the extensive childproofing. There's enough Plexiglas on all four ships to build a subdivision of see-through homes. On the pool decks especially, it feels as if the ships are hermetically sealed. Plus, veranda doors have a two-part locking mechanism, with one of the two parts 6 feet off the floor—causing even adults occasional consternation in trying to operate them.

CABINS

CABINS AND SUITES ARE SPACIOUS, with wood paneling throughout. About three-fourths of cabins are outside; more than half of those have private verandas. The cabin categories range from standard to deluxe, deluxe with veranda, family stateroom, one- and two-bedroom suites, and royal suite.

Cabin design reveals Disney's finely tuned sense of the needs of families and children and offers a cruise-industry first: a split bathroom with a bathtub and shower combo and sink in one room, and toilet, sink, and vanity in another. This configuration, found in all but standard inside cabins, allows any family member to use the facilities without monopolizing them. All bathrooms have tub and shower, except cabins for disabled passengers (shower only).

Decor includes unusual features such as bureaus designed to look like steamer trunks. Cabins also have a direct-dial telephone with voice mail, TV, hair dryer, and a mini-fridge or cooling box. In some cabins, pull-down Murphy beds or drop-down bunk beds (which lower from the ceiling) allow for additional daytime floor space.

We were pretty horrified to discover that duvets have replaced sheets and blankets on the Dream and the Fantasy and may be coming to the Magic and the Wonder. Duvets may be okay for an Alaskan, Baltic, or off-season Mediterranean cruise, but for the Bahamas, the Caribbean, and the Mediterranean during the summer, they're a stupendously dumb idea. What is Disney thinking? You could cook a Christmas goose under one of those things! During our cruise on the Dream, we chucked the duvet in the closet for the duration and requested a sheet (two, actually). Another option is to take the duvet out of its cover and use the cover as a blanket. Cabin stewards frown on this, however, and will usually stuff the duvet back into the cover each morning, forcing you perform a duvet extraction every night before retiring.

Storage is generous, with deep drawers and large closets. On the *Dream* and the *Fantasy*, almost 9 out of 10 of the 1,250 cabins are outside; of those, 90% have a private veranda. Clearly designed for families, including multigenerational ones, the *Dream* and the *Fantasy* have a high percentage of cabins for four or five people, along with 500 connecting cabins. The partition between connecting veranda cabins opens, if needed, to create a larger shared balcony. Every cabin has a 22-inch flat-panel TV on a swivel arm and an iPod docking station. And, in a showcase of Disney Imagineering genius, occupants of inside cabins have a view of the outside—yes, the outside. A large virtual porthole on the back wall of the cabin is connected to high-definition cameras, placed on the exterior of the ship, that will feed live video to each porthole for real-time outside views.

A Maylene, Alabama, reader offers this useful information for families with kids:

> *A big difference between Walt Disney World and Disney Cruise Line is that when it comes to room capacity, infants are counted just like adults. So while a family of five can stay at a Value resort (four adults on the double beds and an infant in a crib), that same family of five must either book a Category 4 (or above) cabin or book a pair of lower-category cabins.*

▐▌ SERVICES *and* AMENITIES

PASSENGERS LAVISHLY PRAISE Disney cast members. They're among the most accommodating you'll ever encounter in travel, and they try hard to smooth your way from boarding to departure. Cruise writer Kay Showker reports, "More than once when I stopped to get my bearings, a Disney cast member was there within seconds to help me."

You'll receive a *Disney Magic Passport*, a purse-sized booklet covering about everything you need to know for your cruise. Daily in your cabin, you'll receive "Personal Navigator," a newsletter listing entertainment and activities, with options for teens, children, adults, and families, as well as information on shore excursions.

DINING

DINING IS DISNEY'S MOST INNOVATIVE AREA. Ships have three family restaurants, plus one adults-only alternative restaurant on the *Magic* and *Wonder* and two on the *Dream* and *Fantasy*. Each night, passengers move to a different family restaurant, each with a different theme and menu. Their table companions and waitstaff move with them. In each restaurant, tableware, linens, menu covers, and waiters' uniforms fit the theme. Themes and names for restaurants and public areas aboard the *Fantasy* largely replicate those of the *Dream*.

On each ship, one luxurious, more formal restaurant is on the rotation. On *Magic*, it's **Lumiere's;** named for the candlestick character in *Beauty and the Beast*, this handsome Art Deco venue serves Continental cuisine. The equivalent restaurant on *Wonder* is the *Little Mermaid*–themed **Triton's;** on the *Dream*, it's **Royal Palace,** and on the *Fantasy*, it's **Royal Court.**

On the *Magic* and *Wonder*, **Parrot Cay** dishes up American and Caribbean-accented food in a colorful, fun, tropical setting that reminds Disney veterans of the *Enchanted Tiki Room*. Parrot Cay is the most popular of the three restaurants for breakfast. Children particularly enjoy the decor and festivity, but the food, although adequate, is a notch below that of the other restaurants. On the *Dream* and *Fantasy*, Parrot Cay is replaced by **Enchanted Garden,** a whimsical, casual restaurant inspired by the gardens of Versailles. Its dining environment transforms from day to night as light fixtures "bloom" and change colors and a sunset spreads over the "sky" on the ceiling.

Animator's Palate reflects the creative genius of Disney animation and is the ships' dining *pièce de résistance*. On the *Magic* and *Wonder*, diners are given the impression that they've entered a black-and-white sketchbook. As the meal progresses, sketches on the walls are transformed through lighting, video, and fiber optics into a full-color extravaganza. Waiters change their costumes from black-and-white to color. Animator's Palate on the *Dream* is similar to the corresponding venues on the other ships, but with interactive animation à la Epcot's *Turtle Talk with Crush*. On the *Fantasy*, guests are asked to draw their own cartoon characters. Then the sketches are collected, and a little while later these characters are brought to life in an animated film projected on the walls of the restaurant. (*Warning:* Do not draw an unflattering representation of a Disney character.) Conversation is often difficult, and the entertainment, though creative, is totally inescapable. Children love it, but adults may find it overwhelming.

Palo, the casual Italian restaurant named for the pole that gondoliers use to navigate Venetian canals, is an intimate adults-only eatery. It's the best on board and has its own kitchen. The sophisticated semicircular room has soft lighting, Venetian glass, inlaid wood, and a backlit bar. Northern Italian cuisine is featured. Food and presentation are excellent. More than two dozen wines are available by the glass for $4.75–$25. There's a $20-per-person cover charge on all four ships; surcharges are listed along with the restaurant descriptions at

disneycruise.com. Service is attentive but leisurely, though it may just seem that way in comparison to the staccato pace in the other restaurants. On days at sea, Palo also serves a Champagne brunch, once again with the $20 surcharge. On weeklong cruises, a high tea is offered for no additional charge.

Palo is exceedingly popular. Make reservations at **disneycruise.com** at least 75 days before your sail date (see page 299). If you forget, make reservations as soon as you board. The restaurant usually fills every night, but some very late or very early seatings sometimes become available after the ship sails. Palo is so superior to the three restaurants on the dining rotation that we check every day for availabilty. By so doing on one seven-day cruise, we were able to eat at Palo three times.

Aboard the *Dream* and *Fantasy*, in addition to Palo, is **Remy,** an adults-only French restaurant that requires a $75 surcharge. Reservations (required) can be made at **disneycruise.com** or onboard. Remy serves eight to nine small courses accompanied by excellent wine pairings (for an additional $99 per person). Other signature features include a tableside trolley for international cheeses, decanting stations for wines, and after-dinner coffee service offering French press and *café grand crème.*

unofficial **TIP**
If you want to eat at all restaurants, reserve Palo or Remy for the night you're scheduled to repeat one of the basic three.

The food and service at Remy are exceptional, but honestly, much of the experience will be lost on anyone lacking a very sophisticated palate, which is most of us. Still, it's great for a one-night splurge, though you can save about $150 by ordering a bottle of wine from the extensive wine list instead of opting for the expensive wine pairings. For those who associate French cuisine with microscopic portions and going away hungry, worry not. Portions at Remy, while not large, are adequate, and the number of courses and intermezzos combines to fill you up by the end. The service, though often baffling, is a wonder. Flatware appears and disappears with astonishing speed. From start to finish, you'll use roughly the same number of utensils as a surgeon does instruments during a C-section. The sophistication of the courses notwithstanding, the atmosphere is friendly, welcoming, and not at all stuffy or intimidating. Waitstaff and sommeliers go to great lengths to educate you concerning the dishes and wines. If you go, allocate at least 2½ hours for the entire meal. In the end, we're glad we did Remy once, but that once was enough. As mentioned previously, Palo is a different animal altogether. We could happily dine there every night.

There are two seatings for dinner at the rotation restaurants. If your children are age 12 or younger and you plan to dine as a family, we recommend the early seating. If your kids are involved in programs where they dine with other children, go with your preference. All three rotation restaurants offer special meals if your picky eaters can't find something they like on the menu.

We view Parrot Cay on the *Magic* and *Wonder* as the most expendable in the rotation, and if you miss it for dinner, you can try it at lunch or breakfast. On a four-day cruise, one restaurant will pop up twice on your rotation. If you plan to dine at Palo, try to schedule your reservation for the night you would've eaten at Parrot Cay.

On the *Dream* and *Fantasy,* the food is better in general than on the *Wonder* and the *Magic,* and the quality of the preparations at each of the three rotation restaurants is pretty much equal. If pressed to single out a restaurant to skip for a night at Palo or Remy, we would recommend blowing off Animator's Palate; if you're keen to see animated entertainment, skip Enchanted Garden.

Wondering how to feed your kids if you dine at Palo or Remy? You have several options: Make a late reservation, then keep your children company (but don't eat) while they dine at the regularly assigned restaurant (this works only if you eat at the first seating); enroll your children in a program where they'll eat with other kids; or take them to **Pluto's Dog House** (poolside) for hot dogs and burgers.

BUFFET AND FAST FOOD Other dining options include **Topsider Buffet** on the *Magic* (**Beach Blanket Buffet** on the *Wonder,* **Cabanas** on the *Dream* and *Fantasy*), an indoor/outdoor cafe serving a buffet breakfast, lunch, and snacks. On the *Magic* and *Wonder,* quick-service food is available at **Pluto's Dog House,** a pool bar and grill for burgers, hot dogs, and sandwiches; **Goofy's Galley,** serving fresh fruit, panini sandwiches, wraps, and salads; **Pinocchio's Pizzeria;** an ice-cream and frozen-yogurt bar; and 24-hour room service. Topsider is the weakest; it's OK for breakfast but long on bulk and short on flavor for lunch. On the *Dream* and *Fantasy,* the same selections are respectively available at **Tow Mater's Grill, Fillmore's Favorites,** and **Luigi's Pizza,** all on the pool deck (Deck 11).

FACILITIES AND ENTERTAINMENT

NIGHTLY ENTERTAINMENT IS UNLIKE any other cruise line's. The **Walt Disney Theatre** stages a different show nightly, with talented actors, singers, and dancers. These family productions are on par with Disney parks' entertainment rather than Broadway and will probably appeal more to children than adults. Longer cruises present a welcome variety show and an end-of-cruise farewell show in addition to some combination of the following presentations:

Disney Dreams has virtually every Disney character and song ever heard and offers a thin plot wherein Peter Pan visits a girl who dreams of Disney's characters. It's pure schmaltz, but audiences give it a standing ovation. At the late show, many kids doze off before the curtain falls.

Disney Wishes (*Dream* and *Fantasy*) is a full-blown musical about three best friends who discover "the secret to being a grown-up is staying connected to their inner child." While visiting Disneyland, they each make a wish to go on the "Ride of Our Lives" in order to find what the future holds. This launches them on an odyssey in which veritable armies of Disney characters materialize to guide them. The most ambitious shipboard production mounted by Disney Cruise Line to date, the 45-minute show includes ensemble dance numbers, elaborate sets, special effects, and of course, a near-lethal dose of Disney sweetness.

Disney's Aladdin—A Musical Spectacular (*Dream* and *Fantasy*) is a seagoing variation of the show of the same name that played at Disney California Adventure theme park. A breezy stage version of the Aladdin story, it features familiar film tunes including "Friend Like

Me" and "Prince Ali," as well as jaw-dropping flying-carpet effects and exquisitely manipulated puppets.

Disney's Believe (*Dream* and *Fantasy*) is the story of a workaholic dad and his daughter's effort to help him understand the power of belief. On the daughter's side are a host of Disney characters including Genie, Mary Poppins, Peter Pan, Baloo, Merlin, Rafiki, and Pocahontas. The choreography is dynamite, and most of the music is drawn from Disney animated features supplemented by original musical compositions.

The Golden Mickeys is an Academy Awards–style tribute to the music and characters of Disney films over the decades.

Mickey's Pirates IN the Caribbean party transforms passengers into pirates for the evening and treats them to a special dinner. The meal is followed by a deck party with Disney characters dressed in pirate garb. The mood of the party changes as Captain Hook, Mr. Smee, and a gang of "bad" pirates take over. In the end, Captain Mickey saves the day.

Twice Charmed: An Original Twist on the Cinderella Story demonstrates that "living happily ever after" is not all it's cracked up to be. Beginning where the original story ended, the musical introduces a wicked Fairy Godfather who sends the mean stepmother back in time to break Cinderella's glass slipper and thus destroy her chances of marrying the prince. It's a weird Disney version of *Back to the Future*, except the stepmother doesn't travel in a DeLorean.

Toy Story—The Musical tunefully chronicles the evolving relationship of Buzz Lightyear and Woody as they transform from jealous adversaries to best friends. *Villains Tonight,* featuring Hades, showcases the Disney villains in music and dance.

On seven-night cruises, *All Aboard: Let the Magic Begin* and *Remember the Magic: A Final Farewell* are added. On the *Dream* and *Fantasy*, *A Fantasy Come True* and *An Unforgettable Journey* serve the same purpose.

First-run movies and classic Disney films are shown daily in the **Buena Vista Theater,** an outdoor venue with full screen and Dolby sound and under the stars on a jumbo 24 x 14–foot LED screen.

unofficial **TIP**
Disney ships have no casinos or libraries.

Studio Sea, modeled after a television- or film-production set, is a family-oriented nightclub offering dance music, cabaret acts, passenger game shows, karaoke, and multimedia entertainment. The Art Deco **Promenade Lounge** offers a haven for reading and relaxing by day, and enjoying cocktails and piano music by night. **Cove Cafe** is a quiet, secluded venue for reading over a designer coffee. *Magic* features **Beat Street,** an adult-oriented evening-entertainment district with shops and three themed nightclubs: **Rockin' Bar D,** with live bands playing rock and roll, Top 40, and country music; **Diversions,** a sports pub offering group sing-alongs and karaoke; and **Sessions,** a casual place to enjoy easy-listening music and jazz. On *Wonder*, Beat Street is replaced with the **Route 66** club complex: **Wavebands** features live bands playing pop and oldies, **Cadillac Lounge** is the place for quiet music. New on the *Wonder* is the **Outlook Cafe,** with a small bar, plenty of seating, and floor-to-ceiling windows that afford incredible views. Adults-only venues on the *Dream* include four lounges: **Skyline,** where virtual cityscapes change daily; **Meridian,** specializing in martinis; **687,** a sports bar; and

Pink, designed to look like the inside of a Champagne bottle. **Evolution** dance club completes the after-dark roster. The *Fantasy* also features a version of Skyline along with **The Tube,** a multipurpose club inspired by the London subway system, hosting dancing and live shows; **O'Gills,** an Irish pub and sports bar; **Ooh La La,** a Victorian, velvet-tufted space specializing in Champagne and fancy (read: expensive) drinks; and **La Piazza,** modeled after an Italian plaza, serving Italian wine, beer, cocktails, and bar food.

CHILDREN'S PROGRAMS

PLAYROOMS AND OTHER KIDS' FACILITIES occupy more than 15,000 square feet of each ship. Age-specific programs are among the most extensive in cruising. They include challenging interactive activities and play areas supervised by trained counselors. Age groups are 3–13 and teens. Babysitting (ages 12 weeks–3 years) is provided in the nursery; hours vary according to the cruise itinerary. Cost is $6 per hour for the first child, $5 per hour for each additional child. Make reservations at **disneycruise.com** at least 75 days before your sail date (see page 299). If you forget, make reservations as soon as you board. On the *Wonder* and *Magic,* the nursery is called **Flounder's Reef;** on the *Dream* and *Fantasy,* it's called the **It's A Small World Nursery.**

The **Oceaneer's Adventure** program encompasses **Oceaneer's Club** (ages 3–12 on *Wonder,* 3–13 on *Magic,* 3–10 on *Dream* and *Fantasy*), themed to resemble Captain Hook's pirate ship, with plenty of activity space; and **Oceaneer's Lab** (ages 3–12 on *Wonder,* 3–13 on *Magic,* and 3–10 on *Dream* and *Fantasy*), with video games, computers, lab equipment, and an area for listening to CDs. **Ocean Quest,** an interactive play area on the *Disney Magic,* features a computer simulator, complete with a replica of the *Magic*'s bridge, that lets kids see what it's like to steer the ship in and out of various ports of call. Kids wear ID bracelets, and parents receive pagers for staying in touch with them. Children in the drop-off program eat dinner together. As with babysitting, you can register your children in advance for the programs described at the Disney Cruise Line website.

Aloft (*Wonder*), **The Stack** (*Magic*), and **Vibe** (*Dream* and *Fantasy*) are teen areas with a coffee-bar theme, featuring a game arcade, videos, and a CD-listening lounge. The venues allow teens to rock out in arguably the most isolated part of the ship (chaperoned, of course). There are also organized activities, including nighttime volleyball. Activities are supervised in a way that makes participants feel unfettered. For example, other than counselors, no adults are allowed in Aloft, The Stack, or Vibe. In addition to the teen haunts, the *Dream* and *Fantasy* also offer **Edge,** an exclusive space for the 11–13 crowd.

SPORTS, FITNESS, AND BEAUTY

OF THREE POOLS, one has a Mickey Mouse motif and waterslide and is intended for families; the second, a little less elaborate, is also set aside for families; the third is adults-only. The *Wonder* also offers a **Splash Zone** for toddlers who are not fully potty-trained and who wear swim diapers; the *Dream* and *Fantasy* offer a similar area. The whimsical venue features spurting water jets, bubble makers, and fountains. Special to the *Dream* and *Fantasy* is **AquaDuck,** a 765-foot water coaster (water jets propel you over the uphills) that winds up and down through four decks and even extends over the side of the ship. The pool area can also be a stage for deck parties and dancing.

The **Sports Deck** has a volleyball court, table tennis, basketball court, and shuffleboard.

Each ship has an open-air walking/jogging track and a fitness center with workout equipment and exercise instruction, plus personal trainers. The spas peddle pricey beauty treatments (along with product sales pitches) and feature saunas and massage rooms. Passengers in concierge-level suites can have a private massage in their suite or veranda (prices vary; a standard 50-minute massage is $118). Spa reservations can be made in advance at **disneycruise.com.** On the *Fantasy* only is **Bibbidi Bobbidi Boutique,** a big-bucks beauty parlor for little princesses. (Boys can be decked out as pirates somewhat more cheaply.)

CASTAWAY CAY

EACH CRUISE INCLUDES A DAY AT CASTAWAY CAY, Disney's 1,000-acre private island. The island's environment and beauty have been preserved, with white-sand beaches surrounded by emerald water. A pier allows access without tendering. An open tram (like those at Disney parks) links the ship to **Scuttle's Cove** family beach. The tram runs every 5 minutes; you could walk the quarter-mile to the beach, but it's inadvisable in the blistering heat. (Bring sunblock and wear a hat.) Strollers are available, as are rental floats, bikes, kayaks, and snorkel gear. Lounge chairs shaded by umbrellas are plentiful, and hammocks swing under the palms, but there's very little shade otherwise.

Disney Imagineers have created shops, restrooms, and pavilions that give the impression they've been there for years. A supervised children's area includes a "dig" at a half-buried whale skeleton. Water sports are offered in a protected lagoon. One snorkeling course is near shore; the other, farther out, requires more endurance. On the distant course, snorkelers see fish they identify from a waterproof card provided with rental equipment; lifeguards watch all snorkelers. A shore excursion provides guests with the opportunity to swim with live stingrays in a private lagoon. The stingray lagoon was relocated in 2010 in order to extend the family beach. Also relocated and enlarged was the teen beach area, with swimming, snorkeling, kayaking, volleyball, tetherball, basketball, pool, and more. Recent additions to Castaway Cay include new restaurants, more private cabanas, and **Pelican Plunge,** a 2,400-square-foot floating platform with an enclosed corkscrew slide, a 140-foot open slide, and a supersized bucket that douses swimmers below. A much-needed improvement is the installation of an aqua-play area for toddlers, featuring a 1,200-square-foot soft, wet deck with fountains and water jets.

The cruise line has planted several "shipwrecks." On one, in about 10 feet of water, snorkelers see Mickey Mouse riding the ship's bow. Rental equipment costs $25 for adults and $10 for children ages 5–9. Nature trails and bike paths are available. The main beach offers kids' activities, live Bahamian music, and shops. Three restaurants serve a buffet lunch of burgers, ribs, hot dogs, baked beans, slaw, corn on the cob, fruit, and potato chips.

A second tram connects to **Serenity Bay,** the adult beach on the island's opposite side. A bar serves drinks, and passengers can enjoy a massage in one of the private cabanas opening on the sea. Passengers must be back aboard by 4:30 p.m. Many cruisers say they would've liked more time on the island.

DISNEY CRUISE LINE *and* *the* ECONOMY

TODAY'S ECONOMIC DOLDRUMS have hit the cruise industry hard, and although the Disney Cruise Line has fared better than most, it's having to work very hard to fill its berths. Throughout the industry, demand has declined and capacity, with the introduction of a number of new ships, has gone up. Disney Cruise Line offers a distinctive product and has a loyal client base. With other lines heavily discounting their cruises, however, the deals are often so good (especially on lines that have good children's programs, like Princess, Royal Caribbean, and Norwegian) that Disney is forced to struggle mightily to hang on to its market share. When you can buy, say, a weeklong Alaska cruise on another line for less than a four-day Disney cruise to Nassau and Castaway Cay, it strains the loyalty of even the most ardent Mouseketeer. Disney, therefore, has been discounting and offering "Kids Sail Free" specials for children who share a cabin with their parents.

To sum it up: Cruises are unequivocally the best deal in travel right now and for the immediate future. Deals abound. Check websites like **cruisecritic.com, cruisemates.com,** and **lastminutetravel.com,** as well as **disneycruise.com,** for the latest discounts.

If you prefer to buy directly from Disney, here's how to get in touch:

Disney Cruise Vacations
Guest Communications
P.O. Box 10238
Lake Buena Vista, FL 32830-0238
☎ 800-951-6499 or 800-951-3532;
fax 407-566-7739; **disneycruise.com**

Disney Cruise Line offers a free planning DVD that tells all you need to know about Disney cruises and then some. To obtain a copy call ☎ 888-DCL-2500, or order online at **disneycruise.com**.

CRUISE–WDW PACKAGES

DISNEY OFFERS PACKAGE VACATIONS that combine any cruise with any length of stay at Walt Disney World. Regarding the Disney World part of the package, an Ithaca, New York, mom complains:

If you're cruising also, you don't get to use the last day of your ticket in the World due to the 11 a.m. bus departure to the terminal.

ADVANCE RESERVATIONS FOR SHORE EXCURSIONS, SPA, PALO, REMY, AND CHILDREN'S PROGRAMS

DISNEY CRUISE LINE OFFERS SHORE EXCURSIONS at each port of call on all of its itineraries. These excursions can be previewed and booked at the Disney Cruise Line website. On the home page, mouse over "Cruises & Destinations," then choose "Port Adventures" from the pop-up menu.

When you can reserve depends on the accommodations you book and whether you've cruised before. Here's the deal:

Concierge and Platinum Castaway Club guests (Categories 1, 2, and 3; Platinum Castaway Club guests have sailed with DCL at least 10 times previously) *paid in full* can book shore excursions, spa treatments, children's programs, and meals at Palo and Remy 120 days before their sail date.

Gold Castaway Club guests (five to nine previous cruises) paid in full can reserve the previous 105 days before their sail date.

unofficial **TIP**
Disney releases bookable activities on a rolling basis, with only a limited number for Concierge and Castaway Club guests in the beginning; they release more as the 75-day mark approaches. So if you can't get an excursion at the 120-, 105, or 90-day mark, try again 75 days before you sail.

Silver Castaway Club guests (one to four previous cruises) paid in full can reserve the previous 90 days before their sail date.

First-time cruisers paid in full can reserve the previous 75 days before their sail date.

A FEW TIPS

1. If you opt for a week that includes a cruise and a Walt Disney World stay, go first to Disney World. Cruising at the end of your vacation will ensure you arrive home rested.

2. At least 75 days before you sail and as soon as your booking is paid in full, reserve meals at Palo and Remy, spa treatments, kids' programs, babysitting, and any shore excursions you can't do without at **disneycruise.com**.

3. Board the ship as early as possible. Check your dining rotation, and change it if desired. If you haven't reserved Palo or Remy, spa treatments, children's programs, or babysitting, do it now.

4. Disney requests that gentlemen wear jackets (no ties required) in the evening at Palo and Remy.

5. If you've purchased a Land/Sea package, complete and return your cruise forms at the hotel. Your shoreside room key card will allow you to bypass lines at the cruise terminal and board the ship directly. Cruise-only passengers can register online at the DCL website.

6. All cabins have a mini-fridge or cooling box; bring your own snacks and drinks.

7. **Sessions** piano bar on the *Magic* (**Cadillac Lounge** on the *Wonder*) is one of the most relaxing and beautiful lounges we've seen on any cruise ship. Make a before- or after-dinner drink there part of your routine. It's on Deck 3, forward.

8. Don't miss the kids' programs.

PART SIX

WALT DISNEY WORLD *with* KIDS

▌! The ECSTASY *and the* AGONY

SO OVERWHELMING IS THE DISNEY MEDIA and advertising presence that any child who watches TV or shops with Mom is likely to get revved up about going to Walt Disney World. Parents, if anything, are even more susceptible. Almost all parents brighten at the prospect of guiding their children through this special place. But the reality of taking a young child (particularly during the summer) can be closer to the agony than to the ecstasy.

A Dayton, Ohio, mother who took her 5-year-old to Disney World one summer recalls:

> I felt so happy and excited before we went. I guess it was all worth it, but when I look back I think I should have had my head examined. The first day we went to the Magic Kingdom, it was packed. By 11 in the morning, we had walked so far and stood in so many lines that we were all exhausted. Kristy cried about going on anything that looked or even sounded scary and was frightened by all of the Disney characters (they're so big!) except Minnie and Snow White.
>
> We got hungry about the same time as everyone else, but the lines for food were too long and my husband said we'd have to wait. By 1 in the afternoon we were just plugging along, not seeing anything we were really interested in, but picking rides because the lines were short, or because whatever it was was air-conditioned. . . . At around 2:30, we finally got something to eat, but by then we were so hot and tired that it felt like we had worked in the yard all day. Kristy insisted on being carried, and we had 50 fights about not going on rides where the lines were too long. At the end, we were so P.O.'d and uncomfortable that we weren't having any fun.

Before you stiffen in denial, let us assure you that this family's experience is not unusual. Most young children are as picky about rides as they are about what they eat, and more than half of all preschoolers are intimidated by the Disney characters. Few humans (of any age) are mentally or physically equipped to march all day in a throng of 50,000 people in the hot Florida sun. And would you be surprised to learn that almost 60% of preschoolers said the thing they liked best about their Disney vacation was the hotel swimming pool?

But even somewhat older kids will surprise you, as this Windsor, Ontario, mom relates:

> *On day three, as we pursued our "Around the World in 80 Minutes" through the World Showcase, our two girls suddenly stopped in their tracks between Italy and Germany. They looked around for a minute, and we asked what was wrong, thinking they might need a bathroom visit. Turns out they'd finally seen something other than characters that appealed to them. "Could we just run around on that grass over there for a few minutes?" they wanted to know. "We won't take too long." So away they went to chase each other on the grass for 10 minutes, and now, 10 years later, that is what they remember about the trip. Ever since, we've tried to include time in each trip plan to "run around on that grass over there," wherever "there" might be.*

*un*official **TIP**
When considering a trip to Walt Disney World, think about whether your kids are old enough to enjoy what can be a very fun, but taxing, trip.

With realistic objectives, a good plan, and a sense of humor, you'll be e-mailing us messages like this one from a Harrisburg, Pennsylvania, mom:

> *I knew it would be fun for my daughter, but what I didn't expect was just how much fun it would be for me.*

REALITY TESTING: WHOSE DREAM IS IT?

REMEMBER WHEN YOU WERE LITTLE and you got that nifty electric train for Christmas, the one Dad wouldn't let you play with? Did you wonder who the train was really for? Ask yourself a similar question about your vacation to Walt Disney World. Whose dream are you trying to make come true: yours or your child's?

Young children read their parents' emotions. When you ask, "Honey, how would you like to go to Disney World?" your child will respond more to your smile and enthusiasm than to any notion of what Disney World is all about. The younger the child, the more this holds true. From many preschoolers, you could elicit the same excitement by asking, "Sweetie, how would you like to go to Cambodia on a dogsled?"

So, is your happy fantasy of introducing your child to Disney magic a pipe dream? Not necessarily, but you have to be practical and open to reality testing. For example, would you increase the probability of a successful visit by waiting a year or two? Is your child adventuresome enough to sample the variety of Disney World? Will your child have sufficient endurance and patience to cope with long lines and large crowds?

RECOMMENDATIONS FOR MAKING THE DREAM COME TRUE

WHEN YOU'RE PLANNING A DISNEY WORLD VACATION with young children, consider the following:

AGE Although Walt Disney World's color and festivity excite all children and specific attractions delight toddlers and preschoolers,

Disney entertainment is generally oriented to older children and adults. Children should be a fairly mature 7 years old to *appreciate* the Magic Kingdom and Disney's Animal Kingdom, a year or two older to get much out of Epcot or Disney's Hollywood Studios.

Readers continually debate how old a child should be or the ideal age to go to Disney World. A Rockaway, New Jersey, mom writes:

> *You were absolutely right about young kids; I found myself rereading your section "The Ecstasy and the Agony." Unfortunately, our experience was pure agony, with the exception of our hotel pool. It was the one and only thing our kids wanted to do. I planned this trip and saved for over a year and cried all week at the disappointment that our kids just wanted to swim.*

A dad from Columbus, Ohio, felt like he was in a maternity ward:

> *We were shocked to see so many newborns as well. I could have sworn that one woman gave birth at the bus stop, her baby was so small.*

But a Cleveland mother takes exception:

> *The best advice for parents with young kids is to remember for whom you're there and if possible accommodate the kids' need to do things again and again. I think you underestimate Disney's appeal to young children. Since we've gotten home, my 4-year-old has said "I don't want to live in Cleveland, I want to live at Disney World!" at least five times a day.*

A mom from New York State also had a positive experience:

> *I think you go overboard in cautioning parents with small children to stay away from WDW. We just went with our daughters, ages 6 and 3, and had a fabulous time. To be sure, our 3-year-old was somewhat intimidated by most rides other than the ones in Fantasyland. But both girls loved meeting all the characters, getting dolled up at the Bibbidi Bobbidi Boutique, and soaking up the Disney magic. Had I waited a year or two, my 6-year-old would've been too old for the Disney-princess stuff.*

A New York City mom had a great vacation—but not exactly the one she'd been expecting:

> *Unfortunately, I was unprepared for traveling with a 2½-year-old. All the indoor rides were deemed too dark and scary, and all she wanted to do was see the characters (which I thought she'd be petrified of!). We had a great trip once I threw all my maps and plans out the window and just went with the flow! Also, three nights was not enough to have a leisurely trip. We were running around way too much. We all would have appreciated more pool time. It was a great trip overall, but I would definitely warn people to think twice before bringing a toddler. It's one exhausting trip!*

An Iowa City, Iowa, mother of three administers some tough love:

> *Get over it! In my opinion, people think too much about the age thing. If taking your 3-year-old to Disney World would make you happy, that's all that counts. End of story. It doesn't matter if the trip*

is really for you or your child—it's all good. You shouldn't have to jump through a bunch of hoops to give yourself permission to go.

A Lawrenceville, Georgia, mother of two toddlers advises maintaining the children's normal schedule:

The first day, we tried your suggestion about an early start; so we woke the children (ages 4 and 2) and hurried them to get going. BAD IDEA with toddlers. This put them off schedule for naps and meals the rest of the day. It's best to let young ones stay on their regular schedule and see Disney at their own pace.

Finally, an Alabama woman encourages parents to be more open-minded about taking toddlers to Disney World:

Parents of toddlers, don't be afraid to bring your little ones! Ours absolutely loved it, and we have priceless photos and videos of our little ones and their grandparents with Mickey and the gang. For all those people in your book who complained about our little sweethearts crying, sorry, but we found your character-hogging, cursing, ill-mannered, cutting-in-line, screaming-in-our-ears-on-the-roller-coasters teens and preteens much more obnoxious.

unofficial **TIP**
Coupled with a sense of humor and a little preparedness on your part, our touring plans and tips for families ensure a super experience at any time of year.

WHEN TO VISIT Avoid the hot, crowded summer months, especially if you have preschoolers. Go in October, November (except Thanksgiving), early December, January, February, or May. If you have children of varied ages and they're good students, take the older ones out of school and visit during the cooler, less congested off-season. Arrange special assignments relating to educational aspects of Disney World. If your children can't afford to miss school, take your vacation as soon as the school year ends. Alternatively, try late August before school starts. Please understand that you don't have to visit during one of the more ideal times of year to have a great vacation.

A Peterborough, England, woman agrees:

We visited WDW at the end of August, and we expected that the crowds would be almost unbearable. However, we were surprised to find that since most local schools were back in session, we could walk on most headliner rides up until late afternoon, and even then there was only a short wait—some rides at Universal Studios didn't even open until 11 a.m. because we were visiting on a low-attendance day! We'd recommend that more people go this time of year, especially those people whose children don't return to school until later.

BUILD NAPS AND REST INTO YOUR ITINERARY The parks are huge: Don't try to see everything in one day. Tour in early morning and return to your hotel around 11:30 a.m. for lunch, a swim, and a nap. Even during off-season, when crowds are smaller and the temperature is more pleasant, the major parks' size will exhaust most children younger than age 8 by lunchtime. Return to the park in late afternoon or early evening and continue touring. A family from Texas underlines the importance of naps and rest:

Despite not following any of your "tours," we did follow the theme of visiting a specific park in the morning, leaving midafternoon for either a nap back at the room or a trip to the hotel pool, and then returning to one of the parks in the evening. On the few occasions when we skipped your advice, I was muttering to myself by dinner. I can't tell you what I was muttering . . . .

Regarding naps, this mom doesn't mince words:

For parents of small kids: Take the book's advice and get out of the park and take the nap, take the nap, TAKE THE NAP! Never in my life have I seen so many parents screaming at, ridiculing, or slapping their kids. (What a vacation!) WDW is overwhelming for kids and adults. Even though the rental strollers recline for sleeping, we noticed that most of the toddlers and preschoolers didn't give up and sleep until 5 p.m., several hours after the fun had worn off, and right about the time their parents wanted them to be awake and polite in a restaurant.

From a Hamburg, New York, mother of a toddler:

Since we were traveling with our 2-year-old, we went to the parks when they opened every morning (usually by 9 a.m.), then followed the advice to return to our hotel for an afternoon nap. If we began lunch in the park by 11:30, our son was down for his nap by 1. This was the best decision we made. We all stayed rested, since one of us would nap in the room and the other would swim or shop during our son's nap. After napping, we were all refreshed and ready to head back to the park. Our son stayed in good spirits throughout the 10-day trip, while his 4-year-old and 7-year-old cousins, who didn't take a break during the day, were exhausted and whiny for half of the vacation. I was worried that 10 days would be too long for a 2-year-old, but going at this pace allowed us to thoroughly cover all of the parks without stress.

And finally, from an Alice, Texas, mom of two school-age children:

Probably the most important tip your guide gave us was going to the hotel to swim and regroup during the day. The parks became unbearable by noon—and so did my husband and boys. The hotel was an oasis that calmed our nerves and refreshed our hearts! After about 3 hours of playtime, we headed out to a different park for dinner and a cool evening of fun.

If you plan to return to your hotel at midday and want your room made up, let housekeeping know.

unofficial **TIP**
If you must rent a car to make returning to your hotel practicable, do it.

WHERE TO STAY The time and hassle involved in commuting to and from the theme parks will be less if your hotel is close by. This doesn't necessarily mean you have to lodge inside Disney World. Because the World is so geographically dispersed, many off-property hotels are closer to the parks than some Disney resorts (see our Hotel Information Chart in Part 3, showing commuting times from Disney and non-Disney hotels). Regardless of where you stay, it's imperative that you take young children out of the parks each day for a few hours of rest. Neglecting to relax can ruin the day—or the vacation—for everyone.

If you have young children, book a hotel that is within a 20-minute driving distance from the theme parks. It's true that you can revive somewhat by retreating to a Disney hotel for lunch or by finding a quiet restaurant in the parks, but there's no substitute for returning to the comfort of your hotel. Regardless of what you've heard, children too large to sleep in a stroller won't relax unless you take them back to your hotel.

> *unofficial* **TIP**
> The way to protect your considerable investment in your Disney vacation is to stay happy and have a good time. You don't have to meet a quota for experiencing attractions. Do what you want.

Thousands of new rooms have been built in and near Walt Disney World, many of them affordable. With some planning, you should have no difficulty finding lodging to meet your requirements.

If you're traveling with children 12 years old and younger and want to stay in the World, we recommend the Polynesian, Grand Floridian, or Wilderness Lodge & Villas resorts (in that order), if they fit your budget. For less expensive rooms, try the Port Orleans Resort. Bargain lodging is available at the All-Star, Art of Animation, and Pop Century resorts. In addition to standard hotel rooms, the All-Star and Art of Animation resorts offer two-room family suites that can sleep as many as six and provide modest kitchens. Log cabins at Fort Wilderness Campground are also a good bet. Outside the World, check our top hotels for families, starting on page 239.

BE IN TOUCH WITH YOUR FEELINGS When you or your children get tired and irritable, call time-out. Trust your instincts. What would feel best? Another ride, an ice-cream break, or going back to the room for a nap?

LEAST COMMON DENOMINATORS Somebody is going to run out of steam first, and when he or she does, the whole family will be affected. Sometimes a snack break will revive the flagging member. Sometimes, however, it's better to return to your hotel. Pushing the tired or discontented beyond their capacity will spoil the day for them—and you. Energy levels vary. Be prepared to respond to members of your group who poop out. *Hint:* "We've driven a thousand miles to take you to Walt Disney World and now you're ruining everything!" is not an appropriate response.

BUILDING ENDURANCE Though most children are active, their normal play usually doesn't condition them for the exertion required to tour a Disney park. Start family walks four to six weeks before your trip to get in shape. A mother from Wescosville, Pennsylvania, reports:

> *We had our 6-year-old begin walking with us a bit every day one month before leaving—when we arrived at Disney World, her little legs could carry her, and she had a lot of stamina.*

A father of two from Albion, Minnesota, had this to say:

> *My wife walked with my son to school every day when it was nice. His stamina was outstanding.*

SETTING LIMITS AND MAKING PLANS In order to avoid arguments and disappointment, establish guidelines for each day and getting everybody committed. Include the following:

1. Wake-up time and breakfast plans

2. When to depart for the park

3. What to take with you

4. A policy for splitting the group or for staying together

5. What to do if the group gets separated or someone is lost

6. How long you intend to tour in the morning and what you want to see, including plans in the event an attraction is closed or too crowded

7. A policy on what you can afford for snacks

8. A time for returning to the hotel to rest

9. When you'll return to the park and how late you'll stay

10. Dinner plans

11. A policy for buying souvenirs, including who pays: Mom and Dad or the kids

12. Bedtimes

BE FLEXIBLE Any day at Disney World includes surprises; be prepared to adjust your plan. Listen to your intuition.

WHAT KIDS WANT According to research by Yesawich, Pepperdine, Brown, and Russell, 71% of children between the ages of 6 and 17 say they need a vacation because school and homework get them down. The chart below shows what kids want and don't want when taking a vacation. Kids surveyed have a lot in common about what they do want, less so concerning what they don't.

WHAT DO KIDS WANT?	WHAT DO KIDS NOT WANT?
To go swimming/have pool time 80%	To get up early 52%
To eat in restaurants 78%	To ride in a car 36%
To stay at a hotel or resort 76%	To play golf 34%
To visit a theme park 76%	To go to a museum 31%
To stay up late 73%	

MAINTAINING SOME SEMBLANCE OF ORDER AND DISCIPLINE OK, OK, wipe that smirk off your face. Order and discipline on the road may seem like an oxymoron to you, but you won't be hooting when your 5-year-old launches a tantrum in the middle of Fantasyland. Your willingness to give this subject serious consideration before you leave home may well be the most important element of your pre-trip preparation.

Discipline and maintaining order are more difficult when traveling than at home because everyone is, as a Boston mom put it, "in and out"—in strange surroundings and out of the normal routine. For children, it's hard to contain excitement and anticipation that pop to the surface in the form of fidgety hyperactivity, nervous energy, and sometimes, acting out. Confinement in a car, plane, or hotel room only exacerbates the situation, and kids often tend to be louder than normal, more aggressive with siblings, and much more inclined to push the envelope of parental patience. Once you're in the theme parks, it doesn't get much better. There's more elbow room, but there are also overstimulation, crowds, heat, and miles of walking. All this, coupled with marginal or inadequate rest, can lead to a meltdown in the most harmonious of families.

Sound parenting and standards of discipline practiced at home, applied consistently, will suffice to handle most situations on vacation. Still, it's instructive to study the hand you're dealt when traveling. For starters, aside from being jazzed and ablaze with adrenaline, your kids may believe that rules followed at home are somehow suspended when traveling. Parents reinforce this misguided intuition by being inordinately lenient in the interest of maintaining peace in the family.

unofficial **TIP**
Just because the kids are on vacation doesn't mean you should let them monopolize your trip—maintain some of your everyday rules, and you'll all have a better time together.

While some of your home protocols (like cleaning your plate and going to bed at a set time) might be relaxed to good effect on vacation, differing from your normal approach to discipline can precipitate major misunderstanding and possibly disaster.

Children, not unexpectedly, are likely to believe that a vacation (especially a vacation to Walt Disney World) is intended expressly for them. This reinforces their focus on their own needs and largely erases any consideration of yours. Such a mind-set dramatically increases their sense of hurt and disappointment when you correct them or deny them something they want. An incident that would hardly elicit a pouty lip at home could well escalate to tears or defiance when traveling. It's important before you depart on your trip, therefore, to discuss your vacation needs with your children, and to explore their wants and expectations as well.

The stakes are high for everyone on a vacation—for you because of the cost in time and dollars, but also because your vacation represents a rare opportunity for rejuvenation and renewal. The stakes are high for your children, too. Children tend to romanticize travel, building anticipation to an almost unbearable level. Discussing the trip in advance can ground expectations to a certain extent, but a child's imagination will, in the end, trump reality every time. The good news is that you can take advantage of your children's emotional state to establish preset rules and conditions for their conduct while on vacation. Because your children want what's being offered *sooooo* badly, they will be unusually accepting and conscientious regarding whatever rules are agreed upon.

According to *Unofficial Guide* child psychologist Karen Turnbow, PhD, successful response to (or avoidance of) behavioral problems on the road begins with a clear-cut disciplinary policy at home. Both at home and on vacation the approach should be the same, and should be based on the following key concepts:

1. LET EXPECTATIONS BE KNOWN Discuss what you expect from your children, but don't try to cover every imaginable situation (that's what lawyers are for—just kidding). Cover expectations regarding compliance with parental directives, treatment of siblings, resolution of disputes, schedules (including morning wake-up and bedtimes), courtesy and manners, staying together, and who pays for what.

2. EXPLAIN THE CONSEQUENCES OF NONCOMPLIANCE Detail very clearly and firmly the consequence of not meeting expectations. This should be very straightforward and unambiguous: "If you do X (or don't do X), this is what will happen."

3. WARNING You're dealing with excited, expectant children, not machines, so it's important to issue a warning before meting out discipline. It's critical to understand that we're talking about one unequivocal warning rather than multiple warnings or nagging. These last undermine your credibility and make your expectations appear relative or less than serious. Multiple warnings or nagging also effectively pass control of the situation from you to your child (who sometimes may continue acting out as an attention-getting strategy).

4. FOLLOW THROUGH If you say you're going to do something, do it. Period. Children must understand that you mean business.

5. CONSISTENCY Inconsistency makes discipline a random event in the eyes of your children. Random discipline encourages random behavior, which translates to a nearly total loss of parental control. Long term, both at home and on the road, your response to a given situation or transgression must be perfectly predictable. Structure and repetition, essential for a child to learn, cannot be achieved in the absence of consistency.

Although the previous methods are the five biggies, there are several corollary concepts and techniques worthy of consideration.

Understand that whining, tantrums, defiance, sibling friction, and even holding up the group are ways in which children communicate with parents. Frequently the object or precipitant of a situation has little or no relation to the unacceptable behavior. A fit may on the surface appear to be about the ice cream you refused to buy little Robby, but there's almost always something deeper, a subtext that is closer to the truth (this is why ill behavior often persists after you give in to a child's demands). As often as not, the real cause is a need for attention. This need is so powerful in some children that they will subject themselves to certain punishment and parental displeasure to garner the attention they crave, even if it's negative.

To get at the root cause of the behavior in question requires both active listening and empowering your child with a "feeling vocabulary." Active listening is a concept that's been around a long time. It involves being alert not only to what a child says, but also to the context in which it's said, to the words used and possible subtext, to the child's emotional state and body language, and even to what's not said. Sounds complicated, but it's basically being attentive to the larger picture and, more to the point, being aware that there's a larger picture.

Helping your child develop a feeling vocabulary consists of teaching your child to use words to describe what's going on. The idea is to teach the child to articulate what's really troubling him, to be able to identify and express emotions and mood states in language. Of course, learning to express feelings is a lifelong learning experience, but it's much less dependent on innate sensitivity than on being provided the tools for expression and being encouraged to use them.

It all begins with convincing your child that you're willing to listen attentively and take what he's saying seriously. By listening to your child, you help him transcend the topical by reframing the conversation to address the underlying emotional state(s). That his brother hit him may have precipitated the mood state, but the act is topical and of secondary importance. What you want is for your child to be able to communicate how that makes him feel, and to get in touch with those emotions. When you reduce an incident (hitting) to the emotions triggered (anger, hurt, rejection), you have the foundation for helping him develop constructive coping strategies. Being in touch with one's feelings and developing constructive coping strategies are essential to emotional well-being, and they also have a positive effect on behavior. A child who can tell his mother why he is distressed is a child who has discovered a coping strategy far more effective (not to mention easier for all concerned) than a tantrum.

unofficial **TIP**
Teaching your kids to tell you clearly what they want or need will help make the trip more enjoyable for everyone.

Children are almost never too young to begin learning a feeling vocabulary. And helping your child to be in touch with—and to communicate—his or her emotions will stimulate you to focus on your feelings and mood states in a similar way. In the end, with persistence and effort, the whole family will achieve a vastly improved ability to communicate.

Until you get the active listening and feeling vocabulary going, be careful not to become part of the problem. There's a whole laundry list of adult responses to bad behavior that only make things worse. Hitting, swatting, yelling, name-calling, insulting, belittling, using sarcasm, pleading, nagging, and inducing guilt (as in "We've spent thousands of dollars to bring you to Disney World and now you're spoiling the trip for everyone!") figure prominently on the list.

Responding to a child appropriately in a disciplinary situation requires thought and preparation. Following are things to keep in mind and techniques to try when your world blows up while waiting in line for Dumbo.

1. BE THE ADULT It's well understood that children can push their parents' buttons faster and more skillfully than just about anyone or anything else. They've got your number, know precisely how to elicit a response, and are not reluctant to go for the jugular. Fortunately (or unfortunately), you're the adult, and to deal with a situation effectively, you've got to act like one. If your kids get you ranting and caterwauling, you effectively abdicate your adult status. Worse, you suggest by way of example that being out of control is an acceptable expression of hurt or anger. No matter what happens, repeat the mantra, "I am the adult in this relationship."

2. FREEZE THE ACTION Being the adult and maintaining control almost always translates to freezing the action, to borrow a sports term. Instead of responding in knee-jerk fashion (that is, at a maturity level closer to your child's than yours), freeze the action by disengaging. Wherever you are or whatever the family is doing, stop in place and concentrate on one thing, and one thing only: getting all involved calmed down. Practically speaking this usually means initiating a time-out. It's essential that you take this action immediately. Grabbing your child by the arm or collar and dragging him toward the car or hotel room only escalates the turmoil by prolonging the confrontation and by adding a coercive physical dimension to an already volatile emotional event. For the sake of everyone involved, including the people around you (as when a toddler throws a tantrum in church), it's essential to retreat to a more private place. Choose the first place available. Firmly sit the child down and refrain from talking to him until you've both cooled off. This might take a little time, but the investment is worthwhile. Truncating the process is like trying to get on your feet too soon after surgery.

3. ISOLATE THE CHILD You'll be able to deal with the situation more effectively and expeditiously if the child is isolated with one parent. Dispatch the uninvolved members of your party for a snack break or have them go on with the activity or itinerary without you (if possible) and arrange to rendezvous later at an agreed time and place. In addition to letting the others get on with their day, isolating the offending child with one parent relieves him of the pressure of being the group's focus of attention and object of anger. Equally important, isolation frees you from the scrutiny and expectations of the others in regard to how to handle the situation.

4. REVIEW THE SITUATION WITH THE CHILD If, as discussed a few pages back, you've made your expectations clear, stated the consequences of failing to meet those expectations, and administered a warning, review the situation with the child and follow through with the discipline warranted. If, as often occurs, things are not so black-and-white, encourage the child to communicate his feelings. Try to uncover what occasioned the acting out. Lectures and accusatory language don't work well here, nor do threats. Dr. Turnbow suggests that a better approach (after the child is calm) is to ask, "What can we do to make this a better day for you?"

5. FREQUENT TANTRUMS OR ACTING OUT The preceding four points relate to dealing with an incident as opposed to a chronic condition. If a child frequently acts out or throws tantrums, you'll need to employ a somewhat different strategy.

Tantrums are cyclical events evolved from learned behavior. A child learns that he can get your undivided attention by acting out. When you respond, whether by scolding, admonishing, threatening, or negotiating, your response further draws you into the cycle and prolongs the behavior. When you accede to the child's demands, you reinforce the effectiveness of the tantrum and raise the cost of capitulation next time around. When a child thus succeeds in monopolizing your attention, he effectively becomes the person in charge.

To break this cycle, you must disengage from the child. The object is to demonstrate that the cause-and-effect relationship (that is, tantrum elicits parental attention) is no longer operative. This can be accomplished by refusing to interact with the child as long as the untoward behavior continues. Tell the child that you're unwilling to discuss his problem until he calms down. You can ignore the behavior, remove yourself from the child's presence (or vice versa), or isolate the child with a time-out. It's important to disengage quickly and decisively with no discussion or negotiation.

Most children don't pick the family vacation as the time to start throwing tantrums. The behavior will be evident before you leave home, and home is the best place to deal with it. Be forewarned, however, that bad habits die hard, and that a child accustomed to getting attention by throwing tantrums will not simply give up after a single instance of disengagement. More likely, the child will at first escalate the intensity and length of his tantrums. By your consistent refusal over several weeks (or even months) to respond to his behavior, however, he will finally adjust to the new paradigm.

Children are cunning as well as observant. Many understand that a tantrum in public is embarrassing to you and that you're more likely to cave in than you would at home. Once again, consistency is the key, along with a bit of anticipation. When traveling, it's not necessary to retreat to the privacy of a hotel room to isolate your child. You can carve out space for a time-out almost anywhere: on a theme park bench, in a park, in your car, in a restroom, even on a sidewalk.

You can often spot the warning signs of an impending tantrum and head it off by talking to the child before he reaches an explosive emotional pitch. And don't forget that tantrums are about getting attention. Giving your child attention when things are on an even keel often preempts acting out.

6. SALVAGE OPERATIONS Who knows what evil lurks in the hearts of children? What's for sure is that they're full of surprises, and sometimes the surprises are not good. If your sweet child manages to pull a stunt of mammoth proportions, what do you do? This happened to an Ohio couple, resulting in the offending kid pretty much being grounded for life. Fortunately there were no injuries or lives lost, but the parents had to determine what to do for the remainder of the vacation. For starters, they split up the group. One parent escorted the offending child back to the hotel, where he was effectively confined to his guest room for the duration. That evening, the parents arranged for in-room sitters for the rest of the stay. Expensive? You bet, but better than watching your whole vacation go down the tubes.

A family at Walt Disney World's Magic Kingdom theme park had a similar experience, although the offense was of a more modest order of magnitude. Because it was their last day of vacation, they elected to place the misbehaver in time-out, in the theme park, for the rest of the day. One parent monitored the culprit while the other parent and the siblings enjoyed the attractions. At agreed times the parents would switch places. Once again, not ideal, but preferable to stopping the vacation.

Parenting Advice: Readers Weigh In

Though the foregoing section was developed by top child psychologists, it rubs some readers the wrong way. Take this teacher from Corryton, Tennessee:

The one thing I don't like is the section on how to make your kids behave. As a preschool teacher, I can honestly say that people who need this advice won't take it anyway—so why bother?

But a North Carolina psychiatrist disagrees:

The section of the Unofficial Guide *dealing with child behavioral issues while traveling is one of the most concise and well-articulated presentations on this subject that I have encountered anywhere. I recommend it to many of my patients who are contemplating traveling with their children.*

A New Hampshire father of two had this to say:

Your advice on touring with children was fabulous. Your book gave us confidence to do the parks without being deer caught in the headlights.

ABOUT THE *UNOFFICIAL GUIDE* TOURING PLANS

PARENTS WHO USE OUR TOURING PLANS are often frustrated by interruptions and delays caused by their young children. Here's what to expect:

1. CHARACTER ENCOUNTERS CAN WREAK HAVOC WITH THE TOURING PLANS. Many children will stop in their tracks whenever they see a Disney character. Attempting to haul your child away before he has satisfied his curiosity is likely to cause anything from whining to full-scale revolt. Either go with the flow or specify a morning or afternoon for photos and autographs. Be aware that queues for autographs can be as long as the queues for major attractions.

2. OUR TOURING PLANS CALL FOR VISITING ATTRACTIONS IN A SEQUENCE, OFTEN SKIPPING ATTRACTIONS ALONG THE WAY. Children don't like to skip anything! If something catches their eye, they want to see it that moment. Some can be persuaded to skip attractions if parents explain their plans in advance. Other kids flip out at skipping something, particularly in Fantasyland. A mom from Charleston, South Carolina, writes:

We didn't have too much trouble following the touring plans at Disney's Hollywood Studios and at Epcot. The Magic Kingdom plan, on the other hand, turned out to be a train wreck. When we were on Dumbo, my 5-year-old saw eight dozen other things in Fantasyland she wanted to see. The long and the short is that after Dumbo, there was no getting her out of there.

A mother of two from Burlington, Vermont, adds:

I found out that my kids were very curious about the castle because we had read Cinderella *at home. Whenever I wanted to leave Fantasyland, I would just say, "Let's go to the castle and see if Cinderella is there." Once we got as far as the front door to the castle, it was no problem going out to the Central Plaza and then to another land.*

3. CHILDREN HAVE AN INSTINCT FOR FINDING RESTROOMS. We have seen adults with maps search interminably for a restroom. Young children, however, including those who can't read, will head for the nearest restroom with the certainty of a homing pigeon. You can be sure your children will ferret out (and want to use) every restroom in the park.

4. IF YOU'RE USING A STROLLER, YOU WON'T BE ABLE TO TAKE IT INTO ATTRACTIONS OR ONTO RIDES. This includes rides such as the Walt Disney World Railroad that are included in the touring plans as in-park transportation.

5. YOU PROBABLY WON'T FINISH THE TOURING PLAN. Varying hours of operation, crowds, your group's size, your children's ages, and your stamina will all affect how much of the plan you'll complete. Tailor your expectations to this reality, or you'll be frustrated, as this mother of two from Nazareth, Pennsylvania, was:

> We don't understand how anyone could fit everything you have on your plans into the time allotted while attending to small children. We found that long lines, potty stops, diaper changes, stroller searches, and autograph breaks ate huge chunks of time. And we were there during the off-season.

While our touring plans allow you to make the most of your time at the parks, it's impossible to define what "most" will be. It differs from family to family. If you have two young children, you probably won't see as much as two adults will. If you have four children, you probably won't see as much as a couple with only two children.

STUFF TO THINK ABOUT

OVERHEATING, SUNBURN, AND DEHYDRATION These are the most common problems of younger children at Disney World. Carry and use sunscreen. Apply it on children in strollers, even if the stroller has a canopy. To avoid overheating, stop for rest regularly—say, in the shade, or in a restaurant or at a show with air-conditioning.

BLISTERS AND SORE FEET All guests should wear comfortable, broken-in shoes and socks that wick away perspiration, like SmartWool socks. If you or your children are susceptible to blisters, bring along some Johnson & Johnson blister bandages. They offer excellent protection, stick great, and won't sweat off. When you feel a "hot spot," stop, air out your foot, and place a blister bandage over the area before a blister forms. The bandages are available at all drugstores. Preschoolers may not say they're developing a blister until it's too late, so inspect their feet two or more times a day. For an expanded discussion about keeping your feet happy, see page 404.

unofficial **TIP**
Keep little ones well covered in sunscreen and hydrated with fluids. Don't count on hydrating young children with soft drinks and stops at water fountains. Carry plastic bottles of water. Squeeze bottles with caps are sold in all major parks for about $3. *Remember:* Excited kids may not tell you when they're thirsty or hot.

FIRST AID Each major theme park has a first-aid center. In the Magic Kingdom, it's at the end of Main Street to your left, between Casey's Corner and The Crystal Palace. At Epcot, it's on the World Showcase side of Odyssey Center. At Disney's Hollywood Studios, it's in the Guest Relations Building inside the main entrance. At Disney's Animal Kingdom, it's in Discovery Island, on your left just before you cross the bridge to Africa, behind Creature Comforts. And in all four parks, First Aid and the Baby Care Center are right next to each other. If you or your children have a medical problem, go to a first-aid center. They're friendlier than most doctor's offices and are accustomed to treating everything from paper cuts to allergic reactions.

CHILDREN ON MEDICATION Some parents of hyperactive children on medication discontinue or decrease the child's dosage at the end of the school year. If you have such a child, be aware that Disney World might overstimulate him or her. Consult your physician before altering your child's medication regimen.

SUNGLASSES If your younger children wear sunglasses, put a strap or string on the frames so the glasses will stay on during rides and can hang from the child's neck while indoors. This works for adults as well.

THINGS YOU FORGOT OR THINGS YOU RAN OUT OF Rain gear, diapers, diaper pins, formula, film, painkillers, topical sunburn treatments, and other sundries are sold at all major theme parks and at Typhoon Lagoon, Blizzard Beach, and Downtown Disney. Rain gear is a bargain, but most other items are pricey. Ask for goods you don't see displayed.

INFANTS AND TODDLERS AT THE THEME PARKS The major parks have centralized facilities for infant and toddler care. Everything necessary for changing diapers, preparing formulas, and warming bottles and food is available. Supplies are for sale, and rockers and special chairs for nursing mothers are provided. At the Magic Kingdom, the Baby Care Center is next to The Crystal Palace at the end of Main Street. At Epcot, the Baby Care Center is in the Odyssey Center, between Test Track in Future World and Mexico in World Showcase. At Disney's Hollywood Studios, the Baby Care Center is in the Guest Relations Building left of the main entrance. At Disney's Animal Kingdom, the Baby Care Center is behind Creature Comforts. Dads are welcome at the centers and can use most services. In addition, many men's restrooms in the major parks have changing tables.

A mom from New Berlin, Wisconsin, offers this tip for families with babies on formula:

> *A note to families with infants: We got hot water from the food vendors at WDW and mixed the formula as we went. It eliminated keeping bottles cold and then warming them up.*

Infants and toddlers are allowed in any attraction that doesn't have minimum height or age restrictions. But as a Minneapolis mother reports, some attractions are better for babies than others:

> *Theater and boat rides are easier for babies (ours was almost a year old, not yet walking). Rides where there's a bar that comes down are doable, but harder. Peter Pan was our first encounter with this type of ride, and we had barely gotten situated when I realized he might fall out of my grasp. The standing auditorium films are too intense; the noise level is deafening and the images inescapable.*

The same mom also advises:

> *We used a baby sling on our trip and thought it was great when standing in lines—much better than a stroller, which you have to park*

before getting in line (and navigate through crowds). The only really great place I found to nurse in MK was a hidden bench in the shade in Adventureland near the Enchanted Tiki Room *and the small shops. It's impractical to go to the baby station every time, so a nursing mom had better be comfortable about nursing in very public situations.*

If you think you might try nursing during a theater attraction, be advised that most shows run about 17–20 minutes. Exceptions are *The Hall of Presidents* at the Magic Kingdom and *The American Adventure* at Epcot, which run 23 and 29 minutes, respectively.

RUNNING OUT OF GAS When Bob was preparing to hike from the Colorado River to the rim of the Grand Canyon—a 5,000-foot ascent—a park ranger told him to mix an electrolyte-replacement powder in his water and eat an energy-boosting snack at least twice every hour. While there's not much ascending to do at Walt Disney World, battling the heat, humidity, and crowds contributes to poop-out, especially where kids are concerned. Limiting calorie consumption to mealtimes just won't get it, as an experienced and wise grandma points out:

Children who get cranky during a visit often do so from all that time and energy expended without food. Feed them! A snack at any price goes a long way to keeping the little ones happy and parents sane. Oh, and the security people are very nice about you taking snacks or drinks in, but DO NOT bring glass containers!

STROLLERS

THE GOOD NEWS: STROLLERS ARE AVAILABLE for rent at all four theme parks and the Downtown Disney area (single stroller, $15 per day with no deposit, $13 per day for the entire stay; double stroller, $31 per day with no deposit, $27 per day for the entire stay; stroller rentals at Downtown Disney require a $100 credit card deposit; double strollers not available at Downtown Disney). Strollers are welcome at Blizzard Beach and Typhoon Lagoon, but no rentals are available. With multiday rentals, you can skip the rental line entirely—just head over to the stroller-handout area, show your receipt, and you'll be wheeling out

of there in no time. If you rent a stroller at the Magic Kingdom and you decide to go to Epcot, Disney's Animal Kingdom, or Disney's Hollywood Studios, turn in your Magic Kingdom stroller and present your receipt at the next park. You'll be issued another stroller at no additional charge.

You can pay in advance for stroller rentals—this allows you to bypass the "paying" line and head straight for the "pickup" line. Disney resort guests can pay in advance at their resort's gift shop. Save receipts! Obtain strollers at the Magic Kingdom entrance, to the left of Epcot's Entrance

Plaza and at Epcot's International Gateway, and at Oscar's Super Service just inside the entrance of Disney's Hollywood Studios. At Disney's Animal Kingdom, they're at Garden Gate Gifts, to the right just inside the entrance. Rental at all parks is fast and efficient, and returning the stroller is a breeze. You can ditch your rental stroller anywhere in the park when you're ready to leave.

Readers inform us that a lively "gray market" for strollers thrives at the parks. Families who arrive late look for families who are heading for the exit and "buy" their stroller at a bargain price. A mom from Chester, New Hampshire, ever vigilant for a bargain, reports:

> We "bought" strollers for $3 when we saw people returning them. Also, we "sold" our strollers for $3 when leaving.

Strollers are a must for infants and toddlers, but we have seen many sharp parents renting strollers for somewhat older children (up to age 5 or so). The stroller spares parents from having to carry children when they sag and provides a convenient place to tote water and snacks.

A family from Tulsa, Oklahoma, recommends springing for a double stroller:

> We rent a double for baggage room or in case the older child gets tired of walking.

But a New Lenox, Illinois, family advocates not leaving anyone out:

> If your kids are 8 or under, RENT STROLLERS for all of them! An 8-year-old will fit in a stroller, and you can fit up to four kids in two doubles. We tried this the first time we visited Disney 10 years ago, when my oldest was 6. My husband suggested getting a stroller for him and the two "babies" (ages 4 and 3). I thought he was nuts but didn't want to argue, and it turned out to be the best idea ever. We plowed through crowds, and the kids didn't get nearly as tired since they could be seated whenever they wanted. It was also a great place to stow heavy gear like video cameras. The Disney strollers are extremely sturdy and can take a lot of abuse—try it!

If you go to your hotel for a break and intend to return to the park, leave your rental stroller by an attraction near the park entrance, marking it with something personal like a bandanna. When you return, your stroller will be waiting.

Rental strollers are too large for all infants and many toddlers. If you plan to rent a stroller for your infant or toddler, bring pillows, cushions, or rolled towels to buttress him in.

Bringing your own stroller is permitted. However, only collapsible strollers are allowed on monorails, parking-lot trams, and buses. Your stroller is unlikely to be stolen, but mark it with your name.

Having her own stroller was indispensable to a Mechanicsville, Virginia, mother of two toddlers:

> How I was going to manage to get the kids from the parking lot to the park was a big worry for me before I made the trip. I didn't read anywhere that it was possible to walk to the entrance of the parks instead of taking the tram, so I wasn't sure I could do it.

Since I have two kids ages 1 and 2, it was easier to walk to the entrance of the park from the parking lot with the kids in my own stroller than to take the kids out of the stroller, fold the stroller (while trying to control the two kids and associated gear), load the stroller and the kids onto the tram, etc. . . . . No matter where I was parked, I could always just walk to the entrance. . . . it sometimes took a while, but it was easier for me.

A Secaucus, New Jersey, mom weighed all the considerations in exemplary type-A fashion:

If your child is under age 2, bring your own stroller. Three reasons to bring your own: First, you have all the way from your car to the TTC [Transportation and Ticket Center] to the monorail (or ferry) to the stroller rental without a stroller, but with your child, diaper bag, and own self and stuff in tow. Not half as bad as doing it in reverse when leaving, when you're exhausted and have added to your luggage with purchases and the toddler who might have walked in wants to be carried out. Second, the WDW stroller is simply too large for most children under age 2 to be comfortable without significant padding. The seat is so low that the child is forced to keep their legs straight out in front of them. Third, despite being sooo big, there's NO PLACE to store anything. The body of the stroller is so low, there's no underneath storage for the diaper bag. There's a small net bag on the back of the carriage, but it seems designed to hold, at most, a small purse. If you hang a diaper bag by its straps from the handle, the stroller will tip backwards very, very easily. And you can't balance it on the top or the canopy won't stay open. It amazed me that the Disney folks didn't provide ample space for all the souvenirs they want you to buy!

Now, if your child is past needing a diaper bag, the WDW strollers seem like a pretty good deal. You won't need the storage space, and they do maneuver very well. They seem especially good for children who no longer need a stroller at home (ages 4–6) but who won't make it walking all day.

If your child is between ages 2 and 3, it's a toss-up. If you're a type-A mom, like me, who carries extra clothes, snacks, toys, enough diapers for three days, along with a pocketbook and extra-jackets-for-everyone-just-in-case, you've probably found a stroller that suits your needs and will be miserable with the WDW kind. If you're a type-B "we can get everything else we need at the park; I'll just throw a diaper in my back pocket" mom, you'll probably be tickled with the WDW strollers. Also consider your toddler's personality. Will his familiar stroller add a level of comfort to a pretty intense experience? Or will he enjoy the novelty of the new wheels?

An Oklahoma mom, however, reports a bad experience with bringing her own stroller:

The first time we took our kids, we had a large stroller (big mistake). It's so much easier to rent one in the park. Large [personally owned] strollers are nearly impossible to get on the buses and are a hassle at the airport. I remember feeling dread when a bus pulled up that was even semifull of people. People look at you like you have a cage full of live chickens when you drag a heavy stroller onto the bus.

PARKING YOUR STROLLER Though most families park their strollers in front of the attraction they're experiencing, a Franklin, Tennessee, family recommends this alternative:

> *Feel free to park your stroller at a central attraction in a land, then retrieve it only when you are leaving the land (with the exception of Epcot). It took us two days to figure out that we didn't need to move the stroller every time we moved.*

STROLLER-RENTAL OPTIONS With Disney pricing its own stroller rentals so high, several Orlando companies have sprung up, able to undercut Disney's prices, provide more comfortable strollers, and deliver them to your hotel. Most of the larger companies offer the same stroller models (the Baby Jogger City Mini Single, for example), so the primary differences between the companies are price and service.

unofficial **TIP**
When you enter a show or board a ride, you must park your stroller, usually in an open area. Bring a cloth or towel to dry it if it rains before you return.

To rate stroller companies, we had mom and *Unofficial Guide* researcher Scarlett Litton, along with **touringplans.com** blogger Shelley Caran, rent the same strollers from each company, use the strollers in the parks, and return them. Our evaluation covers the overall experience, from the ease with which the stroller was rented to the delivery of the stroller, its condition upon arrival, and the return process.

Baby Wheels Orlando (☎ 800-510-2480; **babywheelsorlando .com**) had the best combination of price and service. Upon request, Baby Wheels will include a rain cover and beverage cooler free—both of which are useful during Florida's summer months. A one-day rental is $30, three nights are $40, and five nights are $54. Thus, the break-even point for using Baby Wheels Orlando instead of Disney is four nights. Drop-off and pickup went without incident, and Baby Wheels' customer service is excellent.

We also recommend **Orlando Stroller Rentals, LLC** (☎ 800-281-0884; **orlandostrollerrentals.com**), which is slightly more expensive—rain covers, for instance, are $10—and whose strollers have a few more miles on them. The service is excellent, though.

STROLLER WARS Sometimes strollers disappear while you're enjoying a ride or show. Disney staff will often rearrange strollers parked outside an attraction. This may be done to tidy up or to clear a walkway. Don't assume that your stroller is stolen because it isn't where you left it. It may be neatly arranged a few feet away—or perhaps more than a few feet away, as this Skokie, Illinois, dad reports:

> *The stroller reorganizations while you're on rides are a bit unnerving. More than once, our stroller was moved out of visible distance from the original spot. On one occasion, it was moved to a completely different stroller-parking area near another ride, and no sign or cast member was around to advise where. We had to track a cast member down, and she had to call in to find out where it had been moved. Be prepared for this.*

Sometimes, however, strollers are taken by mistake or ripped off by people not wanting to spend time replacing one that's missing. Don't be alarmed if yours disappears. You won't have to buy it, and you'll be issued a new one. In the Magic Kingdom, replacements are available at Frontier Trading Post in Frontierland, at the Tomorrowland Arcade in Tomorrowland, and at the main rental facility near the park entrance. At Epcot, get replacements at the Entrance Plaza rental headquarters, at the Glas und Porzellan shop in the Germany Pavilion, and at the International Gateway. Strollers at Disney's Hollywood Studios can be replaced at Tatooine Traders. At Disney's Animal Kingdom, they're available at Garden Gate Gifts (just inside the park entrance) and Mombasa Marketplace.

While replacing a stroller is no big deal, it's inconvenient. A Minnesota family complained that their stroller was taken six times in one day at Epcot and five times in a day at Disney's Hollywood Studios. Even with free replacements, larceny on this scale represents a lot of wasted time. Through our own experiments and readers' suggestions, we've developed a technique for

unofficial **TIP**
We suggest that children younger than 8 years be color coded by dressing them in purple T-shirts or equally distinctive clothes.

hanging on to a rented stroller: Affix something personal (but expendable) to the handle. Evidently, most strollers are pirated by mistake (they all look alike) or because it's easier to swipe someone else's than to replace one that has disappeared. Because most stroller "theft" results from confusion or laziness, the average pram-pincher will hesitate to haul off a stroller containing another person's property. We tried several items and concluded that a bright, inexpensive scarf or bandanna tied to the handle works well as identification. A sock partially stuffed with rags or paper works even better (the weirder and more personal the object, the greater the deterrent). A multigenerational family from Utah went a step further and made their stroller difficult to move:

> We "decorated" our stroller with electrical tape to make it stand out. I took a firearm lock (looks like a mini–bike lock) to lock a wheel to the frame while parked. My son added a small cowbell to make it clang if moved. The stroller could then be moved easily for short distances by lifting the back, but trying to go farther would be uncomfortable and noisy.

STROLLERS AS LETHAL WEAPONS A middle-aged couple from Brunswick, Maine, lobbies for a temporary stroller ban:

> As an over-45 couple, we couldn't believe the number and sizes of strollers and those ubiquitous scooters. You had to be constantly vigilant or you would have your heels clipped, foot run over, or path slowed down by them. We've decided that one day a week, in one theme park, there should be a "no wheels" day. (Ah, but we live in Fantasyland!)

You'd be surprised at how many people are injured by strollers pushed by parents who are driving aggressively, in a hurry, or in the ozone. Given the number of strollers, pedestrians, and tight spaces, mishaps are inevitable on both sides. A simple apology and a smile are usually the best remediation.

LOST CHILDREN

ALTHOUGH IT'S AMAZINGLY EASY TO LOSE a child (or two) in the theme parks, it usually isn't a serious problem: Disney employees are schooled in handling the situation. If you lose a child in the Magic Kingdom, report it to a Disney employee, and then check at the Baby Care Center and at City Hall, where lost-children logs are kept. At Epcot, report the loss, then check at the Baby Care Center in the Odyssey Center. At Disney's Hollywood Studios, report the loss at the Guest Service Building, at the entrance end of Hollywood Boulevard. At Disney's Animal Kingdom, go to the Baby Care Center in Discovery Island. Paging isn't used, but in an emergency, an "all-points bulletin" can be issued throughout the park(s) via internal communications. If a Disney employee encounters a lost child, he or she will take the child immediately to the park's Baby Care Center.

Sew a label into each child's shirt that states his or her name, your name, the name of your hotel, and if you have one, your cell phone number. Accomplish the same thing by writing the information on a strip of masking tape. Security professionals suggest the information be printed in small letters and the tape be affixed to the outside of the child's shirt, 5 inches below the armpit. Also, name tags can be obtained at the major theme parks.

A Kingston, Washington, reader recommends recording vital info for each child on a plastic key tag or luggage tag and affixing it to the child's shoe. This reader also snaps a photo of the kids each morning to document what they're wearing. A mother from Rockville, Maryland, reported a strategy one step short of a brand or tattoo:

unofficial **TIP**
We suggest that children younger than 8 years be color coded by dressing them in purple T-shirts or equally distinctive clothes.

> *Traveling with a 3-year-old, I was very anxious about losing him. I wrote my cell phone number on his leg with a permanent marker, and felt much more confident that he'd get back to me quickly if he became lost.*

One way to better keep track of your family is to buy each person a "Disney uniform"—in this case, the same brightly and distinctively colored T-shirt. A Yuma, Arizona, family tried this with great success:

> *We tried the family plan of all of us getting the same shirts (bright red) so that we could easily spot each other in case of separation (VERY easy to do). It was a lifesaver when our 18-month-old decided to get out of the stroller and wander off. As I've heard before, Dumbo seems to draw them in, and lo and behold, guess where we found him (still dragging his leash but with a nice cast member following him). No matter what precautions you may try, it seems there are always those opportunities to lose a child, but the recognizable shirts helped tremendously.*

Finally, from a Swindon, England, mum:

> *In case they got lost, I photo'd my 7-year-old twins every morning so we had a picture of what they were wearing. They wore wristbands with our mobile-phone numbers on them. I made one adult*

responsible for each twin for the morning so that no one assumed someone else was holding their hand; then we switched after lunch. We also taught them if they got lost to shout our first names, not just "Mum" or "Dad."

HOW KIDS GET LOST

CHILDREN GET SEPARATED FROM THEIR PARENTS every day at Disney parks under remarkably similar (and predictable) circumstances:

1. PREOCCUPIED SOLO PARENT The party's only adult is preoccupied with something like buying refreshments, loading the camera, or using the restroom. Junior is there one second and gone the next.

2. THE HIDDEN EXIT Sometimes parents wait on the sidelines while two or more young children experience a ride together. Parents expect the kids to exit in one place and the youngsters pop out elsewhere. Exits from some attractions are distant from entrances. Know exactly where your children will emerge before letting them ride by themselves.

3. AFTER THE SHOW At the end of many shows and rides, a Disney staffer announces, "Check for personal belongings and take small children by the hand." When dozens, if not hundreds, of people leave an attraction simultaneously, it's easy for parents to lose their children unless they have direct contact.

4. RESTROOM PROBLEMS Mom tells 6-year-old Tommy, "I'll be sitting on this bench when you come out of the restroom." Three possibilities: One, Tommy exits through a different door and becomes disoriented (Mom may not know there's another door). Two, Mom decides she also will use the restroom, and Tommy emerges to find her gone. Three, Mom pokes around in a shop while keeping an eye on the bench but misses Tommy when he comes out.

If you can't be with your child in the restroom, make sure there's only one exit. The restroom on a passageway between Frontierland and Adventureland in the Magic Kingdom is the all-time worst for disorienting visitors. Children and adults alike have walked in from the Adventureland side and walked out on the Frontierland side (and vice versa). Adults realize quickly that something is wrong. Children, however, sometimes fail to recognize the problem.

Designate a distinctive meeting spot and give clear instructions: "I'll meet you by this flagpole. If you get out first, stay right here." Have your child repeat the directions back to you. When children are too young to leave alone, sometimes you have to think outside the box, as our Rockville, Maryland, mom (quoted on the previous page) did:

It was very scary for me at times, being alone with children who had just turned 1 and 2. I'm reminded of the time on the trip when I couldn't fit the double stroller into the bathroom. I was at Epcot inside one of the buildings and I had to leave my kids with a WDW employee outside of the restroom because the stroller just wouldn't fit inside with me. Thinking about the incident now makes me laugh. The good news is that I found that most WDW bathrooms can accommodate a front-and-back double stroller inside the handicapped stall with you.

5. PARADES There are many parades and shows at which the audience stands. Children tend to jockey for a better view. By moving a little this way and that, the child quickly puts distance between you and him before either of you notices.

6. MASS MOVEMENTS Be on guard when huge crowds disperse after fireworks or a parade, or at park closing. With 20,000–40,000 people at once in an area, it's very easy to get separated from a child or others in your party. Use extra caution after the evening parade and fireworks in the Magic Kingdom, *Fantasmic!* at Disney's Hollywood Studios, and *IllumiNations* at Epcot. Families should plan where to meet if they get separated.

7. CHARACTER GREETINGS When the Disney characters appear, children can slip out of sight. (See "Then Some Confusion Happened," page 339.)

8. GETTING LOST AT DISNEY'S ANIMAL KINGDOM It's especially easy to lose a child in Animal Kingdom, particularly at the Oasis entryway, on the Maharajah Jungle Trek, and on the Pangani Forest Exploration Trail. Mom and Dad will stop to observe an animal. Junior stays close for a minute or so, and then, losing patience, wanders to the exhibit's other side or to a different exhibit.

Especially in the multipath Oasis, finding a lost child can be maddening, as a Safety Harbor, Florida, mother describes:

> *Manny wandered off in the paths that lead to the jungle village while we were looking at a bird. It reminded me of losing somebody in the supermarket when you run back and forth looking down each aisle but can't find the person you're looking for because they're running around too. I was nutso before we even got to the first ride.*

A mother from Flint, Michigan, came up with yet another way to lose a kid: abandonment.

> *From the minute we hit the park it was gripe, whine, pout, cry, beg, scream, pick, pester, and aggravate. When he went to the restroom for the ninth time before 11 a.m., I thought, "I'm outta here! Let the little snothead walk back to Flint." Unfortunately, I was brought up Catholic with lots of guilt, so I didn't follow through.*

DISNEY, KIDS, *and* SCARY STUFF

DISNEY RIDES AND SHOWS ARE ADVENTURES, and they focus on themes of all adventures: good and evil, death, beauty and ugliness, fellowship and enmity. As you sample the attractions at Walt Disney World, you'll transcend the spinning and bouncing of midway rides to thought-provoking and emotionally powerful entertainment. All the endings are happy, but the adventures' impact, given Disney's gift for special effects, often intimidates and occasionally frightens young children.

There are attractions with menacing witches, burning towns, and ghouls popping out of their graves, all done with humor, provided you're old enough to understand the joke. And bones. There are bones everywhere: human bones, cattle bones, dinosaur bones, even whole skeletons. There's a stack of skulls at the headhunters' camp on the Jungle Cruise, a platoon of skeletons sailing ghost ships in Pirates of the Caribbean, and an assemblage of skulls and skeletons in The Haunted Mansion. Skulls, skeletons, and bones punctuate Peter Pan's Flight and Big Thunder Mountain Railroad. Disney's Animal Kingdom has an entire playground composed exclusively of giant bones and skeletons.

If your child has difficulty coping with the ghouls of The Haunted Mansion, then you should think twice about exposing him at the Studios to machine-gun battles, earthquakes, and the creature from *Alien* in The Great Movie Ride.

You can reliably predict that Walt Disney World will, at one time or another, send a young child into system overload. Be sensitive, alert, and prepared for almost anything, even behavior that is out of character for your child. Most children take Disney's macabre trappings in stride, and others are easily comforted by an arm around the shoulder or a squeeze of the hand. Parents who know that their children tend to become upset should take it slow and easy, sampling benign adventures like the Jungle Cruise, gauging reactions, and discussing with the children how they felt about what they saw.

unofficial **TIP**
Monsters and special effects at Disney's Hollywood Studios are more real and sinister than those in the other parks.

Sometimes young children will rise above their anxiety in an effort to please their parents or siblings. This doesn't necessarily indicate a mastery of fear, much less enjoyment. If children leave a ride in apparently good shape, ask if they would like to go on it again (not necessarily now, but sometime). The response usually will indicate how much they actually enjoyed the experience.

Evaluating a child's capacity to handle the visual and tactile effects of Disney World requires patience, understanding, and experimentation. Each of us has our own demons. If a child balks at or is frightened by a ride, respond constructively. Let your children know that lots of people, adults and children, are scared by what they see and feel. Help them understand that it's OK if they get frightened and that their fear doesn't lessen your love or respect. Take pains not to compound the discomfort by making a child feel inadequate; try not to undermine self-esteem, impugn courage, or ridicule. Most of all, don't induce guilt by suggesting the child's trepidation might be ruining the family's fun. It's also sometimes necessary to restrain older siblings' taunting.

A reader from New York City expresses strong feelings about pressuring children:

> As a psychologist who works with children, I felt ethically torn (and nearly filed a report!) watching parents force their children to go on rides they didn't want to ride (especially the Tower of Terror and DINOSAUR). The Disney staff were more than willing to organize a parental swap to save these children from such abuse!

Continued on page 328

Small-Child Fright-Potential Chart

This is a quick reference to identify attractions to be wary of, and why. The chart represents a generalization, and all kids are different. It relates specifically to kids ages 3–7. On average, children at the younger end of the range are more likely to be frightened than children in their sixth or seventh year.

THE MAGIC KINGDOM

MAIN STREET, U.S.A.

MAIN STREET VEHICLES Not frightening in any respect.

WALT DISNEY WORLD RAILROAD Not frightening in any respect.

ADVENTURELAND

ENCHANTED TIKI ROOM A thunderstorm, loud volume level, and simulated explosions frighten some preschoolers.

JUNGLE CRUISE Moderately intense, some macabre sights. A good test attraction for little ones.

PIRATES OF THE CARIBBEAN Slightly intimidating queuing area; intense boat ride with gruesome (though humorously presented) sights and a short, unexpected slide down a flume.

THE MAGIC CARPETS OF ALADDIN Much like Dumbo. A favorite of young children.

SWISS FAMILY TREEHOUSE May not be suitable for kids who are afraid of heights.

FRONTIERLAND

BIG THUNDER MOUNTAIN RAILROAD Visually intimidating from outside, with moderately intense visual effects. The roller coaster is wild enough to frighten many adults, particularly seniors. Switching-off option provided (see page 334).

COUNTRY BEAR JAMBOREE Not frightening in any respect.

FRONTIERLAND SHOOTIN' ARCADE Not frightening in any respect.

SPLASH MOUNTAIN Visually intimidating from outside, with moderately intense visual effects. The ride culminates in a 52-foot plunge down a steep chute. Switching-off option provided (see page 334).

TOM SAWYER ISLAND AND FORT LANGHORN Some very young children are intimidated by dark walk-through tunnels that can be easily avoided.

LIBERTY SQUARE

THE HALL OF PRESIDENTS Not frightening, but boring for young ones.

THE HAUNTED MANSION Name raises anxiety, as do sounds and sights of waiting area. Intense attraction with humorously presented macabre sights. The ride itself is gentle.

LIBERTY BELLE RIVERBOAT Not frightening in any respect.

FANTASYLAND

DUMBO THE FLYING ELEPHANT A tame midway ride; a great favorite of most young children.

THE BARNSTORMER May frighten some preschoolers.

IT'S A SMALL WORLD Not frightening in any respect.

MAD TEA PARTY Midway-type ride can induce motion sickness in all ages.

THE MANY ADVENTURES OF WINNIE THE POOH Frightens a small percentage of preschoolers.

PETER PAN'S FLIGHT Not frightening in any respect.

PRINCE CHARMING REGAL CARROUSEL Not frightening in any respect.

SEVEN DWARFS MINE TRAIN Not open at press time.

UNDER THE SEA: JOURNEY OF THE LITTLE MERMAID Not open at press time.

TOMORROWLAND

ASTRO ORBITER Visually intimidating from the waiting area, but the ride is relatively tame.

BUZZ LIGHTYEAR'S SPACE RANGER SPIN Dark ride with cartoonlike aliens. May frighten some preschoolers.

MONSTERS, INC. LAUGH FLOOR May frighten a small percentage of preschoolers.

SPACE MOUNTAIN Very intense roller coaster in the dark; the Magic Kingdom's wildest ride and a scary roller coaster by any standard. Switching-off option provided (see page 334).

STITCH'S GREAT ESCAPE! Very intense. May frighten children age 9 and younger. Switching-off option provided (see page 334).

TOMORROWLAND SPEEDWAY Noise of waiting area slightly intimidates preschoolers; otherwise, not frightening.

TOMORROWLAND TRANSIT AUTHORITY PEOPLEMOVER Not frightening in any respect.

WALT DISNEY'S CAROUSEL OF PROGRESS Not frightening in any respect.

EPCOT

FUTURE WORLD

IMAGINATION!: *CAPTAIN EO* Extremely intense visual effects and loudness frighten many young children.

INNOVENTIONS EAST AND WEST Not frightening in any respect.

JOURNEY INTO IMAGINATION WITH FIGMENT Loud noises and unexpected flashing lights startle younger children.

THE LAND: *THE CIRCLE OF LIFE* Not frightening in any respect.

THE LAND: LIVING WITH THE LAND Not frightening in any respect.

THE LAND: SOARIN' May frighten children age 7 and younger. Really a very mellow ride.

MISSION: SPACE Extremely intense space-simulation ride that has been known to frighten guests of all ages. Preshow may also frighten some children. Switching-off option provided (see page 334).

THE SEAS—THE SEAS WITH NEMO & FRIENDS Very sweet but may frighten some toddlers.

Small-Child Fright-Potential Chart *(continued)*

EPCOT *(continued)*

FUTURE WORLD *(continued)*

THE SEAS: MAIN TANK AND EXHIBITS Not frightening in any respect.

THE SEAS: *TURTLE TALK WITH CRUSH* Not frightening in any respect.

SPACESHIP EARTH Dark, imposing presentation intimidates a few preschoolers.

TEST TRACK Intense thrill ride may frighten guests of any age. Switching-off option provided (see page 334).

UNIVERSE OF ENERGY: *ELLEN'S ENERGY ADVENTURE* Dinosaur segment frightens some preschoolers; visually intense, with some intimidating effects.

WORLD SHOWCASE

THE AMERICAN ADVENTURE Not frightening in any respect.

CANADA: *O CANADA!* Not frightening, but audience must stand.

CHINA: *REFLECTIONS OF CHINA* Not frightening in any respect.

FRANCE: *IMPRESSIONS DE FRANCE* Not frightening in any respect.

GERMANY Not frightening in any respect.

ITALY Not frightening in any respect.

JAPAN Not frightening in any respect.

MEXICO: GRAN FIESTA TOUR Not frightening in any respect.

MOROCCO Not frightening in any respect.

NORWAY: MAELSTROM Visually intense in parts. Ride ends with a plunge down a 20-foot flume. A few preschoolers are frightened.

UNITED KINGDOM Not frightening in any respect.

UNITED STATES Not frightening in any respect.

DISNEY'S ANIMAL KINGDOM

THE OASIS Not frightening in any respect.

RAFIKI'S PLANET WATCH Not frightening in any respect.

DISCOVERY ISLAND

THE TREE OF LIFE / *IT'S TOUGH TO BE A BUG!* Very intense and loud, with special effects that startle viewers of all ages and potentially terrify little kids.

CAMP MINNIE-MICKEY

FESTIVAL OF THE LION KING A bit loud, but otherwise not frightening.

AFRICA

KILIMANJARO SAFARIS A "collapsing" bridge and the proximity of real animals make a few young children anxious.

PANGANI FOREST EXPLORATION TRAIL Not frightening in any respect.

WILDLIFE EXPRESS TRAIN Not frightening in any respect.

ASIA

EXPEDITION EVEREST Can frighten guests of all ages. Switching-off option provided (see page 334).

FLIGHTS OF WONDER Swooping birds alarm a few small children.

KALI RIVER RAPIDS Potentially frightening and certainly wet for guests of all ages. Switching-off option provided (see page 334).

MAHARAJAH JUNGLE TREK Some children may balk at the bat exhibit.

DINOLAND U.S.A.

THE BONEYARD Not frightening in any respect.

DINOSAUR High-tech thrill ride rattles riders of all ages. Switching-off option provided (see page 334).

PRIMEVAL WHIRL A beginner roller coaster. Most children age 7 and older will take it in stride. Switching-off option provided (see page 334).

THEATER IN THE WILD / FINDING NEMO—THE MUSICAL Not frightening in any respect, but loud.

TRICERATOP SPIN A midway-type ride that will frighten only a small percentage of younger children.

DISNEY'S HOLLYWOOD STUDIOS

HOLLYWOOD BOULEVARD

THE GREAT MOVIE RIDE Intense in parts, with very realistic special effects and some visually intimidating sights. Frightens many preschoolers.

SUNSET BOULEVARD

FANTASMIC! Terrifies some preschoolers.

ROCK 'N' ROLLER COASTER The wildest coaster at Walt Disney World. May frighten guests of any age. Switching-off option provided (see page 334).

THEATER OF THE STARS / BEAUTY AND THE BEAST—LIVE ON STAGE Not frightening in any respect.

THE TWILIGHT ZONE TOWER OF TERROR Visually intimidating to young children; contains intense and realistic special effects. The plummeting elevator at the ride's end frightens many adults as well as kids. Switching-off option provided (see page 334).

ECHO LAKE

THE AMERICAN IDOL EXPERIENCE At times, the singing may frighten anyone.

INDIANA JONES EPIC STUNT SPECTACULAR! An intense show with powerful special effects, including explosions, but young kids generally handle it well.

Small-Child Fright-Potential Chart (continued)

DISNEY'S HOLLYWOOD STUDIOS (continued)

ECHO LAKE (continued)

STAR TOURS—THE ADVENTURES CONTINUE Extremely intense visually for all ages; too intense for children under age 8. Switching-off option provided (see page 334).

STREETS OF AMERICA

HONEY, I SHRUNK THE KIDS MOVIE SET ADVENTURE Not scary (though oversized).

JIM HENSON'S MUPPET-VISION 3-D Intense and loud, but not frightening.

LIGHTS, MOTORS, ACTION! EXTREME STUNT SHOW Super stunt spectacular; intense with loud noises and explosions, but not threatening in any way.

STUDIO BACKLOT TOUR Sedate and nonintimidating except for Catastrophe Canyon, where an earthquake and a flash flood are simulated. Prepare younger children for this part of the tour.

PIXAR PLACE

TOY STORY MANIA! Dark ride may frighten some preschoolers.

MICKEY AVENUE

WALT DISNEY: ONE MAN'S DREAM Not frightening in any respect.

ANIMATION COURTYARD

DISNEY JUNIOR—LIVE ON STAGE! Not frightening in any respect.

THE MAGIC OF DISNEY ANIMATION Not frightening in any respect.

VOYAGE OF THE LITTLE MERMAID Not frightening in any respect.

Continued from page 323

A visit to Disney World is more than an outing or an adventure for a young child. It's a testing experience, a sort of controlled rite of passage. If you help your little one work through the challenges, the time can be immeasurably rewarding and a bonding experience for you both.

THE FRIGHT FACTOR

WHILE EACH YOUNGSTER IS DIFFERENT, following are seven attraction elements that alone or combined could push a child's buttons and indicate that a certain attraction isn't age appropriate for that child:

1. NAME OF THE ATTRACTION Young children will naturally be apprehensive about something called, say, The Haunted Mansion or Tower of Terror.

2. VISUAL IMPACT OF THE ATTRACTION FROM OUTSIDE Splash Mountain, the Tower of Terror, and Big Thunder Mountain Railroad look scary enough to give adults second thoughts, and they terrify many young children.

3. VISUAL IMPACT OF THE INDOOR-QUEUING AREA The caves at Pirates of the Caribbean and the dungeons and "stretch rooms" of The Haunted Mansion can frighten children.

4. INTENSITY OF THE ATTRACTION Some attractions inundate the senses with sights, sounds, movement, and even smell. Animal Kingdom's *It's Tough to be a Bug!,* for example, combines loud sounds, lights, smoke, and animatronic insects with 3-D cinematography to create a total sensory experience.

A Johnston, Iowa, mom describes the situation well:

> *The 3-D and 4-D experiences are way too scary for even a very brave 5-year-old girl. The shows that blew things on her, shot smells in the air, had bugs flying, etc. scared the bejesus out of her. We escorted her crying from* [It's Tough to Be a Bug!, Mickey's PhilharMagic, and Stitch's Great Escape!].

5. VISUAL IMPACT OF THE ATTRACTION Sights in various attractions range from falling boulders to lurking buzzards, from grazing dinosaurs to waltzing ghosts. What one child calmly absorbs may scare the bejeepers out of another the same age.

6. DARK Many Disney World attractions operate indoors in the dark. For some children, this triggers fear. A child who gets frightened on one dark ride (The Haunted Mansion, for example) may be unwilling to try other indoor rides.

7. THE TACTILE EXPERIENCE OF THE RIDE Some rides are wild enough to cause motion sickness, wrench backs, and discombobulate guests of any age.

As a footnote to the preceding, be aware that gaining the courage and confidence in regard to the attractions is not necessarily an upwardly linear process. A dad from Maryland explains:

> *As a 4-year-old, my daughter absolutely adored The Haunted Mansion. At 5 she was scared to death on it! At 6 she was fine again. Just because a child loves a ride at one age doesn't mean that he or she will love it on the next trip.*

A BIT OF PREPARATION

WE RECEIVE MANY TIPS FROM PARENTS telling how they prepared their young children for the Disney experience. A common strategy is to acquaint children with the characters and stories behind the attractions by reading Disney books and watching Disney videos at home. A more direct approach is to watch videos that show the attractions. Of the latter, a Lexington, Kentucky, mom reports:

> *My timid 7-year-old daughter and I watched rides and shows on YouTube, and we cut out all the ones that looked too scary. At the parks, she still didn't like, and cried at, It's Tough to Be a Bug! Ellen's Energy Adventure made her tense up, but she loved, loved, loved Kali River Rapids.*

A Gloucester, Massachusetts, mom solved the problem on the spot:

My 3½-year-old was afraid of The Haunted Mansion. We just pulled his hat over his face and quietly talked to him while we rode.

If your video store doesn't rent Disney travel DVDs, you can order the free **Walt Disney World Vacation Planning DVD** by calling Disney reservations at ☎ 407-W-DISNEY (934-7639). This DVD isn't as comprehensive as travelogues you might rent, but it's adequate for giving your kids a sense of what they'll see. You can also ask for information on lodging, restaurants, and such. Allow at least one month for delivery. You can also log on to **disneyworld.com** and click on "Free Vacation Planning DVD" to order online. *Note:* Because Disney is in a cost-containment fit, it's possible that the DVD may be discontinued.

Not everything at Disney World is covered in the DVD, but you can find most of what's missing at **YouTube** (see previous page).

ATTRACTIONS THAT EAT ADULTS

YOU MAY SPEND SO MUCH ENERGY worrying about Junior that you forget to take care of yourself. The following attractions can cause motion sickness or other problems for older kids and adults:

POTENTIALLY PROBLEMATIC ATTRACTIONS FOR GROWN-UPS
THE MAGIC KINGDOM
FANTASYLAND Mad Tea Party
FRONTIERLAND Big Thunder Mountain Railroad, Splash Mountain
TOMORROWLAND Space Mountain
EPCOT
FUTURE WORLD Mission: SPACE, Sum of All Thrills, Test Track
DISNEY'S ANIMAL KINGDOM
ASIA Expedition Everest, Kali River Rapids
DINOLAND, U.S.A. DINOSAUR
DISNEY'S HOLLYWOOD STUDIOS
ECHO LAKE Star Tours—The Adventures Continue
SUNSET BOULEVARD Rock 'n' Roller Coaster, The Twilight Zone Tower of Terror

A WORD ABOUT HEIGHT REQUIREMENTS

A NUMBER OF ATTRACTIONS REQUIRE children to meet minimum height and age requirements. If you have children too short or too young to ride, you have several options, including switching off (see page 334). Although the alternatives may resolve some practical and logistical issues, your smaller children may nonetheless be resentful of their older (or taller) siblings who qualify to ride. A mom from Virginia writes of such a situation:

You mention height requirements for rides but not the intense sibling jealousy this can generate. Frontierland was a real problem in that respect. Our very petite 5-year-old, to her outrage, was stuck hanging

Attraction and Ride Restrictions

THE MAGIC KINGDOM	
Big Thunder Mountain Railroad	40" minimum height
Seven Dwarfs Mine Train	(not open at press time)
Space Mountain	44" minimum height
Splash Mountain	40" minimum height
Stitch's Great Escape!	40" minimum height
Tomorrowland Speedway	32" to ride, 54" to drive unassisted

EPCOT	
Mission: SPACE	44" minimum height
Soarin'	40" minimum height
Sum of All Thrills	48" minimum height, 54" for inversions
Test Track	40" minimum height

DISNEY'S ANIMAL KINGDOM	
DINOSAUR	40" minimum height
Expedition Everest	44" minimum height
Kali River Rapids	38" minimum height
Primeval Whirl	48" minimum height

DISNEY'S HOLLYWOOD STUDIOS	
Honey, I Shrunk the Kids Movie Set Adventure	4 years minimum age
Rock 'n' Roller Coaster	48" minimum height
Star Tours—The Adventures Continue	40" minimum height
The Twilight Zone Tower of Terror	40" minimum height

BLIZZARD BEACH WATER PARK	
Chair Lift	32" minimum height
Downhill Double Dipper slide	48" minimum height
Slush Gusher slide	48" minimum height
Summit Plummet slide	48" minimum height
T-Bar (in Ski Patrol Training Camp)	60" maximum height
Tike's Peak children's area	48" maximum height

TYPHOON LAGOON WATER PARK	
Bay Slides	60" minimum height
Crush 'n' Gusher	48" minimum height
Humunga Kowabunga slide	48" minimum height
Ketchakiddee Creek children's area	48" maximum height
Mayday Falls raft ride	No height requirement
Shark Reef saltwater reef swim *unless accompanied by adult:* 10 years minimum age	
Wave Pool	*Adult supervision required*

DISNEYQUEST	
Buzz Lightyear's AstroBlasters	51" minimum height
CyberSpace Mountain	51" minimum height
Mighty Ducks Pinball Slam	48" minimum height
Pirates of the Caribbean—Battle for Buccaneer Gold	35" minimum height

around while our 8-year-old went on Splash Mountain and Big Thunder Mountain with her grandma and granddad, and the nearby alternatives weren't helpful (too long a line for rafts to Tom Sawyer Island, etc.). The best areas had a playground or other quick attractions for short people near the rides with height requirements, like The Boneyard near the DINOSAUR ride at Animal Kingdom.

The reader makes a point, though splitting the group and meeting later can be more complicated than she imagines. If you split up, ask the Disney attendant (called a greeter) at the entrance to the attraction(s) with height requirements how long the wait is. If you tack 5 minutes for riding on to the anticipated wait and add 5 or so minutes to exit and reach the meeting point, you'll have a sense of how long the younger kids (and their supervising adult) will have to do other stuff. Our guess is that even with a long line for the rafts, the reader would've had sufficient time to take her daughter to Tom Sawyer Island while the sibs rode Splash Mountain and Big Thunder Mountain with the grandparents. For sure, she had time to tour the Swiss Family Treehouse in adjacent Adventureland.

For more information, see the chart on the previous page.

WAITING-LINE STRATEGIES *for* ADULTS *with* YOUNG CHILDREN

CHILDREN HOLD UP BETTER through the day if you limit the time they spend in lines. Arriving early and using our touring plans greatly reduce waiting. Here are other ways to reduce stress for children:

1. LINE GAMES Anticipate that children will get restless in line, and plan activities to reduce the stress and boredom. In the morning, have waiting children discuss what they want to see and do during the day. Later, watch for and count Disney characters or play simple games such as 20 Questions. Lines move continuously; games requiring pen and paper are impractical. Waiting in the holding area of a theater attraction is a different story. Here, tic-tac-toe, hangman, drawing, and coloring make the time fly.

A Springfield, Ohio, mom reports on an unexpected but welcome assist from her brother:

I have a bachelor brother who joined my 5-, 7-, and 9-year-olds and me for vacation. Pat surprised all of us with a bunch of plastic animal noses he had in his hip pack. When the kids got restless or cranky in line, he'd turn away and pull out a pig nose or a parrot nose or something. When he turned back around with the nose on, the kids would majorly crack up.

A Waco, Texas, dad broke out the bubbly:

I took bubbles along with us. My boys loved them and so did the other children waiting in line. (I bought wedding-size bottles that would fit into everyone's fanny pack.)

2. LAST-MINUTE ENTRY If an attraction can accommodate many people at once, standing in line is often unnecessary. The Magic Kingdom's *Liberty Belle* Riverboat is an example. The boat holds about 450 people, usually more guests than are waiting in line. Instead of standing in a crowd, grab a snack and sit in the shade until the boat arrives and loading is under way. When the line is almost gone, join it.

At large-capacity theaters like the one for Epcot's *The American Adventure*, ask the greeter how long it will be until guests are admitted for the next show. If it's 15 minutes or more, take a toilet break or get a snack, returning a few minutes before showtime. Food and drink aren't allowed in the attraction; be sure you have time to finish your snack before entering.

ATTRACTIONS YOU CAN USUALLY ENTER AT THE LAST MINUTE
THE MAGIC KINGDOM
Liberty Square *The Hall of Presidents, Liberty Belle* Riverboat
Tomorrowland *Walt Disney's Carousel of Progress*
EPCOT
Future World *The Circle of Life* (except during mealtimes)
World Showcase *The American Adventure, O Canada!, Reflections of China*
DISNEY'S ANIMAL KINGDOM
Asia *Flights of Wonder*
DISNEY'S HOLLYWOOD STUDIOS
Backlot *Studio Backlot Tour*

3. THE HAIL-MARY PASS Certain lines (see chart below) are configured to allow you and your smaller children to pass under the rail to join your partner just before entry or boarding. This technique allows children and one adult to rest, snack, cool off, or potty while another adult or older sibling stands in line.

ATTRACTIONS WHERE YOU CAN USUALLY COMPLETE A HAIL-MARY PASS
THE MAGIC KINGDOM
Adventureland *Swiss Family Treehouse*
Frontierland *Country Bear Jamboree*
Fantasyland *Mad Tea Party, Peter Pan's Flight, Prince Charming Regal Carrousel*
EPCOT
Future World *Living with the Land, Spaceship Earth*
World Showcase *The American Adventure, O Canada!, Reflections of China*
DISNEY'S ANIMAL KINGDOM
DinoLand U.S.A. *TriceraTop Spin*
DISNEY'S HOLLYWOOD STUDIOS
Backlot *Studio Backlot Tour*

4. SWITCHING OFF (A.K.A. THE BABY SWAP) Several attractions have minimum height and/or age requirements. Some couples with children too small or too young forgo these attractions, while others take turns riding. Missing some of Disney's best rides is an unnecessary sacrifice, and waiting in line twice for the same ride is a tremendous waste of time.

ATTRACTIONS WHERE SWITCHING OFF IS COMMON	
THE MAGIC KINGDOM	**DISNEY'S ANIMAL KINGDOM**
Big Thunder Mountain Railroad	DINOSAUR
Seven Dwarfs Mine Train	Expedition Everest
Space Mountain	Kali River Rapids
Splash Mountain	Primeval Whirl
Stitch's Great Escape!	
EPCOT	**DISNEY'S HOLLYWOOD STUDIOS**
Mission: SPACE	Rock 'n' Roller Coaster
Test Track	Star Tours—The Adventures Continue
	The Twilight Zone Tower of Terror

Instead, take advantage of the "switching off" option, also called the Baby Swap. To switch off, there must be at least two adults. Adults and children wait in line together. When you reach a cast member, say you want to switch off. The cast member will allow everyone, including young children, to enter the attraction. When you reach the loading area, one adult rides while the other stays with the kids. Then the riding adult disembarks and takes charge of the children while the other adult rides. A third adult in the party can ride twice, once with each switching-off adult, so that the switching-off adults don't have to ride alone.

On most Fastpass attractions, Disney handles switching off somewhat differently. When you tell the cast member that you want to switch off, he or she will issue you a special "rider exchange" Fastpass good for three people. One parent and the nonriding child (or children) will at that point be asked to leave the line. When those riding reunite with the waiting adult, the waiting adult and two other persons from the party can ride using the special Fastpass. This system eliminates confusion and congestion at the boarding area while sparing the nonriding adult and child the tedium and physical exertion of waiting in line.

5. COMBINING THE FASTPASS SYSTEM WITH SWITCHING-OFF You can incorporate Fastpasses into switching off in order to secure Fastpasses for multiple attractions at the same time. This is an enormous benefit for larger groups.

In the Fastpass system, each ticket is limited to one Fastpass at a time. The holder of the Fastpass for one attraction may not acquire a Fastpass for a second attraction until the return window indicated on the original Fastpass has begun. Only then can a ticket-holder seek a Fastpass for a second attraction, but the "rider exchange" is a game-changer for those who are serious about time efficiency.

Because the rider-exchange pass can be used by the adult holding it as well as by three companions, this yields a "four for the price of one" scenario in terms of Fastpass currency.

An alert reader in Mequon, Wisconsin, discovered this strategy of combining the two time-saving line options to ride more Fastpass attraction headliners:

> *Our group consisted of two adults, two teens, and two young children. We split our tickets into two groups of three and used one group to get Fastpasses for Big Thunder and another group to get Fastpasses for Splash Mountain. When the half with the Big Thunder Fastpasses went to ride, we asked to switch off and obtained a pass good for one adult and up to three other people. My husband used the three Fastpasses to ride with our two teens. Then, with the switch-off pass, I rode again with the teens and one of our younger sons who was willing to ride. We did the same thing on Splash Mountain immediately afterward because the time on our Fastpasses for that ride was already here when we finished riding Big Thunder.*

Depending on size and number of ticket-bearers, this strategy has the potential to hold Fastpasses for as many as five attractions at any given time while still maintaining the ability to get the entire group on each attraction with a single swap. This mass Fastpass acquisition is accomplished by dividing the group's tickets for Fastpasses at different attraction kiosks, but the maximum number of attractions a party can exploit in this way diminishes as the size of the group increases.

Using the strategy to its fullest, a family consisting of two adults and four ticket-bearing children, one of whom is unable or unwilling to ride, can divide their tickets into five groups. One ticket would be used to obtain a Fastpass at Attraction A, another to get a Fastpass at Attraction B. The pattern would continue for acquiring tickets for Attractions C, D, and E simultaneously. With the attraction of the earliest Fastpass time stamp designated Attraction A, an adult wielding the Fastpass for that attraction would request a rider-exchange pass by approaching the cast member at the standby entrance. After securing the exchange pass and giving it to the waiting adult, the riding adult would use his Fastpass to board the ride. Once he rejoins his party, the second adult—accompanied by the three kids who are riding—would present the switch-off pass to the cast member at the Fastpass Return entrance. All four family members would be permitted to enter the Fastpass lane for the ride, while the first adult would remain with the nonriding child. Upon the return of the second group, the same procedure could be followed for the remaining four Fastpass attractions without the family having to wait an extended period for the assigned time-frames.

This scenario may seem unappealing, as it would require an adult who was always willing to ride solo as well as some serious team cooperation in gathering Fastpasses from all corners of the park. For that reason, we see dividing the group's tickets into thirds and using them for three different attractions as a more reasonable option, provided the number of riders in the party doesn't exceed six.

6. LAST-MINUTE COLD FEET If your young child gets cold feet just before boarding a ride where there's no age or height requirement, you usually can arrange a switch-off with the loading attendant. (This happens frequently in Pirates of the Caribbean's dungeon waiting area.)

No law says you have to ride. If you reach the boarding area and someone is unhappy, tell an attendant you've changed your mind and you'll be shown the way out.

7. THROW YOURSELF ON THE GRENADE, MILDRED! For long-suffering parents who are determined to sacrifice themselves on behalf of their children, we provide a Magic Kingdom One-Day Touring Plan called the Dumbo-or-Die-in-a-Day Touring Plan for Parents with Small Children. This plan (see page 823) will ensure that you run yourself ragged. Designed to help you forfeit everything of personal interest for your children's pleasure, the plan guarantees you'll go home battered and exhausted, with extraordinary stories of devotion and perseverance. By the way, it really works. Anyone under age 8 will love it.

▮ The **DISNEY CHARACTERS**

THE LARGE AND FRIENDLY COSTUMED versions of Mickey, Minnie, Donald, Goofy, and others—known as Disney characters—provide a link between Disney animated films and the theme parks. To people emotionally invested, the characters in Disney films are as real as next-door neighbors, never mind that they're drawings on plastic. In recent years, theme park personifications of the characters also have become real to us. It's not a person in a mouse costume; it's Mickey himself. Similarly, meeting Goofy or Snow White is an encounter with a celebrity, a memory to be treasured.

While Disney animated-film characters number in the hundreds, only about 250 have been brought to life in costume. Of these, fewer than a fifth are "greeters" (characters who mix with patrons); the others perform in shows or parades. Originally confined to the Magic Kingdom, characters are now found in all major theme parks and Disney hotels.

We receive hundreds of comments from readers telling us how much the Disney characters enhanced their theme park experience. This e-mail from a Wisconsin mom is representative:

> I can't say enough about the characters and how they react to the children and just people in general. They are obviously highly trained in people skills and just add an extra dimension to the park.

CHARACTER WATCHING Watching characters has become a pastime. Families once were content to meet a character occasionally. They now pursue them relentlessly, armed with autograph books and cameras. Because some characters are only rarely seen, character watching has become character collecting. (To cash in on character collecting, Disney sells autograph books throughout the World.) Mickey, Minnie, and Goofy are a snap to bag; they seem to be everywhere. But some characters, like Tinker Bell and Jiminy Cricket,

unofficial **TIP**
Don't underestimate your child's excitement at meeting the Disney characters—but also be aware that very small children may find the large costumed characters a little frightening.

seldom come out, and quite a few appear only in parades or stage shows. Other characters appear only in a location consistent with their starring role. Cinderella, predictably, reigns at Cinderella Castle in Fantasyland, while Br'er Fox and Br'er Bear frolic in Frontierland near Splash Mountain.

A Brooklyn dad complains that character collecting has gotten out of hand:

> Whoever started the practice of collecting autographs from the characters should be subjected to water torture! We went to WDW 11 years ago with an 8-year-old and an 11-year-old. We would bump into characters, take pictures, and that was it. After a while, our children noticed that some of the other children were getting autographs. We managed to avoid joining in during our first day at the Magic Kingdom and our first day at Epcot, but by day three our children were collecting autographs. But it didn't get too out of hand, since it was limited to accidental character meeting.
>
> This year, when we took our youngest child (who is now 8 years old), he had already seen his siblings' collection and was determined to outdo them. However, rather than random meetings, the characters are now available practically all day long at different locations, according to a printed schedule, which our son was old enough to read. We spent more time standing in line for autographs than we did for the most popular rides!

A family from Birmingham, Alabama, found some benefit in their children's pursuit of characters:

> We had no idea we'd be caught up in this madness, but after my daughters grabbed your guidebook to get Pocahontas to sign it (we had no blank paper), we quickly bought a Disney autograph book and gave in. It was actually the highlight of their trip, and my son even got into the act by helping get places in line for his sisters. They LOVED looking for characters. The possibility of seeing a new character revived my 7-year-old's energy on many occasions. It was an amazing, totally unexpected part of our visit.

PREPARING YOUR CHILDREN TO MEET THE CHARACTERS Almost all characters are quite large, and several, like Br'er Bear, are huge! Small children don't expect this, and preschoolers especially can be intimidated.

Discuss the characters with your children before you go. On first encounter, don't thrust your child at the character. Allow the little one to deal with this big thing from whatever distance feels safe. If two adults are present, one should stay near the youngster while the other approaches the character and demonstrates that it's safe and friendly. Some kids warm to the characters immediately; some never do. Most take a little time and several encounters.

There are two kinds of characters: "furs," or those whose costumes include face-covering headpieces (including animal characters and such humanlike characters as Captain Hook), and "face characters," those for whom no mask or headpiece is necessary. These include

Tiana, Mary Poppins, Ariel, Jasmine, Aladdin, Cinderella, Belle, Snow White, Esmeralda, and Prince Charming.

Only face characters speak. Because cast members couldn't possibly imitate the furs' distinctive cinema voices, Disney has determined that it's more effective to keep such characters silent. Lack of speech notwithstanding, headpiece characters are warm and responsive, and they communicate effectively with gestures. Tell children in advance that these characters don't talk.

Some character costumes are cumbersome and give cast members very poor visibility. (Eyeholes frequently are in the mouth of the costume or even on the neck or chest.) Children who approach the character from the back or side may not be noticed, even if the child touches the character. It's possible in this situation for the character to accidentally step on the child or knock him down. A child should approach a character from the front, but occasionally not even this works. Duck characters (Donald, Daisy, Uncle Scrooge), for example, have to peer around their bills. If a character appears to be ignoring your child, pick up your child and hold her in front of the character until the character responds.

It's OK for your child to touch, pat, or hug the character. Understanding the unpredictability of children, the character will keep his feet still, particularly refraining from moving backward or sideways. Most characters will pose for pictures or sign autographs. Costumes make it difficult for characters to wield a normal pen. If your child collects autographs, carry a pen the width of a Magic Marker.

THE BIG HURT Many children expect to meet Mickey the minute they enter the park and are disappointed if they don't. If your children can't enjoy things until they see Mickey, ask a cast member where to find him. If the cast member doesn't know, he or she can phone to learn exactly where characters are.

"THEN SOME CONFUSION HAPPENED" Children sometimes become lost at character encounters. Usually, there's a lot of activity around a character, with both adults and children touching it or posing for pictures. Most commonly, Mom and Dad stay in the crowd while Junior approaches the character. In the excitement and with the character moving around, Junior heads in the wrong direction to look for Mom and Dad. In the words of a Salt Lake City mom: "Milo was shaking hands with Dopey one minute, then some confusion happened and Milo was gone."

> *unofficial* **TIP**
> If you're using a touring plan and get interrupted, simply skip one step in the plan for every 15 minutes you're delayed, and continue on. Really, it's no big deal.

Families with several young children, and parents who are busy with cameras, can lose a youngster in a heartbeat. We recommend that parents with preschoolers stay with them when they meet characters, stepping back only to take a quick picture.

CHARACTER HOGS While we're on the subject of cameras, give other families a chance. Especially if you're shooting video, consider the perspective of this Houston mom:

> *One of the worst parts to deal with are the people with movie cameras*

> *who take about 3 minutes filming their child with Mickey, asking*
> *everyone else to move. A [photo] camera takes about 2 seconds.*

PLANNUS INTERRUPTUS An admittedly type-A mom from eastern Tennessee was done in by (who else?) Chicken Little:

> *Please caution overplanning parents like me that character meet-and-greets can wreak havoc with the best-laid plans! We were at Disney's Hollywood Studios on my husband's birthday, and our 5-year-old just couldn't pass up Chicken Little and Abbey at the entrance, and Daisy Duck at the Magic Hat. Well, now we were off schedule, and there was no line at The Great Movie Ride beside us, so we rode that. Now we were drifting further and further from the plan. By afternoon, it seems all the adult shows hubby wanted to see were at EXACTLY the same times as the* Little Mermaid *and* Playhouse Disney *shows! As daughter and I dissolved into tears at midday, I realized two things: (1) DO NOT go full-tilt touring for more than two days without a day off in between; and (2) if you have an* Unofficial Guide *touring plan, STICK TO IT! THEY WORK!*

MEETING CHARACTERS FOR FREE

YOU CAN SEE DISNEY CHARACTERS in live shows at all the theme parks and in parades at the Magic Kingdom and Disney's Hollywood Studios. Your daily entertainment schedule lists times. If you want to *meet* characters, get autographs, and take photos, consult the park map or the handout *Times Guide* sometimes provided with it. If there's a particular character you're itching to meet, ask any cast member to call the character hotline and ask if the character is out and about, and if so, where.

unofficial **TIP**
To find out where any character is or will be appearing, call ☎ 407-824-2222.

Disney has several initiatives intended to satisfy its guests' inexhaustible desire to meet characters. Most important, Disney assigned Mickey and a number of other characters to all-day duty in Main Street, U.S.A.'s Town Square Theater in the Magic Kingdom and Camp Minnie-Mickey in Disney's Animal Kingdom. While making the characters more available has taken the guesswork out of finding them, it has robbed encounters of much of their spontaneity. To address this problem, especially at the Magic Kingdom, Disney has put a throng of characters back on the street. At park opening, there are enough characters on hand to satisfy any child's desires. If you line up at one of the permanent character-greeting venues, be aware that lines for face characters move *m-u-c-h* more slowly than do those for nonspeaking characters. Because face characters are allowed to talk, they often engage children in lengthy conversations, much to the dismay of families still in the queue.

AT THE MAGIC KINGDOM Character encounters are more frequent here than anywhere else in Walt Disney World. A character will almost always be next to City Hall on Main Street, and there will usually be one or more in Town Square or near the railroad station. Characters appear in all of the lands but are usually most plentiful around Fantasyland. In Fantasyland, Cinderella regularly greets diners at Cinderella's Royal Table in

the castle. Nearby, check out the Fantasyland Character Festival by the lagoon opposite Dumbo.

With the demolition of Mickey's Toontown Fair and a multiyear expansion of Fantasyland under way, most of Toontown's characters have relocated to other areas of the park. Town Square Theater on Main Street is the main meet-and-greet venue for Mickey and the princesses. Also look for characters in the Central Plaza, outside the Adventureland Veranda, by Splash Mountain in Frontierland, and by *Walt Disney's Carousel of Progress* in Tomorrowland. Because of the construction in Fantasyland, check the daily entertainment schedule when you enter the park for the appearance times and locations of your favorite characters.

unofficial **TIP**
Many kids take special delight in meeting the "face characters," such as Tiana, Jasmine, Aladdin, and Cinderella, who can speak to them and engage them in a way that the mute animal characters can't.

Characters are featured in afternoon and evening parades and also play a major role in Castle Forecourt shows (at the castle entrance on the central-hub side). Find performance times for shows and parades in the daily entertainment schedule (*Times Guide*). Characters sometimes stay to mingle after shows.

AT EPCOT Disney at first didn't think characters would fit the more serious, educational style of Epcot. Later, characters were imported to blunt criticism that Epcot lacked warmth and humor. To integrate them thematically, new and often bizarre costumes were created, but are rarely worn these days. Goofy was seen roaming Future World in a metallic silver cape reminiscent of Buck Rogers. Mickey greeted guests at the United States Pavilion dressed like Ben Franklin.

Today, characters are plentiful at Epcot and usually appear in their normal garb. In Future World, one or more characters, including

Mickey, Minnie, Pluto, Goofy, and Chip 'n' Dale can be found from opening until early evening at the Epcot Character Spot in Innoventions West (waits of an hour or more are not uncommon). In the World Showcase, most pavilions host a character or two. Donald struts his stuff in Mexico, while Mulan and Mushu greet guests in China. Belle and the Beast hang out in France, and Snow White and Dopey are regulars in Germany, as are Jasmine, Aladdin, and the Genie in Morocco. Pooh and friends, Alice in Wonderland, and Mary Poppins appear in the United Kingdom. In addition, character shows are performed daily at the America Gardens Theatre in World Showcase. Check the daily entertainment schedule (*Times Guide*) for times.

unofficial **TIP**
If it's rainy, look for characters on the veranda of Tony's Town Square Restaurant or in the Town Square Theater next to Tony's.

Because Epcot is a more adult park than the Magic Kingdom, characters are often easier to meet. A father from Effingham, Illinois, writes:

Trying to get autographs and pictures with Disney characters in the Magic Kingdom was a nightmare. Every character we saw was mobbed by kids and adults. Our kids had no chance. But at Epcot and Disney's Hollywood Studios, things were much better. We got autographs, pictures, and more involvement. Our kids danced with several characters and received a lot of personal attention.

AT DISNEY'S ANIMAL KINGDOM Camp Minnie-Mickey in Animal Kingdom is designed specifically for meeting characters. Meet Mickey, Minnie, Goofy, and Donald on designated character-greeting "trails." Elsewhere in the park, Pooh, Eeyore, Tigger, and Piglet appear at the river landing opposite Flame Tree Barbecue, and you might encounter a character or two at Rafiki's Planet Watch. Also at Camp Minnie-Mickey is a stage show featuring characters from *The Lion King*.

AT DISNEY'S HOLLYWOOD STUDIOS Characters are likely to turn up anywhere at the Studios but are most frequently found inside the Magic of Disney Animation building, along Pixar Place (leading to the soundstages), by Al's Toy Barn, at Star Tours, and on Streets of America. The main meet-and-greet area, however, is at the giant sorcerer's hat at the end of Hollywood Boulevard, where up to four characters hold court from 9 a.m. until about 1 p.m. Characters are also prominent in shows, with *Voyage of the Little Mermaid* running almost continuously and an abbreviated version of *Beauty and the Beast* performed several times daily at the Theater of the Stars. Check the daily entertainment schedule (*Times Guide*) for showtimes.

CHARACTER DINING

FRATERNIZING WITH CHARACTERS has become so popular that Disney offers character breakfasts, brunches, lunches, and dinners where families can dine in the presence of Mickey, Minnie, Goofy, and other costumed versions of animated celebrities. Aside from grabbing customers from Denny's and Hardee's, character meals provide a controlled setting in which young children can warm to the characters. All meals are attended by several characters. Adult prices apply to persons age 10 or older, children's prices to kids ages 3–9. Children younger than age 3 eat free. For more information on character dining, call ☎ 407-WDW-DINE (939-3463).

Because character dining is very popular, you should arrange Advance Reservations as early as possible by calling ☎ 407-WDW-DINE. Advance Reservations aren't reservations, per se, only a commitment to seat you ahead of walk-in patrons at the scheduled date and time.

unofficial **TIP**
Even with Advance Reservations, expect to wait 10–20 minutes to be seated.

At very popular character meals like the breakfast at Cinderella's Royal Table, you're required to make a for-real reservation and guarantee it with a for-real deposit.

WHAT TO EXPECT

CHARACTER MEALS ARE BUSTLING AFFAIRS held in hotels' or theme parks' largest full-service restaurants. Character breakfasts offer a fixed menu served individually, family-style, or on a buffet. The typical breakfast includes scrambled eggs; bacon, sausage, and ham; hash browns; waffles or French toast; biscuits, rolls, or pastries; and fruit. With family-style service, the meal is served in large skillets or platters at your table. The character breakfast at Cinderella's Royal Table, for example, is served family-style and consists of typical breakfast fare such as eggs, bacon and sausage, and Danish pastries. Seconds (or thirds) are free. Buffets offer much the same fare, but you fetch it yourself.

Character dinners range from a set menu to buffets to ordering off the menu. Character-dinner buffets, such as those at 1900 Park Fare at the Grand Floridian and Chef Mickey's at the Contemporary Resort, offer separate adults' and children's serving lines. Typically, the children's buffet includes hamburgers, hot dogs, pizza, fish sticks, chicken nuggets, macaroni and cheese, and peanut-butter-and-jelly sandwiches. Selections at the adult buffet usually include prime rib or other carved meat, baked or broiled Florida seafood, pasta, chicken, an ethnic dish or two, vegetables, potatoes, and salad.

At all meals, characters circulate around the room while you eat. During your meal, each of the three to five characters present will visit your table, arriving one at a time to cuddle the kids (and sometimes the adults), pose for photos, and sign autographs. Keep autograph books (with pens) and loaded cameras handy. For the best photos, adults should sit across the table from their children. Seat the children where characters can easily reach them. If a table is against a wall, for example, adults should sit with their backs to the wall and children on the aisle.

Theresa Brown posted this great tip for getting the best photos at the independent Disney website **allears.net:**

> *We did several character meals. At first, we would only use our cameras to take pictures of our children with the characters after they had signed the autograph books and were posing with them. But after the second meal, we started snapping away as soon as the characters approached our table. We're so glad we did this, because we captured a very funny sequence of events while at 1900 Park Fare at the Grand*

Floridian. These candid shots tell a funny story showing the playful interaction between my sons and the characters. After that, we started snapping away at all of the character meals, and now that we're back, we see that the candid shots usually gave us better pictures than the posed ones! Of course, you want the posed pictures, but the candid ones just might end up being your favorite memories of the meals!

At some larger restaurants, including 'Ohana at the Polynesian Resort and Chef Mickey's at the Contemporary, character meals involve impromptu parades of characters and children around the room, group singing, napkin waving, and other organized madness.

Servers don't rush you to leave after you've eaten—you can stay as long as you wish to enjoy the characters. Remember, however, that lots of eager kids and adults are waiting not so patiently to be admitted.

WHEN TO GO

ATTENDING A CHARACTER BREAKFAST usually prevents you from arriving at the theme parks in time for opening. Because early morning is best for touring and you don't want to burn daylight lingering over breakfast, we suggest:

1. Go to a character dinner or lunch instead of breakfast; it won't conflict with your touring schedule.

2. Substitute a late character breakfast for lunch. Have a light breakfast early from room service or your cooler to tide you over. Then tour the theme park for an hour or two before breaking off around 10:15 a.m. to go to the character breakfast. Make a big brunch of your character breakfast and skip lunch. You should be fueled until dinner.

3. Go on your arrival or departure day. The day you arrive and check in is usually good for a character dinner. Settle at your hotel, swim, then dine with the characters. This strategy has the added benefit of exposing your children to the characters before chance encounters at the parks. Some children, moreover, won't settle down to enjoy the parks until they have seen Mickey. Departure day also is good for a character meal. Schedule a character breakfast on your check-out day before you head for the airport or begin your drive home.

4. Go on a rest day. If you plan to stay five or more days, you'll probably take a day or half-day from touring to rest or do something else. These are perfect days for a character meal.

HOW TO CHOOSE A CHARACTER MEAL

MANY READERS ASK FOR ADVICE about character meals. This question from a Waterloo, Iowa, mom is typical:

Are all character breakfasts pretty much the same or are some better than others? How should I go about choosing one?

In fact, some *are* better, sometimes much better. When we evaluate character meals, we look for:

1. THE CHARACTERS The meals offer a diverse assortment of characters. Pick a meal that features your kids' favorites. Check out our Character-Meal Hit Parade chart (see pages 346 and 347) to see which characters are assigned to each meal. Most restaurants stick with the same characters. Even so, check the lineup when you call to make Advance Reservations.

2. ATTENTION FROM THE CHARACTERS At all character meals, characters circulate among guests, hugging children, posing for pictures, and signing autographs. How much time a character spends with you and your children depends primarily on the ratio of characters to guests. The more characters and fewer guests, the better. Because many character-meal venues never fill to capacity, the character-to-guest ratios in our Character-Meal Hit Parade chart have been adjusted to reflect an average attendance. Even so, there's quite a range. The best ratio is at Cinderella's Royal Table, where there's about 1 character to every 26 guests.

The worst ratio is theoretically at the Swan resort's Garden Grove, where there could be as few as 1 character for every 198 guests. We say "theoretically," however, because in practice there are far fewer guests at the Garden Grove than at character meals in Disney-owned resorts, and often more characters. During one recent meal, friends of ours were literally the only guests in the restaurant for breakfast and had to ask the characters to leave them alone to eat.

A Jerseyville, Illinois, mom gives the face characters high marks:

> Our 7-year-old daughter wanted to have dinner with Sleeping Beauty, so we scheduled a character dinner with the princesses in the Norway Pavilion. The princesses were so accessible and took their time with our child, answering questions and smiling for pictures. We would definitely recommend that to every parent. In fact, our daughter told us she "had the best day of her life," and parents want to hear that from their child.

An Indiana mother of two relates the importance of keeping tabs on the characters:

> For character meals, take note of which characters are there when you arrive, and mentally check them off as they visit your table. If the last one or two seem slow to arrive, seek out the "character manager" and let him or her know ASAP.

3. THE SETTING Some character meals are in exotic settings. For others, moving the event to an elementary-school cafeteria would be an improvement. Our chart rates each meal's setting with the familiar scale of zero (worst) to five (best) stars. Two restaurants, Cinderella's Royal Table in the Magic Kingdom and Garden Grill Restaurant in the Land Pavilion at Epcot, deserve special mention. Cinderella's Royal Table is on the first and second floors of Cinderella Castle in Fantasyland, offering guests a look inside the castle. Garden Grill is a revolving restaurant overlooking several scenes from the Living with the Land boat ride. Also at Epcot, the popular Princess Storybook Meals are held in the castlelike Akershus Royal Banquet Hall. Though Chef Mickey's at the Contemporary Resort is rather sterile in appearance, it affords a great view of the monorail running through the hotel. Themes and settings of the remaining character-meal venues, while apparent to adults, will be lost on most children.

4. THE FOOD Although some food served at character meals is quite good, most is average (palatable but nothing to get excited about). In

Continued on page 348

Character-Meal Hit Parade

1. CINDERELLA'S ROYAL TABLE MAGIC KINGDOM

MEALS SERVED DAILY Breakfast, lunch, and dinner

SETTING ★★★★

CHARACTERS Cinderella, Fairy Godmother, Aurora, Belle, Jasmine, Snow White

TYPE OF SERVICE Fixed menu

FOOD VARIETY & QUALITY ★★★

NOISE LEVEL Quiet

CHARACTER–GUEST RATIO 1:26

2. AKERSHUS ROYAL BANQUET HALL EPCOT

MEALS SERVED Breakfast, lunch, and dinner

SETTING ★★★★

CHARACTERS 4–6 characters chosen from Alice, Ariel, Belle, Jasmine, Mary Poppins, Mulan, Sleeping Beauty, Snow White

TYPE OF SERVICE Family-style and menu (all you care to eat)

FOOD VARIETY & QUALITY ★★★½

NOISE LEVEL Quiet

CHARACTER–GUEST RATIO 1:54

3. CHEF MICKEY'S CONTEMPORARY

MEALS SERVED Breakfast, dinner

SETTING ★★★

CHARACTERS *Breakfast:* Mickey, Minnie, Donald, Goofy, Pluto (sometimes Chip 'n' Dale) *Dinner:* Mickey, Minnie, Donald, Goofy, Pluto (sometimes Chip 'n' Dale)

TYPE OF SERVICE Buffet

FOOD VARIETY & QUALITY Breakfast ★★★ Dinner ★★★½

NOISE LEVEL Loud

CHARACTER–GUEST RATIO 1:56

4. THE CRYSTAL PALACE MAGIC KINGDOM

MEALS SERVED Breakfast, lunch, and dinner

SETTING ★★★

CHARACTERS Pooh, Eeyore, Piglet, Tigger

TYPE OF SERVICE Buffet

FOOD VARIETY & QUALITY Breakfast ★★½ Lunch and dinner ★★★

NOISE LEVEL Very loud

CHARACTER–GUEST RATIO Breakfast 1:67 Lunch and dinner 1:89

5. 1900 PARK FARE GRAND FLORIDIAN

MEALS SERVED Breakfast, dinner

SETTING ★★★

CHARACTERS *Breakfast:* Mary Poppins, Alice, Mad Hatter, Pooh *Dinner:* Cinderella, Prince Charming, Lady Tremaine, the two stepsisters

TYPE OF SERVICE Buffet

FOOD VARIETY & QUALITY Breakfast ★★★ Dinner ★★★½

NOISE LEVEL Moderate

CHARACTER–GUEST RATIO Breakfast 1:54 Dinner 1:44

6. GARDEN GRILL RESTAURANT   EPCOT

MEAL SERVED Dinner   **SETTING** ★★★★½

CHARACTERS Mickey, Pluto, Chip 'n' Dale

TYPE OF SERVICE Family-style

FOOD VARIETY & QUALITY ★★★½

NOISE LEVEL Very quiet

CHARACTER–GUEST RATIO 1:46

7. TUSKER HOUSE RESTAURANT   DISNEY'S ANIMAL KINGDOM

MEALS SERVED Breakfast, lunch   **SETTING** ★★★

CHARACTERS Donald, Daisy, Mickey, Goofy

TYPE OF SERVICE Buffet

FOOD VARIETY & QUALITY ★★★

NOISE LEVEL Very loud

CHARACTER–GUEST RATIO 1:112

8. CAPE MAY CAFE   BEACH CLUB

MEAL SERVED Breakfast   **SETTING** ★★★

CHARACTERS Goofy, Donald, Minnie

TYPE OF SERVICE Buffet

FOOD VARIETY & QUALITY ★★½

NOISE LEVEL Moderate

CHARACTER–GUEST RATIO 1:67

9. 'OHANA   POLYNESIAN

MEAL SERVED Breakfast   **SETTING** ★★

CHARACTERS Lilo and Stitch, Mickey, Pluto

TYPE OF SERVICE Family-style

FOOD VARIETY & QUALITY ★★½

NOISE LEVEL Moderate

CHARACTER–GUEST RATIO 1:57

10. HOLLYWOOD & VINE   DISNEY'S HOLLYWOOD STUDIOS

MEALS SERVED Breakfast, lunch   **SETTING** ★★½

CHARACTERS June, Leo, Handy Manny, Agent Oso

TYPE OF SERVICE Buffet

FOOD VARIETY & QUALITY ★★★

NOISE LEVEL Moderate

CHARACTER–GUEST RATIO 1:71

11. GARDEN GROVE   SWAN

MEALS SERVED Breakfast (Sat & Sun only), dinner   **SETTING** ★★★

CHARACTERS Rafiki, Timon, Goofy, Pluto

TYPE OF SERVICE Buffet

FOOD VARIETY & QUALITY ★★★½

NOISE LEVEL Moderate

CHARACTER–GUEST RATIO 1:198, but often much better

Continued from page 345

variety, consistency, and quality, restaurants generally do a better job with breakfast than with lunch or dinner (if served). Some restaurants offer a buffet, while others opt for "one-skillet" family-style service, in which all hot items are served from the same pot or skillet. To help you sort it out, we rate the food at each character meal in our chart using the five-star scale.

A Texas mom notes:

> *The family-style meals are much better for character dining. At the buffet, you're scared to leave your table in case you miss a character or other action.*

5. THE PROGRAM Some larger restaurants stage modest performances where the characters dance, head a parade around the room, or lead songs and cheers. For some guests, these activities give the meal a celebratory air; for others, they turn what was already mayhem into absolute chaos. Either way, the antics consume time the characters could spend with families at their table.

6. NOISE If you want to eat in peace, character meals are a bad choice. That said, some are much noisier than others. Our chart gives you an idea of what to expect.

7. WHICH MEAL? Although breakfasts seem to be most popular, character lunches and dinners are usually more practical because they don't interfere with early-morning touring. During hot weather, a character lunch can be heavenly.

8. COST Dinners cost more than lunches and lunches more than breakfasts. Prices for meals (except at Cinderella Castle) vary only about $10 from the least expensive to the most expensive restaurant. Breakfasts run $21–$43 for adults and $11–$28 for kids ages 3–9. For character lunches, expect to pay $26–$46 for adults and $15–$29 for kids. Dinners are $30–$54 for adults and $14–$33 for children. Little ones ages 2 years and younger eat free. The meals at the high end of the price range are at Cinderella's Royal Table in the Magic Kingdom and Akershus Royal Banquet Hall at Epcot. The reasons for the sky-high prices: (1) Cinderella's Royal Table is small but in great demand and (2) the prices at Cinderella's and Akershus include a set of photos of your group taken by a Disney photographer. Whereas photos at other venues are optional, at Cindy's and Akershus you don't have a say in the matter.

BOOSTING SALES OF MEMENTOS AND SOUVENIRS Usually when Disney sees a horse carrying moneybags, it rides the beast until it drops. Disney's latest scheme of bundling photos in the price of character meals at Cinderella's Royal Table extends to Akershus Royal Banquet Hall at Epcot. Adding photos of your group taken by a Disney photographer is Disney's justification for raising the price of the character meals by about 60%. Disney insists that you're getting the photos at a bargain price. This is well and good if you're in the market, but if buying photos was not in your plans, well, they gotcha. It's a matter of some conjecture how far Disney will run with this idea. Maybe next year the price will be $200 and include fanciful medieval costumes for your entire party (charges for the changing room and locker to store your street clothes not included).

9. ADVANCE RESERVATIONS Disney makes Advance Reservations for character meals 180 days before you wish to dine (Disney resort guests can reserve 190 days out, or 10 additional days in advance); moreover, Disney resort guests can make Advance Reservations for all meals during their stay. Advance Reservations for most character meals are easy to obtain even if you call only a couple of weeks before you leave home. Meals at Cinderella's Royal Table are another story. To eat at Cinderella's during summer, holidays, and other peak times, you'll need our strategy (see Part 10), as well as help from Congress and the Pope.

10. CHECKING IT TWICE Disney occasionally shuffles the characters and theme of a character meal. If your little one's heart is set on Pooh and Piglet, getting Hook and Mr. Smee is just a waste of time and money. Reconfirm all character-meal Advance Reservations three weeks or so before you leave home by calling ☎ 407-WDW-DINE.

11. "FRIENDS" For some venues, Disney has stopped specifying characters scheduled for a particular meal. Instead, they say it's a given character "and friends"—for example, "Pooh and friends," meaning Eeyore, Piglet, and Tigger, or some combination thereof, or "Mickey and friends" with some assortment chosen among Minnie, Goofy, Pluto, Donald, Daisy, Chip, and Dale.

12. THE BUM'S RUSH Most character meals are leisurely affairs, and you can usually stay as long as you want. An exception is Cinderella's Royal Table at the Magic Kingdom. Because Cindy's is in such high demand, the restaurant does everything short of pre-chewing your food to move you through, as this European mother of a 5-year-old can attest:

> We dined a lot, did three character meals and a few signature restaurants, and every meal was awesome except for lunch with Cinderella in the castle. While I'd often read it wouldn't be a rushed affair, it was exactly that. We had barely sat down when the appetizers were thrown on our table, the princesses each spent just a few seconds with our daughter—almost no interaction—and the side dishes were cold. We were out of there within 40 minutes and felt very stressed. Considering the price for the meal, I cannot recommend it.

GETTING AN ADVANCE RESERVATION AT CINDERELLA'S ROYAL TABLE

ONCE UPON A TIME, breakfast was the only character meal at Cinderella Castle in the Magic Kingdom. Reservations for every table were gone within minutes of becoming available each morning. Disney responded to this popularity by adding character lunches and dinners—and jacking up the price to almost $60 per adult. As a result, it's now much easier to get into Cinderella's Royal Table for some meals during your stay. If you're visiting during peak periods or you've got to have a reservation at a specific, popular time, see our Advance Reservation tips starting on page 421.

DISNEY'S ROYAL ALTERNATIVES If you're unwilling to fund Cinderella's shoe habit or you simply weren't able to get an Advance Reservation before young Ariel graduates from college, rest assured there are other venues that will feed you in the company of princesses.

Akershus Royal Banquet Hall, in the Norway Pavilion of Epcot's World Showcase, serves family-style breakfast, lunch, and dinner. Disney tends to define princess quite loosely, so you may see any character who's ever donned a dress (with the exception of Cinderella) at this meal. Entrees are a combination of traditional buffet fare and the occasional Scandinavian dish—a nod to the fact that Norway has the only other castle available until the Fantasyland expansion is complete.

Dinner at the Grand Floridian's **1900 Park Fare** features the whole crew from *Cinderella,* including Lady Tremaine and the stepsisters (breakfast is a character buffet with Winnie the Pooh and friends). At $42 per adult and $21 for children age 9 and under, this is a far more economical option for diners wishing to get their princess on, and the stepsisters are an absolute hoot. This meal is also a little more boy-friendly if you're entertaining a mixed crowd. Finally, remember that your princess may be feeding off your own excitement over eating in the Castle—she might be just as happy with a plastic crown purchased in the gift shop and a burger from Cosmic Ray's.

OTHER CHARACTER EVENTS

A CAMPFIRE AND SING-ALONG ARE HELD NIGHTLY (times vary with the season) near the Meadow Trading Post and Bike Barn at Fort Wilderness Resort & Campground. Chip 'n' Dale lead the songs, and a Disney film is shown. The program is free and open to resort guests (☎ 407-824-2900). Another character encounter at Fort Wilderness is **Mickey's Backyard BBQ,** held seasonally on Thursday and Saturday. See page 769 for details.

BABYSITTING

CHILD-CARE CENTERS Child care isn't available inside the theme parks, but three Magic Kingdom resorts connected by monorail or boat (Polynesian, Grand Floridian, and Wilderness Lodge & Villas), four Epcot resorts (the Yacht & Beach Club Resorts, the Swan, and the Dolphin), and Animal Kingdom Lodge, along with the Hilton at Walt Disney World, have child-care centers for potty-trained children older than age 3 (see chart on the facing page). Services vary, but children generally can be left between 4:30 p.m. and midnight. Milk and cookies and blankets and pillows are provided at all centers, and dinner is provided at most. Play is supervised but not organized, and toys, videos, and games are plentiful. Guests at any Disney resort or campground may use the services.

unofficial **TIP**
Child-care clubs close at or before midnight. If you intend to stay out late, in-room babysitting is your best bet.

The most elaborate of the child-care centers (variously called "clubs" or "camps") is **Never Land Club** at the Polynesian Resort. The rate for ages 3–12 is $12 per hour, per child (2-hour minimum).

All the clubs accept reservations (some six months in advance!) with a credit card guarantee. Call the club directly, or reserve through

Babysitting Services

ALL ABOUT KIDS	KID'S NITE OUT	FAIRY GODMOTHERS
☎ 407-812-9300 or 800-728-6506 all-about-kids.com	☎ 407-828-0920 or 800-696-8105 kidsniteout.com	☎ 407-277-3724
HOTELS SERVED All WDW hotels and many outside the WDW area	**HOTELS SERVED** All WDW and Orlando-area hotels	**HOTELS SERVED** All WDW hotels and those in the general WDW area
SITTERS Men and women	**SITTERS** Men and women	**SITTERS** Mothers and grandmothers, female college students
MINIMUM CHARGES 4 hours	**MINIMUM CHARGES** 4 hours	**MINIMUM CHARGES** 4 hours
BASE HOURLY RATES 1 child, $14 2 children, $16 3 children, $18 4 children, $20	**BASE HOURLY RATES** 1 child, $16 2 children, $18.50 3 children, $21 4 children, $23.50	**BASE HOURLY RATES** 1 child, $16 2 children, $16 3 children, $16 4 children, $18
EXTRA CHARGES Transportation fee, $12; starting before 7 a.m. or after 9 p.m., +$2 per hour	**EXTRA CHARGES** Transportation fee, $10; starting before 6:30 a.m. or after 9 p.m., +$2 per hour; additional fee for holidays	**EXTRA CHARGES** Transportation fee, $14; starting after 10 p.m., +$2 per hour
CANCELLATION DEADLINE More than 24 hours before service to avoid cancellation charge	**CANCELLATION DEADLINE** 24 hours before service when reservation is made	**CANCELLATION DEADLINE** 3 hours before service
FORM OF PAYMENT Cash or traveler's checks for actual payment; gratuity in cash; credit card to hold reservation	**FORM OF PAYMENT** AE, D, MC, V; gratuity in cash	**FORM OF PAYMENT** Cash or traveler's checks for actual payment; gratuity in cash
THINGS SITTERS WON'T DO Transport children	**THINGS SITTERS WON'T DO** Transport children in private vehicle, take children swimming, give baths	**THINGS SITTERS WON'T DO** Transport children, give baths. Swimming is at sitter's discretion

Disney at ☎ 407-WDW-DINE. Most clubs require a 24-hour cancellation notice and levy a hefty penalty of 2 hours' time or $22.50 per call for no-shows. A limited number of walk-ins are usually accepted on a first-come, first-served basis.

If you're staying in a Disney resort that doesn't offer a child-care club and you *don't* have a car, then you're better off using in-room babysitting. Trying to take your child to a club in another hotel by Disney bus requires a 50- to 90-minute trip each way. By the time you've deposited your little one, it will almost be time to pick him or her up again.

unofficial TIP
Child-care clubs close at or before midnight. If you intend to stay out late, in-room babysitting is your best bet.

IN-ROOM BABYSITTING Three companies provide in-room sitting in Walt Disney World and surrounding areas. They're **Kid's Nite Out, All About Kids,** and **Fairy Godmothers** (no kidding). Kid's Nite Out also serves hotels in the greater Orlando area, including downtown. All three provide sitters older than age 18 who are insured, bonded, screened, reference-checked, police-checked, and trained in CPR. In addition to caring for your kids in your room, the sitters will, if you direct (and pay), take your children to the theme parks or other venues. All three services offer bilingual sitters.

CHILD-CARE CLUBS*			
HOTEL	**NAME OF PROGRAM**	**AGES**	**PHONE**
ANIMAL KINGDOM LODGE			
Simba's Cubhouse		3–12	☎ 407-938-4785
DOLPHIN AND SWAN			
Camp Dolphin		4–12	☎ 407-934-4241
GRAND FLORIDIAN RESORT & SPA			
Mouseketeer Club		3–12	☎ 407-824-2985
POLYNESIAN RESORT			
Never Land Club		3–12	☎ 407-824-1639
YACHT & BEACH CLUB RESORTS			
Sandcastle Club		3–12	☎ 407-934-3750
WILDERNESS LODGE & VILLAS			
Cub's Den		3–12	☎ 407-824-1083

*Child-care clubs operate afternoons and evenings. Before 4 p.m., call the hotels rather than the numbers listed above. All programs require reservations; call ☎ 407-WDW-DINE (939-3463).

SPECIAL PROGRAMS
for CHILDREN

SEVERAL CHILDREN'S PROGRAMS ARE AVAILABLE at Walt Disney World parks and resorts. While all are undoubtedly fun, we find them somewhat lacking in educational focus.

DISNEY'S FAMILY MAGIC TOUR This is a 1½- to 2-hour guided tour of the Magic Kingdom for the entire family. Even children in strollers (no younger than age 3) are welcome. The tour combines information about the Magic Kingdom with the gathering of clues that ultimately solve "diabolical" problems. There's usually a marginal plot such as saving Wendy from Captain Hook, in which case the character at the end of the tour is Wendy. The tour departs daily at 10 a.m. The cost is about $36 per person with tax, plus a valid Magic Kingdom admission. The maximum group size is 20 persons. Reservations can be made up to one year in advance by calling ☎ 407-WDW-TOUR (939-8687).

DISNEY'S PIRATE ADVENTURE Children ages 4–12 get to don bandannas, hoist the Jolly Roger, and set out on a boat trip to search for buried treasure by following a map. At the final port of call, the kids find the treasure (doubloons, beads, and rubber bugs!) and wolf down PB&J sandwiches. The treasure is split among the kids. The adventure costs about $36 per child with tax and is offered at Port Orleans Riverside (Bayou Pirate Adventure), the Grand Floridian (Pirate Adventure), the Yacht Club (Albatross Cruise), and the Caribbean Beach Resort (Caribbean Pirate Adventure). The Grand Floridian runs the excursion every day except Sunday; the other resorts offer the program three days a week. Call ☎ 407-WDW-PLAY (939-7529) for days offered and other information. Boys and girls alike really love this outing—many report it as the highlight of their vacation. *Note:* No parents allowed.

DISNEY'S THE MAGIC BEHIND OUR STEAM TRAINS Kids must be age 10 or older for this 3-hour tour, presented Monday–Saturday. At the 7:30 a.m. start time, join the crew of the Walt Disney World Railroad as they prepare their steam locomotives for the day. Cost is about $52 per person with tax, plus a valid Magic Kingdom admission. Call ☎ 407-WDW-TOUR for information and reservations.

MY DISNEY GIRL'S PERFECTLY PRINCESS TEA PARTY It certainly takes a princely sum to cover the tab on this Grand Floridian soiree, hosted by Rose Petal, an enchanted storytelling rose. Your little princess gets dressed up in her favorite regal attire and sips tea with Princess Aurora. Girls receive an 18-inch My Disney Girl doll dressed in a matching Princess Aurora gown plus accessories. Other loot includes a ribbon tiara, silver link bracelet, fresh rose, scrapbook set, and "Best Friend" certificate. A luncheon is served as well. The cost is about $314 with tax and gratuity for one adult and one child ages 3–11; add an additional adult for $107 or an additional child for $208. *Note:* **This event is not covered by the Disney Dining Plan.** The tea party is held every Sunday, Monday, and Wednesday–Friday, 10:30 a.m.–noon. Call ☎ 407-939-6397 for reservations and information.

WONDERLAND TEA PARTY Held at 1900 Park Fare restaurant in the Grand Floridian Monday–Friday afternoons at 1:30 p.m. for $43 per child (ages 4–12, with tax), the program consists of decorating (and eating) cupcakes and having lunch and tea with characters from Alice in Wonderland. Reservations can be made by calling ☎ 407-WDW-DINE 180 days in advance.

BIRTHDAYS *and* SPECIAL OCCASIONS

IF SOMEONE IN YOUR FAMILY CELEBRATES A BIRTHDAY while you're at Disney World, don't keep it a secret. A Lombard, Illinois, mom put the word out and was glad she did:

> *My daughter was turning 5 while we were there; our hotel asked me who her favorite character was and did the rest. We came back to our room on her birthday and there were helium balloons, a card, and a Cinderella photo autographed in ink! When we entered the Magic Kingdom, we received an "It's My Birthday Today" pin (FREE!), and at the restaurant she got a huge cupcake with whipped cream, sprinkles, and a candle. IT PAYS TO ASK!*

PART SEVEN

SPECIAL TIPS *for* SPECIAL PEOPLE

WALT DISNEY WORLD *for* SINGLES

DISNEY WORLD IS GREAT FOR SINGLES. It's safe, clean, and low-pressure. Safety and comfort are unsurpassed, especially for women traveling alone. Parking lots are well lit and constantly patrolled.

If you're looking for a place to relax without being hit on, Disney World is perfect. The bars, lounges, and nightclubs are among the most laid-back and friendly you're likely to find. Between the BoardWalk and Downtown Disney, nightlife abounds; virtually every type of entertainment is available at a reasonable price. If you overimbibe and you're a Disney resort guest, Disney buses will return you safely to your hotel.

See "Tips for Going Solo" on the following pages for more ways to enjoy Disney World on your own.

WALT DISNEY WORLD *for* COUPLES

SO MANY COUPLES MARRY OR HONEYMOON in the World that a department was created to tend to their needs. Disney's Fairy Tale Weddings & Honeymoons offers a range of wedding venues and services, plus honeymoon packages.

WEDDINGS

DISNEY'S ESCAPE WEDDING (maximum 18 or fewer guests, plus bride and groom) includes a cake and Champagne toast for the couple and four guests, a personalized wedding website, a Disney wedding certificate, a photographer, an Annual Pass for the bride and groom, and a wedding album. Packages require a four-night stay at a Disney-owned and -operated resort; some ceremony locations have a limit of 10 guests. The cost starts at $4,750; prices also include a musician, cake, bouquet, limousine ride, and wedding coordinator. If you invite more than 18 guests, you must buy one of Disney's customized wedding packages, which start at $12,000 (Monday–Thursday), $15,000 (Friday and Sunday), and $20,000 (Saturday), not including taxes and gratuities.

You can choose from one of the following locations for your ceremony: Disney's Wedding Pavilion near the Grand Floridian Resort & Spa, Sea Breeze Point at the BoardWalk Inn, the Wedding Gazebo at the Yacht Club Resort, Sunset Pointe at the Polynesian Resort, or Sunrise Terrace at the Wilderness Lodge.

unofficial **TIP**
It takes big bucks to marry at Disney World.

If you're short on friends, you can rent Disney characters by the half-hour to attend your wedding reception. At $1,000 per personage, they ain't cheap, but be comforted that they don't eat or drink. In fact, you can't drink either if characters are present—they're not allowed to participate in functions where alcohol is served. For our money, if the choice is between Minnie or a margarita . . .

One of the more improbable services available is bachelor parties (☎ 407-828-3400 for information). What goes on at a Disney bachelor party? Stag *cartoons*?

To marry in the World, you need a marriage license. They're $93.50 at any Florida county courthouse (cash, cashier's checks, money orders, MasterCard, or Visa accepted). There's no waiting period; your license is issued when you apply. If you're a Florida resident, however, you must wait three days after obtaining the license to marry unless you have completed a 4-hour premarital counseling session. The ceremony must occur within 60 days. Blood tests aren't required, but you must present ID (driver's license/nondriver ID, passport, or military ID plus Social Security number). If you were widowed or divorced within 300 days of the wedding, you must produce a certified copy of the deceased spouse's death certificate or your divorce decree. For more information, call the wedding consultant at ☎ 321-939-4610 or 877-566-0969, or visit **disneyweddings.com.**

HONEYMOONS AND VOWS RENEWALS

HONEYMOON PACKAGES ARE ADAPTATIONS of regular Walt Disney Travel Company vacations. No special rooms are included unless you upgrade. Honeymoon features vary according to the package purchased. Vows-renewal packages start at $4,750. For more information, contact Disney's Fairy Tale Weddings & Honeymoons, P.O. Box 10000, Lake Buena Vista, FL 32830-1000; ☎ 800-370-6009; **disneyweddings.com.**

ROMANTIC GETAWAYS

DISNEY WORLD IS A FAVORITE GETAWAY FOR COUPLES, but not all Disney hotels are equally romantic. Some are too family-oriented; others swarm with convention-goers. For romantic (though expensive) lodging, we recommend Animal Kingdom Lodge & Villas, Bay Lake Tower at the Contemporary Resort, the Polynesian Resort, Wilderness Lodge & Villas, the Grand Floridian, BoardWalk Inn & Villas, and the Yacht & Beach Club Resorts.

Tips for Going Solo

Single can mean traveling alone as well as unmarried, and being by yourself doesn't mean you can't have a great time at Disney World. Deb Wills, creator of the all-things-Disney website **allears.net**, offers the following advice:

Some people say visiting Disney World by yourself can't possibly be fun. They couldn't be more wrong! You can have a very magical time exploring the World on your own. Whether you're in Orlando on business and visiting the parks to kill time, or you came to get away from it all, visiting the parks by yourself need not be lonely. It affords you the opportunity to see and do what you want, when you want. For those of you who are hesitating—just do it! You'll be glad you did. Here are ways to maximize your experience when alone at WDW.

- The tendency might be to plan your days full of activity. I suggest the opposite: Don't plan much at all. Keep your schedule as open as you can. One of the best parts about traveling solo is that you can be your own boss. Sleep in, have leisurely morning coffee on the balcony, relax by the pool . . . or not. If you'd rather get up and go early, who's to stop you?

- Put some spontaneity into your day. If you're taking Disney transportation, get on the first park bus that arrives.

- Get on the resort monorail (not the Express!) at the Magic Kingdom, and visit each of the resorts it stops at. Each resort has its own theme and character, with lots to see and explore. The resorts are especially beautiful during the holidays, when all the decorations are in place.

- Did you know that you can walk through the queues and view the preshows of the thrill rides even if you don't intend to ride? Wander through at your own pace; then tell the cast member before boarding that you don't wish to ride, and you'll be shown to a nearby exit. This way you don't have to miss, for example, the very detailed queue of Expedition Everest with its hundreds of unique artifacts.

- If you do want to experience the thrill rides, take advantage of the single-rider lines for the Rock 'n' Roller Coaster, Expedition Everest, and Test Track. They can cut your wait time significantly.

- One of my favorite things to do when I'm traveling solo is play photographer. If you encounter folks taking photos of each other,

The Alligator Bayou section at Port Orleans Riverside, a Moderate Disney resort, also has secluded rooms. In Part Three, Accommodations, we provide recommendations for the best rooms in each Disney resort, taking into consideration view, quiet, and convenience.

ask if they would like to be in one photo, then offer to snap the picture. This is a great way to make friends.

- Get your favorite Disney snack, find a bench, and people-watch. You'll be amazed at what you see: the honeymooning couple wearing bride-and-groom mouse ears, toddlers giving Mickey and the characters their first hugs, grandparents smiling indulgently as their grandchildren smear ice cream all over their faces. If you're missing the smiles of your own children, buy a couple of balloons and give them away. You'll help make the kids near you very, very happy.

- Learn how some of the magic is created. Take a behind-the-scenes tour (see descriptions in Part Nineteen) or one of the Deluxe hotel tours.

- Visit Animal Kingdom Lodge and relax at an animal-viewing area. Find an animal keeper; they'll gladly discuss care of the wild animals at the resort.

- Don't hesitate to strike up conversations with cast members or guests in line with you. Foreign cast members in Epcot's World Showcase are happy to share stories about their homelands.

- With no one pulling to go to Space Mountain, get a snack, or go to the bathroom, you can enjoy a leisurely shop around the World. Some stores (Arribas Brothers in Downtown Disney, and Mitsukoshi Department Store in the Japan section of World Showcase) have really neat displays and exhibits.

- Go to that restaurant you've always wanted to try but your picky eater has always declined. You don't have to order a full meal; try several appetizers or, better yet, just dessert.

- You don't want the folks at home to think you've forgotten them, so go to Innoventions in Epcot to e-mail a photo of yourself to your family.

- Use common sense about your personal security. I feel very comfortable and safe traveling alone at Disney World and have done so many times, but I still don't do things I wouldn't do at home (like announce to anyone listening that I'm traveling solo). If you aren't comfortable walking to your room alone, ask at the front desk for a security escort. Use extra caution in the parking lots at night, just as you would at home.

WALT DISNEY WORLD
"At Large"

YOU'VE JUST SPENT A SMALL FORTUNE for your vacation to Walt Disney World. If you're a person of size, the last thing you want to worry about now is whether you'll have trouble fitting in the ride vehicles. Fortunately, Walt Disney World realizes that its guests come in all shapes and sizes and is quite accommodating. Deb Wills and Debra Martin Koma, authors of *PassPorter's Open Mouse for Walt Disney World and the Disney Cruise Line: Easy Access Vacations for Travelers with Extra Challenges,* offer these suggestions.

- Remember that you'll be on your feet for hours at a time. Be sure to wear comfortable, broken-in shoes. Pay attention to your feet: If you feel a blister starting, take care of it quickly. (Note that each park has a first-aid station where you can find bandages and other necessities. For more on blister prevention, see page 404.)

- If you're prone to chafing, consider bringing a commercial antifriction product (such as Bodyglide) that is designed to control or eliminate rubbing. You can find this and similar products at most pharmacies and sporting-goods stores.

- Know before you go! Not all attractions have the same types of vehicles or seating. Some have bench seats, while others have individual seats; some have overhead harnesses, while others have seat belts or lap bars. Learn what type of seating or vehicle each attraction has before you go so you know what to expect. Check out **allears.net** for the details. If the attraction has a seat belt, pull it all the way out before you sit down to make it easier to strap yourself in. Note that some attractions even have seat-belt extenders—ask a cast member about these.

- Several attractions (Expedition Everest and Test Track, for example) offer a sample ride vehicle for you to try out before you get in line. These are usually discreetly out of view of the general public; ask a cast member for the location.

- Front seats (such as those in the Rock 'n' Roller Coaster and Test Track) often have more legroom.

- In restaurants, look for chairs without arms. If you don't see any, the host or hostess should be able to provide one for you.

- Request a resort hotel room with a king-size bed. Everyone needs a good night's sleep, especially after touring the parks all day. It may cost a bit more, but it will be more than worth it!

WALT DISNEY WORLD *for* EXPECTANT MOTHERS

IT'S SAID THAT A GOOD SHEPHERD will lay down his life for his sheep. Heaven knows we've tried to be good shepherds for you. While researching this guide, we have spun in teacups and been jostled in simulators until we turned green. We have baked in the sun, flapped in the wind, and been drenched in the rain. But we have failed expectant mothers. Try as they might, the authors have never become pregnant. Consequently, the *Unofficial Guide* has never included firsthand information for mothers-to-be. Then to the rescue came Debbie Grubbs, a Colorado reader in her fifth month of pregnancy. She fearlessly waddled all over Disney World, compiling observations and tips for expectant moms. Here are her conclusions:

Generally speaking, pregnant women can experience more attractions than not at Walt Disney World. Therefore, I will outline only those rides that are prohibited to pregnant women and the reasons why. There were several rides that I just knew I could ride even though they were restricted, so I sent my husband and friends to ride first and they reported why they thought I could or could not ride.

Magic Kingdom

Splash Mountain is restricted obviously due to the drop, or so I thought. It turns out that the seat configuration in the "logs" has more to do with it than the drop. The seats are made so that your knees are higher than your rear, causing compression on the abdomen (when it's this large). This is potentially harmful to the baby. As always, better safe than sorry.

Big Thunder Mountain Railroad is also restricted for obvious reasons. It's just not a good idea to ride roller coasters when pregnant.

Mad Tea Party may be OK if you don't spin the cups. We didn't ride this one because my doctor advised me not to ride things with centrifugal [or centripetal] force. Dumbo in Fantasyland and the Astro Orbiter in Tomorrowland are OK, though.

Space Mountain is one of my favorite rides, but a roller coaster nonetheless.

Tomorrowland Speedway is not recommended due to the amount of rear-ending that always occurs from overzealous younger drivers.

Disney's Animal Kingdom

Both DINOSAUR and Primeval Whirl are very jerky and should be avoided.

We think Debbie would've avoided Expedition Everest, too.

Epcot

Mission: SPACE and Test Track are restricted, as are all simulator rides. They're too rough and jerky, much like a roller coaster. [Non-moving seats are available in some simulation attractions—ask a cast member.] Soarin' is fine.

Disney's Hollywood Studios

Tower of Terror is restricted for the drop alone, and Star Tours is restricted because it's a simulator. Although not as rough as Mission: SPACE, Star Tours is still a no-no. The Rock 'n' Roller Coaster is clearly off-limits.

Water Parks

Slides are off-limits. Pregnant women can, however, do Shark Reef at Typhoon Lagoon with an extra-large wet-suit vest. The wave pools and floating creeks are great for getting the weight off your feet.

A mother of three from Bethesda, Maryland, adds:

First, anyone who is pregnant should go to their local golf shop and buy one of those canes that has a seat attached to it. They're lightweight and easy to carry. Without a seat, I would've been a goner.

Second, a pregnant woman must come with some type of support or a BellyBra.

MORE TIPS FOR MOMS-TO-BE

IN ADDITION TO DEBBIE'S TIPS, here are a few of ours:

1. Discuss your Disney World plans with your obstetrician before your trip.

2. Be prepared for a lot of walking. Get in shape by walking at home, gradually building endurance and distance.

3. Get as much rest as you need, even if you have to sacrifice some time at the theme parks. Try to nap each afternoon.

4. Eat properly. Drink plenty of water throughout the day, especially in warmer months.

5. Use in-park transportation whenever available to cut down on walking.

6. Stay in the World if possible. This will make it easier to return to your hotel for rest.

WALT DISNEY WORLD
for SENIORS

SENIOR CITIZENS' PROBLEMS AND CONCERNS are common among Disney visitors of all ages. Older guests do, however, get into predicaments caused by touring with younger people. Pressured by their grandchildren to endure a frantic pace, many seniors concentrate on surviving Disney World rather than enjoying it. Seniors must either set the pace or dispatch the young folks to tour on their own.

An older reader in Alabaster, Alabama, writes:

Being a senior is not for wussies. At Disney World particularly, it requires courage and pluck. Things that used to be easy take a lot of effort, and sometimes your brain has to wait for your body to catch up. Half the time, your grandchildren treat you like a crumbling ruin and then turn around and trick you into getting on a roller coaster in the dark. What you need to tell seniors is that they have to be alert and not trust anyone. Not their children or even the Disney people, and especially not their grandchildren. When your grandchildren want you to go on a ride, don't follow along blindly like a lamb to the slaughter. Make sure you know what the ride is all about. Stand your ground and don't waffle. He who hesitates is launched!

unofficial **TIP**
Because seniors are varied and willing, there are few attractions we suggest that they avoid.

Most seniors we interview enjoy Disney World much more when they tour with folks their own age. If, however, you're considering visiting Disney World with your grandchildren, we recommend making an orientation visit without them first. If you know firsthand what to expect, the easier it'll be to establish limits, maintain control, and set a comfortable pace later on.

If you're *determined* to take the grandkids, read carefully the sections of this book that discuss family touring. (*Hint:* The Dumbo-or-

Die-in-a-Day Touring Plan has been known to bring grown-ups of all ages to their knees.)

Personal taste is more important than age. We hate to see mature visitors pass an exceptional attraction like Splash Mountain because it's a so-called thrill ride. Splash Mountain is a full-blown adventure that gets its appeal more from music and visual effects than from the thrill of the ride. Because you must choose among attractions that might interest you, we provide facts to help you make informed decisions.

GETTING AROUND

MANY SENIORS LIKE TO WALK, but a 7-hour visit to a theme park includes 4–10 miles on foot. If you're not up to that, let someone push you in a rented wheelchair (theme parks: $12 per day with no deposit, $10 per day for multiday rentals; Downtown Disney: $100 rental deposit required). The theme parks also offer fun-to-drive electric carts (electric convenience vehicles, or ECVs) for $50 per day, with a $20 refundable deposit. Don't let your pride keep you from having a good time. Sure, you could march 10 miles if you had to—*but you don't have to!*

Your wheelchair-rental deposit slip is good for a replacement wheelchair in any park during the same day. You can rent a chair at the Magic Kingdom in the morning, return it, go to Epcot, present your deposit slip, and get another chair at no additional charge.

TIMING YOUR VISIT

RETIREES SHOULD MAKE THE MOST of their flexible schedules and go to Disney World in fall or spring (excluding holiday weeks), when the weather is nicest and crowds are thinnest. Crowds are also sparse from late January through early February, but the weather can be unpredictable. If you visit in winter, take coats and sweaters, plus warm-weather clothing. Be prepared for anything from near-freezing rain to afternoons in the 80s.

LODGING

IF YOU CAN AFFORD IT, STAY IN DISNEY WORLD. Rooms are among the Orlando-Kissimmee area's nicest, and transportation is always available to any Disney destination at no additional cost.

Disney hotels reserve rooms close to restaurants and transportation for guests of any age who can't tolerate much walking. They also provide golf carts to pick up and deliver guests at their rooms. Service can vary dramatically depending on the time of day and the number of guests requesting carts. At check-in time (around 3 p.m.), for example, the wait for a ride can be as long as 40 minutes.

Here are four reasons to consider staying in Disney World:

1. The quality of the properties is consistently above average.

2. Buses run only hourly or so for "outside" hotels. Disney buses run about every 20 minutes. Staying in the World guarantees transportation when you need it. On the flip side, the buses that serve out-of-the-World areas usually operate on a fixed schedule so you know exactly what time to be at the loading point.

3. You get free parking in major theme parks' lots.

4. You get preferential tee times on resort golf courses.

All Disney hotels are spread out. It's easy to avoid most stairs, but it's often a long hike to your room from parking lots, bus stops, or public areas. Seniors intending to spend more time at Epcot and Disney's Hollywood Studios than at the Magic Kingdom or Disney's Animal Kingdom should consider the Yacht & Beach Club Resorts, the Swan, the Dolphin, or BoardWalk Inn & Villas.

The Contemporary Resort and the adjacent Bay Lake Tower are good choices for seniors who want to be on the monorail system. So are the Grand Floridian and Polynesian resorts, though they cover many acres, necessitating a lot of walking. For a restful, rustic feeling, choose the Wilderness Lodge & Villas. If you want a kitchen and the comforts of home, book Old Key West Resort, the Beach Club Villas, Animal Kingdom Villas, or BoardWalk Villas. If you enjoy watching birds and animals, try Animal Kingdom Lodge & Villas. Try Saratoga Springs for golf.

RV-ers will find pleasant surroundings at Disney's Fort Wilderness Resort & Campground. Several independent campgrounds are within 30 minutes of Disney World (see page 206). None offers the wilderness setting or amenities that Disney does, but they cost less.

TRANSPORTATION

ROADS IN DISNEY WORLD CAN BE DAUNTING. Armed with a decent sense of direction and a great sense of humor, however, even the most timid driver can get around.

If you drive, parking isn't a problem. Lots are served by trams linking the parking area and the theme park's entrance. Parking for the disabled is available adjacent to each park's entrance. Pay-booth attendants will provide a dashboard ticket and direct you to the reserved spaces. Disney requires that you be recognized officially as disabled to use this parking, but temporarily disabled or injured persons also are permitted access.

SENIOR DINING

EAT BREAKFAST AT YOUR HOTEL RESTAURANT or save money by having juice and rolls in your room. Carry snacks in a fanny pack supplemented by fruit, fruit juice, and soft drinks purchased from vendors. Make Advance Reservations for lunch before noon to avoid the crowds. Follow with an early dinner and be out of the restaurants, ready for evening touring and fireworks, long before the main crowd even thinks about dinner.

We recommend that seniors fit dining and rest into each day. Plan lunch as a break. Sit back, relax, and enjoy. Then return to your hotel for a nap or swim during the hot, crowded hours of the day.

WALT DISNEY WORLD *for* GUESTS *with* SPECIAL NEEDS

DISNEY WORLD IS SO ATTUNED TO GUESTS with physical challenges that unscrupulous people have been known to fake a disability in order to take unfair advantage. If you have a disability, even a re-stricted diet, Disney World is prepared to meet your needs.

Valuable information for trip planning is available at **disneyworld .com.** Each major theme park offers a free booklet describing disabled services and facilities. Disney people are somewhat resistant to mailing you the booklets, but if you're polite and persistent, they can be persuaded. Or get a booklet when entering the theme/water parks, at resort front desks, and at wheelchair-rental locations in the theme parks. More-limited information is available online at **disneyworld .disney.go.com/plain-text.**

For specific requests, such as those for special accommodations at hotels or on the Disney transportation system, call ☎ 407-939-7807 (voice) or 407-939-7670 (TTY). When the recorded menu comes up, press 1. Limit your questions and requests to those regarding disabled services and accommodations (address other questions to ☎ 407-824-4321 or 407-827-5141 [TTY]). If you'll be staying at a Disney resort, let the reservation agent know of any special needs you have when you book your room.

The following equipment, services, and facilities are available at Disney hotels, though not all hotels offer all items:

Accessible vanities	Closed-captioned televisions	Roll-in showers
Bed and bathroom rails	Double peepholes in doors	Rubber bed padding
Braille on signs and elevators	Handheld showerheads	Shower benches
Closed-captioned televisions	Knock and phone alerts	Strobe-light smoke detectors
Double peepholes in doors	Lowered beds	TTYs
Accessible vanities	Portable commodes	Wheelchairs
Bed and bathroom rails	Refrigerators	Wider bathroom doors
Braille on signs and elevators		

Service animals are welcome in all Disney resorts.

Much of the Disney transportation system is disabled-accessible. Monorails can be accessed by ramp or elevator, and all bus routes are served by vehicles with wheelchair lifts, though unusually wide or long wheelchairs (or motorized chairs) may not fit the lift. Watercraft accommodations for wheelchairs are iffier. If you plan to stay at Wilderness Lodge & Villas, Fort Wilderness Campground, or an Epcot resort, call ☎ 407-939-7807 (voice) or 407-939-7670 (TTY) for the latest information on watercraft accessibility.

Food and merchandise locations at theme parks, Downtown Disney, and hotels are generally accessible, but some fast-food queues and shop aisles are too narrow for wheelchairs. At these locations, ask a cast member or member of your party for assistance.

Disabled guests and their families give Disney high marks for accessibility and sensitivity. An Arlington, Virginia, woman writes:

Disney is dynamite in its treatment of handicapped vacationers. My mom has mobility problems that got a lot worse between the time my dad made reservations and the time we arrived, and she was worried about getting around. Disney supplied a free wheelchair, and every bus had kneeling steps for wheelchair users. The disabled brochures for each park were incredibly informative about access for each attraction, and the hosts sprang into action when they saw us coming.

VISITORS WITH DISABILITIES

WHOLLY OR PARTIALLY NONAMBULATORY guests may rent wheelchairs. Most rides, shows, attractions, restrooms, and restaurants accommodate the nonambulatory disabled. If you're in a park and need assistance, go to Guest Relations.

unofficial **TIP**
Park maps issued to each guest on admission are coded to show which attractions accommodate wheelchairs.

A limited number of electric carts or ECVs (electric convenience vehicles) are available for rent. Easy to drive, they give nonambulatory guests tremendous freedom and mobility. For some reason, vehicles at the Magic Kingdom go much faster than those at other parks.

All Disney lots have close-in parking for disabled visitors. Request directions when you pay your parking fee. All monorails and most rides, shows, restrooms, and restaurants accommodate wheelchairs.

Wheelchairs rent for $12 with no deposit required, $10 per day for multiday rentals; ECVs are $70 per day, including a $20 refundable deposit (prices do not include tax). Rentals are available at all Disney World theme parks (see Parts Eleven through Fourteen for specific locations) and Downtown Disney. Wheelchairs are welcome at Blizzard Beach and Typhoon Lagoon water parks but are not available for rent. The rental deposit at Downtown Disney is $100.

Even if an attraction doesn't accommodate wheelchairs, nonambulatory guests may ride if they can transfer from their wheelchair to the ride's vehicle. Disney staff, however, aren't trained or permitted to assist with transfers. Guests must be able to board the ride unassisted or have a member of their party assist them. Either way, members of the nonambulatory guest's party will be permitted to ride with him or her. Because the waiting areas of most attractions won't accommodate wheelchairs, nonambulatory guests and their parties should request boarding instructions as soon as they arrive at an attraction. Almost always, the entire group will be allowed to board without a lengthy wait.

A reader from New Orleans who traveled to Disney World with a nonambulatory friend writes:

I went with a very dear friend of mine who is paraplegic. It was his first trip to WDW, and we were a little apprehensive about how much we'd be able to do. The official pamphlet distributed by the WDW staff is helpful but implies limits to accessibility. After reading it, Brian and I thought we'd end up just looking at the rides, not riding them. The reality is, nonambulatory visitors are able to do much more; one only has to ask the cast members what is really allowed. Brian is a very active person who is able to transfer from his wheelchair without too much difficulty, so we were able to ride almost everything we wanted.

DIETARY RESTRICTIONS Visitors with dietary restrictions can find assistance at Guest Relations in the parks. For Disney World sit-down restaurants outside the parks, call three days ahead for assistance.

Looking for a tasty dessert? Try the **Babycakes NYC** bakery at Downtown Disney Marketplace (☎ 407-938-9044; **babycakesnyc .com**), in the Fresh A-Peel building next to T-REX restaurant. Babycakes' menu features tasty kosher, vegan, and gluten-, wheat-, soy-, egg-, casein- and refined sugar–free baked goods, including cupcakes, cookies, muffins, buns, biscuits, and more. Our favorites are the miniature brownies, whose main ingredient must surely be love, and the "frosting shots"—a generous dollop of flavored icing in a small paper cup. If the manager's in a good mood, we hear that *Unofficial Guide* readers who ask nicely can get a shot for free.

A reader from St. Charles, Illinois, alerted Disney ahead of time with good results:

> *For any families with food allergies, let them know that they are in good hands at Disney! We filled out paperwork ahead of time for each dining reservation. When we arrived, the hostess confirmed our allergies, and then we were met by the head chef. My children were delighted to eat at a restaurant knowing it was safe for them.*

SIGHT- AND/OR HEARING-IMPAIRED GUESTS Guest Relations at the parks provides free assistive-technology devices to visually and hearing-impaired guests ($25–$100 refundable deposit, depending on the device). Sight-impaired guests can customize the given information (such architectural details, restroom locations, and descriptions of attractions and restaurants) through an interactive audio menu that is guided by a GPS system in the device. Hearing-impaired guests can benefit from amplified audio and closed-captioning for attractions loaded into the same device.

Braille guidebooks are available from Guest Relations at all parks ($25 refundable deposit). Some rides provide closed-captioning; many theater attractions provide reflective captioning.

Disney provides sign-language interpretations of live shows at the theme parks on certain designated days of the week:

THE MAGIC KINGDOM: Mondays and Thursdays

EPCOT: Tuesdays and Fridays

DISNEY'S ANIMAL KINGDOM: Saturdays

DISNEY'S HOLLYWOOD STUDIOS: Sundays and Wednesdays

Get confirmation of the interpreted-performance schedule a minimum of a week in advance by calling Disney World information at ☎ 407-824-4321 (voice) or 407-827-5141 (TTY). You'll be contacted before your visit with a show schedule that lists the names, dates, and times of the interpreted performances.

NONAPPARENT DISABILITIES We receive many letters from readers whose traveling companion or child requires special assistance but who, unlike a person in a wheelchair, is not visibly disabled. Autism, for example, makes it very difficult or impossible for someone with the disorder to wait in line for more than a few minutes or in queues surrounded by a crowd.

A trip to Disney World can be nonetheless positive and rewarding for guests with autism and similar conditions. And while any Disney vacation requires planning, a little extra effort to accommodate the affected person will pay large dividends.

THE GUEST ASSISTANCE CARD Visitors with nonapparent disabilities, whether temporary or permanent, should obtain a Guest Assistance Card (GAC), a pass that explains to cast members any special accommodation a guest may need. To request the card, go to the Guest Relations area inside any Disney theme park or just outside the park's gates. If you're requesting the GAC for someone else (your child, for example), he or she must be with you when you make the request.

Having a specific diagnosis doesn't qualify or disqualify someone for a GAC. Rather, the card is issued based on a person's needs—people with the same diagnosis can have very different needs. Also, you don't need a doctor's letter to request a GAC: According to the Americans with Disabilities Act, you cannot be required to provide proof of a disability.

unofficial **TIP**
If you encounter a cast member who is unfamiliar with the Guest Assistance Card, just ask for a manager and explain your situation.

To figure out what those needs are, think about the sorts of things that happen in a day at Disney World and how the following situations, among others, would affect you or someone else with a nonapparent disability:

- Do you have a relative who needs a quiet place to wait or a place away from other people as much as possible? If so, a GAC might help, although not all attractions offer such accommodations.

- Does your ambulatory child need to wait in line in a stroller? Some kids might, either because they can't or won't walk in line or because they need a safe haven where they're not so close to other people. A GAC lets you bring the stroller into lines just as you would a wheelchair. In this case, you'll be issued a red strap, which you'll put around the stroller's handle and show to the first cast member you encounter at each attraction. *Note:* If you or someone else in your party uses a wheelchair or ECV, you don't need a GAC unless you have needs other than access to entrances, lines, and boarding areas.

- Do you, despite being able to walk, need extra time getting into/out of ride vehicles where rides have moving walkways? If so, a GAC might help by letting you board/disembark at designated wheelchair spots.

Guest Relations can add different stamps to a GAC to tell cast members at attractions what assistance the guest requires. You don't need to remember or ask for these specific stamps; just be ready to explain your needs.

The GAC usually covers up to six people (five plus the person with a disability). However, the person whose name is on the card must be present when you use it.

GACs are available at all of the theme parks but not at Downtown Disney or Disney resorts. A card issued at one park is good at all parks and is usually valid for your whole vacation, but theme park GACs are not valid at the water parks. If you obtained a GAC on a previous trip to Walt Disney World, you cannot reuse it. Also, a GAC cannot be obtained in advance of your visit.

Having a GAC doesn't mean that you can go to the front of a line (that privilege is extended only to seriously ill children who are visiting Disney World courtesy of the Make-A-Wish Foundation or similar organizations). Rather, the card is designed to provide "more convenient entrance" into attractions. Note that GACs are not valid at restaurants or character-greeting areas.

To use the GAC, simply show it to the first cast member you see at the attraction. Keep in mind, though, that even with the same attraction, the GAC is not always handled the same way each time. Exactly what happens depends on how busy the attraction is, how many other people with special needs are there at the time, and staffing.

This Seattle mother of two had a great experience using the GAC:

> We ended up getting a Guest Assistance Card for our son who has cystic fibrosis. Let me tell you—that made all the difference in the world. First and most importantly, it made him feel special, and it also made it easier to leave the parks so that he could continue to do all of his required treatments since [because of the touring plans] he realized he wouldn't have to spend so much time waiting in lines.

FRIENDS OF BILL W.

A LINTHICUM, MARYLAND, MOM suggested this:

> We went on this vacation with a recovering alcoholic. He was able to attend daily 3–4 p.m. meetings that were held just outside the park in one of the hotels. It would be helpful if you mentioned that there are meetings available for Alcoholics Anonymous. Disney doesn't sponsor them. This is a very sensitive issue for many who are too afraid to ask for fear of public ridicule. The person in our group took a cab from the resort the first time and never had to after that. There are regulars in the meetings who will pick up anyone from their resorts who needs a ride.

GUESTS WHO DON'T SPEAK ENGLISH

DISNEY HAS DEVELOPED A WIRELESS DEVICE called **Ears to the World** that provides synchronized narration in French, German, Japanese, Portuguese, or Spanish for more than 30 attractions in the major theme parks. The wireless, lightweight headsets provide real-time translation, allowing guests with limited fluency in English to understand the storylines of the designated attractions. The device is available for a $100 refundable deposit at Guest Relations in all parks.

PART EIGHT

ARRIVING *and* GETTING AROUND

GETTING THERE

DIRECTIONS

YOU CAN DRIVE TO ANY Walt Disney World destination via World Drive off US 192; via Epcot Center Drive off Interstate 4, which connects Daytona and Tampa; or from the Hartzog Road/Walt Disney World interchange off FL 429, a.k.a. the Western Beltway (see all maps in this chapter).

unofficial **TIP**
Warning! I-4 is an east–west highway but takes a north–south drop through the Orlando-Kissimmee area. This change in direction complicates getting oriented in and around Disney World. Logic suggests that highways branching off I-4 should run north and south, but most run east and west here.

FROM INTERSTATE 10 Take I-10 east across Florida to I-75 southbound, then take Exit 267A/Tampa onto Florida's Turnpike. Take FL 429 (toll) southbound off the turnpike. Leave FL 429 at Exit 8, the Hartzog Road/Walt Disney World interchange, in the direction of Walt Disney World, and follow the signs to your Disney destination. Also use these directions to reach hotels along US 192, the Irlo Bronson Memorial Highway.

FROM INTERSTATE 75 SOUTHBOUND Exit I-75 southbound onto Florida's Turnpike via Exit 267A/Tampa. Take FL 429 (toll) southbound off the turnpike. Leave FL 429 at Exit 8, the Hartzog Road/Walt Disney World interchange, in the direction of Walt Disney World, and follow the signs to your Disney destination. Also use these directions to reach hotels along US 192, the Irlo Bronson Memorial Highway.

FROM INTERSTATE 95 SOUTHBOUND Follow I-95 south to I-4. Go west on I-4 through Orlando. Take Exit 67/FL 536, marked Epcot/Downtown Disney, and follow the signs. During rush hours take FL 417/Central Florida GreeneWay; take Exit 6 to FL 536 West, and follow the signs.

FROM DAYTONA, SANFORD INTERNATIONAL AIRPORT (SFB), OR ORLANDO Head west on I-4 through Orlando. Take Exit 67/FL 536, marked Epcot/Downtown Disney, and follow the signs.

FROM THE ORLANDO INTERNATIONAL AIRPORT (MCO) There are two routes from the airport to Walt Disney World (see the South Orlando

I-4 & Walt Disney World Area

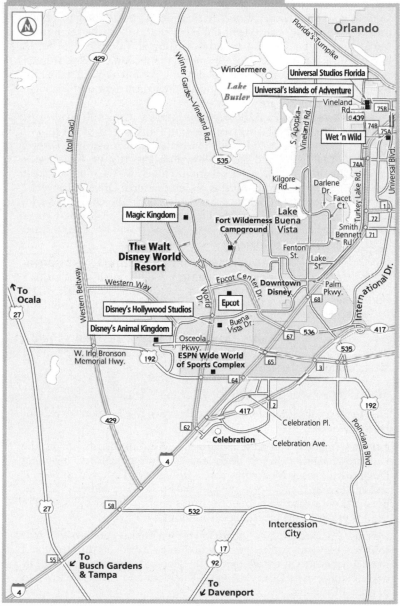

Orlando

Florida's Turnpike

Windermere

Lake Butler

Universal Studios Florida

Universal's Islands of Adventure

Vineland Rd.

Wet 'n Wild

Winter Garden–Vineland Rd.

S. Apopka–Vineland Rd.

Turkey Lake Rd.

International Dr.

Universal Blvd.

429

75B
74B
75A
74A
439

535

Kilgore Rd.→

Darlene Dr.

Facet Ct.

Lake Buena Vista

Smith Bennett Rd.

72
71

Magic Kingdom

Fort Wilderness Campground

The Walt Disney World Resort

(toll road)

Fenton St.

Lake St.

↑To Ocala

27

Western Way

Western Beltway

Epcot Center Dr.

Downtown Disney

Palm Pkwy.

68

Epcot

World Dr.

Disney's Hollywood Studios

Buena Vista Dr.

67   536

417

535

Disney's Animal Kingdom

Osceola Pkwy.

ESPN Wide World of Sports Complex

65

3

W. Irlo Bronson Memorial Hwy.

192

64

429

417

2

62

Celebration Pl.

Poinciana Blvd.

192

Celebration

Celebration Ave.

4

27

58

532

Intercession City

55

To Busch Gardens & Tampa

17

92

To Davenport

4

and Walt Disney World Area map on pages 22 and 23). Both routes take almost exactly the same time to drive, except during rush-hour traffic when Route One via FL 417 is far less congested than Route Two via the Beachline Expressway. Also, Route One eliminates the need to drive on I-4, which is always very congested.

Route One: Drive southwest on FL 417/Central Florida GreeneWay, a toll road. Take Exit 6/International Drive toward FL 535. FL 536 will cross I-4 and become Epcot Center Drive. From here, follow the signs to your Walt Disney World destination. If you're going to a hotel on US 192 (Irlo Bronson Memorial Highway), follow the same route until you reach I-4. Take I-4 west toward Tampa. Take the first US 192 exit if your hotel is on West Irlo Bronson, the second exit if your hotel is on East Irlo Bronson. If your hotel is in Lake Buena Vista, take Exit 6 onto FL 536 as described previously, then turn right on FL 535 to the Lake Buena Vista area.

Route Two: Take FL 528/Beachline Expressway, a toll road, west for about 12 miles to the intersection with I-4. Go west on I-4 to Exit 67/FL 536, marked Epcot/Downtown Disney, and then follow the signs to your Walt Disney World destination. This is also the route to take if your hotel is on International Drive or Universal Boulevard, near Universal Studios, near SeaWorld, or near the Orange County Convention Center. For these destinations, take I-4 east toward Orlando.

unofficial **TIP**
If you take either of these routes from the airport, you'll need money for tolls. Some exits are unmanned and require exact change, so be sure you have at least $2 in quarters. Also, note that while the manned toll booths take bills up to $20, they don't accept credit cards.

FROM MIAMI, FORT LAUDERDALE, AND SOUTH-EASTERN FLORIDA Head north on Florida's Turnpike to I-4 westbound. Take Exit 67/FL 536, marked Epcot/Downtown Disney, and follow the signs.

FROM TAMPA AND SOUTHWESTERN FLORIDA Take I-75 northbound to I-4. Go east on I-4, take Exit 64 onto US 192 West, and follow the signs.

Walt Disney World Exits off I-4

East to west (direction of Orlando to Tampa), five I-4 exits serve Walt Disney World.

EXIT 68 (marked FL 535/Lake Buena Vista) primarily serves the Downtown Disney Resort Area and Downtown Disney, including Downtown Disney Marketplace and Downtown Disney West Side. It also serves non-Disney hotels with a Lake Buena Vista address. This exit puts you on a road with lots of traffic signals. Avoid it unless you're headed to one of the preceding destinations.

EXIT 67 (marked FL 536/Epcot/Downtown Disney) delivers you to a four-lane expressway into the heart of Disney World. It's the fastest and most convenient way for westbound travelers to access almost all Disney destinations except Disney's Animal Kingdom and ESPN Wide World of Sports Complex.

EXIT 65 (marked Osceola Parkway) is the best exit for westbound travelers to access Animal Kingdom, Animal Kingdom Lodge, Pop Century Resort, Art of Animation Resort, All-Star Resorts, and ESPN Wide World of Sports Complex.

EXIT 64 (marked US 192/Magic Kingdom) is the best route for east-bound travelers to all Disney destinations.

EXIT 62 (marked Disney World/Celebration) is the first Disney exit you'll encounter if you're headed eastbound. This four-lane, controlled-access highway connects to the so-called Maingate of Walt Disney World. Accessing Walt Disney World via the next exit, Exit 64, also routes you through the main entrance.

THE I-4 BLUES

OVER MANY YEARS OF COVERING WALT DISNEY WORLD, we've watched I-4 turn from a modern interstate highway into a parking lot. Although the greatest congestion is between the Universal Orlando–International Drive area and downtown Orlando, the section to the southwest serving the tourist areas is becoming a real slog as well. Adding to the problem are construction projects both on the highway itself and at the interchanges. If you're commuting to Walt Disney World from the Universal Florida–International Drive area in particular, try to avoid I-4 during rush hours. If you're going to the airport from the Walt Disney World, Lake Buena Vista, or US 192 areas, use FL 417 rather than the Beachline Expressway. If you're considering a hotel on or near International Drive, try to find one toward the southern end of I-Drive. If the I-4 traffic becomes intolerable, it's pretty easy to commute from the Universal Florida–International Drive area to Walt Disney World via Turkey Lake Road, connecting to Palm Parkway on the northwest side of I-4, or on the southernmost section of I-Drive, connecting to FL 536 on the southeast side of the interstate.

SANFORD INTERNATIONAL AIRPORT

A SHORT DISTANCE NORTHEAST OF ORLANDO is Sanford International Airport (SFB). Small, convenient, and easily accessible, it's totally low-hassle compared with the huge Orlando International Airport (MCO) and its block-long security-checkpoint lines.

The primary domestic carrier serving Sanford International is **Allegiant Air** (☎ 702-505-8888; **allegiantair.com**), with service from large and small airports throughout the eastern United States. European carriers include **ArkeFly** (Netherlands; ☎ 31-0900-2753359; **arkefly .nl**), **Icelandair** (☎ 800-223-5500; **icelandair.com**), **Monarch** (U.K.: ☎ 0871 940 5040; **flymonarch.com**), **Thomas Cook** (U.K.: ☎ 0870 750 0512; **thomascook.com**), and **Thomson Airways** (U.K.: ☎ 0871 231 4787; **flights.thomson.co.uk**). Finally, **SST Air** (☎ 407-407-288-8820; **sstair.com**) offers flights between Orlando and Mexico and Orlando and Brazil.

A reader from Roanoke, Virginia, uses Sanford International frequently, writing:

> *The 45-minute drive to WDW is more than made up for by avoiding the chaos at Orlando International, and it's stress-free.*

SECURITY AT ORLANDO INTERNATIONAL AIRPORT

THIS AIRPORT HANDLES about 34 million passengers a year. It's not unusual to see lines from the checkpoints snaking out of the terminal and into the main shopping corridor and food court. Airport officials sometimes actually shut down moving sidewalks to use them for more queuing space. A number of passengers have reported missing their flights even when they arrived at the airport 90 minutes before departure. System improvements have alleviated some, but by no means all, of the congestion. Most waits to clear security just before we went to press were 25 minutes on average, compared with as many as 55 minutes before the improvements. Even so, there are substantial fluctuations.

GETTING TO WALT DISNEY WORLD FROM THE AIRPORT

YOU HAVE FOUR OPTIONS for getting from Orlando International to Disney World:

1. TAXI Taxis carry four to eight passengers (depending on vehicle type). Rates vary according to distance. If your hotel is in the World, your fare will be about $60, plus tip. For the US 192 Maingate area, it will cost about $55. To International Drive or downtown Orlando, expect to pay in the neighborhood of $33–$39.

unofficial **TIP**
We recommend arriving at Orlando International Airport from 90 minutes to 2 hours before your scheduled departure.

2. SHUTTLE SERVICE Mears Transportation Group (☎ 407-423-5566; **mearstransportation .com**) provides your transportation if your vacation package includes airport transfers. Nonpackage travelers can also use the service. The shuttles collect passengers until they fill a van (or bus). They're then dispatched. Mears charges *per-person* rates (children under age 3 ride free). One-way and round-trip services are available.

FROM THE AIRPORT TO:	ONE-WAY ADULT/CHILD	ROUND-TRIP ADULT/CHILD
INTERNATIONAL DRIVE	$19/$15	$30/$24
DOWNTOWN ORLANDO	$18/$15	$29/$23
WALT DISNEY WORLD–LAKE BUENA VISTA	$21/$17	$34/$27
US 192 MAINGATE AREA	$27/$22	$46/$37

You might have to wait at the airport until a vehicle fills. Once under way, the shuttle will probably stop several times to discharge passengers before reaching your hotel. Obviously, it takes less time to fill a van than a bus, and less time to deliver and unload those passengers.

From your hotel to the airport, you're likely to ride in a van (unless you're part of a tour group, for which Mears might send a bus). Because shuttles make several pickups, they ask you to leave much earlier than you'd depart if you were taking a cab or returning a rental car.

3. TOWN-CAR SERVICE Like a taxi, town-car service will transport you directly from the airport to your hotel. The driver will usually be waiting for you in your airline's baggage-claim area. If saving time and hassle is worth the money, book a town car.

Each town-car service we surveyed offers large, well-appointed late-model sedans, such as the Lincoln Town Car series, or limousines. These hold four persons. To reserve a child's car seat, call ahead. Trunks easily hold golf bags.

Tiffany Towncar Service (☎ 888-838-2161 or 407-370-2196; **tiffanytowncars.com**) provides a prompt, clean ride. The round-trip fee to a Disney or non-Disney resort in a town car is $109 plus tip; one-way is about $60. Tiffany offers a free 30-minute stop at a Publix supermarket en route to your hotel. Also, check Tiffany's website for a coupon worth $5 off a round-trip (valid with online reservations only).

Quicksilver Tours & Transportation (☎ 888-GO-TO-WDW [468-6939] or 407-299-1434; **quicksilver-tours.com**) offers 8-person limos and 10-person vans in addition to town cars. Round-trip rates in a town car range from $110 to $120 depending on location; round-trip rates in a van range from $125 to $135; round-trip limo rate is $240. Like Tiffany, Quicksilver throws in a stop at the supermarket en route.

Mears Transportation Group (☎ 407-423-5566; **mearstranspor tation.com**) also offers a town-car service for around $105 round-trip.

4. RENTAL CARS Short- and long-term rentals are available. Most companies allow drop-off at certain hotels or subsidiary locations in the Disney area if you don't want the vehicle for your entire stay. Likewise, any time during your stay, you can pick up a car at those hotels and locations. Check **mousesavers.com** for rental-car discount codes.

The preferred routes to Walt Disney World, Universal Orlando, SeaWorld, International Drive, and US 192 all involve toll roads. Some roads require exact change to enter or exit via automated gates, and manned toll booths will not accept any denomination bill higher than a $20 bill. So before you leave the airport, make sure you're armed with at least a couple of dollars in quarters and some lower-denomination currency.

DOLLARS AND SENSE Which option is the best deal depends on how many people are in your party and how much you value your time. If you're traveling solo or have only two in your party and you're pretty sure you won't need a rental car, the shuttle is your least expensive bet. A cab for two makes sense if you want to get to your hotel faster than the shuttle can arrange. The cab will cost about $36–$60, including tip. That's $18–$30 per person. The shuttle will cost $20 each (one-way), saving $2–$10 per person. You must decide whether the cab's timeliness and convenience are worth the extra bucks. A one-day car rental costs $40–$70, plus you have to take time to complete the paperwork, get the vehicle, and fill the tank before you return it. The more people in your group, the more economical the cab becomes over the shuttle. Likewise with the rental car, though the cab will get you there faster.

DISNEY'S MAGICAL EXPRESS

DISNEY'S MAGICAL EXPRESS is a free bus service running between Orlando International Airport and most Disney World hotels. Guests with confirmed reservations at most Disney-owned and -operated resorts are eligible, even if their stays have been booked independently of the Walt Disney Travel Company. (The exceptions are guests staying at the Swan, Dolphin, Shades of Green, or any of the independently owned hotels in the Downtown Disney Resort Area.) In addition to transportation, Magical Express provides free luggage-delivery service between your airline and your Disney hotel room, except for flights arriving after 10 p.m., when you'll need to pick up your suitcases from baggage claim.

About two weeks before your departure date, you should receive a document booklet containing your reservation confirmation, transportation vouchers, and special Magical Express luggage tags. Put a tag on any piece of luggage you plan to check with the airline. At the airport, check your bags as you normally would. If all goes well, you'll be reunited with your luggage at your Disney resort hotel room. International travelers must first claim their bags to go through customs and then recheck them; Disney will take over from there.

When you arrive at the terminal, follow the signs to the Magical Express Welcome Center. Here, you'll begin acclimating yourself to Disney regimentation. In other words, you'll wait in your first lines. In front of the queuing area for the Welcome Center, a Disney greeter will ask one or two adults from your party to join the line for initial processing. The rest of your group will sprawl on the floor (there's no seating) and wait for you. This is done in an effort not to jam up the queuing area (which holds only about 300 people) with children and "nonessential" adults. Fortunately, the Welcome Center is adequately staffed, and the line moves quickly. On a weekday, you'll be whisked through in less than 10 minutes; on weekends, especially during crunch time (between 9 a.m. and 5:30 p.m.), it may take upwards of 30 minutes. It's not unusual on a Saturday or Sunday for 10,000 or more guests to move through the Magical Express system.

When you reach the Welcome Center counter, present your document booklet. After your Disney resort reservation is verified, the transportation vouchers in your booklet will be validated. If you accidentally packed your document booklet in your checked baggage, you'll have to ride to Walt Disney World in the back of a stakebed truck carrying goats and free-range chickens (we're kidding; just trying to see if you're paying attention). Actually, if for some reason you can't put your hands on your document booklet, a cast member at the Welcome Center will find your reservation on his computer, reenter all of your information, and get you set up with vouchers for the bus. Furthermore, if you have a Disney resort reservation but you didn't sign up for or know about Magical Express in advance, you can sign up on the spot at the Welcome Center using the same process, but you'll have to handle your own luggage.

After collecting your family, proceed to the bus-queuing area, where you'll present your validated transportation vouchers to a cast member. This queuing area is much larger and can hold maybe 600 or 700 guests. After checking your vouchers, the cast member will direct you to one of five queues depending on your resort destination. Bus routes almost always serve more than one resort (thus, if you're going to the Old Key West Resort, you can expect the bus to also stop at the Port Orleans French Quarter, Port Orleans Riverside, and Saratoga Springs resorts). Each bus holds 55 people, and five buses can load at once. From our observations, you'll be accorded priority attention if you're staying at one of the Deluxe resorts such as the Grand Floridian. Otherwise, a dispatcher controls where the buses are sent based on the number of people in the queue for each route. Buses load slowly—you can't chase people onto a bus the way you'd herd mustangs into a canyon. Once you're under way, it takes about 30 minutes on average to reach the first hotel on the route.

On weekdays, you can expect to reach your hotel anywhere from 70 to 100 minutes from the time you arrived at the Welcome Center; on weekends between 9 a.m. and 5:30 p.m., you're looking at an hour and 45 minutes to 3 hours. In truth, Magical Express functions about as efficiently as possible. But because of certain constraints, such as the number of buses that can be loaded at the same time and uncontrollable variables like the number of arrivals that hit the system at once, Magical Express is subject to being overwhelmed. Remember, though, that with Magical Express you don't have to wait for your luggage at baggage claim. This amounts to about 20 minutes saved that you can net against the overall time it takes to reach your hotel via Magical Express.

Behind the scenes, Disney baggage handlers work with your airline to retrieve suitcases marked with those special tags. All tagged luggage is sent to an airport warehouse, where it's sorted by destination, then loaded onto a truck for delivery. At the resort, the luggage is matched to your reservation. If your room is ready, the luggage is brought up; otherwise it's held by the bellhops until you can check in.

In practice, the logistical challenge of matching totes and tourists is proving to be a bit more than Disney bargained for, with lost and delayed baggage marring the service's reputation. A mother from Baton Rouge, Louisiana, was one of the unlucky ones:

We found out the true meaning of Disney Magical Express: They magically make your luggage disappear. They're still working on the reappear part of the trick. It took about 4 hours for us to get our luggage, which wouldn't have been that bad, except the bellhop showed up at our door with our luggage at 1:30 a.m. After we traveled all day in hopes of getting an early start the next day, this didn't start our trip off well. A word of advice to future travelers: Get your own luggage at the airport!

You can, as the reader suggests, claim your own luggage at baggage claim and bring it to the Magical Express Welcome Center. You'll have to deal with the hassle of dragging your bags around through the various queues, but you'll have the peace of mind of knowing that your luggage is aboard the same bus as you. As noted above, claiming your luggage yourself will add about 20 minutes to the Magical Express process. If you choose to do this, don't attach the Magical Express luggage tags until you reach the Welcome Center. One final word about luggage: Never pack anything in your checked luggage that you might need in the first 24 hours after arriving. This is especially true for documents, medications, eyeglasses or contacts, cell phone chargers, and, for obvious reasons, jewelry.

The night before your flight home, check in with your resort's Airline Check-in Desk to schedule your departure; buses typically leave 3 hours before your flight. You can check your baggage and receive your domestic flight boarding pass at the front desk of your Disney resort. This service is available to all Disney resort guests, even those who have rental cars. Resort check-in counters are open from 5 a.m. until 1 p.m., and you must check in no later than 3 hours before your flight. Participating airlines are **AirTran, Alaska, American, Delta, JetBlue, Southwest, United,** and **US Airways.**

The following comments relating readers' experiences with Disney's Magical Express are representative. First, from a Houston mother of two:

Magical Express was great, but do plan for a couple of hours—like, 3 or 4—before your luggage arrives.

A Provo, Utah, mom loved the Express:

Magical Express was heavenly. Not worrying about lugging six suitcases around and arriving and departing quickly and comfortably was the cherry on top of the vacation.

But a dad from Monroe, Washington, is rethinking the whole deal:

One thing I think you need to stress is planning around the Magical Express. It took over 2 hours to get from the airport to Animal Kingdom Lodge as we were waiting for the bus to fill up, and AKL is the last stop for the drop-off. Luckily, we were able to push our dinner reservations out, but next time I think I'll take a shuttle or a cab.

From a Provo, Utah, dad:

Magical Express got us to the Port Orleans Riverside by about 10 a.m. The line to check in stretched across the entire lobby, and only three clerks were working. It took 90 minutes or more just to get through the line. This is because buses drop whole busloads of guests at once. Non–Magical Express guests are affected, too, if they try to check in just after a Magical Express bus has unloaded.

Regarding the previous comment, always try to find a seat as close to a door as possible. When the bus reaches your resort, you'll be one of the first to get off and one of the first to reach the check-in desk.

A reader from Simsbury, Connecticut, reports:

Disney is a park operator, not a baggage handler. If you check your bags through to your room on Magical Express, don't expect to get them until well after you get to your hotel. Our bags didn't get to the room until 11:30 p.m., almost 6 hours after our plane touched down. On our next visit, we'll handle our luggage ourselves.

A Bloomington, Illinois, couple narrowly made their flight:

Magical Express? Well, that's a misnomer if I've ever heard one. On the way to our resort, we stopped off at three other resorts first, which had us beginning our vacation 30–40 minutes later than we'd hoped. I thought, "Fine, we'll be able to sleep in a little on the last day." Wrong! We stopped at the same three resorts AFTER we were picked up, arriving at the last resort 50 minutes after we had departed. I understand that someone has to be first and someone has to be last, but I thought it was crummy that we drew the short end of the stick both coming and going. We were on the bus on departure day for a total of 1 hour and 40 minutes, and our flight began boarding less than 15 minutes after we reached the gate. That's cutting it a little close in my opinion—and we were picked up 3 hours before our departure time!

A dad from Ontario, Canada, warns:

It should be explained that on the return trip to the airport your bags do not automatically go on the Magical Express—you must get them using claim tickets and put them on the bus yourself. Had it not been for the bus driver, I would have left the resort without my baggage and arrived at the airport thinking that all I had to do was show the driver my claim ticket. The bus driver told me it has happened in the past.

Finally, from a Voorhees, New Jersey, dad:

You may want to add a caveat for Magical Express users arriving late at night: The time that they arrive at their hotel could vary wildly. Since it appears Disney combines a lot of different hotels onto one bus, to make up for the lesser volume of passengers late at night, you may arrive late at your hotel if it's not one of the first stops. I was pleased to walk right onto a bus around 10:50 p.m., just after checking in at the Magical Express desk; we left the airport at 11:07 and arrived at the first resort at 11:39. However, after stopping at four other resorts (not located near one another), I didn't reach Wilderness Lodge until 12:11 a.m.

RENTING A CAR

READERS PLANNING TO STAY IN WALT DISNEY WORLD ask frequently if they'll need a car. If your plans don't include restaurants, attractions, or destinations outside Disney World, then the answer is a very qualified no. But consider the thoughts of this reader from Snohomish, Washington:

We rented a car and were glad we did. It gave us more options, though we used the Disney bus transportation quite extensively. With a car we could drive to the grocery store to restock our snack supply. It also came in handy for our night out. I shudder at how long it might have taken us to get from the Caribbean Beach to the Polynesian to leave our kids at the child-care facility, then back to the Polynesian to get the kids, and then back to the Caribbean Beach.

A dad from Avon Lake, Ohio, adds:

It was unbelievable how often we used our rental car. Although we stayed at the Grand Floridian, we found the monorail convenient only for the Magic Kingdom. Of the six nights we stayed, we used our car five days.

A Portland, Maine, family had a complaint about non-Disney transportation:

We stayed outside WDW and tried to commute on the bus furnished by our hotel. After two days, we gave up and rented a car.

From an Ann Arbor, Michigan, mother of three:

During our stay it was almost impossible to get into any of the Disney restaurants. Purely out of desperation, we rented a car so we could eat outside WDW. We had no problem finding good places to

Rent at the Airport or Off-Site?

If you take a look at the taxes and other fees you're billed when you rent a car at an airport, you might wonder whether a better deal might be available off-site, where many of the extra charges don't apply. Our research team set out to determine whether such deals existed in the Orlando market off airport property.

As in past years, we began by obtaining quotes from the websites of all the car-rental companies in the Orlando airport—for economy cars, midsize vehicles, and minivans—for Saturday–Saturday one-week rentals during every month from June through December, including Thanksgiving and Christmas. We also got quotes for companies near the airport, at major hotels around International Drive, and on Disney property, plus Costco—more than 300 quotes in all. To get the very best prices, we also used car-rental discount codes available at **MouseSavers** (**mousesavers .com**). Our research indicates you'll only need to look at the following rental companies and locations to find the best deals:

1. When it comes to economy cars, **Alamo** and **Dollar** locations at the airport are the two least expensive choices for every week we checked except for holiday weekends. For Alamo, combine coupon code **AD7893SDX** and discount code ID **7014133;** for Dollar, use code **VO5013.** You must enter the discount and coupon codes for Alamo at the same time in order to get the discount; also, you won't see the complete discount until you're almost done booking on the Alamo website.

2. A new face on the Orlando car-rental scene, **Sixt** (**sixt.com**) has the lowest rates on cars during the fall (September–November). Sixt is a

eat at a fraction of what you'd pay inside. With five of us, we saved several times over what we paid for the rental car.

A dad from Vancouver, British Columbia, implores readers to get their act together before they reach the rental counter:

You should strongly encourage readers to decide what options they want beforehand! When I arrived at the Dollar counter at Orlando Airport on a Wednesday night at 6 p.m., there were 20 customers waiting in line and 5 agents. It took 45 minutes before it was my turn. Many of us in line were muttering about the agents trying to upsell, but the real problem was customers who didn't know what they wanted. Everyone in front of me took at least 10 minutes with an agent. One guy spent most of his time talking to someone on his cell phone, trying to decide what to get while the agent waited! When it was my turn, it took me 2 minutes because I knew what I wanted and I had already filled out my rental info online.

PLAN TO RENT A CAR

1. If your hotel is outside Walt Disney World.

2. If your hotel is in the World and you want to dine someplace other than the theme parks and your hotel.

100-year-old German company whose first Florida locations were in Miami and Fort Lauderdale, and it has recently expanded to Orlando. Its website definitely has a translated-from-German feel to it—your user name and password are referred to as your "comfort login," for example. But Sixt's rates often save $300 per week versus Avis and Hertz, so comfort login it is!

3. Looking at minivans? The airport location of **Dollar** (code: **CO5013**) will do right by you almost any time of year. If they're out of cars during your trip, though, check at the **Enterprise** at the Royal Plaza hotel in Downtown Disney.

Except for certain holidays (see facing page), renting a car at the airport is always cheaper than off-site. Off-site rental locations typically have little nearby competition, so they can charge higher rates.

For families, whatever markdowns may be available off-site may not be worth the cab fare and hassle of shuttling kids and luggage back and forth. If, for instance, you're planning on renting around Downtown Disney, you should factor in a $52 cab ride each way from the airport for a family of four. (Orlando's public bus service, **LYNX**, is $2 a person from the airport to Downtown Disney, but you also have to factor in a long walk—a mile to the farthest rental place.)

If you're staying at a hotel with a rental office, it doesn't hurt to call and ask about specials for guests. But in general, the airport is a pretty good deal, unless you're looking at minivans for the holidays.

3. If you plan to return to your hotel for naps or swimming during the day.

4. If you plan to visit other area theme parks or water parks (including Disney's).

Renting a Car at Orlando International Airport

The airport has two terminals: A and B. Airlines serving Orlando are assigned to one or the other. Each terminal has three levels and a parking garage. Ticket counters are on Level Three. Baggage claim is on Level Two. Level One is where car-rental counters are or where you'll catch a courtesy vehicle to an off-site rental company location.

Orlando is the world's largest rental-car market. At last count, 25 companies competed for your business. Twelve—**Advantage, Alamo, Avis, Budget, Dollar, Enterprise, E-Z Rent-A-Car, Hertz, L&M, National, Sixt,** and **Thrifty**—have counters on Level One of both terminals. **Payless** and 12 other companies have locations near the airport and provide courtesy shuttles outside Level One at both terminals. Most shuttles run continuously; you don't have to call for pickup. We prefer using one of the companies inside the airport because (1) you can complete your paperwork while you wait for your checked luggage to arrive at baggage claim and (2) it's a short walk to the garage to pick up your car (no shuttle needed).

If you rent from an on-site company, you'll return your car to the garage adjacent to the terminal where your airline is located. If you return your car to the wrong garage, you'll have to haul your luggage on foot from one side of the airport to the other in order to reach your check-in.

Most rental companies charge about $5–$8 a gallon if they fill the tank. If you plan to drive extensively, prepay for a tank of gas so you can return the car empty. Alternatively, fill up near your hotel on your way back to the airport. If you're taking the FL 417 toll road, turn right at the Airport/Boggy Creek Road exit and drive about a mile to find the closest gas station to Orlando International.

How the Orlando Rental-Car Companies Stack Up

Unofficial Guide readers provide lots of information about the quality of the car and service they receive from Orlando car-rental companies. Most folks are looking for:

1. Quick, courteous, and efficient processing on pickup.

2. A nice, well-maintained, late-model automobile.

3. A car that is clean and odor-free.

4. Quick, courteous, and efficient processing on return.

5. If applicable, an efficient shuttle between the rental agency and airport.

COMPANY	PICKUP EFFICIENCY	CONDITION OF CAR	CLEANLINESS OF CAR	RETURN EFFICIENCY	SHUTTLE EFFICIENCY	OVERALL RATING
ALAMO	88	88	88	94	–	90
AVIS	76	86	92	88	–	86
BUDGET	76	90	92	94	–	88
DOLLAR	82	88	90	96	–	89
ENTERPRISE	86	88	92	94	–	90
HERTZ	80	92	94	92	–	90
L&M	–	–	–	–	–	–
NATIONAL	90	94	96	94	–	94
PAYLESS	70	70	90	80	98	82
SIXT	–	–	–	–	–	–
THRIFTY	72	86	98	74	–	83

Most of our readers rent from Alamo, Avis, Budget, Dollar, Hertz, or National. On a scale of 0 (worst) to 100 (best), the table directly above shows how they rate the Orlando operations of each company, based on the five points listed just above the table. If you'd like to participate in our rental-car survey, please complete and return the form at the back of this book.

For the fourth year in a row, **National Car Rental** ranks highest in overall satisfaction among *Unofficial Guide* readers. That accomplishment is in addition to having fairly low rates. Another great National feature is its automated kiosks—you can rent the car and get keys from a machine at the airport without having to wait in long lines.

If you rent a car, a 6–7% sales tax, $2.05-per-day state surcharge, and 31¢- to $1.45-per-day vehicle-license-recovery fee will be heaped onto your final bill. If you rent from an agency with airport facilities or shuttles, a 10% airport tax will be added. Remember: You can rent a car at your hotel on the day you actually need it.

As a measure of how long you have to stand in line before you're assisted by a rental agent, we observed the number of people in line at each rental-car company's counter from 9:30 a.m. to 4:30 p.m., the period during which most people arrive. Observations were recorded at both Terminals A and B. L&M, a local company, almost never had a line. Customers were processed the moment they walked up. Budget, Avis, Dollar, and National averaged between two and six persons in line, with an average of three agents (four to five agents during the busiest times) working the counter. Alamo averaged a whopping 25 people in line, with three to six (average 4.4) agents. In processing customers, Dollar and Avis were fastest, at 5$\frac{1}{10}$ minutes per renter. Alamo and National each required 6½ minutes, and Budget and L&M came in last at just over 8 minutes.

unofficial **TIP**
To save time in front of the computer, first check **dollar.com** or **thrifty .com** for rates; one of those sites always had the lowest price for every date we checked.

The Insurance Thing

The following reader report is about an incident with Alamo, but we've encountered variations on this scenario all across the nation with a number of different car-rental companies.

unofficial **TIP**
The easiest way to avoid standing in line at a car-rental counter is to sign up for the company's "frequent renter" program before your trip. Most programs are free and allow you to skip long waits in line to receive your car. We've used the free membership programs of Dollar and Budget for years; Alamo, Avis, National, and Hertz have similar no-cost programs.

Our family recently went on a trip to Walt Disney World and had a wonderful time that was marred only by our experience with Alamo Rent A Car. We reserved a car in advance and were quoted an estimated cost. Then, after arriving at the Orlando airport, we went to pick up our rental car. The Alamo desk clerk looked at our auto-insurance card and informed us quite clearly that our insurance wouldn't cover collision damage to the car. Already quite tired following a very early morning and with two kids in tow who were anxious to get to Disney World, we agreed to the extra coverage.

Later, after finding the time to read all the fine print, it became clear that we had paid a good amount of unnecessary insurance fees. The final cost for the car was double the original quote. Following the trip, we spoke with our insurance company; their response concerning rental-car companies was, "Yes, of course we cover collisions." Perhaps had we been more seasoned travelers, we wouldn't have allowed ourselves to be taken advantage of, but hopefully others can learn from our experience.

The point here is not whether Alamo took advantage of the reader, but rather that anyone who rents a car should know what his or her auto insurance does and doesn't cover. If you have the slightest question about your coverage, call your insurance agent. For the record, it's very rare for an auto-insurance policy not to cover a vehicle rented and driven in the United States. A corollary discussion pertains to added coverage from your credit card company if the rental fee is charged on the card. Usually, credit card coverage picks up deductibles and some ancillary charges that your auto-insurance policy doesn't cover. The tune is the same, however: Make sure you understand what is and isn't covered.

GETTING ORIENTED

A GOOD MAP

READERS FREQUENTLY COMPLAIN about signs and maps provided by Disney. While it's easy to find the major theme parks, locating other Disney destinations can be challenging. Many Disney-supplied maps are stylized and hard to read, while others provide incomplete information. The most easily obtained map is in Walt Disney World's "Your Guide to the Magic" guide. Available at any resort or theme park Guest Relations office, the guide provides a reduced version of the Walt Disney World Property Map and information on the Disney transportation system. The guide also covers dining, recreation, and shopping. Unfortunately, Disney isn't very good about updating its property map. New interstate and expressway interchanges take months or even years to show up. For example, the huge new west entrance to Walt Disney World off FL 429, open since 2007, is yet to make an appearance. In fact, FL 429 itself isn't shown! The Disney map is fine for sorting out bus routes, but if you really need to navigate, the maps in this guide are much more current.

A very good map of the Orlando–Kissimmee–Disney World area is free at the **AAA Car Care Center** operated by Goodyear near the Magic Kingdom parking lot.

FINDING YOUR WAY AROUND

WALT DISNEY WORLD IS LIKE ANY BIG CITY. It's easy to get lost. Signs for the theme parks are excellent, but finding a restaurant or hotel is often confusing. The easiest way to orient yourself is to think in terms of five major areas, or clusters (see map on pages 384 and 385):

1. The first encompasses all hotels and theme parks around Seven Seas Lagoon. This includes the Magic Kingdom, hotels connected by the monorail, Shades of Green Resort, and a golf course.

2. The second includes developments on and around Bay Lake: Wilderness Lodge & Villas, Fort Wilderness Campground, and one golf course.

3. Cluster three contains Epcot, Disney's Hollywood Studios, the BoardWalk, ESPN Wide World of Sports, Epcot resort hotels, Pop Century Resort, Art of Animation Resort, and Caribbean Beach Resort.

4. The fourth cluster encompasses Downtown Disney (including Downtown Disney Marketplace and Downtown Disney West Side); Typhoon Lagoon water park; a golf course; the Downtown Disney Resort Area; and the Port Orleans, Saratoga Springs, and Old Key West resorts.

5. The fifth cluster contains Disney's Animal Kingdom; Blizzard Beach water park;

and Animal Kingdom Lodge & Villas, the All-Star Resorts, and Coronado Springs Resort.

HOW *to* TRAVEL *around the* WORLD *(or, The* Real *Mr. Toad's Wild Ride)*

TRYING TO COMMUTE AROUND WALT DISNEY WORLD can be frustrating. A Magic Kingdom street vendor, telling us how to get to Epcot, proposed, "You can take the ferry or the monorail to the Transportation and Ticket Center. Then you can get another monorail, or you can catch the bus, or you can take a tram out to your car and drive over there yourself." What he didn't say was that it would be easier to ride a mule than to take any conceivable combination from this transportation smorgasbord.

unofficial **TIP**
There's no simple way to travel around the World, but there are ways to make it easier. Just give yourself plenty of time.

TRANSPORTATION TRADE-OFFS FOR GUESTS LODGING OUTSIDE WALT DISNEY WORLD

DAY GUESTS (THOSE STAYING OUTSIDE THE WORLD) can use the monorail, bus, and boat systems. Our most important advice for these guests is to park in the lot of the theme park (or other Disney destination) where they plan to finish their day. This is critical if you stay at a park until closing.

Moving Your Car from Lot to Lot on the Same Day

Once you've paid to park in any major theme park lot ($14 per day), show your receipt and you'll be admitted into another park's lot on the same day without further charge. Annual Pass holders and Disney resort guests park free in any theme park lot.

ALL YOU NEED TO KNOW ABOUT DRIVING TO THE THEME PARKS

1. POSITIONING OF THE PARKING LOTS Disney's Animal Kingdom, Disney's Hollywood Studios, and Epcot parking lots are adjacent to each park's entrance. The Magic Kingdom lot is adjacent to the Transportation and Ticket Center (TTC). From the TTC, take a ferry or monorail to the park's entrance.

2. PAYING TO PARK Disney resort guests and Annual Pass holders park free. All others pay. If you pay to park and you move your car during that day, show your receipt and you won't have to pay at the new lot.

3. FINDING YOUR CAR WHEN IT'S TIME TO DEPART Parking lots are huge. Jot down the section and row where you park. If you're driving a rental car, note the license-plate number.

4. GETTING FROM YOUR CAR TO THE PARK ENTRANCE Each lot provides trams to the park entrance or, at the Magic Kingdom, to the TTC.

Continued on page 386

Walt Disney World Touring & Hotel Clusters

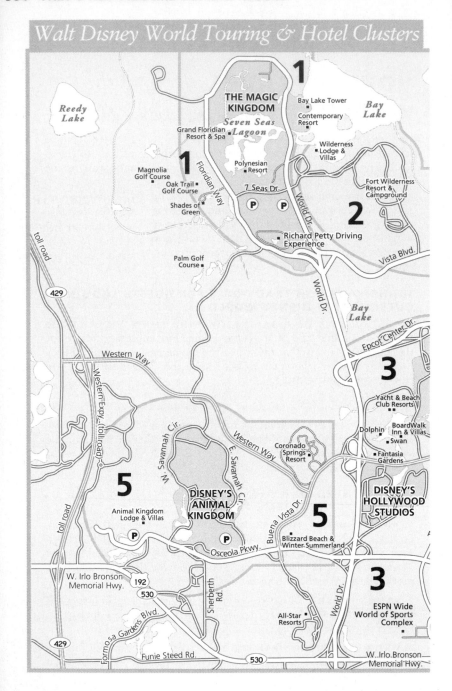

1

THE MAGIC KINGDOM

Seven Seas Lagoon

Reedy Lake

Bay Lake Tower

Contemporary Resort

Bay Lake

Grand Floridian Resort & Spa

Wilderness Lodge & Villas

1

Magnolia Golf Course

Oak Trail Golf Course

Shades of Green

Polynesian Resort

7 Seas Dr.

Fort Wilderness Resort & Campground

2

P

P

Richard Petty Driving Experience

Vista Blvd.

Palm Golf Course

World Dr.

Bay Lake

toll road

Floridian Way

World Dr.

429

Epcot Center Dr.

3

Western Way

Yacht & Beach Club Resorts

Western Expy. (toll road)

BoardWalk Inn & Villas

Dolphin

Swan

W. Savannah Cir.

Western Way

Coronado Springs Resort

Fantasia Gardens

5

E. Savannah Cir.

DISNEY'S ANIMAL KINGDOM

Buena Vista Dr.

5

DISNEY'S HOLLYWOOD STUDIOS

Animal Kingdom Lodge & Villas

P

P

Osceola Pkwy.

Blizzard Beach & Winter Summerland

toll road

W. Irlo Bronson Memorial Hwy.

192

530

Sherberth Rd.

World Dr.

3

ESPN Wide World of Sports Complex

429

Formosa Gardens Blvd.

Funie Steed Rd.

All-Star Resorts

530

W. Irlo Bronson Memorial Hwy.

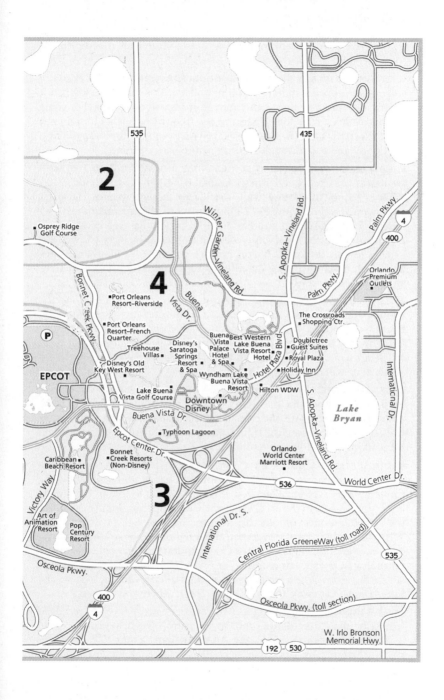

Continued from page 383

If you arrive early in the morning, it may be faster to walk to the entrance (or TTC) than to take the tram.

5. GETTING TO DISNEY'S ANIMAL KINGDOM FOR PARK OPENING If you're staying on-property and are planning to be at this theme park when it opens, take a Disney bus from your resort instead of driving. For some reason, Animal Kingdom's parking lot frequently opens 15 minutes before the park itself—which doesn't leave you enough time to park, hop on a tram, and pass through security before park opening.

6. HOW MUCH TIME TO ALLOT FOR PARKING AND GETTING TO THE PARK ENTRANCE At Epcot and Disney's Animal Kingdom, figure about 10–15 minutes to pay, park, and walk or ride to the entrance. At Disney's Hollywood Studios, allow 8–12 minutes; at the Magic Kingdom, 10–15 minutes to the TTC and another 20–30 to reach the park entrance via the monorail (most of which is waiting to board) or ferry (slower but usually less in demand). If you haven't purchased your theme park admission in advance, tack on another 10–20 minutes before you actually enter the park.

7. COMMUTING FROM PARK TO PARK You can commute among the theme parks via Disney bus, or to and from the Magic Kingdom and Epcot by monorail. You also, of course, can commute in your own car. Using Disney transportation or your car, allow 45–60 minutes entrance to entrance one-way. If you plan to park-hop, leave your car in the lot of the park where you'll finish the day.

8. LEAVING THE PARK AT THE END OF THE DAY If you stay at a park until closing, expect the parking-lot trams, monorails, and ferries to be mobbed. If the wait for the tram is unacceptable, walk to your car, or walk to the first stop on the tram route and wait there for a tram. When someone gets off, you can get on.

9. DINNER AND A QUICK EXIT One way to beat closing crowds at the Magic Kingdom is to arrange reservations for dinner at a restaurant in the Contemporary Resort. When you leave the Magic Kingdom for dinner, move your car from the TTC lot to the Contemporary lot. After dinner, walk (8–10 minutes) or take the monorail back to the Magic Kingdom. When the park closes and everyone else is fighting to board the monorail or ferry, you can stroll back to the Contemporary, claim your car, and get on your way. Use the same strategy at Epcot by arranging a reservation at an Epcot resort. When the park closes after *IllumiNations*, exit via the International Gateway and walk to the resort where you parked.

10. CAR TROUBLE All parking lots have security patrols. If you have a dead battery or minor automotive problem, the patrols will help you.

For more serious trouble, the **AAA Car Care Center** (☎ 407-824-0976), operated by Goodyear near the Magic Kingdom parking lot, will help. Prices for most services are comparable to those at home. The facility stays busy; expect to leave your car unless the fix is simple.

11. SCORING A GREAT PARKING PLACE If you arrive at a park after noon or move your car from park to park, there will be empty parking spaces near the entrance vacated by early guests who have left. Instead of following Disney signage or being directed by staff to a distant space, drive to the front and hunt a space, or use the approach of a Coopersburg, Pennsylvania, couple:

> *After leaving Epcot on our first day for a lunch break, we returned to find a fullish parking lot. We were unhappy because we had left a third-row parking spot. My husband told the attendant that we had left just an hour ago and that there were lots of spaces up front. Without a word of protest, he waved us to the front, and we got the same spot we had left!*

12. AAA PARKING If you purchase certain Walt Disney World vacation packages from AAA, you'll receive a special Diamond parking card. Show it at the parking-fee booth and you'll be directed to a reserved parking area (if capacity allows). Each park's AAA area is handled differently. Parking-lot cast members will instruct you as required.

GOOD FUZZ, BAD FUZZ

FOR AS LONG AS ANYONE CAN REMEMBER, Disney World security imposed little to no restraint on speeding drivers. In more than 20 years, we've received not one letter or e-mail from readers about being pulled over. However, we've been alerted to the increasing presence of Orange County law enforcement busting speeders on Disney World property. So for the lead-footed among you, there will be no more Fairy Godmother treatment, and the character with the flashing blue lights isn't Goofy.

SNEAK ROUTES

SNEAK ROUTE IS A WHITEWATER-PADDLING TERM for an easy way through tough rapids. Unfortunately, not all difficult rapids have a sneak route. For those that don't, there's only one way through: the hard way. As we research this guide, we're constantly looking for ways to avoid traffic snarls. For some roads and areas, there are no alternative routes. For others, we have discovered sneak routes.

THE LIGHTS OF DOWNTOWN DISNEY Although dozens of searchlights blaze at Downtown Disney after dark, what we're talking about here are the many multifunction traffic signals on Buena Vista Drive in front of Downtown Disney. Buena Vista Drive near Downtown Disney is a traffic bottleneck of the first order. Heaven help you if you're traveling from Coronado Springs Resort to Downtown Disney—you'll encounter up to 19 traffic signals in the 5-mile drive, or roughly one every quarter-mile. In the evening especially, this commute can take up to 30 minutes. It wouldn't be so bad if only traffic to Downtown Disney was affected, but because Buena Vista Drive is one of Walt Disney World's most important traffic arteries, the traffic jam is on the order of a blocked coronary ventricle.

Most traffic entering and exiting Walt Disney World from the FL 535 entrance must run this traffic-signal gauntlet, and so too must guests staying at the seven hotels of the Downtown Disney Resort Area and Disney's Saratoga Springs Resort when traveling to Epcot, Disney's Hollywood Studios, the Magic Kingdom, Disney's Animal Kingdom, and Typhoon Lagoon. To avoid the bottlenecked area

International Drive Area Sneak Routes

Windover Dr.

Florida's Turnpike

East to Downtown Orlando

Vineland Rd.

77

4

435

Major Blvd.

Caravan Ct.

Universal Orlando

75B

Oak Ridge Rd.

W. Oak Ridge Rd.

Hollywood Way

Prime Outlets Orlando

Grand National Dr.

International Dr.

Turkey Lake Rd.

Adventure Way

74B

75A

American Way

Kirkman Rd.

Del Verde Way

Wet 'n Wild

International Dr.

Carrier Dr.

Canada Ave.

482

Sand Lake Rd.

74A

Universal Blvd.

Jamaican Ct.

Austrian Ct.

Austrian Row

Official Visitor Center

International Dr.

Samoan Ct.

4

Universal Blvd.

Universal Blvd. W.

Universal Blvd.

Orange County Convention Center

Destination Pkwy.

Hawaiian Ct.

To Orlando International Airport →

528

Sneak route (two-way traffic)

International Drive (area to avoid)

Bridge or overpass

Interstate 4 Exits

77	Florida's Turnpike
75A	Universal Studios/ International Drive
75B	Kirkman Road
74B	Universal Studios
74A	Sand Lake Road
72	FL 528 (Beachline Expressway)
71	Central Florida GreeneWay

72

(no toll)

Beachline Expy. (toll road)

Aquatica

West to Walt Disney World Resort & Tampa

Turkey Lake Rd.

71

Westwood Blvd.

Sea Harbor Dr.

International Dr.

SeaWorld Orlando

Discovery Cove

Central Florida GreeneWay

requires long but nearly traffic-free circumnavigation. Coming from the theme parks, you can bypass the mess by taking I-4 or alternatively by looping around on Bonnet Creek Parkway and Disney Vacation Club Way. If you're going back to an Epcot or Magic Kingdom resort from Downtown Disney, it may be faster to take I-4 West and follow the signs back to Disney property. Any way you look at it, though, it's a small (congested) world.

INTERNATIONAL DRIVE (I-DRIVE) By far the most difficult area to navigate without long traffic delays is International Drive. Most hotels on I-Drive are between Kirkman Road to the north and FL 417/Central Florida GreeneWay to the south. Between Kirkman Road and FL 417, three major roads cross I-Drive. From north to south on I-Drive (in the direction of Disney World), the first major crossroad is Universal Boulevard. Next south is Sand Lake Road (FL 482), pretty squarely in the middle of the hotel district. Then farther south, the Beachline Expressway (FL 528) connects I-4 and the airport.

I-Drive is a mess for a number of reasons: scarcity of left-turn lanes, long multidirectional traffic signals, and, most critically, very limited access to westbound I-4 (toward Disney). From the Orange County Convention Center south to the Beachline Expressway and FL 417/Central Florida GreeneWay, getting on westbound I-4 is straightforward and easy. But in the stretch where the hotels are concentrated (from Kirkman Road to about a mile south of Sand Lake Road), the only way most visitors know to access I-4

unofficial **TIP**
To locate your I-Drive hotel, check **iridetrolley.com** or call ☎ 866-2-i-drive and request the I-Ride Trolley Route Map. It will help you pinpoint your hotel within about 200 yards.

westbound is to fight through the gridlock of the I-Drive–Sand Lake Road intersection en route to the I-4–Sand Lake Road interchange. A long, long traffic signal, a sea of motorists, and insufficient turn lanes make this absolutely grueling.

The object, therefore, is to access I-4 westbound without getting on Sand Lake Road. If your hotel is north of Sand Lake, access Kirkman Road by going north on I-Drive (in the opposite direction of the heaviest traffic) to the Kirkman Road intersection and turning left, or by cutting over to Kirkman via eastbound Carrier Drive. In either case, take Kirkman north over I-4, and at the first traffic signal (at the entrance to Universal Orlando), make a U-turn. This will put you directly onto an I-4 westbound ramp. A second way to access I-4 westbound from this section of I-Drive is to take Universal Boulevard (parallels I-Drive to the east) north. After you cross I-4 onto Universal property, stay left and follow the signs through two left turns to I-4. The signs are small, so stay alert.

If your hotel is south of Sand Lake Road but north of Austrian Court, cut over to Universal Boulevard, which parallels I-Drive to the east. Do this via Austrian Row. Turn right (south) on Universal Boulevard. Continue until you intersect the Beachline Expressway, and then take the Beachline west to I-4 (no toll).

US 192 (IRLO BRONSON MEMORIAL HIGHWAY) US 192, known locally as the Irlo Bronson Memorial Highway, runs east–west along the southern border of Disney World. From the Disney World entrance west on US 192 toward Clermont and east toward Kissimmee is a concentration of hotels. The highway was widened in 2001–02, and, though heavily used, it has ample turn lanes and traffic flows pretty well. The problem is the many long, multidirectional traffic signals.

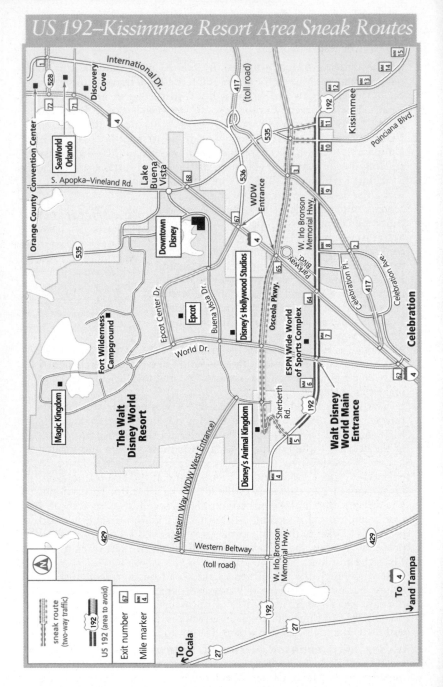

US 192–Kissimmee Resort Area Sneak Routes

Even so, driving US 192 is easy compared with International Drive. Best of all, there are no god-awful intersections like that of I-Drive and Sand Lake Road.

I-4 Sneak Routes

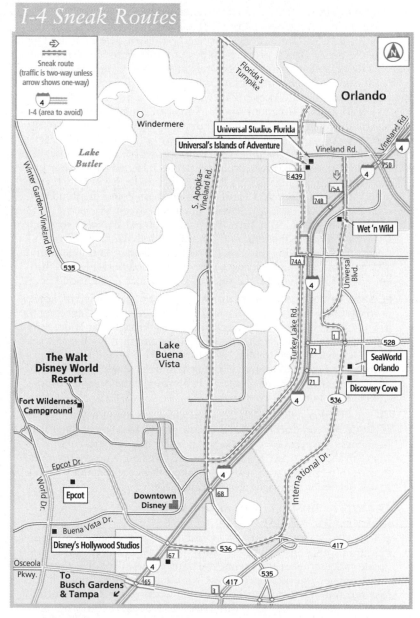

Conspicuous mile markers are posted along US 192. If you know which marker is closest to your hotel, navigation is a snap. The main entrance (Maingate) to Disney World is between Mile Markers 6 and 7, and almost all US 192 hotels and restaurants are between Mile Markers 4 and 15. If your hotel is between Markers 5 and 10, no sneak routes are necessary. If it's between Markers 1 and 5, save time by entering Disney property via Sherberth Road, which runs into Disney's Animal

Kingdom and the west end of Osceola Parkway. This road existed before Animal Kingdom or Osceola Parkway, but there are absolutely no signs on US 192 indicating that Sherberth Road affords a shortcut into and out of Disney property. When you turn onto Sherberth from US 192, bear right almost immediately at the fork. Continue until you reach a major intersection with Disney signage. Turn right and then continue straight to Osceola Parkway and most of Disney World, or go left to Animal Kingdom Lodge. To get to Animal Kingdom, turn right and look immediately for the turn lane that will take you into the theme park's parking lot. Osceola Parkway, a toll road, doesn't levy tolls until it crosses I-4 and leaves Disney property.

If your hotel is between Markers 10 and 15, save time (but pay modest tolls) by taking Osceola Parkway west to Disney World. If your hotel is between Markers 10 and 11, go north on Poinciana Boulevard to access Osceola Parkway. If your hotel is between Markers 11 and 15, go north on FL 535. Turn west onto Osceola Parkway to reach Disney's Animal Kingdom and Disney's Hollywood Studios. For Epcot, the Magic Kingdom, and Downtown Disney, continue on FL 535 past the Osceola Parkway to the intersection with FL 536. Turn left on FL 536 and follow the signs to your Disney destination.

FL 535 (APOPKA–VINELAND ROAD) There are a number of hotels northeast and southwest of I-4 on FL 535 and on streets connecting to it. Though many guests commute to the parks through Disney property via Hotel Plaza Drive to Downtown Disney and then via Buena Vista Drive, it's much easier to take I-4 west from FL 535 and enter Disney property on Epcot Center Drive for Epcot and the Magic Kingdom, and on Osceola Parkway for Disney's Hollywood Studios and Disney's Animal Kingdom.

I-4 Construction at the I-4–US 192 interchange was completed in 2009, so many of the construction-related delays on I-4 have been eliminated. Nevertheless, expect heavy traffic and possible delays westbound on I-4 from 7 to about 9:30 a.m. Eastbound toward Orlando, expect heavy traffic from 4 to 7 p.m. If you want to avoid I-4 altogether, check out our I-4 sneak routes, detailed in the map on the previous page.

TAKING A SHUTTLE BUS FROM YOUR OUT-OF-THE-WORLD HOTEL

MANY INDEPENDENT HOTELS and motels near Disney World provide trams and buses. They're fairly carefree, depositing you near theme park entrances and saving you parking fees. The rub is that they might not get you there as early as you desire (a critical point if you take our touring advice) or be available when you wish to return to your lodging. Each service is different; check details before you make reservations.

Some shuttles go directly to Disney World, while others stop at other hotels en route. This can be a problem if your hotel is the second or third stop on the route. During periods of high demand, buses frequently fill up at the first stop, leaving little or no room for passengers at subsequent stops. Before booking, inquire how many hotels are on the route and the sequence of the stops. The different hotels are often so close together that you can easily walk to the first hotel on the route and board there. Similarly, if there's a large hotel nearby, it might have its own dedicated bus service that is more efficient. Use it instead of the service provided by your hotel. The majority of out-of-the-World shuttles work on a fixed schedule instead of arriving and departing somewhat randomly like the Disney buses. Knowing exactly when a bus will depart makes it easier to plan your day.

A multigenerational family from Seattle shares their experience:

We stayed at a hotel off-site and it was fine, but I think next time we'll stay in the World. The shuttles weren't all that convenient or frequent, so we ended up taking taxis more than we thought we would.

unofficial TIP
Warning: Most shuttles don't add vehicles at park-opening or -closing times. In the mornings, you may not get a seat.

At closing or during a hard rain, more people will be waiting for the shuttle than it can hold, and some will be left behind. Most shuttles return for stranded guests, but guests may wait 20 minutes to more than an hour.

If you're depending on shuttles, leave the park at least 45 minutes before closing. If you stay until closing and don't want to hassle with the shuttle, take a cab. Cab stands are near the Bus Information buildings at Disney's Animal Kingdom, Epcot, Disney's Hollywood Studios, and the TTC. If no cabs are on hand, Bus Information staff will call one. If you're leaving the Magic Kingdom at closing, it's easier to take the monorail to a hotel and hail a cab there rather than at the TTC taxi stand.

THE DISNEY TRANSPORTATION SYSTEM

THE DISNEY TRANSPORTATION SYSTEM (DTS) IS LARGE, diversified, and generally efficient, but it sometimes is overwhelmed, particularly at park-opening and -closing times. If you could be assured of getting on a bus, boat, or monorail at these critical times, we would advise you to leave your car at home. However, when huge crowds want to go somewhere at the same time, delays are unavoidable. In addition, some destinations are served directly, while many others require one or more transfers. Finally, it's sometimes difficult to figure how the buses, boats, and monorails interconnect.

Basically, Disney has a "hub and spoke" system. Hubs include the TTC, Downtown Disney, and all four major theme parks (from 2 hours before official opening time to 2–3 hours after closing). Although there are exceptions, there's direct service from Disney resorts to the major theme parks and Downtown Disney, and between parks.

If a hotel offers boat or monorail service, its bus service will be limited; you'll have to transfer at a hub for many destinations. If you're staying at a Magic Kingdom resort that's served by the monorail (Polynesian, Contemporary–Bay Lake Tower, Grand Floridian), you'll be able to commute efficiently to the Magic Kingdom. If you want to visit Epcot, you must take the monorail to the TTC and transfer to the Epcot monorail. (Guests at the Polynesian can eliminate the transfer by walking 5–10 minutes to the TTC and catching the direct monorail to Epcot.)

Continued on page 396

Door-to-Door Commuting Times to and from the Disney Resorts and Parks

AVERAGE TIME (maximum time) IN MINUTES FROM	TO MAGIC KINGDOM		TO EPCOT		TO DHS		
	YOUR CAR	DISNEY SYSTEM	YOUR CAR	DISNEY SYSTEM	YOUR CAR	DISNEY SYSTEM	
ALL-STAR RESORTS	37 (47)	23 (33)	18 (23)	30 (41)	16 (20)	23 (33)	
ANIMAL KINGDOM	37 (48)	50 (68)	16 (17)	27 (38)	16 (17)	24 (34)	
ANIMAL KINGDOM LODGE & VILLAS	39 (50)	36 (51)	19 (21)	29 (40)	18 (19)	26 (37)	
ART OF ANIMATION RESORT	40 (51)	25 (35)	23 (28)	21 (32)	20 (24)	18 (28)	
BEACH CLUB	36 (46)	23 (33)	16 (21)	18 (29*)	14 (18)	26 (37)	
BLIZZARD BEACH	36 (46)	28 (39)	18 (23)	51 (70)	18 (22)	39 (54)	
BOARDWALK INN & VILLAS	36 (46)	26 (36)	16 (21)	11 (22)	14 (18)	26 (37)	
CARIBBEAN BEACH	37 (47)	31 (43)	18 (23)	35 (49)	15 (19)	23 (33)	
CONTEMPORARY– BAY LAKE	—	12 (17)	21 (26)	21 (29)	23 (27)	29 (39)	
CORONADO SPRINGS	37 (47)	23 (32)	18 (23)	20 (28)	16 (20)	18 (26)	
DHS	36 (46)	25 (35)	19 (24)	25 (35)	—	—	
DOLPHIN	35 (45)	20 (30)	15 (20)	24 (36*)	15 (19)	22 (32)	
DOWNTOWN DISNEY#	38 (49)	47 (65)	20 (25)	46 (64)	17 (22)	56 (77)	
DOWNTOWN DISNEY RESORT AREA	41 (51)	69 (91)	21 (26)	47 (62)	20 (24)	45 (60)	
EPCOT	36 (46)	26 (37)	—	—	19 (23)	21 (30)	
FORT WILDERNESS	37 (47)	17 (27)	18 (23)	49 (67)	19 (23)	39 (54)	
GRAND FLORIDIAN	—	7 (8)	18 (23)	33 (45)	20 (24)	23 (33)	
MAGIC KINGDOM	—	—	26 (39)	33 (45)	22 (29)	24 (34)	
OLD KEY WEST	36 (46)	31 (43)	18 (23)	26 (37)	18 (22)	26 (37)	
POLYNESIAN	—	11 (14)	17 (22)	38 (53**)	19 (23)	19 (29)	
POP CENTURY RESORT	40 (51)	25 (35)	23 (28)	21 (32)	20 (24)	18 (28)	
PORT ORLEANS FRENCH QUARTER	37 (47)	23 (33)	19 (24)	26 (37)	19 (23)	24 (34)	
PORT ORLEANS RIVERSIDE	38 (48)	23 (33)	20 (25)	24 (34)	20 (24)	24 (34)	
SARATOGA SPRINGS	38 (48)	23 (33)	18 (23)	28 (39)	20 (24)	24 (34)	
SHADES OF GREEN	28 (36)	35 (49)	18 (23)	33 (45)	20 (24)	20 (28)	
SWAN	35 (45)	20 (30)	15 (20)	24 (36*)	15 (19)	22 (32)	
TREEHOUSE VILLAS	37 (47)	27 (38)	18 (23)	27 (38)	19 (23)	25 (36)	
TYPHOON LAGOON	37 (47)	41 (56)	18 (23)	51 (70)	15 (19)	62 (85)	
WILDERNESS LODGE	—	20 (35)	20 (25)	33 (45)	22 (26)	37 (52)	
YACHT CLUB	36 (46)	38 (48)	16 (21)	27 (35*)	14 (18)	26 (37)	

Transportation between Downtown Disney and the parks requires transfers at a nearby resort.

* This hotel is within walking distance of Epcot; time given is for boat transportation to the International Gateway (Epcot's rear entrance).

** By foot to Transportation and Ticket Center and then by Epcot monorail

in Your Car versus the Disney Transportation System †

TO ANIMAL KINGDOM		TO TYPHOON LAGOON		TO DOWNTOWN DISNEY		TO BLIZZARD BEACH	
YOUR CAR	**DISNEY SYSTEM**	**YOUR CAR**	**DISNEY SYSTEM**	**YOUR CAR**	**DISNEY SYSTEM**	**YOUR CAR**	**DISNEY SYSTEM**
11 (12)	21 (33)	12 (13)	17 (25)	13 (14)	27 (39)	6 (7)	25 (36)
—	—	17 (19)	45 (63)	19 (21)	42 (58)	10 (13)	21 (30)
9 (10)	10 (17)	19 (21)	44 (62)	22 (24)	41 (57)	11 (14)	27 (39)
14 (16)	19 (31)	12 (14)	36 (51)	15 (16)	27 (39)	10 (12)	37 (52)
17 (18)	24 (36)	9 (10)	29 (41)	10 (11)	22 (33)	12 (13)	28 (40)
10 (13)	26 (38)	13 (14)	60 (83)	14 (15)	61 (84)	—	—
17 (18)	26 (38)	9 (10)	30 (44)	10 (11)	24 (35)	12 (13)	28 (40)
17 (18)	31 (45)	6 (7)	26 (38)	7 (8)	30 (42)	12 (13)	40 (56)
20 (21)	25 (37)	17 (18)	27 (39)	16 (17)	37 (52)	15 (16)	42 (58)
11 (12)	18 (27)	12 (13)	17 (25)	13 (14)	27 (39)	6 (7)	24 (35)
16 (17)	20 (30)	8 (9)	57 (79)	9 (10)	58 (80)	11 (12)	36 (51)
16 (17)	23 (35)	10 (11)	33 (47)	11 (12)	27 (39)	11 (12)	19 (28)
19 (21)	38 (54)	6 (7)	16 (24)	—	—	14 (16)	36 (51)
21 (22)	48 (64)	9 (10)	6 (9)	6 (7)	—	16 (17)	46 (61)
16 (17)	33 (48)	12 (13)	30 (42)	13 (14)	40 (56)	11 (12)	31 (45)
24 (25)	41 (57)	10 (11)	37 (52)	11 (12)	45 (63)	19 (20)	42 (58)
18 (19)	23 (35)	15 (16)	39 (55)	16 (17)	49 (68)	13 (14)	30 (44)
17 (18)	45 (63)	23 (31)	39 (55)	27 (36)	49 (68)	12 (13)	41 (57)
19 (20)	29 (41)	8 (9)	22 (33)	9 (10)	23 (34)	14 (15)	35 (50)
17 (18)	19 (31)	14 (15)	44 (62)	15 (16)	54 (75)	12 (13)	32 (46)
14 (16)	19 (31)	12 (14)	36 (51)	15 (16)	27 (39)	10 (12)	37 (52)
19 (20)	27 (39)	9 (10)	23 (34)	10 (11)	30 (44)	14 (15)	42 (60)
20 (21)	27 (39)	10 (11)	22 (33)	11 (12)	27 (39)	15 (16)	35 (50)
21 (22)	27 (39)	9 (10)	24 (35)	6 (7)	18 (27)	16 (17)	34 (49)
18 (19)	22 (33)	15 (16)	39 (55)	18 (20)	49 (68)	13 (14)	30 (44)
16 (17)	23 (35)	10 (11)	33 (47)	11 (12)	27 (39)	11 (12)	19 (28)
17 (19)	41 (59)	—	—	6 (7)	16 (24)	13 (14)	42 (60)
20 (21)	28 (40)	9 (10)	23 (34)	8 (9)	21 (31)	15 (16)	35 (50)
20 (21)	36 (51)	17 (18)	32 (46)	18 (19)	52 (72)	15 (16)	40 (56)
17 (18)	28 (40)	8 (10)	30 (44)	10 (12)	24 (35)	12 (13)	28 (40)

† Driving time vs. time on DTS. Driving times include time in your car, stops to pay tolls, time to park, and transfers on Disney trams and monorails where applicable.

Continued from page 393

If you're staying at an Epcot resort (Swan, Dolphin, Yacht & Beach Club Resorts, BoardWalk Inn & Villas), you can walk or commute via boat to Epcot's International Gateway (back-door) entrance. Although direct buses link Epcot resorts to the Magic Kingdom and Disney's Animal Kingdom, there's no direct bus to Epcot's main entrance or Disney's Hollywood Studios. To reach the Studios from Epcot resorts, you must take a boat or walk.

*un*official **TIP**
If you want to go from resort to resort or almost anywhere else, you'll have to transfer at a hub.

The Caribbean Beach, Pop Century, Art of Animation, Saratoga Springs, Port Orleans, Coronado Springs, Old Key West, Animal Kingdom Lodge & Villas, and All-Star resorts offer direct buses to all theme parks. The rub is that guests sometimes must walk a long way to bus stops or endure more than a half-dozen additional pick-ups before actually heading for the park(s). Commuting in the morning from these resorts is generally easy, though you may have to ride standing. Returning in the evening, however, can be a different story. Shades of Green runs continuous shuttles from the resort to the TTC, where guests can transfer to their final destinations.

Hotels of the Downtown Disney Resort Area (DDRA) (except the Hilton) terminated their guest-transportation contract with Disney some years ago and provide service through another carrier. The substitute, which we feel doesn't measure up, constitutes a real problem for guests at these hotels. Before booking a hotel in the DDRA, check the nature and frequency of shuttles.

Fort Wilderness guests must use campground buses to reach boat landings or the Settlement Depot and Reception Outpost bus stops. From these points, guests can travel directly by boat to the Magic Kingdom or by bus to other destinations. Except for going to the Magic Kingdom, the best way for Fort Wilderness guests to commute is in their car.

The Disney Transportation System versus Driving Your Own Car

To help you assess your transportation options, we've developed a chart (see pages 394 and 395) comparing the approximate commuting times from Disney resorts to various Walt Disney World destinations, using Disney transportation or your own car.

DISNEY TRANSPORTATION Times on the chart in the DTS columns represent an average-case and worst-case scenario. For example, if you want to go from the Caribbean Beach Resort to Epcot, the chart indicates the times as 35 (49). The first number, 35, indicates how many minutes your commute will take on an average day. It assumes that buses run every 17 minutes, there are no major delays, and everything else is as usual. It represents the average time we observed during our research of the transportation system. For the pessimists, the number in parentheses (49) indicates the worst-case scenario. (*Example:* The bus is pulling away as you arrive at the stop, and you must wait 17 minutes for the next one. When you finally board, the bus makes a number of additional stops before heading for Epcot. Once en route, the bus hits every red light.) When planning your transportation time, you'll do best to assume that your trip will take about the same time as the average in the chart (the first number). If you're running on a rigid schedule and you need to be sure of your arrival time, you can use the maximum time (the second number) to plan conservatively.

By far the biggest influence on your travel time between two points on the DTS is the amount of time you have to wait for your bus to arrive. Once you hop on your bus, the travel time is pretty consistent barring any unusual traffic problems; but your time waiting for the bus can vary greatly. Most cast members will tell you that buses run every 20 minutes. Our data indicates they run slightly more often—about every 17 minutes. The exceptions are at Old Key West and Saratoga Springs, where buses sometimes run every 25 minutes.

Bus schedules are also adjusted based on demand and fuel costs. We observed and timed almost 1,000 bus routes for this edition of the book: The intervals between buses arriving at a resort and those headed for the same destination ranged from 1 minute to 39 minutes! That's an improvement since our last study, when some destinations were served as little as once every 48 minutes. Still, if you've ever waited for an Epcot bus while three empty Downtown Disney buses drive past, you'll realize that Disney still has a lot of opportunity to optimize its bus-routing system.

The first number in the chart expresses the average transportation time, but our data shows that about 20% of the time your actual travel time will be less than half the average. So don't be surprised if your trip from Caribbean Beach Resort to Epcot takes only 15 minutes instead of the 35 (49) listed. Consider yourself lucky and enjoy the extra 20 minutes, doing something fun.

DRIVING YOUR OWN CAR The chart's "Your Car" column indicates the average-case and worst-case scenario for driving. To make these times directly comparable to DTS times, we added the time needed to get from your parked car to the park's entrance. While buses and monorails deposit guests at the park's entrance, those who drive must take a tram from their car to the gate or walk. At the Magic Kingdom, you must take a tram from the parking lot to the TTC, then catch a monorail or ferry to the entrance.

Disney Transportation System for Teenagers

If you're staying at Disney World and have teens in your party, familiarize yourself with the Disney bus system. Safe, clean, and operating until 1 a.m. (later from Downtown Disney) on most nights, buses are a great way for teens to get around.

Walt Disney World Bus Service

Disney buses have an illuminated panel above the windshield that flashes the bus's destination. Also, theme parks have designated waiting areas for each Disney destination. To catch the bus to the Caribbean Beach Resort from Disney's Hollywood Studios, for example, go to the bus stop and wait in the area marked TO THE CARIBBEAN BEACH RESORT. At the resorts, go to any bus stop and wait for the bus displaying your destination on the illuminated panel. Directions to Disney destinations are available when you check in or at your hotel's Guest

Relations desk. Guest Relations can also answer questions about the transportation system.

Service from resorts to major theme parks is fairly direct. You may have intermediate stops, but you won't have to transfer. Service to the water parks and other Disney resorts sometimes requires transfers.

The fastest way to commute among resorts by bus is to take a bus from your resort to one of the major theme parks and transfer there for your resort destination. This works, of course, only when the parks are open (actually, from 2 hours before opening until 2–3 hours after closing). If you're attempting to commute to another resort for a late dinner during the off-season, when parks close early, you'll have to transfer at Downtown Disney. Disney, in its transportation instructions, somewhat disingenuously lists Downtown Disney as the transfer point for all resort-to-resort commuting, hoping that you'll stop and do a little shopping en route. If the theme park buses are running, however, proceed to the theme park closest to your resort and transfer to the bus going to the resort where you'll be dining.

Bus service to the theme parks begins about 7 a.m. on days when the parks' official opening is 9 a.m. Generally, the buses run every 20 minutes. Buses to all four parks deliver you to the park entrance.

Though it's generally true that buses run every 20 minutes, a Kelso, Washington, family notes that they might not be the ones you want:

> It's common for three buses to the same park [that you're not going to] to pass you by while you wait 40 minutes for the bus to the park you're going to. Very frustrating. You need to plan an hour for travel to/from the parks because of the shuttle "variable."

To be on hand for opening time (when official opening is 9 a.m.), catch direct buses to Epcot, Disney's Animal Kingdom, and Disney's Hollywood Studios between 7:30 and 8 a.m. Catch direct buses to the Magic Kingdom between 8 and 8:15 a.m. If you must transfer to reach your park, leave 15–20 minutes earlier. On days when official opening is 7 or 8 a.m., move up your departure time accordingly.

For your return bus trip in the evening, leave the park 40 minutes to an hour before closing to avoid the rush. If you're caught in the exodus, you may be inconvenienced, but you won't be stranded. Buses, boats, and monorails continue to operate for 1–2 hours after the parks close.

Is It High Gas Prices?

Causality is often hard to determine in the mysterious Oz that controls the Disney transportation system. However, a barrage of reader comments and complaints suggests that trying to manage a bus system in the face of high gas prices has led to myriad problems—and much inconvenience to guests.

A woman from Charlotte, North Carolina, offers this:

> The bus service to the parks from Animal Kingdom Lodge was poor in the evenings. We had to wait an hour two times because there were so many people waiting. I think Animal Kingdom Lodge should use the chain system [i.e., create an organized queuing area] like the

Value resorts do to maintain the queue. Guests pushed their way to the front when others had clearly been waiting longer.

From a Decatur, Georgia, reader:

I was really gung-ho about staying on-site and using the buses, but having done it, I would probably not do it again. The buses were just too crowded and unpleasant. Even staying at one of the closest resorts (by bus), we found it took about an hour each way by the time we walked to the bus stations, waited, and walked back to our rooms.

A Tacoma, Washington, reader comments:

Bus service overall: marginal. We may not stay on-property next time due to poor bus service; four years ago, buses were great.

A reader who stayed at Port Orleans reports:

The Disney transportation system was wildly erratic, but we ended up with more luck than not. For every time we had to wait a half-hour at the bus stop, there were two or three times with no wait at all.

If you're planning on riding a bus from Port Orleans Riverside to a park around opening time, going to the West or North bus stop may be your best option. These are the first stops on the route, and the bus is sometimes full or standing-room-only before it gets to all the stops.

From a Huntsville, Alabama, mother of three:

Best advice given was driving to the park instead of relying on buses.

Not All Hubs Are Created Equal

All major theme parks, Downtown Disney, and the TTC are hubs on the bus system. If your route requires you to transfer at a hub, transfer at the closest park or the TTC, except at theme park closing time. Avoid Downtown Disney as a transfer point. Because each bus makes multiple stops within Downtown Disney, it takes 16–25 minutes just to get out of the complex!

Note that with the exception of Fort Wilderness Resort & Campground, buses do not run between the TTC and the Disney resort hotels. If you're commuting from resort to resort, you must transfer at Downtown Disney or one of the major theme parks during park operating hours. If you're parked at the TTC and you want to travel to a Disney resort, go to the right of the Magic Kingdom entrance to catch a bus to your destination.

Downtown Disney Resort Area Bus Service

unofficial **TIP**
There are multiple stops at Downtown Disney, so never use it as a transfer point except as a last resort.

Although they're inside Disney World, the hotels of the Downtown Disney Resort Area provide their own bus service—one that many guests, including a family from Prospect, Connecticut, find lacking:

We were disappointed in the shuttle bus for the DDRA hotels. They don't run often enough, and there's no schedule. The bus at the parks picks up in the middle of busy parking lots. Treats you as second-class *compared to Disney resort guests. Take a cab instead of waiting late at night to get back to your hotel. Costs only $9.*

Walt Disney World Monorail Service

Picture the monorail system as three loops. Loop A is an express route that runs counterclockwise connecting the Magic Kingdom with the TTC. Loop B runs clockwise alongside Loop A, making all stops, with service (in order) to the TTC, Polynesian Resort, Grand Floridian, Magic Kingdom, Contemporary Resort–Bay Lake Tower, and back to the TTC. The long Loop C dips southeast, connecting the TTC with Epcot. The hub for all loops is the TTC (where you usually park to visit the Magic Kingdom).

The monorail serving Magic Kingdom resorts usually starts an hour and a half before official opening. If you're staying at a Magic Kingdom resort and wish to be among the first in the Magic Kingdom when official opening is 9 a.m., board the monorail at these times:

From the Contemporary Resort–Bay Lake Tower	7:45–8 a.m.
From the Polynesian Resort	7:50–8:05 a.m.
From the Grand Floridian Resort & Spa	8–8:10 a.m.

If you're a day guest, you'll be allowed on the monorail at the TTC between 8:15 and 8:30 a.m. when official opening is 9 a.m. If you want to board earlier, walk from the TTC to the Polynesian Resort and board there.

unofficial **TIP**
Monorails run for 1 hour after the Magic Kingdom and Epcot close. If a train is too crowded or you need transportation after the monorails have stopped (for example, during Evening Extra Magic Hours), catch a bus or boat. *Note:* As a safety measure, Disney no longer permits guests to ride in the front of a train.

The monorail connecting Epcot and the TTC begins operating at 7:30 a.m. when Epcot's official opening is 9 a.m. To be at Epcot when it opens, catch the Epcot monorail at the TTC by 8:05 a.m.

While your Park Hopper pass suggests you can flit among parks, getting there is more complicated. For example, you can't go directly from the Magic Kingdom to Epcot. You must catch the express monorail (Loop A) to the TTC and transfer to the Loop C monorail to Epcot. If lines to board either monorail are short, you can usually reach Epcot in 30–40 minutes. But should you want to go to Epcot for dinner (as many do) and you're departing the Magic Kingdom in late afternoon, you may have to wait 30 minutes or longer to board the Loop A monorail. Adding this delay boosts your commute to 50–60 minutes.

PART NINE

BARE NECESSITIES

MONEY, ETC.

CREDIT CARDS

AMERICAN EXPRESS, DINERS CLUB, Discover, Japan Credit Bureau, MasterCard, and Visa are accepted throughout Disney World.

BANKING SERVICES

BANK SERVICE AT THE THEME PARKS is limited to ATMs, which are marked on the park maps and are plentiful throughout Walt Disney World; most MasterCard and Visa cards are accepted. To use an American Express card, you must sign an agreement with Amex before your trip. If your credit card doesn't work in the ATMs, a teller at any **SunTrust Bank** full-service location will process your transaction. The SunTrust closest to Disney World is at 1675 E. Buena Vista Drive, across from Downtown Disney Marketplace; for other Orlando-area branches, visit **suntrust.com.**

CURRENCY EXCHANGE

IN THE MAGIC KINGDOM, it's at Guest Relations in City Hall, on Main Street, U.S.A. In Epcot, it's at Guest Relations on the west side of the Epcot Entrance Plaza.

A LICENSE TO PRINT MONEY

ONE OF DISNEY'S MORE SUBLIME PLOYS for separating you from your money is the printing and issuing of **Disney Dollars.** Available throughout Disney World or in advance by phone (☎ 407-566-4985) in denominations of $1, $5, $10, and $50, each emblazoned with a Disney character, the colorful cash can be used for purchases in Disney World, Disneyland, and Disney stores nationwide. Disney Dollars can also be exchanged one-for-one with U.S. currency, but only while you're in Disney World. Also, you need your sales receipt to exchange for U.S. dollars. Disney money is sometimes a perk (for which you're charged dollar-for-dollar) in Walt Disney Travel Company packages.

While Disney Dollars are one of Disney's better moneymakers, some guests keep the money as souvenirs. Others forget to spend or exchange it before they leave the World, then fail to go to a Disney Store or to exchange it by mail. A Michigan family, however, found a way to make their Disney Dollars useful:

> *Since we had planned on going to Disney a year ahead of time, we asked people giving our children money for birthdays, Christmas, Tooth Fairy, etc., to give Disney Dollars instead. This forced both of our children (ages 5 and 7) to save the money for the trip.*

VISITING MORE THAN ONE PARK IN A SINGLE DAY

IF YOU HAVE A PASS ALLOWING YOU to visit the Magic Kingdom, Epcot, Disney's Animal Kingdom, and Disney's Hollywood Studios in the same day, it will be validated with the date when you enter your first park. To enter another park, present your pass and have the fingertip of your index finger scanned by a biometric reader.

PROBLEMS *and*
UNUSUAL SITUATIONS

ATTRACTIONS CLOSED FOR REPAIRS

FIND OUT IN ADVANCE WHAT RIDES AND ATTRACTIONS may be closed during your visit. For complete refurbishment schedules, check online at **touringplans.com** or use our mobile app, **Lines**.

CAR TROUBLE

SECURITY PATROLS WILL HELP if you lock the keys in your parked car or find the battery dead. For more serious problems, the closest repair facility is the **AAA Car Care Center** near the Magic Kingdom parking lot (☎ 407-824-0976).

The nearest off-World repair center is **Maingate Citgo** (US 192 west of Interstate 4; ☎ 407-396-2721). Disney security can help you find it. Farther away but highly recommended by one of our Orlando-area researchers is **Riker's Automotive & Tire** (5700 Central Florida Parkway, near SeaWorld; ☎ 407-238-9800; **rikersauto.com**). Says our source, "They do great work and are the only car place that has never tried to get extra money out of me because I'm a woman and I know nothing about cars."

GASOLINE

THERE ARE THREE **Hess** gas stations on Disney property. One station is adjacent to the AAA Car Care Center on the exit road from the Transportation and Ticket Center (Magic Kingdom) parking lot. It's also convenient to the Shades of Green, Grand Floridian, and Polynesian resorts. Most centrally located is the station at the corner of Buena Vista Drive and Epcot Resorts Boulevard, near the BoardWalk Inn. A third station, also on Buena Vista Drive, is across from the former Pleasure Island site in Downtown Disney.

LOST AND FOUND

IF YOU LOSE (OR FIND) SOMETHING in the Magic Kingdom, go to City Hall. At Epcot, Lost and Found is in the Entrance Plaza. At

Disney's Hollywood Studios, it's at Hollywood Boulevard Guest Relations, and at Disney's Animal Kingdom, it's at Guest Relations at the main entrance. If you discover your loss after you've left the park(s), call ☎ 407-824-4245 (for all parks). See page 31 for the number(s) to call if you're at the park(s) and discover your loss.

It's unusual for readers to send us tips about Lost and Found, but a mom from Indianapolis sent two!

> Hold on to your things on Space Mountain! My daughter lost her bag going over the first turn, and on an 80-minute-wait time day they had to shut the ride down to retrieve the bag! If you lose something on a ride and it has medication in it, Disney cast members will shut down a ride for 45 seconds to try and retrieve it. If they can't find it or it didn't contain meds, you have to come back to Lost and Found for it at the end of the day.
>
> Also, don't forget to write down the serial numbers on your Park Hopper passes. With the serial number, a cast member can look up when it was last used, giving you an idea of where it was lost.

Lost Disney Resort Room-Key Cards

This isn't a big deal unless you're outside the door to your room fighting an imminent case of Montezuma's revenge (or "Goofy bowels," as it's known in the Kingdom). Duplicate keys can be made at Guest Relations at any of the theme parks or resort hotels. If your room card is set up to use as a charge card, you need to address the problem promptly.

A Grand Haven, Michigan, dad shares his experience:

> When we lost our "keys to the World," I thought we were done for. We walked into Guest Relations (we were in Magic Kingdom at the time), and within 10 minutes we had our old room keys deactivated and new ones in our hands.

MEDICAL MATTERS

HEADACHE RELIEF Aspirin and other sundries are sold at the Emporium on Main Street in the Magic Kingdom (behind the counter; you must ask), at most retail shops in Epcot's Future World and World Showcase, and in Disney's Hollywood Studios and Disney's Animal Kingdom.

ILLNESSES REQUIRING MEDICAL ATTENTION For the locations of the theme park **First Aid** centers, see the respective park chapters.

Off-property, a **Centra Care** walk-in clinic is at 12500 S. Apopka–Vineland Rd. (☎ 407-934-CARE). It's open 8 a.m.–midnight weekdays and 8 a.m.–8 p.m. weekends. Centra Care operates a 24-hour physician-house-call service and runs a free shuttle (☎ 407-938-0650).

A North Carolina family of four had a good experience at **Buena Vista Urgent Care** (8216 World Center Drive, Suite D; ☎ 407-465-1110):

> We started day one needing medical care for our son, who has asthma and had developed croup. We found great care 2 miles down FL 535 at Buena Vista Urgent Care. We waited 20 minutes, and then we were off to the parks. Please add them to your guide.

The Medical Concierge (☎ 407-648-5252; **themedicalconcierge .com**) has board-certified physicians available 24-7 for house calls to your hotel room. They offer in-room X-rays and IV therapy service as well as same-day dental and specialist appointments. They also rent medical equipment. Insurance receipts, insurance billing, and foreign-language interpretation are provided. Walk-in clinics are also available. You can also inquire about transportation arrangements.

DOCS (Doctors on Call Service; ☎ 407-399-DOCS; **doctorsoncall service.com**) offers 24-hour house-call service. All DOCS physicians are certified by the American Board of Medical Specialties. A father of two from O'Fallon, Illinois, gives them a thumbs-up:

> *My wife's cold developed into an ear infection that required medical attention. We opened the medical section of "The Book," and one of your recommended providers, DOCS, was able to respond in 40 minutes. The doctor was fantastic. He had medicine with him and was very professional and friendly. It wasn't a great way to kick off our first night, but the rest of our trip was great.*

Physician Room Service (☎ 407-238-2000; **physicianroomservice .com**) provides board-certified doctor house calls to Walt Disney World–area guest rooms for adults and children.

DENTAL NEEDS Call **Celebration Dental Group** (☎ 407-566-2222).

PRESCRIPTION MEDICINE Two nearby pharmacies are **Walgreens Lake Buena Vista** (☎ 407-238-0600) and **Winn-Dixie Pharmacy Lake Buena Vista** (☎ 407-465-8606). **Turner Drugs** (☎ 407-828-8125) charges $7.50 to deliver a filled prescription to your hotel's front desk. The service is available to Disney and non-Disney hotels in Turner Drugs' area. The fee is charged to your hotel account.

SERGEANT BLISTERBLASTER'S GUIDE TO HAPPY FEET

1. ON YOUR FEET! Get up, La-Z-Boy rider: When you go to Walt Disney World, you'll have to walk a lot farther than to the refrigerator. You can log 5–12 miles a day at the parks, so now's the time to shape up them dogs. Start with short walks around the neighborhood. Increase your distance gradually until you can do 6 miles without CPR.

2. A-TEN-SHUN! During your training program, pay attention when those puppies growl. They'll give you a lot of information about your feet and the appropriateness of your shoes. Listen up! No walking in flip-flops, loafers, or sandals. Wear well-constructed, broken-in running or hiking shoes. If you feel a "hot spot," that means a blister is developing. The most common sites for blisters are heels, toes, and balls of the feet. If you develop a hot spot in the same place every time you walk (a clue!), cover it prophylactically with a Johnson & Johnson blister bandage (in drugstores without a prescription) before you set out. No, Sofa Bunny, I didn't tell you to wear condoms on your feet! *Prophylactically* means to anticipate the problem and treat it in advance.

3. SOCK IT UP, TRAINEE! Good socks are as important as good shoes. When you walk, your feet sweat like a mule in a peat bog, and the moisture only increases friction. To minimize friction, wear a pair of socks, such as SmartWool or CoolMax, that wick perspiration away from your feet (SmartWool makes socks of varying thicknesses).

To further combat moisture, dust your dogs with some antifungal talcum powder.

4. WHO DO YOU THINK YOU ARE, JOHN WAYNE? Don't be a hero. Take care of a foot problem the minute you notice it. Carry a small foot-emergency kit for your platoon. Include gauze, Betadine antibiotic ointment, moleskin or Johnson & Johnson blister bandages, scissors, a sewing needle or such (to drain blisters), and matches to sterilize the needle. Extra socks and talcum powder are optional.

5. BITE THE BULLET! If you develop a hot spot, cover it ASAP with a blister bandage. Cut the material large enough to cover the skin surrounding the spot. If you develop a blister, air out and dry your foot. Next, drain the fluid, but don't remove the top skin. Clean the area with Betadine and place a Johnson & Johnson blister bandage over the blister. The bandages come in several sizes, including specially shaped ones for fingers and toes; they're also good for covering hot spots. If you don't have blister bandages, don't cover the hot spot or blister with Band-Aids; they'll slip and wad up.

6. TAKE CARE OF YOUR PLATOON. If you have young, green troops in your outfit, they might not sound off when a hot spot develops. Stop several times a day and check their feet. If you forgot your emergency kit and a problem arises, call the Disney medics. They have all the stuff you need to keep your command in action.

OK, troops, prepare to move out. Hit the trail and move those feet: left, right, left!

RAIN

WEATHER BAD? Go to the parks anyway. Crowds are lighter, and most attractions and waiting areas are under cover. Showers, especially during warmer months, are short.

> *unofficial* **TIP**
> Rain gear is one of the few bargains at the parks. It isn't always displayed in shops, so you have to ask for it.

Ponchos are about $7, umbrellas about $10. All ponchos sold at Disney World are made of clear plastic, so picking out somebody in your party on a rainy day can be tricky. Walmart sells an inexpensive green poncho that will make your family emerald beacons in a plastic-covered sea of humanity.

Some unusually heavy rain precipitated (no pun intended) dozens of reader suggestions for dealing with soggy days. The best came from this Memphis, Tennessee, mom:

1. Rain gear should include ponchos and umbrellas. Umbrellas make the rain much more bearable. When rain isn't beating down on your ponchoed head, it's easier to ignore.

2. Buy blue ponchos at Walgreens. We could keep track of each other much easier because we had blue ponchos instead of clear ones.

3. If you're using a stroller, bring a plastic sheet or extra poncho to protect it from rain. Ponchos will cover the Disney single rental strollers but not the double strollers. Carry a towel in a plastic bag to wipe off your stroller after experiencing an attraction during a rainfall.

Unofficial Guide fact-checker Connie Wolosyk adds, "It helps to wear a baseball cap under the poncho hood—without it, the hood never covers your head properly, and your face always gets wet."

HOW TO LODGE A COMPLAINT WITH DISNEY

COMPLAINING ABOUT A LEAKY FAUCET or not having enough towels is pretty straightforward, and you usually will find Disney folks highly responsive. However, a more global gripe, or one beyond an on-site manager's ability to resolve, is likely to founder in the labyrinth of Disney bureaucracy.

One of our readers' foremost gripes relates to Disney's unresponsiveness in fielding complaints. A Providence, Rhode Island, dad's remarks are typical:

> It's all warm fuzzies and big smiles until you have a problem. Then everybody plays hide-and-seek. The only thing you know for sure is it's never the responsibility of the Disney person you're talking to.

A Mobile, Alabama, mother echoes his comment:

> I made call after call, with one Disney person passing me on to the next, until finally I ran out of steam. Basically, I had to choose between getting my problem addressed, which was pretty much a full-time job, or going ahead with my vacation.

A Portland, Maine, reader summed it up in quintessential New England style:

> Lodging a complaint with Disney is like shouting at a brick.

Like most companies, Disney would rather hear from you when the message is good. Regarding complaints, Disney prefers to receive them in writing, but by the time you get home and draft a letter, it's often too late to correct the problem. And though Disney would have you believe that it's a touchy-feely outfit, it generally isn't a company that will make things right for you after the fact. You may receive a letter thanking you for writing and expressing regret without acknowledging responsibility (for example, "We're sorry you felt inconvenienced"— as if the perception somehow arose from your imagination). It's unlikely, though, that they'll offer to do anything remedial. That said, if you want to lodge a complaint, write to **Walt Disney World Guest Communications, P.O. Box 10040, Lake Buena Vista, FL 32830-0040.** If you're really steamed, try writing the following higher-ups:

Robert Iger, CEO	**Thomas Staggs,**	**Meg Crofton**
The Walt Disney	**Chairman**	Walt Disney Parks & Resorts
Company	Walt Disney Parks & Resorts	Operations, U.S./France
500 S. Buena Vista St.	500 S. Buena Vista St.	P.O. Box 10040
Burbank, CA 91521	Burbank, CA 91521	Lake Buena Vista, FL 32830

If Disney doesn't respond, you can always go public:

Letters to the Editor
Orlando Sentinel
633 N. Orange Ave., MP-218
Orlando, FL 32801-1349
☎ 407-420-5000; fax 407-420-5286
insight@orlandosentinel.com

If you're at Disney World and you really need to settle an issue, keep your resort general manager's feet to the fire until he hooks you up with the person who can solve it.

SERVICES

MESSAGES

MESSAGES LEFT AT CITY HALL in the Magic Kingdom, Guest Relations at Epcot, Hollywood Boulevard Guest Relations at Disney's Hollywood Studios, or Guest Relations at Disney's Animal Kingdom can be retrieved at any of the four.

PET CARE

ACROSS FROM THE PORT ORLEANS RESORTS, the plush **Best Friends Pet Resort** accommodates up to 270 dogs in a variety of standard and luxury suites, some with private outdoor patios and play yards; the Kitty City pavilion houses up to 30 felines in two- and four-story cat condos. There's also a separate area just for birds and "pocket pets" such as hamsters. Encompassing more than 17,000 square feet of air-conditioned indoor space plus 10,000 square feet of covered outdoor runs and play areas, the resort is open to both Walt Disney World resort guests and visitors staying off-property. For more information, call ☎ 877-4-WDW-PETS (877-493-9738) or visit **bestfriendspetcare.com.** (*Note:* Pet parents must provide written proof of current vaccination from a veterinarian, either at check-in or by fax at 203-840-5266.)

PHOTOPASS

IF THE IDEA OF LUGGING A CAMERA AROUND Walt Disney World makes you think "pack mule" more than "vacation," Disney's willing to take that burden off your back. A service called PhotoPass allows you to collect digital photos taken by Disney photographers around Walt Disney World's theme parks and water parks throughout your vacation. When your trip is complete, all your photos will be available for purchase at **disneyphotopass.com.** Here's how it works:

1. Find a PhotoPass photographer to take your first picture. Photographers can be found throughout the theme parks and water parks, including near park entrances, in restaurants (and during character meals), and around iconic attractions such as Splash Mountain.

2. After snapping the picture, the photographer will hand you a small plastic card with a PhotoPass ID number on it. Keep this card for your entire trip—the ID number uniquely identifies you in the PhotoPass system. Present the card to any other photographer before you have more PhotoPass pictures taken, and all the photos will be linked to that one PhotoPass account.

3. Visit the website within 30 days of your trip and enter your ID number to view your photos. The website allows you to add decorative borders and short captions to your pictures, too, as well as share photos online.

When you receive your PhotoPass card, take a minute to write down its ID number. If the card is later lost or misplaced, you'll be able to retrieve your photos.

Unofficial Guide readers give PhotoPass mixed reviews. Those who favor the service say it frees them from carrying around a camera at all times. But today's multi-megapixel digital cameras and smart phones fit comfortably in your pocket, and most can take short videos as well as photos. The biggest complaint about PhotoPass is the cost: $14.95 for one 5 x 7–inch photo (plus shipping), and $149.95 for a CD with all your photos (advance purchase discounts are sometimes available). An entry-level 10-megapixel digital camera plus memory card costs roughly the same price; what's more, online photo printers such as **snapfish.com** and **photos.walmart.com** offer prints for as little as 9¢ apiece for a 4 x 6 (Snapfish) or 58¢ for a 5 x 7 (Walmart).

A reader from Worcester, Vermont, offers this:

Please warn people that the Disney on-site photographers are very convenient, but (1) they're very expensive, and (2) if you want to get your photos at the parks (necessary if you have a voucher) rather than online, the lines are excessively slow.

EXCUSE ME, BUT WHERE CAN I FIND . . .

RELIGIOUS SERVICES IN THE WALT DISNEY WORLD AREA? See **allears .net/btp/church.htm** for a complete list.

SOMEPLACE TO PUT ALL THESE PACKAGES? Lockers are available on the ground floor of the Main Street railroad station in the Magic Kingdom, to the right of Spaceship Earth in Epcot, and on the Transportation and Ticket Center's east and west ends. At Disney's Hollywood Studios, lockers are to the right of the entrance at Oscar's Classical Car Souvenirs. Disney's Animal Kingdom lockers are to the left inside the entrance. Cost is $7 a day for small lockers and $9 a day for large lockers; prices include a $5 refundable deposit. Lockers at Blizzard Beach and Typhoon Lagoon water parks cost $13 (small) and $15 (large), also with a $5 refundable deposit.

Package Pick-Up is available at each of the major theme parks. Ask the salesperson to send your purchases to Package Pick-Up. When you leave the park, they'll be waiting for you.

unofficial **TIP**
Be aware that Package Pick-Up closes 2 hours before the park. Disney resort guests can have their purchases delivered to their hotel's gift shop.

Epcot has two exits, thus two Package Pick-Ups; specify the main entrance or the International Gateway. If you're staying at a Disney resort, you can also have the packages delivered to your room. If you're leaving within 24 hours, however, take them with you or use the in-park pickup location.

CAMERAS AND FILM? Camera Centers at the major parks sell disposable cameras for about $12 ($19 with flash). Film is sold throughout the World. Developing is available at most Disney hotel gift shops and at Camera Centers. Film processing is no longer available, but Disney will take your digital memory cards and transfer the contents to a CD while you're in the parks. The cost is around $13 for 120 images and around $6.50 for an additional 120 images. Prints are around 75¢ each. You'll need to leave your digital media with Disney while they create the CD, typically around 2–5 hours, so make sure you've got extra media on hand.

A GROCERY STORE? Our first piece of advice is to avoid the **Gooding's Supermarket** in the Crossroads Shopping Center, across FL 535 from the Disney World entrance. While its location makes it undeniably convenient, its selection is poor and you'll find the prices higher and more frightening than the Tower of Terror. For down-to-earth prices, try **Publix** at either the intersection of International Drive and US 192 or near the intersection of Reams Road and FL 535, or **Winn-Dixie** on Apopka–Vineland Road, about a mile north of Crossroads Shopping Center.

We compiled a list of common vacation grocery items and went shopping. No item we bought was on sale. The chart below shows how prices at GardenGrocer (see bottom of page), Gooding's, Publix, and Winn-Dixie compare (Publix and Winn-Dixie are the least expensive).

ITEM	GOODING'S	PUBLIX I-DRIVE	WINN-DIXIE	PUBLIX WINDERMERE	GARDEN GROCER
12 DOUGHNUTS (Krispy Kreme/store brand)	$6.99	$5.49	$4.49	$5.49	$7.98
MAXWELL HOUSE COFFEE (11.5 oz.)	$5.99	$4.92	$4.59	$4.99	$6.19
COFFEE FILTERS (store brand, 200 count)	$2.49	$1.29	$2.19	$1.29	$1.49
1 GALLON MILK (store brand)	$4.49	$3.59	$3.69	$3.59	$4.89
TROPICANA ORANGE JUICE (59 oz.)	$4.99	$3.99	$3.99	$3.99	$5.99
CHEERIOS (8.9 oz.)	$4.99	$3.59	$3.79	$3.99	$4.49
COCA-COLA (12 12-oz. cans)	$5.99	$4.99	$4.99	$4.99	$5.89
LAY'S POTATO CHIPS (10.5 oz.)	$4.29	$4.29	$4.29	$4.29	$5.39
SUGAR (2 lbs., store brand)	$2.99	$2.05	$2.09	$1.89	$3.78
CHIPS AHOY COOKIES (13.72 oz.)	$4.99	$3.59	$3.69	$3.49	$3.99
BUDWEISER (6 12-oz. cans)	$6.49	$6.19	$6.99	$6.19	$6.19**
BANANAS (4 lbs.)	$3.96	$2.76	$2.76	$2.76	$3.56
WONDER WHITE BREAD (20 oz.)	$2.99	$2.89	$2.89	$2.89	$3.69
JIF or SKIPPY CREAMY PEANUT BUTTER (12 oz.)	$4.99*	$2.95	$3.99*	$2.95	$3.59
WELCH'S GRAPE JELLY (18 oz.)	$3.99	$2.09	$2.59	$2.09	$3.49
ORAL-B ADVANTAGE TOOTHBRUSH	$4.59	$3.29	$3.39	$3.29	$2.49
SPF 30 SUNSCREEN (8 oz.)	$15.89	$8.99	$9.99	$7.99	$10.49
TOTAL	**$91.90**	**$66.95**	**$70.90**	**$66.16**	**$83.58**

* Gooding's and Winn-Dixie had only 18-oz. jars.
** GardenGrocer obtains alcohol from other supermarkets.

GROCERY MARKETS THAT DELIVER? If you don't have a car or you don't want to take the time to go to the supermarket, **GardenGrocer** (**gardengrocer.com**) will shop for you and deliver your groceries. The best way to compile your order is on GardenGrocer's website before you leave home. It's simple, and the selection is huge. If there's something you want that's not on their list of available items, they'll try to find it for you (including alcohol). Delivery arrangements are per your instructions. If you're staying at a hotel, you can arrange for your groceries to be left with bell services. For the sake of order-fulfillment accuracy and customer service, GardenGrocer is primarily set up for online ordering. If you can't get online, though, you can order by phone (☎ 866-855-4350). For orders of $200 or more, there's no delivery charge; for orders less than $200, the delivery charge is $12; a minimum order of $40 is required. As of this writing, GardenGrocer is also adding a fuel surcharge of $1.99 to all orders until—and we quote—"gas prices return to $3 per gallon." Also note that Garden Grocer's delivery schedule may fill completely around holidays, at which point they'll stop accepting orders for delivery on those dates.

We get lots of positive reader feedback about GardenGrocer. The following review from an Eagan, Minnesota, family is representative:

> *GardenGrocer was fabulous. I ordered our groceries online about one week before our arrival. I had a few questions, so I called and actually spoke with a human who was very helpful! Our flight got in about 7 p.m., and I called to let them know we were on our way. They arrived about 20 minutes after we did with everything we ordered. We were ready to hit the parks early the next morning!*

You can also order online at the **Gooding's** website (**goodings.com**); a $50 minimum order is required, and a $25 service charge applies (no holiday delivery, and they don't deliver ice cream).

WINE, BEER, AND LIQUOR? Wine and beer are sold in grocery stores. **Gooding's,** on FL 535, used to be well regarded by the *Unofficial* team, but these days their selections are disappointing (not to mention expensive). The best range of adult beverages is sold at the **ABC Fine Wine & Spirits** store less than a mile north of the Crossroads shopping center (11951 S. Apopka–Vineland Road; ☎ 407-239-0775).

PART TEN

DINING *in* AND *around* WALT DISNEY WORLD

DINING *outside* WALT DISNEY WORLD

UNOFFICIAL GUIDE RESEARCHERS LOVE GOOD FOOD and invest a fair amount of time scouting new places to eat. And because food at Walt Disney World is so expensive, we (like you) have an economic incentive for finding palatable meals outside the World. Alas, the area surrounding Disney World is not exactly a culinary nirvana. If you thrive on fast food and the fare at chain restaurants (Denny's, T.G.I. Friday's, The Olive Garden, and the like), you'll be as happy as an alligator at a chicken farm. But if you're in the market for a superlative dining experience, you'll find the pickings outside the World of about the same quality as those inside, only less expensive. Plus, some ethnic cuisines aren't represented in Walt Disney World restaurants.

Among specialty restaurants both in and out of the World, location and price will determine your choice. For instance, both Walt Disney World and adjoining tourist areas have some decent Italian restaurants—which one you select depends on how much money you want to spend and how convenient the place is to reach. Our recommendations for specialty and ethnic fare served outside of Disney World are summarized in the table that starts on page 414.

Better restaurants outside Walt Disney World cater primarily to adults. That's a plus, however, if you're looking to escape children or you want to eat in peace and quiet.

ROOM SERVICE ORLANDO

IF YOU'RE STAYING AT A HOTEL outside Disney World, **Room Service Orlando** (7041 Grand National Drive; ☎ 407-352-1170; **orlandotakeoutexpress.com**) will deliver a meal from your choice of five restaurants: **Café Mineiro, Cariera's Cucina Italiana, Denny's, Kim Wu Chinese Restaurant,** and **TooJay's Gourmet Deli.** The delivery charge is $7 per restaurant for online orders or $8 for phone orders, with a minimum $15 order. Gratuity is added to the bill. Cash, traveler's checks,

In or Out of the World for These Cuisines?

American Good selections both in and out of the World.

Barbecue Better out of the World.

Buffets A toss-up—Disney buffets are expensive, but they offer excellent quality and extensive selections. Out-of-World buffets aren't as upscale but are inexpensive.

Chinese Better out of the World.

Eastern European Passable but not great, in or out of the World.

French Toss-up; reasonably good but expensive both in and out of the World.

Italian Tie on quality; better value out of the World.

Japanese/sushi **Teppan Edo** in the Japan Pavilion at Epcot is tops for teppanyaki (table grilling). For sushi and sashimi, try **Tokyo Dining,** also in Japan, or visit **Kimonos** at the Swan resort.

Mexican **La Hacienda de San Angel** at Epcot is good but expensive, with more-affordable food right next door at the quick-service **La Cantina de San Angel**. For decent Tex-Mex, try **El Patron** outside the World.

Middle Eastern More choice and better value out of the World.

Seafood Toss-up.

Steak/prime rib Try **Shula's Steak House** at the Dolphin or **The Capital Grille** on International Drive out of the World.

MasterCard, Visa, American Express, and Discover are accepted. Hours are 4:30–11 p.m.

DINING AT UNIVERSAL CITYWALK

LIKE DOWNTOWN DISNEY, CityWalk is a combination of entertainment and dining, with a focus on adults. Restaurant tastes run the gamut, from the elegant (**Emeril's Orlando**) to the basic (**NASCAR Sports Grille**)—or, if you prefer, from the sublime to the ridiculous. All the restaurants share one common trait: They're loud. But good food can be found inside some of them.

BOB MARLEY—A TRIBUTE TO FREEDOM ☎ 407-224-3663 A medium-sized (and moderately loud) tribute to the reggae superstar.

BUBBA GUMP SHRIMP CO. ☎ 407-903-0044 This seafood eatery is part of an international chain inspired by the film *Forrest Gump*. Take a wild guess what the specialty here is.

EMERIL'S ORLANDO ☎ 407-224-2424 Chief among your dining options here, this is the Florida outpost of Emeril Lagasse's New Orleans restaurant. Lagasse is on hand here from time to time, though he tends to stay in the kitchen. But even when the celebrity chef isn't around, you're in for some good eating. The food is Louisiana-style with a creative flair.

FUSION BISTRO SUSHI & SAKE BAR ☎ 407-903-7253 Opened in 2010, this restaurant on the upper level of CityWalk is operated by Sushi

House, with other locations in Atlanta and Orlando's Florida Mall. Fusion Bistro's unusual sushi preparations mix traditional Japanese with tastes and ingredients from throughout Eastern Asia and the Pacific Rim, all served in a party atmosphere. The sushi ain't cheap, but because of extended hours, you can get your fix until the wee hours.

HARD ROCK CAFE ☎ 407-351-7625 Serves up so-so burgers, ribs, and other American fare. More remarkable is the extensive collection of music memorabilia, including a pink 1959 Cadillac revolving over the bar. It's the biggest such collection on display anywhere in the Hard Rock chain.

JIMMY BUFFETT'S MARGARITAVILLE ☎ 407-224-2155 A boisterous tribute to the head Parrothead. None of the food, including the cheeseburger, will make you think you're in paradise, but fans don't seem to care. The focal point is a volcano that erupts occasionally, spewing margarita mix instead of lava.

LATIN QUARTER ☎ 407-224-3663 Simple Latin cuisine is served here—beans and rice, plantains, and flan. Most of the patrons come to dance and drink.

NASCAR SPORTS GRILLE ☎ 407-224-7223 A large and noisy tribute to all things motorized. You may find yourself sitting under a full-size race car that from time to time starts up and roars at a too-realistic sound level. The food? See all the logos for oil companies on the walls?

NBA CITY ☎ 407-363-5919 Serves decent theme-restaurant eats. The dining area looks like a miniature basketball arena, and TVs throughout play videos of famous basketball players and key moments in roundball history.

PASTAMORÉ ☎ 407-224-3663 This is the requisite Italian restaurant. The decor is modern and stylish, and the food—with portions big enough to share—is better than average.

PAT O'BRIEN'S ☎ 407-224-2106 This and **CityWalk's Rising Star** are mostly music venues that serve some food. Pat O'Brien's, behind a facade that looks remarkably similar to the New Orleans original, has the best bites (try the jambalaya).

BUFFETS AND MEAL DEALS OUTSIDE WALT DISNEY WORLD

BUFFETS, RESTAURANT SPECIALS, and discount dining abound in the area surrounding Walt Disney World, especially on US 192 (known locally as Irlo Bronson Memorial Highway) and along International Drive. The local visitor magazines, distributed free at non-Disney hotels, among other places, are packed with advertisements and discount coupons for seafood feasts, Chinese buffets, Indian buffets, breakfast buffets, and a host of combination specials for everything from lobster to barbecue. For a family trying to economize, some of the come-ons are mighty sweet. But are these places any good? Is the food fresh, tasty, and appealing? Are the restaurants clean and inviting? Armed with little more than a roll of Tums, the *Unofficial* research team tried all the eateries that advertise heavily in the free tourist magazines. Here's what we discovered.

Continued on page 416

Where to Eat outside Walt Disney World

AMERICAN

J. Alexander's 7335 Sand Lake Road, Orlando; ☎ 407-345-1039; **jalexanders.com;** moderate. Chic but relaxed ambience, contemporary fare such as steaks and seafood, generous portions.

The Ravenous Pig * 1234 N. Orange Ave., Winter Park; ☎ 407-628-2333; **theravenouspig.com;** moderate–expensive. New American cuisine with an award-winning menu that changes frequently depending on seasonal ingredients.

Seasons 52 7700 W. Sand Lake Road, Orlando; ☎ 407-354-5212; **seasons52.com;** moderate–expensive. Delicious, creative New American food that's low in fat and calories. Extensive wine list.

BARBECUE

Bubbalou's Bodacious Bar-B-Que 5818 Conroy Road, Orlando (near Universal Orlando); ☎ 407-295-1212; **bubbalous.com;** inexpensive. Tender, smoky barbecue; tomato-based Killer Sauce.

4 Rivers Smokehouse 1047 S. Dillard St., Winter Garden; ☎ 407-474-8377; **4rsmokehouse.com;** inexpensive. Award-winning beef brisket; fried pickles, cheese grits, fried okra, and collard greens.

CARIBBEAN

Bahama Breeze 8849 International Dr., Orlando; ☎ 407-248-2499; **bahamabreeze.com;** moderate. A creative and tasty version of Caribbean cuisine from the owners of the Olive Garden and Red Lobster chains.

CHINESE

Ming's Bistro * 1212 Woodward St., Orlando; ☎ 407-898-9672; inexpensive. Authentic Chinese, including dim sum, crispy roast pork, and roast duck.

CUBAN/SPANISH

Columbia 649 Front St., Celebration; ☎ 407-566-1505; **columbia restaurant.com;** moderate. Authentic Cuban and Spanish creations, including paella and the famous 1905 Salad.

ETHIOPIAN

Nile Ethiopian Restaurant 7040 International Dr., Orlando; ☎ 407-354-0026; **nile07.com;** inexpensive–moderate. Authentic stews and delicious vegetarian dishes. Bob's favorite Orlando/WDW-area restaurant.

FRENCH

Le Coq au Vin * 4800 S. Orange Ave., Orlando; ☎ 407-851-6980; **lecoqauvinrestaurant.com;** moderate–expensive. Country French cuisine in a relaxed atmosphere. Reservations suggested.

INDIAN

Aashirwad Indian Cuisine 5748 International Drive, Orlando; ☎ 407-370-9830; **aashirwadrestaurant.com;** inexpensive–moderate. Whole spices roasted and ground in the restaurant. Naan, chicken curry, vegetable biryani, tandoori dishes. Daily lunch buffet.

Memories of India 7625 Turkey Lake Road, Orlando; ☎ 407-370-3277; **memoriesofindiacuisine.com;** inexpensive–moderate. Classic tandoori dishes, samosas, *tikka masala,* Sunday Champagne brunch with buffet.

*20 minutes or more from Walt Disney World

ITALIAN

Bice Orlando Ristorante Loews Portofino Bay Hotel, Universal Orlando Resort, 5601 Universal Blvd., Orlando; ☎ 407-503-1415; **orlando.bicegroup.com;** expensive. Authentic Italian; great wines.

Anthony's Coal-Fired Pizza 8031 Turkey Lake Road, Orlando; ☎ 407-363-9466; **anthonyscoalfiredpizza.com;** inexpensive. Pizzas, eggplant, pastas, beer and wine.

JAPANESE/SUSHI

Amura 7786 W. Sand Lake Road, Orlando; ☎ 407-370-0007; **amura .com;** moderate. A favorite sushi bar for locals. The tempura is popular, too.

Hanamizuki 8255 International Drive, Orlando; ☎ 407-363-7200; **hanamizuki.us;** moderate–expensive. Pricey but very authentic.

Nagoya Sushi 7600 Dr. Phillips Blvd., Suite 66, in the very rear of The Marketplace at Dr. Phillips; ☎ 407-248-8558; **nagoyasushi.com;** moderate. A small, intimate restaurant with great sushi and an extensive menu.

MEXICAN

Cantina Laredo 8000 Via Dellagio Way, Orlando; ☎ 407-345-0186; **cantinalaredo.com;** moderate–expensive. Authentic Mexican in an upscale atmosphere.

Chevys Fresh Mex 12547 FL 535, Lake Buena Vista; ☎ 407-827-1052 or 407-827-1119; **chevys.com;** inexpensive–moderate. Conveniently located across from the FL 535 entrance to WDW.

El Patron 12167 S. Apopka–Vineland Road, Orlando; ☎ 407-238-5300; **elpatronrestaurantcantina.com;** inexpensive. Family-owned restaurant serving freshly prepared Mexican dishes. Full bar.

Moe's Southwest Grill 7541-D W. Sand Lake Road, Orlando; ☎ 407-264-9903; **moes.com;** inexpensive. Dependable southwestern fare.

Taquitos Jalisco 1041 S. Dillard St., Winter Garden; ☎ 407-654-0363; inexpensive. Low-key atmosphere; flautas, chicken mole, fajitas, hearty burritos, good vegetarian.

NEW WORLD

Norman's 4012 Central Florida Parkway, in the Ritz-Carlton Orlando; ☎ 407-393-4333; **normans.com;** expensive. Norman Van Aken, dean of New World cuisine, offers a menu that changes often—but you'll always find his sinfully delicious conch chowder. World-class wine menu.

SEAFOOD

Bonefish Grill 7830 W. Sand Lake Road, Orlando; ☎ 407-355-7707; **bonefishgrill.com;** moderate. Casual setting along busy Restaurant Row on Sand Lake Road. Choose your fish, and then choose a favorite sauce to accompany. Also steaks and chicken.

Celebration Town Tavern 721 Front St., Celebration; ☎ 407-566-2526; **thecelebrationtowntavern.com;** moderate. Popular hangout for locals, with New England–style seafood. Clam chowder is a big hit.

Ocean Prime 7339 W. Sand Lake Road, Orlando; ☎ 407-781-4880, **ocean-prime.com;** expensive. Elegant supper-club ambience; classic fare focusing on fresh seafood, perfectly cooked meats. Outdoor dining and piano bar.

Where to Eat outside Walt Disney World (cont'd)

STEAK/PRIME RIB

The Capital Grille Pointe Orlando, 9101 International Drive, Orlando; ☎ 407-370-4392; **thecapitalgrille.com;** expensive. Dry-aged steaks, good wine list, and classic decor.

Del Frisco's* 729 Lee Road, Orlando; ☎ 407-645-4443; **delfriscos orlando.com;** expensive. Family-owned and consistently rated the top steakhouse in Central Florida. Prime steaks, lobster, more than 6,500 bottles of wine in the cellar, world-class selection of single-malt Scotch.

Texas de Brazil 5259 International Drive, Orlando; ☎ 407-355-0355; **texasdebrazil.com;** expensive. All-you-care-to-eat in an upscale Brazilian-style *churrascaria*. Filet mignon, sausage, pork ribs, chicken, lamb, and more. Kids age 6 and under free, ages 7–12 half-price. Salad bar with 40+ options.

Vito's Chop House 8633 International Drive, Orlando; ☎ 407-354-2467; **vitoschophouse.com;** moderate. Surprisingly upscale meat house with a taste of Tuscany.

THAI

Red Bamboo 6803 S. Kirkman Road at International Drive, Orlando; ☎ 407-226-8997; **redbamboothai.com;** moderate. Housed in an unassuming strip-mall location and acclaimed by Orlando dining critics for its authentic Thai dishes. Delicious vegetarian options; impressive wine list. The *Unofficial* research team agrees that this is some of the best Thai food in Orlando. Try the distinctly non-Thai fried cheesecake for dessert.

**20 minutes or more from Walt Disney World*

Continued from page 413

CHINESE SUPER BUFFETS Whoa! Talk about an oxymoron. If you've ever tried preparing Chinese food, especially a stir-fry, you know that split-second timing is required to avoid overcooking. So it should come as no big surprise that Chinese dishes languishing on a buffet lose their freshness, texture, and flavor in a hurry.

For the past few editions of this guide, we were able to find several Chinese buffets that were better than the rest and that we felt comfortable recommending. Unfortunately, however, our endorsements seem to be the kiss of death: We return the next year to discover that quality has slipped precipitously. We attempted to find a new buffet to replace the ones we deleted from the guide, and we can tell you that wasn't fun work. At the end of the day, **Ace Plus Chinese Buffet** (8701 W. Irlo Bronson Memorial Highway; ☎ 407-390-7588; **acepluschinese buffet.com**) is the only Chinese buffet we've elected to list. To call it a *super* buffet might be a stretch, but it's pretty good.

INDIAN BUFFETS Indian food works better on a buffet than Chinese food; in fact, it actually improves as the flavors marry. In the Disney World area, most Indian restaurants offer a buffet at lunch only—not too convenient if you're spending your day at the theme parks. If you're out shopping or taking a day off, these Indian buffets are worth trying:

AASHIRWAD INDIAN CUISINE 5748 International Drive, at the corner of International Drive and Kirkman Road; ☎ 407-370-9830

PUNJAB INDIAN RESTAURANT 7451 International Drive; ☎ 407-352-7887

BRAZILIAN BUFFETS A number of these have sprung up along International Drive. The best of these is **Café Mineiro** (6432 International Drive; ☎ 407-248-2932; **cafemineiroorlando.com**), north of Sand Lake Road.

SEAFOOD AND LOBSTER BUFFETS These affairs don't exactly fall under the category of inexpensive dining. The main draw (no pun intended) is all the lobster you can eat. The problem is that lobsters, like Chinese food, don't wear well on a steam table. After a few minutes on the buffet line, they make better tennis balls than dinner. If, however, there's someone in the kitchen who knows how to steam a lobster, and if you grab your lobster immediately after a fresh batch has been brought out, it'll probably be fine. There are three lobster buffets on US 192 and another two on International Drive. Although all five do a reasonable job, we prefer **Boston Lobster Feast** (6071 W. Irlo Bronson Memorial Highway; ☎ 407-396-2606; and 8731 International Drive, five blocks north of the Convention Center; ☎ 407-248-8606; **bostonlobster feast.com**). Both locations are distinguished by a vast variety of seafood in addition to the lobster. The International Drive location is cavernous and insanely noisy, which is why we prefer the Irlo Bronson location, where you can actually have a conversation over dinner. The International Drive location has ample parking, while parking places are in short supply at the Irlo Bronson restaurant. At about $36.95 for early birds (4–6 p.m.) and $40 after 6 p.m., dining is expensive at both locations.

SALAD BUFFETS The most popular of these in the Walt Disney World area is **Sweet Tomatoes** (6877 S. Kirkman Road, ☎ 407-363-1616; 12561 S. Apopka–Vineland Road, ☎ 407-938-9461; 3236 Rolling Oaks Blvd., off US 192 near the FL 429 western entrance to Walt Disney World, ☎ 407-465-0023; **sweettomatoes.com**). During lunch and dinner, you can expect a line out the door, but fortunately one that moves fast. The buffet features prepared salads and an extensive array of ingredients for building your own. In addition to the rabbit food, Sweet Tomatoes offers a variety of soups, a modest pasta bar, a baked-potato bar, an assortment of fresh fruit, and ice-cream sundaes. Dinner runs $10 for adults, $5 for children ages 6–12, and $3.49 for children ages 3–5. Lunch is $8.79 for adults and the same prices as dinner for children.

BREAKFAST AND ENTREE BUFFETS Most chain steakhouses in the area, including **Ponderosa, Sizzler,** and **Golden Corral,** offer entree buffets. Among them, they have 18 locations in the Walt Disney World area. All serve breakfast, lunch, and dinner. At lunch and dinner, you get the buffet when you buy an entree, usually a steak. Generally speaking, the buffets are less elaborate than a stand-alone buffet but considerably more varied than a salad bar. Breakfast service is a straightforward buffet (that is, you aren't obligated to buy an entree). As for the food, it's chain-restaurant quality but decent all the same. Prices are a bargain, and you can get in and out at lightning speed—important at breakfast when you're trying to get to the theme parks early. Some locations offer lunch and dinner buffets at a set price without your having to buy an entree.

Though you can argue about which chain serves the best steak, Golden Corral wins the buffet contest hands-down, with at least twice as many offerings as its three competitors. While buffets at Golden Corral and Ponderosa are pretty consistent from location to location, the buffets at the different Sizzlers vary a good deal. Our pick of the Sizzlers is the one at 7602 W. Irlo Bronson Memorial Highway (☎ 407-397-0997). In addition to the steakhouses, area **Shoney's** also offer breakfast, lunch, and dinner buffets. Local freebie visitor magazines are full of discount coupons for all of the previous restaurants.

MEAL DEALS Discount coupons are available for a wide range of restaurants, including some wonderful upscale-ethnic places such as **Ming Court** (Chinese; 9188 International Drive, Orlando; ☎ 407-351-9988; **ming-court.com**).

A meat eater's delight is the Feast for Four at **Sonny's Real Pit Bar-B-Q**, a Florida chain that turns out good barbecue. For $40 per family of four, you get sliced pork and beef plus chicken, ribs, your choice of three sides (choose from beans, slaw, fries, among others), garlic bread or cornbread, and soft drinks or tea, all served family-style. The closest Sonny's location to the Walt Disney World and Universal tourist areas is at 7423 S. Orange Blossom Trail in Orlando (☎ 407-859-7197); for a listing of other locations within a wider radius, visit **sonnysbbq.com**. No coupons are available (or needed) for Sonny's, but they're available for the other "meateries."

COUPONS Find discounts and two-for-one coupons for many of the restaurants mentioned in freebie visitor guides available at most hotels outside of Walt Disney World. The **Orlando–Orange County Official Visitors Center** (8723 International Drive; ☎ 407-363-5872; open daily, 8:30 a.m.–6:30 p.m., except Christmas) offers a treasure trove of coupons and free visitor magazines. On the Internet, check out **couponsalacarte.com** and **orlandocoupons.com** for printable coupons.

DINING *in* WALT DISNEY WORLD

THIS SECTION AIMS TO HELP YOU find good food without going broke or tripping over a culinary land mine. More than 100 restaurants operate within the World, including about 75 full-service establishments, 29 of which are inside the theme parks. Disney restaurants offer exceptional variety, serving everything from Moroccan to Texas barbecue. Most restaurants are expensive, and many serve less-than-distinguished fare, but the culinary scene gets better every year.

GETTING IT RIGHT

ALTHOUGH WE WORK HARD to be fair, objective, and accurate, many readers, like this woman from Charleston, West Virginia, think we're too critical of Walt Disney World restaurants:

Get a life! It's crazy and unrealistic to be so snobbish about restaurants at a theme park. Considering the number of people Disney feeds each day, I think they do a darn good job. Also, you act so surprised that the food is expensive. Have you ever eaten at an airport? HELLO IN THERE? . . . Surprise, you're a captive! It's a theme park!

And a mom from Erie, Pennsylvania, struck a practical note:

Most of the food at Walt Disney World is OK. If you pay attention to what other visitors say and what's in the guidebooks, you can avoid the yucky places. It's true that you pay more than you should, but it's more convenient to eat in Walt Disney World than to run around trying to find cheaper restaurants somewhere else. When it comes to Walt Disney World, who needs more running around?

As you may infer from these reader comments, researching and reviewing restaurants is no straightforward endeavor—to the contrary, it's fraught with peril. We have read dining reviews by writers who turn up their noses at anything except four-star French restaurants. We've read reviews absolutely devoid of criticism, written by "experts" unwilling to risk offending the source of their free meals. Finally, we've seen reviews in dining guides that are wholly based on surveys submitted by diners whose credentials for evaluating fine dining are mysterious at best and questionable at least.

How, then, do we go about presenting the best possible dining coverage? At the *Unofficial Guide,* we begin with highly qualified culinary experts and then balance their opinions with those of our readers—which, by the way, don't always coincide. (Likewise, the coauthors' assessments don't always agree with those of our dining experts.)

In the spirit of democracy, we also encourage you to fill out the restaurant surveys in the back of this guide. If you want to share your dining experience in great depth, write to us at the address on page 14 or e-mail us at **unofficialguides@menasharidge.com.**

DISNEY DINING 101

DISNEY DINING PLANS

DISNEY OFFERS SEVERAL DINING PLANS. If you choose to sign up for a plan, you must do so when you book your Disney resort room or package vacation; for this reason, we explore the topic in-depth in Part Three, Accommodations.

IT'S THE ECONOMY, PLUTO

AS TOUGH TIMES AFFECT the number of travelers visiting the World, Disney is scrambling furiously to make up for lost revenue. Unfortunately, this translates to higher and higher prices at Disney restaurants. Main-course prices at some restaurants have risen more than 35%; plus, Disney levies a "dining surcharge" during the summer and other busy times of year. Recently we dined at The Wave restaurant at the Contemporary Resort and ordered a wine that retails for about $10.95 a bottle. It was $9 a glass (!)—about a five-times markup. Believe us—if you rent a car and eat dinner each day at non-Disney restaurants, you'll save enough to more than pay for the rental cost.

These comments from a Tennessee reader spell it out:

The first time we ate at Liberty Tree Tavern a few years ago, the cost was about $23 per person for each adult. This year, the cost would've been about $33 per person with the increased prices and the "holiday dining surcharge" they add during the summer months. This is a nearly 40% price increase over a period of three years for basically the same experience!

And from a New Orleans mom:

Disney keeps pushing prices up and up. For us, the sky is NOT the limit. We won't be back.

BEHIND THE SCENES AT ADVANCE RESERVATIONS

ALTHOUGH THEY'RE CALLED Advance Reservations, most reservations at Disney World don't guarantee you a table at a specific time as they would at your typical hometown restaurant. Disney restaurants operate on what they call a "template system." Instead of scheduling Advance Reservations for actual tables, reservationists fill time slots. The number of slots available is based on the average observed length of time that guests occupy a table at a particular restaurant, adjusted for seasonality.

Here's a rough example of how it works: Let's say Coral Reef Restaurant at Epcot has 40 tables for four and 8 tables for six, and that the average length of time for a family to be seated, order, eat, pay, and depart is 40 minutes. Add 5 minutes to bus the table and set it up for the next guests, and the table is turning every 45 minutes. The restaurant provides Walt Disney World Dining (a.k.a. ☎ 407-WDW-DINE, 939-3463) with a computer template of its capacity, along with the average time the table is occupied. Thus, when WDW-DINE makes Advance Reservations for four people at 6:15 p.m., the system removes one table for four from overall capacity for 45 minutes. The template on the reservationist's computer indicates that the table will not be available for reassignment until 7 p.m. (45 minutes later). So it goes for all tables in the restaurant, each being subtracted from overall capacity for 45 minutes, then listed as available again, and then assigned to other guests and subtracted again, and so on, throughout the meal period. The WDW-DINE hotline tries to fill every time slot for every seat in the restaurant, or come as close to filling every slot as possible. No seats—repeat, none—are reserved for walk-ins.

Templates are filled differently depending on the season and restaurant. Some Disney restaurants charge a no-show fee; this has reduced the no-show rate to as little as 2%, and these restaurants are booked every day according to their actual capacity. The no-show rate is as high as 33% at restaurants that don't charge a no-show penalty, especially during slower times of year. At these, WDW-DINE will overbook the restaurant based on its historical no-show rate, meaning walk-ins stand a decent shot of getting a seat.

With Advance Reservations, your wait will usually be less than 20 minutes during peak hours, and often less than 10 minutes. If you walk in, especially during busier seasons, expect to either wait 40–75 minutes or be told that no tables are available.

GETTING ADVANCE RESERVATIONS
AT POPULAR RESTAURANTS

CINDERELLA'S ROYAL TABLE, in Cinderella Castle in the Magic Kingdom, hosts the immensely popular character breakfast starring Cinderella and other Disney princesses. The toughest character-meal ticket at Disney World is an 8 a.m. Advance Reservation for this venue when the Magic Kingdom opens at 9 a.m. Why? Cinderella's Royal Table is Disney's tiniest character-meal restaurant, accommodating only about 130 diners at a time. During the busiest times of year, demand so outstrips supply for this event that some Disney World visitors find themselves going to unbelievable lengths to secure an Advance Reservation.

unofficial **TIP**
Disney now charges a $10-to-$25-per-person penalty for missing an Advance Reservation at a character meal or Disney Signature restaurant, or if you cancel within 24 hours of the meal.

On the upside, Disney now offers online reservations starting at 6 a.m. Eastern time, a full hour before phone reservations open, at **disneyworld .disney.go.com/reservations/dining.** If you have access to a computer in the morning, this is by far the easiest way to secure a table for any restaurant you like. So that you become familiar with how it works, we suggest trying this site out a couple of days before you actually need to make reservations.

If you're visiting during the off-season and you're not too fussy about which meal you get or what time you eat, our research has found that you can usually book a few weeks out from your desired date (see page 423). If you're visiting Disney World during summer or around a major holiday, or you want to dine at a specific popular time, read on.

The only way to get a table is to obtain an Advance Reservation directly through Disney. Your best chance of getting that reservation is to book online at 6 a.m. Eastern time, exactly 180 days before the day you want to eat. (You'll save time if you set up an account at the website above before the 180-day booking window.) If you live in California and have to get up at 3 a.m. Pacific time to call, Disney couldn't give a mouse's patoot. There's no limit to the number of hoops they can make their patrons jump through if demand exceeds supply.

To be among the fortunate few who score an Advance Reservation during peak times, try the following: First, try on the correct morning. Use a calendar and count backward exactly 180 days from (but not including) the day you wish to dine. (Disney's computers don't understand months, so you can't, for example, try on January 1 to make an Advance Reservation for July 1, because that's more than 180 days.) If you want to eat on May 1, for example, begin your 180-day backward count on April 30. If you count correctly, you'll find that the correct morning to try is November 2. If you don't feel like counting days, call ☎ 407-WDW-DINE and the Disney folks will calculate it for you. Call them during the afternoon, when they're less busy, about 185 days before your trip. Let them know when you'd like your Advance Reservation, and they'll tell you which morning to book.

To get a table, you must be online on Disney's dining-reservations page at almost exactly 6 a.m. Eastern time. Once there, you'll see a place to enter a restaurant name (type "Cinderella's Royal Table"—*without* the quotes), a place to specify the time of your meal, and your party

Advance Reservations: The Official Line

YOU CAN RESERVE THE FOLLOWING up to 180 days in advance:

AFTERNOON TEA AND CHILDREN'S PROGRAMS at the Grand Floridian Resort & Spa

ALL DISNEY TABLE-SERVICE RESTAURANTS and character-dining venues

FANTASMIC! **DINING PACKAGE** at Disney's Hollywood Studios

HOOP-DEE-DOO MUSICAL REVUE at Fort Wilderness Resort & Campground

MICKEY'S BACKYARD BBQ at Fort Wilderness Resort & Campground

SPIRIT OF ALOHA DINNER SHOW at the Polynesian Resort

Guests staying at Walt Disney World resorts—these do *not* include the Swan, the Dolphin, Shades of Green, or the hotels of the Downtown Disney Resort Area—can book their dining 180 days before their arrival date and can book dining reservations for their entire length of stay (up to 10 days).

ADVANCE RESERVATIONS ONLINE

TO RESERVE ONLINE, log on to **disneyworld.disney.go.com/reserva tions/dining.** An e-form will come up where you can enter the name of the restaurant you want to book, your party size, and the date and time for which you'd like to make your reservations. If you're on the Disney Dining Plan and want to use dining credits, there's a prompt for that as well. After selecting a date, you must enter your preferred reservation time or, alternatively, a meal period. If, for example, you select "breakfast" instead of entering a specific time, you're essentially saying that anytime during the hours breakfast is served is fine. If you enter a particular time, say 9:30 a.m., and no tables are available, the online reservation system will display alternative locations at the same time, but it won't show you alternate days for the same location. For instance, if you want Cinderella's Royal Table for breakfast on July 1 and it isn't available, Disney might tell you that The Crystal Palace is; it won't tell you, however, if Cindy's is available on July 2 instead. The advantage of booking online is that you can submit your request an hour earlier than on the phone. The disadvantage is that you can't speak with a live person who can help you explore other options if your preferred reservation time is unavailable. (*Note:* **Disney's online-reservations system opens at 6 a.m. Eastern time—an hour earlier than the phone-reservation system.**)

size; fill these in ahead of time. You'll also see a text box where you can specify the date of your visit. Click on the "Date" text box, enter the date of your visit in MM/DD/YYYY format (for example, 07/01/2012 for July 1, 2012), and press the tab key on your keyboard. (You can also click on the blue calendar icon to flip through a month-by-month calendar, but this is slower.) If your date isn't yet available, a message will appear saying you've chosen a date more than 180 days in advance of today. If this happens, refresh the page within your browser and start over. If you don't see an error message, however, click the "Search for a Table" button to send your request to Disney's computers.

Disney doesn't calibrate its clock with the correct time as determined by the U.S. Naval Observatory or the National Institute of

Advance Reservations: The Unofficial Scoop

USING THE ONLINE ADVANCE RESERVATIONS SYSTEM, we've built profiles of each theme park restaurant, showing how many days in advance (on average) you need to call or click in order to get a seat at any table, at any time. Our results are shown in the tables on the next two pages.

There are many changes from last year's table, almost certainly because Disney is now charging a $10-to-$25-per-person no-show penalty at many popular restaurants. Before this, it was common for people to make reservations at two or more restaurants, often in different theme parks, for the same meal, then show up only at the one most convenient to their schedule that day. This made it difficult for the average guest to get reservations. With the penalty, some restaurants' no-show rate has dropped almost to zero. The penalty ensures that serious diners have some chance to get into Disney's better restaurants.

These days you'll need to reserve only seven breakfast venues in advance most times of the year. The most popular of these is **Cinderella's Royal Table** at the Magic Kingdom. If you don't care what time you eat, you'll need to call about 10 weeks out to get in for breakfast. If you're visiting during a holiday or peak season, or you want a specific time such as 8 a.m., you'll need to call a full 180 days in advance. If Cindy's is unavailable, we recommend **'Ohana** at the Polynesian Resort, which can be booked as little as a week before your trip.

Likewise, only a handful of restaurants require lunch reservations. The most popular is Epcot's **Le Cellier Steakhouse,** in the Canada Pavilion, which fills up about seven weeks in advance. Le Cellier's lunch was popular in 2012 because its dinner is a Disney Signature experience, with much higher prices. (*Note:* Le Cellier's lunch will be a Signature experience in 2013 too.) We suspect that **House of Blues** and **Raglan Road** appear on this list because their management may be setting aside some tables for walk-up guests, making the supply of available reservations artificially low in Disney's reservation system. If you have your heart set on eating lunch at either of these and tables are unavailable online, try calling directly or asking in person.

Dinner reservations are generally easy to get within 60 days at most locations, as long as you're not particular about the time you eat. (If that's critical to your family's happiness, call or click 180 days in advance.) The most in-demand restaurants—**Cítricos, Narcoossee's,** and **Victoria & Albert's**—are all at the Grand Floridian Resort. While they're good dinner choices, we suspect that, as with the House of Blues and Raglan Road, some tables at Cítricos and Narcoossee's are being withheld from Disney's reservation system to accommodate last-minute dining requests from VIPs and guests staying in club-level rooms. Victoria & Albert's, however, is frequently a difficult dinner table to get at any time of evening.

Standards and Technology, but we conducted synchronizing tests and determined that Disney reservation-system clocks are accurate to within a handful of seconds. Several Internet sites will give you the exact time. Our favorite is **atomictime.net,** which offers the exact time in displays that show hours, minutes, and seconds. Once the Atomic Time home page is up, click on "HTML multizone continuous" and look for the Eastern time zone. Using this site or your local time-of-day number from the phone book, synchronize your computer to the

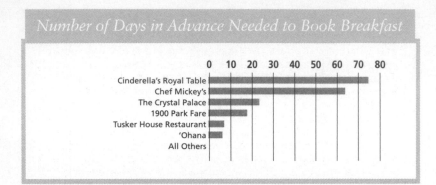

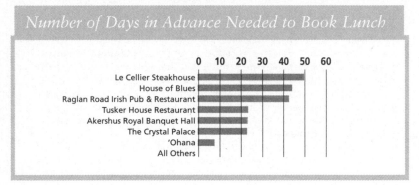

second. About 3 minutes before 6 a.m., start trying to enter your dates to see if they're accepted.

Bear in mind that while you're typing, other guests are trying to make Advance Reservations too, so you want the transaction to go down as quickly as possible. Flexibility on your part counts—it's much harder to get a seating for a large group, so give some thought to breaking your group into numbers that can be accommodated at tables for four. Also make sure that you have your credit card out where you can read it.

All Advance Reservations for Cinderella's Royal Table character meals, the *Fantasmic!* Dining Package, the *Hoop-Dee-Doo Musical Revue,* the *Spirit of Aloha Dinner Show,* and *Mickey's Backyard BBQ* require complete prepayment with a credit card at the time of the booking. The name on the booking can't be changed after the Advance Reservation is made. Reservations may be canceled, with the deposit refunded in full, by calling ☎ 407-WDW-DINE at least 24 hours (Cindy's) or 48 hours (*Fantasmic!* and the dinner shows) before seating time.

While many readers have been successful using our strategies, some have not:

> *I got up extra-early 180 days before our trip to get Thanksgiving reservations at Le Cellier for my husband's birthday. Even though I logged on to Disney's website right at 6 a.m., by the time I got done typing and clicking the only table that was available was for 8:40 p.m.—too late for our children, and we would have missed IllumiNations.*

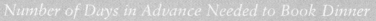

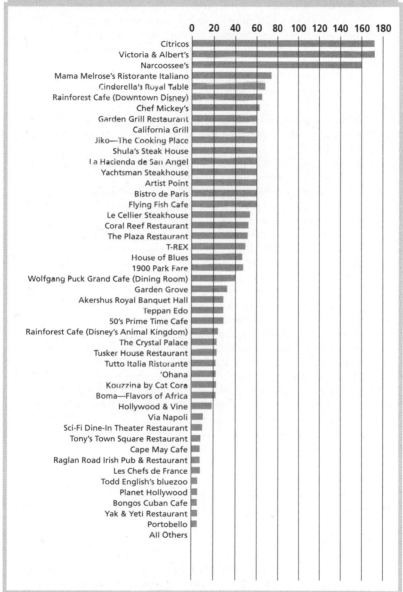

Number of Days in Advance Needed to Book Dinner

Citricos	
Victoria & Albert's	
Narcoossee's	
Mama Melrose's Ristorante Italiano	
Cinderella's Royal Table	
Rainforest Cafe (Downtown Disney)	
Chef Mickey's	
Garden Grill Restaurant	
California Grill	
Jiko—The Cooking Place	
Shula's Steak House	
La Hacienda de San Angel	
Yachtsman Steakhouse	
Artist Point	
Bistro de Paris	
Flying Fish Cafe	
Le Cellier Steakhouse	
Coral Reef Restaurant	
The Plaza Restaurant	
T-REX	
House of Blues	
1900 Park Fare	
Wolfgang Puck Grand Cafe (Dining Room)	
Garden Grove	
Akershus Royal Banquet Hall	
Teppan Edo	
50's Prime Time Cafe	
Rainforest Cafe (Disney's Animal Kingdom)	
The Crystal Palace	
Tusker House Restaurant	
Tutto Italia Ristorante	
'Ohana	
Kouzzina by Cat Cora	
Boma—Flavors of Africa	
Hollywood & Vine	
Via Napoli	
Sci-Fi Dine-In Theater Restaurant	
Tony's Town Square Restaurant	
Cape May Cafe	
Raglan Road Irish Pub & Restaurant	
Les Chefs de France	
Todd English's bluezoo	
Planet Hollywood	
Bongos Cuban Cafe	
Yak & Yeti Restaurant	
Portobello	
All Others	

On most days, a couple hundred users slam Disney's computer system within milliseconds of one another. With this volume, a 20th of a second or less can make the difference between getting a table and not getting one. As it happens, there are variables beyond your control. One is the number of computers through which your request passes before it reaches Disney's reservation system. The explanation is somewhat technical, but the same principle applies whether you're trying to get dining reservations online with Disney or concert seats through Ticketmaster.

When you enter a URL into your web browser, the request for that page gets passed through a series of intermediate computers spread throughout the Internet. The specific route is chosen based on network speed and traffic volume, and preference is given to faster routes. For example, from Len Testa's house in the Greensboro, North Carolina, suburb of Summerfield, the request for Disney's dining page usually goes from his computer to a small Time Warner Cable facility in Greensboro. From there it's routed through Raleigh, North Carolina, to Washington, D.C. From Washington it goes through Chicago, then Denver, and then Las Vegas before finally making it to Disney's computers. (This also tells us that Disney's computers may be hosted somewhere out west—nowhere near Orlando.)

Distance counts too, though we're talking milliseconds. Thus, it takes just a bit longer for a request to reach Disney's computers from Chicago than from Atlanta, and longer yet if you're trying from New York.

If you don't have access to a computer at 6 a.m. on the morning you need to make reservations, Disney's phone agents begin taking calls at 7 a.m. Eastern time. Call ☎ 407-WDW-DINE and follow the prompts to speak to a live person. You may still get placed on hold if call volume is higher than usual, and you'll be an hour behind the early birds with computers. Still, you'll be well ahead of those who couldn't make it up before sunrise.

Also, if you're on the Disney Dining Plan and you want to book the *Fantasmic!* package, Cinderella's Royal Table, or one the dinner shows, you may be better off reserving by phone. The online system may not recognize your table-service credits, but you can book and pay with a credit card and then call ☎ 407-WDW-DINE after 7 a.m. and have them credit the charge for the meal back to your card (a potential hassle if you get an uncooperative cast member). When you get to Walt Disney World, you'll use credits from your dining plan to "pay" for the meal. (Sometimes the online system has glitches and shows no availability; in this case, call after 7 a.m. to confirm if the online system is correct.)

NEVER, NEVER, NEVER, NEVER GIVE UP Not getting what you want the first time you try doesn't mean the end of the story. A mom from Cincinnati recommends persistence in securing Advance Reservations:

> *I was crushed when I called and tried to reserve Chef Mickey's and couldn't. I decided not to give up and would go online once or twice a day to check reservations for Chef Mickey's and the other restaurants I wanted. It took me about a week, but sooner or later I ended up booking every single reservation I wanted except 'Ohana. Bottom line: Keep trying to book reservations even if you don't immediately get what you want. You never know when something may open up.*

IF YOU STILL CAN'T GET AN ADVANCE RESERVATION If you insist on a meal at a specific restaurant but can't get an Advance Reservation, go to the restaurant on the day you wish to dine and try for a table as a walk-in (most full-service restaurants take walk-ins between 2:30 and 4:30

p.m.). This is a long shot, though it's possible during the least busy times of year. There's also a fair shot at success on cold or rainy days during busier seasons, when there's a good chance of no-shows. If you try to walk in then, your chances are best during the last hour of serving.

Landing an Advance Reservation for Cinderella's Royal Table at dinner is somewhat easier than for breakfast or lunch, but the price is a whopping $54 for adults and $33 for children ages 3–9. As at the other two meals, five photos of your group, a photo of Cinderella Castle, and a Cinderella-themed photo holder are included in the price—like it or not. If you're unable to lock up a table for breakfast or lunch, a dinner reservation will at least get your children inside the castle.

A Snellville, Georgia, mom recalls:

> We ate dinner at Cinderella Castle to fulfill my longtime dream. The menu was very limited and expensive. For three people, no appetizers or dessert, the bill was $100.

And no booze—alcohol isn't served in the Magic Kingdom.

CANCELING AN ADVANCE RESERVATION Disney now charges a per-person penalty fee if you fail to show up for an Advance Reservation at a character meal or Disney Signature restaurant, or if you cancel within 24 hours of the meal. Don't worry, however, if you book a table for six and only one of you makes it—you won't be penalized at all as long as at least one person appears for the meal.

A $10 no-show penalty is enforced at the following restaurants, except as noted: **Akershus Royal Banquet Hall, Artist Point, California Grill, Cape May Cafe, Le Cellier Steakhouse, Chef Mickey's, Cítricos, The Crystal Palace, Flying Fish Cafe, Garden Grill Restaurant, Hollywood & Vine, The Hollywood Brown Derby, Jiko—The Cooking Place, Narcoossee's, 1900 Park Fare, 'Ohana, Tusker House Restaurant, Victoria & Albert's** ($25 fee), and **Yachtsman Steakhouse**.

*un***official TIP**
Smoking is banned at all restaurants and lounges on Walt Disney World property. Diners who puff must feed their nicotine fix outdoors—and in the theme parks, that might also mean going to a designated smoking area.

DRESS

DRESS IS INFORMAL AT MOST THEME PARK restaurants, but Disney has a "business casual" dress code for some of its resort restaurants: khakis, dress slacks, jeans, or dress shorts with a collared shirt for men and capris, skirts, dresses, jeans, and dress shorts for women. Restaurants with this dress code are **Jiko—The Cooking Place** at Animal Kingdom Lodge & Villas, the **Flying Fish Cafe** at the BoardWalk, the **California Grill** at the Contemporary Resort, **Bistro de Paris** at Epcot's France Pavilion, **Cítricos** and **Narcoossee's** at the Grand Floridian Resort & Spa, **Artist Point** at Wilderness Lodge, **Yachtsman Steakhouse** at the Yacht Club Resort, **Todd English's bluezoo** and **Shula's Steak House** at the Dolphin, and **Il Mulino New York Trattoria** at the Swan. **Victoria & Albert's** at the Grand Floridian is the only Disney restaurant that requires men to wear a jacket to dinner.

FOOD ALLERGIES AND SPECIAL REQUESTS

IF YOU HAVE FOOD ALLERGIES or observe some specific type of diet like eating kosher, make your needs known when you make your

Advance Reservations. Does it work? Well, a Phillipsburg, New Jersey, mom reports her family's experience:

> *My 6-year-old has many food allergies, and we often have to bring food with us to restaurants when we go out to eat. I was able to make reservations at the Disney restaurants in advance and indicate these allergies to the reservation clerk. When we arrived at the restaurants, the staff was already aware of my child's allergies and assigned our table a chef who double-checked the list of allergies with us. Each member of the waitstaff was also informed of the allergies. The chefs were very nice and made my son feel very special.*

A FEW CAVEATS

BEFORE YOU BEGIN EATING your way through the World, you need to know:

1. Theme park restaurants rush their customers in order to make room for the next group of diners. Dining at high speed may appeal to a family with young, restless children, but for people wanting to relax, it's more like eating in a pressure chamber than fine dining.

2. If you're dining in a theme park and cost is an issue, make lunch your main meal. Entrees are similar to those on the dinner menu, but prices are significantly lower.

3. Disney adds a surcharge of $4 per adult and $2 per child to certain popular restaurants during weeks of peak attendance, including Presidents Day, Easter, Thanksgiving, and Christmas, and every day from mid-June to mid-August. The following restaurants participate in the gouging: **Akershus Royal Banquet Hall** (Princess Storybook Dining), **Biergarten, Boma—Flavors of Africa** (breakfast and dinner), **Cape May Cafe** (breakfast and dinner buffet), **Chef Mickey's** (breakfast and dinner), **Cinderella's Royal Table, The Crystal Palace, Garden Grill Restaurant, Hollywood & Vine** (Play 'n Dine character buffets), the *Hoop-Dee-Doo Musical Revue, Liberty Tree Tavern* (dinner), *Mickey's Backyard BBQ,* **1900 Park Fare** (Supercalifragilistic Breakfast and Cinderella's Happily Ever After Dinner), **'Ohana** (breakfast and dinner), the *Spirit of Aloha Dinner Show,* **Trail's End Restaurant** at Fort Wilderness (an exception: $2 extra for adults and $1 for kids), and **Tusker House Restaurant.** Not to be left out, folks on the Disney Dining Plan pay their own special surcharge—$2 for adults and $1 for kids during peak times—and at every restaurant on the plan.

WALT DISNEY WORLD RESTAURANT CATEGORIES

IN GENERAL, FOOD AND BEVERAGE offerings at Walt Disney World are defined by service, price, and convenience:

FULL-SERVICE RESTAURANTS Full-service restaurants are in all Disney resorts (except the All-Star Resorts, Art of Animation, Port Orleans French Quarter, and Pop Century) and all major theme parks, Downtown Disney Marketplace, and Downtown Disney West Side. Disney operates most of the restaurants in the theme parks and its hotels, while contractors or franchisees operate the restaurants in hotels of the Downtown Disney Resort Area (DDRA), the Swan and Dolphin resorts, and some in Disney's Animal Kingdom, Epcot, the BoardWalk, and Downtown Disney Marketplace–West Side. Advance Reservations (see pages 420–

427) are recommended for most full-service restaurants except those in the DDRA. The restaurants accept American Express, Carte Blanche, Diners Club, Japan Credit Bureau, MasterCard, and Visa.

BUFFETS AND FAMILY-STYLE RESTAURANTS Many of these have Disney characters in attendance, and most have a separate children's menu featuring dishes such as hot dogs, burgers, chicken nuggets, pizza, macaroni and cheese, and spaghetti and meatballs. In addition to the buffets, several restaurants serve a family-style, all-you-can-eat, fixed-price meal.

Walt Disney World Buffets and Family-Style Restaurants

LOCATION	RESTAURANT	CUISINE	MEALS SERVED	CHAR- ACTERS
ANIMAL KINGDOM LODGE	Boma— Flavors of Africa	African (D), American (B)	B, D	No
BEACH CLUB RESORT	Cape May Cafe	American	B, D	Yes (B)
CONTEMPORARY RESORT	Chef Mickey's	American	B, D	Yes
DISNEY'S ANIMAL KINGDOM	Tusker House	African (L, D), American (B)	B, L, D	Yes (B, L)
DISNEY'S HOLLYWOOD STUDIOS	Hollywood & Vine	American	B, L, D	Yes (B, L)
EPCOT	Akershus Royal Banquet Hall	American (B), Norwegian (L, D)	B, L, D	Yes
EPCOT	Biergarten	German	L, D	No
EPCOT	The Garden Grill	American	D	Yes
FORT WILDERNESS	Hoop-Dee-Doo Musical Revue	American	D	No
FORT WILDERNESS	Mickey's Backyard BBQ	American	D	Yes
FORT WILDERNESS	Trail's End Restaurant	American	B***, L, D***	No
GRAND FLORIDIAN	1900 Park Fare	American	B, D	Yes
THE MAGIC KINGDOM	Cinderella's Royal Table	American	B*, L, D	Yes
THE MAGIC KINGDOM	The Crystal Palace	American	B, L, D	Yes
THE MAGIC KINGDOM	Liberty Tree Tavern	American	L, D†	No
POLYNESIAN RESORT	'Ohana	Polynesian	B, D	Yes (B)
POLYNESIAN RESORT	Spirit of Aloha Dinner Show	American	D	No
SWAN	Garden Grove	American	B‡, L‡, D	Yes B**, D
WILDERNESS LODGE	Whispering Canyon Cafe	American	B, L, D	No
YACHT CLUB RESORT	Captain's Grille	American	B*, L, D	No

> * Serves family-style meals only at breakfast.
> ** Character-breakfast buffet served only on weekends.
> *** Serves buffet-style meals only at breakfast and dinner.
> † Serves family-style meals only at dinner.
> ‡ Serves family-style meals only at breakfast and lunch.

Advance Reservations are required for character buffets and recommended for all other buffets and family-style restaurants. Most major credit cards are accepted.

If you want to eat a lot but don't feel like standing in yet another line, then consider one of the all-you-can-eat family-style restaurants. These feature platters of food brought to your table in courses by a server. You can sample everything on the menu and eat as much as you like. You can even go back to a favorite appetizer after you finish the main course. The food tends to be a little better than what you'll find on a buffet line.

The table on the previous page lists buffets and family-style restaurants (where you can belly up for bulk loading) at Walt Disney World.

FOOD COURTS Featuring a collection of counter-service eateries under one roof, food courts can be found at the Moderate resorts (Coronado Springs, Caribbean Beach, Port Orleans) and Value resorts (All-Star, Art of Animation, and Pop Century). (The closest thing to a food court at the theme parks is **Sunshine Seasons** at Epcot; see next page and page 452.) Advance Reservations are neither required nor available at these restaurants.

COUNTER SERVICE Counter-service fast food is available in all theme parks and at Downtown Disney Marketplace, the BoardWalk, and Downtown Disney West Side. The food compares in quality with Captain D's, McDonald's, or Taco Bell but is more expensive, though often served in larger portions.

FAST CASUAL Somewhere between burgers and formal dining are the establishments in Disney's "fast casual" category, including three in the theme parks: **Tomorrowland Terrace Restaurant** in the Magic Kingdom, **Sunshine Seasons** in Epcot, and **Studio Catering Co.** in Disney's Hollywood Studios. Fast-casual restaurants feature menu choices a cut above what you'd normally see at a typical counter-service location. At Sunshine Seasons, for example, chefs will prepare grilled salmon on an open cooking surface while you watch, or you can choose from rotisserie chicken or pork, tasty noodle bowls, or large sandwiches made with artisanal breads. Entrees cost about $2 more on average than traditional counter service, but the variety and food quality more than make up for the difference.

VENDOR FOOD Vendors abound at the theme parks, Downtown Disney Marketplace, Downtown Disney West Side, and the BoardWalk. Offerings include popcorn, ice-cream bars, churros (Mexican pastries), soft drinks, bottled water, and (in theme parks) fresh fruit. Prices include tax; many vendors are set up to accept credit cards, charges to your room at a Disney resort, and the Disney Dining Plan. Others take only cash (look for a sign near the cash register).

THE COST OF COUNTER-SERVICE FOOD

BAGEL OR MUFFIN	$2.59 *(bagel)*, $2.79 *(muffin)*
BROWNIE	$3.29
BURRITO	$7.09–$8.19
CAKE OR PIE	$3.59
CEREAL WITH MILK	$3.19
CHEESEBURGER WITH FRIES	$8.69–$9.19
CHICKEN-BREAST SANDWICH *(grilled)*	$4.75–$10.95 *(basket)*
CHICKEN NUGGETS WITH FRIES	$8.19
CHILDREN'S MEAL	$5.49
CHIPS	$2.69
COOKIES	$2.19
FISH *(fried)* BASKET WITH FRIES	$7.49–$8.99 *(shrimp)*
FRENCH FRIES	$2.49
FRUIT *(whole)*	$1.29
FRUIT CUP/FRUIT SALAD	$3.39
HOT DOG	$6.79 *(basket)*, $8.19 *(with gourmet toppings)*
ICE CREAM/FROZEN NOVELTIES	$3.29
NACHOS WITH CHEESE	$4.50–$7.69
PB&J SANDWICH	$2.49 *(à la carte)*, $5.49 *(kids' meal)*
PIZZA *(personal)*	$8.99–$9.49
POPCORN	$3.25–$4.49
PRETZEL	$3.50–$4.50
SALAD (ENTREE)	$7.19–$8.99
SALAD (SIDE)	$3.00
SMOKED TURKEY LEG	$7.59
SOUP/CHILI	$2.79–$4.49
SUB/DELI SANDWICH	$8.99–$9.99
TACO SALAD	$7.69–$8.19
VEGGIE BURGER	$7.59 *(basket)*

THE COST OF COUNTER-SERVICE DRINKS

DRINKS	SMALL	LARGE
BEER *(one size)* *	$5.25–$7.50	$5.25–$7.50
BOTTLED WATER *(one size)*	$2.50	$2.50
LATTE	$4.39	$5.39
COFFEE *(one size)*	$2.09	$2.09
FLOAT/MILKSHAKE/SUNDAE *(one size)*	$3.99–$4.19	$3.99–$4.19
FRUIT JUICE	$2.59	$2.89
HOT TEA AND COCOA *(one size)*	$2.09	$2.09
MILK	$1.49	$2.19
SOFT DRINKS, ICED TEA, AND LEMONADE	$2.49	$2.89

Refillable souvenir mugs cost $14.50 *(free refills)* at Disney resorts and $10 at water parks.
Each person on a Disney Dining Plan gets a free mug, refillable only at his/her Disney resort.
* Alcoholic beverages not sold in the Magic Kingdom.

HARD CHOICES

DINING DECISIONS WILL DEFINITELY affect your Walt Disney World experience. If you're short on time and you want to see the theme parks, avoid full service. Ditto if you're short on funds. If you do want full service, arrange Advance Reservations—again, they won't actually reserve you a table, but they can minimize your wait.

Integrating Meals into the *Unofficial Guide* Touring Plans

Arrive before the park of your choice opens. Tour expeditiously, using your chosen plan (taking as few breaks as possible), until about 11 or 11:30 a.m. Once the park becomes crowded around midday, meals and other breaks won't affect the plan's efficiency. If you intend to stay in the park for evening parades, fireworks, or other events, eat dinner early enough to be finished in time for the festivities.

Character Dining

A number of restaurants, primarily those that serve all-you-can-eat buffets and family-style meals, offer character dining. At character meals, you pay a fixed price and dine in the presence of one to five Disney characters who circulate throughout the restaurant, hugging children (and sometimes adults), posing for photos, and signing autographs. Character breakfasts, lunches, and dinners are served at restaurants in and out of the theme parks. For an extensive discussion of character dining, see the section starting on page 342 in Part Six, Walt Disney World with Kids.

FULL-SERVICE DINING FOR FAMILIES WITH YOUNG CHILDREN

DISNEY RESTAURANTS OFFER AN EXCELLENT (though expensive) opportunity to introduce young children to the variety and excitement of ethnic food. No matter how formal a restaurant appears, the staff is accustomed to fidgety, impatient, and often boisterous children. **Les Chefs de France** at Epcot, for instance, may be the nation's only French restaurant where most patrons wear shorts and T-shirts and at least two dozen young diners are attired in basic black . . . mouse ears.

unofficial **TIP**
Disney Kids' Meals are for kids ages 3–9.

Almost all Disney restaurants offer children's menus, and all have booster seats and high chairs. Servers understand how tough it may be for children to sit still for an extended period of time, and they'll supply little ones with crackers and rolls and serve your dinner much faster than in comparable restaurants elsewhere. Reader letters suggest that being served too quickly is much more common than having a long wait.

Good Walt Disney World Theme Park Restaurants for Children

In Epcot, preschoolers most enjoy the **Biergarten** in Germany, **San Angel Inn** in Mexico, and **Coral Reef Restaurant** at the Seas with Nemo & Friends Pavilion in Future World. The Biergarten combines a rollicking and noisy atmosphere with good basic food, including roast chicken; a German oompah band entertains, and kids can often participate in Bavarian dancing. San Angel Inn is in the Mexico village marketplace. From the table, children can watch boats on the Gran Fiesta Tour drift beneath a smoking volcano. With a choice of chips, tacos, and other familiar items, picky kids usually have no difficulty finding something to eat. (Be aware, though, that the service here is sometimes glacially slow.) Coral Reef, with tables beside windows looking into The Seas' aquarium, offers a satisfying mealtime diversion for all ages. If your children don't eat fish, Coral Reef also serves beef and chicken.

The Biergarten offers reasonable value, plus good food. The Coral Reef Restaurant and San Angel Inn are overpriced, though the food is palatable.

Cinderella's Royal Table in Cinderella Castle is the big draw in the Magic Kingdom. Interestingly, other Magic Kingdom full-service restaurants hold little appeal for children, but for the best combination of food and entertainment, we recommend booking a character meal at **The Crystal Palace.**

At Disney's Hollywood Studios, all ages enjoy the atmosphere and entertainment at **Hollywood & Vine,** the **Sci-Fi Dine-In Theater Restaurant,** and the **50's Prime Time Cafe.** Unfortunately, the Sci-Fi's food is close to dismal except for dessert, and the Prime Time's is uneven.

The three full-service restaurants at Disney's Animal Kingdom are **Tusker House Restaurant** (actually a buffet); **Rainforest Cafe,** a great favorite of children; and **Yak & Yeti Restaurant.**

QUIET, ROMANTIC PLACES TO EAT

RESTAURANTS WITH GOOD FOOD *and* a couple-friendly ambience are rare in the theme parks. Only a handful of dining locales satisfy both requirements: **Coral Reef Restaurant,** an alfresco table at **Tutto Italia Ristorante,** the terrace at the **Rose & Crown Dining Room,** and the upstairs tables at the France Pavilion's **Bistro de Paris,** all in Epcot; and the corner booths at **The Hollywood Brown Derby** in Disney's Hollywood Studios. Waterfront dining (though not necessarily quiet or romantic) is available at **Fulton's Crab House, Paradiso 37,** and **Portobello** at Downtown Disney and **Narcoossee's** at the Grand Floridian.

*un*official **TIP**
The **California Grill** atop the Contemporary Resort has the best view at Walt Disney World. If window tables aren't available, ask to be served in the adjoining lounge.

Victoria & Albert's at the Grand Floridian is the World's showcase gourmet restaurant; expect to pay big bucks. Other good choices for couples include **Artist Point** at Wilderness Lodge, **Cítricos** at the Grand Floridian, **Shula's Steak House** at the Dolphin, **Jiko—The Cooking Place** at Animal Kingdom Lodge, and **Flying Fish Cafe** at the BoardWalk.

Eating later in the evening and choosing a restaurant we've mentioned will improve your chances for intimate dining; nevertheless, children—well behaved or otherwise—are everywhere at Walt Disney World, and there's no way to escape them. These honeymooners from Slidell, Louisiana, write:

We made dinner reservations at some of the nicer Disney restaurants. We made sure to reserve past dinner hours, and we tried to stress that we were on our honeymoon. In every restaurant we went to, we were seated next to large families. The kids were usually tired and cranky. It's very difficult to enjoy a romantic dinner when there are small children crawling around under your table. We looked around the restaurant and always noticed lots of childless couples. Our suggestion: Seat couples without children together and families with kids elsewhere.

FAST FOOD IN THE THEME PARKS

BECAUSE MOST MEALS DURING a Disney World vacation are consumed on the run while touring, we'll tackle counter-service and vendor foods first. Plentiful in all theme parks are hot dogs, hamburgers, chicken sandwiches, salads, and pizza. They're augmented by special items that relate to the park's theme or the part of the park you're touring. In Epcot's Germany, for example, counter-service bratwurst and beer are sold. In Frontierland in the Magic Kingdom, vendors sell smoked turkey legs. Counter-service prices are fairly consistent from park to park. Expect to pay the same for your coffee or hot dog at Disney's Animal Kingdom as at Disney's Hollywood Studios.

Getting your act together in regard to counter-service restaurants in the parks is more a matter of courtesy than necessity. Rude guests rank fifth among reader complaints. A mother from Fort Wayne, Indiana, points out that indecision can be as maddening as outright discourtesy, especially when you're hungry:

> *Every fast-food restaurant has menu signs the size of billboards, but do you think anybody reads them? People waiting in line spend enough time in front of these signs to memorize them and still don't have a clue what they want when they finally get to the order taker. If by some miracle they've managed to choose between the hot dog and the hamburger, they then fiddle around another 10 minutes deciding what size Coke to order. Tell your readers PULEEEZ get their orders together ahead of time!*

Along similar lines, from an Austin, Texas, reader:

> *We did not get the Disney Dining Plan, but I found it annoying anyway. Whenever we were in line for food, invariably the people in front were on the plan and it took forever to figure out what was included or how many credits the people had.*

A North Carolina reader offers a tip for counter-service food lines:

> *Many counter-service registers serve two queues each, one to the left and one to the right of each register. People are not used to this and will instinctively line up in one queue per register, typically on the right side, leaving the left vacant. We had register operators wave us up to the front several times to start a left queue instead of waiting behind others on the right.*

Healthful Food at Walt Disney World

One of the most commendable developments in food service at Walt Disney World has been the introduction of healthier foods and snacks. People who have diabetes, vegetarians, dieters, those requiring kosher meals, and the like should have no trouble finding something to eat. The same goes for anyone seeking wholesome, nutritious food. Health-conscious choices are available at most fast-food counters and

unofficial **TIP**
Disney continues to work on eliminating added trans fats from foods served in the parks and resorts.

even from vendors. All the major theme parks, for example, have fresh-fruit stands.

Cutting Your Dining Time at the Theme Parks

Even if you confine your meals to vendor and counter-service fast food, you lose a lot of time getting food in the theme parks. Here are some ways to minimize the time you spend hunting and gathering:

1. Eat breakfast before you arrive. Restaurants outside the World offer some outstanding breakfast specials. Plus, some hotels furnish small refrigerators in their guest rooms, or you can rent a fridge or bring a cooler. If you can get by on cold cereal, rolls, fruit, and juice, this will save a ton of time.

2. After a good breakfast, buy snacks from vendors in the parks as you tour, or stuff some snacks in a fanny pack.

3. All theme park restaurants are busiest between 11:30 a.m. and 2:15 p.m. for lunch and 6 and 9 p.m. for dinner. For shorter lines and faster service, don't eat during these hours, especially 12:30–1:30 p.m.

4. Many counter-service restaurants sell cold sandwiches. Buy a cold lunch minus drinks before 11:30 a.m., and carry it in small plastic bags until you're ready to eat (within an hour or so of purchase). Ditto for dinner. Buy drinks at the appropriate time from any convenient vendor.

5. Most fast-food eateries have more than one service window. Regardless of the time of day, check the lines at all windows before queuing. Sometimes a window that's staffed but out of the way will have a much shorter line or none at all. Note, however, that some windows may offer only certain items.

6. If you're short on time and the park closes early, stay until closing and eat dinner outside Disney World before returning to your hotel. If the park stays open late, eat dinner about 4 or 4:30 p.m. at the restaurant of your choice. You should sneak in just ahead of the dinner crowd.

Beyond Counter Service: Tips for Saving Money on Food

Though buying food from counter-service restaurants and vendors will save time and money (compared with full-service dining), additional strategies can bolster your budget and maintain your waistline. Our readers offer the following suggestions for stretching food dollars. A Missouri mom writes:

We arrived at WDW after some days on the beach south of Sarasota. We shopped there and arrived with our steel Coleman cooler well stocked with milk and sandwich fixings. I froze a block of ice in a milk bottle, and we replenished it daily with ice from the resort ice machine. I also froze small packages of deli-type meats for later in the week. We ate cereal, milk, and fruit each morning, with boxed juices. I also had a hot pot to boil water for instant coffee, oatmeal, and soup.

Each child had a belt bag of his own, which he filled from a special box of "goodies" each day. Some things were actual food, like packages of crackers and cheese, packets of peanuts and raisins. Some were worthless junk, like candy and gum. Each child also had a small, rectangular plastic water bottle that could hang on the belt. We filled these at water fountains before getting into lines.

We left the park before noon, ate sandwiches, chips, and soda in the room, and napped. We purchased our evening meal in the park, at a counter-service eatery. We budgeted for both morning and evening snacks from a vendor but often didn't need them.

A Pennsylvania family adds:

Despite the warning against bringing food into the park, we packed a double picnic lunch in a backpack and a small shoulder bag. It cost $195 for the seven of us to tour the park for a day, and I felt that spending another $150 or so on two meals was not in the cards. We froze juice boxes to keep the meat sandwiches cool and had extra juice boxes and peanut butter sandwiches for a late-afternoon snack.

A Whiteland, Indiana, mom suggests:

One must-take item if you're traveling with younger kids is a supply of small paper or plastic cups to split drinks, which are both huge and expensive.

DISNEY DINING SUGGESTIONS

FOLLOWING ARE SUGGESTIONS for dining at each of the major theme parks. If you want to try a full-service restaurant at one of the parks, be aware that the restaurants continue to serve after the park's official closing time. We once showed up at The Hollywood Brown Derby just as Disney's Hollywood Studios closed at 8 p.m. We were seated almost immediately and enjoyed a leisurely dinner while the crowds cleared out.

unofficial **TIP**
Don't worry about dining late if you're depending on Disney transportation: Buses, boats, and monorails run 1–3 hours after the parks close.

THE MAGIC KINGDOM

FOOD AT THE MAGIC KINGDOM has improved noticeably in recent years. **The Crystal Palace** at the end of Main Street offers a good (albeit pricey) buffet chaperoned by Disney characters, while the **Liberty Tree Tavern** in Liberty Square features hearty family-style dining at dinner. **Cinderella's Royal Table,** a full-service restaurant on the second floor of the castle, delivers palatable meals in one of Walt Disney World's most distinctive (and popular) settings.

THE MAGIC KINGDOM

AUTHORS' FAVORITE COUNTER-SERVICE RESTAURANTS

Cosmic Ray's Starlight Cafe (limited kosher items)   *Tomorrowland*
Pecos Bill Tall Tale Inn & Cafe   *Frontierland*

Fast food at the Magic Kingdom is, well, fast food. It's more expensive, of course, than what you'd pay at McDonald's, but what do you expect? On the positive side, portions are large, sometimes large enough for children to share. Overall, the variety of fast-food offerings provides a lot of choice, though the number of selections at any specific eatery remains quite limited. Check our mini-profiles of the park's counter-service restaurants before you queue up.

Our dining recommendations for a day at the Magic Kingdom:

1. Take the monorail to one of the hotels for lunch. The trip takes very little time, and because most guests have left the hotels for the parks, the resorts' restaurants are often uncrowded. The food is better than the Magic Kingdom's; the service is faster; the atmosphere is more relaxed; and beer, wine, and mixed drinks are available.

2. Full-service restaurants that accept Advance Reservations for lunch and/or dinner fill quickly in the summer and during holiday periods. To obtain Advance Reservations, call ☎ 407-939-3463 or hotfoot it to your chosen restaurant as soon as you enter the park. Advance Reservations are explained starting on page 420, and Magic Kingdom full-service and counter-service restaurants are profiled later in this chapter.

3. Of the park's five full-service restaurants, **Liberty Tree Tavern** in Liberty Square is the best. **Tony's Town Square Restaurant** and **The Plaza Restaurant** on Main Street and **Cinderella's Royal Table** in the castle also serve decent food. Because children love Cinderella and everyone's curious about the castle, you need to make Advance Reservations before you leave home if you want to eat a meal at Cinderella's Royal Table (see page 421). Here, Advance Reservations for lunch and for dinner are easier to arrange than for breakfast.

4. A good rule at any full-service restaurant is to keep it simple. Order sandwiches or basic dishes (such as roast turkey and mashed potatoes).

Here are some comments from readers about Magic Kingdom full service and counter-service restaurants. First, regarding Cinderella's Royal Table character meals (each quote is from a different reader):

> *Our whole family did Cinderella's Royal Table for lunch. Our two little boys (ages 3 and 4) loved it even more than their 6-year-old sister. The boys loved all the princesses paying special attention to them since they were the only guys in the whole place. My 3-year-old left with his face covered in princess lipstick and even managed to propose to Cinderella—who, sadly, mentioned she was already married.*

> *The food was OK—a lot of characters: Snow White, Cinderella, Belle, Sleeping Beauty, Fairy Godmother, Mary Poppins. The place was not that big, but the characters spent a lot of time at each table—so much time that we only got to meet Snow White and Belle. The boys were bored. Was not worth the trouble of getting the seating.*

> *Mediocre it was not, and believe me, I've been subjected to plenty of mediocre food. Airport food is mediocre. Convention hall food is mediocre. Cafeteria food is mediocre. Cindy's Royal Table was not in the same category. Our lunch was attractively served and very tasty (I had the pork for lunch). It greatly exceeded my expectations.*

The Crystal Palace gets consistently good reviews from readers. A sampling:

> *The Crystal Palace is highly underrated. We feasted on vegetables, salmon, salads, and fruits. The kids were overjoyed with the characters. . . great way to recharge the batteries.*

unofficial **TIP**
Kosher quick-service meals are available at **Cosmic Ray's** in the Magic Kingdom, as well as at **Pizzafari** in Animal Kingdom, **ABC Commissary** in Disney's Hollywood Studios, and **Liberty Inn** in Epcot.

> *Of all the restaurants we visited, I can't rave enough about The Crystal Palace or Liberty Tree Tavern. The food at both places was great (you just can't beat The Crystal Palace's breakfast buffet!), the service was wonderful, and the characters were awesome.*

As with the previous reader, we also receive many positive comments regarding the Liberty Tree Tavern:

Liberty Tree Tavern—didn't expect much here but made a reservation based on your book. What a surprise. The food was great as well as the atmosphere.

Tony's Town Square Restaurant elicited this appraisal from a Downs, Illinois, reader:

There were only two restaurants on WDW property that we did not speak highly of—until we ate at Tony's—and now there are three. Sheri had the shrimp scampi with asparagus. The shrimp was decent, but the asparagus was so overcooked that not even Viagra would have firmed it up. I had the lasagna, and after one bite I tried to determine whether it was made with Lady or the Tramp.

EPCOT

SINCE THE BEGINNING, dining has been an integral component of Epcot's entertainment product. The importance of dining is reflected in the number of restaurants and their ability to serve consistently interesting and well-prepared meals. This is in stark contrast to the Magic Kingdom, where, until recently, food service was seemingly an afterthought, with quality and selection a distant runner-up to logistical efficiency.

unofficial **TIP**
Epcot has 16 full-service restaurants: 2 in Future World and 14 in World Showcase. With a couple of exceptions, these are among the best restaurants at Walt Disney World, in or out of the theme parks.

For the most part, Epcot's restaurants have always served decent food, though the World Showcase restaurants have occasionally been timid about delivering honest representations of their host nations' cuisine. While these eateries have struggled with authenticity and have sometimes shied away from challenging the meat-and-potatoes sensibilities of the average tourist, they're bolder now, encouraged by Americans' exponentially expanding appreciation of ethnic dining. It's still true that the less adventuresome diner can still find sanitized and homogenized meals, but the same kitchens will serve up the real thing for anyone with a spark of curiosity and daring.

FULL-SERVICE RESTAURANTS IN EPCOT	
FUTURE WORLD	
Coral Reef Restaurant The Seas	Garden Grill Restaurant The Land
WORLD SHOWCASE	
Akershus Royal Banquet Hall Norway	Rose & Crown Dining Room U. K.
Biergarten Germany	San Angel Inn Mexico
Le Cellier Steakhouse Canada	Teppan Edo Japan
Les Chefs de France France	Tokyo Dining Japan
Nine Dragons Restaurant China	Tutto Italia Ristorante Italy
Restaurant Marrakesh Morocco	Via Napoli Italy

EPCOT

AUTHORS' FAVORITE COUNTER-SERVICE RESTAURANTS

Kringla Bakeri og Kafe   *Norway*   Katsura Grill   *Japan*
Sommerfest   *Germany*   Sunshine Seasons   *The Land*

Many Epcot restaurants are overpriced, most conspicuously **Coral Reef Restaurant** (The Seas). Representing decent value with their combination of attractive ambience and well-prepared food are **Les Chefs de France** (France), **Biergarten** (Germany), and **Restaurant Marrakesh** (Morocco). Biergarten and Restaurant Marrakesh also feature live entertainment.

While eating at Epcot can be a consummate hassle, an afternoon without Advance Reservations for dinner in World Showcase is like not having a date on the day of the prom. Each pavilion (except United States) has a beautifully seductive ethnic restaurant or two, offering the gastronomic delights of the world. To tour these exotic settings and not partake is almost beyond the limits of willpower. And while the fare in some World Showcase restaurants isn't always compelling, the overall experience is exhilarating. If you fail to dine in World Showcase, you'll miss one of Epcot's most delightful features.

If you want to sample the ethnic foods of World Showcase without eating in restaurants requiring Advance Reservations, we recommend these counter-service specialties:

FRANCE	**Boulangerie Patisserie** for French pastries
GERMANY	**Sommerfest** for bratwurst and Beck's beer
JAPAN	**Katsura Grill** for noodle dishes, teriyaki, and tempura
MOROCCO	**Tangierine Cafe** for hummus, tabbouleh, and lamb
NORWAY	**Kringla Bakeri og Kafe** for pastries, open-face sandwiches, and Carlsberg beer (our favorite)
UNITED KINGDOM	**Rose & Crown Pub** for Guinness, Harp, and Bass beers

Unofficial Guide readers have diverse opinions of Epcot's full-service restaurants. Concerning the much-hyped Les Chefs de France:

> *Cafeteria food served on linen place mats. An expensive rip-off; food on par with Denny's.*

> *What a joke! Premade food that anyone can get where they live, served by snotty little princesses.*

> *We were very disappointed by Les Chefs de France. We were served cold food—it might as well have been a defrosted frozen dinner. The mashed potatoes tasted like a powdered mix. The service was rushed, the food pedestrian—only the manner was haute.*

Coral Reef Restaurant in The Seas with Nemo & Friends fared a bit better:

> *Food was good; however, service was poor and portions were small and overpriced. Music has added a lot of atmosphere.*

> *You were dead-on; we went this year, and it was fairly disastrous. I think my dinner was prepared under water.*

We were surprised by how much everyone loved Coral Reef. We had great service, and the food was awesome. We had a booth directly in front of the tank and didn't even request it!

Tried Coral Reef for the first time, despite reviews. Waited 40 minutes beyond our reserved time, and the food was mediocre and pricey. Next time I'll cook a burger next to my daughter's goldfish bowl.

Restaurant Marrakesh likewise garnered mixed reviews:

Restaurant Marrakesh is overrated. It may be a walk on the wild side for someone from, say, Wichita, but I can find better and more exotic food at a dozen places in my neighborhood.

(For all you folks in Wichita who are wondering where this reader is from: Arlington, Virginia.) More comments:

It's worth eating here just to see the interior. Going to Epcot and passing this gem up is like going to Paris and skipping Notre Dame.

unofficial **TIP**
If cost is an issue, make lunch your main meal. Entrees are similar to those on the dinner menu, but the prices are significantly lower.

We spent a very memorable lunch at Restaurant Marrakesh. Our son (age 8) loved it when the belly dancer brought him to the floor to dance with her. The portions were very generous, and our waiter, Isaam, took time to speak with us about Moroccan family traditions.

Marrakesh—everything was Moroccan except the food. Not good at all. Very disappointed.

Le Cellier has risen from obscurity to become a Signature Dining experience on the Disney Dining Plan, and one of the most coveted reservations in Epcot:

Le Cellier and the Yachtsman Steakhouse were outstanding. At Le Cellier I didn't even need a knife to cut my steak.

Le Cellier is one of the hardest restaurants for which to get Advance Reservations [see page 423]. It wasn't available any of the 10 days of my trip, and I called more than 90 days in advance.

Akershus Royal Banquet Hall in the Norway Pavilion has become quite the favorite of character-dining enthusiasts:

I took my 4-year-old daughter and 4-year-old niece, and of course they were both obsessed with seeing the princesses. The girls got to see Belle, Ariel, Cinderella, Aurora, and Jasmine. Each princess came to the table one at a time, and the place was not overbooked, so you didn't feel rushed. The food was great, the dessert to die for, and the waitstaff extremely friendly and outgoing. The princesses were really engaged with the girls, and the best thing was that Ariel saw my daughter outside while she was leaving the restaurant. Ariel swooped down and planted a kiss on her cheek—my daughter wouldn't wash her cheek for the rest of the day!

And, finally, about the San Angel Inn:

Expensive, but where else can you drink Corona beer and dine under a moonlit sky at the base of a vaulted pyramid while boats drift by?

But a Bristol, Tennessee, reader complained of cramped conditions:

At San Angel Inn, the tables are so close together you could easily
swipe food off a plate at the next table and they might never notice.

Drinking around the World (Showcase)

A popular adult pastime at Epcot is to make a complete circuit of the
World Showcase, sampling the exceptional alcoholic drinks native to
each nation represented. Perhaps knowing this, Disney has added stand-
alone bars to four pavilions.

LA CAVA DEL TEQUILA, MEXICO Inside the pyramid, La Cava stocks
more than 100 kinds of tequila and mezcal (similar to tequila, with a
smoky flavor), almost a dozen kinds of margaritas, and various light
appetizers. La Cava seats just over 50 people but is far more popular
than that. On weekends and on special events such as the Food & Wine
Festival or Cinco de Mayo, expect a wait to get a table.

La Cava is Len's favorite bar in Walt Disney World. Two things set
La Cava apart from most others on Disney property: First, La Cava
has a dedicated tequila expert on hand most days to explain the different types of tequila and provide tasting notes. (Her name is Hilda,
and she's from the town of Tequila in Jalisco, Mexico—tell her Len
sent you.) Second, the team that runs La Cava is very engaged with
the Disney community via social media, which makes it easy to ask
questions about the drinks and menus. As of this writing, folks who
follow **@cavadeltequila** on Twitter get free chips and salsa.

TUTTO GUSTO WINE CELLAR, ITALY Opened in 2012, Tutto Gusto serves
wine, spirits, and light appetizers in a setting reminiscent of an underground wine cellar. Perhaps learning from La Cava, which opened more
than a year earlier, Tutto Gusto has seating for 113. Our favorite spot is a
small room just inside the entrance, to the right, with a fireplace, a couple
of comfy chairs, and tables big enough to hold your food and drinks.

The menu is divided into four sections: a charcuterie selection, with
five or six cured meats such as prosciutto and various salamis, as well as
five or six cheeses; a small selection of grilled pizzalike flatbreads with
various toppings; four sandwichlike panini served with a small Caesar
salad; and a collection of small plates: vegetables, olives, polenta, and
seafood. There's also a dessert menu—the cannoli are some of the best
we've ever had. The wine list is extensive. Service is good.

Our favorite appetizers are the small plates, many of which are
vegetarian or vegan, and the charcuterie selection. If they're available,
try the *cacciatorini*—dried beef-and-pork sausage flavored with black
pepper and garlic—with a tangy Robiola cheese. Skip the panini (the
bread isn't great) and the flatbreads.

If we have one complaint about Tutto Gusto, it's that the main
door opens directly outside. If you're in the bar before dark, the afternoon sun lights up the entire place like a yellow strobe. The country
that gave us Andrea Palladio should get this architecture right. *Amici*,
please—an awning?

SAKE BAR, JAPAN Not much more than a small circular table at the
far end of the retail space on the first floor of the Japan Pavilion. It's

common to see customers lined up two deep to sip and discuss their favorite rice wines. A decent and affordable selection of sakes can be purchased from a shelf right next to the bar-table. Frankly, we're amazed that this hasn't been expanded into a proper dedicated room.

WEINKELLER, GERMANY Decorated in stone, dark woods, heavy chandeliers, and thick wood tables, Weinkeller serves wines by the glass (around $5) and in flights of three 2-ounce pours (about $10). If you like sweet white wines, this is the place to be. Selections usually include a couple of Rieslings, a Liebfraumilch, dessert wines, and ice wines. The bar has no seating and serves no food, but the wine pours are generous—and that counts for something.

Besides the above, the U.K. Pavilion has had the **Rose & Crown Pub** for years. But with the growing popularity of watering holes in World Showcase, we wouldn't be surprised if Disney added a few more, especially in France.

Along with the spirits and wine, the beer is great (Carlsberg beer in Norway is our favorite), but the price per brew makes the circumnavigation only slightly less expensive than an actual around-the-world tour, as this reader laments:

> As a beer lover, I was looking forward to tasting beers from around the world. That was quickly put to a stop by the $7.25-per-cup cost.

DISNEY'S ANIMAL KINGDOM

BECAUSE TOURING ANIMAL KINGDOM takes less than a day, crowds are heaviest from 9:30 a.m. until about 3:30 p.m. Expect a mob at lunch and thinner crowds at dinner. We recommend you tour early after a good breakfast, then eat a very late lunch or graze on vendor food. If you tour later in the day, eat lunch before you arrive, then enjoy dinner in or out of the theme park. Animal Kingdom full-service and counter-service restaurants are profiled later in this chapter.

unofficial **TIP**
Although grilled meats are available, don't expect a broad choice of exotic dishes in Animal Kingdom.

Animal Kingdom offers a lot of counter-service fast food but has converted **Tusker House** to a buffet-style restaurant and added **Yak & Yeti,** a table-service restaurant, in Asia. You'll find plenty of traditional Disney-theme-park food—hot dogs, hamburgers, and the like—but even the fast food is superior to typical Disney fare. Our two counter-service favorites: **Flame Tree Barbecue** in Discovery Island, with its waterfront dining pavilions, and **Anandapur Local Food Cafes** (just outside Yak & Yeti) for casual Asian dishes from egg rolls to crispy honey chicken.

DISNEY'S ANIMAL KINGDOM

AUTHORS' FAVORITE COUNTER-SERVICE RESTAURANT

Flame Tree Barbecue *Discovery Island*

The third full-service restaurant in Animal Kingdom, **Rainforest Cafe,** has entrances both inside and outside the park (you don't have to purchase theme park admission, in other words, to eat at the restaurant). Both Rainforest Cafes (the other is at Downtown Disney Marketplace) accept Advance Reservations.

DISNEY'S HOLLYWOOD STUDIOS

DINING AT DHS is more interesting than at the Magic Kingdom but less ethnic than at Epcot. The park has five restaurants where Advance Reservations are recommended or required: **The Hollywood Brown Derby, 50's Prime Time Cafe, Sci-Fi Dine-In Theater Restaurant, Mama Melrose's Ristorante Italiano,** and the **Hollywood & Vine** buffet. The upscale Brown Derby is by far the best restaurant at the Studios. For simple Italian food, including pizza, Mama Melrose's is fine; just don't expect anything fancy. At the Sci-Fi Dine-In, you eat in little cars at a simulated drive-in movie from the 1950s. Though you won't find a more entertaining restaurant in Walt Disney World, the food is quite disappointing. Somewhat better is the 50's Prime Time Cafe, where you sit in Mom's time-warp kitchen and scarf down meat loaf while watching clips of classic sitcoms. It's fun and the food is a step up. The best way to experience either restaurant is to stop in for dessert or a drink between 2:30 and 4:30 p.m. Hollywood & Vine features singing and dancing characters from the Disney Channel during breakfast and lunch. DHS full-service and counter-service restaurants are profiled later in this chapter.

DISNEY'S HOLLYWOOD STUDIOS

AUTHORS' FAVORITE COUNTER-SERVICE RESTAURANTS

ABC Commissary *Echo Lake*	Pizza Planet *Streets of America*
Backlot Express *Echo Lake*	Toluca Legs Turkey Company *Sunset Boulevard*

We receive considerable mail from readers recounting their DHS dining experiences. A reader from Sumter, South Carolina, writes:

> We had lunch at the Sci-Fi Dine-In. In the guide you gave it a terrible review, but I've always felt you guys are too hard on the Disney restaurants, so we went ahead and ate there. Well, on this one you were right on target! While the atmosphere was fun and the clips were a hoot, the food was lousy . . . and expensive!

A Mechanicsville, Virginia, family agrees:

> You tried to warn us about the Sci-Fi Dine-In, but my 4-year-old was dying to eat there. The food was even worse than you said, and the cost—$9.50 for basic food!

From an East Lansing, Michigan, woman who'd had it to here with togetherness:

> I disagree with your review of the Sci-Fi Dine-In. After a busy and hot day of touring, it's heaven to be in a dark, air-conditioned room, with no pressure to keep up conversation with the other members of your party, who you could no doubt use a break from after much time spent in line or waiting for the bus together.

The 50's Prime Time Cafe is always a hot topic. First, from a Maryland reader:

> 50's Prime Time Cafe was a fun experience, but again, the food quality was at best mediocre. If my mom really did cook that way, I would've many times run away from home. Our reaction to the poor food quality pushed us quickly into the car and out of WDW. I never

thought I would get down on my knees and kiss the sidewalk outside of a Perkins Pancake House.

But a West Newton, Massachusetts, family loved the Prime Time:

50's Prime Time Cafe: We know you guys didn't rate it very well, but we decided to go against your recommendation and give it a shot. We're so glad we did! For the five of us (ages 16–20), this dining experience was a blast. Our waiter (and big brother for the meal), "Leroy," came and sat at our table and helped us set our places so we wouldn't get in trouble with "Mom." When one member of our party cursed, "Mom" arrived to punish him, making him clear the table onto her tray, which he did shamefully. Overall, the experience was a total kick that we talked about for the rest of the trip.

Other Prime Time advocates had this to say:

Best meal in park, but you must get into character [that is, go along with the role-playing] to have fun.

My teens' favorite restaurant was the 50's Prime Time Cafe. Our waitress gave them a ribbing about their elbows on the table, not pushing their chairs in, and just general grief. They were laughing so hard they had tears in their eyes. It was the only place where they wanted a picture with the restaurant staff.

The Brown Derby was a favorite of a San Diego reader:

Delicious food, great selections, and an excellent end to an evening at the Studios.

While yet another reader made a culinary find at Mama Melrose's Ristorante Italiano:

Great flatbread pizza, although our waiter was as slow as a snail.

Other readers agreed about the slow-service part, not so much about the food:

At Mama Melrose's, we had reservations at 4:20 p.m. for dinner and a show package to see Fantasmic! The food was TERRIBLE and the service was even worse. A person in our party ordered the grilled salmon—it was burned to a crisp. We got no refills on our drinks, and at 5:50 we still had not gotten our dessert (and never did).

If you arrive at Disney's Hollywood Studios without having arranged Advance Reservations for meals, you can make them at the Advance Reservations kiosk at the corner of Hollywood and Sunset boulevards or at the restaurants.

If you have no Advance Reservations and become hungry during meal times, try Pizza Planet (sometimes overlooked by the teeming hordes).

MORE READER COMMENTS ABOUT WALT DISNEY WORLD DINING

EATING IS A POPULAR TOPIC among *Unofficial Guide* readers. In addition to participating in our annual restaurant survey, many readers share their thoughts. The following comments are representative.

Here's a 13-year-old girl from Omaha, Nebraska, who doesn't get her knickers in a twist over one bad meal:

Honestly, when was the last time you came home from Disney World and said, "Gosh, my vacation really sucked because I ate at a bad restaurant"? Disney World is Disney World, no matter what.

A reader from Carbondale, Illinois, exhorts other readers to be adventuresome in their choice of restaurants:

Please advise your readers to try "different" restaurants at Epcot! We had a blast dining at Akershus and Marrakesh! The service was great; food was different but not weird. My husband is a picky eater, but even he was able to say that he tried Norwegian and Moroccan food at the end of our vacation!

Another Illinois reader, this one from Glendale, had a positive experience with Disney food, writing:

In general, we were pleasantly surprised. I expected it to be overpriced, generally bad, and certainly unhealthy. There were a lot of options, and almost all restaurants (including counter service) had generally good food and some healthy options. It's not the place to expect fine cuisine—and is certainly overpriced—but if you understand the parameters, you can eat quite well. One thing I appreciated was having a children's menu that didn't consist only of hot dogs and fries. My children ate well, and we were able to get them a good variety of food, with plenty of fruits and vegetables.

Here's another big thumbs-up from a Troup, Texas, reader for the California Grill:

You recommended the California Grill for the view of the Magic Kingdom fireworks show, but you didn't mention being able to see IllumiNations. We scheduled a 9:15 dinner and arrived early. The staff was extremely helpful and allowed us to have a drink in the lounge area and watch the fireworks at the Magic Kingdom. When we were seated at 8:20, the hostess told us that we had a great view of Epcot and we should watch for the fireworks at 9 o'clock. The food was exceptional, the service was outstanding, and the view was amazing.

Note: Much of *IllumiNations* takes place below tree line, so only the higher aerial fireworks can be seen from the California Grill. Still, it's a treat. A Canadian mom raises a caution, however:

We ate dinner on our last night at the California Grill. It was beautiful and delicious, but it took 3 hours. This is not a great place to take your kids. We were there from 7 to 10 p.m., and it was just too much for them.

A family of five loved Whispering Canyon Cafe at the Wilderness Lodge:

Our best experience for dining was at the Whispering Canyon. My girls (ages 6, 10, and 11) thought the servers were great. They joked with each other, shouted, and laughed with the kids. Our waiter even sat down with our kids and helped my oldest "finish" her salad and showed my youngest how to eat whipped cream off her nose. Out of all the places we ate, this was my kids' (and Mom's and Dad's) favorite. Oh, and the food was pretty good, too.

We've received consistent raves for Boma—Flavors of Africa at Animal Kingdom Lodge:

Please stop telling everyone how wonderful Boma—Flavors of Africa is, because I love it so much there and I don't want everyone to know the secret as it's already difficult to get a table! Prime rib and Zebra Domes—yum!

Sanaa, in the Kidani Village section of Animal Kingdom Lodge, really impressed an Ellicott, Maryland, family:

On another note, Sanaa is one of the best-kept secrets on Disney property. It's a beautiful restaurant with delicious and inexpensive (for Disney) food that you can't find anywhere else in Walt Disney World. We had a fabulous adults-only evening here, but I would bring children here too for an early dinner overlooking the savanna. Disney hit a home run with this place!

A Baltimore reader thinks we've failed to give Wolfgang Puck his due:

Bob, you greatly underestimated the Wolfgang Puck Express Cafe in Marketplace. It's not five-star, but it's a great fast-food alternative. We got yummy gourmet pizzas and rotisserie chicken . . . but the best part was the beer barrels. We ended up eating there on two occasions.

But a mom from New Richmond, Wisconsin, points out that service is important too:

The service at Wolfgang Puck Cafe was terrible. They had no booster seats for smaller children, and it took 30 minutes to get a high chair.

A family from Youngsville, Louisiana, got a leg up on other guests:

The best things we ate were the smoked turkey legs.

A mom from Aberdeen, South Dakota, writes:

When we want great food, we'll be on a different vacation. Who wants to waste fun time with the kids at a sit-down restaurant when you know the food will be mediocre anyway?

A woman from Verona, Wisconsin, offers this:

We think the character meals are underrated in all guidebooks. These meals are in pleasant settings and provide an easy, efficient way for little kids to interact with characters while providing adults with an opportunity to relax. For value and good food, we especially like the breakfasts. Yes, they're a little pricey, but you get more than food.

A Tallahassee, Florida, reader thinks we underrate Cítricos at the Grand Floridian:

How come you gave Cítricos only 3½ stars? We had the most amazing meal ever there! The service was the most outstanding I have ever received, and the food matched. My grandmother had some dietary restrictions; the chef came to our table to talk with her about what she could eat, then sent her out a side dish free of charge. They even let her order from the kids' menu even though she's way over the 9-year-old limit.

(For the record, Cítricos is one of the *Unofficial* team's favorite eateries. The food is indeed excellent, and it's one of the most quiet and sedate restaurants at Walt Disney World.)

A couple from Oxford, England, had a discount coupon and still didn't like Planet Hollywood:

We got $15 off at Planet Hollywood, but it was so noisy with loud music that children were covering their ears—it ruined the meal.

A Pennsylvania Gen Y guy likes PH—and clearly knows how to deal with the LM (loud music, that is):

Planet Hollywood had the best (strongest) mixed drinks, and great ribs and ravioli.

A mother of three from Jamaica, New York, waited 2 hours and 40 minutes for a table at the Rainforest Cafe and still had a good time:

The Rainforest Cafe was an absolute delight. Our 6-year-old sat right next to a gorilla that ranted every few minutes, our 10-month-old loved the huge fish tanks, and they loved the food. Our wait for a table was 2 hours, so we went back to the hotel and returned 2 hours later. We still had to wait 40 minutes, but it was worth it. The gorilla room had more of a jungle feel than the elephant room.

But a Richardson, Texas, family had this to say:

It was wild, wet, and loud, and the service was the worst in WDW.

(We should note that most negative reader comments concerning the Rainforest Cafe pertain to the Downtown Disney location, not the Animal Kingdom location.)

We get lots of comments about the dinosaur-themed T-REX restaurant at Downtown Disney. From a Charlotte, North Carolina, mom:

What an experience! This was a surprise for our dinosaur-loving grandson—I thought he would come out of his skin! No matter how many times the thunderstorm happened, he was just as excited. We had to make complete tours of the restaurant to check out each creature. Well worth the trip.

On the other hand, from a Dartmouth, Nova Scotia, mom . . .

Terrible experience! Bad food, VERY LOUD—we couldn't even hear each other. They put us in the ice-cave room, which has no dinosaur; it felt like I was taking my toddlers to a mini-rave with all the flashing lights. They said we could go around and look at the dinosaurs, but then you were on top of others trying to enjoy their meal. Overpriced. Wouldn't recommend unless you had a die-hard dinosaur fan . . . or request a table outside the ice cave.

But what was a negative for the previous parent was a blessing for a Beaverton, Oregon, mother of two:

I learned that the best place for your kids to have a tantrum is T-REX. No one can hear them screaming!

COUNTER-SERVICE RESTAURANT MINI-PROFILES

TO HELP YOU FIND palatable fast-service food that suits your taste, we've developed mini-profiles of Walt Disney World theme park counter-service restaurants. The restaurants are listed alphabetically by theme park. They're rated for quality and portion size, as well as for value. (The average thumbs-up rating for all Disney restaurants is 84%.) The value rating ranges from A to F, as follows:

A	Exceptional value; a real bargain
B	Good value
C	Fair value; you get exactly what you pay for
D	Somewhat overpriced
F	Extremely overpriced

THE MAGIC KINGDOM

Aloha Isle

QUALITY **Excellent**	VALUE **B+**	PORTION **Medium**	LOCATION **Adventureland**
READER-SURVEY RESPONSES **100%** **0%**		DISNEY DINING PLAN? **No**	

Selections Soft-serve ice cream and sorbet; ice-cream floats; fresh pineapple spears; chips; juice, bottled water, coffee, tea.
Comments The pineapple Dole Whip soft-serve is a must-try.

Casey's Corner

QUALITY **Good**	VALUE **B**	PORTION **Medium**	LOCATION **Main Street, U.S.A.**
READER-SURVEY RESPONSES **83%** **17%**		DISNEY DINING PLAN? **Yes**	

Selections Hot dogs, corn-dog nuggets, fries, and brownies.
Comments Try the barbecue slaw dog, topped with pulled pork, coleslaw, and barbecue sauce. Often crowded.

Columbia Harbour House

QUALITY **Fair**	VALUE **B**	PORTION **Medium**	LOCATION **Liberty Square**
READER-SURVEY RESPONSES **93%** **7%**		DISNEY DINING PLAN? **Yes**	

Selections Healthful options such as grilled salmon with couscous and broccoli and the Lighthouse Sandwich with hummus and broccoli slaw. Other choices: fried fish and shrimp; lobster rolls; chicken nuggets; child's plate with macaroni and cheese, PB&J sandwich, chicken nuggets, or tuna salad with grapes; New England clam chowder; vegetarian chili; coleslaw; garden salad; chocolate cake, apple crisp, strawberry yogurt.
Comments No trans fats in the fried items, and the soups and sandwiches are a cut above most fast-food fare.

Cosmic Ray's Starlight Cafe

QUALITY **Good**	VALUE **B**	PORTION **Large**	LOCATION **Tomorrowland**
READER-SURVEY RESPONSES **83%** **17%**		DISNEY DINING PLAN? **Yes**	

Selections Rotisserie chicken and ribs; burgers (and vegetarian burgers); hot dogs; Greek salad; steak salad; vegetable sandwiches; chicken-noodle soup; chili-cheese fries; carrot cake, triple-chocolate cake, and no-sugar-added mango gelato for dessert. Kosher choices available by request.

Comments Big, noisy place. Inside tables usually available. Plenty of options. Generous toppings bar.

Friar's Nook

QUALITY Good	VALUE B	PORTION Medium–large	LOCATION Fantasyland
READER-SURVEY RESPONSES	Not enough to rate		DISNEY DINING PLAN? Yes

Selections Hot dogs, teriyaki chicken nuggets, Caesar salad with chicken, freshly made potato chips, lemonade slush.

Comments Part of the Fantasyland expansion.

Golden Oak Outpost

QUALITY Good	VALUE B+	PORTION Medium–large	LOCATION Frontierland
READER-SURVEY RESPONSES	92%	8%	DISNEY DINING PLAN? Yes

Selections Chicken nuggets; fried-chicken-breast sandwiches; fries; chocolate cake, carrot cake, and cookies.

Comments Entrees are served with apple slices or French fries.

The Lunching Pad

QUALITY Good	VALUE B–	PORTION Medium	LOCATION Tomorrowland
READER-SURVEY RESPONSES	80%	20%	DISNEY DINING PLAN? Yes

Selections Hot dogs, sweet cream-cheese pretzel, frozen sodas.

Comments Smack in the middle of Tomorrowland, The Lunching Pad now serves "designer dogs": a Philly-cheesesteak hot dog, a Coney Island dog, and a taco dog.

Pecos Bill Tall Tale Inn & Cafe

QUALITY Good	VALUE B	PORTION Medium–large	LOCATION Frontierland
READER-SURVEY RESPONSES	85%	15%	DISNEY DINING PLAN? Yes

Selections One-third-pound Angus cheeseburgers; barbecue-pork sandwiches; veggie burgers; chicken wraps; chicken Caesar salad; taco salad; chili; child's plate with burger or salad with grilled chicken and child's beverage; fries and chili-cheese fries; strawberry yogurt and carrot cake.

Comments Garnish your burger at the fixin's station.

The Pinocchio Village Haus

QUALITY Fair	VALUE C	PORTION Medium	LOCATION Fantasyland
READER-SURVEY RESPONSES	75%	25%	DISNEY DINING PLAN? Yes

Selections Personal pizzas; chicken nuggets; fries; Caesar salad with chicken; meatball sub sandwiches; chicken Parmesan; penne pasta; Mediterranean salad; kids' meals of pizza, mac-and-cheese, or PB&J.

Comments An easy stop for families in Fantasyland, but it's usually crowded. Consider Columbia Harbour House and Pecos Bill Tall Tale Inn & Cafe, both only a few minutes' walk away (and with better food).

Storybook Treats

QUALITY Good	VALUE B	PORTION Medium	LOCATION Fantasyland
READER-SURVEY RESPONSES	95%	5%	DISNEY DINING PLAN? No

Selections Sundaes, including fudge brownie and strawberry shortcake; floats and shakes; cookies; drinks.

Comments An ice-cream stop. Good options and decent value.

Tomorrowland Terrace Restaurant *(open seasonally)*

QUALITY Good	VALUE B	PORTION Medium–large	LOCATION Tomorrowland
READER-SURVEY RESPONSES	71%	29%	DISNEY DINING PLAN? Yes

Selections The menu here changes often, from a burger and a fried-chicken sandwich to pasta Alfredo and a lobster roll with homemade chips. For kids, it's mac-and-cheese, a PB&J sandwich, and chicken nuggets.

Comments Open only during busy park times. Plenty of shaded seating.

Tortuga Tavern *(open seasonally)*

QUALITY Fair	VALUE B	PORTION Medium–large	LOCATION Adventureland
READER-SURVEY RESPONSES	84%	16%	DISNEY DINING PLAN? Yes

Selections Beef taco salad; beef nachos; chicken, beef, or vegetarian burritos; quesadillas and PB&J sandwiches for kids.

Comments Large, shaded eating area. Generous toppings bar with tomatoes, lettuce, cheese, and salsa.

EPCOT

Boulangerie Patisserie

QUALITY Excellent	VALUE B	PORTION Small–medium	LOCATION France
READER-SURVEY RESPONSES	97%	3%	DISNEY DINING PLAN? Yes

Selections Coffee, sweet and savory croissants, pastries, chocolate mousse, sandwiches, baguettes, cheese plate, quiche.

Comments You'll always find a crowd savoring the French pastries at this tucked-away spot. There's no indoor seating, but there are a few shaded outside tables.

La Cantina de San Angel

QUALITY Good	VALUE B	PORTION Medium–large	LOCATION Mexico
READER-SURVEY RESPONSES	67%	33%	DISNEY DINING PLAN? Yes

Selections Chicken or beef tacos, nachos, cheese empanadas, guacamole and chips, churros and frozen fruit pops, margaritas.

Comments The Cantina is a popular spot for a quick meal, with 150 covered outdoor seats.

Crêpes des Chefs de France

QUALITY Excellent	VALUE B+	PORTION Medium	LOCATION France
READER-SURVEY RESPONSES	78%	22%	DISNEY DINING PLAN? No

Selections Crepes filled with chocolate, strawberry preserves, or sugar; ice cream; specialty beer (Kronenbourg 1664); espresso.

Comments These crepes rate high—even with French guests.

Electric Umbrella Restaurant

QUALITY Fair–good	VALUE B–	PORTION Medium	LOCATION Innoventions East
READER-SURVEY RESPONSES	71%	29%	DISNEY DINING PLAN? Yes

Selections Meatball subs, Angus bacon cheeseburgers; mushroom-and-Swiss burgers; Southwest flatbread; Caesar salad; child's plate with cheeseburger or mac-and-cheese; cheesecake, no-sugar-added brownies.

Comments World Showcase has more-interesting fast food.

Fife & Drum Tavern

QUALITY Fair	VALUE C	PORTION Large	LOCATION United States
READER-SURVEY RESPONSES	74%	26%	DISNEY DINING PLAN? Yes

Selections Turkey legs, popcorn, pretzels, ice cream, frozen slushes, beer.

Comments Better for a cold drink or a quick snack than an actual meal. Seating is available in and around the Liberty Inn, behind the Fife & Drum.

Fountain View Ice Cream

QUALITY Fair	VALUE C+	PORTION Medium–large	LOCATION Future World West
READER-SURVEY RESPONSES	88% 👍	12% 👎	DISNEY DINING PLAN? Yes

Selections Ice-cream cones, sundaes, floats; strawberry or mango smoothies; soda, beer, coffee, tea.
Comments Good for a sweet treat on a hot day.

Katsura Grill

QUALITY Good	VALUE B	PORTION Small–medium	LOCATION Japan
READER-SURVEY RESPONSES	82% 👍	18% 👎	DISNEY DINING PLAN? Yes

Selections Udon noodles with beef and tempura shrimp; chicken, beef, or salmon teriyaki; *okonomi yaki* (Japanese vegetable pancake); edamame; sushi; miso soup; green tea; green-tea ice cream and swirl cake; Kirin beer, sake, and plum wine.
Comments The former Yakitori House got a face-lift and new menu items. Pleasant gardens and outdoor seating a little off the World Showcase promenade offer a nice respite, but seating is limited.

Kringla Bakeri og Kafe

QUALITY Good–excellent	VALUE B	PORTION Small–medium	LOCATION Norway
READER-SURVEY RESPONSES	90% 👍	10% 👎	DISNEY DINING PLAN? Yes

Selections Pastries and cakes; rice cream; sandwiches (club, ham-and-apple, roast beef, salmon-and-egg); green salad; espresso, cappuccino, and imported beers (Carlsberg beer for $7.50).
Comments Delicious and different, but pricey. Try the rice cream (not a typo, by the way). Shaded outdoor seating.

Liberty Inn

QUALITY Fair	VALUE C	PORTION Medium	LOCATION United States
READER-SURVEY RESPONSES	67% 👍	33% 👎	DISNEY DINING PLAN? Yes

Selections Bacon cheeseburgers; barbecue pork; hot dogs; veggie burgers; chicken nuggets; grilled-chicken flatbread; chili; iceberg wedge salad; child's plate of chicken nuggets, cheeseburger, or mac-and-cheese.
Comments Try the Angus smokehouse burger, topped with pulled barbecue pork, onion rings, and cheese. Kosher items also available.

Lotus Blossom Cafe

QUALITY Fair	VALUE C	PORTION Medium	LOCATION China
READER-SURVEY RESPONSES	71% 👍	29% 👎	DISNEY DINING PLAN? Yes

Selections Egg rolls, pot stickers, veggie stir-fry, sesame chicken salad, shrimp fried rice, orange chicken, beef-noodle soup bowl.
Comments Middling, overpriced Chinese food.

Promenade Refreshments

QUALITY Fair	VALUE C	PORTION Large	LOCATION World Showcase Promenade
READER-SURVEY RESPONSES	88% 👍	12% 👎	DISNEY DINING PLAN? Yes

Selections Hot dogs, popcorn, pretzels, ice cream, beer.
Comments Best for a quick snack. Seating is limited to nonexistent—be prepared to walk and chew.

Refreshment Outpost

QUALITY Good	VALUE B–	PORTION Small	LOCATION Between Germany and China
READER-SURVEY RESPONSES	88%	12%	DISNEY DINING PLAN? YES

Selections Hot dogs, soft-serve in a waffle cone, floats and sundaes, frozen slushes (frozen soda), coffee or tea, draft Safari Amber beer ($6.25).

Comments Mainly prepackaged food for a quick drink or snack.

Refreshment Port

QUALITY Good	VALUE B	PORTION Medium	LOCATION World Showcase
READER-SURVEY RESPONSES	96%	4%	DISNEY DINING PLAN? Yes

Selections Crispy fried shrimp with *tostones* (green plantains), spicy chicken-and-Cheddar poppers, frozen Bacardi mojito, iced lattes, soft-serve.

Comments Interesting choices for quick service; fun tastes for nibbling and sipping as you begin your walk around World Showcase.

Rose & Crown Pub

QUALITY Good	VALUE C+	PORTION Medium	LOCATION United Kingdom
READER-SURVEY RESPONSES	93%	7%	DISNEY DINING PLAN? No

Selections Fish-and-chips; Scotch egg (hard-boiled, wrapped in sausage, and deep-fried); corned-beef sandwiches; English Bulldog (split sausage stuffed with mashed potatoes, bacon, and Irish Cheddar); Guinness, Harp, and Bass beers, as well as other spirits.

Comments The attractions here are the pub atmosphere and the draft beer. Outside the pub is Yorkshire County Fish Shop (see next page), which serves food to go.

Sommerfest

QUALITY Good	VALUE B–	PORTION Medium	LOCATION Germany
READER-SURVEY RESPONSES	90%	10%	DISNEY DINING PLAN? Yes

Selections Bratwurst and frankfurter sandwiches with kraut; soft pretzels; apple strudel; German wine and beer (Löwenbräu, Franziskaner Weissbier, and Spaten Optimator).

Comments Tucked in the entrance to the Biergarten restaurant, Sommerfest is hard to find from the street. Very limited seating. A good place to grab a cold brew and bratwurst.

Sunshine Seasons

QUALITY Excellent	VALUE A	PORTION Medium	LOCATION The Land
READER-SURVEY RESPONSES	91%	9%	DISNEY DINING PLAN? Yes

Selections Comprises the following four areas: (1) wood-fired grills and rotisseries, with rotisserie half-chicken or slow-roasted pork chop and wood-grilled fish with seasonal vegetables; (2) sandwich shop with made-to-order sandwiches such as oak-grilled veggie flatbread, Reuben panini, and turkey-and-cheese on focaccia; (3) Asian shop, with noodle bowls and various stir-fry combos; (4) soup-and-salad shop, with soups made daily and unusual creations such as seared tuna-noodle salad and roasted-beet-and-goat-cheese salad.

Comments No pizza, no burgers—everything is prepared fresh. Now open for a quick breakfast including oatmeal, croissant sandwiches, and a bacon-sausage-egg platter with a biscuit.

Tangierine Cafe

QUALITY Good	VALUE B	PORTION Medium	LOCATION Morocco
READER-SURVEY RESPONSES	96%	4%	DISNEY DINING PLAN? Yes

Selections Chicken and lamb *shawarma;* hummus; tabbouleh; lentil salad; couscous salad; chicken, lamb, and falafel wraps; marinated olives; child's hamburger or chicken tenders with carrot sticks and apple slices; Moroccan wine and beer; baklava.

Comments No belly dancers as at Restaurant Marrakesh, but the food here is authentic. The best seating is at the outdoor tables.

Yorkshire County Fish Shop

QUALITY Good	VALUE B+	PORTION Medium	LOCATION United Kingdom
READER-SURVEY RESPONSES	91%	9%	DISNEY DINING PLAN? Yes

Selections Fish-and-chips, shortbread, Bass Ale draft.

Comments There's usually a line for the crisp, hot fish-and-chips at this convenient fast-food window attached to the Rose & Crown Pub (see full-service profile on page 490). Outdoor seating overlooks the lagoon.

DISNEY'S ANIMAL KINGDOM
Anandapur Local Food Cafes

QUALITY Fair	VALUE B	PORTION Large	LOCATION Asia
READER-SURVEY RESPONSES	81%	19%	DISNEY DINING PLAN? Yes

Selections Crispy honey chicken with steamed rice, sweet-and-sour chicken, kung pao beef, Mandarin chicken salad, Asian chicken sandwiches, egg rolls, chicken fried rice. Kids' menu includes chicken bites or a cheeseburger with applesauce and carrots.

Comments The crispy honey chicken is the best choice.

Flame Tree Barbecue

QUALITY Excellent	VALUE B–	PORTION Large	LOCATION Discovery Island
READER-SURVEY RESPONSES	97%	3%	DISNEY DINING PLAN? Yes

Selections Half-slab St. Louis–style ribs; smoked half-chicken; smoked beef or pork sandwiches; barbecue-chicken salad; fruit plate with honey yogurt; child's plate of baked chicken drumstick, hot dog, or PB&J sandwich; French fries, coleslaw, and onion rings; Key lime or chocolate mousse; Safari Amber beer, Bud Light, and wine.

Comments One of our favorites for lunch. Try the covered gazebo overlooking the water.

Kusafiri Coffee Shop and Bakery

QUALITY Good	VALUE B	PORTION Medium	LOCATION Africa
READER-SURVEY RESPONSES	86%	14%	DISNEY DINING PLAN? Yes

Selections Fruit turnovers, Danish and other pastries, muffins, croissants, bagels with cream cheese, cookies, brownies, cake, fruit cups, yogurt, coffee, cocoa, and juice.

Comments A good early-morning sugar rush on the way to Kilimanjaro Safaris.

Pizzafari

QUALITY Fair	VALUE B	PORTION Medium	LOCATION Discovery Island
READER-SURVEY RESPONSES	87%	13%	DISNEY DINING PLAN? Yes

Selections Cheese, pepperoni, and veggie personal pizzas served with Caesar salad; antipasto salad; child's mac-and-cheese or cheese pizza; chocolate mousse or no-sugar-added strawberry parfait; beer and wine.

Comments A favorite with children. Hectic at peak mealtimes. The pizza is pretty unimpressive—toppings resemble those on a cheap frozen pizza. Kosher menu is available.

Restaurantosaurus

QUALITY Good	VALUE B+	PORTION Medium–large	LOCATION DinoLand U.S.A.
READER-SURVEY RESPONSES	91% 👍	9% 🗨	DISNEY DINING PLAN? Yes

Selections Angus bacon cheeseburgers; shrimp po'boys; chicken nuggets; grilled-veggie subs; chocolate mousse and cheesecake in a glass; child's cheeseburger, hot dog, or PB&J sandwich; coffee, tea, and cocoa; apple and orange juice; beer.

Comments Good burger-toppings bar.

Royal Anandapur Tea Company

QUALITY Good	VALUE B	PORTION Medium	LOCATION Asia
READER-SURVEY RESPONSES	98% 👍	2% 🗨	DISNEY DINING PLAN? No

Selections Wide variety of hot and iced teas; lattes; coffee, espresso, and cappuccino; pastries.

Comments Halfway between Expedition Everest and Kali River Rapids, this is the kind of small, eclectic, Animal Kingdom–specific food stand that you wish other parks had. Offers nine loose-leaf teas from Asia and Africa, some organic, and many of which can be made either hot or iced. Pastries violate the "never eat anything larger than your head" rule, but everyone knows that doesn't apply when you're on vacation.

Tamu Tamu Eats & Refreshments

QUALITY Good	VALUE C	PORTION Large	LOCATION Africa
READER-SURVEY RESPONSES	81% 👍	19% 🗨	DISNEY DINING PLAN? Yes

Selections Turkey-and-Swiss on focaccia, slow-roasted pulled-beef sandwiches, tandoori chicken salad, soft drinks.

Comments The seating is behind the building and could easily be overlooked.

DISNEY'S HOLLYWOOD STUDIOS

ABC Commissary

QUALITY Fair	VALUE B–	PORTION Medium–large	LOCATION Echo Lake
READER-SURVEY RESPONSES	67% 👍	33% 🗨	DISNEY DINING PLAN? Yes

Selections Asian salads; chicken bleu sandwiches; chicken curry; cheeseburgers with apple slices or fries; fried fish with apple slices or fries; child's chicken nuggets, cheeseburger, or turkey sandwich; chocolate mousse; no-sugar-added strawberry parfait; wine and beer.

Comments Indoors, centrally located, air-conditioned, and usually not too crowded. Hard to find. Offers kosher food.

Backlot Express

QUALITY Fair	VALUE C	PORTION Medium–large	LOCATION Echo Lake
READER-SURVEY RESPONSES	78% 👍	22% 🗨	DISNEY DINING PLAN? Yes

Selections Cheeseburgers with fries or carrot sticks, Southwest salad with chicken, grilled turkey and cheese, chicken nuggets, hot dogs, grilled-vegetable sandwiches, desserts. For children, chicken nuggets or meaty macaroni. Soft drinks and beer.

Comments A big dining space that's often overlooked. Great burger-fixin's bar. Indoor and outdoor seating.

Catalina Eddie's

QUALITY Fair	VALUE B	PORTION Medium–large	LOCATION Sunset Boulevard
READER-SURVEY RESPONSES	75% 👍	25% 🗨	DISNEY DINING PLAN? Yes

Selections Cheese and pepperoni pizzas, hot Italian deli sandwiches, salads, and chocolate fudge cake.

Comments Seldom crowded; picnic tables nearby.

Fairfax Fare

QUALITY Fair	VALUE B	PORTION Medium–large	LOCATION Sunset Boulevard
READER-SURVEY RESPONSES 63%		37%	DISNEY DINING PLAN? Yes

Selections Barbecue chicken and ribs, salads, and pulled-pork sandwiches. "Designer" hot dogs include a version with mac-and-cheese and truffle oil, one with barbecue pork and coleslaw, and the Burrito Dog with lettuce, tomato, Cheddar, jalapeños, and sour cream. For kids, turkey or PB&J sandwiches and mac-and-cheese.

Comments Try one of the designer dogs with a cold beer.

Min and Bill's Dockside Diner

QUALITY Fair	VALUE C	PORTION Small–medium	LOCATION Echo Lake
READER-SURVEY RESPONSES 81%		19%	DISNEY DINING PLAN? Yes

Selections Italian sausage, chicken Caesar sandwiches, frankfurters on a pretzel roll, shakes and soft drinks, chips and cookies, beer.

Comments Walk-up window with limited outdoor seating.

Pizza Planet

QUALITY Good	VALUE B+	PORTION Medium	LOCATION Streets of America
READER-SURVEY RESPONSES 80%		20%	DISNEY DINING PLAN? Yes

Selections Cheese, pepperoni, and vegetarian pizzas; meatball subs; salads; child's meatball sub and cheese pizza; cookies and crisped-rice treats.

Comments *The* pizza place at the Studios.

Rosie's All-American Cafe

QUALITY Fair	VALUE C	PORTION Medium	LOCATION Sunset Boulevard
READER-SURVEY RESPONSES 86%		14%	DISNEY DINING PLAN? Yes

Selections Cheeseburgers; veggie burgers; chicken nuggets; soups; child's mac-and-cheese or chicken nuggets with grapes, carrot sticks, or applesauce; apple pie and chocolate cake.

Comments Backlot Express is a better option for similar fare.

Starring Rolls Cafe

QUALITY Good	VALUE B	PORTION Small–medium	LOCATION Sunset Boulevard
READER-SURVEY RESPONSES 91%		9%	DISNEY DINING PLAN? Yes

Selections Giant deli sandwiches, sushi, oversize pastries and desserts, coffee.

Comments Open for breakfast on some mornings. Slowest service of any counter-service eatery.

Studio Catering Co.

QUALITY Good	VALUE B	PORTION Small–medium	LOCATION Streets of America
READER-SURVEY RESPONSES 93%		7%	DISNEY DINING PLAN? Yes

Selections Grilled-veggie sandwiches, grilled-turkey clubs, buffalo chicken sandwiches, pressed Tuscan deli sandwiches, chicken Caesar wraps, Greek salad. PB&J and chicken nuggets for kids. The adjacent High Octane Refreshments serves cocktails, including a variety of margaritas.

Comments Good place for a break while your kids enjoy the Honey, I Shrunk the Kids Movie Set Adventure. Shady outside seating.

Toluca Legs Turkey Company

QUALITY Good	VALUE B	PORTION Medium–large	LOCATION Sunset Boulevard
READER-SURVEY RESPONSES	80% 👍	20% 👎	DISNEY DINING PLAN? Yes

Selections Smoked turkey legs; hot dogs; coffee, tea, cocoa, bottled soda, and beer.

Comments For fans of the giant turkey legs.

WALT DISNEY WORLD RESTAURANTS:
Rated and Ranked

TO HELP YOU MAKE YOUR DINING CHOICES, we've developed profiles of full-service restaurants at Disney World. Each profile allows you to quickly check the restaurant's cuisine, location, star rating, cost range, quality rating, and value rating. Profiles are listed alphabetically by restaurant.

STAR RATING The star rating represents the entire dining experience: style, service, and ambience, in addition to the taste, presentation, and quality of the food. Five stars is the highest rating and indicates that the restaurant offers the best of everything. Four-star restaurants are above average, and three-star restaurants offer good, though not necessarily memorable, meals. Two-star restaurants serve mediocre fare, and one-star restaurants are below average. Our star ratings don't correspond to ratings awarded by AAA, Mobil, Zagat, or other restaurant reviewers.

COST RANGE The next rating tells how much a full-service entree will cost. Appetizers, sides, soups/salads, desserts, drinks, and tips aren't included. We've rated the cost as inexpensive, moderate, or expensive.

Inexpensive	$15 or less per person
Moderate	$15–$28 per person
Expensive	More than $28 per person

QUALITY RATING The food quality is rated on a scale of one to five stars, five being the best rating attainable. The quality rating is based on the taste, freshness of ingredients, preparation, presentation, and creativity of food served. Price is not a consideration. If you want the best food available and cost is not an issue, you need look no further than the quality ratings.

VALUE RATING If, on the other hand, you're looking for both quality and value, then you should check the value rating, expressed as stars.

PAYMENT All Disney restaurants take American Express, Carte Blanche, Diners Club, Discover, Japan Credit Bureau, MasterCard, and Visa.

READERS' RESTAURANT-SURVEY RESPONSES

FOR EACH DISNEY WORLD RESTAURANT PROFILED, we include the results of last year's Reader-Survey Responses. Results are expressed as a percentage of responding readers who liked the restaurant well enough to eat there again (thumbs-up 👍), as opposed to the percentage of responding readers who had a bad experience and wouldn't go back (thumbs-down 👎). (Readers tend to be less critical than our *Unofficial*

Guide reviewers.) The average thumbs-up rating for all Disney restaurants is 84%. If you'd like to participate in the survey, complete and return the restaurant survey in the back of this book.

In this year's survey, 19 sit-down restaurants merited reader-satisfaction ratings of 90% or greater, up from 15 restaurants last year. Topping the list, with 100% approval, were **Narcoossee's** and **Victoria & Albert's,** both at the Grand Floridian Resort & Spa. Close behind were **Bistro de Paris** at Epcot's France Pavilion, with 96%, and **Boma—Flavors of Africa** at Animal Kingdom Lodge, **ESPN Club** at the BoardWalk complex, and **Tokyo Dining** at Epcot's Japan Pavilion, all three with 95%. Hot on their heels was **Kouzzina by Cat Cora** at the BoardWalk (94%). Remember, though, that the survey reports overall reader satisfaction, not just food quality.

FULL-SERVICE RESTAURANT PROFILES

Akershus Royal Banquet Hall ★★★

NORWEGIAN/BUFFET	EXPENSIVE	QUALITY ★★★	VALUE ★★★★
READER-SURVEY RESPONSES 88%	12%	DISNEY DINING PLAN?	YES

Norway, World Showcase, Epcot; ☎ 407-939-3463

Reservations Required for breakfast; recommended for lunch and dinner, with credit card required to reserve at breakfast and lunch. **Dining Plan credits** 1 per person, per meal. **When to go** Anytime. **Cost range** Breakfast $40 (child $24), lunch $42 (child $25), dinner $47 (child $26). *Note:* Prices increase during peak periods (see page 428). **Service** ★★★★. **Friendliness** ★★★★. **Parking** Epcot lot. **Bar** Full service. **Wine selection** Good. **Dress** Casual. **Disabled access** Yes. **Customers** Theme park guests. **Character breakfast** Daily, 8–11:10 a.m. **Character lunch** Daily, 11:55 a.m.–3:30 p.m. **Character dinner** Daily, 4:55–8:35 p.m.

SETTING AND ATMOSPHERE Home to Princess Storybook Dining for breakfast, lunch, and dinner, the dining room is always full of antsy kids hoping for an audience with the princesses. But there are cocktails for grown-ups (even a shot of Linie Aquavit). Modeled on a 14th-century fortress, Akershus entertains its guests in a great banquet hall under A-framed ceilings and massive iron chandeliers.

HOUSE SPECIALTIES Dinner: *koldtbord* (cold buffet), grilled beef-tenderloin tips, catch of the day, grilled pork tenderloin, pan-seared salmon, traditional *kjottkake* (ground-beef-and-pork dumplings served with mashed potatoes, seasonal vegetables, and lingonberry sauce).

OTHER RECOMMENDATIONS Cold Carlsberg beer on tap.

SUMMARY AND COMMENTS Though the theme is Norwegian, breakfast is all American. Lunch and dinner start at the *koldtbord,* where you'll find a wonderful array of cheeses, meats, seafood, and salads; for lunch, you can also choose from open-faced chicken and beef sandwiches, salmon cakes, mushroom-stuffed pasta, and *kjottkake*. Picky kids will like the cheese ravioli, pizza, and grilled chicken. You can order more than one entree—just ask. Service can sometimes be slow, but the cuisine is above average. As for the prices . . . you're paying for the privilege of princess face time.

Continued on page 462

Walt Disney World Restaurants by Cuisine

CUISINE	LOCATION	OVERALL RATING	COST	QUALITY RATING	VALUE RATING
AFRICAN					
JIKO—THE COOKING PLACE	Animal Kingdom Lodge	★★★★½	Exp	★★★★½	★★★½
BOMA—FLAVORS OF AFRICA	Animal Kingdom Lodge	★★★★	Exp	★★★★	★★★★½
TUSKER HOUSE RESTAURANT	Animal Kingdom	★½	Mod	★	★★
AMERICAN					
CALIFORNIA GRILL	Contemporary	★★★★½	Exp	★★★★½	★★★
THE HOLLYWOOD BROWN DERBY	DHS	★★★★	Exp	★★★★	★★★
ARTIST POINT	Wilderness Lodge	★★★½	Exp	★★★★	★★★
CAPE MAY CAFE	Beach Club	★★★½	Mod	★★★½	★★★★
WHISPERING CANYON CAFE	Wilderness Lodge	★★★	Mod	★★★½	★★★★
CAPTAIN'S GRILLE	Yacht Club	★★★	Mod	★★★½	★★★
THE CRYSTAL PALACE	Magic Kingdom	★★★	Mod	★★★½	★★★
HOUSE OF BLUES	Downtown Disney	★★★	Mod	★★★½	★★★
50'S PRIME TIME CAFE	DHS	★★★	Mod	★★★	★★★
LIBERTY TREE TAVERN	Magic Kingdom	★★★	Mod	★★★	★★★
CINDERELLA'S ROYAL TABLE	Magic Kingdom	★★★	Exp	★★★	★★
T-REX	Downtown Disney	★★★	Mod	★★	★★
THE WAVE . . . OF AMERICAN FLAVORS	Contemporary	★★★	Mod	★★	★★
CHEF MICKEY'S	Contemporary	★★½	Exp	★★★	★★★
ESPN CLUB	BoardWalk	★★½	Mod	★★★	★★★
ESPN WIDE WORLD OF SPORTS CAFE	ESPN Wide World of Sports Complex	★★½	Mod	★★★	★★★
HOLLYWOOD & VINE	DHS	★★½	Mod	★★★	★★★
1900 PARK FARE	Grand Floridian	★★½	Mod	★★★	★★★
BOATWRIGHTS DINING HALL	Port Orleans	★★½	Mod	★★★	★★
GRAND FLORIDIAN CAFE	Grand Floridian	★★½	Mod	★★★	★★
BEACHES & CREAM SODA SHOP	Beach Club	★★½	Inexp	★★½	★★½
PLANET HOLLYWOOD	Downtown Disney	★★½	Mod	★★	★★
RAINFOREST CAFE	Animal Kingdom and Downtown Disney	★★½	Mod	★★	★★

Walt Disney World Restaurants by Cuisine (cont'd)

CUISINE	LOCATION	OVERALL RATING	COST	QUALITY RATING	VALUE RATING
AMERICAN					
GARDEN GROVE	Swan	★★	Mod	★★★	★★
OLIVIA'S CAFE	Old Key West	★★	Mod	★★½	★★
WOLFGANG PUCK GRAND CAFE	Downtown Disney	★★	Exp	★½	★½
SCI-FI DINE-IN THEATER RESTAURANT	DHS	★★	Mod	★★½	★★
GARDEN GRILL RESTAURANT	Epcot	★★	Exp	★★	★★★
BIG RIVER GRILLE & BREWING WORKS	BoardWalk	★★	Mod	★★	★★
THE FOUNTAIN	Dolphin	★★	Mod	★★	★★
THE PLAZA RESTAURANT	Magic Kingdom	★★	Mod	★★	★★
TURF CLUB BAR & GRILL	Saratoga Springs	★★	Mod	★★	★★
TRAIL'S END RESTAURANT	Fort Wilderness Resort	★★	Mod	★★	★★
LAKEVIEW RESTAURANT	Wyndham LBV	★★	Mod	★	★★★
TUSKER HOUSE RESTAURANT	Animal Kingdom	★½	Mod	★	★★
MAYA GRILL	Coronado Springs	★	Mod	★	★
BUFFET					
BOMA—FLAVORS OF AFRICA	Animal Kingdom Lodge	★★★★	Exp	★★★★	★★★★½
CAPE MAY CAFE	Beach Club	★★★½	Mod	★★★½	★★★★
BIERGARTEN	Epcot	★★★½	Exp	★★★	★★★★
THE CRYSTAL PALACE	Magic Kingdom	★★★	Mod	★★★½	★★★
AKERSHUS ROYAL BANQUET HALL	Epcot	★★★	Exp	★★★	★★★★
CHEF MICKEY'S	Contemporary	★★½	Exp	★★★	★★★
HOLLYWOOD & VINE	DHS	★★½	Mod	★★★	★★★
1900 PARK FARE	Grand Floridian	★★½	Mod	★★★	★★★
GARDEN GROVE	Swan	★★	Mod	★★★	★★
TRAIL'S END RESTAURANT	Fort Wilderness Resort	★★	Mod	★★	★★
TUSKER HOUSE RESTAURANT	Animal Kingdom	★½	Mod	★	★★
CHINESE					
NINE DRAGONS RESTAURANT	Epcot	★★★	Mod	★★★	★★

Walt Disney World Restaurants by Cuisine (cont'd)

CUISINE	LOCATION	OVERALL RATING	COST	QUALITY RATING	VALUE RATING
CUBAN					
BONGOS CUBAN CAFE	Downtown Disney	★★	Mod	★★	★★
ENGLISH					
ROSE & CROWN DINING ROOM	Epcot	★★★	Mod	★★★½	★★
FRENCH					
BISTRO DE PARIS	Epcot	★★★★	Exp	★★★★½	★★★
LES CHEFS DE FRANCE	Epcot	★★★	Exp	★★★	★★★
GERMAN					
BIERGARTEN	Epcot	★★★½	Exp	★★★	★★★★
GLOBAL					
PARADISO 37	Downtown Disney	★★½	Inexp	★★★	★★★
GOURMET					
VICTORIA & ALBERT'S	Grand Floridian	★★★★★	Exp	★★★★★	★★★★
INDIAN/AFRICAN					
SANAA	Animal Kingdom Villas–Kidani Village	★★★★	Exp	★★★★	★★★★
IRISH					
RAGLAN ROAD IRISH PUB & RESTAURANT	Downtown Disney	★★★★	Mod	★★★½	★★★
ITALIAN					
TUTTO ITALIA RISTORANTE	Epcot	★★★★	Exp	★★★★	★★★
VIA NAPOLI	Epcot	★★★★	Mod	★★★½	★★★
ANDIAMO ITALIAN BISTRO & GRILLE	Hilton	★★★	Exp	★★★	★★★
IL MULINO NEW YORK TRATTORIA	Swan	★★★	Exp	★★★	★★
MAMA MELROSE'S RISTORANTE ITALIANO	DHS	★★½	Mod	★★★	★★
PORTOBELLO	Downtown Disney	★★½	Exp	★★★	★★
TONY'S TOWN SQUARE RESTAURANT	Magic Kingdom	★★½	Mod	★★★	★★
JAPANESE/SUSHI					
KIMONOS	Swan	★★★★	Mod	★★★★½	★★★
KONA ISLAND SUSHI BAR	Polynesian	★★★★	Mod	★★★★	★★★★
TEPPAN EDO	Epcot	★★★½	Exp	★★★★	★★★
TOKYO DINING	Epcot	★★★	Mod	★★★★	★★★
BENIHANA	Hilton	★★★	Mod	★★★½	★★★

Walt Disney World Restaurants by Cuisine (cont'd)

CUISINE	LOCATION	OVERALL RATING	COST	QUALITY RATING	VALUE RATING
MEDITERRANEAN					
KOUZZINA BY CAT CORA	BoardWalk Inn	★★★★	Mod	★★★★	★★★★
CÍTRICOS	Grand Floridian	★★★½	Exp	★★★★½	★★★
FRESH MEDITERRANEAN MARKET	Dolphin	★★½	Mod	★★½	★★
MEXICAN					
LA HACIENDA DE SAN ANGEL	Epcot	★★★	Exp	★★★½	★★½
SAN ANGEL INN	Epcot	★★★	Exp	★★	★★
MOROCCAN					
RESTAURANT MARRAKESH	Epcot	★★	Mod	★★½	★★
NORWEGIAN					
AKERSHUS ROYAL BANQUET HALL	Epcot	★★★	Exp	★★★	★★★★
POLYNESIAN/PAN-ASIAN					
'OHANA	Polynesian	★★★	Mod	★★★½	★★★
KONA CAFE	Polynesian	★★★	Mod	★★★	★★★★
YAK & YETI RESTAURANT	Animal Kingdom	★★	Exp	★★½	★★
SEAFOOD					
NARCOOSSEE'S	Grand Floridian	★★★★½	Exp	★★★½	★★
FLYING FISH CAFE	BoardWalk	★★★★	Exp	★★★★	★★★
ARTIST POINT	Wilderness Lodge	★★★½	Exp	★★★★	★★★
TODD ENGLISH'S BLUEZOO	Dolphin	★★★	Exp	★★★	★★
FULTON'S CRAB HOUSE	Downtown Disney	★★½	Exp	★★★½	★★
CAP'N JACK'S RESTAURANT	Downtown Disney	★★½	Mod	★★	★★
CORAL REEF RESTAURANT	Epcot	★★½	Exp	★★	★★
SHUTTERS AT OLD PORT ROYALE	Caribbean Beach	★★	Mod	★★½	★★
STEAK					
SHULA'S STEAK HOUSE	Dolphin	★★★★	Exp	★★★★	★★
LE CELLIER STEAKHOUSE	Epcot	★★★½	Exp	★★★½	★★★
YACHTSMAN STEAKHOUSE	Yacht Club	★★★	Exp	★★★½	★★
THE OUTBACK	Buena Vista Palace	★★	Exp	★★★	★★
SHUTTERS AT OLD PORT ROYALE	Caribbean Beach	★★	Mod	★★½	★★

Continued from page 457

Andiamo Italian Bistro & Grille ★★★

ITALIAN	EXPENSIVE	QUALITY ★★★	VALUE ★★★
READER-SURVEY RESPONSES 63% 👍	37% 👎	DISNEY DINING PLAN?	NO

Hilton in the Walt Disney World Resort, Downtown Disney Resort Area;
☎ 407-827-3838

Reservations Accepted. **When to go** Early evening. **Cost range** $17–$38. **Service** ★★★. **Friendliness** ★★★★. **Parking** Valet (free) or hotel lot. **Bar** Full bar. **Wine selection** Good. **Dress** Casual. **Disabled access** Yes. **Customers** Hotel guests. **Dinner** Daily, 5:30–11 p.m.

SETTING AND ATMOSPHERE Casual Italian bistro and wine bar that's suitable for families (kids under age 5 eat free on weekdays).

HOUSE SPECIALTIES Bruschetta, shrimp scampi, pork marsala, filet mignon, pastas from traditional spaghetti and meatballs to pappardelle, angel hair, rigatoni, and lasagna Bolognese.

OTHER RECOMMENDATIONS Broiled salmon with fennel-and-orange butter, osso buco.

SUMMARY AND COMMENTS Better-than-average Italian. Not destination dining, but vacationers at the Downtown Disney resorts can head here for a satisfying meal.

Artist Point ★★★½

AMERICAN	EXPENSIVE	QUALITY ★★★★	VALUE ★★★
READER-SURVEY RESPONSES 81% 👍	19% 👎	DISNEY DINING PLAN?	YES

Wilderness Lodge & Villas; ☎ 407-824-3200

Reservations Required. **Dining Plan credits** 2 per person, per meal. **When to go** Anytime. **Cost range** $28–$43 (child $6–$11). **Service** ★★★★★. **Friendliness** ★★★★★. **Parking** Hotel lot. **Bar** Full service. **Wine selection** All wines from Pacific Northwest. **Dress** Dressy casual. **Disabled access** Yes. **Customers** Hotel guests, locals. **Dinner** Daily, 5:30–9:30 p.m.

SETTING AND ATMOSPHERE Two-story-high paintings depict the landscape of the Pacific Northwest, and out the tall windows you'll see Disney's version of the Pacific Northwest: wildflowers, the lake, a waterfall off high rocks, even an erupting geyser. Cast-iron chandeliers hold 12 lanterns with milk-glass panes; tables are made of heavy wood and engraved with animals native to the Northwest.

HOUSE SPECIALTIES Roasted cedar-plank salmon, kettle-steamed Penn Cove mussels, smoky portobello soup, and berry cobbler.

OTHER RECOMMENDATIONS Grilled buffalo strip loin, pan-seared Alaskan halibut, and house-made potato gnocchi.

SUMMARY AND COMMENTS The cavernous dining room can feel a little sterile, but the food and friendly service warm up the place. The cedar-plank salmon is a must-try, but the buffalo strip loin runs a close second in today's fat- and carb-conscious world. The restaurant offers a terrific all–Pacific Northwest wine list.

Beaches & Cream Soda Shop ★★½

AMERICAN	INEXPENSIVE	QUALITY ★★½	VALUE ★★½
READER-SURVEY RESPONSES 90% 👍	10% 👎	DISNEY DINING PLAN?	YES

Beach Club Resort; ☎ 407-934-8000

Reservations Not accepted. **Dining Plan credits** 1 per person, per meal. **When to go** Anytime. **Cost range** $6.50–$14. **Service** ★★★. **Friendliness** ★★★★. **Parking** Hotel lot. **Bar** Beer only. **Wine selection** None. **Dress** Casual. **Disabled access** Yes. **Customers** Resort guests. **Lunch and dinner** Daily, 11 a.m.–11 p.m.

SETTING AND ATMOSPHERE Casual eats with a retro soda-fountain decor. There's often a line as guests in bathing suits and flip-flops queue up for the hearty burgers (veggie burgers, too) and piles of hot fries.

HOUSE SPECIALTIES Burgers (singles and doubles) and fries; giant hot dogs; hand-scooped ice cream including the gargantuan $24 Kitchen Sink dessert, with five flavors of ice cream smothered in toppings.

OTHER RECOMMENDATIONS Veggie burger, deli turkey sandwich.

SUMMARY AND COMMENTS Grab your burger and sit at a nearby pool-side table.

Benihana ★★★

JAPANESE	MODERATE		QUALITY ★★★½		VALUE ★★★
READER-SURVEY RESPONSES	90%	10%	DISNEY DINING PLAN?		NO

Hilton in the Walt Disney World Resort, Downtown Disney Resort Area; ☎ 407-827-4865

Reservations Recommended. **When to go** Anytime. **Cost range** $17–$43. **Service** ★★★★★. **Friendliness** ★★★★★. **Parking** Hotel lot. **Bar** Full service. **Wine selection** Good. **Dress** Casual. **Disabled access** Yes. **Customers** Hotel guests, some locals. **Dinner** Monday–Thursday, 4–10 p.m.; Friday–Sunday, 2–10 p.m.

SETTING AND ATMOSPHERE Large tables with built-in grills are crammed into small rooms decorated with rice-paper panels and Japanese lanterns. Lighting is low and focused on the stage—the chef's grill.

HOUSE SPECIALTIES Teppanyaki service at large tables (where the chef cooks dinner in front of you). Specialties include tenderloin, ocean scallops, lobster tail, and hibachi vegetables.

OTHER RECOMMENDATIONS Japanese onion soup.

ENTERTAINMENT AND AMENITIES Dinner is the show at this teppanyaki restaurant, where the chef does a lot of noisy chopping and grilling.

SUMMARY AND COMMENTS If you're looking for a nice, quiet dinner, be aware that diners sit at tables of eight, making private conversation almost impossible.

Biergarten ★★★½

GERMAN	EXPENSIVE		QUALITY ★★★		VALUE ★★★★
READER-SURVEY RESPONSES	87%	13%	DISNEY DINING PLAN?		YES

Germany, World Showcase, Epcot; ☎ 407-939-3463

Reservations Accepted. **Dining Plan credits** 1 per person, per meal. **When to go** Lunch or dinner. **Cost range** Lunch $28 (child $15), dinner $40 (child $20). *Note:* Prices increase during peak periods (see page 428). **Service** ★★★★. **Friendliness** ★★★★. **Parking** Epcot lot. **Bar** Full service. **Wine selection** German. **Dress** Casual. **Disabled access** Yes. **Customers** Theme park guests. **Lunch** Daily, noon–3:45 p.m. **Dinner** Daily, 4 p.m.–park closing.

SETTING AND ATMOSPHERE Hungry? This is the place if you want to graze at a hefty German buffet that includes schnitzel, a variety of wursts, spaetzle, roast chicken, and sauerbraten (dinner only). Salads, breads, and desserts round out the offerings. The light level is low, and decor is inspired by a German village town square, with seating at long tables in a tiered dining room that surrounds a stage and dance floor. It's Oktoberfest every day, with a lederhosen-clad oompah band playing on the stage and encouraging diners to sing along and dance.

HOUSE SPECIALTIES Warm German potato salad, beet salad, various sausages and wieners, homemade spaetzle with gravy, and sauerbraten. There's also carved-to-order pork roast with German mustard and breaded pork schnitzel. The buffet is set up on wooden barrels.

OTHER RECOMMENDATIONS Pork-shank gratin with fried onions, braised red cabbage, potato dumplings (dinner only), and beer.

ENTERTAINMENT AND AMENITIES Oompah band and German dancers perform after 1:15 p.m.

SUMMARY AND COMMENTS Unless you have a very big party, you'll be seated with other guests—great fun if you love to socialize. But the lively 25-minute dinner show (one every hour) and noisy dining room are part of the fun, especially for families.

Big River Grille & Brewing Works ★★

AMERICAN	MODERATE	QUALITY ★★	VALUE ★★
READER-SURVEY RESPONSES 91%	9%	DISNEY DINING PLAN?	YES

BoardWalk; ☎ 407-560-0253

Reservations Not accepted. **Dining Plan credits** 1 per person, per meal. **When to go** Anytime. **Cost range** $12–$26 (child $7.59). **Service** ★★★. **Friendliness** ★★★★. **Parking** BoardWalk lot. **Bar** Full service. **Wine selection** Minimal. **Dress** Casual. **Disabled access** Yes. **Customers** Tourists. **Lunch and dinner** Sunday–Thursday, 11 a.m.–11 p.m., Friday and Saturday until midnight.

SETTING AND ATMOSPHERE Industrial cubist murals of factories, machinist-metal and wood chairs and tables, and a midnight-blue neon river that flows along the ceiling of the restaurant set a working-class atmosphere. The place is small—it seems like the huge copper brewing tanks take up more room than that allotted to the diners. Outside seating and service, weather permitting.

HOUSE SPECIALTIES Kobe burger; blackened mahimahi sandwich.

SUMMARY AND COMMENTS Run by a Tennessee company, Big River seems like an afterthought along the BoardWalk and competes with the nearby ESPN Club for the burger-and-brew crowd. But if you're looking for handcrafted beers, this is the place—they serve five beers, including a light lager, a robust ale, and seasonal choices. A good late-night-dining choice.

Bistro de Paris ★★★★

FRENCH	EXPENSIVE	QUALITY ★★★★½	VALUE ★★★
READER-SURVEY RESPONSES 96%	4%	DISNEY DINING PLAN?	NO

France, World Showcase, Epcot; ☎ 407-939-3463

Reservations Required. **When to go** Late dinner. **Cost range** $33–$42. **Service** ★★★★. **Friendliness** ★★★★★. **Parking** Epcot or BoardWalk lot; enter through back gate. **Bar** Full service. **Wine selection** Good but pricey. **Dress** Casual. **Disabled access** Elevator to second level. **Customers** Theme park guests. **Dinner** Daily, 5:30–8:35 p.m.

SETTING AND ATMOSPHERE With attentive and personal service, this is the more upscale of the two restaurants at Epcot's France Pavilion, up a flight of stairs with its own kitchen. Open only for dinner; request a table at the windows to watch the world go by on World Showcase

Lagoon. The quiet dining room, with buttery yellow walls and linen tablecloths, takes you straight to Paris. Seats just 120.

HOUSE SPECIALTIES Maine lobster with sautéed mushrooms, poached egg, and creamy black-truffle bouillon; lamb tenderloin; roasted duck breast with Oriental spices.

SUMMARY AND COMMENTS For a quiet dinner and conversation, this is the spot. Young chef Francesco Santin, who worked at Paul Bocuse's restaurant in Lyon, France, is wowing diners with his authentic, creative French cuisine. He's added delicate starters such as Serrano ham with celery-root rémoulade and artichoke hearts; marinated tuna with lime, herbs, and Mediterranean salad; and fresh goat-cheese terrine with herbs, zucchini salad, and tomato aspic. A new kids' menu includes roasted chicken breast with tomato pasta, filet mignon with mashed potatoes, or pan-roasted snapper with green beans and tomatoes.

Boatwrights Dining Hall ★★½

AMERICAN/CAJUN	MODERATE	QUALITY ★★★	VALUE ★★
READER-SURVEY RESPONSES 67% 👍	33% 👎	DISNEY DINING PLAN? YES	

Port Orleans Resort Riverside; ☎ 407-939-3463

Reservations Accepted. Dining Plan credits 1 per person, per meal. When to go Early evening. Cost range Dinner $16–$28 (child $8.59). Service ★★★. Friendliness ★★★★★. Parking Hotel lot. Bar Full service. Wine selection Fair. Dress Casual. Disabled access Yes. Customers Hotel guests. Dinner Daily, 5–10 p.m.

SETTING AND ATMOSPHERE Cavernous, casual dining room with wood floors and wooden tables set with a boatwright's tool kit that contains condiments. The giant skeleton of a riverboat completes the theme.

HOUSE SPECIALTIES Andouille-crusted catfish; jambalaya with chicken and andouille sausage.

OTHER RECOMMENDATIONS Prime rib, bananas Foster angel-food cake.

SUMMARY AND COMMENTS With 200 seats, Boatwrights serves the masses, and the cuisine (basic fare with a Cajun flair) is pretty homogenized. It's the only table-service restaurant in Port Orleans Resort, so it gets busy and there can be waits. Order a Southern Belle (Southern Comfort and peach schnapps with cranberry juice)—and relax.

Boma—Flavors of Africa ★★★★

AFRICAN	EXPENSIVE	QUALITY ★★★★	VALUE ★★★★½
READER-SURVEY RESPONSES 95% 👍	5% 👎	DISNEY DINING PLAN? YES	

Animal Kingdom Lodge & Villas–Jambo House; ☎ 407-938-3000

Reservations Recommended for dinner. Dining Plan credits 1 per person, per meal. When to go Anytime. Cost range Breakfast $24.50 (child $14), dinner $40 (child $19). *Note:* Prices increase during peak periods (see page 428). Service ★★★★. Friendliness ★★★★. Parking Valet ($12) or hotel lot. Bar Full service. Wine selection All South African. Dress Casual. Disabled access Yes. Customers Hotel guests. Breakfast Daily, 7:30–11 a.m. Dinner Daily, 4:30–10 p.m.

SETTING AND ATMOSPHERE Big dining room with side-by-side food stations that encourage diners to roam about and graze, just like the animals that wander about outside the lodge.

HOUSE SPECIALTIES Watermelon-rind salad, Moroccan seafood salad, roasted meats, Durban spiced roasted chicken, and vegetable skewers.

OTHER RECOMMENDATIONS Sweet-potato pancakes, Zebra Dome dessert, soups and stews.

SUMMARY AND COMMENTS The menu rarely changes, as Boma—Flavors of Africa is a favorite of locals and visitors who return time and again for the salads, roasted meats, and interesting sauces. While Disney calls this a buffet, it's very different from what you'd typically expect (there are no steam tables, for starters). If you like a major bang for your buck, try Boma.

Bongos Cuban Cafe ★★

CUBAN	MODERATE	QUALITY ★★	VALUE ★★
READER-SURVEY RESPONSES 74% 👍	26% 👎	DISNEY DINING PLAN? YES	

Downtown Disney West Side; ☎ 407-828-0999

Reservations Recommended. **Dining Plan credits** 1 per person, per meal. **When to go** Anytime. **Cost range** $14–$35 (child $6–$7). **Service** ★★★★. **Friendliness** ★★★★. **Parking** Downtown Disney lot. **Bar** Full service. **Wine selection** Moderate. **Dress** Casual. **Disabled access** Elevator to second level. **Customers** Gloria Estefan fans and Disney guests. **Lunch and dinner** Sunday–Thursday, 11 a.m.–10:30 p.m., Friday and Saturday until 11:30 p.m.

SETTING AND ATMOSPHERE This multilevel restaurant features an airy environment with a tropical theme built around a three-story pineapple. Other touches include a banana-leaf roof, banana-leaf ceiling fans, and palm tree–shaped columns. Hand-painted murals and mosaics lend an artistic air, and an open wraparound porch provides pleasant outdoor dining.

HOUSE SPECIALTIES *Arroz con pollo* (chicken with rice), *camarones al ajillo* (shrimp in garlic sauce), *ropa vieja* (shredded beef in tomato sauce), and *churrasco* (grilled skirt steak).

ENTERTAINMENT AND AMENITIES Latin music.

SUMMARY AND COMMENTS Gloria Estefan and her husband-producer, Emilio, created this large restaurant that marries salsa music with Cuban cuisine. Any number of mom-and-pop Cuban restaurants in the area do a better and more consistent job with this wonderful cuisine, so if you've never had Cuban food, try it somewhere else. Come here to have a drink with an umbrella in it and listen to music. Upbeat but noisy.

California Grill ★★★★½

AMERICAN	EXPENSIVE	QUALITY ★★★★½	VALUE ★★★
READER-SURVEY RESPONSES 92% 👍	8% 👎	DISNEY DINING PLAN? YES	

Contemporary Resort; ☎ 407-939-3463

Reservations Required. **Dining Plan credits** 2 per person, per meal. **When to go** During evening fireworks. **Cost range** $12–$40 (child $8–$13). **Service** ★★★★★. **Friendliness** ★★★★★. **Parking** Valet ($12) or hotel lot. **Bar** Full service. **Wine selection** Californian. **Dress** Dressy casual. **Disabled access** Yes. **Customers** Hotel guests and locals. **Dinner** Daily, 5:30–10 p.m. **Lounge** Daily, 5 p.m.–10 p.m.

SETTING AND ATMOSPHERE High atop the Contemporary Resort, the award-winning California Grill sets the standard for Disney dining. But expect a boisterous crowd—the noise level makes quiet conversation difficult. Still, the view from the 15th floor is stellar, one of the best spots for watching the Magic Kingdom fireworks. It's so popular that the Grill no longer allows just anyone on the elevator for a ride to the top—you must have a dinner reservation. A show kitchen is the centerpiece of the airy dining room.

HOUSE SPECIALTIES Chef Brian Piasecki takes advantage of seasonal produce, fish, and meats. Sushi chef Yoshie has been there for more than

16 years, creating sublime, artful sushi that's a meal in itself. Oven-fired flatbreads make a meal by themselves, and fans love the grilled pork tenderloin with creamy polenta and Zinfandel glaze, a favorite since day one.

OTHER RECOMMENDATIONS Oak-fired beef filet and any fresh fish on the menu. A beautiful selection of cheeses.

ENTERTAINMENT AND AMENITIES The lights are dimmed during the Magic Kingdom fireworks, and the accompanying music is piped in. You can also step outside onto the 15th-floor deck for a closer look. Other entertainment includes watching the chefs; instead of begging for a window seat, sit at the counter—a chef might slip you a sample.

SUMMARY AND COMMENTS The California Grill still is one of Disney's top dining experiences, more like a hot spot in L.A. or New York City than Disney World. We like the seats at the bar in front of the kitchen, or a coveted window seat. Though it's a sophisticated dining experience, be warned that you'll see plenty of kids in the dining room. But even their menu is upscale, with roasted salmon and oak-fired steak.

Cape May Cafe ★★★½

AMERICAN/BUFFET	MODERATE	QUALITY ★★★½	VALUE ★★★★
READER-SURVEY RESPONSES	89% 👍	11% 👎	DISNEY DINING PLAN? YES

Beach Club Resort; ☎ 407-934-3358

Reservations Recommended. **Dining Plan credits** 1 per person, per meal. **When to go** Anytime. **Cost range** Breakfast $27 (child $13), dinner $37 (child $16). *Note:* Prices increase during peak periods (see page 428). **Service** ★★★★★. **Friendliness** ★★★★★. **Parking** Hotel lot. **Bar** Full service. **Wine selection** Limited. **Dress** Casual. **Disabled access** Yes. **Customers** Theme park and hotel guests. **Breakfast** Daily, 7:30–11 a.m. **Dinner** Daily, 5–10 p.m.

SETTING AND ATMOSPHERE The natural-finish wood furniture and padded booths are executed in a clean, nautical New England style.

HOUSE SPECIALTIES The buffet features peel-and-eat shrimp, tasty (albeit chewy) clams, mussels, snow-crab legs, fish of the day, beef tips, barbecue ribs, chicken, corn on the cob, lots of salads, and a good dessert bar. The kids' bar includes chicken nuggets and mac-and-cheese.

OTHER RECOMMENDATIONS The tart Key lime pie from the dessert bar.

ENTERTAINMENT AND AMENITIES Character breakfast with Goofy, Minnie, and Chip 'n' Dale.

SUMMARY AND COMMENTS Cape May has been a favorite for years because of its consistently good food and efficient service. Advance Reservations are recommended. Because Cape May is within easy walking distance of the World Showcase entrance to Epcot, it's a convenient and affordable place to dine before *IllumiNations*.

Cap'n Jack's Restaurant ★★½

SEAFOOD	MODERATE	QUALITY ★★	VALUE ★★
READER-SURVEY RESPONSES	50% 👍	50% 👎	DISNEY DINING PLAN? YES

Downtown Disney Marketplace; ☎ 407-828-3971

Reservations Not required. **Dining Plan credits** 1 per person, per meal. **When to go** Anytime. **Cost range** $11.50–$25 (child $8.59). **Service** ★★★★★. **Friendliness** ★★★★★. **Parking** Marketplace lot. **Bar** Full service. **Wine selection** Wine available but not a specialty. **Dress** Casual. **Disabled access** Yes. **Customers** Tourists. **Lunch and dinner** Daily, 11:30 a.m.–10:30 p.m.

SETTING AND ATMOSPHERE A nondescript pier house on the edge of Buena Vista Lagoon. It's been here since the 1970s—and looks it.

HOUSE SPECIALTIES Clam chowder, crab cakes. For landlubbers, there's a chicken Parmesan sandwich and beef pot roast.

ENTERTAINMENT AND AMENITIES The lagoon-side setting is nice, and the sunsets are pretty. But there's no outside seating.

SUMMARY AND COMMENTS Back in the 1970s, this was *the* place for sipping drinks and noshing on seafood. Today it's obvious no one's paying much attention to the menu and decor, but it is convenient for shoppers at Downtown Disney Marketplace. Skip the food, sip a cold beer or margarita (or a smoothie if you're a kid), and relax.

Captain's Grille ★★★

AMERICAN	MODERATE	QUALITY ★★★½	VALUE ★★★
READER-SURVEY RESPONSES 91%	9%	DISNEY DINING PLAN?	YES

Yacht Club Resort; ☎ 407-939-3463

Reservations Accepted. **Dining Plan credits** 1 per person, per meal. **When to go** Breakfast or lunch. **Cost range** Breakfast buffet $16, lunch $11.50–$19 (child $8.59), dinner $19–$30. **Service** ★★★★★. **Friendliness** ★★★★★. **Parking** Hotel lot. **Bar** Full service. **Wine selection** Good. **Dress** Casual. **Disabled access** Yes. **Customers** Hotel guests. **Breakfast** Daily, 7:30–11 a.m. **Lunch** Daily, 11:30 a.m.–2 p.m. **Dinner** Daily, 5–9 p.m.

SETTING AND ATMOSPHERE This large dining room—basically the Yacht Club's coffee shop—features a nautical theme with colorful pastels.

HOUSE SPECIALTIES Breakfast features a buffet or an à la carte menu, with such selections as eggs Benedict and French toast. Lunch is coffee-shop fare including New England lobster sliders, burgers, fish-and-chips, and crab cakes. Dinner features standard dishes like grilled New York strip steak, pork chops, fish of the day, and snow-crab legs.

SUMMARY AND COMMENTS Not a dining destination, but it's a favorite of Disney cast members, who like it because it's quiet, the service is quick, and the food is dependable.

Le Cellier Steakhouse ★★★½

STEAK	EXPENSIVE	QUALITY ★★★½	VALUE ★★★
READER-SURVEY RESPONSES 89%	11%	DISNEY DINING PLAN?	YES

Canada, World Showcase, Epcot; ☎ 407-939-3463

Reservations Required. **Dining Plan credits** 2 per person, per meal. **When to go** Before 6 p.m. **Cost range** Lunch $15–$32 (child $9–$11), dinner $25–$44 (child $7–$12). **Service** ★★★★. **Friendliness** ★★★★★. **Parking** Epcot lot. **Bar** Full bar. **Wine selection** Canadian wines are featured. **Dress** Casual. **Disabled access** Yes. **Customers** Theme park guests. **Lunch** Daily, 11:30 a.m.–3 p.m. **Dinner** Daily, 4–8:50 p.m.

SETTING AND ATMOSPHERE Designed to look like a wine cellar, Le Cellier has stayed popular enough that in 2013 it becomes the second Disney Signature restaurant open for both lunch and dinner inside a theme park (the Studios' Hollywood Brown Derby is the other). Chef Al Youngman's cuisine is superb, with Canadian beef now on the menu and starters and sides such as the lobster chopped salad, artisanal cheeses, and classic Canadian *poutine* fries. And, yes, that famous Canadian Cheddar cheese soup stays on the menu. Most of the servers are Canadian and enjoy sharing stories of their home country.

HOUSE SPECIALTIES At lunch, pan-roasted salmon burger, roasted duck meatballs, filet mignon, Canadian Cheddar cheese soup. At dinner, grilled bone-in ribeye, Kurobuta pork, seared Pacific cod.

OTHER RECOMMENDATIONS Potato-leek–goat cheese quiche, braised short rib, and maple crème brûlée. Wonderful selection of dessert wines at dinner.

SUMMARY AND COMMENTS The pricey steaks take center stage at lunch and dinner. You can make a meal of the rich Canadian Cheddar cheese soup or a burger for lunch, but go for the gusto at dinner.

Chef Mickey's ★★½

AMERICAN/BUFFET	EXPENSIVE	QUALITY ★★★	VALUE ★★★
READER-SURVEY RESPONSES 83%	17%	DISNEY DINING PLAN? YES	

Contemporary Resort; ☎ 407-939-3463

Reservations Required. **Dining Plan credits** 1 per person, per meal. **When to go** Early evening. **Cost range** Breakfast $35 (child $19), dinner $40 (child $20). *Note:* Prices increase during peak periods (see page 428). **Service** ★★★★. **Friendliness** ★★★★★. **Parking** Valet ($12) or hotel lot. **Bar** Full service. **Wine selection** Fair. **Dress** Casual. **Disabled access** Yes. **Customers** Theme park guests. **Character breakfast** Daily, 7–11:30 a.m. **Character dinner** Daily, 5–9:30 p.m.

SETTING AND ATMOSPHERE A colorful, open dining room with the monorail running overhead, this is one of the most popular Disney-character restaurants—mostly because you're guaranteed an audience with Mickey Mouse, who dons a chef's toque and visits every single table for photos. (Goofy, Minnie, Donald, and Pluto are on hand, too.) The buffet circles the center of the room. It's loud, crowded, busy, and fun for families. We rarely see anyone here without kids in tow.

HOUSE SPECIALTIES Breakfast: French toast, biscuits and gravy. Dinner: carved meats.

OTHER RECOMMENDATIONS Fresh greens and mixed salads, pasta selections, Parmesan mashed potatoes and gravy. Sundae bar.

ENTERTAINMENT AND AMENITIES Character visits.

SUMMARY AND COMMENTS If you go hungry, this all-you-can-eat buffet is a good value for families; there's plenty for picky eaters, and you can start or end the day with a full tummy and photos of the top Disney characters already checked off your to-do list. Selections at both breakfast and dinner are freshly prepared and served in casseroles and platters on special heated countertops—a small step up from chafing dishes. And no one cares if the kids are loud.

Les Chefs de France ★★★

FRENCH	EXPENSIVE	QUALITY ★★★	VALUE ★★★
READER-SURVEY RESPONSES 85%	15%	DISNEY DINING PLAN? YES	

France, World Showcase, Epcot; ☎ 407-939-3463

Reservations Recommended. **Dining Plan credits** 1 per person, per meal. **When to go** Anytime. **Cost range** Lunch $13–$24 (child $7–$8), dinner $19–$40 (child $7–$8). **Service** ★★★★★. **Friendliness** ★★★★★. **Parking** Epcot lot. **Bar** Beer. **Wine selection** Very good. **Dress** Casual. **Disabled access** Yes. **Customers** Theme park guests. **Lunch** Daily, noon–3 p.m. **Dinner** Daily, 5–9 p.m.

SETTING AND ATMOSPHERE This bustling World Showcase dining room is usually packed and infused with the aroma of buttery croissants—as much a part of the atmosphere here as the carefully placed copies of

Le Monde and the huge, mottled mirrors. White tablecloths and padded banquettes accentuate the classic bistro decor of the main dining room. Another room off to the side is more casual, with a better view of what's going on outside. An Audio-Animatronic version of Remy, the rodent star of Disney/Pixar's *Ratatouille,* visits a few times each day, stopping at tables for brief visits. (He stands just 6 inches tall and fits on a cheese tray.)

HOUSE SPECIALTIES Dishes inspired by three of France's greatest chefs, for whom this restaurant is named: Paul Bocuse, the late Gaston Lenôtre, and Roger Vergé. Sample sautéed scallops, braised beef short ribs, duck breast and leg confit à l'orange, or a silky crème brûlée.

OTHER RECOMMENDATIONS Onion soup topped with Gruyère; chicken crêpes (lunch only); tomato-and-goat-cheese tart.

SUMMARY AND COMMENTS Here's your chance to eat at a restaurant created by three of France's best chefs. Jerome Bocuse, the son of Paul Bocuse, runs the restaurant, and his father still visits from time to time. Executive chef Bruno Vrignon, who trained in Lyon with Bocuse, heads the kitchen team, and the French servers make it an immersion experience. If you're on a budget, go at lunch: Many dinner entrees are available midday at reduced prices. The best deal is the three-course lunch ($24) that starts with French onion soup with Gruyère or lobster bisque and continues with the classic *croque monsieur* (toasted ham-and-cheese sandwich), quiche, or baked macaroni with Gruyère, followed by your choice of dessert.

Cinderella's Royal Table ★ ★ ★

AMERICAN	EXPENSIVE	QUALITY ★ ★ ★	VALUE ★ ★
READER-SURVEY RESPONSES 86% 👍	14% 👎	DISNEY DINING PLAN? YES	

Cinderella Castle, Fantasyland, Magic Kingdom; ☎ 407-939-3463

Reservations Required; credit card required to reserve; must prepay in full. **Dining Plan credits** 2 per person, per meal. **When to go** Early. **Cost range** Character breakfast, $43 adults, $28 children; character lunch, $46 adults, $29 children; character dinner, $54 adults, $33 children. *Note:* Prices increase during peak periods (see page 428). **Service** ★★★★. **Friendliness** ★★★★. **Parking** Magic Kingdom lot. **Bar** None. **Wine selection** None. **Dress** Casual. **Disabled access** Limited. **Customers** Theme park guests. **Character breakfast** Daily, 8:05–10:40 a.m. **Character lunch** Daily, 11:45 a.m.–2:40 p.m. **Character dinner** Daily, 3:50–10 p.m.

SETTING AND ATMOSPHERE A medieval banquet hall, appointed with the requisite banners and Round Table–like regalia, on the second floor of Cinderella Castle. Stained-glass windows overlook Fantasyland, but the view is limited.

HOUSE SPECIALTIES All meals are fixed-price character affairs, with the menus changing periodically. Breakfast is standard-issue. Lunch favorites include pan-seared salmon, pork tenderloin, and the signature Major Domo's Favorite Pie (beef in Cabernet sauce, mashed potatoes, and puff pastry). Dinner fare includes fried chicken, grilled pork chops, braised cobia, and roasted beef tenderloin; kids can choose from a "Minor Domo" pie (a mini–Major Domo), chicken strips, baked pasta, and pretzel dogs.

ENTERTAINMENT AND AMENITIES Assorted princesses attend all three pricey meals. They're expensive not so much because the food is good but because Disney forces you to purchase photos of your group that are bundled into the cost of each meal. No matter—families can't seem to get enough of this "Disney magic." For more on reserving a spot here (and the travails thereof), see page 421.

Cítricos ★★★½

MEDITERRANEAN	EXPENSIVE	QUALITY ★★★★½	VALUE ★★★
READER-SURVEY RESPONSES 89%	11%	DISNEY DINING PLAN?	YES

Grand Floridian Resort & Spa; ☎ 407-939-7429

Reservations Required; credit card required to reserve Chef's Domain. **Dining Plan credits** 2 per person, per meal. **When to go** Anytime. **Cost range** $28–$42 (child $6–$13). **Service** ★★★★★. **Friendliness** ★★★★★. **Parking** Valet ($12); self-parking is deceptively far away. **Bar** Full service. **Wine selection** Very good. **Dress** Dressy casual. **Disabled access** Yes. **Customers** Hotel guests and locals. **Dinner** Daily, 5:30–10 p.m.

SETTING AND ATMOSPHERE The golds and yellows of the Mediterranean color this stylish dining room on the second floor of the Grand Floridian. Diners often find Chef Phillip Ponticelli working his culinary magic in the full-view show kitchen.

HOUSE SPECIALTIES Sautéed shrimp with lemon, feta cheese, tomatoes, and white wine; oak-grilled filet of beef; braised veal shank.

OTHER RECOMMENDATIONS Pan-seared Florida black grouper, braised short ribs, arancini, and Berkshire pork.

SUMMARY AND COMMENTS This is one of the best-kept dining secrets at Disney World. Chef Ponticelli is very hands-on, and his TLC shows. The menu changes with the seasons, so there are always delicious surprises. For an extra-special night, reserve the Chef's Domain, a private room for up to 12 guests where the chef creates a special menu.

Coral Reef Restaurant ★★½

SEAFOOD	EXPENSIVE	QUALITY ★★	VALUE ★★
READER-SURVEY RESPONSES 77%	23%	DISNEY DINING PLAN?	YES

The Seas with Nemo & Friends, Future World, Epcot; ☎ 407-939-3463

Reservations Required. **Dining Plan credits** 1 per person, per meal. **When to go** Lunch. **Cost range** Lunch $17.50–$32 (child $9), dinner $19–$32 (child $9). **Service** ★★★★. **Friendliness** ★★★★. **Parking** Epcot lot. **Bar** Full service. **Wine selection** Good. **Dress** Casual. **Disabled access** Yes. **Customers** Theme park guests. **Lunch** Daily, 11:30 a.m.–3:20 p.m. **Dinner** Daily, 4 p.m.–park closing.

SETTING AND ATMOSPHERE Coral Reef offers one of the best theme park views anywhere: below the water level of the humongous saltwater tank in the Seas with Nemo & Friends. Sharks, rays, and even humans swim by, and every table has a great view. Tiered seating affords perfect views; special lighting fixtures throw ripple patterns on the ceiling, creating an underwater feel.

HOUSE SPECIALTIES Creamy lobster soup, on the menu since the restaurant opened; seared Scottish salmon; grilled New York strip steak; Chocolate Wave dessert. For kids: seared mahimahi, grilled chicken breast, grilled fish of the day, meaty macaroni, and cheese pizza.

SUMMARY AND COMMENTS The quality of the food has dipped, but Coral Reef is the only table-service restaurant in Future World where you can sip a glass of wine and enjoy a decent meal in a quiet, informal setting.

The Crystal Palace ★★★

AMERICAN/BUFFET	MODERATE	QUALITY ★★★½	VALUE ★★★
READER-SURVEY RESPONSES 90% 👍	10% 👎	DISNEY DINING PLAN?	YES

Main Street, U.S.A., Magic Kingdom; ☎ 407-939-3463

Reservations Required. **Dining Plan credits** 1 per person, per meal. **When to go** Anytime. **Cost range** Breakfast $27 (child $15), lunch $29 (child $16), dinner $41 (child $20). *Note:* Prices increase during peak periods (see page 428). **Service** ★★★. **Friendliness** ★★★★. **Parking** Magic Kingdom lot. **Bar** None. **Wine selection** None. **Dress** Casual. **Disabled access** Yes. **Customers** Magic Kingdom guests. **Character breakfast** Daily, 8–10:30 a.m. **Character lunch** Daily, 11:30 a.m.–2:45 p.m. **Character dinner** Daily, 3:15 p.m.–park closing.

SETTING AND ATMOSPHERE A turn-of-the-20th-century glass pavilion awash with sunlight and decorated with plenty of summer greenery. Seating is comfortable, and buffet lines are open and accessible. A low buffet area lets kids help themselves.

HOUSE SPECIALTIES Menu items change often but include waffles and pancakes layered with fresh fruit for breakfast; prime rib, roast pork, and peel-and-eat shrimp for dinner; Thai curry mussels; grilled vegetables with balsamic glaze; pasta with wild mushrooms and chicken; shrimp; and a sundae bar. We love the salads—more than a dozen—from a simple green salad to one with papaya, frisée, and arugula.

ENTERTAINMENT AND AMENITIES Winnie the Pooh and friends dance about and pose with the kids.

SUMMARY AND COMMENTS The best dining value in the Magic Kingdom—go hungry and fill up. The food is consistently fine on the state-of-the-art buffet, which, instead of steam tables, has casserole dishes and pans that sit on special heated countertops. Picky kids get their own buffet with mac-and-cheese and chicken fingers.

ESPN Club ★★½

AMERICAN/SANDWICHES	MODERATE	QUALITY ★★★	VALUE ★★★
READER-SURVEY RESPONSES 95% 👍	5% 👎	DISNEY DINING PLAN?	YES

BoardWalk; ☎ 407-939-1177

Reservations Not accepted. **Dining Plan credits** 1 per person, per meal. **When to go** Anytime. **Cost range** $6.50–$21 (child $8.59). **Service** ★★★. **Friendliness** ★★★★. **Parking** Valet ($12) or BoardWalk lot. **Bar** Full service. **Wine selection** Minimal. **Dress** Casual. **Disabled access** Yes. **Customers** Tourists. **Hours** Daily, 11:30 a.m.–1 a.m.

SETTING AND ATMOSPHERE A sports bar to the nth degree, with basketball-court flooring, sports memorabilia, and more television monitors than a network affiliate. The bar area features satellite sports-trivia video games. A large octagonal space with a wall of TVs serves as the main dining room.

HOUSE SPECIALTIES Red wings (Buffalo-style wings), barbecue pork ribs, Philly cheesesteak, panini-press Reuben, extreme roast-beef sandwich.

SUMMARY AND COMMENTS Family-friendly and affordable. Service is a little more brusque than at other Disney restaurants. Portions are large, and the quality is in line with the price. A good choice for late-night dining or when you have to choose between going out for a bite and staying in the room to catch the big game.

ESPN Wide World of Sports Grill   ★ ★ ½

AMERICAN	MODERATE	QUALITY ★★★	VALUE ★★★
READER-SURVEY RESPONSES 75% 👍	25% 👎	DISNEY DINING PLAN? YES	

ESPN Wide World of Sports Complex; ☎ 407-939-2196

Reservations Not necessary. **Dining Plan credits** 1 per person, per meal. **When to go** When an event is going on. *Note:* You must pay admission to the sports complex to dine. **Cost range** $8–$10 (child $8.59). **Service** ★★★. **Friendliness** ★★½. **Parking** ESPN Wide World of Sports lot. **Bar** Full service. **Wine selection** Minimal. **Dress** Jerseys if you've got 'em. **Disabled access** Yes. **Customers** Sports fans. **Hours** Open only on event days.

SETTING AND ATMOSPHERE Think Hard Rock Cafe with sports memorabilia instead of musical instruments. More than 20 big-screen TVs play whatever games are on.
HOUSE SPECIALTIES Burgers and sandwiches.
ENTERTAINMENT AND AMENITIES Televised sporting events.
SUMMARY AND COMMENTS The food is unpretentious American cuisine — giant burgers and piles of chicken wings. The menu works for hungry fans at the ESPN Wide World of Sports Complex.

50's Prime Time Cafe   ★ ★ ★

AMERICAN	MODERATE	QUALITY ★★★	VALUE ★★★
READER-SURVEY RESPONSES 85% 👍	15% 👎	DISNEY DINING PLAN? YES	

Echo Lake, Disney's Hollywood Studios; ☎ 407-939-3463

Reservations Recommended. **Dining Plan credits** 1 per person, per meal. **When to go** Lunch or dinner. **Cost range** Lunch $13.50–$21 (child $8.59), dinner $15–$21 (child $8.59). **Service** ★★★★★. **Friendliness** ★★★★★. **Parking** DHS lot. **Bar** Full service. **Wine selection** Limited. **Dress** Casual. **Disabled access** Yes. **Customers** Theme park guests. **Lunch** Daily, 11 a.m.–3:55 p.m.; opens at 10:30 a.m. on Sunday and Wednesday. **Dinner** Daily, 4 p.m.–park closing.

SETTING AND ATMOSPHERE Like eating a meal in your own kitchen, 1950s-style: Pastel laminate, gooosenecked lamps, and black-and-white televisions that play vintage sitcoms are the rule.
HOUSE SPECIALTIES Meat loaf, pot roast, fried chicken, and other homey fare. Easy to find something that kids will like.
ENTERTAINMENT AND AMENITIES Fifties sitcom clips on television.
SUMMARY AND COMMENTS Though the restaurant is usually packed and a bit noisy, servers are friendly and keep things moving (and nag you just like Mom did to "take your elbows off the table" or "finish every last bite"). Diners really get a kick out of the classic comedies playing on black-and-white TVs. Skip the appetizers and stick with filling fare like the pot roast or golden fried chicken. Don't miss the PB&J milkshake.

Flying Fish Cafe   ★ ★ ★ ★

SEAFOOD	EXPENSIVE	QUALITY ★★★★	VALUE ★★★
READER-SURVEY RESPONSES 85% 👍	15% 👎	DISNEY DINING PLAN? YES	

BoardWalk; ☎ 407-939-3463

Reservations Required. **Dining Plan credits** 2 per person, per meal. **When to go** Anytime. **Cost range** $29–$42 (child $6–$12). **Service** ★★★★★. **Friendliness** ★★★★★. **Parking** Valet ($12) or BoardWalk lot. **Bar** Full service. **Wine selection** Excellent but pricey. **Dress** Dressy casual. **Disabled access** Good. **Customers** Tourists and locals. **Dinner** Sunday–Thursday, 5:30–10 p.m.; Friday and Saturday, 5:30–10:30 p.m.

SETTING AND ATMOSPHERE Contemporary setting inspired by a 1930s Coney Island roller coaster. (The coaster was actually called the Flying Turns, and one of the cars on the ride was dubbed the Flying Fish.) Booth backs resemble the climbs and swoops of a coaster. On the far wall is a stylized depiction of a Ferris wheel, and whimsical fish fly overhead on a parachute ride. Diners may choose to sit at the counter that overlooks the bar or the open kitchen.

HOUSE SPECIALTIES Chef Tim Keating, a repeat James Beard Foundation finalist, is a big proponent of Florida products. The fare here changes frequently, but you'll always find the potato-wrapped snapper, the restaurant's signature dish, served with creamy leek fondue and a red wine–butter sauce; char-crusted New York strip steak; and lump crab cakes. Desserts are seasonal, but the house-made sorbets and caramelized-banana Napoleon are divine. A good way to sample two of the most popular dishes is the three-course prix fixe tasting menu, which includes both the New York strip and the potato-wrapped snapper.

OTHER RECOMMENDATIONS For a special experience, book the Chef's Tasting Wine Dinner. Sitting at the "Chef's Counter," you watch the chef create the six courses for your meal. Each course is paired with a wine selected by the manager. This experience is designed for ages 14 and up, and you must make reservations at least one day in advance.

SUMMARY AND COMMENTS Locals love the Flying Fish, and for good reason. Though this is food for grown-ups, you'll often see children in the noisy dining room because of the BoardWalk location. If you can't get a table, check on seating availability at the counter.

The Fountain ★★

AMERICAN	MODERATE	QUALITY ★★	VALUE ★★
READER-SURVEY RESPONSES 87% 👍	13% 👎	DISNEY DINING PLAN? NO	

Dolphin Resort; ☎ 407-934-1609

Reservations Not taken. **When to go** Anytime. **Cost range** $7.25–$13.50 (child $8). **Service** ★★★★. **Friendliness** ★★★★. **Bar** Beer and wine only. **Wine selection** Limited. **Parking** Hotel lot ($15). **Dress** Casual. **Disabled access** Yes. **Customers** Hotel guests. **Lunch and dinner** Daily, 11 a.m.–11 p.m.

SETTING AND ATMOSPHERE Informal soda-shop ambience.

HOUSE SPECIALTIES Build-your-own burgers and hot dogs, BLTs, shakes, and ice-cream cones. The PB&J milkshake is worth every calorie.

OTHER RECOMMENDATIONS Seared-salmon salad, tuna-and-Cheddar melt on flatbread.

SUMMARY AND COMMENTS This is the place for Dolphin guests to get a quick bite. Create your own sundae at The Fountain Sweet Treats.

Fresh Mediterranean Market ★★½

MEDITERRANEAN/AMERICAN	MODERATE	QUALITY ★★½	VALUE ★★
READER-SURVEY RESPONSES 71% 👍	29% 👎	DISNEY DINING PLAN? NO	

Dolphin Resort; ☎ 407-934-1609

Reservations Available but not necessary. **When to go** Breakfast or lunch. **Cost range** Breakfast buffet $18 (child $11); lunch $14–$24 (child $12). **Service** ★★★★. **Friendliness** ★★★★. **Parking** Hotel lot ($15). **Bar** Beer, wine, and limited cocktails. **Wine selection** Limited. **Dress** Casual. **Disabled access** Yes. **Customers** Hotel guests. **Breakfast** Daily, 6:30–11 a.m. **Lunch** Monday–Friday, 11:30 a.m.–1 p.m.; Saturday and Sunday, noon–2 p.m. Days of operation may vary according to hotel occupancy.

SETTING AND ATMOSPHERE Brightly colored tiles, light woods, and big windows set the scene. Ask for a veranda table if you want to have a quiet conversation away from the action in the open kitchen.

HOUSE SPECIALTIES Breakfast: fresh fruit and vegetable juices, made-to-order omelets. Lunch: pasta, fish, beef sliders, and generous salads.

OTHER RECOMMENDATIONS Chicken marsala, Italian panini.

SUMMARY AND COMMENTS A pleasant, quiet spot for breakfast or lunch, with a menu that's more healthful than many.

Fulton's Crab House ★ ★ ½

SEAFOOD	EXPENSIVE	QUALITY ★★★½	VALUE ★★
READER-SURVEY RESPONSES 70%	30%	DISNEY DINING PLAN? YES	

Downtown Disney Marketplace; ☎ 407-939-3463

Reservations Accepted. Dining Plan credits 2 per person, per meal. When to go Early evening. Cost range Lunch $10–$18 (child $6–$20), dinner $24–$52 (child $8–$20). Service ★★★★. Friendliness ★★★★. Parking Lot near the old Pleasure Island complex. Bar Full service. Wine selection Good; mostly American. Dress Casual. Disabled access Yes. Customers Locals and Disney guests. Lunch Daily, 11:30 a.m.–3:30 p.m. Dinner Daily, 4–11 p.m.

SETTING AND ATMOSPHERE Separate dining areas include the Market Room, a tribute to New York City's Fulton Fish Market (for which the restaurant is named); the Constellation Room, a semicircular room with a starlit night sky; and the Industry Room, a tribute to the commercial-fishing industry.

HOUSE SPECIALTIES Stone crab; fresh fish flown in daily; fresh oysters; Fulton's crab-and-lobster bisque; cioppino with crab, shrimp, scallops, clams, mussels, and fish in a tomato broth; Alaskan king and Dungeness crab.

OTHER RECOMMENDATIONS Prince Edward Island mussels, Florida little-neck clams, crab and lobster for two, filet mignon, grilled shrimp.

SUMMARY AND COMMENTS Fulton's is a great (but pricey) place to enjoy a beautiful Florida day on the back deck while slurping oysters or digging in to other fresh seafood. You can pretty much get whatever seafood you want, from raw oysters to crab, shrimp, Alaska salmon, and whole Maine lobster. In busy times of year, waits can be long—more than an hour, even on weeknights. But if you don't get fresh seafood back home, go early, request a table on the deck, order a Seafood Tower, and enjoy.

Garden Grill Restaurant ★ ★

AMERICAN	EXPENSIVE	QUALITY ★★	VALUE ★★★
READER-SURVEY RESPONSES 80%	20%	DISNEY DINING PLAN? YES	

The Land, Future World, Epcot; ☎ 407-939-3463

Reservations Required. Dining Plan credits 1 per person, per meal. When to go Dinner. Cost range $35 (child $17). *Note:* Prices increase during peak periods (see page 428). Service ★★★★. Friendliness ★★★★★. Parking Epcot lot. Bar Wine, beer, and some mixed drinks. Wine selection Fair. Dress Casual. Disabled access Yes. Customers Theme park guests. Character dinner Daily, 4:30–8 p.m.

SETTING AND ATMOSPHERE With the popular Soarin' attraction nearby, The Garden Grill stays busy, even though the concept and the dining room are getting a little frayed around the edges. You step on a slowly revolving floor to make your way to tables that revolve above scenes from Living with the Land, the pavilion's ride-through attraction (see page 564). If service is prompt, about the time you finish a meal you've revolved around once, past scenes of a desert, a rainforest, and a farm, along with a few mural-painted walls in between. It's a great place to get photos with the Disney characters—Mickey, Chip 'n' Dale, and others make stops at tables for photo ops and greetings.

HOUSE SPECIALTIES Beef filet, turkey with cranberry-orange relish, and sustainable fish of the day. Dessert is fruit crisp with ice cream. The kids' menu includes mac-and-cheese, chicken drumsticks, potatoes, and vegetables.

ENTERTAINMENT AND AMENITIES The view. Character dining. Complimentary nonalcoholic beverages included with meals.

SUMMARY AND COMMENTS Salads are made with produce grown right in The Land's garden downstairs. More of a low-key destination for filling up and taking photos with the Disney characters than a spot for delicious dining.

Garden Grove ★★

AMERICAN	MODERATE	QUALITY ★★★	VALUE ★★
READER-SURVEY RESPONSES 89% 👍	11% 👎	DISNEY DINING PLAN?	NO

Swan Resort; ☎ 407-934-1609

Reservations Recommended. **When to go** Anytime. **Cost range** Breakfast $9–$16 (child $3.25–$5.50), weekday buffet $19 (child $12), weekend Disney-character breakfast buffet $21 (child $13), lunch $13–$16 (child $6–$7), nightly Disney-character dinner buffet $36 (child $14) **Service** ★★★. **Friendliness** ★★★. **Parking** Valet ($20) or hotel lot ($15). **Bar** Full service. **Wine selection** Good. **Dress** Casual. **Disabled access** Yes. **Customers** Hotel guests, some locals, tourists. **Breakfast, lunch, and dinner** Daily, 6:30 a.m.–9:30 p.m.; weekend character breakfast, Saturday and Sunday, 8–11 a.m.

SETTING AND ATMOSPHERE The spacious dining room has a 25-foot faux oak tree as its centerpiece, and sunlight streams in from the tall windows. At night, the lights are dimmed, the oak tree is full of lanterns and twinkling lights, and street lamps create the pleasant ambience of a nighttime garden.

HOUSE SPECIALTIES For lunch, blackened-shrimp sandwich, Reuben, fresh pasta, fish-and-chips. For dinner, Saturday, Tuesday, and Thursday are Mediterranean-themed (pastas, roasted chicken, eggplant Parmesan); Monday, Wednesday, and Sunday are barbecue night (including prime rib); and Friday is seafood night (raw bar, jumbo scallops, fried-seafood basket, and fish of the day).

OTHER RECOMMENDATIONS Superfoods breakfast menu.

SUMMARY AND COMMENTS Garden Grove's dependable fare isn't worth a special trip unless you want some time with the Disney characters— and it's a bargain compared to other character-dining experiences.

Grand Floridian Cafe ★★½

AMERICAN	MODERATE	QUALITY ★★★	VALUE ★★
READER-SURVEY RESPONSES 84% 👍	16% 👎	DISNEY DINING PLAN?	YES

Grand Floridian Resort & Spa; ☎ 407-824-2496

Reservations Accepted. **Dining Plan credits** 1 per person, per meal. **When to go** Anytime. **Cost range** Breakfast $9–$18 (child $6), lunch $13–$25 (child $8.59), dinner $17–$28 (child $8.50). **Service** ★★★. **Friendliness** ★★★★. **Parking** Valet ($12); self-parking is far away. **Bar** Full service. **Wine selection** Good. **Dress** Casual.

Disabled access Yes. **Customers** Hotel guests. **Breakfast** Daily, 7–11:30 a.m.
Lunch Daily, 11:30 a.m.–2 p.m. **Dinner** Daily, 5–9 p.m.

SETTING AND ATMOSPHERE Basically an upscale coffee shop, the large
dining room—with high ceilings and decorative windows—looks out
on the Grand Floridian's pool and center courtyard.

HOUSE SPECIALTIES Breakfast includes eggs prepared virtually every way
known to mankind, waffles, French toast, and lobster eggs Benedict.
For lunch, there's Cobb salad and the Grand sandwich with ham, turkey, and Boursin cheese sauce. For dinner, choose from salmon, shrimp
pasta, or grilled pork chops.

OTHER RECOMMENDATIONS A hefty Reuben for lunch and a simple New
York strip with mashed potatoes for dinner.

SUMMARY AND COMMENTS A quick place to grab a bite. Scrumptious
desserts by the same team that makes sweets for all the hotel's dining
rooms.

La Hacienda de San Angel ★★★

MEXICAN	EXPENSIVE	QUALITY ★★★½	VALUE ★★½
READER SURVEY RESPONSES	84% 👍 16% 👎	DISNEY DINING PLAN?	YES

Mexico, World Showcase, Epcot; ☎ 407-939-3463

Reservations Required. **Dining Plan credits** 1 per person, per meal. **When to go**
Dinner. **Cost range** $10.75–$26 (child $8–$10). **Service** ★★★★. **Friendliness**
★★★★★. **Parking** Epcot lot. **Bar** Full. **Wine selection** All Mexican. **Dress** Casual.
Disabled access Yes. **Customers** Theme park guests. **Dinner** 4–8:35 p.m.

SETTING AND ATMOSPHERE Traditional Mexican adobe ranch decor. Back
tables have choice views of World Showcase Lagoon and *IllumiNations*.

HOUSE SPECIALTIES If you've ever bought soft tacos off the streets of Mexico, the upscale taquiza appetizer will bring back fond memories . . . at
roughly 10 times the price. They take their margaritas seriously here:
Don't complain that yours isn't strong enough, or they'll remake it for
you and you'll wake up at Betty Ford.

SUMMARY AND COMMENTS Not what you'd typically find at your local
Tex-Mex place. Our favorites are the shrimp tacos and the grilled tilapia with roasted corn and cactus leaves. You can make a meal of appetizers and a margarita—order a bowl of the addictive roasted sweet
peppers with lime and sea salt, share some tacos, and call it happy. If
you're so inclined, ask for the vegetarian menu.

Hollywood & Vine ★★½

AMERICAN	MODERATE	QUALITY ★★★	VALUE ★★★
READER-SURVEY RESPONSES	74% 👍 26% 👎	DISNEY DINING PLAN?	YES

Echo Lake, Disney's Hollywood Studios; ☎ 407-939-3463

Reservations Recommended; credit card required to reserve *Fantasmic!* Dining Package (see page 622). **Dining Plan credits** 1 per person, per meal. **When to go** Anytime. **Cost range** Breakfast buffet $31 (child $17), lunch buffet $35 (child $19), dinner
buffet $29–$35 (child $15–$19), depending on *Fantasmic!* seating. *Note:* Prices for character meals increase during peak periods (see page 428). **Service** ★★★★. **Friendliness**
★★★★★. **Parking** DHS lot. **Bar** Full service. **Wine selection** Limited. **Dress** Casual.
Disabled access Yes. **Customers** Theme park guests. **Character breakfast** Daily,
8–11:20 a.m., **Character lunch** Daily, 11:40 a.m.–2:25 p.m. **Dinner** Daily, 5–9 p.m.

SETTING AND ATMOSPHERE Large Art Deco–style cafeteria with tile
floors, lots of chrome, and huge wall murals with vintage scenes of old

Hollywood and other California landmarks. But breakfast and lunch are known as Disney Junior Play 'n Dine—featuring June from *Little Einsteins,* Special Agent Oso, Jake the Neverland Pirate, and Handy Manny—and that means lots of small children and parents dining at breakfast and lunch. Dinner is subdued.

HOUSE SPECIALTIES Chilled salads, fish of the day, carved and grilled meats, vegetables and pasta, fresh fruits and breads. (Menu changes often.)

SUMMARY AND COMMENTS With all the glass, tile, and chrome, the noise echoes for days.

The Hollywood Brown Derby ★★★★

AMERICAN	EXPENSIVE	QUALITY ★★★★	VALUE ★★★
READER-SURVEY RESPONSES 82% 👍	18% 👎	DISNEY DINING PLAN?	YES

Hollywood Boulevard, Disney's Hollywood Studios; ☎ 407-939-3463

Reservations Accepted; credit card required to reserve *Fantasmic!* Dining Package (see page 428). **Dining Plan credits** 2 per person, per meal. **When to go** Early evening. **Cost range** Lunch and dinner $28–$41 (child $6–$11). **Service** ★★★★★. **Friendliness** ★★★★★. **Parking** DHS lot. **Bar** Full service. **Wine selection** Very good. **Dress** Casual. **Disabled access** Yes. **Customers** Theme park guests. **Lunch** Daily, 11:30 a.m.–3 p.m. **Dinner** Daily, 3:30 p.m.–park closing.

SETTING AND ATMOSPHERE A replica of the original Brown Derby restaurant (not the one shaped like a derby) in California, the elegant sunken dining room has curved booths, tables draped with yards of white linen, and romantic shaded faux candles. Tall palm trees in huge pots stand in the center of the room and reach for the high ceiling.

HOUSE SPECIALTIES Cobb salad (named for Bob Cobb, the original restaurant's owner), duck two ways, and grapefruit cake.

OTHER RECOMMENDATIONS Spit-roasted rack of lamb, Thai noodle bowl with wok-fried coconut tofu, and blue-lump-crab spring-roll appetizer.

SUMMARY AND COMMENTS The Brown Derby is one of the top theme park–dining experiences at Disney. The same menu is in place for both lunch and dinner, so it's pricey for midday dining, but a wonderful way to take a break and regenerate. Decor is so perfect you'll feel as if you're in 1930s Hollywood; everyone really should dress in white ties and long chiffon gowns. Service is outstanding, and the kitchen turns out stellar creations. The kids' menu includes tempura fish strips, grilled cheese on whole wheat, and grilled chicken breast.

House of Blues ★★★

REGIONAL AMERICAN	MODERATE	QUALITY ★★★½	VALUE ★★★
READER-SURVEY RESPONSES 82% 👍	18% 👎	DISNEY DINING PLAN?	YES

Downtown Disney West Side; ☎ 407-934-2623

Reservations Recommended. **Dining Plan credits** 1 per person, per meal. **When to go** Early evening; Sunday gospel brunch. **Cost range** $11–$29 (child $6.25–$6.95); brunch $33.50 (child $17.25). **Service** ★★★★. **Friendliness** ★★★. **Parking** Downtown Disney lot. **Bar** Full service. **Wine selection** Modest. **Dress** Casual. **Disabled access** Good. **Customers** Blues lovers. **Brunch** 2 seatings on Sunday, 10:30 a.m. and 1 p.m. **Lunch and dinner** Sunday–Tuesday, 11:30 a.m.–11 p.m.; Wednesday and Thursday, 11:30 a.m.–midnight; Friday and Saturday, 11:30 a.m.–1 a.m.

SETTING AND ATMOSPHERE You'd think it was a ramshackle hut in the bayou if the place weren't bigger than all of Louisiana. Nearly every available inch of wall space displays some type of voodoo-tinged folk art. The restaurant area is separated from the performance hall, where blues and rock groups perform. A live band often performs in the restaurant on weekends as well.

HOUSE SPECIALTIES Flatbreads, buttermilk fried chicken, Juicy Lucy burger.

OTHER RECOMMENDATIONS Jambalaya, Tennessee-style baby back ribs, shrimp and grits, lobster mac-and-cheese, bourbon bread pudding, molten chocolate cake.

SUMMARY AND COMMENTS The menu got a slight overhaul, and for a themed restaurant, House of Blues does a good job with its food. If you're planning on taking in one of the acts at the performance space next door, you're better off going there first so you can get a good seat, then eating afterward.

Il Mulino New York Trattoria ★★★

ITALIAN	EXPENSIVE	QUALITY ★★★	VALUE ★★
READER-SURVEY RESPONSES 58%	42%	DISNEY DINING PLAN?	NO

Swan Resort; ☎ 407-934-1609

Reservations Accepted. **When to go** Dinner. **Cost range** $16–$45 (child $12–$16). Service ★★. Friendliness ★★. Parking Valet (free with validation) or hotel lot ($15). Bar Full service. Wine selection Good. Dress Dressy casual. Disabled access Yes. Customers Mostly hotel guests and conventioneers. Dinner 5–11 p.m. nightly.

SETTING AND ATMOSPHERE A spin-off of the New York City restaurant, Il Mulino takes an upscale-casual approach to Italian cuisine, with family-style platters for sharing in the noisy dining room. Tables are dark wood. An open kitchen creates a bustle. You can request private dining in one of the smaller rooms.

HOUSE SPECIALTIES The cuisine focuses on Italy's Abruzzi region, with hearty pastas and big cuts of meat. Try the linguine with clam sauce or the seared red snapper.

OTHER RECOMMENDATIONS Tuna carpaccio, pizza with fresh mozzarella, spaghetti carbonara.

SUMMARY AND COMMENTS The tried-and-true menu never changes. Dinner starts with a complimentary taste of Parmesan-topped roasted eggplant, along with ciabatta and focaccia breads and cacciatorini sausages, and ends with a complimentary sip of limoncello, the lemon-flavored Italian liqueur. The dining room's hardwood floors and faux–exposed brick walls create a contemporary space but, unfortunately, don't buffer the noise.

Jiko—The Cooking Place ★★★★½

AFRICAN/FUSION	EXPENSIVE	QUALITY ★★★★½	VALUE ★★★½
READER-SURVEY RESPONSES 90%	10%	DISNEY DINING PLAN?	YES

Animal Kingdom Lodge & Villas–Jambo House; ☎ 407-938-3000

Reservations Required. **Dining Plan credits** 2 per person, per meal. **When to go** Dinner. **Cost range** $28–$43 (child $7–$12). Service ★★★★★. Friendliness ★★★★★. Parking Valet ($12) or hotel lot. Bar Full bar. Wine selection All South African. Dress Dressy casual. Disabled access Good. Customers Hotel guests and locals. Dinner Daily, 5:30–10 p.m.

SETTING AND ATMOSPHERE Jiko has a special ambience, from the young African exchange students who greet guests as they enter to a menu of unusual tastes. Jiko's spacious dining room is inspired by the opening scenes of *The Lion King.* A pair of large wood-burning ovens dominates the center of the room.

HOUSE SPECIALTIES Wood-fired flatbreads; trio of dips with house-made *naan* (Indian flatbread); oak-grilled filet mignon with Cabernet reduction and sweet-corn risotto; maize-crusted corvine.

OTHER RECOMMENDATIONS Grilled wild Gulf shrimp curry, braised beef short ribs, seared Barbary duck breast, and a selection of artisanal cheeses. Kids' menu includes fish, grilled steak, and mac-and-cheese.

SUMMARY AND COMMENTS Jiko has been winning awards and accolades (including AAA's Four Diamond Award) for its interesting fare and stellar wine list—one of the largest collections of South African wines in any North American restaurant, with more than 1,800 bottles. Dishes are beautifully spiced and full of flavor. Start with some flatbread and wrap up with coconut bread pudding or "One Last Cup" (Tanzanian chocolate–Kenya coffee mousse with cinnamon mascarpone). Special menus for the glucose- and lactose-intolerant, vegans, and vegetarians.

Kimonos ★★★★

JAPANESE	MODERATE	QUALITY ★★★★½	VALUE ★★★
READER-SURVEY RESPONSES	72% 👍	28% 👎	DISNEY DINING PLAN? NO

Swan Resort; ☎ 407-934-1609

Reservations Accepted for parties of 6 or more. **When to go** Dinner. **Cost range** Sushi and rolls à la carte, $4.25–$16. **Service** ★★★★★. **Friendliness** ★★★★★. **Parking** Valet ($20) or hotel lot ($15). **Bar** Full service. **Wine selection** Very good. **Dress** Casual. **Disabled access** Yes. **Customers** Hotel guests and locals. **Dinner** Daily, 5:30 p.m.–midnight; bar opens at 5 p.m.

SETTING AND ATMOSPHERE The decor consists of black-lacquered tabletops and counters, tall pillars rising to bamboo rafters with rice-paper lanterns, and elegant kimonos that hang outstretched on the walls and between the dining sections. The chefs will greet you with a friendly welcome, and you'll be offered a hot towel to clean your hands.

HOUSE SPECIALTIES Although sushi and sashimi are the focus, Kimonos also serves hot appetizers, including tempura shrimp and vegetables; Kobe beef and duck satays; spicy Thai egg-drop soup; and miso soup.

SUMMARY AND COMMENTS Sushi fans will find an extensive selection of fresh seafood, including delicacies like sweet shrimp and surf clam that you won't find on every sushi menu. The skill of the sushi artists is as much a joy to watch as is eating the wonderfully fresh creations. There are no full entrees here, just good sushi and appetizers.

Kona Cafe ★★★

POLYNESIAN/PAN-ASIAN	MODERATE	QUALITY ★★★	VALUE ★★★★
READER-SURVEY RESPONSES	93% 👍	7% 👎	DISNEY DINING PLAN? YES

Polynesian Resort; ☎ 407-939-3463

Reservations Accepted. **Dining Plan credits** 1 per person, per meal. **When to go** Anytime. **Cost range** Breakfast $10–$14.50 (child $5), lunch $12–$22 (child $8), dinner $17–$29 (child $8). **Service** ★★★★. **Friendliness** ★★★★★. **Parking** Valet ($12) or hotel lot. **Bar** Full service. **Wine selection** OK. **Dress** Casual. **Disabled access** Yes. **Customers** Mostly hotel guests; some locals. **Breakfast** Daily, 7:30–11:45 a.m. **Lunch** Daily, noon–2:45 p.m. **Dinner** Daily, 5–9:45 p.m.

SETTING AND ATMOSPHERE The casual Kona Cafe has a postmodern decor, with arched railings and grillwork on the ceiling. If you want to escape the Magic Kingdom for a quiet lunch, hop on the monorail or take the resort launch to the Polynesian.

HOUSE SPECIALTIES Breakfast: Tonga toast (a decadent French toast layered with bananas). Lunch: stir-fried Asian noodles, barbecue-pork taco, and sticky wings. Dinner: Kona coffee-rubbed pork chop, gingercrusted ribeye with tamarind jus, and sustainable fish.

OTHER RECOMMENDATIONS Crab cakes, Kilauea torte (chocolate cake with a warm chocolate center), and Kona coffee served in a press pot.

SUMMARY AND COMMENTS This isn't a fancy dining room, but the food is on a higher plane than your average java joint's.

Kona Island Sushi Bar ★★★★

POLYNESIAN/PAN-ASIAN	MODERATE	QUALITY ★★★★	VALUE ★★★★
READER-SURVEY RESPONSES	NOT ENOUGH TO RATE	DISNEY DINING PLAN?	NO

Polynesian Resort; ☎ 407-939-3463

Reservations Not accepted. When to go Dinner. Cost range Sushi $9–$16. Service ★★★★. Friendliness ★★★★. Parking Valet ($12) or hotel lot. Bar Full service. Wine selection OK. Dress Casual. Disabled access Elevator to second level or smooth access from monorail station. Customers Mostly hotel guests; some locals. Breakfast Daily, 6:30–11:30 a.m. (Not a full-service restaurant during these hours—serves pastries and other breakfast snacks.) Dinner Daily, 5–10 p.m.

SETTING AND ATMOSPHERE Kona Island Sushi Bar is very casual, imitating the tones and textures of Kona Cafe but placed in an area of high traffic for the Polynesian. The small eatery seats about 20 diners but accommodates many take-out orders. When eating in, guests can sit right at the bar and watch as the sushi chefs work their culinary magic, or be stationed against a glass wall with views of the resort's monorail stop, tropical gardens, and the ceremonial lighting of the torches on most nights.

HOUSE SPECIALTIES Volcano Roll (spicy tuna and seafood *lau'ai* with tempura crunch), Tuna Poke (traditional Hawaiian *poke* (**POH**-kay) salad with cubed tuna, soy sauce, sesame oil, sea salt, and onions)

OTHER RECOMMENDATIONS Freshly ground Kona coffee—choose from 100% Kona beans in a press pot or a blend of 30% Kona beans and 70% Colombian beans.

SUMMARY AND COMMENTS This is often a good option for last-minute dining plans, lending itself to class and convenience. For diners who shy away from raw fare, cooked items are available on the menu (such as the Kona Crab Cake Roll, Shrimp Tempura Roll, and California Luau Roll). Also, because Kona Island Sushi Bar shares a kitchen with Kona Cafe, any item on the Kona Cafe menu can be ordered from the bar.

Kouzzina by Cat Cora ★★★★

MEDITERRANEAN	MODERATE	QUALITY ★★★★	VALUE ★★★★
READER-SURVEY RESPONSES	94% 👍	6% 👎	DISNEY DINING PLAN? YES

BoardWalk Inn; ☎ 407-939-3463

Reservations Recommended. Dining Plan credits 1 per person, per meal. When to go Breakfast or dinner. Cost range Breakfast $6.50–$14 (child $6.49), dinner $20–$34 (child $7.59) Service ★★★★. Friendliness ★★★★. Parking Valet ($12) or hotel lot. Bar Full service. Wine selection Moderate. Dress Casual. Disabled access Yes. Customers Disney guests, Cat Cora fans. Breakfast Daily, 7:30–11 a.m. Dinner Daily, 5–9:45 p.m.

SETTING AND ATMOSPHERE Kouzzina (Greek for "kitchen") looks like a family-style Greek restaurant you'd find in New York City or L.A., with an open kitchen, wooden floors, big wooden tables, heavy chairs, and a few booths.

HOUSE SPECIALTIES Spanakopita (spinach pie), cinnamon-stewed chicken, fishermen's stew, traditional whole fish, chocolate *budino* cake.

OTHER RECOMMENDATIONS Any of the *mezze* (appetizers), Greek salad, pork tenderloin, *pastitsio* (Greek-style lasagna made with bucatini pasta), Greek doughnuts. For breakfast, turkey–sweet potato hash with two eggs and arugula salad. An olive oil–tasting experience lets you sample two varieties of Greek oil with bread and kalamata olives.

SUMMARY AND COMMENTS When you think "celebrity chef," family-style Kouzzina may not be what comes to mind, but you do get a taste of Cat Cora's recipes. The dining room is a little bare-bones and can get noisy, but it's a fine destination for families.

LakeView Restaurant ★★

AMERICAN	MODERATE	QUALITY ★	VALUE ★★★
READER-SURVEY RESPONSES 21%	79%	DISNEY DINING PLAN? NO	

Wyndham Lake Buena Vista Resort, Downtown Disney; ☎ 407-828-4444

Reservations Accepted. When to go Breakfast or dinner. Cost range Character breakfast $22 ($11 kids ages 3–11), dinner $18–$35 ($6 kids ages 3–11). Service ★★★. Friendliness ★★★. Parking Hotel lot. Bar Limited service. Wine selection Good. Dress Casual. Disabled access Yes. Customers Hotel guests. Breakfast Daily, 7–11 a.m.; character breakfast Tuesday, Thursday, and Saturday, 7:30–10:30 a.m. Dinner Monday–Saturday, 6–10:30 p.m.

SETTING AND ATMOSPHERE Lakefront views.

ENTERTAINMENT AND AMENITIES Disney-character breakfast (usually Goofy and Pluto) three days a week.

SUMMARY AND COMMENTS There's nothing special about the cuisine, but the best reason to dine here is the Disney-character breakfast, with an all-you-can-eat buffet and a kid-sized buffet just for little ones. Dinner is standard hotel fare—burgers, steaks, and salads.

Liberty Tree Tavern ★★★

AMERICAN	MODERATE	QUALITY ★★★	VALUE ★★★
READER-SURVEY RESPONSES 86%	14%	DISNEY DINING PLAN? YES	

Liberty Square, Magic Kingdom; ☎ 407-939-3463

Reservations Accepted. Dining Plan credits 1 per person, per meal. When to go Lunch or dinner. Cost range Lunch $13–$19 (child $8), dinner $32 (child $16). *Note:* Dinner prices increase during peak periods (see page 428). Service ★★★★★. Friendliness ★★★★★. Parking Magic Kingdom lot. Bar None. Wine selection None. Dress Casual. Disabled access Yes. Customers Theme park guests. Lunch Daily, 11:30 a.m.–3 p.m. Character dinner Daily, 4–9 p.m.

SETTING AND ATMOSPHERE Low, exposed-beam ceilings crown rooms framed by pastel-gray chair rails. Colonial-period wall art, much with a nautical theme, accents simple dark-wood tables and chairs with woven seats.

HOUSE SPECIALTIES For lunch: New England–style pot roast, roast turkey, and sandwiches. Family-style character dining at dinner, with all-you-can-eat turkey, carved beef, and smoked pork loin.

OTHER RECOMMENDATIONS Sandwiches and salads are good here, too.

SUMMARY AND COMMENTS Though nothing much changes at Liberty Tree (servers still wear those Colonial-style getups), it's still among the best of the Magic Kingdom's full-service restaurants. Make Advance Reservations here for about an hour or so before parade time—after you eat, you can walk right out and watch the parade. And you can enjoy Thanksgiving turkey and stuffing any day of the year.

Mama Melrose's Ristorante Italiano ★ ★ ½

ITALIAN	MODERATE	QUALITY ★★★	VALUE ★★
READER-SURVEY RESPONSES 82%	18%	DISNEY DINING PLAN?	YES

Streets of America, Disney's Hollywood Studios; ☎ 407-939-3463

Reservations Required; credit card required to reserve *Fantasmic!* Dining Package (see page 622). Dining Plan credits 1 per person, per meal. When to go Lunch or dinner. Cost range $12–$29 (child $8). Service ★★★. Friendliness ★★★★★. Parking DHS lot. Bar Full service. Wine selection Limited. Dress Casual. Disabled access Yes. Customers Theme park guests. Lunch Daily, noon–3:30 p.m. Dinner Daily, 3:30 p.m.–park closing.

SETTING AND ATMOSPHERE Mama Melrose's is inspired by a big-city neighborhood restaurant of the 1930s, with red-and-white checkered tablecloths, red vinyl booths, and grapevines hanging from the rafters. By far the most relaxing restaurant at Disney's Hollywood Studios, Mama Melrose's sports a look as comfortable as an old sweatshirt.

HOUSE SPECIALTIES Caesar salad, crispy calamari, penne alla vodka, and oak-grilled pork chop. Whole-wheat pasta available.

OTHER RECOMMENDATIONS Grilled tuna or four-cheese flatbread.

SUMMARY AND COMMENTS Because of Mama Melrose's out-of-the-way location, you can sometimes just walk in, especially in the evening. Portions here are fairly large; it's possible to dine cheaply on just an appetizer or two. The food won't win any awards—the red sauce is a little heavy, for instance—but for family-style Italian, it's fine.

Maya Grill ★

AMERICAN	MODERATE	QUALITY ★	VALUE ★
READER-SURVEY RESPONSES 57%	43%	DISNEY DINING PLAN?	YES

Coronado Springs Resort; ☎ 407-939-3463

Reservations Accepted. Dining Plan credits 1 per person, per meal. When to go Breakfast or dinner. Cost range Breakfast $6–$16 (child $9), dinner $23–$27 (child $9). Service ★★★. Friendliness ★★★. Parking Hotel lot. Bar Full service. Wine selection Fair. Dress Casual. Disabled access Yes. Customers Hotel guests. Breakfast Daily, 7–11 a.m. Dinner Daily, 5–10 p.m.

SETTING AND ATMOSPHERE The dining room was designed to evoke the ancient world of the Maya, achieving "a harmony of fire, sun, and water." But the idea falls short, with the fire taking the form of "flames" made of fan-blown fabric at the top of two large columns. The kitchen is open to view—but so is the barren and starkly lit walkway outside.

HOUSE SPECIALTIES The breakfast buffet is gone, but the menu now offers everything from a Kobe-beef brunch burger to omelets and pancakes. To suit the resort's convention crowd, the kitchen is leaning toward expensive Tex-Mex–Nuevo Latino dinner fare, such as sirloin or shrimp tacos, chicken with red peppers and an onion cream sauce, and tequila-glazed salmon with chorizo mashed potatoes.

SUMMARY AND COMMENTS The food is ordinary, as is the setting. You're better off eating somewhere else. We hear they may be doing a major overhaul soon.

Narcoossee's ★★★★½

SEAFOOD	EXPENSIVE	QUALITY ★★★½	VALUE ★★
READER-SURVEY RESPONSES	100% ⬤	0% ⬤	DISNEY DINING PLAN? YES

Grand Floridian Resort & Spa; ☎ 407-939-3463

Reservations Required. Dining Plan credits 2 per person, per meal. When to go Early evening. Cost range $22–$58 (child $7–$13). Service ★★★★★. Friendliness ★★★★★. Parking Valet ($12); self-parking is deceptively far away. Bar Full service. Wine selection Good. Dress Dressy casual. Disabled access Yes. Customers Hotel guests and locals. Dinner Daily, 5:30–10 p.m.

SETTING AND ATMOSPHERE Stroll through the grounds of the Grand Floridian and toward the waterfront to this freestanding octagonal building at the edge of Seven Seas Lagoon. The atmosphere is upscale casual, though hardwood floors make it noisy. Diners have great views of the Magic Kingdom and the boats that dock nearby to pick up and drop off guests after a day at the park.

HOUSE SPECIALTIES Maine lobster, crispy whole snapper with basmati rice, and grilled filet mignon. Kids' menu includes grilled steak and oven-baked fish.

OTHER RECOMMENDATIONS Prince Edward Island mussels, jumbo lump crab cakes, and artisanal cheeses.

SUMMARY AND COMMENTS Narcoossee's offers excellent service, a very good wine list—and steep prices. But it is one of the few places at Disney with a seafood-centric menu, and one of the few places where you can get fresh steamed lobster. A splurge for grown-ups. Fun to sit at the bar if you don't have a reservation, and you step out on the porch to watch the nightly Electrical Water Pageant on Seven Seas Lagoon.

Nine Dragons Restaurant ★★★

CHINESE	MODERATE	QUALITY ★★★	VALUE ★★
READER-SURVEY RESPONSES	74% ⬤	26% ⬤	DISNEY DINING PLAN? YES

China, World Showcase, Epcot; ☎ 407-939-3463

Reservations Recommended. Dining Plan credits 1 per person, per meal. When to go Lunch or dinner. Cost range Lunch $13–$22 (child $10), dinner $13–$26 (child $10). Service ★★★. Friendliness ★★★★. Parking Epcot lot. Bar Full service. Wine selection Minimal. Dress Casual. Disabled access Yes. Customers Theme park guests. Lunch Daily, 11:30 a.m.–4 p.m. Dinner Daily, 4:30 p.m.–park closing.

SETTING AND ATMOSPHERE Nine Dragons' attractive interior—subdued wood tones, colorful lanterns, and beautiful backlit glass sculptures from China—and efficient service create a respite from the bustle of World Showcase.

HOUSE SPECIALTIES Roasted Beijing chicken, shrimp and steak, and five-spiced fish.

OTHER RECOMMENDATIONS Vegetarian stir-fry; noodle sampler with fresh vegetables and pork and chicken dipping sauces.

SUMMARY AND COMMENTS Some dishes have a light, contemporary touch, and service is friendly. Though it's pricey for Chinese, the menu is diverse and the food is well prepared.

1900 Park Fare   ★★½

AMERICAN/BUFFET	MODERATE	QUALITY ★★★	VALUE ★★★
READER-SURVEY RESPONSES 81% 👍 19% 👎		DISNEY DINING PLAN? YES	

Grand Floridian Resort & Spa; ☎ 407-824-3000

Reservations Recommended. **Dining Plan credits** 1 per person, per meal. **When to go** Breakfast or dinner. **Cost range** Breakfast $26 (child $15), dinner $42 (child $21). *Note:* Prices increase during peak periods (see page 428). **Service** ★★★★. **Friendliness** ★★★★. **Parking** Valet ($12); self-parking is deceptively far away. **Bar** Full service. **Wine selection** Limited. **Dress** Casual. **Disabled access** Yes. **Customers** Hotel and resort guests. **Character breakfast** Daily, 8–11 a.m. **Character dinner** Daily, 4:30–8:30 p.m.

SETTING AND ATMOSPHERE This bright, cavernous, high-ceilinged room is warmly appointed in pastels. Tables are set with linen. An antique band organ periodically provides musical accompaniment to dining.

HOUSE SPECIALTIES Buffet includes prime rib, salmon, and curry chicken.

OTHER RECOMMENDATIONS Separate buffet for kids includes pasta marinara, mini–corn dogs, chicken nuggets, and mac-and-cheese.

ENTERTAINMENT AND AMENITIES Character dining with Mary Poppins, Winnie the Pooh, Tigger, and Alice at breakfast, Cinderella, Prince Charming, and others at dinner.

SUMMARY AND COMMENTS An OK choice for character dining, but too bright and loud for adults without children. The prime rib is 1900 Park Fare's major draw at dinner, but go someplace else if you prefer your beef on the rare side of medium.

'Ohana   ★★★

POLYNESIAN	MODERATE	QUALITY ★★★½	VALUE ★★★
READER-SURVEY RESPONSES 90% 👍 10% 👎		DISNEY DINING PLAN? YES	

Polynesian Resort; ☎ 407-939-3463

Reservations Recommended. **Dining Plan credits** 1 per person, per meal. **When to go** Breakfast or dinner. **Cost range** Character breakfast $21 (child $12), dinner $33 (child $16). *Note:* Prices increase during peak periods (see page 428). **Service** ★★★★. **Friendliness** ★★★★★. **Parking** Hotel lot. **Bar** Full service. **Wine selection** Limited. **Dress** Casual. **Disabled access** Yes. **Customers** Resort guests. **Character breakfast** Daily, 7:30–11 a.m. **Dinner** Daily, 5–10 p.m.

SETTING AND ATMOSPHERE A large open pit is the centerpiece of the room. Here the grilled foods are prepared with flair, as well as a flare: From time to time the chef will pour some liquid on the fire, causing huge flames to shoot up. This is usually in response to something one of the strolling entertainers has said, evoking a sign from the fire gods. At any given moment, there may be a hula-hoop contest or a coconut race, where kids are invited to push coconuts around the dining room with broomsticks.

HOUSE SPECIALTIES Skewer service is the specialty here—there's no menu. As soon as you're seated, your server will begin to deliver food. First come bread and salad, followed by honey-glazed chicken wings, pork fried dumplings, pineapple-coconut bread, and fresh pineapple. The main course is steak, pork loin, chicken, and grilled peel-and-eat shrimp, accompanied by stir-fried vegetables and egg noodles with pineapple in peanut sauce placed on a lazy Susan in the center of the table.

ENTERTAINMENT AND AMENITIES Strolling singers, games, and Mickey, Pluto, Lilo, and Stitch at breakfast.

SUMMARY AND COMMENTS 'Ohana, which means "family," gets high marks from our readers. The food is good but not superior, but if you love meat and you come hungry, it's a great place to fill up. The method of service and the fact that it just keeps coming make it all taste a little better. Request a seat in the main dining room, where the fire pit is.

Olivia's Cafe ★★

AMERICAN	MODERATE	QUALITY ★★½	VALUE ★★
READER-SURVEY RESPONSES 71% 👍	29% 👎	DISNEY DINING PLAN? YES	

Disney's Old Key West Resort; ☎ 407-939-3463

Reservations Accepted. **Dining Plan credits** 1 per person, per meal. **When to go** Lunch. **Cost range** Breakfast $10–$16 (child $6), lunch $11–$18 (child $6), dinner $16–$29 (child $6). **Service** ★★★★. **Friendliness** ★★★★. **Parking** Hotel lot. **Bar** Full service. **Wine selection** Limited. **Dress** Casual. **Disabled access** Yes. **Customers** Resort guests. **Breakfast** Daily, 7:30–10:30 a.m. **Lunch** Daily, 11:30 a.m.–5 p.m. **Dinner** Daily, 5–10 p.m.

SETTING AND ATMOSPHERE Disneyfied Key West: lots of pastels, mosaic-tile floors, potted palms, tropical trees in the center of the room. There is some outside seating, which looks out over the waterway. Tile, wood siding, and no tablecloths add up to a very noisy dining room that's getting a little worn around the edges. Disney Vacation Club member photos decorate the walls—Disney's Old Key West Resort was one of the first DVC resorts, so members consider Olivia's their home kitchen.

HOUSE SPECIALTIES At breakfast, traditional omelets, banana-bread French toast, and Breakfast Cuban with scrambled eggs, ham, Swiss cheese, and pork loin. At lunch, conch fritters, Duval Street burger topped with grilled shrimp and pepper-Jack cheese, Jamaican jerk chicken sandwich. At dinner, shrimp and grits, prime rib, sustainable fish with black beans and rice, and spiced pecan-crusted mahimahi.

OTHER RECOMMENDATIONS Island barbecue pork ribs; Key lime tart; banana bread pudding sundae.

SUMMARY AND COMMENTS A fun out-of-the-way spot if you have a little extra time to navigate out to Old Key West Resort. The food has a Southern–Key West spin and is well prepared. Service is excellent.

The Outback ★★

STEAK	EXPENSIVE	QUALITY ★★★	VALUE ★★
READER-SURVEY RESPONSES 80% 👍	20% 👎	DISNEY DINING PLAN? NO	

Buena Vista Palace, Downtown Disney Resort Area; ☎ 407-827-2727

Reservations Recommended. **When to go** Very early dinner. **Cost range** $17–$36. **Service** ★★★. **Friendliness** ★★★. **Parking** Valet (free) at the rear of the hotel. **Bar** Full service. **Wine selection** Excellent. **Dress** Casual. **Disabled access** Yes. **Customers** Tourists. **Dinner** Daily, 5:30–11 p.m.

SETTING AND ATMOSPHERE A large open room with a two-story ceiling and a cascading waterfall. Servers wear khaki garb that resembles Australian bush outfits.

HOUSE SPECIALTIES Any of the steaks are a good bet, as is the sustainable catch of the day prepared with a variety of sauces, including Florida citrus salsa and a pink grapefruit, soy, and ginger vinaigrette.

OTHER RECOMMENDATIONS Key West shrimp tacos, braised beef short ribs with brown-butter spaetzle.

SUMMARY AND COMMENTS Not a dining destination (and not to be confused with the steakhouse chain), but if you're in the mood for a decent steak or local fish, give The Outback a try.

Paradiso 37 ★★½

GLOBAL	INEXPENSIVE	QUALITY ★★★	VALUE ★★★
READER-SURVEY RESPONSES	NOT ENOUGH TO RATE	DISNEY DINING PLAN?	YES

Downtown Disney; ☎ 407-934-3700

Reservations Accepted. **When to go** Lunch or dinner. **Dining Plan credits** 1 per person, per meal. **Cost range** $7–$26 (child $7). **Service** ★★★. **Friendliness** ★★★★. **Parking** Downtown Disney lot. **Bar** Full service. **Wine selection** Limited. **Dress** Casual. **Disabled access** Yes. **Customers** Theme park guests, locals. **Lunch and dinner** Sunday–Wednesday, 11:30 a.m.–midnight; Thursday–Saturday, 11:30 a.m.–1 a.m.

SETTING AND ATMOSPHERE Prime location on the waterfront at Downtown Disney. The bar is the centerpiece of a dining room that's deceptively large, with seating for 200-plus on two levels and the best seats outside. Booths, tables, and tall tables. Ambience is festive and casual, with an open kitchen. Food is inspired by street foods of Central, South and North America, from mac-and-cheese bites to enchiladas and barbecue pork.

HOUSE SPECIALTIES Central American "crazy corn" (roasted on the cob with pepper sauce and cheese), Argentinean skirt steak with chimichurri sauce, bottomless homemade salsa and chips, Paradiso 37 cheeseburger, and the "mangled margarita," a combo of a margarita and sangria. (The *37* in the name refers to the number of varieties of tequila.)

OTHER RECOMMENDATIONS Macaroni-and-cheese bites, shrimp ceviche, and citrus barbecue pork ribs.

SUMMARY AND COMMENTS A fresh spot for casual alfresco dining at Downtown Disney, though the setting is better than the food. But it's one of the few Disney spots that cooks burgers medium-rare. And the joint boasts "the coldest beer in the world," served at a crisp 29°F–32°F.

Planet Hollywood ★★½

AMERICAN	MODERATE	QUALITY ★★	VALUE ★★
READER-SURVEY RESPONSES	81% 👍 19% 👎	DISNEY DINING PLAN?	YES

Downtown Disney West Side; ☎ 407-827-7827

Reservations Recommended. **Dining Plan credits** 1 per person, per meal. **When to go** Late lunch. **Cost range** $12–$26 (child $8). **Service** ★★. **Friendliness** ★★. **Parking** Lot near the old Pleasure Island complex. **Bar** Full service. **Wine selection** Limited. **Dress** Casual. **Disabled access** Yes. **Customers** Tourists, locals. **Lunch and dinner** Daily, 11 a.m.–1 a.m.

SETTING AND ATMOSPHERE A large planet-shaped structure "floating" in the lagoon next to the redeveloping Pleasure Island. Planet Hollywood's decor is something of a movie museum, with memorabilia from famous films. Check out artifacts like the bus from the movie *Speed,* Marilyn Monroe's gloves, and the life-size likeness of Robin Williams.

HOUSE SPECIALTIES Pasta, fajitas, huge burgers, dinner salads, and pizzas; for dessert, try the old-fashioned chocolate cake with vanilla ice cream.

OTHER RECOMMENDATIONS Barbecue ribs, World Famous Chicken Crunch; mushroom, onion, and Swiss burger; shrimp Alfredo.

SUMMARY AND COMMENTS PH has gone from a hip dining spot to an afterthought. With more than a dozen Planet Hollywoods around the globe and more on the way, this home base for the chain is resting on its laurels—nothing exciting (including the food).

The Plaza Restaurant ★★

AMERICAN	MODERATE	QUALITY ★★	VALUE ★★
READER-SURVEY RESPONSES	84% 👍	16% 👎	DISNEY DINING PLAN? YES

Main Street, U.S.A., Magic Kingdom; ☎ 407-939-3463

Reservations Required. **Dining Plan credits** 1 per person, per meal. **When to go** Lunch or dinner. **Cost range** $11–$15 (child $8.59). **Service** ★★★★. **Friendliness** ★★★★. **Parking** Magic Kingdom lot. **Bar** None. **Wine selection** None. **Dress** Casual. **Disabled access** Yes. **Customers** Theme park guests. **Lunch and dinner** 11 a.m.–15 minutes before park closing.

SETTING AND ATMOSPHERE Tucked away on a side street at the end of Main Street, U.S.A., as you head to Tomorrowland, the Plaza evokes small-town diners across America. You'll pay top dollar for a tuna-salad sandwich or a burger, but on a hot Florida day it's an air-conditioned paradise.

HOUSE SPECIALTIES Veggie sandwich, club sandwich, chicken-strawberry salad, and ice-cream desserts such as the Plaza banana split or sundae.

OTHER RECOMMENDATIONS Grilled Reuben sandwich, burgers. For kids, grilled cheese, cheeseburger, PB&J.

SUMMARY AND COMMENTS The Victorian-inspired Plaza is a Main Street icon, best known as a spot to escape the Florida heat and enjoy a generous hot-fudge sundae or banana split. You wouldn't head here for a gourmet meal, but the pricey sandwiches taste just fine.

Portobello ★★½

ITALIAN	EXPENSIVE	QUALITY ★★★	VALUE ★★
READER-SURVEY RESPONSES	64% 👍	36% 👎	DISNEY DINING PLAN? YES

Downtown Disney; ☎ 407-934-8888

Reservations Recommended. **Dining Plan credits** 1 per person, per meal. **When to go** Anytime. **Cost range** Lunch $9–$15 (child $5–$13), dinner $11–$40 (child $5–$13). **Service** ★★★. **Friendliness** ★★★★. **Parking** Lot near the old Pleasure Island complex. **Bar** Full service. **Wine selection** Very good; heavily Italian. **Dress** Casual. **Disabled access** Yes. **Customers** Tourists, locals. **Lunch** Daily, 11:30 a.m.–4 p.m. **Dinner** Daily, 4–11 p.m.

SETTING AND ATMOSPHERE Portobello has a faux Tuscan interior designed to look like a "country Italian trattoria." A very *large* trattoria.

HOUSE SPECIALTIES Wood-burning-oven pizzas; farfalle pasta with roasted chicken, snow peas, asparagus, and Parmesan cream sauce.

OTHER RECOMMENDATIONS Filet mignon, local fish, gelatos and sorbets.

SUMMARY AND COMMENTS Wonderful outdoor waterfront seating on the shaded porch. Service is spotty, food is ordinary.

Raglan Road Irish Pub & Restaurant ★★★★

IRISH	MODERATE	QUALITY ★★★½	VALUE ★★★
READER-SURVEY RESPONSES	91% 👍	9% 👎	DISNEY DINING PLAN? YES

Downtown Disney; ☎ 407-938-0300

Reservations Recommended. **Dining Plan credits** 1 per person, per meal. **When to go** Monday–Saturday after 8 p.m. **Cost range** Lunch $9–$25 (child $6.50–$9), dinner $14–$28 (child $7–$9). **Service** ★★★½. **Friendliness** ★★★★★. **Parking**

Marketplace lot or lot near the old Pleasure Island complex. **Bar** Full service specializing in Irish whiskeys and beers. **Wine selection** Better than a pub's but not extensive. **Dress** Casual. **Disabled access** Yes. **Customers** Tourists and locals. **Lunch and dinner** 11 a.m.–11 p.m., with pub food available until closing (1 a.m.–ish).

SETTING AND ATMOSPHERE Many elements of this pub, including the bar, were hand-crafted from hardwoods in Ireland and sent to the United States for reassembly. The venue is huge by Irish-pub standards, but the dark polished-wood paneling, as well as the snugs (small, private cubbyholes), preserves the feel of the traditional pub. The pentagonal main room sits beneath an impressive but very unpublike dome. In the middle of the room is a tall, tablelike platform accessible to Celtic dancers via a permanently attached short staircase. A modest bandstand is situated along the wall in front of a large pseudo-hearth. Branching from the cavernous domed center room are cozy dining areas and snugs.

HOUSE SPECIALTIES Roast loin of ham with cabbage and mashed potatoes, beer-battered fish-and-chips, a froufrou but yummy Shepherd's Pie, chicken-and-wild-mushroom pie. The must-have appetizer is the Dalkey Duo: batter-fried cocktail sausages with a mustard dipping sauce.

ENTERTAINMENT AND AMENITIES Though you could consider a great selection of Irish lagers and stouts an amenity, the real draw here is the knockout Celtic music. A talented band plays Monday–Saturday. Starting in the early evening with a couple of superb acoustic sets, the band plugs in as the diners filter out and the pub crawlers settle in. A Celtic dancer wanders in and dances on the aforementioned table to some of the numbers. (Think *Riverdance*, not rump shaking.)

SUMMARY AND COMMENTS The great thing about Irish pubs is that folks of all ages can have a wonderful time together. The traditional feel-good drinking songs, reels, and sentimental ballads transcend age. A night in a good pub, Raglan Road included, is a joyous and uplifting experience, and as the Irish say, it'll set you right up.

Rainforest Cafe ★★½

AMERICAN	MODERATE	QUALITY ★★	VALUE ★★
READER-SURVEY RESPONSES† 83% 👍	17% 👎	DISNEY DINING PLAN?	YES

†*Average of Animal Kingdom (88% 👍) and Downtown Disney (78% 👍)*

Disney's Animal Kingdom; ☎ 407-938-9100
Downtown Disney Marketplace; ☎ 407-827-8500

Reservations Recommended. **Dining Plan credits** 1 per person, per meal. **When to go** After the lunch crunch, in late afternoon, and before dinner hour. **Cost range** $13–$31 (child $7–$8). **Service** ★★★. **Friendliness** ★★★★. **Parking** Marketplace lot. **Bar** Full bar. **Wine selection** Limited. **Dress** Casual. **Disabled access** Yes. **Customers** Tourists, locals. **Hours** *Disney's Animal Kingdom:* Daily, 8:30 a.m.–park closing; *Downtown Disney Marketplace:* Sunday–Thursday, 11 a.m.–11 p.m.; Friday and Saturday, 11 a.m.–midnight. (Animal Kingdom location serves breakfast; Downtown Disney location does not.)

SETTING AND ATMOSPHERE There's usually a crowd at the Downtown Disney location of this national chain. It sits beneath a giant volcano that can be seen, and heard, erupting all over the Marketplace (the smoke coming from the volcano is nonpolluting, in accordance with the restaurant's conservation theme). Inside is a huge dining room designed to look like a jungle—imagine all the silk plants in the world tacked to the ceiling—complete with animatronic elephants, bats, and monkeys (not the most realistic we've seen). There's occasional thunder and even some rainfall. Large aquariums connected with glass "swim-ways" serve as one of several waiting areas.

HOUSE SPECIALTIES Rasta Pasta with grilled chicken and walnut pesto; turkey wrap; coconut shrimp; slow-roasted pork ribs; brownie cake with ice cream, caramel, and chocolate sauce.

ENTERTAINMENT AND AMENITIES After the wait you endure, a chair and some sustenance are all the entertainment you'll need. If you're willing to pay to avoid the long wait, stop by the day before and buy a Landry's Select Club membership for $25. By presenting your card on the day you want to dine, you'll be seated much faster (and get 10% off retail and other benefits).

SUMMARY AND COMMENTS While we've never been impressed by the Rainforest Cafes, a lot of our readers rave about them. The shopping experience must be the attraction, because it certainly isn't the food: Preparations are spotty, and waits can be horrendous.

Restaurant Marrakesh   ★★

MOROCCAN	MODERATE	QUALITY ★★½	VALUE ★★
READER-SURVEY RESPONSES 84% 👍	16% 👎	DISNEY DINING PLAN? YES	

Morocco, World Showcase, Epcot; ☎ 407-939-3463

Reservations Accepted. **Dining Plan credits** 1 per person, per meal. **When to go** Lunch or dinner. **Cost range** Lunch $15–$22 (child $8), dinner $21–$45 (child $8). **Service** ★★★★. **Friendliness** ★★★★. **Parking** Epcot lot. **Bar** Full service. **Wine selection** Limited. **Dress** Casual. **Disabled access** Yes. **Customers** Theme park guests. **Lunch** Daily, noon–3:15 p.m. **Dinner** Daily, 3:30 p.m.–park closing.

SETTING AND ATMOSPHERE At the very back of the Morocco Pavilion, Marrakesh re-creates a Moroccan palace with tile mosaics, inlaid-wood ceilings, brass chandeliers, subdued lighting, and red Bukhara carpets.

HOUSE SPECIALTIES The appetizer combo is a good way to sample the beef *brewat* (pastry filled with beef, deep-fried, and sprinkled with cinnamon sugar), *bastilla* (a minced-chicken pie sprinkled with cinnamon sugar), and jasmina salad. Follow with lemon chicken or roast lamb shank, and split an order of vegetable couscous.

OTHER RECOMMENDATIONS If you're hungry, curious, or both, try the Royal Feast or Marrakesh Feast with tastes of several courses. The creations are pretty authentic, albeit mildly spiced.

ENTERTAINMENT AND AMENITIES Moroccan band and belly dancing.

SUMMARY AND COMMENTS This is one of the least busy World Showcase restaurants, so it's usually easy to get a table in the spacious dining room. Unlike diners at most Moroccan restaurants, those at Marrakesh sit at tables instead of on the floor, and eat with utensils rather than with their hands. Picky kids can choose from chicken tenders, pasta, and burgers.

Rose & Crown Dining Room   ★★★

ENGLISH	MODERATE	QUALITY ★★★½	VALUE ★★
READER-SURVEY RESPONSES 82% 👍	18% 👎	DISNEY DINING PLAN? YES	

United Kingdom, World Showcase, Epcot; ☎ 407-939-3463

Reservations Accepted. **Dining Plan credits** 1 per person, per meal. **When to go** Lunch or dinner. **Cost range** Lunch $12.50–$23 (child $8.59), dinner $15–$27 (child $8.50). **Service** ★★★★★. **Friendliness** ★★★★★. **Parking** Epcot lot. **Bar** Full bar with Bass, Guinness, and Harp beers on tap. **Wine selection** Limited. **Dress** Casual. **Disabled access** Yes. **Customers** Theme park guests. **Lunch** Daily, noon–3:20 p.m. **Dinner** Daily, 4:30 p.m.–park closing.

SETTING AND ATMOSPHERE The Rose & Crown is both a pub and a dining establishment. The traditional English pub has a large, cozy bar with rich wood appointments, beamed ceilings, and a hardwood floor. The adjoining dining room is rustic and simple.

HOUSE SPECIALTIES Fish-and-chips, bangers and mash (sausage and mashed potatoes), and shepherd's pie (the vegetarian version is delicious, too) washed down with Bass ale.

OTHER RECOMMENDATIONS The appetizer trio with frisée-and-apple salad, Scotch egg, and roasted-shrimp cocktail with Bloody Mary mix ("Mary and the Lads"); sticky toffee pudding.

SUMMARY AND COMMENTS This is a prime spot for viewing *IllumiNations*, so try to get a table on the patio for late evening, order fish-and-chips, and sit back in your front-row seat for the show.

Sanaa ★★★★

INDIAN/AFRICAN	EXPENSIVE	QUALITY ★★★★	VALUE ★★★★
READER-SURVEY RESPONSES 88%		12%	DISNEY DINING PLAN? YES

Animal Kingdom Villas–Kidani Village; ☎ 407-939-3463

Reservations Accepted. **Dining Plan credits** 1 per person, per meal. **When to go** Lunch or dinner. **Cost range** Lunch $10.50–$19 (child $8.59), dinner $15–$29 (child $8.59). **Service** ★★★★. **Friendliness** ★★★★. **Parking** Valet ($12) or garage. **Bar** Full service. **Wine selection** Good. **Dress** Casual. **Disabled access** Yes. **Customers** Theme park guests, locals, Disney Vacation Club guests. **Lunch** Daily, 11:30 a.m.–4 p.m. **Dinner** Daily, 4:30 p.m.–park closing.

SETTING AND ATMOSPHERE One floor down from the Kidani Village lobby, Sanaa's dining room is inspired by Africa's outdoor markets, with baskets, beads, and art on the walls. It's a cozy space, with 9-foot-tall windows that look out on the resort's savanna—giraffes, water buffalo, and other animals wander within yards of you as you dine.

HOUSE SPECIALTIES Indian-style breads (*naan, onion kulcha,* and *paneer paratha*) with green-mango pickle, coriander chutney, and cucumber *raita;* tandoori chicken; sustainable fish with shrimp and scallops.

OTHER RECOMMENDATIONS New York strip steak with warm potato-and-spinach salad; lunchtime burger on naan with minted greens, tomato, and cucumber raita.

SUMMARY AND COMMENTS Sanaa (sah-NAH) is not as upscale as Jiko, the resort's African restaurant (page 479), but the kitchen offers diners a chance to sample and share a variety of Indian-African creations. Diverse Old and New World wines match the cuisine.

San Angel Inn ★★★

MEXICAN	EXPENSIVE	QUALITY ★★	VALUE ★★
READER-SURVEY RESPONSES 80%		20%	DISNEY DINING PLAN? YES

Mexico, World Showcase, Epcot; ☎ 407-939-3463

Reservations Accepted. **Dining Plan credits** 1 per person, per meal. **When to go** Lunch or dinner. **Cost range** Lunch $15–$23 (child $8), dinner $23–$26 (child $8). **Service** ★★★. **Friendliness** ★★★. **Parking** Epcot lot. **Bar** Full service. **Wine selection** Limited. **Dress** Casual. **Disabled access** Yes. **Customers** Theme park guests. **Lunch** Daily, 11:30 a.m.–4 p.m. **Dinner** Daily, 4:30 p.m.–park closing.

SETTING AND ATMOSPHERE Busy San Angel Inn is inside the great Aztec pyramid of the Mexico Pavilion. A romantically crafted open-air cantina, the restaurant overlooks both the Gran Fiesta Tour attraction and the bustling plaza of a small Mexican "village." A recent renovation added white linens, long tables, new chairs, and new tableware inspired by the original San Angel Inn in Mexico City, Mexico.

HOUSE SPECIALTIES New appetizers include *tlacoyos de chilorio,* savory corn cakes topped with refried beans, pork, *queso fresco,* sour cream, and green-tomatillo sauce; and *tacos de filete,* grilled beef tenderloin on a soft flour tortilla with chipotle sauce, scallions, and avocados. Still on the menu is the classic *mole poblano*—chicken with an exotic sauce made from several kinds of peppers and unsweetened Mexican chocolate.

OTHER RECOMMENDATIONS Margaritas; taco and tostada appetizers.

ENTERTAINMENT AND AMENITIES Mariachi or marimba bands in the courtyard.

SUMMARY AND COMMENTS Prices are ridiculously high, but the menu goes beyond typical Mexican selections, offering special and regional dishes that are difficult to find in the United States. We like the appetizers better than the main courses—unusual tacos and tostadas—good for sharing.

Sci-Fi Dine-In Theater Restaurant ★★

AMERICAN	MODERATE	QUALITY ★★½	VALUE ★★
READER-SURVEY RESPONSES	70% 👍 30% 👎	DISNEY DINING PLAN?	YES

Commissary Lane, Disney's Hollywood Studios; ☎ 407-939-3463

Reservations Recommended. **Dining Plan credits** 1 per person, per meal. **When to go** Anytime. **Cost range** $12.50–$25 (child $9). **Service** ★★★★★. **Friendliness** ★★★★★. **Parking** DHS lot. **Bar** Full service. **Wine selection** Limited. **Dress** Casual. **Disabled access** Yes. **Customers** Theme park guests. **Lunch** Sunday and Wednesday, 10:30 a.m.–4 p.m.; Monday and Tuesday and Thursday–Saturday, 11 a.m.–4 p.m. **Dinner** Daily, 4 p.m.–park closing.

SETTING AND ATMOSPHERE Everyone gets a kick out of this unusual dining room—a facsimile of a drive-in from the 1950s, with faux classic cars instead of tables. Hop in, order, and watch campy black-and-white clips. Servers, some on roller skates, take your order from the driver's seat.

HOUSE SPECIALTIES Same menu at lunch and dinner, with everything from burgers to whole-grain pasta and a ribeye steak. While we think the food quality is way out of line with the cost, you can have an adequate meal at the Sci-Fi if you stick with sandwiches (the Reuben is delicious) and other simple fare.

ENTERTAINMENT AND AMENITIES Cartoons and clips of vintage horror and sci-fi movies are shown, such as *Attack of the 50 Foot Woman, Robot Monster,* and *The Blob.*

SUMMARY AND COMMENTS We recommend making late-afternoon or late-evening Advance Reservations and ordering only dessert—the Sci-Fi is an attraction, not a good dining opportunity. If you don't have Advance Reservations, try walking in at 11 a.m. or around 3 p.m.

Shula's Steak House ★★★★

STEAK	EXPENSIVE	QUALITY ★★★★	VALUE ★★
READER-SURVEY RESPONSES	83% 👍 17% 👎	DISNEY DINING PLAN?	NO

Dolphin Resort; ☎ 407-934-1362

Reservations Required. **When to go** Dinner. **Cost range** $24–$85 (sides not included in entree cost). **Service** ★★★★. **Friendliness** ★★★★. **Parking** Valet (free with validation) or hotel lot ($15). **Bar** Full service. **Wine selection** Good; expensive. **Dress** Dressy. **Disabled access** Yes. **Customers** Hotel guests and locals. **Dinner** Daily, 5–11 p.m.

SETTING AND ATMOSPHERE Clubby and masculine, with dark woods and even darker lighting. Large, gilt-framed black-and-white photographs of football players in action offer the only decoration. A favorite of conventioneers on expense accounts.

HOUSE SPECIALTIES In a word, meat—really expensive but very high-quality meat. Only certified Angus beef is served: filet mignon, porterhouse (including a 48-ounce cut), and prime rib.

OTHER RECOMMENDATIONS The steak-tartare appetizer is special, and there are oysters and stone crab in season, as well as a colossal shrimp cocktail and lobster-tail appetizer.

SUMMARY AND COMMENTS This is part of a chain owned by former Miami Dolphins football coach Don Shula. It's classier than it is kitschy, though printing the menu on the side of a football and placing it on a kickoff tee in the center of the table is a bit much. We could also do without the rehearsed spiel from the waiters, who sound completely bored as they present raw examples of the beef selections and a live lobster at each table. Get past that and you're in for some wonderful steaks.

Shutters at Old Port Royale ★★

STEAK AND SEAFOOD	MODERATE	QUALITY ★★½	VALUE ★★
READER-SURVEY RESPONSES	68% 👍 32% 👎	DISNEY DINING PLAN?	YES

Caribbean Beach Resort; ☎ 407-939-3463

Reservations Accepted. **Dining Plan credits** 1 per person, per meal. **When to go** Dinner. **Cost range** $18–$29 (child $8.59). **Service** ★★★. **Friendliness** ★★★★★. **Parking** Hotel lot. **Bar** Full service. **Wine selection** Moderate. **Dress** Casual. **Disabled access** Yes. **Customers** Hotel guests. **Dinner** Daily, 5–10 p.m.

SETTING AND ATMOSPHERE Basically just a table-service restaurant for guests at Caribbean Beach. The small dining areas are claustrophobia-inducing. Nothing about the decor will make you wish you had brought a camera.

HOUSE SPECIALTIES New York strip steak, jerk-crusted tuna, chicken wings with habanero sauce, and pork ribs with chipotle glaze.

OTHER RECOMMENDATIONS Chorizo–black bean soup; pasta with shrimp, chorizo, and goat cheese.

SUMMARY AND COMMENTS You wouldn't come here for dinner if you weren't already staying at the hotel, but if you need to sit down and be waited on, this will meet your needs.

Teppan Edo ★★★½

JAPANESE	EXPENSIVE	QUALITY ★★★★	VALUE ★★★
READER-SURVEY RESPONSES	89% 👍 11% 👎	DISNEY DINING PLAN?	YES

Japan, World Showcase, Epcot; ☎ 407-939-3463

Reservations Recommended. **Dining Plan credits** 1 per person, per meal. **When to go** Lunch or dinner. **Cost range** $17–$30 (child $9.50–$13.50). **Service** ★★★★★. **Friendliness** ★★★★★. **Parking** Epcot lot. **Bar** Full service. **Wine selection** Limited. **Dress** Casual. **Disabled access** Via elevator. **Customers** Theme park guests. **Lunch** Daily, noon–3:45 p.m. **Dinner** Daily, 4 p.m.–park closing.

SETTING AND ATMOSPHERE Six upscale Japanese dining rooms with grills on tables and entertaining teppan chefs chopping, slicing, and dicing.

HOUSE SPECIALTIES Chicken, shrimp, beef, scallops, swordfish, pork loin, and Asian vegetables stir-fried on a teppan grill by a knife-juggling chef.

ENTERTAINMENT AND AMENITIES Watching the teppan chefs.

SUMMARY AND COMMENTS The menu includes sushi and appetizers such as edamame and seaweed salad, but most guests stick to the teppan offerings. Note that diners at the teppan tables are seated with other parties. Still one of the most popular family restaurants at Epcot.

Todd English's bluezoo ★★★

SEAFOOD	EXPENSIVE	QUALITY ★★★	VALUE ★★
READER-SURVEY RESPONSES 57% 👍	43% 💬	DISNEY DINING PLAN? NO	

Dolphin Resort; ☎ 407-934-1111

Reservations Recommended. **When to go** Dinner. **Cost range** $29–$65 (child $10–$16). **Service** ★★★★. **Friendliness** ★★★. **Parking** Valet (free with validation) or hotel lot ($15). **Bar** Full service. **Wine selection** Excellent. **Dress** Dressy casual. **Disabled access** Yes. **Customers** Hotel guests, locals. **Dinner** Daily, 5–11 p.m.

SETTING AND ATMOSPHERE The dreamy dining room is swathed in blues with iridescent bubbles suspended from the lights. The name is courtesy of chef Todd English's son, who as a young boy saw an under-the-sea movie and said it looked like a "blue zoo." Open kitchen, raw bar, and "dancing fish" on a circular rotisserie.

HOUSE SPECIALTIES Clam chowder, grilled fish, 2-pound Maine lobster, and dry-aged beef.

OTHER RECOMMENDATIONS Berkshire pork loin, shake-and-bake fries.

SUMMARY AND COMMENTS Celebrity chef Todd English opened this stylish Florida outpost, frequented by conventioneers who don't mind the high prices ($2.75 for a single oyster, $60 for the 2-pound lobster) or the expensive wine list. Food is sophisticated, but you can make a meal of the simple bowl of clam chowder with salt-cured bacon and the roasted-beet salad with greens, goat-cheese fondue, and walnut vinaigrette.

Tokyo Dining ★★★

JAPANESE	MODERATE	QUALITY ★★★★	VALUE ★★★
READER-SURVEY RESPONSES 95% 👍	5% 💬	DISNEY DINING PLAN? YES	

Japan, World Showcase, Epcot; ☎ 407-939-3463

Reservations Accepted. **Dining Plan credits** 1 per person, per meal. **When to go** Lunch. **Cost range** $17–$28 (child $1.50–$11). **Service** ★★★★. **Friendliness** ★★★. **Parking** Epcot lot. **Bar** Full service. **Wine selection** Limited. **Dress** Casual. **Disabled access** Yes. **Customers** Theme park guests. **Lunch** Daily, noon–3:45 p.m. **Dinner** Daily, 4 p.m.–park close.

SETTING AND ATMOSPHERE Modern Asian decor, a beautifully lighted sushi bar, and well-orchestrated service distinguish this restaurant. There are no seats at the sushi bar, but the sushi chefs are great entertainment for the entire dining room. Tables near the windows have a wonderful second-floor view of World Showcase.

HOUSE SPECIALTIES Grilled meats and seafood; tempura-battered deep-fried foods, featuring chicken, shrimp, scallops, and vegetables; sushi and sashimi; six kinds of sake.

SUMMARY AND COMMENTS Tokyo Dining is a relatively quiet space. The dining room is sleek, the overfriendly servers wear stylish costumes, and the overall experience is relaxing and congenial. Most of the crowd heads to the teppan tables, but you can't beat a window seat here at fireworks time.

Tony's Town Square Restaurant ★★½

ITALIAN	MODERATE		QUALITY ★★★	VALUE ★★
READER-SURVEY RESPONSES	74%	26%	DISNEY DINING PLAN?	YES

Main Street, U.S.A., Magic Kingdom; ☎ 407-939-3463

Reservations Recommended. **Dining Plan credits** 1 per person, per meal. **When to go** Late lunch or early dinner. **Cost range** Lunch $12–$18 (child $8.59), dinner $17–$29 (child $8.59). **Service** ★★★★. **Friendliness** ★★★★★. **Parking** Magic Kingdom lot. **Bar** None. **Wine selection** None. **Dress** Casual. **Disabled access** Yes. **Customers** Theme park guests. **Lunch** Daily, 11:30 a.m.–2:45 p.m. **Dinner** Daily, 5 p.m.–park closing.

SETTING AND ATMOSPHERE Tony's is conveniently located just inside the park on Main Street, with a glass-windowed porch that's wonderful for watching the action outside. The restaurant is a bit worn at the edges, with tile floors, dark woods, and memorabilia from *Lady and the Tramp* on the walls. Ask for a seat on the porch when you book.

HOUSE SPECIALTIES For lunch: chicken calzones, sausage-and-pepperoni flatbread, and spaghetti with meatballs. For dinner: seafood diavolo, braised lamb shank, and New York strip.

SUMMARY AND COMMENTS Tony's does a decent job with pasta. And the chef offers multigrain pasta and keeps gluten-free pasta on hand for diners on special diets. Go at lunch, when the prices aren't so steep.

Trail's End Restaurant ★★

AMERICAN/BUFFET	MODERATE		QUALITY ★★	VALUE ★★
READER-SURVEY RESPONSES	68%	32%	DISNEY DINING PLAN?	YES

Fort Wilderness Resort; ☎ 407-939-3463

Reservations Recommended. **Dining Plan credits** 1 per person, per meal. **When to go** Breakfast or dinner. **Cost range** Breakfast $16 (child $10), lunch $11.50–$17 (child $8.59), dinner $23 (child $13). *Note:* Prices increase during peak periods (see page 428). **Service** ★★★. **Friendliness** ★★★. **Parking** Fort Wilderness lot. **Bar** Full-service bar next door. **Wine selection** Limited. **Dress** Casual. **Disabled access** Yes. **Customers** Fort Wilderness campers, theme park guests. **Breakfast** 7:30–11:30 a.m. **Lunch** 11:30 a.m.–2 p.m. **Dinner** 4:30–9:30 p.m. Sunday–Thursday, 4:30–10 p.m. Friday and Saturday.

SETTING AND ATMOSPHERE At Fort Wilderness, next to the *Hoop-Dee-Doo Musical Revue,* Trail's End is what a restaurant would've looked like had America's settlers built one out of a log cabin. The interior features exposed log beams, oak tabletops, and walls hung with enough old-timey kitchen equipment to start a flea market.

HOUSE SPECIALTIES Breakfast and dinner are served buffet-style; lunch transitions to an à la carte menu. Breakfast features eggs, sausage, bacon, waffles, and biscuits along with fruit and pastries. Lunch includes chili, pan-seared catfish, and spicy grilled shrimp and andouille sausage as well as s'mores and warm sticky-bun sundaes. The dinner lineup is fried chicken, ribs, pasta, fish, carved meats, pizza, and fruit cobbler.

OTHER RECOMMENDATIONS At breakfast there's occasionally a doughnut buffet.

SUMMARY AND COMMENTS The fare isn't much different from what you'd find elsewhere around the parks, and during slow times the food sits quite a while on the steam tables and is not well tended.

T-REX ★★★

AMERICAN	MODERATE	QUALITY ★★	VALUE ★★
READER-SURVEY RESPONSES	80%	20%	DISNEY DINING PLAN? YES

Downtown Disney Marketplace; ☎ 407-828-8739

Reservations Recommended. **Dining Plan credits** 1 per person, per meal. **When to go** Lunch or dinner. **Cost range** $13–$32 (child $7–$8). **Service** ★★★. **Friendliness** ★★★. **Parking** Downtown Disney lot. **Bar** Full service. **Wine selection** Minimal. **Dress** Casual. **Disabled access** Yes. **Customers** Families. **Lunch and dinner** Daily, 11 a.m.–11 p.m.; open until midnight Friday and Saturday.

SETTING AND ATMOSPHERE Sensory overload in a cavernous dining room with life-size robotic dinosaurs, giant fish tanks, bubbling geysers, waterfalls, fossils in the bathrooms, and crystals in the walls. Volume: loud and louder, with meteor showers and growling dinos.

HOUSE SPECIALTIES Tribal Tacos with grilled mahimahi, Ice Age Salmon Salad, and Bronto Burger.

OTHER RECOMMENDATIONS Slow-roasted ribs and Chocolate Extinction fudge cake.

SUMMARY AND COMMENTS Expect a wait unless there's an empty seat at the bar. But nobody's here just for the ordinary, overpriced food—it's nonstop "eatertainment." The coolest spot for dining is the Ice Cave at the back of the restaurant, with glowing blue walls.

Turf Club Bar & Grill ★★

AMERICAN	MODERATE	QUALITY ★★	VALUE ★★
READER-SURVEY RESPONSES	79%	21%	DISNEY DINING PLAN? YES

Disney's Saratoga Springs Resort & Spa; ☎ 407-939-3463

Reservations Accepted. **Dining Plan credits** 1 per person, per meal. **When to go** Lunch or dinner. **Cost range** Lunch $12.50–$19 (child $8.59), dinner $16–$29 (child $8.59). **Service** ★★★. **Friendliness** ★★★★. **Parking** Lot. **Bar** Full service. **Wine selection** Good. **Dress** Casual. **Disabled access** Good. **Customers** Hotel guests. **Lunch** Daily, noon–4 p.m. **Dinner** Daily, 5–9 p.m.

SETTING AND ATMOSPHERE When the weather's nice, ask for an outdoor table; you can spot golfers on the adjacent Lake Buena Vista Golf Course and look across the way to Downtown Disney. Tucked off the lobby of the Saratoga Springs Resort, the dining room is equestrian-themed.

HOUSE SPECIALTIES Steamed mussels, linguine with shrimp, and grilled Caesar salad.

OTHER RECOMMENDATIONS Prime rib with mashed potatoes, maple-whiskey–glazed salmon, or a classic Reuben for lunch; specialty drinks.

SUMMARY AND COMMENTS This out-of-the-way spot is rarely crowded, so it's nice to request an outdoor table on a sunny day and enjoy a drink and appetizers on the shady terrace. The Caesar salad—grilled hearts of romaine lettuce with roasted cherry tomatoes, Caesar dressing, and balsamic-vinegar reduction—is one of the best salads at Disney World.

Tusker House Restaurant ★½

AMERICAN/AFRICAN/BUFFET	MODERATE	QUALITY ★	VALUE ★★
READER-SURVEY RESPONSES	91%	9%	DISNEY DINING PLAN? YES

Africa, Disney's Animal Kingdom; ☎ 407-939-3463

Reservations Required for character meals. **Dining Plan credits** 1 per person, per meal. **When to go** Anytime. **Cost range** Breakfast $25 (child $14), lunch and dinner $26 (child $15). **Service** ★★★. **Friendliness** ★★★. **Parking** Animal Kingdom lot. **Bar** Full-service bar next door. **Dress** Casual. **Disabled access** Yes. **Customers** Theme park guests. **Character breakfast** Daily, 8–10:30 a.m. **Character lunch** Daily, 11:30 a.m.–3:30 p.m. **Dinner** Daily, 4 p.m.–park closing.

SETTING AND ATMOSPHERE Donald's Safari Breakfast features Donald, Daisy, Mickey, and Goofy. The Harambe Village setting is a bit austere and the food unexciting, but it's fine for filling up families and a visit with the Disney characters.

HOUSE SPECIALTIES Carved sirloin, rotisserie pork and chicken, chicken curry, seafood stew, spiced tofu.

OTHER RECOMMENDATIONS African- and Indian-influenced dishes such as chutney, couscous, and curry.

SUMMARY AND COMMENTS The menu mixes comfort food with more-exotic selections for lunch and dinner. The usual bacon, eggs, fruit, and pastries are served for breakfast, with a few African-inspired touches such as beef bobotie quiche and yam casserole.

Tutto Italia Ristorante ★★★★

ITALIAN	EXPENSIVE		QUALITY ★★★★		VALUE ★★★
READER-SURVEY RESPONSES	93%	7%	DISNEY DINING PLAN?		YES

Italy, World Showcase, Epcot; ☎ 407-939-3463

Reservations Recommended. **Dining Plan credits** 1 per person, per meal. **When to go** Midafternoon. **Cost range** Lunch $19.50–$27 (child $9.50), dinner $23–$34 (child $9.50). **Service** ★★★★. **Friendliness** ★★★★. **Parking** Epcot lot. **Bar** Beer and wine only. **Wine selection** All Italian. **Dress** Casual. **Disabled access** Yes. **Customers** Theme park guests. **Lunch** Daily, 11:30 a.m.–3:30 p.m. **Dinner** Daily, 4:30–park closing.

SETTING AND ATMOSPHERE The Roman decor features huge murals of an Italian piazza along the wall behind the upholstered banquettes. The atmosphere is elegant, but the dining room is noisy—nearly always full. If the weather is pleasant, request a table on the piazza. Well-run dining room with excellent service from a mostly young Italian waitstaff.

HOUSE SPECIALTIES Lasagna with meat *ragù*, béchamel, and Parmesan; grilled swordfish steak; baked salmon fillet; braised lamb shank; cannoli.

OTHER RECOMMENDATIONS Any of the pastas.

SUMMARY AND COMMENTS The cavernous dining room recently got a refresh. Tutto Italia is pricey, but the service is professional and friendly, the cuisine is authentic, and the servings are ample.

Via Napoli ★★★★

ITALIAN	MODERATE		QUALITY ★★★½		VALUE ★★★
READER-SURVEY RESPONSES	81%	19%	DISNEY DINING PLAN?		YES

Italy, World Showcase, Epcot; ☎ 407-939-3463

Reservations Recommended. **Dining Plan credits** 1 per person, per meal. **When to go** Lunch or dinner. **Cost range** Entrees $18–$24, pizzas $16 (individual)–$41 (serves 3–5). **Service** ★★★★. **Friendliness** ★★★★. **Parking** Epcot lot. **Bar** Beer and wine only. **Dress** Casual. **Disabled access** Yes. **Customers** Theme park guests. **Lunch** Daily, 11:30 a.m.–3:15 p.m. **Dinner** Daily, 4:30–9 p.m.

SETTING AND ATMOSPHERE The main dining room is cavernous and loud, with tile floors and stucco walls, but there are enough staff and guests moving around that it feels like a bustling Italian market.

Shaded outdoor seating is available, and occasionally pizza by the slice is sold outside.

HOUSE SPECIALTIES The best pizza in Walt Disney World. The rest of the menu is average, with the possible exception of the salads.

SUMMARY AND COMMENTS Because the pies are cooked at inferno-like temperatures, they don't stay in the oven for long and vegetable toppings stay crunchy. The Ortolano (veggie) and four-cheese pies are our favorites.

Victoria & Albert's ★★★★★

GOURMET	EXPENSIVE		QUALITY ★★★★★		VALUE ★★★★
READER-SURVEY RESPONSES	100%	0%	DISNEY DINING PLAN?	NO	

Grand Floridian Resort & Spa; ☎ 407-939-3463

Reservations Mandatory; must confirm by noon the day of your seating; credit card required to reserve; call at least 180 days in advance to reserve. **When to go** Anytime. **Cost range** Fixed price, $125 per person or $185 with wine pairings; Chef's Table and Queen Victoria's Room, $200 or $295 with wine pairings. **Service** ★★★★★. **Friendliness** ★★★★. **Parking** Valet (free); self-parking is deceptively far away. **Wine selection** 700 on the menu, 4,200 more in the cellar. **Dress** Jacket required for men, evening attire for women. **Disabled access** Yes. **Customers** Hotel guests, locals. **Dinner** 2 seatings nightly at 5:45–6:30 p.m. and 9–9:45 p.m., plus 1 seating at 6 p.m. for the Chef's Table. *Note:* No children under age 10 admitted except at Chef's Table.

SETTING AND ATMOSPHERE Frette linens, Riedel crystal, Christofle silver—with only 18 tables in the main dining room and Queen Victoria's Room, a new private space with seating for eight, this is the top dining experience at Disney World. A winner of AAA's Five Diamond Award—the only restaurant in Central Florida so honored—Victoria & Albert's is civilized, lavish, and expensive. Waitstaff in Queen Victoria's Room expertly revive the European art of tableside finishes for each dish.

HOUSE SPECIALTIES The menu changes daily, but Chef Scott Hunnel's favorites include Jamison Farm lamb, Florida seafood, and Japanese Kobe beef. Master pastry chef Erich Herbitschek's desserts are divine.

ENTERTAINMENT AND AMENITIES A harpist or violinist entertains from the foyer. But the best show is in the kitchen when you book the Chef's Table, where Chef Hunnel starts the evening with a Champagne toast and crafts a personal menu.

SUMMARY AND COMMENTS Hunnel and his team prepare modern American cuisine with the best of the best from around the world. While the main dining room and Queen Victoria's Room are whisper-quiet, the convivial Chef's Table is a whole other experience. For foodies, it's a bargain.

The Wave . . . of American Flavors ★★★

NEW AMERICAN	MODERATE		QUALITY ★★		VALUE ★★
READER-SURVEY RESPONSES	89%	11%	DISNEY DINING PLAN?	YES	

Contemporary Resort; ☎ 407-939-3463

Reservations Accepted. **Dining Plan credits** 1 per person, per meal. **When to go** Anytime. **Cost range** Breakfast $9–$12 à la carte, $18.50 buffet (child $6.50), lunch $12–$19 (child $9), dinner $16.50–$30 (child $9). **Service** ★★★. **Friendliness** ★★★. **Parking** Valet ($12) or hotel lot. **Bar** Full service. **Wine selection** All New World screw-caps. **Dress** Casual. **Disabled access** Yes. **Customers** Hotel guests, locals. **Breakfast** Daily, 7:30–11 a.m. **Lunch** Daily, noon–2 p.m. **Dinner** Daily, 5:30–10 p.m.

SETTING AND ATMOSPHERE On the first floor of the Contemporary just past the front desk, The Wave has one of the coolest lounges at Disney World, adjoining a dining room with the feel of an upscale coffee shop—wooden tables and white-linen napkins.

HOUSE SPECIALTIES Unusual drinks like the Antioxidant Cocktail and the strawberry-lychee margarita. For breakfast: a generous buffet, mega-berry smoothie, multigrain pancakes, and make-your-own muesli. For lunch: curry vegetable stew, Reuben, Mediterranean tuna salad. For dinner: sustainable fish and grilled beef tenderloin.

OTHER RECOMMENDATIONS Cabernet-tomato–braised beef short ribs; locally sourced pork tenderloin; oven-roasted chicken with potato waffles.

SUMMARY AND COMMENTS The kitchen continues to create healthful dining options and source local products, setting a good example for other Disney restaurants. Organic beers, organic coffees, hip cocktails, and all-screw-cap wines—focusing on New World wines from Argentina, Australia, Chile, New Zealand, and South Africa—are part of the forward-thinking menu.

Whispering Canyon Cafe ★★★

AMERICAN	MODERATE	QUALITY ★★★½	VALUE ★★★★
READER-SURVEY RESPONSES	79% 👍	21% 👎	DISNEY DINING PLAN? YES

Wilderness Lodge & Villas; ☎ 407-939-3463

Reservations Accepted. Dining Plan credits 1 per person, per meal. When to go Anytime. Cost range Breakfast $10.50–$16.50 (child $6.50–$7.89), lunch $6.50–$19 (child $9), dinner $16–$28.50 (child $9). Service ★★★★. Friendliness ★★★★. Parking Hotel lot. Bar Full service. Wine selection Limited. Dress Casual. Disabled access Yes. Customers Hotel guests. Breakfast Daily, 7:30–11:30 a.m. Lunch Daily, 11:30 a.m.–2:30 p.m. Dinner Daily, 5–10 p.m.

SETTING AND ATMOSPHERE Just off the hotel's atrium lobby, the restaurant looks out on the lobby on one side and a mountain prairie, created by Disney landscapers, on the other. Tables have a barrel-top lazy Susan where food is placed.

HOUSE SPECIALTIES All-you-can-eat skillets with cornbread, pulled pork, smoked pork ribs, beef brisket, roast chicken, mashed potatoes, baked beans, coleslaw, salad, and corn on the cob.

OTHER RECOMMENDATIONS New York strip steak, whiskey-maple–glazed trout, s'mores cheesecake.

SUMMARY AND COMMENTS If you're hungry, the real value here is in the family-style service, with all-you-can-eat servings brought to you on platters and in crocks to pass around to your family. You can always order off the regular menu if you don't feel like sharing, but you may end up paying more for the privilege. Lively dining room with servers who encourage kids to be rowdy—all in good fun.

Wolfgang Puck Grand Cafe ★★

CREATIVE CALIFORNIAN	EXPENSIVE	QUALITY ★½	VALUE ★½
READER-SURVEY RESPONSES	87% 👍	13% 👎	DISNEY DINING PLAN? YES

Downtown Disney West Side; ☎ 407-938-9653

Reservations Recommended. Dining Plan credits 1 per person, per meal (downstairs only). When to go Early evening. Cost range Cafe $13–$29 (child $6–$9), upstairs

$29–$47 (child $10–$18). **Service** ★★★. **Friendliness** ★★★. **Parking** Downtown Disney lot. **Bar** Full service. **Wine selection** Very good. **Dress** Casual in the cafe; collared and sleeved shirts for men and no jeans upstairs. **Disabled access** Yes. **Customers** Tourists, locals. **Hours** *Cafe:* Lunch and dinner daily, 11:30 a.m.–11 p.m. *Upstairs:* Dinner Sunday–Wednesday, 6–9 p.m.; Thursday–Saturday, 6–10 p.m.

SETTING AND ATMOSPHERE This is actually two restaurants in one—four if you count the attached Wolfgang Puck Express and the sushi bar that flows into the restaurant's lounge area. Downstairs is the actual cafe, with several open kitchen areas, colorful tile, and plenty of pictures of Wolfgang Puck hanging around (though you won't find him in the kitchen). The upstairs is a more formal dining room, but in name only. Both spaces are inordinately loud, making conversation difficult.

HOUSE SPECIALTIES Puck's wood-fired pizzas, including barbecue chicken and his signature smoked-salmon pie. Sushi is also a good bet. Upstairs, the menu features fresh fish, chicken, and beef.

SUMMARY AND COMMENTS Quality has really dipped, but in spite of less-than-stellar food, there's usually a crowd. We can always recommend dining at the sushi bar. Or you can skip the entree and go straight for desserts.

Yachtsman Steakhouse ★★★

STEAK	EXPENSIVE		QUALITY	★★★½	VALUE	★★
READER-SURVEY RESPONSES	90% 👍	10% 👎	DISNEY DINING PLAN?	YES		

Yacht Club Resort; ☎ 407-939-3463

Reservations Required. **Dining Plan credits** 2 per person, per meal. **When to go** Dinner. **Cost range** Dinner $29–$47 (child $7–$12). **Service** ★★★★. **Friendliness** ★★★★. **Parking** Hotel lot. **Bar** Full service. **Wine selection** Very good. **Dress** Dressy casual. **Disabled access** Yes. **Customers** Hotel guests and locals. **Dinner** Daily, 5:30–10:30 p.m.

SETTING AND ATMOSPHERE Wood beams, white linens, and a view of the sandy lagoon at the resort make this steakhouse appealing. The menu features seafood, lamb, fowl, and vegetarian creations. The adjacent Crew's Cup Lounge, with dozens of beers and fine wine by the glass, is a fun place to start the evening.

HOUSE SPECIALTIES Start with lobster bisque or a classic Caesar salad. All steaks are cut and trimmed on the premises. The filet mignon, New York strip, and prime rib are just some of the cuts.

OTHER RECOMMENDATIONS Columbia River king salmon; young French red hen; braised beef ravioli; truffle macaroni and cheese; banana Napoleon; trio of Valrhona chocolate. All entrees except the ribeye come with a vegetable, so you can skip the ordinary sides.

SUMMARY AND COMMENTS Yachtsman has a loyal following of locals—die-hard meat lovers who don't mind paying for a good steak. Vintages from every major wine-producing region of the world complement the menu.

Yak & Yeti Restaurant ★★

PAN-ASIAN	EXPENSIVE	QUALITY ★★½	VALUE ★★
READER-SURVEY RESPONSES 79%	21%	DISNEY DINING PLAN?	YES

Asia, Disney's Animal Kingdom; ☎ 407-939-3463

Reservations Recommended. **Dining Plan credits** 1 per person, per meal. **When to go** Dinner. **Cost range** $18–$26 (child $7.50). **Service** ★★★★. **Friendliness** ★★★★. **Parking** Animal Kingdom lot. **Bar** Full service. **Wine selection** Limited. **Dress** Casual. **Disabled access** Yes. **Customers** Theme park guests. **Lunch** Daily, 11 a.m.–3:30 p.m. **Dinner** Daily, 4 p.m.–park closing.

SETTING AND ATMOSPHERE A rustic two-story Nepalese inn . . . with seating for hundreds. Windows on the second floor overlook the Asia section of the park.

HOUSE SPECIALTIES Seared miso salmon, tempura shrimp, and glazed duck; fried wontons with pineapple and cream cheese for dessert.

SUMMARY AND COMMENTS Though this is not fine dining, much of the food, including the seafood and duck, stands out from the usual theme park fare. The steak-and-shrimp combo is also good, but the chicken dishes are just average.

PART ELEVEN

The MAGIC KINGDOM

OPENED IN 1971, THE MAGIC KINGDOM was the first built of Walt Disney World's four theme parks. Many of the attractions found here are originals from that park opening, and a few—including Cinderella Castle, Pirates of the Caribbean, and Splash Mountain—have helped define the basic elements of theme park attractions the world over. Indeed, the Magic Kingdom is undoubtedly what most people think of when they think of Walt Disney World.

Much of the Magic Kingdom was built by the same Disney staff that had built Disneyland almost two decades earlier. The remarkable achievement that Disney wrought in Orlando isn't that they could build a second, equally compelling theme park; rather, it's that they could do so on a much larger scale while keeping many of the fine details that make visiting a Disney park such a completely immersive experience.

NOT TO BE MISSED AT THE MAGIC KINGDOM		
ADVENTURELAND	**FRONTIERLAND**	**SPECIAL EVENTS**
• Pirates of the Caribbean	• Big Thunder Mountain Railroad	• Evening Parade
FANTASYLAND	• Splash Mountain	• *The Magic, The Memories and You!*
• The Many Adventures of Winnie the Pooh	**LIBERTY SQUARE**	**TOMORROWLAND**
• *Mickey's PhilharMagic*	• The Haunted Mansion	• Space Mountain
• Peter Pan's Flight		
• Seven Dwarfs Mine Train		
• Under the Sea: Journey of the Little Mermaid		

ARRIVING

IF YOU DRIVE, the Magic Kingdom **Transportation and Ticket Center (TTC)** parking lot opens about 2 hours before the park's official opening. After paying a fee, you're directed to a parking space, then transported by tram to the TTC, where you catch either a monorail or a ferry to the park's entrance.

If you bring your own stroller, a Ridgewood, New Jersey, family recommends the ferry (which starts operating at about 8:30 a.m.):

The ferry from the TTC to the Magic Kingdom dock is a must if you're using a stroller. You can drive the stroller right onto the ferry and then just head to the back of the ferry to be the first ones off when it docks.

If you're staying at the Contemporary, Bay Lake Tower, Polynesian, or Grand Floridian resorts, you can commute to the Magic Kingdom by monorail (guests at the Contemporary Resort and Bay Lake Tower can walk to the park more quickly). If you're staying at Wilderness Lodge & Villas or Fort Wilderness Resort & Campground, you can take a boat or bus. Guests at other Walt Disney World resorts can reach the park by bus. All Disney lodging guests, whether they arrive by monorail, boat, or bus, are deposited at the park's entrance, bypassing the TTC.

▌ GETTING ORIENTED

AT THE MAGIC KINGDOM, stroller and wheelchair rentals are in the train station; lockers are on the right, just inside the park entrance. On your left as you enter **Main Street, U.S.A.** is **City Hall,** the center for information, lost and found, guided tours, and entertainment schedules.

unofficial **TIP**
If you don't already have a handout guide map of the park, get one at City Hall or the entrance turnstiles.

The guide map found there lists all attractions, shops, and eating places; provides information about first aid, baby care, and assistance for the disabled; and gives tips for good photos. It lists times for the day's special events, live entertainment, Disney-character parades, and concerts, and it also tells when and where to find Disney characters. The guide map is often supplemented by a daily entertainment schedule known as the *Times Guide.* In addition to listing performance times, the *Times Guide* provides info on Disney-character appearances and what Disney calls Special Hours. This term usually refers to attractions that open late or close early and to the operating hours of park restaurants.

Main Street, U.S.A. ends at the **Central Plaza,** a hub from which branch the entrances to five other sections of the Magic Kingdom: **Adventureland, Frontierland, Liberty Square, Fantasyland,** and **Tomorrowland.**

Cinderella Castle, at the entrance to Fantasyland, is the Magic Kingdom's architectural icon and visual center. If you start in Adventureland and go clockwise around the Magic Kingdom, the castle spires will always be roughly on your right; if you start in Tomorrowland and go counterclockwise through the park, the spires will always be roughly on your left. The castle is an excellent meeting place if your group decides to split up during the day or is separated accidentally.

unofficial **TIP**
Because Cinderella Castle is so large, designate a very specific meeting spot, such as the entrance to Cinderella's Royal Table restaurant at the rear of the castle.

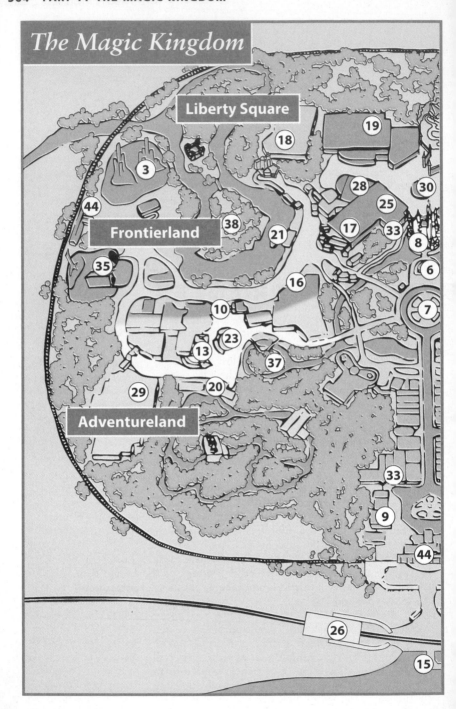

The Magic Kingdom

Liberty Square

Frontierland

Adventureland

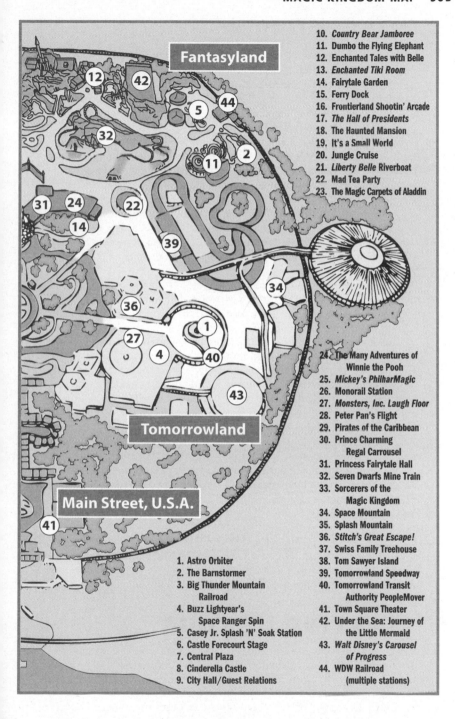

Fantasyland

Tomorrowland

Main Street, U.S.A.

10. *Country Bear Jamboree*
11. Dumbo the Flying Elephant
12. Enchanted Tales with Belle
13. *Enchanted Tiki Room*
14. Fairytale Garden
15. Ferry Dock
16. Frontierland Shootin' Arcade
17. *The Hall of Presidents*
18. The Haunted Mansion
19. It's a Small World
20. Jungle Cruise
21. *Liberty Belle* Riverboat
22. Mad Tea Party
23. The Magic Carpets of Aladdin

24. The Many Adventures of
    Winnie the Pooh
25. *Mickey's PhilharMagic*
26. Monorail Station
27. *Monsters, Inc. Laugh Floor*
28. Peter Pan's Flight
29. Pirates of the Caribbean
30. Prince Charming
    Regal Carrousel
31. Princess Fairytale Hall
32. Seven Dwarfs Mine Train
33. Sorcerers of the
    Magic Kingdom
34. Space Mountain
35. Splash Mountain
36. *Stitch's Great Escape!*
37. Swiss Family Treehouse
38. Tom Sawyer Island
39. Tomorrowland Speedway
40. Tomorrowland Transit
    Authority PeopleMover
41. Town Square Theater
42. Under the Sea: Journey of
    the Little Mermaid
43. *Walt Disney's Carousel
    of Progress*
44. WDW Railroad
    (multiple stations)

1. Astro Orbiter
2. The Barnstormer
3. Big Thunder Mountain
   Railroad
4. Buzz Lightyear's
   Space Ranger Spin
5. Casey Jr. Splash 'N' Soak Station
6. Castle Forecourt Stage
7. Central Plaza
8. Cinderella Castle
9. City Hall/Guest Relations

FANTASYLAND EXPANSION

IN 2010, FANTASYLAND BEGAN the largest themed-land expansion in the Magic Kingdom's history. Scheduled to be completed in 2014, the project will almost double the size of Fantasyland and includes two new headliner rides: **Under the Sea: Journey of the Little Mermaid** and the **Seven Dwarfs Mine Train.** Plus, a new version of the existing **Dumbo** ride has been installed, doubling its capacity. These attractions are described in more detail later in this chapter.

Also in the works is a new castle, modeled after the Beast's fortress in *Beauty and the Beast.* **Beast's Castle** will include a restaurant called **Be Our Guest.** Holding up to 550 diners, it will serve counter-service food during the day and sit-down meals at night. Outside Beast's Castle will be **Belle's Village,** which will bring back a popular interactive storytelling session between Belle and park guests, along with an eatery and a gift shop. Other princesses—Aurora, Cinderella, Rapunzel, and Tiana—will get a dedicated meet-and-greet location, **Princess Fairytale Hall,** across from *Mickey's PhilharMagic* and the Prince Charming Regal Carrousel.

Most of the former land called Mickey's Toontown Fair has been demolished to make way for this expansion. The only attraction to survive the demolition is the **Barnstormer** children's roller coaster. Train service to Fantasyland will also continue to be available.

These changes will increase the number of guests heading to Fantasyland, which was already one of the most crowded lands in the Magic Kingdom. The good news is that the new attractions and restaurants are well designed to handle crowds. The ride vehicles in Under the Sea: Journey of the Little Mermaid, for example, will admit riders almost continuously throughout the day, at a rate of around 2,000 per hour—about the same number of riders that Space Mountain serves per hour. And because the overall size of Fantasyland will almost double, crowds will have more room to spread out.

We've updated our Magic Kingdom touring plans to reflect the latest developments with all the attractions. As with any construction project, plans may change. Check **touringplans.com** for the latest developments and touring plan updates.

DINING IN THE MAGIC KINGDOM

COUNTER-SERVICE RESTAURANTS in the Magic Kingdom are profiled in Part Ten, starting on page 448. For full-service profiles, see the section starting on page 457.

STARTING *the* TOUR

VISITORS SOON FIND THEIR FAVORITE and not-so-favorite attractions in the Magic Kingdom. Our personal experience and research indicate that each visitor differs on which attraction is most enjoyable. Don't dismiss a ride or show until *after* you've tried it.

Take advantage of what Disney does best: the fantasy adventures of Splash Mountain and The Haunted Mansion and the various Audio-Animatronic (talking-robot) attractions, including *The*

Hall of Presidents and Pirates of the Caribbean. Don't burn daylight browsing the shops unless you plan to spend at least 2½ days at the Magic Kingdom, and even then, wait until midday or later. Minimize the time you spend on midway-type rides; you probably have something similar back home. (Don't, however, mistake Space Mountain and Big Thunder Mountain Railroad for amusement-park rides. They may be roller coasters, but they're pure Disney genius.) Eat a good breakfast early, and avoid lines at eateries by snacking during the day on food from vendors or, better yet, from your fanny pack. Fare at most Magic Kingdom eateries is on par with Subway or McDonald's.

MAIN STREET, U.S.A.

BEGIN AND END YOUR VISIT ON MAIN STREET, which may open 30 minutes before and closes 30 minutes–1 hour after the rest of the park. The Walt Disney World Railroad stops at Main Street Station; get on to tour the park or ride to Frontierland or Fantasyland.

Main Street is a Disneyfied turn-of-the-19th-century small-town American street. Its buildings are real, not elaborate props. Attention to detail is exceptional: Furnishings and fixtures are true to the period. Along the street are shops, eating places, City Hall, and a fire station. Occasionally, horse-drawn trolleys, fire engines, and horseless carriages transport visitors along Main Street to the Central Plaza.

Character Greetings *(Fastpass)*

DESCRIPTION AND COMMENTS Meet Mickey, Minnie, and other Disney characters throughout the day at the Town Square Theater on Main Street, to your right as you enter the park. Check the *Times Guide* for details. The Disney princesses will also appear at the Town Square Theater until their permanent meet-and-greet headquarters, Princess Fairytale Hall, is ready in Fantasyland.

TOURING TIPS If the wait to meet Mickey or the princesses appears long, obtain Fastpasses to schedule your visit.

Sorcerers of the Magic Kingdom ★★★

APPEAL BY AGE   TOO NEW TO RATE

What it is Interactive video game in which players must defeat villains spread around different lands. **Scope and scale** Minor attraction. **When to go** Before 11 a.m. or after 8 p.m. **Special comments** Long lines to play. **Authors' rating** Great idea; ★★★. **Duration of presentation** About 2 minutes per step, 4 or 5 steps per game. **Probable waiting time per step** 10–15 minutes.

DESCRIPTION AND COMMENTS Sorcerers of the Magic Kingdom combines aspects of role-playing games such as Dungeons and Dragons with Disney characters and theme park attractions. Your objective: to help the wizard Merlin keep evildoers from taking over the Magic Kingdom. Merlin sends you on adventures in different parts of the park to fight these villains. Each land hosts a different adventure within the game, with different villains in each adventure.

The game is played with a set of trading cards—similar to baseball cards or Magic: The Gathering cards—with a different Disney character on each card. Each character possesses special properties that help it fight

Main Street Services

MOST PARK SERVICES are centered on Main Street, U.S.A., including:	
Baby Care Center Next to The Crystal Palace, left around the Central Plaza (toward Adventureland)	
Banking Services ATMs underneath the Main Street railroad station	
First Aid Next to The Crystal Palace, left around the Central Plaza (toward Adventureland)	
Live Entertainment and Parade Information City Hall, at the railroad-station end of Main Street	
Lost and Found City Hall	
Lost Persons City Hall	
Storage Lockers Underneath the Main Street railroad station (all lockers cleaned out each night)	
Walt Disney World and Local Attraction Information City Hall	
Wheelchair, ECV, and Stroller Rentals Ground floor of the railroad station at the end of Main Street	

certain villains. Pick up the cards (free), plus a map showing where in the park you can play the game, at either the Fire Station on Main Street, U.S.A., or across from Sleepy Hollow Refreshments in Liberty Square.

You'll need your park ticket to pick up your first set of cards and start the game. One card, known as your "key," is special because it links you to your game. You'll need to present your key card when you pick up a set of cards to start your next adventure.

When you pick up your first set of cards, you'll view an instructional video explaining how to use them and the object of the game. Then you'll be sent to another location to start your first adventure. Each location in the park is associated with a unique symbol: an eye, a feather, or Jimmy Page's ZoSo from *Led Zeppelin IV* (just kidding). Look for these symbols on the map to find the best route to your starting point.

Each adventure consists of four or five stops in a particular land. At each stop, another story will play on a computer screen, outlining what your villain is trying to do. Merlin will ask you to cast a spell, using your character cards, to stop the villain. Hold one or more of your cards up to the video display to cast your spell. Cameras in the display read your card, deploy the spell, and show you the results.

The game has three levels: easy, medium, and hard. The easy version is the default and is appropriate for small children; holding up any one

---

DISNEY DISH WITH JIM HILL

SORE ABOUT SORCERERS Because this new and unexpectedly popular interactive adventure is creating traffic jams, Sorcerers of the Magic Kingdom has quickly become something of a touchy subject with the folks in WDW Operations, who've requested that the full rollout of the game's multilevel version be postponed to late 2013 or early 2014. This way, once most of the Fantasyland expansion is opened, guests won't be blocked by would-be wizards awaiting their chance to battle the Disney villains.

of your character cards is enough to defeat any villain. In more-advanced levels of the game, you need to display two or more character cards in specific combinations to defeat a particular villain. Different card combinations produce different spells, and only some spells work on certain characters in those advanced levels.

The audio at each step holds clues to which cards you should use against advanced villains. For example, if a villain says something like "Don't toy with me!" then you should look for cards with characters that are toys, such as the *Toy Story* characters; references to "being spotted" suggest using cards with characters from *101 Dalmatians;* and so on.

The game launched with an initial series of around 70 unique cards; you can obtain 5 new ones per day. Don't worry if you play more than once and end up with duplicate cards—a brisk trading market exists within the park, and it's fairly easy to find someone to trade with. Disney plans to issue new card series over time.

TOURING TIPS Sorcerers is fun and was immediately popular with guests. You'll probably encounter a line of 5–10 people ahead of you at each portal, especially if you play during the afternoon. One complete adventure should take about 30–60 minutes to play, depending on how crowded the park is. If the line to pick up cards is too long at the Main Street Fire Station, try the Liberty Square distribution point.

Transportation Rides

DESCRIPTION AND COMMENTS Trolleys, buses, and the like that add color to Main Street.

TOURING TIPS Will save you a walk to the Central Plaza. Not worth a wait.

Walt Disney World Railroad ★★½

APPEAL BY AGE	PRESCHOOL ★★★★	GRADE SCHOOL ★★½	TEENS ★★★
YOUNG ADULTS ★★★	OVER 30 ★★		SENIORS ★★★

What it is Scenic railroad ride around the perimeter of the Magic Kingdom; provides transportation to Frontierland. **Scope and scale** Minor attraction. **When to go** Anytime. **Special comments** Main Street is usually the least congested station. **Authors' rating** Plenty to see; ★★½. **Duration of ride** About 20 minutes for a complete circuit. **Average wait in line per 100 people ahead of you** 8 minutes; assumes 2 or more trains operating. **Loading speed** Moderate.

DESCRIPTION AND COMMENTS A transportation ride blending an unusual variety of sights and experiences with an energy-saving way to get around the park. The train provides a glimpse of all "lands" except Adventureland, with most of the interesting stuff (Native American village, animatronic animals, frontier structures) on the leg between Frontierland and Fantasyland.

TOURING TIPS Save the train ride until after you've seen the featured attractions, or use it when you need transportation. On busy days, lines form at the Frontierland Station but rarely at the Main Street Station. Strollers aren't allowed on the train. Wheelchair access is available only at the Frontierland station; no word yet on the Fantasyland station's accommodations.

You can't take your rental stroller on the train, but you can obtain a replacement stroller at your destination. Just take your personal belongings, stroller name card, and rental receipt with you on the train.

Finally, note that the railroad shuts down immediately before and during parades. Check your park guide map or *Times Guide* for parade times. Needless to say, this is not the time to queue up for the train.

ADVENTURELAND

ADVENTURELAND IS THE FIRST LAND to the left of Main Street. It combines an African-safari theme with a tropical-island atmosphere.

Enchanted Tiki Room ★★★½

APPEAL BY AGE	PRESCHOOL ★★★	GRADE SCHOOL ★★★	TEENS ★★½
YOUNG ADULTS ★★★	OVER 30 ★★★		SENIORS ★★★

What it is Audio-Animatronic Pacific-island musical-theater show. **Scope and scale** Minor attraction. **When to go** Before 11 a.m. or after 3:30 p.m. **Special comments** Frightens some preschoolers. **Authors' rating** Very, very . . . unusual; ★★★½. **Duration of presentation** 15½ minutes. **Preshow entertainment** Talking birds. **Probable waiting time** 15 minutes.

DESCRIPTION AND COMMENTS A January 2011 fire shut down *The Enchanted Tiki Room—Under New Management!* While repairs were being made, the "management" since 1998—Iago from *Aladdin* and Zazu from *The Lion King*—was laid off. Replacing them were José, Fritz, Michael, and Pierre, the same four crooning, wisecracking parrots that hosted the original version of the attraction, which premiered at Disneyland in 1963. Despite having returned to its roots (egg?), the production remains, well, a featherweight in the Disney galaxy of attractions.

Although readers like the show, they caution that it may be more frightening to younger children than it used to be. Concerning the scary parts, a mother of three from Coleman, Michigan, is outspoken:

The Tiki Room *show was very scary, with a thunder-and-lightning storm and a loud volcano. Can't Disney do anything without scaring young children? It's a bird show!*

A New Jersey dad concurs, commenting:

The Enchanted Tiki Room *is REALLY intense—far more intense than I remember fondly from previous visits. Tiki gods storming and smoking, the whole room plunged into utter darkness, and thunder and lightning that quite literally shakes the benches you're sitting on—our child (age 2½ years) was terrified. Definitely not recommended for very young children.*

TOURING TIPS Usually not too crowded. We go in the late afternoon, when we appreciate sitting in air-conditioned comfort with our brains in park.

Jungle Cruise *(Fastpass)* ★★★

APPEAL BY AGE	PRESCHOOL ★★★★	GRADE SCHOOL ★★★★	TEENS ★★★½
YOUNG ADULTS ★★★½	OVER 30 ★★★½		SENIORS ★★★★

What it is Outdoor safari-themed boat-ride adventure. **Scope and scale** Major attraction. **When to go** Before 10 a.m. or 2 hours before closing, or use Fastpass. **Special comments** A lot of fun to ride at night! **Authors' rating** A long-enduring Disney classic; ★★★. **Duration of ride** 8–9 minutes. **Average wait in line per 100 people ahead of you** 3½ minutes; assumes 10 boats operating. **Loading speed** Moderate.

DESCRIPTION AND COMMENTS An outdoor excursion through jungle waterways. Passengers encounter animatronic elephants, lions, hostile natives, and a menacing hippo. The boatman's spiel adds to the fun. Once one of the most elaborate attractions at the Magic Kingdom, the Jungle Cruise now seems dated. Since the advent of Disney's Animal Kingdom, the attraction's appeal has diminished, but in its defense, you can always depend on the ride's robotic critters being present as you motor past.

A Pelham, Alabama, woman agrees that the Cruise is past its prime:

Jungle Cruise severely needs an update. Our tour guide indulged in annoying comedy to make up for the lack of excitement. I would rather have been eaten by the animatronic hippos.

DISNEY DISH WITH JIM HILL

SHOWDOWN IN THE JUNGLE The Imagineers want to spend a big chunk of the park's annual budget to build a brand-new queuing element for the Jungle Cruise (that is, something similar to The Haunted Mansion's interactive graveyard added in 2011). That idea is at odds with something Operations has long wanted: a separate boat dock for guests in wheelchairs or electric carts. No one knows at this point who's going to win the battle. But Trader Sam sure hopes a few people lose their heads in this behind-the-scenes struggle.

TOURING TIPS A convoluted queuing area makes it very difficult to estimate the length of the wait for the Jungle Cruise. A mother from the Bronx complains:

The line for this ride is extremely deceiving. We got in line toward early evening; it was long but we really wanted to take this ride. Every time the winding line brought us near the loading dock and we thought we were going to get on, we'd discover a whole new section of winding lanes to go through. It was extremely frustrating. We must have waited 20–30 minutes before we finally gave up and got out.

Fortunately, the Jungle Cruise is a Fastpass attraction. Before you get a Fastpass, however, ask a cast member what the estimated wait in the standby line is.

The Magic Carpets of Aladdin ★★★

APPEAL BY AGE   PRESCHOOL ★★★★½   GRADE SCHOOL ★★★★   TEENS ★★★
YOUNG ADULTS ★★½   OVER 30 ★★★   SENIORS ★★½

What it is Elaborate midway ride. **Scope and scale** Minor attraction. **When to go** Before 10 a.m. or in the hour before park closing. **Authors' rating** A visually appealing children's ride; ★★★. **Duration of ride** 1½ minutes. **Average wait in line per 100 people ahead of you** 16 minutes. **Loading speed** Slow.

DESCRIPTION AND COMMENTS The Magic Carpets of Aladdin is a midway ride like Dumbo, except with magic carpets instead of elephants. Copying the water innovation of the One Fish, Two Fish, Red Fish, Blue Fish attraction at Universal's Islands of Adventure, Disney's Aladdin ride has a spitting camel positioned to spray jets of water on carpet riders. Riders can maneuver their carpets up and down and side to side to avoid the water. The front seat controls vehicle height, while the backseat controls tilt—if you let the kids sit up front, prepare to get wet!

TOURING TIPS Like Dumbo, this ride has great eye appeal but extremely limited capacity (that is, it loads slowly). Try to get younger kids on during the first 30 minutes the park is open, or try just before park closing.

Pirates of the Caribbean ★★★★

APPEAL BY AGE	PRESCHOOL ★★★½	GRADE SCHOOL ★★★★	TEENS ★★★★
YOUNG ADULTS ★★★★½	OVER 30 ★★★★½		SENIORS ★★★★½

What it is Indoor pirate-themed boat ride. **Scope and scale** Headliner. **When to go** Before noon or after 5 p.m. **Special comments** Frightens some children. **Authors' rating** Disney Audio-Animatronics at their best; not to be missed; ★★★★. **Duration of ride** About 7½ minutes. **Average wait in line per 100 people ahead of you** 1½ minutes; assumes both waiting lines operating. **Loading speed** Fast.

DISNEY DISH WITH JIM HILL

ARIEL SHE AIN'T If you saw *Pirates of the Caribbean: On Stranger Tides,* you'll remember the murderous mermaids who lived in Whitecap Bay. Well, with the fifth *Pirates* installment sailing into theaters sometime in 2014 or 2015, the Imagineers are looking at adding more of the mythology of the movie series to the attraction that inspired it. Don't be surprised in the next couple of years to spy an HD projection of a sinister mermaid lurking just below the surface of the water, trying to lure you to your doom.

DESCRIPTION AND COMMENTS An indoor cruise through a series of sets that depict a pirate raid on an island settlement, from bombardment of the fortress to debauchery after the victory. Arguably one of the most influential theme park attractions ever created, the Magic Kingdom's version retains the elaborate queuing area, grand scale, and detailed scenes that have awed audiences since its debut in Disneyland in 1967. The wildly successful *Pirates of the Caribbean* movies have boosted the ride's popularity, and guests' demands led to the addition in 2006 of animatronic figures of the movie's Captain Jack Sparrow and Captain Barbossa in key scenes.

Regarding debauchery, Pirates of the Caribbean has been administered a strong dose of political correctness. Even so, a Rockville, Maryland, mother was not prepared for what she saw:

I had not understood that it would be as visually violent and historically accurate as it was. I really didn't look forward to explaining to my son why those women had ropes around their necks and such. I wish I'd been better warned that this isn't the Captain Hook view of piracy, but a much more realistic one.

TOURING TIPS Undoubtedly one of the park's most timeless attractions. Engineered to move large crowds in a hurry, Pirates is a good attraction to see in the late afternoon. It has two covered waiting lines.

Swiss Family Treehouse ★★★

APPEAL BY AGE	PRESCHOOL ★★★	GRADE SCHOOL ★★★	TEENS ★★★
YOUNG ADULTS ★★½	OVER 30 ★★★		SENIORS ★★★

What it is Outdoor walk-through treehouse. **Scope and scale** Minor attraction. **When to go** Anytime. **Special comments** Requires climbing a lot of stairs. **Authors' rating** Incredible detail and execution; ★★★. **Duration of tour** 10–15 minutes. **Average wait in line per 100 people ahead of you** 7 minutes. **Loading speed** N/A.

DESCRIPTION AND COMMENTS An immense replica of the shipwrecked family's treehouse home will turn your children into arboreal architects.

It's the king of all treehouses, with its multiple stories and mechanical wizardry.

TOURING TIPS A self-guided walk-through tour involves a lot of stairs up and down, but no ropes, ladders, or anything fancy. People who stop for extra-long looks or to rest sometimes create bottlenecks that slow the crowd flow. Visit in late afternoon or early evening if you're on a one-day tour, or in the morning of your second day.

▌ FRONTIERLAND

FRONTIERLAND ADJOINS ADVENTURELAND as you move clockwise around the Magic Kingdom. The focus is on the Old West, with stockade-type structures and pioneer trappings.

Big Thunder Mountain Railroad *(Fastpass)* ★★★★

APPEAL BY AGE   PRESCHOOL ★★★½ GRADE SCHOOL ★★★★½ TEENS ★★★★½ YOUNG ADULTS ★★★★   OVER 30 ★★★★½   SENIORS ★★★★

What it is Tame Western mining–themed roller coaster. **Scope and scale** Headliner. **When to go** Before 10 a.m. or in the hour before closing, or use Fastpass. **Special comments** 40" minimum height requirement; children younger than age 7 must ride with an adult. Switching-off option provided (see page 334). **Authors' rating** Great effects; relatively tame ride; not to be missed; ★★★★. **Duration of ride** About 3½ minutes. **Average wait in line per 100 people ahead of you** 2½ minutes; assumes 5 trains operating. **Loading speed** Moderate–fast.

DESCRIPTION AND COMMENTS Roller coaster through and around a Disney "mountain." The idea is that you're on a runaway mine train during the Gold Rush. This coaster is about a 5 on a "scary scale" of 10. A recent refurbishment added air-conditioning to the queue and spruced up these first-rate examples of Disney creativity: a realistic mining town, falling rocks, and an earthquake, all humorously animated with swinging possums, petulant buzzards, and the like. Ride it after dark if you can. Seats in the back offer the best experience.

TOURING TIPS A superb Disney experience, but not too wild a roller coaster. Emphasis is more on the sights than on the thrill of the ride.

Nearby Splash Mountain affects the traffic flow to Big Thunder Mountain Railroad. Adventuresome guests ride Splash Mountain first, then go next door to ride Big Thunder. This means large crowds in Frontierland all day and long waits for Big Thunder Mountain. The best way to experience the Magic Kingdom's "mountains" is to ride Space Mountain one morning as soon as the park opens, then Splash Mountain and Big Thunder Mountain the next morning. If you have only one day, the order should be (1) Space Mountain, (2) Buzz Lightyear (optional), (3) Splash Mountain, and (4) Big Thunder Mountain. If the wait exceeds 30 minutes when you arrive, use Fastpass.

A Midwestern mom offers this tip to families with children who are too short to ride:

If you're switching off on Thunder Mountain or Splash Mountain and have young kids to entertain, there's a fantastic little playground nearby where you can pass the time (and it's a great meeting place when the others get off the ride). It's completely covered and near the restrooms too! It's next to Splash Mountain, under the train tracks.

Guests experience Disney attractions differently. Consider this letter from a lady in Brookline, Massachusetts:

Being senior citizens and having limited time, my friend and I confined our activities to attractions rated as four or five stars for seniors. Because of your recommendation, we waited an hour to board the Big Thunder Mountain Railroad, which you rated a 5 on a scary scale of 10. After living through 3½ minutes of pure terror, I will rate it a 15. We were so busy holding on and screaming and even praying for our safety that we didn't see any falling rocks, a mining town, or an earthquake. The Big Thunder Mountain Railroad should not be recommended for seniors or preschool children.

A woman from Vermont discovered that there's more to consider about Big Thunder than being scared:

Big Thunder Mountain Railroad was rated a 5 on the scary scale. I won't say it warranted a higher scare rating, but it was much higher on the lose-your-lunch meter. One more sharp turn and the kids in front of me would've needed a dip in Splash Mountain!

However, a reader from West Newton, Massachusetts, dubbed the ride "a roller coaster for people who don't like roller coasters."

Country Bear Jamboree ★ ★ ★

APPEAL BY AGE	PRESCHOOL ★★★½	GRADE SCHOOL ★★★	TEENS ★★
YOUNG ADULTS ★★½	OVER 30 ★★★		SENIORS ★★★½

What it is Audio-Animatronic country-hoedown theater show. **Scope and scale** Major attraction. **When to go** Before 11:30 a.m., before a parade, or during the 2 hours before closing. **Authors' rating** Old and worn but pure Disney; ★★★. **Duration of presentation** 15 minutes. **Preshow entertainment** None. **Probable waiting time** This attraction is not terribly popular but has a comparatively small capacity. Waiting time between noon and 5:30 p.m. on a busy day will average 15–30 minutes.

DISNEY DISH WITH JIM HILL

BUFORD'S LAST TRIP TO THE WOODSHED? When *Country Bear Jamboree* returns from its fall 2012 rehab, don't be surprised to find a couple of songs missing. To present a few more shows per day (and make the Frontierland mainstay more politically correct), the Imagineers might ax "Mama, Don't Whip Little Buford" along with other ditties. If so, it'll be unbearable for those of us who've enjoyed the mangy bruins as originally scripted since Walt Disney World opened on October 1, 1971.

DESCRIPTION AND COMMENTS A charming cast of Audio-Animatronic bears sings and stomps in a Western-style hoedown. Although it's one of the Magic Kingdom's most humorous and upbeat shows, *Country Bear Jamboree* has run for so long that the geriatric bears are a step away from assisted living and the fleas all walk with canes. Readers continue to debate the merits of *Country Bear Jamboree*. The following comments are representative. First, from a Sandy Hook, Connecticut, mom:

I know they consider it a classic, and kids always seem to love it, but could they PLEASE update it after half a century?

A woman from Carmel, Indiana, put her experience in perspective:

Here is a half-hour of my life that I cannot get back.

But a Mississippi dad defends the show:

I find it interesting how my reactions and those of my family change to certain attractions. Take Country Bear Jamboree, for instance: In my 30s I enjoyed it mildly but considered it somewhat hokey and lame, yet I thoroughly enjoyed my daughter's intense love of it at ages 3 and 8 on two previous trips. This time, at age 54, I sat up fairly close with my wife and loved it—we even sang along! Of course, this was partly to embarrass my now-16-year-old daughter, who sat hunched down in the very last row. She says we have creeping senility, but I told her, "Just wait till you bring YOUR kids!"

TOURING TIPS The *Jamboree* remains an air-conditioned refuge during summer afternoons, rainy days, and times of peak attendance. On such days, the bears will draw larger crowds from midmorning on.

Frontierland Shootin' Arcade ★ ½

APPEAL BY AGE	PRESCHOOL ★★½	GRADE SCHOOL ★★★½	TEENS ★★★
YOUNG ADULTS ★★★		OVER 30 ★★½	SENIORS ★★

What it is Electronic shooting gallery. **Scope and scale** Diversion. **When to go** Anytime. **Special comments** Costs $1 per play. **Authors' rating** Very nifty shooting gallery; ★½.

DESCRIPTION AND COMMENTS One of a few attractions not included in Magic Kingdom admission. Would-be riflepersons get around 30 shots per $1 play. Each shot is followed by a short delay before the next shot can be taken—this prevents small children from accidentally using all 30 shots in 5 seconds. It's barely noticeable for adults.

TOURING TIPS Not a place to blow your time if you're on a tight schedule. The fun is entirely in the target practice—no prizes can be won.

Splash Mountain *(Fastpass)* ★★★★★

APPEAL BY AGE PRESCHOOL ★★★★†	GRADE SCHOOL ★★★★½	TEENS ★★★★★
YOUNG ADULTS ★★★★★	OVER 30 ★★★★½	SENIORS ★★★★

†*Many preschoolers are too short to ride, and others are intimidated when they see the attraction from the waiting line. Among preschoolers who actually ride, most give it high marks.*

What it is Indoor/outdoor water-flume adventure ride. **Scope and scale** Super-headliner. **When to go** As soon as the park opens, during afternoon or evening parades, or just before closing; or use Fastpass. **Special comments** 40" minimum height requirement; children younger than age 7 must ride with an adult. Switching-off option provided (see page 334). **Authors' rating** A soggy delight, and not to be missed; ★★★★★. **Duration of ride** About 10 minutes. **Average wait in line per 100 people ahead of you** 3½ minutes; assumes ride is operating at full capacity. **Loading speed** Moderate.

DESCRIPTION AND COMMENTS Splash Mountain combines steep chutes and animatronics with at least one special effect for each of the senses. The ride covers more than half a mile, splashing through swamps, caves, and backwoods bayous before climaxing in a five-story plunge and Br'er Rabbit's triumphant return home. More than 100 Audio-Animatronic characters, including Br'er Rabbit (a.k.a. Br'er Hare), Br'er Bear, and Br'er Fox, regale riders with songs, including "Zip-a-Dee-Doo-Dah."

TOURING TIPS This happy, exciting, adventuresome ride vies with Space Mountain in Tomorrowland as the park's most popular attraction.

Crowds build fast in the morning, and waits of more than 2 hours can be expected once the park fills on busy days. Get in line first thing, certainly no later than 45 minutes after the park opens during warmer months. Long lines will persist all day.

If you have only a day to see the Magic Kingdom, ride Space Mountain first, then Buzz Lightyear (also in Tomorrowland), then hotfoot it to Splash Mountain. If the wait is less than 30 minutes, go ahead and ride. Otherwise, get a Fastpass and return later to enjoy Splash Mountain. Fastpass strategies have been incorporated into the Magic Kingdom one-day touring plans (see pages 818–820 and 823). If you have two mornings to devote to the Magic Kingdom, do Space Mountain and Buzz Lightyear one morning, then Splash Mountain and Big Thunder Mountain the next. Spreading your visit over two mornings will eliminate much crisscrossing of the park, as well as the backtracking that's inevitable when you use Fastpass.

As with Space Mountain, hundreds are poised to dash to Splash Mountain when the park opens. The best strategy is to go to the end of Main Street and turn left at The Crystal Palace restaurant. In front of the restaurant is a bridge that provides a shortcut to Adventureland. Stake out a position at the barrier rope. When the park opens, move as fast as you comfortably can and cross the bridge to Adventureland.

Another shortcut: Just past the first group of buildings on your right, roughly across from the Swiss Family Treehouse, is a small passageway containing restrooms and phones. Easy to overlook, it connects Adventureland to Frontierland. Go through here into Frontierland, and take a hard left. As you emerge along the waterfront, Splash Mountain is straight ahead. If you miss the passageway, don't fool around looking for it. Continue straight through Adventureland to Splash Mountain.

Less exhausting in the morning is commuting to Splash Mountain via the Walt Disney World Railroad. Board at Main Street Station and wait for the park to open. The train will pull out of the station a few minutes after the rope drops at the Central Plaza end of Main Street. Ride to Frontierland Station and disembark. As you come down the stairs at the station, the entrance to Splash Mountain will be on your left. Because of the time required to unload at the station, train passengers will arrive at Splash Mountain a little after the lead element from the Central Plaza.

At Splash Mountain, if you ride in the front seat, you almost certainly will get wet. Riders elsewhere get splashed but usually not doused. Since you don't know which seat you'll be assigned, go prepared. On a cool day, carry a plastic garbage bag and tear holes in the bottom and sides to make a water-resistant (not waterproof) sack dress (be sure to tuck the bag under your bottom). Or store a change of clothes, including footwear, in one of the park's rental lockers. Leave your camera with a nonriding member of your group or wrap it in plastic. For any attraction where there's a distinct possibility of getting soaked, wear Tevas or some other type of waterproof sandal, and change back to regular shoes after the ride.

The scariest part of this adventure ride is the steep chute you see when standing in line, but the drop looks worse than it is. Despite reassurances, however, many children wig out when they see it. A mom from Grand Rapids, Michigan, recalls her kids' rather unique reaction:

We discovered after the fact that our children thought they would go under water after the five-story drop and tried to hold their breath throughout the ride in preparation. They were really too preoccupied to enjoy the clever Br'er Rabbit story.

Tom Sawyer Island and Fort Langhorn ★★★

APPEAL BY AGE PRESCHOOL ★★★★ GRADE SCHOOL ★★★★ TEENS ★★★
YOUNG ADULTS ★★★ OVER 30 ★★★ SENIORS ★★★

What it is Outdoor walk-through exhibit and rustic playground. **Scope and scale** Minor attraction. **When to go** Midmorning–late afternoon. **Special comments** Closes at dusk. **Authors' rating** The place for rambunctious kids; ★★★.

DESCRIPTION AND COMMENTS Tom Sawyer Island is a getaway within the park. It has hills to climb; a cave, windmill, and pioneer stockade (Fort Langhorn) to explore; a tipsy barrel bridge to cross; and paths to follow. You can watch riverboats chug past. It's a delight for adults and a godsend for children who have been in tow and closely supervised all day.

TOURING TIPS Tom Sawyer Island isn't one of the Magic Kingdom's more celebrated attractions, but it's one of the park's better-conceived ones. Attention to detail is excellent, and kids revel in its frontier atmosphere. It's a must for families with children ages 5–15. If your group is made up of adults, visit on your second day or on your first day after you've seen the attractions you most wanted to see.

Although children could spend a whole day on the island, plan on at least 20 minutes. Access is by raft from Frontierland; two operate simultaneously, and the trip is pretty efficient, although you may have to stand in line to board both ways.

For a mother from Duncan, South Carolina, Tom Sawyer Island is as much a refuge as an attraction:

In the afternoon when the crowds were at their peak and the weather at its hottest, our organization began to suffer. We retreated over to Tom Sawyer Island, which proved to be a true haven. My husband and I found a secluded bench and regrouped while sipping iced tea and eating delicious soft-serve ice cream. Meanwhile, the kids were able to run freely in the shade.

Walt Disney World Railroad

DESCRIPTION AND COMMENTS Stops in Frontierland on its circle tour of the park. See the description under Main Street, U.S.A. (page 509), for additional details.

TOURING TIPS Pleasant, feet-saving link to Main Street and Fantasyland, but the Frontierland station is more congested than those stations.

LIBERTY SQUARE

LIBERTY SQUARE RE-CREATES AMERICA at the time of the American Revolution. The architecture is Federal or Colonial. The Liberty Tree, a live oak more than 130 years old, lends dignity and grace to the setting.

The Hall of Presidents ★★★

APPEAL BY AGE PRESCHOOL ★★ GRADE SCHOOL ★★★ TEENS ★★★
YOUNG ADULTS ★★★½ OVER 30 ★★★★ SENIORS ★★★★

What it is Audio-Animatronic historical theater presentation. **Scope and scale** Major attraction. **When to go** Anytime. **Authors' rating** Impressive and moving; ★★★.

Duration of presentation Almost 23 minutes. **Preshow entertainment** None. **Probable waiting time** The lines for this attraction look intimidating, but they're usually swallowed up as the theater exchanges audiences. Even during the busiest times, waits rarely exceed 40 minutes.

DESCRIPTION AND COMMENTS In 2009 Barack Obama was added and the entire presentation revamped, including a new narration by Morgan Freeman and a new speech by George Washington. The father of our country joins Presidents Lincoln and Obama as the only chief executives with speaking parts. Although the show is revamped roughly every decade, the presentation remains strongly inspirational and patriotic, highlighting milestones in American history. A very moving show for Americans, coupled with one of Disney's best and most ambitious Audio-Animatronic efforts.

Throughout its periodic refurbishments, we've had a high opinion of *The Hall of Presidents*. That said, we receive a lot of mail from readers who get more than entertainment from it. A woman in St. Louis writes:

We always go to The Hall of Presidents *when my husband gets cranky so he can take a nice nap.*

A young mother in Marion, Ohio, adds:

The Hall of Presidents *is a great place to breast-feed.*

Finally, from a New Jersey teen:

Mom and Dad both fell asleep during The Hall of Presidents. *Only I, a 15-year-old high school freshman, actually paid attention. It's not the most exciting thing in Disney World, but I find it very difficult to fall asleep when Morgan Freeman is speaking. His voice is way too awesome.*

TOURING TIPS Detail and costumes are masterful. This attraction is one of the park's most popular among older visitors. Don't be put off by long lines. The theater holds more than 700 people, thus swallowing large lines at a single gulp when visitors are admitted.

The Haunted Mansion ★★★★

APPEAL BY AGE	PRESCHOOL ★★★	GRADE SCHOOL ★★★★	TEENS ★★★★½
YOUNG ADULTS ★★★★½	OVER 30 ★★★★½		SENIORS ★★★★½

What it is Haunted-house dark ride. **Scope and scale** Major attraction. **When to go** Before 11:30 a.m. or after 8 p.m. **Special comments** Frightens some very young children. **Authors' rating** A masterpiece of detail and not to be missed; ★★★★. **Duration of ride** 7-minute ride plus a 1½-minute preshow. **Average wait in line per 100 people ahead of you** 2½ minutes; assumes both "stretch rooms" operating. **Loading speed** Fast.

DESCRIPTION AND COMMENTS Only slightly scarier than a whoopee cushion, The Haunted Mansion serves up some of the Magic Kingdom's best visual effects. "Doom Buggies" on a conveyor belt transport you through the house from parlor to attic, then through a graveyard. Two new scenes were added in a substantial 2007 refurbishment: an M. C. Escher–like room full of stairs heading in all directions and a montage explaining the fate of the many husbands of the mansion's mistress. However, the storyline remains thin and unemphasized.

Some children become overly anxious about what they think they'll see. Almost nobody is scared by the actual sights.

DISNEY DISH WITH JIM HILL

MORE SPIRITED SURPRISES ON THE WAY With the new interactive graveyard and the now-animated Hitch-hiking Ghosts, you'd think Disney would be done gussy-ing up The Haunted Mansion. Think again. Walt Disney Imagineering (WDI) has recently introduced new guest experiences using radio-frequency identification (RFID). Implemented in various forms all over Walt Disney World, the technology can be used to make a guest's face pop up in the man-sion's portrait gallery or have his or her name appear on a tombstone. If the latter occurs, you'll naturally be charged for the plot and the tomb-stone—it *is* Disney, after all

The Haunted Mansion is one of *Unofficial Guide* writer Eve Zibart's favorite attractions. She says:

This is one of the best attractions in the Magic Kingdom. It's jam-packed with visual puns, special effects, hidden Mickeys, and really lovely Victorian-spooky sets. It's not scary, except in the sweetest of ways, but it will remind you of the days before ghost stories gave way to slasher flicks.

A Temple, Texas, mom isn't convinced:

You say the actual sights aren't really frightening. What isn't *frightening about a hanging corpse, a coffin escapee, and an axe-wielding skeleton bride?*

A new set of interactive elements was added to The Haunted Mansion's outdoor queue in 2011, ensuring that guests have something to occupy them when lines are long. Features include a music-playing monument, an old-fashioned pipe organ, and a ship captain's tomb that squirts water. Dis-neyphiles will recognize the names on many of these new elements as trib-utes to the mansion's designers.

TOURING TIPS Lines here ebb and flow more than those at most other Magic Kingdom hot spots because the Mansion is near *The Hall of Pres-idents* and the *Liberty Belle* Riverboat. These two attractions disgorge 700 and 450 people, respectively, when each show or ride ends, and many of these folks head straight for the Mansion. If you can't go before 11:30 a.m. or after 8 p.m., try to slip in between crowds.

DISNEY DISH WITH JIM HILL

FOR WHOM WILL THE *BELLE* TOIL? With guests complain-ing of how little there is to see during their 17-minute journey around Tom Sawyer Island, WDW Entertain-ment is wondering if the time has come to retire the *Lib-erty Belle* from active service. In 2009, *Tiana's Showboat Jubilee* got an overwhelmingly positive reaction when it was presented at the Magic Kingdom. Should the *Prin-cess and the Frog*–themed show make a comeback, the paddle wheeler could be repurposed as a floating stage.

Liberty Belle Riverboat ★ ★ ½

APPEAL BY AGE	PRESCHOOL ★★★	GRADE SCHOOL ★★★	TEENS ★★½
YOUNG ADULTS ★★★	OVER 30 ★★★		SENIORS ★★★★

What it is Outdoor scenic boat ride. **Scope and scale** Major attraction. **When to go** Anytime. **Authors' rating** Slow, relaxing, and scenic; ★★½. **Duration of ride** About 16 minutes. **Average wait to board** 10–14 minutes.

DESCRIPTION AND COMMENTS Large-capacity paddle-wheel riverboat navigates the waters around Tom Sawyer Island and Fort Langhorn, passing settler cabins, old mining paraphernalia, an Indian village, and a small menagerie of animatronic wildlife. A beautiful craft, the *Liberty Belle* provides a lofty perspective of Frontierland and Liberty Square.

TOURING TIPS The riverboat is a good attraction for the busy middle of the day. If you encounter huge crowds, chances are that the attraction has been inundated by a wave of guests coming from a just-concluded performance of *The Hall of Presidents*.

FANTASYLAND

FANTASYLAND IS THE HEART OF THE MAGIC KINGDOM— a truly enchanting place spread gracefully like a miniature Alpine village beneath the steepled towers of Cinderella Castle.

Much of Fantasyland will be undergoing construction into 2014. While most of the work will be occurring behind existing attractions, you'll almost certainly see construction walls or exterior refurbishment all through Fantasyland until the expansion is complete. Check **touring plans.com** for the latest developments.

DISNEY DISH WITH JIM HILL

OH, DEER "I use antlers in all of my decorating," sings Gaston, Belle's charm-free suitor, in *Beauty and the Beast*. The Imagineers are taking this Disney heel at his word: Covering the walls and ceilings of Gaston's Tavern, his rustic quick-serve restaurant in Fantasyland, will be all sorts of faux deer-related trophies. FYI, Gaston's is slated to become the preferred watering hole of all manner of Disney villains. Don't be surprised to find the dastardly likes of Captain Hook, Cruella de Vil, or the Evil Queen from *Snow White* hanging out and hoisting a glass during a daily event that WDW Entertainment plans on calling "Unhappy Hour."

The expanded Fantasyland is divided into three distinct new sections. Directly behind Cinderella Castle and set upon a snowcapped mountain is **Beast's Castle,** part of a *Beauty and the Beast*–themed area. Most of this section will host dining and shopping, such as the **Be Our Guest** restaurant (see page 506); **Gaston's Tavern,** a small quick-service restaurant; and a gift shop. The far-right corner of Fantasyland—including the new **Dumbo** attraction, the **Barnstormer** kiddie coaster, and the Fantasyland train station—is called **Storybook Circus** as a homage to Disney's *Dumbo* film. These are low-capacity amusement-park rides appropriate for younger children. Finally, the middle of the new Fantasyland territory holds the headliners, including the new Little Mermaid and Seven Dwarfs attractions. Placing these in the middle of the new land should allow good traffic flow either to the left (toward Beast's Castle) for dining, to the right for attractions geared to smaller children, or back to the original part of Fantasyland for classic attractions such as **Peter Pan's Flight** and **The Many Adventures of Winnie the Pooh.**

The Barnstormer ★★

APPEAL BY AGE	PRESCHOOL ★★★★	GRADE SCHOOL ★★★★	TEENS ★★½
YOUNG ADULTS ★★½		OVER 30 ★★★	SENIORS ★★

What it is Small roller coaster. **Scope and scale** Minor attraction. **When to go** Before 10:30 a.m., during parades, or in the evening just before the park closes. **Special comments** 35" minimum height requirement. **Authors' rating** Great for little ones, but not worth the wait for adults; ★★. **Duration of ride** About 53 seconds. **Average wait in line per 100 people ahead of you** 7 minutes. **Loading speed** Slow.

DESCRIPTION AND COMMENTS The Barnstormer is a very small roller coaster. The ride is zippy but supershort. In fact, of the 53 seconds the ride is in motion, 32 seconds are consumed in leaving the loading area, being ratcheted up the first hill, and braking into the off-loading area. The actual time you spend careering around the track is 21 seconds.

A 42-year-old woman from Westport, Connecticut, warns adults that the ride may not be as tame as it looks:

A nightmare that should have gone in your "Eats Adults" section. It looked so innocent—nothing hidden in the dark, over quickly—but my 8-year-old son and I were terrified, and it took me hours to stop feeling nauseated.

Though the reader's point is well taken, The Barnstormer is a fairly benign introduction to the roller-coaster genre and a predictably positive way to help your children step up to more-adventuresome rides. Simply put, a few circuits will increase your little one's confidence and improve his or her chances for enjoying Disney's more adult attractions.

TOURING TIPS The cars of this dinky coaster are too small for most adults and tend to whiplash taller people. This, plus the limited capacity, equals an engineering marvel along the lines of Dumbo. Parties without children should skip this one. If you're touring with children, you have a problem: Like Dumbo, the ride is visually appealing, and all kids want to ride, subjecting the whole family to slow-moving lines. If The Barnstormer is high on your children's hit parade, try to ride as soon as Fantasyland opens.

Dumbo the Flying Elephant *(Fastpass)* ★★★

APPEAL BY AGE	PRESCHOOL ★★★★½	GRADE SCHOOL ★★★★	TEENS ★★½
YOUNG ADULTS ★★½		OVER 30 ★★★	SENIORS ★★½

What it is Disneyfied midway ride. **Scope and scale** Minor attraction. **When to go** Before 10 a.m. or after 9 p.m., or use Fastpass. **Authors' rating** Disney's signature ride for children; ★★★. **Duration of ride** 1½ minutes. **Average wait in line per 100 people ahead of you** 10 minutes. **Loading speed** Slow.

DESCRIPTION AND COMMENTS A tame, happy children's ride based on the lovable flying pachyderm. Parents and children sit inside small fiberglass "elephants" mounted on long metal arms, which spin around a central axis. Controls inside each vehicle allow you to raise the arm, making you spin higher off the ground. Despite being little different from rides at state fairs and amusement parks, Dumbo is the favorite Magic Kingdom attraction of many younger children.

As part of the Fantasyland expansion, Dumbo has moved to the upper-right corner of the land. The attraction's capacity has been doubled with the addition of a second ride—a clone of the first. "Double Dumbo" also includes a covered queue featuring interactive elements (read: things your kids can play with to pass the time in line).

TOURING TIPS If Dumbo is essential to your child's happiness, make it your first stop, preferably within 15 minutes of park opening, or use Fastpass. Disney is installing new games and interactive features at the new queuing area, thus helping keep your antsy ones occupied while they wait in line.

If you want to ride Dumbo twice with a minimal wait, have both adults get in line on the same side of Dumbo, and allow between 32 and 64 people to get between the first adult and child and the second adult. Pass the child to the second adult when the first ride is over.

A mother of two preschoolers from Carmel, Indiana, suggests escaping the Dumbo crowds on a magic carpet:

For the Magic Kingdom Touring Plan for Families with Young Children, how about giving the alternative of The Magic Carpets of Aladdin instead of Dumbo as the first ride? My kids didn't really know Dumbo but wanted a ride like that, so we went to Magic Carpets first, rode twice (there was hardly anyone else there), then went to Fantasyland for Peter Pan and the rest of the touring plan—worked really well.

It's a Small World ★★★

APPEAL BY AGE	PRESCHOOL ★★★★½	GRADE SCHOOL ★★★★	TEENS ★★★
YOUNG ADULTS ★★★	OVER 30 ★★★½		SENIORS ★★★★

What it is World brotherhood–themed indoor boat ride. **Scope and scale** Major attraction. **When to go** Anytime. **Authors' rating** Exponentially "cute"; ★★★. **Duration of ride** About 11 minutes. **Average wait in line per 100 people ahead of you** 3½ minutes; assumes busy conditions with 30 or more boats operating. **Loading speed** Fast.

DESCRIPTION AND COMMENTS Small World is a happy, upbeat indoor attraction with a mind-numbing tune that only a backhoe can remove from your brain. Small boats carry visitors on a tour around the world, with singing and dancing dolls showcasing the dress and culture of each nation. One of Disney's oldest entertainment offerings, It's a Small World first unleashed its brainwashing song and lethally cute ethnic dolls on the real world at the 1964 New York World's Fair. Though it bludgeons you with its sappy redundancy, almost everyone enjoys It's a Small World (at least the first time). It stands, however, along with the *Enchanted Tiki Room* in the "What were they smokin'?" category.

A woman from Holbrook, New York, apparently underwhelmed, suggests that Small World would be much better "if each person got three to four softballs on the way in!"

A Vancouver, British Columbia, teen adds:

The HAPPIEST CRUISE THAT EVER SAILED sign at the entrance to the ride should be replaced with one that says THIS IS YOUR BRAIN ON DRUGS!

TOURING TIPS Cool off here during the heat of the day. With two waiting lines, It's a Small World loads fast and usually is a good bet between 11 a.m. and 5 p.m. If you wear a hearing aid, turn it off.

Mad Tea Party ★★

APPEAL BY AGE **PRESCHOOL** ★★★★ **GRADE SCHOOL** ★★★★ **TEENS** ★★★★
YOUNG ADULTS ★★★½ **OVER 30** ★★★ **SENIORS** ★★

Motion Sickness

What it is Midway-type spinning ride. **Scope and scale** Minor attraction. **When to go** Before 11 a.m. or after 5 p.m. **Special comments** You can make the teacups spin faster by turning the wheel in the center of the cup. **Authors' rating** Fun but not worth the wait; ★★. **Duration of ride** 1½ minutes. **Average wait in line per 100 people ahead of you** 7½ minutes. **Loading speed** Slow.

DESCRIPTION AND COMMENTS Riders whirl feverishly in big teacups. *Alice in Wonderland*'s Mad Hatter provides the theme. Teenagers like to lure adults onto the teacups, then turn the wheel in the middle (making the cup spin faster), until the adults are plastered against the sides and on the verge of throwing up. Unless you aspire to be a living physics experiment, don't even consider getting on this ride with anyone younger than age 21.

A reader we've dubbed Melba the Human Centrifuge advises:

If you want to spin your teacup, do not try to put more than three people in one cup.

TOURING TIPS This ride, well done but not unique, is notoriously slow-loading. Ride the morning of your second day if your schedule is more relaxed.

The Many Adventures of Winnie the Pooh ★★★½
(Fastpass)

APPEAL BY AGE **PRESCHOOL** ★★★★ **GRADE SCHOOL** ★★★★ **TEENS** ★★★
YOUNG ADULTS ★★★ **OVER 30** ★★★½ **SENIORS** ★★★½

What it is Indoor track ride. **Scope and scale** Minor attraction. **When to go** Before 10 a.m. or 2 hours before closing, or use Fastpass. **Authors' rating** As cute as the Pooh Bear himself; not to be missed; ★★★½. **Duration of ride** About 4 minutes. **Average wait in line per 100 people ahead of you** 4 minutes. **Loading speed** Moderate.

DISNEY DISH WITH JIM HILL

BOUNCY, JOUNCY, OUCHY Tigger's Bouncy Place, planned as part of the interactive queue for The Many Adventures of Winnie the Pooh, didn't even make it through the updated dark ride's soft opening in 2010. Why not? Because this series of tiger-striped pads, placed on springs hidden under the Magic Kingdom's pavement, worked a little too well as far as Disney's attorneys were concerned—they were worried that some guests might twist an ankle or break a leg while channeling their inner Tigger.

DESCRIPTION AND COMMENTS Pooh is sunny, upbeat, and fun. You ride a Hunny Pot through the pages of a huge picture book into the Hundred Acre Wood, where you encounter Pooh, Piglet, Eeyore, Owl, Rabbit, Tigger, Kanga, and Roo as they contend with a blustery day. There's even a dream sequence with Heffalumps and Woozles.

A 30-something couple from Lexington, Massachusetts, thinks Pooh has plenty to offer adults:

The attention to detail and special effects make it worth seeing even if you don't have children in your party. The Pooh dream sequence was great!

TOURING TIPS Because of the attraction's relatively low capacity, its daily allocation of Fastpasses is often distributed by early afternoon. For the same reason, your scheduled return time to enjoy the ride might be hours away. It's not unusual to pick up a Fastpass for Winnie the Pooh at 12:30 p.m. with a scheduled return time of 5 p.m. or later.

Mickey's PhilharMagic ★★★★

APPEAL BY AGE	PRESCHOOL ★★★★	GRADE SCHOOL ★★★★½	TEENS ★★★★
YOUNG ADULTS ★★★★½	OVER 30 ★★★★½		SENIORS ★★★★★

What it is 3-D movie. **Scope and scale** Major attraction. **When to go** Before 11 a.m. or during parades. **Special comments** Not to be missed. **Authors' rating** A zany masterpiece; ★★★★. **Duration of presentation** About 12 minutes. **Probable waiting time** 12–30 minutes.

DESCRIPTION AND COMMENTS With *Mickey's PhilharMagic,* each of the four Disney theme parks has a 3-D movie attraction. *PhilharMagic* features an odd collection of Disney characters, mixing Mickey and Donald with Simba and Ariel as well as Jasmine and Aladdin. Presented in a theater large enough to accommodate a 150-foot-wide screen—huge by 3-D movie standards—the 3-D movie is augmented by an arsenal of special effects built into the theater. The plot involves Mickey, as the conductor of the *PhilharMagic,* leaving the theater to solve a mystery. In his absence Donald appears and attempts to take charge, with disastrous results.

The attraction is one of Disney's best 3-D efforts. Brilliantly conceived, furiously paced, and laugh-out-loud funny, *PhilharMagic* incorporates a hit parade of Disney's most beloved characters in a production that will leave you grinning. A North Carolina mother of a 3-year-old, however, accuses us of pulling our punches regarding the show's appropriateness for young children:

Our family found PhilharMagic way too violent (what seemed like minutes on end of Donald getting the crap kicked out of him by various musical instruments). I had to haul my screaming child out of the theater and submit to a therapeutic carousel ride afterwards.

Happily, an Oregon mom has come up with a practical way to nip the willies in the bud:

My advice to parents is simply to have their kids not wear the 3-D glasses. We took my daughter's off right away, and then she began giggling and having a good time watching the movie.

TOURING TIPS Though the other 3-D movies are loud, in-your-face affairs, *Mickey's PhilharMagic* is much softer and cuddlier. Things still pop out of the screen, but they're really not scary. You should still proceed cautiously if you have kids under age 5 in your group, but it's the rare child who is frightened. The show is very popular, but on the other hand, the theater is very large.

Peter Pan's Flight *(Fastpass)* ★★★★

APPEAL BY AGE	PRESCHOOL ★★★★	GRADE SCHOOL ★★★★	TEENS ★★★½
YOUNG ADULTS ★★★★	OVER 30 ★★★★		SENIORS ★★★★

What it is Indoor track ride. **Scope and scale** Minor attraction. **When to go** Before 10 a.m. or after 6 p.m., or use Fastpass. **Authors' rating** Nostalgic, mellow, and well done; not to be missed; ★★★★. Duration of ride A little over 3 minutes. Average wait in line per 100 people ahead of you 5½ minutes. Loading speed Moderate–slow.

DESCRIPTION AND COMMENTS Though not considered a major attraction, Peter Pan's Flight is superbly designed and absolutely delightful, with a happy theme uniting some favorite Disney characters, beautiful effects, and charming music. An indoor attraction, Peter Pan's Flight offers a relaxing ride in a "flying pirate ship" over old London and thence to Never-Never Land, where Peter saves Wendy from walking the plank and Captain Hook rehearses for *Dancing with the Stars* on the snout of the ubiquitous crocodile. Unlike some dark rides, there's nothing here that will jump out at you or frighten young children.

TOURING TIPS Because Peter Pan's Flight is very popular, count on long lines all day. Fortunately, Disney has redesigned much of the queue to run under the roof of the building, out of direct sun and rain. Ride before 10 a.m., during a parade, or just before the park closes; or use Fastpass.

If you use Fastpass, pick up your pass as early in the day as possible. Sometimes Peter Pan exhausts its whole day's supply of Fastpasses by 2 p.m.

Prince Charming Regal Carrousel ★★★

APPEAL BY AGE PRESCHOOL ★★★★½ GRADE SCHOOL ★★★½ TEENS ★★
YOUNG ADULTS ★★★ OVER 30 ★★★ SENIORS ★★★

What it is Merry-go-round. Scope and scale Minor attraction. When to go Before 11 a.m. or after 8 p.m. Special comments Adults enjoy the beauty and nostalgia of this ride. Authors' rating A beautiful ride for children; ★★★. Duration of ride About 2 minutes. Average wait in line per 100 people ahead of you 5 minutes. Loading speed Slow.

DESCRIPTION AND COMMENTS One of the most elaborate and beautiful merry-go-rounds you'll ever have the pleasure of seeing, especially when its lights are on.

A shy and retiring 9-year-old girl from Rockaway, New Jersey, thinks our rating of the carousel for grade schoolers should be higher:

I want to complain. I went on the Prince Charming Regal Carrousel four times and I loved it! Raise those stars right now!

TOURING TIPS Unless young children in your party insist on riding, appreciate this attraction from the sidelines. While lovely to look at, the carousel loads and unloads very slowly.

Princess Fairytale Hall *(opens 2013)* ★★

APPEAL BY AGE NOT YET OPEN

What it is Character-greeting venue. Scope and scale Minor attraction. When to go Before 10:30 a.m. or after 4 p.m. Authors' rating You want princesses? We got 'em! ★★. Duration of ride 7–10 minutes (estimated). Average wait in line per 100 people ahead of you 35 minutes (estimated). Loading speed Slow.

DESCRIPTION AND COMMENTS Scheduled to open on the site of Snow White's Scary Adventures, Princess Fairytale Hall will be the central location for meeting Disney princesses in the Magic Kingdom. While Disney has not yet released details, we think the meet-and-greet process will work similarly to those of other Magic Kingdom character convos: The princesses will occupy a greeting room where 15–20 guests at a time are admitted. They'll be allowed to visit 7–10 minutes—long enough for a photo, an autograph, and a hug from each princess.

TOURING TIPS With all the new attractions in Fantasyland, it's possible that this one will be overlooked in the morning as guests head for the new rides. Check the line on your way out of Fantasyland to see if it's worth a quick stop. If the wait seems too long, consider this advice from a Winchester, Virginia, mom:

The best thing we did with regard to the characters was to have the Winnie the Pooh character dinner at The Crystal Palace. Tigger and Pooh are my kids' favorites, and the characters were VERY attentive; my just-turned 3-year-old was in heaven, and we didn't have to fight crowds.

DISNEY DISH WITH JIM HILL

THE PSYCHIC PRINCESSES NETWORK Princess Fairytale Hall is set to blow some little girls' minds. Thanks to new radio-frequency-identification (RFID) technology being installed all over the parks, a carefully hidden, out-of-the-way prompter will feed the Disney princesses all sorts of information about guests' daughters—info that Mom or Dad shared with WDW reservationists ahead of time. Activated by a Fastpass Plus wristband, RFID will supply princesses with not only a girl's name, but also perhaps her pet's name, her favorite food or color, and maybe even the last ride she experienced. This is Disney magic at a whole new level, thanks to some pretty pricey technology.

On many days, during the first hour the park is open, a multitude of characters roams the Magic Kingdom's streets. It's just like the old days: spontaneous contact and no lines.

Seven Dwarfs Mine Train *(opens 2014)*

APPEAL BY AGE NOT YET OPEN

What it is Indoor/outdoor roller coaster. **Scope and scale** Major attraction. **When to go** Before 10 a.m., during parades, or in the evening. **Special comments** Height requirement (not yet available). **Authors' rating** N/A. **Duration of ride** N/A. **Average wait in line per 100 people ahead of you** N/A. **Loading speed** N/A.

DESCRIPTION AND COMMENTS The land on which the Mine Train sits was originally supposed to be character-greeting areas for Disney princesses and fairies, according to the first press release announcing the project. A legion of parents must have convinced Disney that having a land composed entirely of princesses, fairies, and amusement-park kiddie rides offered nothing to grade-school boys, however, and Disney soon announced changes. (One, the renaming of Cinderella's Golden Carrousel to Prince Charming Regal Carrousel, is laughably transparent.) The Mine Train, however, looks to appeal to the entire family. Although the attraction had not opened as we went to press, the concept art shows a set of small mine trains running through the Seven Dwarfs' workplace and around the forest above the ground. From what we can make out, the experience looks relatively tame—there are no loops, inversions, or rolls in the track, with no massive hills or steep drops. The attraction seems geared to tweens and those slightly younger.

We've also heard that the ride vehicles will "swing" back and forth around the track. We suspect this means your seats pitch left and right while your ride vehicle barrels along—making the ride's tight turns all the more fun.

TOURING TIPS Under the Sea may be the big draw, but we'd bet that the Mine Train will have longer lines throughout the day. If your vacation won't be complete without a comprehensive tour of Fantasyland, see Dumbo and The Barnstormer first, then the Mine Train and Under the Sea. We think the Mine Train will have Fastpass, in which case use it if the line exceeds 30 minutes.

Under the Sea: Journey of the Little Mermaid
(opens late 2012)

APPEAL BY AGE   NOT YET OPEN

What it is Indoor dark ride retelling the film's story. **Scope and scale** Major attraction. **When to go** Before 11 a.m., during parades, or in the evening. **Authors' rating** N/A. **Duration of ride** About 5½ minutes. **Average wait in line per 100 people ahead of you** 3 minutes. **Loading speed** Fast.

DISNEY DISH WITH JIM HILL

WHY DOES THAT FISH LOOK LIKE BARNEY FIFE? Mr. Limpet, the fish character that the late Don Knotts voiced in Warner Bros.' 1964 live-action/animated comedy *The Incredible Mr. Limpet,* will make a blink-and-you'll-miss-him cameo appearance in Journey of the Little Mermaid's "Under the Sea" musical number. Here's hoping that Disney's and WB's lawyers don't raise a stink and that the Imagineers don't try to hide Woody Woodpecker in the kelp as well.

DESCRIPTION AND COMMENTS The centerpiece of the Fantasyland expansion, Under the Sea takes riders through almost a dozen scenes retelling the story of *The Little Mermaid,* this time with Audio-Animatronics, video effects, and a vibrant 3-D set the size of a small theater.

Guests board a clamshell-shaped ride vehicle running along a continuously moving track (similar to The Haunted Mansion's). Then the ride "descends" under water, past Ariel's grotto and on to King Triton's undersea kingdom. The detailed animatronics include Ariel, a school of singing lobsters, octopi, and a conga line of cod. Other scenes hit the film's highlights, including Ariel meeting Prince Eric, her deal with Ursula to become human, and, of course, the couple's happy ending.

TOURING TIPS We estimate that Under the Sea will have a capacity of around 2,000 riders per hour, making it one of the most efficient attractions in the Magic Kingdom. Disney is so sure of its ability to move guests that it isn't making Under the Sea a Fastpass attraction (and at those estimated rates, we agree). While we expect long lines in the first few months the attraction is open, the attraction's sheer capacity means that early mornings, after dinner, and evening Extra Magic Hours should afford shorter waits.

Walt Disney World Railroad

DESCRIPTION AND COMMENTS The railroad stops in Fantasyland on its circle tour of the park. See the description under Main Street, U.S.A. (page 509), for additional details.

TOURING TIPS Pleasant, feet-saving link to Main Street and Frontierland . . . but so crowded in the afternoon during times of peak attendance that you'll almost certainly find it faster to walk anywhere in the park.

TOMORROWLAND

TOMORROWLAND IS A MIX OF rides and experiences relating to technological development and what life will be like in the future. If this sounds like Epcot's theme, it's because Tomorrowland was a breeding ground for ideas that spawned Epcot. Yet Epcot and Tomorrowland are very different in more than scale. Epcot is more educational. Tomorrowland is more for fun, depicting the future as envisioned in science fiction.

An exhaustive renovation of Tomorrowland was completed in 1995. Before refurbishing, Tomorrowland's 24-year-old buildings resembled 1970s motels more than anyone's vision of the future. The current design is ageless, presenting the future as imagined by dreamers and scientists in the 1920s and '30s. Today's Tomorrowland evokes visions of Buck Rogers, fanciful mechanical rockets, and metallic cities spread beneath towering obelisks. Disney calls the renovated Tomorrowland the "Future That Never Was," while *Newsweek* dubbed it "retro-future."

Astro Orbiter ★★

APPEAL BY AGE	PRESCHOOL ★★★½	GRADE SCHOOL ★★★½	TEENS ★★★
YOUNG ADULTS ★★		OVER 30 ★★½	SENIORS ★★

What it is Buck Rogers–style rockets revolving around a central axis. **Scope and scale** Minor attraction. **When to go** Before 11 a.m. or after 5 p.m. **Special comments** This attraction is not as innocuous as it appears. **Authors' rating** Not worth the wait; ★★. **Duration of ride** 1½ minutes. **Average wait in line per 100 people ahead of you** 13½ minutes. **Loading speed** Slow.

Motion Sickness

DESCRIPTION AND COMMENTS Though visually appealing, the Astro Orbiter is still a slow-loading carnival ride. The fat little rocket ships simply fly in circles. The best thing about the Astro Orbiter is the nice view when you're aloft.

TOURING TIPS Expendable on any schedule. If you ride with preschoolers, seat them first, then board. The Astro Orbiter flies higher and faster than Dumbo and frightens some young children. It also apparently messes with some adults. A mother from Lev Hashomnon, Israel, attests:

I think your assessment of Astro Orbiter as "very mild" is way off. I was able to sit through all the "Mountains," the "Tours," and the "Wars" without my stomach reacting even a little, but after Astro Orbiter I thought I would be finished for the rest of the day. Very quickly I realized that my only chance for survival was to pick a point on the toe of my shoe and stare at it (and certainly not lift my eyes out of the "jet") until the ride was over. My 4-year-old was my copilot; she loved the ride (go figure), and she had us up high the whole time. It was a nightmare—people should be forewarned.

Buzz Lightyear's Space Ranger Spin *(Fastpass)* ★★★★

APPEAL BY AGE	PRESCHOOL ★★★★	GRADE SCHOOL ★★★★½	TEENS ★★★★
YOUNG ADULTS ★★★★		OVER 30 ★★★★	SENIORS ★★★★

What it is Whimsical space travel–themed indoor ride. **Scope and scale** Minor attraction. **When to go** Before 10:30 a.m. or after 6 p.m., or use Fastpass. **Authors' rating** Surreal shooting gallery; ★★★★. **Duration of ride** About 4½ minutes. **Average wait in line per 100 people ahead of you** 3 minutes. **Loading speed** Fast.

DESCRIPTION AND COMMENTS This attraction is based on the space-commando character Buzz Lightyear from the film *Toy Story*. The marginal storyline has you and Buzz Lightyear trying to save the universe from the evil Emperor Zurg. The indoor ride is interactive to the extent that you can spin your car and shoot simulated laser cannons at Zurg and his minions.

TOURING TIPS Each car is equipped with two laser cannons and a scorekeeping display. Each scorekeeping display is independent, so you can compete with your riding partner. A joystick allows you to spin the car to line up the various targets. Each time you pull the trigger, you'll release a red laser beam that you can see hitting or missing the target. Most folks' first ride is occupied with learning how to use the equipment (fire off individual shots as opposed to keeping the trigger depressed) and figuring out how the targets work. On the next ride (like certain potato chips, one is not enough), you'll surprise yourself by how much better you do. *Unofficial* readers are unanimous in their praise of Buzz Lightyear. Some, in fact, spend several hours on it, riding again and again. The following comments are representative.

From a Yorktown, Virginia, mom:

I am a 44-year-old woman who has never been fond of shoot-'em-up arcade games, but I decided I'd better check out Buzz Lightyear's Space Ranger Spin after the monorail driver told us that it, along with Space Mountain, were her favorite rides at the Magic Kingdom. What a blast! My husband and I enjoyed it every bit as much as our 10-year-old daughter. After riding it the first time, we couldn't wait to ride it again (and again) in an effort to improve our scores. Alas, I was never able to advance beyond Ranger 1st Class although my husband made it all the way to Space Ace. Warning—Buzz Lightyear is addictive!

And from a Snow Hill, Maryland, dad:

Buzz Lightyear was so much fun it can't be legal! We hit it first on early-entry day and rode it 10 times without stopping. The kids had fun, but it was Dad who spun himself silly trying to shoot the Z's. This is the most unique, creative ride ever devised.

Experience Buzz Lightyear after riding Space Mountain first thing in the morning, or use Fastpass.

Monsters, Inc. Laugh Floor ★★★½

APPEAL BY AGE PRESCHOOL ★★★★½ **GRADE SCHOOL** ★★★★½ **TEENS** ★★★★★
YOUNG ADULTS ★★★★★   **OVER 30** ★★★★   **SENIORS** ★★★★★

What it is Interactive animated comedy routines. **Scope and scale** Major attraction. **When to go** Before 11 a.m. or after 4 p.m. **Special comments** Audience members may be asked to participate in skits. **Authors' rating** Good concept, although the jokes are hit-and-miss; ★★★½. **Duration of presentation** About 15 minutes.

DESCRIPTION AND COMMENTS We learned in Disney/Pixar's *Monsters, Inc.* that children's screams could be converted into electricity, which was used to power a town inhabited by monsters. During the film, the monsters discovered that children's laughter was an even better source of energy. In this attraction, the monsters have set up a comedy club to capture as many laughs as possible. Mike Wazowski, the one-eyed character from the film, emcees the club's three comedy acts. Each consists of an animated monster (most not seen in the film) trying out various bad puns, knock-knock jokes, and Abbott and Costello–like routines. Using the same cutting-edge technology as Epcot's popular *Turtle Talk with Crush,* behind-the-scenes Disney employees voice the characters and often interact with audience members during the skits. As with any comedy club, some performers are funny and some are not. A good thing about this attraction is that Disney has shown a willingness to try new routines and jokes, so the show should remain fresh to repeat visitors.

A Sioux Falls, South Dakota, mom is a big fan:

The Laugh Floor was great. It's amazing how the onscreen characters interact with the audience—I got picked on twice without trying. This should definitely be seen; plus, kids are able to text jokes to Roz.

DISNEY DISH WITH JIM HILL

MONSTERS ON THE MOVE? For a while now, Disney World purists have been complaining that *Monsters, Inc. Laugh Floor,* despite being a fun show, just doesn't fit Tomorrowland's theme. Some Imagineers agree, proposing that this interactive comedy club be moved from the Magic Kingdom to Soundstage One at Disney's Hollywood Studios (DHS). This would not only allow Disney to add a Pixar-themed attraction to the DHS lineup at little cost, but such a move would also free up a valuable chunk of Tomorrowland for a more appropriate sci-fi-/future-themed attraction.

TOURING TIPS The theater holds several hundred people, so there's no need to rush here first thing in the morning. Try to arrive late in the morning after you've visited other Tomorrowland attractions, or after the afternoon parade when guests start leaving the park.

Space Mountain *(Fastpass)* ★★★★

APPEAL BY AGE	PRESCHOOL ★★½†	GRADE SCHOOL ★★★★½	TEENS ★★★★½
YOUNG ADULTS ★★★★½	OVER 30 ★★★★½		SENIORS ★★★

†*Some preschoolers love Space Mountain; others are frightened by it.*

What it is Roller coaster in the dark. **Scope and scale** Super-headliner. **When to go** When the park opens, between 6 and 7 p.m., or during the hour before closing; or use Fastpass. **Special comments** Great fun and action; much wilder than Big Thunder Mountain Railroad. 44" minimum height requirement; children younger than age 7 must be accompanied by an adult. Switching-off option provided (see page 334). **Authors' rating** An unusual roller coaster with excellent special effects; not to be missed; ★★★★. **Duration of ride** Almost 3 minutes. **Average wait in line per 100 people ahead of you** 3 minutes; assumes 2 tracks, with 1 dedicated to Fastpass riders, dispatching at 21-second intervals. **Loading speed** Moderate–fast.

Motion Sickness

DESCRIPTION AND COMMENTS Totally enclosed in a mammoth futuristic structure, Space Mountain has always been the Magic Kingdom's most popular attraction. The theme is a space flight through dark recesses of the galaxy. Effects are superb, and the ride is the fastest and wildest in the Magic

Kingdom. As a roller coaster, Space Mountain is much zippier than Big Thunder Mountain Railroad, but much tamer than the Rock 'n' Roller Coaster at Disney's Hollywood Studios or Expedition Everest at Disney's Animal Kingdom.

DISNEY DISH WITH JIM HILL

GAME ON . . . AND ON . . . AND ON . . . The biggest drawback of the interactive games added to Space Mountain's queue in 2009 is that you start a game and then the line moves. So you start another game . . . and the line moves again. And so on. But what if you could enter the queue and play a single game until you reached the ride's loading area? That's just what the Imagineers are hoping to enable guests to do once WDW's new radio-frequency identification (RFID) comes online. This cutting-edge technology will keep track of exactly where every Disney World visitor is in Space Mountain's queue—meaning no more interrupted play.

Refurbished in 2009, Space Mountain got larger ride vehicles, new lighting and effects, an improved sound system, and a completely redesigned queuing area with interactive games to help pass the time in line. The track was replaced as well but retains the same paths as the old. Then in 2010, a soundtrack was added to the ride that accented high-octane music with sounds of speeding rockets ships and other intergalactic occurrences. It is difficult to know if it's just because of hearing asteroids whiz past your vehicle, but we think the new ride is slightly faster than it was. Roller-coaster aficionados will tell you (correctly) that Space Mountain is a designer version of the Wild Mouse, a midway ride that's been around for at least 50 years. There are no long drops or swooping hills as there are on a traditional roller coaster—only quick, unexpected turns and small drops. Disney's contribution essentially was to add a space theme to the Wild Mouse and put it in the dark. And this does indeed make the Mouse seem wilder.

A family of five from Laramie, Wyoming, has this to say:

The refurbished Space Mountain is fantastic! The cars are much more comfortable, and they've added video-game entertainment near the end of the tunnel portion of the wait.

A Texas mother of two advises working up to Space Mountain:

You might want to start all children off on The Barnstormer, then work up to Thunder Mountain and Space Mountain. We tried Space Mountain first because there was no line, and it ruined the boys for the rest of the trip.

And an Elburn, Illinois, reader recommends special equipment:

They should require you to wear a neck brace on Space Mountain. That ride is painful.

TOURING TIPS People who can handle a fairly wild roller-coaster ride will take Space Mountain in stride. What sets Space Mountain apart is that cars plummet through darkness, with only occasional lighting. Half the fun of Space Mountain is not knowing where the car will go next.

Space Mountain is a favorite of many Magic Kingdom visitors ages 7–60. Each morning before opening, particularly during summer and holiday periods, several hundred Space Mountain "junkies" crowd the rope barriers at the Central Plaza, awaiting the signal to head to the ride's entrance. To get ahead of the competition, be one of the first in the park. Proceed to the end of Main Street and wait at the entrance to Tomorrowland.

Couples touring with children too small to ride Space Mountain can both ride without waiting twice in line by taking advantage of "switching off." Here's how it works: When you enter the Space Mountain line, tell the first Disney attendant (Greeter One) that you want to switch off. The attendant will allow you, your spouse, and your small child (or children) to continue together, phoning ahead to tell Greeter Two to expect you. When you reach Greeter Two (at the turnstile near the boarding area), you'll be given specific directions. One of you will proceed to ride, while the other stays with the kids. Whoever rides will be admitted by the unloading attendant to stairs leading back up to the boarding area. Here you switch off. The second parent rides, and the first parent takes the kids down the stairs to the unloading area where everybody is reunited and exits together. Switching off is also available at Big Thunder Mountain Railroad and Splash Mountain, and for Fastpass users.

Seats are one behind another, as opposed to side by side. Parents whose children meet the height and age requirements for Space Mountain can't sit next to their kids.

If you don't catch Space Mountain first in the morning, use Fastpass or try again during the hour before closing. Often, would-be riders are held in line outside the entrance until all those previously in line have ridden, thus emptying the attraction. The appearance from the outside is that the line is enormous when, in fact, the only people waiting are those visible. This crowd-control technique, known as "stacking," discourages visitors from getting in line. Stacking is used at several Disney rides and attractions during the hour before closing to ensure that the ride will be able to close on schedule. It is also used to keep the number of people who are waiting inside from overwhelming the air-conditioning. Despite the apparently long line, the wait is usually no longer than if you had been allowed to queue inside.

Stitch's Great Escape! ★★

APPEAL BY AGE	PRESCHOOL ★½		GRADE SCHOOL ★★½		TEENS ★★
YOUNG ADULTS ★★		OVER 30 ★★			SENIORS ★★

What it is Theater-in-the-round sci-fi adventure show. **Scope and scale** Major attraction. **When to go** Before 11 a.m. or after 6 p.m.; try during parades. **Special comments** Frightens children of all ages; 40" minimum height requirement. Switching-off option provided (see page 334). **Authors' rating** A cheap coat of paint on a broken car; ★★. **Duration of presentation** About 12 minutes. **Preshow entertainment** About 6 minutes. **Probable waiting time** 12–35 minutes.

DESCRIPTION AND COMMENTS *Stitch's Great Escape!* is a virtual clone of the oft-maligned *Alien Encounter* attraction. Same theater, same teleportation theme, but this time starring the havoc-wreaking little alien from the feature film *Lilo & Stitch*. In this show, Stitch is a prisoner of the galactic authorities and is being transferred to a processing facility en route to his final place of incarceration. He manages to escape by employing an efficient though gross trick, knocking out power to the facility in the process. At this juncture Stitch lumbers around in the dark in much the same way as the theater's previous resident alien.

One wonders why an alien civilization smart enough to master teleportation hasn't yet invented a backup power source.

Guest response to this attraction is so overwhelmingly negative that Disney has been trying to plus it up. This comment from a New South Wales, Australia, reader is typical:

My comments on Stitch's Great Escape! *are . . . It STUNK. It was the worst ride at Walt Disney World.*

The pitch-black darkness in the ride was changed to dim lighting, and several scenes were reworked in an attempt to make it less frightening. Even these measures may not have been enough, because Disney raised the height requirement from 35 inches to 38 inches, then finally to 40 inches (the same as Big Thunder Mountain Railroad) in an attempt to keep out younger children. The fact that Big Thunder is a roller coaster and that this ride doesn't move should be a warning to parents about its fright potential. In our opinion, tinkering at the margins will be futile when it comes to resuscitating this puppy.

TOURING TIPS Disney's press release touting *Stitch* as a child-friendly attraction was about as accurate as Enron's bookkeeping. You're held in your seat by overhead restraints and subjected to something weird clambering around you and whispering to you in a theater darker than a stack of black cats. Stitch is more than enough to scare the pants off many kids ages 6 and younger. *Parents, note:* The overhead restraints will prevent you from leaving your seat to comfort your child if the need arises.

Tomorrowland Speedway ★★

APPEAL BY AGE	PRESCHOOL ★★★★	GRADE SCHOOL ★★★★	TEENS ★★★½
YOUNG ADULTS ★★★★		OVER 30 ★★½	SENIORS ★★★★

What it is Drive-'em-yourself miniature cars. **Scope and scale** Major attraction. **When to go** Before 11 a.m. or after 5 p.m. **Special comments** Kids must be 54" tall to drive unassisted. **Authors' rating** Boring for adults (★★); great for preschoolers. **Duration of ride** About 4¼ minutes. **Average wait in line per 100 people ahead of you** 4½ minutes; assumes 285-car turnover every 20 minutes. **Loading speed** Slow.

Motion Sickness

DESCRIPTION AND COMMENTS An elaborate miniature raceway with gasoline-powered cars that travel up to 7 mph. The raceway, with its sleek cars and racing noises, is quite alluring. The cars poke along on a guide rail, leaving the driver little to do, but teens and many adults still enjoy it.

TOURING TIPS This ride is visually appealing but not a must for grown-ups. The 9-and-under crowd, however, loves it. If your child is too short to drive, ride along and allow him or her to steer the car while you work the foot pedal.

A mom from North Billerica, Massachusetts, writes:

I was truly amazed by the number of adults in line. Please emphasize to your readers that these cars travel on a guided path and are not a whole lot of fun. The only reason I could think of for adults to be in the line would be an insane desire to go on absolutely every ride at Disney World. The other feature about the cars is that they tend to pile up at the end, so it takes almost as long to get off as it did to get on. Parents riding with their preschoolers should keep the car going as slow as possible without stalling. This prolongs the preschooler's joy and decreases the time you'll have to wait at the end.

The line for the Tomorrowland Speedway snakes across a pedestrian bridge to the ride's loading areas. For a shorter wait, turn right off the bridge and head to the first loading area rather than continuing to the second one.

Tomorrowland Transit Authority PeopleMover ★★★

APPEAL BY AGE PRESCHOOL ★★★★ GRADE SCHOOL ★★★½ TEENS ★★★½
YOUNG ADULTS ★★★★ OVER 30 ★★★★ SENIORS ★★★★

What it is Scenic tour of Tomorrowland. **Scope and scale** Minor attraction. **When to go** Anytime, but especially during hot, crowded times of day (11:30 a.m.–4:30 p.m.). **Special comments** A good way to check out the Fastpass line at Space Mountain. **Authors' rating** Scenic and relaxing; ★★★. **Duration of ride** 10 minutes. **Average wait in line per 100 people ahead of you** 1½ minutes; assumes 39 trains operating. **Loading speed** Fast.

DESCRIPTION AND COMMENTS A once-unique prototype of a linear induction–powered mass-transit system, the PeopleMover's tramlike cars carry riders on a leisurely tour of Tomorrowland, including a peek inside Space Mountain. In ancient times, the attraction was called the WEDway PeopleMover ("WED" being the initials of one Walter Elias Disney).

TOURING TIPS A relaxing ride where lines move quickly. It's a good choice during busier times of day.

Walt Disney's Carousel of Progress ★★★

APPEAL BY AGE PRESCHOOL ★★★ GRADE SCHOOL ★★★ TEENS ★★★
YOUNG ADULTS ★★★½ OVER 30 ★★★½ SENIORS ★★★★

What it is Audio-Animatronic theater production. **Scope and scale** Major attraction. **When to go** Anytime. **Authors' rating** Nostalgic, warm, and happy; ★★★. **Duration of presentation** 21 minutes. **Preshow entertainment** Documentary on the attraction's long history. **Probable waiting time** Less than 10 minutes.

DISNEY DISH WITH JIM HILL

A PRAIRIE HOME-OF-THE-FUTURE COMPANION As annual attendance continues to drop at *Walt Disney's Carousel of Progress*, the Imagineers have been fretting about what to do with this theater-go-round presentation. The attraction, last updated in 1994, is sorely in need of makeover, but whom could Disney get to replace the late, great Jean Shepherd as the narrator of this show? Some at WDI have proposed recruiting another radio legend, Garrison Keillor, to be the new voice of Father. So far, however, no one's responded to all those letters sent from Lake Buena Vista to Lake Wobegon asking Keillor to come take a ride on Walt's nearly 50-year-old *Carousel*.

DESCRIPTION AND COMMENTS *Walt Disney's Carousel of Progress* offers a nostalgic look at how technology and electricity have changed the lives of an Audio-Animatronic family over several generations. The family is easy to identify with, and a cheerful, sentimental tune bridges the generations.

TOURING TIPS The *Carousel* handles big crowds effectively and is a good choice during busier times of day.

LIVE ENTERTAINMENT *in* *the* MAGIC KINGDOM

BANDS, DISNEY-CHARACTER APPEARANCES, parades, ceremonies, and singing and dancing further enliven the Magic Kingdom. For specific events the day you visit, check the live-entertainment schedule in your guide map (free as you enter the park or at City Hall) or in the *Times Guide* available along with the guide map. WDW live-entertainment guru Steve Soares usually posts the Magic Kingdom's performance schedule about a week in advance at **wdwent.com**.

Our one-day touring plans exclude live performances in favor of seeing as much of the park as time permits; parades and shows siphon crowds away from popular rides, thus shortening lines. Nonetheless, the color and pageantry of live events are integral to the Magic Kingdom—and a persuasive argument for a second day of touring. Here's a list of some regular performances and events that don't require reservations:

unofficial **TIP**
Be aware: If you're short on time, it's impossible to see Magic Kingdom feature attractions and the live performances.

BAY LAKE AND SEVEN SEAS LAGOON FLOATING ELECTRICAL PAGEANT Usually performed at nightfall (9 p.m. at the Polynesian Resort, 9:15 at the Grand Floridian Resort & Spa, and 10:15 at the Contemporary Resort) on Seven Seas Lagoon and Bay Lake, this is one of our favorites among the Disney extras, but it's necessary to leave the Magic Kingdom to view it. The pageant is a stunning electric-light show aboard small barges and set to nifty electronic music. Leave the Magic Kingdom and take the monorail to the Polynesian, Grand Floridian, or Contemporary.

A couple of 20-somethings from Jersey City, New Jersey, found the pageant less inspiring than did we (but we're sticking to our guns):

> While the Unofficial Guide *described it as "a stunning electric-light show . . . set to nifty electronic music," we found it more akin to a set of Lite-Brites with 1970s Casio-keyboard music. While we did enjoy it, we probably spent more time laughing at how corny it was than anything else.*

CAPTAIN JACK SPARROW'S PIRATE TUTORIAL Meet the legendary pirate and his crew in Adventureland, where would-be knaves and really bad eggs can learn the finer points of this alternative career. Candidates are required to take an oath at the end of the class. (We're not sure whether it's legally binding.) Check the *Times Guide* for schedules.

CASTLE FORECOURT STAGE A new 20-minute forecourt show called *Dream-Along with Mickey* debuted as part of the Year of a Million Dreams campaign. Featuring Mickey, Minnie, Donald, Goofy, and a peck of princesses and other secondary characters, plus human backup dancers, the show is built around the premise that—*quelle horreur!*—Donald doesn't believe in the power of dreams. Crisis is averted through a frenetic whirlwind of song and dance.

The show is performed several times a day according to the season, with showtimes listed in the daily entertainment schedule (*Times Guide*). The Castle Forecourt Stage is elevated well above ground level, so good viewing spots are available all around Main Street's Central Plaza.

DISNEY-CHARACTER SHOWS AND APPEARANCES A number of characters are usually on hand to greet guests when the park opens. Because they snarl pedestrian traffic and stop most children dead in their tracks, this is sort of a mixed blessing. Most days, a character is on duty for photos and autographs from 9 a.m. to 10 p.m. next to City Hall. Mickey and Minnie (and, for a time, the Disney princesses) can be found in Main Street's Town Square Theater, to the right as you enter the park. Your best bet is to check the daily *Times Guide* for character-greeting locations and times. Shows at the Castle Forecourt Stage feature Disney characters several times daily; again, check the schedule.

ENCHANTED TALES WITH BELLE (OPENS 2013) Disney hasn't promoted this interactive storytelling session as much as other parts of the Fantasyland expansion, but something similar was held in another part of Fantasyland for years before the construction. Then, Belle and several helpers selected children from the small amphitheater audience and dressed them up as characters from *Beauty and the Beast*. As Belle would tell the story, the children would act out the roles. There was a 3- to 5-minute meet-and-greet with photo and autograph opportunities afterward. The show was staged six to eight times each day in a small open courtyard between Cinderella Castle and Tomorrowland. We expect Disney to retain many of these details when Enchanted Tales opens in a dedicated location near Beast's Castle in 2013.

FANTASYLAND PAVILION Site of various concerts in Fantasyland.

FLAG RETREAT At 4:45 p.m. daily at Town Square (Walt Disney World Railroad end of Main Street). Sometimes performed with large college marching bands, sometimes with a smaller Disney band.

MAGIC KINGDOM BANDS Banjo, Dixieland, steel drum, marching, and fife-and-drum bands play daily throughout the park.

THE MAGIC, THE MEMORIES AND YOU! In one of the most imaginative shows yet, videos and photos of guests in the park are set to music and projected nightly on Cinderella Castle. The special effects are tremendous: In one vignette, the entire castle appears to shimmer and sway; in another, flames appear throughout the castle's windows to emulate a scene from the Pirates of the Caribbean ride. Throughout the show, images of guests who visited the park that day are displayed. While the show's soundtrack is excessively sentimental (even for Disney), the visuals more than make up for it. We rate this as not to be missed.

MOVE IT! SHAKE IT! CELEBRATE IT! PARADE Starting at the Walt Disney World Railroad end of Main Street, U.S.A., and working toward the Central Plaza, this short walk incorporates about a dozen guests with a handful of floats, Disney characters, and entertainers. Music is provided by one of Disney's latest artists (Miley Cyrus currently), and there's a good amount of interaction between the entertainers and the crowd. Unless you're already on Main Street, however, or too pooped for anything else, we don't recommend making a special trip to view this parade.

TINKER BELL'S FLIGHT This nice special effect in the sky above Cinderella Castle heralds the beginning of the *Wishes* fireworks show (when the park is open late).

TOMORROWLAND FORECOURT STAGE This two-story space near the Astro Orbiter is used primarily for special events. For the time being, Disney has no plans to introduce shows at the venue.

WISHES FIREWORKS SHOW Memorable vignettes and music from beloved Disney films combine with a stellar fireworks display while Jiminy Cricket narrates a lump-in-your-throat story about making wishes come true. For an uncluttered view and lighter crowds, watch from the end of Main Street between The Plaza Restaurant and Tomorrowland Terrace. Another good fireworks-viewing area is the second story of the Main Street railroad station. The spot we'd previously recommended, in the Tomorrowland Terrace area, was apparently so good that Disney decided they could charge for it. To view *Wishes* from this location now costs $27.68 per adult and $14.90 per child. The viewing comes with a dessert buffet and nonalcoholic beverages. Reservations can be made 180 days in advance by calling ☎ 407-WDW-DINE (939-3463).

WISHES FIREWORKS CRUISE For a different view, you can watch the fireworks from Seven Seas Lagoon aboard a chartered pontoon boat. The charter costs $346 and accommodates up to 10 people. Chips, soda, and water are provided; sandwiches and more-substantial food items may be arranged through reservations. Your Disney captain will take you for a little cruise and then position the boat in a perfect place to watch the fireworks. (A major indirect benefit of the charter is that you can enjoy the fireworks without fighting the mob afterward.) Because this is a private charter rather than a tour, only your group will be aboard. Life jackets are provided, but wearing them is at your discretion. To reserve a charter, call ☎ 407-WDW-PLAY (939-7529) at exactly 7 a.m. Eastern time about 180 days before the day you want to cruise. Because the Disney reservations system counts days in a somewhat atypical manner, we recommend phoning about 185 days out to have a Disney agent specify the exact morning to call for reservations.

▮ PARADES

PARADES AT THE MAGIC KINGDOM ARE FULL-FLEDGED spectaculars with dozens of Disney characters and amazing special effects. We rate the afternoon parade as outstanding and the evening parade as not to be missed.

In addition to providing great entertainment, parades lure guests away from the attractions. If getting on rides appeals to you more than watching a parade, you'll find substantially shorter lines just before and during parades. Because the parade route doesn't pass through Adventureland, Tomorrowland, or Fantasyland, attractions in these lands are particularly good bets. Be forewarned: Parades disrupt traffic in the Magic Kingdom. It's nearly impossible, for example, to get to Adventureland from Tomorrowland, or vice versa, during one. Also

Magic Kingdom Parade Route

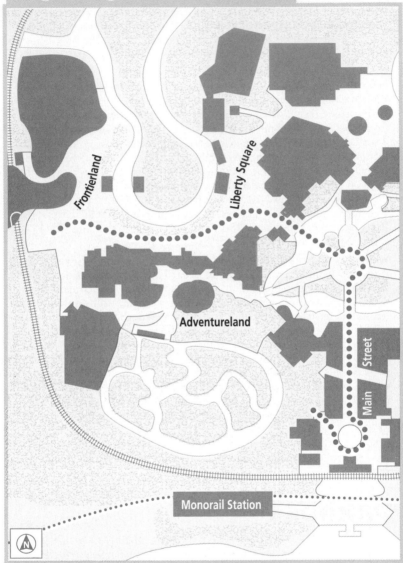

be advised that the Walt Disney World Railroad shuts down during parades, thus making it impossible to access other lands by train.

AFTERNOON PARADE

USUALLY STAGED AT 3 P.M., this parade features bands, floats, and marching Disney characters. A new afternoon parade is introduced every year or two. While some elements—such as Disney characters—

remain constant, the theme, music, and float design change. Seasonal parades during major holidays round out the mix.

EVENING PARADE(S)

THE EVENING PARADE is a high-tech affair that employs electro-luminescent and fiber-optic technologies, light-spreading thermoplastics (don't try this at home!), and clouds of underlit liquid-nitrogen smoke. Don't worry, you won't need a gas mask or lead underwear to watch. For those who flunked chemistry and physics, the parade also offers music, Mickey Mouse, and twinkling lights.

unofficial **TIP**
Call ☎ 407-824-4321 before you go to be sure the evening parade is on.

The evening parade is staged once or twice each evening, depending on the season. During less busy seasons, the parade is presented only on weekends, and sometimes not even then. We rate it as not to be missed.

The **Main Street Electrical Parade** returned to the Magic Kingdom in 2010 after running there from 1977 to 1991; it also ran until recently at Disney California Adventure. It replaces—temporarily, we hear—the popular SpectroMagic parade. There's no word on how long the Electrical Parade will last in its current run, but the soundtrack, a synthesizer-tinged ode to country music, is a classic. In our opinion, the Magic Kingdom's nighttime parade is always the best in Walt Disney World, and the Electrical Parade is the standard against which everything else is judged. If you're at Disney World while the parade is running, make a special trip to see it.

PARADE ROUTE AND VANTAGE POINTS

MAGIC KINGDOM PARADES CIRCLE TOWN SQUARE, head down Main Street, go around the Central Plaza, and cross the bridge to Liberty Square. In Liberty Square, they follow the waterfront and end in Frontierland. Sometimes they begin in Frontierland and run the route in the opposite direction. Most guests watch from the Central Plaza or from Main Street. One of the best and most popular vantage points is the upper platform of the Walt Disney World Railroad station at the Town Square end of Main Street. This is also a good place for watching the *Wishes* fireworks show, as well as for ducking out of the park ahead of the crowd when the fireworks end. The problem is, you have to stake out your position 30–45 minutes before the events begin.

Because most spectators pack Main Street and the Central Plaza, we recommend watching the parade from Liberty Square or Frontierland. Great vantage points frequently overlooked are as follows:

1. Sleepy Hollow snack-and-beverage shop, immediately to your right as you cross the bridge into Liberty Square. If you arrive early, buy refreshments and claim a table by the rail. You'll have a perfect view of the parade as it crosses Liberty Square Bridge, but only when the parade begins on Main Street.

2. The pathway on the Liberty Square side of the moat from Sleepy Hollow snack-and-beverage shop to Cinderella Castle. Any point along this path offers a clear and unobstructed view as the parade crosses Liberty Square Bridge. Once again, this spot works only for parades coming from Main Street.

3. The covered walkway between Liberty Tree Tavern and The Diamond Horseshoe Saloon. This elevated vantage point is perfect (particularly on rainy days) and usually goes unnoticed until just before the parade starts.

4. Elevated wooden platforms in front of the Frontierland Shootin' Arcade, Frontier Trading Post, and the building with the sign reading frontier mercantile. These spots usually get picked off 10–12 minutes before parade time.

5. Benches on the perimeter of the Central Plaza, between the entrances to Liberty Square and Adventureland. Usually unoccupied until after the parade begins, they offer a comfortable resting place and unobstructed (though somewhat distant) view of the parade as it crosses Liberty Square Bridge. What you lose in proximity, you gain in comfort.

6. Liberty Square and Frontierland dockside areas; spots here usually go early.

7. The elevated porch of Tony's Town Square Restaurant on Main Street provides an elevated viewing platform and an easy path to the park exit when the fireworks are over.

Assuming it starts on Main Street (evening parades normally do), the parade takes 16–20 minutes to reach Liberty Square or Frontierland.

On evenings when the parade runs twice, the first parade draws a huge crowd, siphoning guests from attractions. Many folks leave the park after the early parade, with many more departing following the fireworks (which are scheduled on the hour between the two parades).

Continue to tour after the fireworks. This is a particularly good time to ride Splash Mountain and enjoy attractions in Adventureland. If you're touring Adventureland and the parade begins on Main Street, you won't have to assume your viewing position in Frontierland until 15 minutes after the parade kicks off (the time it takes the parade to reach Frontierland). If you watch from the Splash Mountain side of the street and head for the attraction as the last float passes, you'll be able to ride with only a couple minutes' wait. You might even have time to work in a last-minute ride on Big Thunder Mountain Railroad.

unofficial **TIP**
For optimum touring and less congestion, enjoy attractions during the early parade, then break to watch the fireworks.

VANTAGE POINTS FOR FIREWORKS

ANYWHERE ALONG MAIN STREET is fine for the fireworks. If you plan to leave the park immediately afterward, watch from the train-station end to facilitate a quick departure. Our favorite spot if we intend to remain in the park is between The Plaza Restaurant on Main Street and the Tomorrowland Terrace area to its right (if you're facing the castle).

LEAVING THE PARK AFTER EVENING PARADES AND FIREWORKS

ARMIES OF GUESTS leave the Magic Kingdom after evening parades and fireworks. The Disney transportation system (buses, ferries, and monorail) is overwhelmed, causing long waits in boarding areas.

A mother from Kresgeville, Pennsylvania, pleads:

Please stress how terrifying these crowds can be. Our family of five made the mistake of going to the Magic Kingdom the Saturday night before Columbus Day to watch the parade and fireworks. Afterwards, we lingered at The Crystal Palace to wait for the crowds to lessen, but it was no use. We started walking toward the gates and soon became trapped by the throng, not able to go forward or back. There was no way to cross the hordes to get to the dock for our hotel's launch. Our group became separated, and it became a living nightmare. We left the park at 10:30 p.m. and didn't get back to the Polynesian (less than a mile away) until after midnight. How dare they expose children to that nightmare! Even if they were to raise Walt Disney himself from cryogenic sleep and parade him down Main Street, I would never go to the Magic Kingdom on a Saturday night again!

An Oklahoma City dad offers this advice:

Never, never leave the Magic Kingdom just after the 10 p.m. fireworks. I have never seen so many people in one spot before. Go for another ride—no lines because everyone else is trying to get out!

Congestion persists from the end of the early evening parade until closing time. Most folks watch the early parade and then the fireworks a few minutes later. If you're parked at the Transportation and Ticket Center (TTC) and are intent on beating the crowd, view the early parade from the Town Square end of Main Street, leaving the park as soon as the parade ends.

If you're staying at a Disney hotel not served by the monorail and must depend on Disney transportation, watch the early parade and fireworks at the park and then enjoy the attractions until about 20–25 minutes before the late parade is scheduled to begin. At this time, leave the park and catch the Disney bus or boat back to your hotel. Don't cut it too close: Main Street will be so congested that you won't be able to reach the exit.

Here's what happened to a family from Cape Coral, Florida:

We tried to leave the park before the parade began. However, Main Street was already packed and we didn't see any way to get out of the park, so we were stuck. In addition, it was impossible to move across the street, and even the shops were so crowded that it was virtually impossible to maneuver a stroller through them to get close to the entrance.

If you don't have a stroller (or are willing to forgo the $1 return refund for rental strollers), catch the Walt Disney World Railroad in Frontierland and ride to the park exit at Main Street. If you plan to escape by train, don't cut it too close.

If you're on the Tomorrowland side of the park, it's actually possible for you to exit during a parade. Leaving Tomorrowland, cut through Tomorrowland Terrace. Before you reach Main Street, bear left into the side door of the corner shop. Once inside, you'll see that Main Street

*un*official **TIP**
Be aware that the railroad shuts down during parades because the floats must cross the tracks when entering or exiting the parade route in Frontierland.

shops have interior doors allowing you to pass from one shop to the next without having to get on Main Street. Work your way from shop to shop until you reach Town Square (easy, because people will be outside watching the parade). At Town Square, bear left and move to the train station and the park exit.

This strategy won't work if you're on the Adventureland side of the park. You can make your way through Casey's Corner restaurant to Main Street and then work your way through the interior of the Main Street shops, but when you pop out of the Emporium at Town Square, you'll be trapped by the parade. As soon as the last float passes, however, you can bolt for the exit.

Another strategy for beating the masses out of the park (if your car is at the TTC lot) is to watch the early parade and then leave before the fireworks begin. Line up for the ferry. One will depart about every 8–10 minutes. Try to catch the ferry that will be crossing Seven Seas Lagoon while the fireworks are in progress. The best vantage point is on the top deck to the right of the pilothouse as you face the Magic Kingdom; the sight of fireworks silhouetting the castle and reflecting off Seven Seas Lagoon is unforgettable. While there's no guarantee that a ferry will load and depart within 3 or 4 minutes of the fireworks, your chances are about 50–50 of catching it just right. If you're in the front of the line for the ferry and don't want to board the boat that's loading, stop at the gate and let people pass you. You'll be the first to board the next boat.

TRAFFIC PATTERNS *in* *the* MAGIC KINGDOM

WHEN WE RESEARCH THE MAGIC KINGDOM, we study its traffic patterns, asking:

1. WHICH SECTIONS OF THE PARK AND WHICH ATTRACTIONS DO GUESTS VISIT FIRST? When visitors are admitted to the lands during summer and holiday periods, traffic to Tomorrowland and Frontierland is heaviest, followed by Fantasyland, Adventureland, and Liberty Square.

During the school year, when fewer young people are in the park, early-morning traffic is more evenly distributed but remains heaviest in Tomorrowland, Frontierland, and Fantasyland. Our researchers tested the frequent claim that most people turn right into Tomorrowland and tour the Magic Kingdom in a counterclockwise sequence. We found the claim to be baseless.

unofficial **TIP**
As the park fills up, visitors head for the top attractions before lines get long. This, more than anything else, determines morning traffic patterns.

2. HOW LONG DOES IT TAKE FOR THE PARK TO FILL UP? HOW ARE THE VISITORS DISPERSED IN THE PARK? A surge of early birds arrives before or around opening time but is quickly dispersed throughout the empty park. After the initial wave is absorbed, there's a lull lasting about an hour after opening. Then the park is inundated for about 2 hours, peaking between 10 a.m. and noon.

Arrivals continue in a steady but diminishing stream until around 2 p.m. The lines we sampled were longest between 1 and 2 p.m., indicating more arrivals than departures into the early afternoon. For touring purposes, most attractions develop long lines between 10 and 11:30 a.m.

From late morning until early afternoon, guests are equally distributed through all the lands. However, guests concentrate in Fantasyland, Liberty Square, and Frontierland in late afternoon, with a decrease of visitors in Adventureland and Tomorrowland. Adventureland's Jungle Cruise and Tomorrowland's Buzz Lightyear and Space Mountain continue to be crowded, but most other attractions in those lands are readily accessible.

3. HOW DO MOST VISITORS TOUR THE PARK? Do first-time visitors tour differently from repeat guests? Many first-time visitors are guided by friends or relatives familiar with the Magic Kingdom. These tours may or may not follow an orderly sequence. First-time visitors without personal guides tend to be more orderly in their touring. Many first-time visitors, however, are drawn to Cinderella Castle upon entering the park and thus begin their rotation from Fantasyland. Repeat visitors usually go directly to their favorite attractions.

ATTRACTIONS THAT GET CROWDED EARLY	
ADVENTURELAND	Jungle Cruise
FANTASYLAND	Dumbo the Flying Elephant
	The Many Adventures of Winnie the Pooh
	Peter Pan's Flight
	Seven Dwarfs Mine Train
FRONTIERLAND	Big Thunder Mountain Railroad
	Splash Mountain
TOMORROWLAND	Buzz Lightyear's Space Ranger Spin
	Space Mountain

4. HOW DOES FASTPASS AFFECT CROWD DISTRIBUTIONS? The effect is subtle and depends somewhat on the time interval between when the Fastpass is obtained and the Fastpass return period. For example, guests who receive a Fastpass for Splash Mountain at 10 a.m. with an 11:05 a.m.–12:05 p.m. return window tend to tour near Splash Mountain in the interim to minimize the inconvenience of backtracking when it's time to use the pass. However, when the return period is several hours distant, guests don't feel compelled to stay in the immediate area. In general, you won't notice much difference in crowd concentrations because of Fastpass, but empirically speaking, it increases crowds within proximity of the two anchor attractions—Space Mountain and Splash Mountain—throughout the day.

5. HOW DO SPECIAL EVENTS, SUCH AS PARADES AND LIVE SHOWS, AFFECT TRAFFIC PATTERNS? Parades pull huge numbers of guests away from attractions and provide a window of opportunity for experiencing the more popular attractions with less of a wait. Castle Forecourt Stage shows also attract crowds but only slightly affect lines.

6. WHAT ARE THE TRAFFIC PATTERNS NEAR AND AT CLOSING TIME? On our sample days, in busy times and off-season at the park, departures outnumbered arrivals beginning in midafternoon. Many visitors left in late afternoon as the dinner hour approached. When the park closed early, guests departed steadily during the 2 hours before closing, with a huge exodus at closing time. When the park closed late, a huge exodus began immediately after the early-evening parade and fireworks, with a second mass departure after the late parade, continuing until closing. Because Main Street and the transportation services remain open after the other five lands close, crowds leaving at closing mainly affect conditions on Main Street and at the monorail-, ferry-, and bus-boarding areas. In the hour before closing, the other five lands are normally uncrowded.

To get a complete view of the actual traffic patterns while you're in the park, use our mobile app, **Lines** (**touringplans.com/lines**). The app gives you current wait times and future estimates in half-hour increments for today and tomorrow. A quick glance shows how traffic patterns affect wait times throughout the day.

MAGIC KINGDOM TOURING PLANS

STARTING ON PAGE 818, our step-by-step touring plans are field-tested for seeing *as much as possible* in one day with a minimum of time wasted in lines. They're designed to help you avoid crowds and bottlenecks on days of moderate-to-heavy attendance. Understand, however, that there's more to see in the Magic Kingdom than can be experienced in one day. Since we first began covering the Magic Kingdom, four headliner attractions have been added and an entire land created and destroyed. Today, even if you could experience every attraction without any wait, it would still be virtually impossible to see all of the park in a single day.

unofficial **TIP**
Don't worry that other people will be following the plans and render them useless. Fewer than 1 in every 350 people in the park will have been exposed to this info.

On days of lighter attendance (see "Selecting the Time of Year for Your Visit," page 33), our plans will save you time but won't be as critical to successful touring as on busier days.

CHOOSING THE APPROPRIATE TOURING PLAN

WE PRESENT FIVE MAGIC KINGDOM TOURING PLANS:

- Magic Kingdom One-Day Touring Plan for Adults
- Magic Kingdom Authors' Selective One-Day Touring Plan for Adults
- Magic Kingdom One-Day Touring Plan for Parents with Small Children
- Magic Kingdom Two-Day Touring Plan
- Magic Kingdom Dumbo-or-Die-in-a-Day Touring Plan for Parents with Small Children

If you have two days (or two mornings) at the Magic Kingdom, the Two-Day Touring Plan is *by far* the most relaxed and efficient. The two-day plan takes advantage of early morning, when lines are short and the park hasn't filled with guests. This plan works well year-round and eliminates much of the extra walking required by the one-day plans. No matter when the park closes, our two-day plan guarantees the most efficient touring and the least time in lines. The plan is perfect for guests who wish to sample both the attractions and the atmosphere of the Magic Kingdom.

If you have only one day to visit but you wish to see as much as possible, then use the One-Day Touring Plan for Adults. It's exhausting, but it packs in the maximum. If you prefer a more relaxed visit, use the Authors' Selective One-Day Touring Plan. It includes the best the park has to offer (in the authors' opinion), eliminating the less-impressive attractions.

If you have children younger than age 8, adopt the One-Day Touring Plan for Parents with Small Children. It's a compromise, blending the preferences of younger children with those of older siblings and adults. The plan includes many children's rides in Fantasyland but omits roller-coaster rides and other attractions that frighten young children or are off-limits because of height requirements. Or use the One-Day Touring Plan for Adults or the Authors' Selective One-Day Touring Plan for Adults, and take advantage of switching off, a technique whereby children accompany adults to the loading area of a ride with age and height requirements but don't board (see page 334).

unofficial **TIP**
Switching off allows adults to enjoy the more adventuresome attractions while keeping the group together.

The Dumbo-or-Die-in-a-Day Touring Plan for Parents with Small Children is designed for parents who will withhold no sacrifice for their kids. On the Dumbo-or-Die Plan, adults generally stand around, sweat, wipe noses, pay for stuff, and watch the children enjoy themselves. It's great!

"Not a Touring Plan" Touring Plans

For the type-B reader, these touring plans (see page 816) avoid detailed step-by-step strategies for saving every last minute in line. To paraphrase one of our favorite movies, they're more guidelines than actual rules. Use these to avoid the longest waits in line while having maximum flexibility to see whatever interests you in a particular part of the park.

For the Magic Kingdom, these "not" touring plans include advice for adults and parents with one day in the park, for anyone with two days, and for anyone with an afternoon and a full day to tour.

Two-Day Touring Plan for Families with Small Children

If you have young children and are looking for a two-day itinerary, combine the Magic Kingdom One-Day Touring Plan for Parents with Small Children with the second day of the Magic Kingdom Two-Day Touring Plan.

Two-Day Touring Plan for Early-Morning Touring on Day One and Afternoon–Evening Touring on Day Two

Many of you enjoy an early start at the Magic Kingdom on one day, followed by a second day with a lazy, sleep-in morning, resuming your touring in the afternoon and/or evening. If this appeals to you, use the Magic Kingdom One-Day Touring Plan for Adults or the Magic Kingdom One-Day Touring Plan for Parents with Small Children on your early day. Adhere to the touring plan for as long as it feels comfortable (many folks leave after the afternoon parade). On the second day, pick up where you left off. If you intend to use Fastpass on your second day, try to arrive at the park by 1 p.m. or the Fastpasses may be gone. Customize the remaining part of the touring plan to incorporate parades, fireworks, and other live performances according to your preferences.

MAGIC KINGDOM TOURING PLAN COMPANION

WE'VE CONSOLIDATED A GREAT DEAL OF INFORMATION about the Magic Kingdom in the Magic Kingdom Touring Plan Companion, at the back of the guide just after the various touring plans. Like the plans, the companions are designed to clip out and take with you to the park. The Magic Kingdom Touring Plan Companion includes the best days to go, the best times to visit each attraction, the authors' rating, height requirements, small-child fright potential, and info on dining and cool places to take a break.

THE SINGLE-DAY TOURING CONUNDRUM

TOURING THE MAGIC KINGDOM IN A DAY is complicated by the fact that the premier attractions are at almost opposite ends of the park: Splash Mountain and Big Thunder Mountain Railroad in Frontierland, Space Mountain and Buzz Lightyear in Tomorrowland, and Under the Sea: Journey of the Little Mermaid in the top center. It's virtually impossible to ride all five without encountering lines at one or another. If you ride Space Mountain and see Buzz Lightyear immediately after the park opens, for example, you won't have much of a wait, if any. By the time you leave Tomorrowland and hurry to Frontierland, however, the line for Splash Mountain will be substantial. The same situation prevails if you ride the Frontierland duo first: Splash Mountain and Big Thunder Mountain Railroad, no problem; Space Mountain and Buzz Lightyear, however, have fair-sized lines. From 10 minutes after opening until just before closing, lines are long at these headliners.

The best way to ride all five without long waits is to tour the Magic Kingdom over two mornings: Ride Space Mountain first thing one morning, then ride Buzz Lightyear; then ride Under the Sea, Splash Mountain, and Big Thunder Mountain first thing on the other. If you have only one day, be present at opening time. Speed immediately to Space Mountain, then take in Buzz Lightyear. After Buzz Lightyear, rush to Frontierland and scope out the situation at Splash Mountain. If the posted wait time is 30 minutes or less, go ahead and hop in line. If the wait exceeds 30 minutes, get a Fastpass for Splash Mountain, then ride Big Thunder Mountain Railroad. Save Under the Sea for last.

PRELIMINARY INSTRUCTIONS FOR ALL MAGIC KINGDOM TOURING PLANS

ON DAYS OF MODERATE-TO-HEAVY ATTENDANCE, follow your chosen touring plan exactly, deviating only:

1. When you're not interested in an attraction it lists. For example, the plan may tell you to go to Tomorrowland and ride Space Mountain. If you don't enjoy roller coasters, skip this step and proceed to the next.

2. When you encounter a very long line at an attraction the touring plan calls for. Crowds ebb and flow at the park, and an unusually long line may have gathered at an attraction to which you're directed. For example, you arrive at The Haunted Mansion and find extremely long lines. It's possible that this is a temporary situation caused by several hundred people arriving en masse from a recently concluded performance of *The Hall of Presidents* nearby. If this is the case, skip The Haunted Mansion and go to the next step, returning later to retry.

PARK-OPENING PROCEDURES

YOUR SUCCESS DURING your first hour of touring will be affected somewhat by the opening procedure Disney uses that day:

1. All guests are held at the turnstiles until the entire park opens (which may or may not be at the official opening time). If this happens on the day you visit, blow past Main Street and head for the first attraction on the touring plan you're following.

2. Guests are admitted to Main Street a half-hour to an hour before the remaining lands open. Access to other lands will be blocked by a rope barrier at the central-hub end of Main Street. Once admitted, stake out a position at the rope barrier as follows:

   If you're going to Frontierland first (Splash Mountain and Big Thunder Mountain Railroad), stand in front of The Crystal Palace restaurant, on the left at the central-hub end of Main Street. Wait next to the rope barrier blocking the walkway to Adventureland. When the rope is dropped, move quickly to Frontierland by way of Adventureland. This is also the place to line up if your first stop is Adventureland.

   If you're going to Buzz Lightyear and Space Mountain first, wait at the entrance of the bridge to Tomorrowland. When the rope drops, walk quickly across into Tomorrowland.

   If you're going to Fantasyland or Liberty Square first, go to the end of Main Street and line up left of center at the rope.

BEFORE YOU GO

1. Call ☎ 407-824-4321 the day before you go to check official opening time.

2. Purchase admission before you arrive.

3. Get familiar with park-opening procedures (see previous section) and reread the plan you've chosen so you know what you're likely to encounter.

MAGIC KINGDOM ONE-DAY TOURING PLAN
FOR ADULTS *(page 818)*

FOR Adults without young children.

ASSUMES Willingness to experience all major rides (including roller coasters) and shows.

This plan requires a lot of walking and some backtracking to avoid lines. Extra walking and morning hustling will spare you 4 or more hours of standing in line. How far you get depends on how quickly you move from ride to ride, how many times you rest or eat, how quickly the park fills, and what time the park closes.

MAGIC KINGDOM AUTHORS' SELECTIVE ONE-DAY TOURING PLAN FOR ADULTS *(page 819)*

FOR Adults touring without young children.

ASSUMES Willingness to experience all major rides (including roller coasters) and shows.

This plan includes only the attractions we think are best. It requires a lot of walking and some backtracking to avoid lines. How far you get depends on how quickly you move from ride to ride, how many times you rest or eat, how quickly the park fills, and what time the park closes.

MAGIC KINGDOM ONE-DAY TOURING PLAN FOR PARENTS WITH SMALL CHILDREN *(page 820)*

FOR Parents with children younger than age 8.

ASSUMES Periodic stops for rest, restrooms, and refreshments.

This plan represents a compromise between the observed tastes of adults and those of younger children. Included are many amusement-park rides that children may have the opportunity to experience at fairs and amusement parks back home. Although these rides are included in the plan, omit them if possible. These cycle-loading rides often have long lines, consuming valuable touring time:

Dumbo the Flying Elephant	Mad Tea Party
The Magic Carpets of Aladdin	Prince Charming Regal Carrousel

This time could be better spent experiencing the many attractions that better demonstrate the Disney creative genius and are found only in the Magic Kingdom. Try instead either of the one-day plans for adults and take advantage of switching off (see page 334). This allows parents and young children to enter the ride together; at the boarding area, one parent watches the children while the other rides. Families using this plan should review Magic Kingdom attractions in our Small-Child Fright-Potential Chart in Part Six (see pages 324–328).

We recommend taking a break and returning to your hotel for a swim and a nap (even if you're not staying in the World). You won't see as much, but everyone will be more relaxed and happy.

This touring plan requires a lot of walking and some backtracking to avoid long lines. A little extra walking and some morning hustle will spare you 2–3 hours of standing in line. You probably won't complete the tour. How far you get depends on how quickly you move from ride to ride, how many times you rest or eat, how quickly the park fills, and what time the park closes.

To Convert This One-Day Touring Plan into a Two-Day Touring Plan

Follow Steps 1–12 on Day One. Begin Day Two by riding Buzz Lightyear. Skip steps 15–17, then follow steps 18–21. Save Step 12 for after lunch, and end the day with fireworks. Day One works great when morning Extra Magic Hours are offered at the Magic Kingdom.

MAGIC KINGDOM TWO-DAY TOURING PLAN
(pages 821 and 822)

FOR Those wishing to spread their Magic Kingdom visit over two days.

ASSUMES Willingness to experience all major rides (including roller coasters) and shows.

This two-day touring plan takes advantage of early-morning touring. Each day, you should complete the structured part of the plan by about 4 p.m. This leaves plenty of time for live entertainment. If the park is open late (after 8 p.m.), consider returning to your hotel at midday for a swim and a nap. Eat an early dinner outside Walt Disney World, and return refreshed to enjoy the park's nighttime festivities.

MAGIC KINGDOM DUMBO-OR-DIE-IN-A-DAY TOUR-ING PLAN FOR PARENTS WITH SMALL CHILDREN
(page 823)

FOR Adults compelled to devote every waking moment to the pleasure and entertainment of their young children, or rich people who are paying someone else to take their children to the theme park.

PREREQUISITE This plan is designed for days when the Magic Kingdom doesn't close until 9 p.m. or later.

ASSUMES Frequent stops for rest, restrooms, and refreshments.

Note: Name aside, this plan is no joke. Whether you're loving, guilty, masochistic, selfless, or insane, this itinerary will provide a youngster with about as perfect a day as is possible at the Magic Kingdom. Families using this plan should review Magic Kingdom attractions in our Small-Child Fright-Potential Chart in Part Six (see pages 324–328).

unofficial **TIP**
Before entering the park, decide whether you'll return to your hotel for a midday rest.

This plan is a concession to adults determined to give their young children the ultimate Magic Kingdom experience. If you left the kids with a sitter yesterday or wouldn't let little Marvin eat frosting for breakfast, the plan will expiate your guilt.

To Convert This One-Day Touring Plan into a Two-Day Touring Plan

Follow Steps 1–10 on Day One. Begin Day Two with Steps 11–13 and 15, then follow Steps 20, 19, 18, 17, and 14. Eat lunch, then follow steps 21 and 22. Day One works great when morning Extra Magic Hours are offered at the Magic Kingdom.

PART TWELVE

EPCOT

EDUCATION, INSPIRATION, AND CORPORATE IMAGERY are the focus at Epcot, the most adult of the Disney theme parks. What it gains in taking a futuristic, visionary, and technological look at the world, it loses just a bit in warmth, happiness, and charm.

Some people find the attempts at education to be superficial, while others want more entertainment and less education. Most visitors, however, are in between, finding plenty of entertainment *and* education.

Epcot is more than twice as big as the Magic Kingdom or Disney's Hollywood Studios and, though smaller than Disney's Animal Kingdom, has more territory to be covered on foot. Epcot rarely sees the congestion so common in the Magic Kingdom, but it has lines every bit as long as those at the Jungle Cruise or Space Mountain.

unofficial **TIP**
Visitors must be prepared to do considerable walking between attractions and a comparable amount of standing in line.

Epcot's size means you can't see it all in one day without skipping an attraction or two and giving others a cursory glance. A major difference between Epcot and the other parks, however, is that some Epcot attractions can be savored slowly or skimmed, depending on personal interests. For example, the first section of General Motors' Test Track is a thrill ride, the second a collection of walk-through exhibits. Nearly all visitors take the ride, but many people, lacking time or interest, bypass the exhibits.

We rate several Epcot attractions as not to be missed. But part of the enjoyment of the park is that there's something for everyone.

THE EPCOT ACRONYM

IN THE BEGINNING, Epcot was EPCOT. When envisioned by Walt Disney as a utopian working city of the future, EPCOT was the acronym for *E*xperimental *P*rototype *C*ommunity *o*f *T*omorrow. Corporate Disney ultimately altered Walt's vision, and the city became a theme park, but the name remained. And because EPCOT was clearly nothing of the sort, the acronym EPCOT became the name *Epcot*.

OPERATING HOURS

EPCOT HAS TWO THEMED AREAS: **Future World** and **World Showcase**. Each has its own operating hours. Though schedules change throughout the year, Future World always opens before World Showcase in the morning. While most of Future World's attractions stay open until the entire park closes, a few close around 7 p.m. most of the year. World Showcase generally opens 2 hours later than Future World; moreover, some attractions open late or close early.

For park hours during your visit, call ☎ 407-824-4321. For the operating schedules of specific attractions, check the park handout map or the supplemental *Times Guide,* available free throughout the park.

DINING IN EPCOT

COUNTER-SERVICE RESTAURANTS in Epcot are profiled in Part Ten, starting on page 450. For full-service profiles, see the section starting on page 457.

ARRIVING

IF YOU'RE A GUEST AT ONE OF THE EPCOT RESORTS, it will take you about 20–30 minutes to walk from your hotel to the International Gateway (back entrance of Epcot) and from there to the Future World section of the park. Instead of walking, you can catch a boat from your Epcot resort hotel to the International Gateway and then walk about 8 minutes to the Future World section. To reach the front (Future World) entrance of Epcot from the Epcot resorts, either take a boat from your hotel to Disney's Hollywood Studios and transfer to an Epcot bus, take a bus to Downtown Disney and transfer to an Epcot bus, or, best of all, take a cab.

If you're wondering what all the fuss is about, this reader offers a succinct explanation:

Epcot touring plans don't work well if you stay at an Epcot resort. People from the Epcot resorts enter the park at the International Gateway, far away from Test Track [in Future World]. We were first in the park from the International Gateway, but when we got to Test Track the line was already 95 minutes long.

*uno*fficial **TIP**
Plan to arrive at the turnstiles 30–40 minutes before official opening time. Give yourself an extra 10 minutes or so to park and make your way to the entrance.

Arriving at the park by private automobile is easy and direct. Epcot has its own parking lot and, unlike at the Magic Kingdom, there's no need to take a monorail or ferry to reach the entrance. Trams service the parking lot, or you can walk to the front gate. Monorail service connects Epcot with the Transportation and Ticket Center, the Magic Kingdom (transfer required), and Magic Kingdom resorts (transfer required).

For unknown reasons, getting through entrance security at Epcot is more cumbersome and time-consuming than at the other parks. In fact, it's a royal pain, as this unidentified reader relates:

My biggest complaint was the amount of time it took to actually get into Epcot: 35 minutes at 10:30 a.m. to get bags checked (park had

Continued on page 554

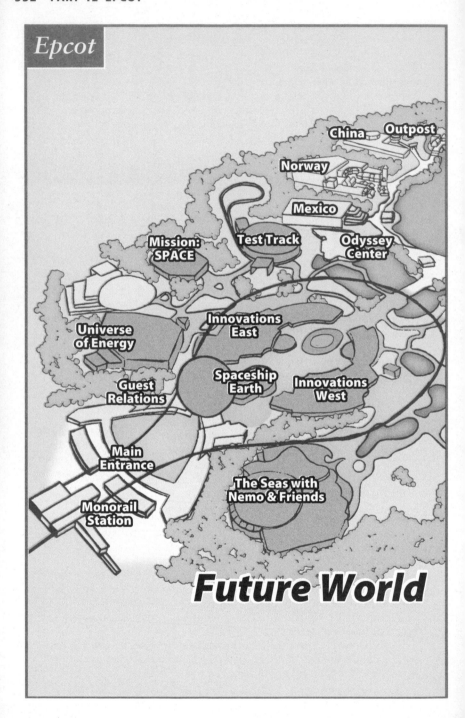

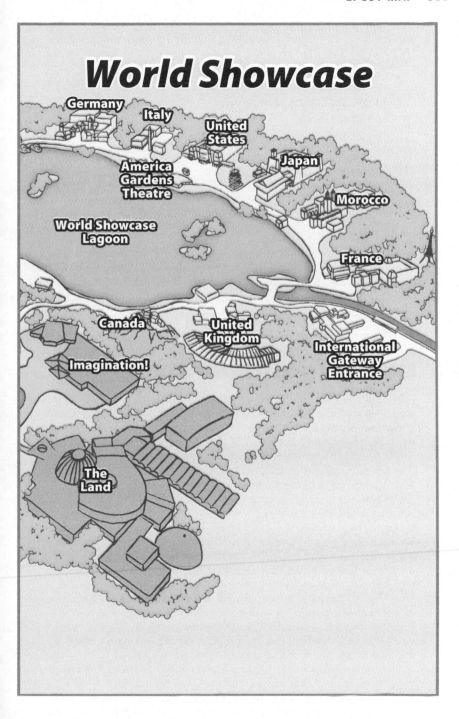

World Showcase

Germany

Italy

United States

Japan

America Gardens Theatre

Morocco

World Showcase Lagoon

France

Canada

United Kingdom

International Gateway Entrance

Imagination!

The Land

NOT TO BE MISSED AT EPCOT		
FUTURE WORLD		
• *Captain EO*	• The Seas Main Tank and Exhibits	• Test Track
• Living with the Land	• Soarin'	
• Mission: SPACE	• Spaceship Earth	
WORLD SHOWCASE		
• *The American Adventure*	• *IllumiNations*	• *Impressions de France*

Continued from page 551

opened at 9) and another 10 minutes to get in. It took nowhere near as long at the other parks, even with the same crowd size.

A Florida mother of a 3-year-old agrees:

Lines were crazy first thing in the morning. Some cast members just glanced in a bag, and others opened every zipper and looked in every crevice of our bags and stroller. One time we got an overzealous employee whose line took 15 minutes—the longest line of the day.

Take these delays into consideration if you're using one of the Epcot touring plans.

GETTING ORIENTED

EPCOT'S THEMED AREAS are distinctly different: **Future World** examines where mankind has come from and where it's going; **World Showcase** features the landmarks, cuisine, and culture of almost a dozen nations and is meant to be a sort of permanent World's Fair.

Navigating Epcot is unlike getting around at the Magic Kingdom. The Magic Kingdom is designed so that nearly every location is part of a specific environment—Liberty Square or Main Street, U.S.A., for example. All environments are visually separated to preserve the integrity of the theme.

Epcot, by contrast, is visually open. And while it seems strange to see a Japanese pagoda and the Eiffel Tower on the same horizon, getting around is fairly simple. An exception is Future World, where the enormous Innoventions East and West buildings hide everything on their opposite sides.

At Epcot, the architectural symbol is **Spaceship Earth.** This shiny, 180-foot geodesic sphere is visible from almost everywhere in the park. Like Cinderella Castle at the Magic Kingdom, Spaceship Earth can help you keep track of where you are in Epcot. But it's in a high-traffic area and isn't centrally located, so it isn't a good meeting place.

Any of the distinctive national pavilions in World Showcase make a good meeting place, but be specific. "Hey, let's meet in Japan!" sounds fun, but each pavilion is a mini-town with buildings, monuments, gardens, and plazas. You could wander quite a while "in Japan" without finding your group. Pick a specific place in Japan—the sidewalk side of the pagoda, for example.

FUTURE WORLD

GLEAMING FUTURISTIC STRUCTURES of immense proportions define the first themed area beyond the main entrance. Broad thoroughfares are punctuated with billowing fountains—all reflected in shiny space-age facades. Everything, including landscaping, is sparkling clean and seems bigger than life. Front and center is **Spaceship Earth,** flanked by **Innoventions East and West,** while pavilions dedicated to mankind's past, present, and future technological accomplishments ring the perimeter of Future World.

Guest Relations

GUEST RELATIONS, left of the geodesic sphere, is Epcot's equivalent of the Magic Kingdom's City Hall. It serves as park headquarters and as Epcot's primary information center. If you wish to eat in one of Epcot's sit-down restaurants and have not made a reservation by calling ☎ 407-WDW-DINE (939-3463), you can make a reservation at Guest Relations or at any other sit-down restaurant in any of the parks. If you're near one of these locations, in-person is often faster than calling.

Spaceship Earth ★★★★

APPEAL BY AGE	PRESCHOOL ★★★★	GRADE SCHOOL ★★★★	TEENS ★★★★
YOUNG ADULTS ★★★★	OVER 30 ★★★★		SENIORS ★★★★½

What it is Educational dark ride through past, present, and future. **Scope and scale** Headliner. **When to go** Before 10 a.m. or after 4 p.m. **Special comments** If lines are long when you arrive, try again after 4 p.m. **Authors' rating** One of Epcot's best; not to be missed; ★★★★. **Duration of ride** About 16 minutes. **Average wait in line per 100 people ahead of you** 3 minutes. **Loading speed** Fast.

DESCRIPTION AND COMMENTS This ride spirals through the 18-story interior of Epcot's premier landmark, taking visitors past animatronic scenes depicting mankind's developments in communications, from cave painting to printing to television to space communications and computer networks. The ride shows an amazing use of the geodesic sphere's interior.

Spaceship Earth's scenes are periodically redone to keep things fresh. The most recent include a 1970s-era computer room and a home garage showing what looks suspiciously like the invention of the Apple personal computer (perhaps a homage to Steve Jobs, who before his death was Disney's largest individual shareholder). Interactive video screens on the ride vehicles allow you to customize the ride's ending animated video. A post-show area with games and interactive exhibits rounds out the attraction.

Apart from going deaf, a family of five from Columbus, Ohio, wrote approvingly of Spaceship Earth's makeover:

We loved the [updated] Spaceship Earth—the kids thought it was hilarious at the end with the new interactive video screen. I did think the volume was too high, however. I felt like the voice was screaming in my ear the whole ride.

TOURING TIPS Because it's near Epcot's main entrance, Spaceship Earth is inundated with arriving guests throughout the morning. If you're interested in riding Test Track, postpone Spaceship Earth until, say, after 4 p.m. Spaceship Earth loads continuously and quickly. If the line runs only along the right side of the sphere, you'll board in less than 15 minutes.

Future World Services

EPCOT'S SERVICE FACILITIES in Future World include the following:

Baby Care Center	On the World Showcase side of the Odyssey Center
Banking Services	ATMs outside the main entrance, on the Future World bridge, and in World Showcase at the Germany Pavilion
Dining Reservations	At Guest Relations, to the left of Spaceship Earth
First Aid	Next to the Baby Care Center on the World Showcase side of the Odyssey Center
Live Entertainment Information	At Guest Relations
Lost and Found	At the main entrance at the gift shop
Lost Persons	At Guest Relations and the Baby Care Center on the World Showcase side of the Odyssey Center
Walt Disney World and Local Attraction Information	At Guest Relations
Wheelchair, ECV, and Stroller Rentals	Inside the main entrance and to the left, toward the rear of the Entrance Plaza

Most Epcot services are concentrated in Future World's Entrance Plaza, near the main gate

Innoventions East and West ★★★½

APPEAL BY AGE	PRESCHOOL ★★★½	GRADE SCHOOL ★★★★	TEENS ★★★½
YOUNG ADULTS ★★★		OVER 30 ★★★	SENIORS ★★★

What it is Static and hands-on exhibits relating to products and technologies of the near future. **Scope and scale** Major diversion. **When to go** On your second day at Epcot or after you've seen all the major attractions. **Special comments** Most exhibits demand time and participation to be rewarding—there's not much gained here by a quick walk-through. **Authors' rating** Something for everyone; ★★★½.

DESCRIPTION AND COMMENTS Innoventions—a huge, busy collection of hands-on walk-through exhibits sponsored by corporations—consists of two huge, crescent-shaped, glass-walled structures separated by a central plaza. Dynamic, interactive, and forward-looking, the area resembles a high-tech trade show. Electronics and entertainment technology exhibits play a prominent role, as do ecology and "how things work" displays.

Each major exhibit is sponsored by a different manufacturer or research lab, and most emphasize the effect of the product(s) or technology on daily living. Exhibits change periodically, and there's a definite trend toward larger, more elaborate affairs—almost mini-attractions. The newer exhibits are more compelling, but they require waiting in line to be admitted. For example, a current exhibit on saving for retirement includes a short game show–type activity complete with a computerized piggy bank you carry around. Other hands-on interactive exhibits cover recycling and protecting your home from severe weather.

Our favorite attraction is Raytheon's **Sum of All Thrills,** a roller-coaster simulator in which you design the coaster track on a computer, then climb aboard a giant robotic arm to experience your creation. We're so impressed, we've given it its own attraction review and added a step devoted to it in our Epcot touring plans.

A father of three from Tulsa, Oklahoma, liked Innoventions:

The best things at Epcot for my kids were the hands-on exhibits at Innoven-
tions. We bumped into the computer games there as we were passing
through en route to something else (I don't remember what, because we
never got there).

TOURING TIPS Spend time at Innoventions on your second day at Epcot.
If you have only one day, visit late if you have the time and endurance.
(The one exception to this is Sum of All Thrills, which you should visit
in the morning after Soarin', Test Track, and Mission: SPACE.)

Although many of these productions are worthwhile, the quest capacity of each theater is so small that long lines form. A couple of exhibits,
such as Where's the Fire?—an interactive program about fire safety—are
worth 15 minutes of waiting in line, but they're the exception. We suggest skipping exhibits with waits of more than 10 minutes or experiencing them first thing in the morning on your second day, when there are
no lines.

CLUB COOL

DESCRIPTION AND COMMENTS Attached to the fountain side of Innoventions West is a retail space–soda fountain called Club Cool. It doesn't
look like much, but inside, this Coca-Cola–sponsored exhibit provides
free unlimited samples of soft drinks from around the world. Some of
the selections will taste like medicine to an American, but others will
please. Because it's centrally located in Future World, it makes a good
meeting or break place, and you can slake your thirst while you wait
for the rest of your party.

Sum of All Thrills ★★★★

APPEAL BY AGE	PRESCHOOL ★★★	GRADE SCHOOL ★★★★	TEENS ★★★★
YOUNG ADULTS ★★★★		OVER 30 ★★★★	SENIORS ★★★

What it is Combination hands-on exhibit and ride simulator. **Scope and scale** Minor
attraction. **When to go** Before 11 a.m. or after 6 p.m. **Special comments** 48" minimum
height requirement, 54" for track designs with inversions. **Authors' rating** Way cool;
★★★★. **Duration of attraction** 15 minutes. **Average wait in line per 100 people
ahead of you** 40 minutes; assumes all simulators operating. **Loading speed** Slow.

DISNEY DISH WITH JIM HILL

A FAREWELL TO ARMS The Kuka arms that drive Sum of
All Thrills are incredibly cool, but this attraction isn't the
one the Imagineers originally had in mind for this technology. They had an *Incredibles*-themed headliner mapped
out, featuring a battle with the menacing Omnidroids
from the 2004 Disney/Pixar film. But then Kuka cut a deal
with Universal Studios to use its robotics wizardry to
power another film-based blockbuster: Harry Potter and the Forbidden
Journey at Islands of Adventure (see page 687).

DESCRIPTION AND COMMENTS Sum of All Thrills is a design-your-own-
roller-coaster simulator in which you use a computer program to specify the drops, curves, and loops of a coaster track before boarding an
industrial robotic arm to experience your creation. Three vehicle options
are available: bobsled, roller coaster, and jet aircraft. It's possible to

program actual loops into both the coaster and jet courses, and the robot arm will swing you upside down.

In addition to the vehicle, you also select the kinds of turns, loops, and hills in your track design. Choices range from mild, broad curves to extreme multiple-loop inversions. Using computer-design tools, you can further customize these components by changing the height and width of each piece as you go. This customization makes it easy to ride Sum of All Thrills many times without experiencing the same track twice. It's a great addition to Epcot.

TOURING TIPS Not a high-capacity attraction, but also not on most guests' radar. Ride as early in the morning as possible.

Universe of Energy: *Ellen's Energy Adventure* ★★★★

APPEAL BY AGE	PRESCHOOL ★★★	GRADE SCHOOL ★★★½	TEENS ★★★
YOUNG ADULTS ★★★	OVER 30 ★★★½		SENIORS ★★★½

What it is Combination ride–theater presentation about energy. **Scope and scale** Major attraction. **When to go** Before 11:15 a.m. or after 4:30 p.m. **Special comments** Don't be dismayed by long lines; 580 people enter the pavilion each time the theater changes audiences. **Authors' rating** The most distinctive theater in Walt Disney World; ★★★★. **Duration of presentation** About 26½ minutes. **Preshow entertainment** 8 minutes. **Probable waiting time** 20–40 minutes.

DESCRIPTION AND COMMENTS Audio-Animatronic dinosaurs and the unique traveling theater make this pavilion one of Future World's most popular. Because this is a theater with a ride component, the line doesn't move while the show is in progress. When the theater empties, however, a large chunk of the line will disappear as people are admitted for the next show. Visitors are seated in what appears to be an ordinary theater while they watch a film about energy sources. Then the theater seats divide into six 97-passenger traveling cars that glide among the swamps and reptiles of a prehistoric forest. Special effects include the feel of warm, moist air from the swamp and the smell of sulphur from an erupting volcano.

The accompanying film is a humorous and upbeat flick starring Ellen DeGeneres and Bill Nye that sugarcoats the somewhat ponderous discussion of energy. For kids, Universe of Energy remains a toss-up. The dinosaurs frighten some preschoolers, and kids of all ages lose the thread during the educational segments.

TOURING TIPS This attraction draws large crowds beginning early in the morning. Because Universe of Energy can operate more than one show at a time, lines are generally tolerable.

Mission: SPACE *(Fastpass)* ★★★★

APPEAL BY AGE	PRESCHOOL ★★★	GRADE SCHOOL ★★★★	TEENS ★★★★½
YOUNG ADULTS ★★★★	OVER 30 ★★★★		SENIORS ★★★

Motion Sickness

What it is Space-flight-simulator ride. **Scope and scale** Super-headliner. **When to go** First hour the park is open, or use Fastpass. **Special comments** Not recommended for pregnant women or people prone to motion sickness or claustrophobia; 44" minimum height requirement; a gentler nonspinning version is also available. **Authors' rating** Impressive; not to be missed; ★★★★. **Duration of ride** About 5 minutes plus preshow. **Average wait in line per 100 people ahead of you** 4 minutes.

DESCRIPTION AND COMMENTS Mission: SPACE, among other things, is Disney's reply to all the cutting-edge attractions introduced over the past few years by crosstown rival Universal. The first truly groundbreaking Disney attraction since The Twilight Zone Tower of Terror, Mission: SPACE was one of the hottest tickets at Walt Disney World until two guests died after riding it in 2005 and 2006. While neither death was linked directly to the attraction, the negative publicity caused many guests to skip it entirely. In response, Disney added a tamer nonspinning version of Mission: SPACE in 2006.

Disney's lawyers probably clocked as much time as the ride engineers in designing the "lite" version. Even before you walk into the building, you're asked whether you want your ride with or without spin. Choose the spinning version and you're on the "orange" team; the "green" team trains on the no-spin side. Either way, you're immediately handed the appropriate "launch ticket" containing the first of myriad warnings about the attraction, as this *Unofficial Guide* reader discovered:

Since I hadn't done Mission: SPACE before, I chose the more intense version and was handed the orange launch ticket to read. Basically, it explained that if I had ever had a tonsillectomy, or even a mild case of pattern baldness, I should take the less intense ride.

We've had a good deal of reader mail about the no-spin version. The following comment is typical. A couple from Chicago had this to say:

For Mission: SPACE in Epcot, I tried convincing my husband to take the less intense version of the ride but he didn't think it was going to be that bad. Oh, but it was! I felt sick to my stomach after that ride.

Guests for both versions of the attraction enter the International Space Training Center, where they're introduced to the deep-space exploration program and then divided into groups for flight training. After orientation, they're strapped into space capsules for a simulated flight, where, of course, the unexpected happens. Each capsule accommodates a crew consisting of a group commander, pilot, navigator, and engineer, with a guest functioning in each role. The crew's skill and finesse (or, more often, lack thereof) in handling their respective responsibilities have no effect on the outcome of the flight. The capsules are small, and both ride versions are amazingly realistic. The nonspinning version doesn't subject your body to g-forces, but it does bounce and toss you around in a manner roughly comparable to other Disney motion simulators.

TOURING TIPS In minutes, Disney can reconfigure the ride's four centrifuges to either version of the attraction based on guest demand. In general, the kinder, gentler version has a wait time of about half that of its more harrowing counterpart.

Having experienced the industrial-strength version of Mission: SPACE under a variety of circumstances, we've always felt icky when riding it on an empty stomach, especially first thing in the morning. We came up with a number of potential explanations for this phenomenon, involving everything from low blood sugar and inner-ear disorders to some of us just not being astronaut material. Understandably disturbed by the latter possibility, we looked around for an expert opinion to explain what we were feeling. The number of organizations with experience studying the effects of high-g (high-gravity) forces on humans is limited to a select few: NASA, the Air Force, and Mad Tea Party cast members were the first to come to mind. As NASA is a codeveloper of Mission: SPACE, we called them. Amazingly, a spokesman told us that NASA no longer does much high-g training these days. And the agency was reluctant to pass along anything resembling medical advice to the general public.

Fortunately, a longtime friend put us in touch with a real NASA astronaut who was willing to share (anonymously) some ideas on what causes the nausea, as well as tips astronauts use to prevent it. Our astronaut guesses, as we do, that low blood sugar is the culprit behind the queasiness and suggests eating a normal meal 1–2 hours before experiencing the ride. Try to avoid milk and tomatoes beforehand; they're difficult to keep down and, as our contact noted with the voice of experience, particularly unpleasant if they make a return trip. A banana, we hear, is a good choice for your preflight meal. Also, we were told, one trick astronauts use to avoid nausea while in these simulators is to keep a piece of hard candy or a mint in their mouths; it's not clear, though, whether the candy helps keep blood-sugar levels high or is just a placebo. If all else fails, there are airsickness bags in each simulator.

Make a restroom stop before you get in line; you'll think your bladder has been to Mars and back for real before you get out of this attraction. Fastpass is generally needed only during times of peak attendance, and then only if you intend to ride during the middle of the day; mornings and dinnertimes should have shorter waits.

There's nothing our readers enjoy more than kibitzing about rides that can make you puke, and Mission: SPACE has vaulted to the top of this particular heap. First from a Yakima, Washington, reader:

Mission: SPACE is awesome, the best attraction yet. It didn't have nearly the wait Test Track had. We spoke to a number of people who didn't ride as they were intimidated by the number of Disney warning announcements regarding motion sickness.

From Wilton, Connecticut, this 12-year-old's mom had a somewhat different experience:

It was the worst motion sickness my mom ever had at a theme park—Mom had to use an airsick bag 20 minutes after leaving the ride, then had to return to the hotel to lie down. Warn future readers!!!

On a lighter note, a woman from Lisbon, Connecticut, used Mission: SPACE as her own personal relationship lab:

We now understand why husbands and wives will probably never go to space together after I (the "navigator") pushed his (the "pilot's") button during the flight. I couldn't help being a backseat driver. He wasn't pushing the button— we could have crashed!

TEST TRACK PAVILION

DESCRIPTION AND COMMENTS This pavilion, presented by General Motors, comprises the Test Track ride and Inside Track, a collection of transportation-themed stationary exhibits and multimedia presentations. The pavilion is the last on the left before crossing into the World Showcase. Many readers tell us that Test Track "is one big commercial" for General Motors. We agree that promotional hype is more heavy-handed here than in most other business-sponsored attractions. But Test Track is nonetheless one of the most creatively conceived and executed attractions in Walt Disney World.

Test Track *(Fastpass)* ★★★½

APPEAL BY AGE PRESCHOOL ★★★★   GRADE SCHOOL ★★★★½ TEENS ★★★★★
YOUNG ADULTS ★★★★½   OVER 30 ★★★★½   SENIORS ★★★★

What it is Automobile test-track simulator ride. **Scope and scale** Super-headliner.
When to go The first 30 minutes the park is open or just before closing, or use Fastpass. **Special comments** 40" minimum height requirement. **Authors' rating** Not to
be missed; ★★★½. **Duration of ride** About 4 minutes. **Average wait in line per
100 people ahead of you** 4½ minutes. **Loading speed** Moderate–fast.

DESCRIPTION AND COMMENTS Visitors test a future-model car at high
  speeds through hairpin turns, up and down steep hills, and over rough
  terrain. The six-guest vehicle is a motion simulator that rocks and pitches.
  Unlike the Star Tours simulator, however, the Test Track model is affixed
  to a track and actually travels. Though reader comments on Test Track
  have been mixed, most like it. From a Westford, Massachusetts, family:

  *Test Track was the favorite ride at WDW of all five members of our party. Even
  my mom (age 56), who has always refused to go on roller coasters, was
  coaxed onto Test Track and loved it. Five stars from one preschooler, three
  over-30s, and a senior citizen!*

  But a Monona, Wisconsin, couple were somewhat underwhelmed:

  *Based on the loud whoosh coming from the ride, the buildup in the preshow
  area, and your comments, we expected a much more intense experience.
  Compared to the Tower of Terror, Test Track is a Sunday drive in the park.*

TOURING TIPS Some great technology is at work here. Test Track is so complex, in fact, that keeping it running is a constant struggle. When it's
  working properly, it's one of the park's better attractions. But as a London, Ontario, mom reports, "working properly" seems to be a challenge:

  *Test Track breaks down more than any other ride I've ever seen. We went
  back there over and over again, got Fastpasses, got in line, and then had to
  get out. Fastpass lines would have a 40-minute wait because no one got to
  ride at the proper time. What's wrong with that ride?*

  A repeat visitor from East Aurora, New York, suggests that all is not
  lost when the ride breaks down:

  *If the ride breaks down or does not run normally (e.g., it goes very slowly
  around the lateral curves), tell a cast member at the end of your ride. They
  will most likely give you a slip that allows you to skip the line and ride again.
  This happened to us twice during the busiest time of the year, and we were
  able to ride again with no problem.*

  If you use Fastpass, be aware that the daily allocation of passes is often distributed by 4:30 p.m. If all the Fastpasses are gone, another time-
  saving technique is to join the singles line, a separate line for individuals
  who don't object to riding alone. The objective is to fill the odd spaces
  left by groups that don't fill up the ride vehicle. Because there are not
  many singles and most groups are unwilling to split up, singles lines are
  usually much shorter than the regular line.

IMAGINATION! PAVILION

DESCRIPTION AND COMMENTS Multiattraction pavilion on the west side
  of Innoventions West and down the walk from The Land. Outside is
  an "upside-down waterfall" and one of our favorite Future World

landmarks, the "jumping water," a fountain that hops over the heads of unsuspecting passersby.

TOURING TIPS We recommend late-morning touring. See individual attractions for specifics.

Honey, I Shrunk the Audience ★★★★½
Captain EO ★★★★

APPEAL BY AGE	PRESCHOOL ★★★★½	GRADE SCHOOL ★★★★	TEENS ★★★
YOUNG ADULTS ★★	OVER 30 ★★½		SENIORS ★★

(The Smithsonian hadn't sent back our archive request for EO's Appeal by Age ratings before we went to press.)

What they are 3-D films with special effects. **Scope and scale** Headliners. **When to go** Before noon or after 4 p.m. **Special comments** Adults shouldn't be put off by the sci-fi theme of either film (or rock music, for *Captain EO*). The high decibels and *Honey*'s tactile effects frighten some young children. **Authors' rating** *Honey:* An absolute hoot! ★★★★½. *EO:* ★★★★. Both presentations are not to be missed. **Duration of presentation** About 17 minutes. **Preshow entertainment** 8 minutes. **Probable waiting time** 15 minutes (at suggested times).

DISNEY DISH WITH JIM HILL

COULD *EO*'S EXIT SIGNAL DREAMFINDER'S RETURN? Though the Imagination! Pavilion's 3-D theater saw a brief rise in attendance following the return of *Captain EO* in July 2010, the crowds have definitely thinned at this point. Now the Imagineers are planning to shut down this Michael Jackson movie and do something that Disney theme park fans have been screaming for: Bring back Dreamfinder and Figment in an all-new 4-D production rumored to be inspired by Disneyland Paris's *CinéMagique*. When? As soon as Disney can find a corporate sponsor to underwrite the production costs. (No breath-holding, please.)

DESCRIPTION AND COMMENTS In response to Michael Jackson's death in 2009, Disney brought back his 3-D space-themed musical film presentation *Captain EO* for a "limited engagement" in its theme parks; at Epcot, that engagement is still ongoing, having supplanted *Honey, I Shrunk the Audience. Captain EO* originally ran here from 1986 to 1994; we don't know how long the current run will last, but we've heard Disney will yank the film as soon as its audience numbers begin to drop. Both films share exceptionally loud soundtracks and a propensity to frighten young kids.

HONEY, I SHRUNK THE AUDIENCE As a 3-D offshoot of Disney's feature film *Honey, I Shrunk the Kids,* this presentation features an array of special effects, including simulated explosions, smoke, fiber optics, lights, water spray, and moving seats. The attraction is played strictly for laughs—a commodity that's in short supply when it comes to Epcot entertainment.

CAPTAIN EO The ultimate music video. Starring the late Michael Jackson and directed by Francis Ford Coppola, this 3-D space fantasy is more than a film; it's a happening. Action on the screen is augmented by lasers, fiber optics, cannons, and a host of other special effects in the theater, as well as by some audience participation. There's not much of a story, but there's plenty of music and dancing performed by some of the most unlikely creatures ever to shake a tail feather.

TOURING TIPS Shows usually begin on the hour and half-hour. The sound level is earsplitting, frightening some young children. Many adults report that the loud soundtrack is distracting, even uncomfortable. While *Honey, I Shrunk the Audience* is a huge hit, it overwhelms some preschoolers. A dad from Lexington, South Carolina, writes:

Honey, I Shrunk the Audience is too intense for kids. Our 4-year-old took off his 3-D glasses 5 minutes into the movie. Because of this experience, he wouldn't wear glasses in the Muppet movie at Disney's Hollywood Studios.

A Tucson, Arizona, mom tells of a similar reaction:

Our 3- and 4-year-olds loved all the rides. They giggled through Thunder Mountain three times, squealed with delight on Splash Mountain, thought Space Mountain was the coolest, and begged to ride Star Tours over and over. They even "fought ghosts" at The Haunted Mansion. But Honey, I Shrunk the Audience dissolved them into sobbing, sniveling, shaking, terrified preschoolers.

Try to work either film into your touring before noon. The venue is to the left of Journey into Imagination (see below); you don't have to ride to enter the theater. Avoid seats in the first several rows; if you sit too close to the screen, the 3-D images don't focus properly.

Journey into Imagination with Figment   ★★½

APPEAL BY AGE	PRESCHOOL ★★★½	GRADE SCHOOL ★★★½	TEENS ★★★
YOUNG ADULTS ★★★	OVER 30 ★★★		SENIORS ★★★

What it is Dark fantasy-adventure ride. **Scope and scale** Major-attraction wannabe. **When to go** Anytime. **Authors' rating** ★★½. **Duration of ride** About 6 minutes. **Average wait in line per 100 people ahead of you** 2 minutes. **Loading speed** Fast.

DESCRIPTION AND COMMENTS This attraction replaced its dull and vacuous predecessor in the fall of 1999 and was retooled again in 2002 to add the ever-popular purple dragon Figment. Journey into Imagination takes you on a tour of the zany Imagination Institute. Sometimes you're a passive observer and sometimes you're a test subject as the ride provides a glimpse of the fictitious lab's inner workings. Stimulating all your senses and then some, it hits you with optical illusions, an experiment in which noise generates colors, a room that defies gravity, and other brain teasers. All along the way, Figment makes surprise appearances. After the ride, you can adjourn to an interactive exhibit area offering the latest in unique, hands-on imagery technology.

Reader responses to Figment and Company are pretty consistent. First, from a Brooklyn, New York, family:

Figment was just plain weird—talking about five senses, then only introducing three, then the dragon singing . . . huh?

And from a Franklin, Tennessee, family of three:

You should put a bold notation next to the Figment attraction stating it should be experienced only if you are a HUGE Figment fan. We didn't even know who Figment was, and we all hated this attraction. After the Figment disaster, I had to hide from my husband the fact that I was selecting the next attraction based on your touring plan. He was convinced after the plan sent us to Figment that all touring plans were a waste of time.

Pleasant rather than exciting, the ride falls short of the promise suggested by its name. Will you go to sleep? No. Will you find it amusing? Probably. Will you remember it tomorrow? Only Figment knows.

TOURING TIPS The standby wait for this attraction rarely exceeds 15 minutes. You can enjoy the interactive exhibit without taking the ride, so save it for later in the day.

THE LAND PAVILION

DESCRIPTION AND COMMENTS The Land is a huge themed area containing three attractions and several restaurants. When the pavilion was originally built, its emphasis was on farming, but it now focuses on the environment.

TOURING TIPS This is a good place to grab a fast-food lunch. If you're coming here to see the attractions, however, stay away during mealtimes.

The Circle of Life ★★★½

APPEAL BY AGE	PRESCHOOL ★★★	GRADE SCHOOL ★★★	TEENS ★★★
YOUNG ADULTS ★★★		OVER 30 ★★★	SENIORS ★★★

What it is Film exploring humans' relationship with their environment. **Scope and scale** Minor attraction. **When to go** Before 11 a.m. or after 2 p.m. **Authors' rating** Inspiring and enlightening; ★★★½. **Duration of presentation** About 20 minutes. **Preshow entertainment** Ecological slide show and trivia. **Probable waiting time** 10–15 minutes.

DESCRIPTION AND COMMENTS This playful yet educational film, starring Pumbaa, Simba, and Timon from Disney's animated feature *The Lion King*, spotlights the environmental interdependency of all creatures, demonstrating how easily the ecological balance can be upset. The message is sobering, but one that enlightens.

A reader e-mailed us this comment:

> The Circle of Life *is somewhat hypocritical. Simba berates Timon and Pumbaa because they don't understand the ecological impact of putting up a resort. Hello—am I missing something, or didn't Disney do just that?*

TOURING TIPS Every visitor should see this film. To stay ahead of the crowd, see it in late afternoon. Long lines usually occur at mealtimes.

Living with the Land *(Fastpass seasonally)* ★★★★

APPEAL BY AGE	PRESCHOOL ★★★½	GRADE SCHOOL ★★★½	TEENS ★★★½
YOUNG ADULTS ★★★★		OVER 30 ★★★★	SENIORS ★★★★

What it is Indoor boat-ride adventure chronicling the past, present, and future of farming and agriculture in the United States. **Scope and scale** Major attraction. **When to go** Before 10:30 a.m. or after 5 p.m., or use Fastpass if available. **Special comments** Go early in the morning and save other Land attractions (except for Soarin') for later in the day. The ride is on the pavilion's lower level. **Authors' rating** Informative without being dull; not to be missed; ★★★★. **Duration of ride** About 14 minutes. **Average wait in line per 100 people ahead of you** 3 minutes; assumes 15 boats operating. **Loading speed** Moderate.

DESCRIPTION AND COMMENTS The boat ride takes visitors through swamps, past inhospitable farm environments, and through a futuristic greenhouse where real crops such as giant pumpkins are grown using the latest agricultural technologies.

Many Epcot guests who read about Living with the Land in guidebooks decide it sounds too dry and educational for their tastes. A woman from Houston writes:

I had a bad attitude about Living with the Land, as I heard it was an agricultural exhibit. I just didn't think I was up for a movie about wheat farming. Wow, was I surprised.

TOURING TIPS See this attraction before the lunch crowd hits The Land's restaurants, or use Fastpass if it's available. If you have a special interest in the agricultural techniques being demonstrated, take the **Behind the Seeds at Epcot** tour (see page 704).

Soarin' *(Fastpass)* ★★★★½

APPEAL BY AGE PRESCHOOL ★★★ GRADE SCHOOL ★★★★★ TEENS ★★★★★
YOUNG ADULTS ★★★★★ OVER 30 ★★★★★ SENIORS ★★★★★

What it is Flight-simulator ride. **Scope and scale** Super-headliner. **When to go** First 30 minutes the park is open, or use Fastpass. **Special comments** Entrance on the lower level of the Land Pavilion. May induce motion sickness; 40" minimum height requirement. Switching-off option provided (see page 334). **Authors' rating** Exciting and mellow at the same time; not to be missed; ★★★★½. **Duration of ride** 5½ minutes. **Average wait in line per 100 people ahead of you** 4 minutes; assumes 2 concourses operating. **Loading speed** Moderate.

DISNEY DISH WITH JIM HILL

SOARIN' OVER . . . SHANGHAI For a while now, the Imagineers have been rumored to be working on a new ride film for Soarin', the original of which debuted at Disney California Adventure in 2001. As it turns out, the rumors are true—but the film is slated to premiere at Shanghai Disneyland when it opens in December 2015. What's more, the film will be China-specific, built around IMAX HD footage captured during low-level flyovers of such landmarks as the Great Wall, the Forbidden City, and the Three Gorges Dam. As for a stateside Soarin' movie, word around WDI is to look for it in 2016.

Motion Sickness

DESCRIPTION AND COMMENTS Soarin' is a thrill ride for all ages, as exhilarating as a hawk on the wing and as mellow as swinging in a hammock. If you've ever experienced flying dreams, you'll have a sense of how Soarin' feels.

Once you enter the main theater, you're secured in a seat not unlike those on inverted roller coasters. When everyone is in place, the rows of seats swing into position, making you feel as if the floor has dropped away, and you're suspended with your legs dangling. Thus hung out to dry, you embark on a simulated hang-glider tour with IMAX-quality images projected all around you and with the flight simulator moving in sync with the movie. The images are well chosen and drop-dead beautiful. Special effects include wind, sound, and even smell. The ride itself is thrilling but perfectly smooth. We think Soarin' is a must-experience for guests of any age who meet the height requirement. And yes, we've interviewed senior citizens who tried it and were crazy about it.

But a North Carolina mom says, "Wait a minute!

Soarin' was VERY cool but definitely on the scary side for people afraid of heights or who don't like that "unsteady" feeling. While we were "soaring" up I was fine, but when we were going down I had to continually say to myself, "This is only an illusion, I cannot fall out, this is only an illusion. . . . "

TOURING TIPS Soarin's addition to the Epcot lineup takes some of the pressure off the park's other two big attractions. Keep in mind, however, that Test Track and Mission: SPACE serve up a little too much thrill for some guests. Soarin', conversely, is an almost platonic ride for any age. For that reason, it has climbed to the top of the hit parade. See it before 10:30 a.m., or use Fastpass; expect all passes to be gone after 2 p.m. on days of moderate attendance or as early as noon on busier days.

THE SEAS WITH NEMO & FRIENDS PAVILION

THIS AREA ENCOMPASSES one of America's top marine aquariums, a ride that tunnels through the aquarium, an interactive animated film, and a number of first-class educational walk-through exhibits. Altogether it's a stunning package, one we rate as not to be missed. A comprehensive makeover featuring characters from Disney/Pixar's animated feature *Finding Nemo* brought whimsy and much-needed levity to what theretofore was educationally brilliant but somewhat staid.

The Seas Main Tank and Exhibits ★★★½

APPEAL BY AGE	PRESCHOOL ★★★★	GRADE SCHOOL ★★★★	TEENS ★★★★
YOUNG ADULTS ★★★★		OVER 30 ★★★★	SENIORS ★★★★

What it is A huge saltwater aquarium, plus exhibits on oceanography, ocean ecology, and sea life. **Scope and scale** Major attraction. **When to go** Before 11:30 a.m. or after 5 p.m. **Authors' rating** An excellent marine exhibit; not to be missed; ★★★½. **Average wait in line per 100 people ahead of you** 3½ minutes. **Loading speed** Fast.

DESCRIPTION AND COMMENTS The Seas is among Future World's most ambitious offerings. Scientists and divers conduct actual marine experiments in a 200-foot-diameter, 27-foot-deep main tank containing fish, mammals, and crustaceans in a simulation of an ocean ecosystem. Visitors can watch the activity through 8-inch-thick windows below the surface (including some in the Coral Reef restaurant). On entering The Seas, you're directed to the loading area for The Seas with Nemo & Friends, an attraction that conveys you via a Plexiglas tunnel through The Seas' main tank. Following the ride, you disembark at Sea Base Alpha, where you can enjoy the attractions mentioned previously. (If the wait for the ride is too long, it's possible to head straight for the exhibits by going through the pavilion's exit, around back, and to the left of the main entrance.)

The Seas' fish population is substantial, but the strength of this attraction lies in the dozen or so exhibits offered after the ride. Visitors can view fish-breeding experiments, watch short films about sea life, and more. A delightful exhibit showcases clownfish (Nemo), regal blue tang (Dory), and other species featured in *Finding Nemo*. Other highlights include a haunting, hypnotic jellyfish tank; a sea horse aquarium; a stingray exhibit; and a manatee tank.

About two-thirds of the main aquarium is home to reef species, including sharks, rays, and a number of fish that you've seen in quiet repose on your dinner plate. The other third, separated by an inconspicuous divider, houses bottle-nosed dolphins and sea turtles. As you face the main aquarium, the most glare-free viewing windows for the dolphins are on the ground floor to the left by the escalators. For the reef species, it's the same floor on the right by the escalators. Stay as long as you wish.

TOURING TIPS With The Seas with Nemo & Friends and *Turtle Talk with Crush*, The Seas is one of Epcot's more popular venues. We recommend experiencing the ride and *Turtle Talk* in the morning before the park gets crowded, saving the excellent exhibits for later.

The Seas with Nemo & Friends ★★★

APPEAL BY AGE   PRESCHOOL ★★★★   GRADE SCHOOL ★★★★   TEENS ★★★
YOUNG ADULTS ★★★   OVER 30 ★★★½   SENIORS ★★★★

What it is Ride through a tunnel in The Seas' main tank. **Scope and scale** Major attraction. **When to go** Before 11 a.m. or after 5 p.m. **Authors' rating** ★★★. **Duration of ride** 4 minutes. **Average wait in line per 100 people ahead of you** 3½ minutes. **Loading speed** Fast.

DESCRIPTION AND COMMENTS The Seas with Nemo & Friends is a high-tech ride featuring characters from the animated hit *Finding Nemo*. The ride likewise deposits you at the heart of The Seas, where the exhibits, *Turtle Talk with Crush,* and viewing platforms for the main aquarium are.

Upon entering The Seas, you're given the option of experiencing the ride or proceeding directly to the exhibit area. If you choose the ride, you'll be ushered to its loading area, where you'll be made comfortable in a "clamobile" for your journey through the aquarium. The attraction features technology that makes it seem as if the animated characters are swimming with live fish. Very cool. Almost immediately you meet Mr. Ray and his class and learn that Nemo is missing. The remainder of the odyssey consists of finding Nemo with the help of Dory, Bruce, Marlin, Squirt, and Crush, all characters from the animated feature. Unlike the film, however, the ride ends with a musical finale.

A mom from Asheville, North Carolina, warns about underestimating the scare factor:

> You need to change the fear rating for The Seas with Nemo & Friends! It's scary—sharks, jellyfish, and anglerfish, along with growling, etc. My 8-year-old hated it!

TOURING TIPS The earlier you experience the ride, the better (ditto for *Turtle Talk with Crush*). If waits are intolerable, come back after 5 p.m. or so.

Turtle Talk with Crush ★★★★

APPEAL BY AGE   PRESCHOOL ★★★★½   GRADE SCHOOL ★★★★½   TEENS ★★★★
YOUNG ADULTS ★★★★   OVER 30 ★★★★   SENIORS ★★★★

What it is An interactive animated film. **Scope and scale** Minor attraction. **When to go** Before 11 a.m. or after 5 p.m. **Authors' rating** A real spirit-lifter; ★★★★. **Duration of presentation** 17 minutes. **Preshow entertainment** None. **Probable waiting time** 10–20 minutes before 11 a.m. and after 5 p.m.; as much as 40–60 minutes during the more crowded part of the day.

DESCRIPTION AND COMMENTS *Turtle Talk with Crush* is an interactive theater show starring the 153-year-old surfer-dude turtle from *Finding Nemo*. Although it starts like a typical Disney-theme-park movie, *Turtle Talk* quickly turns into a surprise interactive encounter as the on-screen Crush begins to have actual conversations with guests in the audience. Real-time computer graphics are used to accurately move Crush's mouth when forming words, and he's voiced by a guy who went to the *Fast Times at Ridgemont High* school of diction.

A mom from Henderson, Colorado, has a crush on Crush:

Turtle Talk with Crush is a must-see. Our 4-year-old was picked out of the crowd by Crush, and we were just amazed by the technology that allowed one-on-one conversation. It was adorable and enjoyed by everyone from Grammy and Papa to the 4-year-old!

TOURING TIPS The interactive technology behind *Turtle Talk* proved so successful in drawing crowds that a follow-up attraction, *Monsters, Inc. Laugh Floor,* debuted in the Magic Kingdom's Tomorrowland in 2007. *Turtle Talk* has also moved to a new, larger theater in an attempt to shorten waits, which sometimes exceeded an hour. Still, the attraction's capacity is relatively small, so you'll want to get here as early as you can to avoid long lines.

The "Mom, I Can't Believe It's Disney!" Fountain ★ ★ ★ ★

APPEAL BY AGE	PRESCHOOL ★ ★ ★ ★ ★	GRADE SCHOOL ★ ★ ★ ★ ★	TEENS ★ ★ ★ ★
YOUNG ADULTS ★ ★ ★ ★		OVER 30 ★ ★ ★ ★	SENIORS ★ ★ ★ ★ ★

What it is Combination fountain and shower. **Scope and scale** Diversion. **When to go** When it's hot. **Special comments** Secretly installed by Martians during *IllumiNations*. **Authors' rating** Yes! ★ ★ ★ ★. **Duration of experience** Indefinite. **Probable waiting time** None.

DESCRIPTION AND COMMENTS This simple fountain on the walkway linking Future World to World Showcase isn't much to look at, but it offers a truly spontaneous experience—rare in Walt Disney World, where everything is controlled, from the snow peas in your stir-fry to how frequently the crocodile yawns in the Jungle Cruise.

Spouts of water erupt randomly from the sidewalk. You can frolic in the water or let it cascade down on you, or blow up your britches. On a broiling Florida day, when you think you might spontaneously combust, fling yourself into the fountain and cut loose. Dance, skip, sing, jump, splash, cavort, roll around, stick your toes down the spouts, or catch the water in your mouth as it descends. You can do all of this with your clothes on or, depending on your age, with your clothes off.

TOURING TIPS We don't know if the fountain's creator has been drummed out of the corps by the Disney Tribunal of People Who Sit on Sticks (probably), but we're grateful for his courage in introducing one thing that's not super-controlled. We do know your kids will be right in the middle of this thing before your brain sounds the alert. *Our advice:* Pack a few pairs of dry shorts and turn the kids loose. You might even want to bring a spare pair for yourself. Or maybe not.

WORLD SHOWCASE

EPCOT'S SECOND THEMED AREA, World Showcase is an ongoing World's Fair encircling a picturesque 40-acre lagoon. The cuisine, culture, history, and architecture of almost a dozen countries are permanently displayed in individual national pavilions spaced along a 1.2-mile promenade. Pavilions replicate familiar landmarks and present representative street scenes from the host countries.

World Showcase features some of the loveliest gardens in the United States. In Germany, France, United Kingdom, Canada, and, to a lesser extent, China, they're sometimes tucked away and out of sight of pedestrian traffic on the World Showcase promenade. They're best appreciated during daylight hours, as a Clio, Michigan, woman explains:

> Make sure to visit World Showcase in the daylight in order to view the beautiful gardens. We were sorry that we didn't do this because we were following the guide and riding the rides that we could have done later in the dark.

Most adults enjoy World Showcase, but many children find it boring. To make it more interesting to children, most Epcot retail shops sell **Passport Kits** for about $10. Each kit contains a blank passport and stamps for every World Showcase country. As kids accompany their folks to each country, they tear out the appropriate stamp and stick it in the passport. The kit also contains basic information on the nations and a Mickey Mouse button. Disney has built a lot of profit into this little product, but guests—namely, parents—don't seem to mind the cost. As this dad from Birmingham, Alabama, relates, the Passport Kit helps get the kids through World Showcase with a minimum of impatience, whining, and tantrums:

unofficial **TIP**
If you don't want to spring for the Passport Kit, the Disney folks will be happy to stamp an autograph book or just about anything else— even your forehead.

> Adding stamps from the Epcot countries was the only way I was able to see all the displays with cheerful children.

Children also enjoy **Kidcot Fun Stops** (see page 579), designed to make World Showcase more interesting for the 5- to 12-year-old set. The stops are usually nothing more than a large table on the sidewalk at each pavilion. Tables are staffed by Disney cast members who stamp passports and lead modest craft projects relating to the host countries. A mom from Billerica, Massachusetts, is a fan of the Fun Stops:

> The Kidcot project at Epcot was amazing! Our 2- and 5-year-olds loved making masks and collecting stamps.

An adult version of passport-stamp collecting is known as **Drinking around the World** (see page 441), an activity enthusiastically endorsed by a woman from party-hearty New Orleans:

> We drank a beer in each country at Epcot—Dad was the designated driver—and posed for photos in each, and it quickly became hilarious, as were the progression-of-drunkenness photos that followed. I recommend it as a great adult alternative to that [passport] thing.

World Showcase offers some of the most diverse and interesting shopping at Walt Disney World. For more information, see Part Twenty-Two, Shopping in and out of Walt Disney World.

Agent P's World Showcase Adventure ★★★★

APPEAL BY AGE   PRESCHOOL ★★★½   GRADE SCHOOL ★★★★½   TEENS ★★★
YOUNG   ADULTS   ★★★   OVER   30   ★★★½   SENIORS   ★★

What it is Interactive scavenger hunt in select World Showcase pavilions. **Scope and scale** Minor attraction. **When to go** Anytime. **Authors' rating** One of our favorite additions to the parks; ★★★★. **Duration of presentation** Allow 30 minutes per adventure. **Preshow entertainment** None. **Probable waiting time** None.

DESCRIPTION AND COMMENTS In their eponymous Disney Channel show, Phineas and Ferb have a pet platypus named Perry. In the presence of humans, Perry doesn't do a whole lot. (To be fair, we're not experts on typical platypus behavior, but read on.) When the kids aren't looking, though, Perry takes on the role of Agent P—a fedora-wearing, James Bond–esque secret agent who battles the evil Dr. Doofenshmirtz to prevent world domination (or at least domination of the "tri-state area" in which the show is based).

In Agent P's World Showcase Adventure, you're a secret agent helping Perry, and you receive a mobile phone–like device before you're dispatched on a mission to your choice of seven World Showcase pavilions. Once you arrive at the pavilion, the device's video screen and audio provide various clues to help you solve a set of simple puzzles necessary for defeating Doofenshmirtz's plan. As you discover each clue, you'll find special effects such as talking statues and flaming lanterns, plus live "secret agents" stationed in the pavilions just for this attraction. For example, in a prior version of the game you were instructed to utter the phrase "Danger is my cup of tea" to someone working behind the counter at the United Kingdom's tea shop; he or she would respond by handing you a Twinings tea packet on which was printed a clue to solve a puzzle.

Agent P makes static World Showcase pavilions more interactive and kid-friendly. The adventures have simple clues, fast pacing, and neat rewards for solving the puzzles. Len's teenage daughter, Hannah, will happily spend an entire afternoon in World Showcase playing this game and drinking Japanese sodas. Don't be surprised if, having completed one pavilion's adventure, your child wants to do the same.

This attraction opened in 2009 as the Kim Possible World Showcase Adventure and was rethemed to *Phineas and Ferb* in 2012. Reader reviews have been uniformly positive since its Kim Possible debut, and we expect the same with Agent P.

TOURING TIPS Playing the game is free, and no deposit is required for the device. You'll need a valid theme park ticket to sign up before you play, and you can choose both the time and location of your adventure. Register at Future World's Innoventions East or West building, or along the Odyssey Bridge connecting Future World to World Showcase. Before heading off to your chosen country, pick up your device at the Italy, Norway, or United Kingdom Pavilion or the east side of the main walkway from Future World to World Showcase.

Each group can have up to three devices for the same adventure. Because you're working with a device about the size of a cell phone, it's best to have one device for every two people in your group.

From a Fairlawn, New Jersey, dad:

[Agent P's] World Showcase Adventure should be renamed "How to Keep the Tweens Out of Your Hair While You Enjoy World Showcase."

A Tucker, Georgia, mother of a 7-year-old is also a fan:

My daughter and I thoroughly enjoyed [Agent P's] World Showcase Adventure. The interactivity was clever and exciting, the clues were challenging yet simple enough for a child to figure out, plus NO LINES!

A reader from Wauwatosa, Wisconsin, recounts:

From your description, it didn't sound like much fun [Really? —The Authors], but my 4- and 7-year-olds LOVED it. We did three adventures in a row, then returned two days later and did another.

Now, moving clockwise around the World Showcase promenade, here are the nations represented and their attractions:

MEXICO PAVILION

DESCRIPTION AND COMMENTS Pre-Columbian pyramids dominate the architecture of this exhibit. One forms the pavilion's facade, and the other overlooks the restaurant and plaza alongside the boat ride—**Gran Fiesta Tour**—inside the pavilion.

TOURING TIPS A romantic and exciting testimony to Mexico's charms, the pyramids contain a large number of authentic and valuable artifacts. Many people zip past these treasures without stopping to look. The village scene inside the pavilion is beautiful and exquisitely detailed. A retail shop occupies most of the left half of the inner pavilion, while Mexico's Kidcot stop is in the first entryway inside the pyramid. On the opposite side of the main floor is **La Cava del Tequila,** a bar serving more than 70 varieties of tequila as well as margaritas and appetizers.

Gran Fiesta Tour Starring the Three Caballeros ★★½

APPEAL BY AGE	PRESCHOOL ★★★★	GRADE SCHOOL ★★★½	TEENS ★★★
YOUNG ADULTS ★★★	OVER 30 ★★★		SENIORS ★★★

What it is Indoor scenic boat ride. Scope and scale Minor attraction. When to go Before noon or after 5 p.m. Authors' rating Visually appealing, light, and relaxing; ★★½. Duration of ride About 7 minutes (plus 1½-minute wait to disembark). Average wait in line per 100 people ahead of you 4½ minutes; assumes 16 boats in operation. Loading speed Moderate.

DESCRIPTION AND COMMENTS The Gran Fiesta Tour replaces this pavilion's first boat ride, El Río del Tiempo. The new incarnation adds animated versions of Donald Duck, José Carioca, and Panchito—an avian singing group called The Three Caballeros, from Disney's 1944 film of the same name—to spice up what was often characterized as a slower-paced Mexican-style It's a Small World.

The ride's premise is that the Caballeros are scheduled to perform at a fiesta, but Donald has gone missing. Large video screens show Donald enjoying Mexico's pyramids, monuments, and water sports while José and Panchito search other Mexican points of interest. Everyone is reunited in time for a rousing concert near the end of the ride. Along the way, guests are treated to detailed scenes in eye-catching colors, and an improved music system. At the risk of sounding like the Disney geeks we are, we must point out that Panchito is technically the only Mexican Caballero; José Carioca is from Brazil, and Donald is from Burbank. In any case, more of the ride's visuals seem to be on the left side of the boat; have small children sit nearer the left to keep their attention, and listen for Donald's humorous monologue as you wait to disembark at the end of the ride.

A family of three from Fanwood, New Jersey, thinks Disney blew it with the Gran Fiesta Tour:

The Gran Fiesta Tour was dreadful. If the idea was to rid the ride of derogatory Mexican stereotypes, the designers woefully missed the mark.

A Wilmington, Delaware, woman blames the attraction's lack of appeal on . . . who else?

Donald Duck has ruined even the minimal value of the Mexico ride.

TOURING TIPS The ride tends to get busier during early afternoon.

NORWAY PAVILION

DESCRIPTION AND COMMENTS The Norway Pavilion is complex, beautiful, and architecturally diverse. Surrounding a courtyard is an assortment of traditional Scandinavian buildings, including a replica of the 14th-century Akershus Castle, a wooden stave church (go inside—the doors open!), red-tiled cottages, and replicas of historic buildings representing the traditional designs of Bergen, Alesund, and Oslo. Attractions include an adventure boat ride in the mold of Pirates of the Caribbean, a movie about Norway, and a gallery of art and artifacts. The pavilion houses **Akershus Royal Banquet Hall,** a sit-down eatery that hosts princess character meals for breakfast, lunch, and dinner; breakfast here is one of the most popular character meals in all of Walt Disney World. **Kringla Bakeri og Kafe,** an open-air cafe attached to a bakery, caters to those on the run. Shoppers will find abundant native handicrafts.

Maelstrom *(Fastpass)* ★★★

| APPEAL BY AGE | PRESCHOOL ★★★ | GRADE SCHOOL ★★★½ | TEENS ★★★½ |
| YOUNG ADULTS ★★★½ | | OVER 30 ★★★½ | SENIORS ★★★½ |

What it is Indoor adventure boat ride. **Scope and scale** Major attraction. **When to go** Before noon or after 4:30 p.m., or use Fastpass. **Special comments** Animatronic polar bears may frighten a few small children. **Authors' rating** Too short but has its moments; ★★★. **Duration of ride** 4½ minutes, followed by a 5-minute film with a short wait in between; about 14 minutes for all. **Average wait in line per 100 people ahead of you** 4 minutes; assumes 12 or 13 boats operating. **Loading speed** Fast.

DESCRIPTION AND COMMENTS In one of Disney World's shorter water rides, guests board dragon-headed ships for a voyage through the fabled rivers and seas of Viking history and legend. They brave trolls, fjords, waterfalls, and a storm at sea. A second-generation Disney water ride, the Viking voyage assembles an impressive array of special effects, combining visual, tactile, and auditory stimuli in a fast-paced and often humorous odyssey. Afterward, guests see a 5-minute film on Norway. We don't have any major problems with Maelstrom, but a vocal minority of our readers consider the ride too brief.

TOURING TIPS Sometimes, several hundred guests from a recently concluded screening of *Reflections of China* arrive at Maelstrom en masse. Should you encounter this horde, postpone Maelstrom. If you don't want to see the Norway film, not to worry; you'll be given the opportunity to exit before the film begins.

CHINA PAVILION

DESCRIPTION AND COMMENTS A half-sized replica of the Temple of Heaven in Beijing identifies this pavilion. Gardens and reflecting ponds simulate those found in Suzhou, and an art gallery features a lotus-blossom gate and formal saddle roof line. The China Pavilion offers two restaurants: the **Lotus Blossom Cafe,** a fast-food eatery, and **Nine Dragons Restaurant,** a full-service establishment (Advance Reservations recommended) that serves lamentably lackluster Chinese food in a lovely setting. **The Joy of Tea,** a tea stand and specialty-drink vendor, will feed your caffeine addiction until you can make it to Morocco's espresso bar.

DISNEY DISH WITH JIM HILL

HEIGH-HO HEADS EAST Walt Disney Pictures is at work on a unique new action-adventure film, *Order of the Seven,* which reimagines the Seven Dwarfs as Shaolin monks defending an Englishwoman who runs afoul of a wicked empress in 19th-century Hong Kong. Once this Michael Gracey production premieres in 2014, Disney envisions hiring some martial-arts masters to reprise the monks at Epcot in an *Order of the Seven* kung fu demonstration staged daily at the China Pavilion.

The pavilion also hosts regularly updated exhibits on Chinese history, culture, or trend-setting developments. Past exhibits have covered everything from China's indigenous peoples to the layout of Hong Kong Disneyland. The current exhibit features a look at Chinese funeral sculptures, including miniature clay warriors who protect the tombs' occupants.

Reflections of China   ★ ★ ★ ½

APPEAL BY AGE	PRESCHOOL ★ ★	GRADE SCHOOL ★ ★ ★	TEENS ★ ★ ★
YOUNG ADULTS ★ ★ ★ ½	OVER 30 ★ ★ ★ ★		SENIORS ★ ★ ★ ½

What it is Film about the Chinese people and culture. **Scope and scale** Major attraction. **When to go** Anytime. **Special comments** Audience stands throughout performance. This beautifully produced film was introduced in 2003. **Authors' rating** ★ ★ ★ ½. **Duration of presentation** About 14 minutes. **Preshow entertainment** None. **Probable waiting time** 10 minutes.

DESCRIPTION AND COMMENTS Pass through the Hall of Prayer for Good Harvest to view the Circle-Vision 360 film *Reflections of China.* Warm and appealing, it's a brilliant (albeit politically sanitized) introduction to the people and natural beauty of China.

TOURING TIPS The pavilion is truly beautiful—serene yet exciting. *Reflections of China* plays in a theater where guests must stand, but the film can usually be enjoyed anytime without much waiting. If you're touring World Showcase in a counterclockwise rotation and plan next to go to Norway and ride Maelstrom, position yourself on the far left of the theater (as you face the attendant's podium). After the show, be one of the first to exit. Hurry to Maelstrom as fast as you can to arrive ahead of the several hundred other *Reflections of China* patrons who will be right behind you.

GERMANY PAVILION

DESCRIPTION AND COMMENTS A clock tower, adorned with boy and girl figures, rises above the *platz* (plaza) marking the Germany Pavilion. Dominated by a fountain depicting St. George's victory over the dragon, the platz is encircled by buildings in the style of traditional German architecture. The main attraction is the **Biergarten,** a buffet restaurant that serves traditional German food and beer (Advance Reservations are required; see full profile on page 457 of Part Ten). Yodeling, folk dancing, and oompah-band music are part of the mealtime festivities.

The latest addition to the Germany Pavilion is **Karamell-Küche** ("Caramel Kitchen"), offering small caramel-covered sweets including apples, fudge, and cupcakes. We love coming here for a midday snack to tide us over before dinner. Also be sure to check out the large and elaborate model railroad just beyond the restrooms as you walk from Germany toward Italy.

TOURING TIPS The pavilion is pleasant and festive. Tour anytime.

ITALY PAVILION

DESCRIPTION AND COMMENTS The entrance to Italy is marked by an 83-foot-tall campanile (bell tower) said to mirror the tower in St. Mark's Square in Venice. Left of the campanile is a replica of the 14th-century Doge's Palace, also in the famous square. The pavilion has a waterfront on the lagoon where gondolas are tied to striped moorings.

TOURING TIPS Streets and courtyards in the Italy Pavilion are among the most realistic in World Showcase. For a quick lunch, **Via Napoli** occasionally offers pizza by the slice, and the new **Tutto Gusto Wine Cellar** serves appetizer plates along with libations. Because there's no film or ride, you can tour the rest of the pavilion at any hour.

UNITED STATES PAVILION

The American Adventure ★★★★

APPEAL BY AGE	PRESCHOOL ★★½		GRADE SCHOOL ★★★		TEENS ★★★
YOUNG ADULTS ★★★½		OVER 30 ★★★★		SENIORS	★★★★

What it is Patriotic mixed-media and Audio-Animatronic theater presentation on U.S. history. **Scope and scale** Headliner. **When to go** Anytime. **Authors' rating** Disney's best historic/patriotic attraction; not to be missed; ★★★★. **Duration of presentation** About 29 minutes. **Preshow entertainment** Voices of Liberty choral singing. **Probable waiting time** 25 minutes.

DESCRIPTION AND COMMENTS The United States Pavilion consists (not surprisingly) of a fast-food restaurant and a patriotic show.

The American Adventure production is a composite of everything Disney does best. Housed in an imposing brick structure reminiscent of colonial Philadelphia, the 29-minute show is a stirring, but sanitized, rendition of American history narrated by an animatronic Mark Twain (who carries a smoking cigar) and Ben Franklin (who climbs a set of stairs to visit Thomas Jefferson). Behind a stage (almost half the size of a football field) is a 28 x 155–foot rear-projection screen (the largest ever used) on which motion picture images are interwoven with action on stage.

Though the production rouses patriotic emotion in some viewers, others find it deadly dull. A man from Fort Lauderdale, Florida, writes:

I've always disagreed with you about The American Adventure. *I saw it about 10 years ago and snoozed through it. We tried it again since you said it was updated. It was still ponderous. Casey used the time for a nap, and I was checking my watch, waiting for it to be over. I'll try it again in 10 years.*

An Erie, Pennsylvania, couple resented Disney's squeaky-clean version of American history:

Our biggest gripe was with The American Adventure. *What was that supposed to be? My husband and I were actually embarrassed by that show. They glossed over the dark points of American history and neatly cut out the audio about who bombed Pearl Harbor (after all, Japan is right next door and everyone is happy at WDW). Why do they not focus on the natural beauty of America, the ethnic diversity, immigration, contributions to the world society? No, it's a condensed and Disneyfied history lesson that made us want to pretend to be Canadians after seeing it.*

But an Iowa City, Iowa, father of three thinks a lot of people are missing the point:

Cramming all of American history into a 20-minute flick is no easy task, and face it, a theme park is hardly the place for a wholly objective, serious critique of the United States. I think that it's perfectly appropriate for the film, as an attraction in Epcot, to emphasize what's good about the United States.

TOURING TIPS Architecturally, the U.S. Pavilion isn't as interesting as most others in World Showcase. But the presentation, our researchers believe, is the very best patriotic attraction in the Disney repertoire. It usually plays to capacity audiences from around 1:30 to 3:30 p.m., but it isn't hard to get into. Because of the theater's large capacity, the wait during busy times of day seldom approaches an hour and averages 25–40 minutes. Because of its theme, the presentation is decidedly less compelling to non-Americans.

The adjacent **Liberty Inn** serves a quick, nonethnic fast-food meal.

DISNEY DISH WITH JIM HILL

SAKE TO ME! With the enormous success of the Mexico Pavilion's La Cava del Tequila and La Hacienda de San Angel, WDW officials are seriously rethinking their approach to World Showcase–area eateries. Given that guests are willing to pay top dollar for fine spirits and spectacular views, Disney's restaurant-development team is mulling over a new outdoor eatery for the Japan Pavilion. It would be built right along the edge of World Showcase Lagoon and offer guests a prime view of *IllumiNations,* as well as a wide variety of sushi and sake.

JAPAN PAVILION

DESCRIPTION AND COMMENTS The five-story, blue-roofed pagoda, inspired by a 17th-century shrine in Nara, sets this pavilion apart. A hill garden behind it features waterfalls, rocks, flowers, lanterns, paths, and rustic bridges. The building on the right (as one faces the entrance) was inspired by the ceremonial and coronation hall at the Imperial Palace at Kyoto. It contains restaurants and a large retail store. Through the center entrance and to the left is the **Bijutsu-kan Gallery,** exhibiting colorful displays from Japanese pop culture. Recent subjects have included everything from postwar tin toys to comics devoted to heroes with "animal spirits."

TOURING TIPS Tasteful and elaborate, the pavilion creatively blends simplicity, architectural grandeur, and natural beauty. Tour anytime.

MOROCCO PAVILION

DESCRIPTION AND COMMENTS The bustling market, winding streets, lofty minarets, and stuccoed archways re-create the romance and intrigue of Marrakesh and Casablanca. Attention to detail makes Morocco one of the most exciting World Showcase pavilions. It also has a museum of Moorish art and **Restaurant Marrakesh,** which serves some exotic North African specialties.

Another interesting item in Morocco is the water wheel in World Showcase Lagoon that provides irrigation to the flowerbeds opposite the pavilion. Unlike the "scoop and dump" mechanisms most people are familiar with, the water here is actually carried inside the wheel. Through a complex combination of baffles, chambers, and gravity, the water emerges at the highest point of the circle through a spout perpendicular to the wheel's motion. One can only imagine the number of late, espresso-filled nights it took to come up with this design.

TOURING TIPS Morocco has neither a ride nor a theater. Tour anytime.

FRANCE PAVILION

DESCRIPTION AND COMMENTS Naturally, a replica of the Eiffel Tower (a big one) is this pavilion's centerpiece. In the foreground, streets recall *la belle époque,* France's "beautiful time" between 1870 and 1910. The sidewalk cafe and restaurant are very popular, as is the pastry shop. This probably explains why readers rank the France Pavilion as the best in World Showcase.

A group from Chicago found that the pavilion's realism exceeds what was intended:

There were no public restrooms in the France part of Epcot—just like Paris. We had to go to Morocco to find facilities.

Impressions de France ★★★½

APPEAL BY AGE	PRESCHOOL ★★	GRADE SCHOOL ★★★	TEENS ★★★
YOUNG ADULTS ★★★½	OVER 30 ★★★½		SENIORS ★★★★

What it is Film essay on the French people and country. **Scope and scale** Major attraction. **When to go** Anytime. **Authors' rating** Exceedingly beautiful film; not to be missed; ★★★½. **Duration of presentation** About 18 minutes. **Preshow entertainment** None. **Probable waiting time** 15 minutes (at suggested times).

DESCRIPTION AND COMMENTS *Impressions de France* is an 18-minute movie projected over 200 degrees onto five screens. Unlike at China and Canada, the audience sits to view this well-made film introducing France's people, cities, and natural wonders.

TOURING TIPS The film usually begins on the hour and half-hour. Detail and the evocation of a bygone era enrich the atmosphere of this pavilion. Streets are small and become quite congested when visitors queue for the film.

UNITED KINGDOM PAVILION

DESCRIPTION AND COMMENTS A variety of period architecture attempts to capture Britain's city, town, and rural atmospheres. One street alone has a thatched-roof cottage, a four-story timber-and-plaster building, a pre-Georgian plaster building, a formal Palladian exterior of dressed stone, and a city square with a Hyde Park bandstand (whew!).

The pavilion is composed mostly of shops. **The Rose & Crown Pub and Dining Room** feature dining on the water side of the promenade. For fast food, try **Yorkshire County Fish Shop.**

TOURING TIPS There are no attractions here, hence minimal congestion, so tour anytime. Mary Poppins, Alice in Wonderland, and/or Pooh can occasionally be found in the character-greeting area; check the *Times Guide* for a schedule. Advance Reservations aren't required for the pub section of the Rose & Crown, making it a nice place to stop for a beer.

CANADA PAVILION

DESCRIPTION AND COMMENTS Canada's cultural, natural, and architectural diversity are reflected in this large and impressive pavilion. Thirty-foot-tall totem poles embellish a Native American village at the foot of a magnificent château-style hotel. Nearby is a rugged stone building said to be modeled after a famous landmark near Niagara Falls and reflecting Britain's influence on Canada. **Le Cellier,** a steakhouse on the pavilion's lower level, is one of Disney World's highest-rated restaurants. It almost always requires Advance Reservations; you'd have to be incredibly lucky to get a walk-in spot, but it doesn't hurt to ask.

O Canada! ★★★½

APPEAL BY AGE	PRESCHOOL ★★½	GRADE SCHOOL ★★★	TEENS ★★★½
YOUNG ADULTS ★★★½	OVER 30 ★★★★		SENIORS ★★★★

What it is Film essay on the Canadian people and their country. **Scope and scale** Major attraction. **When to go** Anytime. **Special comments** Audience stands during performance. **Authors' rating** Makes you want to catch the first plane to Canada; ★★★½. **Duration of presentation** About 18 minutes. **Preshow entertainment** None. **Probable waiting time** 10 minutes.

DESCRIPTION AND COMMENTS *O Canada!* showcases Canada's natural beauty and population diversity and demonstrates the immense pride Canadians have in their country. An updated film replaced the decades-old original in 2007. Starring Martin Short, it features additional clips and dialogue interspersed with some of the original film's scenes. Visitors leave the theater through **Victoria Gardens,** which was inspired by the famed Butchart Gardens of British Columbia.

Readers have reacted positively to the new film. This comment from a Texas mom is typical:

The updated O Canada! *movie is a great improvement. The narration was entertaining enough to keep our 8-year-old from being bored, and the scenery was amazing.*

Speaking of Canada's immense pride, cast members often run a preshow quiz on Canadian trivia outside the theater before the show. Helpful tips for Americans: Canada's capital is Ottawa; its $1 coin is nicknamed the Loonie, after the bird engraved on it; and the $2 coin is the Toonie—not, unfortunately, the Doubloonie.

TOURING TIPS This large-capacity attraction (guests must stand) gets fairly heavy late-morning attendance, as Canada is the first pavilion encountered as one travels counterclockwise around World Showcase Lagoon.

LIVE ENTERTAINMENT
in EPCOT

LIVE ENTERTAINMENT IN EPCOT is more diverse than in the Magic Kingdom. In World Showcase, it reflects the nations represented. Future World provides a perfect setting for new and experimental offerings. Information about live entertainment on the day you visit is contained in the Epcot guide map, often supplemented by a *Times Guide*. WDW live-entertainment guru Steve Soares usually posts the Epcot performance schedule about a week in advance at **wdwent.com.**

Following are some of the venues, performers, and performances you'll encounter:

AMERICA GARDENS THEATRE This large amphitheater, near the U.S. Pavilion, faces World Showcase Lagoon. International talent plays limited engagements there. Many shows spotlight the music, dance, and costumes of the performer's home country. Other programs feature Disney characters.

AROUND THE WORLD SHOWCASE Impromptu performances take place in and around the World Showcase pavilions. They include a strolling mariachi group in Mexico; street actors in Italy; a fife-and-drum corps or singing group (The Voices of Liberty) at the U.S. Pavilion; traditional songs, drums, and dances in Japan; white-faced mimes in France; street comedy in the United Kingdom; and bagpipes in Canada, among other offerings. Street entertainment occurs about every half-hour.

Live entertainment in World Showcase exceeded the expectations of a mother from Rhode Island and led her son to develop a new talent:

You should stress in the new edition that Epcot's World Showcase is really quite lively now. Street performances are scheduled throughout the day in the different pavilions. The schedules were printed on the daily map we picked up at the ticket booth.

My 2-year-old was taken with the Chinese acrobats and the Chinese variety performers. We must have watched their shows four times each! As I write this, he's balancing an empty trash can on his feet.

And an Ayden, North Carolina, woman offers this:

I don't feel that you emphasize the street shows at Epcot enough. My husband and I loved the Japanese drumming, the Chinese and Moroccan acrobats, and the street players in Great Britain. These activities were much more indicative of foreign cultures than the rides.

We think the reader's right on target.

DINNER AND LUNCH SHOWS Restaurants in World Showcase serve healthy portions of live entertainment to accompany the victuals. Find folk dancing and an oompah band in Germany, singing waiters in Italy, and belly dancers in Morocco. Shows are performed only at dinner in Italy, but at both lunch and dinner in Germany and Morocco. Advance Reservations are required.

DISNEY CHARACTERS Once believed to be inconsistent with Epcot's educational focus, Disney characters have now been imported in significant numbers. Characters appear throughout Epcot (see page 341) and in live shows at the America Gardens Theatre and the Showcase Plaza between Mexico and Canada. Times are listed in the *Times Guide* available upon entry and at Guest Relations. Finally, **Garden Grill Restaurant** in the Land Pavilion and **Akershus Royal Banquet Hall** in Norway offer character meals.

IN FUTURE WORLD A musical crew of drumming janitors work near the front entrance and at Innoventions Plaza (between the two Innoventions buildings and by the fountain) according to the daily entertainment schedule. They're occasionally complemented by an electric-keyboard band playing what today's kids would call "oldies."

INNOVENTIONS FOUNTAIN SHOW Numerous times each day, the fountain between the two Innoventions buildings comes alive with pulsating, arching plumes of water synchronized to a musical score. Because no schedule of performances is posted, the fountain show comes as a surprise to many readers, such as this man from Berwickshire, England:

> *You don't mention one of the newer joys of Epcot, so the musical fountain came as a real surprise and treat. I sat down and listened to it from start to finish on two different occasions. The music is catchy, and played through the stereo speakers, the soaring effects of both music and water are really beautiful.*

KIDCOT FUN STOPS World Showcase pavilions have areas called Kidcot Fun Stops, where younger children can hear a story or make some small craft representative of the host nation. The Fun Stops are informal, usually set up right on the walkway. During busy times of the year, you'll find Fun Stops at each country in World Showcase; at slower times, only a couple of zones operate. Parents from Nanticoke, Pennsylvania, who thought Epcot would be a drag for their kids, were surprised by their experience:

> *Unfortunately we saved Epcot for the last day, thinking the children (ages 5 and 6) would be bored. This was a mistake. They wanted to sit for every storyteller. And the best part was the Kidcot Fun Stops in each pavilion. Imagine, something free at Disney World. It's only a stick, but it has a little something from each country added by the child at his whim. They had a ball.*

ILLUMINATIONS

EPCOT'S GREAT OUTDOOR SPECTACLE integrates fireworks, laser lights, neon, and music in a stirring tribute to the nations of the world. It's the climax of every Epcot day.

DISNEY DISH WITH JIM HILL

WDW ABOUT TO GET MORE COLORFUL Steve Davison, Disney Vice President of Parades and Spectaculars, is facing an unusual dilemma. The visionary who created Disney California Adventure's super-popular *World of Color* nighttime show is now charged with deciding which Disney World theme park will inherit DCA's lighted-fountain-and-mist-screen technology. Should it be Disney's Hollywood Studios, which has been itching to update its now-14-year-old *Fantasmic!*? Or Epcot, where *IllumiNations* premiered in 1999? We should know shortly: Davison is reportedly working on two new U.S. projects likely to be officially announced in early 2013.

Unlike earlier incarnations of *IllumiNations*, this version has a plot as well as a theme and is loaded with symbolism. We'll provide the CliffsNotes version here, because it all sort of runs together in the show itself. The show kicks off with colliding stars that suggest the Big Bang, following which "chaos reigns in the universe." This display is soon replaced by twittering songbirds and various other manifestations signaling the nativity of the Earth. Next comes a brief history of time, from the dinosaurs to ancient Rome, all projected in images on a huge, floating globe. Man's art and inspiration then flash across the globe "in a collage of creativity." All this stimulates the globe to unfold "like a massive flower," bringing on the fireworks crescendo heralding the dawn of a new age. Although only the artistically sensitive will be able to differentiate all this from, say, the last 5 minutes of any Bruce Willis movie, we thought you'd like to know what Disney says is happening.

Getting Out of Epcot after *IllumiNations* (Read This before Selecting a Viewing Spot)

Decide how quickly you want to leave the park after the show, then pick your vantage point. *IllumiNations* ends the day at Epcot. When it's over, only a couple of gift shops remain open. Because there's nothing to do, everyone leaves at once. This creates a great snarl at Package Pick-Up, the Epcot monorail station, and the Disney bus stop. It also pushes to the limit the tram system hauling guests to their cars in the parking lot. Stroller return, however, is extraordinarily efficient and doesn't cause any delay.

If you're staying at an Epcot resort (Swan, Dolphin, Yacht & Beach Club Resorts, and BoardWalk Inn & Villas), watch the show from somewhere on the southern (U.S. Pavilion) half of World Showcase Lagoon and then leave through the International Gateway between France and the United Kingdom. You can walk or take a boat back to your hotel from the International Gateway. If you have a car and are visiting Epcot in the evening for dinner and *IllumiNations,* park at the Yacht Club or Beach Club. After the show, duck out the International Gateway and be on the road to your hotel in 15 minutes. We should warn you that there's a manned security gate at the entrances to most of the Epcot resorts, including the Yacht and Beach clubs. You will, of course, be admitted if you have legitimate business, such as dining at one of the hotel restaurants, or, if you park at the BoardWalk Inn & Villas (requiring a slightly longer walk to Epcot), going to the clubs and restaurants at the BoardWalk. If you're staying at any other Disney hotel and you don't have a car, the fastest way home is to join the mass exodus through the main gate after *IllumiNations* and catch a bus or the monorail.

Those who have a car in the Epcot lot have a more problematic situation. To beat the crowd, find a viewing spot at the end of World Showcase Lagoon nearest Future World (and the exits). Leave as soon as *IllumiNations* concludes, trying to exit ahead of the crowd (note that thousands of people will be doing exactly the same thing). To get a good vantage point between Mexico and Canada on the northern end of the lagoon, stake out your spot 60–100 minutes before the show (45–90 minutes during less-busy periods). Conceivably, you may squander more time holding your spot before *IllumiNations* than you would if you watched from the less-congested southern end of the lagoon and took your chances with the crowd upon departure.

More groups get separated and more children get lost following *IllumiNations* than at any other time. In summer, you'll be walking in a throng of up to 30,000 people. If you're heading for the parking lot, anticipate this congestion and preselect a point in the Epcot entrance area where you can meet if someone gets separated from the group. We recommend the fountain just inside the main entrance. Everyone in your party should be told not to exit through the turnstiles until all noses have been counted. It can be a nightmare if the group gets split up and you don't know whether the others are inside or outside the park.

For those with a car, the main problem is reaching the parking lot. Once you're there, traffic leaves the parking lot pretty well. If you paid close attention to where you parked, consider skipping the tram and walking. If you walk, watch your children closely and hang on to them for all they're worth. The parking lot is pretty wild at this time of night, with hundreds of moving cars.

Good Locations for Viewing *IllumiNations* and Other World Showcase Lagoon Performances

The best place to be for any presentation on World Showcase Lagoon is in a seat on the lakeside veranda of **La Cantina de San Angel** in Mexico. Come early (at least 90 minutes before *IllumiNations*) and relax with a cold drink or snack while you wait for the show.

A woman from Pasadena, California, nailed down the seat but missed the relaxation. She writes:

> *Stake out a prime site for* IllumiNations *at least 2 hours ahead, and be prepared to defend it. We got a lakeside table at the Cantina de San Angel at 6:30 p.m. and had a great view of* IllumiNations. *Unfortunately, we had to put up with troops of people asking us to share our table and trying to wedge themselves between our table and the fence.*

La Hacienda de San Angel in Mexico and the **Rose & Crown Pub** in the United Kingdom also have lagoon-side seating. Because of a small wall at the Rose & Crown, however, the view isn't quite as good as from the Cantina. If you want to combine dinner at either location with *IllumiNations,* make a dinner reservation for about 1 hour and 15 minutes before showtime. Report a few minutes early for your seating and tell the host that you want a table outside where you can view *IllumiNations* during or after dinner. Our experience is that the staff will bend over backward to accommodate you. If you aren't able to obtain a table outside, eat inside, then hang out until showtime. When the lights dim, indicating the start of *IllumiNations,* you'll be allowed to join the diners to watch the show.

Because most guests run for the exits after a presentation and islands in the southern (U.S. Pavilion) half of the lagoon block the view from some places, the most popular spectator positions are along the northern waterfront from Norway and Mexico to Canada and the United Kingdom. Although the northern half of the lagoon unquestionably offers excellent viewing, it's usually necessary to claim a spot 60–100 minutes before *IllumiNations* begins. For those who are late finishing dinner or don't

unofficial **TIP**
Because most of *Illumi Nations'* action is significantly above ground level, you don't need to be right on the rail or have an unobstructed view of the water to enjoy it.

want to spend an hour or more standing by a rail, here are some good viewing spots along the southern perimeter (moving counterclockwise from the United Kingdom to Germany) that often go unnoticed until 10–30 minutes before showtime:

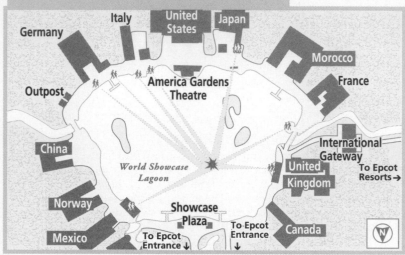

Where to View IllumiNations

1. **International Gateway Island** The pedestrian bridge across the canal near International Gateway spans an island that offers great viewing. This island normally fills 30 minutes or more before showtime.

2. **Second-floor (Restaurant-level) Deck of the Mitsukoshi Building in Japan** An Asian arch slightly blocks your sight line, but this covered deck offers a great vantage point, especially if the weather is iffy. Only the Hacienda de San Angel in Mexico is more protected. If you take up a position on the Mitsukoshi deck and find the wind blowing directly at you, you can be reasonably sure that the smoke from the fireworks won't be far behind.

3. **Gondola Landing at Italy** An elaborate waterfront promenade offers excellent viewing. Claim a spot at least 30 minutes before showtime.

4. **The Boat Dock Opposite Germany** Another good vantage point, the dock generally fills 30 minutes before *IllumiNations. Note:* This area may be exposed to more smoke from the fireworks because of Epcot's prevailing winds.

5. **Waterfront Promenade by Germany** Views are good from the 90-foot-long lagoon-side walkway between Germany and China.

Do these suggestions work every time? No. A dad from San Ramon, California, writes:

Your recommendations for IllumiNations *didn't work out in the time frame you mentioned. People had the area staked out 2 hours ahead.*

None of the viewing locations are reservable, and good spots go early on busier nights. But speaking personally, we refuse to hold down a slab of concrete for 2 hours before *IllumiNations* as some people do. Most nights, you can find an acceptable vantage point 15–30 minutes before the show.

It's important not to position yourself under a tree, awning, or anything that blocks your overhead view. If *IllumiNations* is a top priority for you and you want to be certain of getting a good viewing position, claim your place an hour or more before showtime.

A New Yorker who staked out his turf well in advance made this suggestion for staying comfortable until showtime:

> *Your excellent guide also served as a seat cushion while I waited seated on the ground. Make future editions thicker for greater comfort.*

ILLUMINATIONS CRUISE

FOR A REALLY GOOD VIEW, you can charter a pontoon boat for $346 with tax. Captained by a Disney cast member, the boat holds up to 10 guests. Your captain will take you for a little cruise and then position the boat in a perfect place to watch *IllumiNations*. Chips, soda, and water are provided; sandwiches and more-substantial food items may be arranged through Disney reservations or Yacht Club Private Dining at ☎ 407-934-3160. Cruises depart from Bayside Marina. A major indirect benefit of the charter is that you can enjoy *IllumiNations* without fighting the mob afterward. Because this is a private charter rather than a tour, only your group will be aboard. Life jackets are provided, but you can wear them at your discretion. Because there are few boats, charters sell out fast. To reserve, call ☎ 407-WDW-PLAY (939-7529) at exactly 7 a.m. Eastern time 180 days before the day you want to charter. Because the Disney reservations system counts days in a somewhat atypical manner, we recommend phoning about 185 days out to have a Disney agent specify the exact morning to call for reservations. Similar charters are available on the Seven Seas Lagoon to watch the Magic Kingdom fireworks.

TRAFFIC PATTERNS
in EPCOT

IN THE MAGIC KINGDOM, Main Street, U.S.A., with its shops and eateries, serves as a huge gathering place when the park opens and funnels visitors to the Central Plaza, where entrances branch off to the lands. Thus, crowds are first welcomed and entertained (on Main Street), then distributed almost equally to the lands.

At Epcot, by contrast, Spaceship Earth, the park's premier landmark and one of its headliner attractions, is just inside the main entrance. When visitors enter the park, they almost irresistibly head for it. Hence, a bottleneck forms less than 75 yards from the turnstiles as soon as the park opens.

Early-morning crowds form in Future World because most of the park's rides and shows are there. Except at Mission: SPACE, Soarin', and Test Track, visitors are fairly equally distributed among Future World attractions. Mission: SPACE, Soarin', and Test Track are the major early-morning magnets. These three biggies will draw so many guests that the other attractions in Future World don't develop long waits until 11 a.m. or later.

Between 9 and 11 a.m., crowds build in Future World. Even when World Showcase opens (usually 11 a.m. but sometimes earlier), more people are entering Future World than are leaving for the Showcase. Attendance continues building in Future World between noon and 2 p.m. World Showcase attendance builds rapidly as lunchtime approaches. Exhibits at the far end of World Showcase Lagoon report capacity audiences from about noon through 6:30 or 7:30 p.m.

The Magic Kingdom's premier attractions are situated on the far perimeters of its lands to distribute crowds evenly. Epcot's cluster of attractions in Future World holds the greater part of the throng in the smaller part of the park. World Showcase has only two major draws— Maelstrom in Norway and *The American Adventure*—but these are not in the same league as the three super-headliners in Future World, and consequently you have no compelling reason to rush to see them. The bottom line: Crowds build all morning and into early afternoon in Future World. Not until the evening meal approaches do crowds equalize in Future World and World Showcase. Evening crowds in World Showcase, however, don't compare in size with morning and midday crowds in Future World. Attendance throughout Epcot is normally lighter in the evening.

unofficial **TIP**
Visitors aware of the congestion at Spaceship Earth can take advantage of the excellent opportunities it provides for escaping waits at other Future World attractions.

Some guests leave Epcot in the early evening, but most of them exit en masse after *IllumiNations*. Upward of 30,000 people head for the parking lot and monorail station at once. Still, this congestion doesn't compare with the post-fireworks gridlock at the Magic Kingdom. One primary reason for the easier departure from Epcot is that its parking lot is adjacent to the park, not separated from it by a lake as at the Magic Kingdom. At the Magic Kingdom, departing visitors form bottlenecks at the monorail to the Transportation and Ticket Center and main parking lot. At Epcot, they proceed directly to their cars.

To get a complete view of the actual traffic patterns while you're in the park, use our mobile app, **Lines** (**touringplans.com/lines**). The app gives you current wait times and future estimates in half-hour increments for today and tomorrow. A quick glance shows how traffic patterns affect wait times throughout the day.

▮ EPCOT TOURING PLANS

TOURING EPCOT IS MUCH MORE STRENUOUS and demanding than touring the other theme parks. Epcot requires about twice as much walking. And, unlike the Magic Kingdom, Epcot has no effective in-park transportation; wherever you want to go, it's always quicker to walk. Our plans will help you avoid crowds and bottlenecks on days of moderate-to-heavy attendance, but they can't shorten the distance you have to walk. (Wear comfortable shoes.) On days of lighter attendance, when crowd conditions aren't a critical factor, the plans will help you organize your tour. We offer four touring plans:

- Epcot One-Day Touring Plan
- Epcot Authors' Selective One-Day Touring Plan

- Epcot One-Day Touring Plan for Parents with Small Children
- Epcot Two-Day Early-Riser Touring Plan

The One-Day Touring Plan packs as much as possible into one long day and requires a lot of hustle and stamina. The Authors' Selective One-Day Touring Plan eliminates some lesser (in the authors' opinion) attractions and offers a somewhat more relaxed tour if you have only one day. The One-Day Touring Plan for Parents with Small Children gives little ones the best of Epcot while also building in needed rest time. Finally, the Two-Day Early-Riser Touring Plan is the most efficient, eliminating 90% of the backtracking and extra walking required by the other plans while still providing a comprehensive tour.

"Not a Touring Plan" Touring Plans

For the type-B reader, these touring plans (see page 816) avoid detailed step-by-step strategies for saving every last minute in line. For Epcot, these "not" touring plans include advice for adults and parents with one day in the park, for anyone with two days, and for anyone with an afternoon and a full day to tour.

BEFORE YOU GO

1. Call ☎ 407-824-4321 in advance for the hours of operation on the day of your visit.

2. Make reservations at the Epcot full-service restaurant(s) of your choice 180 days before your visit.

EPCOT ONE-DAY TOURING PLAN *(page 824)*

FOR Adults and children age 8 or older.

ASSUMES Willingness to experience all major rides and shows.

This plan requires a lot of walking and some backtracking in order to avoid long waits in line. A little extra walking and some early-morning hustle will spare you 2–3 hours of standing in line. You might not complete the tour. How far you get depends on how quickly you move from attraction to attraction, how many times you rest and eat, how quickly the park fills, and what time it closes.

This plan is not recommended for families with very young children. If you're touring with young children and have only one day, use the Epcot Authors' Selective One-Day Touring Plan or the Epcot One-Day Touring Plan for Parents with Small Children. Break after lunch and relax at your hotel, returning to the park in late afternoon. If you can allocate two days to Epcot, use the Epcot Two-Day Early-Riser Touring Plan.

EPCOT AUTHORS' SELECTIVE ONE-DAY TOURING PLAN *(page 825)*

FOR All parties.

ASSUMES Willingness to experience major rides and shows.

This touring plan includes only what the authors believe is the best Epcot has to offer. Families with children younger than age 8 should review Epcot attractions in our Small-Child Fright-Potential Chart in Part Six (see pages 324–328). Rent a stroller for any child small enough to fit in one, and take your young children back to the hotel for a nap after lunch. If you can allocate two days to Epcot, use the Epcot Two-Day Early-Riser Touring Plan (see below).

EPCOT ONE-DAY TOURING PLAN FOR PARENTS WITH SMALL CHILDREN *(page 826)*

FOR Parents with children younger than age 8.

This touring plan is for parents and kids who want to experience Epcot's best attractions in a single day. It's the most popular Epcot touring plan at **touringplans.com.**

The plan includes a midday break of 3–4 hours. Make time for this break by skipping intense attractions such as Test Track and Mission: SPACE, and by forgoing many World Showcase exhibits. Regarding World Showcase, we encourage families to sign up for a free interactive game called Agent P's World Showcase Adventure (see page 569), which most kids find endlessly entertaining.

Families with children younger than age 8 should review Epcot attractions in our Small-Child Fright-Potential Chart in Part Six (see pages 324–328). Rent a stroller for any child small enough to fit in one.

EPCOT TWO-DAY EARLY-RISER TOURING PLAN *(pages 827 and 828)*

FOR All parties.

This is the most efficient of the Epcot touring plans. It takes advantage of easy touring made possible by morning's light crowds. Most folks will complete each day of the plan by midafternoon. While the plan doesn't include *IllumiNations* or other evening festivities, these activities, along with dinner at an Epcot restaurant, can be added at your discretion.

Families with children younger than age 8 should review Epcot attractions in our Small-Child Fright-Potential Chart in Part Six (see pages 324–328). Rent a stroller for any child small enough to fit in one.

PART THIRTEEN

DISNEY'S ANIMAL KINGDOM

WITH ITS LUSH FLORA, WINDING STREAMS, meandering paths, and exotic setting, Disney's Animal Kingdom is a stunningly beautiful theme park. The landscaping alone conjures images of rainforest, veldt, and formal gardens. Soothing, mysterious, and exciting, every vista is a feast for the eye. Add to this loveliness a population of more than 1,000 animals, replicas of Africa's and Asia's most intriguing architecture, and a diverse array of singularly original attractions, and you have the most distinctive of all the Disney theme parks. In Animal Kingdom, Disney has created an environment to savor.

At 500 acres, Animal Kingdom is five times the size of the Magic Kingdom and almost twice the size of Epcot. But as is the case with Disney's Hollywood Studios, most of Animal Kingdom's vast geography is accessible only on guided tours or as part of attractions. Animal Kingdom consists of six sections, or "lands": **The Oasis, Discovery Island, DinoLand U.S.A., Camp Minnie-Mickey, Africa,** and **Asia.** (A seventh section, **Rafiki's Planet Watch,** is touted as a land by Disney but doesn't really qualify as such in our eyes.)

Its size notwithstanding, Animal Kingdom features a limited number of attractions. To be exact, there are seven rides, several walk-through exhibits, an indoor theater, four amphitheaters, a conservation exhibit, and a children's playground.

Animal Kingdom's opening was seen as Disney taking dead aim at Busch Gardens in Tampa, a theme park known for its exceptional zoological exhibits, and one that had seen a marked increase in attendance in the 1990s with the addition of numerous thrill rides. Up to that time, Disney had preferred the neatly controlled movements of Audio-Animatronic animals to the unpredictable behaviors of real critters.

unofficial **TIP**
Three attractions—
DINOSAUR, Expedition Everest, and **Kilimanjaro Safaris**—are among the best in the Disney repertoire.

Unfortunately for Disney, however, the combination of creative natural-habitat zoological exhibits and coasters developed by Busch Gardens became immensely popular, and as any student of the Walt Disney Company can attest, there's nothing like a successful competitor to make the Disney folks change their tune. So, all the press releases

NOT TO BE MISSED AT DISNEY'S ANIMAL KINGDOM	
AFRICA	• Kilimanjaro Safaris
ASIA	• Expedition Everest
CAMP MINNIE-MICKEY	• *Festival of the Lion King*
DINOLAND U.S.A.	• DINOSAUR • *Finding Nemo—The Musical*
DISCOVERY ISLAND	• *It's Tough to Be a Bug!*

aside, Disney's Animal Kingdom was designed as a combination of nat-ural-habitat zoological exhibits and thrill rides. Big surprise!

Even if the recipe was copied, the Disney version serves up more than its share of innovations, particularly when it comes to the wildlife habitats. For starters, there's lots of space, thus allowing for the sweep-ing vistas that Discovery Channel viewers would expect in, say, an African veldt setting. Then there are the enclosures, natural in appear-ance, with few or no apparent barriers between you and the animals. The operative word, of course, is *apparent*. That flimsy stand of bam-boo separating you from a gorilla is actually a neatly disguised set of steel rods embedded in concrete. The Imagineers even take a crack at certain animals' stubborn unwillingness to be on display: A lion that would rather sleep out of sight under a bush, for example, is lured to center stage with nice, cool, climate-controlled artificial rocks.

Animal Kingdom has received mixed reviews since it opened in 1998. Guests complain loudly about the park layout and the neces-sity of backtracking through Discovery Island in order to access the various themed areas. Congested walkways, lack of shade, and insuf-ficient air-conditioning also rank high on the gripe list. However, most of the attractions (with one or two notable exceptions) have been well received. Also praised are the natural-habitat animal exhibits as well as the park architecture and landscaping. We marvel at the fact that readers of similar backgrounds come away with such vastly differing opinions. A 36-year-old mother of three, for example, exclaims:

Animal Kingdom is a monstrous disappointment! Disney should be ashamed to have their name on it!

Meanwhile, a 34-year-old mom with two children reports:

Animal Kingdom was our favorite theme park at Disney World. We spent four evenings out of our seven-day vacation there.

In truth, Animal Kingdom is a park to linger over and savor—two things that Disney, with its crowds, lines, and regimentation, has con-ditioned us not to do. But many people intuit that Animal Kingdom must be approached in a different way, including this mother of three (ages 5, 7, and 9) from Hampton Bay, New York:

Despite the crowds, we really enjoyed Animal Kingdom. In order to enjoy it, you really must have the right attitude. It's an educational experience, not a thrill park. Talk to the cast members and you won't regret it. We spoke to a cast member who played games with the kids—my daughter found a drawer full of butterflies, and the boys located a hidden ostrich egg and lion skull.

A family from the Southwest agrees, writing:

Animal Kingdom with kids should be approached as you would bird-watching, fossil hunting, or nature walks. To enjoy it, you need to slow down, stop and look, and, especially, engage the cast members. Encourage your children to ask questions; the answers are educational, enlightening, and a wonderful alternative to standing in a hot queue.

Finally, from a Crofton, Maryland, mother of two:

We took your advice and did a slow day at Animal Kingdom. We stumbled upon the Discovery Club for kids, and they ended up being the best part of our trip. We hunted for each of the areas, got stamps at each station, and learned so much.

ARRIVING

DISNEY'S ANIMAL KINGDOM IS OFF OSCEOLA PARKWAY in the southwest corner of Walt Disney World and is not too far from Blizzard Beach, Coronado Springs Resort, and the All-Star Resorts. Animal Kingdom Lodge is about a mile away from the park on its west side. From Interstate 4, take Exit 64B, US 192, to the so-called Walt Disney World main entrance (World Drive) and follow the signs to Animal Kingdom. Animal Kingdom has its own vast pay parking lot with close-in parking for the disabled. Once parked, you can walk to the entrance or catch a ride on one of Disney's trademark trams.

The park is connected to other Walt Disney World destinations by the Disney bus system. If you're staying at a Disney resort and plan to arrive at Animal Kingdom before park opening, use Disney transportation rather than taking your own car. The Animal Kingdom parking lot often opens only 15 minutes before the park, causing long lines and frustration for drivers.

unofficial **TIP**
Take a picture of the row you're parked in with your cell phone or digital camera.

OPERATING HOURS

ANIMAL KINGDOM'S OPENING TIME corresponds to that of the other parks. Thus, you can expect a 9 a.m. opening during less busy times of the year and an 8 a.m. opening during holidays and high season. This park usually closes well before the others in Disney World, however—as early as 5 p.m., in fact, during off-season. More common is a 6 or 7 p.m. closing.

Park-opening procedures at Animal Kingdom vary. Sometimes guests arriving before the official opening time are admitted to The Oasis and Discovery Island. The remainder of the park is roped off until official opening time. The rest of the time, those arriving early are held at the entrance turnstiles.

unofficial **TIP**
Arrive, admission in hand, 40 minutes before official opening during the summer and holiday periods, and 30 minutes before official opening the rest of the year.

During the financial turmoil of the last few years, Disney has laid off a number of cast members and trotted out several cost-cutting initiatives. One of these is to delay the daily opening of Kali River Rapids in Asia, as well as the Boneyard playground, the Wildlife Express Train, and Conservation

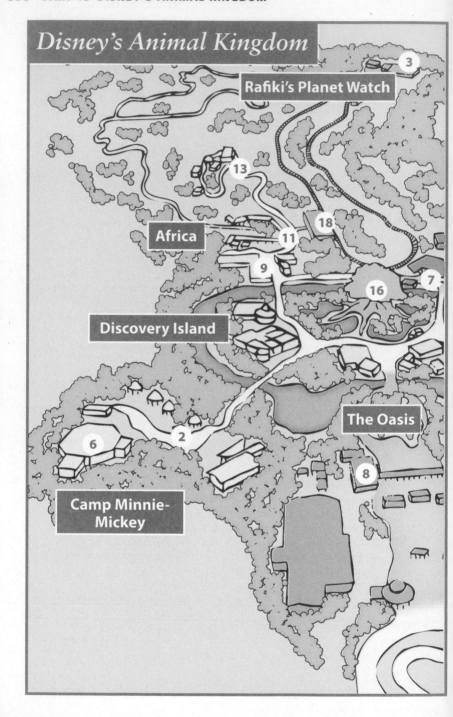

Disney's Animal Kingdom

Rafiki's Planet Watch

3

13

18

Africa

11

9

16

7

Discovery Island

The Oasis

2

6

8

Camp Minnie-
Mickey

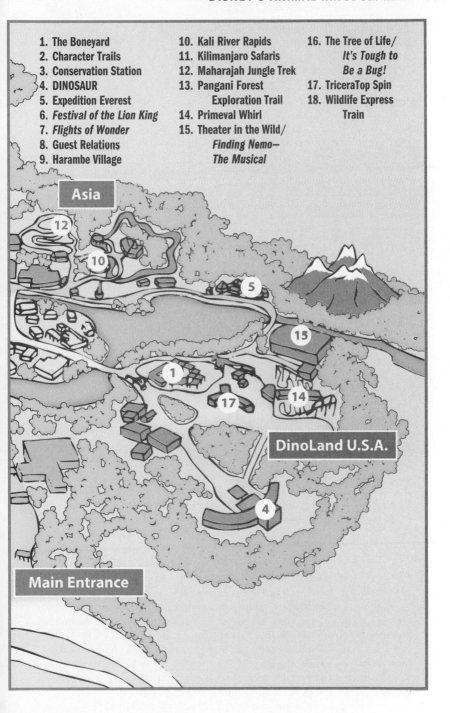

1. The Boneyard
2. Character Trails
3. Conservation Station
4. DINOSAUR
5. Expedition Everest
6. *Festival of the Lion King*
7. *Flights of Wonder*
8. Guest Relations
9. Harambe Village

10. Kali River Rapids
11. Kilimanjaro Safaris
12. Maharajah Jungle Trek
13. Pangani Forest
    Exploration Trail
14. Primeval Whirl
15. Theater in the Wild/
    *Finding Nemo—
    The Musical*

16. The Tree of Life/
    *It's Tough to
    Be a Bug!*
17. TriceraTop Spin
18. Wildlife Express
    Train

Asia

DinoLand U.S.A.

Main Entrance

Disney's Animal Kingdom Services

MOST OF THE PARK'S SERVICE FACILITIES are inside the main entrance and on Discovery Island as follows:

Baby Care Center	On Discovery Island, behind Creature Comforts
Banking Services	ATMs at the main entrance, by the turnstiles, and near DINOSAUR in DinoLand U.S.A.
Film and Cameras	Just inside the main entrance at Garden Gate Gifts, in Africa at Duka La Filimu and Mombasa Marketplace, and at other retail shops throughout the park
First Aid	On Discovery Island, next to the Creature Comforts Shop
Guest Relations/Information	Inside the main entrance to the left
Live Entertainment and Parade Information	Included in the park guide map, available free at Guest Relations
Lost and Found	Inside the main entrance to the left
Lost Persons	Can be reported at Guest Relations and at the Baby Care Center on Discovery Island
Storage Lockers	Inside the main entrance to the left
Wheelchair, ECV, and Stroller Rentals	Inside the main entrance, to the right

Station until 30 minutes or so after the rest of Animal Kingdom opens. It's not clear whether these delayed openings are temporary or permanent, seasonal or year-round.

On holidays and other days of projected heavy attendance, Disney will open the park 30–60 minutes early.

Many guests wrap up their tour and leave by 3:30 or 4 p.m. Lines for the major rides and the 3-D movie in The Tree of Life will usually thin appreciably between 4 p.m. and closing time. If you arrive at 2 p.m. and take in a couple of stage shows (described later), waits should be tolerable by the time you hit The Tree of Life and the rides.

Animal Kingdom has joined the other three major theme parks in the Extra Magic Hours early-entry program. Even with Expedition Everest open, getting up early to participate in the program doesn't really save you any time standing in line. Our testing has shown that the additional attendance on early-entry days totally nullifies any advantage associated with being admitted an hour early—the time required to see the same set of attractions is almost exactly equal to the time required on a non-early-entry day. Our advice is to get an extra hour of sleep and visit when early entry is not in effect.

Evening Extra Magic Hours are another story. In early 2011, Disney quietly changed Animal Kingdom's schedule so that it no longer includes evening Extra Magic Hours. As we were going to press, no evening hours were scheduled through January 2012. As compensation, the park has two morning EMH sessions per week. We're not sure whether this is a temporary move or a permanent change; your best bet is to check the Disney website as you plan your visit.

Kilimanjaro Safaris and the Pangani Forest Exploration Trail close around 30–60 minutes before sunset. Thus, as days get shorter with the change of seasons, the attractions close earlier in the day. In the fall, when the clocks are rolled back, Disney closes all animal exhibits as early as 4:45 p.m.

GETTING ORIENTED

AT THE ENTRANCE PLAZA ARE TICKET KIOSKS fronting the main entrance. To your right, before the turnstiles, is an ATM. After you pass through the turnstiles, wheelchair and stroller rentals are to your right. Guest Relations—the park headquarters for information, handout park maps, entertainment schedules (*Times Guides*), missing persons, and lost and found—is to the left. Nearby are restrooms, public phones, and rental lockers. Beyond the entrance plaza, you enter **The Oasis,** a lushly vegetated network of converging pathways winding through a landscape punctuated with streams, waterfalls, and misty glades and inhabited by what Disney calls "colorful and unusual animals."

The park is arranged somewhat like the Magic Kingdom, in a hub-and-spoke configuration. The lush, tropical Oasis serves as Main Street, funneling visitors to **Discovery Island** at the center of the park. Dominated by the park's central icon, the 14-story hand-carved **Tree of Life,** Discovery Island is the park's retail and dining center. From Discovery Island, guests can access the respective themed areas of **Africa, Camp Minnie-Mickey, Asia,** and **DinoLand U.S.A.** Discovery Island additionally hosts a theater attraction in The Tree of Life, and a number of short nature trails.

Even if you dawdle in the shops and linger over the wildlife exhibits, you should easily be able to take in Animal Kingdom in one day.

DINING IN DISNEY'S ANIMAL KINGDOM

COUNTER-SERVICE RESTAURANTS in Animal Kingdom are profiled in Part Ten, starting on page 453. For full-service profiles, see the section starting on page 457.

The OASIS

> *unofficial* **TIP**
> Animal-watching Disney-style requires a sharp eye and a bit of effort.

THOUGH THE FUNCTIONAL PURPOSE of The Oasis is the same as that of Main Street in the Magic Kingdom—that is, to funnel guests to the center of the park—it also serves as what Disney calls a "transitional experience." In plain English, this means that it sets the stage and gets you into the right mood to enjoy Disney's Animal Kingdom. You'll know the minute you pass through the turnstiles that this is not just another Main Street. Where Main Street, Hollywood Boulevard, and the Epcot entrance plaza direct you like an arrow straight into the heart of the respective parks, The Oasis immediately envelops you in an environment that is replete with choices. There's no one broad thoroughfare, but rather multiple paths. Each will deliver you to Discovery Island at the center of the park, but which path you choose and what you see along the way is up to you. Nothing obvious clues you in about where you're going—there's no Cinderella Castle or giant golf ball to beckon you. Instead you'll find a lush, green, canopied landscape with streams, grottoes, and waterfalls, an environment that promises adventure without revealing its nature.

The natural-habitat zoological exhibits in The Oasis are representative of those throughout the park. Although extraordinarily lush and beautiful, the exhibits are primarily designed for the comfort and well-being of the animals.

A sign will identify the animal(s) in each exhibit, but there's no guarantee the animals will be immediately visible. Because most habitats are large and provide ample terrain for the occupants to hide, you must linger and concentrate, looking for small movements in the vegetation. When you do spot the animal, you may make out only a shadowy figure, or perhaps only a leg or a tail.

TOURING TIPS The Oasis is a place to linger and appreciate, and although this is exactly what the designers intended, it will be largely lost on Disney-conditioned guests who blitz through at warp speed to queue up for the big attractions. If you're a blitzer in the morning, plan to spend some time in The Oasis on your way out of the park. The Oasis usually closes 30–60 minutes after the rest of the park.

DISCOVERY ISLAND

DISCOVERY ISLAND IS AN ISLAND of tropical greenery and whimsical equatorial African architecture, executed in vibrant hues of teal, yellow, red, and blue. Connected to the other lands by bridges, the island is the hub from which guests can access the park's various themed areas. A village is arrayed in a crescent around the base of Animal Kingdom's signature landmark, **The Tree of Life.** Towering 14 stories above the village, it's this park's version of Cinderella Castle or Spaceship Earth. Flanked by pools, meadows, and exotic gardens populated by a diversity of birds and animals, The Tree of Life houses a theater attraction inspired by the Disney/Pixar film *A Bug's Life.*

As you enter Discovery Island via the bridge from The Oasis and the park entrance, you'll see The Tree of Life directly ahead at the 12 o'clock position. The bridge to Asia is to the right of the tree at the 2 o'clock position, with the bridge to DinoLand U.S.A. at roughly 4 o'clock. The bridge connecting The Oasis to Discovery Island is at the 6 o'clock position; the bridge to Camp Minnie-Mickey is at 8 o'clock; and the bridge to Africa is at 11 o'clock.

Discovery Island is the park's central shopping, dining, and services headquarters. It's here that you'll find the **First Aid** and **Baby Care** centers. For the best selection of Disney trademark merchandise, try the **Island Mercantile** shop. Counter-service food and snacks are available, but there are no full-service restaurants on Discovery Island (the three full-service restaurants in the park are the **Rainforest Cafe,** to the left of the main entrance; **Tusker House Restaurant,** in Africa; and **Yak & Yeti Restaurant,** in Asia).

The Tree of Life / *It's Tough to Be a Bug!*   ★★★★

APPEAL BY AGE	PRESCHOOL ★★★	GRADE SCHOOL ★★★★	TEENS ★★★★
YOUNG ADULTS ★★★★		OVER 30 ★★★★	SENIORS ★★★★

What it is 3-D theater show. **Scope and scale** Major attraction. **When to go** Before noon or after 4 p.m. **Special comments** The theater is inside the tree. **Authors'**

rating Zany and frenetic and not to be missed; ★★★★. **Duration of presentation** About 8 minutes. **Probable waiting time** 12–30 minutes.

DISNEY DISH WITH JIM HILL

HIGH ART All you folks of a certain age who loved Cheech and Chong in your ill-spent youth will undoubtedly recognize the voice of Chili, the Chilean tarantula in this Animal Kingdom show. He's voiced by Cheech Marin, who over the past 25 years has gone from playing a stereotypical stoner to voicing characters for Disney and Pixar. Marin was Tito in *Oliver & Company,* Banzai in *The Lion King,* and Ramon in *Cars* and *Cars 2.*

DESCRIPTION AND COMMENTS The Tree of Life, apart from its size, is quite a work of art. Although from afar it's certainly magnificent and imposing, it's not until you examine the tree at close range that you truly appreciate its rich detail. What appears to be ancient gnarled bark is, in fact, hundreds of carvings depicting all manner of wildlife, each integrated seamlessly into the trunk, roots, and limbs of the tree. A stunning symbol of the interdependence of all living things, The Tree of Life is the most visually compelling structure to be found in any Disney park.

In sharp contrast to the grandeur of the tree is the subject of the attraction housed within its trunk. Called *It's Tough to Be a Bug!,* this humorous 3-D presentation is about the difficulties of being a very small creature. Contrasting with the relatively serious tone of Disney's Animal Kingdom in general, *It's Tough to Be a Bug!* stands virtually alone in providing some much-needed levity and whimsy. The show is similar to *Mickey's Philhar-Magic* at the Magic Kingdom in that it combines a 3-D film with an arsenal of tactile and visual special effects. We rate *Bug* as not to be missed.

TOURING TIPS Although it's in the most eye-popping structure in the park, *It's Tough to Be a Bug!* is rarely crowded even on the busiest days, and Fastpass is almost never needed. Go in the morning after Kilimanjaro Safaris, Kali River Rapids, Expedition Everest, and DINOSAUR. If you miss the *Bug* in the morning, try again in the late afternoon.

Be advised that *It's Tough to Be a Bug!* is very intense and that the special effects will do a number on young children as well as anyone who is squeamish about insects. A mother of two from Williamsville, New York, shared this experience:

> It's Tough to Be a Bug! *was my girls' first Disney experience, and almost their last. The storyline was nebulous and difficult to follow—all they were aware of was the torture of sitting in a darkened theater being overrun with bugs. Total chaos, the likes of which I've never experienced, was breaking out around us. A constant stream of parents headed to the exits with terrorized children. Those that were left behind were screaming and crying as well. The 11-year-old refused to talk for 20 minutes after the fiasco, and the 3½-year-old wanted to go home—not back to the hotel, but* home.

Most readers, however, loved the bugs, including this mom from Brentwood, Tennessee:

> Comments from your readers make It's Tough to Be a Bug! sound worse than Stitch's Great Escape! It's not. It's intense, but mostly funny. The bugs are cartoonlike instead of realistic and icky, so I can't understand what all the fuss is about. Kids think nothing of walking up to a mouse the size of a porta-john but go nuts over some cartoon bugs. Get a grip!

CAMP MINNIE-MICKEY

THIS LAND IS DESIGNED to be the Disney characters' Animal Kingdom headquarters. A small land, Camp Minnie-Mickey has a rustic, woodsy theme like that of a summer camp. In addition to a character meeting-and-greeting area, Camp Minnie-Mickey is home to a live stage production featuring Disney characters.

DISNEY DISH WITH JIM HILL

ANIMAL KINGDOM SINGS THE (AVATAR) BLUES James Cameron never does anything small. So when work begins on the building that will be the centerpiece of Animal Kingdom's forthcoming *Avatar* "land," expect to see one truly massive structure looming over the trees on the west side of the park. If all goes according to plan, the Imagineers will make use of the hi-def digital-projection system that powers the Magic Kingdom's *The Magic, The Memories and You!* to make it appear as if clouds are moving across the surface of Pandora.

Situated in a cul-de-sac, Camp Minnie-Mickey is a pedestrian nightmare. Lines for the stage show and from the character-greeting areas spill out into the congested walkways, making movement almost impossible. To compound the problem, hundreds of parked strollers clog the paths, squeezing the flow of traffic to a trickle. Meanwhile, hordes of guests trying to enter Camp Minnie-Mickey collide with guests trying to exit on the bridge connecting the camp to Discovery Island. It's a planning error of the first order, one that seems totally avoidable in a theme park with as much usable acreage as Animal Kingdom.

Character Trails

DESCRIPTION AND COMMENTS Characters can be found at the end of each of several "character trails." Each trail has its own private reception area and, of course, its own queue. A sign in front of each queue tells you to which character the path leads. The most typical lineup has Mickey, Minnie, Goofy, and Pluto at one queue each. Other frequently seen characters include Winnie the Pooh, Eeyore, Pocahontas, Timon, and Baloo. Disney will occasionally supplement these with characters from its latest film, if the movie has anything to do with nature, animals, or the environment. Mickey and Minnie are constants.

TOURING TIPS Characters usually appear an hour after the rest of the park opens. Waiting in line to see them can be very time-consuming. We recommend visiting early in the morning or late in the afternoon. Because there are fewer attractions at Animal Kingdom than at the other parks, expect to find a disproportionate number of guests in Camp Minnie-Mickey. If the place is really mobbed, you may want to consider meeting the characters in one of the other parks. Ditto for the stage show.

Festival of the Lion King ★★★★

APPEAL BY AGE PRESCHOOL ★★★★½	GRADE SCHOOL ★★★★½	TEENS ★★★★½
YOUNG ADULTS ★★★★½	OVER 30 ★★★★½	SENIORS ★★★★★

What it is Theater-in-the-round stage show. **Scope and scale** Major attraction. **When to go** Before 11 a.m. or after 4 p.m. **Special comments** Performance times are listed in the handout park map or *Times Guide*. **Authors' rating** Upbeat and spectacular; not to be missed; ★★★★. **Duration of presentation** 30 minutes. **Preshow entertainment** None. **When to arrive** 20–30 minutes before showtime.

DESCRIPTION AND COMMENTS This energetic production, inspired by Disney's *Lion King* feature, is part stage show, part parade, part circus. Guests are seated in four sets of bleachers surrounding the stage and organized into separate cheering sections, which are called on to make elephant, warthog, giraffe, and lion noises (you won't be alone if you don't know how to make a giraffe or warthog noise). There's a great deal of parading around, some acrobatics, and a lot of singing and dancing. By our count, every tune from *The Lion King* is belted out and reprised several times. No joke—if you don't know the words to all the songs by the end of the show, you must have been asleep.

Unofficial Guide readers are almost unanimous in their praise of *Festival of the Lion King*. This letter from a Naples, Florida, mom is typical:

> Festival of the Lion King *is a spectacular show with singers, dancers, fire twirlers, acrobats, robotics, and great set design. My whole family agreed this was the best thing we experienced at Animal Kingdom.*

TOURING TIPS This show is both popular and difficult to see. Your best bet is to go to the first show in the morning or to one of the last two performances in the evening. To see the show during the more crowded midday, you'll need to queue up at least 35–45 minutes before showtime. To minimize standing in the hot sun, refrain from hopping in line until the Disney people begin directing guests to the far-right queue. If you have small children or short adults in your party, sit higher up in the bleachers. The first five rows in particular have very little rise, making it difficult for those in rows two through five to see.

▌ AFRICA

AFRICA IS THE LARGEST of Animal Kingdom's lands, and guests enter through Harambe, a Disneyfied version of a modern rural African town. A market is equipped with modern cash registers; dining options consist of a sit-down buffet, limited counter service, and snack stands. What distinguishes Harambe is its understatement: Far from the stereotypical great-white-hunter image of an African town, Harambe is definitely (and realistically) not exotic. The buildings, while interesting, are architecturally simple. Though better maintained and more idealized than the real McCoy, Disney's Harambe would be a lot more at home in Kenya than the Magic Kingdom's Main Street would be in Missouri.

Harambe serves as the gateway to the African veldt habitat, Animal Kingdom's largest and most ambitious zoological exhibit. Access to the veldt is via the **Kilimanjaro Safaris** attraction, at the end of Harambe's main drag near the fat-trunked baobab tree. Harambe is also the departure point for the train to **Rafiki's Planet Watch** and **Conservation Station**, the park's veterinary headquarters.

Kilimanjaro Safaris *(Fastpass)* ★★★★★

APPEAL BY AGE   PRESCHOOL ★★★★½   GRADE SCHOOL ★★★★½   TEENS ★★★★½
YOUNG ADULTS ★★★★★   OVER 30 ★★★★½   SENIORS ★★★★★

What it is Ride through an African wildlife reservation. **Scope and scale** Super-headliner. **When to go** As soon as the park opens or in the 2 hours before closing, or use Fastpass. **Authors' rating** Truly exceptional; not to be missed; ★★★★★. **Duration of ride** About 20 minutes. **Average wait in line per 100 people ahead of you** 4 minutes; assumes full-capacity operation with 18-second dispatch interval. **Loading speed** Fast.

DISNEY DISH WITH JIM HILL

TAKING THE *KILL* **OUT OF** *KILIMANJARO* So why did the Imagineers finally opt to drop the "Poachers have captured Little Red!" storyline? For starters, blame former Disney CEO Michael Eisner, who reportedly just couldn't stand the sight of all those cast members' kids crying when they spied the plastic carcass of big dead Big Red (Little Red's mother) during a sneak peek of the safaris back before Animal Kingdom officially opened. Once Eisner ordered that prop removed, the endangered-baby-elephant storyline never really jelled. After years of head-scratching, the Imagineers sent Little Red and those poachers packing for good in anticipation of the attraction's new zebra habitat.

DESCRIPTION AND COMMENTS The park's premier zoological attraction, Kilimanjaro Safaris offers an exceptionally realistic, albeit brief, imitation of an actual African photo safari. Thirty-two guests at a time board tall, open safari vehicles and are dispatched into a simulated African veldt habitat. Animals such as zebras, wildebeests, impalas, Thomson's gazelles, giraffes, and even rhinos roam apparently free, while predators such as lions, as well as potentially dangerous large animals like hippos, are separated from both prey and guests by all-but-invisible, natural-appearing barriers. Although the animals have more than 100 acres of savanna, woodland, streams, and rocky hills to call home, careful placement of water holes, forage, and salt licks ensures that the critters are hanging out by the road when safari vehicles roll by.

A scripted storyline formerly had an onboard guide pointing out and identifying various animals for guests while also communicating by radio with a game warden about elephant poachers in the vicinity. Toward the end of the ride, the safari vehicle chased the poachers. The poaching narrative was recently scrapped to make way for a new zebra savanna, scheduled for completion in late 2012.

Having traveled in Kenya and Tanzania, I (Bob) will tell you that Disney has done an amazing job of replicating the sub-Saharan east-African landscape. The main difference that an east African would notice is that Disney's version is greener and, generally speaking, less barren. As on a real African safari, what animals you see, and how many, is pretty much a matter of luck. We've experienced Kilimanjaro Safaris more than 100 times and had a different experience on each trip.

In 2011 Disney introduced the **Wild Africa Trek,** a behind-the-scenes tour of the Animal Kingdom that takes you through much of the Kilimanjaro Safaris' animal enclosures. As you drive past the hippo pool or over the crocodile pool, look up for a series of rope bridges towering far above the ground. You may see Trekkers on tour. See page 705 of Part Nineteen for a complete description.

TOURING TIPS Kilimanjaro Safaris is Animal Kingdom's number-two draw behind Expedition Everest. This is good news: By distributing guests more evenly throughout the park, Expedition Everest makes it unnecessary to run to Kilimanjaro Safaris first thing in the morning. Our

Animal Kingdom touring plan has you obtain Fastpasses for the safaris just before lunch. While your Fastpass return window approaches, you'll have plenty of time to eat and tour the rest of Africa. Before Expedition Everest, seeing the Safaris early meant backtracking to Africa later in the day to see exhibits and attractions that were not open first thing in the morning; our touring plan eliminates all of that extra walking, too.

Waits for Kilimanjaro Safaris diminish in late afternoon, sometimes as early as 3:30 p.m. but more commonly somewhat later. As noted previously, Kilimanjaro Safaris is a Fastpass attraction. If the wait exceeds 30 minutes when you arrive, by all means use Fastpass. The downside to Fastpass, and the reason we prefer that you ride around lunchtime, is that there aren't many other attractions in Africa to occupy your attention while you wait for your Fastpass return time. This means you'll probably be touring somewhere far removed when it's time to backtrack to Safaris.

If you want to take photos, be advised that the vehicle isn't guaranteed to stop at any location, although the drivers try their best to do so when big animals are sighted. Be prepared to snap at any time. Also, don't worry about the ride itself: It really isn't very rough. Finally, the only thing that a young child might find intimidating is crossing an "old bridge" that seems to collapse under your truck.

Pangani Forest Exploration Trail   ★★★★

**APPEAL BY AGE   PRESCHOOL ★★★★   GRADE SCHOOL ★★★★   TEENS ★★★½
YOUNG ADULTS ★★★★   OVER 30 ★★★★   SENIORS ★★★★**

What it is Walk-through zoological exhibit. **Scope and scale** Major attraction. **When to go** Anytime. **Authors' rating ★★★★. Duration of tour** About 20–25 minutes.

DESCRIPTION AND COMMENTS As the trail winds between the domain of two troops of lowland gorillas, it's hard to see what, if anything, separates you from the primates. Also on the trail are a hippo pool with an underwater viewing area, and a naked-mole-rat exhibit. A highlight of the trail is an exotic-bird aviary so craftily designed that you can barely tell you're in an enclosure.

TOURING TIPS The Pangani Forest Exploration Trail is lush, beautiful, and jammed to the gills with people much of the time. Guests exiting the safari can choose between returning to Harambe or walking the Pangani Forest Exploration Trail. Many opt for the trail. Thus, when the safari is operating at full tilt, it spews hundreds of guests every couple of minutes onto the Exploration Trail. The one-way trail in turn becomes so clogged that nobody can move or see much of anything. After a minute or two, however, you catch the feel of the mob moving forward in small lurches. From then on you shift, elbow, grunt, and wriggle your way along, every so often coming to an animal exhibit. Here you endeavor to work your way close to the rail but are opposed by people trapped against the rail who are trying to rejoin the surging crowd. The animals, as well as their natural-habitat enclosures, are pretty nifty if you can fight your way close enough to see them.

Clearly this attraction is either badly designed, misplaced, or both. Your only real chance for enjoying it is to walk through before 10 a.m. (that is, before the safari hits full stride) or after 2:30 p.m.

Another strategy, especially if you're more into the wildlife than the thrill rides, is to head for Kilimanjaro Safaris as soon as the park opens and get a Fastpass instead of riding. Early in the morning, the return window will be short—just long enough, in fact, for an uncrowded, leisurely tour of the Pangani Forest Exploration Trail before you go on safari.

RAFIKI'S PLANET WATCH

THIS AREA ISN'T REALLY a "land" and not really an attraction either. Our best guess is that Disney uses the name as an umbrella for Conservation Station, the petting zoo, and the environmental exhibits accessible from Harambe via the Wildlife Express Train. Presumably, Disney hopes that invoking Rafiki (a beloved character from *The Lion King*) will stimulate guests to make the effort to check out things in this far-flung outpost of the park.

Conservation Station and Affection Section ★★★

APPEAL BY AGE	PRESCHOOL ★★★½	GRADE SCHOOL ★★★½	TEENS ★★★
YOUNG ADULTS ★★★	OVER 30 ★★★		SENIORS ★★★

What it is Behind-the-scenes educational exhibit and petting zoo. **Scope and scale** Minor attraction. **When to go** Anytime. **Special comments** Opens 30 minutes after the rest of the park. **Authors' rating** Not bad; ★★★. **Probable waiting time** None.

DESCRIPTION AND COMMENTS Conservation Station is Animal Kingdom's veterinary and conservation headquarters. On the perimeter of the African section of the park, Conservation Station is, strictly speaking, a backstage, working facility. Here guests can meet wildlife experts, observe some of the Station's ongoing projects, and learn about the behind-the-scenes operations of the park. The Station includes a rehabilitation area for injured animals and a nursery for recently born (or hatched) critters. Vets and other experts are on hand to answer questions.

While there are several permanent exhibits, including Affection Section (an animal-petting area), what you see at Conservation Station will largely depend on what's going on when you arrive. On most days when we visit, there isn't enough happening to warrant waiting in line twice (coming and going) for the train. Most of our readers tell us that Conservation Station is not worth the hassle. A Tinley Park, Illinois, mom writes:

Skip Conservation Station at Animal Kingdom. Between the train ride to get to it and being there, we wasted a precious 1½ hours!

A Denver family had a better experience:

We really enjoyed Conservation Station at Animal Kingdom. We saw a 13-foot python eating a rat!

And a reader from Kent in the United Kingdom was amused by both the goings-on and the other guests:

The most memorable part of Animal Kingdom for me was watching a veterinary surgeon and his team at Conservation Station perform an operation on a rat snake that had inadvertently swallowed a golf ball, presumably believing it to be an egg! This operation took about an hour and caused at least one onlooker to pass out.

You can access Conservation Station by taking the Wildlife Express Train directly from Harambe. To return to the center of the park, continue the loop from Conservation Station back to Harambe.

TOURING TIPS To enjoy Conservation Station, you have to invest a little effort and be inquisitive. Because it's so removed from the rest of the park, you'll never bump into it unless you take the train.

Habitat Habit!

DESCRIPTION AND COMMENTS Listed on park maps as an attraction is Habitat Habit!, on the pedestrian path between the train station and Conservation Station. It consists of a tiny collection of signs about wild-life and a few cotton-top tamarins. To call it an attraction is absurd.

Wildlife Express Train ★★

APPEAL BY AGE	PRESCHOOL ★★★½	GRADE SCHOOL ★★★	TEENS ★★★
YOUNG ADULTS ★★½		OVER 30 ★★★	SENIORS ★★★

What it is Scenic railroad ride to Rafiki's Planet Watch and Conservation Station. **Scope and scale** Minor attraction. **When to go** Anytime. **Special comments** Opens 30 minutes after the rest of the park. **Authors' rating** Ho-hum; ★★. **Duration of ride** About 5–7 minutes one-way. **Average wait in line per 100 people ahead of you** 9 minutes. **Loading speed** Moderate.

DESCRIPTION AND COMMENTS This ride snakes behind the African wild-life reserve as it makes its loop connecting Harambe to Rafiki's Planet Watch and Conservation Station. En route, you see the nighttime enclo-sures for the animals that populate Kilimanjaro Safaris. Similarly, return-ing to Harambe, you see the backstage areas of Asia. Regardless of which direction you're heading, the sights aren't especially interesting.

TOURING TIPS Most guests will embark for Rafiki's Planet Watch and Con-servation Station after experiencing Kilimanjaro Safaris and the Pan-gani Forest Exploration Trail. Thus, the train begins to get crowded between 10 and 11 a.m.

ASIA

CROSSING THE ASIA BRIDGE FROM DISCOVERY ISLAND, you enter Asia through the village of Anandapur, a veritable collage of Asian themes inspired by the architecture and ruins of India, Thailand, Indonesia, and Nepal. Situated near the bank of the Chakranadi River (translation: "the river that runs in circles") and surrounded by lush vegetation, Anandapur provides access to a gibbon exhibit and to Asia's two feature attractions, the **Kali River Rapids** whitewater-raft ride and **Expedition Everest.** Also in Asia is *Flights of Wonder,* an educational production about birds.

Expedition Everest—yep, another mountain, and at 200 feet, the tallest in Florida—is a super-headliner roller coaster. You board an old mountain railway destined for the foot of Mount Everest that ends up racing both forward and backward through caverns and frigid can-yons en route to paying a social call on the Abominable Snowman. Expedition Everest is billed as a "family thrill ride," which means sim-ply that it's more like Big Thunder Mountain Railroad than like the Rock 'n' Roller Coaster.

Expedition Everest *(Fastpass)* ★★★★½

APPEAL BY AGE	PRESCHOOL ★★★	GRADE SCHOOL ★★★★½	TEENS ★★★★★
YOUNG ADULTS ★★★★★		OVER 30 ★★★★★	SENIORS ★★★★

What it is High-speed outdoor roller coaster through Nepalese mountain village. **Scope and scale** Super-headliner. **When to go** Before 9:30 a.m. or after 3 p.m., or use Fastpass. **Special comments** 44" minimum height requirement. Switching-off option provided (see page 334). **Authors' rating** Contains some of the park's most stunning visual elements; not to be missed; ★★★★½. **Duration of ride** 3½ minutes. **Average wait in line per 100 people ahead of you** Just under 4 minutes; assumes 2 tracks operating. **Loading speed** Moderate–fast.

DISNEY DISH WITH JIM HILL

SIMPLY PANDORABLE In addition to the bizarre computer-generated critters of the upcoming *Avatar* "land," Animal Kingdom may be getting some cuddly new for-real residents in the near future. To commemorate the opening of the $4 billion Shanghai Disney Resort in late 2012, the Chinese government will reportedly partner with Disney to bring giant pandas to the park. Look for these cute-times-infinity creatures to set up housekeeping just north of Expedition Everest.

DESCRIPTION AND COMMENTS The first true roller coaster in Disney's Animal Kingdom, Expedition Everest earned the park's longest waits in line from the moment it opened—and for good reason. Your journey begins in an elaborate waiting area modeled after a Nepalese village; then you board an old train headed for the top of Mount Everest. Throughout the waiting area are posted notes from previous expeditions, some with cryptic observations regarding a mysterious creature said to guard the mountain. These ominous signs are ignored (as if you have a choice!), resulting in a high-speed encounter with the Abominable Snowman himself.

The ride consists of tight turns (some while traveling backward), hills, and dips, but no loops or inversions. From your departure at the loading station through your first high-speed descent, you'll see some of the most spectacular panoramas available in Walt Disney World. On a clear day, you'll be able to view the arrangement of the buildings at Coronado Springs, Epcot's Spaceship Earth, and possibly downtown Orlando. But look quickly, because you'll immediately be propelled, projectile-like, through the inner and outer reaches of the mountain. The final drop and last few turns are among the best-designed coaster effects Disney has ever made. A few minor criticisms: At a couple of points, your vehicle is stopped while the ride's track is reconfigured, affecting the attraction's continuity. And while the Audio-Animatronic Yeti is undoubtedly impressive, he breaks down more than a 30-year old Fiat. Most days Disney just simulates the Yeti moving by flashing a strobe light on his motionless body. But don't let these small shortcomings stop you from riding.

The coaster reaches a top speed of around 50 mph, just about twice that of Space Mountain, so expect to see the usual warnings for health and safety. The first few seats of these vehicles offer the best front-seat experience of any Disney coaster, indoor or out. If at all possible, ask to sit up front. Also, look for the animal poop on display in the Fastpass return line—a deliberate attempt at verisimilitude, or did Disney run out of money for ride props and use whatever they could find? You decide.

As you might expect for a super-headliner attraction, Expedition Everest is the subject of much reader mail. A Seattle family rated Expedition Everest four thumbs up:

Expedition Everest is tremendous. It has enough surprises and runaway speed to make it one of the more enjoyable thrill rides in the whole Orlando area.

For a Kettering, Ohio, mom, it was a multigenerational happening:

Expedition Everest alone is worth the cost of park admission—we had three generations on the ride, and everybody loved it!

A Macon, Georgia, teen recruited the aged:

Expedition Everest was so smooooth! I went right out and brought my granny back to ride it. She didn't throw up or anything!

Beating the morning crowds to Expedition Everest is also a hot topic. From a Yonkers, New York, man:

At Animal Kingdom the first ride we rode was Expedition Everest. When the park opened, the Disney people walked the crowd through Asia to the ride. We went right toward DinoLand and followed the path around the lake to Everest. We arrived about 90 seconds ahead of the crowd being walked in and were the first to ride. Upon exiting we noticed the line was already enormous, and, to our delight, the wait at the other major rides was negligible.

Finally, a mom from Fishers, Indiana, wonders where you can get a little butt-time:

They need benches near Expedition Everest—there was nowhere to sit with babies while others in our party rode it over and over. We sat on a rock!

A multigenerational family from Brookfield, Connecticut, had great luck with the singles line, writing:

The single-rider line at Expedition Everest is amazing! I went there without my mother and daughter and rode seven times in a row. I think my longest wait was 3–5 minutes, but often I just walked on!

TOURING TIPS Get Fastpasses for Everest first thing in the morning. Alternatively, ride immediately after the park opens or the last hour the park is open. If using Fastpass in the morning, try to tour DinoLand U.S.A. before you return; Kali River Rapids and *Flights of Wonder* don't usually open with the rest of Asia, so you'll backtrack less if you can get the must-see attractions in DinoLand covered early.

Flights of Wonder ★★★★

APPEAL BY AGE	PRESCHOOL ★★★★	GRADE SCHOOL ★★★★	TEENS ★★★★
YOUNG ADULTS ★★★★		OVER 30 ★★★★	SENIORS ★★★★

What it is Stadium show about birds. **Scope and scale** Major attraction. **When to go** Anytime. **Special comments** Performance times listed in handout park map or *Times Guide.* **Authors' rating** Unique; ★★★★. **Duration of presentation** 30 minutes. **Preshow entertainment** None. **When to arrive** 20–30 minutes before showtime.

DESCRIPTION AND COMMENTS *Flights of Wonder* is well paced and showcases a surprising number of bird species. The focus is on the natural talents and characteristics of the various species, so don't expect to see any parrots riding bicycles—the birds' natural behaviors far surpass any tricks learned from humans. A Brattleboro, Vermont, reader found *Flights of Wonder* especially compelling, writing:

The ornithologist guide is not only a wealth of information but a talented, comedic entertainer. The birds are thrilling, and we especially appreciated the fact that their antics were not the results of training against the grain but actual survival techniques the birds use in the wild.

Flights of Wonder exceeded the expectations of a Colorado Springs family with two elementary-school-age kids:

A coworker with kids the same age as ours said her kids loved Flights of Wonder. *Midway through the show I stopped taking pictures of the birds and began taking pictures of the expressions of amazement and joy on the faces of my kids and husband.*

TOURING TIPS *Flights of Wonder* plays at the stadium near the Asia Bridge on the walkway into Asia. Though the stadium is covered, it's not air-conditioned; thus, early-morning and late-afternoon performances are more comfortable. To play it safe, arrive about 10–15 minutes before showtime.

Kali River Rapids *(Fastpass)* ★★★½

APPEAL BY AGE   PRESCHOOL ★★★★   GRADE SCHOOL ★★★★½   TEENS ★★★★½
YOUNG ADULTS ★★★★   OVER 30 ★★★★   SENIORS ★★★★

What it is Whitewater-raft ride. **Scope and scale** Headliner. **When to go** Before 10:30 a.m. or after 4:30 p.m., or use Fastpass. **Special comments** You're guaranteed to get wet. Opens 30 minutes after the rest of the park. 38" minimum height requirement. Switching-off option available (see page 334). **Authors' rating** Short but scenic; ★★★½. **Duration of ride** About 5 minutes. **Average wait in line per 100 people ahead of you** 5 minutes. **Loading speed** Moderate.

DESCRIPTION AND COMMENTS Whitewater-raft rides have been a hot-weather favorite of theme park patrons for more than 20 years. The ride itself consists of an unguided trip down an artificial river in a circular rubber raft with a top-mounted platform seating 12 people. The raft essentially floats free in the current and is washed downstream through rapids and waves. Because the river is fairly wide, with numerous currents, eddies, and obstacles, there's no telling exactly where the raft will drift. Thus, each trip is different and exciting.

What distinguishes Kali River Rapids from other theme park raft rides is Disney's trademark attention to visual detail. Where many raft rides essentially plunge down a concrete ditch, Kali River Rapids flows through a dense rainforest and past waterfalls, temple ruins, and bamboo thickets, emerging into a cleared area where greedy loggers have ravaged the forest, and finally drifting back under the tropical canopy as the river cycles back to Anandapur. Along the way, your raft runs a gauntlet of raging cataracts, logjams, and other dangers.

The queuing area, which winds through an ancient Southeast Asian temple, is one of the most striking and visually interesting settings of any Disney attraction. And though the sights on the raft trip itself are also first-class, the attraction is marginal in two important respects. First, it's only about 3½ minutes on the water, and second, well . . . it's a weenie ride. Sure, you get wet, but otherwise the drops and rapids aren't all that exciting, as this Kansas family points out:

It was boiling hot, so we were happy about the prospect of being drenched. We couldn't believe how short and dull the ride was. At the end, we all looked at each other and said, "Is that IT?" We couldn't believe we'd stood in line, sweating half to death, for 75 minutes just for that.

How wet do you get? A Plymouth, Michigan, reader has the answer:

Beware! Rather than just getting a little wet like on Splash Mountain, you get soaked to the skin—beyond the fun kind of wet. Poncho sales were brisk the day we were there.

You can use Fastpass to ride later in the day when it's a little warmer. A family from Humble, Texas, who rode early in the morning on a cool day, shares this:

Our plan hit a definite wall upon experiencing Kali River Rapids as number two on the schedule. We didn't read about the precautions for this ride in your book until after riding. The 6-year-old and mom were COMPLETELY drenched—so much so that we actually had to leave the park and go back to our room at Port Orleans to change clothes. Since the temperature was around 60 degrees that morning, we were pretty miserable by the time we got back to our room. Needless to say, our schedule was shot by that time. We wouldn't recommend Kali River Rapids so early in the morning when the weather is chilly.

TOURING TIPS This attraction is hugely popular on hot summer days. Ride Kali River Rapids before 11 a.m., after 4:30 p.m., or use Fastpass. Again, you'll probably get drenched on this ride—we recommend wearing shorts to the park and bringing along a jumbo-sized trash bag or bin liner, as well as a smaller plastic bag. Before boarding the raft, take off your socks and punch a hole in your jumbo bag for your head. Though you can also cut holes for your arms, you'll probably stay drier with your arms inside the bag. Use the smaller plastic bag to wrap around your shoes. If you're worried about mussing your 'do, bring a third bag for your head.

A Shaker Heights, Ohio, family who donned our garbage-bag couture discovered that staying dry on Kali River Rapids is not without its social consequences:

I must tell you that the Disney cast members and the other people in our raft looked at us like we had just beamed down from Mars. Plus, we didn't cut arm holes in our trash bags because we thought we'd stay drier that way. Only problem was once we sat down we couldn't fasten our seat belts. One cast member asked sarcastically whether we needed wet suits and snorkels. After a lot of wiggling and adjusting and helping each other, we finally got belted in, and off we went looking like sacks of fertilizer with little heads perched on top. Very embarrassing, but we stayed nice and dry.

Other tips for staying dry (well, *drier*) include wearing as little as the law and Disney allow and storing a change of clothes in a park rental locker. Sandals are the perfect footwear, but if you're wearing closed shoes, try to prop your feet up above the bottom of the raft.

Maharajah Jungle Trek ★★★★

APPEAL BY AGE	PRESCHOOL ★★★★	GRADE SCHOOL ★★★★	TEENS ★★★★
YOUNG ADULTS ★★★★		OVER 30 ★★★★	SENIORS ★★★★

What it is Walk-through zoological exhibit. **Scope and scale** Headliner. **When to go** Anytime. **Special comments** Opens 30 minutes after the rest of the park. **Authors' rating** A standard-setter for natural habitat design; ★★★★. **Duration of tour** About 20–30 minutes.

DESCRIPTION AND COMMENTS The Maharajah Jungle Trek is a zoological nature walk similar to the Pangani Forest Exploration Trail, but with an Asian setting and Asian animals. You start with Komodo dragons and then work up to Malayan tapirs. Next is a cave with fruit bats. Ruins of the maharaja's palace provide the setting for Bengal tigers. From the top of a parapet in the palace you can view a herd of blackbuck antelope and Asian deer. The trek concludes with an aviary.

Labyrinthine, overgrown, and elaborately detailed, the temple ruin would be a compelling attraction even without the animals. Throw in a few bats, bucks, and Bengals and you're in for a treat.

Most readers agree. A Washington, D.C., couple chimed in with this:

We went on the Maharajah Jungle Trek, which was absolutely amazing. We were able to see all the animals, which were awake by that time (9:30 a.m.), including the elusive tigers. The part of the jungle trek with the birds was fabulous. If you looked, you could spot hundreds of birds, some of which were eating on the ground a mere 3 feet away from us. Take your time walking through the jungle, since most of the animals are not obvious to the breezing eye and you must look for them.

TOURING TIPS The Jungle Trek doesn't get as jammed up as the Pangani Forest Exploration Trail and is a good choice for midday touring when most other attractions are crowded. The downside, of course, is that the exhibit showcases tigers, tapirs, and other creatures that might not be as active in the heat of the day as mad dogs and Englishmen.

DINOLAND U.S.A.

THIS MOST TYPICALLY DISNEY of Animal Kingdom's lands is a cross between an anthropological dig and a quirky roadside attraction. Accessible via the bridge from Discovery Island, DinoLand U.S.A. is home to a children's play area, a nature trail, a 1,500-seat amphitheater, and **DINOSAUR,** one of Animal Kingdom's three thrill rides.

Also in DinoLand are a couple of natural-history exhibits, including **Dino-Sue,** an exact replica of the largest, most complete *Tyrannosaurus rex* discovered to date. Named after the fossil hunter Sue Hendrickson, the replica (like the original) is 40 feet long and 13 feet tall. And no, it doesn't dance, sing, or whistle, but it will get your attention nonetheless.

The Boneyard ★★★½

APPEAL BY AGE	PRESCHOOL ★★★★½		GRADE SCHOOL ★★★★	TEENS ★★
YOUNG ADULTS ★★		OVER 30 ★★½		SENIORS ★★

What it is Elaborate playground. **Scope and scale** Diversion. **When to go** Anytime. **Special comments** Opens 30 minutes after the rest of the park. **Authors' rating** Stimulating fun for children; ★★★½. **Duration of visit** Varies. **Probable waiting time** None.

DESCRIPTION AND COMMENTS This attraction is an elaborate playground, particularly appealing to kids age 12 and younger, but visually appealing to all ages. Arranged in the form of a rambling open-air dig site, The Boneyard offers plenty of opportunity for exploration and letting off steam. Playground equipment consists of the skeletons of *Triceratops, Tyrannosaurus rex, Brachiosaurus,* and the like, on which children can swing, slide, and climb. In addition, there are sandpits where little ones can scrounge around for bones and fossils.

TOURING TIPS Not the cleanest Disney attraction, but certainly one where younger children will want to spend some time. And aside from being dirty, or at least sandy, The Boneyard gets mighty hot in the Florida sun. Keep your kids well hydrated, and drag them into the shade from time to time. Try to save the playground until after you've experienced the main attractions. Because The Boneyard is so close to the center of the park, it's easy to stop in whenever your kids get antsy. While the little ones clamber around on giant femurs and ribs, you can sip a tall cool one in the shade (still keeping an eye on them, of course).

As a Michigan family attests, kids love The Boneyard:

The highlight for our kids was The Boneyard, especially the dig site. They just kept digging and digging to uncover the bones of the woolly mammoth. It was also in the shade, and there were places for parents to sit, making it a wonderful resting place.

And so do parents. From the father of a 4-year-old:

You should give playgrounds like The Boneyard higher ratings. After having our 4-year-old wait in lines for two days straight, she was thrilled to run around for 2 hours in The Boneyard without waiting for anything. Perhaps calling it a diversion is accurate, but it was a priceless diversion for us.

Be aware that The Boneyard rambles over about a half acre and is multistoried. It's pretty easy to lose sight of a small child in the playground. Fortunately, there's only one entrance and exit. A mother of two from Stillwater, Minnesota, found the playground too large for her liking:

If you're a parent who likes to have your eyes on your kids at all times, you won't like The Boneyard. Kids climb to the top of the slides, then you can't see them and you don't know what chute they'll be exiting from.

DINOSAUR *(Fastpass)* ★★★★½

APPEAL BY AGE	PRESCHOOL ★★½	GRADE SCHOOL ★★★½	TEENS ★★★★½
YOUNG ADULTS ★★★★★		OVER 30 ★★★★	SENIORS ★★★★½

What it is Motion-simulator dark ride. **Scope and scale** Super-headliner. **When to go** Before 10:30 a.m. or in the hour before closing, or use Fastpass. **Special comments** 40" minimum height requirement. Switching-off option provided (see page 334). **Authors' rating** Really improved; not to be missed; ★★★★½. **Duration of ride** 3½ minutes. **Average wait in line per 100 people ahead of you** 3 minutes; assumes full-capacity operation with 18-second dispatch interval. **Loading speed** Fast.

DISNEY DISH WITH JIM HILL

BUT CAN HE CHECK YOUR PC FOR VIRUSES? Disney is looking to offer park guests all sorts of high-tech gewgaws as it rolls out its next-generation radio-frequency-identification (RFID) technology. One of the weirder ideas is an Aladar avatar—a computer-generated version of the iguanodon protagonist from the 2000 Disney Animation Studios release *Dinosaur*—that guests can "capture" via RFID in their wristbands as they roll through DINOSAUR. Apparently, the Imagineers are looking to repurpose some of the animation created for the film in such a way that guests will be able to download an interactive iguanodon when they get home.

DESCRIPTION AND COMMENTS DINOSAUR is a combination track ride and motion simulator. In addition to moving along a cleverly hidden track, the ride vehicle also bucks and pitches (the simulator part) in sync with the visuals and special effects. The plot has you traveling back in time on a mission of rescue and conservation. Your objective: to haul back a living dinosaur before the species becomes extinct. Whoever is operating the clock, however, cuts it a little close, and you arrive on the prehistoric scene just as a giant asteroid is hurtling toward Earth. General mayhem ensues as you evade carnivorous predators, catch Barney, and get the heck out of Dodge before the asteroid hits.

DINOSAUR is a technological clone of the *Indiana Jones* ride at Disneyland. A good effort, although not quite as visually interesting as *Indiana Jones,* DINOSAUR serves up nonstop action from beginning to end with brilliant visual effects. Elaborate even by Disney standards, the attraction provides a tense, frenetic ride that's embellished by the entire Imagineering arsenal of high-tech gimmickry. The ride *is* jerky, but it's not too rough for seniors. The menacing dinosaurs, however, along with the intensity of the experience, make DINOSAUR a no-go for younger kids.

To its credit, Disney is unafraid to keep DINOSAUR a dark, fast ride. A mother from Kansasville, Wisconsin, liked it a lot, commenting:

DINOSAUR is the best ride at WDW. Our group of 10, ranging in age from 65 (grandma) to 8 (grandson), immediately—and unanimously!—got back in line immediately after finishing.

Others, like this Illinois family of four, got back in line also—for the bus to their hotel:

The scariness of DINOSAUR cannot be underestimated. We saw young kids in tears as they were coming off this ride, and it got mixed reviews within our own family. They snap the souvenir picture as the dinosaur is jumping out at you. We have the most awesome family picture: two of us laughing, two of us recoiling in terror!

And from a Michigan family:

Our 7-year-old son withstood every ride Disney threw at him, from Space Mountain to Tower of Terror. DINOSAUR, however, did him in. By the end, he was riding with his head down, scared to look around.

TOURING TIPS Disney situated DINOSAUR in such a remote corner of the park that guests have to poke around to find it. This, in conjunction with the overwhelming popularity of Kilimanjaro Safaris and Expedition Everest, makes DINOSAUR the easiest super-headliner attraction at Disney World to get on. We recommend, nonetheless, that you ride early after obtaining Fastpasses for Expedition Everest.

Primeval Whirl ★★★

APPEAL BY AGE	PRESCHOOL ★★	GRADE SCHOOL ★★★★	TEENS ★★★★
YOUNG ADULTS ★★★½		OVER 30 ★★★	SENIORS ★★½

What it is Small coaster. **Scope and scale** Minor attraction. **When to go** During the first 2 hours the park is open, in the hour before park closing. **Special comments** 48" minimum height requirement. Switching-off option provided (see page 334). **Authors' rating** "Wild mouse" on steroids; ★★★. **Duration of ride** Almost 2½ minutes. **Average wait in line per 100 people ahead of you** 4½ minutes. **Loading speed** Slow.

DESCRIPTION AND COMMENTS Primeval Whirl is a small coaster with short drops and curves, and it runs through the jaws of a dinosaur, among other things. What makes this coaster different is that the cars also spin.

You can't control the spinning—it starts and stops according to how the ride is programmed. Sometimes the spin is braked to a jarring halt after half a revolution, and sometimes it's allowed to make one or two complete turns. The complete spins are fun, but the screeching-stop half-spins are almost painful. If you subtract the time it takes to ratchet up the first hill, the actual ride time is about 90 seconds.

TOURING TIPS As for Space Mountain, the ride is duplicated side-by-side, but with only one queue. When it runs smoothly, about 700 people per side can whirl in an hour—a goodly number for this type of attraction, but not enough to preclude long waits on busy-to-moderate days. If you want to ride, try to get on before 11 a.m.

Theater in the Wild / *Finding Nemo—The Musical*
★★★★

APPEAL BY AGE PRESCHOOL ★★★★ GRADE SCHOOL ★★★★ TEENS ★★★★
YOUNG ADULTS ★★★★   OVER 30 ★★★★   SENIORS ★★★★

What it is Enclosed venue for live stage shows. **Scope and scale** Major attraction. **When to go** Anytime. **Special comments** Performance times are listed in the handout park map or *Times Guide*. **Authors' rating** Not to be missed; ★★★★. **Duration of presentation** About 35 minutes. **When to arrive** 30 minutes before showtime.

DISNEY DISH WITH JIM HILL

A TIGHT-LIPPED APPROACH Michael Curry, the puppeteering genius behind many of the actor-operated dimensional characters in Disney's *The Lion King* on Broadway, had a simple request for the creative team of *Finding Nemo—The Musical*: "Let's not go backwards." Guests, he reasoned, understand that actors give voice and movement to the puppets on stage; therefore, there's no need to burden the performers with the task of moving their puppets' lips in perfect sync to the dialogue. Curry even included a few puppets whose mouths don't move at all so that the live actors' performances can shine through.

DESCRIPTION AND COMMENTS Another chapter in the Pixar-ization of Disney theme parks, *Finding Nemo* is arguably the most elaborate live show in any Disney World theme park. Incorporating dancing, special effects, and sophisticated digital backdrops of the undersea world, it features on-stage human performers retelling Nemo's story with colorful, larger-than-life puppets. To be fair, "puppets" doesn't adequately convey the size or detail of these props, many of which are as big as a car and require two people to manipulate. An original musical score was written for the show, which is a must-see for most Animal Kingdom guests. A few scenes, such as one in which Nemo's mom is eaten, may be too intense for some very small children. Some of the midshow musical numbers slow the pace, so the main concern for parents is whether the kids can sit still for an entire show. With that in mind, we advise parents to catch an afternoon performance—around 3 p.m. would be great—after seeing the rest of Animal Kingdom. If the kids get restless, you can either leave the show and catch the afternoon parade, or end your day at the park.

New Jersey drama critics have their own way with words, as this family of five demonstrates:

The Finding Nemo musical is da bomb! The musical was amazing! It's a flaw-less package of puppetry, effects, music, and lots of Disney magic! Even if you don't have kids in your party, go see it!

TOURING TIPS To get a seat, show up 20–25 minutes in advance for morning and late-afternoon shows, and 30–35 minutes in advance for shows scheduled between noon and 4:30 p.m. Access to the theater is via a relatively narrow pedestrian path—if you arrive as the previous show is letting out, you'll feel like a salmon swimming upstream.

TriceraTop Spin ★ ★

APPEAL BY AGE	PRESCHOOL ★ ★ ★ ★	GRADE SCHOOL ★ ★ ★ ★	TEENS ★ ★ ★
YOUNG ADULTS ★ ★		OVER 30 ★ ★ ½	SENIORS ★ ★

What it is Hub-and-spoke midway ride. **Scope and scale** Minor attraction. **When to go** First 90 minutes the park is open or the hour before park closing. **Authors' rating** Dumbo's prehistoric forebear; ★ ★. **Duration of ride** 1½ minutes. **Average wait in line per 100 people ahead of you** 10 minutes. **Loading speed** Slow.

DESCRIPTION AND COMMENTS Another Dumbo-like ride. Here you spin around a central hub until a dinosaur pops out of the top of the hub. You'd think with the collective imagination of the Walt Disney Company, they'd come up with something a little more creative.

TOURING TIPS An attraction for the children, except they won't appreciate the long wait for this slow-loading ride.

LIVE ENTERTAINMENT *in* DISNEY'S ANIMAL KINGDOM

WDW LIVE-ENTERTAINMENT GURU Steve Soares usually posts the Animal Kingdom performance schedule about a week in advance at **wdwent.com.**

AFTERNOON PARADE Mickey's Jammin' Jungle Parade is comparable to the parades at the other parks, complete with floats, Disney characters (especially those from *The Lion King, The Jungle Book,* and *Song of the South*), skaters, acrobats, and stilt walkers.

Though subject to change, the parade starts in Africa, crosses the bridge to Discovery Island, proceeds counterclockwise around the island, and then crosses the bridge to Asia. In Asia, the parade turns left and follows the walkway paralleling the river back to Africa. The walking path between Africa and Asia has several small cutouts that offer good views of the parade and excellent sun protection. As it's used mainly as a walkway, the path is also relatively uncrowded. (*Note:* The paths on Discovery Island get very crowded, making it easy to lose members of your party.)

Here's our advice for watching the festivities:

The parade both begins and ends near the entrance to Camp Minnie-Mickey on Discovery Island. From Camp Minnie-Mickey, the route goes counterclockwise around Discovery Island and over the bridge to Asia (the parade doesn't enter DinoLand U.S.A. at all). Once over the bridge to Asia, the parade turns left and heads for Africa, where it turns left again at the Dawa Bar in the village of Harambe, crosses the bridge to Discovery Island, and heads back to Camp Minnie-Mickey.

Don't be concerned if you find a huge group when the parade emerges. As soon as the parade gets out of sight, the crowd should break up and leave the area relatively deserted. Because most guests don't realize that the parade returns, few are on hand when the parade rumbles through the second time en route to going offstage. Therefore, if you make your way to Camp Minnie-Mickey about 20 minutes after the parade time listed in the handout *Times Guide,* you should be able to score yourself an excellent vantage point at the last minute.

ANIMAL ENCOUNTERS Throughout the day, Disney staff conduct impromptu short lectures on specific animals at the park. Look for a cast member in safari garb holding a bird, reptile, or small mammal.

GOODWILL AMBASSADORS A number of Asian and African cast members are on hand throughout the park. Gracious and knowledgeable, they're delighted to discuss their native countries and the wildlife in them. Look for these ambassadors in Harambe and along the Pangani Forest Exploration Trail in Africa, and in Anandapur and along the Maharajah Jungle Trek in Asia. They can also be found near the main entrance and at The Oasis.

KIDS' DISCOVERY CLUB Activity stations offer kids ages 4–8 a structured learning experience as they tour Animal Kingdom. Set up along walkways in six themed areas, Discovery Club stations are manned by cast members who supervise a different activity at each station. A souvenir logbook, available free, is stamped at each station when the child completes a craft or exercise. Kids enjoy collecting the stamps and noodling puzzles in the logbook while in attraction lines.

STAGE SHOWS These are performed daily at the Lion King Theater in Camp Minnie-Mickey, at the Theater in the Wild in DinoLand U.S.A., and at the stadium in Asia. Shows at Camp Minnie-Mickey and DinoLand U.S.A. feature the Disney/Pixar characters.

STREET PERFORMERS Can be found most of the time at Camp Minnie-Mickey, at Harambe in Africa, and at Anandapur in Asia.

Far and away the most intriguing of these performers is the one you can't see—at least not at first. Totally bedecked in foliage and luxuriant vines is a stilt walker named **DiVine,** who blends so completely with Animal Kingdom's dense flora that you never notice her until she moves. We've seen guests standing less than a foot away gasp in amazement as DiVine brushes them with a leafy tendril. Usually found on the path between Asia and Africa, DiVine is a must-see. If you don't encounter her, ask a cast member when and where she can be found. Video of her is available at **YouTube** (go to **youtube.com** and search for "DiVine Disney's Animal Kingdom"), and excellent photographs of her are featured at **arondaparks.com/DeVine.htm.**

TRAFFIC PATTERNS *in* DISNEY'S ANIMAL KINGDOM

THE FIVE CROWD MAGNETS ARE *It's Tough to Be a Bug!* in The Tree of Life, Kilimanjaro Safaris in Africa, DINOSAUR in DinoLand U.S.A., and Kali River Rapids and Expedition Everest in Asia.

Because the park hosts large crowds with only a relative handful of attractions, expect for all attractions to be extremely busy, and for Expedition Everest and Kilimanjaro Safaris to be mobbed. Most guests arrive in the morning, with a sizable number on hand before opening and a larger wave arriving before 10 a.m. Guests continue to stream in through the late morning and into the early afternoon, with crowds peaking at around 2 p.m. From about 2:30 p.m. on, departing guests outnumber arriving guests by a wide margin, as guests who arrived early complete their tour and leave. Crowds thin appreciably by late afternoon and continue to decline into the early evening.

unofficial **TIP**
If you visit during late afternoon, you'll almost certainly have to return another afternoon to finish seeing everything.

Because the number of attractions, including theater presentations, is limited, most guests complete a fairly comprehensive tour in two-thirds of a day if they arrive early. Thus, generally speaking, your best bet for easy touring is either to be on hand when the park opens or to arrive at about 3 p.m. (if the park stays open until 7 or 8 p.m.), when the early birds are heading for the exits.

How guests tour Animal Kingdom depends on their prior knowledge of the park and its attractions. Newbies make their way to Discovery Island and depend on their park map to decide what to do next. Animal Kingdom experts make straight for Kilimanjaro Safaris in Africa and Expedition Everest in Asia. Kali River Rapids in Asia and *It's Tough to Be a Bug!* in The Tree of Life are also early-morning favorites.

With so many guests heading first thing for either Kilimanjaro Safaris in Africa or Expedition Everest in Asia, the remaining lands and attractions are lightly trafficked backwaters until late morning. As the day wears on, the masses who have experienced Kilimanjaro Safaris and Expedition Everest turn their attention to other shows and attractions, and the crowds become more equally distributed. Less-popular attractions now don't experience high traffic until 11:30.

To get a complete view of the actual traffic patterns while you're in the park, use our mobile app, **Lines** (**touringplans.com/lines**). It gives you current wait times and future estimates in half-hour increments for today and tomorrow. A quick glance shows how traffic patterns affect wait times throughout the day.

DISNEY'S ANIMAL KINGDOM TOURING PLAN

TOURING ANIMAL KINGDOM is not as complicated as touring the other parks because it has fewer attractions. Also, most rides, shows, and exhibits are oriented to the entire family, eliminating differences of opinion regarding how to spend the day. Here, the whole family can pretty much see and enjoy everything together.

Because there are fewer attractions than at the other parks, expect the crowds at Animal Kingdom to be more concentrated. If a line seems unusually long, ask a cast member what the estimated wait is. If the wait exceeds your tolerance, try the same attraction again after 3 p.m., while a show is in progress at the Theater in the Wild in DinoLand U.S.A., or while some special event is going on.

unofficial **TIP**
For the time being, the limited number of attractions in Animal Kingdom can work to your advantage.

"Not a Touring Plan" Touring Plans

For the type-B reader, these touring plans (see page 817) avoid detailed step-by-step strategies for saving every last minute in line. For Animal Kingdom, these "not" touring plans include advice for adults and parents with one day in the park, for anyone with two days, and for anyone with an afternoon and a full day to tour.

BEFORE YOU GO

1. Call ☎ 407-824-4321 before you go for the park's operating hours.

2. Purchase your admission before arrival.

DISNEY'S ANIMAL KINGDOM ONE-DAY TOURING PLAN *(page 829)*

THIS TOURING PLAN ASSUMES a willingness to experience all major rides and shows. Be forewarned that Expedition Everest, DINOSAUR, Kali River Rapids, and Primeval Whirl are sometimes frightening to children under age 8. Similarly, the theater attractions at The Tree of Life might be too intense for some preschoolers. When you're following the touring plan, simply skip any attraction you don't wish to experience.

Many readers have asked us whether fewer animals are visible from Kilimanjaro Safaris around lunchtime than at park opening, out of concern that the animals might be less active in the midday heat. To help answer that question, we sent a team of researchers to ride continuously during one week in the summer and had them count the number of animals visible at different times of day. We subdivided our counting into large animals (elephants, hippos, and lions, for example), small (deer and other ungulates), and birds. Our results indicate that you'll probably see the same number of animals regardless of when you visit. As we mention in the Kilimanjaro Safaris review, this finding is almost certainly due to Disney's deliberate placement of water, food, and shade near the safari vehicles.

PART FOURTEEN

DISNEY'S HOLLYWOOD STUDIOS

FORMERLY KNOWN AS DISNEY-MGM STUDIOS, Disney's Hollywood Studios was hatched from a corporate rivalry and a wild, twisted plot. At a time when The Walt Disney Company was weak and fighting off "greenmail"—hostile-takeover bids—Universal's parent company at the time, MCA, announced it was going to build an Orlando clone of its wildly successful Universal Studios Hollywood theme park. Behind the scenes, MCA was courting the real estate–rich Bass brothers of Texas, hoping to secure their investment in the project. The Basses, however, defected to the Disney camp and were front and center when Michael Eisner suddenly announced that Disney, too, would build a movie theme park in Florida. A construction race ensued, but Universal, in the middle of developing new attraction technologies, was no match for Disney, which could import proven concepts and attractions from its other parks. In the end, Disney's Hollywood Studios opened May 1, 1989, more than a year before Universal Studios Florida.

THE END OF THE MGM CONNECTION

SO WHAT HAPPENED TO "DISNEY-MGM STUDIOS"? Disney purchased Pixar Animation Studios after partnering with the company on a series of highly successful films, including *Toy Story; A Bug's Life; Monsters, Inc.; Finding Nemo;* and *The Incredibles.* The cost of continuing an association with MGM, coupled with Pixar's arguably greater popularity, probably convinced Disney to rename the theme park. But rather than replace *MGM* with *Pixar,* Disney decided that *Hollywood* represented a more generic reference to moviemaking. In practice, however, many folks drop the *Hollywood* entirely, referring to the park simply as "Disney Studios" or "The Studios."

WHAT'S OFFERED AT THE STUDIOS TODAY

DHS'S SOUNDSTAGES and facilities produced many television shows and films, both live-action and animated, in the park's early years. The 2003 Disney film *Brother Bear* was largely drawn—by hand!—in the Magic of Disney Animation attraction, and cinema buffs will recognize DHS's landscape in the background of Jim Varney's magnum opus, *Ernest Saves Christmas.* TV series filmed here span everything from the

NOT TO BE MISSED AT DISNEY'S HOLLYWOOD STUDIOS	
• *Fantasmic!*	• Studio Backlot Tour
• *Jim Henson's Muppet-Vision 3-D*	• Toy Story Mania!
• Rock 'n' Roller Coaster	• *Voyage of the Little Mermaid*
• Star Tours—The Adventures Continue	• The Twilight Zone Tower of Terror

ABC hit *Who Wants to Be a Millionaire?* to the Hulk Hogan fiasco *Thunder in Paradise.*

In addition, DHS once hosted a variety of attractions that explained how TV shows and movies are made. The *Monster Sound Show,* which ran during the Studios' first decade, used audience volunteers to show how sound effects were added to films; the contemporaneous *SuperStar Television* reenacted famous TV scenes using "green screen" technology and theme park guests as actors.

Today, the *Studios* in "Disney's Hollywood Studios" is of little significance. Movie production left here long ago; it's been more than a decade since any television production of note has taken place; and only a handful of attractions remain that offer a peek behind the scenes, such as the Studio Backlot Tour and the *Indiana Jones Epic Stunt Spectacular!* Unfortunately—for those who loved its creative aspects, that is—DHS is now simply an amusement park whose theme is movies and TV.

While many of the current attractions are entertaining, Disney's self-promotion is often blatant, inescapable, and distracting. The primary goal of any new DHS development, it seems, is to market an upcoming Disney film, TV franchise, or musical act. Most visitors are willing to forgive Disney its excesses, but hardcore devotees lament these changes and remember how good the Studios was when education was the goal instead of the medium.

HOW MUCH TIME TO ALLOCATE

WHEREAS IT'S IMPOSSIBLE to see all of Epcot or the Magic Kingdom in one day, DHS is doable: There's far less ground to cover by foot, trams carry guests through much of the backlot, and attractions are concentrated in an area about the size of Main Street, Tomorrowland, and Frontierland combined.

One fly in the ointment, however, is the park's perverse way of scheduling live shows. A Hoover, Alabama, mom explains:

> DHS was a big negative. The way the shows were scheduled and staggered, it was impossible to get from one to another in time.

A West Chester, Pennsylvania, mother of two adds:

> If I had it to do over, I'd skip the Studios. The shows were good, but we kept missing showtimes because either all the shows started at the same time or the walk between them was too long with little ones. We missed Disney Junior three times by just a few seconds.

Because DHS is smaller, it's more affected by large crowds. Our touring plan will help you stay a step ahead of the mob and minimize

Disney's Hollywood Studios

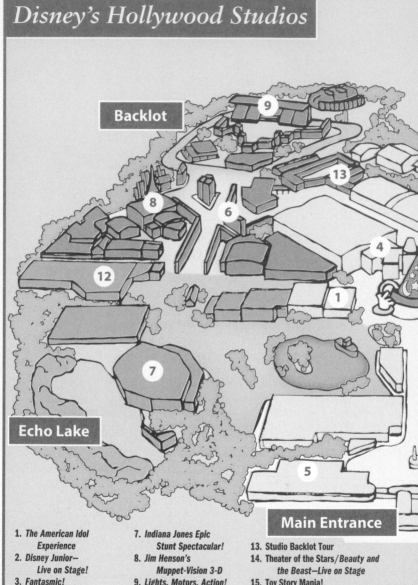

Backlot

Echo Lake

Main Entrance

1. *The American Idol Experience*
2. *Disney Junior— Live on Stage!*
3. *Fantasmic!*
4. *The Great Movie Ride*
5. Guest Relations
6. Honey, I Shrunk the Kids Movie Set Adventure
7. *Indiana Jones Epic Stunt Spectacular!*
8. *Jim Henson's Muppet-Vision 3-D*
9. *Lights, Motors, Action! Extreme Stunt Show*
10. The Magic of Disney Animation
11. Rock 'n' Roller Coaster
12. Star Tours—The Adventures Continue/ Jedi Training Academy
13. Studio Backlot Tour
14. Theater of the Stars/*Beauty and the Beast—Live on Stage*
15. Toy Story Mania!
16. The Twilight Zone Tower of Terror
17. *Voyage of the Little Mermaid*
18. *Walt Disney: One Man's Dream*

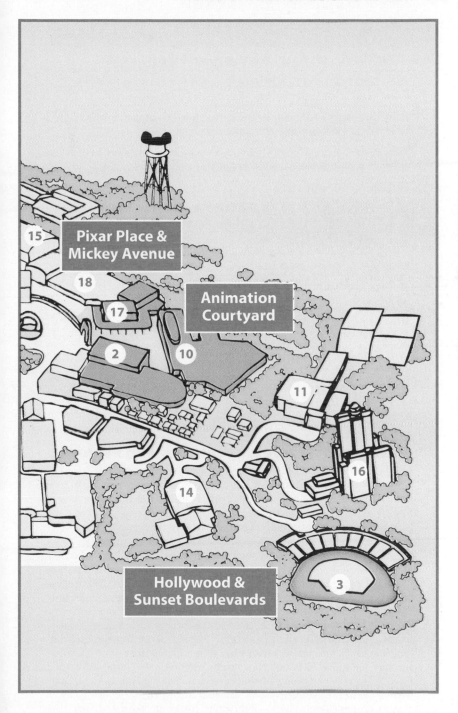

Pixar Place &
Mickey Avenue

Animation
Courtyard

Hollywood &
Sunset Boulevards

Hollywood Boulevard Services

MOST OF DHS'S SERVICES are on Hollywood Boulevard, including:
Baby Care Center At Guest Relations; baby food and other necessities available at Oscar's Super Service
Banking Services ATM outside the park to the right of the turnstiles and on Streets of America near Pizza Planet restaurant
Film At The Darkroom on the right side of Hollywood Boulevard as you enter the park, just past Oscar's Super Service
First Aid At Guest Relations
Live Entertainment, Parade, and Character Information Available free at Guest Relations and elsewhere in the park
Lost and Found At Package Pick-Up, to the right of the entrance
Lost Persons Report lost persons at Guest Relations
Storage Lockers Rental lockers to the right of the main entrance, on the left of Oscar's Classic Car Souvenirs
Walt Disney World and Local Attraction Information At Guest Relations
Wheelchair, ECV, and Stroller Rentals To the right of the entrance, at Oscar's Super Service

waiting in line. It'll also help with the show-schedule problem, but even when the park is crowded, you can see almost everything in a day.

DISNEY'S HOLLYWOOD STUDIOS IN THE EVENING

BECAUSE DHS CAN BE SEEN in as few as 8 hours, many guests who arrive early in the morning run out of things to do by 5 p.m. or so and leave. Their departure greatly thins crowds and makes the Studios ideal for evening touring. Lines for most attractions are bearable, and the park is cooler and more comfortable. The *Indiana Jones Epic Stunt Spectacular!* and productions at other outdoor theaters are infinitely more enjoyable during the evening than in the sweltering heat of the day.

DHS is the home of *Fantasmic!* (see page 621), the most dazzling nighttime-entertainment event in the Disney repertoire. Staged at least twice weekly, weather permitting (three to seven-plus times a week during busier times), in its own theater behind The Twilight Zone Tower of Terror, *Fantasmic!* is not to be missed. Unfortunately, evening crowds increase substantially when *Fantasmic!* is performed; some guests stay longer at DHS, and others arrive after dinner from other parks expressly to see the show. Although the crowds thin in the late afternoon, they build again as performance time approaches, making *Fantasmic!* a challenge to get into. Also adversely affected are Rock 'n' Roller Coaster and, to a lesser extent, The Twilight Zone Tower of Terror, both near the entrance to *Fantasmic!* Crowd levels throughout the remainder of the park, including at Toy Story Mania!, remain generally light.

ARRIVING AT DISNEY'S HOLLYWOOD STUDIOS

DHS HAS ITS OWN PARKING LOT and is served by the Disney transportation system. If you drive, Disney's ubiquitous trams will convey you to the ticketing area and entrance gate.

GETTING ORIENTED AT
DISNEY'S HOLLYWOOD STUDIOS

GUEST RELATIONS, on your left as you enter, serves as the park headquarters and information center, similar to City Hall in the Magic Kingdom and Guest Relations at Epcot and Disney's Animal Kingdom. Go there for a map of the Studios, a schedule of live performances (*Times Guide*), lost persons, Package Pick-Up, lost and found (on the right side of the entrance), baby-care facilities, and general information, or in an emergency. To the right of the entrance are locker, stroller, and wheelchair rentals.

About half of the complex is set up as a theme park. As at the Magic Kingdom, you enter the park and pass down a main street. In this case, it's the **Hollywood Boulevard** of the 1930s and '40s. At the end of Hollywood Boulevard is a replica of the famed **Chinese Theater.** Lording over the plaza in front of the theater is a 122-foot-tall replica of the sorcerer hat Mickey Mouse wore in the animated classic *Fantasia.* Besides providing photo ops, the hat is the park's most central landmark, making it a good meeting place if your group gets separated. (*Fun fact:* Mickey would have to be 350 feet tall to wear the hat.)

Though modest in size, the open-access areas of the Studios are confusingly arranged (a product of the park's hurried expansion in the early 1990s). As you face the hat, two guest areas—**Sunset Boulevard** and the **Animation Courtyard**—branch off Hollywood Boulevard to the right. Branching left off Hollywood Boulevard is the **Echo Lake** area. **Streets of America** wraps around the back of **Echo Lake**, while **Pixar Place**'s attractions are behind the Chinese Theater and to the left of the Animation Courtyard. Between Pixar Place and the Animation Courtyard is **Mickey Avenue** with its lone minor attraction.

Still farther to the rear is a limited-access area consisting of soundstages, technical facilities, wardrobe shops, administrative offices, and sets. These are accessible on a guided tour by tram and foot.

DINING IN DISNEY'S HOLLYWOOD STUDIOS

COUNTER-SERVICE RESTAURANTS in DHS are profiled in Part Ten, starting on page 454. For full-service profiles, see the section starting on page 457.

DISNEY'S HOLLYWOOD
STUDIOS ATTRACTIONS

HOLLYWOOD BOULEVARD

THIS PALM-LINED THOROUGHFARE re-creates Tinseltown's main drag during the Golden Age of Hollywood. Most service facilities are here, interspersed with eateries and shops. Merchandise includes Disney trademark items, movie-related souvenirs, and one-of-a-kind collectibles obtained from studio auctions and estate sales.

Hollywood characters and roving performers entertain on the boulevard, and daily parades and other happenings pass this way.

The Great Movie Ride ★★★½

APPEAL BY AGE	PRESCHOOL ★★★	GRADE SCHOOL ★★★½	TEENS ★★★½
YOUNG ADULTS ★★★½		OVER 30 ★★★½	SENIORS ★★★★

What it is Indoor movie-history ride. **Scope and scale** Headliner. **When to go** Before 11 a.m. or after 4:30 p.m. **Special comments** Elaborate, with several surprises. **Authors' rating** Unique; ★★★½. **Duration of ride** About 19 minutes. **Average wait in line per 100 people ahead of you** 2 minutes; assumes all trains operating. **Loading speed** Fast.

DISNEY DISH WITH JIM HILL

ONE SET OF THEME PARK RIGHTS TO RULE THEM ALL For the past few years, both Disney and Universal have been wooing *Lord of the Rings* director Peter Jackson in hopes of getting the theme park rights to his high-grossing trilogy of films. WDI wants to use the cinematic versions of J. R. R. Tolkien's characters to update a scene in The Great Movie Ride, whereas Universal is looking to use the films as a springboard for a brand-new "land" at Islands of Adventure, done in the highly detailed style of The Wizarding World of Harry Potter. Jackson, to his credit, has reportedly postponed making any decisions on this issue until he finishes production of his two-part *Hobbit* movie.

DESCRIPTION AND COMMENTS Entering through a re-creation of Hollywood's Chinese Theater, guests board vehicles for a fast-paced tour of soundstage sets from classic films, including *Casablanca, Tarzan, The Wizard of Oz, Alien,* and *Raiders of the Lost Ark.* Each set is populated with Disney Audio-Animatronic characters, as well as the occasional human, all augmented by sound and lighting effects. One of Disney's larger and more ambitious dark rides, The Great Movie Ride encompasses 95,000 square feet and showcases some of the most famous scenes in filmmaking. Life-size animatronic sculptures of stars, including Gene Kelly, John Wayne, James Cagney, and Julie Andrews, inhabit some of the largest sets ever constructed for a Disney ride.

A Tennessee family thinks the attraction needs some freshening up:

As someone who attended the grand opening of DHS in 1989, I think The Great Movie Ride seems stuck in the 1980s.

A teenage girl from Fanwood, New Jersey, agrees (with attitude):

A big suggestion for Disney: Update The Great Movie Ride, for goodness' sake! Start by getting rid of scenes from movies no one remembers or knows—Footlight Parade? What?—and put in scenes from recent films that are sure to become tomorrow's classics: The Dark Knight, Slumdog Millionaire, Across the Universe . . . *I could very easily go on.*

TOURING TIPS It's rare to see a wait of more than 30 minutes at The Great Movie Ride except during Christmas. Part of the reason is that it's an interval-loading, high-capacity attraction, and part of the reason is that the films shown (as the previous reader asserts) probably don't ring a bell with anyone under age 40. For what it's worth, actual wait times usually run about one-third shorter than the times posted.

SUNSET BOULEVARD

EVOKING THE 1940s, Sunset Boulevard—the first right off Hollywood Boulevard—provides another venue for dining, shopping, and street entertainment.

Fantasmic! ★★★★★

APPEAL BY AGE   PRESCHOOL ★★★★   GRADE SCHOOL ★★★★½   TEENS ★★★★½
YOUNG ADULTS ★★★★★   OVER 30 ★★★★½   SENIORS ★★★★½

What it is Mixed-media nighttime spectacular. **Scope and scale** Super-headliner. **When to go** Staged 2–7+ nights a week depending on the season. **Special comments** Disney's very best nighttime event. **Authors' rating** Not to be missed; ★★★★★. **Duration of presentation** 25 minutes. **Probable waiting time** 50–90 minutes for a seat, 35–40 minutes for standing room.

DESCRIPTION AND COMMENTS *Fantasmic!* is presented one or more times each evening when the park is open late. Off Sunset Boulevard behind the Tower of Terror, this mixed-media show is staged on an island opposite the 6,900-seat Hollywood Hills Amphitheater. By far the largest theater facility ever created by Disney, the amphitheater can accommodate an additional 3,000 standing guests for an audience of nearly 10,000.

Fantasmic! is the most innovative outdoor spectacle ever attempted at any theme park. Starring Mickey Mouse in his role as the Sorcerer's Apprentice from *Fantasia*, the production uses lasers, images projected on a shroud of mist, fireworks, lighting effects, and music in combinations so stunning you can scarcely believe what you're seeing. The plot is simple: good versus evil. The story gets lost in all the special effects at times, but no matter; it's the spectacle, not the storyline, that's powerful.

A mom from Pearland, Texas, found *Fantasmic!* too intense for her young child:

Fantasmic! *should come with a warning label. The show features a multitude of characters in various vignettes interspersed with water and laser-light interludes as Mickey begins his fanciful dream. The dream becomes a nightmare as the villains take over Mickey's imagination. The combination of characters, their larger-than-life laser visages, loud and ominous music, and thundering explosions with blinding flashes of light, fire, and sparks sent hordes of parents with screaming children fleeing for the exits.*

We don't receive many reports of young children being terrified by *Fantasmic!*, but the reader's point is well taken. Spend some time preparing your kids for what they will see. You can mitigate the fright factor somewhat by sitting back a bit. Also, hang on to your kids after *Fantasmic!* and give them instructions for regrouping should you get separated.

TOURING TIPS As a day-capping event, *Fantasmic!* is to the Studios what *IllumiNations* is to Epcot. While it's hard to imagine a 10,000-person stadium running out of space, that's just what happens almost every time the show is staged. On evenings when there are two performances, the second show will always be less crowded. If you attend the first (or only) scheduled performance, then show up at least an hour in advance. If you opt for the second show, arrive 50 minutes early.

From a Yorktown, Virginia, mom:

You seriously underestimated the time when people should arrive to see Fantasmic! if they want to get a seat. The stadium was already full when we arrived, 45 minutes before the show was scheduled to start, and the remaining seats filled up quickly—and this was during the off-season on a slow day.

A Cross Junction, Virginia, woman offers this tip:

It's a good idea to buy deli sandwiches outside the park, pack them with snacks and water in your backpack, and get a seat early.

A multigenerational family from Barrie, Ontario, makes this suggestion for guests who are short on nature's upholstery:

Bring pillows or towels to sit on. We were sitting on those benches from 6 p.m. for the 7:30 show, and boy, did our rears hurt by the end!

Rainy and windy conditions sometimes cause *Fantasmic!* to be cancelled. Unfortunately, Disney officials usually don't make a final decision about whether to proceed or cancel until just before showtime. We've seen guests wait stoically for over an hour with no assurance that their patience and sacrifice will be rewarded. We don't recommend arriving more than 20 minutes before showtime on rainy or especially windy nights. On nights like these, pursue your own agenda until 10 minutes or so before showtime, then head to the stadium to see what happens.

A Franklin, Tennessee, family of five describes what you might be in for on a rainy night and offers Disney a suggestion:

The week we were there, it rained every afternoon for several hours, and the Fantasmic! audience had to sit in the rain for 60–90 minutes until Disney figured out whether they would do the show. (Most times, it was cancelled—so they got soaked for nothing.) With Fastpass, this wait would be unnecessary—just have guests go to kiosks at their convenience during the day, put in their pass, and get a "reservation" for Fantasmic! Then the guests could enjoy the park or choose to stay dry until 15–20 minutes before showtime, giving Disney time to make announcements about the show's status.

A Wisconsin family reports that rain isn't the only thing that can have a dampening effect on *Fantasmic!*:

On a night with even a slight breeze, the mist from the water on which the projections are cast drifts over the theater and gets you wet. We were sprayed with a mist of cold water for 25 minutes. The show was hard to enjoy when it was already cool and then this cold spray of water was added. I don't know how many rows behind us were affected, but it was very uncomfortable.

Exiting *Fantasmic!* via the show's single exit can be hair-raising, as this retired elementary-school teacher attests:

It was like a cattle stampede, but at a snail's pace! Twice I almost ran over toddlers whose mothers didn't have the sense or energy to carry them.

Finally, a couple from Alberta, Canada, sums it up for all of us:

For a show so deservedly hyped, I would hope WDW finds ways to make seeing it less stressful.

FANTASMIC! DINING PACKAGE If you eat lunch or dinner at **Hollywood & Vine, The Hollywood Brown Derby,** or **Mama Melrose's Ristorante Italiano,** you can obtain a voucher for the members of your dining party to enter *Fantasmic!* via a special entrance and sit in a reserved section of seats. In return for your patronage of the restaurant, you can avoid 30–90 minutes waiting in the regular line to be admitted.

You must call ☎ 407-WDW-DINE (939-3463) 180 days in advance and request the *Fantasmic!* Dining Package for the night you want to see the show. This is a real reservation, not an Advance Reservation, and must be guaranteed with a credit card at the time of booking. There's no additional charge for the package itself, but there is a $10 charge for canceling a reservation with less than 48 hours' notice.

Included in the package are fixed-price menus for all three restaurants as follows; respective prices are for adults and kids ages 3–9: *Hollywood & Vine:* lunch, $26–$35/$15–$20, dinner, $30–$40/$15–$19; *The Hollywood Brown Derby:* lunch and dinner, $50–$57/$13–$19; *Mama Melrose's:* lunch and dinner, $35–$39/$13–$19. Nonalcoholic drinks and tax are included; park admission and gratuity are not. Prices fluctuate according to season, so call WDW-DINE if you want to know exactly what the dinner charge will be for a particular date.

You'll receive your vouchers at the restaurant. After dinner, report to the Highlands Gate on Sunset Boulevard—between Theater of the Stars and the Once Upon a Time store—30–45 minutes before showtime. A cast member will collect your vouchers and escort you to the reserved-seating section of the amphitheater. Though you're required to arrive early, you can be seated immediately. The reserved seats are off to the far right, though they afford a good line of sight. You won't have specific assigned seats in the reserved section. It's first-come, first-served, so arrive early for the best choice; try to sit in the middle three or four sections, preferably a bit off-center. Finally, understand that if *Fantasmic!* is canceled due to weather or other circumstances, you won't receive a refund or even a voucher for another performance.

Rock 'n' Roller Coaster *(Fastpass)* ★★★★

| APPEAL BY AGE | PRESCHOOL ★ | GRADE SCHOOL ★★★★½ | TEENS ★★★★★ |
| YOUNG ADULTS ★★★★★ | | OVER 30 ★★★★★ | SENIORS ★★★ |

What it is Rock music–themed roller coaster. **Scope and scale**Headliner. **When to go** Before 10 a.m. or in the hour before closing, or use Fastpass. **Special comments**48" minimum height requirement; children younger than age 7 must ride with an adult. Switching-off option provided (see page 334). Note that this attraction has a single-rider line. **Authors' rating**Disney's wildest American coaster; not to be missed; ★★★★. **Duration of ride**Almost 1½ minutes. **Average wait in line per 100 people ahead of you**2½ minutes; assumes All trains operating. **Loading speed**Moderate–fast.

Motion Sickness

DESCRIPTION AND COMMENTS When it opened in 1999, Rock 'n' Roller Coaster was Disney's answer to the coaster proliferation at Universal's Islands of Adventure and Busch Gardens. Exponentially wilder than Space Mountain or Big Thunder Mountain in the Magic Kingdom, Rock 'n' Roller Coaster is an attraction for fans of high-speed thrill rides. Although the rock icons and synchronized music add measurably to the experience, the ride itself, as opposed to sights and sounds along the way, is the focus. Rock 'n' Roller Coaster's loops, corkscrews, and drops make Space Mountain seem like It's a Small World. What really makes this metal coaster unusual, however, is that first, it's in the dark (like Space Mountain, only with

Southern California nighttime scenes instead of space), and second, you're launched up the first hill like a jet off a carrier deck. By the time you crest the hill, you'll have gone from 0 to 57 mph in less than three seconds. When you enter the first loop, you'll be pulling 5 g's—2 more than astronauts experience at liftoff on a space shuttle.

Reader opinions of Rock 'n' Roller Coaster are predictably mixed, colored invariably by how the reader feels about roller coasters. First, from a mother of two from High Mills, New York:

You can't warn people enough about Rock 'n' Roller Coaster. My daughter and I refused to go on it at all. My 9-year-old son, who had no problems with any ride, including Tower of Terror, went on with my husband first thing in the morning. My son came off so shaken he was "done for" the rest of the day. My husband just closed his eyes and hoped for the best.

And from a Longmont, Colorado, dad:

Rock 'n' Roller Coaster: The first 15 seconds of this ride are spectacular. I've never experienced anything like the initial take-off.

From an Australian couple who traveled a long way to ride a coaster:

My wife and I are definitely not roller-coaster people. However, we found Rock 'n' Roller Coaster quite exhilarating—and because it's dark, we didn't always realize that we were being thrown upside down. We rode it twice!

DISNEY DISH WITH JIM HILL

CHILL LIKE A ROCK STAR Imagineers have hatched an update to the queue for Rock 'n' Roller Coaster that involves adding a "green room" (the backstage area where performers hang out before they go onstage). Here guests can go to relax, have a beverage, and even play a game of Guitar Hero before they're told, "Your limousine is here. Please head into the studio so your manager can explain how you're getting to tonight's concert."

TOURING TIPS This ride is not for everyone. If Space Mountain or Big Thunder pushes your limits, stay away from Rock 'n' Roller Coaster.

Expect long lines except in the first 30 minutes after opening and during the late-evening performance of *Fantasmic!* Ride as soon as possible in the morning, or use Fastpass.

If you're on hand when the park opens, position yourself on the far left side of Sunset Boulevard as close to the rope barrier as possible. If there's already a crowd at the rope, you can usually work yourself forward by snaking along the wall of the Beverly Sunset Shop. Once in position, wait for the rope drop. When the park opens, cast members will walk the rope up the street toward Rock 'n' Roller Coaster and Tower of Terror. Stay on the far-left sidewalk and you'll be among the first to make the left turn to the entrance of the coaster. Usually the Disney people get out of the way and allow you to run the last 100 feet or so.

A good strategy for riding both the Tower of Terror and Rock 'n' Roller Coaster with minimum waits is to rush first thing after opening to Rock 'n' Roller Coaster and obtain Fastpasses, then line up for the Tower of Terror. Most days, by the time you finish experiencing the Tower of Terror, it will be time to use your Fastpass for Rock 'n' Roller Coaster. If the Tower of Terror, the Rock 'n' Roller Coaster, and the popular Toy Story Mania! are all must-sees for you, check out our recommendations for how to experience all three in our Toy Story Mania! touring tips on page 633.

Theater of the Stars / *Beauty and the Beast*
—*Live on Stage* ★★★★

APPEAL BY AGE   PRESCHOOL ★★★★   GRADE SCHOOL ★★★★   TEENS ★★★★
YOUNG ADULTS ★★★★   OVER 30 ★★★★   SENIORS ★★★★½

What it is Live Hollywood-style musical, usually featuring Disney characters; performed in an open-air theater. **Scope and scale** Major attraction. **When to go** Anytime; evenings are cooler. **Special comments** Performances are listed in the daily *Times Guide*. **Authors' rating** Excellent; ★★★★. **Duration of presentation** 25 minutes. **Preshow entertainment** None. **When to arrive** 20–30 minutes before showtime.

DISNEY DISH WITH JIM HILL

THIS COULD GET HAIRY WDW Entertainment is looking to ease this 20-plus-year-old musical out of the 1,500-seat Theater of the Stars and bring in an all-new production based on 2010's *Tangled*. Among the ideas being considered to bring this film to life as a musical is turning the backmost wall of the set into a massive video screen. This is a staging technique previously used on the Disney Cruise Line, but never for a show inside a Disney theme park.

DESCRIPTION AND COMMENTS Theater of the Stars combines Disney characters with singers and dancers in upbeat and humorous Hollywood musicals. The *Beauty and the Beast* show, in particular, is outstanding. The theater offers a clear field of vision from almost every seat. Best, a canopy protects the audience from the Florida sun (or rain), but the theater still gets mighty hot in the summer.

TOURING TIPS Unless you visit during the cooler months, see this show in the late afternoon or the evening. The production is so popular that you should show up 25–35 minutes early to get a seat.

The Twilight Zone Tower of Terror
(*Fastpass*) ★★★★★

APPEAL BY AGE   PRESCHOOL ★★½   GRADE SCHOOL ★★★★   TEENS ★★★★★
YOUNG ADULTS ★★★★★   OVER 30 ★★★★★   SENIORS ★★★★

What it is Sci-fi–themed indoor thrill ride. **Scope and scale** Super-headliner. **When to go** Before 9:30 a.m. or after 6 p.m., or use Fastpass. **Special comments** 40" minimum height requirement. Switching-off option provided (see page 334). **Authors' rating** Walt Disney World's best attraction; not to be missed; ★★★★★. **Duration of ride** About 4 minutes plus preshow. **Average wait in line per 100 people ahead of you** 4 minutes; assumes all elevators operating. **Loading speed** Moderate.

DESCRIPTION AND COMMENTS The Tower of Terror is a different species of Disney thrill ride, though it borrows elements of The Haunted Mansion at the Magic Kingdom. The story is that you're touring a once-famous Hollywood hotel gone to ruin. As at Star Tours, the queuing area immerses guests in the adventure as they pass through the hotel's once-opulent public rooms. From the lobby, guests are escorted into the hotel's library, where Rod Serling, speaking from an old black-and-white television, greets the guests and introduces the plot.

The Tower of Terror is a whopper at 13-plus-stories tall. Breaking tradition in terms of visually isolating themed areas, it lets you see the entire Studios from atop the tower . . . but you have to look quick.

The ride vehicle, one of the hotel's service elevators, takes guests to see the haunted hostelry. The tour begins innocuously, but at about the fifth floor things get pretty weird. Guests are subjected to a full range of eerie effects as they cross into the Twilight Zone. The climax of the adventure occurs when the elevator reaches the top floor—the 13th, of course—and the cable snaps.

The Tower of Terror is an experience to savor. Though the final plunges (yep, plural) are calculated to thrill, the meat of the attraction is its extraordinary visual and audio effects. There's richness and subtlety here, enough to keep the ride fresh and stimulating after many repetitions. Disney has also programmed random lift-and-drop sequences into the mix, making the attraction faster and keeping you guessing about when, how far, and how many times the elevator will fall. Visual and auditory effects are incorporated as well.

A senior from the United Kingdom tried the Tower of Terror and liked it very much, writing:

I was thankful I had read your review of the Tower of Terror, or I would certainly have avoided it. As you say, it's so full of magnificent detail that it's worth riding even if you don't fancy the drops involved.

The Tower has great potential for terrifying young children and rattling more-mature visitors. If you have teenagers in your party, use them as experimental probes. If they report back that they really, really liked the Tower of Terror, run like hell in the opposite direction.

TOURING TIPS If you're on hand when the park opens and want to ride Tower of Terror first, position yourself on the middle right side of Sunset Boulevard as close to the rope barrier as possible. Once in position, wait for the rope drop. When the park opens, cast members will walk the rope up the street toward Rock 'n' Roller Coaster and Tower of Terror. Just stay on the outside of the far-right sidewalk, and you'll be among the first to make the right turn to the entrance of the tower. Usually the Disney people get out of the way and allow you to run the last 100 feet or so. Also, be aware that about 65% of the folks waiting for the rope walk will head for Rock 'n' Roller Coaster. If you're not positioned on the far right, it will be hard to move through the crowd to make a right turn into Tower of Terror.

To save time, when you enter the library waiting area, stand in the far back corner across from the door where you entered and at the opposite end of the room from the TV. When the doors to the loading area open, you'll be one of the first admitted.

If you have young children (or anyone) who are apprehensive about this attraction, ask the attendant about switching off (see page 334).

A good strategy for riding both Tower of Terror and Rock 'n' Roller Coaster with minimum waits is to rush first thing after opening to Rock 'n' Roller Coaster and obtain Fastpasses, then line up for the Tower of Terror. Most days, by the time you finish experiencing the Tower of Terror, it will be time to use your Fastpass for Rock 'n' Roller Coaster. Factoring a ride on the overwhelmingly popular Toy Story Mania! into the equation requires a different strategy. See our touring plan on page 830.

ECHO LAKE

AN ACTUAL MINIATURE LAKE near the middle of the Studios, to the left of Hollywood Boulevard, Echo Lake pays homage to its real-life California counterpart, which served as the backdrop to many early motion picture. It also provides a visual transition from Hollywood Boulevard's retro theming to Streets of America's film-set ambience.

The American Idol Experience ★★★★

APPEAL BY AGE	PRESCHOOL ★★★	GRADE SCHOOL ★★★★	TEENS ★★★★
YOUNG ADULTS ★★★★		OVER 30 ★★★★	SENIORS ★★★

What it is Theme park version of the TV show. **Scope and scale** Major attraction. **When to go** Anytime. **Special comments** Guests must be at least age 14 to perform. **Author's rating** Even if you don't watch the show, you'll find someone to cheer for; ★★★★. **Duration of presentation** 20 minutes for daytime preliminary shows, 40 minutes for the nighttime finale. **When to arrive** 20–30 minutes before showtime.

DESCRIPTION AND COMMENTS Based on the long-running TV talent search, *The American Idol Experience* is your chance to unleash your song stylings on the world. Your path to superstardom goes like this:

Guests audition a cappella in front of a judge, just as in *American Idol's* first shows of the season. Those who make the cut move on to a second audition and sing, karaoke-style, to a prerecorded track. The judges' picks from this round get to perform in one of the preliminary shows, held several times a day.

During the preliminaries, each contestant repeats his or her song from the second audition in front of a live audience of theme park guests. As with *Idol*, three judges—in this case, Disney cast members—provide feedback. For the most part, the panel uses gentle humor to tell you not to quit your day job, although the judge who stands in for former *Idol* host Simon Cowell does let fly the occasional zinger ("I can picture you on the cover of *Rolling Stone* . . . standing next to someone who can sing on-key").

Audience members decide the preliminary winners, who meet for one last showdown at night. The winner of the finale gets a "Dream Ticket"—a front-of-the-line pass to try out for the real *American Idol* in his or her hometown.

TOURING TIPS The last show of the day offers (ostensibly) the best talent but runs twice as long as the daytime shows. If you don't want to commit to the entire show inside the auditorium, the final show (usually scheduled around 7 p.m.) can be viewed from outside on a JumboTron screen. This is a wise option (as is catching one of the daytime shows) for those who have to leave for a dinner reservation or line up early for *Fantasmic!* For complete details on auditioning and eligibility, go to **tinyurl.com /americanidolexperience.**

Indiana Jones Epic Stunt Spectacular! ★★★★

APPEAL BY AGE	PRESCHOOL ★★★½	GRADE SCHOOL ★★★★	TEENS ★★★★
YOUNG ADULTS ★★★★		OVER 30 ★★★★	SENIORS ★★★★

What it is Movie-stunt demonstration and action show. **Scope and scale** Headliner. **When to go** First 3 morning shows or last evening show. **Special comments** Performance times posted on a sign at the entrance to the theatre. **Authors' rating** Done on a grand scale; ★★★★. **Duration of presentation** 30 minutes. **Preshow entertainment** Selection of "extras" from audience. **When to arrive** 20–30 minutes before showtime.

DESCRIPTION AND COMMENTS Coherent and educational, though some-what unevenly paced, the popular production showcases professional stunt men and women who demonstrate dangerous stunts with a behind-the-scenes look at how they're done. Sets, props, and special effects are very elaborate.

While most live shows at Walt Disney World are revised from time to time, the *Epic Stunt Spectacular!*, as a Hamden, Connecticut, man laments, has not changed for years:

The show is the same as it's been since it opened, but the acting grows tired.

TOURING TIPS The Stunt Theater holds 2,000 people; capacity audiences are common. The first performance is always the easiest to see. If the first show is at 10 a.m. or earlier, you can usually walk in, even if you arrive 5 minutes late. For the second performance, show up about 15–20 minutes ahead of time. For the third and subsequent shows, arrive 20–30 minutes early. If you plan to tour during late afternoon and eve-ning, attend the last scheduled performance. If you want to beat the crowd out of the stadium, sit on the far right (as you face the staging area) and near the top.

To be chosen from the audience to be an "extra" in the stunt show, arrive early, sit down front, and display unbridled enthusiasm. A woman from Richmond, Virginia, explains:

After the first performance, I realized the best way to get picked was to stand up, wave my arms, and shout when the "casting director" called for volun-teers. (Sitting toward the front helps, too.)

Jedi Training Academy ★★★★

APPEAL BY AGE	PRESCHOOL ★★★★	GRADE SCHOOL ★★★★	TEENS ★★★★
YOUNG ADULTS ★★★★		OVER 30 ★★★★	SENIORS ★★★★

What it is Outdoor stage show. **Scope and scale** Minor attraction. **When to go** First 2 shows of the day. **Special comments** To sign up your children to go on stage, visit the old *Sounds Dangerous* building early in the morning; spots are first-come, first-served. **Authors' rating** A treat for young *Star Wars* lovers; ★★★★. **Duration of show** About 15 minutes. **When to arrive** 15 minutes before showtime.

DESCRIPTION AND COMMENTS *Jedi Training Academy* is staged several times daily to the left of the Star Tours building entrance, opposite Back-lot Express. If you want your young Skywalkers-in-training to appear on stage, visit the sign-up area at the site of the now-closed *Sounds Danger-ous with Drew Carey* show (across from Star Tours) as early in the morn-ing as possible. Spots go quickly and are first-come, first-served.

A Windham, New Hampshire, mother of three describes a common conundrum:

I'm guessing many families will have to chose between racing to Toy Story Mania! to ride or get Fastpasses (or both) or racing to sign up for Jedi Train-ing Academy (children MUST be present at sign-up). We hopped on TSM, grabbed a few Fastpasses for later, then crossed the park to sign up for Jedi Training Academy. By the time we got there, we were pushed to the 2:20 p.m. show, which eliminated the possibility of leaving for a nap after lunch.

Once on stage, these miniature Jedi are trained in the ways of The Force and do battle against Darth Vader. If all this sounds too intense, it's not—Storm Troopers provide comic relief, and just as in the movies, the good guys always win.

TOURING TIPS Surprisingly popular, given that Disney hasn't promoted it at the same level of hype as other shows. If you plan to watch during summer afternoons, grab drinks at Backlot Express, right next door, about 20 minutes before the show starts.

Star Tours—The Adventures Continue
(Fastpass) ★★★★

| APPEAL BY AGE | PRESCHOOL ★★★★ | GRADE SCHOOL ★★★★ | TEENS ★★★★ |
| YOUNG ADULTS ★★★★ | | OVER 30 ★★★★ | SENIORS ★★★½ |

What it is Indoor space-flight-simulation ride. **Scope and scale** Headliner. **When to go** First 90 minutes after opening, or use Fastpass. **Special comments** Expectant mothers and anyone prone to motion sickness are advised against riding. Too intense for many children younger than age 8; 40" minimum height requirement. **Authors' rating** A classic adventure; ★★★★. **Duration of ride** About 7 minutes. **Average wait in line per 100 people ahead of you** 5 minutes; assumes all simulators operating. **Loading speed** Moderate–fast.

Motion Sickness

DESCRIPTION AND COMMENTS Based on the *Star Wars* movie series, this was Disney's first modern simulator ride. Guests ride in a flight simulator modeled after those used for training pilots and astronauts. Star Tours completed its first major overhaul in decades in 2011, with a new story based on the "pod racing" scene from *Star Wars Episode 1: The Phantom Menace*. The new version has lots of dips, turns, twists, and climbs as your vehicle goes through an intergalactic version of the chariot race in *Ben-Hur*. The new ride film is projected in high-definition 3-D and has more than 50 combinations of opening and ending scenes. You could ride Star Tours all day without seeing the same film segment twice.

An interactive show, *Jedi Training Academy* (see facing page), is staged several times daily to the left of the Star Tours building entrance.

TOURING TIPS Expect waits not to exceed 35–45 minutes except on unusually busy days. For the first couple of hours the park is open, expect a wait of 25 minutes or less. Even so, ride before 11 a.m., or use Fastpass. If you have young children (or anyone) who are apprehensive about this attraction, ask the attendant about switching off (see page 334). Watch for throngs arriving from performances of the *Indiana Jones Epic Stunt Spectacular!* If you encounter a long line, try again later.

STREETS OF AMERICA

FORMERLY A WALK-THROUGH backlot movie set, Streets of America is now a designated themed area, or "land," that is home to four attractions. The backlot street sets remain intact and serve as the primary pedestrian thoroughfare.

Honey, I Shrunk the Kids Movie Set Adventure ★★½

| APPEAL BY AGE | PRESCHOOL ★★★★½ | GRADE SCHOOL ★★★★ | TEENS ★★★ |
| YOUNG ADULTS ★★ | | OVER 30 ★★½ | SENIORS ★★ |

What it is Small but elaborate playground. **Scope and scale** Diversion. **When to go** Before 11 a.m. or after dark. **Special comments** Opens an hour later than the rest of the park; kids must be age 10 or younger to play. **Authors' rating** Great for young children, more of a curiosity for adults; ★★½. **Duration of presentation** Varies. **Average wait in line per 100 people ahead of you** 20 minutes.

DESCRIPTION AND COMMENTS This elaborate playground appeals to kids age 11 and younger. The story is that you've been "miniaturized" and must make your way through a yard full of 20-foot-tall blades of grass, giant ants, lawn sprinklers, and other oversize props. There are also tunnels, slides, and rope ladders to play on. All areas are padded, and cast members are on hand to maintain some semblance of control.

TOURING TIPS While this attraction undoubtedly looked good on paper, it has problems that are hard to "miniaturize" in practice. First of all, it's nowhere near large enough to accommodate all the kids who would like to play. Only 240 people are allowed "on the set" at a time, and many of these are supervising parents or curious adults who hopped in line without knowing what they were waiting for. Frequently by 10:30 or 11 a.m., the playground is full, with dozens waiting outside (some impatiently).

Also, kids get to play as long as parents allow. This creates uneven traffic flow and unpredictable waits. If it weren't for the third flaw—that the attraction is poorly ventilated (as hot and sticky as an Everglades swamp)—there's no telling when anyone would leave.

A Tolland, Connecticut, mom found the playground exasperating:

We let the kids hang out here because we thought it would be relaxing. NOT! You have three choices: (1) Let your kids go anywhere and hope if they try to get out without your permission, someone will stop them. (2) Go everywhere with your kids—this takes a lot of stamina, some athleticism, and a high tolerance for humiliation (you look pretty stupid coming down those slides). (3) Try to visually keep track of your kids. This is impossible, so you'll be either on the edge of or in the middle of an anxiety attack the whole time you're there.

On the other hand, a mom from Shawnee Mission, Kansas, loved it:

Some of the things your book said to skip were our favorites (at least for the kids). We thought the playground from Honey, I Shrunk the Kids *was great—definitely worth seeing.*

If you visit during warmer months and want your children to experience the playground, get them in and out before 11 a.m.—by late morning, this attraction is way too hot and crowded for anyone to enjoy. Access is via Streets of America or Pixar Place.

Jim Henson's Muppet-Vision 3-D ★★★★½

APPEAL BY AGE	PRESCHOOL ★★★★	GRADE SCHOOL ★★★★	TEENS ★★★★
YOUNG ADULTS ★★★★		OVER 30 ★★★★	SENIORS ★★★★

What it is 3-D movie starring the Muppets. **Scope and scale** Major attraction. **When to go** Before 11 a.m. or after 3 p.m. **Authors' rating** Uproarious; not to be missed; ★★★★½. **Duration of presentation** 17 minutes. **Preshow entertainment** Muppets on television. **Probable waiting time** 12 minutes.

DESCRIPTION AND COMMENTS *Muppet-Vision 3-D* provides a total sensory experience, with wild 3-D action augmented by auditory, visual, and tactile special effects. If you're tired and hot, this zany presentation will make you feel brand-new. Arrive early and enjoy the hilarious video preshow.

TOURING TIPS This production is popular, but the theater's capacity is almost always sufficient. Waits peak around lunchtime, and it's unusual to see a wait of more than 20 minutes except during holidays. Watch for throngs arriving from performances of the *Indiana Jones Epic Stunt Spectacular!* If you encounter a long line, try again later.

Lights, Motors, Action! Extreme Stunt Show ★★★½

APPEAL BY AGE PRESCHOOL ★★★½ GRADE SCHOOL ★★★★½ TEENS ★★★★½ YOUNG ADULTS ★★★★ OVER 30 ★★★★ SENIORS ★★★★

What it is Auto stunt show. **Scope and scale** Headliner. **When to go** First show of the day. **Authors' rating** Good stunt work, slow pace; ★★★½. **Duration of presentation** 25–30 minutes. **Preshow entertainment** Selection of audience volunteers. **When to arrive** 25–30 minutes before showtime.

DESCRIPTION AND COMMENTS This show, which originated at Disneyland Paris, features cars and motorcycles in a blur of chases, crashes, jumps, and explosions The secrets behind the special effects are explained after each stunt sequence, with replays and different camera views shown on an enormous movie screen; the replays also serve to pass the time needed to place the next stunt's props into position. While the stunt driving is excellent, the show plods between tricks, and you'll probably have had your fill by the time the last stunt ends. Expect about 6–8 minutes of real action in a show that runs 25–30 minutes.

TOURING TIPS At the end of the Streets of America, *Lights, Motors, Action!* presents two to five shows daily. It's popular, but its remoteness—it's the most distant attraction from the park entrance—helps distribute and moderate the crowds. Seating is in a 3,000-person stadium, so it's not difficult to find a seat except on the busiest days.

A family of four from Mount Pleasant, South Carolina, notes that it's easier to get into the stadium than out:

When we exited the 3,000-seat arena (which was full the day we visited), it was horrible! The cast members directed us all to the same exit, and it was a HUGE bottleneck that took us 20 minutes to break free from.

Studio Backlot Tour ★★★★

APPEAL BY AGE PRESCHOOL ★★★½ GRADE SCHOOL ★★★★½ TEENS ★★★★ YOUNG ADULTS ★★★★ OVER 30 ★★★★ SENIORS ★★★★

What it is Combination tram and walking tour of modern film and video production. **Scope and scale** Headliner. **When to go** Anytime. **Special comments** Use the restroom before getting in line. **Authors' rating** Educational and fun; not to be missed; ★★★★. **Duration of presentation** About 30 minutes. **Preshow entertainment** A video before the special-effects segment and another video in the tram boarding area.

DISNEY DISH WITH JIM HILL

SO LONG BACKLOT, HELLO BLACKTOP If you love the Studio Backlot Tour, you might better get in a few extra trips the next time you're in the park. The Imagineers have penciled in this corner of the Studios as a possible location for the WDW version of Radiator Springs Racers, the centerpiece attraction of Cars Land, the Pixar-themed area that opened at Disney California Adventure in 2012. Given that Cars Land is in the American Southwest, there's a very good chance that Catastrophe Canyon will survive this radical retheming in some form. But as for the rest of DHS's backlot, it's most likely going bye-bye.

DESCRIPTION AND COMMENTS A substantial part of the Studios was a film- and TV-production facility, although no actual production takes place these days. Nonetheless, visitors to DHS can take a backstage tour to learn about production methods and technologies.

The tour begins on the edge of the backlot with the special-effects walking segment, then continues with the tram segment. To reach the Studio Backlot Tour, turn right off Hollywood Boulevard through the Studio Arch into the Animation Courtyard. Bear left at the corner where *Voyage of the Little Mermaid* is situated. Follow the street until you see a redbrick warehouse on your right. Go through the door and up the ramp.

The first stop is a special-effects water tank where technicians explain the mechanical and optical tricks that "turn the seemingly impossible into on-screen reality." Included are rain effects and a naval battle.

A prop room separates the special-effects tank and the tram tour. Trams depart about once every 4 minutes on busy days, winding among production and shop buildings before stopping at the wardrobe and crafts shops. Still seated on the tram, you look through large windows to see craftspeople at work.

The tour continues through the backlot, where western desert canyons exist side by side with New York City brownstones. The tour's highlight is Catastrophe Canyon, an elaborate special-effects movie set where a thunderstorm, earthquake, oil-field fire, and flash flood are simulated.

A reader from Cherry Hill, New Jersey, found the tour lacking:

I was extremely disappointed to discover how much the Studio Backlot Tour has been shortened. The tram ride is hardly worth the time, as most of the Backlot is now gone. Catastrophe Canyon is tired and in need of refurbishment. And the special-effects/behind-the-scenes walking tour, which I thought was a great experience when I was a young teen, is also no more.

TOURING TIPS Because the Studio Backlot Tour is one of Disney's most efficient attractions, you'll rarely wait more than 15 minutes (usually less than 10). Take the tour at your convenience, but preferably before 5 p.m., when the various workshops shut down for the day.

PIXAR PLACE

THE WALKWAY BETWEEN *Voyage of the Little Mermaid* and the Studio Backlot Tour holds the popular Toy Story Mania! attraction. To emphasize the importance of the *Toy Story* franchise, this section of the park is called Pixar Place.

Toy Story Mania! *(Fastpass)* ★ ★ ★ ★ ½

| APPEAL BY AGE | PRESCHOOL ★★★★★ | GRADE SCHOOL ★★★★★ | TEENS ★★★★★ |
| YOUNG ADULTS ★★★★★ | | OVER 30 ★★★★★ | SENIORS ★★★★½ |

What it is 3-D ride through indoor shooting gallery. **Scope and scale** Headliner. **When to go** Before 10:30 a.m. or after 6 p.m., or use Fastpass (if available). **Authors' rating** Not to be missed; ★★★★½. **Duration of ride** About 6H minutes. **Average wait in line per 100 people ahead of you** 4½ minutes. **Loading speed** Fast.

DESCRIPTION AND COMMENTS Toy Story Mania! ushers in a whole new generation of Disney attraction: the "virtual dark ride." Since Disneyland opened in 1955, ride vehicles have moved past two- and three-dimensional sets often populated by Audio-Animatronic (AA) figures. These amazingly detailed sets and robotic figures defined the Disney Imagineering genius in attractions such as Pirates of the Caribbean, The Haunted Mansion, and Peter Pan's Flight. Now for Toy Story Mania!, the elaborate sets and endearing AA characters are gone. Imagine long corridors, totally empty, covered with reflective material. There's almost nothing there . . . until you put on your 3-D glasses. Instantly, the corridor is full and brimming with color and activity, thanks to projected computer-graphic (CG) images.

Conceptually, this is an interactive shooting gallery much like Buzz Lightyear's Space Ranger Spin (see page 528), but in Toy Story Mania!, your ride vehicle passes through a totally virtual midway, with booths offering such games as ring tossing and ball throwing. You use a cannon on your ride vehicle to play as you move along from booth to booth. Unlike the laser guns in Buzz Lightyear, however, the pull-string cannons in Toy Story Mania! take advantage of CG image technology to toss rings, shoot balls, even throw eggs and pies. Each game booth is manned by a *Toy Story* character who is right beside you in 3-D glory, cheering you on. In addition to 3-D imagery, you experience vehicle motion, wind, and water spray.

The ride begins with a training round to familiarize you with the games, then continues through a number of "real" games in which you compete against your riding mate. The technology has the ability to self-adjust the level of difficulty, and there are plenty of easy targets for small children to reach. *Tip:* Let the pull-string retract all the way back into the cannon before pulling it again.

Finally, and also of note, a new generation of "living character" AA figures has been introduced in the preshow queuing area. A 6-foot-tall Mr. Potato Head breaks new ground for an AA character by interacting with and talking to guests in real time (similar to *Turtle Talk with Crush*).

Reader reviews of Toy Story Mania! have been over-the-top enthusiastic. This praise from a Fanwood, New Jersey, reader is typical:

Toy Story Mania! is the best ride at Disney—well worth the 70-minute wait. Five stars from one teen and two over-30s!

TOURING TIPS Because it's a ton of fun and it has a relatively low rider-per-hour capacity, Toy Story Mania! is the biggest bottleneck in Walt Disney World, surpassing even Test Track at Epcot. The only way to get aboard without a horrendous wait is to be one of the first through the turnstiles when the park opens and zoom to the attraction. Another alternative is to obtain Fastpasses for Toy Story Mania! as soon as the park opens and then backtrack to ride the Rock 'n' Roller Coaster and Tower of Terror. Don't think you'll have all day to procure Fastpasses, though: Even on days of moderate attendance, all Fastpasses for the day are usually gone by 11 a.m. Also, expect long queues at the Fastpass kiosks.

Following are reports from readers. From a St. Louis mom:

"Mania" is right—we got there when the park opened, and the wait was already 60 minutes, or 15 minutes for a Fastpass. On our second day at DHS, our strategy was for me to get Fastpasses while hubby stayed with the kids. By myself I was able to dart through the crowd to the rope, then on to Toy Story Mania! at rope drop. The wait for this ride was 150 minutes later that day!

A Nashville, Tennessee, mom recalls a similar experience:

Toy Story Mania! was already swamped fairly early in the day. We had to resort to getting some of the last Fastpasses, and it elongated our day to wait until our return time came up. But oh my gosh, what fun! It was worth the wait!

And from a Boston reader:

Toy Story Mania! was great, but the line was a nightmare. I had to duck out and use the ladies' room when I saw what the main queue room looked like!

MICKEY AVENUE

DESIGNATED AS A NEW THEMED AREA in 2011, Mickey Avenue hosts one minor attraction on the pedestrian promenade that connects Pixar Place and the Animation Courtyard.

Walt Disney: One Man's Dream ★ ★ ★

APPEAL BY AGE	PRESCHOOL ★ ★	GRADE SCHOOL ★ ★ ★	TEENS ★ ★ ★ ½
YOUNG ADULTS ★ ★ ★ ★		OVER 30 ★ ★ ★ ★	SENIORS ★ ★ ★ ★

What it is Tribute to Walt Disney. **Scope and scale** Minor attraction. **When to go** Anytime. **Authors' rating** Excellent; ★★★. **Duration of presentation** 25 minutes. **Preshow entertainment** Disney memorabilia. **Probable waiting time** For the film, 10 minutes.

DESCRIPTION AND COMMENTS Launched in 2001 to celebrate the 100th anniversary of Disney's birth, *One Man's Dream* consists of an exhibit area showcasing Disney memorabilia and recordings, followed by a film documenting Disney's life. On display are a replica of Walt's California office, various innovations in animation developed by Disney, and early models and working plans for Walt Disney World as well as various Disney theme parks around the world. The film provides a personal glimpse of Disney and offers insights regarding both his successes and failures.

TOURING TIPS Give yourself some time here. Every minute spent among these extraordinary artifacts will enhance your visit, taking you back to a time when the creativity and vision that created Walt Disney World were personified by one struggling entrepreneur.

ANIMATION COURTYARD

THIS AREA IS TO THE RIGHT of the big blue sorcerer's hat in the middle of the park. It holds two large theaters used for live stage shows, plus a separate attraction focusing on Disney animation. Spend any time here, and you'll slowly realize it's just a big swath of asphalt in desperate need of some landscaping or a water feature.

Disney Junior—Live on Stage! ★ ★ ★ ★

APPEAL BY AGE	PRESCHOOL ★ ★ ★ ★ ½	GRADE SCHOOL ★ ★ ★ ★	TEENS ★ ½
YOUNG ADULTS ★ ★		OVER 30 ★ ★ ½	SENIORS ★ ★ ½

What it is Live show for children. **Scope and scale** Minor attraction. **When to go** Per the daily entertainment schedule. **Special comments** Audience sits on the floor. **Authors' rating** A must for families with preschoolers; ★★★★. **Duration of presentation** 20 minutes. **When to arrive** 20–30 minutes before showtime.

DESCRIPTION AND COMMENTS The show features characters from the Disney Channel's *Little Einsteins, Mickey Mouse Clubhouse, Jake and the Never Land Pirates,* and *Handy Manny,* plus other Disney Channel characters. Reengineered in 2011, *Disney Junior* uses elaborate puppets instead of live characters on stage. A simple plot serves as the platform for singing, dancing, some great puppetry, and a great deal of audience participation. The characters, who ooze love and goodness, rally throngs of tots and preschoolers to sing and dance along with them. All the jumping, squirming, and high-stepping is facilitated by having the audience sit on the floor so that kids can spontaneously erupt into motion when the mood strikes. Even for adults without children, it's a treat to watch the tykes rev up.

Disney Junior will be the highlight of a preschooler's day, as a Thomasville, North Carolina, mom attests:

Disney Junior was fantastic! My 3-year-old loved it. The children danced, sang, and had a great time.

TOURING TIPS The show is staged in a huge building to the right of The Magic of Disney Animation—get here at least 25 minutes before showtime, then pick a spot on the floor and take a breather until the performance begins.

The Magic of Disney Animation ★★½

APPEAL BY AGE	PRESCHOOL ★★★	GRADE SCHOOL ★★★½	TEENS ★★★½
YOUNG ADULTS ★★★½		OVER 30 ★★★½	SENIORS ★★★½

What it is Overview of Disney animation process, with limited hands-on demonstrations. **Scope and scale** Minor attraction. **When to go** Before 11 a.m. or after 5 p.m. **Special comments** Opens an hour later than the rest of the park. **Authors' rating** Not as good as previous renditions; ★★½. **Duration of presentation** 20 minutes. **Preshow entertainment** Gallery of animation art in waiting area. **Average wait in line per 100 people ahead of you** 7 minutes.

DESCRIPTION AND COMMENTS The consolidation of Walt Disney Animation Studios in Burbank, California, has left this attraction without a story to tell. Park guests can still get a general overview of the Disney animation process but will not see the detailed work of actual artists, as was possible in previous versions.

The revamped attraction starts in a small theater, where the audience is introduced to a cast-member host and Mushu, the dragon from Mulan. Between the host's speech, Mushu's constant interruptions, and a very brief taped segment with real Disney animators, guests are hard-pressed to learn anything about actual animation. The audience is shown a plug for current Disney animated releases, which falls flat.

The audience then moves to another room, this one with floor seating, where another cast member describes what used to be the walking tour of the actual animation studio. The cast member supplies bits of Disney-character trivia—for example, Buzz Lightyear's original name was Lunar Larry—and fields questions from the audience, but one learns nothing truly enlightening.

Afterward, guests have the option of exiting the attraction participating in some interactive games, or attending the Animation Academy (the limited space is on a first-come, first-served basis). This is by far the most interesting part of the attraction, but not designed for all guests. The animator works quickly, which seems to frustrate younger guests who need more time or assistance. For those who keep up with the animator, this part gives a good idea of how difficult hand-drawn animation really is.

Judging by its low wait times, the tour may be in need of yet another overhaul. A mother of two from Oak Ridge, North Carolina, writes:

The new Animation tour is missing the essence of Disney animation, with little to no mention of the modern classics that helped revitalize Disney. The new version is a shell of its former self. It's hard to avoid the word lame.

TOURING TIPS Some days, the animation tour doesn't open until 10 or 11 a.m., by which time the park is pretty full. The tour is a relatively small-volume attraction, and lines can build on busy days by mid- to late morning. Character greetings take place at the end of most tours. If you want to meet characters without taking the tour, go through the Animation Gallery gift shop and head to the back of the store. A path leads directly from the shop to the characters.

Voyage of the Little Mermaid ★★★★

APPEAL BY AGE	PRESCHOOL ★★★★	GRADE SCHOOL ★★★★	TEENS ★★★
YOUNG ADULTS ★★★★	OVER 30 ★★★★		SENIORS ★★★★

What it is Musical stage show featuring characters from the Disney movie *The Little Mermaid*. **Scope and scale** Major attraction. **When to go** Before 9:45 a.m. or just before closing. **Authors' rating** Romantic, lovable, and humorous in the best Disney tradition; not to be missed; ★★★★. **Duration of presentation** 15 minutes. **Preshow entertainment** Taped ramblings about the decor in the preshow holding area. **Probable waiting time** Before 9:30 a.m., 10–30 minutes; after 9:30 a.m., 35–70 minutes.

DESCRIPTION AND COMMENTS *Voyage of the Little Mermaid* is a winner, appealing to every age. Sweet but not saccharine, the *Little Mermaid* show is the most tender and romantic entertainment offered anywhere in Walt Disney World. The story is simple and engaging, the special effects impressive, and the Disney characters memorable.

We get a lot of mail from Europeans who complain about the "soppy sentimentality" of Americans in general and of Disney attractions in particular. These comments of a man from Bristol, England, are typical:

Americans have an ability to think as a child and so enjoy the soppiness of The Little Mermaid. English cynicism made it hard for us at times to see Disney stories as anything other than gushing, namby-pamby, and full of stereotypes. Other Brits might also find the sentimentality cloying. Maybe you should prepare them for the need to rethink their wry outlook on life temporarily.

TOURING TIPS Except during the busiest holiday periods, it's unusual for anyone in line not to be admitted to the next showing of *Mermaid*. Typical waits are under 25 minutes most of the year.

When you enter the preshow lobby, stand near the doors to the theater. When they open, go inside, pick a row of seats, and let 6–10 people enter the row ahead of you. The strategy is twofold: to obtain a good seat and be near the exit.

Finally, a Charlotte, North Carolina, mom takes exception to our fright-potential assessment:

The Guide let me down on the Little Mermaid show—the huge sea witch portrayed in laser lights, cartoon, and live action TERRIFIED my 3-year-old. Your description led me to believe it was all sweetness and romance.

LIVE ENTERTAINMENT *at* DISNEY'S HOLLYWOOD STUDIOS

THE STUDIOS' LIVE-ENTERTAINMENT ROSTER includes theater shows, musical acts, roaming bands of street performers, a daily afternoon parade, and *Fantasmic!* (see page 621), a nighttime water, fireworks, and laser show that draws rave reviews. Of all of these, the theater shows, musical acts, and street performers are generally as good as or better than comparable acts at the other Disney parks. You can read on for the details, but we'd be remiss if we didn't tell you to catch a show of **Mulch, Sweat, & Shears,** a group of landscaping "brothers" who make up a cover band that plays everything from AC/DC to Journey. Guests standing near the front may be invited into the act.

AFTERNOON PARADE Staged once a day, the parade begins near the park's entrance, continues down Hollywood Boulevard, and circles in front of the giant hat. From there, it passes in front of the now-closed *Sounds Dangerous with Drew Carey* and ends by Star Tours. An alternate route begins at the far end of Sunset Boulevard and turns right, onto Hollywood Boulevard.

unofficial **TIP**
If you're anywhere on the route when the parade begins, stay put and enjoy it. Our favorite vantage point is the steps of the theater next to the site of the old *Sounds Dangerous* show.

The Studios' latest parade, **Pixar Pals Countdown to Fun,** features floats and characters from Pixar's films including *Toy Story; A Bug's Life; The Incredibles; Ratatouille; Monsters, Inc.;* and *Up.* Clocking in at slightly less than 10 minutes, it's essentially a cut-rate version of the previous Studios parade, with slightly rethemed floats and a couple of new songs. The afternoon parades at Animal Kingdom and the Magic Kingdom are better.

DISNEY CHANNEL ROCKS! We can't fault Disney for trying to cash in on the success of its movie franchises, including *High School Musical, The Cheetah Girls,* and *Camp Rock.* The performers sing and dance their way through songs from Disney's original movies and TV shows with an enthusiasm suggesting they all had Mountain Dew for breakfast (and we mean that in a good way). Problem is, Disney doesn't give them anything in the way of a venue or script to work with. Their stage is essentially a repurposed parade float on which some lights and colored tape have been strung. The performers' singing and dancing are wasted on the show designer's lack of creativity. We're holding out for a *Phineas and Ferb* rock opera (ideally released on the medium God intended: a vinyl double album).

DISNEY DISH WITH JIM HILL

A CALL FOR SUGGESTIONS For two months of the year, thanks to the Osborne Family Spectacle of Dancing Lights, the Studios' Streets of America is the busiest, most densely packed part of the park. It's those other 10 months that bother Entertainment staffers, who are itching to come up with yet another compelling seasonal celebration to draw crowds to this underutilized section of DHS. Among the ideas that management has nixed are a month-long Easter-parade celebration and a Halloween event involving guests trick-or-treating along New York Street, where Disney characters give out candy from each door. Got any better ideas? A running of the bulls?

DISNEY CHARACTERS Find characters in front of the Sorcerer's Hat, in front of the Magic of Disney Animation building, at the *Cars* Meet and Greet (near Mama Melrose's in Streets of America), in the

Animation Courtyard, along Pixar Place, and in parades. Characters from *Monsters, Inc.* can sometimes be found near the Studio Backlot Tour. Check the *Times Guide* for times and locations of character appearances.

STREET ENTERTAINMENT The Studios has one of the best collections of roving street performers in all of Walt Disney World. Appearing primarily on Hollywood and Sunset boulevards, the cast of characters includes Hollywood stars and wannabes, their agents, directors, and gossip columnists. If you're looking for a spot to rest and a bit of entertainment, grab a drink and seek out these performers. Just keep in mind that the performers aren't shy about asking you to join in their antics.

DISNEY'S HOLLYWOOD STUDIOS TOURING PLAN

TOURING THE STUDIOS CENTERS primarily around Toy Story Mania! and the fact that it simply cannot handle the number of guests who want to ride. A wonderful attraction for small children, it's therefore the first choice for families with young kids.

"Not a Touring Plan" Touring Plans

For the type-B reader, these touring plans (see page 817) avoid detailed step-by-step strategies for saving every last minute in line. For DHS, these "not" touring plans include advice for adults and parents with one day in the park, for anyone with two days, and for anyone with an afternoon and a full day to tour.

BEFORE YOU GO

1. Call ☎ 407-824-4321 or visit **disneyworld.com** to verify the park's hours.

2. Buy your admission before you arrive.

3. Make lunch and dinner Advance Reservations or reserve the *Fantasmic!* Dining Package (if desired) before you arrive, by calling ☎ 407-WDW-DINE (939-3463).

4. The schedule of live entertainment changes from week to week and even from day to day. Review the handout daily *Times Guide,* available free throughout Disney's Hollywood Studios.

DISNEY'S HOLLYWOOD STUDIOS
ONE-DAY TOURING PLAN *(page 830)*

WE'VE TESTED MANY VARIATIONS of this touring plan since Toy Story Mania! opened, and the current version is the best. Readers often ask why we recommend getting a Fastpass for TSM instead of riding first thing, or why we recommend TSM for Fastpass instead of, say, Rock 'n' Roller Coaster or Tower of Terror.

The answer lies in its relatively low ride capacity. Before Toy Story Mania! opened, we'd heard unofficially that it was going to handle around 1,600 guests per hour—to put that in perspective, the Magic Kingdom's Space Mountain handles around 1,900. Since opening, however, TSM struggles to serve around 960 guests per hour, or roughly half the guests Space Mountain does. The result is that stand-by waits build immediately. More importantly, Fastpasses at TSM get distributed faster than at any other attraction in Walt Disney World. Getting Fastpasses for TSM first is therefore the best option, since that guarantees you a short wait and you can usually still get other passes in the morning.

While we're on the subject, we'd like to thank Lou Mongello, author of the fabulous *Walt Disney World Trivia* book series, for noticing the insane speed of Toy Story Mania!'s Fastpass distribution and suggesting the analysis that led to the current touring plan.

PART FIFTEEN

UNIVERSAL ORLANDO

WHEN UNIVERSAL STUDIOS FLORIDA opened in 1990, it competed directly with Disney's Hollywood Studios. Both parks offered movie- and television-themed rides and shows, while other attractions provided an educational, behind-the-scenes introduction to the cinematic arts. And both had working film- and TV-production facilities.

unofficial **TIP**
Universal Studios is less congested than Disney's Hollywood Studios because it's almost double the size.

In the summer of 1999, Universal launched its second major theme park, **Universal's Islands of Adventure,** which competes directly with Walt Disney World's Magic Kingdom. Universal Studios Florida, Islands of Adventure, the three Universal hotels, and the **CityWalk** dining, nightlife, and shopping complex are collectively known as **Universal Orlando.** Both theme parks and their respective attractions are profiled in the next two chapters.

The parks have gone in different directions since then. For example, Disney essentially abandoned its production facilities long ago, but even now on any day at Universal, crews will be shooting on its backlot in full view of guests who care to watch. Universal Orlando has also added more attractions, the most famous of which is the groundbreaking Wizarding World of Harry Potter at Islands of Adventure. Construction is under way now to expand Potter attractions to both Universal parks, and these may set the standard for years to come for immersive themed entertainment.

In contrast, only one truly innovative attraction has opened at Disney Studios in the past decade: 2008's Toy Story Mania! Not even the most ardent Disney supporter would argue that Disney is as invested in the Studios as Universal is in its parks.

A UNIVERSAL PRIMER

UNIVERSAL ON THE WEB

IF, JUDGING FROM the plenitude of independent Disney World websites, you expect a similar number of such sites for Universal, you'd be wrong. Though some of the Disney sites mentioned in Part 1 (see pages

29–33) cover Universal in some (usually minimal) way, independent Universal sites, especially for Universal Orlando, are practically non-existent. Of the independent Disney sites that deal with Universal, we recommend **mousesavers.com** for hotel and admission bargains as well as some good touring tips concerning the Wizarding World of Harry Potter. For more-comprehensive information and discussion, try **disboards.com,** which has a discussion board dedicated to Universal. For crowd projections and touring tips, check our own **touringplans.com.** News and park developments are available at **orlandosentinel.com,** and **jimhill media.com** offers insider information on attractions, new technologies, and changes in the parks. Finally, there's the official Universal Orlando website, **universalorlando.com.**

COST

UNIVERSAL'S ADMISSION POLICY largely emulates Disney's Magic Your Way program (see page 50). A one-day, one-park Base Ticket is only slightly more expensive at Disney; multiday single-park Base Tickets, however, are significantly less expensive at Universal. Park-hopping (or "Park-to-Park," in Universal parlance) passes are much more expensive at Disney, where, for example, a four-day Park Hopper ticket costs about twice what you'd pay at Universal.

UNIVERSAL VS. WALT DISNEY WORLD ADMISSIONS *(prices include tax)*
UNIVERSAL ONE-DAY BASE TICKET: *adults* $91   *ages 3–9* $84
WDW ONE-DAY BASE TICKET: *adults* $95   *ages 3–9* $88
UNIVERSAL TWO-DAY BASE TICKET: *adults* $124   *ages 3–9* $113
WDW TWO-DAY BASE TICKET: *adults* $187   *ages 3–9* $175
UNIVERSAL THREE-DAY BASE TICKET: *adults* $145   *ages 3–9* $132
WDW THREE-DAY BASE TICKET: *adults* $258   *ages 3–9* $241
UNIVERSAL FOUR-DAY BASE TICKET: *adults* $155   *ages 3–9* $142
WDW FOUR-DAY BASE TICKET: *adults* $273   *ages 3–9* $255
UNIVERSAL ONE-DAY PARK-TO-PARK: *adults* $128   *ages 3–9* $121
WDW ONE-DAY PARK HOPPER: *adults* $132   *ages 3–9* $126
UNIVERSAL TWO-DAY PARK-TO-PARK: *adults* $145   *ages 3–9* $134
WDW TWO-DAY PARK HOPPER: *adults* $248   *ages 3–9* $235
UNIVERSAL THREE-DAY PARK-TO-PARK: *adults* $161   *ages 3–9* $148
WDW THREE-DAY PARK HOPPER: *adults* $318   *ages 3–9* $301
UNIVERSAL FOUR-DAY PARK-TO-PARK: *adults* $166   *ages 3–9* $152
WDW FOUR-DAY PARK HOPPER: *adults* $333   *ages 3–9* $315
UNIVERSAL PREFERRED ANNUAL PASS: $277
COMPARABLE WDW PASS: $611
UNIVERSAL PREMIUM ANNUAL PASS: $426
COMPARABLE WDW PASS: $744

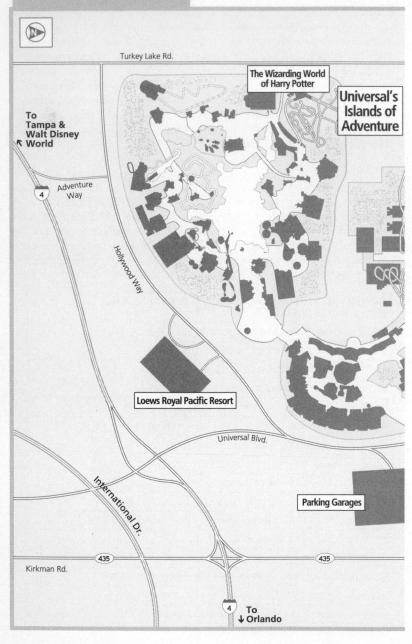

Universal Orlando

N

Turkey Lake Rd.

The Wizarding World
of Harry Potter

Universal's
Islands of
Adventure

To
Tampa &
Walt Disney
World

Adventure
Way

4

Hollywood Way

Loews Royal Pacific Resort

Universal Blvd.

International Dr.

Parking Garages

435

435

Kirkman Rd.

4 To
↓ Orlando

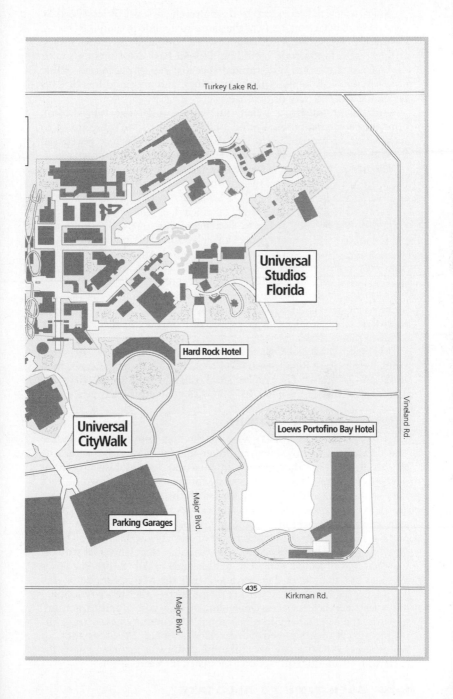

As at Disney, passes expire 14 days after the first use. Prices listed on page 641 are what you'd pay at the gate and include tax; unlike Disney, however, Universal offers discounts when you purchase passes online at **universalorlando.com,** including $20-per-pass discounts on multi-day tickets plus other time-limited specials. Passes purchased online are printable, can be used at the turnstiles, and are good for 14 days beginning with the day of first use.

Undercover Tourist, a ticket discounter (**undercovertourist.com**), offer the most deeply discounted Universal tickets we're aware of to subscribers of **MouseSavers** (**mousesavers.com**). Tickets purchased through the MouseSavers Newsletter include tax and free shipping.

The five-park, 14-day **Orlando Flex Ticket** allows unlimited entry to Universal Studios, Universal's Islands of Adventure, SeaWorld, Aquatica, and Wet 'n Wild and costs $292.82 for adults and $271.58 for children ages 3–9, tax included. The six-park, 14-day **Orlando Flex Ticket Plus,** providing unlimited entry to Universal Studios, Universal's Islands of Adventure, SeaWorld, Aquatica, Wet 'n Wild, and Busch Gardens, costs $334.41 for adults and $312.05 for children. All Orlando Flex Tickets can be purchased online at the websites of the participating parks, or you can buy them at a discount at **orlando funtickets.com.** Flex Tickets are a good deal only if you visit each of the included theme parks.

unofficial **TIP**
In order, Mondays, Sundays, and Saturdays are the best days to visit Universal Orlando.

The main Universal Orlando information number is ☎ 407-363-8000. Reach Guest Relations at ☎ 407-224-4233; order tickets by mail at ☎ 877-247-5561. The numbers for Lost and Found are ☎ 407-224-4244 (Universal Studios) and 407-224-4245 (Islands of Adventure).

A WORD ABOUT CROWDS

YOU'VE PROBABLY READ ABOUT the huge crowds that inundate The Wizarding World of Harry Potter at Islands of Adventure. The reports are true, but they present an unbalanced view of the crowds at the Universal parks overall. To get a quantitative grip on crowding, let's look at attendance figures compared with the size of the parks. On a day of average attendance, Universal Studios sees about 160 guests per acre, while Disney's Hollywood Studios sees about 263. Because both parks contain almost the same number of attractions, this means Disney Studios is 64% more crowded on an average day than Universal Studios. Contrasting the Magic Kingdom with Islands of Adventure, the latter averages 164 guests per day, per acre, while the Magic Kingdom—the attendance leader of all the world's theme parks—registers a whopping 435 guests per day, per acre. Depending on how you define attractions, however, the Magic Kingdom has about 31 (counting new attractions in the as-yet-uncompleted Fantasyland) versus 21 at Islands of Adventure. Even so, there are still more than twice as many guests for each Magic Kingdom attraction as for each IOA attraction.

HOW MUCH TIME TO ALLOCATE

TOURING UNIVERSAL STUDIOS, including one meal, takes about 8–10 hours. One reader laments:

There's a lot more "standing" at Universal Studios, and it isn't as organized as DHS. Many of the attractions don't open until 10 a.m. We weren't able to see nearly as many attractions at Universal as we were at DHS during the same amount of time. The one plus at Universal Studios is that there seems to be more property, and things are spaced out better so you have more elbow room.

As the reader observes, many Universal Studios attractions don't open until 10 a.m. or later. Most theater attractions don't schedule performances until 11 a.m. or after. This means that early in the day, all park guests are concentrated among the limited number of attractions in operation.

As a postscript, you won't have to worry about any of this if you use our Universal Studios touring plans. We'll keep you one jump ahead of the crowd and make sure that any given attraction is running by the time you get there.

LODGING AT UNIVERSAL ORLANDO

UNIVERSAL CURRENTLY has three operating resort hotels. The 750-room **Loews Portofino Bay Hotel** is a gorgeous property set on an artificial bay and themed like an Italian coastal town. The 650-room **Hard Rock Hotel** is an ultracool "Hotel California" replica, and the 1,000-room, Polynesian-themed **Loews Royal Pacific Resort** is sumptuously decorated and richly appointed. The Portofino and the Hard Rock are on the pricey side, and the Royal Pacific ain't exactly cheap. Scheduled to open in 2014, the **Cabana Bay Beach Resort** will be Universal's largest hotel, with 1,800 moderate- and value-priced rooms.

unofficial **TIP**
Get to the parks with your admission already purchased about 30–45 minutes before official opening time. Arrive 45–60 minutes before official opening time if you need to buy admission.

Like Disney, Universal offers a number of incentives for visitors to stay at its hotels. Perks available that mirror those offered by the Mouse include free parking, delivery to your on-site hotel room of purchases made in the parks, tickets and reservation information from hotel concierges, priority dining reservations at Universal restaurants, and the ability to charge purchases to your room account.

In addition, Universal offers complimentary transportation by bus or water taxi to Universal Studios, Islands of Adventure, CityWalk, SeaWorld, Aquatica (SeaWorld's water park), and Wet 'n Wild. Hotel guests may use the Universal Express program without limitation all day long. Universal lodging guests are also eligible for "next available" table privileges at CityWalk restaurants and similar priority admission to Universal Orlando theme park shows. The most valuable perk to most Universal resort guests, however, is admission to The Wizarding World of Harry Potter at Islands of Adventure 1 hour before the general public.

ARRIVING AT UNIVERSAL ORLANDO

THE UNIVERSAL ORLANDO COMPLEX can be accessed from eastbound I-4 by taking Exit 75A and turning left at the top of the ramp onto Universal Boulevard. If you're traveling westbound on I-4, use Exit

74B and then turn right on Hollywood Way. There are also entrances off Kirkman Road to the east, Turkey Lake Road to the north, and Vineland Road to the west. Universal Boulevard connects the International Drive area to Universal via an overpass bridging I-4. Turkey Lake and Vineland roads are particularly good alternatives when I-4 is gridlocked.

Two multistory parking garages hold 20,000 cars; signs from all four entrances route you to the parking structures. Parking is $15 for cars and $20 for RVs, trailers, and other large rigs. Regular parking drops to $5 between 6 p.m. and 10 p.m. and is free after 10 p.m. Preferred parking is offered during the day for $20, but we've scored spaces just as good or better using the regular parking, especially when we've arrived before 10:30 a.m. An advantage of preferred parking, however, is that you'll park faster because the ratio of cars choosing preferred to regular is about 1 to 13. In addition to the garages, valet parking is available at CityWalk for $15 for a visit of up to 2 hours or $25 for longer than that. If you're a Universal hotel guest, park in the hotel lot and walk, take a free water taxi to CityWalk, or catch a shuttle bus to the Studios.

The two rectangular garages lie along a north–south axis, with the pedestrian walkways leading to the theme parks running along the west, or long, side of each building. Because the garages are two-thirds as wide as they are long, the farther your parking place is from the west side, the worse it will be. This is why preferred parking is often not as close as regular parking—with the former, you'll be closer to the covered walkways to the parks, but if your particular space is toward the east side of the garage, you'll end up farther away than a guest who chose regular parking and was assigned a space closer to the west side of the structure.

Given that it's hard to find your car among 20,000 others, we strongly recommend that you write down the name and number of your section, level, and row. Sections are named for movies—Jurassic Park, King Kong, and the like. The first numeral of the number following the section name tells you what deck level you're on, and the remaining numbers specify the row. So if a sign tells you that you're on King Kong 410, you're in the King Kong section on the fourth floor in Row 10.

From the garages, moving sidewalks deliver you to CityWalk. From here, you can access the main entrances of both Universal Studios Florida and Islands of Adventure. Unlike at Disney parks, there are no trams, so depending on where in the garage your car is parked, you'll have an 8- to 20-minute hike to the theme park entrances even if you use the (sometimes) moving walkways.

If you're staying at Walt Disney World and you don't have a car, **Mears Transportation** will shuttle you from your hotel to Universal and back for $19. Pickup and return times are at your convenience. To schedule a shuttle, call ☎ 407-423-5566.

UNIVERSAL EXPRESS

LIKE DISNEY'S FASTPASS, Universal Express is a system whereby any guest can schedule an appointment to experience an attraction later in the day with little or no waiting. Unlike Fastpass, Universal Express is not free. Two versions are available, both of which require you to cough up more money beyond your park admission:

Universal Express is available to all guests at Universal hotels, who can access the Express lines all day long simply by flashing their hotel keys. This can be especially valuable during peak season.

Guests not staying at a Universal hotel can purchase the **Universal Express Plus** pass for an extra $21–$64 (depending on the season), which provides line-cutting privileges at each Universal Express attraction at a given park.

The Plus feature is good for only one day at one park—in other words, no park-hopping—and for one ride only on each participating attraction. The number of Plus passes is limited each day, and they can sell out. Increase your chances of securing passes by buying and printing them at home off Universal's website. Speaking of participating attractions, more than 90% of rides and shows are covered by Universal Express, a much higher percentage than those covered by Fastpass at Disney World.

You can also purchase Universal Express Plus at the theme parks' ticket windows, just outside the front gates. Inside Universal Studios, it's available at Nickstuff; inside Islands of Adventure, you can buy it at Jurassic Outfitters, Toon Extra, and the Marvel Alterniverse Store. Universal Express Plus is also available up to eight months in advance at **universalorlando.com.** You must know what date you plan on using it, because different dates have different prices.

When we tested Express Plus one recent summer, we discovered that Universal employees very rarely scrutinize the pass and that we could use it several times on most attractions, as long as we waited 15 minutes or so between attempts. Although the pass has a bar code, it was never scanned, nor did we see any scanning devices at the entrances of the attractions.

A New York mom had a trouble-free experience but questions the value of the investment:

> We bought Universal's Express Plus, but it was neither necessary nor consistently effective. Arriving at park opening, we were able to see many attractions right away without needing the passes at all. They helped on about three attractions between the two parks—a poor return for an investment of $156, but it was like life insurance: a good thing to have "just in case." On Dudley Do-Right, we still had to wait 30 minutes even with Universal Express Plus, whereas with Disney's free Fastpass we never waited more than 5 minutes for an attraction. The only aspect of UEP that was better than FP is that touring order was unaffected: UEP could be used whenever you first approached an attraction instead of your having to come back later.

IS UNIVERSAL EXPRESS PLUS WORTH IT? The answer depends on the season you visit, hours of park operation, and crowd levels. For the first three years The Wizarding World of Harry Potter is open, crowd levels are expected to increase dramatically at Islands of Adventure while remaining steady at Universal Studios. In the Studios, only one attraction,

Hollywood Rip Ride Rockit, might be hard to ride without your waiting an inordinate amount of time, but it's not a Universal Express Plus attraction. If, however, you arrive 30 minutes before park opening and use our touring plan (page 831), you should experience "The Triple R" with a minimal wait. For the Studios, therefore, you shouldn't need Universal Express Plus.

Islands of Adventure is a different story. Because of all the hoopla surrounding Harry Potter and the lack of high-capacity theater shows at IOA to siphon off crowds (one show at IOA compared with six at the Studios), rides here are sure to be inundated. Using our touring plan (page 832) will cut your waiting to a minimum, so we encourage you to try it first. The beauty of Universal Express Plus is that you can purchase it in the park if waits for the rides become intolerable.

UNIVERSAL EXPRESS PROGRAM AVAILABLE TO UNIVERSAL RESORT GUESTS This program allows Universal resort guests to bypass the regular line anytime and as often as desired by simply showing their room key. This perk far surpasses any benefit accorded to guests of Disney resorts. Be aware that neither Hollywood Rip Ride Rockit at Universal Studios nor Harry Potter and the Forbidden Journey at Islands of Adventure is a Universal Express attraction. As mentioned before, however, Universal hotel guests are eligible to enter The Wizarding World of Harry Potter 1 hour before the park opens to the public.

A father from Snellville, Georgia, did the math and discovered that it was cheaper for his family to stay at a Universal resort than buy Universal Express Plus:

> The benefits of that room key alone can be worth the price, with early entry to The Wizarding World and unlimited Express privileges at both parks. We got a room at the Royal Pacific Resort for $349 on a Saturday night, which allowed us to use Universal Express Saturday and Sunday. The room cost $43.63 per person per day, while an [à la carte] Express pass this same weekend would have cost $55.99 per person per day, and we still would have had to pay for a hotel.

How Universal Express Affects Crowd Conditions at the Attractions

This system dramatically affects crowd movement (and touring plans) in the Universal parks. A woman from Yorktown, Virginia, writes:

> People in the Express line were let in at a rate of about 10 to 1 over the regular-line folks. This created bottlenecks and long waits for people who didn't have the Express privilege at the very times when it's supposed to be easier to get around!

SINGLES LINES

THERE'S YET ANOTHER OPTION: the singles line. Several attractions have this special line for guests riding alone. As Universal employees will tell you, this line is often even faster than the Express line. We strongly recommend you use the singles line whenever possible, as it will decrease your overall wait and leave more time for repeat rides or just bumming around the parks.

LOCKERS

UNIVERSAL HAS INSTITUTED a mandatory locker system at its big thrill rides. Lockers outside these attractions are free for the first 45 minutes, then $2 for each hour after that, with a $14 maximum.

The locker banks are easy to find; each bank has a small computer in the center. When the sun is bright, the screen is almost impossible to read, so have someone block the sun or use a different computer. After selecting your language, you press your thumb onto the keypad and have your fingerprint scanned. We've seen people walk off cursing at this step, having repeated it over and over with no success. Most patrons press their thumb down too hard. The computer cannot read your thumbprint if it's squished together, so take a deep breath and just place your thumb on the scanner.

After your thumb scans, you'll receive a locker number. Write it down! When you return from your ride, go to the same kiosk machine, enter your locker number, and scan your thumb again. At Guest Relations, family-sized lockers are available for $8 for the entire day, but remember that only the person who used his or her thumb to get the locker can retrieve anything from it.

UNIVERSAL, KIDS, AND SCARY STUFF

ALTHOUGH THERE'S PLENTY FOR YOUNGER CHILDREN to enjoy at the Universal parks, most major attractions can potentially make kids under age 8 wig out. At Universal Studios Florida, forget *Disaster!*, Hollywood Rip Ride Rockit, Men in Black Alien Attack, Revenge of the Mummy, The Simpsons Ride, *Terminator 2: 3-D,* and *TWISTER ... Ride It Out.* The first part of the E.T. Adventure ride is a little intense for a few preschoolers, but the end is all happiness and harmony. Interestingly, very few families report problems with *Beetlejuice's Graveyard Revue* or *Universal Orlando's Horror Make-Up Show.* Anything we haven't listed is pretty tame.

At Universal's Islands of Adventure, watch out for The Amazing Adventures of Spider-Man, Doctor Doom's Fearfall, Dragon Challenge, Harry Potter and the Forbidden Journey, The Incredible Hulk Coaster, Jurassic Park River Adventure, and *Poseidon's Fury.* Popeye & Bluto's Bilge-Rat Barges is wet and wild, but most younger children handle it well. Dudley Do-Right's Ripsaw Falls is a toss-up, to be considered only if your kids like water-flume rides. The *Eighth Voyage of Sindbad Stunt Show* includes some explosions and startling special effects, but again, kids tolerate it well. Nothing else should pose a problem.

CHILD SWAP "Switching off" at Universal is similar to Disney's version. The entire family goes through the whole line together before being split into riding and nonriding groups near the loading platform. The nonriding parent and child(ren) wait in a designated room, usually with some sort of entertainment (for example, Forbidden Journey at IOA shows the first 20 minutes of *Harry Potter and the Sorcerer's Stone* on a loop), a place to sit down, and sometimes restrooms with changing tables. At any theme park, the best tip we can give is to ask the greeter in front of the attraction what you're supposed to do.

QUITTING TIME

BECAUSE THE PARKING for both Universal theme parks and the CityWalk shopping, dining, and entertainment complex is consolidated in the same parking structure, chaos ensues when the parks close. An Orlando woman, obviously very perturbed, comments thusly:

> *Universal needs to change the hours when each park closes! Both Universal Studios and Islands of Adventure share the same parking lot. IT MAKES NO SENSE for the two theme parks to close at the same time (especially since Islands has no night finale). I cannot even explain the amount of people. It was insane at closing (and other people were coming IN to go to CityWalk so it was SUCH a big mess)! There was less of a crowd coming out of Epcot on July 4! I think they really need to rethink their hours, especially on weekends in the summer!*

IMPACT WRESTLING AND BLUE MAN GROUP

UNIVERSAL ORLANDO OFFERS TWO theater productions. At Soundstage 21, guests can sit in on the taping of Spike TV's *Impact Wrestling* program, while Universal Studios' Sharp Aquos Theatre, near CityWalk, is home to **Blue Man Group.** Tickets for the latter can be purchased online or at the Universal Box Office. No admission fee is charged for the rasslin'.

Impact Wrestling

About five shows are filmed each month, usually with audience seating at 6:30 p.m. and taping starting at 7 p.m. For the uninitiated, *Impact,* like any good pro-wrestling show, is more brawl than sporting event; whether you consider it good theater is a matter of taste. Wrestlers include Kurt Angle, Ric Flair, Jeff Hardy, Hulk Hogan, Mickie James, AJ Styles, and Rob Van Dam, among others. If you go, you can pretty much depend on witnessing great athleticism, terrible acting, horrifying staged brutality, and a down-to-earth introduction to chaos theory. It's as American as bluegrass banjo, and a perfect show to see on a first date. The taping calendar can be found online at **universalorlando.com/shows/impact_wrestling.aspx.** Arrive an hour early to score the best seats. Universal suggests that children be at least age 14 to attend, although younger kids are permitted.

Blue Man Group

Blue Man Group gives Orlando its first large-scale introduction to that nebulous genre called "performance art." If the term confuses you, relax—it won't hurt a bit. Blue Man Group serves up a stunning show that can be appreciated by folks of all ages. The 1-hour, 45-minute production was updated and reimagined in 2012 to reflect cultural changes in the use of technology in daily life.

The three blue men are just that—blue—and bald and mute. Wearing black clothing and skull caps slathered with bright-blue grease paint, they deliver a fast-paced show that uses music (mostly percussion) and multimedia effects to make light of contemporary art and life in the information age. The Universal act is just one expression of a franchise that started with three friends in New York's East

Village. Now you can catch their zany, wacky, smart stuff in New York, Las Vegas, Boston, Chicago, and Berlin, among other places.

Funny, sometimes poignant, and always compelling, Blue Man Group pounds out vital, visceral tribal rhythms on complex instruments (made of PVC pipes) that could pass for industrial intestines, and makes seemingly spontaneous eruptions of visual art rendered with marshmallows and a mysterious goo. The weekly supplies include 25½ pounds of Cap'n Crunch, 60 Twinkies, 75 gallons of Jell-O, 996 marshmallows, 9½ gallons of paint, and 185 miles—yes, miles—of rolled recycled paper. If all this sounds silly, it is, but it's also strangely thought-provoking and deals with topics such as the value of modern art, the ubiquity and addictiveness of smartphones, DNA, the persistence of vision, the way rock music moves you, and how we're all connected. (*Hint:* It's not the Internet.)

A live percussion band backs Blue Man Group with a relentless and totally engrossing industrial dance riff. The band resides in long, dark alcoves above the stage. At just the right moments, the lofts are lit to reveal a group of pulsating neon-colored skeletons.

Audience participation completes the Blue Man experience. The blue men often move into the audience to bring audience members on stage. At the end of the show, the entire audience is involved in an effort to move a sea of paper across the theater. And a lot of folks can't help standing up to dance—and laugh. Magicians for the creative spirit that resides in us all, Blue Man Group makes everyone a co-conspirator in a joyous explosion of showmanship.

This show is decidedly different and requires an open mind to be appreciated. It also helps to be a little loose, because, like it or not, everybody gets sucked into the production and leaves the theater a little bit lighter in spirit. If you don't want to be pulled onstage to become a part of the improvisation, don't sit in the first half-dozen or so rows.

The Universal Box Office (☎ 888-340-5476 or 407-224-3200) is open 7 a.m.–7 p.m. EST, or you can buy tickets online at **universal orlando.com**. Advance tickets at the Universal Orlando website run $69–$84, $34 for children; tickets purchased at the box office are $10 higher. The current ticket price for kids is a time-limited special and may revert to the old $49–$64 range at any time. The show is staged in the Sharp Aquos Theatre, which can be accessed from inside or outside Universal Studios theme park. We recommend seats at least 15 rows back from the stage.

PART SIXTEEN

UNIVERSAL STUDIOS FLORIDA

UNIVERSAL CITY STUDIOS INC. HAS RUN a behind-the-scenes tour and movie-themed tourist attraction in Hollywood for nearly 50 years, predating all Disney parks except Disneyland. In the early 1980s, Universal announced plans to build a new theme park complex in Florida. But while Universal labored over its new project, Disney jumped into high gear and rushed its own studios and theme park into the market, beating Universal by more than a year.

Universal Studios Florida opened in June 1990. At the time, it was almost four times the size of Disney's Hollywood Studios (which has since expanded to become the larger of the two parks), and much more of the facility was accessible to visitors. Like its sister park in Los Angeles, Universal Studios Florida is spacious, beautifully landscaped, meticulously clean, and delightfully varied in its entertainment. Rides are exciting and innovative and, as with many Disney rides, focus on familiar and/or beloved movie characters or situations.

While these rides incorporate state-of-the-art technology and live up to their billing in terms of creativity and uniqueness, some lack the capacity to handle the number of guests who frequent major Florida tourist destinations. If a ride has great appeal but can accommodate only a small number of guests per ride or per hour, long lines form. (It isn't unusual for the wait to exceed an hour and a quarter for E.T. Adventure, for example.) Happily, most shows and theater performances at Universal Studios Florida take place in venues that accommodate large numbers of people. Since many shows run continuously, waits usually don't exceed twice the show's performance time (15–30 minutes).

Universal Studios Florida is laid out in an upside-down-L configuration. Beyond the main entrance, a wide boulevard stretches past several shows and rides to the park's New York section. Branching off this

NOT TO BE MISSED AT UNIVERSAL STUDIOS FLORIDA		
• *Disaster!*	• Revenge of the Mummy	• The Simpsons Ride
• Hollywood Rip Ride Rockit	• *Shrek 4-D*	
• Men in Black Alien Attack	• *Terminator 2: 3-D*	

pedestrian thoroughfare to the right are four streets that access other areas of the park and intersect a promenade circling a large lake.

The park is divided into six sections: **Hollywood, New York, Production Central, San Francisco, Woody Woodpecker's KidZone,** and **World Expo.** Where one section begins and another ends is blurry, but no matter. Guests orient themselves by the major rides, sets, and landmarks and refer, for instance, to "New York," "the waterfront," "over by E.T.," or "by Mel's Diner." The area of Universal Studios Florida open to visitors is about the size of Epcot.

UNIVERSAL UNDERCOVER WITH JIM HILL

BYE-BYE SHARK, HELLO SLUG AND JIGGERS JAWS fans are still mourning the loss of the fishy thrill ride based on the 1975 thriller. Harry Potter fans, on the other hand, are ecstatic: In place of Amity, Universal is developing a full-scale version of Diagon Alley, the magical city-within-a-city where the witches and wizards of London do their shopping. Expected highlights include a super-size version of Ollivanders, the wand shop that's one of the more popular features of IOA's Wizarding World of Harry Potter, and the Gringotts roller coaster, where guests will hurtle through the high-security vaults and darkened caverns below the best-known bank among the sorcerer set.

Dining at Universal Studios is on par with that at Disney's Hollywood Studios. Our favorites include **Finnegan's Bar & Grill,** with a fun setting and good burgers and fish-and-chips; **Lombard's Seafood Grille,** the park's premier restaurant (but not in the same league as DHS's Hollywood Brown Derby); and **Universal Studios' Classic Monsters Cafe,** a pizza-and-chicken place that shows promotional trailers for 1950s and '60s horror movies. For something quick and satisfying, there's usually a **Nathan's Famous Hot Dogs** stand at Central Park in the New York section of the studios. For milkshakes made the old-fashioned way, try **Schwab's Pharmacy** on Hollywood Boulevard.

Services and amenities include stroller and wheelchair rental, lockers, diaper-changing and infant-nursing facilities, car assistance, and foreign-language assistance. Most of the park is accessible to disabled guests, and TDDs are available for the hearing-impaired. Almost all services are in the **Front Lot,** just inside the main entrance.

UNIVERSAL STUDIOS FLORIDA ATTRACTIONS

Animal Actors on Location (Universal Express)   ★★★

APPEAL BY AGE	PRESCHOOL ★★★★	GRADE SCHOOL ★★★★	TEENS ★★★
YOUNG ADULTS ★★★		OVER 30 ★★★	SENIORS ★★★★

What it is Animal-tricks and comedy show. **Scope and scale** Major attraction. **When to go** After you've experienced all rides. **Authors' rating** Cute li'l critters; ★★★. **Duration of presentation** 20 minutes. **Probable waiting time** 25 minutes.

Universal Studios Florida

1. *Animal Actors on Location*
2. *Beetlejuice's Graveyard Revue*
3. *The Blues Brothers*
4. *A Day in the Park with Barney*
5. Despicable Me
6. *Disaster!*
7. *E.T. Adventure*
8. *Fear Factor Live*
9. Fievel's Playland
10. Hollywood Rip Ride Rockit
11. *Lucy—A Tribute*
12. Men in Black Alien Attack
13. Revenge of the Mummy
14. *Shrek 4-D*
15. The Simpsons Ride
16. *Terminator 2: 3-D*
17. *TWISTER . . . Ride It Out*
18. *Universal's Cinematic Spectacular* (seasonal)
19. *Universal Orlando's Horror Make-Up Show*
20. Woody Woodpecker's Nuthouse Coaster, Curious George Goes to Town

Parade Route: ••••••••••••

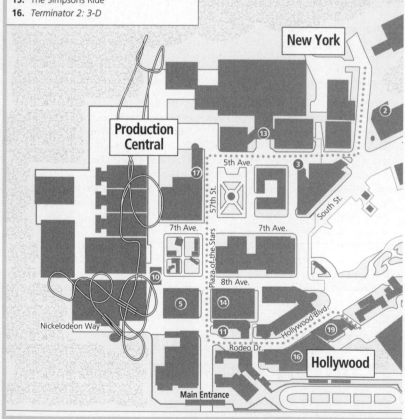

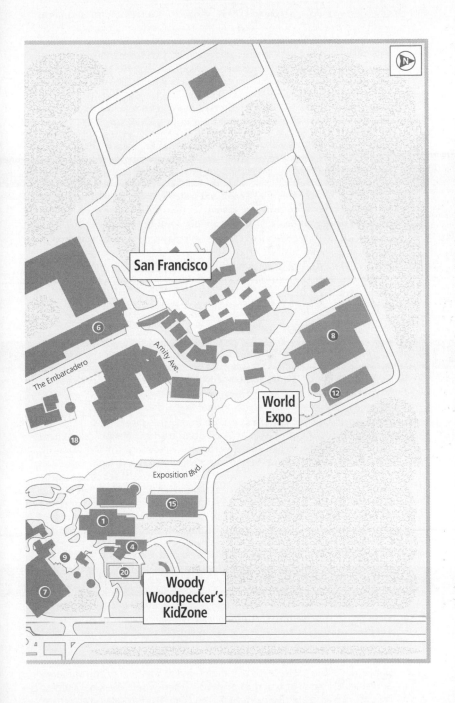

DESCRIPTION AND COMMENTS This show integrates video segments with live sketches, jokes, and animal tricks performed onstage. The idea is to create eco-friendly family entertainment. Several of the animal thespians are veterans of television and movies; many were rescued from shelters. Audience members can participate as well—where else will you get the chance to hold an 8-foot albino reticulated python in your lap?

TOURING TIPS Check the daily entertainment schedule for showtimes. You shouldn't have any trouble getting in.

Beetlejuice's Graveyard Revue (Universal Express) ★★★½

APPEAL BY AGE	PRESCHOOL ★★★★	GRADE SCHOOL ★★★★	TEENS ★★★★
YOUNG ADULTS ★★★★		OVER 30 ★★★★	SENIORS ★★★★

What it is Rock-and-roll stage show. **Scope and scale** Almost major attraction. **When to go** At your convenience. **Authors' rating** Capable of waking the dead; ★★★½. **Duration of presentation** 18 minutes. **Probable waiting time** None.

DESCRIPTION AND COMMENTS This high-powered musical revue stars Beetlejuice, Frankenstein, the Bride of Frankenstein, Wolfman, Dracula, and a pair of fly girls called Hip and Hop. Featuring contemporary dance and pop songs rather than classic rock, the show is high-energy, silly, bawdy, and generally funnier than it has any right to be.

TOURING TIPS Mercifully, this attraction is under cover.

The Blues Brothers ★★★½

APPEAL BY AGE	PRESCHOOL ★★★	GRADE SCHOOL ★★★½	TEENS ★★★½
YOUNG ADULTS ★★★½		OVER 30 ★★★★	SENIORS ★★★★

What it is Blues concert. **Scope and scale** Diversion. **When to go** Scheduled showtimes. **Special comments** A party in the street. **Authors' rating** Energetic; ★★★½. **Duration of presentation** 15 minutes. **Probable waiting time** None.

DESCRIPTION AND COMMENTS An impromptu concert featuring live singing and sax playing with a background track. The show takes place on a stoop in the street scene, across from Revenge of the Mummy. Jake and Elwood pull up in the famous police cruiser from the *Blues Brothers* movie and hop on stage. They turn the city set into a scene from a musical and get audience members dancing in the streets.

TOURING TIPS The concert is a great pick-me-up, and the short running time keeps the energy high. If you arrive early, you might be able to find a seat on a stoop across the street . . . but why would you want to sit?

A Day in the Park with Barney (Universal Express) ★★★★

APPEAL BY AGE	PRESCHOOL ★★★★★	GRADE SCHOOL ★★★	TEENS ★★
YOUNG ADULTS ★★★		OVER 30 ★★★	SENIORS ★★★

What it is Live character stage show. **Scope and scale** Major children's attraction. **When to go** Anytime. **Authors' rating** A great hit with preschoolers; ★★★★. **Duration of presentation** 20 minutes, plus 5-minute preshow and character greeting after the show. **Probable waiting time** 15 minutes.

DESCRIPTION AND COMMENTS Barney, the cuddly purple dinosaur of public-television fame, leads a sing-along with the help of the audience and sidekicks Baby Bop and BJ. A short preshow gets the kids lathered up before they enter Barney's Park (the theater). Interesting theatrical effects include wind, falling leaves, clouds and stars in the simulated sky, and snow. After the show, Barney exits momentarily to allow parents and children to gather along the stage. He then returns and moves from child to child, hugging each and posing for photos.

TOURING TIPS If your child likes Barney, this show is a must. It's happy and upbeat, and the character greeting that follows is the best organized we've seen in any theme park. There's no line and no fighting for Barney's attention—just relax by the rail and await your hug.

Despicable Me *(Universal Express)* ★★★★

APPEAL BY AGE **PRESCHOOL** ★★★★ **GRADE SCHOOL** ★★★★ **TEENS** ★★★★
YOUNG ADULTS ★★★★ **OVER 30** ★★★★ **SENIORS** ★★★★

What it is Motion simulator 3-D ride. **Scope and scale** Major attraction. **When to go** The first hour after park opening or after 5 p.m. **Special comments** Expect *long* waits in line. **Authors' rating** Great fun; ★★★★. **Duration of ride** 5 minutes. **Average wait in line per 100 people ahead of you** 7 minutes; assumes all simulators in use. **Loading speed** Moderate–slow.

Motion Sickness

DESCRIPTION AND COMMENTS Universal is hoping the third time's the charm with this motion-simulator system, which premiered as the Funtastic World of Hanna-Barbera when the park opened in 1990; was used again in Jimmy Neutron's Nicktoon Blast, which replaced the former in 2003; and is being retained for the attraction's third incarnation as Despicable Me, which opened in summer 2012.

As with the former attractions, Despicable Me involves the motion simulators moving and reacting in sync with a cartoon projected on an IMAX-like screen. Though the simulators have been updated, the most significant upgrade is incorporated in the projection system, which employs high-definition 3-D digital technology. The storyline combines elements from the animated movie *Despicable Me*, starring Gru, the archvillain, along with his adopted daughters and his diminutive yellow minions. During the queue and preshow, you visit Gru's house and are then ushered into his lab, where you're turned into a minion. The ride ends with a 3-minute dance party that you join as you exit.

TOURING TIPS All new attractions draw large crowds, and Despicable Me won't be any different. Compounding the crowding is the ride's location just inside the main entrance. If you're on hand at park opening and ride Despicable Me first, you'll have a short wait. However, you'll set yourself up for a long wait at nearby Hollywood Rip Ride Rockit. If the coaster is a priority for you, ride it first, returning to Despicable Me immediately afterward. If by that time the wait is intolerable, try again in the late afternoon. Stationary seating is available for those prone to motion sickness and for children less than 40 inches tall.

Disaster! (Universal Express) ★★★★

APPEAL BY AGE **PRESCHOOL** ★★★ **GRADE SCHOOL** ★★★★ **TEENS** ★★★★
YOUNG ADULTS ★★★★ **OVER 30** ★★★★ **SENIORS** ★★★★

What It is Combination theater presentation and adventure ride. **Scope and scale** Major attraction. **When to go** In the morning or late afternoon. **Special comments** May frighten young children. **Authors' rating** Shaken, not stirred; not to be missed; ★★★★. **Duration of presentation** 20 minutes. **Loading speed** Moderate. **Probable waiting time** 18 minutes.

DESCRIPTION AND COMMENTS Guests are recruited for roles in a film called *Mutha Nature*, directed by the overbearing and conceited Frank

Kincaid (Christopher Walken) and starring an unnamed actor you'll recognize as Dwayne "The Rock" Johnson. After the recruiting, the audience enters a soundstage where a number of seemingly random scenes are filmed starring the guests-cum-volunteers. The filming demonstrates various techniques for integrating sets, blue screens, and matte painting with live-action stunts. Next, guests board a faux subway where they experience a simulated earthquake. Following the quake, while the subway returns to the station, guests view a finished cut of *Mutha Nature* that incorporates all the soundstage shots.

TOURING TIPS Experience *Disaster!* after tackling the park's other rides.

E.T. Adventure *(Universal Express)* ★★★½

APPEAL BY AGE	PRESCHOOL ★★★★	GRADE SCHOOL ★★★★	TEENS ★★★
YOUNG ADULTS ★★★	OVER 30 ★★★★		SENIORS ★★★★

What it is Indoor adventure ride based on the beloved movie. **Scope and scale** Major attraction. **When to go** During the first 90 minutes the park is open. **Authors' rating** A happy reunion; ★★★½. **Duration of ride** 4½ minutes. **Average wait in line per 100 people ahead of you** 5 minutes. **Loading speed** Moderate.

DESCRIPTION AND COMMENTS Guests aboard a bicycle-like conveyance escape with E.T., The Extra-Terrestrial, from earthly law enforcement officials and journey to his home planet. The attraction is similar to Peter Pan's Flight at the Magic Kingdom but longer, with more elaborate special effects and a wilder ride.

TOURING TIPS Most preschoolers and grade-school children love E.T. We think it's worth a 20- to 30-minute wait, but nothing longer. Lines build quickly after 10:30 a.m., and waits can be more than 2 hours on busy days. Ride in the morning or late afternoon.

A mother from Columbus, Ohio, writes about horrendous lines at E.T.:

The line for E.T. took 2 hours! The rest of the family waiting outside thought that we had gone to E.T.'s planet for real.

A woman from Richmond, Virginia, thinks the way Universal represents the waiting time is deceptive:

When you see people in line outside and the sign says 10-MINUTE WAIT FROM THIS POINT, *it means 10 minutes until you're* inside the building. *But there's a very long wait inside before you get to the moving vehicles.*

Fear Factor Live (Universal Express) ★★★★

APPEAL BY AGE	PRESCHOOL ★	GRADE SCHOOL ★★	TEENS ★★★★
YOUNG ADULTS ★★★	OVER 30 ★★★		SENIORS ★★

What it is Live version of the gross-out-stunt television show on NBC. **Scope and scale** Headliner. **When to go** 6–8 shows daily; crowds are smallest at the first and second-to-last shows. **Authors' rating** Ewwww; ★★★★. **Duration of presentation** 30 minutes. **Probable waiting time** 25 minutes.

DESCRIPTION AND COMMENTS *Fear Factor Live* is a stage version of NBC's on-again, off-again reality ickfest, which clawed its way back to prime time for a blessedly brief run in 2011–12. In the theme park iteration, six volunteers compete for one prize; this varies but is always a package that contains at least $400 worth of Universal goodies ranging from park tickets to T-shirts. Contestants must be 18 years or older (with a photo ID to prove it) and weigh at least 110 pounds. Those demented enough to volunteer should arrive at least 75 minutes before showtime to sign papers and complete some obligatory training for the specific competitive events.

Anyone who doesn't wish to compete in the stage show itself can sign up for the Critter Challenge or the Food Challenge. With an adult's permission, volunteers as young as age 16 can compete in the latter.

The stage show is performed in a covered theater and consists of three different challenges. In the first, all six contestants are suspended two-and-a-half stories in the air and try to hang on to a bar as long as possible. The difficulty is compounded by heavy-duty fans blasting the contestants' faces while they hold on for dear life (are we having fun yet?). Only four people go on to the next round, and the person who hangs on to the bar the longest gets to choose his or her partner for the next event.

Once the first two contestants are eliminated, it's time for a brief intermission called the Desert Hat Ordeal. This involves a brave audience member–lunatic who has signed up for the Critter Challenge. Prepared with eye goggles and a mouthpiece, the volunteer is put in a chair with a glass case over his or her head. A wheel is spun to determine what will be crawling over the volunteer's head; the creepy-crawly choices include spiders, snakes, roaches, and scorpions. The only incentive to participate is a free photo of the ordeal for contestants to take to their therapists.

Back at the main competition, the four remaining contestants are split into two teams to compete in the Eel Tank Relay. This consists of one team member grabbing beanbags out of a tank full of eels and throwing them to his or her partner to catch in a bucket. Audience members drench the contestants with high-powered water guns, further spicing up the event. The duo who buckets the most beanbags wins, going on to compete against each other in the final round for the $400 prize package.

As the stage is prepared for the finale, the folks who volunteered for the Food Challenge steel themselves for the Guess What's Crawling to Dinner event. Here four contestants are split into two teams and invited to drink a mixture of curdled milk, mystery meat, and various live bugs that are all blended together on stage. The team that drinks the most of the mixture within the time limit wins a glamorous plastic mug that says, "I Ate a Bug," a convenient euphemism for "I have the brain of a nematode."

The last event has the two remaining contestants scramble up a wall to retrieve flags, jump into a car that is lifted in the air, then jump out of the car to retrieve more flags. When the required climbing, jumping, and flag-grabbing are accomplished, the first player to remove a rocket launcher from the backseat of the car and hit a target on the stage wall wins.

TOURING TIPS If you've ever wanted a chance to test your mettle (sanity?), *Fear Factor Live* may be your big chance. Participants for the physical stunts are chosen early in the morning and between performances outside the theater, so head there first thing if you want to be a contestant. The first challenge—hanging from the bar—requires exceptional upper-body strength. In the several performances we observed, the first two contestants eliminated were almost always women; in fact, the only way women usually make it to the second round is when there are three or four (very rare) female contestants to start with. The victims—er, contestants—for the skeevier stunts, like the bug-smoothie drinking, are chosen directly from the audience. Sit close to the front and wave your hands like crazy when it comes time for selection. Finally (and seriously), this show is too intense and gross for kids age 8 and under.

An extremely relevant query from two University of Iowa students:

We're thinking about volunteering to drink the bug smoothie and want to know if it's better to chew the bugs or just chug the smoothie and hope they

*die after crawling around for a while in your stomach. Also, do you recom-
mend holding your nose?*

We recommend practicing both options at home, preferably while
heavily medicated and under the supervision of a psychiatrist.

Fievel's Playland ★ ★ ★ ★

| APPEAL BY AGE | PRESCHOOL ★ ★ ★ ★ | GRADE SCHOOL ★ ★ ★ ★ | TEENS – |
| YOUNG ADULTS | – | OVER 30 – | SENIORS – |

What it is Children's play area with waterslide. **Scope and scale** Minor attraction.
When to go Anytime. **Authors' rating** A much-needed attraction for preschoolers;
★ ★ ★ ★. **Probable waiting time** 20–30 minutes for the waterslide; otherwise, no
waiting. **Loading speed** Slow for the waterslide.

DESCRIPTION AND COMMENTS This whimsical playground in Woody
   Woodpecker's KidZone features ordinary household items reproduced
   on a giant scale, as a mouse would experience them. Preschoolers and
   grade-schoolers can climb nets, walk through a huge boot, splash in a
   sardine-can fountain, seesaw on huge spoons, and climb onto a cow
   skull. Most of the playground is reserved for preschoolers, but a combo
   waterslide and raft ride is open to all ages.

TOURING TIPS Fievel's Playland entails no waiting, so you can stay as long
   as you want. Younger children love the oversize items, and there's
   enough to keep teens and adults busy while little ones let off steam.
   The waterslide–raft ride is open to everyone but is extremely slow-loading
   and carries only 300 riders per hour. With an average wait of 20–30 minutes, we don't think the 16-second ride is worth the trouble. Also, you're
   highly likely to get soaked.

Lack of shade is a major shortcoming of the entire attraction—the
   playground is scorching during the heat of the day.

Hollywood Rip Ride Rockit ★ ★ ★ ★

| APPEAL BY AGE | PRESCHOOL – | GRADE SCHOOL ★ ★ ★ ★ | TEENS ★ ★ ★ ★ ½ |
| YOUNG ADULTS ★ ★ ★ ★ ½ | | OVER 30 ★ ★ ★ ★ ½ | SENIORS ★ ★ ★ ½ |

What it is High-tech roller coaster. **Scope and scale** Headliner. **When to go** Immediately after park opening. **Special comments** 51" minimum height requirement; expect
long waits in line. **Authors' rating** Woo-hoo! Not to be missed; ★ ★ ★ ★. **Duration of
ride** 2½ minutes. **Average wait in line per 100 people ahead of you** 6–8 minutes.
Loading speed Moderate.

Motion Sickness

DESCRIPTION AND COMMENTS Opened in the summer of
2009, Hollywood Rip Ride Rockit is Universal Studios' candidate
for the most technologically advanced coaster in the world.
Well, we know how long that distinction will last, but for sure
this ride has some features we've never seen before. Let's start
with the basics: Rip Ride Rockit is a sit-down X-Car coaster that runs on
a 3,800-foot steel track, with a maximum height of 167 feet and a top
speed of 65 miles an hour. Manufactured by German coaster maker Mau-
rer Söhne, X-Car vehicles are more maneuverable than most other kinds
and use less restrictive restraints, making for an exhilarating ride.

You ascend—vertically—at 11 feet per second to crest the 17-story-tall
first hill, the highest point reached by any roller coaster in Orlando. The
drop is almost vertical, too, launching you into Double Take, a loop inversion in which you begin on the inside of the loop, twist to the outside at
the top (so you're upright), and then twist back inside the loop for the

descent. Double Take stands 136 feet tall, and its loop is 103 feet in diameter at its widest point. You next hurl (no, not that kind of hurl!) into a stretch of track shaped like a musical treble clef. As on Double Take, the track configuration on Treble Clef is a first. Another innovation is Jump Cut, a spiraling negative-gravity maneuver. Usually on coasters, you experience negative gravity on long, steep vertical drops; with Jump Cut you feel like you're in a corkscrew inversion, but you never actually go upside down. Other high points include a 95-degree turn, a downhill into an "underground chasm" (gotta love those Universal PR wordsmiths!), and a final incline loop banked at 150 degrees.

The ride starts in the Production Central area; weaves into the New York area near *TWISTER . . . Ride It Out*, popping out over the heads of guests in the square below; and then storms out and over the lagoon separating Universal Studios from Islands of Adventure.

Each train consists of two cars, with riders arranged two across in three rows per car. Each row is outfitted with color-changing LEDs and high-end audio and video technology for each seat. Like Rock 'n' Roller Coaster at Disney's Hollywood Studios, the "Triple R" features a musical soundtrack, but in this case you can choose the genre of music you want to hear as you ride: classic rock, country, disco, pop, or rap. When it's over, Universal flogs a digital-video "rip" of your ride, complete with the soundtrack you chose, that you can upload to websites such as YouTube.

From a Whalton, England, mom:

A fabulous, gut-wrenching coaster that thrilled the socks off my 8- and 9-year-olds. (Mum found it a bit too brutal to repeat.) At the end of the ride you'll be offered a video and photo package for about $50. You get the impression that your whole terrifying, toe-curling experience on the ride will be videoed; in fact, it's only a few seconds at the beginning, which is a bit disappointing.

A perhaps-jaded Easton, Connecticut, coaster aficionado offers this:

The loud music blasting in our ears cancelled out the sound of the coaster. If only they had a "None of the Above: Silence" button as a selection. The singles-line hint was a real time-saver.

When Hollywood Rip Ride Rockit premiered in 2009, it was pretty smooth. Alas, the wheels on the cars haven't held up well in the hot Florida sun. While perfectly safe, Rip Ride Rockit now subjects you to a lot of side-to-side jarring. To crib a phrase from Ike and Tina Turner's version of "Proud Mary," some folks like it easy . . . and some folks like it *rough*.

TOURING TIPS Rip Ride Rockit can put more trains on the tracks simultaneously than any other coaster in Florida, which means on paper that it should be able to handle about 1,850 riders per hour. In practice, you'll wait about 6–8 minutes for every 100 people in the queue ahead of you, indicating an hourly capacity of 1,500 riders. Because the ride is so close to the Universal Studios entrance, it's a crowd magnet, creating bottlenecks from park opening on. Your only chance to ride without a long wait is to be one of the first to enter the park when it opens.

Lucy—A Tribute ★★★

| APPEAL BY AGE | PRESCHOOL ★ | GRADE SCHOOL ★★ | TEENS ★★ |
| YOUNG ADULTS ★★★ | OVER 30 ★★★ | | SENIORS ★★★ |

What it is Walk-through exhibit about Lucille Ball. **Scope and scale** Diversion. **When to go** Anytime. **Authors' rating** A touching remembrance; ★★★. **Probable waiting time** None.

DESCRIPTION AND COMMENTS The life and career of Lucille Ball are spotlighted, with emphasis on her role as Lucy Ricardo in *I Love Lucy*. Well designed and informative, the exhibit succeeds admirably in recalling the talent and temperament of the beloved redhead.

TOURING TIPS See Lucy during the hot, crowded midafternoon. Adults could easily stay 15–30 minutes. Kids get restless after a few minutes.

Men in Black Alien Attack (Universal Express) ★★★★½

APPEAL BY AGE	PRESCHOOL†	GRADE SCHOOL ★★★★★	TEENS ★★★★★
YOUNG ADULTS ★★★★★		OVER 30 ★★★★★	SENIORS ★★★★

†Due to height requirement, sample size is too small for an accurate rating.

What it is Interactive dark thrill ride. **Scope and scale** Super-headliner. **When to go** During the first 90 minutes the park is open. **Special comments** May induce motion sickness. 42" minimum height requirement. Switching-off option provided (see page 334). **Authors' rating** Buzz Lightyear on steroids; not to be missed; ★★★★½. **Duration of ride** 2½ minutes. **Average wait in line per 100 people ahead of you** 5 minutes. **Loading speed** Moderate–fast.

UNIVERSAL UNDERCOVER WITH JIM HILL

LOOK FOR THE HIDDEN STEVE Back in 2000, when the Universal Creative team was developing Men in Black Alien Attack, they wanted to honor Steven Spielberg, *Men in Black*'s executive producer. Keep a sharp eye out for an alien seated on a park bench, hiding behind a newspaper—not only is that target worth a lot of points, but the head-on-a-stick that the alien uses as a disguise bears an uncanny resemblance to Mr. Spielberg.

DESCRIPTION AND COMMENTS Men in Black Alien Attack brings together Will Smith and Rip Torn (as Agent J and MIB director Zed) for an interactive sequel to the hit film. The storyline has you volunteering as a Men in Black (MIB) trainee. After an introduction warning that aliens "live among us" and articulating MIB's mission to round them up, Zed expounds on the finer points of alien spotting and familiarizes you with your training vehicle and your weapon, an alien "zapper." You then load up and are dispatched on an innocuous training mission that immediately deteriorates into a situation where only you can prevent aliens from taking over the universe. If you saw the movie, you understand that the aliens are mostly giant bugs and that zapping them involves blasting them into myriad gooey body parts. Thus, the meat of the ride (pardon the pun) consists of careening around Manhattan in your MIB vehicle and shooting aliens. The technology at work is similar to that used in the Spider-Man attraction at Islands of Adventure, which is to say that it's both a wild ride and one where movies, sets, robotics, and your vehicle are all integrated into a fairly seamless package.

Men in Black is interactive in that your marksmanship and ability to blast yourself out of some tricky situations will determine how the story ends. Also, you're awarded a personal score (as at the Magic Kingdom's Buzz Lightyear's Space Ranger Spin) and a score for your car. There are about three dozen possible outcomes and literally thousands of different ride experiences determined by your pluck, performance, and, in the final challenge, your intestinal fortitude.

TOURING TIPS Each alien figure has sensors that activate special effects and respond to your zapper. Aim for the eyes and keep shooting until the aliens' eyes turn red. Also, many of the aliens shoot back, causing your vehicle to veer or spin; in the mayhem, you might fail to notice that another vehicle runs beside you on a dual track. At a certain point, you can shoot the flashing "vent" on top of this other car and make its occupants spin around. Of course, they can do the same to you.

There are many possible endings, but the long lines at this headliner attraction will probably dissuade you from experiencing all but one or two. Avoid a long wait and ride during the first 90 minutes the park is open.

Revenge of the Mummy *(Universal Express)* ★★★★½

APPEAL BY AGE	PRESCHOOL ★★	GRADE SCHOOL ★★★★	TEENS ★★★★★
YOUNG ADULTS ★★★★½		OVER 30 ★★★★	SENIORS ★★★½

What it is Combination dark ride and roller coaster. **Scope and scale** Super-headliner. **When to go** The first hour the park is open or after 6 p.m. **Special comments** 48" minimum height requirement. **Authors' rating** Killer! Not to be missed; ★★★★½. **Duration of ride** 3 minutes. **Average wait in line per 100 people ahead of you** 7 minutes. **Loading speed** Moderate.

DESCRIPTION AND COMMENTS It's hard to wrap your mind around this attraction, but trust us when we say you're in for a very strange experience. Here, quoting Universal, are some of the things you can look forward to:

- Authentic Egyptian catacombs.
- High-velocity show-immersion system. [Huh? quickie baptism?]
- Magnet-propulsion launch wave system.
- A "Brain Fire" [!] that hovers [over guests] with temperatures soaring to 2,000°F.
- Canopic jars containing grisly remains.

When you read between the lines, Revenge of the Mummy is an indoor dark ride based on the *Mummy* flicks, where guests fight off "deadly curses and vengeful creatures" while flying through Egyptian tombs and other spooky places on a high-tech roller coaster. The special effects are cutting-edge, integrating the best technology from such attractions as *Terminator 2: 3-D* and The Amazing Adventures of Spider-Man (the ride), with groundbreaking visuals. It's really cool.

The queuing area serves to establish the storyline: You're in a group touring a set from the *Mummy* films when you enter a tomb where the fantasy world of film gives way to the real thing. Along the way, you're warned about a possible curse. The visuals are rich and compelling as the queue makes its way to the loading area where you board a clunky, Jeep-like vehicle. The ride begins as a slow, very elaborate dark ride, passing through various chambers, including one where flesh-eating scarab beetles descend on you. Suddenly your vehicle stops, then drops backward and rotates. Here's where the "magnet-propulsion launch wave system" comes in. In more ordinary language, this means you're shot at high speed up the first hill of the roller coaster part of the ride. We won't divulge too much, but the coaster part of the ride offers its own panoply of surprises (there are no barrel rolls or upside-down stuff, however). And though it's a wild ride by anyone's definition, the emphasis remains as much on the visuals, robotics, and special effects as on the ride itself.

TOURING TIPS The newer Hollywood Rip Ride Rockit and Despicable Me have diminished the early-morning crowds. Nevertheless, try to ride during the first hour the park is open. If lines are long, one fallback is to use the singles line, which is often more expedient than Universal Express. Concerning motion sickness, if you can ride Space Mountain without ill effect, you should be fine on Revenge of the Mummy. Switching off is available (see page 334). Finally, note that the Mummy's queue contains enough scary stuff to frighten little kids all on its own.

Shrek 4-D (Universal Express) ★ ★ ★ ★ ½

APPEAL BY AGE	PRESCHOOL ★★★★	GRADE SCHOOL ★★★★★	TEENS ★★★★★
YOUNG ADULTS ★★★★★	OVER 30 ★★★★★		SENIORS ★★★★★

What it is 3-D movie. **Scope and scale** Headliner. **When to go** The first hour the park is open or after 4 p.m. **Authors' rating** Warm, fuzzy, sometimes smelly mayhem; not to be missed; ★★★★½. **Duration of presentation** 20 minutes. **Probable waiting time** 16 minutes.

DESCRIPTION AND COMMENTS Based on characters from the hit movie *Shrek,* the preshow presents the villain from the movie, Lord Farquaad, as he appears on various screens to describe his posthumous plan to reclaim his lost bride, Princess Fiona, who married Shrek. The plan is posthumous since Lord Farquaad ostensibly died in the movie, and it's his ghost making the plans, but never mind. Guests then move into the main theater, don their 3-D glasses, and recline in seats equipped with "tactile transducers" and "pneumatic air propulsion and water spray nodules capable of both vertical and horizontal motion." As the 3-D film plays, guests are also subjected to smells relevant to the on-screen action (oh boy).

Technicalities aside, *Shrek 4-D* is a real winner. It's frantic, laugh-out-loud funny, and iconoclastic. Concerning the last, the film takes a good poke at Disney, with Pinocchio, the Three Little Pigs, and Tinker Bell (among others) all sucked into the mayhem. The quality and 3-D effects are great, and like the feature film, it's sweet without being sappy. Plus, in contrast to Disney's *Honey, I Shrunk the Audience* or *It's Tough to Be a Bug!*, *Shrek 4-D* doesn't generally scare kids under age 7.

TOURING TIPS Universal claims it can move 2,400 guests an hour through *Shrek 4-D.* However, the show's popularity means that waits in line may exceed an hour. Bear that in mind when scheduling your day.

The Simpsons Ride *(Universal Express)* ★ ★ ★ ★

APPEAL BY AGE	PRESCHOOL –	GRADE SCHOOL ★★★★	TEENS ★★★★
YOUNG ADULTS ★★★★	OVER 30 ★★★★		SENIORS ★★★½

What it is Mega–simulator ride. **Scope and scale** Super-headliner. **When to go** During the first hour the park is open. **Special comments** 40" minimum height requirement; not recommended for pregnant women or people prone to motion sickness. Switching-off option provided (see page 334). **Authors' rating** Despicable Me with attitude; not to be missed; ★★★★. **Duration of ride** 4 minutes and 20 seconds, plus preshow. **Average wait in line per 100 people ahead of you** 5 minutes. **Loading speed** Moderate.

Motion Sickness

DESCRIPTION AND COMMENTS The Simpsons Ride is based on the Fox animated series that is now TV's longest-running sitcom. Featuring the voices of Dan Castellaneta (Homer), Julie Kavner (Marge), Nancy Cartwright (Bart), Yeardley Smith (Lisa), and other cast members, the attraction takes a wild, humorous poke at thrill rides, dark rides, and live shows "that make up a fantasy amusement park dreamed up by the show's cantankerous Krusty the Clown."

Two preshows involve *Simpsons* characters speaking sequentially on different video screens around the line area. Their comments help define the characters for guests who are unfamiliar with the TV show. The attraction is a simulator ride similar to Star Tours at DHS and Despicable Me at Universal, but with a larger screen more like that of Soarin' at Epcot. The visuals aren't as sharp as Soarin's, but they're sharp enough.

The storyline has the conniving Sideshow Bob secretly arriving at Krustyland, the aforementioned amusement park, and plotting his revenge on Krusty and Bart, who, in a past *Simpsons* episode, revealed that Sideshow Bob had committed a crime for which he'd framed Krusty. Sideshow Bob gets even by making things go wrong with the attractions that the Simpsons (and you) are riding.

Like the show on which it's based, The Simpsons Ride definitely has an edge, and more than a few wild hairs. Like *Shrek 4-D,* it operates on several levels. There will be jokes and visuals that you'll get but will fly over your children's heads—and most assuredly vice versa.

A mom from Huntington, New York, had this to say:

> *I'm not a fan of wild motion simulators, but I was fine on this ride. The field of vision makes it very engrossing, like Soarin'. However, our family still rates Star Tours higher than The Simpsons Ride, as participating in the Star Tours simulation was most like actually being a character in the original* Star Wars *movie!*

UNIVERSAL UNDERCOVER WITH JIM HILL

D'OH!-HO-HO Don't tell Disney's legal department, but the setting that Homer and Marge float through as they experience "Captain Dinosaur's Pirate Rip-Off" ride is an exact replica of the "we take the town" sequence in Pirates of the Caribbean at the Magic Kingdom. The only difference is that you travel backwards through these well-known scenes, moving from the auction scene back to the Wicked Wench instead of the other way around.

TOURING TIPS Arrive at the park before opening and make The Simpsons Ride your fourth stop after riding Despicable Me, Hollywood Rip Ride Rockit, and Revenge of the Mummy. Though not as rough and jerky as its predecessor, Back to the Future—The Ride, it's a long way from being tame. Skip it if you're an expectant mom or prone to motion sickness. Some parents may find the humor a little too coarse for their younger children.

Street Scenes ★★★★★

**APPEAL BY AGE   PRESCHOOL ★★★   GRADE SCHOOL ★★★★★   TEENS ★★★★★
YOUNG ADULTS ★★★★★   OVER 30 ★★★★★   SENIORS ★★★★★**

What it is Elaborate outdoor sets for making films. **Scope and scale** Diversion. **When to go** Anytime. **Special comments** You'll see most sets without special effort as you tour the park. **Authors' rating** One of the park's great assets; ★★★★★ **Probable waiting time** None.

DESCRIPTION AND COMMENTS Unlike at DHS, all Universal Studios Florida's backlot sets are accessible for guest inspection. They include a New York City street, San Francisco's waterfront, a New England coastal town, Rodeo Drive, and Hollywood Boulevard.

TOURING TIPS You'll see most as you walk through the park.

Terminator 2: 3-D (Universal Express) ★★★★

| APPEAL BY AGE | PRESCHOOL ★★★ | GRADE SCHOOL ★★★★ | TEENS ★★★★ |
| YOUNG ADULTS ★★★★★ | | OVER 30 ★★★★★ | SENIORS ★★★★ |

What it is 3-D thriller mixed-media presentation. **Scope and scale** Super-headliner. **When to go** After 3:30 p.m. **Special comments** The nation's best theme park theater attraction; very intense for some preschoolers and grade-schoolers. **Authors' rating** Furiously paced and not to be missed; ★★★★. **Duration of presentation** 20 minutes, including 8-minute preshow. **Probable waiting time** 20–40 minutes.

DESCRIPTION AND COMMENTS The evil "cop" from *Terminator 2* battles Arnold Schwarzenegger's T-100 cyborg character. In case you missed the *Terminator* flicks, here's a refresher: A bad robot arrives from the future to kill a nice boy. Another bad robot—who has been reprogrammed to be good—pops up to save the boy. The bad robot chases the boy and the good robot, menacing the audience in the process.

    The attraction, like the films, is all action, and you really don't need to understand much. What's interesting is that it uses 3-D film and a theater full of sophisticated technology to integrate the real with the imaginary. Images seem to move in and out of the film, not only in the manner of traditional 3-D, but also in actuality. Remove your 3-D glasses momentarily and you'll see that the guy on the motorcycle is actually onstage.

    We've watched this type of presentation evolve, pioneered by Disney's *Captain EO; Honey, I Shrunk the Audience;* and *Muppet-Vision 3-D. Terminator 2: 3-D,* however, goes way beyond lasers, with moving theater seats, blasts of hot air, and spraying mist. It creates a multidimensional space that blurs the boundary between entertainment and reality. Is it seamless? Not quite, but it's close. We rank *Terminator 2: 3-D* as not to be missed.

TOURING TIPS The 700-seat theater changes audiences about every 19 minutes. Even so, because the show is popular, expect to wait about 30 minutes. *Terminator 2: 3-D* has been eclipsed somewhat by newer attractions like Hollywood Rip Ride Rockit, The Simpsons Ride, and Despicable Me. We suggest that you save *Terminator* and other theater presentations until you've experienced all the rides. Families with young children should know that the violence characteristic of the *Terminator* movies is largely absent from the attraction. There's suspense and action but not much blood and guts.

TWISTER . . . Ride It Out (Universal Express) ★★★½

| APPEAL BY AGE | PRESCHOOL ★★ | GRADE SCHOOL ★★★★ | TEENS ★★★★ |
| YOUNG ADULTS ★★★★ | | OVER 30 ★★★★ | SENIORS ★★★ |

What it is Theater presentation featuring special effects from the movie *Twister*. **Scope and scale** Major attraction. **When to go** Should be your first show after experiencing all rides. **Special comments** High potential for frightening young children. **Authors' rating** Gusty; ★★★½. **Duration of presentation** 15 minutes. **Probable waiting time** 26 minutes.

DESCRIPTION AND COMMENTS *TWISTER* combines an elaborate set and special effects, climaxing with a five-story-tall simulated tornado created by circulating more than 2 million cubic feet of air per minute.

TOURING TIPS The wind, pounding rain, and freight-train sound of the tornado are deafening, and the entire presentation is exceptionally intense. Schoolchildren are mightily impressed, while younger children

UNIVERSAL UNDERCOVER WITH JIM HILL

BILL AND HELEN, HUG IT OUT! By the end of production on *Twister* in 1996, Bill Paxton and Helen Hunt had come to hate each other. When Universal Orlando executives approached them about lending their talents to TWISTER . . . *Ride It Out,* they agreed to do so only if they could shoot their scenes on different days and never appear on camera together. That's why in the preshow, they're always on opposite sides of the room and seen on different monitors.

are terrified and overwhelmed. Unless you want the kids hopping in your bed whenever they hear thunder, try this attraction yourself first.

Universal Orlando's Horror Make-Up Show (Universal Express) ★★★½

APPEAL BY AGE	PRESCHOOL ★★★	GRADE SCHOOL ★★★★	TEENS ★★★★
YOUNG ADULTS ★★★★		OVER 30 ★★★★	SENIORS ★★★★

What it is Theater presentation on the art of makeup. **Scope and scale** Major attraction. **When to go** After you've experienced all rides. **Special comments** May frighten young children. **Authors' rating** A gory knee-slapper; ★★★½. **Duration of presentation** 25 minutes. **Probable waiting time** 20 minutes.

DESCRIPTION AND COMMENTS Lively, well-paced look at how makeup artists create film monsters, realistic wounds, severed limbs, and other unmentionables. Funnier and more upbeat than many other Universal Studios presentations, the show also presents a wealth of fascinating information. It's excellent and enlightening, if somewhat gory.

TOURING TIPS Exceeding most guests' expectations, the *Horror Make-Up Show* is the sleeper attraction at Universal. Its humor and tongue-in-cheek style transcend the gruesome effects, and most folks (including preschoolers) take the blood and guts in stride.

It's the exception that proves the rule, as this reader relates:

My 7- and 9-year-olds had no problem with Terminator *but were scared by the* Horror Make-Up Show *(despite my telling them the guy really was not cutting anyone's arm off!). We ended up leaving before the show was over.*

Universal's Cinematic Spectacular: 100 Years of Movie Memories ★★★½ (seasonal when park is open late)

APPEAL BY AGE	PRESCHOOL ★★★	GRADE SCHOOL ★★★★	TEENS ★★★½
YOUNG ADULTS ★★★★		OVER 30 ★★★★	SENIORS ★★★★

What it is Fireworks, dancing fountains, and movies. **Scope and scale** Major attraction. **When to go** 1 show a day, usually at park closing. **Authors' rating** Good effort; ★★★½. **Special comments** Movie trailers galore. **Duration of presentation** 15–20 minutes. **Probable waiting time** None.

DESCRIPTION AND COMMENTS This is Universal Studios' new nighttime event, shown on the lagoon in the middle of the park. The presentation, a celebration of the last 100 years of Universal motion pictures, is built around three large water screens flanked by colorful fountains (roughly similar to Disneyland's *World of Color*—check YouTube for the idea). During the 17-minute show, montages of various movie genres are projected onto water screens. Enhanced by the fountains, special water effects, fireworks, and Morgan Freeman's sonorous narration, the clips make for an entertaining show.

The show premiered in May 2012, with reviews generally either mixed or positive. This mother of two had a positive experience:

"My family really enjoyed the show. It didn't have the same emotional impact as [Disney's] Wishes, but it was entertaining. There were so many great movies we hadn't thought about in ages! I wouldn't make a special trip to see it, but it was nice to have a night event to end the day. We'll definitely stay for the Cinematic Spectacular on our next trip."

TOURING TIPS The ends of the lagoon are not recommended for viewing. The best spot is directly across the lagoon from Richter's Burger Co., where the sidewalk makes a small protrusion into the water. Because acquiring a spot here can be very difficult, we recommend arriving at least 45 minutes ahead of time.

Before the show begins, realize that not all of the movie clips may be suitable for young viewers. The horror montage, for example, mixes excerpts from hoary black-and-white monster movies with potentially fright-inducing clips from films like *The Birds, Halloween, Psycho, The Silence of the Lambs,* and *Tales from the Crypt.*

Woody Woodpecker's Nuthouse Coaster and Curious George Goes to Town ★★★

APPEAL BY AGE	PRESCHOOL ★★★★	GRADE SCHOOL –	TEENS –
YOUNG ADULTS –	OVER 30 –		SENIORS –

What it is Interactive playground and kids' roller coaster. **Scope and scale** Minor attraction. **When to go** Anytime. **Authors' rating** The place for rambunctious kids; ★★★.**Average wait in line per 100 people ahead of you** 5 minutes for the coaster. **Loading speed** For the coaster, *slooow.*

DESCRIPTION AND COMMENTS These two kid-friendly attractions reside, along with Fievel's Playland (see page 660), in Woody Woodpecker's KidZone. The Nuthouse Coaster is small enough for kids to enjoy but sturdy enough for adults, though its moderate speed might unnerve some smaller children (the minimum height to ride is 36 inches). Adjacent is Curious George Goes to Town, an interactive playground that exemplifies the Universal obsession with wet stuff; in addition to innumerable spigots, pipes, and spray guns, two giant roof-mounted buckets periodically dump a thousand gallons of water on unsuspecting visitors below. Kids who want to stay dry can mess around in the foamball playground, also equipped with chutes, tubes, and ball-blasters.

TOURING TIPS Visit after you've experienced all the major attractions.

LIVE ENTERTAINMENT *at* UNIVERSAL STUDIOS FLORIDA

IN ADDITION TO THE SHOWS PROFILED PREVIOUSLY, Universal Studios offers a wide range of street entertainment. Costumed comic book and cartoon characters (Shrek, Donkey, SpongeBob SquarePants, Woody Woodpecker) roam the park for photo ops supplemented by look-alikes of movie stars, both living and deceased, plus the Frankenstein monster, who can be said to be neither. Musical acts also pop up.

In 2012 the Studios introduced the Disney-like **Universal's Superstar Parade,** featuring dancers and performers, four large and elaborate floats inspired by cartoons and animated features, and a very mixed bag of street-prowling Universal characters. The parade stops twice for a highly choreographed ensemble number. Though impressive in its scope and coordination, the performance is well-nigh impossible to take in from any given viewing spot. The same floats are trotted out individually at various times of day for mini-shows and character meet-and-greets.

The parade begins at the gate between Louie's Pizza, in the New York section of the park, and Beetlejuice's Graveyard Revue, in San Francisco. From there it proceeds along 5th Avenue, past Revenge of the Mummy. At the end of 5th Avenue, the parade takes a left onto Plaza of the Stars and heads toward the front of the park, where it makes another left onto Hollywood Boulevard, from whence it disappears backstage across from Mel's Diner. The best viewing spots are along 5th Avenue, on the front steps of faux buildings in New York.

UNIVERSAL STUDIOS FLORIDA TOURING PLAN

BUYING ADMISSION TO UNIVERSAL STUDIOS FLORIDA

ONE OF OUR BIG GRIPES ABOUT UNIVERSAL STUDIOS is that there are never enough ticket windows open in the morning to accommodate the crowds. You can arrive 30 minutes before official opening time and still be in line to buy your admission when the park opens. Therefore, we strongly recommend that you buy your admission in advance. Passes are available online or by mail from Universal Studios at ☎ 800-711-0080. They're also sold at the concierge desk or attractions box office of many Orlando-area hotels. If your hotel doesn't offer tickets, try Guest Services at the DoubleTree Universal hotel (☎ 407-351-1000), at the intersection of Major Boulevard and Kirkman Road.

Many hotels that sell Universal admissions don't issue actual passes. Instead, the purchaser gets a voucher that can be redeemed for a pass at the theme park. Fortunately, the voucher-redemption window is separate from the park's ticket-sales operation.

UNIVERSAL STUDIOS FLORIDA ONE-DAY TOURING PLAN *(page 831)*

THIS PLAN IS FOR ALL VISITORS. If a ride or show is listed that you don't want to experience, skip that step and proceed to the next. Move quickly from attraction to attraction and, if possible, don't stop for lunch until after Step 9. Minor street shows occur at various times and places throughout the day; check the daily schedule for details.

PART SEVENTEEN

UNIVERSAL'S ISLANDS *of* ADVENTURE

WHEN UNIVERSAL'S ISLANDS OF ADVENTURE (IOA) opened in 1999, it provided Universal with enough critical mass to actually compete with Disney. Doubly interesting is that the second Universal park is a direct competitor to Disney's Magic Kingdom, the most-visited theme park in the world. How direct a competitor is it? See below for a comparison.

And though Universal played second fiddle to Disney for many years, times have changed: Universal's Islands of Adventure is a state-of-the-art park competing with a Disney park that is more than 35 years old and did not add a new super-headliner attraction for many years until the still-ongoing expansion of Fantasyland got under way in 2010.

unofficial **TIP**
Roller coasters at Islands of Adventure are the real deal—not for the faint of heart or for little ones.

Incidentally, 2010 marked IOA's coming-out party. In one of the greatest seismic shifts in theme park history, Universal secured the rights to build a Harry Potter–themed area within the park. Harry P. is possibly the only fictional character extant capable of trumping Mickey Mouse, and Universal has gone all-out, under J. K. Rowling's watchful and exacting eye, to create a setting and attractions designed to be the envy of the industry.

Disney and Universal officially downplay their fierce competition, pointing out that any new theme park or attraction makes Central Florida a more marketable destination. Behind closed doors, however, the two companies share a Pepsi-versus-Coke rivalry that keeps both working hard to gain a competitive edge. The good news is that all this translates into better and better attractions for you to enjoy.

IOA AND THE MAGIC KINGDOM AT A GLANCE	
ISLANDS OF ADVENTURE	**MAGIC KINGDOM**
• Seven "islands" (*includes Port of Entry*)	• Six "lands" (*includes Main Street*)
• Two adult roller-coaster attractions	• Two adult roller-coaster attractions
• A Dumbo-type ride	• Dumbo the Flying Elephant
• One flume ride	• One flume ride
• Toon Lagoon character area	• Main Street, U.S.A. character greeting

NOT TO BE MISSED AT UNIVERSAL'S ISLANDS OF ADVENTURE	
• The Amazing Adventures of Spider-Man	• The Incredible Hulk Coaster
• Dragon Challenge	• Jurassic Park River Adventure
• Harry Potter and the Forbidden Journey	• *Poseidon's Fury*

BEWARE OF THE WET AND WILD

ALTHOUGH WE'VE DESCRIBED Universal's Islands of Adventure as a direct competitor to the Magic Kingdom, know this: Whereas most Magic Kingdom attractions are designed to be enjoyed by guests of any age, attractions at Islands of Adventure are created largely for an under-40 population. The roller coasters at Universal are serious with a capital S, making Space Mountain and Big Thunder Mountain look about as frightening as Dumbo. In fact, seven of the nine top attractions at IOA are thrill rides; of these, three will not only scare the bejeepers out of you but will also drench you with water.

For families, there are three interactive playgrounds as well as six rides that young children will enjoy. Of the thrill rides, only the two in Toon Lagoon (described later) are marginally appropriate for little kids, and even on these rides your child needs to be fairly stalwart.

GETTING ORIENTED *at* UNIVERSAL'S ISLANDS *of* ADVENTURE

BOTH UNIVERSAL THEME PARKS are accessed via the Universal CityWalk entertainment complex. After crossing CityWalk from the parking garages, bear right to Universal Studios Florida or left to Universal's Islands of Adventure.

Islands of Adventure is arranged much like Epcot's World Showcase, in a large circle surrounding a lagoon, but it evinces the same sort of thematic continuity present in the Magic Kingdom. Each "land," or "island" in this case, is self-contained and visually consistent in its theme.

You first encounter the Moroccan-style **Port of Entry,** where you'll find Guest Services, lockers, stroller and wheelchair rentals, ATM banking, lost and found, and shopping. From the Port of Entry, moving clockwise around the lagoon, you can access **Marvel Super Hero Island, Toon Lagoon, Jurassic Park, The Wizarding World of Harry Potter, The Lost Continent,** and **Seuss Landing.** There is no in-park transportation to move you between lands.

DECISIONS, DECISIONS

WHEN IT COMES TO TOURING IOA efficiently, you have two basic choices, and as you might expect, there are trade-offs. The Wizarding World of Harry Potter sucks up guests like a Hoover. If you're keen to experience **Harry Potter and the Forbidden Journey** without suffering 1–2 hours in line, you need to be at the turnstiles waiting to be admitted at least 30 minutes before the park opens. Once admitted, move as

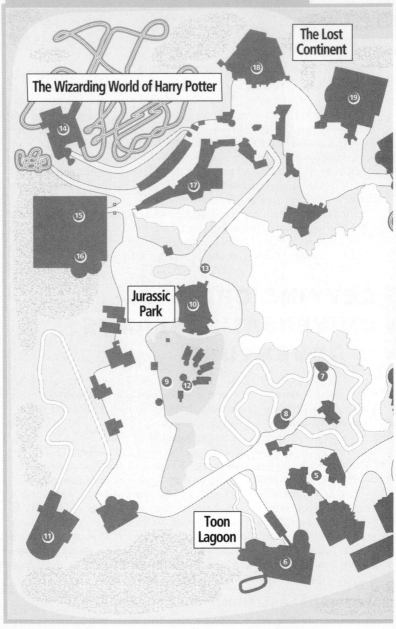

Universal's Islands of Adventure

The Lost Continent

The Wizarding World of Harry Potter

Jurassic Park

Toon Lagoon

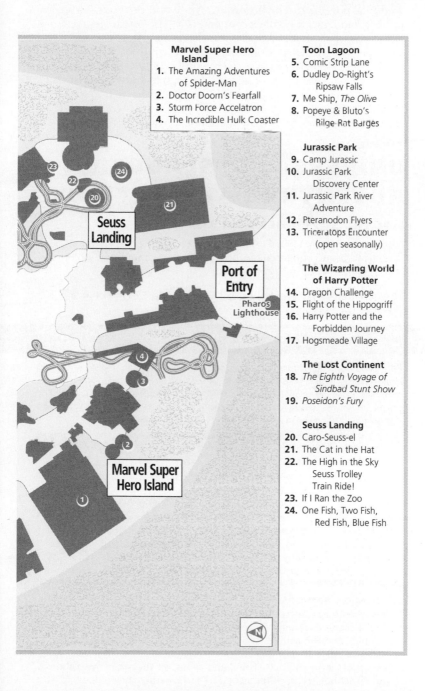

Marvel Super Hero Island
1. The Amazing Adventures of Spider-Man
2. Doctor Doom's Fearfall
3. Storm Force Accelatron
4. The Incredible Hulk Coaster

Toon Lagoon
5. Comic Strip Lane
6. Dudley Do-Right's Ripsaw Falls
7. Me Ship, *The Olive*
8. Popeye & Bluto's Bilge-Rat Barges

Jurassic Park
9. Camp Jurassic
10. Jurassic Park Discovery Center
11. Jurassic Park River Adventure
12. Pteranodon Flyers
13. Triceratops Encounter (open seasonally)

The Wizarding World of Harry Potter
14. Dragon Challenge
15. Flight of the Hippogriff
16. Harry Potter and the Forbidden Journey
17. Hogsmeade Village

The Lost Continent
18. *The Eighth Voyage of Sindbad Stunt Show*
19. *Poseidon's Fury*

Seuss Landing
20. Caro-Seuss-el
21. The Cat in the Hat
22. The High in the Sky Seuss Trolley Train Ride!
23. If I Ran the Zoo
24. One Fish, Two Fish, Red Fish, Blue Fish

Seuss Landing

Port of Entry

Pharos Lighthouse

Marvel Super Hero Island

swiftly as possible to The Wizarding World and then ride Forbidden Journey and Dragon Challenge, in that order. If you can get them out of the way in about an hour, you'll find much of the remainder of the park sparsely populated. Come back to The Wizarding World later in the day to explore Hogsmeade and the shops.

If you can't be at the park when it opens, skip Potterville first thing and enjoy other attractions in IOA. You'll still be able to visit The Wizarding World later in the day, but you probably won't be able to experience the attractions there without exceedingly long waits.

UNIVERSAL'S ISLANDS *of* ADVENTURE ATTRACTIONS

MARVEL SUPER HERO ISLAND

THIS ISLAND, WITH ITS FUTURISTIC AND RETRO-FUTURE design and comic-book signage, offers shopping, dining, and attractions based on Marvel Comics characters.

The Amazing Adventures of Spider-Man ★★★★★
(Universal Express)

APPEAL BY AGE	PRESCHOOL ★★★	GRADE SCHOOL ★★★★★	TEENS ★★★★★
YOUNG ADULTS ★★★★★		OVER 30 ★★★★★	SENIORS ★★★★

What it is Indoor adventure simulator ride based on Spider-Man. **Scope and scale** Super-headliner. **When to go** During the first 40 minutes the park is open. **Special comments** 40" minimum height requirement. **Authors' rating** One of the best attractions anywhere; not to be missed; ★★★★★. **Duration of ride** 4½ minutes. **Probable waiting time per 100 people ahead of you** 5 minutes. **Loading speed** Fast.

UNIVERSAL UNDERCOVER WITH JIM HILL

WHERE'S WALDO—UH, STAN? Marvel Comics founder Stan Lee angles for a cameo appearance in any film featuring the characters he helped create, so the Universal Creative team decided to get in on the fun by folding him into the recently retooled Spider-Man ride. Lee appears in the crowd in three scenes: as Spidey and Doc Ock duke it out in New York City's Theater District, in the street below you as your vehicle is flung in the air by a gravity gun, and finally as the stolen Statue of Liberty is being flown back into place.

DESCRIPTION AND COMMENTS Already considered by many to be the best theme park attraction on the planet, The Amazing Adventures of Spider-Man—covering 1½ acres and combining moving ride vehicles, 3-D film, and live action—was enhanced in 2012 with a complete high-definition digital upgrade. Thirteen reanimated 3-D scenes fuse almost seamlessly with the actual sets and props, so that in many instances guests cannot tell until the action begins whether they're looking at a movie screen or an actual brick wall. The total package is astonishing—frenetic yet fluid, and visually rich. The ride is wild yet very smooth. Although the attractions are not directly comparable, Spider-Man is technologically ahead of The Twilight Zone Tower of Terror at Disney's Hollywood Studios—which is to say it will leave you in awe.

The storyline is that you're a reporter for the *Daily Bugle* newspaper (where Peter Parker, a.k.a. Spider-Man, works as a mild-mannered photographer), when it's discovered that evildoers have stolen—we promise we're not making this up—the Statue of Liberty. You're drafted on the spot by your cantankerous editor to go get the story. After speeding around and being thrust into a battle between good and evil, you experience a 400-foot "sensory drop" from a skyscraper roof all the way to the pavement. Because the ride is so wild and the action so continuous, it's hard to understand the plot, but you're so thoroughly entertained that you don't really care. Plus, you'll want to ride again and again. Eventually, with repetition, the storyline will begin to make sense.

TOURING TIPS If you were on hand at park opening, ride after experiencing Harry Potter and the Forbidden Journey, Dragon Challenge, and The Incredible Hulk Coaster. If you elect to bypass all the congestion at Forbidden Journey, ride after Dragon Challenge and the Hulk. If you arrived more than 15 minutes after park opening, skip Wizarding World attractions and ride Spider-Man after the Hulk.

Doctor Doom's Fearfall *(Universal Express)* ★ ★ ★

APPEAL BY AGE	PRESCHOOL –	GRADE SCHOOL ★ ★ ★	TEENS ★ ★ ★ ★
YOUNG ADULTS ★ ★ ★ ★		OVER 30 ★ ★ ★	SENIORS –

What it is Lunch liberator. **Scope and scale** Headliner. **When to go** During the first 40 minutes the park is open. **Special comments** 52" minimum height requirement. **Authors' rating** More bark than bite; ★ ★ ★. **Duration of ride** 40 seconds. **Probable waiting time per 100 people ahead of you** 18 minutes. **Loading speed** Slow.

DESCRIPTION AND COMMENTS Here you are (again), strapped into a seat with your feet dangling and blasted 200 feet up in the air and then allowed to partially free-fall back down. Imagine the midway game wherein a macho guy swings a sledgehammer, propelling a metal sphere up a vertical shaft to ring a bell—on this ride, you're the metal sphere.

That prospect sounds much worse than it actually is. The scariest part of the ride by far is the apprehension that builds as you sit, strapped in, waiting for the thing to launch. Blasting up and falling down are actually very pleasant.

TOURING TIPS We've seen glaciers that move faster than the line for Doctor Doom's Fearfall. If you want to ride without investing half a day, be one of the first in the park to ride. Fortunately, if you're on hand at opening time, being among the first isn't too difficult (mainly because the nearby Wizarding World, Hulk, and Spider-Man attractions are bigger draws).

The Incredible Hulk Coaster ★ ★ ★ ★ ½
(Universal Express)

APPEAL BY AGE	PRESCHOOL ★	GRADE SCHOOL ★ ★ ★ ★ ★	TEENS ★ ★ ★ ★ ★
YOUNG ADULTS ★ ★ ★ ★		OVER 30 ★ ★ ★ ★	SENIORS ★ ★ ★

What it is Roller coaster. **Scope and scale** Super-headliner. **When to go** During the first 40 minutes the park is open. **Special comments** 54" minimum height requirement. **Authors' rating** A coaster-lover's coaster; not to be missed; ★ ★ ★ ★ ½. **Duration of ride** 2¼ minutes. **Probable waiting time per 100 people ahead of you** 9 minutes. **Loading speed** Moderate.

DESCRIPTION AND COMMENTS There is, as always, a storyline, but for this attraction it's of no importance whatsoever. What you need to know about this attraction is simple. You'll be shot like a cannonball from 0 to 40 mph in 2 seconds, and then you'll be flung upside down 100 feet off the ground, which will, of course, induce weightlessness. From there it's a mere six rollovers punctuated by two plunges into holes in the ground before you're allowed to get out and throw up.

Seriously, the Hulk is a great roller coaster, one of the best in Florida, providing a ride comparable to that of Montu (Busch Gardens) with the added thrill of an accelerated launch (instead of the more typical uphill crank). Plus, like Montu, this coaster has a smooth ride.

TOURING TIPS Arrive before park opening. When admitted, ride after experiencing Harry Potter and the Forbidden Journey and Dragon Challenge. If you want to stay clear of the crowds at Forbidden Journey, ride after Dragon Challenge. If you arrived more than 15 minutes after park opening, skip the Wizarding World attractions and ride the Hulk first thing. Universal provides electronic lockers near the entrance of the Hulk to deposit any items that might depart your person during the Hulk's seven inversions. The locker is free for the first 45 minutes; thereafter you'll have to pay a $2-per-hour rental charge. When you reach the boarding area, note that the Hulk has a separate line for those who want to ride in the first row.

Storm Force Accelatron *(Universal Express)* ★★★

APPEAL BY AGE	PRESCHOOL ★★★★	GRADE SCHOOL ★★★	TEENS ★★★
YOUNG ADULTS ★★★		OVER 30 ★★★	SENIORS ★★★

What it is Covered spinning ride. **Scope and scale** Minor attraction. **Special comments** May induce motion sickness. **When to go** During the first hour the park is open. **Authors' rating** Teacups in the dark; ★★★. **Duration of ride** 1½ minutes. **Probable waiting time per 100 people ahead of you** 21 minutes. **Loading speed** Slow.

DESCRIPTION AND COMMENTS Storm Force is a spiffed-up version of Disney's nausea-inducing Mad Tea Party. Here, you spin to the accompaniment of a simulated thunderstorm and swirling sound and light. A storyline loosely ties this midway-type ride to the Marvel Super Hero Island area, but it's largely irrelevant and offers no advice on keeping your lunch down.

TOURING TIPS Ride early or late to avoid long lines. If you're prone to motion sickness, keep your distance.

TOON LAGOON

TOON LAGOON IS CARTOON ART TRANSLATED into real buildings and settings. Whimsical and gaily colored, with rounded and exaggerated lines, Toon Lagoon is Universal's answer to the old Mickey's Toontown Fair in the Magic Kingdom—only you have about a 60% chance of drowning at Universal's version.

Comic Strip Lane

What it is Walk-through exhibit and shopping and dining venue. **Scope and scale** Diversion. **When to go** Anytime.

DESCRIPTION AND COMMENTS This is the main street of Toon Lagoon. Here you can visit the domains of such vintage characters as Beetle

Bailey, Hagar the Horrible, Krazy Kat, The Family Circus, and Blondie and Dagwood. Shops and eateries tie into the funny-papers theme.

TOURING TIPS This is a great place for photo ops with cartoon characters in their own environment. It's also a great place to drop a few bucks in the diners and shops—but you probably already figured that out.

Dudley Do-Right's Ripsaw Falls ★★★½
(Universal Express)

APPEAL BY AGE	PRESCHOOL ★★★	GRADE SCHOOL ★★★★	TEENS ★★★★
YOUNG ADULTS ★★★		OVER 30 ★★★★	SENIORS ★★★

What it is Flume ride. **Scope and scale** Major attraction. **When to go** Before 11 a.m. **Special comments** 44" minimum height requirement. **Authors' rating** A minimalist Splash Mountain; ★★★½. **Duration of ride** 5 minutes. **Probable waiting time per 100 people ahead of you** 9 minutes. **Loading speed** Moderate.

UNIVERSAL UNDERCOVER WITH JIM HILL

RIPPING ON A RIVAL Universal Creative has always enjoyed poking fun at Disney—for instance, tossing a pair of Mickey ears into the floating wreckage in the now-closed JAWS ride. But for the finale of Dudley Do-Right's Ripsaw Falls, the team outdid itself, lifting an entire scene from Pirates of the Caribbean: A jailed Snidely Whiplash tries to persuade a not-so-eager beaver to hand over the keys to his cell.

DESCRIPTION AND COMMENTS Inspired by the *Rocky and Bullwinkle* cartoons, this ride features Canadian Mountie Dudley Do-Right as he tries to save Nell from the evil Snidely Whiplash. Storyline aside, it's a flume ride, with the inevitable big drop at the end. Universal claims this is the first flume ride to "send riders plummeting 15 feet below the surface of the water." Actually, though, you're just plummeting into a tunnel.

The only problem with this attraction is that everyone inevitably compares it to Splash Mountain at the Magic Kingdom. The flume is as good as Splash Mountain's, and the final drop is a whopper, but the theming and the visuals aren't even in the same league. The art, sets, audio, and jokes at Dudley Do-Right are minimalist at best; it's Dudley's 2-D approach versus Splash Mountain's 3-D presentation. Taken on its own terms, however, Dudley Do-Right is a darn good flume ride.

TOURING TIPS This ride will get you wet, but on average not as wet as you might expect. If you want to stay dry, however, arrive prepared with a poncho or at least a big garbage bag with holes cut out for your head and arms. After riding, take a moment to gauge the timing of the water cannons that go off along the exit walk. This is where you can really get drenched. Ride after experiencing the Marvel Super Hero rides.

Me Ship, *The Olive* ★★★

APPEAL BY AGE	PRESCHOOL ★★★★	GRADE SCHOOL ★★★★	TEENS ½
YOUNG ADULTS ½		OVER 30 ½	SENIORS –

What it is Interactive playground. **Scope and scale** Minor attraction. **When to go** Anytime. **Authors' rating** Colorful and appealing for kids; ★★★.

DESCRIPTION AND COMMENTS *The Olive* is Popeye's three-story boat come to life as an interactive playground. Younger children can scramble around in Swee'Pea's Playpen, while older sibs shoot water cannons at riders trying to survive the adjacent Bilge-Rat Barges.

TOURING TIPS If you're into the big rides, save this for later in the day.

Popeye & Bluto's Bilge-Rat Barges ★★★★
(Universal Express)

APPEAL BY AGE   PRESCHOOL ★★★   GRADE SCHOOL ★★★★★   TEENS ★★★★
YOUNG ADULTS ★★★★   OVER 30 ★★★★   SENIORS ★★★

What it is Whitewater-raft ride. **Scope and scale** Major attraction. **When to go** Before 11 a.m. **Special comments** 42" minimum height requirement. **Authors' rating** Bring your own soap; ★★★★. **Duration of ride** 4½ minutes. **Probable waiting time per 100 people ahead of you** 5 minutes. **Loading speed** Moderate.

DESCRIPTION AND COMMENTS This sweetly named whitewater-raft ride includes an encounter with an 18-foot-tall octopus. Engineered to ensure that everyone gets drenched, the attraction even provides water cannons for highly intelligent nonparticipants ashore to fire at those aboard. The rapids are rougher and more interesting, and the ride longer, than Animal Kingdom's Kali River Rapids. But nobody surpasses Disney for visuals and theming.

TOURING TIPS If you didn't drown on Dudley Do-Right, here's a second chance. You'll get a lot wetter from the knees down on this ride, so use your poncho or garbage bag and ride barefoot with your britches rolled up. Experience the barges in the morning after the Marvel Super Hero attractions and Dudley Do-Right. If you've forgotten your wet wear, you might want to put off riding until last thing before leaving the park. Most preschoolers enjoy the barges. Kids who are frightened react more to the way the rapids look than to the roughness of the ride.

JURASSIC PARK

JURASSIC PARK (for anyone who's been asleep for 20 years) is a Steven Spielberg film franchise about a theme park with real dinosaurs. Jurassic Park at Universal's Islands of Adventure is a real theme park (or at least a section of one) with fictitious dinosaurs.

> **UNIVERSAL UNDERCOVER WITH JIM HILL**
>
>
>
> **FORWARD TO THE PAST** Dino-flavored fun abounds in this far-flung corner of IOA, but if the Creative team has its way, you'll be able to hop in a jeep and drive into the jungle one of these days. You'll roll past some of the best-known sets from the *Jurassic Park* movies—until, of course, something goes horribly wrong and you're menaced by (what else?) animatronic raptors, T. rexes, and spinosauruses. The expansion pad for the proposed attraction has been in place since IOA opened. The only thing reportedly standing in this ride's way is a catalytic event—say, the long-delayed production of *Jurassic Park 4*.

Camp Jurassic ★★★

APPEAL BY AGE   PRESCHOOL ★★★   GRADE SCHOOL ★★★   TEENS –
YOUNG ADULTS –   OVER 30 –   SENIORS –

What it is Interactive play area. **Scope and scale** Minor attraction. **When to go** Anytime. **Authors' rating** Creative playground, confusing layout; ★★★.

DESCRIPTION AND COMMENTS Camp Jurassic is a great place for children to cut loose. Sort of a Jurassic version of Tom Sawyer Island, it allows kids to explore lava pits, caves, mines, and a rainforest.

TOURING TIPS Camp Jurassic will fire the imaginations of the under-13 set. If you don't impose a time limit on the exploration, you could be here awhile. The layout of the play area is confusing and intersects the queuing area for Pteranodon Flyers.

Jurassic Park Discovery Center ★★★

APPEAL BY AGE	PRESCHOOL ★★★	GRADE SCHOOL ★★★★	TEENS ★★★
YOUNG ADULTS ★★★		OVER 30 ★★★	SENIORS ★★★

What it is Interactive natural-history exhibit. **Scope and scale** Minor attraction. **When to go** Anytime. **Authors' rating** Definitely worth checking out; ★★★.

DESCRIPTION AND COMMENTS This interactive educational exhibit mixes fiction from the movie *Jurassic Park*, such as using fossil DNA to bring dinosaurs to life, with skeletal remains and other paleontological displays. One exhibit lets guests watch an animatronic raptor being hatched. Another allows you to digitally "fuse" your DNA with a dinosaur's to see what the resultant creature would look like.

TOURING TIPS Cycle back after experiencing all the rides or on a second day. Most folks can digest this exhibit in 10–15 minutes.

Jurassic Park River Adventure ★★★★
(Universal Express)

APPEAL BY AGE	PRESCHOOL ★★★	GRADE SCHOOL ★★★★★	TEENS ★★★★★
YOUNG ADULTS ★★★★		OVER 30 ★★★★	SENIORS ★★★★

What it is Indoor-outdoor adventure river-raft ride based on the *Jurassic Park* movies. **Scope and scale** Super-headliner. **When to go** Before 11 a.m. **Special comments** 42" minimum height requirement. **Authors' rating** Better than its Hollywood cousin; not to be missed; ★★★★. **Duration of ride** 6½ minutes. **Probable waiting time per 100 people ahead of you** 5 minutes. **Loading speed** Fast.

DESCRIPTION AND COMMENTS Guests board boats for a water tour of Jurassic Park. Everything is tranquil as the tour begins, and the boat floats among large herbivorous dinosaurs such as brontosauruses and stegosauruses. Then, as word comes in that some of the carnivores have escaped their enclosure, the tour boat is accidentally diverted into Jurassic Park's maintenance facilities. Here, the boat and its riders are menaced by an assortment of hungry meat-eaters led by the ubiquitous T-Rex. At the climactic moment, the boat and its passengers escape by plummeting over an 85-foot drop.

TOURING TIPS Though the boats make a huge splash at the bottom of the 85-foot drop, you don't get all that wet. Once you're under way, there's a little splashing but nothing major until the big drop at the end of the ride. Fortunately, not all that much water lands in the boat.

A Honolulu reader thinks Jurassic Park doesn't pass the smell test:

The Jurassic Park ride is a lot of fun—so fun, in fact, that you won't realize how truly HEINOUS the water that drenches you during the climactic splashdown is until much later. We sat in the front row for the ride and got soaked. Three hours later, my girlfriend and I realized we reeked.

Young children must endure a double whammy on this ride. First, they're stalked by giant, salivating (sometimes spitting) reptiles, and then they're sent catapulting over the falls. Unless your children are fairly hardy, wait a year or two before you spring the River Adventure on them.

Because the Jurassic Park section of IOA is situated next to The Wizarding World of Harry Potter, the boat will experience heavy crowds earlier in the day. Try to ride before 11 a.m.

Pteranodon Flyers ½

APPEAL BY AGE	PRESCHOOL ★★★	GRADE SCHOOL ★★★	TEENS ★
YOUNG ADULTS ★		OVER 30 ★	SENIORS ★

What it is Slow as Christmas. **Scope and scale** Minor attraction. **When to go** When there's no line. **Special comments** Adults and older children must be accompanied by a child between 36" and 52" tall. **Authors' rating** All sizzle, no steak; ½. **Duration of ride** 1¼ minutes. **Probable waiting time per 100 people ahead of you** 28 minutes. **Loading speed** More sluggish than a hog in quicksand.

DESCRIPTION AND COMMENTS This is Islands of Adventure's biggest blunder. Engineered to accommodate only 170 persons per hour—about half the hourly capacity of Dumbo!—the ride dangles you on a swing below a track that passes over a small part of Jurassic Park. We recommend skipping this one. Why? Because the Jurassic period will probably end before you reach the front of the line! And your reward for all that waiting? A 1-minute-and-15-second ride.

TOURING TIPS Photograph the pteranodon as it flies overhead. You're probably looking at something that will someday be extinct.

Triceratops Encounter ★★★½
(open seasonally)

APPEAL BY AGE	PRESCHOOL ★★★	GRADE SCHOOL ★★★★	TEENS ★★★
YOUNG ADULTS ★★★½		OVER 30 ★	SENIORS ★★

What it is Prehistoric petting zoo. **Scope and scale** Minor attraction. **When to go** After experiencing all the rides. **Special comments** Expect long waits in line. **Authors' rating** Clever and different; ★★★½. **Duration of experience** 5 minutes. **Probable waiting time per 100 people ahead of you** 30 minutes.

DESCRIPTION AND COMMENTS Triceratops Encounter was one of the original Islands of Adventure attractions. Presumably because of its low capacity and staffing requirements, it was taken out of operation several years ago. In 2010 it was revived, but who knows for how long. Guests are ushered in groups into a "feed and control" station, where they can view and pet a 24-foot-long animatronic triceratops. While the trainer lectures about the creature's behaviors, habits, and lifestyle, the dinosaur breathes, blinks, chews, and flinches at the touch of the guests.

TOURING TIPS Nothing is certain, but this is one of only a couple of IOA attractions where you won't get wet. Just to sure, though, we suggest you stand along the side of the beast rather than near the head or tail. Though not a major attraction, Triceratops Encounter is well executed. Make it your first show/exhibit after experiencing the rides.

THE WIZARDING WORLD OF HARRY POTTER

IN WHAT MAY PROVE TO BE the competitive coup of all time between theme park archrivals Disney and Universal, the latter inked a deal with Warner Brothers Entertainment to create a "fully immersive" Harry Potter–themed environment based on the bestselling children's books by J. K. Rowling and the companion blockbuster movies from Warner Brothers. The books have been translated into 68 languages, with more than 400 million copies sold in more than 200 territories around the world. The movies have made more than $5.4 billion worldwide, making Harry Potter the largest-grossing film franchise in history. The project was blessed by Rowling, who is known for tenaciously protecting the integrity of her work. In the case of the films, she demanded that Warner Brothers be true, to an almost unprecedented degree, to the books on which the films were based.

The 20-acre Wizarding World is an amalgamation of landmarks, creatures, and themes that are faithful to the films and books. You access the area through an imposing gate that opens onto **Hogsmeade,** depicted in winter and covered in snow. This is The Wizarding World's primary shopping and dining venue. Exiting Hogsmeade, you first glimpse the towering castle housing **Hogwarts School of Witchcraft and Wizardry,** flanked by the **Forbidden Forest** and **Hagrid's Hut.** The grounds and interior of the castle house part of the queue for the super-headliner **Harry Potter and the Forbidden Journey.** Universal has gone all-out on the castle, with the intention of creating an icon even more beloved and powerful than Cinderella Castle at Disney's Magic Kingdom.

"What a Long Strange Trip It's Been"

That Grateful Dead lyric is awfully appropriate when recounting the evolution of The Wizarding World. A Harry Potter theme park (or themed area) has been the chop-licking dream of the amusement industry for a decade. First, of course, there were the books, which against all odds trumped texting and TV to lure a broad age range of youth back to the printed page. Next came the movies. In securing the film rights, Warner Brothers, along with several unsuccessful suitors, learned the most important thing about exploiting the Harry Potter phenomenon: J. K. Rowling is boss.

As the Potter books, films, and characters took the world by storm, entertainment conglomerates began approaching Rowling about theme park rights. When she spurned a Universal Studios concept for a show based on the Potter characters, industry observers were certain that she had struck a deal with Disney. In fact, Disney was in talks with Rowling about a stand-alone Harry Potter theme park and had fielded a team to develop concepts for Rowling's inspection. For her part, Rowling had no problem visualizing what she wanted in a theme park, but from

---

UNIVERSAL UNDERCOVER WITH JIM HILL

A WHOLE LOTTA POTTER Given how hugely popular The Wizarding World of Harry Potter has grown in three short years, it doesn't take a soothsayer to predict it'll get a whole lot bigger in the not-so-distant future. What is currently The Lost Continent will be subsumed, enabling Hogsmeade to expand. The creative team also reportedly has a Whomping Willow spinner ride and Shrieking Shack walk-though attraction in the works. Plus, Universal reportedly hopes to link The Wizarding World to the upcoming Diagon Alley at the Studios with a working version of the Hogwarts Express.

Disney's point of view, what Rowling wanted was operationally problematic, if not altogether impossible. Never an entity to concede control, Disney walked.

Universal caught Rowling on the rebound and brought her to Orlando to tour Islands of Adventure. Among other things, they squired her around the Lost Continent section of the park, impressing her with its detailed theme execution and showing her how with a little imagination it could be rethemed. Rowling saw the potential but wasn't much more flexible with Universal than she was with Disney. From her perspective, getting a themed area right couldn't be any harder than getting a movie right, so she insisted that Stuart Craig, her trusted production designer for the films, be responsible for faithfully re-creating sets from the movies. Universal, on fire to land Harry Potter, became convinced that the collaboration could work.

But theme parks and movies are two very different things. With a film, a set has to look good only for a few moments and then it's on to something else. With a theme park, a set has to look good 12–16 hours a day, in all manner of weather, and with tens of thousands of tourists rambling through it in need of food, drink, restrooms, protection from rain, and places to rest. In developing The Wizarding World, Rowling's insistence on authenticity occasioned conundrums not anticipated by the theme park designers, who, for example, logically assumed that guests would like to see the interior of Hagrid's Hut. No problem—a walkthrough attraction will serve nicely. Of course, there's the Americans with Disabilities Act, so we'll need ramps both in and out of the hut. No way, say the movie people: Hagrid's Hut in the films had steps, so the theme park version must have them, too.

One piece of information that Universal didn't get across well in its marketing blitz for The Wizarding World is that the "land" is not a stand-alone park but part of a bigger one. Drawing conclusions to the contrary were many Potterphiles who had been exposed to the relentless promotion. So as opening day approached, Universal braced itself for blowback from guests who expected Harry Potter and nothing but.

Bone Up

We don't have room to explain all the Potter allusions and icons incorporated into The Wizarding World. Because they so accurately replicate scenes from the books and films, it helps immeasurably to be well versed in all things Harry. If it's been a while since you've seen one of the movies or read one of the novels, you can brush up by watching the first four flicks in the series, in particular *Harry Potter and the Sorcerer's Stone* (*Harry Potter and the Philosopher's Stone* outside of India and the United States) and *Harry Potter and the Goblet of Fire*. For an easy memory jog, check out the films' trailers at **YouTube.** If you know nothing at all about Harry Potter, you'll still have fun, but to truly appreciate the nuance and detail, we suggest you hit the books.

Getting In

Wizarding World crowds will certainly be larger during summer and holidays, but because The Wizarding World is new and proving popular beyond all expectations, you'll encounter lines even at slower times of year. In the summer of 2012, guests were allowed through the turnstiles

30–60 minutes before official opening time. Universal hotel guests formed a line on the right side of Port of Entry (IOA's main entrance plaza) and were admitted to The Wizarding World through the Hogsmeade main gate; day guests (the general public) were directed left to The Wizarding World's border with Jurassic Park. Here, on the Jurassic Park side of the bridge leading to The Wizarding World, day guests could obtain a pass to enter The Wizarding World later.

Wizarding World crowd management has been a work-in progress for Universal. Trying to ride herd on tens of thousands of guests, all wanting to alight in the same few acres of the park, has been a monumental challenge. A variety of measures have been tried, abandoned, modified, and run up the flagpole yet again, all with mixed success. Now, with three years of Wizarding World operation under its belt, Universal has settled on a flexible system with three basic crowd-control options predicated on the expected level of attendance for any given day; which level will be readily apparent as you approach. No matter the crowd level, if you're staying in one of Universal's three on-site hotels and you have early-entry privileges for The Wizarding World, use them, arriving as early during the early-entry period as possible.

CROWD-CONTROL OPTION ONE is for off season and slow days. On these days you can enter and depart The Wizarding World as you please. The waits for the rides will still be more than an hour at times, but gaining entry to the themed area itself is not an issue.

Sometimes Option One will be in force in the morning, transitioning to Option Two as crowds build over the course of the day.

CROWD-CONTROL OPTION TWO is for days when attendance is high and the park is nearly full to capacity—for example, during spring break or on the days before or after a major holiday. It is at this level that barricades are placed at both entrances to The Wizarding World. You can go to either entrance and obtain a free pass (not unlike a Fastpass at Walt Disney World) to come back at a designated time. This way you can enjoy other areas of the park while waiting for your scheduled time in The Wizarding World. At the specified time, return to either entrance and present your pass to the barricade crew.

Because the Hogsmeade main entrance is marginally closer to the park entrance, a majority of day guests hustle there to obtain their return passes. To avoid congestion at the main entrance, instead cross the bridge that directly connects The Lost Continent to Jurassic Park, and then turn right to reach the Jurassic Park bridge entrance to Harryville. Far fewer guests will be vying for return passes here than at the Hogsmeade entrance.

Once admitted to The Wizarding World, you will still have to wait for each ride, store, and concession, as well as for the area's one restaurant. It's common when Option Two is in effect for the entrance barricades to be removed during the last hour or two the park is open, thus presenting the opportunity to come and go as you please.

CROWD-CONTROL OPTION THREE is for when the park is at full capacity, usually during major holidays. On these days, the barricades around The Wizarding World are in place all day, and the demand to get in is much higher.

On an Option Three day, you'll be directed toward the Jurassic Park entrance to The Wizarding World. There, you can obtain a pass with a designated return time as described under Option Two.

Be forewarned that on Option Three days, return passes are fully distributed by noon or earlier. This means that if you aren't in line to enter Islands of Adventure before the park opens, you might not be able to enter The Wizarding World at all. We strongly counsel you to arrive an hour before opening on these busiest of days and, once admitted, immediately obtain a return pass.

On Option Two and Option Three days, don't leave The Wizarding World until you've done and seen everything of interest. This advice applies to both day guests and hotel guests. Don't defer anything for later in the day or depend on being able to get back in. Eat before or after your visit. If you leave The Wizarding World, you'll have to get a new pass or wait an indeterminate time in the standby line to reenter.

VARIATIONS On days when the park is projected to be at or close to full capacity, day guests are sometimes admitted to the park before official opening and directed clockwise around the lagoon to obtain a return ticket. On days when attendance is less than expected, Universal might start the day running Option Two and later remove the barricades, allowing for free access.

The return time on your pass depends on crowd conditions and how many Universal resort guests are in The Wizarding World before the park opens to the general public. Another factor that will affect your wait is how well Harry Potter and the Forbidden Journey is operating, since this is what those in line are waiting for. If the ride comes up on schedule and runs trouble-free, everything runs smoothly. If Forbidden Journey experiences problems, though, especially first thing in the morning, it jams things up for everyone.

If you leave The Wizarding World, the only way to get back in is to obtain another pass (providing they haven't all been distributed), unless the entrance barriers have been removed, thus allowing free access. This is true for hotel guests as well as day guests.

Crowds finally dissipate between 7 and 8 p.m., except on Option Three days. An extra bonus for visiting late is enjoying the exquisite lighting and magical nighttime personality of The Wizarding World. Forbidden Journey will accommodate anyone already in line at park closing, and many of the Hogsmeade shops remain open awhile after the park closes.

Gentlemen, Start Your Broomsticks

The Wizarding World is in the northwest corner of Islands of Adventure, between The Lost Continent and Jurassic Park. From the IOA entrance, the most direct route there is through Port of Entry then right, through Seuss Landing and The Lost Continent, to the Hogsmeade main gate. The alternative route is to cross the bridge connecting The Lost Continent with Jurassic Park, then turn right after entering the latter area.

For the moment, though, let's begin our exploration at The Wizarding World's main entrance, on the Lost Continent side of the themed area. Passing beneath a stone archway, you enter the village of **Hogsmeade**. The **Hogwarts Express** locomotive sits belching steam on your right (but it doesn't actually go anywhere). The setting is rendered in exquisite detail: Stone cottages and shops have steeply pitched slate roofs, bowed multipaned windows, gables, and tall, crooked chimneys. Add cobblestone streets and gas street lamps, and Hogsmeade is as reminiscent of David Copperfield or Sherlock Holmes as of Harry Potter.

On your left, opposite the locomotive and station, is **Zonko's**, a novelty shop specializing in such necessities as Shrunken Heads, Extendable Ears, and Screaming Yo-yos. If your sweet tooth is on a rampage, the shop also sells sweets such as Nosebleed Nougat, U-No-Poo, and our personal favorite, Puking Pastilles. (Not only the attractions but all the merchandise and food had to meet with the approval of the redoubtable Ms. Rowling. As you can imagine, this was a painstaking process that resulted in stuff still floating around on container ships mere days before The Wizarding World's scheduled opening.)

Connected to Zonko's through an interior passage is **Honeydukes**. For those whose appetites have recovered from disgorging their Puking Pastilles, Honeydukes offers another opportunity to expand your midriff, specializing in Acid Pops (no flashbacks, guaranteed), Tooth Splintering Strong Mints, and Fizzing Whizzbees. Across the street from Honeydukes, next to the train station, is the entrance to the **Dragon Challenge** roller coasters (see page 691).

Next door to Honeydukes and set back from the main street is **Three Broomsticks,** a rustic tavern serving English staples such as fish-and-chips, shepherd's pie, Cornish pasties, and turkey legs. The menu is mostly familiar, eschewing dishes with fanciful, incomprehensible names. Kids' fare includes the obligatory mac-and-cheese and chicken fingers. To the rear of the tavern is the **Hog's Head** pub, which serves a nice selection of beer as well as The Wizarding World's signature non-alcoholic brew, Butterbeer (see page 687). Three Broomsticks and the Hog's Head were carved out of The Lost Continent's popular Enchanted Oak Tavern, which was Potterfied pretty effectively in its reincarnation, although a good deal of seating capacity was sacrificed—the restaurant and pub combined seat only 123. To dine at Three Broomsticks anytime from its opening until roughly 8 p.m., you'll have to wait in a long queue during busier times of year. In the summer of 2012, waiting times for Three Broomsticks were upwards of 70 minutes most of the day. This, coupled with the facts that (1) one usually can't reenter The Wizarding World without starting over and (2) no other food is available in the themed area save some meager vendor snacks, means that many guests are left without a practical alternative for getting something to eat. What's more, Three Broomsticks doesn't participate in any of Universal's meal plans.

The only restrooms in The Wizarding World, labeled PUBLIC CONVENIENCES, are in the middle of Hogsmeade. Remember where they are—especially if you're planning to ride Forbidden Journey or Dragon Challenge and you're prone to motion sickness.

Roughly across the street from the pub, you'll find benches in the shade at the **Owlery,** where animatronic owls (complete with lifelike poop) ruffle and hoot from the rafters. Next to the Owlery is the **Owl Post,** a functioning post office where any postcards you mail will be delivered with a Hogsmeade postmark. The Owl Post also sells stationery, toy owls, and the like. Here, once again, a nice selection of owls preens on the timbers overhead. You access the Owl Post in either of two ways: through an interior door following the wand-choosing demonstration at Ollivanders (see below), or through **Dervish and Banges,** a magic-supplies shop that's interconnected with the Owl Post. You can't enter through the Owl Post front door, which serves exclusively as an exit. Because it's so difficult to get into the Owl Post, IOA sometimes stations a team member outside to stamp your postcards with the Wizarding World postmark.

Next to the Owl Post is the previously mentioned **Ollivanders,** a musty little shop stacked to the ceiling with boxes of magic wands. Here, following a script from the Potter books, you can pick out a wand or, in an interactive experience, let it pick you. This is one of the most truly imaginative elements of The Wizarding World: A Wandkeeper sizes you up and presents a wand, inviting you to try it out; your attempted spells produce unintended, unwanted, and highly amusing consequences. Ultimately, a wand chooses you, with all the attendant special effects. It's great fun, but the tiny shop can accommodate only about 24 guests at a time. Usually just one person in each group gets to be chosen by a wand, and then the whole group is dispatched to the Owl Post and Dervish and Banges to make purchases. Wands cost $29.99. The wand experience is second in popularity only to Harry Potter and the Forbidden Journey—lines build quickly after opening, and there's little to no shade. If Ollivanders is a priority, go there first thing in the morning or after 7:30 p.m. The average wait time during summer and other busy periods is 45–85 minutes between 9:30 a.m. and 7:30 p.m. If you're just looking to buy a wand without the interactive experience, a cart is usually set up between Filch's Emporium of Confiscated Goods and the Flight of the Hippogriff exit, with little to no wait.

At the far end of the village, the massive **Hogwarts** castle comes into view, set atop a rock face and towering over Hogsmeade and the entire Wizarding World. Follow the path through the castle's massive gates to the entrance of Harry Potter and the Forbidden Journey. Below the castle and to the right, at the base of the cliff, are the **Forbidden Forest, Hagrid's Hut,** and the **Flight of the Hippogriff** children's roller coaster. In the village, near the gate to Hogwarts Castle, is **Filch's Emporium of Confiscated Goods,** which offers all manner of Potter-themed gear, including Quidditch clothing, magical-creature toys, film-inspired chess sets, and, of course, Death Eater masks (breath mints extra).

In keeping with the stores depicted in the Potter films, the shopping venues in The Wizarding World are small and intimate—so intimate, in fact, that they feel congested when they're serving only 12–20 shoppers. With so many avid Potter fans, lines for the shops develop most days by 9:30 or 10 a.m., creating a phenomenon we've never seen in our 28 years of covering theme parks: The lines for the shops are longer than the lines for Dragon Challenge and Flight of the Hippogriff—at 11 a.m., there was frequently a 30- to 40-minute wait to get into the shops, compared with a less-than-20-minute wait to ride the coasters. Filch's Emporium is the only shop in The Wizarding World that you can enter during high season without waiting in line; problem is, it doubles as the exit for Forbidden Journey. As throngs of riders flow out continuously, trying to enter Filch's is not unlike swimming upstream to spawn. If you have the persistence of a salmon, it's doable, and a whole lot better than standing in lines for the other shops. Because the stores are so jammed, IOA sells some Potter merchandise, including wands, through street vendors and in Port of Entry shops.

At the end of the village and to the left is the walkway to **Jurassic Park,** the themed area contiguous to The Wizarding World.

The Butterbeer Craze

Butterbeer is a nonalcoholic, cream soda–like beverage served from a tap, with a butterscotch-y head that's added after the drink is poured. There's also a frozen version that's sort of like a slushie. Both were invented for The Wizarding World and had to meet J. K. Rowling's stringent specifications, which, among other things, required natural sugar (don't ask for Butterbeer Lite). We didn't expect to like it but were pleasantly surprised: It's tasty and refreshing, albeit *really* sweet. Twelve ounces of the soda in a plastic cup goes for $2.99, while the frozen version is $3.99. The same soda in a Harry Potter souvenir cup sells for $9.50.

It seems everyone in the park is dead-set on trying Butterbeer. Unfortunately, it's sold only at **Three Broomsticks** and the **Hog's Head** pub, and by a single street vendor—and that means, once again, long lines. Most folks buy from the vendor, many waiting 30 minutes or more to be served. One Butterbeer queue, totally out of sight from the street, forms on the patio behind the Hog's Head: To find the patio, go down the alley between the restrooms and the Dogweed & Death Cap Exotic Plants Shop. The wait here is usually only about 10 minutes or less, with most of your time spent in the quaint air-conditioned pub. Once served, you can relax with your drink at a table in the pub or out on the patio. In addition to Butterbeer, there's a pumpkin-juice drink that comes in a bottle with a pumpkin cap; it's sold by several street vendors and is much easier to get, though not as well received. At Rowling's behest, no brand-name soft drinks are available in The Wizarding World—if you want a Coke, you have to go to The Lost Continent or Jurassic Park.

Wizarding World Entertainment

Nearly every retail space sports some sort of animatronic or special-effects surprise. At **Dervish and Banges,** the fearsome *Monster Book of Monsters* rattles around and snarls at you as Nimbus 2001 brooms strain at their tethers overhead. At the Hog's Head pub, the titular porcine part, mounted behind the bar, similarly thrashes and growls. Street entertainment at the Forbidden Journey end of Hogsmeade includes the **Hogwarts Choir,** accompanied by frogs sitting on pillows, and the **Triwizard Spirit Rally,** featuring dancing, martial arts, and acrobatics. Performances run about 15 minutes—which, given the absolute lack of shade, is about all that anybody can stand.

Harry Potter and the Forbidden Journey ★★★★½

APPEAL BY AGE	PRESCHOOL –	GRADE SCHOOL ★★★★★	TEENS ★★★★★
YOUNG ADULTS ★★★★★		OVER 30 ★★★★★	SENIORS ★★★★★

What It Is Motion-simulator dark ride. **Scope and scale** Super-headliner. **When to go** Immediately after park opening. **Special comments** Expect *long* waits in line; 48" minimum height requirement. **Authors' rating** Marvelous for muggles; not to be missed; ★★★★½. **Duration of ride** 4¼ minutes. **Probable waiting time per 100 people ahead of you** 4 minutes. **Loading speed** Fast.

Motion Sickness

DESCRIPTION AND COMMENTS The big banana of The Wizarding World, this ride provides the only opportunity to actually come in contact with the Harry Potter characters. Half the attraction is a series of preshows that set the stage for the main event, a dark ride. Incorporated into the queue, the shows compose an integral element of the overall experience—not merely something to keep you occupied while you wait for the main event. You can get on the ride in only 10–25 minutes using the singles line, but everyone should go through the main queue at least once.

From Hogsmeade you reach the attraction through the imposing Winged Boar gates and progress along a winding path. Entering the castle on a lower level, you walk through a sort of dungeon festooned with various icons and prop replicas from the Potter flicks, including the Mirror of Erised from *Harry Potter and the Sorcerer's Stone*. You later emerge back outside and into the Hogwarts greenhouses. Cleverly conceived and executed, with some strategically placed mandrakes to amuse you, the greenhouses compose the larger part of the Forbidden Journey's queuing area. If you're among the first in the park and you hustle to the attraction, you'll move through this area pretty quickly. Otherwise . . . well, we hope you like plants. The greenhouses are not air-conditioned, but fans move the (hot) air around. Blessedly, there are water fountains, but, alas, no restrooms—you'll need to take care of business before you get in line.

Having finally escaped horticulture purgatory, you reenter the castle, moving along its halls and passageways. One chamber you'll probably remember from the films is a multistory gallery of portraits, many of whose subjects come alive when they take a notion. You'll recognize the Fat Lady but will see for the first time the four founders of Hogwarts: Helga Hufflepuff holding her famous cup, Godric Gryffindor and Rowena Ravenclaw nearby, and the tall, moving portrait of Salazar Slytherin straight ahead. The founders argue about Quidditch and Dumbledore's controversial decision to host an open house at Hogwarts for muggles (garden-variety mortals). Don't rush through the gallery—the effects are very cool, and the conversation is essential to understanding the rest of the attraction.

Next up, after you've navigated some more passages, is Dumbledore's office, where the chief wizard appears on a balcony and welcomes you to Hogwarts. The headmaster's appearance is your introduction to Musion Eyeliner technology—a high-definition video-projection system that produces breathtakingly realistic, three-dimensional, life-size moving holograms. The technology uses a special foil that reflects images from HD projectors, producing holographic images of variable sizes and incredible clarity. After his welcoming remarks, Dumbledore dispatches you to the Defence Against the Dark Arts classroom to hear a presentation on the history of Hogwarts. The classroom is recognizable from the Potter films, although in this version there are no desks.

As you gather to await the lecture, Harry, Ron Weasley, and Hermione Granger pop out from beneath an invisibility cloak. They suggest you ditch the lecture in favor of joining them for a proper tour of Hogwarts, including a Quidditch match. After some repartee among the characters and a couple of special-effects surprises, it's off to the Hogwarts Official Attraction Safety Briefing and Boarding Instructions Chamber—OK, we made up the name, but you get the picture. The briefing and instructions are presented by animated portraits, including an etiquette teacher. Later on, even the famed Sorting Hat gets into the act. All this leads to the Room of Requirement, where hundreds of candles float overhead. This is where you board the ride.

After all the high-tech stuff in your queuing odyssey, you'll naturally expect to be wowed by your ride vehicle. Surely it's a Nimbus 3000 turbo-broom, a Phoenix, a Hippogriff, or at least the Weasleys' flying car. But no, what you'll ride on the most technologically advanced theme park attraction in America is . . . a *bench*? Yep, a bench. Not that there's anything wrong with a bench. We're just saying that maybe the well ran a little dry in the imagination department.

As benches go, though, it's a doozy, mounted on a Kuka robotic arm. When not engaged in Quidditch matches, a Kuka arm is a computer-controlled robotic arm similar to the kind used in heavy manufacturing. If you think about pictures you've seen of automotive assembly plants, Kuka arms are like those long metal appendages that come in to complete welds, move heavy stuff around, or fasten things. With the right programming, the arms can handle just about any repetitive industrial tasks thrown at them (see **kuka-robotics.com** for more info).

Bear with us for a moment; you know how we *Unofficials* like technical stuff. When you put a Kuka arm on a ride platform, it provides six axes—six degrees of freedom, with synchronized motion that can be programmed to replicate all the sensations of flying, including broad swoops, steep dives, sharp turns, sudden stops, and fast acceleration. Here's where it gets really good: Up to now, when Kuka arms and similar robotic systems have been employed in theme park rides, the arm has been anchored to a stationary platform. In Forbidden Journey, the arm is mounted on a ride vehicle that moves you through a series of action scenes projected all around you. The movement of the arm is synchronized to create the motion that corresponds to what's happening in the film. When everything works right, it's mind-blowing.

When the ride was being designed, it was assumed that Kuka's robotic programming could easily produce the various movements called for in each scene. What nobody considered, however, is that the program was designed for maximum industrial efficiency. If, to correspond to the action in a given scene, the Kuka arm had to simulate 22 different motions, the software—not knowing a theme park ride from a diesel assembly line—would think, "OK, let's knock these 22 movements down to 13 and save half a minute." Because this would throw the timing of everything out of whack, Universal ended up having to create a program that would behave as it was told and not be so anal about efficiency. For you, the practical implication of all this is an extraordinary attraction with more gremlins than inhabit the dark-arts lab. If all goes well, however, you'll soar over Hogwarts Castle, get tossed into a Quidditch match, spar with the Whomping Willow, narrowly evade an attacking dragon, and fight off Dementors.

Having experienced Forbidden Journey for ourselves, we have two primary bones to pick. First, Islands of Adventure team members rush you through the queue. To understand the storyline and get the most out of the attraction, you really need to see and hear the entire presentation in each of the preshow rooms. This won't happen unless, contrary to the admonishments of the team members, you just park yourself and watch a full run-through of each preshow. Try to find a place to stop where you can let those behind you pass and where you're as far away from any team members as possible. As long as you're not creating a logjam, the team members will leave you alone as often as not.

Another alternative is to tell the greeter at the castle entrance that you want to take the **castle-only tour.** This self-guided experience lets guests who don't want to ride view the many features of the castle via a different queue. You can pause as long as you desire in each of the various chambers and savor the preshows without being herded along. At the end, if you decide to ride, ask to be guided to the singles line—using this strategy, you'll maximize your enjoyment of the castle while minimizing your wait for the ride. Note that the castle-only tour is often unavailable on peak-attendance days and might be deep-sixed for good should Forbidden Journey someday become a Universal Express attraction.

Another gripe: The dialogue in the preshows is delivered in English accents of varying degrees of intelligibility, and at a very brisk pace. Add an echo effect owing to the cavernous nature of the preshow rooms, and it can be quite difficult for Yanks to understand what's being said. This is especially evident in the staccato repartee between Harry, Ron, and Hermione in the Defense Against the Dark Arts classroom.

TOURING TIPS Harry Potter and the Forbidden Journey has quickly become the most popular attraction at Islands of Adventure, and arguably the most in-demand theme park attraction in America. The only way to ride without a prohibitive wait is to be one of the first through the turnstiles in the morning or to visit after 7:30 or 8 in the evening.

Upon entering Forbidden Journey's outside queue, you have two choices: left line or right line. They are unmarked, but the right line is for those who have bags or loose items and therefore require a locker (no charge). Our wait-time research has shown that in some cases, not needing a locker can save you as much as 30 minutes of standing in line. If you do need to stow your stuff, be aware that the Forbidden Journey locker area is small, crowded, and confusing. It may make more sense to pay the $3 to stash your things in the lockers beside Dragon Challenge.

Universal warns you to secure or leave behind loose objects, which most people interpret to mean eyeglasses, purses, ball caps, and the like. However, the ride makes a couple of moves that will empty your trousers faster than a master pickpocket—ditto and worse for shirt pockets. When these moves occur, your stuff will clatter around like quarters in a slot-machine tray. Much better to use the small compartment built into the seat back for keys, coins, phone, wallet, and pocket Bible. Be prepared, however: Team members don't give you much time to stow or retrieve your things.

The single-rider line is likewise unmarked, as relatively few guests use it. Typically, on most attractions, the wait in the singles line is one-third the wait of the standby line. At Forbidden Journey it can be as much as one-tenth. Because the ride experience is individual (you can't see the other riders, including members of your party), the singles line is a great option. To get in the singles line, enter the left (no-bags) line and stay to the left all the way into Hogwarts Castle. After you pass the locker area, take the first left into the single-rider line.

If you see a complete iteration of each preshow in the queue and then experience the ride, you'll invest 25–35 minutes even if you don't have to wait. If you elect to skip the preshows (the Gryffindor Common Room, where you receive safety and loading directions, is mandatory) and use the singles line, you can get on in about 10–25 minutes at any time of day. At a time when the posted wait in the regular line was 2 hours, we rode and were out the door in 15 minutes using the singles line.

Many riders experience some degree of motion sickness on Forbidden Journey. It's possible that Universal will tone down the ride or introduce a tamer version as Disney did with Mission: SPACE at Epcot, but don't count on it. The best defense against motion sickness is not to ride on an empty stomach. If you start getting queasy, fix your gaze on your feet and try to exclude as much from your peripheral vision as possible.

If you have a child who doesn't meet the minimum height requirement of 48 inches, a child-swapping option is provided at the loading area. If you ride with a child who meets the minimum height, be advised that the seats on each bench are compartmentalized—your child will not be able to see you or hold your hand.

In response to many larger guests being denied rides, the seats on Forbidden Journey have been redesigned to accommodate a wide variety of body shapes and sizes. All benches now have specially modified seats at either end. Though these new seats allow many more people to ride, it's still possible that guests of size can't fit in them. The best way to figure out whether you can fit in a regular seat or one of the modified ones is to sit in one of the test seats outside the queue or just inside the castle. After sitting down, pull down on the safety harness as far as you can. One of three safety lights will illuminate: A green light indicates you can fit into any seat, a yellow light means you should ask for one of the modified seats on the outside of the bench, and a red light means the harness can't engage enough for you to experience the ride safely.

In addition, IOA team members select guests of all sizes "at random" to plop in the test seats, but they're just being politically correct: They're really looking for large people or those who have a certain body shape. Team members handle the situation as diplomatically as possible, but if they suspect you're not the right size, you'll be asked to sit down for a test. This is the time to suck it in to the max. To ride, the overhead restraint has to click three times; once again, it's body shape rather than weight (unless you're over 300 pounds) that's key. Most team members will let you try a second time if you don't achieve three clicks on the first go. Passing the test by inhaling sharply is not recommended unless you can also hold your breath for the entire 4½ minutes of the ride.

With The Wizarding World and especially Forbidden Journey soaking up so many guests in IOA, the waits for attractions in the other themed areas are minimal up to around 11 a.m. (providing Forbidden Journey doesn't break down)—so there's no reason to pay the big extra bucks for Universal Express Plus. The Wizarding World even sucks people out of Universal Studios next door, making Universal Express nonessential there as well.

Dragon Challenge *(Universal Express)* ★★★★½

APPEAL BY AGE	PRESCHOOL –	GRADE SCHOOL ★★★★	TEENS ★★★★
YOUNG ADULTS ★★★★		OVER 30 ★★★★	SENIORS ★★

What it is Roller coaster. **Scope and scale** Headliner. **When to go** Immediately after Harry Potter and the Forbidden Journey. **Special comments** 54" minimum height requirement. **Authors' rating** As good as the Hulk coaster; not to be missed; ★★★★½. **Duration of ride** 2½ minutes. **Probable waiting time per 100 people ahead of you** 9 minutes. **Loading speed** Moderate.

DESCRIPTION AND COMMENTS This high-tech coaster launches two trains— Chinese Fireball and Hungarian Horntail—moments apart on tracks that are closely intertwined. The tracks are configured so that you get a different experience on each.

Previously the two trains barreled toward each other in what appeared to be an imminent collision, closing in at one point to only a foot or so apart. In 2012, however, there were two incidents in which loose objects from one train hit and injured riders on the other train. Following a thorough investigation (and a lawsuit), Universal permanently altered the launch so that the trains are now dispatched sequentially instead of simultaneously, resulting in more of a chase than a race and eliminating the danger of loose stuff popping passengers in the chops. If you're speculating on the nature of the objects involved, consider riders trying to take pictures with their phones—what could possibly go wrong?

Because this is an inverted coaster, your view of the action is limited unless you're sitting in the front row. (Thus, most passengers on the pre-2012 version of the ride missed seeing all those near-collisions.) But don't worry; regardless of where you sit, there's plenty to keep you busy. Dragon Challenge is the highest coaster in the park and also claims the longest drop at 115 feet, plus five inversions. As on the Hulk, it's a smooth ride all the way.

Coaster cadets argue about which seat on which train provides the wildest ride. We prefer the front row on either train, but coaster loonies hype the front row of Fireball and the last row of Horntail.

Dragon Challenge, formerly Dueling Dragons and part of The Lost Continent, was renamed and incorporated into The Wizarding World in 2010. The storyline is that you're preparing to compete in the Triwizard Tournament from *Harry Potter and the Goblet of Fire*. As you wind through the long, long queue, you pass through tournament tents and dark passages that are supposed to be under the stadium. You'll see the Goblet of Fire on display and hear the distant roar of the crowd in the supposed stadium above you.

TOURING TIPS The good news about this ride is that you won't get wet unless you wet yourself. The bad news is that the queuing area for Dragon Challenge is the longest, most convoluted affair we've ever seen, winding endlessly through a maze of faux subterranean passages. After what feels like a comprehensive tour of Mammoth Cave, you finally emerge at the loading area, where you must choose between Chinese Fireball or Hungarian Horntail. Of course, at this critical juncture, you're as blind as a mole rat from being in the dark for so long. Our advice is to follow the person in front of you until your eyes adjust to the light.

Waits for Dragon Challenge, one of the best coasters in the country, rarely exceed 30 minutes before 11 a.m. Ride after experiencing Harry Potter and the Forbidden Journey. Warn anyone waiting for you that you might be a while. Even if there's no line to speak of, it takes 10–12 minutes just to navigate the passages and not much less time to exit after riding. If lines are short, however, park employees will open special doors marked REENTRY TO CHINESE FIREBALL or REENTRY TO HUNGARIAN HORNTAIL (depending on what coaster you just rode) that allow you to get right back to the head of the queue and ride again. Finally, if you don't have time to ride both coasters, the *Unofficial* crew unanimously prefers Chinese Fireball.

Flight of the Hippogriff *(Universal Express)* ★★½

APPEAL BY AGE	PRESCHOOL ★★★★	GRADE SCHOOL ★★★★	TEENS ★★
YOUNG ADULTS ★★		OVER 30 ★	SENIORS ★

What it is Kiddie roller coaster. **Scope and scale** Minor attraction. **When to go** First 90 minutes the park is open. **Special comments** 36" minimum height requirement. **Authors' rating** A good beginner coaster; ★★½. **Duration of ride** 1 minute. **Probable waiting time per 100 people ahead of you** 14 minutes. **Loading speed** Slow.

DESCRIPTION AND COMMENTS Previously called the Flying Unicorn, this coaster underwent a name and theme change when it was incorporated into The Wizarding World. Below and to the right of Hogwarts Castle, next to Hagrid's Hut, the Hippogriff is short and sweet but not worth much of a wait. Fortunately, waits usually don't exceed 20 minutes, even in the non-Express line.

TOURING TIPS Have your kids ride soon after the park opens while older sibs enjoy Dragon Challenge. Even if you don't ride, it's worth a stroll to see Hogwarts Castle from the cliff bottom and to check out Hagrid's Hut, above the path for the regular line.

THE LOST CONTINENT

The Eighth Voyage of Sindbad Stunt Show (Universal Express) ★★

APPEAL BY AGE   PRESCHOOL ★★★   GRADE SCHOOL ★★★★   TEENS ★★★
YOUNG ADULTS ★★★   OVER 30 ★★★   SENIORS ★★★

What it is Theater stunt show. **Scope and scale** Major attraction. **When to go** Any time on the daily entertainment schedule. **Authors' rating** Lame-o; ★★. **Duration of presentation** 17 minutes. **Probable waiting time** 15 minutes.

DESCRIPTION AND COMMENTS A story about Sindbad the Sailor is the glue that (loosely) binds this stunt show featuring water explosions, 10-foot-tall circles of flame, and various other eruptions and perturbations. Not unlike an action movie that substitutes a mind-numbing succession of explosions, crashes, and special effects for plot and character development, the production is so vacuous and redundant (not to mention silly) that it's hard to get into the spirit of the thing. When our researchers went to review *Sindbad,* one team member passed, explaining that the show is like a colonoscopy—once every 10 years is enough.

TOURING TIPS See *The Eighth Voyage* after you've experienced the rides and the better-rated shows.

Poseidon's Fury (Universal Express) ★★★★

APPEAL BY AGE   PRESCHOOL ★★   GRADE SCHOOL ★★★★   TEENS ★★★★
YOUNG ADULTS ★★★★   OVER 30 ★★★★   SENIORS ★★★★

What it is High-tech theater attraction. **Scope and scale** Headliner. **When to go** After experiencing all the rides. **Special comments** Audience stands throughout. **Authors' rating** Not to be missed; ★★★★. **Duration of presentation** 17 minutes, including preshow. **Probable waiting time** 25 minutes.

DESCRIPTION AND COMMENTS In the first incarnation of this story, the Greek gods Poseidon and Zeus duked it out, with Poseidon as the heavy. Poseidon fought with water, and Zeus fought with fire, though both sometimes resorted to laser beams and smoke machines. In the current incarnation, the rehabilitated Poseidon now tussles with an evil wizardish guy—named Lord Darkenon, of all things—and they fight with fire, water, lasers, smoke machines, and angry lemurs. (Just seeing if you're paying attention.) As you might have inferred, the story is somewhat incoherent, but the special effects are still amazing, and the theming of the preshow area is quite imposing. The plot unfolds in installments as you pass through a couple of antechambers and finally into the main theater. Though the production plods a bit at first, it wraps up with quite an impressive flourish. There's some great technology at work here. *Poseidon* is far and away the best of the Islands of Adventure theater attractions (it only has to compete with *Sindbad*).

TOURING TIPS If you're still wet from Dudley Do-Right, the Bilge-Rat Barges, and the Jurassic Park River Adventure, you might be tempted to cheer the evil wizard's flame jets in hopes of finally drying out. Our money, however, is on Poseidon—it's legal in Florida for theme parks to get you wet, but setting you on fire is frowned upon.

Frequent explosions and noise may frighten younger children. Catch *Poseidon* after getting your fill of the rides.

SEUSS LANDING

THIS 10-ACRE THEMED AREA is based on Dr. Seuss's famous children's books. As at the old Mickey's Toontown Fair in the Magic Kingdom, the buildings and attractions replicate a whimsical, brightly colored cartoon style with exaggerated features and rounded lines. Seuss Landing has four rides and an interactive play area, **If I Ran the Zoo,** populated by Seuss creatures.

UNIVERSAL UNDERCOVER WITH JIM HILL

NOT EGG-XACTLY A HIT Someone in Universal Creative thought it would be neat to put a Green Eggs and Ham Cafe in Seuss Landing, serving the actual foodstuffs enshrined in the 1960 book. Well, as it turns out, Sam I Am, *nobody* likes greens eggs and ham—even if the eggs are only tinted with food coloring. IOA janitors attest to finding trashcans near the eatery overflowing with green-egg-and-ham sandwiches that guests took one bite of and tossed.

Caro-Seuss-el *(Universal Express)* ★★★½

APPEAL BY AGE	PRESCHOOL ★★★★		GRADE SCHOOL ★★★★		TEENS –
YOUNG ADULTS –		OVER 30 –			SENIORS –

What it is Merry-go-round. **Scope and scale** Minor attraction. **When to go** Before 11 a.m. **Authors' rating** Wonderfully whimsical; ★★★½. **Duration of ride** 2 minutes. **Probable waiting time per 100 people ahead of you** 9 minutes. **Loading speed** Slow.

DESCRIPTION AND COMMENTS Totally outrageous, this full-scale, 56-mount merry-go-round is made up entirely of Dr. Seuss characters.

TOURING TIPS Even if you're too old or you don't want to ride, Caro-Seuss-el is worth an inspection. Whatever your age, chances are good you'll see some old friends.

The Cat in the Hat *(Universal Express)* ★★★½

APPEAL BY AGE	PRESCHOOL ★★★★		GRADE SCHOOL ★★★★		TEENS ★★★
YOUNG ADULTS ★★★★		OVER 30 ★★★★			SENIORS ★★★★

What it is Indoor adventure ride. **Scope and scale** Major attraction. **When to go** Before 11:30 a.m. **Authors' rating** Dr. S. would be proud; ★★★½. **Duration of ride** 3½ minutes. **Probable waiting time per 100 people ahead of you** 5 minutes. **Loading speed** Moderate.

DESCRIPTION AND COMMENTS Guests ride on "couches" through 18 different sets inhabited by animatronic Seuss characters, including The

Cat in the Hat, Thing 1 and Thing 2, and the beleaguered goldfish who tries to maintain order in the midst of bedlam. Well done overall, with nothing that should frighten younger children.

TOURING TIPS This is fun for all ages. Try to ride early.

A father of three from Natick, Massachusetts, thinks we're off-base when we say that nothing should frighten younger children:

> The Cat in the Hat ride has quite the fright potential. Besides all the things popping out at you, it whips you around very wildly. My wife took my fairly advanced 3½-year-old daughter on the ride, and she was screaming her head off. Nearly two years later, she still reminds me of the scary Cat in the Hat ride (it hasn't affected her love for the books, though!).

The High in the Sky Seuss Trolley Train Ride!   ★★★½
(Universal Express)

APPEAL BY AGE	PRESCHOOL ★★★★	GRADE SCHOOL ★★★½	TEENS ★
YOUNG ADULTS ★★½	OVER 30 ★★½		SENIORS ★★★

What it is Elevated train. **Scope and scale** Major attraction. **When to go** Before 11:30 a.m. **Special comments** A relaxed look at the park; 34" minimum height requirement. **Authors' rating** ★★★½. **Duration of ride** 3½ minutes. **Probable waiting time per 100 people ahead of you** 9 minutes. **Loading speed** Molasses.

DESCRIPTION AND COMMENTS Trains putter along elevated tracks while a voice reads a Dr. Seuss story over the train's speakers. As each train makes its way through Seuss Landing, it passes a series of animatronic characters in scenes that are part of the story being told. Little tunnels and a few mild turns make this a charming ride.

There are two tracks at the station. As you face the platform, to your left is the Beech track, which is aquamarine; to your right is the Star track, which is purple. Each track offers a different story.

TOURING TIPS The line for this ride is much less charming than the attraction. The trains are small, fitting about 20 people, and the loading speed is glacial. Save High in the Sky for the end of the day or ride first thing in the morning.

One Fish, Two Fish, Red Fish, Blue Fish   ★★★½
(Universal Express)

APPEAL BY AGE	PRESCHOOL ★★★★	GRADE SCHOOL ★★★★	TEENS ★★★
YOUNG ADULTS ★★★	OVER 30 ★★★		SENIORS ★★★

What it is Wet version of Dumbo the Flying Elephant. **Scope and scale** Minor attraction. **When to go** Before 10 a.m. **Authors' rating** Who says you can't teach an old ride new tricks?; ★★★½. **Duration of ride** 2 minutes. **Probable waiting time per 100 people ahead of you** 9 minutes. **Loading speed** Slow.

DESCRIPTION AND COMMENTS Imagine Dumbo with Seuss-style fish instead of elephants and you've got half the story—the other half involves yet another opportunity to drown. Guests steer their fish up or down 15 feet in the air while traveling in circles. At the same time, they try to avoid streams of water projected from "squirt posts." A catchy song provides clues to help you avoid the squirting.

Though the ride is ostensibly for kids, the song and the challenge of steering your fish away from the water make it fun for all ages.

TOURING TIPS We don't know what it is about this theme park and water, but you'll get wetter than at a full-immersion baptism.

UNIVERSAL'S ISLANDS *of* ADVENTURE TOURING PLAN

ROLLING THE DICE WITH HARRY POTTER

THE WIZARDING WORLD, and Harry Potter and the Forbidden Journey in particular, create some real challenges when trying to develop an optimum touring plan for IOA. Some of this will sort itself out over time, but for The Wizarding World's third year:

- The 20-acre section of the park will be completely overrun by crowds.
- The science and innovation behind Forbidden Journey are remarkable, but the ride is subject to malfunctions.
- Because of Forbidden Journey's several preshows, it takes about 25 minutes to experience, even if you don't have to wait.

If you try to enjoy Forbidden Journey first thing after the park opens, and if the ride operates as designed, you're golden. You'll be off to other must-see attractions before the park gets crowded. If, on the other hand, the ride suffers technical difficulties, you may be stuck there a long while, during which time the crowds will have spread to other areas of IOA. By the time you exit the Forbidden Journey, there will be long lines for all of the park's other popular attractions.

If The Wizarding World is your top priority, experience it early in the morning and take your chances with crowds in the other parts of the parks later on. If Harry isn't such a hot button, skip The Wizarding World and enjoy short waits at IOA's other top attractions.

Following are what the first two alternatives look like in the first five steps of a touring plan:

PLAN A: HARRY POTTER OR BUST	PLAN B: EASY TOURING
1. Harry Potter and the Forbidden Journey	1. The Incredible Hulk Coaster
2. Dragon Challenge	2. Spider-Man
3. The Incredible Hulk Coaster	3. Dr. Doom's Fearfall
4. Spider-Man (*skip Dr. Doom's Fearfall*)	4. Popeye & Bluto's Bilge-Rat Barges
5. Popeye & Bluto's Bilge-Rat Barges	5. Dudley Do-Right's Ripsaw Falls

UNIVERSAL'S ISLANDS OF ADVENTURE ONE-DAY TOURING PLAN *(page 832)*

THIS TOURING PLAN is for groups of all sizes and ages and includes thrill rides that may induce motion sickness or get you wet. If the plan calls for you to experience an attraction that doesn't interest you, simply skip it and go to the next step. Be aware that the plan calls for some backtracking. If you have young children in your party, customize the plan to fit their needs and take advantage of switching off at thrill rides.

PART EIGHTEEN

SEAWORLD ORLANDO

SEAWORLD IS A WORLD-CLASS marine-life theme park near the intersection of I-4 and the Beachline Expressway (FL 528). It's about 8 miles east of Walt Disney World. Open daily at 9 a.m. and closing between 6 and 11 p.m. depending on the season, SeaWorld charges about $87 for adults and $79 for children ages 3–9 at the gate (prices include tax). If you buy online at the website below, the same tickets will cost you about $77 and $69, respectively. An added bonus for buying online is that you receive a second day's admission free. Several multipark tickets are available as well, including the six-park **Orlando Flex Plus Ticket,** which includes admission to SeaWorld, Aquatica, Universal Studios, Islands of Adventure, Wet 'n Wild, and Busch Gardens. Parking is $14 per car, $18 per RV or camper; preferred parking costs $20 For additional information, call ☎ 407-351-3600 or 888-800-5447, or visit **seaworld.com/orlando.**

unofficial **TIP**
You can't take prepackaged sandwiches or drinks into SeaWorld or Aquatica water park.

Figure on 8–9 hours to see everything, 6 or so if you stick to the big deals. **Discovery Cove** (see page 700), another SeaWorld park, is directly across Central Florida Parkway.

SeaWorld is about the size of the Magic Kingdom and requires about the same amount of walking. In terms of size, quality, and creativity, it's unequivocally on par with Disney's major theme parks. Unlike Walt Disney World, SeaWorld primarily features stadium shows and walk-through exhibits. This means you'll spend about 80% less time waiting in line during 8 hours at SeaWorld than you would for the same-length visit at a Disney park.

Because lines, except those for Journey to Atlantis, Kraken, and Manta (see next page), aren't much of a problem at SeaWorld, you can tour at almost any time of day. If you visit in the morning, arrive early. Morning arrivals tend to create long waits at the ticket windows, so consider buying your admission in advance. Like those at other area parks, SeaWorld's turnstiles often open at

unofficial **TIP**
If you don't purchase your admission in advance, take advantage of the automatic admission machines to the right of the main entrance. If you have a credit card, the machines are faster than standing in line at the ticket windows.

either 8:30 a.m. or 8:45 a.m., depending on the season, which means you can enter the park before the scheduled 9 a.m. opening.

A mother of two correctly points out that crowds at SeaWorld on some days can be as daunting as those at the Disney parks:

> *Your reference to crowds at SeaWorld should be changed. We were there on a Sunday and it was extremely crowded, so crowded that we were not able to see everything, even the major attractions. Waits were way too long for us to consider the rides.*

A daily entertainment schedule is printed on a place mat–sized map of the park. The featured shows are as follows:

- *A'Lure: The Call of the Ocean* (Cirque du Soleil–type revue)
- *Blue Horizons* (whale, dolphin, and bird show)
- *Clyde and Seamore Take Pirate Island* (sea-lion, walrus, and otter show)
- *One Ocean* (Shamu and killer-whale show)
- *Pets Ahoy!* (show with performing domestic animals)

You'll notice immediately as you check the performance times that the shows are scheduled so that it's almost impossible to see them back to back. *One Ocean,* for example, might run from 5 to 5:25 p.m. Ideally, you'd like to bop over to *Clyde and Seamore,* which begins at 5:30 p.m. Unfortunately, five minutes isn't enough time to exit Shamu Stadium and cross the park to the Sea Lion and Otter Stadium. SeaWorld, of course, planned it this way so you'd stay longer. A Cherry Hill, New Jersey, visitor confirms this rather major problem, complaining:

> *The shows were timed so we could not catch all the major ones in a 7-hour visit.*

Trying to sort out a game plan for seeing the shows while you're on the run is somewhat exasperating. A better alternative is to visit **seaworld.com/orlando** and, under "Park Info," click on "Park Hours and Show Schedules." Here you can see the show roster for the day of your visit and plan your touring itinerary in advance.

Much of the year, you can get a seat for the stadium shows by showing up 10 or so minutes in advance. When the park is crowded, however, you need to be at the stadiums at least 20 minutes in advance (30 minutes in advance for a good seat). All of the stadiums have "splash zones," specified areas where you're likely to be drenched with ice-cold salt water by whales, dolphins, and sea lions. Trust us when we say you should take these seriously. You don't have to be in the tank for Shamu to douse you.

Journey to Atlantis, Kraken, and **Manta** are SeaWorld's entries into the theme park super-attraction competition. Occupying the equivalent of six football fields, Journey to Atlantis is the world's first attraction to combine elements of a high-speed water ride and a roller coaster. (By the way, you'll get soaked.) Kraken is currently the second-longest roller coaster in Orlando.

STAR RATINGS FOR SEAWORLD ATTRACTIONS	
★★★★★	**Manta** (roller coaster)
★★★★½	*One Ocean* (high-tech Shamu and killer-whale show)
★★★★	**Kraken** (roller coaster)
★★★★	*TurtleTrek* (IMAX-style 3-D film about sea turtles)
★★★½	*Clyde and Seamore Take Pirate Island* (sea-lion, walrus, and otter show)
★★★½	**Shamu's Happy Harbor** (children's play area)
★★★½	**Shark Encounter**
★★★½	**Wild Arctic** (simulation ride and Arctic-wildlife viewing)
★★★	*A'Lure: The Call of the Ocean* (Cirque du Soleil–type presentation)
★★★	*Blue Horizons* (whale, dolphin, and bird show)
★★★	**Pacific Point Preserve** (sea lions and seals)
★★★	*Pets Ahoy!* (show with performing birds, cats, dogs, and a pig)
★★½	**Journey to Atlantis** (combination roller coaster–flume ride)
★★	**Skytower** (400-foot-tall observation tower)
N/A	*Antarctica: Empire of the Penguin* (opens spring 2013)

Opened in 2009, Manta is a steel coaster that arranges riders four across, lying facedown and parallel to the track, beneath the expanse of a giant manta ray–shaped carriage. The coaster is said to emulate the movements of a manta ray, but if that's the case, it's a mighty frisky ray. The coaster soars and swoops through a pretzel loop, a 360-degree inline roll, and two corkscrews—not to mention a first drop of 113 feet. Manta reaches a height of 140 feet and speeds of more than 55 mph. But don't worry: Lying facedown puts you in the perfect position to throw up. Actually, the ride is very smooth. If you get sick, it'll be from the bugs you pick out of your teeth (keep your mouth closed at all times—you're supposed to be a ray, not a bat). The queuing area is a stunning underwater exhibit featuring 300 rays from five different species; several fish keep the rays company. Manta is a huge hit—roller-coaster buffs almost unanimously rank it as the top coaster in Florida.

Catch all three rides just after the park opens, or prepare to wait.

SeaWorld offers quite a few guided tours. Most include the major shows, a glimpse behind the scenes, rides (without waiting) on Journey to Atlantis and Kraken, and some seal, ray, and dolphin feeding. The tour guides, both personable and well informed, are a font of interesting and useful information. We learned on a recent tour, for example, that in the United States, more people are killed each year by vending machines than by sharks. Think about that next time you buy a Coke.

DISCOVERY COVE

ALSO OWNED BY SEAWORLD, this intimate park is a welcome departure from the hustle and bustle of other Orlando parks. Its slower pace could be the overstimulated family's ticket back to mental health.

unofficial **TIP**
With a focus on personal guest service and one-on-one animal encounters, Discovery Cove admits only 1,200 guests per day.

The main draw at Discovery Cove is the chance to swim with an **Atlantic bottlenose dolphin** from among the 45 here. The 50-minute experience (30 minutes in the water) is open to visitors age 6 and up who are comfortable in the water. The experience begins with an orientation led by trainers and an opportunity for participants to ask questions. Next, small groups wade into shallow water to get an introduction to the dolphin in its habitat. The experience culminates with two to three guests and a trainer swimming into deeper water for closer interaction with the dolphin.

Other exhibits at Discovery Cove include the **Grand Reef,** the **Freshwater Oasis,** and the **Explorer's Aviary.** Snorkel or swim in the Grand Reef, which houses thousands of exotic fish as well as an underwater shipwreck and hidden grottoes. The Freshwater Oasis is a swimming and wading experience where you can get up close and personal with otters and marmosets. In the Explorer's Aviary, you can touch and feed gorgeous tropical birds. The park is threaded by the **Wind-Away River,** in which you can float or swim, and dotted with beaches that serve as pathways to the attractions.

All guests are required to wear flotation vests when swimming, and lifeguards are omnipresent. You'll need your swimsuit, pool shoes, and a cover-up. On rare days when it's too cold to swim in Orlando, guests are provided with free wet suits. Discovery Cove also provides fish-friendly sunscreen samples; guests may not use their own sunscreen.

Discovery Cove is open 9 a.m.–5:30 p.m. daily. Admission is limited, so purchase tickets well in advance; call ☎ 877-557-7404 or visit **discoverycove.com.** Prices vary seasonally from $212 per person to $414, including tax (no children's discount). Admission includes the dolphin swim, self-parking, Continental breakfast, a substantial lunch, snacks and drinks, and use of beach umbrellas, lounge chairs, towels, lockers, swim and snorkel gear, and unlimited admission to SeaWorld and Aquatica water park (see page 722) for 14 days surrounding your visit to Discovery Cove.

For an additional $59 per person, you can take a 25-minute underwater stroll on the bottom of the Grand Reef aquarium. Participants wear diving helmets, and no experience or scuba certification is necessary. The helmets are large enough to accommodate eyeglasses. Minimum age is 10 years.

PART NINETEEN

BEHIND *the* SCENES *at* WALT DISNEY WORLD

IF YOU'RE INTERESTED IN THE MOUSE'S INNARDS—um, make that inner workings—a number of guided tours offer a glimpse of what goes on behind the scenes. Reservations must be guaranteed with a credit card, and you need to cancel within 48 hours if you want a full refund. Many tours require that you buy park admission separately; we've noted where it isn't mandatory. Prices listed include sales tax; discounts on some tours are available to Walt Disney World Annual Pass holders, Disney Vacation Club members, and Disney Visa Card holders.

unofficial **TIP**
The walking tours involve a considerable amount of walking, standing, and time spent outdoors (depending on the tour).

Certain tours are available only on certain days of the week (see chart on the next two pages). For reservations and more information, call ☎ 407-WDW-TOUR (939-8687). Customized VIP tours are also available; call ☎ 407-560-4033 for details.

MULTIPARK TOURS

THE 7-HOUR **Backstage Magic** tour ($244) goes behind the scenes at all the WDW parks, including a backstage look at Mickey's Jammin' Jungle Parade at Disney's Animal Kingdom. Includes lunch; guests must be at least 16 years old to participate. Park admission is not required.

Disney's Holiday D-Lights (4½ hours, $212) and **Disney's Yuletide Fantasy** (3 hours, $90) explore the myriad ways in which Walt Disney World transforms for the Christmas season. Neither tour requires park admission; guests must be at least age 16. For 2013 tour dates, call ☎ 407-WDW-TOUR close to the holidays.

BEHIND *the* SCENES *at the* MAGIC KINGDOM

AS ITS NAME MAKES CLEAR, **Disney's Keys to the Kingdom** takes guests behind the scenes at the Magic Kingdom. This fascinating guided

Behind-the-Scenes Tours at Walt Disney World

	TOUR LENGTH	COST	MINIMUM AGE
MULTIPARK TOURS			
Backstage Magic	7 hours	$244	16
Disney's Holiday D-Lights	4½ hours	$212	16
Disney's Yuletide Fantasy	3 hours	$90	16
THE MAGIC KINGDOM			
Disney's Family Magic Tour	1½–2 hours	$36	None
Disney's Keys to the Kingdom	4½–5 hours	$79	16
Disney's The Magic Behind Our Steam Trains	3 hours	$52	10
Pirates and Pals Fireworks Voyage	1–3 hours	$58	None
Walt Disney: Marceline to Magic Kingdom Tour	2–3 hours	$32	12
EPCOT			
Around the World at Epcot	2 hours	$105	16
Behind the Seeds at Epcot	1 hour	$19 adults, $15 ages 3–9	None
Dolphins in Depth	3 hours	$207	13
Epcot DiveQuest	3 hours	$186	10
Gardens of the World	3 hours	$64	16
Seas Aqua Tour	2½ hours	$150	8
The UnDISCOVERed Future World	4 hours	$59	16
DISNEY'S ANIMAL KINGDOM			
Backstage Safari	3 hours	$77	16
Wild Africa Trek	3 hours	$201	8
Wild by Design	3 hours	$64	14
FORT WILDERNESS CAMPGROUND			
Disney's Wilderness Back Trail Adventure	2 hours	$96	16

tour provides a detailed look at the park's logistical, technical, and operational sides. Included are the parade-assembly area, the waste-treatment plant, and the utilidor network beneath the park. The program ($79 per person) includes lunch and runs about 4½–5 hours; children must be at least 16 years old to participate. For those interested in the tour, a reader from Ludington, Michigan, warns:

> Keys to the Kingdom is not for the faint of heart. This is a 4-hour walking tour with only one 15-minute break, plus a few minutes to sit awhile on Pirates of the Caribbean, The Haunted Mansion, and the Tomorrowland Transit Authority PeopleMover.

Disney's The Magic Behind Our Steam Trains, a 3-hour tour for children age 10 and up, takes a backstage look at the steam locomotives of the Walt Disney World Railroad. Cost is $52 per person. A less costly tour is **Disney's Family Magic Tour,** an interactive romp through the

FOCUS	DAYS AVAILABLE
Peeks behind the scenes at every Disney World park	M–F
Close-up look at Disney World holiday spectacles	Seasonal
Another look at holiday productions	Seasonal
Following clues in a sort of treasure hunt	Daily
Park's logistical, technical, and operational sides	Daily
Steam locomotives of the Walt Disney World Railroad	M, Tu, Th, Sa
Cruise around Seven Seas Lagoon	Daily
Examination of Walt Disney's career and vision	M, W, F
Taking a spin around the World Showcase on Segways	Daily
Vegetable gardens in the Land Pavilion	Daily
Visiting the dolphin-research facility at The Seas	M–F
Swimming with the fish at The Seas	Tu–Sa
Epcot horticultural tour	Seasonal
Swimming in the main tank at The Seas	Tu–Sa
The history of Epcot	M, W, F
Observing how the animals are housed and cared for	M, W, Th, F
Enhanced safari and adventure activities with meal	Daily
Inside look at the creation of Animal Kingdom	M, W, Th, F
Segway romp on campground trails and paths	Tu, F, Sa

park following clues in a sort of treasure hunt. The 1½- to 2-hour tour is offered daily for $36. **Walt Disney: Marceline to Magic Kingdom Tour** (2–3 hours, $32 age 12 and older) is a guided walking tour that interprets the Magic Kingdom as a "walking timeline" of Disney's life (Marceline, Missouri, was his childhood hometown).

The Contemporary Resort's **Pirates and Pals Fireworks Voyage** (1–3 hours, $58) offers daily sailings with a unique view of the Magic Kingdom fireworks from Seven Seas Lagoon. Your guide, Patch, sings pirate songs and delights the kids with Disney trivia. On select nights, the voyage also includes a viewing of the Floating Electrical Pageant.

▌ **BEHIND** *the* **SCENES** *at* **EPCOT**

A TOUR CALLED **The UnDISCOVERed Future World** traces the history of Epcot, including Walt Disney's original concept. The tour takes guests to backstage areas and lasts a bit over 4 hours. The cost is $59; guests must be at least 16 years old to participate.

Behind the Seeds at Epcot is shorter and takes guests to vegetable gardens and aquaculture farms in the Land Pavilion. The quality of the experience—a cross between science lecture and Willy Wonka factory tour—depends heavily on the tour guide's presentation and enthusiasm. You're not permitted to touch or sample the plants shown on the tour, but it's hard to resist the urge. Behind the Seeds requires same-day reservations; make them on the lower level of The Land (to the far right of the fast-food windows). The cost of the hour-long tour is $19 for adults and $15 for children ages 3–9.

On the 2-hour **Around the World at Epcot** tour, guests can take a Segway Personal Transporter for a spin around the World Showcase after mastering the machine during an hour-long indoor riding lesson. The cost is $105 per person. **Disney's Wilderness Back Trail Adventure** ($96) is a 2-hour Segway romp on the trails and walking paths of Fort Wilderness Campground. For all four programs, guests must be at least 16 years old and weigh less than 250 pounds. Finally, **Gardens of the World** (3 hours, $64; age 16 and older), a seasonal horticultural tour, coincides with the annual Epcot International Flower & Garden Festival (see page 45).

EPCOT DIVEQUEST

THE SOGGIEST BEHIND-THE-SCENES experience available any-where is **Epcot DiveQuest,** in which open water scuba–certified divers (age 10 and up; kids age 12 and younger must be accompanied by an adult) can swim around with the fish at The Seas with Nemo & Friends Pavilion. Offered twice a day, Tuesday–Saturday, at 4:30 and 5:30 p.m., each tour lasts about 3 hours, including a 40-minute dive. Cost is $186 per diver and includes all gear, a souvenir T-shirt, a dive-log stamp, and refreshments. For recorded information, call ☎ 407-560-5590. Theme park admission is not required, but proof of dive certification is.

DOLPHINS IN DEPTH

THIS TOUR (FOR GUESTS AGE 13 AND OLDER) visits the dolphin-research facility at The Seas with Nemo & Friends. There you'll witness a training session, then wade into the water for a photo (but not a swim) with the two dolphins. Cost for the 3-hour experience is $207; children under age 18 must be accompanied by an adult; expectant mothers may not participate. Theme park admission is not required. Wet suits are provided. Only eight guests per day can participate; call ☎ 407-WDW-TOUR when you're ready to book.

If you really dig dolphins, keep in mind that for $212–$414 (tax included), you can visit SeaWorld's **Discovery Cove** and actually swim with a dolphin. Though the experience is only about an hour long, the ticket entitles visitors to an entire day at Discovery Cove. For more information, see page 700.

SEAS AQUA TOUR

THIS TOUR IS SORT OF a watered-down (rimshot) version of Epcot DiveQuest. The 2½-hour tour lets you swim with goggles, a mini–air tank, and a flotation vest in the main tank for 30 minutes and explore backstage areas at The Seas with Nemo & Friends. It costs $150, accepts guests as young as 8 years old, and doesn't require separate park admission. Children under age 18 must be accompanied by an adult. Gear, refreshments, a T-shirt, and a group photo are included.

BEHIND *the* SCENES *at* DISNEY'S ANIMAL KINGDOM

IN THE 3-HOUR **Backstage Safari** tour, animal keepers and vets discuss conservation, animal nutrition, behavioral studies, and medicine, among other topics. Limited to guests age 16 and older, the Backstage Safari costs $77. You'll see animal enclosures, feed bins, medical facilities, and labs, but not many animals.

Wild by Design offers an inside look at the creation of Animal Kingdom, explaining how architecture, functionality, habitats, themes, and storytelling are combined to provide a complete theme park experience. The tour also runs 3 hours and costs $64 per person; it's open to guests age 14 and older.

The **Wild Africa Trek** takes groups of up to 12 on to newly created forest hiking trails, on suspension bridges high above hippo and crocodile pools, and on a private safari complete with a gourmet camp meal. Possibly our favorite tour of the last couple of years, the Wild Africa Trek lasts 3 hours and costs $201 per person. Open to guests age 8 and older. Extensive walking is required, and there's a maximum weight limit for the safety gear. A host of other warnings applies, so call Disney for details.

PART TWENTY

The
WATER PARKS

▐█ YOU'RE SOAKING *in* IT!

DISNEY HAS TWO WATER PARKS, and there are two competitive water parks in the area. At Disney World, **Typhoon Lagoon** is the more diverse splash pad, while **Blizzard Beach** takes the prize for the greater number of slides and the more bizarre theme. Outside the World are **Wet 'n Wild** and **Aquatica by SeaWorld**, both on International Drive.

At both Disney water parks, the following rules and prices apply: One cooler per family or group is allowed, but no glass and no alcoholic beverages; towels are $2; lockers are $13 small, $15 large (includes $5 refundable deposit); life jackets are available at no cost.

Guests can use automated ticket-vending machines to purchase admission at Blizzard Beach and Typhoon Lagoon. These machines use touch-screen technology and are intended to reduce the amount of time spent standing in line at ticket windows. Admission, including tax, runs $59 for adults and $50 for children ages 3–9. Parking is free.

WATCH THE WEATHER

IF YOU BUY YOUR WALT DISNEY WORLD admission tickets before leaving home and you're considering the Water Park Fun and More (WPFAM) add-on (see page 52), you might want to wait until you arrive and have some degree of certainty about the weather during your stay. You can add the WPFAM option at any Disney resort or Guest Relations window at the theme parks. This is true regardless of whether you purchased your Base Tickets separately or as part of a package.

We get a lot of questions about the water parks during cold-weather months. Orlando-area temperatures can vary from the high 40s to the low 80s during December, January, and February. When it's warmer out, these months can serve up a dandy water-park experience, as this Batavia, Ohio, reader confirms:

Going to Blizzard Beach in December was the best decision ever! We went on December 12, and there was no one there. They told us at the entrance that if the park didn't reach 100—yes, I said 100—people by noon, they would be closing. I guess they got to 101, because it stayed open but was virtually empty. There was no wait for anything

*all day! In June we waited in line for an hour for Summit Plummet,
but in December it was just the amount of time it took to walk up the
stairs. We had the enormous wave pool to ourselves. We did everything in the entire park and ate lunch in less than 3 hours. It was perfect. The weather was slightly chilly at 71 degrees, and overcast with
very light rain, but the water was heated, so we were fine.*

EXTRA MAGIC HOURS

LIKE THE FOUR MAJOR DISNEY PARKS, the swimming parks
participate in the Extra Magic Hours program. Each day, Disney
resort guests can enter either of the water parks 1 hour before the park
is open to the public. On select days during the summer and some
spring holiday periods, evening Extra Magic Hours are offered at
Typhoon Lagoon only on two to five designated evenings a month; on
these days, Typhoon Lagoon stays open until 9 p.m., 2 hours beyond
the normal closing time. For our money, Typhoon Lagoon is the best
possible place to be on a hot Florida summer evening. As a postscript,
Disney is cutting costs left and right. Don't be surprised if Extra Magic
Hours goes the way of the dodo.

BLIZZARD BEACH

BLIZZARD BEACH IS DISNEY'S MORE EXOTIC water-adventure
park and, like Typhoon Lagoon, it arrived with its own legend. This
time, the story goes, an entrepreneur tried to open a ski resort in Florida
during a particularly savage winter. Alas, the snow melted; the palm
trees grew back; and all that remained of the ski resort was its Alpine
lodge, the ski lifts, and, of course, the mountain. Plunging off the moun
tain are ski slopes and bobsled runs transformed into waterslides.
Visitors to Blizzard Beach catch the thaw—icicles drip and patches of
snow remain. The melting snow has formed a lagoon (the wave pool),
fed by gushing mountain streams.

Like Typhoon Lagoon, Blizzard Beach is distinguished by its landscaping and the attention paid to executing its theme. As you enter
Blizzard Beach, you face the mountain. Coming
off the highest peak and bisecting the area at
the mountain's base are two long slides. To the
left of the slides is the wave pool. To the right
are the children's swimming area and the ski lift.
Surrounding the layout like a moat is a tranquil
stream for floating in tubes.

unofficial **TIP**
Picnic areas are scattered
around the park, as
are pleasant places for
sunbathing.

On either side of the highest peak are tube, raft, and body slides.
Including the two slides coming off the peak, Blizzard Beach has 17
slides. Among them is **Summit Plummet,** Disney World's longest speed
slide, which begins with a 120-foot free fall, and the **Teamboat Springs**
water-bobsled run, 1,200 feet long.

One reader reports that the Blizzard Beach slides picked her husband's pocket:

*Our family absolutely loved Summit Plummet, but it claimed all four
of our park passes/room-key cards as its victims. My husband had*

Blizzard Beach Attractions

CHAIR LIFT UP MT. GUSHMORE Height requirement: 32 inches. Great ride even if you only go up for the view. When the park is packed, use the singles line.

CASTAWAY CREEK No height requirement. Lazy river circling the park; grab a tube.

DOWNHILL DOUBLE DIPPER Height requirement: 48 inches. Side-by-side tube-racing slides. At 25 mph, the tube zooms through water curtains and free falls. It's a lot of fun, but rough.

MELT-AWAY BAY No height requirement. Wave pool with gentle, bobbing waves. Great for younger swimmers.

RUNOFF RAPIDS No height requirement. Three corkscrew tube slides to choose from. The center slide is for solo raft rides; the other two slides offer one- or two-person tubes. The dark, enclosed tube makes you feel as if you were flushed down a toilet.

SKI PATROL TRAINING CAMP Height requirement: 60 inches for T-Bar. A place for preteens to train for the big rides.

SLUSH GUSHER Height requirement: 48 inches. A 90-foot double-humped slide. Ladies, cling to those tops—all others, hang on to live.

SNOW STORMERS No height requirement. Three mat-slide flumes; down you go on your belly.

SUMMIT PLUMMET Height requirement: 48 inches. A 120-foot free fall, at 60 mph. Needless to say, this ride is very intense. Make sure your child knows what to expect. Being over 48 inches tall doesn't guarantee an enjoyable experience. If you think you'd enjoy washing out of a 12th-floor window during a heavy rain, then this slide is for you.

TEAMBOAT SPRINGS No height requirement. 1,200-foot group whitewater-raft flume. Wonderful ride for the whole family.

TIKE'S PEAK 4 feet and under only. Kid-sized version of Blizzard Beach. This is the place for little ones.

TOBOGGAN RACERS No height requirement. Eight-lane race course. You go down the flume on a mat. Less intense than Snow Stormers.

the four cards in an exterior pocket of his swimsuit, secured closed by Velcro AND a snap. But after doing Summit Plummet and Slush Gusher twice apiece and Teamboat Springs once, he looked down, noticed the pocket flapping open, and found all four cards missing! So we had to cancel all the cards (they had charging privileges) and couldn't purchase any food or drinks while we were there (we didn't bring any cash because we planned to charge with our cards)!

A couple from Bowie, Maryland, came away with battle scars:

Summit Plummet gave me a bunch of bruises. Even my husband hurt for a few days. It wasn't a fun ride, and we both agree that it wasn't worth waiting in line for. Basically, you drop until you hit the slide, and that is why everyone comes off rubbing their butts. They say you go 60 mph on a 120-foot drop. I'll never do it again.

For our money, the most exciting and interesting slides are the **Slush Gusher** and Teamboat Springs on the front right of the mountain, and **Runoff Rapids** on the back side of the mountain. Slush Gusher is an undulating speed slide that we consider as exciting as the more vertical Summit Plummet without being as bone-jarring. On Teamboat Springs, you ride in a raft that looks like a children's round blow-up wading pool.

Runoff Rapids is accessible from a path that winds around the far left bottom of the mountain. The rapids consist of three corkscrew tube slides, one of which is enclosed and dark. As at Teamboat Springs, you'll go much faster on a two- or three-person tube than on a one-person tube. If you lean so that you enter curves high and come out low, you'll really fly. Because we like to

unofficial **TIP**
The more people you load into the raft, the faster it goes. If you have only a couple in it, the slide is kind of a snore.

steer the tube and go fast, we much prefer the open slides (where we can see) to the dark, enclosed tube. We thought crashing through the pitch-dark tube felt disturbingly like being flushed down a toilet.

The **Snow Stormers'** mat slides on the front of the mountain are fun but not as fast or as interesting as Runoff Rapids or **Downhill Double Dipper** on the far left front. The **Toboggan Racers** at the front and center of the mountain consists of eight parallel slides where riders are dispatched in heats to race to the bottom. The ride itself is no big deal, and the time needed to get everybody lined up ensures that you'll wait extra-long to ride. A faster, more exciting race venue can be found on the side-by-side slides of the undulating Downhill Double Dipper. Competitors here can reach speeds of up to 25 miles an hour.

A ski lift carries guests to the mountaintop (you can also walk up), where they can choose from Summit Plummet, Slush Gusher, or Teamboat Springs. For all other slides at Blizzard Beach, the only way to reach the top is on foot. If you're among the first in the park and don't have to wait to ride, the ski lift is fun and provides a bird's-eye view of the park. After riding once to satisfy your curiosity, however, you're better off taking the stairs to the top. The following attractions have a minimum height restriction of 48 inches: Slush Gusher, Summit Plummet, and Downhill Double Dipper.

The wave pool, called **Melt-Away Bay,** has gentle, bobbing waves. The float creek, **Cross Country Creek,** circles the park, passing through the mountain. The children's areas, **Tike's Peak** and **Ski Patrol Training Camp,** are creatively designed, nicely isolated, and, like the rest of the park, visually interesting.

Like Typhoon Lagoon, Blizzard Beach is a bit convoluted in its layout. With slides on both the front and back of the mountain, it isn't always easy to find a path leading to where you want to go.

At the ski resort's now-converted base area are shops; counter-service food; restrooms; and tube, towel, and locker rentals. Blizzard Beach has its own parking lot but no lodging, though Disney's All-Star and Coronado Springs resorts are almost within walking distance. Disney resort guests can commute to the park aboard Disney buses.

Because it's novel and has popular slides, Blizzard Beach fills early during hotter months. To stake out a nice sunning spot and to enjoy the slides without long waits, arrive at least 35 minutes before the official opening time (check **wdwinfo.com** for hours before you go).

TYPHOON LAGOON

TYPHOON LAGOON IS COMPARABLE in size to Blizzard Beach. Eleven waterslides and streams, some as long as 420 feet, drop from

Typhoon Lagoon Attractions

CASTAWAY CREEK **No height requirement.** Half-mile lazy river in a tropical setting. Wonderful!

CRUSH 'N' GUSHER **Height requirement: 48 inches** Water roller coaster where you can choose from among three slides: Banana Blaster, Coconut Crusher, and Pineapple Plunger, ranging from 410 to 420 feet long. This thriller leaves you wondering what exactly happened—if you make it down in one piece, that is, it's not for the faint of heart. If your kids are new to water-park rides, this is not the place to break them in, even if they're tall enough to ride.

GANG PLANK FALLS **No height requirement.** Whitewater-raft flume in a multiperson tube.

HUMUNGA KOWABUNGA **Height requirement: 48 inches.** Speed slides that hit 30 mph. A five-story drop in the dark rattles the most courageous rider. Women should ride this one in a one-piece swimsuit.

KEELHAUL FALLS **No height requirement.** Fast whitewater ride in a single-person tube.

KETCHAKIDDEE CREEK **Height requirement: 48 inches and under only.** Toddlers and preschoolers love this area reserved only for them. Say "splish-splash" and have lots of fun.

MAYDAY FALLS **No height requirement.** Wild single-person tube ride. *Hang on!*

SHARK REEF **No height requirement; kids under age 10 must be accompanied by an adult.** After you're equipped with fins, mask, snorkel, and a life vest, you get a brief lesson on snorkeling. Then off you go for about 60 feet to the other side of the saltwater pool, where you swim with small, colorful fish; rays; and very small leopard and hammerhead sharks. If you don't want to swim with the fish, visit the underwater-viewing chamber anytime during the day. Surface Air Snorkeling, a scubalike pursuit involving a "pony" tank, small regulator, and buoyancy vest, is also offered. Participants must be at least 5 years old. To sign up and get more information, visit the kiosk near the entrance to Shark Reef.

STORM SLIDES **No height requirement.** Three body-slides down and through Mount Mayday.

SURF POOL **No height requirement.** World's largest inland surf facility, with waves up to 6 feet high. Adult supervision is required. Monday–Friday, in the early morning before the park opens (hours vary), surfing lessons are offered (surfboard provided). Cost is $150 for 2½ hours; minimum age is 8; class size is 12. Call ☎ 407-WDW-PLAY (939-7529). The price doesn't include park admission.

the top of a 100-foot-tall man-made mountain. Landscaping and an aftermath-of-a-typhoon theme add interest and a sense of adventure to the wet rides.

Guests enter Typhoon Lagoon through a misty rainforest, then emerge in a ramshackle tropical town where concessions and services are situated. Special sets make every ride an odyssey as swimmers encounter bat caves, lagoons and pools, spinning rocks, formations of dinosaur bones, and many other imponderables.

Typhoon Lagoon has its own parking lot but no lodging. Disney resort and campground guests can commute to the water park on Disney buses.

If you indulge in all features of Typhoon Lagoon, admission is a fair value. If you go primarily for the slides, you'll have only 2 early-morning hours to enjoy them before the wait becomes prohibitive. Speaking of crowds, a Maryland family tried a little experiment and reports the following:

We did Typhoon Lagoon one morning and it was fun. So we theo-rized that since it was crowded midday, that maybe it clears out late afternoon. My wife took our oldest there at 3 p.m. on Friday and said it was wide open—they rode waterslides without any wait at all for 2 hours and loved it.

Typhoon Lagoon provides water adventure for all ages. Activity pools for young children and families feature geysers, tame slides, bubble jets, and fountains. For the older and more adventurous are the enclosed **Humunga Kowabunga** speed slides, the corkscrew **Storm Slides,** and three whitewater-raft rides: **Gang Plank Falls, Keelhaul Falls,** and **Mayday Falls.** Billed as a "water roller coaster," **Crush 'n' Gusher** consists of a series of flumes and spillways that course through an abandoned tropical fruit–processing plant. It features tubes that hold one or two people, and you can choose from three different routes: Banana Blaster, Coconut Crusher, and Pineapple Plunger, ranging between 410 and 420 feet long. The minimum height requirement is 48 inches. Of all the Typhoon Lagoon slides, only Crush 'n' Gusher and the Humunga Kowabunga speed slides (where you can hit 30 miles an hour) have a minimum height requirement of 48 inches. Slower metabolisms will enjoy the scenic, meandering, 2,000-foot-long **Castaway Creek,** which floats tubers through hidden grottoes and rainforests. And, of course, the sedentary will usually find plenty of sun to sleep in. Typhoon Lagoon's **Surf Pool** and **Shark Reef** are unique, the former being the world's largest inland surf facility, with waves up to 6 feet high (enough, so Disney says, to "encompass an ocean liner"). Shark Reef is a saltwater snorkeling pool where guests can swim among real fish.

SHARK REEF

FINS, MASK, SNORKEL, AND WET-SUIT VEST ARE PROVIDED free in the wooden building beside the diving pool. After you obtain the proper equipment (no forms or money involved), you shower and then report to a snorkeling instructor. After a brief lesson, you swim about 60 feet to the other side of the pool. You're not allowed to paddle aimlessly but must traverse the pool more or less directly.

The reef is fun in early morning. Equipment collection, shower, instruction, and the quick swim can be accomplished without much hassle. Also, because few guests are present, attendants are more flexible about your lingering in the pool or making minor departures from the charted course.

unofficial **TIP**
Try Shark Reef in the morning—afternoons can get crowded, and you may be ushered out of the pool more quickly than in the early hours.

Later, as crowds build, it becomes increasingly difficult and time-consuming to provide the necessary instruction. The result is platoons of would-be frogmen restlessly awaiting their snorkeling lesson. Guests are grouped in impromptu classes with the entire class briefed and then launched together. What takes four or five minutes shortly after opening can take more than an hour by 11 a.m.

By far the most prevalent species in the pool is the dual-finned *Homo sapiens.* Other denizens include small, colorful tropical fish; some diminutive rays; and a few very small leopard and hammerhead sharks. In terms of numbers, it would be unusual to cross the pool and not see some fish. On the other hand, you aren't exactly bumping into them.

It's very important to fit your diving mask on your face so that it seals around the edges. Brush your hair from your forehead and sniff a couple of times once the mask is in place, to create a vacuum. Mustaches often prevent the mask from sealing properly. The first indication that your mask isn't correctly fitted will be salt water in your nose.

If you don't want to swim with fish early in the morning or fight crowds later in the day, visit the underwater viewing chamber, accessible anytime without waiting, special equipment, showers, instruction, or water in your nose.

SURF POOL

WHILE BLIZZARD BEACH and Wet 'n Wild have wave pools, Typhoon Lagoon has a Surf Pool. Most people will encounter larger waves here than they have in the ocean. The surf machine puts out a wave about every 90 seconds (just about how long it takes to get back in position if you caught the previous wave). Perfectly formed and ideal for riding, each wave is about 5–6 feet from trough to crest. Before you join the fray, watch two or three waves from shore. Since each wave breaks in almost the same spot, you can get a feel for position and timing. Observing other surfers is also helpful.

unofficial **TIP**
A final warning: The Surf Pool has a knack for loosening watchbands, stripping jewelry, and sucking stuff out of your pockets. Don't take anything out there except your swimsuit (and hang on to that).

The best way to ride the waves is to swim about three-fourths of the way to the wall at the wave-machine end of the Surf Pool. When the wave comes (you'll both feel and hear it), swim vigorously toward the beach, attempting to position yourself one-half to three-fourths of a body length below the breaking crest. The waves are so perfectly engineered that they will either carry you forward or bypass you. Unlike an ocean wave, they won't slam you down.

A teenage girl from Urbana, Illinois, notes that the primary hazard in the Surf Pool is colliding with other surfers and swimmers:

The Surf Pool was nice except that I kept landing on really hairy fat guys whenever the big waves came.

A reader from Somerset, New Jersey, alerted us to yet another problem:

Typhoon Lagoon is a great family water park—our unexpected favorite. However, please tell your readers not to sit on the bottom of the wave pool—I got a horrible scratch/raspberry and saw about five others with similar injuries. The waves are stronger than they look.

Sitting on the bottom also disturbs the hippos.

The best way to avoid collisions while surfing is to paddle out far enough that you'll be at the top of the wave as it breaks. This tactic eliminates the possibility of anyone landing on you from above and assures maximum forward visibility. A corollary to this: The worst place to swim is where the wave actually breaks. You'll look up to see a 6-foot wall of water carrying eight dozen screaming surfers bearing down on you. This is the time to remember every submarine movie you've ever seen. . . . Dive! Dive! Dive!

On weekdays in the early morning before the park opens (hours vary), you can take surfing lessons (with a surfboard) from Craig Carroll's **Cocoa Beach Surf School.** Practice waves range from 3 to 6 feet tall. Most of the school's students are first-timers. Cost is $150 per person, and equipment is provided. For reservations and information, call ☎ 407-WDW-PLAY (939-7529).

TYPHOON LAGOON *versus* BLIZZARD BEACH

MANY WALT DISNEY WORLD GUESTS aren't interested in leaving the World. For them, the question is: Which is better, Typhoon Lagoon or Blizzard Beach? Our readers answer.

A mother of four from Winchester, Virginia, gives her opinion:

At Blizzard Beach, the family raft ride is great, but the kids' area is poorly designed. As a parent, when you walk your child to the top of a slide or the tube ride, they're lost to your vision as they go down because of the fake snowdrifts. There are no direct ways down to the end of the slides, so little ones are left standing unsupervised while parents scramble down from the top. The Typhoon Lagoon kids' area is far superior in design.

unofficial **TIP**
If you're into slides, Blizzard Beach is tops among the Disney water parks.

A couple from Woodridge, Illinois, writes:

We liked Blizzard Beach much more. It seems like they took everything from Typhoon Lagoon and made it better and faster. Summit Plummet was awesome—a total rush. Worth the half-hour wait. The toboggan and bobsled rides were really exciting—the bobsled really throws you around. The family tube ride was really good—much better and much longer than the one at Typhoon Lagoon. Tube rides were great, especially in the enclosed tube. If you have time to go to only one water park, go to Blizzard Beach.

A hungry reader from Aberdeen, New Jersey, complains:

At Blizzard Beach, there's only one main place to get food (most of the other spots are more for snacks). At lunchtime, it took almost 45 minutes to get some sandwiches and drinks.

WHEN *to* GO

unofficial **TIP**
During summer and holiday periods, Typhoon Lagoon and Blizzard Beach sometimes fill to capacity and close their gates before 11 a.m.

THE BEST WAY TO AVOID STANDING IN LINES is to visit the Disney water parks when they're less crowded. Our research, conducted over many weeks in the parks, indicates that tourists, not locals, make up the majority of visitors on any given day. And because weekends are popular travel days, the water parks tend to be less crowded then. In fact, of the weekend days we evaluated, the parks never reached full capacity;

during the week, conversely, one or both parks closed every Thursday we monitored, and both closed at least once every other weekday. If you're a Disney resort guest, by all means use your morning Extra Magic Hours privileges whenever offered; otherwise, we recommend going on a Monday or Friday.

From a mom from Manlius, New York, here's what *crowded* means:

Because we had the all-inclusive pass, we also visited Typhoon Lagoon, arriving before opening so we could stake out a shady spot. The kids loved it until the lines got long (11 a.m.–noon), but I hated it. It made Coney Island seem like a deserted island in the Bahamas. Floating on Castaway Creek was really unpleasant. Whirling around in a chlorinated, concrete ditch with some stranger's feet in my face, periodically getting squirted by waterguns, passing under cascades of cold water, and getting hung up by the crowd is not at all relaxing for me. My husband and I then decided to "bob" in the Surf Pool. After about 10 minutes of being tossed around like corks in boiling water, he turned a little green around the gills, and we sought the peace of our shady little territory which, in our absence, had become much, much smaller. The kids, however, loved the body slides and the surf waves.

A visitor from Middletown, New York, had a somewhat better experience at Typhoon Lagoon:

On our second trip to Typhoon Lagoon, we dispensed with the locker rental (having planned to stay for only the morning when it was least crowded), and at park's opening just took right off for the Storm Slides before the masses arrived—it was perfect! We must have ridden the slides at least five times before any kind of line built up, and then we were also able to ride the tube and raft rides (Keelhaul and Mayday Falls) in a similar uncrowded, quick fashion because everyone else was busy getting their lockers! We also experienced the Shark Reef, snorkeling three times with minimal crowds that day, because, I think, most people overlook this attraction. Shark Reef is fun and a great way to cool off since their water temp is well below the wave pool's.

If your schedule is flexible, a good time to visit the swimming parks is midafternoon to late in the day when the weather has cleared after a storm. The parks usually close during bad weather. If the storm is prolonged, most guests leave for their hotels. When Typhoon Lagoon or Blizzard Beach reopens after inclement weather has passed, you almost have a whole park to yourself.

PLANNING YOUR DAY *at* DISNEY WATER PARKS

DISNEY WATER PARKS ARE ALMOST AS LARGE and elaborate as the major theme parks. You must be prepared for a lot of walking, exercise, sun, and jostling crowds. If your group really loves the water, schedule your visit early in your vacation. If you go at the beginning of your stay, you'll have more flexibility if you want to return.

To have a great day and beat the crowds, consider:

1. GETTING INFORMATION Call ☎ 407-wdw-magic (939-6244) or check **disneyworld.com** the night before to verify when your chosen park opens.

2. TO PICNIC OR NOT TO PICNIC Decide whether you want to carry a picnic lunch. Guests are permitted to take lunches and beverage coolers into the parks. However, alcoholic beverages and glass containers of any kind are forbidden.

3. GETTING STARTED If you're going to Blizzard Beach or Typhoon Lagoon, get up early, have breakfast, and arrive at the park 40 minutes before opening. If you have a car, drive instead of taking a Disney bus.

4. FOLLOW A GOOD TOURING PLAN We've added two new touring plans designed to help you avoid the crowds and bottlenecks at the Disney water parks (see pages 833 and 834). If you're attending on a day of moderate-to-heavy attendance (see the Crowd Calendar at our website), consider using one of these battle-tested plans. More are available at **touringplans.com.**

5. ATTIRE Wear your bathing suit under shorts and a T-shirt so you don't need to use lockers or dressing rooms. Regarding women's bathing suits, be advised that it's extremely common for women of all ages to part company with the top of their two-piece suit on the slides. Wear shoes. Paths are relatively easy on bare feet, but there's a lot of ground to cover. If you have tender feet, wear your shoes as you move around the park, removing them when you raft, slide, or go into the water. Shops in the parks sell sandals, Reef Runners, and other protective footwear that can be worn in and out of the water.

6. WHAT TO BRING You'll need a towel, suntan lotion, and money. Since wallets and purses get in the way, lock them in your car's trunk or leave them at your hotel. Carry enough money for the day and your Disney resort ID (if you have one) in a plastic bag or Tupperware container. Though nowhere is completely safe, we felt very comfortable hiding our plastic money bags in our cooler. Nobody disturbed our stuff, and our cash was much easier to reach than if we'd stashed it in a locker across the park. If you're carrying a wad or you worry about money anyway, rent the locker.

A Canadian reader offers another option if you don't feel comfortable stashing your valuables:

As our admission was from an all-inclusive ticket, I was concerned about our multiday passes being stolen or lost, yet I didn't want the hassle of a locker. Once inside, I noticed several guests wearing small plastic boxes on strings around their necks, and was pleased to find these for sale in the gift shop. They're waterproof and available in two sizes for around $5, with the smallest being just big enough for passes, credit cards, and a bit of money. I would've spent nearly as much on a locker rental, so I was able to enjoy the rest of the day with peace of mind.

7. WHAT NOT TO BRING Personal swim gear (fins, masks, rafts, and the like) isn't allowed. Everything you need is provided or available to rent. If you forget your towel, you can rent one (cheap!). If you forget your swimsuit or lotion, they're for sale. Personal flotation devices (life jackets) are available at no cost.

8. ADMISSIONS Buy your admission in advance or about 45 minutes before official opening time. If you're staying at a Disney property, you may be entitled to a discount; bring your hotel or campground ID. Guests staying five or more days should consider the **Plus Pack** add-on, which provides admission to both Disney swimming parks.

9. LOCKERS Rental lockers are $13 per day for a small one and $15 per day for a large, $5 of which is refunded when you return your key. Small lockers are roomy enough for one person or a couple, but a family will generally need a large locker. Though you can access your locker freely all day, not all lockers are conveniently located.

Getting a locker at Blizzard Beach or Typhoon Lagoon is truly competitive. When the gates open, guests race to the locker rental desk. Once there, the rental procedure is somewhat slow. If you aren't among the first in line, you can waste a lot of time waiting to be served. We recommend you skip the locker. Carry only as much cash as you'll need for the day in a watertight container you can stash in your cooler. Ditto for personal items including watches and eyeglasses. With planning, you can manage nicely without the locker and save time and hassle in the bargain.

10. TUBES Tubes for bobbing on the waves, floating in the creeks, and riding the tube slides are available for free.

11. GETTING SETTLED Establish your base for the day. There are many beautiful sunning and lounging spots scattered throughout both Disney swimming parks. Arrive early, and you can almost have your pick. The breeze is best along the beaches of the surf pools at Blizzard Beach and Typhoon Lagoon. At Typhoon Lagoon, if there are children younger than age 6 in your party, choose an area to the left of Mount Mayday (ship on top) near the children's swimming area.

Also available are flat lounges (nonadjustable) and chairs (better for reading), shelters for guests who prefer shade, picnic tables, and a few hammocks.

The best spectator sport at Typhoon Lagoon is the bodysurfing in the Surf Pool. It's second only to being out there yourself. With this in mind, position yourself to have an unobstructed view of the waves.

If you've got money to burn, a handful of private covered seating areas are available at both Disney water parks for up to six guests at $319 per day. That includes your own lounge chairs, tables, towels, private lockers, a refillable drink mug, and a cabana boy who'll be at your beck and call. These seating areas are first-come, first-served.

unofficial **TIP**
When lines for the slides become intolerable, head for the surf or wave pool or the tube-floating streams.

12. A WORD ABOUT THE SLIDES Waterslides come in many shapes and sizes. Some are steep and vertical, some long and undulating. Some resemble corkscrews; others imitate the pool-and-drop nature of whitewater streams. Depending on the slide, swimmers ride mats, inner tubes, or rafts. On the body slides, swimmers slosh to the bottom on the seat of their pants.

Modern traffic engineering bows to old-fashioned queuing. At the waterslides, it's just one person, one raft (or tube) at a time, and the swimmer on deck can't go until the person preceding him or her is safely out of the way. Thus, the slides' hourly capacity is limited compared with the continuously loading rides in the major theme parks. Because a certain interval between swimmers is required for safety, the only way to increase capacity is to increase the number of slides and rapids rides.

Though Typhoon Lagoon and Blizzard Beach are huge parks with many slides, they're overwhelmed almost daily by armies of guests. If your main reason for going to Typhoon Lagoon or Blizzard Beach is the slides, and you hate long lines, be among the first guests to enter the park. Go directly to the slides and ride as many times as you can before the park fills.

For maximum speed on a body slide, cross your legs at the ankles and cross your arms over your chest. When you take off, arch your back so almost all of your weight is on your shoulder blades and heels (the less contact with the surface, the less resistance). Steer by shifting most of your upper-body weight onto one shoulder blade. For top speed on turns, weight the shoulder blade on the outside of each curve. If you want to go slowly, distribute your weight equally as if you were lying on your back in bed. For curving slides, maximize speed by hitting the entrance to each curve high and exiting the curve low.

Some slides and rapids have a minimum height requirement. Riders for Humunga Kowabunga at Typhoon Lagoon and for Slush Gusher and Summit Plummet at Blizzard Beach, for example, must be 4 feet tall. Pregnant women and persons with back problems or other health difficulties shouldn't ride.

13. FLOATING STREAMS Disney's Blizzard Beach and Typhoon Lagoon, Aquatica, and the independent Wet 'n Wild offer mellow floating streams. A great idea, the floating streams are long, tranquil inner-tube rides that give you the illusion that you're doing something while you're being sedentary. For wimps, wussies, and exhausted people of all ages, floating streams are an answered prayer.

Disney's streams flow ever so slowly around the entire park, through caves, beneath waterfalls, past gardens, and under bridges. They offer a relaxing alternative to touring a park on foot.

Floating streams can be reached from several put-in and take-out points. There are never lines; just wade into the creek and plop into one of the inner tubes floating by. Ride the current all the way around, or get out at any exit. It takes 30–35 minutes to float the full circuit.

Predictably, there will be guests on whom the subtlety of floating streams is lost. They'll be screaming and splashing. Let them pass, stopping a few moments, if needed, to distance yourself from them.

14. LUNCH If you didn't bring a picnic, you can buy food. Quality is comparable to fast food; prices (as you might expect) are a bit high.

15. MORE OPTIONS If you really are a water puppy, consider returning to your hotel for a heat-of-the-day nap and coming back to the water park for some early-evening swimming. Special lighting after dusk makes Typhoon Lagoon and Blizzard Beach enchanting; crowds tend to be lighter, too. If you leave the park and want to return, keep your admission ticket and have your hand stamped. If you're staying in a hotel served by Disney buses, older children can return on their own to the water parks, giving Mom and Dad a little private quiet time.

16. BAD WEATHER Thunderstorms are common in Florida. On summer afternoons, storms can be a daily occurrence. Water parks close during a storm. Most storms, however, are short-lived, allowing the water park to resume normal operations. If a storm is severe and prolonged, it can cause a great deal of inconvenience. In addition to the park's closing, guests compete aggressively for shelter, and Disney resort guests may have to joust for seats on a bus back to the hotel.

unofficial **TIP**
Because Florida is so flat, approaching weather can be seen from atop the slide platforms at the swimming parks. Especially if you're dependent on Disney buses, leave the park early when you see a storm moving in.

We recommend you monitor the local weather forecast the day before you go, checking again in the morning before leaving for the water park. Scattered thundershowers are to be expected, but moving storm fronts are to be avoided.

17. ENDURANCE The water parks are large and require almost as much walking as one of the theme parks. Add to this wave surfing, swimming, and all the climbing required to reach the slides, and you'll be pooped by day's end. Unless you spend your hours like a lizard on a rock, don't expect to return to the hotel with much energy. Consider something low-key for the evening. You'll probably want to hit the hay early.

18. LOST CHILDREN AND LOST ADULTS It's easier to lose a child or become separated from your party at one of the water parks than it is at a major theme park. Upon arrival, pick a very specific place to meet should you get separated. If you split up on purpose, set times for checking in. Lost-children stations at the water parks are so out of the way that neither you nor your lost child will find them without help from a Disney cast member. Explain to your children how to recognize cast members (by their distinctive name tags) and how to ask for help.

WATER-PARK TOURING PLANS

ONE-DAY TOURING PLANS for Blizzard Beach and Typhoon Lagoon can be found on pages 833 and 834, respectively. These plans are for parents with small children; touring plans for adults, along with our online reader survey, can be found at **touringplans.com**. We'd love to hear from families who've tried these plans.

The plans presented here include all the slides, flumes, and rides appropriate for kids in both parks. Having brought our own children to these parks, we've also included tips on which slides to try first in case this is your child's first water-park experience. For example, at Typhoon Lagoon we suggest the family whitewater-rafting ride Gang

Plank Falls as the first attraction. If your child enjoys that, we list Keelhaul Falls as the next step up in waterslides. If that seems a bit much, however, the touring plan recommends the Ketchakiddee Creek play area as an alternative.

WET 'n WILD

unofficial **TIP**
Wet 'n Wild, though clean, is cluttered and not very appealing to the eye.

WET 'N WILD (on International Drive in Orlando, one block east of I-4 at Exit 75A; ☎ 800-992-WILD or 407-351-1800; **wetnwildorlando.com**) is a non-Disney water-park option. Unlike Typhoon Lagoon and Blizzard Beach, in which scenic man-made mountains and integrated themes create a colorful atmosphere, Wet 'n Wild's only themes appear to be concrete, plastic, and water. Fortunately, the thrill, scope, and diversity of its rides make Wet 'n Wild an excellent alternative to the Disney swimming parks. Besides, contrary to what some Disney execs might believe, their water isn't any wetter.

Mears Transportation operates a shuttle to Wet 'n Wild that stops three times a day at Disney hotels. It's the same shuttle that commutes between Walt Disney World and Universal Orlando. Cost is $19 for guests age 3 and older. If you're staying in Walt Disney World, in Lake Buena Vista, or along US 192, you'll need a car. If you're staying on International Drive, you can take the **International Drive trolley** (visit **iridetrolley.com** for schedules and fees). If you drive, a large Wet 'n Wild parking lot charges $12 per day for cars and vans and $16 for RVs. Parking is ample; just be sure to hold the kids' hands when crossing the street.

You can buy your Wet 'n Wild tickets at the main gate or at **wetn wildorlando.com/tickets.** Prices are about $52 for adults and $46 for children ages 3–9, and $52 for weekday season passes, but call or check online for special deals and discounts. For the same price as a single-day ticket, Wet 'n Wild offers a Length of Stay pass on its website that is good for 14 consecutive days. Ticket prices are similar to those of the Disney parks, but if you attend during the summer, the park is open late (hours vary, from 9:30 a.m. until 9 p.m. at the latest; call or visit the website for details), allowing visitors to hit the slides in the morning, go back to their hotels for lunch and a nap, and then return for a dip at night. Disney water parks typically close by 6 or 7 p.m.

When you get hungry, the main food pavilions are the centrally located **Bubba's BBQ, Manny's Pizza,** and **Surf Grill,** together offering such staples as burgers, pizza, and barbecued-pork sandwiches as well as more-nutritious (and nontraditional) items such as veggie burgers and tabbouleh. Wait times are long, and prices are high but not outrageous. For guests whose budgets and impatience thresholds are less flexible, feel free to bring in a cooler of lunch fixings (remember, glass containers and alcoholic beverages are prohibited, but you can purchase beer inside).

All the slides outside the **Blastaway Beach** kids' park have a 48-inch height requirement except for multipassenger slides, for which the minimum height is 36 inches if an adult accompanies the short rider;

the only exceptions to this are the rides at the **Wake Zone**, with a height requirement of 51 inches (The Wild One) and 56 inches (Knee Ski and Wake Skating).

BODY AND MAT SLIDES

SLIDES AT WET 'N WILD INCLUDE **Mach 5, The Bomb Bay, Der Stuka,** and **The Storm.** The Mach 5 tower, to the left of the park entrance, consists of three mat slides. The mats increase your speed and eliminate the chafing often experienced on body slides. To go even faster, try to get a newer mat with a smoother bottom. They're easily distinguishable: The new mats have white handles, while the old mats have blue ones.

unofficial **TIP**
Although ride attendants say that all three of the Mach 5 slides are equal, the center slide appears to be the zippiest route to the bottom.

Among the body slides (those without mats or rafts) are The Bomb Bay and Der Stuka, twin speed flumes with pitches up to 79 degrees that descend from the top of a six-story tower. On The Bomb Bay you stand on a pair of doors that open, dropping you into the chute. You have to work up the nerve to launch yourself on Der Stuka. The lack of a fully enclosed tube (such as the one on the Humunga Kowabunga speed slide at Typhoon Lagoon) adds the (perhaps justifiable) fear of falling off the 250-foot slides, but their ability to float your stomach somewhere near your teeth is a pretty unforgettable thrill.

The Storm body slide, near The Bomb Bay and Der Stuka, is a hybrid ride: half slide, half toilet bowl. The steep slide creates enough momentum to launch riders into a few laps around the bowl below before they begin slipping toward the hole in the center, eventually falling into a 6-foot-deep pool. The ride is exhilarating and disorienting; when the lifeguard at the ending pool begins hollering, just stumble toward his voice and give him a thumbs-up.

RAFT AND TUBE RIDES

THE HEADLINERS AT WET 'N WILD are the raft and tube rides, including **Brain Wash, Disco H2O, The Surge, The Black Hole,** the **Bubba Tub, The Flyer,** and **The Blast.** Brain Wash is an extreme six-story tube ride with a 53-foot vertical drop into a 65-foot funnel; tubes hold two or four riders. Disco H2O holds up to four people in one raft, ushering them down a long tube into a 1970s-era nightclub complete with lights, music, and a disco ball. The basic design of the ride is similar to that of The Storm (a long tube into a bowl), only not as frantic and disorienting; the disco theme, coupled with the fluidity of the ride, makes it a main draw.

The Surge launches from the same tower as Disco H2O and uses the same four-person rafts. Riders spin down the open-air course, drifting high onto the walls on each banked corner. To reach the top of the walls, try to go with a full raft—as with all raft rides, the more riders squeezed in, the faster you'll all go. Directly across from The Surge's splashdown pool is the entrance for The Black Hole. Bring a partner for this one; The Black Hole requires two riders on each raft, and honestly, who wants to embark into endless murk without some company? As impressive as the ride seems from afar, the anxiety created by the gaping entrance is the most exciting part of the ride. Yes, it's dark—a piece of green track lighting runs the length of the entire course—but besides the darkness, the ride lacks the dips and turns found on the other slides. If you're claustrophobic and scared of the dark, this isn't the ride for you; if tight spaces and inky blackness don't give you a rush, then this ride isn't for you either.

The three gentler raft rides are The Flyer, The Blast, and the Bubba Tub. The first two launch from the same tower as the Mach 5, but their entrance is accessible through the Blastaway Beach kids' area. At the base of the entrance are one- and two-person rafts; these are only for The Blast, so don't carry them up to the tower to the Flyer entrance. The Flyer is a calmer, toboggan-style ride in which riders sit one behind the other; it's suitable for families with smaller children. The Blast is a themed ride, like Disco H20, and is the wettest you can get without swimming. The theme of The Blast appears to be a broken waterworks, complete with spinning dials and broken pipes, all painted in comic book red and yellow. From mist to falling water to spraying pipes, this is the best way to cool off at Wet 'n Wild. The Bubba Tub, across the park from The Flyer and The Blast, is a long, straight track with three hummocks to impede momentum, but with a full tube of four people, you hit the "tub" at a pretty good clip.

OTHER ATTRACTIONS

THE CENTRAL FIXTURE AT WET 'N WILD, the **Surf Lagoon** wave pool, is on par with Blizzard Beach's. Unlike at Typhoon Lagoon, there's no surfing in this wave pool, but you can rent tubes at the main rental stand or go bobbing with your body. The wave-making machine takes long breaks every day, so when you walk by and see waves, be sure to wade in.

Another any-time-of-day option is the **Lazy River.** Don't be fooled by the name, though: The circuit is short, the current fast—nothing lazy about it. Don't even bother trying to walk upstream to catch a tube; it's better to swim down the river or wait patiently until one passes within reach.

Wet 'n Wild's 1-acre **Blastaway Beach** is a small-fry version of the adult menu. It's to the left of the main gate; look for the oversize sand castle capped off with a big blue bucket. The bucket actually fills with water and tips over, soaking the people in front of the castle. Blastaway Beach, which replaced the former children's area in 2012, is the largest water-park playground in Florida. The giant sandcastle alone spans two pools (upper and lower), covering over 15,000 square feet with over 85,000 gallons of water powering over 100 soakers, jets, waterfalls, and water cannons; 15 slides; and the aforementioned bucket.

WAKE ZONE

THE MOST DISTINCTIVE OFFERING AT WET 'N WILD is the Wake Zone, on a lake that's roughly the same size as the rest of the park and offering three different activities: wakeboarding, kneeboarding, and tubing. The lines can be considerable, especially since the attraction only runs from noon to dusk and is open on weekends only from mid-March to June, daily during the summer, and weekends only from September to mid-October. Be sure to call before going to Wet 'n Wild to see if the area is open that day. To avoid lines, wander over to the Wake Zone at least 20 minutes before noon.

At the boarding area, you can choose either a wakeboard or a kneeboard. Helmets and life jackets, provided free at the entrance, are required; the height requirement is 56 inches. The ride is basically a cable with hanging towlines that, like a T-bar at a ski resort, pull riders along the half-mile loop. You board from a slightly submerged dock where you grab the towline as it passes overhead. Brace yourself—towlines have a tendency to jerk. Keep your arms rigid and the nose of the board up. There are no instructors, so watch the other riders and chat up the good ones for tips while you're in line. If you fall down while riding, get out of the cable's path and swim to shore. If you fall where no dock is nearby, a Jet Ski will come and pick you up.

The name of the tubing ride is **The Wild One.** For an extra fee ($6 per person), a Jet Ski will pull you around the lake while you sit in an inner tube. The ride lasts five minutes, but it's worth the money if you've never been tubing before.

▌ **AQUATICA** *by* **SEAWORLD**

AQUATICA IS ACROSS INTERNATIONAL DRIVE from the back side of SeaWorld. From Kissimmee, Walt Disney World, and Lake Buena Vista, take I-4 east, exit onto the Central Florida Parkway, and then bear left on International Drive. From Universal Studios, take I-4 west to FL 528 and from there exit onto International Drive. Admission prices are comparable to those of the Disney water parks: $53 for adults and $48 for kids, including tax; tickets purchased online are a flat $48 for adults and $43 for kids. Standard parking is $12 ($16 for RVs, $16 for preferred parking, $25 for valet parking). If you don't want to wait in a queue to purchase tickets, buy them in advance at **aquaticabyseaworld .com,** or use the credit-card ticket machines to the left of Aquatica's main entrance.

Aquatica is comparable in size to the other water theme parks in the area. Attractively landscaped with palms, ferns, and tropical flowers, it's far less themed than Disney's Typhoon Lagoon and Blizzard Beach but much greener and more aesthetically appealing than Wet 'n Wild. Promotional material suggests that Aquatica is unique by virtue of combining SeaWorld's signature marine-animal exhibits with the expected water-park assortment of wave pools, slides, and creek floats. Marine exhibits, however, start and end with a float-through tank of tropical fish and a pool of black-and-white Commerson's dolphins. Print, web, and television ads for the park show guests viewing the dolphins while descending through a see-through tube on the **Dolphin Plunge** body slide—a corkscrewing romp through a totally dark tube until you blast through the clear tube at the end. The reality, however, is that you're flushed through the clear tube so fast, and with so much water splashing around your face, that it's pretty much impossible to see anything. At Aquatica, the best option by far is to view the dolphins from the walkway surrounding the exhibit or from the subsurface viewing windows.

A Yorkshire, England, woman reacted to the Dolphin Plunge:

The slide had the longest queue in the park. We queued for the best part of an hour and all agreed that it was a waste of time! You can barely see through the transparent *part of the tube where the dolphins are (if you're lucky!), the slide is short, and the see-through bit lasts about 2 seconds!*

SeaWorld's promotion hype, coupled with the location of the Plunge just inside the park entrance and the slide's low carrying capacity (about 280 persons per hour), ensures that the slide stays mobbed all day. To experience the slide without a long wait, be on hand at park opening and ride first thing.

Other slides include **Tassie's Twisters,** in which an enclosed tube slide spits you into an open bowl where you careen around the bowl's edge much in the manner of the ball in a roulette wheel. Close to the Dolphin Plunge, Tassie's Twisters should be your second early-morning stop. Next, head over to **Walhalla Wave** and **HooRoo Run,** both on the park's far right side. Both slides use circular rafts that can accommodate up to three people. Walhalla Wave splashes down an enclosed twisting tube, while HooRoo Run is an open-air run down a steep, straight, undulating slide. The same entrance serves both slides. Line up for Walhalla (vastly more popular) on the right, for HooRoo on the left. Make Walhalla your third slide of the day, followed by HooRoo.

Then pass along the right side of the children's adventure area, **Walkabout Waters,** to **Taumata Racer,** the park's highest-capacity slide with eight enclosed corkscrewing tubes. The remaining slide is **Whanau Way,** all the way across the park to the left of the entrance. Sporting one corkscrew and a few twists, Whanau Way employs tubes that can carry one or two people. Because it's hard to see from the park entrance, Whanau Way doesn't attract long lines until midmorning.

Taken as a whole, the slides at Aquatica are not nearly as interesting, thrilling, or imaginative as those of its competitors, and aside from whisking you through a dolphin tank, they don't break any new ground. Also, all the slides except HooRoo Run have you launching yourself down a black hole, making every ride seem like the one before it. Dark slides are an essential part of every water-park lineup, but to have all slides dark save one makes for a very homogenized experience.

In addition to the slides, Aquatica offers side-by-side wave pools, **Cutback Cove** and **Big Surf Shores.** This arrangement allows one cove to serve up body-surfing waves while the other puts out gently bobbing floating waves. A spacious beach arrayed around the coves is the park's primary sunning venue. Shady spots, courtesy of beach umbrellas, ring the perimeter of the area for the sun-sensitive.

Loggerhead Lane and **Roa's Rapids** are the two floating streams. The former is a slow and gentle tube journey that circumnavigates the Tassie's Twisters slide. Its claim to fame is a section of the float where a Plexiglas tunnel passes through the Fish Grotto, a tank populated by hundreds of exotic tropical fish. Unique to Aquatica, Roa's Rapids is a much longer course with a very swift current. (The other water parks have floating creeks, but most are leisurely affairs where you can fall asleep in your tube.) Buoyancy vests are available, but most adults float or swim the stream. The name notwithstanding, there are no rapids, but the flow is constricted from time to time, considerably increasing the already fast speed of the current. There's only one place to get in and out, so if you miss the takeout, you're in for another lap.

When it comes to children's water attractions, Aquatica more than equals the other area parks. In the back of the park, to the right of the wave pools, is **Kata's Kookaburra Cove,** featuring a wading pool and slides for the preschool crowd. But the real pièce de résistance is **Walkabout Waters.** If you have children under age 10, this alone may be worth the price of admission. In a calf-deep 15,000-square-foot pool, it's an immense three-story interactive playground set with slides, stairs, rope bridges, landings, and more. Water sprays, spritzes, pulsates, and plops at you from every conceivable angle. Randomly placed plastic squirting devices allow kids to take aim at unsuspecting adults, but the kids disperse quickly when either of two huge buckets dumps hundreds of gallons of water down on the entire structure. It's impossible not to get wet. It's also impossible not to have fun.

As at the other water parks, there are lockers, towels, wheelchairs, and strollers to rent, gift shops to browse, and places to eat. The three restaurants are **WaterStone Grill,** offering specialty sandwiches, fried fish, wraps, and salads; **Banana Beach,** an all-you-can-eat venue dishing up burgers, hot dogs, and chicken; and **Mango Market,** a diminutive eatery serving pizza, wraps, and salads. WaterStone Grill and Mango Market serve beer.

PART TWENTY-ONE

BEYOND
the PARKS

◾ DOWNTOWN DISNEY

DOWNTOWN DISNEY IS A SHOPPING, dining, and entertainment development strung along the banks of Village Lake. On the far right is the **Downtown Disney Marketplace;** on the far left is **Downtown Disney West Side.** See pages 750 and 751 for a map of the area.

DOWNTOWN DISNEY MARKETPLACE

ALTHOUGH THE MARKETPLACE OFFERS interactive fountains, a couple of playgrounds, a lakeside amphitheater, and watercraft rentals, it's primarily a shopping and dining venue. The centerpiece of shopping is the 50,000-square-foot **World of Disney,** the largest store in the world selling Disney-trademark merchandise.

At **Disney's Design-a-Tee** you can create customized T-shirts, and **Mickey's Pantry** offers Disney home and kitchen products, including the Donald Duck Press (joke!). Another noteworthy retailer is the **LEGO Imagination Center,** showcasing a number of huge and unbelievable sculptures made entirely of LEGO "bricks." Spaceships, sea serpents, sleeping tourists, and dinosaurs are just a few of the sculptures on display. **Once Upon a Toy** is a toys, games, and collectibles superstore. Rounding out the selection are stores specializing in resort wear, athletic attire and gear, Christmas decorations, Disney art and collectibles, and handmade craft items. Most retail establishments are open from 9:30 a.m. until 11:30 p.m. Detailed coverage of shopping opportunities follows in Part Twenty-Two.

Rainforest Cafe and **T-REX** are the headliner restaurants at the Marketplace. The others are **Pollo Campero,** a Latin chicken eatery; **Cap'n Jack's Restaurant; Earl of Sandwich,** for deli Dagwoods; **Wolfgang Puck Express Cafe;** and **Ghirardelli Soda Fountain & Chocolate Shop.** Full-service restaurants are profiled in Part Ten, Dining in and around Walt Disney World.

WHITHER PLEASURE ISLAND?

FORMERLY DISNEY'S NIGHTTIME-ENTERTAINMENT complex, Pleasure Island effectively shut down in September 2008 when its six admission-charging nightclubs closed. Disney plans to replace these with a more family-oriented mix of shops and restaurants. Remaining open during the transition are **Fulton's Crab House** and **Portobello** restaurants, along with **Raglan Road,** an Irish pub and restaurant featuring live Celtic music; **Fuego by Sosa Cigars,** a posh cigar bar; **Curl by Sammy Duvall,** a surf shop; and all outdoor food-and-beverage locations. Part of the development is **Paradiso 37,** featuring the cuisines of the Americas (that would be North, Central, and South) served both indoors and out. Disney remains mum regarding the future of the four former nightclubs that have not been demolished.

DOWNTOWN DISNEY WEST SIDE

THE WEST SIDE IS THE NEWEST ADDITION to Downtown Disney and offers a broad range of entertainment, dining, and shopping. Restaurants include the **House of Blues,** which serves Cajun specialties; **Planet Hollywood,** offering movie memorabilia and basic American fare; **Bongos Cuban Cafe,** serving Cuban favorites; and **Wolfgang Puck Grand Cafe,** featuring California cuisine. All four West Side restaurants are profiled in Part Ten, Dining in and around Walt Disney World.

West Side shopping is some of the most interesting in Disney World. For instance, there's **Pop Gallery,** selling high-end paintings and sculptures, and **D-Street,** offering "cutting edge" (that is, bizarre) apparel and Vinylmation figurines (see page 746). Other shops include a **Harley-Davidson** showroom and a designer-sunglasses studio.

In the entertainment department are **DisneyQuest,** an interactive theme park contained in a building; the **House of Blues,** a concert and dining venue; and a 24-screen **AMC** movie theater. New to the West Side in 2012 is **Splitsville,** an upscale bowling, billiards, and dining venue covering 45,000 square feet on two levels. If you feel like getting high, try **Characters in Flight,** where you ascend 400 feet over Downtown Disney in a tethered balloon (the characters are painted on the balloon—don't expect to float around up there with Br'er Fox). The weather-dependent ride operates 8:30 a.m.–midnight, lasts 8–10 minutes, and costs $18 for adults (age 10 and up) and $12 for kids (ages 3–9). It's also wheelchair-accessible.

The West Side is also home to **Cirque du Soleil La Nouba,** an amazing production show with a cast of more than 70 performers and musicians. The House of Blues concert hall and *La Nouba* are described in Part Twenty-Three, Nightlife in and out of Walt Disney World. A discussion of DisneyQuest follows.

DISNEYQUEST

FOR MORE THAN THREE DECADES, major theme parks have experimented with attractions based on motion-simulation and virtual-reality technologies. Among other things, these technologies have allowed thrill rides with the punch of a roller coaster to be engineered and operated in spaces as small as a one-car garage. Analogous to the computer industry, where the power of a room-filling mainframe is now available in an iPhone, Disney is pioneering the concept of a theme park in a box, or in the case of DisneyQuest, a modest five-story building.

Opened in 1998, DisneyQuest contains all the elements of the larger Disney theme parks. An entrance area facilitates your transition into the park environment and leads to the gateways of four distinct themed lands, here referred to as zones. As at other Disney parks, almost everything is included in the price of your admission.

It takes about 2–5 hours to experience DisneyQuest once you get in, depending on the crowd. Disney claims to limit the number of guests admitted to ensure that each person has a positive experience. Well, so does the Super Bowl, and that's how big the crowd feels at DisneyQuest. Once the complex hits capacity, newly arriving guests are lined up outside to wait until departing guests make some room.

DisneyQuest is aimed at a youthful audience, say, 8–35 years of age, though younger and older patrons will enjoy much of what it offers. Those who haunt the video arcades at shopping malls will be most at home here. And similar to what occurs at most malls, when late afternoon turns to evening, the median age at DisneyQuest also rises toward adolescents and teens who have been released from parental supervision for a while.

unofficial **TIP**
Weekday mornings are the least crowded times to visit DisneyQuest.

You begin your experience in the **Departure Lobby,** adjacent to admission sales. From the Departure Lobby you enter a "Cyberlator," a "transitional attraction" (read: elevator) hosted by the Genie from *Aladdin*, that delivers you to an entrance plaza called Ventureport. From here you can enter the four zones. As in the larger parks, each zone is distinctively themed. Some zones cover more than one floor, so, looking around, you can see things going on both above and below you. The four zones, in no particular order, are **Explore Zone, Score Zone, Create Zone,** and **Replay Zone.**

Though most kids and adolescents aren't going to care, the zone layout at DisneyQuest may confuse adults trying to orient themselves. Don't count on trapping certain kids in certain zones either, or planning a rendezvous inside one without designating a specific location. Each zone spreads out over multiple levels, with stairways, elevators, slides, and walkways linking them in a variety of ways. Still, as we said, the labyrinthine design of the place won't bother most youngsters, who are usually happy just to wander (or dash madly) between games and rides.

Admission to DisneyQuest is $47 for adults and $41 for children ages 3–9, including tax. The facility is open Sunday–Thursday, 11:30 a.m.–10 p.m.; Friday and Saturday, 11:30 a.m.–11 p.m. For more information, call ☎ 407-828-4600.

Explore Zone

The gateway to Explore Zone is the tiger's-head cave from *Aladdin*. You can descend to the attractions area via elevators or ramps. The headline attraction in Explore Zone is the **Virtual Jungle Cruise,** in which you paddle a six-person raft. The raft is a motion simulator perched on top of blue air bags that replicate the motion of water. Responding to the film of the river projected before you, you can choose from among several routes through the rapids. The motion simulator responds to sensors on your paddle, so the ride you experience simulates the course you choose. As if navigating the river isn't enough, man-eating dinosaurs and a cataclysmic comet are tossed in for good measure. Another

Explore Zone attraction, **Aladdin's Magic Carpet Ride,** is a virtual-reality trip through the streets of Agrabah. On **Pirates of the Caribbean—Battle for Buccaneer Gold,** you fight pirates attacking your ship. The entire battle takes place in 3-D on a motion-base platform, which shudders with every hit by the pirates' cannonballs.

Score Zone

Here you pass through a slash in a giant comic book to enter a themed area based on comic book characters and competition. The big deals here are enlarged, high-tech versions of electronic and video games where you pit your skill and reflexes against other players. The headliner is **Mighty Ducks Pinball Slam,** where you stand atop a mammoth hockey puck. By manipulating a joystick, you control the motion of your puck as it bounces around a virtual-reality pinball machine. In **Ride the Comix,** you don virtual-reality headgear to ride off into comic-book scenes and do battle with archvillains. In **Invasion! An Alien ExtraTERRORestrial Encounter,** you and your friends team up to steer a spaceship over an alien planet, rescue the human colonists there, and destroy the enemy.

Create Zone

A digital artist's palette serves as the entrance to Create Zone. Featured here is **CyberSpace Mountain,** an attraction where you can design your own roller coaster—including 360-degree loops—and then go for a virtual-reality motion-simulator ride on your creation. Also in the Create Zone is **Animation Academy,** a sort of crash tutorial in Disney animation.

Replay Zone

Replay Zone draws its theme from a 1950s view of the future. Basically, it's three levels of classic midway games with a few futuristic twists. The balls on the **Skeeball** games, for example, glow in the dark. Winners of the various games earn redemption tickets, which can be redeemed for midway-type prizes. The pièce de résistance of Replay Zone is **Buzz Lightyear's AstroBlasters,** a fancy version of bumper cars. Here, guests pilot two-person bumper bubbles that suck up grapefruit-sized balls from the floor and fire them from an air cannon at other vehicles. Direct hits cause the other vehicles to spin momentarily out of control.

Reader response to DisneyQuest is very mixed, as evidenced by the following comments.

From a Pennsylvania family with kids ages 11 and 13:

Our only really big disappointment was DisneyQuest. My husband and daughters paid $32 to get in because the guy at the window told us that fee covered nearly all the experiences. Once inside, they found that at least half the stuff they wanted to do cost mega-extra-bucks. It's truly an offensive deal for people who have already spent scads in their darned parks.

But for a Cleveland family of five, DisneyQuest was a slam dunk:

Your description and reader feedback had us a little skeptical. But with another cold day on hand, we gave it a shot. If you have right-brained (creative) kids, you can't miss. Your book said 2–5 hours for DQ. We had dinner reservations that forced a cutoff at 7 hours, otherwise we could have pulled an all-nighter with them! The interactive stuff was fascinating. I think DQ provides parents the best chance to see their kids' brains and personalities in action.

A family from Columbia, Maryland, offers this advice to parents with babies and toddlers:

Alert your readers to bring a baby carrier–backpack to DisneyQuest. You're there for several hours, and absolutely no strollers are allowed in the entire building.

ESPN WIDE WORLD *of* SPORTS COMPLEX

THIS 220-ACRE, STATE-OF-THE-ART competition and training center consists of a 9,500-seat ballpark, a fieldhouse, and dedicated venues for baseball, softball, tennis, track and field, beach volleyball, and 27 other sports. From Little League Baseball to rugby to beach volleyball, the complex hosts a mind-boggling calendar of professional and amateur competitions.

In late winter and early spring, the complex is the spring-training home of the Atlanta Braves. While Disney guests are welcome at the ESPN Wide World of Sports as paying spectators (prices vary according to event), none of the facilities are available for guests unless they're participants in a scheduled, organized competition. To learn which sporting events, including Major League Baseball exhibition games, are scheduled during your visit, call ☎ 407-939-GAME (4263) or check the online calendar at **disneyworldsports.com.**

Admission is $17 adults, $12 children ages 3–9 (prices include tax). Some events carry an extra charge. There's a restaurant, the **ESPN Wide World of Sports Grill,** but no on-site lodging.

Off Osceola Parkway, on Victory Way, the ESPN Wide World of Sports Complex has its own parking lot and is accessible via the Disney transportation system.

The DISNEY WILDERNESS PRESERVE

ABOUT 40–60 MINUTES SOUTH of Walt Disney World is the Disney Wilderness Preserve, a wetlands-restoration area operated by The Nature Conservancy in partnership with Disney. At 12,000 acres, this is as real as Disney gets. There are hiking trails and an interpretive center. Trails wind through grassy savannas, beneath ancient cypress trees, and along the banks of pristine Lake Russell. More than 1,000 species of plants and animals call the preserve home. Birds include the bald eagle, red-cockaded woodpecker, Florida scrub-jay, wood stork, sandhill crane, northern harrier, and crested caracara. Other wildlife includes the southeastern big-eared bat, Sherman's fox squirrel, the eastern indigo snake, and the gopher tortoise. The Florida panther has been spotted here as well. The preserve is open Monday–Friday, 9 a.m.–5 p.m., except for major holidays; admission is free, but donations are welcome. For more information and directions, call ☎ 407-935-0002 or visit **tinyurl.com/disneywildernesspreserve**.

WALT DISNEY WORLD SPEEDWAY

ADJACENT TO THE TRANSPORTATION and ticket center parking lot sits the Walt Disney World Speedway, a 1-mile tri-oval course. If you're a NASCAR fan, check out the **Richard Petty Driving Experience,** where you can ride in a two-seater stock car for $105 (3 laps) or learn to drive one for $478 (8 laps), $904 (18 laps), $1,383 (30 laps), or $2,235 (50 laps); prices include tax. There's also a teen (ages 14–19) ride-along for $31 when a parent purchases the full-price riding option. For information call ☎ 800-BE-PETTY (237-3889) or check out **drivepetty.com**.

Also at the speedway is the **Indy Racing Experience.** Usually starting in the afternoon when the Richard Petty folks have finished, this experience features sleeker, faster open-wheeled cars like those seen in the Indianapolis 500. You can ride in a modified two-seat Indy car or drive one of the single-seat cars. The cost is $425 (tax included) for eight laps. For information call ☎ 317-243-7171, ext. 106, or 888-357-5002, ext. 106, or visit **indyracingexperience.com**.

For either driving course, you'll be paired with an experienced instructor who'll show you how the car handles, how the various gauges and pedals work, and most importantly, where to change into the flame-retardant driving suit you'll be wearing. If you choose to drive, the instructor will drive a pace car ahead of you and (we're told) will happily go as fast as you can demonstrate you're comfortable with—up to 180 mph in the Indy cars.

Both the Richard Petty and Indy experiences are by reservation only. Plan on arriving an hour before your appointment to fill out paperwork and go through an orientation session. To drive any of these cars, you must be age 18 or older, have a valid driver's license, and be able to operate a stick shift; for the Indy course, you must also be shorter than 6 feet 5 inches and weigh less than 250 pounds. Richard Petty riders must be at least age 14; Indy riders must meet the same age, height, and weight requirements as drivers. The Indy Racing Experience is closed around some major holidays and when Disney hosts PGA golf events, so check the website for schedules before you go.

For those more interested in how cool they look than how fast they go, there's the **Exotic Driving Experience,** which takes you six laps around the 1-mile track and incorporates the high banks of the speedway plus a Formula One–style street course. Prices range from $199 to $389 plus tax, depending on the car; choices include a Ferrari 458 Italia, two variations on the Lamborghini Gallardo, a Porsche 997 S, and an Audi R8. Drivers must be age 18 or older, but there's a $99 ride-along option for those age 14 and older. For more information and online reservations, call ☎ 855-822-0149 or go to **exoticdriving.com.**

WALT DISNEY WORLD RECREATION

MOST WALT DISNEY WORLD GUESTS never make it beyond the theme parks, the water parks, or Downtown Disney. Those who do, however, will discover an extraordinary selection of recreational opportunities ranging from guided fishing adventures and water-skiing outings to hayrides, horseback riding, fitness-center workouts, and miniature golf. If you can do it at a resort, it's probably available at Walt Disney World.

Boat, bike, and fishing-equipment rentals are handled on an hourly basis. Just show up at the rental office during operating hours and they'll fix you up. The same goes for various fitness centers in the resort hotels. Golf, tennis, fishing expeditions, water-ski excursions, hayrides, trail rides, and most spa services must be scheduled in advance. Though every resort features an extensive selection of recreational options, those resorts on a navigable body of water offer the greatest variety. Also, the more upscale a resort, the more likely it is to have such amenities as a fitness center and spa. In addition, you can rent boats and other recreational equipment at Downtown Disney Marketplace.

WALT DISNEY WORLD GOLF

RECENT YEARS HAVE BROUGHT a stream of big changes to Walt Disney World golf. Until 2007, the resort had six golf courses, all expertly designed and meticulously maintained. Now there are five, since the closing of the **Eagle Pines** course. Nothing is changing for the **Magnolia, Oak Trail,** and **Palm** courses, across Floridian Way from the Polynesian Resort. They envelop the Shades of Green resort's recreational complex, and the pro shops and support facilities adjoin the hotel proper (for active and retired military personnel only). It's also business as usual for the **Lake Buena Vista Golf Course** at Disney's Saratoga Springs Resort & Spa, near the Downtown Disney Marketplace and across the lake from the redeveloping Pleasure Island.

On the other hand, **Osprey Ridge Golf Course,** near Fort Wilderness Resort & Campground, has been a moving target. The Tom Fazio–designed course was originally set to close in mid-2010, slated to be replaced by a new course on a site shared by the new Four Seasons Resort and Golden Oak, a Disney-owned luxury residential development. Current plans call for Osprey Ridge to be renovated substantially and its management turned over to Four Seasons. The course may close temporarily during renovations, which should be completed in time for the resort's grand opening in 2014.

The Magnolia and Palm have completed substantial renovations and upgrades over the past few years. These two 36-hole courses host the annual Children's Miracle Network Classic, one of the longest-running stops on the PGA Tour. Oak Trail is a nine-hole, par-36 course for beginners. The other four courses are designed for the mid-handicap player and, while interesting, are quite forgiving. All courses are popular, with morning tee times at a premium, especially from January through April. In addition to the golf courses, there are driving ranges and putting greens at each location.

Peak season for all courses is January–May, and off-season is May–October. Off-season and afternoon twilight rates are available. Carts are required (except at Oak Trail) and are included in the greens fee. Tee times may be reserved 90 days in advance by Disney resort guests and 60 days in advance by day guests with a credit card. Proper golf attire, including spikeless shoes, is required. A collared shirt and Bermuda-length shorts or slacks meet the requirements.

Besides the ability to book tee times farther in advance, guests of Walt Disney World–owned resorts get other benefits that may sway a golfer's lodging decision. These include discounted greens fees, free club rental, and charge privileges. The single most important, and least known, benefit is the provision of free round-trip taxi transportation between the golf courses and your hotel, which lets you avoid moving your car or dragging your clubs

unofficial **TIP**
To avoid the crowds, play on a Monday, Tuesday, or Wednesday, and sign up for a late-afternoon tee time.

on Disney buses. The cabs, which make access to the courses much simpler, are paid by vouchers happily supplied to hotel guests. Perhaps as a sign of tough economic times, Walt Disney World recently introduced discounted two-day, two-round passes at its four championship courses, taking about 30% off rates that are already good values.

The following chart summarizes prices for daily play at all Disney courses except Oak Trail. Fees are raised annually, usually at the beginning of October; the cost of replaying the same course on the same day (if space is available) is half the full rate.

TYPE OF ADMISSION	OPENING–10 A.M.	10 A.M.–3 P.M.	3 P.M.–CLOSING
Resort guest	$89	$59	$49
Resort guest, 2-round pass	$140	N/A	N/A
Day guest	$104	$59	$49
Day guest, 2-round pass	$180	N/A	N/A

For more information, call ☎ 407-938-GOLF (4653) or visit **disneyworld.disney.go.com/golf/course-rates.**

Lake Buena Vista Golf Course ★★★

ESTABLISHED 1971   DESIGNER Joe Lee   STATUS Resort

2200 Club Lake Drive, Lake Buena Vista, FL 32830; ☎ 407-938-GOLF

TEES
- BLUE: 6,745 yards, par 72, USGA 72.3, slope 133
- WHITE: 6,281 yards, par 72, USGA 70.1, slope 130
- GOLD: 5,910 yards, par 72, USGA 68.5, slope 125
- RED: 5,177 yards, par 72, USGA 69.7, slope 119

FACILITIES Pro shop, GPS, driving range, practice green, locker rooms, snack bar, food and beverage cart, and club and shoe rentals.

COMMENTS There are several memorable holes here, but this layout is the only one at Disney with housing on it—a lot of housing—which detracts from the golf experience. The course is geographically unique among the other layouts, tucked behind Saratoga Springs, and has a swampy feel reminiscent of the area's pre-Disney wetlands, with trees dripping Spanish moss. Narrow fairways and small greens emphasize accuracy over length.

Magnolia Golf Course ★ ★ ★ ½

ESTABLISHED 1970   DESIGNER Joe Lee   STATUS Resort

1950 W. Magnolia/Palm Drive, Lake Buena Vista, FL 32830; ☎ 407-938-GOLF

TEES
- BLACK: 7,488 yards, par 72, USGA 76.0, slope 141
- BLUE: 7,073 yards, par 72, USGA 74.0, slope 137
- WHITE: 6,558 yards, par 72, USGA 71.6, slope 130
- GOLD: 6,027 yards, par 72, USGA 69.0, slope 121
- RED: 5,127 yards, par 72, USGA 69.6, slope 126

FACILITIES Pro shop, GPS-equipped golf carts, driving range, practice green, locker rooms, food and beverage cart, and club and shoe rentals.

COMMENTS Another fine Joe Lee creation, Magnolia is Disney's longest course and features a whopping 97 bunkers, including the famous one in the shape of Mickey Mouse's head. But the layout is slightly less challenging than the Palm's. Ten holes were lengthened and all greens resurfaced with TifEagle turf in 2005 as part of an "extreme makeover." This refurbishment added 300 yards to the already long course, and at more than 7,500 yards, it will be the longest most guests ever have the opportunity to play. Like the Palm, this course hosts the PGA Tour.

Oak Trail Golf Course ★ ★ ½

ESTABLISHED 1980   DESIGNER Ron Garl   STATUS Resort

1950 W. Magnolia/Palm Drive, Lake Buena Vista, FL 32830; ☎ 407-938-GOLF

TEES
- WHITE: 2,913 yards, par 36
- RED: 2,532 yards, par 36

FEES Adult, $38; junior (age 17 and under), $20. Pull carts, $6 (course is walking only). Replaying the course costs an additional $19 for adults and $10 for junior players.

FACILITIES Pro shop, driving range, practice green, locker rooms, food and beverage cart, and club and shoe rentals.

COMMENTS This Ron Garl nine-holer is a "real" course, not an executive par-3 like many nine-hole designs. Geared toward introducing children to the game, it also makes a good quick-fix or warm-up before a round, and the walking-only layout is the only such routing at Walt Disney World.

Osprey Ridge Golf Course ★ ★ ★ ½

ESTABLISHED 1992   DESIGNER Tom Fazio   STATUS Resort

3451 Golf View Drive, Lake Buena Vista, FL 32830; ☎ 407-938-GOLF

TEES
- TALON: 7,039 yards, par 72, USGA 73.7, slope 127
- CREST: 6,629 yards, par 72, USGA 71.7, slope 124
- WINGS: 5,996 yards, par 72, USGA 68.8, slope 117
- FEATHERS: 5,283 yards, par 72, USGA 70.2, slope 124

FACILITIES Pro shop, GPS-equipped golf carts, driving range, practice green, locker rooms, Sand Trap Bar & Grill, food and beverage cart, and club and shoe rentals.

COMMENTS This Tom Fazio layout is a thoroughly modern course whose construction involved a large amount of earth-moving. Its main characteristics are large, rolling mounds and elevated tees and greens. The greens are huge, almost to the point of being bizarre, making them easy to hit but leaving approaches at four-putt distances where you almost cannot hit the ball hard enough to get it to the hole.

Palm Golf Course ★★★★

ESTABLISHED 1970   DESIGNER Joe Lee   STATUS Resort

1950 W. Magnolia/Palm Drive, Lake Buena Vista, FL 32830; ☎ 407-938-GOLF

TEES
- BLUE: 6,991 yards, par 72, USGA 73.7, slope 131
- WHITE: 6,479 yards, par 72, USGA 71.4, slope 125
- GOLD: 6,006 yards, par 72, USGA 69.2, slope 118
- RED: 5,262 yards, par 72, USGA 70.5, slope 126

FACILITIES Pro shop, GPS-equipped golf carts, driving range, practice green, locker rooms, food and beverage cart, and club and shoe rentals.

COMMENTS Designed by Joe Lee, this is Disney's best course. Home to a PGA Tour event, the Palm has numerous lakes coming into play on nine holes, and sand everywhere, with 94 hazards. The highlight, however, is a set of excellent greens—a real surprise given the heavy volume of play. The defining characteristic is a set of holes where water separates tees from landing areas and landing areas from greens, a wet take on desert-style target golf. The signature 18th, with its island green, caps a fine set of finishing holes and has been ranked as high as fourth in difficulty among all holes on the PGA Tour's many venues. But four sets of well-spaced tees make the course playable for all abilities.

GOLF *beyond*
WALT DISNEY WORLD

GRAND CYPRESS GOLF CLUB

THE GREATER ORLANDO AREA has enough high-quality courses (more than 150 of them!) to rival better-known golfing Meccas such as Scottsdale, Arizona, and Palm Springs, California. But unlike these destinations, with their endless private country clubs, Orlando is unique because almost all its courses are open for some sort of public play.

Of the many courses and resorts in the area, one stands head and shoulders above the rest, especially because it actually abuts Walt Disney World. Not only is the location of this course excellent, but the sprawling 1,500-acre **Grand Cypress Resort** is superb in every other respect, with top-notch lodging, dining, and grounds, and an enormous fantasy-pool complex. Hotel choices are the full-service **Hyatt Regency,** which just finished renovating its guest rooms, or the **Villas at Grand Cypress,** an enclave of upscale rental homes. But the standout feature is the golf, which would be worth a trip regardless of where the resort was. The facilities are first-rate, from the luxurious clubhouse to the GPS-equipped carts. The golf club is also home to an excellent instructional facility, the **Grand Cypress Academy of Golf.**

Grand Cypress Golf Club, New Course ★★★★

ESTABLISHED 1988 DESIGNER Jack Nicklaus STATUS Resort (Guests Only)

1 N. Jacaranda, Orlando, FL 32836; ☎ 407-239-4700 or 877-330-7377; grandcypress.com

TEES
- BLUE: 6,720 yards, par 72, USGA 71.9, slope 121
- WHITE: 6,106 yards, par 72, USGA 69.0, slope 115
- WHITE (ladies): 6,106 yards, par 72, USGA 74.7, slope 124
- RED: 5,242 yards, par 72, USGA 69.2, slope 112

FEES $150–$175 ($120 in summer).

FACILITIES Pro shop, driving range, practice greens, locker rooms, restaurant, food and beverage cart, GPS-equipped golf carts, and club and shoe rentals.

COMMENTS The New Course is Jack Nicklaus's homage to the famous Old Course at St. Andrews, Scotland, the birthplace of golf. The first and last two holes are near-replicas of those at the Old Course; other features, such as the famous Swilcan Bridge and some of the huge bunkers, are re-created here. In between are Nicklaus's original holes, done in a links style, with double greens; pot bunkers; tall rough; and wide, hard fairways. As on most Scottish links courses, there are no trees, and the wind will play havoc with your shots when it's blowing. If you've never had a chance to play Scottish courses, the New is a reasonable facsimile that captures the spirit and history of the sport's earliest form.

Grand Cypress Golf Club, ★★★★½
North, South, and East Courses

ESTABLISHED 1986 DESIGNER Jack Nicklaus STATUS Resort (Guests Only)

1 N. Jacaranda, Orlando, FL 32836; ☎ 407-239-4700 or 877-330-7377; grandcypress.com

NORTH/SOUTH TEES
- GOLD: 7,208 yards, par 72, USGA 75.9, slope 142
- BLUE: 6,643 yards, par 72, USGA 73.0, slope 138
- WHITE: 6,066 yards, par 72, USGA 70.1, slope 131
- WHITE (ladies): 6,106 yards, par 72, USGA 75.7, slope 130
- RED: 5,513 yards, par 72, USGA 72.8, slope 130

SOUTH/EAST TEES
- GOLD: 6,953 yards, par 72, USGA 74.5, slope 138
- BLUE: 6,392 yards, par 72, USGA 71.7, slope 135
- WHITE: 5,840 yards, par 72, USGA 68.9, slope 129
- WHITE (ladies): 5,840 yards, par 72, USGA 74.5, slope 140
- RED: 5,038 yards, par 72, USGA 69.7, slope 125

EAST/NORTH TEES

- GOLD: 6,985 yards, par 72, USGA 74.6, slope 138
- BLUE: 6,389 yards, par 72, USGA 71.5, slope 133
- WHITE: 5,882 yards, par 72, USGA 69.0, slope 129
- WHITE (ladies): 5,882 yards, par 72, USGA 75.2, slope 137
- RED: 5,047 yards, par 72, USGA 69.9, slope 125

FEES $150–$175 ($120 in summer).

FACILITIES Pro shop, driving range, practice greens, locker rooms, restaurant, food and beverage cart, carts equipped with GPS, and club rentals ($65) and shoe rentals ($20).

COMMENTS This course can be played in three different 18-hole combinations, but the South (renovated by Jack Nicklaus in the summer of 2007) is the very best nine at the resort, so try to book either North/South or South/East. The North/South combination hosted the LPGA Tournament of Champions from 1994 to 1996, as well as the PGA Tour Skills Challenge and the Shark Shootout. The course is one of the most beautiful in Orlando, and water is found on 13 of the holes, creating additional peril. There are many unique and interesting holes, several with true risk–reward choices such as shortcuts over lakes. The undulating greens are guarded by pot bunkers and grass depressions and are kept in superb shape. Unlike the New Course, this group of courses provides very few opportunities to bump and run the ball onto the green.

OTHER STANDOUT COURSES IN ORLANDO

IN ADDITION TO THE GRAND CYPRESS COURSES, the ones we've profiled in the following section also stand out and are worth leaving Walt Disney World to play. No new courses of note have opened since Rees Jones's **Waldorf Astoria Golf Club,** just outside of Walt Disney World, opened in 2009. New to Orlando visitors, however, is the **Windermere Country Club,** which recently opened its doors to nonmembers. Along with the Grand Cypress Golf Club, Windermere is partnering with the three hotels at Universal Orlando—the Loews Portofino Bay Hotel, the Hard Rock Hotel, and the Loews Royal Pacific Resort—to offer special rates and preferred access to guests.

The next seismic shift in the golf landscape will occur in late 2012, when the courses of the massive **Streamsong Resort,** on 16,000 acres midway between Orlando and Tampa, are scheduled to open. Currently under construction are two courses by the world's two most highly acclaimed design firms, Tom Doak's Renaissance Golf and the duo of Bill Coore and Ben Crenshaw.

Arnold Palmer's Bay Hill Club & Lodge ★★★★

ESTABLISHED 1961 DESIGNER Dick Wilson STATUS Resort

9000 Bay Hill Blvd., Orlando, FL 32819; ☎ 407-876-2429 or 888-422-9445; bayhill.com

TEES

- YELLOW: 6.437 yards, par 72, USGA 71.3, slope 129
- BLUE: 6,895 yards, par 72, USGA 72.3, slope 127
- GREEN: 7,381 yards, par 72, USGA 73.9, slope 136

FEES Golf packages with lodging (for two) from $499 per night in summer to $598 per night in peak season.

FACILITIES Lodging, pro shop, driving range, practice greens, locker rooms, restaurant, beverage cart, and shoe rentals.

COMMENTS Bay Hill is famous in the golf world as the home club of The King, Arnold Palmer, and is the site of his invitational tournament each year. You have to stay to play, and the luxury resort—much improved after a $7 million face-lift in 2009—features a spa, fine dining, and a comprehensive golf academy. When he is in town, which is most of the time, Palmer makes a point of stopping by the clubhouse daily, and half the attraction of staying and playing here is to see him. The other half is the course. It consists of three nines, but it's the Challenger–Champion combination that is the most popular, and the one on which the PGA Tour event is played. This combo starts off with a roar, featuring the toughest opening hole on the PGA Tour, an uphill, 441-yard, dogleg left that is heavily bunkered, both in the fairway and around the green. Recent renovations by Palmer have made the course better than ever, lifted it upward in all the major golf rankings, and include entirely new and better greens and tees throughout, plus substantial changes to eight holes.

CHAMPIONSGATE GOLF CLUB

THREE MILES FROM WALT DISNEY WORLD and close to Celebration lies one of the city's premier golf destinations. The complex includes an Omni hotel and the Florida headquarters of the world-renowned David Leadbetter Golf Academy. But the centerpieces of the $800 million, 1,500-acre facility are the two Greg Norman–designed courses. For more information, visit **championsgategolf.com.**

ChampionsGate International Course ★★★★

ESTABLISHED 2000   DESIGNER Greg Norman   STATUS Public

1400 Masters Blvd., ChampionsGate, FL 33896; ☎ 407-787-4653 or 888-558-9301

TEES
- BLACK: 7,363 yards, par 72, USGA 76.8, slope 143
- BLUE: 6,792 yards, par 72, USGA 74.1, slope 137
- WHITE: 6,239 yards, par 72, USGA 71.5, slope 132
- GOLD: 5,618 yards, par 72, USGA 68.0, slope 117

FEES $46–$140. Discounts available for Omni hotel guests.

FACILITIES Pro shop, driving range, practice greens, locker rooms, restaurant, GPS-equipped carts, beverage cart, and club and shoe rentals.

COMMENTS The tougher and more highly ranked of ChampionsGate's two layouts, with a USGA rating of 76.8, the International lives up to its name by re-creating the feel of the championship courses of the British Isles. Laid out in a links style, the course has carpetlike fairways framed by the stark, unfinished look of brown dunes, mounds, and severe pot bunkers.

ChampionsGate National Course ★★★½

ESTABLISHED 2000   DESIGNER Greg Norman   STATUS Public

1400 Masters Blvd., ChampionsGate, FL 33896; ☎ 407-787-4653 or 888-558-9301

TEES
- BLACK: 7,128 yards, par 72, USGA 75.2, slope 138
- BLUE: 6,427 yards, par 72, USGA 71.9, slope 133

- WHITE: 5,937 yards, par 72, USGA 69.1, slope 124
- GOLD: 5,150 yards, par 72, USGA 65.3, slope 111

FEES $35–$120 Florida residents, $60–$140 nonresidents. Discounts available for Omni hotel guests.

FACILITIES Pro shop, driving range, practice greens, locker rooms, restaurant, GPS-equipped carts, beverage cart, and club and shoe rentals.

COMMENTS The kinder, gentler course at ChampionsGate, the National is a resort-style layout that ambles through 200 acres of citrus groves in a traditional parkland routing with far less water than the International. Deep greens welcome bump-and-run shots, and the length is manageable from every set of tees.

Falcon's Fire Golf Club ★★★★

ESTABLISHED 1993 DESIGNER Rees Jones STATUS Public

3200 Seralago Blvd., Kissimmee, FL 34746; ☎ 407-239-5445; falconsfire.com

TEES

- GOLD: 7.006 yards, par 72, USGA 73.2, slope 135
- BLUE: 6,435 yards, par 72, USGA 71.0, slope 130
- WHITE: 5,962 yards, par 72, USGA 68.5, slope 126
- RED: 5,388 yards, par 72, USGA 71.0, slope 123

FEES $39–$139 ($35 for guests age 15 and under). Fees include carts.

FACILITIES Pro shop, driving range, practice greens, restaurant, GPS-equipped carts, beverage cart, and club rentals.

COMMENTS A top-to-bottom million-dollar renovation completed in October 2009 raised the Orlando-area profile of this still-bargain-priced daily-fee course. Features include all-new and much faster greens, plus completely renovated and reshaped bunkers throughout. The Rees Jones design features plenty of water hazards, especially on the harder back nine, and remains a course suitable for all abilities—and, conveniently, is just 3 miles from Walt Disney World. A similarly comprehensive renovation of the large clubhouse was completed in 2010.

ORANGE COUNTY NATIONAL GOLF CENTER

FIVE MILES NORTH OF DISNEY, in Winter Garden, lies Orlando's premier daily-fee public facility, winner of numerous industry awards and consistently named among the nation's top public clubs by most golf publications. Forty-five holes (including a nine-hole short course) and one of the country's best practice facilities (42 acres) occupy 922 verdant acres, without homes or other distractions—just pure golf. It's also easily the region's best value, with inexpensive on-site lodging and two-night, three-round packages ($148–$178 depending on season). For more information, visit **ocngolf.com**.

Crooked Cat ★★★★

EST. 1997 DESIGNERS Isao Aoki, Davis Harman, and Phil Ritson STATUS Public

16301 Phil Ritson Way, Winter Garden, FL 34787; ☎ 407-656-2626 or 888-727-3672

TEES

- Q-SCHOOL: 7,493 yards, par 72, USGA 76.0, slope 139
- CHAMPIONSHIP: 6,927 yards, par 72, USGA 73.7, slope 132
- BACK: 6,432 yards, par 72, USGA 71.4, slope 126
- MIDDLE: 6,020 yards, par 72, USGA 66.8, slope 122
- FORWARD: 5,112 yards, par 72, USGA 69.6 slope 120

FEES $29–$89, varying by time of day, day of week, and time of year. Discounts for Florida and Orange County residents and guests age 17 and under.

FACILITIES Lodging, GPS, pro shop, driving range, practice greens, locker rooms, restaurant, beverage cart, and club and shoe rentals.

COMMENTS Variety is the spice of life, and this partner to the very modern Panther Lake is a throwback to Scottish style links courses, with few trees, wide fairways, and heather mixed in the rough. Large, sloped greens welcome bump-and-run shots but are protected by deep bunkers of both grass and sand. Crooked Cat is as well maintained as its sibling.

Panther Lake ★ ★ ★ ★ ½

EST. 1997   DESIGNERS Isao Aoki, Davis Harman, and Phil Ritson   STATUS Public

16301 Phil Ritson Way, Winter Garden, FL 34787; ☎ 407-656-2626 or 888-727-3672

TEES

- Q-SCHOOL: 7,350 yards, par 72, USGA 76, slope 139
- CHAMPIONSHIP: 6,849 yards, par 72, USGA 73.2, slope 132
- BACK: 6,394 yards, par 72, USGA 71.2, slope 127
- MIDDLE: 6,011 yards, par 72, USGA 69.2, slope 120
- FORWARD: 5,319 yards, par 72, USGA 70.8, slope 123

FEES $29–$89, varying by time of day, day of week, and time of year. Discounts for Florida and Orange County residents and guests age 17 and under.

FACILITIES Lodging, GPS, pro shop, driving range, practice greens, locker rooms, restaurant, beverage cart, and club and shoe rentals.

COMMENTS Panther Lake was the nation's first course designed to showcase 18 signature holes, and no expense was spared to make the course beautiful, just as none is spared to keep it in excellent condition. The front nine is carved from Florida wetlands with water at every turn, while the much-different back has a Carolinas-like style with surprising elevation changes, stands of pines and oaks, and hard-to-hold greens emphasizing accuracy.

REUNION RESORT

REUNION IS NOW A WYNDHAM GRAND RESORT, but little else has changed. This 2,300-acre resort and residential golf community has three courses, designed by Arnold Palmer, Tom Watson, and Jack Nicklaus. In 2007, Reunion saw the addition of Annika Sorenstam's **Annika Academy.** (Sorenstam, now retired after the greatest career in women's golf, lives here part-time, shows up occasionally, and focuses on this single location.) Reunion is the region's largest golf destination outside of Walt Disney World itself. For more information, visit **reunion resort.com.**

Nicklaus Course   ★ ★ ★ ★

ESTABLISHED 2006   DESIGNER Jack Nicklaus   STATUS Resort (Guests Only)

7593 Gathering Drive, Reunion, FL 34747; ☎ 407-396-3199 or 888-418-9611

TEES

- GOLD: 7,244 yards, par 72, USGA 76.7, slope 147
- BLUE: 6,537 yards, par 72, USGA 72.6, slope 142
- WHITE: 6,260 yards, par 72, USGA 71.3, slope 140
- RED: 5,055 yards, par 72, USGA 65.4, slope 116

FEES Golf available only as part of inclusive lodging packages starting at $171 per day, with one round per night.

FACILITIES Lodging, pro shop, driving range, practice greens, locker rooms, restaurant, beverage cart, and club and shoe rentals.

COMMENTS Nicklaus went for a flat parkland design here. This doesn't mean the course is easy, however, as he used a target-style layout, with forced carries of the tees to small landing areas in the fairways; small greens; and the constant temptation to go for it with risk–reward gambles over a variety of hazards, including water and sand. Water is in play on fully half the holes, and since the course is built through a bird sanctuary, it's quiet and pristine and a world apart from the city's hustle and bustle.

Palmer Course   ★ ★ ★ ★

ESTABLISHED 2004   DESIGNER Arnold Palmer   STATUS Resort (Guests Only)

7593 Gathering Drive, Reunion, FL 34747; ☎ 407-396-3199 or 888-418-9611

TEES

- BLACK: 6,916 yards, par 72, USGA 73.4, slope 137
- GOLD: 6,419 yards, par 72, USGA 70.9, slope 132
- BLUE: 6,058 yards, par 72, USGA 69.2, slope 128
- WHITE: 5,529 yards, par 72, USGA 67.0, slope 116
- RED: 4,802 yards, par 72, USGA 63.3, slope 106

FEES Golf available only as part of inclusive lodging packages starting at $171 per day, with one round per night.

FACILITIES Lodging, pro shop, driving range, practice greens, locker rooms, restaurant, beverage cart, and club and shoe rentals.

COMMENTS Palmer frames vast green fairways with numerous shapely white bunkers, and there's plenty of water, so much so that the course needs elaborate boardwalk-style cart bridges to whisk guests around. Still, the possibility for lost balls is offset by very generous fairways, with lots of room for errant drives, and this is the easiest of the three layouts here.

Watson Course   ★ ★ ★ ★

ESTABLISHED 2004   DESIGNER Tom Watson   STATUS Resort (Guests Only)

7593 Gathering Drive, Reunion, FL 34747; ☎ 407-396-3199 or 888-418-9611

TEES

- BLACK: 7,154 yards, par 72, USGA 74.7, slope 140
- GOLD: 6,697 yards, par 72, USGA 72.2, slope 131
- BLUE: 6,319 yards, par 72, USGA 70.6, slope 124

- WHITE: 5,990 yards, par 72, USGA 69.4, slope 120
- RED: 5,395 yards, par 72, USGA 66.3, slope 114

FEES Golf available only as part of inclusive lodging packages starting at $171 per day, with one round per night.

FACILITIES Lodging, pro shop, driving range, practice greens, locker rooms, restaurant, beverage cart, and club and shoe rentals.

COMMENTS Tom Watson is said to have made more than 40 site visits during construction to ensure that his British Isles–inspired master-piece here was built correctly. Greens are huge but undulating, so getting on is no insurance against three- (or four-) putting. Bunkers are everywhere, from fairways hazards to greenside pot bunkers; from the back, where all the hazards come into play, this is one of Orlando's stiffest tests, yet the course gets appreciably easier as you move to shorter tees.

THE BEST OF THE REST

Shingle Creek Golf Club ★★★★

ESTABLISHED 2003   DESIGNER David Harman   STATUS Public

9939 Universal Blvd., Orlando, FL 32819; ☎ 407-996-9933 or 866-996-9933; shinglecreekgolf.com

TEES

- BLACK: 7,149 yards, par 72, USGA 74.7, slope 133
- GOLD: 6,659 yards, par 72, USGA 72.1, slope 130
- BLUE: 6,359 yards, par 72, USGA 70.4, slope 128
- SILVER: 5,813 yards, par 72, USGA 68.2, slope 119
- IVORY: 5,099 yards, par 72, USGA 69.5 slope 122

FEES $99–$135; twilight, $55–$75. Further discounts for resort guests; golf and lodging packages also available.

FACILITIES Lodging, pro shop, driving range, practice greens, locker rooms, restaurant, GPS-equipped carts, beverage cart, and club and shoe rentals.

COMMENTS Hotelier Harris Rosen runs the state's largest privately owned hotel company, and the flagship Shingle Creek Resort opened in 2006. The $300 million, 1,500-room property includes a golf course by David Harman of nearby Orange County National fame, and the layout quickly won a place among *Golfweek's* Top 40 Best New Courses in the United States after it opened in late 2003. The main feature is the namesake creek, originating some 10 miles north as part of the headwaters of the Everglades and meandering through the design, surrounded by native oaks and pines. Even in peak season, Shingle Creek has quickly become one of the very best golf values in the Orlando region, even more so for resort guests.

Waldorf Astoria Golf Club ★★★★

ESTABLISHED 2009   DESIGNER Rees Jones   STATUS Resort

14224 Bonnet Creek Resort Lane, Orlando, FL 32821; ☎ 407-597-3782; waldorfastoriagolfclub.com

TEES

- BLACK: 7,108 yards, par 72, USGA 74.9, slope 134
- BLUE: 6,661 yards, par 72, USGA 72.9, slope 131

- WHITE: 6,309 yards, par 72, USGA 71.4, slope 127
- GREEN: 5,990 yards, par 72, USGA 69.7, slope 125
- SILVER: 5,089 yards, par 72, USGA 70.8, slope 127

FEES $95–$200 peak season, $90–$160 midseason.

FACILITIES Lodging, pro shop, driving range, practice greens, locker rooms, restaurant, GPS-equipped carts, beverage cart, and club and shoe rentals.

COMMENTS The 482-acre Bonnet Creek Resort encompasses two hotels: a 497-room Waldorf Astoria and a 1,000-room Hilton, both of which opened in October 2009. The Rees Jones–designed Waldorf Astoria course, finished in spring 2009 but wisely allowed to mature and grow in until the hotels were ready, combines a classic parkland routing, where holes are separated by stands of towering pines, with the omnipresent lakes for which Florida golf is known. Several holes wrap dramatically along the shore or feature greens set against the water—in fact, only one hole from the 12th to 18th holes (17) is dry. Private lessons are available.

Windermere Country Club ★★★

ESTABLISHED 1986 DESIGNER Ward Northrup STATUS Semiprivate

2710 Butler Bay Drive N., Windermere, FL 34786; ☎ 407-876-4410; windermeregolf.com

TEES

- BLUE: 6,641 yards, par 72, USGA 71.6, slope 136
- WHITE: 6,259 yards, par 72, USGA 69.9, slope 131
- GOLD: 5,933 yards, par 72, USGA 68.3, slope 128
- RED: 5,375 yards, par 72, USGA 71.7, slope 127

FEES $49–$99; twilight, $24–$54.

FACILITIES Pro shop, driving range, practice greens, locker rooms, restaurant, carts, beverage cart, and club rentals.

COMMENTS Windermere is a private club that has begun allowing unrestricted outside play and also offers special deals to guests of the three resort hotels within Universal Studios. Secluded, quiet, and parklike, the course is well maintained and offers a genteel "member for a day" experience. It was also recently renovated, including the greens and practice facilities. Short by modern standards, it's challenging nonetheless: 13 holes have lakes in play, and the layout is heavily bunkered.

▮ MINIATURE GOLF

YEARS AGO, THE DISNEY INTELLIGENCE PATROL (DIP) noticed that as many as 113 guests a day were sneaking out of Walt Disney World to play Goofy Golf. Applying the logic of the boy who jammed his finger in the dike, Disney feared a hemorrhage of patrons from the theme parks. The thought of those truant guests making instant millionaires of miniature-golf entrepreneurs on International Drive was enough to give a fat mouse ulcers.

The response to this assault on Disney's market share was **Fantasia Gardens Miniature Golf,** an 11-acre complex with two 18-hole dink-and-putt golf courses. One is an "adventure" course, themed after

Disney's animated film *Fantasia*. The other, geared more toward older children and adults, is an innovative approach-and-putt course with sand traps and water hazards.

Fantasia Gardens is beautifully landscaped and creatively executed. It features fountains, animated statues, topiaries, flower beds, and a multitude of other imponderables that you're unlikely to find at most mini-golf courses.

Fantasia Gardens is on Epcot Resorts Boulevard, across the street from the Swan resort; it's open daily, 10 a.m.–11 p.m. To reach the course via Disney transportation, take a bus or boat to the Swan. The cost to putt, including tax, is $12.78 for adults and $10.65 for children ages 3–9. In case you arrive hungry or naked, Fantasia Gardens has a snack bar and gift shop. For more information, call ☎ 407-WDW-PLAY (939-7529).

In 1999, Disney opened **Winter Summerland,** a second miniature-golf facility next to the Blizzard Beach water park. Winter Summerland offers two 18-hole courses—one has a "blizzard in Florida" theme, while the other sports a tropical-holiday theme. The Winter Summerland courses are much easier than the Fantasia courses, which makes them a better choice for families with preteen children. Operating hours and cost are the same as for Fantasia Gardens.

PART TWENTY-TWO

SHOPPING
in and out of
WALT DISNEY WORLD

◾ HEY, BIG SPENDER

THE *UNOFFICIAL GUIDE* aims to help you see as much as possible, not buy as much as possible. But we acknowledge that for many people, a vacation is an extended shopping spree. If you're among these shoppers, you'll love exploring the stores at and around Walt Disney World. You'll notice that our touring plans keep you on track to see attractions, dissuading you somewhat from shopping. However, to give you a notion of what shopping means to an enthusiast, we share this letter from a Los Angeles couple:

> Although your book discourages it, the shopping is a divine experience at WDW for those who like to shop. One doesn't shop in WDW for bargains (that's what flea markets, garage sales, and Target are for), but Disney buyers obtain a large selection of above-average to excellent-quality merchandise, much of it not available anywhere else (not even at a Disney Store or in a catalog). They're marketing geniuses! Not even the largest shops have all the merchandise they have to offer, hence, a shopper can make little discoveries in almost every shop. That, coupled with congenial, helpful Disney staff and services like complimentary hotel delivery, makes shopping an attraction of its own at WDW.

And a woman from Suffolk, Virginia, offers this:

> Let readers know if they're into shopping to allot at least 6 hours for Downtown Disney Marketplace and West Side.

Central Florida is a shopper's Mecca. With more than 52 million square feet of retail space, Orlando now has nine first-rate malls and three top shopping outlets, and millions of visitors from around the globe have retailers scrambling to keep up with demand.

Beyond the ubiquitous mouse ears and T-shirts, avid shoppers can find a wide array of items, from hard-to-find imports at Epcot's World Showcase to designer bargains from hundreds of off-price outlets. We figure you haven't come to Orlando *just* for the shopping, so we'll whittle down our lists to the best of the best. We'll take a look at all four Disney theme parks and Downtown Disney, then head for the other shopping hot spots around Central Florida.

There are too many shops to mention every single one, but we'll tell you what's special and point out the smart buys—along with the overpriced merchandise. We'll also tell you where to locate hard-to-find goods. If a shop has a special, not-to-be-missed quality, we've marked it with a ★ .

PIN MANIA

CALL IT A HOBBY OR AN OBSESSION—serious pin traders show up at the theme parks decked out in vests, hats, and sashes decorated with collectible Disney pins, always on the lookout for the one that got away. The mania started in October 1999 with the launch of Disney's Millennium Celebration, and today Disney churns out thousands of pins annually at its resorts around the world. The pins generally sell for around $8–$20, with one for every occasion, from new attractions to special events. The spot for the largest collection of pins is **Disney's Pin Traders** at Downtown Disney Marketplace.

Disney Pinformation

Since pin trading is such a serious business, here's a primer on Disney's pin-trading etiquette, courtesy of **disneypins.com:**

1. Pins should be in good, undamaged condition.

2. You can trade pins only one at a time. The back of the pin must be attached.

3. Guests may trade a maximum of two pins per cast member.

4. Don't touch a cast member's, or another individual's, pins or lanyard. If you want to view a pin up close, just ask the person you're trading with for a closer look.

5. Pins must represent a Disney event, location, character, or icon.

6. "Name pins" cannot be traded with cast members.

7. If the cast member already has the same pin that you want to trade, don't even bother trying.

8. You may trade only one pin of the same style with a particular cast member.

9. Don't try to buy a pin from a cast member—not acceptable.

10. Some cast members have what's called a "showcase" pin on their lanyard. These pins are just for show, and cast members are not allowed to trade them. Sorry!

There's a real camaraderie in the chase. Most agree there's no great monetary gain in the trade, just lots of fun. But there is "pin etiquette" (see "Disney Pinformation," above). For instance, pins must be cloisonné, semicloisonné, or hard-enamel metal and must be traded one at a time, hand-to-hand.

Many Disney cast members wear lanyards festooned with the ubiquitous pins and happily trade with park visitors. Cast members wearing pin-trading lanyards can be found at all four theme parks, Downtown Disney, and some resorts.

A Michigan mom has the pin-trading thing figured out:

I'm both a bargain geek and a Disney geek. I got a grab bag of 20 tradable pins for $1 each on eBay, plus I learned a trading tip this year: At Guest Services at every park, there's a book with many pages of pins to look at. My daughter scored a hard-to-find Perry the Platypus pin!

And a Bloomfield Hills, Michigan, reader suggests:

If you're buying pins to trade, buy a set. The per-pin price is much cheaper.

THEME PARK SHOPS WITH THE BEST DISNEY STUFF
THE MAGIC KINGDOM **Emporium** Main Street, U.S.A. (largest selection at Magic Kingdom)
EPCOT **MouseGear** Future World (largest selection at Epcot)
DISNEY'S ANIMAL KINGDOM **Island Mercantile and Disney Outfitters** Discovery Island **Serka Zong Bazaar** Asia
DISNEY'S HOLLYWOOD STUDIOS **Animation Gallery** Animation Courtyard **Mickey's of Hollywood** Hollywood Boulevard

VINYLMATION

ANOTHER DISNEY COLLECTING CRAZE involves 3- and 9-inch vinyl figures in the shape of Mickey Mouse. Some are completely blank, allowing you to make your own design with markers and stickers. Others are already decorated with a variety of motifs, representing the Disney parks, Disney movie characters (from Mr. Incredible to WALL-E), and even an "urban" theme. The limited-release 3-inch figures are sold in opaque boxes, so you don't know what you get until it's opened. (For this reason, you can't return limited-edition Vinylmation merchandise.) There are 10–12 3-inch figures in each series, and the last design is kept a secret, adding to the intrigue of the collectible. Much like the pins, guests can trade Vinylmation with other guests and cast members. Though Vinylmation is sold throughout the parks, the biggest and most comprehensive selection is available at **D-Street** in Downtown Disney West Side, where you can also spend time at the Vinylmation Creation Station decorating your own blank figure with pens, markers, stickers, jewels, and more.

SHOPPING *in* WALT DISNEY WORLD

TIPS FOR DISNEY SHOPPING

AFTER EXHAUSTIVE RESEARCH in all four Disney theme parks, water parks, and resorts, we can assure you that Disney-brand merchandise is pretty much the same wherever you go. In fact, maybe too much the same, as a Denver family laments:

One problem is the homogenization of merchandise throughout the resort. This not only undermines the opportunity to find truly unique gifts and products in the shops, but it also dilutes or destroys critical theming—the dinosaur stores in DinoLand U.S.A., for instance, now contain very little actual dinosaur merchandise.

The only big differences are a handful of items with logos for specific resorts or theme parks. So if you're short on time, save your shopping spree for one favorite theme park or for the **World of Disney** shop in Downtown Disney Marketplace, the largest Disney-character shop in the world.

Much like the merchandise, prices rarely differ across Disney property. A beach towel, for instance, was the same price at every location we checked. Ditto for sale merchandise: If it's on sale at one store, it's on sale in all stores (though you may not be able to find it at all locations).

unofficial **TIP**
Beyond Epcot, shopping is hit-and-miss in the other three theme parks. You'll find the same basic Disney merchandise everywhere, with specialty items for each park tossed in. Nevertheless, amid all the Disney goods are some unusual shops.

If you're staying at a Disney hotel, you can have your packages delivered to your resort from any of the four Disney parks. Packages will be delivered to your hotel's gift shop by noon of the following day, so this service is unavailable if you're checking out of your room the same day. Same-day pickup inside the theme parks is available. For a nominal charge, you can ship items to your home.

If you remember on your flight home that you forgot to buy mouse ears for your nephew, call Walt Disney World Mail Order Merchandise on weekdays at ☎ 407-363-6200, or visit the Disney Catalog online at **disneyparks.com/store**. Most trademark merchandise sold at Walt Disney World is available.

I NEED . . .

Where at Walt Disney World is the best selection of a particular item? Here are a few recommendations:

BATHING SUITS

- **Beach Club Marketplace,** Beach Club Resort
- **Calypso Trading Post,** Caribbean Beach Resort
- **Curl by Sammy Duvall,** Downtown Disney

MEN'S CLOTHING

- **D-Street,** Downtown Disney West Side • **ESPN Club,** BoardWalk
- **Mouse About Town,** Disney's Hollywood Studios
- **Team Mickey,** Downtown Disney Marketplace

WOMEN'S CLOTHING

- **Bou-Tiki,** Polynesian Resort • **Tren-D,** Downtown Disney Marketplace

SPORTSWEAR

- **ESPN Club,** BoardWalk • **Team Mickey,** Downtown Disney Marketplace

JEWELRY

- **Mitsukoshi Department Store** (pearls and watches), Japan Pavilion, Epcot World Showcase
- **Uptown Jewelers,** Magic Kingdom
- **World of Disney** (Disney-themed jewelry), Downtown Disney Marketplace

DOWNTOWN DISNEY

IF SHOPPING IS AN ESSENTIAL PART of your Disney vacation, we recommend that your first stop be Downtown Disney, which comprises two shopping areas, each with its own special feel: the **Marketplace** and **West Side.** (**Pleasure Island,** the onetime nightlife district, has largely closed but still has a few shops. Disney plans to remake the area with a mix of dining and shopping.) If you have time constraints and need to limit your shopping spree to a single stop, this is it.

> *unofficial* **TIP**
> Except for specialty items, like silk rugs from the Japan Pavilion at Epcot, you can find a little bit of everything at Downtown Disney.

Downtown Disney stretches along the shore of Lake Buena Vista at the intersection of Buena Vista Drive and Hotel Plaza Boulevard. It's a pleasant walk from the Marketplace on the east end to the West Side. The West Side has smaller shops with trendy merchandise; the Marketplace is loaded with Disney merchandise and a smattering of non-Disney products. So what you're shopping for determines the best place to park—free parking on a surface lot spreads from one end to the other.

The Marketplace

Hours at the Marketplace vary among shops, but most stores open at 9:30 a.m. Beat the crowds by arriving right when everything opens—it's usually nearly empty then, so you'll have at least an hour or two to enjoy the shops without the lines or flocks of other shoppers. There are more than 15 shops and 10 places to eat, including **Rainforest Cafe** and **T-REX.** Wheelchair and stroller rentals are available at Guest Relations (between Arribas Brothers and Team Mickey). It's a comfortable place to stroll and people-watch. Near the central area is a carousel that runs daily; it's decorated with hand-painted renderings of the Marketplace shops. Cost is $2 per ride (there's also a kiddie train ride for $2). If you don't mind the kids getting wet, check out the free "Fun Fountain" in the back of the Marketplace. Streams of water squirt out of the spongy sidewalk, soaking energetic youngsters on hot summer days.

The Marketplace is accessible by Disney bus or boat. A few lockers are available on the dock close to Cap'n Jack's Restaurant.

Longtime Marketplace shoppers have complained that the merchandise is "too Disney" and that all the unusual shops have disappeared and been replaced with Disney shops. You'll still find non-Disney merchandise (like clothes and swimwear), just not in the abundance of the old Marketplace.

TOP SHOPS AT THE MARKETPLACE

ARRIBAS BROTHERS There's beautiful (and expensive) glassware and crystal at every turn, including an area dedicated to sparkling Swarovski pieces. *Not* the place to take rambunctious kids.

THE ART OF DISNEY Sells a small number of limited-edition animation cels, as well as giclée prints and pricey Disney creations from pottery to crystal. Most of the merchandise is high-quality and therefore expensive, but you'll find a few affordable souvenirs in the mix.

BASIN Browse among wooden tubs filled with soaps and lotions, then scoop your own bath salts or build your own gift basket. All the store's products are chemical-free and made with natural ingredients.

★ **DISNEY'S DAYS OF CHRISTMAS** This shop is just plain fun, with hundreds of holiday decorations from ornaments to stockings to stuffed animals wearing their Christmas Day best. We especially like the stations for engraving, embroidery, and ornament personalization. A hot seller in all the Christmas shops is the Disney monorail train (also carried at some toy stores).

DISNEY'S DESIGN-A-TEE A store where guests can create custom T-shirts and personalized merchandise. Next door is **Disney's Wonderful World of Memories,** which offers stationery and scrapbook materials, as well as customizable ear hats—themes include sports, princesses, brides, grooms, and more.

DISNEY'S PIN TRADERS The spot for the largest collection of pins, with tables for trading and two Internet stations for visiting the official pin-trading website (**disneypins.com**).

GOOFY'S CANDY CO. An interactive show kitchen with sweets . . . lots of sweets!

GHIRARDELLI SODA FOUNTAIN AND CHOCOLATE SHOP You can smell the chocolate when you walk in, and most of the time a cast member is on hand to dole out free samples. Chocolate souvenirs abound, but treat yourself to a "world famous" sundae topped with the decadent hot fudge made daily at the shop. The line for ice cream often winds out the door—it's that good.

★ **LEGO IMAGINATION CENTER** This is an ideal rest stop for parents, and you don't even have to go inside the store. A hands-on outdoor play area has bins of LEGOs that the kids can go crazy with while Mom and Dad take a break. Inside is all the latest LEGO paraphernalia. Check out the "sea monster" across from the store "swimming" in Lake Buena Vista.

Downtown Disney

Downtown Disney West Side

Parking

1. Cirque du Soleil *La Nouba*
2. DisneyQuest
3. Splitsville
4. House of Blues
5. Wolfgang Puck Grand Cafe
6. Bongos Cuban Cafe
7. AMC Downtown Disney 24 Theatres
8. *Specialty shopping:*
   Blink by Wet Seal
   Disney's Candy Cauldron
   D-Street
   Hoypoloi
   Orlando Harley-Davidson
   Pop Gallery
   Sosa Family Cigars
   Sunglass Icon

9. Wetzel's Pretzels/Häagen-Dazs
10. Characters in Flight
11. Planet Hollywood
12. Curl by Sammy Duvall
13. Paradiso 37
14. Apricot Lane Boutique
15. Fuego by Sosa Cigars
16. Raglan Road/Cookes of Dublin
17. Portobello

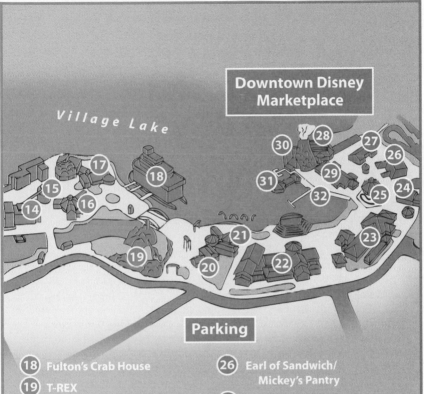

Downtown Disney
Marketplace

Village Lake

Parking

18 Fulton's Crab House

19 T-REX

20 Babycakes NYC/Fresh A-Peel/
Pollo Campero

21 LEGO Imagination Center

22 World of Disney

23 *Specialty shopping:*
Arribas Brothers
Basin
Ghirardelli Soda Fountain
& Chocolate Shop
Rawlings Making the Game
Ridemakerz
Team Mickey Athletic Club
Tren-D

24 Once Upon a Toy

25 Disney's Pin Traders

26 Earl of Sandwich/
Mickey's Pantry

27 Wolfgang Puck Express Cafe

28 *Specialty shopping:*
The Art of Disney
Disney's Design-a-Tee
Disney's Wonderful World
of Memories

29 *Specialty shopping:*
Goofy's Candy Co.
littlemissmatched
Marketplace Fun Finds

30 Rainforest Cafe

31 Cap'n Jack's Restaurant

32 Cap'n Jack's Marina

LITTLEMISSMATCHED Little fashion plates will have fun browsing the selection of funky printed socks, bags, and clothes. Socks are sold three to a pack in different patterns that you can mix and match.

MARKETPLACE FUN FINDS Disney-character merchandise organized into price points, including plush toys, clothing, and housewares.

MICKEY'S PANTRY A small shop with Disney home products, kitchen gadgets, cookbooks, and appliances. Also home to the **Spice & Tea Exchange,** which offers an assortment of teas and gourmet seasonings.

ONCE UPON A TOY Five rooms of toys, from build-your-own Mr. Potato Heads and light sabers to a room dedicated to video games. Several favorites, including *Star Wars, Toy Story,* and *Transformers* toys, are on the shelves. Also for sale are miniature play sets of Cinderella Castle; plush animals; and plenty of pirate, princess, and fairy items.

RIDEMAKERZ Inside Team Mickey Athletic Club (below), this toy store specializes in radio-controlled cars and trucks that kids build and customize themselves.

TEAM MICKEY ATHLETIC CLUB From soccer to basketball to golf to surfing, this shop features sports apparel. Not all of it has Mickey Mouse or Goofy logos—instead, there's a decent selection of college- and professional-team-logo sportswear and ESPN-themed gear. You'll also find plenty of sports memorabilia such as jerseys and sports balls. Baseball fans should check out the **Rawlings Making the Game** kiosk at the front of the store—there you can get an engraved baseball bat or the authentic helmet of a Major League Baseball all-star.

TREN-D A fun, funky, urban-inspired boutique with fashion apparel and accessories, plus exclusive items from cutting-edge designers.

★ **WORLD OF DISNEY** It's a superstore with 12 rooms—50,000 square feet—stacked with Disney merchandise. World of Disney is also home to one of Disney World's two **Bibbidi Bobbidi Boutiques,** sort-of salons that can turn your snot-nosed tomboy into a little princess (the second location is inside Cinderella Castle in the Magic Kingdom). At the boutique, girls can try on various princess costumes before repairing to the beauty parlor for hairstyling, makeup, a manicure, and even a princess gown, depending on which of the three packages you choose. Girls can choose between three hairstyles—Disney Diva, Pop Princess, or Fairytale Princess. At 2 p.m. daily, the newly minted princesses and divas are invited to participate in the Princess Parade. Holding onto a rope adorned with bells, the girls are walked from World of Disney to the carousel in Downtown Disney and given a personalized certificate. Call the boutique at ☎ 407-WDW-STYLE for more details.

Bibbidi Bobbidi Boutique costs a bundle, but this Northport, Alabama, mother of a 4-year-old thought it was worth it:

> *Yes, we spent $200, but the look on my daughter's face was priceless as she walked to the castle to eat. Everyone spoke to her, calling her "Princess." There hasn't been a day in three months since we've been home that she has not asked to go back.*

If you don't have $200 in loose change lying around, there are alternatives, as a dollar-conscious Kalamazoo, Michigan, mom explains:

The tip that tickled me the most in your book, which we have used every year, is taking little girls to the Harmony Barber Shop [on Main Street, U.S.A.] to get their hair done. I think I spent about $12, including tip. You don't need reservations, and in my opinion they do a better job than Bibbidi Bobbidi Boutique. We never waited more than an hour for my daughter to have her hair done. They put it into a teased bun and use brightly colored paints and colorful confetti to match whatever princess dress she had on. I understand that Disney doesn't want the barber shop to compete with the BBB, so I don't know if I want you telling anyone this great secret or not!

Pleasure Island . . . or What's Left of It

This nighttime-entertainment complex largely shut down in September 2008. Restaurants and stores are slated to replace the clubs, but in the meantime a few shops remain that are worth a look. **Apricot Lane Boutique** features brand-name denim, women's apparel, and a selection of gifts including Vera Bradley totes. The small shop adjacent to **Raglan Road Irish Pub & Restaurant** stocks a nice selection of Irish goods (surprise, surprise) ranging from kitschy to cute. **Curl by Sammy Duvall** offers men's, women's, and children's summer clothing, along with watches, sunglasses, and lots of bathing suits. **Fuego by Sosa Cigars** is an upscale cigar bar.

As a side note, some shops in Downtown Disney contain props from the old clubs of Pleasure Island. One such example is the split zebra cabinet in D-Street, a remnant from the Adventurer's Club.

Downtown Disney West Side

The West Side opens daily at 10:30 a.m. This is the hip extension of the Marketplace, with shops that are full of fun tchotchkes for compulsive buyers.

TOP SHOPS ON DOWNTOWN DISNEY WEST SIDE

BLINK BY WET SEAL The latest in denim for young women.

DISNEY'S CANDY CAULDRON Watch as gooey treats are made in the open kitchen. You can buy everything from jelly beans to caramel apples and cotton candy—more than 200 sweets are on the shelves.

D-STREET The newest addition to the West Side, this shop offers an eclectic mix of urban-chic apparel for men and women. It also houses the largest and most extensive collection of Vinylmation figurines, apparel, and accessories, plus a Vinylmation Creation Station where you can customize blank figures with markers.

★ **HOYPOLOI** Not a set of mouse ears in sight, but one of our favorite shops, with one-of-a-kind pieces of art from various regions of the United States—Zen water fountains, contemporary art, blown glass, wooden boxes, and Judaica including mezuzahs and menorahs.

ORLANDO HARLEY-DAVIDSON Sit on a real Harley and shop for Harley outerwear, including men's and women's T-shirts and (of course) leather jackets. You can even customize your own leather vest.

POP GALLERY The sister store to Hoypoloi, this gallery-like shop features a wide variety of contemporary art, including limited-edition sculptures and paintings, high-end gift items, and even a small collection of inexpensive souvenirs such as art-instruction kits and brightly painted ceramic piggy banks.

SOSA FAMILY CIGARS They hand-roll 'em here and feature premium imports, including Arturo Fuente, Cuesta-Rey, Diamond Crown, La Gloria Cubana, Macanudo, Puros Indios, Padrón, Partagas, and Sosa. A walk-in humidor stores the top brands.

SUNGLASS ICON Designer sunglasses and eyewear.

THE MAGIC KINGDOM

BECAUSE THE MAGIC KINGDOM is usually the most crowded theme park, you're best off browsing the shops in the early afternoon, when attractions are crowded. Much of the non-Disney merchandise that was once available here has disappeared from the shelves. For instance, longtime visitors may remember Liberty Square's Olde World Antiques, which sold unique brass, silver, and pewter, but today it's a shop full of Disney Christmas ornaments. Or remember when the Yankee Trader stocked soufflé dishes and escargot holders? Now it's mostly kitchenware.

MAIN STREET, U.S.A. Because this area stays open an hour after the official park closing, you could save your shopping time until the end of the day; just be prepared for crowds. Two shops here are of note: If you want a monogrammed mouse-ears hat,

unofficial **TIP**
Store your purchases in lockers at the Main Street rail station while you tour, or have them forwarded from shops to Package Pick-Up and retrieve them when you leave the park.

★ **The Chapeau on Main Street** has scores of them, along with a nice selection of other Disney-themed hats. At **The Emporium,** a Disney superstore, you can browse among four huge rooms categorized by kids' apparel, adult apparel, toys and costumes, and souvenirs. It's one-stop shopping if time is of the essence.

Fun for browsing is **Crystal Arts.** Glassblowers entertain, and the merchandise includes jewelry, swords, Disney figurines, and traditional glass and crystal. Occupying prime real estate on the corner of Town Square, **Main Street Confectionery** is the biggest candy shop in all four theme parks, with every sweet imaginable. Watch as cast members make fudge and dip apples in caramel. For expensive jewelry, lots of Disney pins, and Lenox and Armani figurines, as well as some handbags and accessories, check out **Uptown Jewelers.** Lots of parents bring babies and toddlers to the **Harmony Barber Shop** (open daily, 9 a.m.–6 p.m.; make reservations in advance by calling 407-WDW-DINE) for their first haircut, but anyone can stop in for a trim. For interactive spending, let the artists at **The Shadow Box,** a tiny kiosk in the alcove between Crystal Arts and Uptown Jewelers, snip your silhouette out of black paper (similar kiosks can be found in Liberty Square). Inside the Main Street Cinema you'll find yet another **Art of Disney** that replicates the merchandise found in the other Art of Disney stores around the parks, including the new collectible fad Vinylmation (see page 746). **Box Office Gifts,** inside Town Square Theatre near the entrance to the park, sells a small selection of pins, as well as film and photo supplies, including picture frames and scrapbooks. It's also where you purchase the photos cast members take of you and your family as you enter the park.

ADVENTURELAND Across from The Magic Carpets of Aladdin, **Agrabah Bazaar** and the adjacent **Zanzibar Trading Co.** specialize in safari-themed clothing and toys, Aladdin merchandise, and moderately priced imports from Africa. The shops are worth a look solely for their wide selection of beautifully handcrafted African sculptures, masks, and pottery. Near Pirates of the Caribbean, the **Plaza del Sol Caribe Bazaar** carries an ample selection of Pirates merchandise, including costumes, play sets, men's and women's T-shirts, swords, eye patches, and Jack Sparrow dreadlocks. Young pirate wannabes can join Captain Jack's crew at **The Pirates League** in the same plaza, where three packages offer buccaneer make-overs and souvenir portraits. **Island Supply Company,** across from the Swiss Family Treehouse, carries men's and women's clothing from such designers as O'Neill, Roxy, and Quiksilver.

FRONTIERLAND The **Frontier Trading Post** has been converted into a Disney pin-trading shop; **Big Al's,** a small kiosk across the way, sells a very limited selection of frontier-themed items. Those who forget to try the fudge at the Main Street Confectionery have another chance at the **Prairie Outpost,** a small bakery and candy shop. **Briar Patch** is a small store that sells kids' apparel and hats for the whole family. **Splash Mountain Shop** sells hats, Magic Kingdom merchandise, personalized accessories, and Vinylmation.

LIBERTY SQUARE Heritage House sells patriotic-themed souvenirs, T-shirts, and seasonal mementos. **Ye Olde Christmas Shoppe** is a repeat of the holiday shops in all the other Disney parks. **Yankee Trader Gourmet Shop,** near The Haunted Mansion, stocks primarily house-wares such as character aprons, plates, and picture frames.

FANTASYLAND Shops are themed to the attractions, like **Hundred Acre Goods** at The Many Adventures of Winnie the Pooh and **Seven Dwarfs' Mine** near Snow White's Scary Adventures. A favorite of little girls is ★ **Castle Couture,** with a large selection of princess costumes—Belle, Snow White, Cinderella, and others. A second **Bibbidi Bobbidi Boutique** is in the breezeway of Cinderella Castle. Reservations are strongly recommended; call ☎ 407-WDW-STYLE.

TOMORROWLAND The sci-fi stock in **Merchant of Venus** is limited to items with a Disney tie-in. You'll find a large selection of Vinylmation, as well as a sampling of *Star Wars,* Power Rangers, and Pirates of the Caribbean products. A corner of the store is occupied by a photo station, where guests can have their faces transplanted onto a character from a favorite *Star Wars* or Disney scene. The adjacent **Mickey's Star Traders** is a general Walt Disney World souvenir shop. While the decor has a Tomorrowland theme, there's no space- or future-themed merchandise here. Neither shop is a must-see unless you're killing time. **Space Mountain Shop,** at the exit of the iconic attraction, features apparel and accessories and a large selection of cell-phone, tablet, and e-reader accessories.

EPCOT

WE ENJOY WANDERING IN AND OUT of the shops in the 11 World Showcase pavilions, looking for unusual finds and bargains. Often you'll see sale items, especially in the shops in France and Italy, but most of the imported merchandise is relatively expensive. However, the Epcot shops may be among the few places in the United States that carry some of the merchandise found here.

Aside from World Showcase, two stores in Future World are worth a mention: **MouseGear,** on the east side of Future World, is the biggest Disney shop in any of the four theme parks. You can find almost any Disney merchandise here, and there's an enormous selection of adult and children's clothing. Prices and selection are about the same as at other Disney merchandise shops. On the other side of Future World is **The Art of Disney,** featuring Vinylmation figures, framed artwork, Giuseppe Armani and Lenox figurines, and character models.

Walking clockwise around World Showcase, you'll find:

★ **MEXICO** The foyer of this pavilion is home to the **Animales Fantásticos: Spirits in Wood** kiosk, which sells hand-carved and hand-painted animal sculptures in brilliant fluorescent colors. You can watch an artist paint and sand individual creations as you browse—and browsing is what we suggest: Even the smallest items (we're talking a 2-inch-long turtle) are in the $15-and-up neighborhood. From there, let your eyes adjust to the dim light in the **Plaza de los Amigos,** a lovely re-creation of a charming Mexican city at dusk; here, a live mariachi band often entertains passersby. Carts and kiosks are piled with blankets, sombreros, paper flowers, and tambourines. Sure, the merchandise may be cheaper south of the border, but these prices aren't bad: Piñatas are wildly popular, starting at about $10, while blankets start at $20. Or pick up a good bottle of tequila or hot sauce to pack home. Two shops along the perimeter are **La Princesa Cristal** (a small crystal shop) and an unnamed store that sells leather handbags, wallets, and jewelry. **La Cava del Tequila** is a new bar serving more than 70 varieties of tequila, plus margaritas and appetizers.

★ **NORWAY The Puffin's Roost** is a series of small shopping galleries with popular imports such as trolls (from $15) and wooden Christmas ornaments ($4 and up). Other hard-to-find imports include Laila perfume and body lotion as well as Helly Hansen and Dale of Norway clothing, including thick woolen sweaters. You'll also find sterling-silver jewelry, butterfly pins, and classic Viking hats (with or without braids).

★ **CHINA** This pavilion features one of our favorite shops, piled with imports from real silk kimonos to cloisonné and thick silk rugs. **House of Good Fortune** is more like a rambling department store than a shop. You'll find everything here from silk fans to $4,000 jade sculptures to antique furniture. The silk dresses and robes are competitively priced in the $100 range. Darling handbags are $10 and up, and silk ties are $19. We always admire the handwoven pure-silk carpets, starting around $320 for a 2-foot rug and topping out around $2,500 for a 4 x 8–foot rug. The prices are comparable to what you'd pay in a retail shop—if you could find one that imports carpets like these.

Village Traders, a shop between China and Germany, sells African woodcarvings that are as unusual as they come. Every day, an artist carves new creations using a special tool called a *ngomo*. Guests can even commission individual sculptures if they're willing to pay extra for the privilege.

★ **GERMANY** Shops interconnect on both sides of the cobblestoned central plaza and purvey an impressive collection of imports. Tiny **Das Kaufhaus** stocks a nice selection of Adidas sportswear. Next door is **Volkskunst,** where the walls are covered with Schneider cuckoo clocks and the shelves are stocked with limited-edition steins and glassware. Next is **Der Teddybär,** featuring Engel-Puppen dolls and Steiff plush toys, among other delights for kids. Across the plaza, **Kunstarbeit in Kristall** carries a fabulous collection of Swarovski crystal, including pins, glassware, and Arribas Brothers collectibles (check out the limited-edition $37,500 replica of Cinderella Castle, blinged out with more than 20,000 Swarovski crystals). Next is the **Weinkeller,** with nearly 300 varieties of German wine. Step through the door to **Die Weihnachts Ecke,** where Christmas ornaments and handmade nutcrackers are on display year-round. Anyone with a sweet tooth will go crazy just smelling the newest addition to Germany's lineup, **Karamell-Küche.** Treats are made in-house with Werther's Original caramel, from caramel apples to cookies and candies made or drizzled with caramel. You'll also find an impressive selection of Werther's Original candies.

★ **ITALY Il Bel Cristallo** showcases Puma sportswear, Bulgari and Ferragamo fragrances, Giuseppe Armani figurines from Florence, elaborate Venetian masks, and a small selection of Christmas decorations in the back room. Across the walkway, **Enoteca Castello** offers a small wine room with tastings, along with Perugina candies, olive oils, pastas, and Murano glass.

THE AMERICAN ADVENTURE Heritage Manor Gifts carries patriotic gifts with a twist, such as American-made candy, regional souvenirs, and lots of American flag–inspired apparel.

★ **JAPAN** A U.S. branch of Japan's 300-year-old **Mitsukoshi Department Store** stretches along one entire side of the pavilion. Kid-friendly merchandise—Hello Kitty, Naruto, and Yu-Gi-Oh!—fills the front, with kimonos, slippers, handbags, and lots more at the back of the store. Mitsukoshi's expanded culinary display includes a sake-tasting bar, along with chopsticks, pretty rice bowls, a large variety of teas and teapots, and imported snacks. Pricey Mikimoto pearls (rings, necklaces, earrings, and bracelets) are showcased in a separate room. And tourists line up for an oyster guaranteed to have a pearl in its shell (pearls are polished for you by the salesperson).

★ **MOROCCO** Several shops wend through this pavilion: **Tangier Traders** sells traditional Moroccan clothing, shoes, and fezzes; **Marketplace in the Medina** peddles straw bags, glass tea sets, ceramic-tile furniture, and belly-dancing kits; **The Brass Bazaar** features brass, of course, and ceramic and wooden kitchenware (not dishwasher safe); **Casablanca Carpets** offers a wider variety of Moroccan rugs, as well as decorative pieces such as abstract-shaped lamps, sequined pillows, and incense holders; and **Medina Arts,** which as of late appears to be an extension of the merchandise sold at the Brass Bazaar, stocks larger pottery and ceramic pieces.

★ **FRANCE** We always find a few moments to browse in **Plume et Palette,** a perfume shop with more than 100 imports. You'll find scents by Dior, Chanel, Givenchy, and other top names. Famed design house **Givenchy** recently opened a 300-square-foot cosmetics shop here—the only retail location in the United States to offer the full line of Givenchy makeup and skin-care products, as well as a large selection of fragrances. Cross over to **Les Vins de France** and **L'Esprit de la Provence,** two stores in one, with a wine room and a small selection of Provençal goods. At the back of the pavilion, **Souvenirs de France** offers T-shirts, traditional berets, Aristocats merchandise, and Eiffel Tower collectibles.

★ **UNITED KINGDOM** A handful of interesting imports is scattered throughout a half-dozen small shops. **The Toy Soldier** stocks costumes, books, and plush toys featuring English characters from favorite films, as well as British rock-and-roll-themed items, including Beatles merchandise. You'll find plenty of Alice in Wonderland, Peter Pan, and Winnie the Pooh merchandise here. Stop in **The Crown & Crest** to look up your family name in the coat-of-arms book, and the shop will create your family's insignia in a beautiful frame of choice. At the adjacent **Sportsman's Shoppe,** you'll find plenty of football (soccer) apparel, balls, and books.

Across the street, you'll find **The Queen's Table,** a gift shop with British-themed hats, clothing, glassware, and more. **Lords and Ladies,** a quaint store, offers lotions, soaps, scarves, jewelry, and perfume from the United Kingdom. **The Tea Caddy** stocks Twinings tea, biscuits, and candies.

★ **CANADA** There's not much shopping here, but **Northwest Mercantile** has a wide selection of merchandise, including NHL jerseys, T-shirts, sweatshirts, aprons, and pajamas. Bottles of ice wine and maple syrup make nice souvenirs for foodies.

DISNEY'S ANIMAL KINGDOM

THOUGH DISNEY MERCHANDISE DOMINATES, Animal Kingdom has a fair selection of animal-themed items. The largest cluster of shops is in the centrally located Discovery Island: **Disney Outfitters** carries men's, women's, and children's clothing and animal-themed items, as well as a selection of Disney souvenirs. Check out the carved animal totem poles in the center of the room. **Island Mercantile** offers more (yawn) Disney-character merchandise; and **Creature Comforts** is the best stop for children's clothing and toys.

In Africa, ★ **Mombasa Marketplace** and the adjoining **Ziwani Traders** showcases reasonably priced African-themed pottery, musical instruments, South African wines, and housewares, plus plenty of plush animal toys and a large selection of Animal Kingdom–themed merchandise. Asia has several open-air kiosks, but the main attraction in shopping is the ★ **Bhaktapur Market,** next to Yak & Yeti Restaurant. The venue is small but packed with extraordinary themed merchandise, including cast-iron teapots and tea sets; sushi kits and Asian cookbooks; bonsai kits; origami; and some beautiful Southeast Asian–inspired clothing, PJs, and shoes for women and children. At Expedition Everest's exit is

Serka Zong Bazaar, where the merchandise is more interesting than that of most post-attraction shops. Although mostly Disney branded, the goods don't scream Mickey Mouse. The selection is mostly Everest- and Yeti-themed, with T-shirts, apparel, collectibles, and historical books and videos for those interested in the legend of the Yeti.

Chester & Hester's Dinosaur Treasures in DinoLand U.S.A. is worth a look simply to check out the amusing architecture. The atmosphere inside is reminiscent of a dollar store (although the prices can't compare)—the merchandise is now mostly Disney-branded souvenirs. **The Dino Institute Shop** has dino-themed clothing, dinosaur figurines, books, and toys.

DISNEY'S HOLLYWOOD STUDIOS

ON HOLLYWOOD BOULEVARD, just to the left of the park entrance, is a California Mission–style house called ★ **Sid Cahuenga's One-of-a-Kind,** which is loosely inspired by junk shops in southern California, the land of movie stars. You'll find plenty of autographed photos of film and TV stars, old movie posters, even costumes worn by celebrities on daytime soaps and in recent and vintage films.

Other shops on the right side of the street include **The Darkroom,** for Kodak cameras, film, and accessories; **Celebrity 5 & 10,** with men's, women's, and children's T-shirts and other small souvenirs; and **L.A. Prop Cinema Storage,** full of kids' clothing (mostly for girls), PJs, and lots of toys and plushes (there's also a substantial infant area). **Adrian & Edith's Head to Toe** has an embroidery station where you can get any Disney item embroidered with a name, phrase, or character of your choice. (One caveat: The item needs to have been purchased on Disney property and be unworn.) On the left side of the street, **Mickey's of Hollywood** carries plush toys, watches, T-shirts, hats, sunglasses, and more—virtually none without a Disney logo—while **Keystone Clothiers** offers an array of Disney wear for grown-ups. There's plenty to look at but not much to recommend.

On Sunset Boulevard, **Sunset Club Couture** carries a sizable stock of Disney jewelry and scads of watches, as well as clothing and Disney collectibles. **Mouse About Town** features men's apparel and accessories. **Legends of Hollywood,** also on the boulevard, is home to souvenirs and other gifts.

Elsewhere in the park: ★ **Animation Gallery** in the Animation Courtyard carries an impressive collection of paintings, sculptures, and other artwork. You'll pay the same price here as in all the other Disney art galleries. You can pick up a hat or trench coat just like Harrison Ford's, or an Indy-style T-shirt, action figure, or Mickey plush at the **Indiana Jones Adventure Outpost** outside the amphitheater. **Stage 1 Company Store** carries a wide variety of Muppet- and *Phineas and Ferb*–themed merchandise; *Star Wars* fans will eat their hearts out at ★ **Tatooine Traders,** where everything from light-saber key chains to $200 glass light-saber collectibles is for sale. **In Character,** next to *Voyage of the Little Mermaid,* is the best spot in the Studios for Disney-princess dress-up clothes and accessories for little ones. The new **Toy Story Dept.,** across from Toy Story Mania!, offers Toy Story and Disney/Pixar souvenirs and toys.

DISNEY OUTLET STORES

ORLANDO IS HOME to two **Disney's Character** stores at each of the **Orlando Premium Outlets**—one at the north end of International Drive (☎ 407-354-3255; **premiumoutlets.com/orlando**), and another off Vineland Avenue (☎ 407-477-0222). The I-Drive store, **Disney's Character Warehouse** (in the complex's Mall 1), gets liquidation merchandise directly from Walt Disney World stores, so you never know what you'll find. **Disney's Character Premiere** outlet, at the Vineland location, has even more sale-price souvenirs of similar selection and vintage.

A Kentucky family had a hard time getting to the I-Drive location:

> *Avoid International Drive between the Beachline Expressway and Oak Ridge Road. After crawling for what seemed like an hour, we reached Premium Outlets. Take Interstate 4 directly to the Oak Ridge Road exit. It's much faster.*

SHOPPING *beyond* WALT DISNEY WORLD

CELEBRATION

"THE TOWN THAT DISNEY BUILT," near Walt Disney World off US 192 (**celebrationfl.com**), gets its fair share of tourists who like to stroll the sidewalks. No one shop is worth going out of the way for, but you'll find good restaurants here (including Italian, Spanish, and American), as well as a two-screen theater and a handful of shops. Because Celebration is an upscale community, the shops are all high-end.

Celebration residents often gather on the patio of **Starbucks** for a freshly brewed cuppa joe. Specialty stores include **Market Street Gallery,** with year-round Christmas décor, candles, jewelry, and gifts for the home; **Sanrio Surprises,** dedicated to all things Hello Kitty; **Lollipop Cottage,** a children's clothing shop; **Woof Gang Bakery,** which sells fun items for furry friends, including fresh-baked treats; **Confetti,** a monogramming and personalized-stationery store that also sells candies and other snacks; **Unique Boutique,** an affordably priced shop with small-label designer items; **Soft as a Grape,** offering casual clothing for the whole family; **Jewel Box,** featuring fine jewelry, diamonds, and watches; and **Kilwin's Chocolates & Ice Cream,** an extraordinary confectionery.

UNIVERSAL CITYWALK

WHILE DOWNTOWN DISNEY is 120 acres (with a strolling area equivalent to about 10 city blocks), CityWalk (**citywalk.com**) comprises 30 acres in a relatively compact area between the two Universal theme parks. It features 10 shops to Downtown Disney's 32.

At both destinations, the shopping complements the restaurants and clubs. Without question, Disneyphiles will prefer Downtown Disney, where at least a third of the shops are Disney-themed. CityWalk is most comparable to the West Side at Downtown Disney—fun for browsing and impulse buys. Our favorites **The Endangered Species Store,** which offers wildlife-themed items, colorful skirts and dresses, and accessories; **Fresh Produce,** featuring swimsuits, comfy shorts, T-shirts, bags, and more; **Katie's Candy Company,** selling handmade fudge and other goodies, as well as bulk brand-name candies; and **Quiet Flight Surf Shop,** with merchandise from beachy brands such as Billabong, Element, Hurley, Nixon, Oakley, Quicksilver, Reef, Rip Curl, Roxy, Volcom, and Von Zipper.

For jewelry, **Fossil** has a notable collection of watches, as well as sunglasses and leather goods. **The Universal Studios Store** offers one-stop shopping for all theme park merchandise.

INTERNATIONAL DRIVE

"I-DRIVE" IS THE HEART of Central Florida's tourist district, jammed with hotels, motels, discount stores, and restaurants. Locals generally avoid the area except for the outlet malls (which we'll discuss separately).

*un**official* **TIP** CityWalk is open 11 a.m.–2 a.m. (although some stores may close earlier). Parking, though plentiful in the Universal garage, costs a steep $12 before 6 p.m. but only $3 in the evening.

On the more refined south end of International Drive is **Pointe Orlando** (9101 International Drive; ☎ 407-248-2838; **pointeorlando .com**), with a handful of stores. This complex gets a lot of its business from the convention center, less than a mile away, rather than from locals. Hours are Monday–Saturday, noon–10 p.m; Sunday, noon–8 p.m. (Bars and restaurants stay open later.)

Clothing stores at Pointe Orlando include **Chico's; Armani Exchange; Tropical Clothiers; Hollister; Tommy Bahama; Flow** and **Flow Boutique; Design by U,** with custom-embroidery options; **Synergy,** carrying Life Is Good merchandise; and **Victoria's Secret.**

Among the specialty shops are **Artsy Abode,** with Vera Bradley merchandise and Pandora jewelry; **Brighton Collectibles,** for small leather goods and watches; **Tharoo & Co.** jewelry boutique; **Image Leather,** featuring Italian-lambskin leather goods; **Mindful Minerals,** a natural-skin-care line; **Sunglass Hut,** offering shades from Ray-Ban and Prada; and **Bath & Body Works.** Pointe Orlando prices are full retail, but there are always sales.

*un**official* **TIP** If you're picky, a major department store's end-of-season sales often yield deals as good as or better than an outlet store's.

OUTLETS

LIKE EVERY MAJOR TOURIST DESTINA-TION in the United States, Central Florida has hundreds of factory-outlet stores, most of them near major attractions. Having spent many hours checking prices and merchandise, we generally conclude that at most stores you'll save about 20% on desirable merchandise and up to 75% on last-season (or older) stock. Some stores in the outlet malls are full retail or sell a few brands at a 20% discount and the rest at full price.

Orlando Premium Outlets–International Drive (☎ 407-352-9600; **primeoutlets.com/orlando;** open Monday–Saturday, 10 a.m.–11 p.m.; Sunday, 10 a.m.–9 p.m.), on the north end of I-Drive, features 175 of the world's hottest designers and brand names, among them **BCBG Max Azria Factory Store, Hugo Boss Factory Store, Ed Hardy, Ed Hardy Outlet, Kenneth Cole, Juicy Couture, Michael Kors, Saks Fifth Avenue**

OFF 5TH, Sean John Factory Store, St. John, Tommy Hilfiger, Under Armour, Victoria's Secret Outlet, and the only **Neiman Marcus Last Call Clearance Center** in Central Florida.

★ The second location, **Orlando Premium Outlets–Vineland Avenue** (☎ 407-238-7787; open Monday–Saturday, 10 a.m.–11 p.m.; Sunday, 10 a.m.–9 p.m.), is off I-4 (Exit 68) at Vineland, near Lake Buena Vista. An impressive array of 150 stores includes **Banana Republic Factory Store, Barneys New York Outlet, Brooks Brothers, Fendi, Giorgio Armani, Joe's Jeans, Nautica, Nike Factory Store, Kate Spade, Polo Ralph Lauren Factory Store, Salvatore Ferragamo, 7 For All Mankind,** and **Tory Burch.** You'll also find **Disney's Character Premiere,** featuring plenty of Disney merchandise, plus a food court and a convenient parking garage.

Festival Bay Mall (☎ 407-351-7718; **shopfestivalbaymall.com**), nearby on International Drive, includes **Bass Pro Shops Outdoor World, BCBG Max Azria, Rainbow, Ron Jon Surf Shop, Sheplers Western Wear,** and a handful of small shops. Other big draws are **Monkey Joe's,** an indoor kids' play area filled with inflatable gyms; a 20-screen movie theater; and a **Vans Skatepark.**

Another popular outlet center is **Lake Buena Vista Factory Stores** (☎ 407-238-9301; **lbvfs.com**), on FL 535 near Walt Disney World (take Exit 68 off I-4, then go 2 miles south on FL 535). Hours are Monday–Saturday, 10 a.m.–9 p.m.; Sunday, 10 a.m.–7 p.m. We were a little disappointed by the inventory, and the discounts were mostly in the 10–20% range. Key tenants include **Converse, Eddie Bauer, Gap Outlet, Izod, Levi's, LOFT Outlet, Nike Factory Store, Nine West, Old Navy, Oshkosh B'Gosh, Samsonite, Tommy Hilfiger, VF Outlet,** and **Reebok.**

TRADITIONAL SHOPPING

THE PREMIER SHOPPING EXPERIENCE in Central Florida is **The Mall at Millenia** (☎ 407-363-3555; **mallatmillenia.com**), anchored by **Bloomingdale's, Macy's,** and **Neiman Marcus.** Other stores include **Cartier, Burberry, Crate & Barrel, Tiffany & Co., Gucci,** and **Louis Vuitton.** Clothing options include **Anthropologie, lululemon athletica, Burberry, Betsey Johnson, Henri Bendel,** and **Urban Outfitters.** Hours are Monday–Saturday, 10 a.m.–9 p.m.; Sunday, noon–7 p.m.

★ **The Florida Mall** (☎ 407-851-6255; **simon.com**) is the biggest in the area, with about 200 shops, including **Coach, Saks Fifth Avenue, Macy's, M•A•C Cosmetics, Nordstrom,** and **Sephora.** Go early and park near one of the major stores you want to explore. The mall is at 8001 S. Orange Blossom Trail, at the corner of Sand Lake Road (FL 482) and South Orange Blossom Trail (US 441); hours are Monday–Saturday, 10 a.m.–9 p.m.; Sunday, noon–6 p.m.

PART TWENTY-THREE

NIGHTLIFE
in and out of
WALT DISNEY WORLD

WALT DISNEY WORLD
at NIGHT

DISNEY SO CLEVERLY CONSPIRES to exhaust you during the day that the thought of night activity sends most visitors into shock. Walt Disney World, however, offers much for the hearty and the nocturnal to do in the evenings.

IN THE THEME PARKS

EPCOT'S MAJOR EVENING EVENT is *IllumiNations,* a laser and fireworks show at World Showcase Lagoon. Showtime is listed in the daily entertainment schedule (*Times Guide*).

In the Magic Kingdom are the popular evening parade(s); *The Magic, The Memories and You!,* in which digital photos of Walt Disney World guests are projected onto Cinderella Castle; and the *Wishes* fireworks show. Consult the *Times Guide* for performances.

On selected nights when the park is open late, Disney's Hollywood Studios features *Fantasmic!,* a laser, special-effects, and water spectacular (see page 621). The *Times Guide* lists showtimes.

Disney's Animal Kingdom offers no nighttime entertainment.

AT THE HOTELS

A SORT OF MAIN STREET ELECTRICAL PARADE on barges, the **Floating Electrical Pageant** stars creatures of the sea. This nightly spectacle, with background music played on a doozy of a synthesizer, is one of our favorite Disney productions. The first performance of the short but captivating show is at 9 p.m. off the Polynesian Resort docks. From there, it circles around and repeats at the Grand Floridian Resort & Spa at 9:15 p.m., heading afterward to Fort Wilderness Resort & Campground, Wilderness Lodge & Villas, and the Contemporary Resort–Bay Lake Tower.

For something more elaborate, consider a dinner theater. If you want to go honky-tonkin', the Buena Vista Palace, Hilton, and Royal Plaza hotels at the Downtown Disney Resort Area have lively (all right, all right, *relatively* lively) bars.

Speaking of bars, Disney hotels, the BoardWalk, and Downtown Disney have them, too. Be prepared, however, for an odd wrinkle, as described by this reader:

> I understand Disney is all about kids, but we tried to go into a resort bar at 8 p.m. for some drinks, and there were three children running wild playing Duck-Duck-Goose. This would not fly in any bar at home, but we were told there was nothing to be done, as "It's Disney."

If you're into family films, all Disney resorts offer outdoor movies each evening. The largest, most permanent screen is at Fort Wilderness Resort & Campground. Other resorts use inflatable screens set up near their pools. Movie schedules are available at the front desk.

AT ANIMAL KINGDOM LODGE For children, there's African storytelling around a campfire each night, followed by a movie shown by the pool. In addition, kids can march around the lobby each evening at 8 p.m. during the **Zawadi Primal Parade.** Finally, guests can view animals after dark using night-vision goggles.

AT THE BOARDWALK **Jellyrolls** features dueling pianos and sing-alongs. **Big River Grille & Brewing Works** is Disney's first and only brewpub (see dining profile on page 464). Completing the BoardWalk's entertainment mix are the **ESPN Club,** a sports bar; the **Atlantic Dance Hall,** an upscale but largely deserted dance club; and several restaurants. Access is by foot from Epcot, by ferry from Disney's Hollywood Studios, and by bus from other Disney World locations. The *Unofficial Guide* research team rates Jellyrolls as its second favorite of all Disney nightspots (**Raglan Road Irish Pub & Restaurant** at Downtown Disney is our top pick). It's raucous, frequently hilarious, and positively rejuvenating. The piano players are outstanding. Best of all, it's strictly for adults.

AT CORONADO SPRINGS RESORT Perhaps Disney's hippest nightspot is the 5,000-square-foot **Rix Lounge,** a Vegas-ultralounge clone. DJs spin Top 40 tracks from 9 p.m. to 2 a.m.; a percussion band performs on select evenings. Few locals or resort guests have discovered Rix, so the place is frequently dead unless there's a big meeting or trade show at Coronado Springs. Also at this resort is the **Laguna Bar,** a romantic outdoor-terrace affair arrayed alongside the lake.

AT FORT WILDERNESS RESORT & CAMPGROUND The free nightly campfire program begins with a sing-along led by Chip 'n' Dale and progresses to cartoons and a Disney movie. For Disney lodging guests only.

AT DOWNTOWN DISNEY

PLEASURE ISLAND Walt Disney World's nighttime-entertainment complex cashed in its chips in the fall of 2008. Gone for good are the BET Soundstage Club, Mannequins Dance Palace, Motion, 8 TRAX, the Comedy Warehouse, and the much-loved Adventurers Club. This last so exemplified Disney whimsy that everyone thought it would surely escape the ax. No such luck. All the Pleasure Island restaurants survived, though, as did a few shops. For now, the only live-music venue is **Raglan Road Irish Pub & Restaurant** (see page 488).

DOWNTOWN DISNEY MARKETPLACE It's flog-your-wallet each night at the Marketplace, with shops open until 11:30 p.m.

DOWNTOWN DISNEY WEST SIDE This 70-acre shopping, restaurant, and nightlife complex is to the left of Pleasure Island. This area features a 24-screen **AMC** movie complex; **DisneyQuest,** a pay-for-play indoor theme park (see page 726); a permanent showplace for **Cirque du Soleil**'s extraordinary *La Nouba* (see profile below); and a **House of Blues** concert hall with a seating capacity of 2,000. Dining options include **Planet Hollywood;** a 450-seat Cajun restaurant at **House of Blues; Wolfgang Puck Grand Cafe** (serving California fare); and **Bongos Cuban Cafe,** owned by Gloria and Emilio Estefan. The complex is accessible via Disney buses from most Disney World locations.

Cirque du Soleil *La Nouba* ★★★★★

APPEAL BY AGE   UNDER 21 ★★★★   21–37 ★★★★★
38–50 ★★★★   51 AND UP ★★★★½

Type of show Circus as theater. **Tickets and information** ☎ 407-939-7600; **cirque dusoleil.com/lanouba. Admission cost** *Category Front & Center:* $132.06 adults, $108.63 children ages 3–9; *Category 1:* $120.35 adults, $94.79 children; *Category 2:* $94.79 adults, $76.69 children; *Category 3:* $77.75 adults, $61.77 children. Box Office *Only:* $56.45 adults, $45.80 children (to buy tickets at this level, you must call or visit the box office directly). All prices include tax. **Cast size** 72. **Night of lowest attendance** Thursday. **Usual showtimes** Tuesday–Saturday, 6 p.m. and 9 p.m. **Authors' rating** ★★★★★. **Duration of presentation** 1 hour, 45 minutes (no intermission) plus preshow.

DESCRIPTION AND COMMENTS *La Nouba* is a far cry from a traditional circus but retains all the fun and excitement of it. It is whimsical, mystical, and sophisticated, yet pleasing to all ages. The action takes place on an elaborate stage that incorporates almost every part of the theater. The original musical score is exotic, like the show.

Note: In the following paragraphs, we get into how the show *feels* and why it's special. If you don't care how it feels, or if you're not up to slogging through a boxcar of adjectives, just trust us when we tell you that *La Nouba* is great. See it.

La Nouba is a most difficult show to describe. To categorize it as a circus doesn't begin to cover its depth, though its performers could perform with distinction in any circus on earth. *La Nouba* is more, much more, than a circus. It combines elements of classical Greek theater, mime, the English morality play, Dalí surrealism, Fellini characterization, and Chaplin comedy. *La Nouba* is at once an odyssey, a symphony, and an exploration of human emotions.

The show pivots on its humor, which is sometimes black, and engages the audience with its unforgettable characters. Though light and uplifting, it is also poignant and dark. Simple in presentation, it is at the same time extraordinarily intricate, always operating on multiple levels of meaning. As you laugh and watch the amazingly talented cast, your mind enters a dimension seldom encountered in a waking state. The presentation begins to register in your consciousness more as a seamless dream than as a stage production. You're moved, lulled, and soothed as well as excited and entertained. The sensitive, the imaginative, the literate, and those who love good theater and art will find nothing in all of Disney World that compares with *La Nouba*.

Thus far, as the following comments suggest, we have not received one negative comment about *La Nouba*.

From an Iowa City, Iowa, couple:

In terms of shows and attractions, Cirque du Soleil was absolutely wonderful and anyone with the time should make an attempt to go. I could go on and on about it, but I think just "GO!" is enough.

The comments of a mom from Kansasville, Wisconsin, whose teens reluctantly consented to attend the show:

Even my hard-to-impress MTV-generation teens were awestruck.

Finally, from an Andover, Massachusetts, mother:

One of the true highlights of the trip was seeing Cirque du Soleil. The ticket prices were a bit steep and I debated doing it. But I thought it might be enjoyable for my non-Disney-loving husband and decided it was no more expensive than the rest of the trip. In fact, we all loved it, and it was the best money we spent.

TOURING TIPS Be forewarned that the audience is an integral part of *La Nouba* and that at almost any time you might be plucked from your seat to participate. Our advice is to loosen up and roll with it. If you don't want to get involved, politely but firmly decline to be conscripted. Then fix a death grip on the arms of your chair. Tickets for reserved seats can be purchased in advance at the Cirque box office or over the phone, using your credit card. Don't wait until the last minute; book well in advance from home.

House of Blues

Type of show Live concerts with an emphasis on rock and blues. **Tickets and information** ☎ 407-934-BLUE (2583); **hob.com. Admission cost with taxes** About $8–$95, depending on who's performing. **Nights of lowest attendance** Monday and Tuesday. **Usual showtimes** Vary between 7 p.m. and 9:30 p.m., depending on who's performing.

DESCRIPTION AND COMMENTS The House of Blues, developed by original Blues Brother Dan Aykroyd, features a restaurant and blues bar, as well as the concert hall. The restaurant serves Thursday–Saturday, 11 a.m.–1:30 a.m., which makes it one of the few late-night-dining options in Walt Disney World. Live music cranks up every night at 10:30 p.m. in the restaurant–blues bar, but even before then, the joint is way beyond 110 decibels. The music hall next door features concerts by an eclectic array of musicians and groups. During one visit, the show bill listed gospel, blues, funk, ska, dance, salsa, rap, zydeco, hard rock, groove rock, and reggae groups over a two-week period.

TOURING TIPS Prices vary from night to night according to the fame and drawing power of the featured band. Tickets ranged from $8 to $62 during our visits but go higher when a really big name is scheduled.

The music hall is set up like a nightclub, with tables and bar stools for only about 150 people and standing room for a whopping 1,850 people. Folks dance when there's room and sometimes when there isn't. The tables and stools are first-come, first-served, with doors opening an hour before showtime on weekdays and 90 minutes before showtime on weekends. Acoustics are good, and the showroom is small enough to provide a relatively intimate concert experience. All shows are all ages unless otherwise indicated.

Sunday night at the House of Blues is Service Industry Night (a.k.a. SIN), when hospitality-industry employees (read: Disney cast members) get in free; other folks are welcome but pay a cover of $8 (age 21 and older). A Florida Gen Y reader describes it:

Ahh, SIN night . . . there's always a DJ who will play club music, and all the times I went it was packed. It's more of a club atmosphere, and both floors are open for people to dance and mingle, but it's still a great time for tourists if they want to stay on-property and dance all night. Basically, each Sunday night is a huge party there.

WALT DISNEY WORLD DINNER THEATERS

SEVERAL DINNER-THEATER SHOWS play each night at Walt Disney World, and unlike other Disney dining venues, they make hard reservations instead of Advance Reservations, meaning you must guarantee your reservation ahead of time with a credit card. You'll receive a confirmation number and be told to pick up your tickets at a Disney-hotel Guest Relations desk. Unless you cancel your tickets at least 48 hours before your reservation time, your credit card will still be charged the full amount. Dinner-show reservations can be made 180 days in advance; call ☎ 407-939-3463. While getting reservations for the *Spirit of Aloha Dinner Show* isn't terribly tough, booking the *Hoop-Dee-Doo Musical Revue* is a trick of the first order.

> *unofficial* **TIP**
> To make reservations for the *Hoop-Dee-Doo Musical Revue,* call as soon as you're certain of the dates of your visit. The earlier you call, the better your seats will be.

A couple from Bismarck, North Dakota, explains:

> *I'm glad we made our reservations so early (a year in advance). I was able to reserve space for us at* Spirit of Aloha *at the Polynesian and the* Hoop-Dee-Doo Musical Revue. *At both of these, they seat you according to when you made your reservation. At the* Hoop-Dee-Doo Musical Revue, *we had a front-center table. We were so close to the stage, we could see how many cavities the performers had!*

If you can't get reservations and want to see one of the shows:

1. Call ☎ 407-939-3463 at 9 a.m. each morning while you're at Disney World to make a same-day reservation. There are three performances each night, and for all three combined, only 3–24 people total will be admitted with same-day reservations.

2. Arrive at the show of your choice 45 minutes before showtime (early and late shows are your best bets) and put your name on the standby list. If someone with reservations fails to show, you may be admitted.

Borrowing a page from Vegas strip joints where nearsighted old coots are charged extra to sit way up front, Disney offers tiered seating for the *Hoop-Dee-Doo Musical Revue* and the *Spirit of Aloha Dinner Show*. The best seats are in Category 1. Next comes Category 2, with seats off to the side or behind Category 1. Finally, Category 3 seats are at the Orlando Greyhound station, where you watch the show on a video feed. Just making sure you're still with us—actually, they're farther still to the side or back, or on another level from the stage. For both the *Spirit of Aloha Dinner Show* and the *Hoop-Dee-Doo Musical Revue*, there's a good view from almost all seats, so you can decide if sitting closer to the action is worth the extra bucks.

Hoop-Dee-Doo Musical Revue

Pioneer Hall, Fort Wilderness Campground ☎ 407-939-3463. **Showtimes** 5, 7:15, and 9:30 p.m. nightly. **Cost** $55–$68 adults, $28–$35 children ages 3–9. Prices include tax and gratuity. **Discounts** Seasonal. **Type of seating** Tables of various sizes to fit the number in each party, set in an Old West–style dance hall. **Menu** All-you-can-eat barbecue ribs, fried chicken, corn, and strawberry shortcake. **Vegetarian alternative** On request (at least 24 hours in advance). **Beverages** Unlimited beer, wine, sangria, and soft drinks.

DESCRIPTION AND COMMENTS Six Wild West performers arrive by stagecoach (sound effects only) to entertain the crowd inside Pioneer Hall. There isn't much of a plot, just corny jokes interspersed with song or dance. The humor is of the *Hee Haw* ilk, but it's presented enthusiastically.

Audience participation includes sing-alongs, hand clapping, and a finale that uses volunteers to play parts on stage. Performers are accompanied by a banjo player and pianist who also play quietly while the food is being served. The fried chicken and corn on the cob are good, the ribs a bit tough though tasty. With the all-you-can-eat policy, at least you can get your money's worth by stuffing yourself silly.

Traveling to Fort Wilderness and absorbing the rustic atmosphere of Pioneer Hall augments the adventure. For repeat Disney World visitors, an annual visit to the revue is a tradition of sorts. Plus, warts and all, the revue is all Disney, and for some folks that's enough. The fact that performances sell out far in advance gives the experience a special aura.

Most of our readers enjoy the *Hoop-Dee-Doo Musical Revue,* but not all, as this letter from a Texas family attests:

What is all the hoop-dee-doo with the Hoop-Dee-Doo Musical Revue? *The food was OK, if "gut busting" fare is your idea of a fine night out, and the entertainment was pleasant. As a dinner theater, however, our family of three found it unexceptional in every respect but its cost. Had your review of the* Revue *tempered its enthusiasm (much as you present its Polynesian counterpart), we probably would've canceled our reservation, pocketed the $100, and spent the evening joyously stunned by another glorious light-and-fireworks spectacle.*

More typical are the remarks of a Cambridge, Massachusetts, mom:

The kids in our group (ages 3–8) thought the Hoop-Dee-Doo Musical Revue *was just terrific. They watched intently the whole time, laughing hysterically. With them having such a good time, how could the adults not enjoy themselves? But I wouldn't recommend the show for adults on their own. One thing we adults appreciated was the lack of commercialism: no movie tie-in, no merchandise sales. The entire experience, including its setting in the rustic Fort Wilderness campground, brought us back to simpler days and gave the kids exposure to entertainment before there were special effects.*

If you go to *Hoop-Dee-Doo,* allow plenty of driving time (about an hour) to get there. Or do as this California dad suggests:

To go to the Hoop-Dee-Doo Musical Revue *at Fort Wilderness, take the boat from the Magic Kingdom rather than any bus. This is contrary to the "official" directions. The boat dock is a short walk from Pioneer Hall in Fort Wilderness, while the bus goes to the main Fort Wilderness parking lot, where one has to transfer to another bus to Pioneer Hall.*

Boat service may be suspended during thunderstorms, so if it's raining or it looks like it's about to rain, Disney will provide bus service from the parks.

Mickey's Backyard BBQ

Fort Wilderness Campground ☎ 407-939-3463. **Showtimes** Thursday and Saturday at 5, 6:30, and 7 p.m. **Cost** $51–$55 adults, $30–$32 children ages 3–9. Prices include tax and gratuity. **Type of seating** Picnic tables. **Menu** Baked chicken, barbecue pork ribs, burgers, hot dogs, corn, beans, mac-and-cheese, salads and slaw, bread, and watermelon and ice-cream bars for dessert. **Vegetarian alternatives** On request. **Beverages** Unlimited beer, wine, lemonade, and iced tea.

DESCRIPTION AND COMMENTS Situated along Bay Lake and held in a covered pavilion next to the site of the old River Country swimming park, *Mickey's Backyard BBQ* features Mickey, Minnie, Chip 'n' Dale, and Goofy, along with a country band and line dancing. Though the pavilion gets some breeze off Bay Lake, we recommend going during the spring or fall, if possible. The food is pretty good, as is, fortunately, the insect control.

The barbecue was previously offered only seasonally, from March through December, but is now year-round. Even so, dates are usually not entered into the WDW-DINE reservations system until about six months in advance. Once the dates are in the system, you can make an Advance Reservation for anytime during the dinner show's season.

The easiest way to get to the barbecue is to take a boat from the Magic Kingdom or from one of the Disney resorts on the Magic Kingdom monorail. Give yourself at least 45 minutes if you plan to arrive by boat. Ferry service may be suspended during thunderstorms, so if it's raining or it looks like it's about to rain, Disney will provide bus service from the parks.

Spirit of Aloha Dinner Show

Disney's Polynesian Resort ☎ 407-939-3463. **Showtimes** Tuesday–Saturday, 5:15 and 8 p.m. **Cost** $59–$72 adults, $30–$37 children ages 3–9. Prices include tax and gratuity. **Discounts** Seasonal. **Type of seating** Long rows of tables, with some separation between individual parties. The show is performed on an outdoor stage, but all seating is covered. Ceiling fans provide some air movement, but it can get warm, especially at the early show. **Menu** Tropical fruit, roasted chicken, island pork ribs, mixed vegetables, rice, and pineapple bread; chicken tenders, PB&J sandwiches, mac-and-cheese, and hot dogs are also available for children. **Vegetarian alternative** On request. **Beverages** Beer, wine, and soft drinks.

DESCRIPTION AND COMMENTS This show features South Seas–island native dancing followed by an all-you-can-eat "Polynesian-style" meal. The dancing is interesting and largely authentic, and the dancers are attractive though definitely PG-rated in the Disney tradition. We think the show has its moments and the meal is adequate, but neither is particularly special.

The show follows (tenuously) the common "girl leaves home for the big city, forgets her roots, and must rediscover them" theme. The performers are uniformly attractive ("Studmuffins!" said a female *Unofficial* researcher when asked about the men), and the dancing is very good. The story, however, never really makes sense as anything other than a slender thread between musical numbers. Our show lasted for more than 2 hours and 15 minutes.

The food does little more than illustrate how difficult it must be to prepare the same meal for hundreds of people simultaneously. The roasted chicken is better than the ribs, but neither is anything special. We conditionally recommend *Spirit of Aloha* for special occasions, when the people celebrating get to go on stage. But go to the early show and get dessert somewhere else in the World.

A well-traveled couple from Fond du Lac, Wisconsin, comments:

> Spirit of Aloha *was a beautiful presentation, better than some shows we have seen in Hawaii! The food, however, lacked in all areas. Better food has come out of Disney kitchens. During our visit, the fruit platter was chintzy, the honey-roasted chicken was a bit fatty, and the pineapple cake was dry.*

▮▮ UNIVERSAL CITYWALK

CITYWALK WAS UNIVERSAL ORLANDO'S ANSWER to Pleasure Island. Now, with Pleasure Island defunct, CityWalk takes its place as the preeminent nightlife venue. In addition to a number of restaurants, you'll find **CityWalk's Rising Star,** a karaoke club where singers are backed by a live band; reggae at **Bob Marley—A Tribute to Freedom;** a **Pat O'Brien's** dueling-pianos club; a **Hard Rock Cafe** and **Hard Rock Live** concert venue; **Jimmy Buffett's Margaritaville;** the **Latin Quarter,** for Nuevo Latino music, food, and dancing; the **Red Coconut Club,** a two-story upscale cocktail lounge with live music and dancing; and a dance club called **The Groove,** with high-tech lighting and visual effects. If you do decide to dine at CityWalk, your options include **Bubba Gump Shrimp Co., Bob Marley—A Tribute to Freedom, CityWalk's Rising Star, Emeril's Orlando, Hard Rock Cafe, Jimmy Buffett's Margaritaville,** the **Latin Quarter, NASCAR Sports Grille, NBA City, Pastamoré,** and **Pat O'Brien's** (for more on CityWalk restaurants, see page 412). For dancing, try **Bob Marley—A Tribute to Freedom, The Groove,** the **Latin Quarter,** or the **Red Coconut Club.** And if you're in the mood for live music, check out **Bob Marley—A Tribute to Freedom, Jimmy Buffett's Margaritaville, Pat O'Brien's,** or the **Red Coconut Club.**

There's no admission charge to enjoy the shops, restaurants, and street entertainment. As for the clubs, you can buy a **CityWalk Party Pass** for about $12 that admits you to all of them, or if you prefer, you can pay a cover charge (usually about $7) at each club you visit. In addition to the clubs, shops, and restaurants, there's a 20-screen **AMC Universal Cineplex** movie theater. Add a movie to your pass for a total cost of $15.

APPENDIX

READERS' QUESTIONS *to* *the* AUTHORS

FOLLOWING ARE QUESTIONS AND COMMENTS from *Unofficial Guide* readers. Some frequently asked questions are addressed in every edition of the *Guide*.

QUESTION:

When you do your research, are you admitted to the parks free? Do the Disney people know you're there?

ANSWER:

We pay the regular admission, and usually the Disney people don't know we're on-site. Similarly, both in and out of Walt Disney World, we pay for our own meals and lodging.

QUESTION:

How often is the Unofficial Guide *revised?*

ANSWER:

We publish a new edition once a year, but we revise every time we go to press, usually twice a year.

QUESTION:

Where can I find information about what's changed at Walt Disney World in between published editions of the Unofficial Guide?

ANSWER:

We post important information online at **touringplans.com**.

QUESTION:

Do you write each new edition from scratch?

ANSWER:

Nope. When it comes to a destination the size of Walt Disney World, it's hard enough to keep up with what's new. Moreover, we put a lot of effort into communicating the most useful information in the clearest possible language. If an attraction or hotel has not changed, we're reluctant to tinker with its coverage for the sake of freshening the writing.

QUESTION:

I've never read any other Unofficial Guides. *Are they all as critical as* The Unofficial Guide to Walt Disney World?

ANSWER:

What some readers perceive as critical we see as objective and constructive. Our job is to prepare you for both the best and worst of Walt Disney World. As it happens, some folks are very passionate about what one reader calls "the inherent goodness of Disney." These readers might be more comfortable with press releases or the *Official Guide* than with the strong consumer viewpoint represented in our guide. That said, some readers take us to task for being overly positive.

QUESTION:

How many people have you surveyed for your age-group ratings regarding the attractions?

ANSWER:

Since the first *Unofficial Guide* was published in 1985, we've interviewed or surveyed slightly more than 41,000 Walt Disney World patrons. Even with such a large survey population, however, we continue to find certain age groups underrepresented. Specifically, we'd love to hear more from seniors about their experiences with coasters and other thrill rides.

QUESTION:

Do you stay in Walt Disney World? If not, where?

ANSWER:

We stay at Walt Disney World lodging properties quite often. Since we began writing about Walt Disney World in 1982, we've stayed at all the Disney resorts and more than 75 different properties in various locations around Orlando, Lake Buena Vista, and Kissimmee.

QUESTION:

Bob, what's your favorite Florida attraction?

ANSWER:

What attracts me (as opposed to my favorite attraction) is **Juniper Springs,** a stunningly beautiful stream about 1½ hours north of Orlando in the Ocala National Forest. Originating in a limestone aquifer, the crystal-clear water erupts from the ground and begins a 10-mile journey to the creek's mouth at Lake George. Winding through palm, cypress, and live oak, the stream is more exotic than the Jungle Cruise, and alive with birds, turtles, and alligators. Put in at the Juniper Springs Recreation Area on FL 40, 36 miles east of Ocala. The 7-mile trip to the FL 19 bridge takes about 4½ hours. Canoe rentals and shuttle service are available at the recreation area. Call ☎ 352-625-3147 for more information.

▋ READERS' COMMENTS

OUR READERS LOVE TO SHARE TIPS. From a St. Louis mom:

When dining at Downtown Disney, it's best to arrive before 7 p.m. We ate there twice and had no problem getting seated immediately, but after 7 p.m. everywhere was packed.

And from an Ann Arbor, Michigan, mother of three:

Even though we stayed on Disney property, we stopped off on US 192 and loaded up on the local freebie visitor magazines and coupon books. We estimate they saved us over $200, mostly on food.

An Iowa City, Iowa, couple offers this observation about being in touch with your feelings:

We didn't build rest breaks into our plans but were willing to say, "OK, I'm just not having fun right now; we should leave the park," and go on to something else (like a water park, hotel pool, or shopping trip to Downtown Disney). This is a skill I would like to see more people develop. I can't count the number of people or families I saw who were obviously not having fun.

A woman from Suwanee, Georgia, offers a suggestion for the perfect Disney vacation:

Your book made our trip a much more successful one. It also frustrated our male adults, who erroneously believed this was a trip for their enjoyment. We followed your advice to get up early and see as much as possible before an early lunch. But the men refused to go back to the hotel for a nap and a meal outside the park, so we fought the crowds until 3 or 4 p.m., by which time everyone was exhausted and cranky. My mother and I decided our next trip will include your guidebook and the children—but no men!

A Norwalk, Ohio, mom searched for happy feet:

*On the subject of footwear, support is just as important as comfort. On one trip I wore Keds—big mistake. My shins ached unbelievably before the end of the second day. From then on I was a die-hard tennis-shoe girl, until I discovered FitFlops [go to **fitflop.com /page/retailer** for stores]. You get the support of a tennis shoe with the comfort of a flip-flop.*

From a Greenville, Kentucky, mom who wasn't able to take advantage of the free-admission promotion on her daughter's birthday:

We were disappointed that a birth certificate was the only acceptable ID for my daughter. We had certified shot records and they still wouldn't accept them.

A reader from Crofton, Maryland, discovered that the best bargains on Disney merchandise can turn up in unexpected places:

People who want to save $$$ on Disney trinkets and aren't fussy about selection really should go to the Disney shop at Orlando Premium Outlets. I bought a talking Goofy doll for my nephew and was *very pleased with the $19.99 price, which was significantly lower than the list price. However, the VERY SAME doll was only $9.99 at (of all places!) Publix grocery store! In fact, Publix has loads of cute dolls, T-shirts, keychains, and other gifts at great prices!*

A Midwestern mom loved getting in the game, writing:

It was a thrill for me to stand behind the ropes and wait till the park officially opened—to hear the music and announcements, then hurry with the throngs to the first ride. It was so exciting! My husband wasn't so thrilled. He teased me for days about running over old ladies and little children—I didn't run! I was speed-walking!

Henry Ford famously said, "You can have any color car you want, as long as it's black." A hungry (and persistent) Fairfax, Vermont, reader found that mind-set alive and well at his Disney resort's food court:

The real difficulty of our stay began when I made the ill-advised decision to request a hamburger at the food court. I was first given a cheeseburger. I then informed the cast member that I requested a hamburger. She placed the burger back under the heat lamp, and I proceeded to watch the person at the grill place cheese on all 14 burgers that had just been put on the grill. Sensing my unease, another cast member asked me what I had ordered. I informed him that I was waiting for a hamburger. He then reached under the heat lamp and proceeded to give me the original cheeseburger. Had I realized that, at that very moment, fate had determined that I was not to enjoy a hamburger on this night, then I would have given up. Sadly, I did not come to this realization at that time. Instead, I chose to "spit into the wind" and insist on getting my hamburger. Thus, I watched as another 14 burgers were placed on the grill. I could almost taste the reward for my patience . . . until I saw the cast member delicately place cheese on each and every one of the new burgers. Alas, my quest for a burger ended, and my call to Pizza Hut delivery was made.

A Lafayette, Louisiana, dad overheard this comment:

The "out of the mouths of babes" award goes to a very cute little blonde girl, about 3 years old. We were racing past her and the rest of the goats standing in the regular line for the Kilimanjaro Safaris. She asked her mother, "Why do they get to go?" and Mom said, "They have Fastpasses." The girl immediately replied, "Well, why did we get Slow Passes?" Good question, kid.

A father of two from Widnes, England, knows who butters his bread:

While we did not make the early starts, the guide still managed to advise of enough shortcuts that enabled us to keep everyone happy. (Let's face it—I'm talking about my wife.)

A Columbia, Missouri, woman offers advice for wives with anxious husbands:

A smartphone is the best thing in the world for keeping your husband busy in line. As long as mine had that phone, he could check e-mail, check dinner plans, and take and send pictures of the kids to family back home. He never complained about waiting in line, ever.

A Cleveland dad complains about folks from the East Coast:

We would not go again during "Jersey Week." I was sick of tank top–wearing fathers yelling "ANTNEE, git ovah heah!"

A Nashville, Tennessee, family of three report a tough reentry:

My wife and I were so depressed when we had to adjust to reality after a week of being in Disney's alternate universe. We think Disney needs to offer some sort of debriefing or transition program to ease its visitors back into the real world. Perhaps they could send Mickey and Minnie over to make blueberry pancakes the morning after you return.

A Denver reader bursts our bubble (we thought we were Disney's favorites):

WDW cast members have an interesting reaction to the Guide. *In one case, with the book in hand, we got an almost vampire-vs.-holy-water reaction from one CM (who then asked if he could take a quick peek).*

A mom from Brighton, Michigan, was searching for quiet in all the wrong places:

Disney is so much flash and sparkle without a lot of time for reflection. They had to fill every quiet minute throughout the park with noise, music, talking, animation, flashing lights, etc.—as if they were afraid we'd get bored if we stopped to think. Next year we plan to go to Costa Rica instead.

An Atlanta reader relates the story of a dirty bird and a solicitous cast member:

While riding Splash Mountain, a mother and teenage son in our boat had brought ponchos (smart move), and the son took his off before we got out of the boat, just in time for a bird to poop on him. He went to buy a clean shirt in the gift shop, and when the cast member found out what happened, he gave the kid a free shirt. I thought that was very nice!

From a husband and wife, also from Atlanta:

My brother-in-law, Pat, and his wife were planning a trip to Disney for the first time with their 4-year-old daughter. My other brother-in-law, Robert, who has three kids and has taken them to Disney twice, asked Pat if he had taken the "Disney test": Take a $100 bill, throw it in the toilet, and flush. If you can do this without flinching, you're ready for Disney.

A mom from Flower Mound, Texas, boils our windy 850-page guide down to one paragraph, and she's pretty much right-on:

If you get just the following two things from the Guide, *they're worth the cost of the entire book—especially when you put them together: (1)*

Get to the parks early. You won't believe what a difference it makes. The parks are wonderful in the morning. (2) The afternoon break is essential! I wouldn't even consider a WDW trip without it. If your kids are under 10 years old, turn out the lights, shut the curtains, and make them sleep. It's the difference between disaster and delight!

A dad from Westminster, Colorado, rethought his game plan:

The book was a home run. My first thought was to just go with the flow—why ruin a vacation by being so regimented? After reading the guide, I figured it would be best to be "in the know" rather than "with the flow."

A Texas woman never says never:

As I walked out of the Magic Kingdom for the last time, I promised I wouldn't wait so long to visit again.

And finally, this Hawaii woman either is a record-holder of some sort or forgot to proofread before she hit SEND:

We've used the book for more than 90 years and love it. Keep up the good work!

And so it goes. . . .

ACCOMMODATIONS INDEX

Note: Page numbers of profiles are in **boldface** type.

See also the Restaurant Index on pages 784–787 and the Subject Index on pages 788–815.

See also the Restaurant Index on pages 784–787 and the Subject Index on pages 788–815.

See also the Restaurant Index on pages 784–787 and the Subject Index on pages 788–815.

See also the Restaurant Index on pages 784–787 and the Subject Index on pages 788–815.

See also the Restaurant Index on pages 784–787 and the Subject Index on pages 788–815.

See also the Restaurant Index on pages 784–787 and the Subject Index on pages 788–815.

See also the Restaurant Index on pages 784–787 and the Subject Index on pages 788–815.

RESTAURANT INDEX

Note: Page numbers of restaurant profiles are in **boldface** type.

See also the Accommodations Index on pages 777–783 and the Subject Index on pages 788–815.

See also the Accommodations Index on pages 777–783 and the Subject Index on pages 788–815.

See also the Accommodations Index on pages 777–783 and the Subject Index on pages 788–815.

SUBJECT INDEX

See also the Accommodations Index on pages 777–783 and the Restaurant Index on pages 784–787.

See also the Accommodations Index on pages 777–783 and the Restaurant Index on pages 784–787.

See also the Accommodations Index on pages 777–783 and the Restaurant Index on pages 784–787.

See also the Accommodations Index on pages 777–783 and the Restaurant Index on pages 784–787.

See also the Accommodations Index on pages 777–783 and the Restaurant Index on pages 784–787.

See also the Accommodations Index on pages 777–783 and the Restaurant Index on pages 784–787.

See also the Accommodations Index on pages 777–783 and the Restaurant Index on pages 784–787.

See also the Accommodations Index on pages 777–783 and the Restaurant Index on pages 784–787.

See also the Accommodations Index on pages 777–783 and the Restaurant Index on pages 784–787.

See also the Accommodations Index on pages 777–783 and the Restaurant Index on pages 784–787.

See also the Accommodations Index on pages 777–783 and the Restaurant Index on pages 784–787.

See also the Accommodations Index on pages 777–783 and the Restaurant Index on pages 784–787.

See also the Accommodations Index on pages 777–783 and the Restaurant Index on pages 784–787.

See also the Accommodations Index on pages 777–783 and the Restaurant Index on pages 784–787.

See also the Accommodations Index on pages 777–783 and the Restaurant Index on pages 784–787.

TOURING PLANS

"Not a Touring Plan"
TOURING PLANS

IT'S EASIER TO DEVISE a good touring plan than an optimal one. Or maybe we've been doing this so long we've finally achieved Zen enlightenment. Either way, below are the simple rules we use when friends ask us for touring plans that don't sound like a space-shuttle launch checklist. Use these when you don't want the regimentation of a step-by-step plan but you do want to avoid long waits in line. Skip attractions that don't suit you, and use Fastpass if waits seem too long.

MAGIC KINGDOM

FOR PARENTS OF SMALL CHILDREN WITH ONE DAY TO TOUR, ARRIVING AT PARK OPENING See Fantasyland first. See Frontierland and some of Adventureland, then take a midday break. Return to the park and complete your tour of Adventureland. Next see Liberty Square and Tomorrowland. End on Main Street for parades and fireworks.

FOR ADULTS WITH ONE DAY TO TOUR, ARRIVING AT PARK OPENING First see Space Mountain and Buzz Lightyear in Tomorrowland, then Fantasyland, Frontierland, Adventureland, Liberty Square, and the rest of Tomorrowland. End on Main Street for parades and fireworks.

FOR PARENTS AND ADULTS WITH TWO DAYS TO TOUR *Note:* Day One works great for Disney resort guests on Extra Magic Hour mornings. Start Day One in Fantasyland, then tour Frontierland and Pirates of the Caribbean in Adventureland. Take a midday break and return to Adventureland. Next see Liberty Square and the evening parade. See fireworks from Main Street. Begin Day Two in Tomorrowland. See any missed Adventureland or Frontierland attractions before leaving the park around midday.

FOR PARENTS AND ADULTS WITH AN AFTERNOON AND A FULL DAY For the afternoon, get Fastpasses, if possible, for any Frontierland and Adventureland headliners you can; save other headliners for later in the evening. Tour Liberty Square, Adventureland, and Frontierland, then see the evening parade and fireworks. On your full day of touring, see Fantasyland, and Tomorrowland (use Fastpass for Space Mountain), then catch any missed attractions from the previous afternoon.

EPCOT

FOR PARENTS AND ADULTS WITH ONE DAY TO TOUR, ARRIVING AT PARK OPENING Obtain Fastpasses for Soarin' first, then see Test Track and Mission: SPACE. See remaining Future World West attractions, then tour Future World East. Tour World Showcase clockwise, starting in Mexico.

FOR PARENTS AND ADULTS WITH ONE DAY TO TOUR, ARRIVING LATE MORNING Try to obtain Fastpasses for Soarin', Test Track, or Mission: SPACE (in that order). See Future World East attractions, then Future World West. Tour World Showcase counterclockwise, starting in Canada.

FOR PARENTS AND ADULTS WITH TWO DAYS TO TOUR On Day One, see Future World East attractions and Mexico through the United States in World Showcase. On Day Two, tour Future World West and Canada through Japan.

DISNEY'S ANIMAL KINGDOM

FOR PARENTS AND ADULTS ARRIVING AT PARK OPENING Obtain Fastpasses for Expedition Everest in Asia, then begin a land-by-land counterclockwise tour of the park, starting in DinoLand U.S.A. Work in shows as you near them, but leave *Finding Nemo—The Musical* for last.

FOR PARENTS AND ADULTS ARRIVING LATE MORNING Obtain Fastpasses for Kilimanjaro Safaris, then begin a counterclockwise tour of the park starting in Africa, saving Kali River Rapids and Expedition Everest for last.

DISNEY'S HOLLYWOOD STUDIOS

FOR PARENTS ARRIVING AT PARK OPENING Ride Toy Story Mania!, then head to Animation Courtyard to begin a counterclockwise tour of the park starting with *Voyage of the Little Mermaid*. Work in other shows as you near them. End the day on Sunset Boulevard for *Fantasmic!*

FOR ADULTS ARRIVING AT PARK OPENING Obtain Fastpasses for Toy Story Mania!, then begin a counterclockwise tour of the park with Rock 'n' Roller Coaster, Tower of Terror, and The Great Movie Ride. End the day in Animation Courtyard for Voyage of the Little Mermaid and The Magic of Disney Animation. Work in other shows as you near them. End the day on Sunset Boulevard for *Fantasmic!*

FOR PARENTS AND ADULTS ARRIVING LATE MORNING Try to get Fastpasses for Rock 'n' Roller Coaster or Tower of Terror (in that order). Start clockwise tour of park with Studio Backlot Tour, working in shows as you near them. Save Toy Story Mania! for last, grab a bite to eat, and see *Fantasmic!*

unofficial **TIP**
In the parks? Help other *Unofficial Guide* readers plan their next move by sending any wait times you notice to **touringplans.com /lines** from your smartphone. You can also view current and future wait times here.

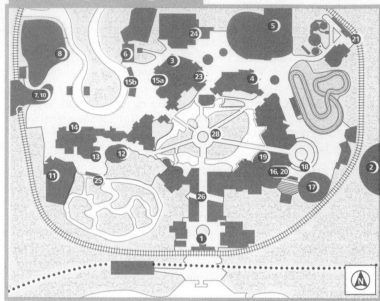

The Magic Kingdom

Magic Kingdom One-Day Touring Plan for Adults

1. Arrive at the entrance to the Magic Kingdom 50 minutes (Disney resort guests) to 70 minutes (non–Disney resort guests) before opening. Get guide maps and the *Times Guide*.
2. As soon as the park opens, ride Space Mountain in Tomorrowland.
3. Ride Peter Pan's Flight in Fantasyland.
4. Ride Winnie the Pooh.
5. Ride Under the Sea: Journey of the Little Mermaid (opens winter 2012).
6. See The Haunted Mansion in Liberty Square.
7. Obtain Fastpasses for Splash Mountain in Frontierland.
8. Ride Big Thunder Mountain Railroad.
9. Eat lunch. The best nearby counter-service restaurant is Pecos Bill Tall Tale Inn & Cafe in Frontierland.
10. Ride Splash Mountain using the Fastpasses obtained earlier.
11. Ride Pirates of the Caribbean.
12. Explore the Swiss Family Treehouse.
13. See *Enchanted Tiki Room*.
14. In Frontierland, see *Country Bear Jamboree*.
15. In Liberty Square, experience *The Hall of Presidents* **(15a)** and ride the *Liberty Belle* Riverboat **(15b)**, in any order.

16. In Tomorrowland, obtain Fastpasses for Buzz Lightyear's Space Ranger Spin.
17. See *Walt Disney's Carousel of Progress*.
18. Take a round-trip on the Tomorrowland Transit Authority PeopleMover.
19. See *Monsters, Inc. Laugh Floor*.
20. Ride Buzz Lightyear using the Fastpasses obtained earlier.
21. Take a round-trip on the Walt Disney World Railroad from the Fantasyland station. There's a walkway to the station from Tomorrowland, just past the left side of Space Mountain.
22. Eat dinner.
23. See *Mickey's PhilharMagic*.
24. Ride It's a Small World.
25. In Adventureland, take the Jungle Cruise.
26. Tour Main Street, U.S.A., and meet any characters that interest you. Check the *Times Guide* for greeting locations and times.
27. Revisit any favorite attractions or see any missed attractions.
28. Check the *Times Guide* for performance times for the evening parade and fireworks. A good viewing spot is between The Plaza Restaurant and Tomorrowland Terrace Restaurant.

You can customize this touring plan and get up-to-the-minute attraction wait times at **touringplans.com**.

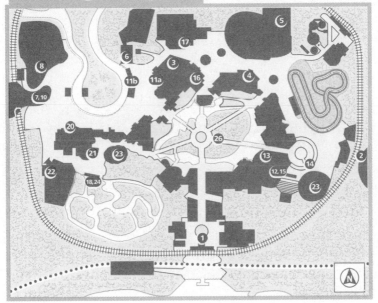

The Magic Kingdom

Magic Kingdom
Authors' Selective One-Day Touring Plan for Adults

1. Arrive at the entrance to the Magic Kingdom 50 minutes (Disney resort guests) to 70 minutes (non–Disney resort guests) before opening. Get guide maps and the *Times Guide.*
2. As soon as the park opens, ride Space Mountain in Tomorrowland.
3. Ride Peter Pan's Flight in Fantasyland.
4. Ride Winnie the Pooh.
5. Ride Under the Sea: Journey of the Little Mermaid (opens winter 2012).
6. See The Haunted Mansion in Liberty Square.
7. Obtain Fastpasses for Splash Mountain in Frontierland.
8. Ride Big Thunder Mountain Railroad.
9. Eat lunch. The best nearby counter-service restaurant is Pecos Bill Tall Tale Inn & Cafe in Frontierland.
10. Ride Splash Mountain using the Fastpasses obtained earlier.
11. In Liberty Square, experience *The Hall of Presidents* **(11a)** and ride the *Liberty Belle* Riverboat **(11b)**, in any order.
12. In Tomorrowland, obtain Fastpasses for Buzz Lightyear's Space Ranger Spin.
13. See *Monsters, Inc. Laugh Floor.*
14. Take a round-trip on the Tomorrowland Transit Authority PeopleMover.
15. Ride Buzz Lightyear using the Fastpasses obtained earlier.
16. In Fantasyland, see *Mickey's PhilharMagic.*
17. Ride It's a Small World.
18. Obtain Fastpasses for the Jungle Cruise in Adventureland.
19. Eat dinner.
20. In Frontierland, see *Country Bear Jamboree.*
21. See *Enchanted Tiki Room.*
22. Ride Pirates of the Caribbean.
23. Explore the Swiss Family Treehouse.
24. Take the Jungle Cruise using the Fastpasses obtained earlier.
25. Revisit any favorite attractions or see any missed attractions.
26. Check the *Times Guide* for performance times for the evening parade and fireworks. A good viewing spot is between The Plaza Restaurant and Tomorrowland Terrace Restaurant.

You can customize this touring plan and get up-to-the-minute attraction wait times at **touringplans.com.**

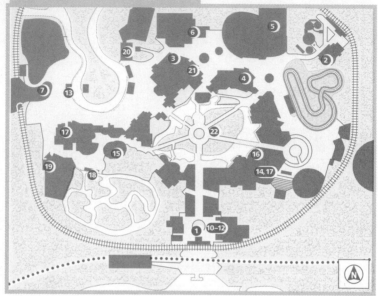

The Magic Kingdom

Magic Kingdom
One-Day Touring Plan for Parents with Small Children
(Review the Small-Child Fright-Potential Chart on pages 324–328.)

1. Arrive at the entrance to the Magic Kingdom 50 minutes (Disney resort guests) to 70 minutes (non–Disney resort guests) before opening. Rent strollers before the park opens. Get guide maps and the *Times Guide*.

2. As soon as the park opens, ride Dumbo the Flying Elephant in Fantasyland.

3. Ride Peter Pan's Flight in Fantasyland.

4. Ride Winnie the Pooh.

5. Ride Under the Sea: Journey of the Little Mermaid (opens winter 2012).

6. Ride It's a Small World.

7. Ride Splash Mountain in Frontierland.

8. Eat lunch. The best nearby counter-service restaurant is Pecos Bill Tall Tale Inn & Cafe in Frontierland.

9. Leave the park for a midday break. Allow at least 3 hours for the break. When the park is open past 8 p.m., a 4-hour break is possible.

10. Return to the park and obtain Fastpasses to meet the Disney princesses at the Town Square Theater on Main Street.

11. Meet Mickey Mouse at the Town Square Theater.

12. Meet the Disney princesses using the Fastpasses obtained earlier.

13. In Frontierland, take the raft over to Tom Sawyer Island. Allow at least 30 minutes to explore the island.

14. In Tomorrowland, obtain Fastpasses for Buzz Lightyear's Space Ranger Spin.

15. Eat dinner.

16. See *Monsters, Inc. Laugh Floor.*

17. Ride Buzz Lightyear using the Fastpasses obtained earlier.

18. In Adventureland, take the Jungle Cruise.

19. Ride Pirates of the Caribbean.

20. See The Haunted Mansion in Liberty Square.

21. See *Mickey's PhilharMagic* in Fantasyland, if time permits.

22. Check the *Times Guide* for performance times for the evening parade and fireworks. A good viewing spot is between The Plaza Restaurant and Tomorrowland Terrace Restaurant.

You can customize this touring plan and get up-to-the-minute attraction wait times at **touringplans.com**.

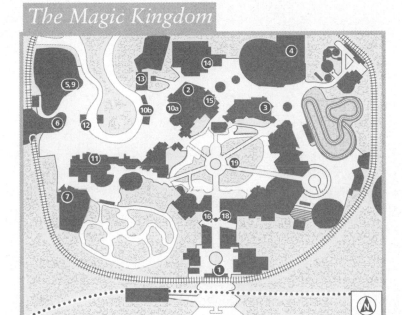

The Magic Kingdom

Magic Kingdom Two-Day Touring Plan: Day One

1. Arrive at the entrance to the Magic Kingdom 50 minutes (Disney resort guests) to 70 minutes (non–Disney resort guests) before opening. Rent strollers before the park opens. Get guide maps and the *Times Guide*.

2. As soon as the park opens, ride Peter Pan's Flight in Fantasyland.

3. Ride Winnie the Pooh.

4. Ride Under the Sea: Journey of the Little Mermaid (opens winter 2012).

5. Obtain Fastpasses for Big Thunder Mountain Railroad in Frontierland.

6. Ride Splash Mountain, also in Frontierland.

7. Experience Pirates of the Caribbean in Adventureland.

8. Eat lunch.

9. Ride Big Thunder Mountain Railroad using the Fastpasses obtained earlier.

10. In Liberty Square, experience *The Hall of Presidents* **(10a)** and ride the *Liberty Belle* Riverboat **(10b)**, in any order.

11. See *Country Bear Jamboree* in Frontierland.

12. Take the raft over to Tom Sawyer Island. Allow at least 30 minutes to explore the island.

13. See The Haunted Mansion in Liberty Square.

14. In Fantasyland, see It's a Small World.

15. See *Mickey's PhilharMagic*.

16. Tour Main Street, U.S.A., and meet any characters that interest you. Check the *Times Guide* for greeting locations and times.

17. Shop, see live entertainment, or revisit favorite attractions.

18. See the evening parade on Main Street.

19. See the evening fireworks on Main Street. A good viewing spot is to the right of the Central Plaza, on the walkway toward Tomorrowland.

You can customize this touring plan and get up-to-the-minute attraction wait times at **touringplans.com**.

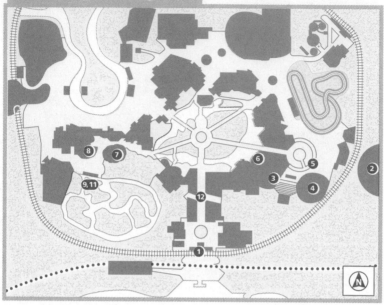

The Magic Kingdom

Magic Kingdom Two-Day Touring Plan: Day Two

1. Arrive at the entrance to the Magic Kingdom 50 minutes (Disney resort guests) to 70 minutes (non–Disney resort guests) before opening. Rent strollers before the park opens. Get guide maps and the *Times Guide.*

2. As soon as the park opens, ride Space Mountain in Tomorrowland.

3. Ride Buzz Lightyear's Space Ranger Spin. Ride again, if desired.

4. See *Walt Disney's Carousel of Progress.*

5. Ride the Tomorrowland Transit Authority PeopleMover.

6. See *Monsters, Inc. Laugh Floor.*

7. In Adventureland, explore the Swiss Family Treehouse.

8. See *Enchanted Tiki Room.*

9. Obtain Fastpasses for the Jungle Cruise.

10. Eat lunch.

11. Ride the Jungle Cruise using the Fastpasses obtained earlier.

12. Shop, see live entertainment, or revisit favorite attractions.

You can customize this touring plan and get up-to-the-minute attraction wait times at **touringplans.com.**

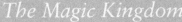

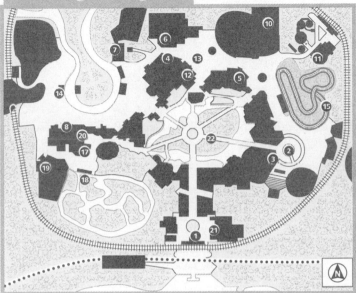

Magic Kingdom Dumbo-or-Die-in-a-Day Touring Plan for Parents with Small Children

(Review the Small-Child Fright-Potential Chart on pages 324–328.
Interrupt the touring plan for lunch, rest, and dinner.)

1. Arrive at the entrance to the Magic Kingdom 50 minutes (Disney resort guests) to 70 minutes (non–Disney resort guests) before opening. Rent strollers before the park opens. Get guide maps and the *Times Guide*.
2. As soon as the park opens, ride the Astro Orbiter in Tomorrowland.
3. Ride Buzz Lightyear's Space Ranger Spin, also in Tomorrowland.
4. In Fantasyland, ride Peter Pan's Flight.
5. Ride Winnie the Pooh.
6. Ride It's a Small World.
7. In Liberty Square, see The Haunted Mansion.
8. See *Country Bear Jamboree* in Frontierland.
9. Eat lunch and take a midday break of at least 3 hours outside the park.
10. Return to the park and Ride Under the Sea: Journey of the Little Mermaid in Fantasyland (opens winter 2012). (To save walking, you could take the Walt Disney World Railroad from Main Street, U.S.A., to Fantasyland.)
11. Ride Dumbo the Flying Elephant. Ride again, if desired.
12. See *Mickey's PhilharMagic*.
13. Ride the Prince Charming Regal Carrousel.
14. Take the raft over to Tom Sawyer Island. Allow at least 30 minutes to explore.
15. Ride the Tomorrowland Speedway in Tomorrowland.
16. Eat dinner.
17. In Adventureland, see *Enchanted Tiki Room*.
18. Take the Jungle Cruise.
19. Ride Pirates of the Caribbean.
20. Ride The Magic Carpets of Aladdin.
21. On Main Street, meet Mickey Mouse and the Disney princesses at the Town Square Theater.
22. Check the *Times Guide* for performance times for the evening parade and fireworks. A good viewing spot is between The Plaza Restaurant and Tomorrowland Terrace Restaurant.

You can customize this touring plan and get up-to-the-minute attraction wait times at **touringplans.com**.

Epcot One-Day Touring Plan

(Interrupt the touring plan for lunch, dinner, and *IllumiNations*.)

1. Arrive 40 minutes before opening time. Get guide maps and the *Times Guide*.
2. As soon as the park opens, obtain Fastpasses for Soarin'.
3. In Future World East, ride Test Track.
4. Ride Mission: SPACE. Do not use Fastpass.
5. In Innoventions East, ride Sum of All Thrills.
6. Return to the Land Pavilion and ride Soarin' using the Fastpasses obtained earlier. Now might be a good time to obtain additional Fastpasses for Soarin' if you want to ride again.
7. Ride Living with the Land in the Land Pavilion.
8. See The Seas with Nemo & Friends and *Turtle Talk with Crush*.
9. Ride Journey into Imagination with Figment.
10. See Captain EO.
11. Eat lunch. The best nearby counter-service restaurant is Sunshine Seasons, in The Land.
12. Ride Spaceship Earth.
13. Ride *Ellen's Energy Adventure* in Future World East.
14. Tour the exhibits in Innoventions East.
15. If you have children, sign up for Agent P's World Showcase Adventure on the walk to World Showcase.
16. Take the Gran Fiesta Tour boat ride in Mexico.
17. Ride Maelstrom and tour the stave church in Norway.
18. See *Reflections of China*.
19. Tour Germany.
20. Visit Italy.
21. See *The American Adventure*.
22. Explore Japan.
23. Visit Morocco, including the small museum on the left side of the pavilion.
24. See *Impressions de France*.
25. Eat dinner.
26. Visit the United Kingdom.
27. Tour Canada and see *O Canada!*
28. See *IllumiNations*. Prime viewing spots are along the lagoon between Canada and France.

You can customize this touring plan and get up-to-the-minute attraction wait times at **touringplans.com**.

Epcot

Epcot

Epcot Authors' Selective One-Day Touring Plan

(Interrupt the touring plan for lunch, dinner, and *IllumiNations*.)

1. Arrive 40 minutes before opening time. Rent strollers before the park opens, if needed. Get guide maps and the *Times Guide*.

2. As soon as the park opens, obtain Fastpasses for Soarin'.

3. In Future World East, ride Test Track.

4. Ride Mission: SPACE. Do not use Fastpass.

5. In Innoventions East, ride Sum of All Thrills

6. Return to the Land Pavilion and ride Soarin' using the Fastpasses obtained earlier. Now might be a good time to obtain additional Fastpasses for Soarin' if you want to ride again.

7. Ride Living with the Land.

8. See The Seas with Nemo & Friends and *Turtle Talk with Crush*.

9. See *Captain EO*.

10. Eat lunch. The best nearby counter-service restaurant is Sunshine Seasons, in The Land.

11. Ride Spaceship Earth.

12. Ride *Ellen's Energy Adventure* in Future World East.

13. Tour Canada and see *O Canada!*

14. See *Impressions de France.*

15. Visit Morocco, including the small museum on the left side of the pavilion.

16. Explore Japan.

17. See *The American Adventure.*

18. Visit Italy.

19. Tour Germany.

20. See *Reflections of China.*

21. Ride Maelstrom and tour the stave church in Norway.

22. Take the Gran Fiesta Tour boat ride in Mexico.

23. Eat dinner.

24. See *IllumiNations*. Prime viewing spots are along the lagoon between Canada and France.

You can customize this touring plan and get up-to-the-minute attraction wait times at **touringplans.com.**

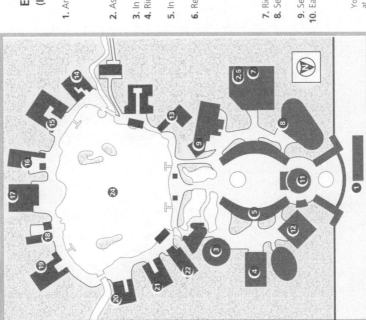

Epcot

Epcot One-Day Touring Plan for Parents with Small Children

(Review the Small-Child Fright-Potential Chart on pages 324–328.)

1. Arrive 40 minutes before opening. Rent strollers before the park opens, if needed. Get guide maps and the *Times Guide.*

2. As soon as the park opens, ride Soarin' in the Land Pavilion. If your children aren't yet tall enough, skip this step.

3. Ride Living with the Land.

4. See *The Circle of Life.*

5. Ride Journey into Imagination with Figment.

6. See *Captain EO.*

7. See The Seas with Nemo & Friends and catch *Turtle Talk with Crush.*

8. Eat lunch. The best nearby spot for lunch is Sunshine Seasons, in The Land.

9. Return to your hotel for a midday break of 3–4 hours.

10. Return to Epcot and ride Spaceship Earth.

11. Ride *Ellen's Energy Adventure* in Future World East.

12. Sign up for Agent P's World Showcase Adventure on the way to World Showcase.

13. See *O Canada!* in the Canada Pavilion.

14. Eat dinner.

15. See *The American Adventure* in the United States Pavilion.

16. Ride Maelstrom in Norway.

17. Take the Gran Fiesta Tour boat ride in the Mexico Pavilion.

18. See *IllumiNations.* Prime viewing spots are along the lagoon between Canada and France.

You can customize this touring plan and get up-to-the-minute attraction wait times at **touringplans.com.**

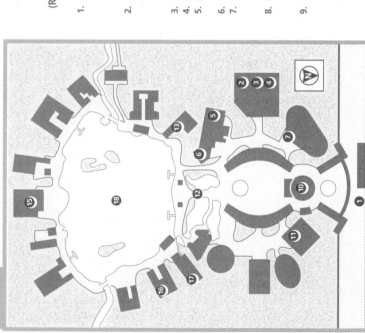

Epcot Two-Day Early-Riser Touring Plan

(Parents with young children should review the Small-Child Fright-Potential Chart on pages 324–328.)

Day One

1. Arrive 40 minutes before official opening time. Get guide maps and the *Times Guide*.
2. At the Land Pavilion, ride Soarin'.
3. Ride Living with the Land. If you want to ride Soarin' again, get Fastpasses now.
4. See *The Circle of Life*.
5. Make dinner reservations at Guest Relations or by calling ☎ 407-WDW-DINE (939-3463).
6. See The Seas with Nemo & Friends and *Turtle Talk with Crush*.
7. Ride Journey into Imagination with Figment.
8. See *Captain EO*.
9. If you have small children, sign up for Agent P's World Showcase Adventure on the way to World Showcase. Ask for a mission in either the United Kingdom or France.
10. Start a counterclockwise tour of World Showcase with the film *O Canada!* in Canada.
11. Explore the United Kingdom.
12. See *Impressions de France*.
13. Continue around the lagoon, or visit the exhibits in Innoventions West.

You can customize this touring plan and get up-to-the-minute attraction wait times at **touringplans.com**.

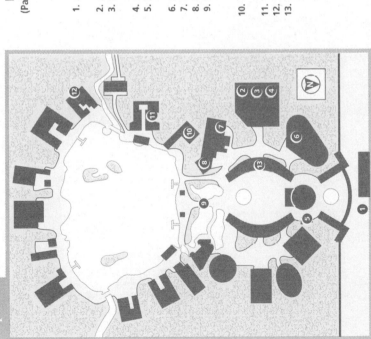

Epcot

Epcot Two-Day Early-Riser Touring Plan

(Parents with young children should review the Small-Child Fright-Potential Chart on pages 324–328.)

Day Two

1. Arrive 40 minutes before official opening time. Get guide maps and the *Times Guide.*
2. Ride Test Track. Use Fastpass if wait exceeds 30 minutes.
3. Ride Mission: SPACE.
4. Tour Innoventions East and ride Sum of All Thrills.
5. See the Universe of Energy.
6. Ride Spaceship Earth.
7. Take the Gran Fiesta Tour boat ride at the Mexico Pavilion in World Showcase. This begins a clockwise tour of World Showcase.
8. Ride Maelstrom at Norway. Use Fastpass if wait exceeds 20 minutes.
9. See *Reflections of China.*
10. Visit Germany.
11. Visit Italy.
12. See *The American Adventure.*
13. Visit Japan.
14. Visit Morocco, including the small museum on the left side of the pavilion.
15. If you have kids, try Agent P's World Showcase Adventure in Japan.
16. Eat dinner and enjoy *IllumiNations.*

You can customize this touring plan and get up-to-the-minute attraction wait times at **touringplans.com.**

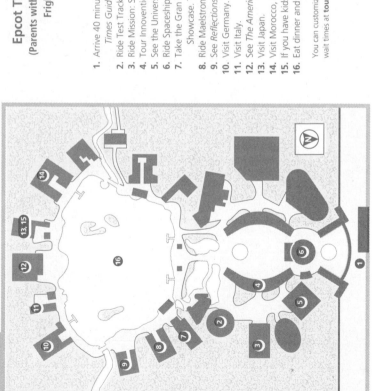

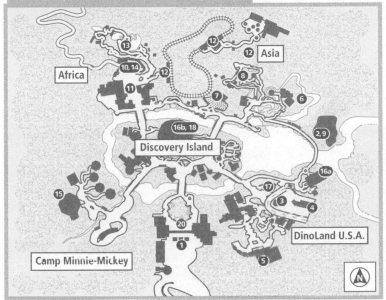

Disney's Animal Kingdom

Africa

Asia

Discovery Island

DinoLand U.S.A.

Camp Minnie-Mickey

Disney's Animal Kingdom One-Day Touring Plan

1. Arrive 30–40 minutes prior to opening.
2. Send one member of your party to obtain Fastpasses for Expedition Everest. The group should meet up at TriceraTop Spin.
3. Ride TriceraTop Spin if you have young children in your group.
4. Ride Primeval Whirl.
5. Follow the signs to DINOSAUR, and ride.
6. Ride Kali River Rapids.
7. See *Flights of Wonder*. If wait exceeds 20 minutes, walk the Maharajah Jungle Trek first, then see the show.
8. Walk the Maharajah Jungle Trek if you haven't already done so.
9. Return to Expedition Everest and ride.
10. Visit Africa, and send one member of your party to obtain Fastpasses for Kilimanjaro Safaris.
11. Eat lunch.
12. Take the Wildlife Express Train from Africa to Conservation Station and Rafiki's Planet Watch. Tour the areas and take the train back to Africa.

13. Walk the Pangani Forest Exploration Trail in Africa.
14. Experience Kilimanjaro Safaris using the Fastpasses that you obtained in Step 10.
15. See *Festival of the Lion King* at Camp Minnie-Mickey.
16. See *Finding Nemo—The Musical* at Theater in the Wild in DinoLand U.S.A. (**16a**) if next show is within 25 minutes. Otherwise, see *It's Tough to Be a Bug!* on Discovery Island (**16b**). Also check out exhibits at The Tree of Life.
17. If you have the time and interest, check out The Boneyard in DinoLand U.S.A.
18. If you've not already done so, see *It's Tough to Be a Bug!* and the exhibits at The Tree of Life on Discovery Island.
19. Shop, snack, or repeat any attractions you especially enjoyed.
20. Visit the zoological exhibits at The Oasis.

You can customize this touring plan and get up-to-the-minute attraction wait times at **touringplans.com**.

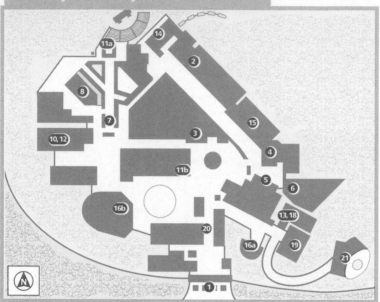

Disney's Hollywood Studios

Disney's Hollywood Studios One-Day Touring Plan

1. Arrive at the park 30–40 minutes before official opening time. Get guide maps and the *Times Guide*.
2. As soon as the park opens, ride Toy Story Mania! on Pixar Place.
3. Ride The Great Movie Ride.
4. See *Voyage of the Little Mermaid*.
5. If you have small children, see *Disney Junior—Live on Stage!*
6. Take The Magic of Disney Animation tour.
7. Explore the Streets of America on the way to *Muppet-Vision 3-D.*
8. See *Muppet-Vision 3-D.*
9. Eat lunch.
10. Obtain Fastpasses for Star Tours— The Adventures Continue.
11. Work in the *Lights, Motors, Action! Extreme Stunt Show* **(11a)** and *The American Idol Experience* **(11b)**. Consult the *Times Guide* for show schedules.

12. In Echo Lake, ride Star Tours— The Adventures Continue.
13. Send one member of your party to obtain Fastpasses for Rock 'n' Roller Coaster on Sunset Boulevard.
14. Take the Studio Backlot Tour.
15. See *Walt Disney: One Man's Dream.*
16. Work in *Beauty and the Beast—Live on Stage* **(16a)** and the *Indiana Jones Epic Stunt Spectacular!* **(16b)**. Consult the *Times Guide* for show schedules.
17. Eat dinner.
18. Ride Rock 'n' Roller Coaster using the Fastpasses obtained earlier.
19. Ride The Twilight Zone Tower of Terror, also on Sunset Boulevard.
20. Tour Hollywood and Sunset boulevards.
21. Enjoy *Fantasmic!* Plan on arriving around 1 hour early to get good seats, or 30 minutes early for standing-room only.

You can customize this touring plan and get up-to-the-minute attraction wait times at **touringplans.com**.

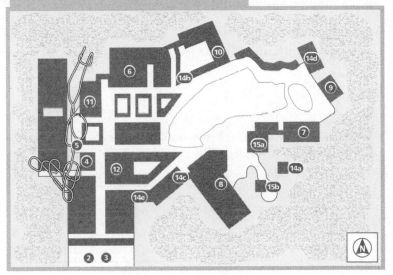

Universal Studios Florida
One-Day Touring Plan

1. Call ☎ 407-363-8000 the day before your visit for the official opening time.
2. Arrive 50 minutes before opening and pick up a map and entertainment schedule.
3. Line up at the turnstile. Ask if any rides or shows are closed, and adjust touring plan.
4. Ride Despicable Me.
5. Ride Hollywood Rip Ride Rockit.
6. Ride Revenge of the Mummy.
7. Ride The Simpsons Ride.
8. Ride E.T. Adventure (expendable if there are no young kids in your group).
9. Ride Men in Black Alien Attack.
10. Experience *Disaster!*
11. See *TWISTER . . . Ride It Out.*
12. See *Shrek 4-D.*
13. Take a break for lunch.
14. See *Animal Actors on Location* **(14a)**, *Beetlejuice's Graveyard Revue* **(14b)**, *Universal Orlando's Horror Make-Up Show* **(14c)**, and *Fear Factor Live* **(14d)** as convenient according to the daily entertainment schedule. See *Terminator 2: 3-D* **(14e)** after 3:30 p.m.
15. Take preschoolers to see Barney **(15a)** after riding E.T., and then head for Woody Woodpecker's KidZone **(15b).**
16. Revisit favorite rides and shows. See any live performances you may have missed.

You can customize this touring plan and get up-to-the-minute attraction wait times at **touringplans.com.**

Universal's Islands of Adventure

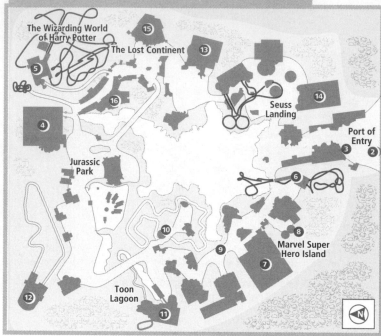

Universal's Islands of Adventure One-Day Touring Plan

1. Call ☎ 407-363-8000 the day before your visit for the official opening time.
2. Arrive at least 60 minutes before opening time, and pick up a map and daily entertainment schedule.
3. Line up at the turnstiles. Ask if any attractions are closed; adjust touring plan accordingly.
4. Hurry to Harry Potter and the Forbidden Journey as soon as you clear the turnstiles, and ride. Be warned that even without much waiting, you'll invest at least 35–40 minutes here.
5. Ride Dragon Challenge if the wait is 30 minutes or less. Otherwise, skip to Step 6.
6. At Marvel Super Hero Island, ride The Incredible Hulk Coaster.
7. Exit left and experience The Adventures of Spider-Man.
8. On exiting Spider-Man, backtrack right and ride Doctor Doom's Fearfall. Skip it if the wait exceeds 20 minutes.
9. Depart Super Hero Island and cross into Toon Lagoon.
10. On your right, ride Popeye & Bluto's Bilge-Rat Barges.
11. Continue your clockwise circuit of the park. Ride Dudley Do-Right's Ripsaw Falls.
12. Continue around the lagoon to Jurassic Park. Ride Jurassic Park River Adventure.
13. Pass through The Wizarding World to The Lost Continent. Experience *Poseidon's Fury*.
14. Continue clockwise to Seuss Landing and ride The Cat in the Hat.
15. Check the daily entertainment schedule for performances of *The Eighth Voyage of Sindbad Stunt Show* in The Lost Continent. See the show when convenient.
16. Return to The Wizarding World and explore Hogsmeade.
17. Revisit favorite rides and check out attractions you may have missed.

You can customize this touring plan and get up-to-the-minute attraction wait times at **touringplans.com**.

Blizzard Beach

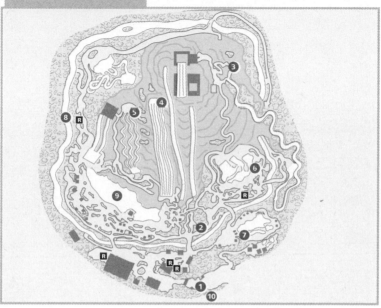

Blizzard Beach One-Day Touring Plan for Parents with Small Children

1. Arrive at the park entrance 30 minutes before park opening. Take care of locker and towel rentals at Lottawatta Lodge, to your left as you enter the park. Find a spot to stow the remainder of your gear, noting any nearby landmarks to help you find your way back.
2. Take the chair lift up Mt. Gushmore to the Green Slope. *Note:* It might be faster (but more tiring) to walk to the top.
3. Raft down Teamboat Springs. Repeat as desired while the park is still uncrowded.
4. If your kids are up for it, try the Toboggan Racers next.
5. If the kids enjoyed the Toboggan Racers, try the Snow Stormers next.
6. Visit the Ski Patrol Training Camp.
7. Ride Tike's Peak.
8. Grab some tubes and ride the Cross Country Creek.
9. Swim in Melt-Away Bay's Wave Pool as long as desired.

You can customize this touring plan and get up-to-the-minute attractionwait times at **touringplans.com**.

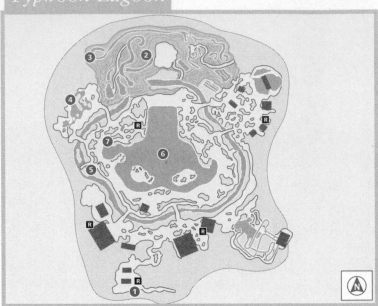

Typhoon Lagoon One-Day Touring Plan for Parents with Small Children

1. Arrive at the park entrance 30 minutes before park opening. Take care of locker and towel rentals at Singapore Sal's, to your right after you've walked through the winding entrance path and emerged into the park. Find a spot to stow the remainder of your gear, noting any nearby landmarks to help you find your way back.
2. Ride Gang Plank Falls. Repeat as desired.

3. If your kids enjoyed Gang Plank Falls, the next step up in slides is Keelhaul Falls—try it if it seems appropriate.
4. Enjoy the Ketchakiddee Creek play area.
5. Grab some tubes and ride Castaway Creek. A complete circle takes 20–25 minutes.
6. Swim in the Surf Pool as long as desired.
7. Ride the Bay Slides in the Surf Pool.
8. Repeat any favorite attractions as desired.

You can customize this touring plan and get up-to-the-minute attraction wait times at **touringplans.com**.

✂ MAGIC KINGDOM **TOURING PLAN COMPANION**

ATTRACTION | RECOMMENDED VISITATION TIMES | AUTHOR'S RATING

Astro Orbiter | Before 11 a.m., after 5 p.m. | ★★

The Barnstormer | Before 10:30 a.m., during parades, just before park closing | ★★

Big Thunder Mountain Railroad *(Fastpass)* | Before 10 a.m., hour before closing | ★★★★
   Special comments 40" minimum height; expectant mothers should not ride

Buzz Lightyear's *Space* **Ranger Spin** *(Fastpass)* | Before 10:30 a.m., after 6 p.m. | ★★★★

Country Bear Jamboree | Before 11:30 a.m., before parades, 2 hours before closing | ★★★

Dumbo the Flying Elephant *(Fastpass)* | Before 10 a.m., after 9 p.m. | ★★★

Enchanted Tiki Room | Before 11 a.m., after 3:30 p.m. | ★★★½

Frontierland Shootin' Arcade | Anytime | ★½

The Hall of Presidents | Anytime | ★★★

The Haunted Mansion | Before 11:30 a.m., after 8 p.m. | ★★★★ |
   Special comment Fright potential

It's a Small World | Anytime | ★★★

Jungle Cruise *(Fastpass)* | Before 10 a.m., 2 hours before closing | ★★★

Liberty Belle **Riverboat** | Anytime | ★★½

Mad Tea Party | Before 11 a.m., after 5 p.m. | ★★ | *Special comments* Expectant mothers
   should not ride; motion-sickness potential

The Magic Carpets of Aladdin | Before 10 a.m., hour before closing | ★★★

The Many Adventures of Winnie the Pooh *(Fastpass)* | Before 10 a.m.,
   2 hours before closing | ★★★½

Mickey's PhilharMagic | Before 11 a.m., during parades | ★★★★

Monsters, Inc. Laugh Floor | Before 11 a.m., after 4 p.m. | ★★★½

Peter Pan's Flight *(Fastpass)* | Before 10 a.m., after 6 p.m. | ★★★★

Pirates of the Caribbean | Before noon, after 5 p.m. | ★★★★

Prince Charming Regal Carrousel | Before 11 a.m., after 8 p.m. | ★★★

Princess Fairytale Hall *(opens 2013)* | Before 10:30 a.m., after 4 p.m. | ★★

Seven Dwarfs Mine Train *(opens 2014)* | Before 10 a.m., during parades, in the evening | N/A

Sorcerers of the Magic Kingdom | Before 11 a.m., after 8 p.m. | ★★★

Space Mountain *(Fastpass)* | At opening, 6–7 p.m., hour before closing | ★★★★
   Special comments 44" minimum height; expectant mothers should not ride

Splash Mountain *(Fastpass)* | At opening, during parades, just before closing | ★★★★★
   Special comments 40" minimum height; expectant mothers should not ride

Stitch's Great Escape! | Before 11 a.m., during parades, after 6 p.m. | ★★
   Special comments Fright potential; 40" minimum height

Swiss Family Treehouse | Anytime | ★★★ | *Special comments* Lots of stairs;
   fright potential due to height

Tom Sawyer Island and Fort Langhorn | Midmorning–late afternoon | ★★★
   Special comments Closes at dusk

Tomorrowland Speedway | Before 11 a.m., after 5 p.m. | ★★
   Special comments 54" minimum height requirement to drive; expectant mothers should not ride

Tomorrowland Transit Authority PeopleMover | Anytime | ★★★
   Special comment Good on hot, crowded days

Under the Sea: Journey of the Little Mermaid *(opens late 2012)* | Before 11 a.m.,
   during parades, in the evening | N/A

Walt Disney's Carousel of Progress | Anytime | ★★★
   Special comment Good during busy times

Walt Disney World Railroad | Anytime | ★★½

DINING INFORMATION—Counter Service

RESTAURANT | LOCATION | QUALITY | VALUE

Aloha Isle | Adventureland | Excellent | **B+** | *Selections* Ice cream, sorbet, fresh fruit, soft drinks

Casey's Corner | Main Street, U.S.A. | Good | **B** | *Selections* Hot dogs, corn-dog nuggets, fries

DINING INFORMATION—Counter Service *(continued)*

RESTAURANT | LOCATION | QUALITY | VALUE

Columbia Harbour House | Liberty Square | Fair | **B** | *Selections* Grilled salmon, fried fish and shrimp, chicken nuggets, sandwiches, soups, salads, kids' meals

Cosmic Ray's Starlight Cafe | Tomorrowland | Good | **B** | *Selections* Burgers (veggie available), rotisserie chicken and ribs, sandwiches, soups, some kosher

Friar's Nook | Fantasyland | Good | **B** | *Selections* Hot dogs, chicken nuggets, homemade potato chips, chicken Caesar salad, frozen drinks

Golden Oak Outpost | Frontierland | Good | **B+** | *Selections* Chicken nuggets, fried-chicken-breast sandwiches, fries, baked goods

The Lunching Pad | Tomorrowland | Good | **B–** | *Selections* Hot dogs, dessert pretzels, frozen sodas

Pecos Bill Tall Tale Inn & Cafe | Frontierland | Good | **B** | *Selections* Burgers, barbecue-pork sandwiches, chicken wraps, taco salad, chili, kids' meals

The Pinocchio Village Haus | Fantasyland | Fair | **C** | *Selections* Personal pizzas, meatball sub sandwiches, chicken Parmesan, chicken nuggets, salads, kids' meals

Storybook Treats | Fantasyland | Good | **B** | *Selections* Ice cream and other sweets

Tomorrowland Terrace Restaurant *(open seasonally)* | Tomorrowland | Good | **B** | *Selections* Burgers, chicken sandwiches, lobster rolls, pasta, kids' meals

Tortuga Tavern *(open seasonally)* | Adventureland | Fair | **B** | *Selections* Tacos, taco salad, burritos, quesadillas

DINING INFORMATION—Full Service

RESTAURANT | MEALS SERVED | LOCATION | PRICE | QUALITY | VALUE

Cinderella's Royal Table | B-L-D | Fantasyland | Expensive | ★★★ | ★★
Selections Beef tenderloin, Major Domo's Favorite Pie (beef in Cabernet sauce, mashed potatoes, and puff pastry), grilled pork chops, seafood, kids' menu

The Crystal Palace | B-L-D | Main Street, U.S.A. | Moderate | ★★★½ | ★★★
Selections Buffet (items change often); *best dining value in the Magic Kingdom*

Liberty Tree Tavern | L-D | Liberty Square | Moderate | ★★★ | ★★★
Selections Roasted meats, sandwiches, salads; all-you-can-eat character dinner

The Plaza Restaurant | L-D | Main Street, U.S.A. | Moderate | ★★ | ★★
Selections Sandwiches, salads, ice cream

Tony's Town Square Restaurant | L-D | Main Street, U.S.A. | Moderate | ★★★ | ★★
Selections Chicken calzones, sausage-and-pepper flatbread, pasta, New York strip

Advance Reservations recommended for Magic Kingdom full-service restaurants; call ☎ *407-WDW-DINE (939-3463).*

GOOD REST AREAS IN THE MAGIC KINGDOM

PLACE | LOCATION | NOTES

Covered tables | Adventureland | Across from Swiss Family Treehouse; has padded seats, nearby refreshments

Covered porch with rocking chairs on Tom Sawyer Island | Frontierland
Across the water from the Liberty Belle Riverboat dock; bring refreshments from Frontierland

Shaded benches | Liberty Square | Between Central Plaza and entrance to Liberty Square, on left

Cul-de-sac | Main Street, U.S.A. | Between the china shop and Main Street Market House on right-hand side of street as you face the castle; nearby refreshments

Quiet seating area | Tomorrowland | Near restrooms on the right as you approach Space Mountain—look for pay phones, and there's a covered seating area farther back of that corridor; refreshments nearby

EPCOT **TOURING PLAN COMPANION**

ATTRACTION | RECOMMENDED VISITATION TIMES | AUTHOR'S RATING

Agent P's World Showcase Adventure | World Showcase, various pavilions
Anytime | ★★★★

The American Adventure | United States, World Showcase | Anytime | ★★★★

The Circle of Life | The Land, Future World | Before 11 a.m., after 2 p.m. | ★★★½

Gran Fiesta Tour Starring the Three Caballeros | Mexico, World Showcase
Before noon, after 5 p.m. | ★★½

Honey, I Shrunk the Audience / Captain EO | Imagination! Pavilion, Future World
Before noon, after 4 p.m. | ★★★★½ / ★★★★ | *Special comment* Fright potential

Impressions de France | France, World Showcase | Anytime | ★★★½

Innoventions East and West | Future World | Second day or after major attractions | ★★★½

Journey into Imagination with Figment | Imagination!, Future World | Anytime | ★★½

Living with the Land *(Fastpass seasonally)* | The Land, Future World | Before 10:30 a.m.,
after 5 p.m. | ★★★★

Maelstrom *(Fastpass)* | Norway, World Showcase | Before noon, after 4:30 p.m. | ★★★

Mission: SPACE *(Fastpass)* | Future World | First hour the park is open | ★★★★
Special comments 44" minimum height; expectant mothers should not ride; motion-sickness potential

The "Mom, I Can't Believe It's Disney!" Fountain | Future World | When it's hot | ★★★★

O Canada! | Canada, World Showcase | Anytime | ★★★½

Reflections of China | China, World Showcase | Anytime | ★★★½
Special comments Audience stands throughout performance

The Seas Main Tank and Exhibits | The Seas with Nemo & Friends, Future World
Before 11:30 a.m., after 5 p.m. | ★★★½

The Seas with Nemo & Friends | The Seas with Nemo & Friends, Future World
Before 11 a.m., after 5 p.m. | ★★★

Soarin' *(Fastpass)* | The Land, Future World | First 30 minutes the park is open | ★★★★½
Special comments 40" minimum height; motion-sickness potential

Spaceship Earth | Future World | Before 10 a.m., after 4 p.m. | ★★★★

Sum of All Thrills | Innoventions, Future World | Before 11 a.m., after 6 p.m. | ★★★★
Special comments 48" minimum height, 54" for coaster-track designs with inversions

Test Track *(Fastpass)* | Test Track, Future World | First 30 minutes the park is open, just before
closing | ★★★½ | *Special comments* 40" minimum height; expectant mothers should not ride

Turtle Talk with Crush | The Seas with Nemo & Friends, Future World | Before 11 a.m., after 5 p.m.
★★★★

Universe of Energy: *Ellen's Energy Adventure* | Future World | Before 11:15 a.m., after 4:30 p.m.
★★★★

DINING INFORMATION—Counter Service

RESTAURANT | LOCATION | QUALITY | VALUE | SELECTIONS

Boulangerie Patisserie | France, World Showcase | Excellent | **B** | *Selections* Croissants, pastries,
cheese plate, sandwiches, quiche, coffee

La Cantina de San Angel | Mexico, World Showcase | Good | **B** | *Selections* Chicken and beef
tacos, nachos, cheese empanadas, margaritas

Crêpes des Chefs de France | France, World Showcase | Excellent | **B+** | *Selections* Dessert crêpes,
ice cream, specialty beer, espresso

Electric Umbrella Restaurant | Innoventions East, Future World | Fair–good | **B–**
Selections Burgers, chicken nuggets, Caesar and Greek salads, kids' meals

Fife & Drum Tavern | United States, World Showcase | Fair | **C** | *Selections* Turkey legs, pretzels,
ice cream, frozen slushes, beer

Fountain View Ice Cream | Future World West | Fair | **C+** | *Selections* Ice cream, smoothies, sodas

Katsura Grill | Japan, World Showcase | Excellent | **B** | *Selections* Beef, chicken, or salmon teriyaki;
noodles; sushi; miso soup; beer, sake, green tea

Kringla Bakeri og Kafe | Norway, World Showcase | Good–excellent | **B** | *Selections* Pastries,
sandwiches, green salad, rice cream, beer

Liberty Inn | United States, World Showcase | Fair | **C** | *Selections* Burgers, hot dogs, chili,
chicken nuggets, salads, kids' meals, some kosher

Lotus Blossom Cafe | China, World Showcase | Fair | **C** | *Selections* Egg rolls, pot stickers,
stir-fries, fried rice, orange chicken, noodle bowls

Promenade Refreshments | World Showcase Promenade | Fair | **C** | *Selections* Hot dogs,
pretzels, popcorn, ice cream, beer

Refreshment Outpost | Between Germany and China | Good | **B–** | *Selections* Hot dogs,
ice cream, frozen slushes, coffee and tea, beer

DINING INFORMATION—Counter Service *(continued)*

RESTAURANT | LOCATION | QUALITY | VALUE | SELECTIONS

Refreshment Port | World Showcase | Good | **B** | *Selections* Fried shrimp with *tostones* (plantains), spicy chicken-and-cheddar poppers, frozen mojitos, ice cream

Rose & Crown Pub | United Kingdom, World Showcase | Good | **C+** | *Selections* Fish-and-chips, Scotch eggs, British Bulldog (split sausage stuffed with mashed potatoes, bacon, and cheese), British beers

Sommerfest | Germany, World Showcase | Good | **B–** | *Selections* Bratwurst and frankfurter sandwiches with kraut, apple strudel, beer

Sunshine Seasons | The Land, Future World | Excellent | **A** | *Selections* Rotisserie meats, salads, sandwiches, soups, Asian noodle bowls and stir-fries, quick breakfast

Tangierine Cafe | Morocco, World Showcase | Good | **B** | *Selections* Chicken and lamb *shawarma*, lentil and couscous salads, hummus, wraps, kids' meals, wine and beer

Yorkshire County Fish Shop | United Kingdom, World Showcase | Good | **B+**
Selections Fish-and-chips, shortbread, draft ale

DINING INFORMATION—Full Service

RESTAURANT | MEALS SERVED | LOCATION | PRICE | QUALITY | VALUE

Akershus Royal Banquet Hall | B-L-D | Norway, World Showcase | Expensive | ★★★ | ★★★★
Selections *Koldtbord* (Norwegian buffet), grilled pork chop, mustard-glazed salmon

Biergarten | L-D | Germany, World Showcase | Expensive | ★★★ | ★★★★
Selections Buffet with schnitzel, sausages, spaetzle, roast chicken

Bistro de Paris | D | France, World Showcase | Expensive | ★★★½ | ★★
Selections Roasted duck breast, Maine lobster, lamb tenderloin

Le Cellier Steakhouse | L-D | Canada, World Showcase | Expensive | ★★★½ | ★★★
Selections Canadian Cheddar cheese soup, steaks, seafood

Les Chefs de France | L-D | France, World Showcase | Expensive | ★★★ | ★★★
Selections Duck à l'orange, braised beef short ribs, French onion soup, crêpes

Coral Reef Restaurant | L-D | The Seas with Nemo & Friends, Future World | Expensive | ★★
| ★★ | *Selections* Creamy lobster soup, seared Scottish salmon, steaks, kids' menu

Garden Grill Restaurant | D | The Land, Future World | Expensive | ★★ | ★★★
Selections Beef filet, fish of the day, kids' menu with chicken drumstick, potatoes, and veggies

La Hacienda de San Angel | D | Mexico, World Showcase | Expensive | ★★½ | ★★½
Selections Soft-taco appetizer, shrimp tacos, grilled tilapia with roasted corn and cactus leaves

Nine Dragons Restaurant | L-D | China, World Showcase | Moderate | ★★★ | ★★
Selections Roasted Beijing chicken, shrimp and steak, five-spiced fish, noodles, veggie stir-fry

Restaurant Marrakesh | L-D | Morocco, World Showcase | Moderate | ★★½ | ★★
Selections *Bastilla* (minced-chicken pie), lemon chicken, roast lamb, couscous

Rose & Crown Dining Room | L-D | United Kingdom, World Showcase | Moderate |
★★★½ | ★★ | *Selections* Fish-and-chips, bangers and mash (sausage and mashed potatoes), shepherd's pie

San Angel Inn | L-D | Mexico, World Showcase | Expensive | ★★ | ★★ | *Selections* *Mole poblano* (chicken in chile-chocolate sauce), *tacos de filete* (grilled beef tenderloin and chipotle sauce on a soft flour tortilla), *tlacoyos de chilorio* (corn cakes with refried beans, pork, and cheese)

Teppan Edo | L-D | Japan, World Showcase | Expensive | ★★★★ | ★★★
Selections Chicken, shrimp, beef, pork, scallops, swordfish, and veggies stir-fried on teppan grill

Tokyo Dining | L-D | Japan, World Showcase | Moderate | ★★★★ | ★★★
Selections Grilled meats and seafood, tempura, sushi, and sashimi

Tutto Italia Ristorante | L-D | Italy, World Showcase | Expensive | ★★★★ | ★★★
Selections Lasagna, grilled swordfish steak, baked salmon fillet, braised lamb shank

Via Napoli | L-D | Italy, World Showcase | Moderate | ★★★½ | ★★★
Selections Wood-fired pizzas, pastas, salads, sandwiches

*Advance Reservations recommended for Epcot full-service restaurants;
call ☎ 407-WDW-DINE (939-3463).*

GOOD REST AREAS IN EPCOT

PLACE | LOCATION | NOTES

Benches | The Seas with Nemo & Friends, Future World | Air-conditioned

Benches | Innoventions East and West, Future World | Air-conditioned; usually not crowded

Covered gazebo | In garden behind shops on left side of United Kingdom, World Showcase
Often empty; refreshments nearby

Rotunda and lobby | United States, World Showcase | Ample room; air-conditioned;
refreshments nearby; usually quiet unless singers are performing

DISNEY'S ANIMAL KINGDOM
TOURING PLAN COMPANION

ATTRACTION | RECOMMENDED VISITATION TIMES | AUTHOR'S RATING

The Boneyard | Anytime | ★★★½

Camp Minnie-Mickey Character Trails | Early morning, late afternoon | N/A

Conservation Station and Affection Section | Anytime | ★★★

DINOSAUR *(Fastpass)* | Before 10:30 a.m., hour before closing | ★★★★½
  Special comments Fright potential; 40" minimum height; expectant mothers should not ride

Expedition Everest *(Fastpass)* | Before 9:30 a.m., after 3 p.m. | ★★★★½
  Special comments 44" minimum height; expectant mothers should not ride

Festival of the Lion King | Before 11 a.m., after 4 p.m. | ★★★★

Flights of Wonder | Anytime | ★★★★

Kali River Rapids *(Fastpass)* | Before 10:30 a.m., after 4:30 p.m. | ★★★½
  Special comments You'll get wet; 38" minimum height; expectant mothers should note that ride is bouncy

Kilimanjaro Safaris *(Fastpass)* | Park opening, 2 hours before closing | ★★★★★

Maharajah Jungle Trek | Anytime | ★★★★

The Oasis | Anytime | N/A

Pangani Forest Exploration Trail | Anytime | ★★★★

Primeval Whirl | First 2 hours park is open, hour before closing | ★★★
  Special comments 48" minimum height; expectant mothers should not ride

Theater In the Wild / *Finding Nemo—The Musical* | Anytime | ★★★★

The Tree of Life / *It's Tough to Be a Bug!* | Before noon., after 4 p.m. | ★★★★
  Special comment Fright potential

TriceraTop Spin | First 90 minutes park is open, hour before closing | ★★

Wildlife Express Train | Anytime | ★★

DINING INFORMATION—Counter Service

RESTAURANT | LOCATION | QUALITY | VALUE

Anandapur Local Food Cafes | Asia | Fair | **B** | *Selections* Crispy honey chicken with steamed rice, kung pao beef, sweet-and-sour chicken, Mandarin chicken salad, Asian chicken sandwiches, egg rolls, fried rice, kids' meals

Flame Tree Barbecue | Discovery Island | Excellent | **B−** | *Selections* Barbecue beef or pork sandwiches; ribs; barbecue-chicken salad; fruit plate; child's plate of baked chicken drumstick, hot dog, or PB&J sandwich; beer and wine

Kusafiri Coffee Shop and Bakery | Africa | Good | **B** | *Selections* Pastries, yogurt, coffee, cocoa, juice

Pizzafari | Discovery Island | Fair | **B** | *Selections* Cheese, pepperoni, and veggie pizzas; salads; kids' meals; beer and wine

Restaurantosaurus | DinoLand U.S.A. | Good | **B+** | *Selections* Cheeseburgers, shrimp po'boys, chicken nuggets, chocolate mousse, cheesecake, kids' meals, beer and soft drinks

Royal Anandapur Tea Company | Asia | Good | **B** | *Selections* Hot and iced teas, coffee, lattes, pastries

Tamu Tamu Eats & Refreshments | Africa | Good | **C** | *Selections* Turkey-and-Swiss on focaccia, slow-roasted pulled-beef sandwiches, tandoori chicken salad, soft drinks

DINING INFORMATION—Full Service

RESTAURANT | MEALS SERVED | LOCATION | PRICE | QUALITY | VALUE

Rainforest Cafe | B-L-D | Park entrance | Moderate | ★★ | ★★ *Selections* Pasta with grilled chicken, turkey wraps, coconut shrimp, ribs, brownie cake

Tusker House Restaurant | B-L-D | Africa | Moderate | ★ | ★★
  Selections Rotisserie chicken, couscous, curry, roasted meats

Yak & Yeti Restaurant | L-D | Asia | Expensive | ★★½ | ★★ *Selections* Seared miso salmon, glazed duck, tempura shrimp

Advance Reservations recommended for Animal Kingdom full-service restaurants; call ☎ 407-WDW-DINE (939-3463).

GOOD REST AREAS IN
DISNEY'S ANIMAL KINGDOM
PLACE | LOCATION | NOTES

Walkway between Africa and Asia | Between Africa and Asia | Plenty of shaded rest spots, some overlooking running streams; refreshments nearby; a favorite of *Unofficial Guide* researchers

Gazebo behind Flame Tree Barbecue | Discovery Island | Follow the path toward the water, along the left side of Flame Tree Barbecue; gazebo has ceiling fans

Outdoor covered benches near exit from DINOSAUR | DinoLand U.S.A. | Gazebo-like structure with nearby water fountain

Tusker House Restaurant | Africa | Note how the panoramic photos are made

DISNEY'S HOLLYWOOD STUDIOS TOURING PLAN COMPANION

ATTRACTION | RECOMMENDED VISITATION TIMES | AUTHOR'S RATING

The American Idol Experience | Anytime | ★★★★

Disney Junior—Live on Stage! | Per entertainment schedule | ★★★★

Fantasmic! | Evening, 2–7+ times a week, depending on season | ★★★★★

The Great Movie Ride | Before 11 a.m., after 4:30 p.m. | ★★★½

Honey, I Shrunk the Kids Movie Set Adventure | Before 11 a.m., after dark | ★★½
Special comment Kids must be age 10 or younger to play

Indiana Jones Epic Stunt Spectacular! | First 3 morning shows or last evening show
★★★★

Jedi Training Academy | First 2 shows of the day | ★★★★

Jim Henson's Muppet-Vision 3-D | Before 11 a.m., after 3 p.m. | ★★★★½

Lights, Motors, Action! Extreme Stunt Show | First show of the day | ★★★½

The Magic of Disney Animation | Before 11 a.m., after 5 p.m. | ★★½

Rock 'n' Roller Coaster *(Fastpass)* | Before 10 a.m., hour before closing | ★★★★
Special comments 48" minimum height; expectant mothers should not ride;
kids under age 7 must ride with an adult

Star Tours—The Adventures Continue *(Fastpass)* | First 90 minutes after opening |
★★★★ *Special comments* Fright potential; 40" minimum height; expectant mothers should
not ride; motion-sickness potential

Studio Backlot Tour | Anytime | ★★★★

Theater of the Stars / Beauty and the Beast—Live on Stage | Anytime | ★★★★

Toy Story Mania! *(Fastpass)* | Before 10:30 a.m., after 6 p.m. | ★★★★½

The Twilight Zone Tower of Terror *(Fastpass)* | Before 9:30 a.m., after 6 p.m. |
★★★★★ | *Special comments* 40" minimum height; expectant mothers should not ride

Voyage of the Little Mermaid | Before 9:45 a.m., just before closing | ★★★★

Walt Disney: One Man's Dream | Anytime | ★★★

DINING INFORMATION—Counter Service

RESTAURANT | LOCATION | QUALITY | VALUE

ABC Commissary | Echo Lake | Fair | **B–** | *Selections* Asian salads, chicken curry, burgers,
kids' meals, some kosher

Backlot Express | Echo Lake | Fair | **C** | *Selections* Burgers, fries, chicken nuggets, hot dogs,
child's plate with chicken nuggets or meaty macaroni

Catalina Eddie's | Sunset Boulevard | Fair | **B** | *Selections* Pizzas, sandwiches, salads,
chocolate fudge cake

Fairfax Fare | Sunset Boulevard | Fair | **B** | *Selections* Barbecue chicken, ribs, and pulled-pork
sandwiches; "designer" hot dogs; salads; kids' meals

Min and Bill's Dockside Diner | Echo Lake | Fair | **C** | *Selections* Italian sausage,
chicken Caesar sandwich, shakes, beer and soft drinks, chips, cookies

Pizza Planet | Streets of America | Good | **B+** | *Selections* Pizza, subs, salads, cookies

Rosie's All-American Cafe | Sunset Boulevard | Fair | **C** | *Selections* Burgers,
chicken nuggets, soups, child's mac-and-cheese or chicken nuggets

Starring Rolls Cafe | Sunset Boulevard | Good | **B** | *Selections* Sandwiches, salads, sushi,
pastries, baked goods, coffee

Studio Catering Co. | Streets of America | Good | **B** | *Selections* Veggie sandwiches,
chicken Caesar wraps, buffalo chicken sandwiches, kids' meals

Toluca Legs Turkey Company | Sunset Boulevard | Good | **B** | *Selections* Smoked turkey
legs, hot dogs, coffee and soft drinks

DINING INFORMATION—Full Service

RESTAURANT | MEALS SERVED | LOCATION | PRICE | QUALITY | VALUE

50's Prime Time Cafe | L-D | Echo Lake | Moderate | ★★★ | ★★★ *Selections* Meat loaf, pot roast, chicken, other homey fare

Hollywood & Vine | B-L-D | Echo Lake | Moderate | ★★★ | ★★★ *Selections* Fresh fish of the day, carved and grilled meats, vegetables and pasta, fresh fruits and breads

The Hollywood Brown Derby | L-D | Hollywood Boulevard | Expensive | ★★★★ | ★★★ *Selections* Cobb salad, duck two ways, grapefruit cake

Mama Melrose's Ristorante Italiano | L-D | Streets of America | Moderate | ★★★ | ★★ *Selections* Caesar salad, crispy calamari, penne alla vodka, oak-grilled pork chop

Sci-Fi Dine-In Theater Restaurant | L-D | Commissary Lane | Moderate | ★★½ | ★★ *Selections* Sandwiches, burgers, salads, shakes; pasta, ribs, steak

Advance Reservations recommended for DHS full-service restaurants; call ☎ *407-WDW-DINE (939-3463).*

GOOD REST AREAS IN DISNEY'S HOLLYWOOD STUDIOS

PLACE | LOCATION | NOTES

Covered seating behind Toluca Legs Turkey Company | Sunset Boulevard Refreshments nearby; ample seating

Studios Catering Co. | Backlot | Ample covered seating; refreshments nearby

Benches along Echo Lake | Echo Lake | Some are shaded; refreshments nearby

Tune In Lounge | Echo Lake, next to 50's Prime Time Cafe | Air-conditioned bar; nonalcoholic drinks and food from 50's Prime Time Cafe also available. (Thanks to Matt Hochberg of **studioscentral.com** for this tip.)

If you'd like to express your opinion about Walt Disney World or this guidebook, fill out the online survey at **touringplans.com/walt-disney-world/survey,** or complete the one below and mail it to:

Unofficial Guide Reader Survey
P.O. Box 43673
Birmingham, AL 35243

Inclusive dates of your visit: _____

Your hometown: _____

Your e-mail address: _____

Members of your party:	Person 1	Person 2	Person 3	Person 4	Person 5	Person 6
Gender:	M F	M F	M F	M F	M F	M F
Age:	_____	_____	_____	_____	_____	_____

How many times have you been to Walt Disney World? _____

CAR RENTALS Did you rent a car? If so, from what company? _____
Concerning your rental car, on a scale with
5 being best and 1 worst, how would you rate: Condition of the car? _____
                                                 Cleanliness of the car? _____
Pickup-processing efficiency? _____   Airport-shuttle efficiency?_____
Return-processing efficiency?_____

LODGING On your most recent trip, where did you stay?
_____

Have you stayed at any other hotels in the past 12 months? Yes ____ No ____
Please indicate the hotels you have stayed at in the past year, or write in others.
Write in _____

❏ Best Western	❏ Fairfield Inn	❏ Hyatt	❏ Quality	❏ Ritz-Carlton
❏ Days Inn	❏ Hampton Inn	❏ Holiday Inn	❏ Radisson	❏ Super 8
❏ Embassy Suites	❏ Hilton	❏ Marriott	❏ Ramada Inn	

Please tell us how important the following amenities were in your selection of a Walt Disney World–area resort/hotel. Select up to five amenities, and rank them in order of importance using 1 for the most important and 5 for the least. Feel free to add others.

- cost_____
- bar _____
- distance to parks _____
- in-room dining/
room service_____
- food court _____
- shuttle service to parks _____

- sit-down restaurant _____
- room size_____
- fine dining_____
- multiple bedroom suites _____
- spa/fitness center _____
- in-room kitchen _____
- pool _____

- shuttle to/from airport _____
- architecture/theme _____
- kids' activity center _____
- location inside WDW _____
- other _____
- other _____
- other _____

On a scale with 5 being best and 1 being worst, please indicate how satisfied you were with your accommodations. Feel free to add other items you feel are important.
When rating food services, please rate only meals eaten at your resort.

- cleanliness of room_____
- size and layout of pool _____
- comfort of beds/pillows_____
- crowd level at the pool _____
- room size and layout _____
- cleanliness of pool area _____
- quietness of room _____
- shuttle to/from airport _____

- ability to find your room, etc.
_____
- check-in/out process_____
- shuttle to/from parks _____
- accessibility, friendliness, and knowledge of staff _____
- recreational amenities (fitness center, sports, etc.)
_____

- overall food-court experience
_____
- overall food-court value
_____
- child care _____
- overall experience with full-service restaurant _____
- overall layout of the resort
- overall value of full-service restaurant _____

Please circle the number that best describes how satisfied you were with your total resort experience during this trip.

1 Very dissatisfied	**2** Somewhat dissatisfied	**3** Neither satisfied or dissatisfied
4 Somewhat satisfied	**5** Very satisfied	

Continued on next page

LODGING *(continued)* Please circle the number that best describes how satisfied you were with your total resort experience during this trip.

1 Very dissatisfied   **2** Somewhat dissatisfied   **3** Neither satisfied or dissatisfied

4 Somewhat satisfied   **5** Very satisfied

Would you stay at this resort again? Yes ❑   No ❑

How likely are you to recommend this resort to a friend?

❑ Will definitely recommend   ❑ May recommend   ❑ Neutral

❑ Probably won't recommend   ❑ Definitely will not recommend

DINING Concerning your dining experiences:

How many restaurant meals (including fast food) did you average per day?_____

How much (approximately) did your party spend on meals per day? _____

Favorite restaurant outside Walt Disney World? _____

Did you purchase the Disney Dining Plan? Yes ❑ No ❑

PARK TOURING On a scale with 5 being best and 1 being worst, please rate how the touring plans worked:

	PARK	NAME OF PLAN	RATING
The Magic Kingdom			
Epcot			
Disney's Animal Kingdom			
Disney's Hollywood Studios			
Universal Studios Florida			
Islands of Adventure			

TRAVEL AGENT If you used a travel agent, what was name of the agent?

_____

What was name of the agency?_____

Would you consider this agent an expert on Disney World? Yes ❑ No ❑

Would you use this agent for your next Disney World trip? Yes ❑ No ❑

OTHER How did you hear about this guide? _____

Please rate any other guidebooks or websites you used on this trip using the scale of 5-as-best and 1-as-worst.

	NAME	RATING
guidebooks		
Web sites		

Using the same scale, how would you rate this *Unofficial Guide*?_____

Which other *Unofficial Guides* have you used? _____

Use the space below and add another sheet to include any additional comments you'd like to share with us about your Walt Disney World vacation or about the *Unofficial Guide:* _____

_____
_____
_____
_____
_____

WALT DISNEY WORLD RESTAURANT SURVEY

TELL US ABOUT YOUR WALT DISNEY WORLD dining experiences. Listed below are all counter-service and full-service restaurants. Beside each restaurant is a thumbs-up and thumbs-down symbol. If you enjoyed the restaurant enough that you'd like to eat there again, circle the thumbs-up symbol. If not, circle the thumbs-down symbol.

WALT DISNEY WORLD COUNTER-SERVICE RESTAURANTS
(in alphabetical order):

ABC Commissary Disney's Hollywood Studios	👍 👎
Anandapur Local Food Cafes Disney's Animal Kingdom	👍 👎
Aloha Isle The Magic Kingdom	👍 👎
Backlot Express Disney's Hollywood Studios	👍 👎
Boulangerie Patisserie France Pavilion, Epcot	👍 👎
La Cantina de San Angel Mexico Pavilion, Epcot	👍 👎
Casey's Corner The Magic Kingdom	👍 👎
Catalina Eddie's Disney's Hollywood Studios	👍 👎
Columbia Harbour House The Magic Kingdom	👍 👎
Cosmic Ray's Starlight Cafe The Magic Kingdom	👍 👎
Crêpes des Chefs de France France Pavilion, Epcot	👍 👎
Electric Umbrella Restaurant Innoventions East, Epcot	👍 👎
Fairfax Fare Disney's Hollywood Studios	👍 👎
Fife & Drum Tavern United States Pavilion, Epcot	👍 👎
Flame Tree Barbecue Disney's Animal Kingdom	👍 👎
Fountain View Ice Cream Future World, Epcot	👍 👎
Friar's Nook The Magic Kingdom	👍 👎
Golden Oak Outpost The Magic Kingdom	👍 👎
Katsura Grill Japan Pavilion, Epcot	👍 👎
Kringla Bakeri og Kafe Norway Pavilion, Epcot	👍 👎
Kusafiri Coffee Shop and Bakery Disney's Animal Kingdom	👍 👎
Liberty Inn United States Pavilion, Epcot	👍 👎
Lotus Blossom Cafe China Pavilion, Epcot	👍 👎
The Lunching Pad The Magic Kingdom	👍 👎
Min and Bill's Dockside Diner Disney's Hollywood Studios	👍 👎
Pecos Bill Tall Tale Inn & Cafe The Magic Kingdom	👍 👎
The Pinocchio Village Haus The Magic Kingdom	👍 👎
Pizzafari Disney's Animal Kingdom	👍 👎

Pizza Planet Disney's Hollywood Studios 👍 👎

Promenade Refreshments World Showcase, Epcot 👍 👎

Refreshment Outpost World Showcase, Epcot 👍 👎

Refreshment Port World Showcase, Epcot 👍 👎

Restaurantosaurus Disney's Animal Kingdom 👍 👎

Rose & Crown Pub United Kingdom Pavilion, Epcot 👍 👎

Rosie's All-American Cafe Disney's Hollywood Studios 👍 👎

Royal Anandapur Tea Company Disney's Animal Kingdom 👍 👎

Sommerfest Germany Pavilion, Epcot 👍 👎

Starring Rolls Cafe Disney's Hollywood Studios 👍 👎

Storybook Treats The Magic Kingdom 👍 👎

Studio Catering Co. Disney's Hollywood Studios 👍 👎

Sunshine Seasons The Land, Epcot 👍 👎

Tamu Tamu Eats & Refreshments Disney's Animal Kingdom 👍 👎

Tangierine Cafe Morocco Pavilion, Epcot 👍 👎

Toluca Legs Turkey Company Disney's Hollywood Studios 👍 👎

Tortuga Tavern The Magic Kingdom 👍 👎

Tomorrowland Terrace Restaurant The Magic Kingdom 👍 👎

Yorkshire County Fish Shop United Kingdom Pavilion, Epcot 👍 👎

WALT DISNEY WORLD FULL-SERVICE RESTAURANTS
(in alphabetical order):

Akershus Royal Banquet Hall Norway Pavilion, Epcot 👍 👎

Andiamo Italian Bistro & Grille Hilton, Downtown Disney 👍 👎

Artist Point Wilderness Lodge Resort 👍 👎

Beaches & Cream Soda Shop Beach Club Resort 👍 👎

Benihana Hilton, Downtown Disney 👍 👎

Biergarten Germany Pavilion, Epcot 👍 👎

Big River Grille & Brewing Works BoardWalk 👍 👎

Bistro de Paris France Pavilion, Epcot 👍 👎

Boatwrights Dining Hall Port Orleans Resort 👍 👎

Boma—Flavors of Africa Animal Kingdom Lodge & Villas 👍 👎

Bongos Cuban Cafe Downtown Disney West Side 👍 👎

California Grill Contemporary Resort 👍 👎

Cape May Cafe Beach Club Resort 👍 👎

Cap'n Jack's Restaurant   Downtown Disney Marketplace   👍 👎

Captain's Grille   Yacht Club Resort   👍 👎

Le Cellier Steakhouse   Canada Pavilion, Epcot   👍 👎

Chef Mickey's   Contemporary Resort   👍 👎

Les Chefs de France   France Pavilion, Epcot   👍 👎

Cinderella's Royal Table   The Magic Kingdom   👍 👎

Citricos   Grand Floridian Resort & Spa   👍 👎

Coral Reef Restaurant   The Seas with Nemo & Friends, Epcot   👍 👎

The Crystal Palace   The Magic Kingdom   👍 👎

ESPN Club   BoardWalk   👍 👎

ESPN Wide World of Sports Grill   ESPN Wide World of Sports   👍 👎

50's Prime Time Cafe   Disney's Hollywood Studios   👍 👎

Flying Fish Cafe   BoardWalk   👍 👎

The Fountain   Dolphin Resort   👍 👎

Fresh Mediterranean Market   Dolphin Resort   👍 👎

Fulton's Crab House   Downtown Disney   👍 👎

Garden Grill Restaurant   The Land, Epcot   👍 👎

Garden Grove   Swan Resort   👍 👎

Grand Floridian Cafe   Grand Floridian Resort & Spa   👍 👎

La Hacienda de San Angel   Mexico Pavilion, Epcot   👍 👎

Hollywood & Vine   Disney's Hollywood Studios   👍 👎

The Hollywood Brown Derby   Disney's Hollywood Studios   👍 👎

House of Blues   Downtown Disney West Side   👍 👎

Il Mulino New York Trattoria   Swan Resort   👍 👎

Jiko—The Cooking Place   Animal Kingdom Lodge & Villas   👍 👎

Kimonos   Swan Resort   👍 👎

Kona Cafe   Polynesian Resort   👍 👎

Kona Island Sushi Bar   Polynesian Resort   👍 👎

Kouzzina by Cat Cora   BoardWalk   👍 👎

LakeView Restaurant   Wyndham Lake Buena Vista Resort   👍 👎

Liberty Tree Tavern   The Magic Kingdom   👍 👎

Mama Melrose's Ristorante Italiano   Disney's Hollywood Studios   👍 👎

Maya Grill   Coronado Springs Resort   👍 👎

Narcoossee's   Grand Floridian Resort & Spa   👍 👎

Nine Dragons Restaurant   China Pavilion, Epcot   👍 👎

1900 Park Fare   Grand Floridian Resort & Spa   👍 👎

'Ohana   Polynesian Resort   👍 👎

Olivia's Cafe   Disney's Old Key West Resort   👍 👎

The Outback   Buena Vista Palace, Downtown Disney   👍 👎

Paradiso 37   Downtown Disney   👍 👎

Planet Hollywood   Downtown Disney West Side   👍 👎

The Plaza Restaurant   The Magic Kingdom   👍 👎

Portobello   Downtown Disney   👍 👎

Raglan Road   Downtown Disney   👍 👎

Rainforest Cafe   Disney's Animal Kingdom and Downtown Disney   👍 👎

Restaurant Marrakesh   Morocco Pavilion, Epcot   👍 👎

Rose & Crown Dining Room   United Kingdom Pavilion, Epcot   👍 👎

San Angel Inn   Mexico Pavilion, Epcot   👍 👎

Sanaa   Animal Kingdom Villas–Kidani Village   👍 👎

Sand Trap Bar & Grill   adjacent to Osprey Ridge Golf Course   👍 👎

Sci-Fi Dine-In Theater Restaurant   Disney's Hollywood Studios   👍 👎

Shula's Steak House   Dolphin Resort   👍 👎

Shutters at Old Port Royale   Caribbean Beach Resort   👍 👎

Teppan Edo   Japan Pavilion, Epcot   👍 👎

Todd English's bluezoo   Dolphin Resort   👍 👎

Tokyo Dining   Japan Pavilion, Epcot   👍 👎

Tony's Town Square Restaurant   The Magic Kingdom   👍 👎

T-REX   Downtown Disney Marketplace   👍 👎

Trail's End Restaurant   Fort Wilderness Resort   👍 👎

Turf Club Bar & Grill   Disney's Saratoga Springs Resort   👍 👎

Tusker House Restaurant   Disney's Animal Kingdom   👍 👎

Tutto Italia Ristorante   Italy Pavilion, Epcot   👍 👎

Via Napoli   Italy Pavilion, Epcot   👍 👎

Victoria & Albert's   Grand Floridian Resort & Spa   👍 👎

The Wave . . . of American Flavors   Contemporary Resort   👍 👎

Whispering Canyon Cafe   Wilderness Lodge Resort   👍 👎

Wolfgang Puck Grand Cafe   Downtown Disney West Side   👍 👎

Yachtsman Steakhouse   Yacht Club Resort   👍 👎

Yak & Yeti Restaurant   Disney's Animal Kingdom   👍 👎